OFFICIAL
NBA REGISTER

1996-97 EDITION

Editors/Official NBA Register
MARK BONAVITA
MARK BROUSSARD
SEAN STEWART

Contributing Editors/Official NBA Register
CHRIS EKSTRAND
JOHN HAREAS
JAN HUBBARD
DAVE SLOAN

PUBLISHING CO.

Efrem Zimbalist III, President and Chief Executive Officer, Times Mirror Magazines; **Francis X. Farrell,** Senior Vice President, Publisher; **John D. Rawlings,** Senior Vice President, Editorial Director; **John Kastberg,** Vice President, General Manager; **Kathy Kinkeade,** Vice President, Operations; **Mike Nahrstedt,** Managing Editor; **Dave Sloan,** Associate Editor; **Craig Carter,** Statistical Editor; **Mark Bonavita and Sean Stewart,** Assistant Editors; **Fred Barnes,** Director of Graphics; **Marilyn Kasal,** Production Manager; **Michael Behrens and Christen Webster,** Macintosh Production Artists.

A Times Mirror
Company

Certain statistical data have been selected, compiled and exclusively supplied by NBA Properties, Inc. Elias Sports Bureau, New York, is the official statistician of the NBA.

All photos supplied by NBA Photos.

Published by The Sporting News Publishing Co., 10176 Corporate Square Dr., Suite 200, St. Louis, MO 63132. Printed in the U.S.A.

ISBN: 0-89204-560-4 (perfect-bound)   10 9 8 7 6 5 4 3 2 1
      0-89204-562-0 (comb-bound)

CONTENTS

EXPLANATION OF FOOTNOTES AND ABBREVIATIONS

* Led league.
† Tied for league lead.
‡ College freshman or junior varsity statistics; not counted toward totals.
... Statistic unavailable, unofficial or mathematically impossible to calculate.
— Statistic inapplicable.

POSITIONS: C: center. **F:** forward. **G:** guard.

STATISTICS: APG: Assists per game. **Ast.:** Assists. **Blk.:** Blocked shots. **Def.:** Defensive rebounds. **Dq.:** Disqualifications. **FGA:** Field goals attempted. **FGM:** Field goals made. **FTA:** Free throws attempted. **FTM:** Free throws made. **G:** Games. **L:** Losses. **Min.:** Minutes. **Off.:** Offensive rebounds. **Pct.:** Percentage. **PF:** Personal fouls. **PPG:** Points per game. **Pts.:** Points. **Reb.:** Rebounds. **RPG:** Rebounds per game. **Stl.:** Steals. **TO:** Turnovers. **Tot.:** Total. **W:** Wins.

LEAGUES/ORGANIZATIONS: AABA: All-America Basketball Alliance. **ABA:** American Basketball Association. **ABL:** American Basketball League. **BAA:** Basketball Association of America. **CBA:** Continental Basketball Association. **EBL:** Eastern Basketball League. **IL:** Inter-State League. **MBL:** Metropolitan Basketball League. **NAIA:** National Association of Intercollegiate Athletics. **NBA:** National Basketball Association. **NBL:** National Basketball League or National League. **NCAA:** National Collegiate Athletic Association. **NIT:** National Invitation Tournament. **NYSL:** New York State League. **PBLA:** Professional Basketball League of America. **WBA:** Western Basketball Association.

TEAMS: Ala.: Alabama. **Al.:** Albany. **Amw. Zaragoza:** Amway Zaragoza. **And.:** Anderson. **Ark.:** Arkansas. **Atl.:** Atlanta. **Bakers.:** Bakersfield. **Balt.:** Baltimore. **Bay St.:** Bay State. **B., Bos.:** Boston. **Buck. Beer Bolo.:** Buckler Beer Bologna. **Buff.:** Buffalo. **Cha., Char.:** Charlotte. **Ch., Chi.:** Chicago. **Chip. Panionios:** Chipita Panionios. **Cin.:** Cincinnati. **Cl., Clev.:** Cleveland. **Col.:** Columbus. **Dal., Dall.:** Dallas. **Den.:** Denver. **Det.:** Detroit. **Fargo/Moor., F./M.:** Fargo-Moorhead. **Ft. Wayne, F.W.:** Fort Wayne. **Frank. & Marsh.:** Franklin & Marshall. **George Wash.:** George Washington. **Gold. St., G.S.:** Golden State. **G.R., Gr. Rap.:** Grand Rapids. **Grupo Ifa Espa.:** Grupo Ifa Espanol's. **Hfrd.:** Hartford. **Hou.:** Houston. **Ind.:** Indiana. **K.C.:** Kansas City. **K.C./O., K.C./Omaha:** Kansas City/Omaha. **L.A.:** Los Angeles. **L.A.C., LA Clip.:** Los Angeles Clippers. **La Cr.:** La Crosse. **L.A.L., LA Lak.:** Los Angeles Lakers. **Il Mess. Roma:** Il Messaggero Roma. **Mil.:** Milwaukee. **Min., Minn.:** Minnesota. **Neptunas Klaib.:** Neptunas Klaibeda. **N.J.:** New Jersey. **N.O.:** New Orleans. **N.Y.:** New York. **N.C.:** North Carolina. **Okla. C., O.C.:** Oklahoma City. **Or., Orl.:** Orlando. **Penn.:** Pennsylvania. **Pens.:** Pensacola. **Pfizer R. Calabria:** Pfizer Reggio Calabria. **Phi., Phil.:** Philadelphia. **Phoe.:** Phoenix. **Pitt.:** Pittsburgh. **Port.:** Portland. **Quad C., Q.C.:** Quad City. **Rancho San.:** Rancho Santiago. **Rap. C., R.C.:** Rapid City. **Roch.:** Rochester. **Rock.:** Rockford. **S.A., San Ant.:** San Antonio. **Sac.:** Sacramento. **S.F., San Fran.:** San Francisco. **Sav.:** Savannah. **Sea.:** Seattle. **Shamp. C. Cantu:** Shampoo Clear Cantu. **Shb.:** Sheboygan. **Sioux F.:** Sioux Falls. **St.L.:** St. Louis. **Syr., Syrac.:** Syracuse. **Team. Fabriano:** Teamsystem Fabriano. **Tele. Brescia:** Telemarket Brescia. **Teore. Milan:** Teorematur Milan. **Top.:** Topeka. **Tri C.:** Tri-Cities. **Tul.:** Tulsa. **Va.:** Virginia. **W.:** Warren. **Wash.:** Washington. **Wash. & Jeff.:** Washington & Jefferson. **Wis., Wisc.:** Wisconsin. **Yak.:** Yakima.

BASEBALL STATISTICS: A.A.: American Association. **A:** Assists. **AB:** At-bats. **A.L.:** American League. **Avg.:** Average. **BB:** Bases on balls. **E:** Errors. **East.:** Eastern League. **ER:** Earned runs. **ERA:** Earned-run average. **G:** Games. **H:** Hits. **HR:** Home runs. **Int'l.:** International. **IP:** Innings pitched. **L:** Losses. **N.L.:** National League. **NYP:** New York-Pennsylvania. **OF:** Outfield. **Pct.:** Winning percentage. **PO:** Putouts. **Pos.:** Position. **R:** Runs. **RBI:** Runs batted in. **SB:** Stolen bases. **SO:** Strikeouts. **South.:** Southern Association. **SS:** Shortstop. **Sv.:** Saves. **W:** Wins. **1B:** First base. **2B:** Doubles or second base. **3B:** Triples or third base.

ON THE COVER: Shawn Kemp led the SuperSonics to the NBA Finals and was named to the All-NBA second team for the third consecutive season. (Photo by Sam Forencich/NBA Photos.)

Spine photo of David Robinson by Vincent Manniello/NBA Photos.

ABDUL-RAUF, MAHMOUD　　　　G　　　　　　　　　KINGS

PERSONAL: Born March 9, 1969, in Gulfport, Miss. ... 6-1/162. ... Name pronounced MOCK-mood AHB-dool rah-OOF. ... Formerly known as Chris Jackson.
HIGH SCHOOL: Gulfport (Miss.).
COLLEGE: Louisiana State.
TRANSACTIONS/CAREER NOTES: Selected after sophomore season by Denver Nuggets in first round (third pick overall) of 1990 NBA Draft. ... Traded by Nuggets to Sacramento Kings for G Sarunas Marciulionis and 1996 second-round draft choice (June 13, 1996).

COLLEGIATE RECORD

NOTES: The Sporting News All-America first team (1989). ... The Sporting News All-America second team (1990).

Season Team	G	Min.	FGM	FGA	Pct.	FTM	FTA	Pct.	Reb.	Ast.	Pts.	RPG	APG	PPG
88-89—Louisiana State............	32	1180	359	739	.486	163	200	.815	108	130	965	3.4	4.1	30.2
89-90—Louisiana State............	32	1202	305	662	.461	191	210	.910	81	102	889	2.5	3.2	27.8
Totals	64	2382	664	1401	.474	354	410	.863	189	232	1854	3.0	3.6	29.0

Three-point field goals: 1988-89, 84-for-216 (.389). 1989-90, 88-for-246 (.358). Totals, 172-for-462 (.372).

NBA REGULAR-SEASON RECORD

HONORS: NBA Most Improved Player (1993). ... NBA All-Rookie second team (1991).

Season Team	G	Min.	FGM	FGA	Pct.	FTM	FTA	Pct.	Off.	Def.	Tot.	Ast.	St.	Blk.	TO	Pts.	RPG	APG	PPG
90-91—Denver	67	1505	417	1009	.413	84	98	.857	34	87	121	206	55	4	110	942	1.8	3.1	14.1
91-92—Denver	81	1538	356	845	.421	94	108	.870	22	92	114	192	44	4	117	837	1.4	2.4	10.3
92-93—Denver	81	2710	633	1407	.450	217	232	.935	51	174	225	344	84	8	187	1553	2.8	4.2	19.2
93-94—Denver	80	2617	588	1279	.460	219	229	*.956	27	141	168	362	82	10	151	1437	2.1	4.5	18.0
94-95—Denver	73	2082	472	1005	.470	138	156	.885	32	105	137	263	77	9	119	1165	1.9	3.6	16.0
95-96—Denver	57	2029	414	955	.434	146	157	*.930	26	112	138	389	64	3	115	1095	2.4	6.8	19.2
Totals	439	12481	2880	6500	.443	898	980	.916	192	711	903	1756	406	38	799	7029	2.1	4.0	16.0

Three-point field goals: 1990-91, 24-for-100 (.240). 1991-92, 31-for-94 (.330). 1992-93, 70-for-197 (.355). 1993-94, 42-for-133 (.316). 1994-95, 83-for-215 (.386). 1995-96, 121-for-309 (.392). Totals, 371-for-1048 (.354).
Personal fouls/disqualifications: 1990-91, 149/2. 1991-92, 130/0. 1992-93, 179/0. 1993-94, 150/1. 1994-95, 126/0. 1995-96, 117/0. Totals, 851/3.

NBA PLAYOFF RECORD

Season Team	G	Min.	FGM	FGA	Pct.	FTM	FTA	Pct.	Off.	Def.	Tot.	Ast.	St.	Blk.	TO	Pts.	RPG	APG	PPG
93-94—Denver	12	339	57	154	.370	29	31	.935	3	15	18	30	5	1	14	155	1.5	2.5	12.9
94-95—Denver	3	76	12	33	.364	14	14	1.000	2	3	5	5	2	0	8	40	1.7	1.7	13.3
Totals	15	415	69	187	.369	43	45	.956	5	18	23	35	7	1	22	195	1.5	2.3	13.0

Three-point field goals: 1993-94, 12-for-37 (.324). 1994-95, 2-for-12 (.167). Totals, 14-for-49 (.286).
Personal fouls/disqualifications: 1993-94, 29/0. 1994-95, 8/0. Totals, 37/0.

ADAMS, MICHAEL　　　　　　G

PERSONAL: Born January 19, 1963, in Hartford, Conn. ... 5-10/162.
HIGH SCHOOL: Hartford (Conn.) Public.
COLLEGE: Boston College.
TRANSACTIONS/CAREER NOTES: Selected by Sacramento Kings in third round (66th pick overall) of 1985 NBA Draft. ... Played in United States Basketball League with Springfield Fame (1985 and 1986). ... Waived by Kings (December 17, 1985). ... Played in Continental Basketball Association with Bay State Bombardiers (1985-86). ... Signed as free agent by Washington Bullets (May 13, 1986). ... Waived by Bullets (September 25, 1986). ... Re-signed by Bullets (September 29, 1986). ... Waived by Bullets (October 28, 1986). ... Re-signed by Bullets (November 21, 1986). ... Traded by Bullets with F Jay Vincent to Denver Nuggets for F Mark Alarie and G Darrell Walker (November 2, 1987). ... Traded by Nuggets with 1991 first-round draft choice and future considerations to Bullets for 1991 first-round draft choice (June 11, 1991). ... Traded by Bullets to Charlotte Hornets for 1996 and 1997 second-round draft choices (August 2, 1994). ... Rights renounced by Hornets (July 11, 1996).

COLLEGIATE RECORD

Season Team	G	Min.	FGM	FGA	Pct.	FTM	FTA	Pct.	Reb.	Ast.	Pts.	RPG	APG	PPG
81-82—Boston College	26	379	51	103	.495	36	61	.590	30	40	138	1.2	1.5	5.3
82-83—Boston College	32	1075	195	405	.481	127	157	.809	86	170	517	2.7	5.3	16.2
83-84—Boston College	30	1026	195	429	.455	130	172	.756	102	105	520	3.4	3.5	17.3
84-85—Boston College	31	1044	193	413	.467	89	119	.748	102	160	475	3.3	5.2	15.3
Totals	119	3524	634	1350	.470	382	509	.750	320	475	1650	2.7	4.0	13.9

CBA REGULAR-SEASON RECORD

NOTES: CBA Rookie of the Year (1986). ... CBA All-League second team (1986). ... CBA All-Defensive second team (1986).

Season Team	G	Min.	FGM	FGA	Pct.	FTM	FTA	Pct.	Reb.	Ast.	Pts.	RPG	APG	PPG
85-86—Bay State	38	1526	262	558	.470	125	164	.762	149	320	670	3.9	8.4	17.6

Three-point field goals: 1985-86, 21-for-71 (.296).

NBA REGULAR-SEASON RECORD

RECORDS: Holds single-game record for most three-point field goals attempted in one half—13 (April 12, 1991, vs. Los Angeles Clippers). ... Shares single-game records for most three-point field goals attempted—20 (April 12, 1991, vs. Los Angeles Clippers); and most three-point field goals made in one half—7 (January 21, 1989, vs. Milwaukee).

Season Team	G	Min.	FGM	FGA	Pct.	FTM	FTA	Pct.	Off.	Def.	Tot.	Ast.	St.	Blk.	TO	Pts.	RPG	APG	PPG
									REBOUNDS								**AVERAGES**		
85-86—Sacramento	18	139	16	44	.364	8	12	.667	2	4	6	22	9	1	11	40	0.3	1.2	2.2
86-87—Washington	63	1303	160	393	.407	105	124	.847	38	85	123	244	85	6	81	453	2.0	3.9	7.2
87-88—Denver	82	2778	416	927	.449	166	199	.834	40	183	223	503	168	16	144	1137	2.7	6.1	13.9
88-89—Denver	77	2787	468	1082	.433	322	393	.819	71	212	283	490	166	11	180	1424	3.7	6.4	18.5
89-90—Denver	79	2690	398	989	.402	267	314	.850	49	176	225	495	121	3	141	1221	2.8	6.3	15.5
90-91—Denver	66	2346	560	1421	.394	465	529	.879	58	198	256	693	147	6	240	1752	3.9	10.5	26.5
91-92—Washington	78	2795	485	1233	.393	313	360	.869	58	252	310	594	145	9	212	1408	4.0	7.6	18.1
92-93—Washington	70	2499	365	831	.439	237	277	.856	52	188	240	526	100	4	175	1035	3.4	7.5	14.8
93-94—Washington	70	2337	285	698	.408	224	270	.830	37	146	183	480	96	6	167	849	2.6	6.9	12.1
94-95—Charlotte	29	443	67	148	.453	25	30	.833	6	23	29	95	23	1	26	188	1.0	3.3	6.5
95-96—Charlotte	21	329	37	83	.446	26	35	.743	5	17	22	67	21	4	25	114	1.0	3.2	5.4
Totals	653	20446	3257	7849	.415	2158	2543	.849	416	1484	1900	4209	1081	67	1402	9621	2.9	6.4	14.7

Three-point field goals: 1985-86, 0-for-3. 1986-87, 28-for-102 (.275). 1987-88, 139-for-379 (.367). 1988-89, 166-for-466 (.356). 1989-90, 158-for-432 (.366). 1990-91, 167-for-564 (.296). 1991-92, 125-for-386 (.324). 1992-93, 68-for-212 (.321). 1993-94, 55-for-191 (.288). 1994-95, 29-for-81 (.358). 1995-96, 14-for-41 (.341). Totals, 949-for-2857 (.332).

Personal fouls/disqualifications: 1985-86, 9/0. 1986-87, 88/0. 1987-88, 138/0. 1988-89, 149/0. 1989-90, 133/0. 1990-91, 162/1. 1991-92, 162/1. 1992-93, 146/0. 1993-94, 140/0. 1994-95, 41/0. 1995-96, 25/0. Totals, 1193/2.

NBA PLAYOFF RECORD

Season Team	G	Min.	FGM	FGA	Pct.	FTM	FTA	Pct.	Off.	Def.	Tot.	Ast.	St.	Blk.	TO	Pts.	RPG	APG	PPG
									REBOUNDS								**AVERAGES**		
86-87—Washington ..	3	82	8	25	.320	1	3	.333	0	7	7	10	7	0	5	19	2.3	3.3	6.3
87-88—Denver	11	406	47	130	.362	36	41	.878	9	27	36	64	18	2	23	147	3.3	5.8	13.4
88-89—Denver	2	75	15	36	.417	7	8	.875	5	12	17	9	3	0	8	47	8.5	4.5	23.5
89-90—Denver	3	105	13	34	.382	7	8	.875	0	6	6	18	4	0	8	39	2.0	6.0	13.0
94-95—Charlotte	1	11	2	5	.400	0	0	...	0	1	1	2	0	0	0	4	1.0	2.0	4.0
Totals	20	679	85	230	.370	51	60	.850	14	53	67	103	32	2	44	256	3.4	5.2	12.8

Three-point field goals: 1986-87, 2-for-9 (.222). 1987-88, 17-for-54 (.315). 1988-89, 10-for-22 (.455). 1989-90, 6-for-20 (.300). 1994-95, 0-for-2. Totals, 35-for-107 (.327).

Personal fouls/disqualifications: 1986-87, 6/0. 1987-88, 19/0. 1988-89, 6/0. 1989-90, 10/0. Totals, 41/0.

NBA ALL-STAR GAME RECORD

Season Team	Min.	FGM	FGA	Pct.	FTM	FTA	Pct.	Off.	Def.	Tot.	Ast.	PF	Dq.	St.	Blk.	TO	Pts.
								REBOUNDS									
1992 —Washington	14	4	8	.500	0	0	...	1	0	1	1	1	0	4	0	1	9

Three-point field goals: 1992, 1-for-3 (.333).

ADDISON, RAFAEL   F   HORNETS

PERSONAL: Born July 22, 1964, in Jersey City, N.J. ... 6-8/241. ... Name pronounced ra-FL-el.
HIGH SCHOOL: Snyder (Jersey City, N.J.).
COLLEGE: Syracuse.
TRANSACTIONS/CAREER NOTES: Selected by Phoenix Suns in second round (39th pick overall) of 1986 NBA Draft. ... Played in Italy (1987-88 through 1990-91 and 1993-94). ... Signed as free agent by New Jersey Nets (October 4, 1991). ... Signed as free agent by Detroit Pistons (July 27, 1994). ... Waived by Pistons (April 19, 1995). ... Signed as unrestricted free agent by Charlotte Hornets (September 27, 1995).

COLLEGIATE RECORD

Season Team	G	Min.	FGM	FGA	Pct.	FTM	FTA	Pct.	Reb.	Ast.	Pts.	RPG	APG	PPG
												AVERAGES		
82-83—Syracuse	31	572	110	211	.521	41	63	.651	98	37	261	3.2	1.2	8.4
83-84—Syracuse	32	1104	229	410	.559	107	128	.836	192	71	565	6.0	2.2	17.7
84-85—Syracuse	31	1110	235	452	.520	101	139	.727	180	79	571	5.8	2.5	18.4
85-86—Syracuse	32	1012	205	385	.532	69	87	.793	179	133	479	5.6	4.2	15.0
Totals	126	3798	779	1458	.534	318	417	.763	649	320	1876	5.2	2.5	14.9

NBA REGULAR-SEASON RECORD

Season Team	G	Min.	FGM	FGA	Pct.	FTM	FTA	Pct.	Off.	Def.	Tot.	Ast.	St.	Blk.	TO	Pts.	RPG	APG	PPG
									REBOUNDS								**AVERAGES**		
86-87—Phoenix	62	711	146	331	.441	51	64	.797	41	65	106	45	27	7	54	359	1.7	0.7	5.8
91-92—New Jersey	76	1175	187	432	.433	56	76	.737	65	100	165	68	28	28	46	444	2.2	0.9	5.8
92-93—New Jersey	68	1164	182	411	.443	57	70	.814	45	87	132	53	23	11	64	428	1.9	0.8	6.3
94-95—Detroit	79	1776	279	586	.476	74	99	.747	67	175	242	109	53	25	76	656	3.1	1.4	8.3
95-96—Charlotte	53	516	77	165	.467	17	22	.773	25	65	90	30	9	9	27	171	1.7	0.6	3.2
Totals	338	5342	871	1925	.452	255	331	.770	243	492	735	305	140	80	267	2058	2.2	0.9	6.1

Three-point field goals: 1986-87, 16-for-50 (.320). 1991-92, 14-for-49 (.286). 1992-93, 7-for-34 (.206). 1994-95, 24-for-83 (.289). 1995-96, 0-for-9. Totals, 61-for-225 (.271).

Personal fouls/disqualifications: 1986-87, 75/1. 1991-92, 109/1. 1992-93, 125/0. 1994-95, 236/2. 1995-96, 74/0. Totals, 619/4.

NBA PLAYOFF RECORD

Season Team	G	Min.	FGM	FGA	Pct.	FTM	FTA	Pct.	Off.	Def.	Tot.	Ast.	St.	Blk.	TO	Pts.	RPG	APG	PPG
									REBOUNDS								**AVERAGES**		
91-92—New Jersey	1	9	2	7	.286	0	0	...	0	0	0	1	0	0	0	5	0.0	1.0	5.0
92-93—New Jersey	5	53	7	21	.333	3	3	1.000	3	3	6	5	3	0	3	17	1.2	1.0	3.4
Totals	6	62	9	28	.321	3	3	1.000	3	3	6	6	3	0	3	22	1.0	1.0	3.7

Three-point field goals: 1991-92, 1-for-2 (.500).
Personal fouls/disqualifications: 1992-93, 3/0.

ITALIAN LEAGUE RECORD

Season Team	G	Min.	FGM	FGA	Pct.	FTM	FTA	Pct.	Reb.	Ast.	Pts.	RPG	APG	PPG
												AVERAGES		
87-88—Livorno	36	1398	368	722	.510	130	170	.765	214	69	949	5.9	1.9	26.4
88-89—Livorno	40	1517	405	790	.513	189	240	.788	235	66	1056	5.9	1.7	26.4

Season Team	G	Min.	FGM	FGA	Pct.	FTM	FTA	Pct.	Reb.	Ast.	Pts.	AVERAGES RPG	APG	PPG
89-90—Livorno	40	1569	434	778	.558	199	235	.847	261	88	1157	6.5	2.2	28.9
90-91—Livorno	30	1142	287	508	.565	121	149	.812	201	42	771	6.7	1.4	25.7
93-94—Benetton	14	449	71	151	.470	19	28	.679	49	14	170	3.5	1.0	12.1
Totals	160	6075	1565	2949	.531	658	822	.800	960	279	4103	6.0	1.7	25.6

ALEXANDER, CORY   G   SPURS

PERSONAL: Born June 22, 1973, in Waynesboro, Va. ... 6-1/190. ... Full name: Cory Lynn Alexander.
HIGH SCHOOL: Oak Hill Academy (Mouth of Wilson, Va.).
COLLEGE: Virginia.
TRANSACTIONS/CAREER NOTES: Selected after junior season by San Antonio Spurs in first round (29th pick overall) of 1995 NBA Draft.

COLLEGIATE RECORD

NOTES: Broke ankle (1993-94); granted extra year of eligibility.

Season Team	G	Min.	FGM	FGA	Pct.	FTM	FTA	Pct.	Reb.	Ast.	Pts.	AVERAGES RPG	APG	PPG
91-92—Virginia	33	1037	127	338	.376	72	105	.686	106	145	370	3.2	4.4	11.2
92-93—Virginia	31	1118	213	470	.453	93	132	.705	107	144	583	3.5	4.6	18.8
93-94—Virginia	1	11	0	4	.000	0	2	.000	1	2	0	1.0	2.0	0.0
94-95—Virginia	20	692	119	263	.452	61	87	.701	84	110	333	4.2	5.5	16.7
Totals	85	2858	459	1075	.427	226	326	.693	298	401	1286	3.5	4.7	15.1

Three-point field goals: 1991-92, 44-for-149 (.295). 1992-93, 64-for-174 (.368). 1993-94, 0-for-2. 1994-95, 34-for-97 (.351). Totals, 142-for-422 (.336).

NBA REGULAR-SEASON RECORD

Season Team	G	Min.	FGM	FGA	Pct.	FTM	FTA	Pct.	REBOUNDS Off.	Def.	Tot.	Ast.	St.	Blk.	TO	Pts.	AVERAGES RPG	APG	PPG
95-96—San Antonio	60	560	63	155	.406	16	25	.640	9	33	42	121	27	2	68	168	0.7	2.0	2.8

Three-point field goals: 1995-96, 26-for-66 (.394).
Personal fouls/disqualifications: 1995-96, 94/0.

NBA PLAYOFF RECORD

Season Team	G	Min.	FGM	FGA	Pct.	FTM	FTA	Pct.	REBOUNDS Off.	Def.	Tot.	Ast.	St.	Blk.	TO	Pts.	AVERAGES RPG	APG	PPG
95-96—San Antonio	9	70	10	24	.417	5	7	.714	4	5	9	9	2	0	6	26	1.0	1.0	2.9

Three-point field goals: 1995-96, 1-for-5 (.200).
Personal fouls/disqualifications: 1995-96, 8/0.

ALLEN, JEROME   G   PACERS

PERSONAL: Born January 28, 1973, in Philadelphia. ... 6-4/184. ... Full name: Jerome Byron Allen.
HIGH SCHOOL: Episcopal Academy (Merion Station, Pa.).
COLLEGE: Pennsylvania.
TRANSACTIONS/CAREER NOTES: Selected by Minnesota Timberwolves in second round (49th pick overall) of 1995 NBA Draft. ... Rights renounced by Timberwolves (July 25, 1996). ... Signed as free agent by Indiana Pacers (August 17, 1996).

COLLEGIATE RECORD

Season Team	G	Min.	FGM	FGA	Pct.	FTM	FTA	Pct.	Reb.	Ast.	Pts.	AVERAGES RPG	APG	PPG
91-92—Pennsylvania	26	795	108	263	.411	65	95	.684	93	82	318	3.6	3.2	12.2
92-93—Pennsylvania	27	912	129	305	.423	46	69	.667	128	133	354	4.7	4.9	13.1
93-94—Pennsylvania	28	929	124	309	.401	107	136	.787	127	130	405	4.5	4.6	14.5
94-95—Pennsylvania	28	934	143	333	.429	84	118	.712	134	160	411	4.8	5.7	14.7
Totals	109	3570	504	1210	.417	302	418	.722	482	505	1488	4.4	4.6	13.7

Three-point field goals: 1991-92, 37-for-117 (.316). 1992-93, 50-for-127 (.394). 1993-94, 50-for-146 (.342). 1994-95, 41-for-129 (.318). Totals, 178-for-519 (.343).

NBA REGULAR-SEASON RECORD

Season Team	G	Min.	FGM	FGA	Pct.	FTM	FTA	Pct.	REBOUNDS Off.	Def.	Tot.	Ast.	St.	Blk.	TO	Pts.	AVERAGES RPG	APG	PPG
95-96—Minnesota	41	362	36	105	.343	26	36	.722	5	20	25	49	21	5	34	108	0.6	1.2	2.6

Three-point field goals: 1995-96, 10-for-33 (.303).
Personal fouls/disqualifications: 1995-96, 42/0.

ALSTON, DERRICK   F

PERSONAL: Born August 20, 1972, in Bronx, N.Y. ... 6-11/225. ... Full name: Derrick Samuel Alston.
HIGH SCHOOL: Hoboken (N.J.).
COLLEGE: Duquesne.
TRANSACTIONS/CAREER NOTES: Selected by Philadelphia 76ers in second round (33rd pick overall) of 1994 NBA Draft. ... Rights renounced by 76ers (July 31, 1996).

COLLEGIATE RECORD

Season Team	G	Min.	FGM	FGA	Pct.	FTM	FTA	Pct.	Reb.	Ast.	Pts.	AVERAGES RPG	APG	PPG
90-91—Duquesne	28	807	128	239	.536	61	102	.598	175	36	317	6.3	1.3	11.3

Season Team	G	Min.	FGM	FGA	Pct.	FTM	FTA	Pct.	Reb.	Ast.	Pts.	AVERAGES RPG	APG	PPG
91-92—Duquesne	28	918	154	277	.556	82	156	.526	225	43	390	8.0	1.5	13.9
92-93—Duquesne	28	960	214	380	.563	128	223	.574	261	30	557	9.3	1.1	19.9
93-94—Duquesne	30	1080	245	424	.578	149	248	.601	218	41	639	7.3	1.4	21.3
Totals	114	3765	741	1320	.561	420	729	.576	879	150	1903	7.7	1.3	16.7

Three-point field goals: 1991-92, 0-for-1. 1992-93, 1-for-1. 1993-94, 0-for-1. Totals, 1-for-3 (.333).

NBA REGULAR-SEASON RECORD

Season Team	G	Min.	FGM	FGA	Pct.	FTM	FTA	Pct.	REBOUNDS Off.	Def.	Tot.	Ast.	St.	Blk.	TO	Pts.	AVERAGES RPG	APG	PPG
94-95—Philadelphia	64	1032	120	258	.465	59	120	.492	98	121	219	33	39	35	53	299	3.4	0.5	4.7
95-96—Philadelphia	73	1614	198	387	.512	55	112	.491	127	175	302	61	56	52	59	452	4.1	0.8	6.2
Totals	137	2646	318	645	.493	114	232	.491	225	296	521	94	95	87	112	751	3.8	0.7	5.5

Three-point field goals: 1994-95, 0-for-4. 1995-96, 1-for-3 (.333). Totals, 1-for-7 (.143).
Personal fouls/disqualifications: 1994-95, 107/1. 1995-96, 191/1. Totals, 298/2.

AMAECHI, JOHN   F

PERSONAL: Born November 26, 1970, in Boston. ... 6-10/270. ... Name pronounced uh-MAY-chee.
HIGH SCHOOL: St. John's (Toledo, Ohio).
COLLEGE: Vanderbilt, then Penn State.
TRANSACTIONS/CAREER NOTES: Not drafted by an NBA franchise. ... Signed as free agent by Cleveland Cavaliers (October 5, 1995). ... Waived by Cavaliers (July 31, 1996).

COLLEGIATE RECORD

Season Team	G	Min.	FGM	FGA	Pct.	FTM	FTA	Pct.	Reb.	Ast.	Pts.	AVERAGES RPG	APG	PPG
90-91—Vanderbilt	24	311	26	57	.456	14	25	.560	65	6	66	2.7	0.3	2.8
91-92—Penn State						Did not play—transfer student.								
92-93—Penn State	27	897	114	241	.473	130	182	.714	206	20	373	7.6	0.7	13.8
93-94—Penn State	25	837	124	243	.510	171	245	.698	223	37	423	8.9	1.5	16.9
94-95—Penn State	32	1108	168	300	.560	176	260	.677	316	55	514	9.9	1.7	16.1
Totals	108	3153	432	841	.514	491	712	.690	810	118	1376	7.5	1.1	12.7

Three-point field goals: 1992-93, 15-for-48 (.313). 1993-94, 4-for-15 (.267). 1994-95, 2-for-6 (.333). Totals, 21-for-69 (.304).

NBA REGULAR-SEASON RECORD

Season Team	G	Min.	FGM	FGA	Pct.	FTM	FTA	Pct.	REBOUNDS Off.	Def.	Tot.	Ast.	St.	Blk.	TO	Pts.	AVERAGES RPG	APG	PPG
95-96—Cleveland	28	357	29	70	.414	19	33	.576	13	39	52	9	6	11	34	77	1.9	0.3	2.8

Personal fouls/disqualifications: 1995-96, 49/1.

NBA PLAYOFF RECORD

Season Team	G	Min.	FGM	FGA	Pct.	FTM	FTA	Pct.	REBOUNDS Off.	Def.	Tot.	Ast.	St.	Blk.	TO	Pts.	AVERAGES RPG	APG	PPG
95-96—Cleveland	1	2	0	1	.000	0	0	...	0	0	0	0	0	0	0	0	0.0	0.0	0.0

AMAYA, ASHRAF   F   BULLETS

PERSONAL: Born November 23, 1971, in Oak Park, Ill. ... 6-8/230. ... Name pronounced AHSH-rahf uh-MY-ah.
HIGH SCHOOL: Walter Lutheran (Melrose Park, Ill.).
COLLEGE: Southern Illinois.
TRANSACTIONS/CAREER NOTES: Not drafted by an NBA franchise. ... Signed as free agent by Houston Rockets (October 7, 1993). ... Waived by Rockets (November 2, 1993). ... Played in Continental Basketball Association with Fort Wayne Fury (1993-94) and Quad City Thunder (1993-94). ... Signed as free agent by Vancouver Grizzlies (October 5, 1995). ... Rights renounced by Grizzlies (July 16, 1996). ... Signed as free agent by Washington Bullets (September 4, 1996).

COLLEGIATE RECORD

Season Team	G	Min.	FGM	FGA	Pct.	FTM	FTA	Pct.	Reb.	Ast.	Pts.	AVERAGES RPG	APG	PPG
89-90—Southern Illinois	33	802	89	149	.597	67	116	.578	209	4	245	6.3	0.1	7.4
90-91—Southern Illinois	32	1081	188	313	.601	115	191	.602	266	13	491	8.3	0.4	15.3
91-92—Southern Illinois	30	1117	207	361	.573	165	229	.721	308	30	583	10.3	1.0	19.4
92-93—Southern Illinois	33	1116	198	378	.524	142	206	.689	354	18	545	10.7	0.5	16.5
Totals	128	4116	682	1201	.568	489	742	.659	1137	65	1864	8.9	0.5	14.6

Three-point field goals: 1990-91, 0-for-1. 1991-92, 4-for-19 (.211). 1992-93, 7-for-26 (.269). Totals, 11-for-46 (.239).

CBA REGULAR-SEASON RECORD

Season Team	G	Min.	FGM	FGA	Pct.	FTM	FTA	Pct.	Reb.	Ast.	Pts.	AVERAGES RPG	APG	PPG
93-94—Q.C.-Ft. Wayne	18	415	46	102	.451	30	47	.638	110	6	123	6.1	0.3	6.8

Three-point field goals: 1993-94, 1-for-1.

NBA REGULAR-SEASON RECORD

Season Team	G	Min.	FGM	FGA	Pct.	FTM	FTA	Pct.	REBOUNDS Off.	Def.	Tot.	Ast.	St.	Blk.	TO	Pts.	AVERAGES RPG	APG	PPG
95-96—Vancouver	54	1104	121	252	.480	97	149	.651	114	189	303	33	22	10	57	339	5.6	0.6	6.3

Three-point field goals: 1995-96, 0-for-1.
Personal fouls/disqualifications: 1995-96, 151/3.

A

ANDERSON, GREG   F/C   SPURS

PERSONAL: Born June 22, 1964, in Houston. ... 6-10/250. ... Full name: Gregory Wayne Anderson. ... Nickname: Cadillac.
HIGH SCHOOL: E.E. Worthing (Houston).
COLLEGE: Houston.
TRANSACTIONS/CAREER NOTES: Selected by San Antonio Spurs in first round (23rd pick overall) of 1987 NBA Draft. ... Traded by Spurs with G Alvin Robertson and future considerations to Milwaukee Bucks for F Terry Cummings and future considerations (May 28, 1989). ... Traded by Bucks to New Jersey Nets for G Lester Conner (January 11, 1991). ... Traded by Nets to Denver Nuggets in three-way deal in which Nuggets sent F Terry Mills to Nets and G Walter Davis to Portland Trail Blazers, and Trail Blazers sent G Drazen Petrovic to Nets (January 23, 1991); Nuggets also received 1992 first-round draft choice from Nets and 1993 second-round draft choice from Trail Blazers, and Trail Blazers also received 1992 second-round draft choice from Nuggets. ... Rights renounced by Nuggets (October 5, 1992). ... Played in Italy (1992-93). ... Signed as free agent by Detroit Pistons (September 8, 1993). ... Rights renounced by Pistons (September 29, 1994). ... Signed as free agent by Atlanta Hawks (December 15, 1994). ... Signed as unrestricted free agent by Spurs (September 29, 1995).

COLLEGIATE RECORD

Season Team	G	Min.	FGM	FGA	Pct.	FTM	FTA	Pct.	Reb.	Ast.	Pts.	RPG	APG	PPG
83-84—Houston	35	414	49	101	.485	19	36	.528	123	2	117	3.5	0.1	3.3
84-85—Houston	30	931	197	344	.573	69	129	.535	244	20	463	8.1	0.7	15.4
85-86—Houston	28	1055	215	376	.572	106	181	.586	360	19	536	12.9	0.7	19.1
86-87—Houston	30	1057	215	409	.526	116	192	.604	318	18	546	10.6	0.6	18.2
Totals	123	3457	676	1230	.550	310	538	.576	1045	59	1662	8.5	0.5	13.5

HONORS: NBA All-Rookie team (1988).

NBA REGULAR-SEASON RECORD

Season Team	G	Min.	FGM	FGA	Pct.	FTM	FTA	Pct.	Off.	Def.	Tot.	Ast.	St.	Blk.	TO	Pts.	RPG	APG	PPG
87-88—San Antonio	82	1984	379	756	.501	198	328	.604	161	352	513	79	54	122	143	957	6.3	1.0	11.7
88-89—San Antonio	82	2401	460	914	.503	207	403	.514	255	421	676	61	102	103	180	1127	8.2	0.7	13.7
89-90—Milwaukee	60	1291	219	432	.507	91	170	.535	112	261	373	24	32	54	80	529	6.2	0.4	8.8
90-91—Mil-NJ-Den	68	924	116	270	.430	60	115	.522	97	221	318	16	35	45	84	292	4.7	0.2	4.3
91-92—Denver	82	2793	389	854	.456	167	268	.623	337	604	941	78	88	65	201	945	11.5	1.0	11.5
93-94—Detroit	77	1624	201	370	.543	88	154	.571	183	388	571	51	55	68	94	491	7.4	0.7	6.4
94-95—Atlanta	51	622	57	104	.548	34	71	.479	62	126	188	17	23	32	32	148	3.7	0.3	2.9
95-96—San Antonio	46	344	24	47	.511	6	25	.240	29	71	100	10	9	24	22	54	2.2	0.2	1.2
Totals	548	11983	1845	3747	.492	851	1534	.555	1236	2444	3680	336	398	513	836	4543	6.7	0.6	8.3

Three-point field goals: 1987-88, 1-for-5 (.200). 1988-89, 0-for-3. 1990-91, 0-for-1. 1991-92, 0-for-4. 1993-94, 1-for-3 (.333). 1995-96, 0-for-1. Totals, 2-for-17 (.118).

Personal fouls/disqualifications: 1987-88, 228/1. 1988-89, 221/2. 1989-90, 176/3. 1990-91, 140/3. 1991-92, 263/3. 1993-94, 234/4. 1994-95, 103/0. 1995-96, 66/0. Totals, 1431/16.

NBA PLAYOFF RECORD

Season Team	G	Min.	FGM	FGA	Pct.	FTM	FTA	Pct.	Off.	Def.	Tot.	Ast.	St.	Blk.	TO	Pts.	RPG	APG	PPG
87-88—San Antonio	3	95	17	36	.472	4	9	.444	6	15	21	3	2	4	10	38	7.0	1.0	12.7
89-90—Milwaukee	4	101	13	19	.684	7	14	.500	6	18	24	0	1	4	4	33	6.0	0.0	8.3
94-95—Atlanta	3	39	1	5	.200	3	4	.750	1	12	13	2	2	2	0	5	4.3	0.7	1.7
95-96—San Antonio	6	34	0	5	.000	1	2	.500	2	7	9	0	2	1	4	1	1.5	0.0	0.2
Totals	16	269	31	65	.477	15	29	.517	15	52	67	5	7	11	18	77	4.2	0.3	4.8

Personal fouls/disqualifications: 1987-88, 10/1. 1989-90, 19/2. 1994-95, 9/0. 1995-96, 5/0. Totals, 43/3.

ITALIAN LEAGUE RECORD

Season Team	G	Min.	FGM	FGA	Pct.	FTM	FTA	Pct.	Reb.	Ast.	Pts.	RPG	APG	PPG
92-93—Phonola Caserta	28	949	175	324	.540	97	143	.678	381	6	447	13.6	0.2	16.0

ANDERSON, KENNY   G   TRAIL BLAZERS

PERSONAL: Born October 9, 1970, in Queens, N.Y. ... 6-1/168. ... Full name: Kenneth Anderson.
HIGH SCHOOL: Archbishop Molloy (Queens, N.Y.).
COLLEGE: Georgia Tech.
TRANSACTIONS/CAREER NOTES: Selected after sophomore season by New Jersey Nets in first round (second pick overall) of 1991 NBA Draft. ... Traded by Nets with G/F Gerald Glass to Charlotte Hornets for G Kendall Gill and G Khalid Reeves (January 19, 1996). ... Signed as free agent by Portland Trail Blazers (July 23, 1996).
MISCELLANEOUS: New Jersey Nets all-time assists leader with 2,363 (1991-92 through 1995-96).

COLLEGIATE RECORD

NOTES: THE SPORTING NEWS All-America second team (1990, 1991).

Season Team	G	Min.	FGM	FGA	Pct.	FTM	FTA	Pct.	Reb.	Ast.	Pts.	RPG	APG	PPG
89-90—Georgia Tech	35	1321	283	549	.515	107	146	.733	193	285	721	5.5	8.1	20.6
90-91—Georgia Tech	30	1167	278	636	.437	155	187	.829	171	169	776	5.7	5.6	25.9
Totals	65	2488	561	1185	.473	262	333	.787	364	454	1497	5.6	7.0	23.0

Three-point field goals: 1989-90, 48-for-117 (.410). 1990-91, 65-for-185 (.351). Totals, 113-for-302 (.374).

NBA REGULAR-SEASON RECORD

Season Team	G	Min.	FGM	FGA	Pct.	FTM	FTA	Pct.	Off.	Def.	Tot.	Ast.	St.	Blk.	TO	Pts.	RPG	APG	PPG
91-92—New Jersey	64	1086	187	480	.390	73	98	.745	38	89	127	203	67	9	97	450	2.0	3.2	7.0

– 8 –

Season Team	G	Min.	FGM	FGA	Pct.	FTM	FTA	Pct.	Off.	Def.	Tot.	Ast.	St.	Blk.	TO	Pts.	RPG	APG	PPG
92-93—New Jersey.....	55	2010	370	850	.435	180	232	.776	51	175	226	449	96	11	153	927	4.1	8.2	16.9
93-94—New Jersey.....	82	3135	576	1381	.417	346	423	.818	89	233	322	784	158	15	266	1538	3.9	9.6	18.8
94-95—New Jersey.....	72	2689	411	1031	.399	348	414	.841	73	177	250	680	103	14	225	1267	3.5	9.4	17.6
95-96—N.J.-Char........	69	2344	349	834	.418	260	338	.769	63	140	203	575	111	14	146	1050	2.9	8.3	15.2
Totals	342	11264	1893	4576	.414	1207	1505	.802	314	814	1128	2691	535	63	887	5232	3.3	7.9	15.3

Three-point field goals: 1991-92, 3-for-13 (.231). 1992-93, 7-for-25 (.280). 1993-94, 40-for-132 (.303). 1994-95, 97-for-294 (.330). 1995-96, 92-for-256 (.359). Totals, 239-for-720 (.332).

Personal fouls/disqualifications: 1991-92, 68/0. 1992-93, 140/1. 1993-94, 201/0. 1994-95, 184/1. 1995-96, 178/1. Totals, 771/3.

NBA PLAYOFF RECORD

Season Team	G	Min.	FGM	FGA	Pct.	FTM	FTA	Pct.	Off.	Def.	Tot.	Ast.	St.	Blk.	TO	Pts.	RPG	APG	PPG
91-92—New Jersey.....	3	24	3	9	.333	2	2	1.000	1	2	3	3	1	0	1	8	1.0	1.0	2.7
93-94—New Jersey.....	4	181	19	54	.352	22	33	.667	2	10	12	27	9	0	9	63	3.0	6.8	15.8
Totals	7	205	22	63	.349	24	35	.686	3	12	15	30	10	0	10	71	2.1	4.3	10.1

Three-point field goals: 1993-94, 3-for-10 (.300).

Personal fouls/disqualifications: 1991-92, 1/0. 1993-94, 11/0. Totals, 12/0.

NBA ALL-STAR GAME RECORD

Season Team	Min.	FGM	FGA	Pct.	FTM	FTA	Pct.	Off.	Def.	Tot.	Ast.	PF	Dq.	St.	Blk.	TO	Pts.
1994 —New Jersey........	16	3	10	.300	0	0	...	1	3	4	3	2	0	0	0	4	6

Three-point field goals: 1994, 0-for-1.

ANDERSON, NICK — G — MAGIC

PERSONAL: Born January 20, 1968, in Chicago. ... 6-6/228. ... Full name: Nelison Anderson.

HIGH SCHOOL: Prosser Vocational (Chicago), then Neal F. Simeon (Chicago).

COLLEGE: Illinois.

TRANSACTIONS/CAREER NOTES: Selected after junior season by Orlando Magic in first round (11th pick overall) of 1989 NBA Draft.

MISCELLANEOUS: Orlando Magic all-time leading scorer with 8,302 points and all-time steals leader with 748 (1989-90 through 1995-96).

COLLEGIATE RECORD

Season Team	G	Min.	FGM	FGA	Pct.	FTM	FTA	Pct.	Reb.	Ast.	Pts.	RPG	APG	PPG
86-87—Illinois						Did not play—ineligible.								
87-88—Illinois	33	909	223	390	.572	77	120	.642	217	53	525	6.6	1.6	15.9
88-89—Illinois	36	1125	262	487	.538	99	148	.669	285	72	647	7.9	2.0	18.0
Totals	69	2034	485	877	.553	176	268	.657	502	125	1172	7.3	1.8	17.0

Three-point field goals: 1987-88, 2-for-6 (.333). 1988-89, 24-for-66 (.364). Totals, 26-for-72 (.361).

NBA REGULAR-SEASON RECORD

Season Team	G	Min.	FGM	FGA	Pct.	FTM	FTA	Pct.	Off.	Def.	Tot.	Ast.	St.	Blk.	TO	Pts.	RPG	APG	PPG
89-90—Orlando...........	81	1785	372	753	.494	186	264	.705	107	209	316	124	69	34	138	931	3.9	1.5	11.5
90-91—Orlando...........	70	1971	400	857	.467	173	259	.668	92	294	386	106	74	44	113	990	5.5	1.5	14.1
91-92—Orlando...........	60	2203	482	1042	.463	202	303	.667	98	286	384	163	97	33	125	1196	6.4	2.7	19.9
92-93—Orlando...........	79	2920	594	1324	.449	298	402	.741	122	355	477	265	128	56	164	1574	6.0	3.4	19.9
93-94—Orlando...........	81	2811	504	1054	.478	168	250	.672	113	363	476	294	134	33	165	1277	5.9	3.6	15.8
94-95—Orlando...........	76	2588	439	923	.476	143	203	.704	85	250	335	314	125	22	141	1200	4.4	4.1	15.8
95-96—Orlando...........	77	2717	400	904	.442	166	240	.692	92	323	415	279	121	46	141	1134	5.4	3.6	14.7
Totals	524	16995	3191	6857	.465	1336	1921	.695	709	2080	2789	1545	748	268	987	8302	5.3	2.9	15.8

Three-point field goals: 1989-90, 1-for-17 (.059). 1990-91, 17-for-58 (.293). 1991-92, 30-for-85 (.353). 1992-93, 88-for-249 (.353). 1993-94, 101-for-314 (.322). 1994-95, 179-for-431 (.415). 1995-96, 168-for-430 (.391). Totals, 584-for-1584 (.369).

Personal fouls/disqualifications: 1989-90, 140/0. 1990-91, 145/0. 1991-92, 132/0. 1992-93, 200/1. 1993-94, 148/1. 1994-95, 124/0. 1995-96, 135/0. Totals, 1024/2.

NBA PLAYOFF RECORD

NOTES: Holds NBA Finals single-game record for most three-point field goals attempted—12 (June 11, 1995, at Houston).

Season Team	G	Min.	FGM	FGA	Pct.	FTM	FTA	Pct.	Off.	Def.	Tot.	Ast.	St.	Blk.	TO	Pts.	RPG	APG	PPG
93-94—Orlando...........	3	120	13	34	.382	9	12	.750	2	8	10	10	5	2	5	43	3.3	3.3	14.3
94-95—Orlando...........	21	814	107	239	.448	43	63	.683	21	79	100	65	33	10	30	298	4.8	3.1	14.2
95-96—Orlando...........	11	418	55	127	.433	28	45	.622	16	39	55	21	21	5	21	156	5.0	1.9	14.2
Totals	35	1352	175	400	.438	80	120	.667	39	126	165	96	59	17	56	497	4.7	2.7	14.2

Three-point field goals: 1993-94, 8-for-20 (.400). 1994-95, 41-for-107 (.383). 1995-96, 18-for-63 (.286). Totals, 67-for-190 (.353).

Personal fouls/disqualifications: 1993-94, 8/0. 1994-95, 49/0. 1995-96, 22/0. Totals, 79/0.

ANDERSON, WILLIE — G

PERSONAL: Born January 8, 1967, in Greenville, S.C. ... 6-8/200. ... Full name: Willie Lloyd Anderson. ... Brother of Shandon Anderson, guard/forward with Utah Jazz.

HIGH SCHOOL: East Atlanta.

COLLEGE: Georgia.

TRANSACTIONS/CAREER NOTES: Selected by San Antonio Spurs in first round (10th pick overall) of 1988 NBA Draft. ... Selected by Toronto Raptors from Spurs in NBA expansion draft (June 24, 1995). ... Traded by Raptors with F/C Victor Alexander to New York Knicks for G/F Doug Christie, C/F Herb Williams and cash (February 18, 1996). ... Rights renounced by Knicks (July 14, 1996).

MISCELLANEOUS: Member of bronze-medal-winning U.S. Olympic team (1988).

A

COLLEGIATE RECORD

Season Team	G	Min.	FGM	FGA	Pct.	FTM	FTA	Pct.	Reb.	Ast.	Pts.	RPG	APG	PPG
												AVERAGES		
84-85—Georgia	13	80	19	39	.487	5	8	.625	19	4	43	1.5	0.3	3.3
85-86—Georgia	29	493	99	197	.503	48	61	.787	98	141	246	3.4	4.9	8.5
86-87—Georgia	30	1047	187	374	.500	77	97	.794	123	150	476	4.1	5.0	15.9
87-88—Georgia	35	1161	241	482	.500	91	116	.784	177	139	583	5.1	4.0	16.7
Totals	107	2781	546	1092	.500	221	282	.784	417	434	1348	3.9	4.1	12.6

Three-point field goals: 1986-87, 25-for-64 (.391). 1987-88, 10-for-44 (.227). Totals, 35-for-108 (.324).

NBA REGULAR-SEASON RECORD

HONORS: NBA All-Rookie first team (1989).

Season Team	G	Min.	FGM	FGA	Pct.	FTM	FTA	Pct.	Off.	Def.	Tot.	Ast.	St.	Blk.	TO	Pts.	RPG	APG	PPG
									REBOUNDS								AVERAGES		
88-89—San Antonio	81	2738	640	1285	.498	224	289	.775	152	265	417	372	150	62	261	1508	5.1	4.6	18.6
89-90—San Antonio	82	2788	532	1082	.492	217	290	.748	115	257	372	364	111	58	198	1288	4.5	4.4	15.7
90-91—San Antonio	75	2592	453	991	.457	170	213	.798	68	283	351	358	79	46	167	1083	4.7	4.8	14.4
91-92—San Antonio	57	1889	312	685	.455	107	138	.775	62	238	300	302	54	51	140	744	5.3	5.3	13.1
92-93—San Antonio	38	560	80	186	.430	22	28	.786	7	50	57	79	14	6	44	183	1.5	2.1	4.8
93-94—San Antonio	80	2488	394	837	.471	145	171	.848	68	174	242	347	71	46	153	955	3.0	4.3	11.9
94-95—San Antonio	38	556	76	162	.469	30	41	.732	15	40	55	52	26	10	38	185	1.4	1.4	4.9
95-96—Tor.-N.Y.	76	2060	288	660	.436	132	163	.810	48	198	246	197	75	59	143	742	3.2	2.6	9.8
Totals	527	15671	2775	5888	.471	1047	1333	.785	535	1505	2040	2071	580	338	1144	6688	3.9	3.9	12.7

Three-point field goals: 1988-89, 4-for-21 (.190). 1989-90, 7-for-26 (.269). 1990-91, 7-for-35 (.200). 1991-92, 13-for-56 (.232). 1992-93, 1-for-8 (.125). 1993-94, 22-for-68 (.324). 1994-95, 3-for-19 (.158). 1995-96, 34-for-120 (.283). Totals, 91-for-353 (.258).

Personal fouls/disqualifications: 1988-89, 295/8. 1989-90, 252/3. 1990-91, 226/4. 1991-92, 151/2. 1992-93, 52/0. 1993-94, 187/1. 1994-95, 71/1. 1995-96, 230/5. Totals, 1464/24.

NBA PLAYOFF RECORD

Season Team	G	Min.	FGM	FGA	Pct.	FTM	FTA	Pct.	Off.	Def.	Tot.	Ast.	St.	Blk.	TO	Pts.	RPG	APG	PPG
									REBOUNDS								AVERAGES		
89-90—San Antonio	10	375	87	168	.518	29	36	.806	16	38	54	52	9	4	26	205	5.4	5.2	20.5
90-91—San Antonio	4	159	33	68	.485	8	13	.615	2	17	19	19	6	2	13	76	4.8	4.8	19.0
92-93—San Antonio	10	219	37	82	.451	15	17	.882	4	19	23	28	9	2	12	95	2.3	2.8	9.5
93-94—San Antonio	4	106	14	37	.378	4	7	.571	3	5	8	12	5	2	4	33	2.0	3.0	8.3
94-95—San Antonio	11	97	9	20	.450	2	3	.667	5	7	12	10	5	0	8	20	1.1	0.9	1.8
95-96—New York	4	64	7	22	.318	6	7	.857	2	7	9	1	4	0	6	21	2.3	0.3	5.3
Totals	43	1020	187	397	.471	64	83	.771	32	93	125	122	38	10	69	450	2.9	2.8	10.5

Three-point field goals: 1989-90, 2-for-5 (.400). 1990-91, 2-for-10 (.200). 1992-93, 6-for-11 (.545). 1993-94, 1-for-1. 1994-95, 0-for-1. 1995-96, 1-for-6 (.167). Totals, 12-for-34 (.353).

Personal fouls/disqualifications: 1989-90, 40/2. 1990-91, 16/0. 1992-93, 23/0. 1993-94, 7/0. 1994-95, 12/0. 1995-96, 10/0. Totals, 108/2.

ANTHONY, GREG   G   GRIZZLIES

PERSONAL: Born November 15, 1967, in Las Vegas. ... 6-1/176. ... Full name: Gregory C. Anthony.
HIGH SCHOOL: Rancho (North Las Vegas).
COLLEGE: Portland, then UNLV.
TRANSACTIONS/CAREER NOTES: Selected by New York Knicks in first round (12th pick overall) of 1991 NBA Draft. ... Selected by Vancouver Grizzlies from Knicks in NBA expansion draft (June 24, 1995).
MISCELLANEOUS: Vancouver Grizzlies all-time assists leader with 476 (1995-96).

COLLEGIATE RECORD

NOTES: Member of NCAA Division I championship team (1990).

Season Team	G	Min.	FGM	FGA	Pct.	FTM	FTA	Pct.	Reb.	Ast.	Pts.	RPG	APG	PPG
												AVERAGES		
86-87—Portland	28	923	147	369	.398	100	144	.694	121	112	429	4.3	4.0	15.3
87-88—UNLV						Did not play—transfer student.								
88-89—UNLV	36	1025	155	350	.443	107	153	.699	102	239	464	2.8	6.6	12.9
89-90—UNLV	39	1160	145	317	.457	101	148	.682	116	289	436	3.0	7.4	11.2
90-91—UNLV	35	1100	141	309	.456	79	102	.775	89	310	406	2.5	8.9	11.6
Totals	138	4208	588	1345	.437	387	547	.707	428	950	1735	3.1	6.9	12.6

Three-point field goals: 1986-87, 35-for-95 (.368). 1988-89, 47-for-125 (.376). 1989-90, 45-for-120 (.375). 1990-91, 45-for-114 (.395). Totals, 172-for-454 (.379).

NBA REGULAR-SEASON RECORD

Season Team	G	Min.	FGM	FGA	Pct.	FTM	FTA	Pct.	Off.	Def.	Tot.	Ast.	St.	Blk.	TO	Pts.	RPG	APG	PPG
									REBOUNDS								AVERAGES		
91-92—New York	82	1510	161	435	.370	117	158	.741	33	103	136	314	59	9	98	447	1.7	3.8	5.5
92-93—New York	70	1699	174	419	.415	107	159	.673	42	128	170	398	113	12	104	459	2.4	5.7	6.6
93-94—New York	80	1994	225	571	.394	130	168	.774	43	146	189	365	114	13	127	628	2.4	4.6	7.9
94-95—New York	61	943	128	293	.437	60	76	.789	7	57	64	160	50	7	57	372	1.0	2.6	6.1
95-96—Vancouver	69	2096	324	781	.415	229	297	.771	29	145	174	476	116	11	160	967	2.5	6.9	14.0
Totals	362	8242	1012	2499	.405	643	858	.749	154	579	733	1713	452	52	546	2873	2.0	4.7	7.9

Three-point field goals: 1991-92, 8-for-55 (.145). 1992-93, 4-for-30 (.133). 1993-94, 48-for-160 (.300). 1994-95, 56-for-155 (.361). 1995-96, 90-for-271 (.332). Totals, 206-for-671 (.307).

Personal fouls/disqualifications: 1991-92, 170/0. 1992-93, 141/0. 1993-94, 163/1. 1994-95, 99/1. 1995-96, 137/1. Totals, 710/3.

NBA PLAYOFF RECORD

Season Team	G	Min.	FGM	FGA	Pct.	FTM	FTA	Pct.	Off.	Def.	Tot.	Ast.	St.	Blk.	TO	Pts.	RPG	APG	PPG
									REBOUNDS								AVERAGES		
91-92—New York	12	213	19	46	.413	20	33	.606	4	13	17	41	16	1	13	63	1.4	3.4	5.3

Season Team	G	Min.	FGM	FGA	Pct.	FTM	FTA	Pct.	Off.	Def.	Tot.	Ast.	St.	Blk.	TO	Pts.	RPG	APG	PPG
									REBOUNDS								AVERAGES		
92-93—New York	15	240	24	60	.400	8	14	.571	4	26	30	52	13	1	11	59	2.0	3.5	3.9
93-94—New York	25	436	45	128	.352	14	24	.583	9	18	27	59	19	8	31	122	1.1	2.4	4.9
94-95—New York	11	135	15	38	.395	10	11	.909	2	8	10	15	2	2	6	47	0.9	1.4	4.3
Totals	63	1024	103	272	.379	52	82	.634	19	65	84	167	50	12	61	291	1.3	2.7	4.6

Three-point field goals: 1991-92, 5-for-12 (.417). 1992-93, 3-for-14 (.214). 1993-94, 18-for-61 (.295). 1994-95, 7-for-23 (.304). Totals, 33-for-110 (.300).

Personal fouls/disqualifications: 1991-92, 28/0. 1992-93, 26/0. 1993-94, 55/0. 1994-95, 27/0. Totals, 136/0.

ARMSTRONG, B.J. G WARRIORS

PERSONAL: Born September 9, 1967, in Detroit. ... 6-2/185. ... Full name: Benjamin Roy Armstrong Jr.
HIGH SCHOOL: Brother Rice (Birmingham, Mich.).
COLLEGE: Iowa.
TRANSACTIONS/CAREER NOTES: Selected by Chicago Bulls in first round (18th pick overall) of 1989 NBA Draft. ... Selected by Toronto Raptors from Bulls in NBA expansion draft (June 24, 1995). ... Traded by Raptors to Golden State Warriors for C Victor Alexander, F/C Carlos Rogers and draft rights to F Dwayne Whitfield, F Martin Lewis and C Michael McDonald (September 18, 1995).
MISCELLANEOUS: Member of NBA championship teams (1991, 1992, 1993).

COLLEGIATE RECORD

Season Team	G	Min.	FGM	FGA	Pct.	FTM	FTA	Pct.	Reb.	Ast.	Pts.	RPG	APG	PPG
												AVERAGES		
85-86—Iowa	29	232	32	66	.485	19	21	.905	16	41	83	0.6	1.4	2.9
86-87—Iowa	35	995	153	295	.519	100	126	.794	89	148	434	2.5	4.2	12.4
87-88—Iowa	34	1023	203	421	.482	124	146	.849	74	155	592	2.2	4.6	17.4
88-89—Iowa	32	1015	195	403	.484	160	192	.833	79	173	596	2.5	5.4	18.6
Totals	130	3265	583	1185	.492	403	485	.831	258	517	1705	2.0	4.0	13.1

Three-point field goals: 1986-87, 28-for-54 (.519). 1987-88, 62-for-137 (.453). 1988-89, 46-for-116 (.397). Totals, 136-for-307 (.443).

NBA REGULAR-SEASON RECORD

NOTES: Led NBA with .453 three-point field-goal percentage (1993).

Season Team	G	Min.	FGM	FGA	Pct.	FTM	FTA	Pct.	Off.	Def.	Tot.	Ast.	St.	Blk.	TO	Pts.	RPG	APG	PPG
									REBOUNDS								AVERAGES		
89-90—Chicago	81	1291	190	392	.485	69	78	.885	19	83	102	199	46	6	83	452	1.3	2.5	5.6
90-91—Chicago	82	1731	304	632	.481	97	111	.874	25	124	149	301	70	4	107	720	1.8	3.7	8.8
91-92—Chicago	82	1875	335	697	.481	104	129	.806	19	126	145	266	46	5	94	809	1.8	3.2	9.9
92-93—Chicago	82	2492	408	818	.499	130	151	.861	27	122	149	330	66	6	83	1009	1.8	4.0	12.3
93-94—Chicago	82	2770	479	1007	.476	194	227	.855	28	142	170	323	80	9	131	1212	2.1	3.9	14.8
94-95—Chicago	82	2577	418	894	.468	206	233	.884	25	161	186	244	84	8	103	1150	2.3	3.0	14.0
95-96—Golden State	82	2262	340	727	.468	234	279	.839	22	162	184	401	68	6	128	1012	2.2	4.9	12.3
Totals	573	14998	2474	5167	.479	1034	1208	.856	165	920	1085	2064	460	44	729	6364	1.9	3.6	11.1

Three-point field goals: 1989-90, 3-for-6 (.500). 1990-91, 15-for-30 (.500). 1991-92, 35-for-87 (.402). 1992-93, 63-for-139 (.453). 1993-94, 60-for-135 (.444). 1994-95, 108-for-253 (.427). 1995-96, 98-for-207 (.473). Totals, 382-for-857 (.446).

Personal fouls/disqualifications: 1989-90, 105/0. 1990-91, 118/0. 1991-92, 88/0. 1992-93, 169/0. 1993-94, 147/1. 1994-95, 159/0. 1995-96, 147/0. Totals, 933/1.

NBA PLAYOFF RECORD

Season Team	G	Min.	FGM	FGA	Pct.	FTM	FTA	Pct.	Off.	Def.	Tot.	Ast.	St.	Blk.	TO	Pts.	RPG	APG	PPG
									REBOUNDS								AVERAGES		
89-90—Chicago	16	217	21	62	.339	22	24	.917	3	17	20	29	10	0	12	64	1.3	1.8	4.0
90-91—Chicago	17	273	35	70	.500	20	25	.800	5	22	27	43	19	1	13	93	1.6	2.5	5.5
91-92—Chicago	22	434	63	139	.453	30	38	.789	2	22	24	47	14	0	18	161	1.1	2.1	7.3
92-93—Chicago	19	643	88	168	.524	20	22	.909	6	22	28	62	19	2	14	217	1.5	3.3	11.4
93-94—Chicago	10	360	55	106	.519	36	44	.818	2	22	24	25	8	0	9	153	2.4	2.5	15.3
94-95—Chicago	10	288	36	79	.456	18	22	.818	4	14	18	27	6	0	6	103	1.8	2.7	10.3
Totals	94	2215	298	624	.478	146	175	.834	22	119	141	233	76	3	72	791	1.5	2.5	8.4

Three-point field goals: 1989-90, 0-for-4. 1990-91, 3-for-5 (.600). 1991-92, 5-for-17 (.294). 1992-93, 21-for-41 (.512). 1993-94, 7-for-12 (.583). 1994-95, 13-for-29 (.448). Totals, 49-for-108 (.454).

Personal fouls/disqualifications: 1989-90, 22/0. 1990-91, 13/0. 1991-92, 33/0. 1992-93, 49/0. 1993-94, 21/0. 1994-95, 21/0. Totals, 159/0.

NBA ALL-STAR GAME RECORD

Season Team	Min.	FGM	FGA	Pct.	FTM	FTA	Pct.	Off.	Def.	Tot.	Ast.	PF	Dq.	St.	Blk.	TO	Pts.
								REBOUNDS									
1994 —Chicago	22	5	9	.556	0	0	...	1	0	1	4	1	0	0	0	1	11

Three-point field goals: 1994, 1-for-2 (.500).

ARMSTRONG, DARRELL G MAGIC

PERSONAL: Born June 22, 1968, in Gastonia, N.C. ... 6-1/180.
HIGH SCHOOL: Ashbrook (Gastonia, N.C.).
COLLEGE: Fayetteville State.
TRANSACTIONS/CAREER NOTES: Not drafted by an NBA franchise. ... Played in Global Basketball Association (1991-92). ... Played in United States Basketball League with Atlanta Trojans (1992 through 1994). ... Played in Global Basketball Association with South Georgia (1992-93). ... Played in Continental Basketball Association with Capital Region Pontiacs (1992-93). ... Played in Spain (1994-95). ... Signed by Orlando Magic for remainder of season (April 8, 1995).

COLLEGIATE RECORD

Season Team	G	Min.	FGM	FGA	Pct.	FTM	FTA	Pct.	Reb.	Ast.	Pts.	AVERAGES		
												RPG	APG	PPG
87-88—Fayetteville State							Did not play.							
88-89—Fayetteville State	27	662	131	255	.514	93	116	.802	80	58	369	3.0	2.1	13.7
89-90—Fayetteville State	27	800	125	235	.532	83	106	.783	140	125	350	5.2	4.6	13.0
90-91—Fayetteville State	24	643	117	233	.502	115	152	.757	86	113	393	3.6	4.7	16.4
Totals	78	2105	373	723	.516	291	374	.778	306	296	1112	3.9	3.8	14.3

Three-point field goals: 1988-89, 14-for-40 (.350). 1989-90, 17-for-40 (.425). 1990-91, 44-for-107 (.411). Totals, 75-for-187 (.401).

CBA REGULAR-SEASON RECORD

Season Team	G	Min.	FGM	FGA	Pct.	FTM	FTA	Pct.	Reb.	Ast.	Pts.	AVERAGES		
												RPG	APG	PPG
92-93—Capital Region	2	13	1	3	.333	0	0	...	1	1	2	0.5	0.5	1.0

Three-point field goals: 1992-93, 0-for-2.

NBA REGULAR-SEASON RECORD

Season Team	G	Min.	FGM	FGA	Pct.	FTM	FTA	Pct.	REBOUNDS			Ast.	St.	Blk.	TO	Pts.	AVERAGES		
									Off.	Def.	Tot.						RPG	APG	PPG
94-95—Orlando...........	3	8	3	8	.375	2	2	1.000	1	0	1	3	1	0	1	10	0.3	1.0	3.3
95-96—Orlando...........	13	41	16	32	.500	4	4	1.000	0	2	2	5	6	0	6	42	0.2	0.4	3.2
Totals	16	49	19	40	.475	6	6	1.000	1	2	3	8	7	0	7	52	0.2	0.5	3.3

Three-point field goals: 1994-95, 2-for-6 (.333). 1995-96, 6-for-12 (.500). Totals, 8-for-18 (.444).
Personal fouls/disqualifications: 1994-95, 3/0. 1995-96, 4/0. Totals, 7/0.

SPANISH LEAGUE RECORD

Season Team	G	Min.	FGM	FGA	Pct.	FTM	FTA	Pct.	Reb.	Ast.	Pts.	AVERAGES		
												RPG	APG	PPG
94-95—Coren Orense	38	1481	309	631	.490	176	293	.601	170	94	936	4.5	2.5	24.6

ASKEW, VINCENT ° G/F NETS

PERSONAL: Born February 28, 1966, in Memphis. ... 6-6/235. ... Full name: Vincent Jerome Askew.
HIGH SCHOOL: Frayser (Memphis).
COLLEGE: Memphis.
TRANSACTIONS/CAREER NOTES: Selected after junior season by Philadelphia 76ers in second round (39th pick overall) of 1987 NBA Draft. ... Waived by 76ers (December 22, 1987). ... Played in Continental Basketball Association with Savannah Spirits (1987-88) and Albany Patroons (1988-89 through 1990-91). ... Signed as free agent by Washington Bullets (September 23, 1988). ... Waived by Bullets (October 12, 1988). ... Played in Italy (1988-89 and 1992-93). ... Played in World Basketball League with Memphis Rockers (1990). ... Signed as free agent by Golden State Warriors (April 6, 1991). ... Signed as free agent by Sacramento Kings (October 2, 1992). ... Traded by Kings to Seattle SuperSonics for 1993 conditional second-round draft choice (November 25, 1992). ... Traded by SuperSonics to New Jersey Nets for G Greg Graham (July 16, 1996).

COLLEGIATE RECORD

Season Team	G	Min.	FGM	FGA	Pct.	FTM	FTA	Pct.	Reb.	Ast.	Pts.	AVERAGES		
												RPG	APG	PPG
84-85—Memphis	35	1177	115	225	.511	59	93	.634	117	170	289	3.3	4.9	8.3
85-86—Memphis	34	1094	150	306	.490	70	86	.814	228	99	370	6.7	2.9	10.9
86-87—Memphis	34	1164	187	387	.483	122	155	.787	170	129	512	5.0	3.8	15.1
Totals	103	3435	452	918	.492	251	334	.751	515	398	1171	5.0	3.9	11.4

Three-point field goals: 1986-87, 16-for-42 (.381).

CBA REGULAR-SEASON RECORD

NOTES: CBA Most Valuable Player (1990, 1991). ... CBA All-League first team (1990, 1991). ... CBA All-Defensive team (1991).

Season Team	G	Min.	FGM	FGA	Pct.	FTM	FTA	Pct.	Reb.	Ast.	Pts.	AVERAGES		
												RPG	APG	PPG
87-88—Savannah	5	35	5	10	.500	0	0	...	4	0	10	0.8	0.0	2.0
88-89—Albany	29	989	196	372	.527	152	225	.676	267	76	544	9.2	2.6	18.8
89-90—Albany	56	2271	590	1143	.516	301	402	.749	435	247	*1484	7.8	4.4	26.5
90-91—Albany	53	2017	441	832	.530	293	392	.747	494	301	1175	9.3	5.7	22.2
Totals	143	5312	1232	2357	.523	746	1019	.732	1200	624	3213	8.4	4.4	22.5

Three-point field goals: 1988-89, 0-for-4. 1989-90, 3-for-9 (.333). 1990-91, 3-for-5. Totals, 3-for-18 (.167).

NBA REGULAR-SEASON RECORD

Season Team	G	Min.	FGM	FGA	Pct.	FTM	FTA	Pct.	REBOUNDS			Ast.	St.	Blk.	TO	Pts.	AVERAGES		
									Off.	Def.	Tot.						RPG	APG	PPG
87-88—Philadelphia	14	234	22	74	.297	8	11	.727	6	16	22	33	10	6	12	52	1.6	2.4	3.7
90-91—Golden State ...	7	85	12	25	.480	9	11	.818	7	4	11	13	2	0	6	33	1.6	1.9	4.7
91-92—Golden State ...	80	1496	193	379	.509	111	160	.694	89	144	233	188	47	23	84	498	2.9	2.4	6.2
92-93—Sac.-Sea.	73	1129	152	309	.492	105	149	.705	62	99	161	122	40	19	69	411	2.2	1.7	5.6
93-94—Seattle	80	1690	273	567	.481	175	211	.829	60	124	184	194	73	19	70	727	2.3	2.4	9.1
94-95—Seattle	71	1721	248	504	.492	176	238	.740	65	116	181	176	49	15	85	703	2.5	2.5	9.9
95-96—Seattle	69	1725	215	436	.493	123	161	.764	65	153	218	163	47	15	96	582	3.2	2.4	8.4
Totals	394	8080	1115	2294	.486	707	941	.751	354	656	1010	889	268	95	422	3006	2.6	2.3	7.6

Three-point field goals: 1991-92, 1-for-10 (.100). 1992-93, 2-for-6 (.333). 1993-94, 6-for-31 (.194). 1994-95, 31-for-94 (.330). 1995-96, 29-for-86 (.337). Totals, 69-for-227 (.304).
Personal fouls/disqualifications: 1987-88, 12/0. 1990-91, 21/1. 1991-92, 128/1. 1992-93, 135/2. 1993-94, 145/0. 1994-95, 191/1. 1995-96, 178/0. Totals, 810/5.

NBA PLAYOFF RECORD

									REBOUNDS								AVERAGES		
Season Team	G	Min.	FGM	FGA	Pct.	FTM	FTA	Pct.	Off.	Def.	Tot.	Ast.	St.	Blk.	TO	Pts.	RPG	APG	PPG
90-91—Golden State...	6	41	6	15	.400	3	6	.500	5	6	11	2	2	0	0	15	1.8	0.3	2.5
91-92—Golden State...	4	30	1	8	.125	0	0	...	3	1	4	5	0	0	2	2	1.0	1.3	0.5
92-93—Seattle	12	103	23	41	.561	16	23	.696	10	9	19	9	1	1	62	62	1.6	0.8	5.2
93-94—Seattle	5	95	10	28	.357	16	19	.842	2	4	6	9	2	0	2	36	1.2	1.8	7.2
94-95—Seattle	4	93	12	29	.414	2	3	.667	11	4	15	8	3	0	3	30	3.8	2.0	7.5
95-96—Seattle	19	345	24	70	.343	17	28	.607	5	36	41	26	13	8	28	71	2.2	1.4	3.7
Totals	50	707	76	191	.398	54	79	.684	36	60	96	59	21	9	42	216	1.9	1.2	4.3

Three-point field goals: 1993-94, 0-for-1. 1994-95, 4-for-5 (.800). 1995-96, 6-for-23 (.261). Totals, 10-for-29 (.345).
Personal fouls/disqualifications: 1990-91, 6/0. 1991-92, 3/0. 1992-93, 12/0. 1993-94, 10/0. 1994-95, 14/1. 1995-96, 50/0. Totals, 95/1.

ITALIAN LEAGUE RECORD

												AVERAGES		
Season Team	G	Min.	FGM	FGA	Pct.	FTM	FTA	Pct.	Reb.	Ast.	Pts.	RPG	APG	PPG
88-89—Bologna Arimo	20	703	142	258	.550	93	122	.762	138	20	380	6.9	1.0	19.0
92-93—Sid. Regg. Emilia...........	2	73	15	28	.536	10	12	.833	13	2	41	6.5	1.0	20.5
Totals	22	776	157	286	.549	103	134	.769	151	22	421	6.9	1.0	19.1

ASKINS, KEITH   G/F   HEAT

PERSONAL: Born December 15, 1967, in Athens, Ala. ... 6-8/224. ... Full name: Keith Bernard Askins.
HIGH SCHOOL: Athens (Ala.).
COLLEGE: Alabama.
TRANSACTIONS/CAREER NOTES: Not drafted by an NBA franchise. ... Signed as free agent by Miami Heat (August 7, 1990).

COLLEGIATE RECORD

												AVERAGES		
Season Team	G	Min.	FGM	FGA	Pct.	FTM	FTA	Pct.	Reb.	Ast.	Pts.	RPG	APG	PPG
86-87—Alabama	32	432	38	80	.475	16	29	.552	95	8	94	3.0	0.3	2.9
87-88—Alabama	30	805	58	139	.417	43	62	.694	147	13	171	4.9	0.4	5.7
88-89—Alabama	31	741	87	175	.497	24	35	.686	131	20	241	4.2	0.6	7.8
89-90—Alabama	35	978	117	268	.437	61	93	.656	180	46	346	5.1	1.3	9.9
Totals	128	2956	300	662	.453	144	219	.658	553	87	852	4.3	0.7	6.7

Three-point field goals: 1986-87, 2-for-7 (.286). 1987-88, 12-for-27 (.444). 1988-89, 43-for-96 (.448). 1989-90, 51-for-140 (.364). Totals, 108-for-270 (.400).

NBA REGULAR-SEASON RECORD

									REBOUNDS								AVERAGES		
Season Team	G	Min.	FGM	FGA	Pct.	FTM	FTA	Pct.	Off.	Def.	Tot.	Ast.	St.	Blk.	TO	Pts.	RPG	APG	PPG
90-91—Miami	39	266	34	81	.420	12	25	.480	30	38	68	19	16	13	11	86	1.7	0.5	2.2
91-92—Miami	59	843	84	205	.410	26	37	.703	65	77	142	38	40	15	47	219	2.4	0.6	3.7
92-93—Miami	69	935	88	213	.413	29	40	.725	74	124	198	31	31	29	37	229	2.9	0.4	3.3
93-94—Miami	37	319	36	88	.409	9	10	.900	33	49	82	13	11	1	21	85	2.2	0.4	2.3
94-95—Miami	50	854	81	207	.391	46	57	.807	86	112	198	39	35	17	25	229	4.0	0.8	4.6
95-96—Miami	75	1897	157	391	.402	45	57	.789	113	211	324	121	48	61	82	458	4.3	1.6	6.1
Totals	329	5114	480	1185	.405	167	226	.739	401	611	1012	261	181	136	223	1304	3.1	0.8	4.0

Three-point field goals: 1990-91, 6-for-25 (.240). 1991-92, 25-for-73 (.342). 1992-93, 22-for-65 (.338). 1993-94, 4-for-21 (.190). 1994-95, 21-for-78 (.269). 1995-96, 99-for-237 (.418). Totals, 177-for-499 (.355).
Personal fouls/disqualifications: 1990-91, 46/0. 1991-92, 109/0. 1992-93, 141/2. 1993-94, 57/0. 1994-95, 109/0. 1995-96, 271/6. Totals, 733/8.

NBA PLAYOFF RECORD

									REBOUNDS								AVERAGES		
Season Team	G	Min.	FGM	FGA	Pct.	FTM	FTA	Pct.	Off.	Def.	Tot.	Ast.	St.	Blk.	TO	Pts.	RPG	APG	PPG
91-92—Miami	3	48	5	11	.455	0	2	.000	4	5	9	3	1	0	1	13	3.0	1.0	4.3
93-94—Miami	1	6	0	1	.000	0	0	...	1	0	1	0	0	0	2	0	1.0	0.0	0.0
95-96—Miami	3	48	4	11	.364	3	3	1.000	3	5	8	2	1	0	4	13	2.7	0.7	4.3
Totals	7	102	9	23	.391	3	5	.600	8	10	18	5	2	0	7	26	2.6	0.7	3.7

Three-point field goals: 1991-92, 3-for-5 (.600). 1995-96, 2-for-6 (.333). Totals, 5-for-11 (.455).
Personal fouls/disqualifications: 1991-92, 7/0. 1995-96, 9/0. Totals, 16/0.

AUGMON, STACEY   G/F   PISTONS

PERSONAL: Born August 1, 1968, in Pasadena, Calif. ... 6-8/205. ... Full name: Stacey Orlando Augmon. ... Name pronounced AWG-mon.
HIGH SCHOOL: John Muir (Pasadena, Calif.).
COLLEGE: UNLV.
TRANSACTIONS/CAREER NOTES: Selected by Atlanta Hawks in first round (ninth pick overall) of 1991 NBA Draft. ... Traded by Hawks with F Grant Long to Detroit Pistons for four conditional draft choices (July 15, 1996).
MISCELLANEOUS: Member of bronze-medal-winning U.S. Olympic team (1988).

COLLEGIATE RECORD

NOTES: THE SPORTING NEWS All-America first team (1991). ... Member of NCAA Division I championship team (1990).

												AVERAGES		
Season Team	G	Min.	FGM	FGA	Pct.	FTM	FTA	Pct.	Reb.	Ast.	Pts.	RPG	APG	PPG
86-87—UNLV..............................						Did not play—ineligible.								
87-88—UNLV	34	884	117	204	.574	75	116	.647	206	64	311	6.1	1.9	9.1
88-89—UNLV	37	1091	210	405	.519	106	160	.663	274	101	567	7.4	2.7	15.3

A

Season Team	G	Min.	FGM	FGA	Pct.	FTM	FTA	Pct.	Reb.	Ast.	Pts.	AVERAGES		
												RPG	APG	PPG
89-90—UNLV	39	1246	210	380	.553	118	176	.670	270	143	554	6.9	3.7	14.2
90-91—UNLV	35	1062	220	375	.587	101	139	.727	255	125	579	7.3	3.6	16.5
Totals	145	4283	757	1364	.555	400	591	.677	1005	433	2011	6.9	3.0	13.9

Three-point field goals: 1987-88, 2-for-2. 1988-89, 41-for-98 (.418). 1989-90, 16-for-50 (.320). 1990-91, 38-for-81 (.469). Totals, 97-for-231 (.420).

NBA REGULAR-SEASON RECORD

HONORS: NBA All-Rookie first team (1992).

Season Team	G	Min.	FGM	FGA	Pct.	FTM	FTA	Pct.	REBOUNDS			Ast.	St.	Blk.	TO	Pts.	AVERAGES		
									Off.	Def.	Tot.						RPG	APG	PPG
91-92—Atlanta	82	2505	440	899	.489	213	320	.666	191	229	420	201	124	27	181	1094	5.1	2.5	13.3
92-93—Atlanta	73	2112	397	792	.501	227	307	.739	141	146	287	170	91	18	157	1021	3.9	2.3	14.0
93-94—Atlanta	82	2605	439	861	.510	333	436	.764	178	216	394	187	149	45	147	1212	4.8	2.3	14.8
94-95—Atlanta	76	2362	397	876	.453	252	346	.728	157	211	368	197	100	47	152	1053	4.8	2.6	13.9
95-96—Atlanta	77	2294	362	738	.491	251	317	.792	137	167	304	137	106	31	138	976	3.9	1.8	12.7
Totals	390	11878	2035	4166	.488	1276	1726	.739	804	969	1773	892	570	168	775	5356	4.5	2.3	13.7

Three-point field goals: 1991-92, 1-for-6 (.167). 1992-93, 0-for-4. 1993-94, 1-for-7 (.143). 1994-95, 7-for-26 (.269). 1995-96, 1-for-4 (.250). Totals, 10-for-47 (.213).

Personal fouls/disqualifications: 1991-92, 161/0. 1992-93, 141/1. 1993-94, 179/0. 1994-95, 163/0. 1995-96, 188/1. Totals, 832/2.

NBA PLAYOFF RECORD

Season Team	G	Min.	FGM	FGA	Pct.	FTM	FTA	Pct.	REBOUNDS			Ast.	St.	Blk.	TO	Pts.	AVERAGES		
									Off.	Def.	Tot.						RPG	APG	PPG
92-93—Atlanta	3	93	14	31	.452	8	12	.667	3	5	8	5	4	0	4	36	2.7	1.7	12.0
93-94—Atlanta	11	324	46	89	.517	27	38	.711	13	16	29	28	7	2	15	119	2.6	2.5	10.8
94-95—Atlanta	3	52	6	14	.429	9	12	.750	3	4	7	5	3	0	2	21	2.3	1.7	7.0
95-96—Atlanta	10	314	35	72	.486	33	40	.825	9	27	36	27	11	6	17	103	3.6	2.7	10.3
Totals	27	783	101	206	.490	77	102	.755	28	52	80	65	25	8	38	279	3.0	2.4	10.3

Three-point field goals: 1995-96, 0-for-1.
Personal fouls/disqualifications: 1992-93, 7/0. 1993-94, 26/0. 1994-95, 8/0. 1995-96, 26/0. Totals, 67/0.

AVENT, ANTHONY   F

PERSONAL: Born October 18, 1969, in Rocky Mount, N.C. ... 6-9/235. ... Name pronounced AY-vent.
HIGH SCHOOL: M.X. Shabazz (Newark, N.J.).
COLLEGE: Seton Hall.
TRANSACTIONS/CAREER NOTES: Selected by Atlanta Hawks in first round (15th pick overall) of 1991 NBA Draft. ... Draft rights traded by Hawks to Milwaukee Bucks in three-way deal in which Denver Nuggets sent C Blair Rasmussen to Hawks and Bucks sent draft rights to F Kevin Brooks to Nuggets (July 1, 1991); Nuggets also received 1994 second-round draft choice and other considerations from Bucks. ... Played in Italy (1991-92). ... Traded by Bucks to Orlando Magic for F/C Anthony Cook and conditional 1994 first-round draft choice (January 15, 1994). ... Traded by Magic to Vancouver Grizzlies for F Larry Stewart and G Kevin Pritchard (November 1, 1995). ... Rights renounced by Grizzlies (July 16, 1996).

COLLEGIATE RECORD

Season Team	G	Min.	FGM	FGA	Pct.	FTM	FTA	Pct.	Reb.	Ast.	Pts.	AVERAGES		
												RPG	APG	PPG
87-88—Seton Hall					Did not play—ineligible.									
88-89—Seton Hall	38	395	68	149	.456	32	49	.653	114	12	168	3.0	0.3	4.4
89-90—Seton Hall	28	842	119	244	.488	55	89	.618	262	47	293	9.4	1.7	10.5
90-91—Seton Hall	34	1114	228	395	.577	150	200	.750	335	53	606	9.9	1.6	17.8
Totals	100	2351	415	788	.527	237	338	.701	711	112	1067	7.1	1.1	10.7

ITALIAN LEAGUE RECORD

Season Team	G	Min.	FGM	FGA	Pct.	FTM	FTA	Pct.	Reb.	Ast.	Pts.	AVERAGES		
												RPG	APG	PPG
91-92—Phonola Caserta	15	450	84	158	.532	29	41	.707	154	7	197	10.3	0.5	13.1

NBA REGULAR-SEASON RECORD

Season Team	G	Min.	FGM	FGA	Pct.	FTM	FTA	Pct.	REBOUNDS			Ast.	St.	Blk.	TO	Pts.	AVERAGES		
									Off.	Def.	Tot.						RPG	APG	PPG
92-93—Milwaukee	82	2285	347	802	.433	112	172	.651	180	332	512	91	57	73	140	806	6.2	1.1	9.8
93-94—Mil.-Orl.	74	1371	150	398	.377	89	123	.724	144	194	338	65	33	31	85	389	4.6	0.9	5.3
94-95—Orlando	71	1066	105	244	.430	48	75	.640	97	196	293	41	28	50	53	258	4.1	0.6	3.6
95-96—Vancouver	71	1586	179	466	.384	57	77	.740	108	247	355	69	30	42	107	415	5.0	1.0	5.8
Totals	298	6308	781	1910	.409	306	447	.685	529	969	1498	266	148	196	385	1868	5.0	0.9	6.3

Three-point field goals: 1992-93, 0-for-2.
Personal fouls/disqualifications: 1992-93, 237/0. 1993-94, 147/0. 1994-95, 170/1. 1995-96, 202/3. Totals, 756/4.

NBA PLAYOFF RECORD

Season Team	G	Min.	FGM	FGA	Pct.	FTM	FTA	Pct.	REBOUNDS			Ast.	St.	Blk.	TO	Pts.	AVERAGES		
									Off.	Def.	Tot.						RPG	APG	PPG
93-94—Orlando	2	40	6	13	.462	7	8	.875	8	3	11	1	0	0	1	19	5.5	0.5	9.5
94-95—Orlando	7	40	3	7	.429	3	4	.750	4	4	8	0	0	1	2	9	1.1	0.0	1.3
Totals	9	80	9	20	.450	10	12	.833	12	7	19	1	0	1	3	28	2.1	0.1	3.1

Three-point field goals: 1994-95, 0-for-1.
Personal fouls/disqualifications: 1993-94, 2/0. 1994-95, 11/0. Totals, 13/0.

BAKER, VIN   F   BUCKS

PERSONAL: Born November 23, 1971, in Lake Wales, Fla. ... 6-11/250. ... Full name: Vincent Lamont Baker.
HIGH SCHOOL: Old Saybrook (Conn.).
COLLEGE: Hartford.
TRANSACTIONS/CAREER NOTES: Selected by Milwaukee Bucks in first round (eighth pick overall) of 1993-NBA Draft.

COLLEGIATE RECORD

Season Team	G	Min.	FGM	FGA	Pct.	FTM	FTA	Pct.	Reb.	Ast.	Pts.	RPG	APG	PPG
89-90—Hartford	28	374	58	94	.617	16	41	.390	82	7	132	2.9	0.3	4.7
90-91—Hartford	29	899	216	440	.491	137	202	.678	302	18	569	10.4	0.6	19.6
91-92—Hartford	27	997	281	638	.440	142	216	.657	267	36	745	9.9	1.3	27.6
92-93—Hartford	28	1019	305	639	.477	150	240	.625	300	54	792	10.7	1.9	28.3
Totals	112	3289	860	1811	.475	445	699	.637	951	115	2238	8.5	1.0	20.0

Three-point field goals: 1991-92, 41-for-214 (.192). 1992-93, 32-for-119 (.269). Totals, 73-for-333 (.219).

NBA REGULAR-SEASON RECORD

HONORS: NBA All-Rookie first team (1994).

Season Team	G	Min.	FGM	FGA	Pct.	FTM	FTA	Pct.	Off.	Def.	Tot.	Ast.	St.	Blk.	TO	Pts.	RPG	APG	PPG
93-94—Milwaukee	82	2560	435	869	.501	234	411	.569	277	344	621	163	60	114	162	1105	7.6	2.0	13.5
94-95—Milwaukee	82	*3361	594	1229	.483	256	432	.593	289	557	846	296	86	116	221	1451	10.3	3.6	17.7
95-96—Milwaukee	82	3319	699	1429	.489	321	479	.670	263	545	808	212	68	91	216	1729	9.9	2.6	21.1
Totals	246	9240	1728	3527	.490	811	1322	.613	829	1446	2275	671	214	321	599	4285	9.2	2.7	17.4

Three-point field goals: 1993-94, 1-for-5 (.200). 1994-95, 7-for-24 (.292). 1995-96, 10-for-48 (.208). Totals, 18-for-77 (.234).
Personal fouls/disqualifications: 1993-94, 231/3. 1994-95, 277/5. 1995-96, 272/3. Totals, 780/11.

NBA ALL-STAR GAME RECORD

Season Team	Min.	FGM	FGA	Pct.	FTM	FTA	Pct.	Off.	Def.	Tot.	Ast.	PF	Dq.	St.	Blk.	TO	Pts.
1995 —Milwaukee	11	0	2	.000	2	4	.500	2	0	2	0	1	0	0	1	1	2
1996 —Milwaukee	14	2	5	.400	2	2	1.000	1	1	2	2	4	0	1	0	0	6
Totals	25	2	7	.286	4	6	.667	3	1	4	2	5	0	1	1	1	8

BARDO, STEVE   G

PERSONAL: Born April 5, 1968, in Henderson, Ky. ... 6-6/200. ... Full name: Stephen Dean Bardo.
HIGH SCHOOL: Carbondale (Ill.).
COLLEGE: Illinois.
TRANSACTIONS/CAREER NOTES: Selected by Atlanta Hawks in second round (41st pick overall) of 1990 NBA Draft. ... Waived by Hawks (October 19, 1990). ... Played in Continental Basketball Association with Quad City Thunder (1990-91 and 1991-92), Wichita Falls Texans (1991-92 and 1992-93) and Chicago Rockers (1994-95). ... Played in United States Basketball League with Atlanta Eagles (1991). ... Signed as free agent by San Antonio Spurs (September 5, 1991). ... Waived by Spurs (November 12, 1991). ... Signed by Spurs to 10-day contract (February 19, 1992). ... Released by Spurs (February 27, 1992). ... Signed as free agent by Dallas Mavericks (October 1, 1992). ... Waived by Mavericks (January 6, 1993). ... Signed as free agent by Philadelphia 76ers (October 6, 1994). ... Waived by 76ers (October 27, 1994). ... Signed as free agent by Detroit Pistons (October 5, 1995). ... Waived by Pistons (January 5, 1996).

COLLEGIATE RECORD

Season Team	G	Min.	FGM	FGA	Pct.	FTM	FTA	Pct.	Reb.	Ast.	Pts.	RPG	APG	PPG
86-87—Illinois	31	630	42	102	.412	34	50	.680	92	85	119	3.0	2.7	3.8
87-88—Illinois	33	820	80	178	.449	53	87	.609	138	125	216	4.2	3.8	6.5
88-89—Illinois	36	1000	94	212	.443	76	96	.792	144	148	293	4.0	4.1	8.1
89-90—Illinois	29	944	99	225	.440	55	78	.705	178	137	281	6.1	4.7	9.7
Totals	129	3394	315	717	.439	218	311	.701	552	495	909	4.3	3.8	7.0

Three-point field goals: 1986-87, 1-for-3 (.333). 1987-88, 3-for-8 (.375). 1988-89, 29-for-59 (.492). 1989-90, 28-for-64 (.438). Totals, 61-for-134 (.455).

CBA REGULAR-SEASON RECORD

NOTES: CBA Defensive Player of the Year (1993, 1994). ... CBA All-League first team (1993). ... CBA All-League second team (1992, 1994). ... CBA All-Defensive team (1992, 1993, 1994).

Season Team	G	Min.	FGM	FGA	Pct.	FTM	FTA	Pct.	Reb.	Ast.	Pts.	RPG	APG	PPG
90-91—Quad City	56	1847	310	685	.453	191	243	.786	266	277	823	4.8	4.9	14.7
91-92—Quad C.-W.F.	38	1393	244	526	.464	166	210	.790	235	229	669	6.2	6.0	17.6
92-93—Wichita Falls	35	1472	247	537	.460	181	229	.790	221	254	680	6.3	7.3	19.4
93-94—Wichita Falls	31	1238	226	453	.499	145	175	.829	176	202	628	5.7	6.5	20.3
94-95—Chicago	26	1034	178	385	.462	120	146	.822	109	139	522	4.2	5.3	20.1
Totals	186	6984	1205	2586	.466	803	1003	.801	1007	1101	3322	5.4	5.9	17.9

Three-point field goals: 1990-91, 12-for-43 (.279). 1991-92, 15-for-43 (.349). 1992-93, 5-for-39 (.128). 1993-94, 31-for-71 (.437). 1994-95, 46-for-102 (.451). Totals, 109-for-298 (.366).

NBA REGULAR-SEASON RECORD

Season Team	G	Min.	FGM	FGA	Pct.	FTM	FTA	Pct.	Off.	Def.	Tot.	Ast.	St.	Blk.	TO	Pts.	RPG	APG	PPG
91-92—San Antonio	1	1	0	0	...	0	0	...	0	1	1	0	0	0	0	0	1.0	0.0	0.0
92-93—Dallas	23	175	19	62	.306	12	17	.706	10	27	37	29	8	3	17	51	1.6	1.3	2.2
95-96—Detroit	9	123	9	23	.391	4	6	.667	2	20	22	15	4	1	5	22	2.4	1.7	2.4
Totals	33	299	28	85	.329	16	23	.696	13	47	60	44	12	4	22	73	1.8	1.3	2.2

Three-point field goals: 1992-93, 1-for-6 (.167). 1995-96, 0-for-4. Totals, 1-for-10 (.100).
Personal fouls/disqualifications: 1992-93, 28/0. 1995-96, 17/1. Totals, 45/1.

BARKLEY, CHARLES   F   ROCKETS

PERSONAL: Born February 20, 1963, in Leeds, Ala. ... 6-6/252. ... Full name: Charles Wade Barkley.
HIGH SCHOOL: Leeds (Ala.).
COLLEGE: Auburn.
TRANSACTIONS/CAREER NOTES: Selected after junior season by Philadelphia 76ers in first round (fifth pick overall) of 1984 NBA Draft. ... Traded by 76ers to Phoenix Suns for G Jeff Hornacek, F Tim Perry and C Andrew Lang (June 17, 1992). ... Traded by Suns with 1999 second-round draft choice to Houston Rockets for G Sam Cassell, F Robert Horry, F Chucky Brown and F Mark Bryant (August 19, 1996).
MISCELLANEOUS: Member of gold-medal-winning U.S. Olympic teams (1992, 1996).

COLLEGIATE RECORD

Season Team	G	Min.	FGM	FGA	Pct.	FTM	FTA	Pct.	Reb.	Ast.	Pts.	AVERAGES RPG	APG	PPG
81-82—Auburn	28	746	144	242	.595	68	107	.636	275	30	356	9.8	1.1	12.7
82-83—Auburn	28	782	161	250	.644	82	130	.631	266	49	404	9.5	1.8	14.4
83-84—Auburn	28	794	162	254	.638	99	145	.683	265	58	423	9.5	2.1	15.1
Totals	84	2322	467	746	.626	249	382	.652	806	137	1183	9.6	1.6	14.1

NBA REGULAR-SEASON RECORD

RECORDS: Holds single-game records for most offensive rebounds in one quarter—11; and most offensive rebounds in one half—13 (March 4, 1987, vs. New York).
HONORS: NBA Most Valuable Player (1993). ... IBM Award, for all-around contributions to team's success (1986, 1987, 1988). ... All-NBA first team (1988, 1989, 1990, 1991, 1993). ... All-NBA second team (1986, 1987, 1992, 1994, 1995). ... All-NBA third team (1996). ... NBA All-Rookie team (1985).
NOTES: Led NBA with 333 personal fouls (1986).

Season Team	G	Min.	FGM	FGA	Pct.	FTM	FTA	Pct.	REBOUNDS Off.	Def.	Tot.	Ast.	St.	Blk.	TO	Pts.	AVERAGES RPG	APG	PPG
84-85—Philadelphia	82	2347	427	783	.545	293	400	.733	266	437	703	155	95	80	209	1148	8.6	1.9	14.0
85-86—Philadelphia	80	2952	595	1041	.572	396	578	.685	354	672	1026	312	173	125	*350	1603	12.8	3.9	20.0
86-87—Philadelphia	68	2740	557	937	.594	429	564	.761	*390	604	994	331	119	104	322	1564	*14.6	4.9	23.0
87-88—Philadelphia	80	3170	753	1283	.587	714	*951	.751	*385	566	951	254	100	103	304	2264	11.9	3.2	28.3
88-89—Philadelphia	79	3088	700	1208	.579	602	799	.753	*403	583	986	325	126	67	254	2037	12.5	4.1	25.8
89-90—Philadelphia	79	3085	706	1177	.600	557	744	.749	361	548	909	307	148	50	243	1989	11.5	3.9	25.2
90-91—Philadelphia	67	2498	665	1167	.570	475	658	.722	258	422	680	284	110	33	210	1849	10.1	4.2	27.6
91-92—Philadelphia	75	2881	622	1126	.552	454	653	.695	271	559	830	308	136	44	233	1730	11.1	4.1	23.1
92-93—Phoenix	76	2859	716	1376	.520	445	582	.765	237	691	928	385	119	74	233	1944	12.2	5.1	25.6
93-94—Phoenix	65	2298	518	1046	.495	318	452	.704	198	529	727	296	101	37	206	1402	11.2	4.6	21.6
94-95—Phoenix	68	2382	554	1141	.486	379	507	.748	203	553	756	276	110	45	150	1561	11.1	4.1	23.0
95-96—Phoenix	71	2632	580	1160	.500	440	566	.777	243	578	821	262	114	56	218	1649	11.6	3.7	23.2
Totals	890	32932	7393	13445	.550	5502	7454	.738	3569	6742	10311	3495	1451	818	2934	20740	11.6	3.9	23.3

Three-point field goals: 1984-85, 1-for-6 (.167). 1985-86, 17-for-75 (.227). 1986-87, 21-for-104 (.202). 1987-88, 44-for-157 (.280). 1988-89, 35-for-162 (.216). 1989-90, 20-for-92 (.217). 1990-91, 44-for-155 (.284). 1991-92, 32-for-137 (.234). 1992-93, 67-for-220 (.305). 1993-94, 48-for-178 (.270). 1994-95, 74-for-219 (.338). 1995-96, 49-for-175 (.280). Totals, 452-for-1680 (.269).
Personal fouls/disqualifications: 1984-85, 301/5. 1985-86, 333/8. 1986-87, 252/5. 1987-88, 278/6. 1988-89, 262/3. 1989-90, 250/2. 1990-91, 173/2. 1991-92, 196/2. 1992-93, 196/0. 1993-94, 160/1. 1994-95, 201/3. 1995-96, 208/3. Totals, 2810/40.

NBA PLAYOFF RECORD

NOTES: Shares single-game playoff records for most free throws made in one half—19 (June 5, 1993, vs. Seattle); and most field goals made in one half—15 (May 4, 1994, at Golden State).

Season Team	G	Min.	FGM	FGA	Pct.	FTM	FTA	Pct.	REBOUNDS Off.	Def.	Tot.	Ast.	St.	Blk.	TO	Pts.	AVERAGES RPG	APG	PPG
84-85—Philadelphia	13	408	75	139	.540	40	63	.635	52	92	144	26	23	15	35	194	11.1	2.0	14.9
85-86—Philadelphia	12	497	104	180	.578	91	131	.695	60	129	189	67	27	15	65	300	15.8	5.6	25.0
86-87—Philadelphia	5	210	43	75	.573	36	45	.800	27	36	63	12	4	8	22	123	12.6	2.4	24.6
88-89—Philadelphia	3	135	29	45	.644	22	31	.710	8	27	35	16	5	2	11	81	11.7	5.3	27.0
89-90—Philadelphia	10	419	88	162	.543	65	108	.602	66	89	155	43	8	7	30	247	15.5	4.3	24.7
90-91—Philadelphia	8	326	74	125	.592	49	75	.653	31	53	84	48	15	3	25	199	10.5	6.0	24.9
92-93—Phoenix	24	1026	230	482	.477	168	218	.771	93	233	326	102	39	25	50	638	13.6	4.3	26.6
93-94—Phoenix	10	425	110	216	.509	42	55	.764	34	96	130	48	25	9	27	276	13.0	4.8	27.6
94-95—Phoenix	10	390	91	182	.500	66	90	.733	39	95	134	32	13	11	25	257	13.4	3.2	25.7
95-96—Phoenix	4	164	31	70	.443	37	47	.787	18	36	54	15	4	4	6	102	13.5	3.8	25.5
Totals	99	4000	875	1676	.522	616	863	.714	428	886	1314	409	163	99	296	2417	13.3	4.1	24.4

Three-point field goals: 1984-85, 4-for-6 (.667). 1985-86, 1-for-15 (.067). 1988-89, 1-for-5 (.200). 1989-90, 6-for-18 (.333). 1990-91, 2-for-5 (.100). 1992-93, 10-for-45 (.222). 1993-94, 14-for-40 (.350). 1994-95, 9-for-35 (.257). 1995-96, 3-for-12 (.250). Totals, 50-for-196 (.255).
Personal fouls/disqualifications: 1984-85, 49/0. 1985-86, 52/2. 1986-87, 21/0. 1988-89, 9/0. 1989-90, 36/0. 1990-91, 23/0. 1992-93, 73/0. 1993-94, 26/0. 1994-95, 28/0. 1995-96, 15/0. Totals, 332/2.

NBA ALL-STAR GAME RECORD

NOTES: NBA All-Star Game Most Valuable Player (1991).

Season	Team	Min.	FGM	FGA	Pct.	FTM	FTA	Pct.	REBOUNDS Off.	Def.	Tot.	Ast.	PF	Dq.	St.	Blk.	TO	Pts.
1987	—Philadelphia	16	2	6	.333	3	6	.500	1	3	4	1	2	0	1	0	0	7
1988	—Philadelphia	15	1	4	.250	2	2	1.000	1	2	3	0	2	0	1	1	3	4
1989	—Philadelphia	20	6	11	.545	5	8	.625	3	2	5	0	0	0	2	1	1	17
1990	—Philadelphia	22	7	12	.583	2	3	.667	2	2	4	0	1	0	1	2	2	17
1991	—Philadelphia	35	7	15	.467	3	6	.500	8	14	22	4	5	0	1	1	3	17
1992	—Philadelphia	28	6	14	.429	0	0	...	2	7	9	1	3	0	0	0	3	12
1993	—Phoenix	34	5	11	.455	5	7	.714	4	4	8	3	3	0	4	0	4	16
1994	—Phoenix							Selected, did not play—injured.										
1995	—Phoenix	23	7	12	.583	0	0	...	5	4	9	2	1	0	2	0	2	15
1996	—Phoenix	16	4	6	.667	0	0	...	0	0	0	1	1	0	0	0	2	8
Totals		209	45	91	.495	20	32	.625	22	38	60	16	18	0	12	4	20	113

Three-point field goals: 1987, 0-for-2. 1988, 0-for-1. 1990, 1-for-1. 1992, 0-for-1. 1993, 1-for-2 (.500). 1995, 1-for-4 (.250). Totals, 3-for-12 (.250).

BARROS, DANA   G   CELTICS

PERSONAL: Born April 13, 1967, in Boston. ... 5-11/163. ... Full name: Dana Bruce Barros.
HIGH SCHOOL: Xaverian Brothers (Westwood, Mass.).
COLLEGE: Boston College.
TRANSACTIONS/CAREER NOTES: Selected by Seattle SuperSonics in first round (16th pick overall) of 1989 NBA Draft. ... Traded by SuperSonics with F Eddie Johnson and option to switch 1994 first-round draft choices to Charlotte Hornets for G Kendall Gill (September 1, 1993). ... Traded by Hornets with F Sidney Green, draft rights to G Greg Graham and option to switch 1994 first-round draft choices to Philadelphia 76ers for G Hersey Hawkins (September 3, 1993). ... Signed as unrestricted free agent by Boston Celtics (September 22, 1995).

B

COLLEGIATE RECORD

Season Team	G	Min.	FGM	FGA	Pct.	FTM	FTA	Pct.	Reb.	Ast.	Pts.	RPG	APG	PPG
85-86—Boston College	28	971	158	330	.479	68	86	.791	78	97	384	2.8	3.5	13.7
86-87—Boston College	29	1145	194	424	.458	85	100	.850	85	110	543	2.9	3.8	18.7
87-88—Boston College	33	1223	242	504	.480	130	153	.850	113	135	723	3.4	4.1	21.9
88-89—Boston College	29	1096	230	484	.475	120	140	.857	103	96	692	3.6	3.3	23.9
Totals	119	4435	824	1742	.473	403	479	.841	379	438	2342	3.2	3.7	19.7

Three-point field goals: 1986-87, 70-for-173 (.405). 1987-88, 109-for-240 (.454). 1988-89, 112-for-261 (.429). Totals, 291-for-674 (.432).

NBA REGULAR-SEASON RECORD

RECORDS: Holds career record for most consecutive games with one or more three-point field goal made—89 (December 23, 1994-January 10, 1996).
HONORS: NBA Most Improved Player (1995).
NOTES: Led NBA with .446 three-point field-goal percentage (1992).

Season Team	G	Min.	FGM	FGA	Pct.	FTM	FTA	Pct.	Off.	Def.	Tot.	Ast.	St.	Blk.	TO	Pts.	RPG	APG	PPG
89-90—Seattle	81	1630	299	738	.405	89	110	.809	35	97	132	205	53	1	123	782	1.6	2.5	9.7
90-91—Seattle	66	750	154	311	.495	78	85	.918	17	54	71	111	23	1	54	418	1.1	1.7	6.3
91-92—Seattle	75	1331	238	493	.483	60	79	.760	17	64	81	125	51	4	56	619	1.1	1.7	8.3
92-93—Seattle	69	1243	214	474	.451	49	59	.831	18	89	107	151	63	3	58	541	1.6	2.2	7.8
93-94—Philadelphia	81	2519	412	878	.469	116	145	.800	28	168	196	424	107	5	167	1075	2.4	5.2	13.3
94-95—Philadelphia	82	3318	571	1165	.490	347	386	.899	27	247	274	619	149	4	242	1686	3.3	7.5	20.6
95-96—Boston	80	2328	379	806	.470	130	147	.884	21	171	192	306	58	3	120	1038	2.4	3.8	13.0
Totals	534	13119	2267	4865	.466	869	1011	.860	163	890	1053	1941	504	21	820	6159	2.0	3.6	11.5

Three-point field goals: 1989-90, 95-for-238 (.399). 1990-91, 32-for-81 (.395). 1991-92, 83-for-186 (.446). 1992-93, 64-for-169 (.379). 1993-94, 135-for-354 (.381). 1994-95, 197-for-425 (.464). 1995-96, 150-for-368 (.408). Totals, 756-for-1821 (.415).
Personal fouls/disqualifications: 1989-90, 97/0. 1990-91, 40/0. 1991-92, 84/0. 1992-93, 78/0. 1993-94, 96/0. 1994-95, 159/1. 1995-96, 116/1. Totals, 670/2.

NBA PLAYOFF RECORD

Season Team	G	Min.	FGM	FGA	Pct.	FTM	FTA	Pct.	Off.	Def.	Tot.	Ast.	St.	Blk.	TO	Pts.	RPG	APG	PPG
90-91—Seattle	3	25	9	13	.692	3	4	.750	1	3	4	5	3	0	3	23	1.3	1.7	7.7
91-92—Seattle	7	96	21	40	.525	0	0	...	1	6	7	8	4	0	6	52	1.0	1.1	7.4
92-93—Seattle	16	136	22	47	.468	6	8	.750	0	12	12	12	5	0	8	55	0.8	0.8	3.4
Totals	26	257	52	100	.520	9	12	.750	2	21	23	25	12	0	17	130	0.9	1.0	5.0

Three-point field goals: 1990-91, 2-for-5 (.400). 1991-92, 10-for-17 (.588). 1992-93, 5-for-16 (.313). Totals, 17-for-38 (.447).
Personal fouls/disqualifications: 1990-91, 1/0. 1991-92, 11/0. 1992-93, 6/0. Totals, 18/0.

NBA ALL-STAR GAME RECORD

Season Team	Min.	FGM	FGA	Pct.	FTM	FTA	Pct.	Off.	Def.	Tot.	Ast.	PF	Dq.	St.	Blk.	TO	Pts.
1995 —Philadelphia	11	2	5	.400	0	0	...	0	1	1	3	0	0	0	0	0	5

Three-point field goals: 1995, 1-for-3 (.333).

BARRY, BRENT   G   CLIPPERS

PERSONAL: Born December 31, 1971, in Roseville Park, N.Y. ... 6-6/185. ... Full name: Brent Robert Barry. ... Son of Rick Barry, forward with San Francisco/Golden State Warriors and Houston Rockets of NBA (1965-66, 1966-67 and 1972-73 through 1979-80), Oakland Oaks, Washington Capitols and New York Nets of American Basketball Association (1968-69 through 1971-72) and member of Naismith Memorial Basketball Hall of Fame; brother of Jon Barry, guard with Atlanta Hawks; and brother of Drew Barry, guard with Seattle SuperSonics.
HIGH SCHOOL: De La Salle Catholic (Concord, Calif.).
COLLEGE: Oregon State.
TRANSACTIONS/CAREER NOTES: Selected by Denver Nuggets in first round (15th pick overall) of 1995 NBA Draft. ... Draft rights traded by Nuggets with F Rodney Rogers to Los Angeles Clippers for G Randy Woods and draft rights to F Antonio McDyess (June 28, 1995).

COLLEGIATE RECORD

Season Team	G	Min.	FGM	FGA	Pct.	FTM	FTA	Pct.	Reb.	Ast.	Pts.	RPG	APG	PPG
90-91—Oregon State						Did not play—redshirted.								
91-92—Oregon State	31	545	57	136	.419	22	33	.667	47	70	161	1.5	2.3	5.2
92-93—Oregon State	23	607	55	134	.410	40	47	.851	49	83	165	2.1	3.6	7.2
93-94—Oregon State	27	959	144	289	.498	85	112	.759	141	94	411	5.2	3.5	15.2
94-95—Oregon State	27	1012	181	352	.514	153	186	.823	159	104	567	5.9	3.9	21.0
Totals	108	3123	437	911	.480	300	378	.794	396	351	1304	3.7	3.3	12.1

Three-point field goals: 1991-92, 25-for-77 (.325). 1992-93, 15-for-64 (.234). 1993-94, 38-for-104 (.365). 1994-95, 52-for-132 (.394). Totals, 130-for-377 (.345).

HONORS: Slam-Dunk Championship winner (1996). ... NBA All-Rookie second team (1996).

Season Team	G	Min.	FGM	FGA	Pct.	FTM	FTA	Pct.	REBOUNDS Off.	Def.	Tot.	Ast.	St.	Blk.	TO	Pts.	AVERAGES RPG	APG	PPG
95-96—L.A. Clippers...	79	1898	283	597	.474	111	137	.810	38	130	168	230	95	22	120	800	2.1	2.9	10.1

Three-point field goals: 1995-96, 123-for-296 (.416).
Personal fouls/disqualifications: 1995-96, 196/2.

B

BARRY, JON   G   HAWKS

PERSONAL: Born July 25, 1969, in Oakland. ... 6-5/204. ... Full name: Jon Alan Barry. ... Son of Rick Barry, forward with San Francisco/Golden State Warriors and Houston Rockets of NBA (1965-66, 1966-67 and 1972-73 through 1979-80), Oakland Oaks, Washington Capitols and New York Nets of American Basketball Association (1968-69 through 1971-72), and member of Naismith Memorial Basketball Hall of Fame; and brother of Brent Barry, guard with Los Angeles Clippers; and brother of Drew Barry, guard with Seattle SuperSonics.
HIGH SCHOOL: De La Salle Catholic (Concord, Calif.).
JUNIOR COLLEGE: Paris (Texas) Junior College.
COLLEGE: Pacific, then Georgia Tech.
TRANSACTIONS/CAREER NOTES: Selected by Boston Celtics in first round (21st pick overall) of 1992 NBA Draft. ... Traded by Celtics to Milwaukee Bucks for F Alaa Abdelnaby (December 4, 1992). ... Signed as unrestricted free agent by Golden State Warriors (October 4, 1995). ... Rights renounced by Warriors (July 21, 1996). ... Signed as free agent by Atlanta Hawks (August 13, 1996).

COLLEGIATE RECORD

Season Team	G	Min.	FGM	FGA	Pct.	FTM	FTA	Pct.	Reb.	Ast.	Pts.	AVERAGES RPG	APG	PPG
87-88—Pacific	29	809	100	269	.372	53	71	.746	74	108	275	2.6	3.7	9.5
88-89—Paris Junior College					Did not play.									
89-90—Paris Junior College	30	...	204	358	.570	58	73	.795	108	90	513	3.6	3.0	17.1
90-91—Georgia Tech	30	1088	180	405	.444	41	56	.732	110	110	478	3.7	3.7	15.9
91-92—Georgia Tech	35	1231	201	468	.429	101	145	.697	152	207	602	4.3	5.9	17.2
Junior college totals	30	...	204	358	.570	58	73	.795	108	90	513	3.6	3.0	17.1
4-year-college totals	94	3128	481	1142	.421	195	272	.717	336	425	1355	3.6	4.5	14.4

Three-point field goals: 1987-88, 22-for-59 (.373). 1990-91, 77-for-209 (.368). 1991-92, 99-for-265 (.374). Totals, 198-for-533 (.371).

NBA REGULAR-SEASON RECORD

Season Team	G	Min.	FGM	FGA	Pct.	FTM	FTA	Pct.	REBOUNDS Off.	Def.	Tot.	Ast.	St.	Blk.	TO	Pts.	AVERAGES RPG	APG	PPG
92-93—Milwaukee	47	552	76	206	.369	33	49	.673	10	33	43	68	35	3	42	206	0.9	1.4	4.4
93-94—Milwaukee	72	1242	158	382	.414	97	122	.795	36	110	146	168	102	17	83	445	2.0	2.3	6.2
94-95—Milwaukee	52	602	57	134	.425	61	80	.763	15	34	49	85	30	4	41	191	0.9	1.6	3.7
95-96—Golden State	68	712	91	185	.492	31	37	.838	17	46	63	85	33	11	42	257	0.9	1.3	3.8
Totals	239	3108	382	907	.421	222	288	.771	78	223	301	406	200	35	208	1099	1.3	1.7	4.6

Three-point field goals: 1992-93, 21-for-63 (.333). 1993-94, 32-for-115 (.278). 1994-95, 16-for-48 (.333). 1995-96, 44-for-93 (.473). Totals, 113-for-319 (.354).
Personal fouls/disqualifications: 1992-93, 57/0. 1993-94, 110/0. 1994-95, 54/0. 1995-96, 51/1. Totals, 272/1.

BECK, COREY   G

PERSONAL: Born May 27, 1971, in Memphis. ... 6-2/190. ... Full name: Corey Laveon Beck.
HIGH SCHOOL: Fairley (Memphis).
JUNIOR COLLEGE: South Plains.
COLLEGE: Arkansas.
TRANSACTIONS/CAREER NOTES: Not drafted by an NBA franchise. ... Signed as free agent by Charlotte Hornets (October 4, 1995). ... Waived by Hornets (November 2, 1995). ... Played in Continental Basketball Association with Sioux Falls Skyforce (1995-96). ... Re-signed by Hornets for remainder of season (December 23, 1995). ... Waived by Hornets (January 5, 1996).

COLLEGIATE RECORD

NOTES: Member of NCAA Division I championship team (1994).

Season Team	G	Min.	FGM	FGA	Pct.	FTM	FTA	Pct.	Reb.	Ast.	Pts.	AVERAGES RPG	APG	PPG
90-91—South Plains College	29	...	128	246	.520	102	150	.680	187	176	368	6.4	6.1	12.7
91-92—Arkansas				Did not play—transfer student.										
92-93—Arkansas	30	770	64	129	.496	82	122	.672	115	107	210	3.8	3.6	7.0
93-94—Arkansas	34	876	88	174	.506	118	177	.667	131	169	299	3.9	5.0	8.8
94-95—Arkansas	39	1134	102	207	.493	80	119	.672	186	207	308	4.8	5.3	7.9
Junior college totals	29	...	128	246	.520	102	150	.680	187	176	368	6.4	6.1	12.7
4-year-college totals	103	2780	254	510	.498	280	418	.670	432	483	817	4.2	4.7	7.9

Three-point field goals: 1992-93, 0-for-2. 1993-94, 5-for-11 (.455). 1994-95, 24-for-49 (.490). Totals, 29-for-62 (.468).

CBA REGULAR-SEASON RECORD

NOTES: Member of CBA championship team (1996).

Season Team	G	Min.	FGM	FGA	Pct.	FTM	FTA	Pct.	Reb.	Ast.	Pts.	AVERAGES RPG	APG	PPG
95-96—Sioux Falls	43	748	95	209	.455	55	83	.663	93	147	250	2.2	3.4	5.8

Three-point field goals: 1995-96, 5-for-23 (.217).

NBA REGULAR-SEASON RECORD

Season Team	G	Min.	FGM	FGA	Pct.	FTM	FTA	Pct.	REBOUNDS Off.	Def.	Tot.	Ast.	St.	Blk.	TO	Pts.	AVERAGES RPG	APG	PPG
95-96—Charlotte	5	33	2	8	.250	1	2	.500	3	4	7	5	1	0	4	5	1.4	1.0	1.0

Personal fouls/disqualifications: 1995-96, 8/0.

BENJAMIN, BENOIT — C

PERSONAL: Born November 22, 1964, in Monroe, La. ... 7-0/265. ... Full name: Lenard Benoit Benjamin. ... Name pronounced ba-NOYT.
HIGH SCHOOL: Carroll (Monroe, La.).
COLLEGE: Creighton.
TRANSACTIONS/CAREER NOTES: Selected after junior season by Los Angeles Clippers in first round (third pick overall) of 1985 NBA Draft. ... Traded by Clippers to Seattle SuperSonics for C Olden Polynice, 1991 first-round draft choice and 1993 or 1994 first-round draft choice (February 20, 1991). ... Traded by SuperSonics with G Doug Christie to Los Angeles Lakers for F/C Sam Perkins (February 22, 1993). ... Traded by Lakers to New Jersey Nets for C Sam Bowie and 1988 second-round draft choice (June 21, 1993). ... Selected by Vancouver Grizzlies from Nets in NBA expansion draft (June 24, 1995). ... Traded by Grizzlies to Milwaukee Bucks for G Eric Murdock and C Eric Mobley (November 27, 1995). ... Rights renounced by Bucks (July 11, 1996).
MISCELLANEOUS: Los Angeles Clippers franchise all-time blocked shots leader with 1,117 (1985-86 through 1990-91).

COLLEGIATE RECORD

Season Team	G	Min.	FGM	FGA	Pct.	FTM	FTA	Pct.	Reb.	Ast.	Pts.	RPG	APG	PPG
82-83—Creighton	27	871	162	292	.555	76	116	.655	259	28	400	9.6	1.0	14.8
83-84—Creighton	30	1112	190	350	.543	107	144	.743	295	55	487	9.8	1.8	16.2
84-85—Creighton	32	1193	258	443	.582	172	233	.738	451	68	688	14.1	2.1	21.5
Totals	89	3176	610	1085	.562	355	493	.720	1005	151	1575	11.3	1.7	17.7

NBA REGULAR-SEASON RECORD

Season Team	G	Min.	FGM	FGA	Pct.	FTM	FTA	Pct.	Off.	Def.	Tot.	Ast.	St.	Blk.	TO	Pts.	RPG	APG	PPG
85-86—L.A. Clippers	79	2088	324	661	.490	229	307	.746	161	439	600	79	64	206	145	878	7.6	1.0	11.1
86-87—L.A. Clippers	72	2230	320	713	.449	188	263	.715	134	452	586	135	60	187	184	828	8.1	1.9	11.5
87-88—L.A. Clippers	66	2171	340	693	.491	180	255	.706	112	418	530	172	50	225	223	860	8.0	2.6	13.0
88-89—L.A. Clippers	79	2585	491	907	.541	317	426	.744	164	532	696	157	57	221	237	1299	8.8	2.0	16.4
89-90—L.A. Clippers	71	2313	362	688	.526	235	321	.732	156	501	657	159	59	187	187	959	9.3	2.2	13.5
90-91—LAC-Seattle	70	2236	386	778	.496	210	295	.712	157	566	723	119	54	145	235	982	10.3	1.7	14.0
91-92—Seattle	63	1941	354	740	.478	171	249	.687	130	383	513	76	39	118	175	879	8.1	1.2	14.0
92-93—Sea.-L.A.L.	59	754	133	271	.491	69	104	.663	51	158	209	22	31	48	78	335	3.5	0.4	5.7
93-94—New Jersey	77	1817	283	589	.480	152	214	.710	135	364	499	44	35	90	97	718	6.5	0.6	9.3
94-95—New Jersey	61	1598	271	531	.510	133	175	.760	94	346	440	38	23	64	125	675	7.2	0.6	11.1
95-96—Van.-Mil.	83	1896	294	590	.498	140	194	.722	141	398	539	64	45	85	144	728	6.5	0.8	8.8
Totals	780	21629	3558	7161	.497	2024	2803	.722	1435	4557	5992	1065	517	1576	1830	9141	7.7	1.4	11.7

Three-point field goals: 1985-86, 1-for-3 (.333). 1986-87, 0-for-2. 1987-88, 0-for-8. 1988-89, 0-for-2. 1989-90, 0-for-1. 1991-92, 0-for-2. 1995-96, 0-for-3. Totals, 1-for-21 (.048).
Personal fouls/disqualifications: 1985-86, 286/5. 1986-87, 251/7. 1987-88, 203/2. 1988-89, 221/4. 1989-90, 217/3. 1990-91, 184/1. 1991-92, 185/1. 1992-93, 134/0. 1993-94, 198/0. 1994-95, 151/3. 1995-96, 224/1. Totals, 2254/27.

NBA PLAYOFF RECORD

Season Team	G	Min.	FGM	FGA	Pct.	FTM	FTA	Pct.	Off.	Def.	Tot.	Ast.	St.	Blk.	TO	Pts.	RPG	APG	PPG
90-91—Seattle	5	163	20	41	.488	29	32	.906	7	26	33	1	3	13	11	69	6.6	0.2	13.8
91-92—Seattle	9	161	23	41	.561	9	18	.500	10	36	46	5	5	13	8	55	5.1	0.6	6.1
93-94—New Jersey	4	108	7	17	.412	7	8	.875	5	16	21	1	2	8	5	21	5.3	0.3	5.3
Totals	18	432	50	99	.505	45	58	.776	22	78	100	7	10	34	24	145	5.6	0.4	8.1

Three-point field goals: 1991-92, 0-for-1.
Personal fouls/disqualifications: 1990-91, 17/1. 1991-92, 20/0. 1993-94, 16/0. Totals, 53/1.

BENNETT, ELMER — G

PERSONAL: Born February 13, 1970, in Evanston, Ill. ... 6-0/171. ... Full name: Elmer James Bennett.
HIGH SCHOOL: Bellaire (Texas).
COLLEGE: Notre Dame.
TRANSACTIONS/CAREER NOTES: Selected by Atlanta Hawks in second round (38th pick overall) of 1992 NBA Draft. ... Waived by Hawks (November 3, 1992). ... Played in Continental Basketball Association with Rochester Renegade (1992-93), Grand Rapids Hoops (1992-93 and 1993-94), Fargo-Moorhead Fever (1993-94) and Oklahoma City Cavalry (1994-95). ... Signed as free agent by Portland Trail Blazers (October 4, 1994). ... Waived by Trail Blazers (October 24, 1994). ... Played in Italy (1994-95). ... Signed by Cleveland Cavaliers to first of two consecutive 10-day contracts (January 26, 1995). ... Signed as free agent by Philadelphia 76ers (October 5, 1995). ... Waived by 76ers (November 20, 1995).

COLLEGIATE RECORD

Season Team	G	Min.	FGM	FGA	Pct.	FTM	FTA	Pct.	Reb.	Ast.	Pts.	RPG	APG	PPG
88-89—Notre Dame	30	436	67	146	.459	25	39	.641	36	59	165	1.2	2.0	5.5
89-90—Notre Dame	29	716	112	233	.481	84	114	.737	45	106	317	1.6	3.7	10.9
90-91—Notre Dame	32	1127	161	389	.414	106	144	.736	95	147	460	3.0	4.6	14.4
91-92—Notre Dame	33	1187	195	441	.442	112	159	.704	119	204	546	3.6	6.2	16.5
Totals	124	3466	535	1209	.443	327	456	.717	295	516	1488	2.4	4.2	12.0

Three-point field goals: 1988-89, 5-for-14 (.357). 1989-90, 9-for-25 (.360). 1990-91, 32-for-87 (.368). 1991-92, 44-for-133 (.331). Totals, 90-for-259 (.347).

CBA REGULAR-SEASON RECORD

Season Team	G	Min.	FGM	FGA	Pct.	FTM	FTA	Pct.	Reb.	Ast.	Pts.	RPG	APG	PPG
92-93—Roch.-Gr. Rap.	29	354	52	125	.416	27	45	.600	34	66	135	1.2	2.3	4.7
93-94—Gr. Rap.-F./M.	16	211	31	76	.408	11	14	.786	16	37	78	1.0	2.3	4.9
94-95—Oklahoma City	30	1076	186	388	.479	101	138	.732	90	273	513	3.0	9.1	17.1
Totals	75	1641	269	589	.457	139	197	.706	140	376	726	1.9	5.0	9.7

Three-point field goals: 1992-93, 4-for-19 (.211). 1993-94, 5-for-19 (.263). 1994-95, 40-for-113 (.354). Totals, 49-for-151 (.325).

B

Season Team	G	Min.	FGM	FGA	Pct.	FTM	FTA	Pct.	Reb.	Ast.	Pts.	AVERAGES		
												RPG	APG	PPG
94-95—Scavolini Pesaro............	5	164	26	66	.394	20	24	.833	13	26	82	2.6	5.2	16.4

NBA REGULAR-SEASON RECORD

Season Team	G	Min.	FGM	FGA	Pct.	FTM	FTA	Pct.	REBOUNDS			Ast.	St.	Blk.	TO	Pts.	AVERAGES		
									Off.	Def.	Tot.						RPG	APG	PPG
94-95—Cleveland	4	18	6	11	.545	3	4	.750	0	1	1	3	4	0	3	15	0.3	0.8	3.8
95-96—Philadelphia	8	66	4	17	.235	3	4	.750	1	4	5	8	1	1	7	11	0.6	1.0	1.4
Totals	12	84	10	28	.357	6	8	.750	1	5	6	11	5	1	10	26	0.5	0.9	2.2

Three-point field goals: 1994-95, 0-for-2.
Personal fouls/disqualifications: 1994-95, 3/0. 1995-96, 6/0. Totals, 9/0.

B

BENNETT, MARIO   F   SUNS

PERSONAL: Born August 1, 1973, in Denton, Texas. ... 6-10/235. ... Full name: Mario Marcell Bennett.
HIGH SCHOOL: Denton (Texas).
COLLEGE: Arizona State.
TRANSACTIONS/CAREER NOTES: Selected after junior season by Phoenix Suns in first round (27th pick overall) of 1995 NBA Draft.

COLLEGIATE RECORD

Season Team	G	Min.	FGM	FGA	Pct.	FTM	FTA	Pct.	Reb.	Ast.	Pts.	AVERAGES		
												RPG	APG	PPG
91-92—Arizona State.................	33	889	159	277	.574	86	140	.614	224	28	411	6.8	0.8	12.5
92-93—Arizona State.................					Did not play—knee injury.									
93-94—Arizona State.................	21	706	134	226	.593	67	132	.508	180	32	340	8.6	1.5	16.2
94-95—Arizona State.................	33	1132	247	417	.592	115	234	.491	271	79	617	8.2	2.4	18.7
Totals	87	2727	540	920	.587	268	506	.530	675	139	1368	7.8	1.6	15.7

Three-point field goals: 1991-92, 7-for-22 (.318). 1993-94, 5-for-16 (.313). 1994-95, 8-for-30 (.267). Totals, 20-for-68 (.294).

NBA REGULAR-SEASON RECORD

Season Team	G	Min.	FGM	FGA	Pct.	FTM	FTA	Pct.	REBOUNDS			Ast.	St.	Blk.	TO	Pts.	AVERAGES		
									Off.	Def.	Tot.						RPG	APG	PPG
95-96—Phoenix	19	230	29	64	.453	27	42	.643	21	28	49	6	11	11	11	85	2.6	0.3	4.5

Three-point field goals: 1995-96, 0-for-1.
Personal fouls/disqualifications: 1995-96, 46/0.

NBA PLAYOFF RECORD

Season Team	G	Min.	FGM	FGA	Pct.	FTM	FTA	Pct.	REBOUNDS			Ast.	St.	Blk.	TO	Pts.	AVERAGES		
									Off.	Def.	Tot.						RPG	APG	PPG
95-96—Phoenix	2	8	2	4	.500	0	0	...	2	1	3	0	0	0	2	4	1.5	0.0	2.0

BENOIT, DAVID   F   NETS

PERSONAL: Born May 9, 1968, in Lafayette, La. ... 6-8/220. ... Name pronounced ben-WAH.
HIGH SCHOOL: Lafayette (La.).
JUNIOR COLLEGE: Tyler (Texas) Junior College.
COLLEGE: Alabama.
TRANSACTIONS/CAREER NOTES: Not drafted by an NBA franchise. ... Played in Spain (1990-91). ... Signed as free agent by Utah Jazz (August 7, 1991). ... Signed as free agent by New Jersey Nets (August 7, 1996).

COLLEGIATE RECORD

Season Team	G	Min.	FGM	FGA	Pct.	FTM	FTA	Pct.	Reb.	Ast.	Pts.	AVERAGES		
												RPG	APG	PPG
86-87—Tyler J.C.						Statistics unavailable.								
87-88—Tyler J.C.						Statistics unavailable.								
88-89—Alabama	31	913	136	268	.507	62	84	.738	248	20	335	8.0	0.6	10.8
89-90—Alabama	35	920	156	303	.515	46	60	.767	212	29	367	6.1	0.8	10.5
Totals	66	1833	292	571	.511	108	144	.750	460	49	702	7.0	0.7	10.6

Three-point field goals: 1988-89, 1-for-3 (.333). 1989-90, 9-for-20 (.450). Totals, 10-for-23 (.435).

SPANISH LEAGUE RECORD

Season Team	G	Min.	FGM	FGA	Pct.	FTM	FTA	Pct.	Reb.	Ast.	Pts.	AVERAGES		
												RPG	APG	PPG
90-91—Malaga	34	1235	302	609	.496	128	165	.776	349	22	749	10.3	0.6	22.0

NBA REGULAR-SEASON RECORD

Season Team	G	Min.	FGM	FGA	Pct.	FTM	FTA	Pct.	REBOUNDS			Ast.	St.	Blk.	TO	Pts.	AVERAGES		
									Off.	Def.	Tot.						RPG	APG	PPG
91-92—Utah	77	1161	175	375	.467	81	100	.810	105	191	296	34	19	44	71	434	3.8	0.4	5.6
92-93—Utah	82	1712	258	592	.436	114	152	.750	116	276	392	43	45	43	90	664	4.8	0.5	8.1
93-94—Utah	55	1070	139	361	.385	68	88	.773	89	171	260	23	23	37	37	358	4.7	0.4	6.5
94-95—Utah	71	1841	285	587	.486	132	157	.841	96	272	368	58	45	47	75	740	5.2	0.8	10.4
95-96—Utah	81	1961	255	581	.439	87	112	.777	90	272	383	82	43	49	71	661	4.7	1.0	8.2
Totals	366	7745	1112	2496	.446	482	609	.791	496	1203	1699	240	175	220	344	2857	4.6	0.7	7.8

Three-point field goals: 1991-92, 3-for-14 (.214). 1992-93, 34-for-98 (.347). 1993-94, 12-for-59 (.203). 1994-95, 38-for-115 (.330). 1995-96, 64-for-192 (.333). Totals, 151-for-478 (.316).
Personal fouls/disqualifications: 1991-92, 124/0. 1992-93, 201/2. 1993-94, 115/0. 1994-95, 183/1. 1995-96, 166/2. Totals, 789/5.

NBA PLAYOFF RECORD

Season Team	G	Min.	FGM	FGA	Pct.	FTM	FTA	Pct.	Off.	Def.	Tot.	Ast.	St.	Blk.	TO	Pts.	RPG	APG	PPG
									REBOUNDS								AVERAGES		
91-92—Utah	13	257	36	84	.429	11	11	1.000	18	32	50	6	6	5	10	89	3.8	0.5	6.8
92-93—Utah	5	136	13	41	.317	9	13	.692	7	17	24	5	3	6	2	37	4.8	1.0	7.4
93-94—Utah	16	357	48	122	.393	16	25	.640	23	44	67	10	7	11	16	115	4.2	0.6	7.2
94-95—Utah	5	167	21	45	.467	6	9	.667	7	21	28	4	2	4	10	59	5.6	0.8	11.8
95-96—Utah	14	259	33	70	.471	7	9	.778	6	31	37	7	1	3	14	87	2.6	0.5	6.2
Totals	53	1176	151	362	.417	49	67	.731	61	145	206	32	19	29	52	387	3.9	0.6	7.3

Three-point field goals: 1991-92, 6-for-13 (.462). 1992-93, 2-for-9 (.222). 1993-94, 3-for-16 (.188). 1994-95, 11-for-25 (.440). 1995-96, 14-for-28 (.500). Totals, 36-for-91 (.396).

Personal fouls/disqualifications: 1991-92, 30/0. 1992-93, 17/0. 1993-94, 31/0. 1994-95, 10/0. 1995-96, 17/0. Totals, 105/0.

BEST, TRAVIS　　　　　G　　　　　PACERS　　B

PERSONAL: Born July 12, 1972, in Springfield, Mass. ... 5-11/182. ... Full name: Travis Eric Best.
HIGH SCHOOL: Springfield (Mass.) Central.
COLLEGE: Georgia Tech.
TRANSACTIONS/CAREER NOTES: Selected by Indiana Pacers in first round (23rd pick overall) of 1995 NBA Draft.

COLLEGIATE RECORD

Season Team	G	Min.	FGM	FGA	Pct.	FTM	FTA	Pct.	Reb.	Ast.	Pts.	RPG	APG	PPG
												AVERAGES		
91-92—Georgia Tech	35	1227	151	336	.449	72	98	.735	89	198	430	2.5	5.7	12.3
92-93—Georgia Tech	30	1075	163	345	.472	82	109	.752	94	176	488	3.1	5.9	16.3
93-94—Georgia Tech	29	1087	180	390	.462	123	142	.866	104	167	532	3.6	5.8	18.3
94-95—Georgia Tech	30	1115	209	469	.446	116	137	.847	95	151	607	3.2	5.0	20.2
Totals	124	4504	703	1540	.456	393	486	.809	382	692	2057	3.1	5.6	16.6

Three-point field goals: 1991-92, 56-for-145 (.386). 1992-93, 80-for-175 (.457). 1993-94, 49-for-144 (.340). 1994-95, 73-for-192 (.380). Totals, 258-for-656 (.393).

NBA REGULAR-SEASON RECORD

Season Team	G	Min.	FGM	FGA	Pct.	FTM	FTA	Pct.	Off.	Def.	Tot.	Ast.	St.	Blk.	TO	Pts.	RPG	APG	PPG
									REBOUNDS								AVERAGES		
95-96—Indiana	59	571	69	163	.423	75	90	.833	11	33	44	97	20	3	63	221	0.7	1.6	3.7

Three-point field goals: 1995-96, 8-for-25 (.320).
Personal fouls/disqualifications: 1995-96, 80/0.

NBA PLAYOFF RECORD

Season Team	G	Min.	FGM	FGA	Pct.	FTM	FTA	Pct.	Off.	Def.	Tot.	Ast.	St.	Blk.	TO	Pts.	RPG	APG	PPG
									REBOUNDS								AVERAGES		
95-96—Indiana	5	84	11	22	.500	6	7	.857	3	8	11	9	6	0	10	29	2.2	1.8	5.8

Three-point field goals: 1995-96, 1-for-6 (.167).
Personal fouls/disqualifications: 1995-96, 10/0.

BLAYLOCK, MOOKIE　　　　　G　　　　　HAWKS

PERSONAL: Born March 20, 1967, in Garland, Texas. ... 6-1/185. ... Full name: Daron Oshay Blaylock.
HIGH SCHOOL: Garland (Texas).
JUNIOR COLLEGE: Midland (Texas).
COLLEGE: Oklahoma.
TRANSACTIONS/CAREER NOTES: Selected by New Jersey Nets in first round (12th pick overall) of 1989 NBA Draft. ... Traded by Nets with F Roy Hinson to Atlanta Hawks for G Rumeal Robinson (November 3, 1992).

NOTES: The Sporting News All-America second team (1989). ... Holds NCAA Division I single-season record for most steals—150 (1988). ... Holds NCAA Division I single-game record for most steals—13 (December 12, 1987, vs. Centenary and December 17, 1988, vs. Loyola Marymount).

COLLEGIATE RECORD

Season Team	G	Min.	FGM	FGA	Pct.	FTM	FTA	Pct.	Reb.	Ast.	Pts.	RPG	APG	PPG
												AVERAGES		
85-86—Midland College	34	...	254	449	.566	62	84	.738	109	158	570	3.2	4.6	16.8
86-87—Midland College	33	...	258	500	.516	60	83	.723	138	161	647	4.2	4.9	19.6
87-88—Oklahoma	39	1347	241	524	.460	78	114	.684	162	232	638	4.2	5.9	16.4
88-89—Oklahoma	35	1359	272	598	.455	65	100	.650	164	233	700	4.7	6.7	20.0
Junior college totals	67	...	512	949	.540	122	167	.731	247	319	1217	3.7	4.8	18.2
4-year-college totals	74	2706	513	1122	.457	143	214	.668	326	465	1338	4.4	6.3	18.1

Three-point field goals: 1987-88, 78-for-201 (.388). 1988-89, 91-for-245 (.371). Totals, 169-for-446 (.379).

NBA REGULAR-SEASON RECORD

HONORS: NBA All-Defensive first team (1994, 1995). ... NBA All-Defensive second team (1996).

Season Team	G	Min.	FGM	FGA	Pct.	FTM	FTA	Pct.	Off.	Def.	Tot.	Ast.	St.	Blk.	TO	Pts.	RPG	APG	PPG
									REBOUNDS								AVERAGES		
89-90—New Jersey	50	1267	212	571	.371	63	81	.778	42	98	140	210	82	14	111	505	2.8	4.2	10.1
90-91—New Jersey	72	2585	432	1039	.416	139	176	.790	67	182	249	441	169	40	207	1017	3.5	6.1	14.1
91-92—New Jersey	72	2548	429	993	.432	126	177	.712	101	168	269	492	170	40	152	996	3.7	6.8	13.8
92-93—Atlanta	80	2820	414	964	.429	123	169	.728	89	191	280	671	203	23	187	1069	3.5	8.4	13.4
93-94—Atlanta	81	2915	444	1079	.412	116	159	.730	117	307	424	789	212	44	196	1118	5.2	9.7	13.8
94-95—Atlanta	80	3069	509	1198	.425	156	214	.729	117	276	393	616	200	26	242	1373	4.9	7.7	17.2
95-96—Atlanta	81	2893	455	1123	.405	127	170	.747	110	222	332	478	212	17	188	1268	4.1	5.9	15.7
Totals	516	18097	2895	6967	.416	850	1146	.742	643	1444	2087	3697	1248	204	1283	7346	4.0	7.2	14.2

Three-point field goals: 1989-90, 18-for-80 (.225). 1990-91, 14-for-91 (.154). 1991-92, 12-for-54 (.222). 1992-93, 118-for-315 (.375). 1993-94, 114-for-341 (.334). 1994-95, 199-for-555 (.359). 1995-96, 231-for-623 (.371). Totals, 706-for-2059 (.343).

Personal fouls/disqualifications: 1989-90, 110/0. 1990-91, 180/0. 1991-92, 182/1. 1992-93, 156/0. 1993-94, 144/0. 1994-95, 164/3. 1995-96, 151/1. Totals, 1087/5.

NBA PLAYOFF RECORD

Season Team	G	Min.	FGM	FGA	Pct.	FTM	FTA	Pct.	REBOUNDS Off.	Def.	Tot.	Ast.	St.	Blk.	TO	Pts.	AVERAGES RPG	APG	PPG
91-92—New Jersey	4	148	17	55	.309	3	4	.750	5	11	16	31	15	2	7	38	4.0	7.8	9.5
92-93—Atlanta	3	99	9	25	.360	5	6	.833	2	11	13	13	3	4	11	27	4.3	4.3	9.0
93-94—Atlanta	11	415	48	141	.340	25	30	.833	16	39	55	98	24	5	32	143	5.0	8.9	13.0
94-95—Atlanta	3	121	18	49	.367	7	11	.636	7	6	13	17	4	0	9	54	4.3	5.7	18.0
95-96—Atlanta	10	426	61	145	.421	16	24	.667	13	30	43	64	22	8	29	171	4.3	6.4	17.1
Totals	31	1209	153	415	.369	56	75	.747	43	97	140	223	68	19	88	433	4.5	7.2	14.0

Three-point field goals: 1991-92, 1-for-6 (.167). 1992-93, 4-for-12 (.333). 1993-94, 22-for-64 (.344). 1994-95, 11-for-28 (.393). 1995-96, 33-for-84 (.393). Totals, 71-for-194 (.366).
Personal fouls/disqualifications: 1991-92, 16/0. 1992-93, 9/0. 1993-94, 22/0. 1994-95, 6/0. 1995-96, 15/0. Totals, 68/0.

NBA ALL-STAR GAME RECORD

Season Team	Min.	FGM	FGA	Pct.	FTM	FTA	Pct.	REBOUNDS Off.	Def.	Tot.	Ast.	PF	Dq.	St.	Blk.	TO	Pts.
1994 —Atlanta	16	2	5	.400	0	0	...	0	1	1	2	3	0	0	0	1	5

Three-point field goals: 1994, 1-for-2 (.500).

BLOUNT, CORIE   F   LAKERS

PERSONAL: Born January 4, 1969, in Monrovia, Calif. ... 6-10/242. ... Full name: Corie Kasoun Blount. ... Name pronounced BLUNT.
HIGH SCHOOL: Monrovia (Calif.).
JUNIOR COLLEGE: Rancho Santiago Community College (Calif.).
COLLEGE: Cincinnati.
TRANSACTIONS/CAREER NOTES: Selected by Chicago Bulls in first round (25th pick overall) of 1993 NBA Draft. ... Traded by Bulls to Los Angeles Lakers for cash (June 30, 1995).

COLLEGIATE RECORD

NOTES: Broke foot during 1988-89 season; granted extra year of eligibility.

Season Team	G	Min.	FGM	FGA	Pct.	FTM	FTA	Pct.	Reb.	Ast.	Pts.	AVERAGES RPG	APG	PPG
88-89—Rancho Santiago C.C.	4	...	8	16	.500	3	5	.600	15	2	19	3.8	0.5	4.8
89-90—Rancho Santiago C.C.	34	...	200	373	.536	72	123	.585	279	56	472	8.2	1.6	13.9
90-91—Rancho Santiago C.C.	37	...	301	511	.589	121	182	.665	333	108	723	9.0	2.9	19.5
91-92—Cincinnati	34	864	114	238	.479	50	90	.556	213	69	278	6.3	2.0	8.2
92-93—Cincinnati	21	588	104	189	.550	30	53	.566	170	47	238	8.1	2.2	11.3
Junior college totals	75		509	900	.566	196	310	.632	627	166	1214	8.4	2.2	16.2
4-year-college totals	55	1452	218	427	.511	80	143	.559	383	116	516	7.0	2.1	9.4

Three-point field goals: 1991-92, 0-for-2.

NBA REGULAR-SEASON RECORD

Season Team	G	Min.	FGM	FGA	Pct.	FTM	FTA	Pct.	REBOUNDS Off.	Def.	Tot.	Ast.	St.	Blk.	TO	Pts.	AVERAGES RPG	APG	PPG
93-94—Chicago	67	690	76	174	.437	46	75	.613	76	118	194	56	19	33	52	198	2.9	0.8	3.0
94-95—Chicago	68	889	100	210	.476	38	67	.567	107	133	240	60	26	33	59	238	3.5	0.9	3.5
95-96—L.A. Lakers	57	715	79	167	.473	25	44	.568	69	101	170	42	25	35	47	183	3.0	0.7	3.2
Totals	192	2294	255	551	.463	109	186	.586	252	352	604	158	70	101	158	619	3.1	0.8	3.2

Three-point field goals: 1994-95, 0-for-2. 1995-96, 0-for-2. Totals, 0-for-4.
Personal fouls/disqualifications: 1993-94, 93/0. 1994-95, 146/0. 1995-96, 109/2. Totals, 348/2.

NBA PLAYOFF RECORD

Season Team	G	Min.	FGM	FGA	Pct.	FTM	FTA	Pct.	REBOUNDS Off.	Def.	Tot.	Ast.	St.	Blk.	TO	Pts.	AVERAGES RPG	APG	PPG
94-95—Chicago	8	20	0	3	.000	0	0	...	1	4	5	0	0	0	1	0	0.6	0.0	0.0

Three-point field goals: 1994-95, 0-for-1.
Personal fouls/disqualifications: 1994-95, 5/0.

BOGUES, MUGGSY   G   HORNETS

PERSONAL: Born January 9, 1965, in Baltimore. ... 5-3/141. ... Full name: Tyrone Curtis Bogues. ... Name pronounced BOAGS.
HIGH SCHOOL: Dunbar (Baltimore).
COLLEGE: Wake Forest.
TRANSACTIONS/CAREER NOTES: Selected by Washington Bullets in first round (12th pick overall) of 1987 NBA Draft. ... Played in United States Basketball League with Rhode Island Gulls (1987). ... Selected by Charlotte Hornets from Bullets in NBA expansion draft (June 23, 1988).
MISCELLANEOUS: Charlotte Hornets all-time assists leader with 5,084 and all-time steals leader with 983 (1988-89 through 1995-96).

COLLEGIATE RECORD

NOTES: Frances Pomeroy Naismith Award winner (1987).

Season Team	G	Min.	FGM	FGA	Pct.	FTM	FTA	Pct.	Reb.	Ast.	Pts.	AVERAGES RPG	APG	PPG
83-84—Wake Forest	32	312	14	46	.304	9	13	.692	21	53	37	0.7	1.7	1.2
84-85—Wake Forest	29	1025	81	162	.500	30	44	.682	69	207	192	2.4	7.1	6.6
85-86—Wake Forest	29	1101	132	290	.455	65	89	.730	90	245	329	3.1	8.4	11.3

Season Team	G	Min.	FGM	FGA	Pct.	FTM	FTA	Pct.	Reb.	Ast.	Pts.	AVERAGES RPG	APG	PPG
86-87—Wake Forest	29	1130	159	318	.500	75	93	.806	110	276	428	3.8	9.5	14.8
Totals	119	3568	386	816	.473	179	239	.749	290	781	986	2.4	6.6	8.3

Three-point field goals: 1986-87, 35-for-79 (.443).

NBA REGULAR-SEASON RECORD

Season Team	G	Min.	FGM	FGA	Pct.	FTM	FTA	Pct.	REBOUNDS Off.	Def.	Tot.	Ast.	St.	Blk.	TO	Pts.	AVERAGES RPG	APG	PPG
87-88—Washington	79	1628	166	426	.390	58	74	.784	35	101	136	404	127	3	101	393	1.7	5.1	5.0
88-89—Charlotte	79	1755	178	418	.426	66	88	.750	53	112	165	620	111	7	124	423	2.1	7.8	5.4
89-90—Charlotte	81	2743	326	664	.491	106	134	.791	48	159	207	867	166	3	146	763	2.6	10.7	9.4
90-91—Charlotte	81	2299	241	524	.460	86	108	.796	58	158	216	669	137	3	120	568	2.7	8.3	7.0
91-92—Charlotte	82	2790	317	671	.472	94	120	.783	58	177	235	743	170	6	156	730	2.9	9.1	8.9
92-93—Charlotte	81	2833	331	730	.453	140	168	.833	51	247	298	711	161	5	154	808	3.7	8.8	10.0
93-94—Charlotte	77	2746	354	751	.471	125	155	.806	78	235	313	780	133	2	171	835	4.1	10.1	10.8
94-95—Charlotte	78	2629	348	730	.477	160	180	.889	51	206	257	675	103	0	132	862	3.3	8.7	11.1
95-96—Charlotte	6	77	6	16	.375	2	2	1.000	6	1	7	19	2	0	6	14	1.2	3.2	2.3
Totals	644	19500	2267	4930	.460	837	1029	.813	438	1396	1834	5488	1110	29	1110	5396	2.8	8.5	8.4

Three-point field goals: 1987-88, 3-for-16 (.188). 1988-89, 1-for-13 (.077). 1989-90, 5-for-26 (.192). 1990-91, 0-for-12. 1991-92, 2-for-27 (.074). 1992-93, 6-for-26 (.231). 1993-94, 2-for-12 (.167). 1994-95, 6-for-30 (.200). 1995-96, 0-for-1. Totals, 25-for-163 (.153).
Personal fouls/disqualifications: 1987-88, 138/1. 1988-89, 141/1. 1989-90, 168/1. 1990-91, 160/2. 1991-92, 156/0. 1992-93, 179/0. 1993-94, 147/1. 1994-95, 151/0. 1995-96, 4/0. Totals, 1244/6.

NBA PLAYOFF RECORD

Season Team	G	Min.	FGM	FGA	Pct.	FTM	FTA	Pct.	REBOUNDS Off.	Def.	Tot.	Ast.	St.	Blk.	TO	Pts.	AVERAGES RPG	APG	PPG
87-88—Washington	1	2	0	0	...	0	0	...	0	0	0	2	0	0	1	0	0.0	2.0	0.0
92-93—Charlotte	9	346	39	82	.476	10	14	.714	6	30	36	70	24	0	17	88	4.0	7.8	9.8
94-95—Charlotte	4	145	14	45	.311	5	5	1.000	3	3	6	25	4	0	9	34	1.5	6.3	8.5
Totals	14	493	53	127	.417	15	19	.789	9	33	42	97	28	0	27	122	3.0	6.9	8.7

Three-point field goals: 1992-93, 0-for-2. 1994-95, 1-for-3 (.333). Totals, 1-for-5 (.200).
Personal fouls/disqualifications: 1992-93, 21/0. 1994-95, 8/0. Totals, 29/0.

BONNER, ANTHONY   F

PERSONAL: Born June 8, 1968, in St. Louis. ... 6-8/225.
HIGH SCHOOL: Vashon (St. Louis).
COLLEGE: St. Louis.
TRANSACTIONS/CAREER NOTES: Selected by Sacramento Kings in first round (23rd pick overall) of 1990 NBA Draft. ... Rights renounced by Kings (September 15, 1993). ... Signed as free agent by New York Knicks (October 5, 1993). ... Played in Italy (1995-96). ... Signed by Orlando Magic for remainder of season (April 15, 1996). ... Signed to play with PAOK (Greece) during 1996-97 season.

COLLEGIATE RECORD

NOTES: Led NCAA Division I with 13.8 rebounds per game (1990).

Season Team	G	Min.	FGM	FGA	Pct.	FTM	FTA	Pct.	Reb.	Ast.	Pts.	AVERAGES RPG	APG	PPG
86-87—St. Louis	35	1066	138	233	.592	84	127	.661	337	46	360	9.6	1.3	10.3
87-88—St. Louis	28	942	154	287	.537	77	129	.597	245	32	385	8.8	1.1	13.8
88-89—St. Louis	37	1246	228	407	.560	117	201	.582	386	92	573	10.4	2.5	15.5
89-90—St. Louis	33	...	254	508	.500	142	205	.693	456	95	654	13.8	2.9	19.8
Totals	133	...	774	1435	.539	420	662	.634	1424	265	1972	10.7	2.0	14.8

Three-point field goals: 1989-90, 4-for-12 (.333).

NBA REGULAR-SEASON RECORD

Season Team	G	Min.	FGM	FGA	Pct.	FTM	FTA	Pct.	REBOUNDS Off.	Def.	Tot.	Ast.	St.	Blk.	TO	Pts.	AVERAGES RPG	APG	PPG
90-91—Sacramento	34	750	103	230	.448	44	76	.579	59	102	161	49	39	5	41	250	4.7	1.4	7.4
91-92—Sacramento	71	2287	294	658	.447	151	241	.627	192	293	485	125	94	26	133	740	6.1	1.6	9.4
92-93—Sacramento	70	1764	229	497	.461	143	241	.593	188	267	455	96	86	17	105	601	6.5	1.4	8.6
93-94—New York	73	1402	162	288	.563	50	105	.476	150	194	344	88	76	13	89	374	4.7	1.2	5.1
94-95—New York	58	1126	88	193	.456	44	67	.657	113	149	262	80	48	23	79	221	4.5	1.4	3.8
95-96—Orlando	4	43	5	15	.333	3	7	.429	6	13	19	4	3	0	3	13	4.8	1.0	3.3
Totals	318	7372	881	1881	.468	435	737	.590	708	1018	1726	442	346	84	450	2199	5.4	1.4	6.9

Three-point field goals: 1991-92, 1-for-4 (.250). 1992-93, 0-for-7. 1994-95, 1-for-5 (.200). Totals, 2-for-16 (.125).
Personal fouls/disqualifications: 1990-91, 62/0. 1991-92, 194/0. 1992-93, 183/1. 1993-94, 175/3. 1994-95, 159/0. 1995-96, 11/0. Totals, 784/4.

NBA PLAYOFF RECORD

Season Team	G	Min.	FGM	FGA	Pct.	FTM	FTA	Pct.	REBOUNDS Off.	Def.	Tot.	Ast.	St.	Blk.	TO	Pts.	AVERAGES RPG	APG	PPG
93-94—New York	13	118	10	22	.455	7	13	.538	15	13	28	2	5	0	13	27	2.2	0.2	2.1
94-95—New York	6	38	6	11	.545	3	6	.500	4	4	8	2	1	1	3	15	1.3	0.3	2.5
95-96—Orlando	4	16	1	3	.333	1	2	.500	2	0	2	1	0	0	0	3	0.5	0.3	0.8
Totals	23	172	17	36	.472	11	21	.524	21	17	38	5	6	1	16	45	1.7	0.2	2.0

Three-point field goals: 1994-95, 0-for-1.
Personal fouls/disqualifications: 1993-94, 22/0. 1994-95, 6/0. 1995-96, 3/0. Totals, 31/0.

ITALIAN LEAGUE RECORD

Season Team	G	Min.	FGM	FGA	Pct.	FTM	FTA	Pct.	Reb.	Ast.	Pts.	AVERAGES RPG	APG	PPG
95-96—Buckler Beer Bologna.....	12	393	90	152	.592	20	43	.465	114	14	200	9.5	1.2	16.7

BOOKER, MELVIN   G

PERSONAL: Born August 20, 1972, in Pascagoula, Miss. ... 6-2/185. ... Full name: Melvin Jermaine Booker.
HIGH SCHOOL: Moss Point (Miss.).
COLLEGE: Missouri.
TRANSACTIONS/CAREER NOTES: Not drafted by an NBA franchise. ... Played in Continental Basketball Association with Hartford Hellcats (1994-95), Pittsburgh Piranhas (1994-95) and Grand Rapids Mackers (1995-96). ... Signed by Houston Rockets to first of two consecutive 10-day contracts (March 5, 1996). ... Re-signed by Rockets for remainder of season (March 27, 1996). ... Rights renounced by Rockets (July 16, 1996).

COLLEGIATE RECORD

Season Team	G	Min.	FGM	FGA	Pct.	FTM	FTA	Pct.	Reb.	Ast.	Pts.	RPG	APG	PPG
90-91—Missouri	30	856	89	205	.434	51	76	.671	66	105	248	2.2	3.5	8.3
91-92—Missouri	30	996	124	261	.475	53	69	.768	114	118	348	3.8	3.9	11.6
92-93—Missouri	33	1157	164	374	.439	143	175	.817	142	122	522	4.3	3.7	15.8
93-94—Missouri	32	1114	189	375	.504	135	164	.823	121	143	579	3.8	4.5	18.1
Totals	125	4123	566	1215	.466	382	484	.789	443	488	1697	3.5	3.9	13.6

Three-point field goals: 1990-91, 19-for-55 (.345). 1991-92, 47-for-108 (.435). 1992-93, 51-for-141 (.362). 1993-94, 66-for-163 (.405). Totals, 183-for-467 (.392).

CBA REGULAR-SEASON RECORD

Season Team	G	Min.	FGM	FGA	Pct.	FTM	FTA	Pct.	Reb.	Ast.	Pts.	RPG	APG	PPG
94-95—Hartford-Pittsburgh	33	690	81	194	.418	41	55	.745	68	92	221	2.1	2.8	6.7
95-96—Grand Rapids	49	1303	225	463	.486	158	191	.827	162	235	670	3.3	4.8	13.7
Totals	82	1993	306	657	.466	199	246	.809	230	327	891	2.8	4.0	10.9

Three-point field goals: 1994-95, 18-for-61 (.295). 1995-96, 62-for-137 (.453). Totals, 80-for-198 (.405).

NBA REGULAR-SEASON RECORD

Season Team	G	Min.	FGM	FGA	Pct.	FTM	FTA	Pct.	Off.	Def.	Tot.	Ast.	St.	Blk.	TO	Pts.	RPG	APG	PPG
95-96—Houston	11	131	16	50	.320	9	11	.818	1	8	9	21	5	1	12	44	0.8	1.9	4.0

Three-point field goals: 1995-96, 3-for-19 (.158).
Personal fouls/disqualifications: 1995-96, 18/0.

BOWIE, ANTHONY   G

PERSONAL: Born November 9, 1963, in Tulsa, Okla. ... 6-6/200. ... Full name: Anthony Lee Bowie. ... Name pronounced BOO-ee.
HIGH SCHOOL: East Central (Tulsa, Okla.).
JUNIOR COLLEGE: Seminole (Okla.) Junior College.
COLLEGE: Oklahoma.
TRANSACTIONS/CAREER NOTES: Selected by Houston Rockets in third round (66th pick overall) of 1986 NBA Draft. ... Waived by Rockets (November 4, 1986). ... Re-signed by Rockets (June 11, 1987). ... Waived by Rockets (November 5, 1987). ... Played in Continental Basketball Association with Quad City Thunder (1987-88, 1988-89 and 1991-92). ... Signed as free agent by New Jersey Nets (July 19, 1988). ... Waived by Nets (November 1, 1988). ... Signed by San Antonio Spurs to first of two consecutive 10-day contracts (March 20, 1989). ... Re-signed by Spurs for remainder of season (April 9, 1989). ... Traded by Spurs to Rockets for cash (August 15, 1989). ... Waived by Rockets (July 5, 1990). ... Played in Italy (1990-91). ... Signed as free agent by Chicago Bulls (October 2, 1991). ... Waived by Bulls (October 30, 1991). ... Signed as free agent by Orlando Magic (December 31, 1991). ... Signed to play with Stefanel Milan (Italy) for 1996-97 season.

COLLEGIATE RECORD

Season Team	G	Min.	FGM	FGA	Pct.	FTM	FTA	Pct.	Reb.	Ast.	Pts.	RPG	APG	PPG
82-83—Seminole J.C.	40	...	...	...	...	...	...	...	...	...	712	...	...	17.8
83-84—Seminole J.C.	38	...	...	...	...	...	...	...	...	...	707	...	...	18.6
84-85—Oklahoma	37	1282	202	392	.515	92	119	.773	215	196	496	5.8	5.3	13.4
85-86—Oklahoma	35	1170	202	402	.502	63	78	.808	161	166	467	4.6	4.7	13.3
Junior college totals	78	...	...	...	...	...	...	...	...	...	1419	...	...	18.2
4-year-college totals	72	2452	404	794	.509	155	197	.787	376	362	963	5.2	5.0	13.4

CBA REGULAR-SEASON RECORD

NOTES: CBA Most Valuable Player (1989). ... CBA All-League first team (1989).

Season Team	G	Min.	FGM	FGA	Pct.	FTM	FTA	Pct.	Reb.	Ast.	Pts.	RPG	APG	PPG
87-88—Quad City	37	1028	205	388	.528	75	83	.904	163	105	492	4.4	2.8	13.3
88-89—Quad City	53	1959	456	936	.487	171	213	.803	363	238	1097	6.8	4.5	20.7
91-92—Quad City	23	841	197	384	.513	75	86	.872	174	77	475	7.6	3.3	20.7
Totals	113	3828	858	1708	.502	321	382	.840	700	420	2064	6.2	3.7	18.3

Three-point field goals: 1987-88, 7-for-23 (.304). 1988-89, 14-for-58 (.241). 1991-92, 6-for-13 (.462). Totals, 27-for-94 (.288).

NBA REGULAR-SEASON RECORD

Season Team	G	Min.	FGM	FGA	Pct.	FTM	FTA	Pct.	Off.	Def.	Tot.	Ast.	St.	Blk.	TO	Pts.	RPG	APG	PPG
88-89—San Antonio	18	438	72	144	.500	10	15	.667	25	31	56	29	18	4	22	155	3.1	1.6	8.6
89-90—Houston	66	918	119	293	.406	40	54	.741	36	82	118	96	42	5	59	284	1.8	1.5	4.3
91-92—Orlando	52	1721	312	633	.493	117	136	.860	70	175	245	163	55	38	107	758	4.7	3.1	14.6
92-93—Orlando	77	1761	268	569	.471	67	84	.799	36	158	194	175	54	14	84	618	2.5	2.3	8.0
93-94—Orlando	70	948	139	289	.481	41	49	.837	29	91	120	102	32	12	58	320	1.7	1.5	4.6
94-95—Orlando	77	1261	177	369	.480	61	73	.836	54	85	139	159	47	21	86	427	1.8	2.1	5.5
95-96—Orlando	74	1078	128	272	.471	40	46	.870	40	83	123	105	34	10	55	308	1.7	1.4	4.2
Totals	434	8125	1215	2569	.473	376	457	.823	290	705	995	829	282	104	471	2870	2.3	1.9	6.6

Three-point field goals: 1988-89, 1-for-5 (.200). 1989-90, 6-for-21 (.286). 1991-92, 17-for-44 (.386). 1992-93, 15-for-48 (.313). 1993-94, 1-for-18 (.056). 1994-95, 12-for-40 (.300). 1995-96, 12-for-31 (.387). Totals, 64-for-207 (.309).
Personal fouls/disqualifications: 1988-89, 43/1. 1989-90, 80/0. 1991-92, 101/1. 1992-93, 131/0. 1993-94, 81/0. 1994-95, 138/1. 1995-96, 112/0. Totals, 686/3.

B

Season Team	G	Min.	FGM	FGA	Pct.	FTM	FTA	Pct.	REBOUNDS Off.	Def.	Tot.	Ast.	St.	Blk.	TO	Pts.	AVERAGES RPG	APG	PPG
89-90—Houston	2	4	0	1	.000	0	0	...	0	0	0	0	0	0	0	0	0.0	0.0	0.0
93-94—Orlando	2	13	0	1	.000	0	0	...	0	0	0	0	0	0	0	0	0.0	0.0	0.0
94-95—Orlando	17	118	21	42	.500	8	9	.889	4	8	12	18	1	1	8	55	0.7	1.1	3.2
95-96—Orlando	12	152	13	27	.481	4	4	1.000	3	14	17	14	3	2	5	30	1.4	1.2	2.5
Totals	33	287	34	71	.479	12	13	.923	7	22	29	32	4	3	13	85	0.9	1.0	2.6

Three-point field goals: 1994-95, 5-for-7 (.714).
Personal fouls/disqualifications: 1989-90, 1/0. 1993-94, 3/0. 1994-95, 23/0. 1995-96, 16/0. Totals, 43/0.

ITALIAN LEAGUE RECORD

Season Team	G	Min.	FGM	FGA	Pct.	FTM	FTA	Pct.	Reb.	Ast.	Pts.	AVERAGES RPG	APG	PPG
90-91—Ranger Varese	21	770	152	258	.589	88	112	.786	110	36	452	5.2	1.7	21.5

B

BOYCE, DONNIE　　　　　　　G　　　　　　　HAWKS

PERSONAL: Born September 2, 1973, in Chicago. ... 6-5/196. ... Full name: Donald Nathaniel Boyce.
HIGH SCHOOL: Proviso East (Maywood, Ill.).
COLLEGE: Colorado.
TRANSACTIONS/CAREER NOTES: Selected by Atlanta Hawks in second round (42nd pick overall) of 1995 NBA Draft. ... Waived by Hawks (July 19, 1996). ... Re-signed as free agent by Hawks (August 5, 1996).

COLLEGIATE RECORD

Season Team	G	Min.	FGM	FGA	Pct.	FTM	FTA	Pct.	Reb.	Ast.	Pts.	AVERAGES RPG	APG	PPG
91-92—Colorado	28	938	163	389	.419	66	117	.564	133	87	417	4.8	3.1	14.9
92-93—Colorado	27	896	184	404	.455	124	194	.639	168	96	515	6.2	3.6	19.1
93-94—Colorado	26	893	189	471	.401	165	233	.708	173	116	582	6.7	4.5	22.4
94-95—Colorado	26	801	157	384	.409	125	177	.706	170	106	481	6.5	4.1	18.5
Totals	107	3528	693	1648	.421	480	721	.666	644	405	1995	6.0	3.8	18.6

Three-point field goals: 1991-92, 25-for-90 (.278). 1992-93, 23-for-73 (.315). 1993-94, 39-for-123 (.317). 1994-95, 42-for-133 (.316). Totals, 129-for-419 (.308).

NBA REGULAR-SEASON RECORD

Season Team	G	Min.	FGM	FGA	Pct.	FTM	FTA	Pct.	REBOUNDS Off.	Def.	Tot.	Ast.	St.	Blk.	TO	Pts.	AVERAGES RPG	APG	PPG
95-96—Atlanta	8	41	9	23	.391	2	4	.500	5	5	10	3	3	1	6	24	1.3	0.4	3.0

Three-point field goals: 1995-96, 4-for-8 (.500).
Personal fouls/disqualifications: 1995-96, 2/0.

NBA PLAYOFF RECORD

Season Team	G	Min.	FGM	FGA	Pct.	FTM	FTA	Pct.	REBOUNDS Off.	Def.	Tot.	Ast.	St.	Blk.	TO	Pts.	AVERAGES RPG	APG	PPG
95-96—Atlanta	1	2	0	2	.000	0	0	...	0	0	0	0	0	0	0	0	0.0	0.0	0.0

Three-point field goals: 1995-96, 0-for-2.

BRADLEY, SHAWN　　　　　　C　　　　　　　NETS

PERSONAL: Born March 22, 1972, in Landstuhl, West Germany. ... 7-6/248. ... Full name: Shawn Paul Bradley.
HIGH SCHOOL: Emery County (Castle Dale, Utah).
COLLEGE: Brigham Young.
TRANSACTIONS/CAREER NOTES: Selected after freshman season by Philadelphia 76ers in first round (second pick overall) of 1993 NBA Draft. ... Traded by 76ers with F Tim Perry and G Greg Graham to New Jersey Nets for F Derrick Coleman, F Sean Higgins and G Rex Walters (November 30, 1995).

COLLEGIATE RECORD

NOTES: Shares NCAA Division I single-game record for most blocked shots—14 (December 7, 1990, vs. Eastern Kentucky). ... Led NCAA Division I with 5.2 blocked shots per game (1991).

Season Team	G	Min.	FGM	FGA	Pct.	FTM	FTA	Pct.	Reb.	Ast.	Pts.	AVERAGES RPG	APG	PPG
90-91—Brigham Young	34	984	187	361	.518	128	185	.692	262	41	503	7.7	1.2	14.8
91-92—Brigham Young						Did not play—on Mormon mission.								
92-93—Brigham Young						Did not play—on Mormon mission.								
Totals	34	984	187	361	.518	128	185	.692	262	41	503	7.7	1.2	14.8

Three-point field goals: 1990-91, 1-for-1.

NBA REGULAR-SEASON RECORD

HONORS: NBA All-Rookie second team (1994).
NOTES: Led NBA with 338 personal fouls and 18 disqualifications (1995).

Season Team	G	Min.	FGM	FGA	Pct.	FTM	FTA	Pct.	REBOUNDS Off.	Def.	Tot.	Ast.	St.	Blk.	TO	Pts.	AVERAGES RPG	APG	PPG
93-94—Philadelphia	49	1385	201	491	.409	102	168	.607	98	208	306	98	45	147	148	504	6.2	2.0	10.3
94-95—Philadelphia	82	2365	315	693	.455	148	232	.638	243	416	659	53	54	274	142	778	8.0	0.6	9.5
95-96—Phil.-N.J.	79	2329	387	873	.443	169	246	.687	221	417	638	63	49	288	179	944	8.1	0.8	11.9
Totals	210	6079	903	2057	.439	419	646	.649	562	1041	1603	214	148	709	469	2226	7.6	1.0	10.6

Three-point field goals: 1993-94, 0-for-3. 1994-95, 0-for-3. 1995-96, 1-for-4 (.250). Totals, 1-for-10 (.100).
Personal fouls/disqualifications: 1993-94, 170/3. 1994-95, 338/18. 1995-96, 286/5. Totals, 794/26.

BRAGG, MARQUES — F

PERSONAL: Born March 24, 1970, in East Orange, N.J. ... 6-8/230. ... Name pronounced mar-KEYS.
HIGH SCHOOL: Clifford J. Scott (East Orange, N.J.).
COLLEGE: Providence.
TRANSACTIONS/CAREER NOTES: Not drafted by an NBA franchise. ... Played in United States Basketball League with Philadelphia Spirit (1992) and Jersey Turnpikes (1995). ... Played in France (1992-93 and 1993-94). ... Played in Continental Basketball Association with Grand City Rapids (1994-95). ... Signed as free agent by Minnesota Timberwolves (October 5, 1995). ... Rights renounced by Timberwolves (July 11, 1996).

COLLEGIATE RECORD

Season Team	G	Min.	FGM	FGA	Pct.	FTM	FTA	Pct.	Reb.	Ast.	Pts.	RPG	APG	PPG
88-89—Providence	14	...	13	28	.464	6	15	.400	17	4	32	1.2	0.3	2.3
89-90—Providence	28	...	60	107	.561	39	88	.443	111	11	159	4.0	0.4	5.7
90-91—Providence	32	...	162	270	.600	66	145	.455	280	35	390	8.8	1.1	12.2
91-92—Providence	30	867	124	230	.539	92	170	.541	249	42	340	8.3	1.4	11.3
Totals	104		359	635	.565	203	418	.486	657	92	921	6.3	0.9	8.9

FRENCH LEAGUE RECORD

Season Team	G	Min.	FGM	FGA	Pct.	FTM	FTA	Pct.	Reb.	Ast.	Pts.	RPG	APG	PPG
93-94—Gravelines	20	...	...	...	...	...	...	...	205	40	310	10.3	2.0	15.5

CBA REGULAR-SEASON RECORD

NOTES: CBA Newcomer of the Year (1995). ... CBA All-League first team (1995).

Season Team	G	Min.	FGM	FGA	Pct.	FTM	FTA	Pct.	Reb.	Ast.	Pts.	RPG	APG	PPG
94-95—Grand Rapids	56	2184	445	845	.527	217	347	.625	486	118	1108	8.7	2.1	19.8

Three-point field goals: 1994-95, 1-for-7 (.143).

NBA REGULAR-SEASON RECORD

Season Team	G	Min.	FGM	FGA	Pct.	FTM	FTA	Pct.	Off.	Def.	Tot.	Ast.	St.	Blk.	TO	Pts.	RPG	APG	PPG
95-96—Minnesota	53	369	54	120	.450	23	41	.561	38	41	79	8	17	8	26	131	1.5	0.2	2.5

Personal fouls/disqualifications: 1995-96, 71/0.

BRANDON, TERRELL — G — CAVALIERS

PERSONAL: Born May 20, 1970, in Portland, Ore. ... 5-11/180. ... Full name: Thomas Terrell Brandon. ... Name pronounced tur-RELL.
HIGH SCHOOL: Grant (Portland, Ore.).
COLLEGE: Oregon.
TRANSACTIONS/CAREER NOTES: Selected after junior season by Cleveland Cavaliers in first round (11th pick overall) of 1991 NBA Draft.

COLLEGIATE RECORD

Season Team	G	Min.	FGM	FGA	Pct.	FTM	FTA	Pct.	Reb.	Ast.	Pts.	RPG	APG	PPG
88-89—Oregon						Did not play—ineligible.								
89-90—Oregon	29	1067	190	401	.474	97	129	.752	106	174	518	3.7	6.0	17.9
90-91—Oregon	28	1108	273	556	.491	159	187	.850	101	141	745	3.6	5.0	26.6
Totals	57	2175	463	957	.484	256	316	.810	207	315	1263	3.6	5.5	22.2

Three-point field goals: 1989-90, 41-for-94 (.436). 1990-91, 40-for-119 (.336). Totals, 81-for-213 (.380).

HONORS: NBA All-Rookie second team (1992).

NBA REGULAR-SEASON RECORD

Season Team	G	Min.	FGM	FGA	Pct.	FTM	FTA	Pct.	Off.	Def.	Tot.	Ast.	St.	Blk.	TO	Pts.	RPG	APG	PPG
91-92—Cleveland	82	1605	252	601	.419	100	124	.806	49	113	162	316	81	22	136	605	2.0	3.9	7.4
92-93—Cleveland	82	1622	297	621	.478	118	143	.825	37	142	179	302	79	27	107	725	2.2	3.7	8.8
93-94—Cleveland	73	1548	230	548	.420	139	162	.858	38	121	159	277	84	16	111	606	2.2	3.8	8.3
94-95—Cleveland	67	1961	341	762	.448	159	186	.855	35	151	186	363	107	14	144	889	2.8	5.4	13.3
95-96—Cleveland	75	2570	510	1096	.465	338	381	.887	47	201	248	487	132	33	142	1449	3.3	6.5	19.3
Totals	379	9306	1630	3628	.449	854	996	.857	206	728	934	1745	483	112	640	4274	2.5	4.6	11.3

Three-point field goals: 1991-92, 1-for-23 (.043). 1992-93, 13-for-42 (.310). 1993-94, 7-for-32 (.219). 1994-95, 48-for-121 (.397). 1995-96, 91-for-235 (.387). Totals, 160-for-453 (.353).
Personal fouls/disqualifications: 1991-92, 107/0. 1992-93, 122/1. 1993-94, 108/0. 1994-95, 118/0. 1995-96, 146/1. Totals, 601/2.

NBA PLAYOFF RECORD

Season Team	G	Min.	FGM	FGA	Pct.	FTM	FTA	Pct.	Off.	Def.	Tot.	Ast.	St.	Blk.	TO	Pts.	RPG	APG	PPG
91-92—Cleveland	12	157	22	55	.400	3	4	.750	4	18	22	30	3	1	11	47	1.8	2.5	3.9
92-93—Cleveland	8	132	20	46	.435	9	9	1.000	4	13	17	17	7	3	14	51	2.1	2.1	6.4
93-94—Cleveland	3	56	12	19	.632	2	3	.667	1	3	4	5	1	0	1	26	1.3	1.7	8.7
95-96—Cleveland	3	125	21	47	.447	13	15	.867	1	8	9	24	4	1	11	58	3.0	8.0	19.3
Totals	26	470	75	167	.449	27	31	.871	10	42	52	76	15	5	37	182	2.0	2.9	7.0

Three-point field goals: 1991-92, 0-for-3. 1992-93, 2-for-5 (.400). 1995-96, 3-for-9 (.333). Totals, 5-for-17 (.294).
Personal fouls/disqualifications: 1991-92, 17/0. 1992-93, 6/0. 1993-94, 1/0. 1995-96, 10/0. Totals, 34/0.

B

NBA ALL-STAR GAME RECORD

Season Team	Min.	FGM	FGA	Pct.	FTM	FTA	Pct.	REBOUNDS Off.	Def.	Tot.	Ast.	PF	Dq.	St.	Blk.	TO	Pts.
1996 —Cleveland............	20	4	10	.400	2	2	1.000	1	0	1	3	1	0	1	1	3	11

Three-point field goals: 1996, 1-for-4 (.250).

BREAUX, TIM — F — GRIZZLIES

PERSONAL: Born September 19, 1970, in Baton Rouge, La. ... 6-7/235. ... Full name: Timothy Breaux. ... Name pronounced BROH.
HIGH SCHOOL: Zachary (La.).
COLLEGE: Wyoming.
TRANSACTIONS/CAREER NOTES: Not drafted by an NBA franchise. ... Played in Continental Basketball Association with Sioux Falls Skyforce (1992-93). ... Did not play professional basketball (1993-94). ... Signed as free agent by Houston Rockets (August 26, 1994). ... Traded by Rockets with F Pete Chilcutt, 1996 first- and second-round draft choices and 1997 conditional second-round draft choice to Vancouver Grizzlies for two 1996 second-round draft choices (June 19, 1996).

B

COLLEGIATE RECORD

Season Team	G	Min.	FGM	FGA	Pct.	FTM	FTA	Pct.	Reb.	Ast.	Pts.	AVERAGES RPG	APG	PPG
88-89—Wyoming.....................	31	809	93	200	.465	64	99	.646	108	24	269	3.5	0.8	8.7
89-90—Wyoming.....................	29	868	133	330	.403	63	101	.624	116	55	371	4.0	1.9	12.8
91-92—Wyoming.....................	29	1017	165	313	.527	113	171	.661	130	53	472	4.5	1.8	16.3
Totals	89	2694	391	843	.464	240	371	.647	354	132	1112	4.0	1.5	12.5

Three-point field goals: 1988-89, 19-for-52 (.365). 1989-90, 42-for-115 (.365). 1991-92, 29-for-65 (.446). Totals, 90-for-232 (.388).

CBA REGULAR-SEASON RECORD

NOTES: Named to CBA All-Rookie second team (1993).

Season Team	G	Min.	FGM	FGA	Pct.	FTM	FTA	Pct.	Reb.	Ast.	Pts.	AVERAGES RPG	APG	PPG
92-93—Sioux Falls....................	50	1368	273	589	.464	128	165	.776	116	83	683	2.3	1.7	13.7

Three-point field goals: 1992-93, 9-for-34 (.265).

NBA REGULAR-SEASON RECORD

Season Team	G	Min.	FGM	FGA	Pct.	FTM	FTA	Pct.	REBOUNDS Off.	Def.	Tot.	Ast.	St.	Blk.	TO	Pts.	AVERAGES RPG	APG	PPG
94-95—Houston.........	42	340	45	121	.372	32	49	.653	16	18	34	15	11	4	16	128	0.8	0.4	3.0
95-96—Houston.........	54	570	59	161	.366	28	45	.622	22	38	60	24	11	8	30	161	1.1	0.4	3.0
Totals	96	910	104	282	.369	60	94	.638	38	56	94	39	22	12	46	289	1.0	0.4	3.0

Three-point field goals: 1994-95, 6-for-25 (.240). 1995-96, 15-for-46 (.326). Totals, 21-for-71 (.296).
Personal fouls/disqualifications: 1994-95, 25/0. 1995-96, 42/0. Totals, 67/0.

BRICKOWSKI, FRANK — F/C — CELTICS

PERSONAL: Born August 14, 1959, in Bayville, N.Y. ... 6-9/248. ... Full name: Francis Anthony Brickowski. ... Name pronounced breh-KOW-ski.
HIGH SCHOOL: Locust Valley (N.Y.).
COLLEGE: Penn State.
TRANSACTIONS/CAREER NOTES: Selected by New York Knicks in third round (57th pick overall) of 1981 NBA Draft. ... Played in Italy (1981-82). ... Played in France (1982-83). ... Draft rights renounced by Knicks (June 30, 1983). ... Played in Israel (1983-84). ... Signed as free agent by Seattle SuperSonics (September 23, 1984). ... Signed as veteran free agent by Los Angeles Lakers (October 8, 1986). ... SuperSonics agreed not to exercise their right of first refusal in exchange for 1988 third-round draft choice and cash. ... Traded by Lakers with C Petur Gudmundsson, 1987 first-round draft choice, 1990 second-round draft choice and cash to San Antonio Spurs for C/F Mychal Thompson (February 13, 1987). ... Traded by Spurs to Milwaukee Bucks for G Paul Pressey (August 1, 1990). ... Traded by Bucks with conditional first-round draft choice to Charlotte Hornets for C Mike Gminski (February 24, 1994). ... Signed as unrestricted free agent by Sacramento Kings (August 19, 1994). ... Traded by Kings to Seattle SuperSonics for G Sarunas Marciulionis and F Byron Houston (September 18, 1995). ... Rights renounced by SuperSonics (July 16, 1996). ... Signed as free agent by Boston Celtics (August 1, 1996).

COLLEGIATE RECORD

Season Team	G	Min.	FGM	FGA	Pct.	FTM	FTA	Pct.	Reb.	Ast.	Pts.	AVERAGES RPG	APG	PPG
77-78—Penn State.....................	25	266	37	81	.457	21	25	.840	64	11	95	2.6	0.4	3.8
78-79—Penn State.....................	24	349	49	99	.495	38	48	.792	109	23	136	4.5	1.0	5.7
79-80—Penn State.....................	27	692	111	213	.521	82	105	.781	202	43	304	7.5	1.6	11.3
80-81—Penn State.....................	24	615	131	218	.601	49	63	.778	150	50	311	6.3	2.1	13.0
Totals	100	1922	328	611	.537	190	241	.788	525	127	846	5.3	1.3	8.5

ITALIAN LEAGUE RECORD

Season Team	G	Min.	FGM	FGA	Pct.	FTM	FTA	Pct.	Reb.	Ast.	Pts.	AVERAGES RPG	APG	PPG
81-82—Cagiva G. Varese	35	1158	204	375	.544	84	123	.683	296	18	492	8.5	0.5	14.1

NBA REGULAR-SEASON RECORD

NOTES: Tied for NBA lead with 11 disqualifications (1988).

Season Team	G	Min.	FGM	FGA	Pct.	FTM	FTA	Pct.	REBOUNDS Off.	Def.	Tot.	Ast.	St.	Blk.	TO	Pts.	AVERAGES RPG	APG	PPG
84-85—Seattle	78	1115	150	305	.492	85	127	.669	76	184	260	100	34	15	100	385	3.3	1.3	4.9
85-86—Seattle	40	311	30	58	.517	18	27	.667	16	38	54	21	11	7	23	78	1.4	0.5	2.0
86-87—L.A.L.-S.A.	44	487	63	124	.508	50	70	.714	48	68	116	17	20	6	32	176	2.6	0.4	4.0
87-88—San Antonio....	70	2227	425	805	.528	268	349	.768	167	316	483	266	74	36	207	1119	6.9	3.8	16.0
88-89—San Antonio....	64	1822	337	654	.515	201	281	.715	148	258	406	131	102	35	165	875	6.3	2.0	13.7
89-90—San Antonio....	78	1438	211	387	.545	95	141	.674	89	238	327	105	66	37	93	517	4.2	1.3	6.6
90-91—Milwaukee	75	1912	372	706	.527	198	248	.798	129	297	426	131	86	43	160	942	5.7	1.7	12.6

B

Season Team	G	Min.	FGM	FGA	Pct.	FTM	FTA	Pct.	Off.	Def.	Tot.	Ast.	St.	Blk.	TO	Pts.	RPG	APG	PPG
91-92—Milwaukee	65	1556	306	584	.524	125	163	.767	97	247	344	122	60	23	112	740	5.3	1.9	11.4
92-93—Milwaukee	66	2075	456	836	.545	195	268	.728	120	285	405	196	80	44	202	1115	6.1	3.0	16.9
93-94—Mil.-Char.	71	2094	368	754	.488	195	254	.768	85	319	404	222	80	27	181	935	5.7	3.1	13.2
94-95—Sacramento.....								Did not play—shoulder injury.											
95-96—Seattle	63	986	123	252	.488	61	86	.709	26	125	151	58	26	8	78	339	2.4	0.9	5.4
Totals	714	16023	2841	5465	.520	1491	2014	.740	1001	2375	3376	1369	639	281	1353	7221	4.7	1.9	10.1

Three-point field goals: 1984-85, 0-for-4. 1986-87, 0-for-4. 1987-88, 1-for-5 (.200). 1988-89, 0-for-2. 1989-90, 0-for-2. 1990-91, 0-for-2. 1991-92, 3-for-6 (.500). 1992-93, 8-for-26 (.308). 1993-94, 4-for-20 (.200). 1995-96, 32-for-79 (.405). Totals, 48-for-150 (.320).

Personal fouls/disqualifications: 1984-85, 171/1. 1985-86, 74/2. 1986-87, 118/4. 1987-88, 275/11. 1988-89, 252/10. 1989-90, 226/4. 1990-91, 255/4. 1991-92, 223/11. 1992-93, 235/8. 1993-94, 242/6. 1995-96, 185/4. Totals, 2256/65.

NBA PLAYOFF RECORD

Season Team	G	Min.	FGM	FGA	Pct.	FTM	FTA	Pct.	Off.	Def.	Tot.	Ast.	St.	Blk.	TO	Pts.	RPG	APG	PPG
87-88—San Antonio....	3	113	22	44	.500	13	19	.684	7	15	22	14	6	2	9	58	7.3	4.7	19.3
89-90—San Antonio....	10	161	31	54	.574	17	26	.654	16	28	44	11	8	1	15	79	4.4	1.1	7.9
90-91—Milwaukee	3	110	24	45	.533	7	14	.500	5	21	26	3	1	2	6	55	8.7	1.0	18.3
95-96—Seattle	21	206	16	38	.421	3	4	.750	2	28	30	11	7	5	20	41	1.4	0.5	2.0
Totals	37	590	93	181	.514	40	63	.635	30	92	122	39	22	10	50	233	3.3	1.1	6.3

Three-point field goals: 1987-88, 1-for-1. 1990-91, 0-for-2. 1995-96, 6-for-22 (.273). Totals, 7-for-25 (.280).
Personal fouls/disqualifications: 1987-88, 12/0. 1989-90, 31/0. 1990-91, 16/1. 1995-96, 55/1. Totals, 114/2.

BROOKS, SCOTT   G   MAVERICKS

PERSONAL: Born July 31, 1965, in French Camp, Calif. ... 5-11/165. ... Full name: Scott William Brooks.
HIGH SCHOOL: East Union (Manteca, Calif.).
JUNIOR COLLEGE: San Joaquin Delta College (Calif.).
COLLEGE: Texas Christian, then UC Irvine.
TRANSACTIONS/CAREER NOTES: Not drafted by an NBA franchise. ... Played in Continental Basketball Association with Albany Patroons (1987-88). ... Played in World Basketball League with Fresno Flames (1988). ... Signed as free agent by Philadelphia 76ers (September 23, 1988). ... Traded by 76ers to Minnesota Timberwolves for 1990 second-round draft choice (June 25, 1990). ... Traded by Timberwolves to Houston Rockets for 1995 second-round draft choice (September 25, 1992). ... Traded by Rockets to Dallas Mavericks for G Morlon Wiley and 1995 second-round draft choice (February 23, 1995).
MISCELLANEOUS: Member of NBA championship team (1994).

COLLEGIATE RECORD

Season Team	G	Min.	FGM	FGA	Pct.	FTM	FTA	Pct.	Reb.	Ast.	Pts.	RPG	APG	PPG
84-85—San Joaquin	31	...	158	301	.525	90	102	.882	45	206	406	1.5	6.6	13.1
83-84—Texas Christian	27	...	46	87	.529	10	14	.714	32	37	102	1.2	1.4	3.8
85-86—UC Irvine	30	945	100	223	.448	78	88	.886	70	95	308	2.3	3.2	10.3
86-87—UC Irvine	28	1027	206	431	.478	142	168	.845	50	105	665	1.8	3.8	23.8
Junior college totals	31	...	158	301	.525	90	102	.882	45	206	406	1.5	6.6	13.1
4-year-college totals	85	...	352	741	.475	230	270	.852	152	237	1075	1.8	2.8	12.6

Three-point field goals: 1985-86, 30-for-80 (.375). 1986-87, 111-for-257 (.432). Totals, 141-for-337 (.418).

NOTES: CBA All-Rookie team (1988).

CBA REGULAR-SEASON RECORD

Season Team	G	Min.	FGM	FGA	Pct.	FTM	FTA	Pct.	Reb.	Ast.	Pts.	RPG	APG	PPG
87-88—Albany	52	1155	160	365	.438	106	132	.803	94	116	451	1.8	2.2	8.7

Three-point field goals: 1987-88, 25-for-76 (.329).

NBA REGULAR-SEASON RECORD

Season Team	G	Min.	FGM	FGA	Pct.	FTM	FTA	Pct.	Off.	Def.	Tot.	Ast.	St.	Blk.	TO	Pts.	RPG	APG	PPG
88-89—Philadelphia	82	1372	156	371	.420	61	69	.884	19	75	94	306	69	3	65	428	1.1	3.7	5.2
89-90—Philadelphia	72	975	119	276	.431	50	57	.877	15	49	64	207	47	0	38	319	0.9	2.9	4.4
90-91—Minnesota	80	980	159	370	.430	61	72	.847	28	44	72	204	53	5	51	424	0.9	2.6	5.3
91-92—Minnesota	82	1082	167	374	.447	51	63	.810	27	72	99	205	66	7	51	417	1.2	2.5	5.1
92-93—Houston	82	1516	183	385	.475	112	135	.830	22	77	99	243	79	2	72	519	1.2	3.0	6.3
93-94—Houston	73	1225	142	289	.491	74	85	.871	10	92	102	149	51	2	55	381	1.4	2.0	5.2
94-95—Hou.-Dal.	59	808	126	275	.458	64	79	.810	14	52	66	116	34	4	47	341	1.1	2.0	5.8
95-96—Dallas..............	69	716	134	293	.457	59	69	.855	11	30	41	100	42	3	43	352	0.6	1.4	5.1
Totals	599	8674	1186	2633	.450	532	629	.846	146	491	637	1530	441	27	422	3181	1.1	2.6	5.3

Three-point field goals: 1988-89, 55-for-153 (.359). 1989-90, 31-for-79 (.392). 1990-91, 45-for-135 (.333). 1991-92, 32-for-90 (.356). 1992-93, 41-for-99 (.414). 1993-94, 23-for-61 (.377). 1994-95, 25-for-69 (.362). 1995-96, 25-for-62 (.403). Totals, 277-for-748 (.370).
Personal fouls/disqualifications: 1988-89, 116/0. 1989-90, 105/0. 1990-91, 122/1. 1991-92, 82/0. 1992-93, 136/0. 1993-94, 98/0. 1994-95, 56/0. 1995-96, 53/0. Totals, 768/1.

NBA PLAYOFF RECORD

Season Team	G	Min.	FGM	FGA	Pct.	FTM	FTA	Pct.	Off.	Def.	Tot.	Ast.	St.	Blk.	TO	Pts.	RPG	APG	PPG
88-89—Philadelphia	3	21	1	6	.167	2	2	1.000	0	4	4	5	0	0	1	5	1.3	1.7	1.7
89-90—Philadelphia	9	99	6	19	.316	6	9	.667	2	6	8	16	3	0	7	21	0.9	1.8	2.3
92-93—Houston..........	12	197	16	42	.381	10	13	.769	1	9	10	31	9	0	13	47	0.8	2.6	3.9
93-94—Houston..........	5	23	5	6	.833	0	1	.000	1	1	2	3	0	0	0	11	0.4	0.6	2.2
Totals	29	340	28	73	.384	18	25	.720	4	20	24	55	12	0	21	84	0.8	1.9	2.9

Three-point field goals: 1988-89, 1-for-2 (.500). 1989-90, 3-for-7 (.429). 1992-93, 5-for-13 (.385). 1993-94, 1-for-1. Totals, 10-for-23 (.435).
Personal fouls/disqualifications: 1988-89, 4/0. 1989-90, 13/0. 1992-93, 21/0. 1993-94, 3/0. Totals, 41/0.

BROWN, CHUCKY　　　　　　　F　　　　　　　SUNS

PERSONAL: Born February 29, 1968, in New York. ... 6-8/215. ... Full name: Clarence Brown.
HIGH SCHOOL: North Brunswick (Leland, N.C.).
COLLEGE: North Carolina State.
TRANSACTIONS/CAREER NOTES: Selected by Cleveland Cavaliers in second round (43rd pick overall) of 1989 NBA Draft. ... Waived by Cavaliers (December 2, 1991). ... Signed as free agent by Los Angeles Lakers (December 5, 1991). ... Played in Italy (1992-93). ... Signed as free agent by New Jersey Nets (October 7, 1992). ... Signed as free agent by Dallas Mavericks (November 12, 1993). ... Waived by Mavericks (November 23, 1993). ... Signed as free agent by Miami Heat (October 4, 1994). ... Waived by Heat (November 1, 1994). ... Played in Continental Basketball Association with Grand Rapids Hoops (1993-94) and Yakima Sun Kings (1993-94 and 1994-95). ... Signed by Houston Rockets to first of two consecutive 10-day contracts (February 2, 1995). ... Re-signed by Rockets for remainder of season (February 25, 1995). ... Traded by Rockets with G Sam Cassell, F Robert Horry and F Mark Bryant to Phoenix Suns for F Charles Barkley and 1999 second-round draft choice (August 19, 1996).
MISCELLANEOUS: Member of NBA championship team (1995).

COLLEGIATE RECORD

Season Team	G	Min.	FGM	FGA	Pct.	FTM	FTA	Pct.	Reb.	Ast.	Pts.	RPG	APG	PPG
85-86—N.C. State	31	310	38	80	.475	21	34	.618	67	13	97	2.2	0.4	3.1
86-87—N.C. State	34	629	81	138	.587	61	80	.763	145	12	223	4.3	0.4	6.6
87-88—N.C. State	32	1024	226	395	.572	77	121	.636	193	27	530	6.0	0.8	16.6
88-89—N.C. State	31	1051	210	383	.548	81	125	.648	274	42	507	8.8	1.4	16.4
Totals	128	3014	555	996	.557	240	360	.667	679	94	1357	5.3	0.7	10.6

Three-point field goals: 1986-87, 0-for-1. 1987-88, 1-for-6 (.167). 1988-89, 6-for-21 (.286). Totals, 7-for-28 (.250).

NBA REGULAR-SEASON RECORD

									REBOUNDS								AVERAGES		
Season Team	G	Min.	FGM	FGA	Pct.	FTM	FTA	Pct.	Off.	Def.	Tot.	Ast.	St.	Blk.	TO	Pts.	RPG	APG	PPG
89-90—Cleveland	75	1339	210	447	.470	125	164	.762	83	148	231	50	33	26	69	545	3.1	0.7	7.3
90-91—Cleveland	74	1485	263	502	.524	101	144	.701	78	135	213	80	26	24	94	627	2.9	1.1	8.5
91-92—Clev.-L.A.L.	42	431	60	128	.469	30	49	.612	31	51	82	26	12	7	29	150	2.0	0.6	3.6
92-93—New Jersey	77	1186	160	331	.483	71	98	.724	88	144	232	51	20	24	56	391	3.0	0.7	5.1
93-94—Dallas	1	10	1	1	1.000	0	1	1.000	0	1	1	0	0	0	0	3	1.0	0.0	3.0
94-95—Houston	41	814	105	174	.603	38	62	.613	64	125	189	30	11	14	29	249	4.6	0.7	6.1
95-96—Houston	82	2019	300	555	.541	104	150	.693	134	307	441	89	47	38	94	705	5.4	1.1	8.6
Totals	392	7284	1099	2138	.514	470	668	.704	478	911	1389	326	149	133	371	2670	3.5	0.8	6.8

Three-point field goals: 1989-90, 0-for-7. 1990-91, 0-for-4. 1991-92, 0-for-3. 1992-93, 0-for-5. 1994-95, 1-for-3 (.333). 1995-96, 1-for-8 (.125). Totals, 2-for-30 (.067).
Personal fouls/disqualifications: 1989-90, 148/0. 1990-91, 130/0. 1991-92, 48/0. 1992-93, 112/0. 1993-94, 2/0. 1994-95, 105/0. 1995-96, 163/0. Totals, 708/0.

NBA PLAYOFF RECORD

									REBOUNDS								AVERAGES		
Season Team	G	Min.	FGM	FGA	Pct.	FTM	FTA	Pct.	Off.	Def.	Tot.	Ast.	St.	Blk.	TO	Pts.	RPG	APG	PPG
91-92—L.A. Lakers	3	44	8	19	.421	3	6	.500	3	8	11	2	0	2	1	19	3.7	0.7	6.3
92-93—New Jersey	4	62	9	22	.409	6	7	.857	3	6	9	1	3	3	2	24	2.3	0.3	6.0
94-95—Houston	21	326	34	76	.447	25	37	.676	20	45	65	7	9	2	12	94	3.1	0.3	4.5
95-96—Houston	8	168	25	45	.556	15	18	.833	6	18	24	5	3	0	4	65	3.0	0.6	8.1
Totals	36	600	76	162	.469	49	68	.721	32	77	109	15	15	7	19	202	3.0	0.4	5.6

Three-point field goals: 1991-92, 0-for-1. 1994-95, 1-for-2 (.500). Totals, 1-for-3 (.333).
Personal fouls/disqualifications: 1991-92, 3/0. 1992-93, 2/0. 1994-95, 46/2. 1995-96, 17/0. Totals, 68/2.

ITALIAN LEAGUE RECORD

Season Team	G	Min.	FGM	FGA	Pct.	FTM	FTA	Pct.	Reb.	Ast.	Pts.	RPG	APG	PPG
92-93—Panna Firenze	3	111	16	36	.444	11	17	.647	22	3	47	7.3	1.0	15.7

CBA REGULAR-SEASON RECORD

NOTES: CBA All-League first team (1995).

Season Team	G	Min.	FGM	FGA	Pct.	FTM	FTA	Pct.	Reb.	Ast.	Pts.	RPG	APG	PPG
93-94—Gr. Rap.-Yakima	46	1372	251	513	.489	110	150	.733	278	60	612	6.0	1.3	13.3
94-95—Yakima	31	1107	262	459	.571	122	162	.753	171	51	659	5.5	1.6	21.3
Totals	77	2479	513	972	.528	232	312	.744	449	111	1271	5.8	1.4	16.5

Three-point field goals: 1993-94, 0-for-4. 1994-95, 13-for-32 (.406). Totals, 13-for-36 (.362).

BROWN, DEE　　　　　　　G　　　　　　　CELTICS

PERSONAL: Born November 29, 1968, in Jacksonville. ... 6-2/192. ... Full name: DeCovan Kadell Brown.
HIGH SCHOOL: The Bolles School (Jacksonville).
COLLEGE: Jacksonville.
TRANSACTIONS/CAREER NOTES: Selected by Boston Celtics in first round (19th pick overall) of 1990 NBA Draft.

COLLEGIATE RECORD

Season Team	G	Min.	FGM	FGA	Pct.	FTM	FTA	Pct.	Reb.	Ast.	Pts.	RPG	APG	PPG
86-87—Jacksonville	21	186	28	65	.431	13	22	.591	28	17	71	1.3	0.8	3.4
87-88—Jacksonville	28	764	108	239	.452	54	66	.818	125	56	282	4.5	2.0	10.1
88-89—Jacksonville	30	1133	219	447	.490	108	131	.824	228	112	589	7.6	3.7	19.6
89-90—Jacksonville	29	1052	231	466	.496	69	101	.683	192	151	561	6.6	5.2	19.3
Totals	108	3135	586	1217	.482	244	320	.763	573	336	1503	5.3	3.1	13.9

Three-point field goals: 1986-87, 2-for-12 (.167). 1987-88, 12-for-45 (.267). 1988-89, 43-for-101 (.426). 1989-90, 30-for-80 (.375). Totals, 87-for-238 (.366).

B

NBA REGULAR-SEASON RECORD

HONORS: Slam-Dunk Championship winner (1991). ... NBA All-Rookie first team (1991).

Season Team	G	Min.	FGM	FGA	Pct.	FTM	FTA	Pct.	Off.	Def.	Tot.	Ast.	St.	Blk.	TO	Pts.	RPG	APG	PPG
90-91—Boston	82	1945	284	612	.464	137	157	.873	41	141	182	344	83	14	137	712	2.2	4.2	8.7
91-92—Boston	31	883	149	350	.426	60	78	.769	15	64	79	164	33	7	59	363	2.5	5.3	11.7
92-93—Boston	80	2254	328	701	.468	192	242	.793	45	201	246	461	138	32	136	874	3.1	5.8	10.9
93-94—Boston	77	2867	490	1021	.480	182	219	.831	63	237	300	347	156	47	126	1192	3.9	4.5	15.5
94-95—Boston	79	2792	437	977	.447	236	277	.852	63	186	249	301	110	49	146	1236	3.2	3.8	15.6
95-96—Boston	65	1591	246	616	.399	135	158	.854	36	100	136	146	80	12	74	695	2.1	2.2	10.7
Totals	414	12332	1934	4277	.452	942	1131	.833	263	929	1192	1763	600	161	678	5072	2.9	4.3	12.3

Three-point field goals: 1990-91, 7-for-34 (.206). 1991-92, 5-for-22 (.227). 1992-93, 26-for-82 (.317). 1993-94, 30-for-96 (.313). 1994-95, 126-for-327 (.385). 1995-96, 68-for-220 (.309). Totals, 262-for-781 (.335).

Personal fouls/disqualifications: 1990-91, 161/0. 1991-92, 74/0. 1992-93, 203/2. 1993-94, 207/3. 1994-95, 181/0. 1995-96, 119/0. Totals, 945/5.

NBA PLAYOFF RECORD

Season Team	G	Min.	FGM	FGA	Pct.	FTM	FTA	Pct.	Off.	Def.	Tot.	Ast.	St.	Blk.	TO	Pts.	RPG	APG	PPG
90-91—Boston	11	284	53	108	.491	28	34	.824	9	36	45	41	11	6	22	134	4.1	3.7	12.2
91-92—Boston	6	120	22	44	.500	4	6	.667	3	9	12	31	1	4	7	48	2.0	5.2	8.0
92-93—Boston	4	133	15	41	.366	14	14	1.000	2	4	6	15	2	4	6	45	1.5	3.8	11.3
94-95—Boston	4	172	26	62	.419	14	16	.875	6	14	20	19	5	1	7	75	5.0	4.8	18.8
Totals	25	709	116	255	.455	60	70	.857	20	63	83	106	19	15	42	302	3.3	4.2	12.1

Three-point field goals: 1990-91, 0-for-5. 1991-92, 0-for-3. 1992-93, 1-for-7 (.143). 1994-95, 9-for-26 (.346). Totals, 10-for-41 (.244).
Personal fouls/disqualifications: 1990-91, 32/0. 1991-92, 16/2. 1992-93, 11/0. 1994-95, 13/1. Totals, 72/3.

BROWN, MIKE   F/C

PERSONAL: Born July 19, 1963, in Newark, N.J. ... 6-10/260. ... Full name: Michael Brown.
HIGH SCHOOL: Clifford J. Scott (East Orange, N.J.).
COLLEGE: George Washington.
TRANSACTIONS/CAREER NOTES: Selected by Chicago Bulls in third round (69th pick overall) of 1985 NBA Draft. ... Played in Italy (1985-86 and 1995-96). ... Selected by Charlotte Hornets from Bulls in NBA expansion draft (June 23, 1988). ... Traded by Hornets to Utah Jazz for F Kelly Tripucka (June 23, 1988). ... Traded by Jazz to Minnesota Timberwolves for C Felton Spencer (June 30, 1993). ... Signed by Philadelphia 76ers for remainder of season (December 12, 1995). ... Waived by 76ers (January 4, 1996).

COLLEGIATE RECORD

Season Team	G	Min.	FGM	FGA	Pct.	FTM	FTA	Pct.	Reb.	Ast.	Pts.	RPG	APG	PPG
81-82—George Wash.	27	926	174	350	.497	73	141	.518	230	27	421	8.5	1.0	15.6
82-83—George Wash.	29	1058	192	369	.520	112	171	.655	298	40	496	10.3	1.4	17.1
83-84—George Wash.	29	1049	190	355	.535	187	256	.730	351	51	567	12.1	1.8	19.6
84-85—George Wash.	26	937	154	321	.480	124	191	.649	287	56	432	11.0	2.2	16.6
Totals	111	3970	710	1395	.509	496	759	.653	1166	174	1916	10.5	1.6	17.3

ITALIAN LEAGUE RECORD

Season Team	G	Min.	FGM	FGA	Pct.	FTM	FTA	Pct.	Reb.	Ast.	Pts.	RPG	APG	PPG
85-86—Filanto Desio	30	1080	255	415	.614	142	185	.768	362	...	655	12.1	...	21.8
95-96—Teamsystem Bologna	4	130	20	38	.526	8	13	.615	28	3	48	7.0	0.8	12.0

NBA REGULAR-SEASON RECORD

Season Team	G	Min.	FGM	FGA	Pct.	FTM	FTA	Pct.	Off.	Def.	Tot.	Ast.	St.	Blk.	TO	Pts.	RPG	APG	PPG
86-87—Chicago	62	818	106	201	.527	46	72	.639	71	143	214	24	20	7	59	258	3.5	0.4	4.2
87-88—Chicago	46	591	78	174	.448	41	71	.577	66	93	159	28	11	4	38	197	3.5	0.6	4.3
88-89—Utah	66	1051	104	248	.419	92	130	.708	92	166	258	41	25	17	77	300	3.9	0.6	4.5
89-90—Utah	82	1397	177	344	.515	157	199	.789	111	262	373	47	32	28	88	512	4.5	0.6	6.2
90-91—Utah	82	1391	129	284	.454	132	178	.742	109	228	337	49	29	24	82	390	4.1	0.6	4.8
91-92—Utah	82	1783	221	488	.453	190	285	.667	187	289	476	81	42	34	105	632	5.8	1.0	7.7
92-93—Utah	82	1551	176	409	.430	113	164	.689	147	244	391	64	32	23	95	465	4.8	0.8	5.7
93-94—Minnesota	82	1921	111	260	.427	77	118	.653	119	328	447	72	51	29	75	299	5.5	0.9	3.6
94-95—Minnesota	27	213	10	40	.250	15	27	.556	9	36	45	10	7	0	16	35	1.7	0.4	1.3
95-96—Philadelphia	9	162	9	16	.563	8	17	.471	14	23	37	3	3	2	6	26	4.1	0.3	2.9
Totals	620	10878	1121	2464	.455	871	1261	.691	925	1812	2737	419	252	168	641	3114	4.4	0.7	5.0

Three-point field goals: 1987-88, 0-for-1. 1989-90, 1-for-2 (.500). 1991-92, 0-for-1. 1992-93, 0-for-1. 1993-94, 0-for-2. 1994-95, 0-for-1. Totals, 1-for-8 (.125).
Personal fouls/disqualifications: 1986-87, 129/2. 1987-88, 85/0. 1988-89, 133/0. 1989-90, 187/0. 1990-91, 166/0. 1991-92, 196/1. 1992-93, 190/1. 1993-94, 218/4. 1994-95, 35/0. 1995-96, 24/1. Totals, 1363/9.

NBA PLAYOFF RECORD

Season Team	G	Min.	FGM	FGA	Pct.	FTM	FTA	Pct.	Off.	Def.	Tot.	Ast.	St.	Blk.	TO	Pts.	RPG	APG	PPG
86-87—Chicago	1	3	0	1	.000	0	0	...	0	0	0	0	1	0	1	0	0.0	0.0	0.0
87-88—Chicago	1	4	0	0	...	1	2	.500	0	0	0	1	1	0	1	1	0.0	1.0	1.0
88-89—Utah	2	11	0	2	.000	0	0	...	0	2	2	0	0	0	0	0	1.0	0.0	0.0
89-90—Utah	5	67	7	15	.467	4	5	.800	5	5	10	3	1	1	5	18	2.0	0.6	3.6
90-91—Utah	9	223	27	56	.482	32	38	.842	20	46	66	5	3	1	12	86	7.3	0.6	9.6
91-92—Utah	16	274	30	75	.400	32	41	.780	22	43	65	11	2	2	16	92	4.1	0.7	5.8
92-93—Utah	5	93	13	25	.520	7	11	.636	4	12	16	2	0	1	5	33	3.2	0.4	6.6
Totals	39	675	77	174	.443	76	97	.784	51	108	159	22	8	5	39	230	4.1	0.6	5.9

Personal fouls/disqualifications: 1986-87, 1/0. 1988-89, 3/0. 1989-90, 11/0. 1990-91, 36/1. 1991-92, 43/0. 1992-93, 9/0. Totals, 103/1.

BROWN, P.J.　　　　　　　　F　　　　　　　　HEAT

PERSONAL: Born October 14, 1969, in Detroit. ... 6-11/240. ... Full name: Collier Brown Jr.
HIGH SCHOOL: Winnfield (La.) Senior.
COLLEGE: Louisiana Tech.
TRANSACTIONS/CAREER NOTES: Selected by New Jersey Nets in second round (29th pick overall) of 1992 NBA Draft. ... Played in Greece (1992-93). ... Signed as free agent by Miami Heat (July 18, 1996).

COLLEGIATE RECORD

Season Team	G	Min.	FGM	FGA	Pct.	FTM	FTA	Pct.	Reb.	Ast.	Pts.	RPG	APG	PPG
88-89—Louisiana Tech	32	569	61	147	.415	25	44	.568	178	36	149	5.6	1.1	4.7
89-90—Louisiana Tech	27	672	94	204	.461	48	81	.593	230	29	239	8.5	1.1	8.9
90-91—Louisiana Tech	31	936	170	315	.540	98	150	.653	301	58	445	9.7	1.9	14.4
91-92—Louisiana Tech	31	931	151	309	.489	84	115	.730	308	53	395	9.9	1.7	12.7
Totals	121	3108	476	975	.488	255	390	.654	1017	176	1228	8.4	1.5	10.1

Three-point field goals: 1988-89, 2-for-3 (.667). 1989-90, 3-for-5 (.600). 1990-91, 7-for-20 (.350). 1991-92, 9-for-25 (.360). Totals, 21-for-53 (.396).

GREEK LEAGUE RECORD

Season Team	G	Min.	FGM	FGA	Pct.	FTM	FTA	Pct.	Reb.	Ast.	Pts.	RPG	APG	PPG
92-93—Panionios	26	...	164	299	.549	107	151	.709	357	...	441	13.7	...	17.0

NBA REGULAR-SEASON RECORD

Season Team	G	Min.	FGM	FGA	Pct.	FTM	FTA	Pct.	Off.	Def.	Tot.	Ast.	St.	Blk.	TO	Pts.	RPG	APG	PPG
93-94—New Jersey	79	1950	167	402	.415	115	152	.757	188	305	493	93	71	93	72	450	6.2	1.2	5.7
94-95—New Jersey	80	2466	254	570	.446	139	207	.672	178	309	487	135	69	135	80	651	6.1	1.7	8.1
95-96—New Jersey	81	2942	354	798	.444	204	265	.770	215	345	560	165	79	100	133	915	6.9	2.0	11.3
Totals	240	7358	775	1770	.438	458	624	.734	581	959	1540	393	219	328	285	2016	6.4	1.6	8.4

Three-point field goals: 1993-94, 1-for-6 (.167). 1994-95, 4-for-24 (.167). 1995-96, 3-for-15 (.200). Totals, 8-for-45 (.178).
Personal fouls/disqualifications: 1993-94, 177/1. 1994-95, 262/8. 1995-96, 249/5. Totals, 688/14.

NBA PLAYOFF RECORD

Season Team	G	Min.	FGM	FGA	Pct.	FTM	FTA	Pct.	Off.	Def.	Tot.	Ast.	St.	Blk.	TO	Pts.	RPG	APG	PPG
93-94—New Jersey	4	56	2	9	.222	8	8	1.000	4	4	8	3	0	2	3	12	2.0	0.8	3.0

Personal fouls/disqualifications: 1993-94, 13/0.

BROWN, RANDY　　　　　　　　G　　　　　　　　BULLS

PERSONAL: Born May 22, 1968, in Chicago. ... 6-2/191.
HIGH SCHOOL: Collins (Chicago).
JUNIOR COLLEGE: Howard County (Texas).
COLLEGE: Houston, then New Mexico State.
TRANSACTIONS/CAREER NOTES: Selected by Sacramento Kings in second round (31st pick overall) of 1991 NBA Draft. ... Signed as unrestricted free agent by Chicago Bulls (October 5, 1995).
MISCELLANEOUS: Member of NBA championship team (1996).

COLLEGIATE RECORD

Season Team	G	Min.	FGM	FGA	Pct.	FTM	FTA	Pct.	Reb.	Ast.	Pts.	RPG	APG	PPG
86-87—Houston	28	578	42	83	.506	21	36	.583	75	81	105	2.7	2.9	3.8
87-88—Houston	29	998	64	142	.451	75	100	.750	83	162	203	2.9	5.6	7.0
88-89—Howard County College..							Did not play.							
89-90—New Mexico St.	31	907	131	294	.446	131	184	.712	106	109	409	3.4	3.5	13.2
90-91—New Mexico St.	29	917	110	276	.399	121	175	.691	116	187	351	4.0	6.4	12.1
4-year-college totals	117	3400	347	795	.436	348	495	.703	380	539	1068	3.2	4.6	9.1

Three-point field goals: 1986-87, 0-for-2. 1987-88, 0-for-4. 1989-90, 16-for-42 (.381). 1990-91, 10-for-36 (.278). Totals, 26-for-84 (.310).

NBA REGULAR-SEASON RECORD

Season Team	G	Min.	FGM	FGA	Pct.	FTM	FTA	Pct.	Off.	Def.	Tot.	Ast.	St.	Blk.	TO	Pts.	RPG	APG	PPG
91-92—Sacramento	56	535	77	169	.456	38	58	.655	26	43	69	59	35	12	42	192	1.2	1.1	3.4
92-93—Sacramento	75	1726	225	486	.463	115	157	.732	75	137	212	196	108	34	120	567	2.8	2.6	7.6
93-94—Sacramento	61	1041	110	251	.438	53	87	.609	40	72	112	133	63	14	75	273	1.8	2.2	4.5
94-95—Sacramento	67	1086	124	287	.432	55	82	.671	24	84	108	133	99	19	78	317	1.6	2.0	4.7
95-96—Chicago	68	671	78	192	.406	28	46	.609	17	49	66	73	57	12	31	185	1.0	1.1	2.7
Totals	327	5059	614	1385	.443	289	430	.672	182	385	567	594	362	91	346	1534	1.7	1.8	4.7

Three-point field goals: 1991-92, 0-for-6. 1992-93, 2-for-6 (.333). 1993-94, 0-for-4. 1994-95, 14-for-47 (.298). 1995-96, 1-for-11 (.091). Totals, 17-for-74 (.230).
Personal fouls/disqualifications: 1991-92, 68/0. 1992-93, 206/4. 1993-94, 132/2. 1994-95, 153/0. 1995-96, 88/0. Totals, 647/6.

NBA PLAYOFF RECORD

Season Team	G	Min.	FGM	FGA	Pct.	FTM	FTA	Pct.	Off.	Def.	Tot.	Ast.	St.	Blk.	TO	Pts.	RPG	APG	PPG
95-96—Chicago	16	112	16	28	.571	9	12	.750	3	7	10	7	5	1	7	44	0.6	0.4	2.8

Three-point field goals: 1995-96, 3-for-6 (.500).
Personal fouls/disqualifications: 1995-96, 18/0.

BRYANT, MARK   F/C   SUNS

PERSONAL: Born April 25, 1965, in Glen Ridge, N.J. ... 6-9/245. ... Full name: Mark Craig Bryant.
HIGH SCHOOL: Columbia (Maplewood, N.J.).
COLLEGE: Seton Hall.
TRANSACTIONS/CAREER NOTES: Selected by Portland Trail Blazers in first round (21st pick overall) of 1988 NBA Draft. ... Signed as unrestricted free agent by Houston Rockets (September 29, 1995). ... Traded by Rockets with G Sam Cassell, F Robert Horry and F Chucky Brown to Phoenix Suns for F Charles Barkley and 1999 second-round draft choice (August 19, 1996).

COLLEGIATE RECORD

Season Team	G	Min.	FGM	FGA	Pct.	FTM	FTA	Pct.	Reb.	Ast.	Pts.	RPG	APG	PPG
84-85—Seton Hall	26	774	122	257	.475	74	114	.649	177	16	318	6.8	0.6	12.2
85-86—Seton Hall	30	901	169	323	.523	82	121	.678	226	16	420	7.5	0.5	14.0
86-87—Seton Hall	28	891	171	345	.496	127	180	.706	198	23	470	7.1	0.8	16.8
87-88—Seton Hall	34	1105	267	473	.564	163	218	.748	311	32	698	9.1	0.9	20.5
Totals	118	3671	729	1398	.521	446	633	.705	912	87	1906	7.7	0.7	16.2

Three-point field goals: 1986-87, 1-for-1. 1987-88, 1-for-2 (.500). Totals, 2-for-3 (.667).

NBA REGULAR-SEASON RECORD

Season Team	G	Min.	FGM	FGA	Pct.	FTM	FTA	Pct.	Off.	Def.	Tot.	Ast.	St.	Blk.	TO	Pts.	RPG	APG	PPG
88-89—Portland	56	803	120	247	.486	40	69	.580	65	114	179	33	20	7	41	280	3.2	0.6	5.0
89-90—Portland	58	562	70	153	.458	28	50	.560	54	92	146	13	18	9	25	168	2.5	0.2	2.9
90-91—Portland	53	781	99	203	.488	74	101	.733	65	125	190	27	15	12	33	272	3.6	0.5	5.1
91-92—Portland	56	800	95	198	.480	40	60	.667	87	114	201	41	26	8	30	230	3.6	0.7	4.1
92-93—Portland	80	1396	186	370	.503	104	148	.703	132	192	324	41	37	23	65	476	4.1	0.5	6.0
93-94—Portland	79	1441	185	384	.482	72	104	.692	117	198	315	37	32	29	66	442	4.0	0.5	5.6
94-95—Portland	49	658	101	192	.526	41	63	.651	55	106	161	28	19	16	39	244	3.3	0.6	5.0
95-96—Houston	71	1587	242	446	.543	127	177	.718	131	220	351	52	31	19	85	611	4.9	0.7	8.6
Totals	502	8028	1098	2193	.501	526	772	.681	706	1161	1867	272	198	123	384	2723	3.7	0.5	5.4

Three-point field goals: 1990-91, 0-for-1. 1991-92, 0-for-3. 1992-93, 0-for-1. 1993-94, 0-for-1. 1994-95, 1-for-2 (.500). 1995-96, 0-for-2. Totals, 1-for-10 (.100).
Personal fouls/disqualifications: 1988-89, 144/3. 1989-90, 93/0. 1990-91, 120/0. 1991-92, 105/0. 1992-93, 226/1. 1993-94, 187/0. 1994-95, 109/1. 1995-96, 234/4. Totals, 1218/9.

NBA PLAYOFF RECORD

Season Team	G	Min.	FGM	FGA	Pct.	FTM	FTA	Pct.	Off.	Def.	Tot.	Ast.	St.	Blk.	TO	Pts.	RPG	APG	PPG
89-90—Portland	13	160	18	33	.545	6	8	.750	9	20	29	3	3	2	12	42	2.2	0.2	3.2
90-91—Portland	14	137	10	22	.455	14	16	.875	14	18	32	2	2	1	4	34	2.3	0.1	2.4
91-92—Portland	12	116	10	29	.345	3	4	.750	11	18	29	1	3	0	9	23	2.4	0.1	1.9
92-93—Portland	4	83	17	37	.459	5	5	1.000	10	8	18	0	0	3	6	39	4.5	0.0	9.8
93-94—Portland	4	64	5	17	.294	0	0	—	6	6	12	2	2	2	3	10	3.0	0.5	2.5
94-95—Portland	2	6	1	2	.500	0	2	.000	1	1	2	0	0	0	1	2	1.0	0.0	1.0
95-96—Houston	8	145	21	35	.600	12	15	.800	7	20	27	4	1	2	3	54	3.4	0.5	6.8
Totals	57	711	82	175	.469	40	50	.800	58	91	149	12	11	10	37	204	2.6	0.2	3.6

Three-point field goals: 1993-94, 0-for-2.
Personal fouls/disqualifications: 1989-90, 27/1. 1990-91, 25/0. 1991-92, 22/0. 1992-93, 14/0. 1993-94, 7/0. 1994-95, 1/0. 1995-96, 21/0. Totals, 117/1.

BUECHLER, JUD   G/F   BULLS

PERSONAL: Born June 19, 1968, in San Diego. ... 6-6/228. ... Full name: Judson Donald Buechler. ... Name pronounced BUSH-ler.
HIGH SCHOOL: Poway (Calif.).
COLLEGE: Arizona.
TRANSACTIONS/CAREER NOTES: Selected by Seattle SuperSonics in second round (38th pick overall) of 1990 NBA Draft. ... Draft rights traded by SuperSonics to New Jersey Nets in exchange for Nets agreement not to select G/F Dennis Scott in 1990 draft (June 27, 1990). ... Claimed off waivers by San Antonio Spurs (November 12, 1991). ... Waived by Spurs (December 17, 1991). ... Signed as free agent by Golden State Warriors (December 22, 1991). ... Signed as free agent by Chicago Bulls (September 16, 1994).
MISCELLANEOUS: Member of NBA championship team (1996).

COLLEGIATE RECORD

Season Team	G	Min.	FGM	FGA	Pct.	FTM	FTA	Pct.	Reb.	Ast.	Pts.	RPG	APG	PPG
86-87—Arizona	30	474	54	111	.486	16	28	.571	68	35	134	2.3	1.2	4.5
87-88—Arizona	36	422	64	124	.516	38	58	.655	87	41	170	2.4	1.1	4.7
88-89—Arizona	33	962	139	229	.607	84	103	.816	219	51	363	6.6	1.5	11.0
89-90—Arizona	32	1072	182	338	.538	88	115	.765	264	129	477	8.3	4.0	14.9
Totals	131	2930	439	802	.547	226	304	.743	638	256	1144	4.9	2.0	8.7

Three-point field goals: 1986-87, 10-for-25 (.400). 1987-88, 4-for-9 (.444). 1988-89, 1-for-5 (.200). 1989-90, 25-for-66 (.379). Totals, 40-for-105 (.381).

NBA REGULAR-SEASON RECORD

Season Team	G	Min.	FGM	FGA	Pct.	FTM	FTA	Pct.	Off.	Def.	Tot.	Ast.	St.	Blk.	TO	Pts.	RPG	APG	PPG
90-91—New Jersey	74	859	94	226	.416	43	66	.652	61	80	141	50	33	15	56	232	1.9	0.7	3.1
91-92—NJ-SA-GS	28	290	29	71	.408	12	21	.571	18	34	52	23	19	7	13	70	1.9	0.8	2.5
92-93—Golden State	70	1287	176	403	.437	65	87	.747	81	114	195	94	47	19	55	437	2.8	1.3	6.2

Season Team	G	Min.	FGM	FGA	Pct.	FTM	FTA	Pct.	Off.	Def.	Tot.	Ast.	St.	Blk.	TO	Pts.	RPG	APG	PPG
93-94—Golden State...	36	218	42	84	.500	10	20	.500	13	19	32	16	8	1	12	106	0.9	0.4	2.9
94-95—Chicago	57	605	90	183	.492	22	39	.564	36	62	98	50	24	12	30	217	1.7	0.9	3.8
95-96—Chicago	74	740	112	242	.463	14	22	.636	45	66	111	56	34	7	39	278	1.5	0.8	3.8
Totals	339	3999	543	1209	.449	166	255	.651	254	375	629	290	165	61	175	1340	1.9	0.9	4.0

Three-point field goals: 1990-91, 1-for-4 (.250). 1991-92, 0-for-1. 1992-93, 20-for-59 (.339). 1993-94, 12-for-29 (.414). 1994-95, 15-for-48 (.313). 1995-96, 40-for-90 (.444). Totals, 88-for-231 (.381).

Personal fouls/disqualifications: 1990-91, 79/0. 1991-92, 31/0. 1992-93, 98/0. 1993-94, 24/0. 1994-95, 64/0. 1995-96, 70/0. Totals, 366/0.

NBA PLAYOFF RECORD

Season Team	G	Min.	FGM	FGA	Pct.	FTM	FTA	Pct.	Off.	Def.	Tot.	Ast.	St.	Blk.	TO	Pts.	RPG	APG	PPG
94-95—Chicago	10	104	9	21	.429	2	4	.500	11	9	20	5	4	3	3	20	2.0	0.5	2.0
95-96—Chicago	17	127	18	38	.474	2	4	.500	2	8	10	6	7	0	8	46	0.6	0.4	2.7
Totals	27	231	27	59	.458	4	8	.500	13	17	30	11	11	3	11	66	1.1	0.4	2.4

Three-point field goals: 1994-95, 0-for-2. 1995-96, 8-for-21 (.381). Totals, 8-for-23 (.348).

Personal fouls/disqualifications: 1994-95, 15/0. 1995-96, 13/0. Totals, 28/0.

BULLARD, MATT   F   HAWKS

PERSONAL: Born June 5, 1967, in West Des Moines, Iowa. ... 6-10/235. ... Full name: Matthew Gordon Bullard. ... Name pronounced BULL-ard.

HIGH SCHOOL: Valley (West Des Moines, Iowa).

COLLEGE: Colorado, then Iowa.

TRANSACTIONS/CAREER NOTES: Not drafted by an NBA franchise. ... Signed as free agent by Houston Rockets (August 22, 1990). ... Traded by Rockets with F Robert Horry and two future second-round draft choices to Detroit Pistons for F Sean Elliott (February 4, 1994); trade voided when Elliott failed physical (February 7, 1994). ... Signed as free agent by Atlanta Hawks (October 5, 1995).

MISCELLANEOUS: Member of NBA championship team (1994).

COLLEGIATE RECORD

Season Team	G	Min.	FGM	FGA	Pct.	FTM	FTA	Pct.	Reb.	Ast.	Pts.	RPG	APG	PPG
85-86—Colorado......................	28	869	142	235	.604	72	88	.818	179	86	356	6.4	3.1	12.7
86-87—Colorado......................	28	938	182	349	.521	95	128	.742	280	61	464	10.0	2.2	16.6
87-88—Iowa						Did not play—transfer student.								
88-89—Iowa	20	498	66	117	.564	32	40	.800	123	37	181	6.2	1.9	9.1
89-90—Iowa	18	366	72	166	.434	36	50	.720	53	24	205	2.9	1.3	11.4
Totals	94	2671	462	867	.533	235	306	.768	635	208	1206	6.8	2.2	12.8

Three-point field goals: 1986-87, 5-for-26 (.192). 1988-89, 17-for-43 (.395). 1989-90, 25-for-71 (.352). Totals, 47-for-140 (.336).

NBA REGULAR-SEASON RECORD

Season Team	G	Min.	FGM	FGA	Pct.	FTM	FTA	Pct.	Off.	Def.	Tot.	Ast.	St.	Blk.	TO	Pts.	RPG	APG	PPG
90-91—Houston..........	18	63	14	31	.452	11	17	.647	6	8	14	2	3	0	3	39	0.8	0.1	2.2
91-92—Houston..........	80	1278	205	447	.459	38	50	.760	73	150	223	75	26	21	56	512	2.8	0.9	6.4
92-93—Houston..........	79	1356	213	494	.431	58	74	.784	66	156	222	110	30	11	57	575	2.8	1.4	7.3
93-94—Houston..........	65	725	78	226	.345	20	26	.769	23	61	84	64	14	6	28	226	1.3	1.0	3.5
95-96—Atlanta	46	460	66	162	.407	16	20	.800	18	42	60	18	17	11	24	174	1.3	0.4	3.8
Totals	288	3882	576	1360	.424	143	187	.765	186	417	603	269	90	49	168	1526	2.1	0.9	5.3

Three-point field goals: 1990-91, 0-for-3. 1991-92, 64-for-166 (.386). 1992-93, 91-for-243 (.374). 1993-94, 50-for-154 (.325). 1995-96, 26-for-72 (.361). Totals, 231-for-638 (.362).

Personal fouls/disqualifications: 1990-91, 10/0. 1991-92, 129/1. 1992-93, 129/0. 1993-94, 67/0. 1995-96, 50/0. Totals, 385/1.

NBA PLAYOFF RECORD

Season Team	G	Min.	FGM	FGA	Pct.	FTM	FTA	Pct.	Off.	Def.	Tot.	Ast.	St.	Blk.	TO	Pts.	RPG	APG	PPG
92-93—Houston..........	12	169	20	42	.476	6	6	1.000	4	19	23	13	4	5	9	61	1.9	1.1	5.1
93-94—Houston..........	10	55	4	19	.211	6	8	.750	2	8	10	0	1	2	0	16	1.0	0.0	1.6
95-96—Atlanta	4	51	4	12	.333	2	4	.500	0	6	6	0	0	2	2	14	1.5	0.0	3.5
Totals	26	275	28	73	.384	14	18	.778	6	33	39	13	5	9	11	91	1.5	0.5	3.5

Three-point field goals: 1992-93, 15-for-28 (.536). 1993-94, 2-for-10 (.200). 1995-96, 4-for-8 (.500). Totals, 21-for-46 (.457).

Personal fouls/disqualifications: 1992-93, 11/0. 1993-94, 6/0. 1995-96, 6/0. Totals, 23/0.

BURRELL, SCOTT   G/F   HORNETS

PERSONAL: Born January 12, 1971, in New Haven, Conn. ... 6-7/226. ... Full name: Scott David Burrell.

HIGH SCHOOL: Hamden (Conn.).

COLLEGE: Connecticut.

TRANSACTIONS/CAREER NOTES: Selected by Charlotte Hornets in first round (20th pick overall) of 1993 NBA Draft.

COLLEGIATE RECORD

Season Team	G	Min.	FGM	FGA	Pct.	FTM	FTA	Pct.	Reb.	Ast.	Pts.	RPG	APG	PPG
89-90—Connecticut	32	826	88	228	.386	66	106	.623	177	57	262	5.5	1.8	8.2
90-91—Connecticut	31	1075	136	309	.440	84	142	.592	234	95	393	7.5	3.1	12.7
91-92—Connecticut	30	1059	175	386	.453	77	126	.611	183	87	488	6.1	2.9	16.3
92-93—Connecticut	26	861	145	353	.411	79	104	.760	156	54	419	6.0	2.1	16.1
Totals	119	3821	544	1276	.426	306	478	.640	750	293	1562	6.3	2.5	13.1

Three-point field goals: 1989-90, 20-for-64 (.313). 1990-91, 37-for-108 (.343). 1991-92, 61-for-154 (.396). 1992-93, 50-for-145 (.345). Totals, 168-for-471 (.357).

Season Team	G	Min.	FGM	FGA	Pct.	FTM	FTA	Pct.	Off.	Def.	Tot.	Ast.	St.	Blk.	TO	Pts.	RPG	APG	PPG
93-94—Charlotte	51	767	98	234	.419	46	70	.657	46	86	132	62	37	16	45	244	2.6	1.2	4.8
94-95—Charlotte	65	2014	277	593	.467	100	144	.694	96	272	368	161	75	40	85	750	5.7	2.5	11.5
95-96—Charlotte	20	693	92	206	.447	42	56	.750	26	72	98	47	27	13	43	263	4.9	2.4	13.2
Totals	136	3474	467	1033	.452	188	270	.696	168	430	598	270	139	69	173	1257	4.4	2.0	9.2

Three-point field goals: 1993-94, 2-for-6 (.333). 1994-95, 96-for-235 (.409). 1995-96, 37-for-98 (.378). Totals, 135-for-339 (.398).
Personal fouls/disqualifications: 1993-94, 88/0. 1994-95, 187/1. 1995-96, 76/2. Totals, 351/3.

RECORD AS BASEBALL PLAYER

TRANSACTIONS/CAREER NOTES: Threw right, batted right. ... Selected by Seattle Mariners organization in first round (26th pick overall) of free-agent draft (June 5, 1989). ... Selected by Toronto Blue Jays organization in fifth round of free-agent draft (June 4, 1990). ... On St. Catharines temporary inactive list (June 17-30, 1991). ... On Myrtle Beach temporary inactive list (April 9-June 30, 1992). ... On Dunedin disabled list (August 27, 1992-remainder of season). ... On Syracuse temporary inactive list (April 8-July 2, 1993). ... On Syracuse restricted list (July 2, 1993).

Year Team (League)	W	L	Pct.	ERA	G	GS	CG	ShO	Sv.	IP	H	R	ER	BB	SO
1990—St. Catharines (NYP)	1	4	.200	5.86	7	7	0	0	0	27⅔	29	20	18	15	24
1991—St. Catharines (NYP)	0	2	.000	1.50	2	2	0	0	0	6	3	3	1	3	5
Myrtle Beach (S. Atl.)	1	0	1.000	2.00	5	5	0	0	0	27	18	6	6	13	31
1992—								Did not play.							

BC

BURROUGH, JUNIOR   F   CELTICS

PERSONAL: Born January 18, 1973, in Charlotte. ... 6-8/252. ... Full name: Thomas Harold Burrough.
HIGH SCHOOL: West Charlotte (Charlotte), then Oak Hill Academy (Mouth of Wilson, Va.).
COLLEGE: Virginia.
TRANSACTIONS/CAREER NOTES: Selected by Boston Celtics in second round (33rd pick overall) of 1995 NBA Draft.

COLLEGIATE RECORD

Season Team	G	Min.	FGM	FGA	Pct.	FTM	FTA	Pct.	Reb.	Ast.	Pts.	RPG	APG	PPG
91-92—Virginia	33	996	166	372	.446	105	151	.695	192	8	437	5.8	0.2	13.2
92-93—Virginia	31	887	178	406	.438	97	152	.638	224	20	453	7.2	0.6	14.6
93-94—Virginia	31	977	179	442	.405	95	149	.638	218	28	465	7.0	0.9	15.0
94-95—Virginia	34	1079	236	471	.501	142	200	.710	295	55	615	8.7	1.6	18.1
Totals	129	3939	759	1691	.449	439	652	.673	929	111	1970	7.2	0.9	15.3

Three-point field goals: 1991-92, 0-for-1. 1992-93, 0-for-4. 1993-94, 12-for-37 (.324). 1994-95, 1-for-4 (.250). Totals, 13-for-46 (.283).

NBA REGULAR-SEASON RECORD

Season Team	G	Min.	FGM	FGA	Pct.	FTM	FTA	Pct.	Off.	Def.	Tot.	Ast.	St.	Blk.	TO	Pts.	RPG	APG	PPG
95-96—Boston	61	495	64	170	.376	61	93	.656	45	64	109	15	15	10	40	189	1.8	0.2	3.1

Personal fouls/disqualifications: 1995-96, 74/0.

BUTLER, MITCHELL   G/F   TRAIL BLAZERS

PERSONAL: Born December 15, 1970, in Los Angeles. ... 6-5/210. ... Full name: Mitchell Leon Butler.
HIGH SCHOOL: Oakwood (North Hollywood, Calif.).
COLLEGE: UCLA.
TRANSACTIONS/CAREER NOTES: Not drafted by an NBA franchise. ... Signed as free agent by Washington Bullets (October 5, 1993). ... Traded by Bullets with F Rasheed Wallace to Portland Trail Blazers for G Rod Strickland and F Harvey Grant (July 15, 1996).

COLLEGIATE RECORD

Season Team	G	Min.	FGM	FGA	Pct.	FTM	FTA	Pct.	Reb.	Ast.	Pts.	RPG	APG	PPG
89-90—UCLA	33	596	78	145	.538	45	72	.625	94	46	203	2.8	1.4	6.2
90-91—UCLA	32	696	103	188	.548	45	72	.625	94	48	252	2.9	1.5	7.9
91-92—UCLA	33	845	108	221	.489	32	71	.451	140	60	263	4.2	1.8	8.0
92-93—UCLA	32	920	129	252	.512	41	78	.526	171	75	305	5.3	2.3	9.5
Totals	130	3057	418	806	.519	163	293	.556	499	229	1023	3.8	1.8	7.9

Three-point field goals: 1989-90, 2-for-11 (.182). 1990-91, 6-for-25 (.240). 1991-92, 15-for-57 (.263). 1992-93, 6-for-34 (.176). Totals, 29-for-127 (.228).

NBA REGULAR-SEASON RECORD

Season Team	G	Min.	FGM	FGA	Pct.	FTM	FTA	Pct.	Off.	Def.	Tot.	Ast.	St.	Blk.	TO	Pts.	RPG	APG	PPG
93-94—Washington	75	1321	207	418	.495	104	180	.578	106	119	225	77	54	20	87	518	3.0	1.0	6.9
94-95—Washington	76	1554	214	508	.421	123	185	.665	43	127	170	91	61	10	106	597	2.2	1.2	7.9
95-96—Washington	61	858	88	229	.384	48	83	.578	29	89	118	67	41	12	67	237	1.9	1.1	3.9
Totals	212	3733	509	1155	.441	275	448	.614	178	335	513	235	156	42	260	1352	2.4	1.1	6.4

Three-point field goals: 1993-94, 0-for-5. 1994-95, 46-for-141 (.326). 1995-96, 13-for-60 (.217). Totals, 59-for-206 (.286).
Personal fouls/disqualifications: 1993-94, 131/1. 1994-95, 155/0. 1995-96, 104/0. Totals, 390/1.

CAFFEY, JASON   F   BULLS

PERSONAL: Born June 12, 1973, in Mobile, Ala. ... 6-8/256. ... Full name: Jason Andre Caffey.
HIGH SCHOOL: Davidson (Mobile, Ala.).
COLLEGE: Alabama.
TRANSACTIONS/CAREER NOTES: Selected by Chicago Bulls in first round (20th pick overall) of 1995 NBA Draft.
MISCELLANEOUS: Member of NBA championship team (1996).

COLLEGIATE RECORD

Season Team	G	Min.	FGM	FGA	Pct.	FTM	FTA	Pct.	Reb.	Ast.	Pts.	AVERAGES RPG	APG	PPG
91-92—Alabama	30	331	31	73	.425	10	30	.333	67	10	72	2.2	0.3	2.4
92-93—Alabama	29	847	169	326	.518	80	130	.615	252	39	421	8.7	1.3	14.5
93-94—Alabama	29	784	140	269	.520	90	143	.629	183	20	371	6.3	0.7	12.8
94-95—Alabama	31	933	148	291	.509	79	145	.545	249	51	375	8.0	1.6	12.1
Totals	119	2895	488	959	.509	259	448	.578	751	120	1239	6.3	1.0	10.4

Three-point field goals: 1991-92, 0-for-1. 1992-93, 3-for-11 (.273). 1993-94, 1-for-2 (.500). 1994-95, 0-for-4. Totals, 4-for-18 (.222).

NBA REGULAR-SEASON RECORD

Season Team	G	Min.	FGM	FGA	Pct.	FTM	FTA	Pct.	REBOUNDS Off.	Def.	Tot.	Ast.	St.	Blk.	TO	Pts.	AVERAGES RPG	APG	PPG
95-96—Chicago	57	545	71	162	.438	40	68	.588	51	60	111	24	12	7	48	182	1.9	0.4	3.2

Three-point field goals: 1995-96, 0-for-1.
Personal fouls/disqualifications: 1995-96, 91/3.

CAGE, MICHAEL   F/C   76ERS

PERSONAL: Born January 28, 1962, in West Memphis, Ark. ... 6-9/248. ... Full name: Michael Jerome Cage.
HIGH SCHOOL: West Memphis (Ark.).
COLLEGE: San Diego State.
TRANSACTIONS/CAREER NOTES: Selected by Los Angeles Clippers in first round (14th pick overall) of 1984 NBA Draft. ... Traded by Clippers to Seattle SuperSonics for draft rights to G Gary Grant and 1989 first-round draft choice (June 28, 1988). ... Signed as unrestricted free agent by Cleveland Cavaliers (August 2, 1994). ... Signed as free agent by Philadelphia 76ers (August 22, 1996).

C

COLLEGIATE RECORD

Season Team	G	Min.	FGM	FGA	Pct.	FTM	FTA	Pct.	Reb.	Ast.	Pts.	AVERAGES RPG	APG	PPG
80-81—San Diego State.............	27	1031	115	206	.558	65	86	.756	355	11	295	13.1	0.4	10.9
81-82—San Diego State.............	29	1076	123	252	.488	72	109	.661	256	44	318	8.8	1.5	11.0
82-83—San Diego State.............	28	1070	191	335	.570	165	221	.747	354	31	547	12.6	1.1	19.5
83-84—San Diego State.............	28	1085	250	445	.562	186	251	.741	352	12	686	12.6	0.4	24.5
Totals	112	4262	679	1238	.548	488	667	.732	1317	98	1846	11.8	0.9	16.5

NBA REGULAR-SEASON RECORD

NOTES: Led NBA with 13.03 rebounds per game (1988).

Season Team	G	Min.	FGM	FGA	Pct.	FTM	FTA	Pct.	REBOUNDS Off.	Def.	Tot.	Ast.	St.	Blk.	TO	Pts.	AVERAGES RPG	APG	PPG
84-85—L.A. Clippers ...	75	1610	216	398	.543	101	137	.737	126	266	392	51	41	32	81	533	5.2	0.7	7.1
85-86—L.A. Clippers ...	78	1566	204	426	.479	113	174	.649	168	249	417	81	62	34	106	521	5.3	1.0	6.7
86-87—L.A. Clippers ...	80	2922	457	878	.521	341	467	.730	354	568	922	131	99	67	171	1255	*11.5	1.6	15.7
87-88—L.A. Clippers ...	72	2660	360	766	.470	326	474	.688	371	567	938	110	91	58	160	1046	*13.0	1.5	14.5
88-89—Seattle	80	2536	314	630	.498	197	265	.743	276	489	765	126	92	52	124	825	9.6	1.6	10.3
89-90—Seattle	82	2595	325	645	.504	148	212	.698	306	515	821	70	79	45	94	798	10.0	0.9	9.7
90-91—Seattle	82	2141	226	445	.508	70	112	.625	177	381	558	89	85	58	83	522	6.8	1.1	6.4
91-92—Seattle	82	2461	307	542	.566	106	171	.620	266	462	728	92	99	55	78	720	8.9	1.1	8.8
92-93—Seattle	82	2156	219	416	.526	61	130	.469	268	391	659	69	76	46	59	499	8.0	0.8	6.1
93-94—Seattle	82	1708	171	314	.545	36	74	.486	164	280	444	45	77	38	51	378	5.4	0.5	4.6
94-95—Cleveland	82	2040	177	340	.521	53	88	.602	203	361	564	56	61	67	56	407	6.9	0.7	5.0
95-96—Cleveland	82	2631	220	396	.556	50	92	.543	288	441	729	53	87	79	54	490	8.9	0.6	6.0
Totals	959	27026	3196	6196	.516	1602	2396	.669	2967	4970	7937	973	949	631	1117	7994	8.3	1.0	8.3

Three-point field goals: 1985-86, 0-for-3. 1986-87, 0-for-3. 1987-88, 0-for-1. 1988-89, 0-for-4. 1990-91, 0-for-3. 1991-92, 0-for-5. 1992-93, 0-for-1. 1993-94, 0-for-1. 1994-95, 0-for-2. 1995-96, 0-for-1. Totals, 0-for-24.
Personal fouls/disqualifications: 1984-85, 164/1. 1985-86, 176/1. 1986-87, 221/1. 1987-88, 194/1. 1988-89, 184/1. 1989-90, 232/1. 1990-91, 194/0. 1991-92, 237/0. 1992-93, 183/0. 1993-94, 179/0. 1994-95, 149/1. 1995-96, 215/0. Totals, 2328/7.

NBA PLAYOFF RECORD

Season Team	G	Min.	FGM	FGA	Pct.	FTM	FTA	Pct.	REBOUNDS Off.	Def.	Tot.	Ast.	St.	Blk.	TO	Pts.	AVERAGES RPG	APG	PPG
88-89—Seattle	8	175	24	40	.600	9	22	.409	22	24	46	5	7	3	8	57	5.8	0.6	7.1
90-91—Seattle	5	80	6	14	.429	13	17	.765	9	12	21	2	3	2	3	25	4.2	0.4	5.0
91-92—Seattle	9	197	19	34	.559	1	1	1.000	18	33	51	4	6	8	8	39	5.7	0.4	4.3
92-93—Seattle	19	378	42	80	.525	7	18	.389	47	64	111	10	13	7	16	91	5.8	0.5	4.8
93-94—Seattle	5	93	6	16	.375	2	6	.333	10	17	27	4	4	5	3	14	5.4	0.8	2.8
94-95—Cleveland	4	81	8	18	.444	0	2	.000	8	10	18	3	2	4	1	16	4.5	0.8	4.0
95-96—Cleveland	3	101	8	14	.571	3	5	.600	13	15	28	2	2	5	0	19	9.3	0.7	6.3
Totals	53	1105	113	216	.523	35	71	.493	127	175	302	30	37	34	39	261	5.7	0.6	4.9

Three-point field goals: 1988-89, 0-for-1. 1994-95, 0-for-1. Totals, 0-for-2.
Personal fouls/disqualifications: 1988-89, 14/0. 1990-91, 12/0. 1991-92, 22/0. 1992-93, 43/1. 1993-94, 15/0. 1994-95, 9/0. 1995-96, 5/0. Totals, 120/1.

CALDWELL, ADRIAN   F/C   PACERS

PERSONAL: Born July 4, 1966, in Falls County, Texas. ... 6-9/265. ... Full name: Adrian Bernard Caldwell.
HIGH SCHOOL: West Oso (Corpus Christi, Texas).
JUNIOR COLLEGE: Navarro College (Texas).
COLLEGE: Southern Methodist, then Lamar.
TRANSACTIONS/CAREER NOTES: Not drafted by an NBA franchise. ... Signed as free agent by Houston Rockets (August 2, 1989). ... Waived by Rockets (August 23, 1991). ... Played in Italy (1991-92 and 1992-93). ... Played in Continental Basketball Association with Sioux Falls Skyforce (1993-94 and 1994-95). ... Signed as free agent by Rockets (September 20, 1994). ... Waived by Rockets (November 29, 1994). ... Signed as free agent by Indiana Pacers (October 4, 1995).

COLLEGIATE RECORD

Season Team	G	Min.	FGM	FGA	Pct.	FTM	FTA	Pct.	Reb.	Ast.	Pts.	RPG	APG	PPG
84-85—Navarro College.............						Statistics unavailable.								
85-86—Navarro College.............						Statistics unavailable.								
86-87—South. Methodist...........	28	300	22	45	.489	15	44	.341	68	18	59	2.4	0.6	2.1
87-88—Lamar............................						Did not play—transfer student.								
88-89—Lamar............................	26	839	151	266	.568	80	178	.449	260	51	382	10.0	2.0	14.7
Junior college totals	...	...	...	...	...	...	...	...	...	...	...	...	...	...
4-year-college totals	54	1139	173	311	.556	95	222	.428	328	69	441	6.1	1.3	8.2

NBA REGULAR-SEASON RECORD

Season Team	G	Min.	FGM	FGA	Pct.	FTM	FTA	Pct.	REBOUNDS Off.	Def.	Tot.	Ast.	St.	Blk.	TO	Pts.	AVERAGES RPG	APG	PPG
89-90—Houston..........	51	331	42	76	.553	13	28	.464	36	73	109	7	11	18	32	97	2.1	0.1	1.9
90-91—Houston..........	42	343	35	83	.422	7	17	.412	43	57	100	8	19	10	30	77	2.4	0.2	1.8
94-95—Houston..........	7	30	1	4	.250	3	6	.500	1	9	10	0	1	0	1	5	1.4	0.0	0.7
95-96—Indiana..........	51	327	46	83	.554	18	36	.500	42	68	110	6	9	5	35	110	2.2	0.1	2.2
Totals	151	1031	124	246	.504	41	87	.471	122	207	329	21	40	33	98	289	2.2	0.1	1.9

Three-point field goals: 1990-91, 0-for-1.
Personal fouls/disqualifications: 1989-90, 69/0. 1990-91, 35/0. 1994-95, 6/0. 1995-96, 73/0. Totals, 183/0.

NBA PLAYOFF RECORD

Season Team	G	Min.	FGM	FGA	Pct.	FTM	FTA	Pct.	REBOUNDS Off.	Def.	Tot.	Ast.	St.	Blk.	TO	Pts.	AVERAGES RPG	APG	PPG
89-90—Houston..........	1	1	0	0	...	0	0	...	0	0	0	0	0	0	0	0	0.0	0.0	0.0
95-96—Indiana...........	1	3	1	1	1.000	0	0	...	0	1	1	0	0	0	0	2	1.0	0.0	2.0
Totals	2	4	1	1	1.000	0	0	...	0	1	1	0	0	0	0	2	0.5	0.0	1.0

ITALIAN LEAGUE RECORD

Season Team	G	Min.	FGM	FGA	Pct.	FTM	FTA	Pct.	Reb.	Ast.	Pts.	RPG	APG	PPG
91-92—Shamp. Clear Cantu	30	1065	198	348	.569	65	123	.528	357	27	461	11.9	0.9	15.4
92-93—Shamp. Clear Cantu	30	1013	179	312	.574	71	118	.602	332	18	429	11.1	0.6	14.3
Totals	60	2078	377	660	.571	136	241	.564	689	45	890	11.5	0.8	14.8

CBA REGULAR-SEASON RECORD

Season Team	G	Min.	FGM	FGA	Pct.	FTM	FTA	Pct.	Reb.	Ast.	Pts.	RPG	APG	PPG
93-94—Sioux Falls.....................	17	458	51	102	.500	34	63	.540	150	18	136	8.8	1.1	8.0
94-95—Sioux Falls.....................	28	977	130	214	.607	84	137	.613	329	25	344	11.8	0.9	12.3
Totals	45	1435	181	316	.573	118	200	.590	479	43	480	10.6	1.0	10.7

Three-point field goals: 1994-95, 0-for-1.

CAMPBELL, ELDEN   F/C   LAKERS

PERSONAL: Born July 23, 1968, in Los Angeles. ... 6-11/250. ... Full name: Elden Jerome Campbell.
HIGH SCHOOL: Morningside (Inglewood, Calif.).
COLLEGE: Clemson.
TRANSACTIONS/CAREER NOTES: Selected by Los Angeles Lakers in first round (27th pick overall) of 1990 NBA Draft.

COLLEGIATE RECORD

Season Team	G	Min.	FGM	FGA	Pct.	FTM	FTA	Pct.	Reb.	Ast.	Pts.	RPG	APG	PPG
86-87—Clemson	31	534	107	193	.554	59	84	.702	126	20	273	4.1	0.6	8.8
87-88—Clemson	28	808	217	345	.629	91	147	.619	207	15	525	7.4	0.5	18.8
88-89—Clemson	29	814	205	373	.550	95	138	.688	222	34	507	7.7	1.2	17.5
89-90—Clemson	35	1038	225	431	.522	124	207	.599	281	44	575	8.0	1.3	16.4
Totals	123	3194	754	1342	.562	369	576	.641	836	113	1880	6.8	0.9	15.3

Three-point field goals: 1987-88, 0-for-4. 1988-89, 2-for-5 (.400). 1989-90, 1-for-1. Totals, 3-for-10 (.300).

NBA REGULAR-SEASON RECORD

NOTES: Tied for NBA lead with 300 personal fouls (1996).

Season Team	G	Min.	FGM	FGA	Pct.	FTM	FTA	Pct.	REBOUNDS Off.	Def.	Tot.	Ast.	St.	Blk.	TO	Pts.	AVERAGES RPG	APG	PPG
90-91—L.A. Lakers	52	380	56	123	.455	32	49	.653	40	56	96	10	11	38	16	144	1.8	0.2	2.8
91-92—L.A. Lakers	81	1876	220	491	.448	138	223	.619	155	268	423	59	53	159	73	578	5.2	0.7	7.1
92-93—L.A. Lakers	79	1551	238	520	.458	130	204	.637	127	205	332	48	59	100	69	606	4.2	0.6	7.7
93-94—L.A. Lakers	76	2253	373	808	.462	188	273	.689	167	352	519	86	54	146	98	934	6.8	1.1	12.3
94-95—L.A. Lakers	73	2076	360	785	.459	193	290	.666	168	277	445	92	69	132	98	913	6.1	1.3	12.5
95-96—L.A. Lakers	82	2699	447	888	.503	249	349	.713	162	461	623	181	88	212	137	1143	7.6	2.2	13.9
Totals	443	10835	1694	3615	.469	930	1388	.670	819	1619	2438	476	344	787	491	4318	5.5	1.1	9.7

Three-point field goals: 1991-92, 0-for-2. 1992-93, 0-for-3. 1993-94, 0-for-2. 1994-95, 0-for-1. 1995-96, 0-for-5. Totals, 0-for-13.
Personal fouls/disqualifications: 1990-91, 71/1. 1991-92, 203/1. 1992-93, 165/0. 1993-94, 241/2. 1994-95, 246/4. 1995-96, 300/4. Totals, 1226/12.

NBA PLAYOFF RECORD

Season Team	G	Min.	FGM	FGA	Pct.	FTM	FTA	Pct.	REBOUNDS Off.	Def.	Tot.	Ast.	St.	Blk.	TO	Pts.	AVERAGES RPG	APG	PPG
90-91—L.A. Lakers	14	138	25	38	.658	7	15	.467	8	21	29	3	6	8	6	57	2.1	0.2	4.1
91-92—L.A. Lakers	4	117	14	37	.378	12	18	.667	9	16	25	6	3	6	4	40	6.3	1.5	10.0

C

Season Team	G	Min.	FGM	FGA	Pct.	FTM	FTA	Pct.	REBOUNDS Off.	Def.	Tot.	Ast.	St.	Blk.	TO	Pts.	AVERAGES RPG	APG	PPG
92-93—L.A. Lakers	5	178	29	69	.420	12	24	.500	17	25	42	7	6	12	12	70	8.4	1.4	14.0
94-95—L.A. Lakers	10	376	64	132	.485	29	44	.659	26	47	73	16	4	30	15	157	7.3	1.6	15.7
95-96—L.A. Lakers	4	129	20	39	.513	8	16	.500	3	29	32	8	1	9	10	48	8.0	2.0	12.0
Totals	37	938	152	315	.483	68	117	.581	63	138	201	40	20	65	47	372	5.4	1.1	10.1

Three-point field goals: 1995-96, 0-for-1.

Personal fouls/disqualifications: 1990-91, 23/1. 1991-92, 14/0. 1992-93, 15/0. 1994-95, 44/2. 1995-96, 17/1. Totals, 113/4.

CARR, ANTOINE   F   JAZZ

PERSONAL: Born July 23, 1961, in Oklahoma City. ... 6-9/255. ... Full name: Antoine Labotte Carr. ... Name pronounced an-TWON.
HIGH SCHOOL: Wichita (Kan.) Heights.
COLLEGE: Wichita State.
TRANSACTIONS/CAREER NOTES: Selected by Detroit Pistons in first round (eighth pick overall) of 1983 NBA Draft. ... Played in Italy (1983-84). ... Draft rights traded by Pistons with F Cliff Levingston and 1986 and 1987 second-round draft choices to Atlanta Hawks for F Dan Roundfield (June 18, 1984). ... Traded by Hawks with G Sedric Toney and future considerations to Sacramento Kings for G Kenny Smith and G Mike Williams (February 13, 1990). ... Traded by Kings to San Antonio Spurs for C Dwayne Schintzius and 1994 second-round draft choice (September 23, 1991). ... Signed as free agent by Utah Jazz (October 29, 1994). ... Rights renounced by Jazz (May 10, 1995). ... Re-signed as free agent by Jazz (October 4, 1995).

C

COLLEGIATE RECORD

NOTES: THE SPORTING NEWS All-America first team (1983).

Season Team	G	Min.	FGM	FGA	Pct.	FTM	FTA	Pct.	Reb.	Ast.	Pts.	AVERAGES RPG	APG	PPG
79-80—Wichita State	29	818	178	355	.501	86	129	.667	171	64	442	5.9	2.2	15.2
80-81—Wichita State	33	1030	211	360	.586	101	132	.765	241	94	523	7.3	2.8	15.8
81-82—Wichita State	28	785	179	316	.566	91	115	.791	196	46	449	7.0	1.6	16.0
82-83—Wichita State	22	727	195	339	.575	104	136	.765	168	39	497	7.6	1.8	22.6
Totals	112	3360	763	1370	.557	382	512	.746	776	243	1911	6.9	2.2	17.1

Three-point field goals: 1982-83, 3-for-5 (.600).

ITALIAN LEAGUE RECORD

Season Team	G	Min.	FGM	FGA	Pct.	FTM	FTA	Pct.	Reb.	Ast.	Pts.	AVERAGES RPG	APG	PPG
83-84—Milano	27	956	242	434	.558	86	137	.628	237	...	570	8.8	...	21.1

NBA REGULAR-SEASON RECORD

Season Team	G	Min.	FGM	FGA	Pct.	FTM	FTA	Pct.	REBOUNDS Off.	Def.	Tot.	Ast.	St.	Blk.	TO	Pts.	AVERAGES RPG	APG	PPG
84-85—Atlanta	62	1195	198	375	.528	101	128	.789	79	153	232	80	29	78	108	499	3.7	1.3	8.0
85-86—Atlanta	17	258	49	93	.527	18	27	.667	16	36	52	14	7	15	14	116	3.1	0.8	6.8
86-87—Atlanta	65	695	134	265	.506	73	103	.709	60	96	156	34	14	48	40	342	2.4	0.5	5.3
87-88—Atlanta	80	1483	281	517	.544	142	182	.780	94	195	289	103	38	83	116	705	3.6	1.3	8.8
88-89—Atlanta	78	1488	226	471	.480	130	152	.855	106	168	274	91	31	62	82	582	3.5	1.2	7.5
89-90—Atlanta-Sac. ...	77	1727	356	721	.494	237	298	.795	115	207	322	119	30	68	125	949	4.2	1.5	12.3
90-91—Sacramento ...	77	2527	628	1228	.511	295	389	.758	163	257	420	191	45	101	171	1551	5.5	2.5	20.1
91-92—San Antonio....	81	1867	359	732	.490	162	212	.764	128	218	346	63	32	96	114	881	4.3	0.8	10.9
92-93—San Antonio....	71	1947	379	705	.538	174	224	.777	107	281	388	97	35	87	96	932	5.5	1.4	13.1
93-94—San Antonio....	34	465	78	160	.488	42	58	.724	12	39	51	15	9	22	15	198	1.5	0.4	5.8
94-95—Utah	78	1677	290	546	.531	165	201	.821	81	184	265	67	24	68	87	746	3.4	0.9	9.6
95-96—Utah	80	1532	233	510	.457	114	144	.792	71	129	200	74	28	65	78	580	2.5	0.9	7.3
Totals	800	16861	3211	6323	.508	1653	2118	.780	1032	1963	2995	948	322	793	1046	8081	3.7	1.2	10.1

Three-point field goals: 1984-85, 2-for-6 (.333). 1986-87, 1-for-3 (.333). 1987-88, 1-for-4 (.250). 1988-89, 0-for-1. 1989-90, 0-for-7. 1990-91, 0-for-3. 1991-92, 1-for-5 (.200). 1992-93, 0-for-5. 1993-94, 0-for-1. 1994-95, 1-for-4 (.250). 1995-96, 0-for-3. Totals, 6-for-42 (.143).
Personal fouls/disqualifications: 1984-85, 219/4. 1985-86, 51/1. 1986-87, 146/1. 1987-88, 272/7. 1988-89, 221/0. 1989-90, 247/6. 1990-91, 315/14. 1991-92, 264/5. 1992-93, 264/5. 1993-94, 75/0. 1994-95, 253/4. 1995-96, 264/4. Totals, 2581/51.

NBA PLAYOFF RECORD

Season Team	G	Min.	FGM	FGA	Pct.	FTM	FTA	Pct.	REBOUNDS Off.	Def.	Tot.	Ast.	St.	Blk.	TO	Pts.	AVERAGES RPG	APG	PPG
86-87—Atlanta	9	162	39	56	.696	26	32	.813	11	16	27	13	3	8	10	104	3.0	1.4	11.6
87-88—Atlanta	12	210	36	68	.529	9	14	.643	12	29	41	15	4	17	10	81	3.4	1.3	6.8
88-89—Atlanta	5	81	13	21	.619	8	11	.727	5	3	8	7	0	4	4	34	1.6	1.4	6.8
91-92—San Antonio	3	109	24	44	.545	10	16	.625	8	15	23	3	2	11	4	59	7.7	1.0	19.7
92-93—San Antonio	8	171	39	74	.527	6	10	.600	13	25	38	9	3	9	7	84	4.8	1.1	10.5
93-94—San Antonio	3	37	5	11	.455	8	9	.889	1	0	1	3	1	2	0	18	0.3	1.0	6.0
94-95—Utah	5	114	14	31	.452	20	24	.833	3	12	15	7	3	5	4	48	3.0	1.4	9.6
95-96—Utah	18	339	46	97	.474	17	25	.680	11	23	34	21	4	14	16	109	1.9	1.2	6.1
Totals	63	1223	216	402	.537	104	141	.738	64	123	187	78	20	70	55	537	3.0	1.2	8.5

Three-point field goals: 1988-89, 0-for-1. 1991-92, 1-for-2 (.500). Totals, 1-for-3 (.333).
Personal fouls/disqualifications: 1986-87, 36/1. 1987-88, 47/2. 1988-89, 13/0. 1991-92, 14/1. 1992-93, 28/1. 1993-94, 7/0. 1994-95, 26/2. 1995-96, 66/2. Totals, 237/9.

CARR, CHRIS   G   TIMBERWOLVES

PERSONAL: Born March 12, 1974, in Ironton, Mo. ... 6-5/207. ... Full name: Chris Dean Carr.
HIGH SCHOOL: Arcadia Valley (Pilot Knob, Mo.).
COLLEGE: Southern Illinois.
TRANSACTIONS/CAREER NOTES: Selected after junior season by Phoenix Suns in second round (56th pick overall) of 1995 NBA Draft. ... Signed as free agent by Minnesota Timberwolves (July 19, 1996).

COLLEGIATE RECORD

												AVERAGES		
Season Team	G	Min.	FGM	FGA	Pct.	FTM	FTA	Pct.	Reb.	Ast.	Pts.	RPG	APG	PPG
92-93—Southern Illinois.............	31	353	52	88	.591	18	33	.545	110	15	122	3.5	0.5	3.9
93-94—Southern Illinois.............	30	946	156	301	.518	88	109	.807	197	55	424	6.6	1.8	14.1
94-95—Southern Illinois.............	32	1069	250	521	.480	165	214	.771	232	68	705	7.3	2.1	22.0
Totals	93	2368	458	910	.503	271	356	.761	539	138	1251	5.8	1.5	13.5

Three-point field goals: 1992-93, 0-for-4. 1993-94, 24-for-74 (.324). 1994-95, 40-for-101 (.396). Totals, 64-for-179 (.358).

NBA REGULAR-SEASON RECORD

									REBOUNDS								AVERAGES		
Season Team	G	Min.	FGM	FGA	Pct.	FTM	FTA	Pct.	Off.	Def.	Tot.	Ast.	St.	Blk.	TO	Pts.	RPG	APG	PPG
95-96—Phoenix	60	590	90	217	.415	49	60	.817	27	75	102	43	10	5	40	240	1.7	0.7	4.0

Three-point field goals: 1995-96, 11-for-42 (.262).
Personal fouls/disqualifications: 1995-96, 77/1.

NBA PLAYOFF RECORD

									REBOUNDS								AVERAGES		
Season Team	G	Min.	FGM	FGA	Pct.	FTM	FTA	Pct.	Off.	Def.	Tot.	Ast.	St.	Blk.	TO	Pts.	RPG	APG	PPG
95-96—Phoenix	3	36	9	14	.643	4	5	.800	3	4	7	4	2	1	4	24	2.3	1.3	8.0

Three-point field goals: 1995-96, 2-for-3 (.667).
Personal fouls/disqualifications: 1995-96, 6/0.

C

CASSELL, SAM   G   SUNS

PERSONAL: Born November 18, 1969, in Baltimore. ... 6-3/195. ... Full name: Samuel James Cassell. ... Name pronounced cah-SELL.
HIGH SCHOOL: Dunbar (Baltimore).
JUNIOR COLLEGE: San Jacinto College (Texas).
COLLEGE: Florida State.
TRANSACTIONS/CAREER NOTES: Selected by Houston Rockets in first round (24th pick overall) of 1993 NBA Draft. ... Traded by Rockets with F Robert Horry, F Chucky Brown and F Mark Bryant to Phoenix Suns for F Charles Barkley and 1999 second-round draft choice (August 19, 1996).
MISCELLANEOUS: Member of NBA championship teams (1994, 1995).

COLLEGIATE RECORD

												AVERAGES		
Season Team	G	Min.	FGM	FGA	Pct.	FTM	FTA	Pct.	Reb.	Ast.	Pts.	RPG	APG	PPG
89-90—San Jacinto College........	38	1061	296	597	.496	136	170	.800	208	200	810	5.5	5.3	21.3
90-91—San Jacinto College........	31	864	233	471	.495	198	246	.805	157	237	727	5.1	7.6	23.5
91-92—Florida State	31	1046	206	454	.454	100	142	.704	141	119	570	4.5	3.8	18.4
92-93—Florida State	35	1298	234	466	.502	123	162	.759	152	170	641	4.3	4.9	18.3
Junior college totals	69	1925	529	1068	.495	334	416	.803	365	437	1537	5.3	6.3	22.3
4-year-college totals	66	2344	440	920	.478	223	304	.734	293	289	1211	4.4	4.4	18.3

Three-point field goals: 1991-92, 58-for-164 (.354). 1992-93, 50-for-131 (.382). Totals, 108-for-295 (.366).

NBA REGULAR-SEASON RECORD

									REBOUNDS								AVERAGES		
Season Team	G	Min.	FGM	FGA	Pct.	FTM	FTA	Pct.	Off.	Def.	Tot.	Ast.	St.	Blk.	TO	Pts.	RPG	APG	PPG
93-94—Houston..........	66	1122	162	388	.418	90	107	.841	25	109	134	192	59	7	94	440	2.0	2.9	6.7
94-95—Houston..........	82	1882	253	593	.427	214	254	.843	38	173	211	405	94	14	167	783	2.6	4.9	9.5
95-96—Houston..........	61	1682	289	658	.439	235	285	.825	51	137	188	278	53	4	157	886	3.1	4.6	14.5
Totals	209	4686	704	1639	.430	539	646	.834	114	419	533	875	206	25	418	2109	2.6	4.2	10.1

Three-point field goals: 1993-94, 26-for-88 (.295). 1994-95, 63-for-191 (.330). 1995-96, 73-for-210 (.348). Totals, 162-for-489 (.331).
Personal fouls/disqualifications: 1993-94, 136/1. 1994-95, 209/3. 1995-96, 166/2. Totals, 511/6.

NBA PLAYOFF RECORD

									REBOUNDS								AVERAGES		
Season Team	G	Min.	FGM	FGA	Pct.	FTM	FTA	Pct.	Off.	Def.	Tot.	Ast.	St.	Blk.	TO	Pts.	RPG	APG	PPG
93-94—Houston	22	478	63	160	.394	64	74	.865	19	40	59	93	21	5	47	207	2.7	4.2	9.4
94-95—Houston..........	22	485	74	169	.438	71	85	.835	8	34	42	89	21	2	33	243	1.9	4.0	11.0
95-96—Houston	8	206	26	81	.321	23	29	.793	1	16	17	34	6	1	18	83	2.1	4.3	10.4
Totals	52	1169	163	410	.398	158	188	.840	28	90	118	216	48	8	98	533	2.3	4.2	10.3

Three-point field goals: 1993-94, 17-for-45 (.378). 1994-95, 24-for-60 (.400). 1995-96, 8-for-29 (.276). Totals, 49-for-134 (.366).
Personal fouls/disqualifications: 1993-94, 62/1. 1994-95, 66/1. 1995-96, 20/0. Totals, 148/2.

CAUSWELL, DUANE   C   KINGS

PERSONAL: Born May 31, 1968, in Queens Village, N.Y. ... 7-0/240.
HIGH SCHOOL: Benjamin Cardozo (Bayside, N.Y.).
COLLEGE: Temple.
TRANSACTIONS/CAREER NOTES: Selected by Sacramento Kings in first round (18th pick overall) of 1990 NBA Draft. ... Traded by Kings with 1994, 1995 and 1996 second-round draft choices to Detroit Pistons for C Olden Polynice and F David Wood (February 16, 1994); trade voided when Causwell failed physical (February 19, 1994).

COLLEGIATE RECORD

												AVERAGES		
Season Team	G	Min.	FGM	FGA	Pct.	FTM	FTA	Pct.	Reb.	Ast.	Pts.	RPG	APG	PPG
86-87—Temple...........................						Did not play—redshirted.									
87-88—Temple...........................	33	399	27	55	.491	13	30	.433	85	3	67	2.6	0.1	2.0

Season Team	G	Min.	FGM	FGA	Pct.	FTM	FTA	Pct.	Reb.	Ast.	Pts.	AVERAGES RPG	APG	PPG
88-89—Temple	30	1081	128	249	.514	84	123	.683	267	19	340	8.9	0.6	11.3
89-90—Temple	12	416	52	107	.486	31	52	.596	99	9	135	8.3	0.8	11.3
Totals	75	1896	207	411	.504	128	205	.624	451	31	542	6.0	0.4	7.2

Three-point field goals: 1988-89, 0-for-1.

NBA REGULAR-SEASON RECORD

Season Team	G	Min.	FGM	FGA	Pct.	FTM	FTA	Pct.	REBOUNDS Off.	Def.	Tot.	Ast.	St.	Blk.	TO	Pts.	AVERAGES RPG	APG	PPG
90-91—Sacramento	76	1719	210	413	.508	105	165	.636	141	250	391	69	49	148	96	525	5.1	0.9	6.9
91-92—Sacramento	80	2291	250	455	.549	136	222	.613	196	384	580	59	47	215	124	636	7.3	0.7	8.0
92-93—Sacramento	55	1211	175	321	.545	103	165	.624	112	191	303	35	32	87	58	453	5.5	0.6	8.2
93-94—Sacramento	41	674	71	137	.518	40	68	.588	68	118	186	11	19	49	33	182	4.5	0.3	4.4
94-95—Sacramento	58	820	76	147	.517	57	98	.582	57	117	174	15	14	80	33	209	3.0	0.3	3.6
95-96—Sacramento	73	1044	90	216	.417	70	96	.729	86	162	248	20	27	78	53	250	3.4	0.3	3.4
Totals	383	7759	872	1689	.516	511	814	.628	660	1222	1882	209	188	657	397	2255	4.9	0.5	5.9

Three-point field goals: 1991-92, 0-for-1. 1992-93, 0-for-1. 1994-95, 0-for-1. 1995-96, 0-for-1. Totals, 0-for-4.
Personal fouls/disqualifications: 1990-91, 225/4. 1991-92, 281/4. 1992-93, 192/7. 1993-94, 109/2. 1994-95, 146/4. 1995-96, 173/2. Totals, 1126/23.

NBA PLAYOFF RECORD

Season Team	G	Min.	FGM	FGA	Pct.	FTM	FTA	Pct.	REBOUNDS Off.	Def.	Tot.	Ast.	St.	Blk.	TO	Pts.	AVERAGES RPG	APG	PPG
95-96—Sacramento	2	25	1	3	.333	3	4	.750	1	4	5	1	0	0	2	5	2.5	0.5	2.5

Three-point field goals: 1995-96, 0-for-1.
Personal fouls/disqualifications: 1995-96, 3/0.

CEBALLOS, CEDRIC   F   LAKERS

C

PERSONAL: Born August 2, 1969, in Maui, Hawaii. ... 6-7/225. ... Full name: Cedric Z. Ceballos. ... Name pronounced SED-rick seh-BAHL-ose.
HIGH SCHOOL: Dominquez (Compton, Calif.).
JUNIOR COLLEGE: Ventura (Calif.) College.
COLLEGE: Cal State Fullerton.
TRANSACTIONS/CAREER NOTES: Selected by Phoenix Suns in second round (48th pick overall) of 1990 NBA Draft. ... Traded by Suns to Los Angeles Lakers for 1995 first-round draft choice (September 23, 1994).

COLLEGIATE RECORD

Season Team	G	Min.	FGM	FGA	Pct.	FTM	FTA	Pct.	Reb.	Ast.	Pts.	AVERAGES RPG	APG	PPG
86-87—Ventura College						Statistics unavailable.								
87-88—Ventura College						Statistics unavailable.								
88-89—Cal State Fullerton	29	986	241	545	.442	117	174	.672	256	43	615	8.8	1.5	21.2
89-90—Cal State Fullerton	29	1071	247	509	.485	144	215	.670	362	50	669	12.5	1.7	23.1
Totals	58	2057	488	1054	.463	261	389	.671	618	93	1284	10.7	1.6	22.1

Three-point field goals: 1988-89, 16-for-58 (.276). 1989-90, 31-for-96 (.323). Totals, 47-for-154 (.305).

NBA REGULAR-SEASON RECORD

HONORS: Slam-Dunk Championship winner (1992).

Season Team	G	Min.	FGM	FGA	Pct.	FTM	FTA	Pct.	REBOUNDS Off.	Def.	Tot.	Ast.	St.	Blk.	TO	Pts.	AVERAGES RPG	APG	PPG
90-91—Phoenix	63	730	204	419	.487	110	166	.663	77	73	150	35	22	5	69	519	2.4	0.6	8.2
91-92—Phoenix	64	725	176	365	.482	109	148	.736	60	92	152	50	16	11	71	462	2.4	0.8	7.2
92-93—Phoenix	74	1607	381	662	*.576	187	258	.725	172	236	408	77	54	28	106	949	5.5	1.0	12.8
93-94—Phoenix	53	1602	425	795	.535	160	221	.724	153	191	344	91	59	23	93	1010	6.5	1.7	19.1
94-95—L.A. Lakers	58	2029	497	977	.509	209	292	.716	169	295	464	105	60	19	143	1261	8.0	1.8	21.7
95-96—L.A. Lakers	78	2628	638	1203	.530	329	409	.804	215	321	536	119	94	22	167	1656	6.9	1.5	21.2
Totals	390	9321	2321	4421	.525	1104	1494	.739	846	1208	2054	477	305	108	649	5857	5.3	1.2	15.0

Three-point field goals: 1990-91, 1-for-6 (.167). 1991-92, 1-for-6 (.167). 1992-93, 0-for-2. 1993-94, 0-for-9. 1994-95, 58-for-146 (.397). 1995-96, 51-for-184 (.277). Totals, 111-for-353 (.314).
Personal fouls/disqualifications: 1990-91, 70/0. 1991-92, 52/0. 1992-93, 103/1. 1993-94, 124/0. 1994-95, 131/1. 1995-96, 144/0. Totals, 624/2.

NBA PLAYOFF RECORD

Season Team	G	Min.	FGM	FGA	Pct.	FTM	FTA	Pct.	REBOUNDS Off.	Def.	Tot.	Ast.	St.	Blk.	TO	Pts.	AVERAGES RPG	APG	PPG
90-91—Phoenix	3	24	7	12	.583	2	6	.333	3	2	5	2	2	0	1	16	1.7	0.7	5.3
91-92—Phoenix	8	188	44	80	.550	20	30	.667	20	31	51	12	6	6	11	108	6.4	1.5	13.5
92-93—Phoenix	16	185	40	70	.571	16	22	.727	13	24	37	13	5	7	5	96	2.3	0.8	6.0
93-94—Phoenix	10	212	43	93	.462	15	18	.833	16	28	44	8	8	2	11	101	4.4	0.8	10.1
94-95—L.A. Lakers	10	340	48	126	.381	28	38	.737	11	50	61	18	12	7	21	142	6.1	1.8	14.2
95-96—L.A. Lakers	4	142	30	62	.484	11	12	.917	11	22	33	5	4	1	8	76	8.3	1.3	19.0
Totals	51	1091	212	443	.479	92	126	.730	74	157	231	58	37	23	57	539	4.5	1.1	10.6

Three-point field goals: 1993-94, 0-for-2. 1994-95, 18-for-50 (.360). 1995-96, 5-for-16 (.313). Totals, 23-for-68 (.338).
Personal fouls/disqualifications: 1991-92, 14/0. 1992-93, 12/0. 1993-94, 9/0. 1994-95, 21/0. 1995-96, 9/0. Totals, 65/0.

NBA ALL-STAR GAME RECORD

Season Team	Min.	FGM	FGA	Pct.	FTM	FTA	Pct.	REBOUNDS Off.	Def.	Tot.	Ast.	PF	Dq.	St.	Blk.	TO	Pts.
1995 —Los Angeles						Selected, did not play—injured.											

CHAPMAN, REX   G

PERSONAL: Born October 5, 1967, in Bowling Green, Ky. ... 6-4/195. ... Full name: Rex Everett Chapman. ... Son of Wayne Chapman, guard with Kentucky Colonels, Denver Rockets and Indiana Pacers of American Basketball Association (1968-69 through 1971-72).
HIGH SCHOOL: Apollo (Owensboro, Ky.).
COLLEGE: Kentucky.
TRANSACTIONS/CAREER NOTES: Selected after sophomore season by Charlotte Hornets in first round (eighth pick overall) of 1988 NBA Draft. ... Traded by Hornets to Washington Bullets for F Tom Hammonds (February 19, 1992). ... Traded by Bullets with draft rights to G Terrence Rencher to Miami Heat for draft rights to F Jeff Webster and draft rights to C Ed Stokes (June 28, 1995). ... Rights renounced by Heat (July 17, 1996).

COLLEGIATE RECORD

| | | | | | | | | | | | | AVERAGES | | |
Season Team	G	Min.	FGM	FGA	Pct.	FTM	FTA	Pct.	Reb.	Ast.	Pts.	RPG	APG	PPG
86-87—Kentucky	29	962	173	390	.444	50	68	.735	66	103	464	2.3	3.6	16.0
87-88—Kentucky	32	1108	231	461	.501	81	102	.794	93	117	609	2.9	3.7	19.0
Totals	61	2070	404	851	.475	131	170	.771	159	220	1073	2.6	3.6	17.6

Three-point field goals: 1986-87, 68-for-176 (.386). 1987-88, 66-for-159 (.415). Totals, 134-for-335 (.400).

NBA REGULAR-SEASON RECORD

HONORS: NBA All-Rookie second team (1989).

| | | | | | | | | | REBOUNDS | | | | | | | | AVERAGES | | |
Season Team	G	Min.	FGM	FGA	Pct.	FTM	FTA	Pct.	Off.	Def.	Tot.	Ast.	St.	Blk.	TO	Pts.	RPG	APG	PPG
88-89—Charlotte	75	2219	526	1271	.414	155	195	.795	74	113	187	176	70	25	113	1267	2.5	2.3	16.9
89-90—Charlotte	54	1762	377	924	.408	144	192	.750	52	127	179	132	46	6	100	945	3.3	2.4	17.5
90-91—Charlotte	70	2100	410	922	.445	234	282	.830	45	146	191	250	73	16	131	1102	2.7	3.6	15.7
91-92—Char.-Wash.	22	567	113	252	.448	36	53	.679	10	48	58	89	15	8	45	270	2.6	4.0	12.3
92-93—Washington	60	1300	287	602	.477	132	163	.810	19	69	88	116	38	10	79	749	1.5	1.9	12.5
93-94—Washington	60	2025	431	865	.498	168	206	.816	57	89	146	185	59	8	117	1094	2.4	3.1	18.2
94-95—Washington	45	1468	254	639	.398	137	159	.862	23	90	113	128	67	15	62	731	2.5	2.8	16.2
95-96—Miami	56	1865	289	679	.426	83	113	.735	22	123	145	166	45	10	79	786	2.6	3.0	14.0
Totals	442	13306	2687	6154	.437	1089	1363	.799	302	805	1107	1242	413	98	726	6944	2.5	2.8	15.7

Three-point field goals: 1988-89, 60-for-191 (.314). 1989-90, 47-for-142 (.331). 1990-91, 48-for-148 (.324). 1991-92, 8-for-29 (.276). 1992-93, 43-for-116 (.371). 1993-94, 64-for-165 (.388). 1994-95, 86-for-274 (.314). 1995-96, 125-for-337 (.371). Totals, 481-for-1402 (.343).
Personal fouls/disqualifications: 1988-89, 167/1. 1989-90, 113/0. 1990-91, 167/1. 1991-92, 51/0. 1992-93, 119/1. 1993-94, 83/0. 1994-95, 85/0. 1995-96, 117/0. Totals, 902/3.

NBA PLAYOFF RECORD

| | | | | | | | | | REBOUNDS | | | | | | | | AVERAGES | | |
Season Team	G	Min.	FGM	FGA	Pct.	FTM	FTA	Pct.	Off.	Def.	Tot.	Ast.	St.	Blk.	TO	Pts.	RPG	APG	PPG
95-96—Miami	3	88	12	28	.429	0	0	...	0	6	6	5	3	0	1	27	2.0	1.7	9.0

Three-point field goals: 1995-96, 3-for-13 (.231).
Personal fouls/disqualifications: 1995-96, 6/0.

CHEANEY, CALBERT   G/F   BULLETS

PERSONAL: Born July 17, 1971, in Evansville, Ind. ... 6-7/215. ... Full name: Calbert N. Cheaney. ... Name pronounced CHAIN-ee.
HIGH SCHOOL: Harrison (Evansville, Ind.).
COLLEGE: Indiana.
TRANSACTIONS/CAREER NOTES: Selected by Washington Bullets in first round (sixth pick overall) of 1993 NBA Draft.

COLLEGIATE RECORD

NOTES: The Sporting News College Player of the Year (1993). ... Naismith Award winner (1993). ... Wooden Award winner (1993). ... The Sporting News All-America first team (1993). ... The Sporting News All-America third team (1991).

| | | | | | | | | | | | | AVERAGES | | |
Season Team	G	Min.	FGM	FGA	Pct.	FTM	FTA	Pct.	Reb.	Ast.	Pts.	RPG	APG	PPG
89-90—Indiana	29	928	199	348	.572	72	96	.750	133	48	495	4.6	1.7	17.1
90-91—Indiana	34	1029	289	485	.596	113	141	.801	188	47	734	5.5	1.4	21.6
91-92—Indiana	34	991	227	435	.522	112	140	.800	166	48	599	4.9	1.4	17.6
92-93—Indiana	35	1181	303	552	.549	132	166	.795	223	84	785	6.4	2.4	22.4
Totals	132	4129	1018	1820	.559	429	543	.790	710	227	2613	5.4	1.7	19.8

Three-point field goals: 1989-90, 25-for-51 (.490). 1990-91, 43-for-91 (.473). 1991-92, 33-for-86 (.384). 1992-93, 47-for-110 (.427). Totals, 148-for-338 (.438).

NBA REGULAR-SEASON RECORD

| | | | | | | | | | REBOUNDS | | | | | | | | AVERAGES | | |
Season Team	G	Min.	FGM	FGA	Pct.	FTM	FTA	Pct.	Off.	Def.	Tot.	Ast.	St.	Blk.	TO	Pts.	RPG	APG	PPG
93-94—Washington	65	1604	327	696	.470	124	161	.770	88	102	190	126	63	10	108	779	2.9	1.9	12.0
94-95—Washington	78	2651	512	1129	.454	173	213	.812	105	216	321	177	80	21	151	1293	4.1	2.3	16.6
95-96—Washington	70	2324	426	905	.471	151	214	.706	67	172	239	154	67	18	129	1055	3.4	2.2	15.1
Totals	213	6579	1265	2730	.463	448	588	.762	260	490	750	457	210	49	388	3127	3.5	2.1	14.7

Three-point field goals: 1993-94, 1-for-23 (.043). 1994-95, 96-for-283 (.339). 1995-96, 52-for-154 (.338). Totals, 149-for-460 (.324).
Personal fouls/disqualifications: 1993-94, 148/0. 1994-95, 215/0. 1995-96, 205/1. Totals, 568/1.

CHILCUTT, PETE F GRIZZLIES

PERSONAL: Born September 14, 1968, in Sumter, S.C. ... 6-10/235. ... Full name: Peter Shawn Chilcutt.
HIGH SCHOOL: Tuscaloosa Academy (Eutaw, Ala.).
COLLEGE: North Carolina.
TRANSACTIONS/CAREER NOTES: Selected by Sacramento Kings in first round (27th pick overall) of 1991 NBA Draft. ... Traded by Kings with 1994 second-round draft choice and conditional first-round draft choice to Detroit Pistons for C Olden Polynice (February 20, 1994). ... Rights renounced by Pistons (September 29, 1994). ... Played in Italy (1994-95). ... Signed as free agent by Houston Rockets (November 29, 1994). ... Traded by Rockets with F Tim Breaux, 1996 first- and second-round draft choices and 1997 conditional second-round draft choice to Vancouver Grizzlies for two 1996 second-round draft choices (June 19, 1996).
MISCELLANEOUS: Member of NBA championship team (1995).

COLLEGIATE RECORD

Season Team	G	Min.	FGM	FGA	Pct.	FTM	FTA	Pct.	Reb.	Ast.	Pts.	RPG	APG	PPG
86-87—North Carolina							Did not play—redshirted.							
87-88—North Carolina	34	573	66	117	.564	36	51	.706	110	43	168	3.2	1.3	4.9
88-89—North Carolina	37	750	110	205	.537	33	53	.623	200	51	256	5.4	1.4	6.9
89-90—North Carolina	34	917	132	257	.514	30	42	.714	225	47	306	6.6	1.4	9.0
90-91—North Carolina	35	937	175	325	.538	65	85	.765	231	47	420	6.6	1.3	12.0
Totals	140	3177	483	904	.534	164	231	.710	766	188	1150	5.5	1.3	8.2

Three-point field goals: 1987-88, 0-for-1. 1988-89, 3-for-8 (.375). 1989-90, 12-for-30 (.400). 1990-91, 5-for-19 (.263). Totals, 20-for-58 (.345).

NBA REGULAR-SEASON RECORD

Season Team	G	Min.	FGM	FGA	Pct.	FTM	FTA	Pct.	Off.	Def.	Tot.	Ast.	St.	Blk.	TO	Pts.	RPG	APG	PPG
91-92—Sacramento	69	817	113	250	.452	23	28	.821	78	109	187	38	32	17	41	251	2.7	0.6	3.6
92-93—Sacramento	59	834	165	340	.485	32	46	.696	80	114	194	64	22	21	54	362	3.3	1.1	6.1
93-94—Sac.-Det.	76	1365	203	448	.453	41	65	.631	129	242	371	86	53	39	74	450	4.9	1.1	5.9
94-95—Houston	68	1347	146	328	.445	31	42	.738	106	211	317	66	25	43	61	358	4.7	1.0	5.3
95-96—Houston	74	651	73	179	.408	17	26	.654	51	105	156	26	19	14	22	200	2.1	0.4	2.7
Totals	346	5014	700	1545	.453	144	207	.696	444	781	1225	280	151	134	252	1621	3.5	0.8	4.7

Three-point field goals: 1991-92, 2-for-2. 1993-94, 3-for-15 (.200). 1994-95, 35-for-86 (.407). 1995-96, 37-for-98 (.378). Totals, 77-for-201 (.383).
Personal fouls/disqualifications: 1991-92, 70/0. 1992-93, 102/2. 1993-94, 164/2. 1994-95, 117/0. 1995-96, 65/0. Totals, 518/4.

NBA PLAYOFF RECORD

Season Team	G	Min.	FGM	FGA	Pct.	FTM	FTA	Pct.	Off.	Def.	Tot.	Ast.	St.	Blk.	TO	Pts.	RPG	APG	PPG
94-95—Houston	20	323	31	64	.484	14	17	.824	15	43	58	18	7	4	11	90	2.9	0.9	4.5
95-96—Houston	1	10	1	4	.250	0	2	.000	2	1	3	0	0	0	1	2	3.0	0.0	2.0
Totals	21	333	32	68	.471	14	19	.737	17	44	61	18	7	4	12	92	2.9	0.9	4.4

Three-point field goals: 1994-95, 14-for-36 (.389). 1995-96, 0-for-1. Totals, 14-for-37 (.378).
Personal fouls/disqualifications: 1994-95, 39/0.

ITALIAN LEAGUE RECORD

Season Team	G	Min.	FGM	FGA	Pct.	FTM	FTA	Pct.	Reb.	Ast.	Pts.	RPG	APG	PPG
94-95—Trieste	9	321	51	111	.459	23	28	.821	82	6	136	9.1	0.7	15.1

CHILDRESS, RANDOLPH G TRAIL BLAZERS

PERSONAL: Born September 21, 1972, in Washington, D.C. ... 6-2/188. ... Name pronounced CHILL-dress.
HIGH SCHOOL: Flint Hill Prep (Oakton, Va.).
COLLEGE: Wake Forest.
TRANSACTIONS/CAREER NOTES: Selected by Detroit Pistons in first round (19th pick overall) of 1995 NBA Draft. ... Draft rights traded by Pistons with F Bill Curley to Portland Trail Blazers for F Otis Thorpe (September 20, 1995).

COLLEGIATE RECORD

Season Team	G	Min.	FGM	FGA	Pct.	FTM	FTA	Pct.	Reb.	Ast.	Pts.	RPG	APG	PPG
90-91—Wake Forest	29	708	123	274	.449	95	123	.772	62	65	405	2.1	2.2	14.0
91-92—Wake Forest							Did not play—knee injury.							
92-93—Wake Forest	30	1030	184	380	.484	128	158	.810	84	126	592	2.8	4.2	19.7
93-94—Wake Forest	29	1017	158	381	.415	176	223	.789	99	114	567	3.4	3.9	19.6
94-95—Wake Forest	32	1216	183	418	.438	184	221	.833	115	167	644	3.6	5.2	20.1
Totals	120	3971	648	1453	.446	583	725	.804	360	472	2208	3.0	3.9	18.4

Three-point field goals: 1990-91, 64-for-166 (.386). 1992-93, 96-for-217 (.442). 1993-94, 75-for-204 (.368). 1994-95, 94-for-245 (.384). Totals, 329-for-832 (.395).

NBA REGULAR-SEASON RECORD

Season Team	G	Min.	FGM	FGA	Pct.	FTM	FTA	Pct.	Off.	Def.	Tot.	Ast.	St.	Blk.	TO	Pts.	RPG	APG	PPG
95-96—Portland	28	250	25	79	.316	22	27	.815	1	18	19	32	8	1	28	85	0.7	1.1	3.0

Three-point field goals: 1995-96, 13-for-47 (.277).
Personal fouls/disqualifications: 1995-96, 22/0.

C

CHILDS, CHRIS   G   KNICKS

PERSONAL: Born November 20, 1967, in Bakersfield, Calif. ... 6-3/195.
HIGH SCHOOL: Foothill (Bakersfield, Calif.).
COLLEGE: Boise State.
TRANSACTIONS/CAREER NOTES: Not drafted by an NBA franchise. ... Played in Continental Basketball Association with Columbus Horizon (1989-90 and 1990-91), Rapid City Thrillers (1989-90), La Crosse Catbirds (1990-91), Rockford Lightning (1990-91 and 1991-92), Bakersfield Jammers (1991-92) and Quad City Thunder (1992-93 and 1993-94). ... Played in United States Basketball League with Miami Tropics (1993, 1994). ... Signed as free agent by San Antonio Spurs (August 16, 1993). ... Waived by Spurs (October 25, 1993). ... Signed as free agent by New Jersey Nets (July 29, 1994). ... Signed as free agent by New York Knicks (July 14, 1996).

COLLEGIATE RECORD

Season Team	G	Min.	FGM	FGA	Pct.	FTM	FTA	Pct.	Reb.	Ast.	Pts.	RPG	APG	PPG
85-86—Boise State	28	792	109	264	.413	72	91	.791	87	84	300	3.1	3.0	10.7
86-87—Boise State	30	945	153	344	.445	109	132	.826	77	87	462	2.6	2.9	15.4
87-88—Boise State	30	944	147	316	.465	81	95	.853	79	99	429	2.6	3.3	14.3
88-89—Boise State	30	929	131	295	.444	97	121	.802	101	122	411	3.4	4.1	13.7
Totals	118	3610	540	1219	.443	359	439	.818	344	392	1602	2.9	3.3	13.6

Three-point field goals: 1985-86, 10-for-31 (.323). 1986-87, 47-for-116 (.405). 1987-88, 54-for-120 (.450). 1988-89, 52-for-119 (.437). Totals, 163-for-386 (.422).

CBA REGULAR-SEASON RECORD

NOTES: CBA Playoff Most Valuable Player (1994). ... Member of CBA championship team (1994).

Season Team	G	Min.	FGM	FGA	Pct.	FTM	FTA	Pct.	Reb.	Ast.	Pts.	RPG	APG	PPG
89-90—Columbus-Rapid City	21	531	55	136	.404	38	46	.826	61	158	158	2.9	7.5	7.5
90-91—Col.-La Crosse-Rockford	33	717	100	228	.439	84	105	.800	94	165	297	2.8	5.0	9.0
91-92—Bakersfield-Rockford	47	1379	205	443	.463	159	183	.869	174	357	585	3.7	7.6	12.4
92-93—Quad City	50	1624	226	497	.455	130	157	.828	173	292	597	3.5	5.8	11.9
93-94—Quad City	56	2143	368	772	.477	246	281	.875	220	423	1003	3.9	7.6	17.9
Totals	207	6394	954	2076	.460	657	772	.851	722	1395	2640	3.5	6.7	12.8

Three-point field goals: 1989-90, 10-for-30 (.333). 1990-91, 13-for-41 (.317). 1991-92, 16-for-64 (.250). 1992-93, 15-for-62 (.242). 1993-94, 21-for-88 (.239). Totals, 75-for-285 (.264).

NBA REGULAR-SEASON RECORD

Season Team	G	Min.	FGM	FGA	Pct.	FTM	FTA	Pct.	REBOUNDS Off.	Def.	Tot.	Ast.	St.	Blk.	TO	Pts.	RPG	APG	PPG
94-95—New Jersey	53	1021	106	279	.380	55	73	.753	14	55	69	219	42	3	76	308	1.3	4.1	5.8
95-96—New Jersey	78	2408	324	778	.416	259	304	.852	51	194	245	548	111	8	230	1002	3.1	7.0	12.8
Totals	131	3429	430	1057	.407	314	377	.833	65	249	314	767	153	11	306	1310	2.4	5.9	10.0

Three-point field goals: 1994-95, 41-for-125 (.328). 1995-96, 95-for-259 (.367). Totals, 136-for-384 (.354).
Personal fouls/disqualifications: 1994-95, 116/1. 1995-96, 246/3. Totals, 362/4.

CHRISTIE, DOUG   G/F   RAPTORS

PERSONAL: Born May 9, 1970, in Seattle. ... 6-6/205. ... Full name: Douglas Dale Christie. ... Name pronounced CHRIS-tee.
HIGH SCHOOL: Rainier Beach (Seattle).
COLLEGE: Pepperdine.
TRANSACTIONS/CAREER NOTES: Selected by Seattle SuperSonics in first round (17th pick overall) of 1992 NBA Draft. ... Traded by SuperSonics with C Benoit Benjamin to Los Angeles Lakers for F/C Sam Perkins (February 22, 1993). ... Traded by Lakers to New York Knicks for two future second-round draft choices (October 13, 1994). ... Traded by Knicks with C/F Herb Williams and cash to Toronto Raptors for G Willie Anderson and F/C Victor Alexander (February 18, 1996).

COLLEGIATE RECORD

Season Team	G	Min.	FGM	FGA	Pct.	FTM	FTA	Pct.	Reb.	Ast.	Pts.	RPG	APG	PPG
88-89—Pepperdine						Did not play—ineligible.								
89-90—Pepperdine	28	687	84	167	.503	70	98	.714	115	112	250	4.1	4.0	8.9
90-91—Pepperdine	28	913	188	401	.469	143	187	.765	145	134	536	5.2	4.8	19.1
91-92—Pepperdine	31	1058	211	453	.466	144	193	.746	183	149	606	5.9	4.8	19.5
Totals	87	2658	483	1021	.473	357	478	.747	443	395	1392	5.1	4.5	16.0

Three-point field goals: 1989-90, 12-for-47 (.255). 1990-91, 17-for-65 (.262). 1991-92, 40-for-120 (.333). Totals, 69-for-232 (.297).

NBA REGULAR-SEASON RECORD

Season Team	G	Min.	FGM	FGA	Pct.	FTM	FTA	Pct.	REBOUNDS Off.	Def.	Tot.	Ast.	St.	Blk.	TO	Pts.	RPG	APG	PPG
92-93—L.A. Lakers	23	332	45	106	.425	50	66	.758	24	27	51	53	22	5	50	142	2.2	2.3	6.2
93-94—L.A. Lakers	65	1515	244	562	.434	145	208	.697	93	142	235	136	89	28	140	672	3.6	2.1	10.3
94-95—New York	12	79	5	22	.227	4	5	.800	3	10	13	8	2	1	13	15	1.1	0.7	1.3
95-96—N.Y.-Tor.	55	1036	150	337	.445	69	93	.742	34	120	154	117	70	19	95	415	2.8	2.1	7.5
Totals	155	2962	444	1027	.432	268	372	.720	154	299	453	314	183	53	298	1244	2.9	2.0	8.0

Three-point field goals: 1992-93, 2-for-12 (.167). 1993-94, 39-for-119 (.328). 1994-95, 1-for-7 (.143). 1995-96, 46-for-106 (.434). Totals, 88-for-244 (.361).
Personal fouls/disqualifications: 1992-93, 53/0. 1993-94, 186/2. 1994-95, 18/1. 1995-96, 141/5. Totals, 398/8.

NBA PLAYOFF RECORD

Season Team	G	Min.	FGM	FGA	Pct.	FTM	FTA	Pct.	REBOUNDS Off.	Def.	Tot.	Ast.	St.	Blk.	TO	Pts.	RPG	APG	PPG
92-93—L.A. Lakers	5	39	4	11	.364	0	0	...	1	3	4	6	2	2	4	9	0.8	1.2	1.8
94-95—New York	2	6	0	4	.000	0	0	...	0	0	0	0	0	0	1	0	0.0	0.0	0.0
Totals	7	45	4	15	.267	0	0	...	1	3	4	6	2	2	5	9	0.6	0.9	1.3

Three-point field goals: 1992-93, 1-for-3 (.333).
Personal fouls/disqualifications: 1992-93, 5/0. 1994-95, 3/0. Totals, 8/0.

CHURCHWELL, ROBERT   G/F

PERSONAL: Born February 20, 1972, in South Bend, Ind. ... 6-7/195.
HIGH SCHOOL: Gonzaga (Washington, D.C.).
COLLEGE: Georgetown.
TRANSACTIONS/CAREER NOTES: Not drafted by an NBA franchise. ... Played in Continental Basketball Association with Chicago Rockers (1994-95 and 1995-96). ... Signed by Golden State Warriors to first of three consecutive 10-day contracts (March 14, 1996). ... Re-signed by Warriors for remainder of season (April 3, 1996). ... Rights renounced by Warriors (July 21, 1996).

COLLEGIATE RECORD

Season Team	G	Min.	FGM	FGA	Pct.	FTM	FTA	Pct.	Reb.	Ast.	Pts.	RPG	APG	PPG
90-91—Georgetown	32	903	114	277	.412	37	60	.617	154	50	268	4.8	1.6	8.4
91-92—Georgetown	32	865	120	243	.494	57	75	.760	153	42	308	4.8	1.3	9.6
92-93—Georgetown	33	1020	148	329	.450	67	92	.728	201	58	380	6.1	1.8	11.5
93-94—Georgetown	31	857	115	270	.426	53	72	.736	160	40	300	5.2	1.3	9.7
Totals	128	3645	497	1119	.444	214	299	.716	668	190	1256	5.2	1.5	9.8

Three-point field goals: 1990-91, 3-for-12 (.250). 1991-92, 11-for-29 (.379). 1992-93, 17-for-46 (.370). 1993-94, 17-for-43 (.395). Totals, 48-for-130 (.369).

NOTES: CBA All-Rookie second team (1995).

CBA REGULAR-SEASON RECORD

Season Team	G	Min.	FGM	FGA	Pct.	FTM	FTA	Pct.	Reb.	Ast.	Pts.	RPG	APG	PPG
94-95—Chicago	56	1682	291	598	.487	113	151	.748	272	104	722	4.9	1.9	12.9
95-96—Chicago	52	1456	262	544	.482	132	156	.846	220	122	658	4.2	2.3	12.7
Totals	108	3138	553	1142	.484	245	307	.798	492	226	1380	4.6	2.1	12.8

Three-point field goals: 1994-95, 27-for-91 (.297). 1995-96, 2-for-17 (.118). Totals, 29-for-108 (.269).

NBA REGULAR-SEASON RECORD

Season Team	G	Min.	FGM	FGA	Pct.	FTM	FTA	Pct.	Off.	Def.	Tot.	Ast.	St.	Blk.	TO	Pts.	RPG	APG	PPG
95-96—Golden State	4	20	3	8	.375	0	0	...	0	3	3	1	0	0	2	6	0.8	0.3	1.5

Personal fouls/disqualifications: 1995-96, 1/0.

CLAXTON, CHARLES   C

PERSONAL: Born December 13, 1970, in St. Thomas, Virgin Islands. ... 7-0/265. ... Full name: Charles Claxton Jr.
HIGH SCHOOL: Carol City (Miami).
COLLEGE: Georgia.
TRANSACTIONS/CAREER NOTES: Selected after junior season by Phoenix Suns in second round (50th pick overall) of 1994 NBA Draft. ... Returned to college for his senior season (1994-95). ... Signed as free agent by Cleveland Cavaliers (October 10, 1995). ... Waived by Cavaliers (October 16, 1995). ... Signed as free agent by Boston Celtics (October 24, 1995). ... Waived by Celtics (November 27, 1995).

COLLEGIATE RECORD

Season Team	G	Min.	FGM	FGA	Pct.	FTM	FTA	Pct.	Reb.	Ast.	Pts.	RPG	APG	PPG
90-91—Georgia						Did not play—redshirted.								
91-92—Georgia	29	644	109	208	.524	55	102	.539	190	51	273	6.6	1.8	9.4
92-93—Georgia	29	637	133	236	.564	68	141	.482	192	12	334	6.6	0.4	11.5
93-94—Georgia	30	728	132	239	.552	63	149	.423	236	18	327	7.9	0.6	10.9
94-95—Georgia	28	769	124	226	.549	89	166	.536	222	21	340	7.9	0.8	12.1
Totals	116	2778	498	909	.548	275	558	.493	840	102	1274	7.2	0.9	11.0

Three-point field goals: 1994-95, 3-for-10 (.300).

NBA REGULAR-SEASON RECORD

Season Team	G	Min.	FGM	FGA	Pct.	FTM	FTA	Pct.	Off.	Def.	Tot.	Ast.	St.	Blk.	TO	Pts.	RPG	APG	PPG
95-96—Boston	3	7	1	2	.500	0	2	.000	2	0	2	0	0	1	1	2	0.7	0.0	0.7

Personal fouls/disqualifications: 1995-96, 4/0.

COKER, JOHN   C   SUNS

PERSONAL: Born October 28, 1971, in Richland, Wash. ... 7-1/253. ... Full name: John Michael Coker.
HIGH SCHOOL: Olympic (Bremerton, Wash.).
COLLEGE: Boise State.
TRANSACTIONS/CAREER NOTES: Not drafted by an NBA franchise. ... Signed as free agent by Phoenix Suns (September 25, 1995).

COLLEGIATE RECORD

Season Team	G	Min.	FGM	FGA	Pct.	FTM	FTA	Pct.	Reb.	Ast.	Pts.	RPG	APG	PPG
90-91—Boise State						Did not play—redshirted.								
91-92—Boise State	11	98	14	25	.560	1	5	.200	17	3	29	1.5	0.3	2.6
92-93—Boise State	22	298	65	125	.520	18	26	.692	86	13	148	3.9	0.6	6.7
93-94—Boise State	30	866	231	403	.573	59	117	.504	203	39	521	6.8	1.3	17.4
94-95—Boise State	21	573	129	244	.529	76	112	.679	153	17	334	7.3	0.8	15.9
Totals	84	1835	439	797	.551	154	260	.592	459	72	1032	5.5	0.9	12.3

							REBOUNDS								AVERAGES		
Season Team	G	Min.	FGM	FGA	Pct.	FTM	FTA	Pct.	Off.	Def.	Tot.	Ast.	St.	Blk.	TO	Pts.	RPG APG PPG
95-96—Phoenix	5	11	4	5	.800	0	0	...	2	0	2	1	0	1	0	8	0.4 0.2 1.6

Personal fouls/disqualifications: 1995-96, 1/0.

COLEMAN, DERRICK F 76ERS

PERSONAL: Born June 21, 1967, in Mobile, Ala. ... 6-10/260. ... Full name: Derrick D. Coleman.
HIGH SCHOOL: Northern (Detroit).
COLLEGE: Syracuse.
TRANSACTIONS/CAREER NOTES: Selected by New Jersey Nets in first round (first pick overall) of 1990 NBA Draft. ... Traded by Nets with F Sean Higgins and G Rex Walters to Philadelphia 76ers for C Shawn Bradley, F Tim Perry and G Greg Graham (November 30, 1995).

COLLEGIATE RECORD

NOTES: THE SPORTING NEWS All-America first team (1990). ... 1986-87 minutes played totals are missing one game.

											AVERAGES		
Season Team	G	Min.	FGM	FGA	Pct.	FTM	FTA	Pct.	Reb.	Ast.	Pts.	RPG	APG	PPG
86-87—Syracuse	38	1163	173	309	.560	107	156	.686	333	45	453	8.8	1.2	11.9
87-88—Syracuse	35	1133	176	300	.587	121	192	.630	384	76	474	11.0	2.2	13.5
88-89—Syracuse	37	1226	227	395	.575	171	247	.692	422	106	625	11.5	2.9	16.9
89-90—Syracuse	33	1166	194	352	.551	188	263	.715	398	95	591	12.1	2.9	17.9
Totals	143	4688	770	1356	.568	587	858	.685	1537	322	2143	10.8	2.3	15.0

Three-point field goals: 1987-88, 1-for-6 (.167). 1988-89, 0-for-8. 1989-90, 15-for-41 (.366). Totals, 16-for-55 (.291).

NBA REGULAR-SEASON RECORD

HONORS: NBA Rookie of the Year (1991). ... All-NBA third team (1993, 1994). ... NBA All-Rookie first team (1991).

								REBOUNDS								AVERAGES		
Season Team	G	Min.	FGM	FGA	Pct.	FTM	FTA	Pct.	Off.	Def.	Tot.	Ast.	St.	Blk.	TO	Pts.	RPG	APG	PPG
90-91—New Jersey	74	2602	514	1100	.467	323	442	.731	269	490	759	163	71	99	217	1364	10.3	2.3	18.4
91-92—New Jersey	65	2207	483	958	.504	300	393	.763	203	415	618	205	54	98	248	1289	9.6	3.2	19.8
92-93—New Jersey	76	2759	564	1226	.460	421	521	.808	247	605	852	276	92	126	243	1572	11.3	3.7	20.7
93-94—New Jersey	77	2778	541	1209	.447	439	567	.774	262	608	870	262	68	142	208	1559	11.3	3.4	20.2
94-95—New Jersey	56	2103	371	875	.424	376	490	.767	167	424	591	187	35	94	172	1146	10.6	3.4	20.5
95-96—Philadelphia	11	294	48	118	.407	20	32	.625	13	59	72	31	4	10	28	123	6.6	2.9	11.2
Totals	359	12743	2521	5486	.460	1879	2445	.769	1161	2601	3762	1124	324	569	1116	7053	10.5	3.2	19.7

Three-point field goals: 1990-91, 13-for-38 (.343). 1991-92, 23-for-76 (.303). 1992-93, 23-for-99 (.233). 1993-94, 38-for-121 (.315). 1994-95, 28-for-120 (.234). 1995-96, 7-for-21 (.334). Totals, 132-for-475 (.278).
Personal fouls/disqualifications: 1990-91, 217/3. 1991-92, 168/2. 1992-93, 210/1. 1993-94, 209/2. 1994-95, 162/2. 1995-96, 30/0. Totals, 996/10.

NBA PLAYOFF RECORD

								REBOUNDS								AVERAGES		
Season Team	G	Min.	FGM	FGA	Pct.	FTM	FTA	Pct.	Off.	Def.	Tot.	Ast.	St.	Blk.	TO	Pts.	RPG	APG	PPG
91-92—New Jersey	4	162	36	74	.486	16	21	.762	13	32	45	21	7	4	11	89	11.3	5.3	22.3
92-93—New Jersey	5	225	50	94	.532	29	36	.806	13	54	67	23	6	13	13	134	13.5	4.7	26.8
93-94—New Jersey	4	173	27	68	.397	39	50	.780	19	38	57	10	2	5	18	98	14.3	2.6	24.5
Totals	13	560	113	236	.479	84	107	.786	45	124	169	54	15	22	42	321	13.1	4.2	24.7

Three-point field goals: 1991-92, 1-for-6 (.167). 1992-93, 5-for-12 (.417). 1993-94, 5-for-9 (.556). Totals, 11-for-27 (.408).
Personal fouls/disqualifications: 1991-92, 12/0. 1992-93, 18/0. 1993-94, 12/0. Totals, 42/0.

NBA ALL-STAR GAME RECORD

								REBOUNDS								
Season Team	Min.	FGM	FGA	Pct.	FTM	FTA	Pct.	Off.	Def.	Tot.	Ast.	PF	Dq.	St.	Blk.	TO Pts.
1994 —New Jersey........	18	1	6	.167	0	0	...	1	2	3	1	3	0	1	1	0 2

Three-point field goals: 1994, 0-for-2.

COLES, BIMBO G WARRIORS

PERSONAL: Born April 22, 1968, in Covington, Va. ... 6-2/182. ... Full name: Vernell Eufaye Coles.
HIGH SCHOOL: Greenbriar East (Lewisburg, W.Va.).
COLLEGE: Virginia Tech.
TRANSACTIONS/CAREER NOTES: Selected by Sacramento Kings in second round (40th pick overall) of 1990 NBA Draft. ... Draft rights traded by Kings to Miami Heat for G Rory Sparrow (June 27, 1990). ... Traded by Heat with F/C Kevin Willis to Golden State Warriors for G Tim Hardaway and F/C Chris Gatling (February 22, 1996).
MISCELLANEOUS: Member of bronze-medal-winning U.S. Olympic team (1988). ... Selected by California Angels organization in 54th round of free-agent draft (June 4, 1990); did not sign. ... Miami Heat all-time assists leader with 1,946 (1990-91 through 1995-96).

COLLEGIATE RECORD

											AVERAGES		
Season Team	G	Min.	FGM	FGA	Pct.	FTM	FTA	Pct.	Reb.	Ast.	Pts.	RPG	APG	PPG
86-87—Virginia Tech	28	752	101	245	.412	78	109	.716	85	112	280	3.0	4.0	10.0
87-88—Virginia Tech	29	990	241	544	.443	200	270	.741	103	172	702	3.6	5.9	24.2
88-89—Virginia Tech	27	924	249	547	.455	157	200	.785	111	141	717	4.1	5.2	26.6
89-90—Virginia Tech	31	1147	280	693	.404	158	214	.738	147	122	785	4.7	3.9	25.3
Totals	115	3813	871	2029	.429	593	793	.748	446	547	2484	3.9	4.8	21.6

Three-point field goals: 1986-87, 0-for-14. 1987-88, 20-for-62 (.323). 1988-89, 62-for-166 (.373). 1989-90, 67-for-218 (.307). Totals, 149-for-460 (.324).

NBA REGULAR-SEASON RECORD

								REBOUNDS								AVERAGES		
Season Team	G	Min.	FGM	FGA	Pct.	FTM	FTA	Pct.	Off.	Def.	Tot.	Ast.	St.	Blk.	TO	Pts.	RPG	APG	PPG
90-91—Miami	82	1355	162	393	.412	71	95	.747	56	97	153	232	65	12	98	401	1.9	2.8	4.9

C

Season Team	G	Min.	FGM	FGA	Pct.	FTM	FTA	Pct.	Off.	Def.	Tot.	Ast.	St.	Blk.	TO	Pts.	RPG	APG	PPG
									REBOUNDS								**AVERAGES**		
91-92—Miami	81	1976	295	649	.455	216	262	.824	69	120	189	366	73	13	167	816	2.3	4.5	10.1
92-93—Miami	81	2232	318	686	.464	177	220	.805	58	108	166	373	80	11	108	855	2.0	4.6	10.6
93-94—Miami	76	1726	233	519	.449	102	131	.779	50	109	159	263	75	12	107	588	2.1	3.5	7.7
94-95—Miami	68	2207	261	607	.430	141	174	.810	46	145	191	416	99	13	156	679	2.8	6.1	10.0
95-96—Mia.-G.S.	81	2615	318	777	.409	168	211	.796	49	211	260	422	94	17	171	892	3.2	5.2	11.0
Totals	469	12111	1587	3631	.437	875	1093	.801	328	790	1118	2072	486	78	807	4231	2.4	4.4	9.0

Three-point field goals: 1990-91, 6-for-34 (.176). 1991-92, 10-for-52 (.192). 1992-93, 42-for-137 (.307). 1993-94, 20-for-99 (.202). 1994-95, 16-for-76 (.211). 1995-96, 88-for-254 (.346). Totals, 182-for-652 (.279).
Personal fouls/disqualifications: 1990-91, 149/0. 1991-92, 151/3. 1992-93, 199/4. 1993-94, 132/0. 1994-95, 185/1. 1995-96, 253/5. Totals, 1069/13.

NBA PLAYOFF RECORD

Season Team	G	Min.	FGM	FGA	Pct.	FTM	FTA	Pct.	Off.	Def.	Tot.	Ast.	St.	Blk.	TO	Pts.	RPG	APG	PPG
									REBOUNDS								**AVERAGES**		
91-92—Miami	3	45	7	10	.700	8	10	.800	2	5	7	6	3	0	5	23	2.3	2.0	7.7
93-94—Miami	5	140	25	47	.532	18	23	.783	2	12	14	17	7	1	11	69	2.8	3.4	13.8
Totals	8	185	32	57	.561	26	33	.788	4	17	21	23	10	1	16	92	2.6	2.9	11.5

Three-point field goals: 1991-92, 1-for-1. 1993-94, 1-for-4 (.250). Totals, 2-for-5 (.400).
Personal fouls/disqualifications: 1991-92, 5/0. 1993-94, 15/0. Totals, 20/0.

CONLON, MARTY   F   BUCKS

C

PERSONAL: Born January 19, 1968, in Bronx, N.Y. ... 6-11/245. ... Full name: Martin McBride Conlon.
HIGH SCHOOL: Archbishop Stepinac (White Plains, N.Y.).
COLLEGE: Providence.
TRANSACTIONS/CAREER NOTES: Not drafted by an NBA franchise. ... Played in Continental Basketball Association with Rockford Lightning (1990-91 and 1993-94). ... Signed as free agent by Seattle SuperSonics (October 1, 1991). ... Signed as free agent by Sacramento Kings (October 1, 1992). ... Waived by Kings (November 2, 1993). ... Signed by Charlotte Hornets to first of two consecutive 10-day contracts (February 2, 1994). ... Re-signed by Hornets for remainder of season (February 25, 1994). ... Claimed off waivers by Washington Bullets (March 24, 1994). ... Signed as unrestricted free agent by Milwaukee Bucks (August 3, 1994).

COLLEGIATE RECORD

Season Team	G	Min.	FGM	FGA	Pct.	FTM	FTA	Pct.	Reb.	Ast.	Pts.	RPG	APG	PPG
													AVERAGES	
86-87—Providence	34	487	43	96	.448	64	77	.831	100	16	150	2.9	0.5	4.4
87-88—Providence	11	282	45	88	.511	55	66	.833	62	19	145	5.6	1.7	13.2
88-89—Providence	29	885	154	294	.524	91	125	.728	202	60	415	7.0	2.1	14.3
89-90—Providence	29	866	136	271	.502	138	187	.738	220	72	425	7.6	2.5	14.7
Totals	103	2520	378	749	.505	348	455	.765	584	167	1135	5.7	1.6	11.0

Three-point field goals: 1987-88, 0-for-3. 1988-89, 16-for-42 (.381). 1989-90, 15-for-48 (.313). Totals, 31-for-93 (.333).

CBA REGULAR-SEASON RECORD

Season Team	G	Min.	FGM	FGA	Pct.	FTM	FTA	Pct.	Reb.	Ast.	Pts.	RPG	APG	PPG
													AVERAGES	
90-91—Rockford	41	1104	215	342	.629	118	157	.752	286	72	548	7.0	1.8	13.4
93-94—Rockford	21	796	169	284	.595	82	105	.781	203	82	420	9.7	3.9	20.0
Totals	62	1900	384	626	.613	200	262	.763	489	154	968	7.9	2.5	15.6

Three-point field goals: 1990-91, 0-for-3.

NBA REGULAR-SEASON RECORD

Season Team	G	Min.	FGM	FGA	Pct.	FTM	FTA	Pct.	Off.	Def.	Tot.	Ast.	St.	Blk.	TO	Pts.	RPG	APG	PPG
									REBOUNDS								**AVERAGES**		
91-92—Seattle	45	381	48	101	.475	24	32	.750	33	36	69	12	9	7	27	120	1.5	0.3	2.7
92-93—Sacramento	46	467	81	171	.474	57	81	.704	48	75	123	37	13	5	28	219	2.7	0.8	4.8
93-94—Char.-Wash.	30	579	95	165	.576	43	53	.811	53	86	139	34	9	8	33	233	4.6	1.1	7.8
94-95—Milwaukee	82	2064	344	647	.532	119	194	.613	160	266	426	110	42	18	123	815	5.2	1.3	9.9
95-96—Milwaukee	74	958	153	327	.468	84	110	.764	58	119	177	68	20	11	79	395	2.4	0.9	5.3
Totals	277	4449	721	1411	.511	327	470	.696	352	582	934	261	93	49	290	1782	3.4	0.9	6.4

Three-point field goals: 1992-93, 0-for-4. 1993-94, 0-for-2. 1994-95, 8-for-29 (.276). 1995-96, 5-for-30 (.167). Totals, 13-for-65 (.200).
Personal fouls/disqualifications: 1991-92, 40/0. 1992-93, 43/0. 1993-94, 69/1. 1994-95, 218/3. 1995-96, 126/1. Totals, 496/5.

NBA PLAYOFF RECORD

Season Team	G	Min.	FGM	FGA	Pct.	FTM	FTA	Pct.	Off.	Def.	Tot.	Ast.	St.	Blk.	TO	Pts.	RPG	APG	PPG
									REBOUNDS								**AVERAGES**		
91-92—Seattle	1	1	0	1	.000	2	2	1.000	0	1	1	0	0	0	0	2	1.0	0.0	2.0

COOK, ANTHONY   F/C

PERSONAL: Born March 19, 1967, in Los Angeles. ... 6-9/240. ... Full name: Anthony Lacquise Cook.
HIGH SCHOOL: Van Nuys (Calif.).
COLLEGE: Arizona.
TRANSACTIONS/CAREER NOTES: Selected by Phoenix Suns in first round (24th pick overall) of 1989 NBA Draft. ... Played in Greece (1989-90). ... Draft rights traded by Suns to Detroit Pistons for G Micheal Williams and draft rights to F Kenny Battle (June 27, 1989). ... Traded by Pistons to Denver Nuggets for future second-round draft choice (September 28, 1990). ... Traded by Nuggets with G Todd Lichti and 1994 second-round draft choice to Orlando Magic for F/C Brian Williams (August 19, 1993). ... Traded by Magic with conditional 1994 first-round draft choice to Milwaukee Bucks for F Anthony Avent (January 15, 1994). ... Rights renounced by Bucks (July 5, 1994). ... Played in France (1994-95). ... Signed as free agent by Portland Trail Blazers (October 1, 1995). ... Waived by Trail Blazers (January 5, 1996).

COLLEGIATE RECORD

Season Team	G	Min.	FGM	FGA	Pct.	FTM	FTA	Pct.	Reb.	Ast.	Pts.	RPG	APG	PPG
													AVERAGES	
85-86—Arizona	32	833	73	146	.500	48	73	.658	137	41	194	4.3	1.3	6.1

Season Team	G	Min.	FGM	FGA	Pct.	FTM	FTA	Pct.	Reb.	Ast.	Pts.	AVERAGES		
												RPG	APG	PPG
86-87—Arizona	30	969	118	246	.480	54	100	.540	217	18	290	7.2	0.6	9.7
87-88—Arizona	38	1169	201	325	.618	126	176	.716	269	15	528	7.1	0.4	13.9
88-89—Arizona	33	1066	237	377	.629	104	166	.627	238	12	578	7.2	0.4	17.5
Totals	133	4037	629	1094	.575	332	515	.645	861	86	1590	6.5	0.6	12.0

Three-point field goals: 1987-88, 0-for-1.

NBA REGULAR-SEASON RECORD

Season Team	G	Min.	FGM	FGA	Pct.	FTM	FTA	Pct.	REBOUNDS			Ast.	St.	Blk.	TO	Pts.	AVERAGES		
									Off.	Def.	Tot.						RPG	APG	PPG
90-91—Denver	58	1121	118	283	.417	71	129	.550	134	192	326	26	35	72	50	307	5.6	0.4	5.3
91-92—Denver	22	115	15	25	.600	4	6	.667	13	21	34	2	5	4	3	34	1.5	0.1	1.5
92-93—Denver						Did not play—knee injury.													
93-94—Orl.-Mil.	25	203	26	54	.481	10	25	.400	20	36	56	4	3	14	12	62	2.2	0.2	2.5
95-96—Portland	11	60	7	16	.438	1	4	.250	5	7	12	2	0	1	1	15	1.1	0.2	1.4
Totals	116	1499	166	378	.439	86	164	.524	172	256	428	34	43	91	66	418	3.7	0.3	3.6

Three-point field goals: 1990-91, 0-for-3. 1993-94, 0-for-1. 1995-96, 0-for-2. Totals, 0-for-6.
Personal fouls/disqualifications: 1990-91, 100/1. 1991-92, 10/0. 1993-94, 22/0. 1995-96, 8/0. Totals, 140/1.

FRENCH LEAGUE RECORD

Season Team	G	Min.	FGM	FGA	Pct.	FTM	FTA	Pct.	Reb.	Ast.	Pts.	AVERAGES		
												RPG	APG	PPG
94-95—Levallois	17	...	...	...	...	...	...	...	143	30	225	8.4	1.8	13.2

CORBIN, TYRONE   F

PERSONAL: Born December 31, 1962, in Columbia, S.C. ... 6-6/225. ... Full name: Tyrone Kennedy Corbin.
HIGH SCHOOL: A.C. Flora (Columbia, S.C.).
COLLEGE: DePaul.
TRANSACTIONS/CAREER NOTES: Selected by San Antonio Spurs in second round (35th pick overall) of 1985 NBA Draft. ... Waived by Spurs (January 21, 1987). ... Signed as free agent by Cleveland Cavaliers (January 24, 1987). ... Traded by Cavaliers with G Kevin Johnson, F/C Mark West, 1988 first- and second-round draft choices and 1989 second-round draft choice to Phoenix Suns for F Larry Nance, F Mike Sanders and 1988 first-round draft choice (February 25, 1988). ... Selected by Minnesota Timberwolves from Suns in NBA expansion draft (June 15, 1989). ... Traded by Timberwolves to Utah Jazz for F Thurl Bailey and 1992 second-round draft choice (November 25, 1991). ... Traded by Jazz with 1995 second-round draft choice to Atlanta Hawks for F Adam Keefe (September 16, 1994). ... Traded by Hawks to Sacramento Kings for G Spud Webb (June 29, 1995). ... Traded by Kings with F/G Walt Williams to Miami Heat for G/F Billy Owens and G/F Kevin Gamble (February 22, 1996). ... Rights renounced by Heat (July 17, 1996).

COLLEGIATE RECORD

Season Team	G	Min.	FGM	FGA	Pct.	FTM	FTA	Pct.	Reb.	Ast.	Pts.	AVERAGES		
												RPG	APG	PPG
81-82—DePaul	28	602	43	103	.417	56	78	.718	172	30	142	6.1	1.1	5.1
82-83—DePaul	33	1060	124	263	.471	102	132	.773	262	39	350	7.9	1.2	10.6
83-84—DePaul	30	1070	166	316	.525	93	125	.744	223	89	425	7.4	3.0	14.2
84-85—DePaul	29	1004	189	354	.534	83	102	.814	236	69	461	8.1	2.4	15.9
Totals	120	3736	522	1036	.504	334	437	.764	893	227	1378	7.4	1.9	11.5

NBA REGULAR-SEASON RECORD

Season Team	G	Min.	FGM	FGA	Pct.	FTM	FTA	Pct.	REBOUNDS			Ast.	St.	Blk.	TO	Pts.	AVERAGES		
									Off.	Def.	Tot.						RPG	APG	PPG
85-86—San Antonio	16	174	27	64	.422	10	14	.714	11	14	25	11	11	2	12	64	1.6	0.7	4.0
86-87—S.A.-Clev.	63	1170	156	381	.409	91	124	.734	88	127	215	97	55	5	66	404	3.4	1.5	6.4
87-88—Clev.-Phoe.	84	1739	257	525	.490	110	138	.797	127	223	350	115	72	18	104	625	4.2	1.4	7.4
88-89—Phoenix	77	1655	245	454	.540	141	179	.788	176	222	398	118	82	13	92	631	5.2	1.5	8.2
89-90—Minnesota	82	3011	521	1083	.481	161	209	.770	219	385	604	216	175	41	143	1203	7.4	2.6	14.7
90-91—Minnesota	82	3196	587	1311	.448	296	371	.798	185	404	589	347	162	53	209	1472	7.2	4.2	18.0
91-92—Min.-Utah	80	2207	303	630	.481	174	201	.866	163	309	472	140	82	20	97	780	5.9	1.8	9.8
92-93—Utah	82	2555	385	766	.503	180	218	.826	194	325	519	173	108	32	108	950	6.3	2.1	11.6
93-94—Utah	82	2149	268	588	.456	117	144	.813	150	239	389	122	99	24	92	659	4.7	1.5	8.0
94-95—Atlanta	81	1389	205	464	.442	78	114	.684	98	164	262	67	55	16	74	502	3.2	0.8	6.2
95-96—Sac.-Mia.	71	1284	155	351	.442	100	120	.833	81	163	244	84	63	20	67	413	3.4	1.2	5.8
Totals	800	20529	3109	6617	.470	1484	1832	.796	1492	2575	4067	1490	964	244	1064	7703	5.1	1.9	9.6

Three-point field goals: 1985-86, 0-for-1. 1986-87, 1-for-4 (.250). 1987-88, 1-for-6 (.167). 1988-89, 0-for-2. 1989-90, 2-for-10 (.200). 1991-92, 0-for-4. 1992-93, 0-for-5. 1993-94, 6-for-29 (.207). 1994-95, 14-for-56 (.250). 1995-96, 3-for-18 (.167). Totals, 27-for-146 (.185).
Personal fouls/disqualifications: 1985-86, 21/0. 1986-87, 129/0. 1987-88, 181/2. 1988-89, 222/2. 1989-90, 288/5. 1990-91, 257/3. 1991-92, 193/1. 1992-93, 252/3. 1993-94, 212/0. 1994-95, 161/1. 1995-96, 147/1. Totals, 2063/18.

NBA PLAYOFF RECORD

Season Team	G	Min.	FGM	FGA	Pct.	FTM	FTA	Pct.	REBOUNDS			Ast.	St.	Blk.	TO	Pts.	AVERAGES		
									Off.	Def.	Tot.						RPG	APG	PPG
85-86—San Antonio	1	14	0	4	.000	0	0	...	0	1	1	1	0	0	0	0	1.0	1.0	0.0
88-89—Phoenix	12	310	45	86	.523	19	25	.760	43	42	85	26	24	4	14	109	7.1	2.2	9.1
91-92—Utah	16	447	69	137	.504	42	54	.778	39	49	88	17	12	3	17	180	5.5	1.1	11.3
92-93—Utah	5	161	24	52	.462	9	13	.692	16	22	38	9	3	1	7	59	7.6	1.8	11.8
93-94—Utah	16	413	41	106	.387	14	15	.933	25	54	79	15	21	3	11	100	4.9	0.9	6.3
94-95—Atlanta	3	79	12	26	.462	8	9	.889	6	4	10	2	2	1	2	34	3.3	0.7	11.3
95-96—Miami	2	34	1	5	.200	3	4	.750	4	3	7	1	2	0	1	5	3.5	0.5	2.5
Totals	55	1458	192	416	.462	95	120	.792	133	175	308	71	64	12	52	487	5.6	1.3	8.9

Three-point field goals: 1991-92, 0-for-2. 1993-94, 4-for-12 (.333). 1994-95, 2-for-6 (.333). Totals, 6-for-20 (.300).
Personal fouls/disqualifications: 1988-89, 37/0. 1991-92, 45/0. 1992-93, 15/0. 1993-94, 31/0. 1994-95, 10/0. 1995-96, 3/0. Totals, 141/0.

COURTNEY, JOE   F

PERSONAL: Born October 17, 1969, in Jackson, Miss. ... 6-9/235. ... Full name: Joseph Pierre Courtney.
HIGH SCHOOL: Callaway (Jackson, Miss.).
COLLEGE: Mississippi State, then Southern Mississippi.
TRANSACTIONS/CAREER NOTES: Not drafted by an NBA franchise. ... Signed as free agent by Chicago Bulls (October 6, 1992). ... Waived by Bulls (October 28, 1992). ... Played in Continental Basketball Association with Sioux Falls Skyforce (1992-93), Rockford Lightning (1992-93 and 1994-95) and Mexico Aztecas (1994-95). ... Re-signed by Bulls to first of two consecutive 10-day contracts (January 12, 1993). ... Signed by Golden State Warriors for remainder of season (April 14, 1993). ... Signed as free agent by Phoenix Suns (September 3, 1993). ... Claimed off waivers by Milwaukee Bucks (March 2, 1994). ... Signed as free agent by Bulls (September 9, 1994). ... Waived by Bulls (October 14, 1994). ... Signed as free agent by Charlotte Hornets (November 2, 1994). ... Waived by Hornets (November 16, 1994). ... Signed as free agent by Cleveland Cavaliers (October 5, 1995). ... Waived by Cavaliers (March 5, 1996).

COLLEGIATE RECORD

Season Team	G	Min.	FGM	FGA	Pct.	FTM	FTA	Pct.	Reb.	Ast.	Pts.	RPG	APG	PPG
87-88—Mississippi State	28	449	49	112	.438	24	29	.828	73	10	122	2.6	0.4	4.4
88-89—Mississippi State	13	101	14	35	.400	12	17	.706	43	2	40	3.3	0.2	3.1
89-90—Southern Miss						Did not play—transfer student.								
90-91—Southern Miss	28	327	48	104	.462	18	33	.545	84	12	114	3.0	0.4	4.1
91-92—Southern Miss	29	710	102	210	.486	44	64	.688	154	34	248	5.3	1.2	8.6
Totals	98	1587	213	461	.462	98	143	.685	354	58	524	3.6	0.6	5.3

Three-point field goals: 1991-92, 0-for-1.

NOTES: CBA All-Rookie first team (1993).

CBA REGULAR-SEASON RECORD

Season Team	G	Min.	FGM	FGA	Pct.	FTM	FTA	Pct.	Reb.	Ast.	Pts.	RPG	APG	PPG
92-93—Sioux F.-Rock.	44	1046	208	365	.570	121	158	.766	255	40	537	5.8	0.9	12.2
94-95—Rockford-Mexico	37	1164	264	497	.531	96	128	.750	235	72	624	6.4	1.9	16.9
Totals	81	2210	472	862	.548	217	286	.759	490	112	1161	6.0	1.4	14.3

Three-point field goals: 1994-95, 0-for-6.

NBA REGULAR-SEASON RECORD

Season Team	G	Min.	FGM	FGA	Pct.	FTM	FTA	Pct.	REBOUNDS Off.	Def.	Tot.	Ast.	St.	Blk.	TO	Pts.	RPG	APG	PPG
92-93—Chi.-Gold.St.	12	104	13	32	.406	7	9	.778	4	15	19	3	5	5	6	33	1.6	0.3	2.8
93-94—Phoe.-Mil.	52	345	67	148	.453	32	47	.681	28	28	56	15	10	12	21	168	1.1	0.3	3.2
95-96—Cleveland	23	200	15	35	.429	8	18	.444	24	25	49	9	5	6	17	38	2.1	0.4	1.7
Totals	87	649	95	215	.442	47	74	.635	56	68	124	27	20	23	44	239	1.4	0.3	2.7

Three-point field goals: 1993-94, 2-for-3 (.667).
Personal fouls/disqualifications: 1992-93, 17/0. 1993-94, 44/0. 1995-96, 35/0. Totals, 96/0.

CROTTY, JOHN   G

PERSONAL: Born July 15, 1969, in Orange, N.J. ... 6-1/185. ... Full name: John Kevin Crotty.
HIGH SCHOOL: Christian Brothers Academy (Lincroft, N.J.).
COLLEGE: Virginia.
TRANSACTIONS/CAREER NOTES: Not drafted by an NBA franchise. ... Played in Global Basketball Association with Greenville Spinners (1991-92). ... Signed as free agent by Utah Jazz (September 4, 1992). ... Signed as free agent by Cleveland Cavaliers (October 23, 1995). ... Rights renounced by Cavaliers (August 13, 1996). ... Signed to play with Bologna (Italy) during 1996-97 season.

COLLEGIATE RECORD

Season Team	G	Min.	FGM	FGA	Pct.	FTM	FTA	Pct.	Reb.	Ast.	Pts.	RPG	APG	PPG
87-88—Virginia	31	717	59	163	.362	51	87	.586	70	92	195	2.3	3.0	6.3
88-89—Virginia	33	1143	136	309	.440	113	169	.669	85	208	426	2.6	6.3	12.9
89-90—Virginia	32	1176	156	401	.389	134	191	.702	94	214	512	2.9	6.7	16.0
90-91—Virginia	33	1138	176	397	.443	115	148	.777	78	169	513	2.4	5.1	15.5
Totals	129	4174	527	1270	.415	413	595	.694	327	683	1646	2.5	5.3	12.8

Three-point field goals: 1987-88, 26-for-75 (.347). 1988-89, 41-for-112 (.366). 1989-90, 66-for-194 (.340). 1990-91, 46-for-136 (.338). Totals, 179-for-517 (.346).

NBA REGULAR-SEASON RECORD

Season Team	G	Min.	FGM	FGA	Pct.	FTM	FTA	Pct.	REBOUNDS Off.	Def.	Tot.	Ast.	St.	Blk.	TO	Pts.	RPG	APG	PPG
92-93—Utah	40	243	37	72	.514	26	38	.684	4	13	17	55	11	0	30	102	0.4	1.4	2.6
93-94—Utah	45	313	45	99	.455	31	36	.861	11	20	31	77	15	1	27	132	0.7	1.7	2.9
94-95—Utah	80	1019	93	231	.403	98	121	.810	27	70	97	205	39	6	70	295	1.2	2.6	3.7
95-96—Cleveland	58	617	51	114	.447	62	72	.861	20	34	54	102	22	6	51	172	0.9	1.8	3.0
Totals	223	2192	226	516	.438	217	267	.813	62	137	199	439	87	13	178	701	0.9	2.0	3.1

Three-point field goals: 1992-93, 2-for-14 (.143). 1993-94, 11-for-24 (.458). 1994-95, 11-for-36 (.306). 1995-96, 8-for-27 (.296). Totals, 32-for-101 (.317).
Personal fouls/disqualifications: 1992-93, 29/0. 1993-94, 36/0. 1994-95, 105/0. 1995-96, 60/0. Totals, 230/0.

NBA PLAYOFF RECORD

Season Team	G	Min.	FGM	FGA	Pct.	FTM	FTA	Pct.	REBOUNDS Off.	Def.	Tot.	Ast.	St.	Blk.	TO	Pts.	RPG	APG	PPG
92-93—Utah	1	3	2	2	1.000	0	0		1	0	1	1	0	0	0	4	1.0	1.0	4.0
93-94—Utah	8	38	4	11	.364	2	2	1.000	0	3	3	9	1	0	1	12	0.4	1.1	1.5
94-95—Utah	3	24	2	3	.667	3	5	.600	0	0	0	6	1	0	0	7	0.0	2.0	2.3
95-96—Cleveland	2	9	0	0	...	2	2	1.000	1	0	1	1	1	1	1	2	0.5	0.5	1.0
Totals	14	74	8	16	.500	7	9	.778	2	3	5	17	3	1	2	25	0.4	1.2	1.8

Three-point field goals: 1993-94, 2-for-2.
Personal fouls/disqualifications: 1993-94, 6/0. 1994-95, 2/0. Totals, 8/0.

C

CUMMINGS, TERRY   F   BUCKS

PERSONAL: Born March 15, 1961, in Chicago. ... 6-9/250. ... Full name: Robert Terrell Cummings.
HIGH SCHOOL: Carver (Chicago).
COLLEGE: DePaul.
TRANSACTIONS/CAREER NOTES: Selected after junior season by San Diego Clippers in first round (second pick overall) of 1982 NBA Draft. ... Clippers franchise moved from San Diego to Los Angeles for 1984-85 season. ... Traded by Clippers with G Craig Hodges and G/F Ricky Pierce to Milwaukee Bucks for F Marques Johnson, C/F Harvey Catchings, G/F Junior Bridgeman and cash (September 29, 1984). ... Traded by Bucks with future considerations to San Antonio Spurs for G Alvin Robertson, F/C Greg Anderson and future considerations (May 28, 1989). ... Signed as unrestricted free agent by Milwaukee Bucks (November 2, 1995).

COLLEGIATE RECORD

NOTES: THE SPORTING NEWS All-America first team (1982).

Season Team	G	Min.	FGM	FGA	Pct.	FTM	FTA	Pct.	Reb.	Ast.	Pts.	RPG	APG	PPG
79-80—DePaul	28	...	154	303	.508	89	107	.832	263	40	397	9.4	1.4	14.2
80-81—DePaul	29	994	151	303	.498	75	100	.750	260	47	377	9.0	1.6	13.0
81-82—DePaul	28	1031	244	430	.567	136	180	.756	334	57	624	11.9	2.0	22.3
Totals	85	...	549	1036	.530	300	387	.775	857	144	1398	10.1	1.7	16.4

NBA REGULAR-SEASON RECORD

HONORS: NBA Rookie of the Year (1983). ... All-NBA second team (1985). ... All-NBA third team (1989). ... NBA All-Rookie team (1983).

Season Team	G	Min.	FGM	FGA	Pct.	FTM	FTA	Pct.	Off.	Def.	Tot.	Ast.	St.	Blk.	TO	Pts.	RPG	APG	PPG
82-83—San Diego	70	2531	684	1309	.523	292	412	.709	303	441	744	177	129	62	204	1660	10.6	2.5	23.7
83-84—San Diego	81	2907	737	1491	.494	380	528	.720	323	454	777	139	92	57	218	1854	9.6	1.7	22.9
84-85—Milwaukee	79	2722	759	1532	.495	343	463	.741	244	472	716	228	117	67	190	1861	9.1	2.9	23.6
85-86—Milwaukee	82	2669	681	1438	.474	265	404	.656	222	472	694	193	121	51	191	1627	8.5	2.4	19.8
86-87—Milwaukee	82	2770	729	1426	.511	249	376	.662	214	486	700	229	129	81	172	1707	8.5	2.8	20.8
87-88—Milwaukee	76	2629	675	1392	.485	270	406	.665	184	369	553	181	78	46	170	1621	7.3	2.4	21.3
88-89—Milwaukee	80	2824	730	1563	.467	362	460	.787	281	369	650	198	106	72	201	1829	8.1	2.5	22.9
89-90—San Antonio	81	2821	728	1532	.475	344	440	.780	226	451	677	219	110	52	202	1818	8.4	2.7	22.4
90-91—San Antonio	67	2195	503	1039	.484	164	240	.683	194	327	521	157	61	30	131	1177	7.8	2.3	17.6
91-92—San Antonio	70	2149	514	1053	.488	177	249	.711	247	384	631	102	58	34	115	1210	9.0	1.5	17.3
92-93—San Antonio	8	76	11	29	.379	5	10	.500	6	13	19	4	1	1	2	27	2.4	0.5	3.4
93-94—San Antonio	59	1133	183	428	.428	63	107	.589	132	165	297	50	31	13	59	429	5.0	0.8	7.3
94-95—San Antonio	76	1273	224	464	.483	72	123	.585	138	240	378	59	36	19	95	520	5.0	0.8	6.8
95-96—Milwaukee	81	1777	270	584	.462	104	160	.650	162	283	445	89	56	30	69	645	5.5	1.1	8.0
Totals	992	30476	7428	15280	.486	3089	4378	.706	2876	4926	7802	2025	1125	615	2019	17985	7.9	2.0	18.1

Three-point field goals: 1982-83, 0-for-1. 1983-84, 0-for-3. 1984-85, 0-for-1. 1985-86, 0-for-2. 1986-87, 0-for-3. 1987-88, 1-for-3 (.333). 1988-89, 7-for-15 (.467). 1989-90, 19-for-59 (.322). 1990-91, 7-for-33 (.212). 1991-92, 5-for-13 (.385). 1993-94, 0-for-2. 1995-96, 1-for-7 (.143). Totals, 40-for-142 (.282).
Personal fouls/disqualifications: 1982-83, 294/10. 1983-84, 298/6. 1984-85, 264/4. 1985-86, 283/4. 1986-87, 296/3. 1987-88, 274/6. 1988-89, 265/5. 1989-90, 286/1. 1990-91, 225/5. 1991-92, 210/4. 1992-93, 17/0. 1994-95, 188/1. 1995-96, 263/2. Totals, 3300/51.

NBA PLAYOFF RECORD

Season Team	G	Min.	FGM	FGA	Pct.	FTM	FTA	Pct.	Off.	Def.	Tot.	Ast.	St.	Blk.	TO	Pts.	RPG	APG	PPG
84-85—Milwaukee	8	311	86	149	.577	48	58	.828	21	49	70	20	12	7	26	220	8.8	2.5	27.5
85-86—Milwaukee	14	510	130	253	.514	43	62	.694	33	105	138	42	20	16	39	303	9.9	3.0	21.6
86-87—Milwaukee	12	443	105	215	.488	57	83	.687	29	66	95	28	12	13	15	267	7.9	2.3	22.3
87-88—Milwaukee	5	193	50	89	.562	29	44	.659	12	27	39	13	9	3	12	129	7.8	2.6	25.8
88-89—Milwaukee	5	124	25	69	.362	14	16	.875	19	14	33	7	3	0	4	64	6.6	1.4	12.8
89-90—San Antonio	10	375	103	195	.528	42	52	.808	31	63	94	22	7	4	19	249	9.4	2.2	24.9
90-91—San Antonio	4	124	25	49	.510	9	18	.500	14	23	37	4	3	2	9	59	9.3	1.0	14.8
91-92—San Antonio	3	122	34	66	.515	10	20	.500	15	19	34	7	4	4	7	78	11.3	2.3	26.0
92-93—San Antonio	10	138	31	70	.443	5	8	.625	17	22	39	5	3	1	8	67	3.9	0.5	6.7
93-94—San Antonio	4	72	11	22	.500	10	12	.833	10	15	25	2	5	3	4	32	6.3	0.5	8.0
94-95—San Antonio	15	135	18	48	.375	22	30	.733	12	19	31	4	5	1	7	58	2.1	0.3	3.9
Totals	90	2547	618	1225	.504	289	403	.717	213	422	635	154	83	54	150	1526	7.1	1.7	17.0

Three-point field goals: 1984-85, 0-for-1. 1988-89, 0-for-1. 1989-90, 1-for-5 (.200). 1990-91, 0-for-1. 1991-92, 0-for-1. 1992-93, 0-for-1. 1994-95, 0-for-1. Totals, 1-for-11 (.091).
Personal fouls/disqualifications: 1984-85, 33/1. 1985-86, 52/0. 1986-87, 51/1. 1987-88, 16/0. 1988-89, 16/0. 1989-90, 39/0. 1990-91, 13/0. 1991-92, 9/0. 1992-93, 27/0. 1993-94, 10/0. 1994-95, 25/0. Totals, 291/2.

NBA ALL-STAR GAME RECORD

Season Team	Min.	FGM	FGA	Pct.	FTM	FTA	Pct.	Off.	Def.	Tot.	Ast.	PF	Dq.	St.	Blk.	TO	Pts.
1985 —Milwaukee	16	7	17	.412	3	4	.750	4	3	7	0	1	0	0	1	0	17
1989 —Milwaukee	19	4	9	.444	2	2	1.000	2	3	5	1	4	0	3	1	0	10
Totals	35	11	26	.423	5	6	.833	6	6	12	1	5	0	3	2	0	27

CURRY, DELL   G   HORNETS

PERSONAL: Born June 25, 1964, in Harrisonburg, Va. ... 6-5/200. ... Full name: Wardell Stephen Curry.
HIGH SCHOOL: Fort Defiance (Va.).
COLLEGE: Virginia Tech.
TRANSACTIONS/CAREER NOTES: Selected by Utah Jazz in first round (15th pick overall) of 1986 NBA Draft. ... Traded by Jazz with F/C Kent Benson and future second-round draft considerations to Cleveland Cavaliers for C Darryl Dawkins, C Mel Turpin and future second-round draft considerations (October 8, 1987). ... Selected by Charlotte Hornets from Cavaliers in NBA expansion draft (June 23, 1988).
MISCELLANEOUS: Selected by Baltimore Orioles organization in 14th round of free-agent baseball draft (June 3, 1985); did not sign. ... Charlotte Hornets all-time leading scorer with 8,341 points (1988-89 through 1995-96).

COLLEGIATE RECORD

NOTES: THE SPORTING NEWS All-America second team (1986).

Season Team	G	Min.	FGM	FGA	Pct.	FTM	FTA	Pct.	Reb.	Ast.	Pts.	AVERAGES RPG	APG	PPG
82-83—Virginia Tech	32	1024	198	417	.475	68	80	.850	95	107	464	3.0	3.3	14.5
83-84—Virginia Tech	35	1166	293	561	.522	88	116	.759	143	96	674	4.1	2.7	19.3
84-85—Virginia Tech	29	968	225	467	.482	75	99	.758	169	91	529	5.8	3.1	18.2
85-86—Virginia Tech	30	1117	305	577	.529	112	142	.789	203	113	722	6.8	3.8	24.1
Totals	126	4275	1021	2022	.505	343	437	.785	610	407	2389	4.8	3.2	19.0

Three-point field goals: 1984-85, 4-for-7 (.571).

NBA REGULAR-SEASON RECORD

HONORS: NBA Sixth Man Award (1994).

Season Team	G	Min.	FGM	FGA	Pct.	FTM	FTA	Pct.	REBOUNDS Off.	Def.	Tot.	Ast.	St.	Blk.	TO	Pts.	AVERAGES RPG	APG	PPG
86-87—Utah	67	636	139	326	.426	30	38	.789	30	48	78	58	27	4	44	325	1.2	0.9	4.9
87-88—Cleveland	79	1499	340	742	.458	79	101	.782	43	123	166	149	94	4	44	571	2.1	1.9	11.9
88-89—Charlotte	48	813	256	521	.491	40	46	.870	26	78	104	50	42	4	44	571	2.2	1.0	11.9
89-90—Charlotte	67	1860	461	990	.466	96	104	.923	31	137	168	159	98	26	100	1070	2.5	2.4	16.0
90-91—Charlotte	76	1515	337	715	.471	96	114	.842	47	152	199	166	75	25	80	802	2.6	2.2	10.6
91-92—Charlotte	77	2020	504	1038	.486	127	152	.836	57	202	259	177	93	20	134	1209	3.4	2.3	15.7
92-93—Charlotte	80	2094	498	1102	.452	136	157	.866	51	235	286	180	87	23	129	1227	3.6	2.3	15.3
93-94—Charlotte	82	2173	533	1171	.455	117	134	.873	71	191	262	221	98	27	120	1335	3.2	2.7	16.3
94-95—Charlotte	69	1718	343	778	.441	95	111	.856	41	127	168	113	55	18	98	935	2.4	1.6	13.6
95-96—Charlotte	82	2371	441	974	.453	146	171	.854	68	196	264	176	108	25	130	1192	3.2	2.1	14.5
Totals	727	16699	3852	8357	.461	962	1128	.853	465	1489	1954	1449	777	194	987	9453	2.7	2.0	13.0

Three-point field goals: 1986-87, 17-for-60 (.283). 1987-88, 28-for-81 (.346). 1988-89, 19-for-55 (.345). 1989-90, 52-for-147 (.354). 1990-91, 32-for-86 (.372). 1991-92, 74-for-183 (.404). 1992-93, 95-for-237 (.401). 1993-94, 152-for-378 (.402). 1994-95, 154-for-361 (.427). 1995-96, 164-for-406 (.404). Totals, 787-for-1994 (.395).
Personal fouls/disqualifications: 1986-87, 86/0. 1987-88, 128/0. 1988-89, 68/0. 1989-90, 148/0. 1990-91, 125/0. 1991-92, 156/1. 1992-93, 150/1. 1993-94, 161/0. 1994-95, 144/1. 1995-96, 173/2. Totals, 1339/5.

NBA PLAYOFF RECORD

Season Team	G	Min.	FGM	FGA	Pct.	FTM	FTA	Pct.	REBOUNDS Off.	Def.	Tot.	Ast.	St.	Blk.	TO	Pts.	AVERAGES RPG	APG	PPG
86-87—Utah	2	4	0	3	.000	0	1	.000	0	0	0	0	0	0	0	0	0.0	0.0	0.0
87-88—Cleveland	2	17	1	4	.250	0	0	...	1	0	1	2	0	1	0	2	0.5	1.0	1.0
92-93—Charlotte	9	222	42	97	.433	9	11	.818	11	21	32	18	13	0	13	99	3.6	2.0	11.0
94-95—Charlotte	4	107	16	34	.471	10	11	.909	5	4	9	6	0	0	6	51	2.3	1.5	12.8
Totals	17	350	59	138	.428	19	23	.826	17	25	42	26	13	1	19	152	2.5	1.5	8.9

Three-point field goals: 1986-87, 0-for-1. 1987-88, 0-for-1. 1992-93, 6-for-21 (.286). 1994-95, 9-for-21 (.429). Totals, 15-for-44 (.341).
Personal fouls/disqualifications: 1986-87, 1/0. 1987-88, 1/0. 1992-93, 19/0. 1994-95, 11/0. Totals, 32/0.

CURRY, MIKE   F   PISTONS

PERSONAL: Born August 22, 1968, in Anniston, Ala. ... 6-5/210. ... Full name: Michael Curry.
HIGH SCHOOL: Glenn Hills (Augusta, Ga.).
COLLEGE: Georgia Southern.
TRANSACTIONS/CAREER NOTES: Not drafted by an NBA franchise. ... Played in Continental Basketball Association with Capital Region Pontiacs (1992-93) and Omaha Racers (1995-96). ... Signed as free agent by Philadelphia 76ers (October 7, 1993). ... Waived by 76ers (December 29, 1993). ... Played in Italy (1993-94). ... Played in Spain (1994-95). ... Signed by Washington Bullets to 10-day contract (January 12, 1996). ... Signed by Detroit Pistons to first of two consecutive 10-day contracts (January 31, 1996). ... Re-signed by Pistons for remainder of season (February 22, 1996).

COLLEGIATE RECORD

Season Team	G	Min.	FGM	FGA	Pct.	FTM	FTA	Pct.	Reb.	Ast.	Pts.	AVERAGES RPG	APG	PPG
86-87—Georgia Southern	31	594	59	116	.509	31	45	.689	87	29	149	2.8	0.9	4.8
87-88—Georgia Southern	31	836	82	151	.543	33	51	.647	154	44	198	5.0	1.4	6.4
88-89—Georgia Southern	29	1014	117	219	.534	75	108	.694	211	89	309	7.3	3.1	10.7
89-90—Georgia Southern	28	926	164	264	.621	137	170	.806	196	58	465	7.0	2.1	16.6
Totals	119	3370	422	750	.563	276	374	.738	648	220	1121	5.4	1.8	9.4

Three-point field goals: 1987-88, 1-for-6 (.167). 1988-89, 0-for-3. 1989-90, 0-for-3. Totals, 1-for-12 (.083).

CBA REGULAR-SEASON RECORD

Season Team	G	Min.	FGM	FGA	Pct.	FTM	FTA	Pct.	Reb.	Ast.	Pts.	AVERAGES RPG	APG	PPG
92-93—Capital Region	36	1391	268	482	.556	161	200	.805	179	75	698	5.0	2.1	19.4
95-96—Omaha	11	404	84	153	.549	46	61	.754	37	44	237	3.4	4.0	21.5
Totals	47	1795	352	635	.554	207	261	.793	216	119	935	4.6	2.5	19.9

Three-point field goals: 1992-93, 1-for-7 (.143). 1995-96, 23-for-55 (.418). Totals, 24-for-62 (.388).

ITALIAN LEAGUE RECORD

Season Team	G	Min.	FGM	FGA	Pct.	FTM	FTA	Pct.	Reb.	Ast.	Pts.	AVERAGES RPG	APG	PPG
93-94—S. Clear	15	581	110	206	.534	72	87	.828	74	21	323	4.9	1.4	21.5

Season Team	G	Min.	FGM	FGA	Pct.	FTM	FTA	Pct.	REBOUNDS Off.	Def.	Tot.	Ast.	St.	Blk.	TO	Pts.	AVERAGES RPG	APG	PPG
93-94—Philadelphia....	10	43	3	14	.214	3	4	.750	0	1	1	1	1	0	3	9	0.1	0.1	0.9
95-96—Was.-Det........	46	783	73	161	.453	45	62	.726	27	58	85	27	24	2	24	211	1.8	0.6	4.6
Totals	56	826	76	175	.434	48	66	.727	27	59	86	28	25	2	27	220	1.5	0.5	3.9

Three-point field goals: 1993-94, 0-for-2. 1995-96, 20-for-53 (.377). Totals, 20-for-55 (.364).
Personal fouls/disqualifications: 1995-96, 92/1.

NBA PLAYOFF RECORD

Season Team	G	Min.	FGM	FGA	Pct.	FTM	FTA	Pct.	REBOUNDS Off.	Def.	Tot.	Ast.	St.	Blk.	TO	Pts.	AVERAGES RPG	APG	PPG
95-96—Detroit	3	43	3	7	.429	0	0	...	1	2	3	1	1	0	0	6	1.0	0.3	2.0

Three-point field goals: 1995-96, 0-for-1.
Personal fouls/disqualifications: 1995-96, 5/0.

SPANISH LEAGUE RECORD

Season Team	G	Min.	FGM	FGA	Pct.	FTM	FTA	Pct.	Reb.	Ast.	Pts.	AVERAGES RPG	APG	PPG
94-95—Valvi Girona................	38	...	...	...	...	...	...	...	128	60	672	3.4	1.6	17.7

CVETKOVIC, RASTKO   C

PERSONAL: Born June 22, 1970, in Belgrade, Yugoslavia. ... 7-1/260. ... Name pronounced: ROSS-co svet-KO-vich ... Son of Vladimir Cvetkovic, member of Yugoslavian Olympic basketball team (1964 and 1968).
HIGH SCHOOL: 14 Belgrade (Yugoslavia).
COLLEGE: Did not attend college.
TRANSACTIONS/CAREER NOTES: Played in Yugoslavia (1986-87 through 1994-95). ... Not drafted by an NBA franchise. ... Signed as free agent by Denver Nuggets (September 26, 1995). ... Rights renounced by Nuggets (July 17, 1996).

NBA REGULAR-SEASON RECORD

Season Team	G	Min.	FGM	FGA	Pct.	FTM	FTA	Pct.	REBOUNDS Off.	Def.	Tot.	Ast.	St.	Blk.	TO	Pts.	AVERAGES RPG	APG	PPG
95-96—Denver............	14	48	5	16	.313	0	4	.000	4	7	11	3	2	1	3	10	0.8	0.2	0.7

Three-point field goals: 1995-96, 0-for-1.
Personal fouls/disqualifications: 1995-96, 11/0.

CD

DANILOVIC, SASHA   G   HEAT

PERSONAL: Born February 26, 1970, in Sarajevo, Bosnia. ... 6-6/200. ... Name pronounced da-NILL-oh-vich.
TRANSACTIONS/CAREER NOTES: Selected by Golden State Warriors in second round (43rd pick overall) of 1992 NBA Draft. ... Played in Italy (1992-93 through 1994-95). ... Rights traded by Warriors with F Billy Owens to Miami Heat for C Rony Seikaly (November 2, 1994).
MISCELLANEOUS: Member of silver-medal-winning Yugoslavian Olympic team (1996).

ITALIAN LEAGUE RECORD

Season Team	G	Min.	FGM	FGA	Pct.	FTM	FTA	Pct.	Reb.	Ast.	Pts.	AVERAGES RPG	APG	PPG
92-93—Knorr Bologna................	28	993	217	381	.570	172	207	.831	103	42	652	3.7	1.5	23.3
93-94—Buckler Beer Bologna.....	26	864	217	341	.636	181	223	.812	85	28	654	3.3	1.1	25.2
94-95—Buckler Beer Bologna.....	27	952	256	414	.618	228	261	.874	89	38	786	3.3	1.4	29.1
Totals	81	2809	690	1136	.607	581	691	.841	277	108	2092	3.4	1.3	25.8

NBA REGULAR-SEASON RECORD

Season Team	G	Min.	FGM	FGA	Pct.	FTM	FTA	Pct.	REBOUNDS Off.	Def.	Tot.	Ast.	St.	Blk.	TO	Pts.	AVERAGES RPG	APG	PPG
95-96—Miami	19	542	83	184	.451	55	72	.764	12	34	46	47	15	3	37	255	2.4	2.5	13.4

Three-point field goals: 1995-96, 34-for-78 (.436).
Personal fouls/disqualifications: 1995-96, 49/0.

NBA PLAYOFF RECORD

Season Team	G	Min.	FGM	FGA	Pct.	FTM	FTA	Pct.	REBOUNDS Off.	Def.	Tot.	Ast.	St.	Blk.	TO	Pts.	AVERAGES RPG	APG	PPG
95-96—Miami	3	60	9	18	.500	3	3	1.000	1	0	1	4	1	0	3	25	0.3	1.3	8.3

Three-point field goals: 1995-96, 4-for-10 (.400).
Personal fouls/disqualifications: 1995-96, 8/0.

DARE, YINKA   C   NETS

PERSONAL: Born October 10, 1972, in Kano, Nigeria. ... 7-0/265. ... Name pronounced DAR-ay.
HIGH SCHOOL: Milford (Conn.) Academy.
COLLEGE: George Washington.
TRANSACTIONS/CAREER NOTES: Selected after sophomore season by New Jersey Nets in first round (14th pick overall) of 1994 NBA Draft.

COLLEGIATE RECORD

Season Team	G	Min.	FGM	FGA	Pct.	FTM	FTA	Pct.	Reb.	Ast.	Pts.	AVERAGES RPG	APG	PPG
92-93—George Wash................	30	831	140	254	.551	86	182	.473	308	3	366	10.3	0.1	12.2
93-94—George Wash................	28	838	164	305	.538	100	172	.581	284	15	428	10.1	0.5	15.3
Totals	58	1669	304	559	.544	186	354	.525	592	18	794	10.2	0.3	13.7

NBA REGULAR-SEASON RECORD

Season Team	G	Min.	FGM	FGA	Pct.	FTM	FTA	Pct.	Off.	Def.	Tot.	Ast.	St.	Blk.	TO	Pts.	RPG	APG	PPG
									REBOUNDS								AVERAGES		
94-95—New Jersey.....	1	3	0	1	.000	0	0	...	0	1	1	0	0	0	1	0	1.0	0.0	0.0
95-96—New Jersey.....	58	626	63	144	.438	38	62	.613	56	125	181	0	8	40	72	164	3.1	0.0	2.8
Totals	59	629	63	145	.434	38	62	.613	56	126	182	0	8	40	73	164	3.1	0.0	2.8

Personal fouls/disqualifications: 1994-95, 2/0. 1995-96, 117/3. Totals, 119/3.

DAVIS, ANTONIO   F/C   PACERS

PERSONAL: Born October 31, 1968, in Oakland. ... 6-9/230. ... Full name: Antonio Lee Davis.
HIGH SCHOOL: McClymonds (Oakland).
COLLEGE: Texas-El Paso.
TRANSACTIONS/CAREER NOTES: Selected by Indiana Pacers in second round (45th pick overall) of 1990 NBA Draft. ... Played in Greece (1990-91 and 1991-92). ... Played in Italy (1992-93).

COLLEGIATE RECORD

Season Team	G	Min.	FGM	FGA	Pct.	FTM	FTA	Pct.	Reb.	Ast.	Pts.	RPG	APG	PPG
												AVERAGES		
86-87—Texas-El Paso	28	240	11	32	.344	13	30	.433	51	4	35	1.8	0.1	1.3
87-88—Texas-El Paso	30	907	108	183	.590	63	115	.548	195	20	279	6.5	0.7	9.3
88-89—Texas-El Paso	32	1014	162	298	.544	135	218	.619	255	14	459	8.0	0.4	14.3
89-90—Texas-El Paso	32	991	119	228	.522	106	165	.642	243	21	344	7.6	0.7	10.8
Totals	122	3152	400	741	.540	317	528	.600	744	59	1117	6.1	0.5	9.2

Three-point field goals: 1988-89, 0-for-1. 1989-90, 0-for-1. Totals, 0-for-2.

ITALIAN LEAGUE RECORD

Season Team	G	Min.	FGM	FGA	Pct.	FTM	FTA	Pct.	Reb.	Ast.	Pts.	RPG	APG	PPG
												AVERAGES		
92-93—Philips Milano	29	892	121	195	.621	81	130	.623	286	5	323	9.9	0.2	11.1

NBA REGULAR-SEASON RECORD

Season Team	G	Min.	FGM	FGA	Pct.	FTM	FTA	Pct.	Off.	Def.	Tot.	Ast.	St.	Blk.	TO	Pts.	RPG	APG	PPG
									REBOUNDS								AVERAGES		
93-94—Indiana...........	81	1732	216	425	.508	194	302	.642	190	315	505	55	45	84	107	626	6.2	0.7	7.7
94-95—Indiana...........	44	1030	109	245	.445	117	174	.672	105	175	280	25	19	29	64	335	6.4	0.6	7.6
95-96—Indiana...........	82	2092	236	482	.490	246	345	.713	188	313	501	43	33	66	87	719	6.1	0.5	8.8
Totals	207	4854	561	1152	.487	557	821	.678	483	803	1286	123	97	179	258	1680	6.2	0.6	8.1

Three-point field goals: 1993-94, 0-for-1. 1995-96, 1-for-2 (.500). Totals, 1-for-3 (.333).
Personal fouls/disqualifications: 1993-94, 189/1. 1994-95, 134/2. 1995-96, 248/6. Totals, 571/9.

NBA PLAYOFF RECORD

Season Team	G	Min.	FGM	FGA	Pct.	FTM	FTA	Pct.	Off.	Def.	Tot.	Ast.	St.	Blk.	TO	Pts.	RPG	APG	PPG
									REBOUNDS								AVERAGES		
93-94—Indiana...........	16	401	48	89	.539	37	66	.561	37	69	106	7	11	18	22	134	6.6	0.4	8.4
94-95—Indiana...........	17	367	32	71	.451	37	59	.627	38	59	97	7	9	11	23	101	5.7	0.4	5.9
95-96—Indiana...........	5	127	13	25	.520	13	15	.867	12	19	31	3	3	6	10	39	6.2	0.6	7.8
Totals	38	895	93	185	.503	87	140	.621	87	147	234	17	23	35	55	274	6.2	0.4	7.2

Three-point field goals: 1993-94, 1-for-1.
Personal fouls/disqualifications: 1993-94, 47/0. 1994-95, 61/0. 1995-96, 12/0. Totals, 120/0.

DAVIS, DALE   F   PACERS

PERSONAL: Born March 25, 1969, in Toccoa, Ga. ... 6-11/230. ... Full name: Elliott Lydell Davis.
HIGH SCHOOL: Stephens County (Toccoa, Ga.).
COLLEGE: Clemson.
TRANSACTIONS/CAREER NOTES: Selected by Indiana Pacers in first round (13th pick overall) of 1991 NBA Draft.

COLLEGIATE RECORD

Season Team	G	Min.	FGM	FGA	Pct.	FTM	FTA	Pct.	Reb.	Ast.	Pts.	RPG	APG	PPG
												AVERAGES		
87-88—Clemson	29	714	91	171	.532	45	89	.506	223	10	227	7.7	0.3	7.8
88-89—Clemson	29	736	146	218	.670	93	144	.646	258	16	385	8.9	0.6	13.3
89-90—Clemson	35	1077	205	328	.625	127	213	.596	395	21	537	11.3	0.6	15.3
90-91—Clemson	28	971	191	359	.532	119	205	.580	340	37	501	12.1	1.3	17.9
Totals	121	3498	633	1076	.588	384	651	.590	1216	84	1650	10.0	0.7	13.6

Three-point field goals: 1989-90, 0-for-1. 1990-91, 0-for-2. Totals, 0-for-3.

NBA REGULAR-SEASON RECORD

Season Team	G	Min.	FGM	FGA	Pct.	FTM	FTA	Pct.	Off.	Def.	Tot.	Ast.	St.	Blk.	TO	Pts.	RPG	APG	PPG
									REBOUNDS								AVERAGES		
91-92—Indiana...........	64	1301	154	279	.552	87	152	.572	158	252	410	30	27	74	49	395	6.4	0.5	6.2
92-93—Indiana...........	82	2264	304	535	.568	119	225	.529	291	432	723	69	63	148	79	727	8.8	0.8	8.9
93-94—Indiana...........	66	2292	308	582	.529	155	294	.527	280	438	718	100	48	106	102	771	10.9	1.5	11.7
94-95—Indiana...........	74	2346	324	576	.563	138	259	.533	259	437	696	58	72	116	124	786	9.4	0.8	10.6
95-96—Indiana...........	78	2617	334	599	.558	135	289	.467	252	457	709	76	56	112	119	803	9.1	1.0	10.3
Totals	364	10820	1424	2571	.554	634	1219	.520	1240	2016	3256	333	266	556	473	3482	8.9	0.9	9.6

Three-point field goals: 1991-92, 0-for-1. 1993-94, 0-for-1. 1994-95, 0-for-1. Totals, 0-for-3.
Personal fouls/disqualifications: 1991-92, 191/2. 1992-93, 274/5. 1993-94, 214/1. 1994-95, 222/2. 1995-96, 238/0. Totals, 1139/10.

NBA PLAYOFF RECORD

Season Team	G	Min.	FGM	FGA	Pct.	FTM	FTA	Pct.	Off.	Def.	Tot.	Ast.	St.	Blk.	TO	Pts.	RPG	APG	PPG
									REBOUNDS								AVERAGES		
91-92—Indiana...........	3	69	4	10	.400	0	0	...	5	14	19	2	0	5	1	8	6.3	0.7	2.7

D

Season Team	G	Min.	FGM	FGA	Pct.	FTM	FTA	Pct.	Off.	Def.	Tot.	Ast.	St.	Blk.	TO	Pts.	RPG	APG	PPG
92-93—Indiana	4	117	8	12	.667	1	4	.250	4	28	32	4	4	4	3	17	8.0	1.0	4.3
93-94—Indiana	16	578	56	106	.528	11	36	.306	63	96	159	11	18	17	30	123	9.9	0.7	7.7
94-95—Indiana	17	490	56	105	.533	23	47	.489	53	83	136	6	7	14	22	135	8.0	0.4	7.9
95-96—Indiana	5	184	16	31	.516	4	11	.364	20	36	56	4	3	6	10	36	11.2	0.8	7.2
Totals	45	1438	140	264	.530	39	98	.398	145	257	402	27	32	46	66	319	8.9	0.6	7.1

Three-point field goals: 1993-94, 0-for-1.

Personal fouls/disqualifications: 1991-92, 8/0. 1992-93, 15/0. 1993-94, 52/0. 1994-95, 56/0. 1995-96, 16/0. Totals, 147/0.

DAVIS, HUBERT　　　　　　　G　　　　　　　RAPTORS

PERSONAL: Born May 17, 1970, in Winston-Salem, N.C. ... 6-5/183. ... Full name: Hubert Ira Davis Jr. ... Nephew of Walter Davis, forward/guard with Phoenix Suns, Denver Nuggets and Portland Trail Blazers (1977-78 through 1991-92).
HIGH SCHOOL: Lake Braddock Secondary School (Burke, Va.).
COLLEGE: North Carolina.
TRANSACTIONS/CAREER NOTES: Selected by New York Knicks in first round (20th pick overall) of 1992 NBA Draft. ... Traded by Knicks to Toronto Raptors for 1997 first-round draft choice (July 24, 1996).

COLLEGIATE RECORD

Season Team	G	Min.	FGM	FGA	Pct.	FTM	FTA	Pct.	Reb.	Ast.	Pts.	RPG	APG	PPG
88-89—North Carolina	35	248	44	86	.512	24	31	.774	27	9	116	0.8	0.3	3.3
89-90—North Carolina	34	725	111	249	.446	59	74	.797	60	52	325	1.8	1.5	9.6
90-91—North Carolina	35	851	161	309	.521	81	97	.835	85	66	467	2.4	1.9	13.3
91-92—North Carolina	33	1095	241	474	.508	140	169	.828	76	52	707	2.3	1.6	21.4
Totals	137	2919	557	1118	.498	304	371	.819	248	179	1615	1.8	1.3	11.8

Three-point field goals: 1988-89, 4-for-13 (.308). 1989-90, 44-for-111 (.396). 1990-91, 64-for-131 (.489). 1991-92, 85-for-198 (.429). Totals, 197-for-453 (.435).

NBA REGULAR-SEASON RECORD

Season Team	G	Min.	FGM	FGA	Pct.	FTM	FTA	Pct.	Off.	Def.	Tot.	Ast.	St.	Blk.	TO	Pts.	RPG	APG	PPG
92-93—New York	50	815	110	251	.438	43	54	.796	13	43	56	83	22	4	45	269	1.1	1.7	5.4
93-94—New York	56	1333	238	505	.471	85	103	.825	23	44	67	165	40	4	76	614	1.2	2.9	11.0
94-95—New York	82	1697	296	617	.480	97	120	.808	30	80	110	150	35	11	87	820	1.3	1.8	10.0
95-96—New York	74	1773	275	566	.486	112	129	.868	35	88	123	103	31	8	63	789	1.7	1.4	10.7
Totals	262	5618	919	1939	.474	337	406	.830	101	255	356	501	128	27	271	2492	1.4	1.9	9.5

Three-point field goals: 1992-93, 6-for-19 (.316). 1993-94, 53-for-132 (.402). 1994-95, 131-for-288 (.455). 1995-96, 127-for-267 (.476). Totals, 317-for-706 (.449).

Personal fouls/disqualifications: 1992-93, 71/1. 1993-94, 118/0. 1994-95, 146/1. 1995-96, 120/1. Totals, 455/3.

NBA PLAYOFF RECORD

Season Team	G	Min.	FGM	FGA	Pct.	FTM	FTA	Pct.	Off.	Def.	Tot.	Ast.	St.	Blk.	TO	Pts.	RPG	APG	PPG
92-93—New York	7	96	14	25	.560	2	3	.667	1	5	6	5	6	0	9	31	0.9	0.7	4.4
93-94—New York	23	396	44	121	.364	23	32	.719	5	16	21	26	5	3	23	121	0.9	1.1	5.3
94-95—New York	11	184	17	48	.354	2	2	1.000	0	7	7	9	1	5	9	46	0.6	0.8	4.2
95-96—New York	8	145	17	31	.548	9	11	.818	4	8	12	4	0	0	7	53	1.5	0.5	6.6
Totals	49	821	92	225	.409	36	48	.750	10	36	46	44	12	8	48	251	0.9	0.9	5.1

Three-point field goals: 1992-93, 1-for-2 (.500). 1993-94, 10-for-35 (.286). 1994-95, 10-for-27 (.370). 1995-96, 10-for-19 (.526). Totals, 31-for-83 (.373).

Personal fouls/disqualifications: 1992-93, 8/0. 1993-94, 43/0. 1994-95, 20/0. 1995-96, 12/0. Totals, 83/0.

DAVIS, MARK　　　　　　　G/F　　　　　　　TIMBERWOLVES

PERSONAL: Born April 26, 1973, in Thibodaux, La. ... 6-7/210. ... Full name: Mark Anthony Davis.
HIGH SCHOOL: Thibodaux (La.).
JUNIOR COLLEGE: Howard College (Texas).
COLLEGE: Texas Tech.
TRANSACTIONS/CAREER NOTES: Selected by Minnesota Timberwolves in second round (48th pick overall) of 1995 NBA Draft.

COLLEGIATE RECORD

Season Team	G	Min.	FGM	FGA	Pct.	FTM	FTA	Pct.	Reb.	Ast.	Pts.	RPG	APG	PPG
91-92—Howard College	30	...	158	303	.521	90	159	.566	184	80	406	6.1	2.7	13.5
92-93—Howard College	28	...	211	369	.572	158	237	.667	233	95	588	8.3	3.4	21.0
93-94—Texas Tech	28	995	186	375	.496	130	197	.660	227	109	519	8.1	3.9	18.5
94-95—Texas Tech	30	971	199	399	.499	102	166	.614	254	142	520	8.5	4.7	17.3
Junior college totals	58	...	369	672	.549	248	396	.626	417	175	994	7.2	3.0	17.1
4-year-college totals	58	1966	385	774	.497	232	363	.639	481	251	1039	8.3	4.3	17.9

Three-point field goals: 1993-94, 17-for-54 (.315). 1994-95, 20-for-60 (.333). Totals, 37-for-114 (.325).

NBA REGULAR-SEASON RECORD

Season Team	G	Min.	FGM	FGA	Pct.	FTM	FTA	Pct.	Off.	Def.	Tot.	Ast.	St.	Blk.	TO	Pts.	RPG	APG	PPG
95-96—Minnesota	57	571	55	149	.369	74	116	.638	56	69	125	47	40	22	68	188	2.2	0.8	3.3

Three-point field goals: 1995-96, 4-for-13 (.308).

Personal fouls/disqualifications: 1995-96, 92/1.

DAVIS, TERRY   F/C   MAVERICKS

PERSONAL: Born June 17, 1967, in Danville, Va. ... 6-10/250. ... Full name: Terry Raymond Davis.
HIGH SCHOOL: George Washington (Danville, Va.).
COLLEGE: Virginia Union.
TRANSACTIONS/CAREER NOTES: Not drafted by an NBA franchise. ... Signed as free agent by Miami Heat (September 28, 1989). ... Signed as unrestricted free agent by Dallas Mavericks (August 6, 1991).

COLLEGIATE RECORD

Season Team	G	Min.	FGM	FGA	Pct.	FTM	FTA	Pct.	Reb.	Ast.	Pts.	RPG	APG	PPG
85-86—Virginia Union	27	...	42	91	.462	26	43	.605	116	...	110	4.3	...	4.1
86-87—Virginia Union	32	...	135	259	.521	98	142	.690	360	23	368	11.3	0.7	11.5
87-88—Virginia Union	31	...	257	454	.566	191	267	.715	338	...	705	10.9	...	22.7
88-89—Virginia Union	31	1034	272	442	.615	148	217	.682	369	40	692	11.9	1.3	22.3
Totals	121	...	706	1246	.567	463	669	.692	1183	...	1875	9.8	...	15.5

Three-point field goals: 1988-89, 0-for-1.

NBA REGULAR-SEASON RECORD

Season Team	G	Min.	FGM	FGA	Pct.	FTM	FTA	Pct.	Off.	Def.	Tot.	Ast.	St.	Blk.	TO	Pts.	RPG	APG	PPG
89-90—Miami	63	884	122	262	.466	54	87	.621	93	136	229	25	25	28	68	298	3.6	0.4	4.7
90-91—Miami	55	996	115	236	.487	69	124	.556	107	159	266	39	18	28	36	300	4.8	0.7	5.5
91-92—Dallas	68	2149	256	531	.482	181	285	.635	228	444	672	57	26	29	117	693	9.9	0.8	10.2
92-93—Dallas	75	2462	393	863	.455	167	281	.594	259	442	701	68	36	28	160	955	9.3	0.9	12.7
93-94—Dallas	15	286	24	59	.407	8	12	.667	30	44	74	6	9	1	5	56	4.9	0.4	3.7
94-95—Dallas	46	580	49	113	.434	42	66	.636	63	93	156	10	6	3	30	140	3.4	0.2	3.0
95-96—Dallas	28	501	55	108	.509	27	47	.574	43	74	117	21	10	4	25	137	4.2	0.8	4.9
Totals	350	7858	1014	2172	.467	548	902	.608	823	1392	2215	226	130	121	441	2579	6.3	0.6	7.4

Three-point field goals: 1989-90, 0-for-1. 1990-91, 1-for-2 (.500). 1991-92, 0-for-5. 1992-93, 2-for-8 (.250). 1994-95, 0-for-2. Totals, 3-for-18 (.167).
Personal fouls/disqualifications: 1989-90, 171/2. 1990-91, 129/2. 1991-92, 202/1. 1992-93, 199/3. 1993-94, 27/0. 1994-95, 76/2. 1995-96, 66/2. Totals, 870/12.

DAY, TODD   G/F   CELTICS   D

PERSONAL: Born January 7, 1970, in Decatur, Ill. ... 6-6/188. ... Full name: Todd Fitzgerald Day.
HIGH SCHOOL: Hamilton (Memphis).
COLLEGE: Arkansas.
TRANSACTIONS/CAREER NOTES: Selected by Milwaukee Bucks in first round (eighth pick overall) of 1992 NBA Draft. ... Traded by Bucks with C Alton Lister to Boston Celtics for G Sherman Douglas (November 26, 1995).

NOTES: The Sporting News All-America second team (1992).

COLLEGIATE RECORD

Season Team	G	Min.	FGM	FGA	Pct.	FTM	FTA	Pct.	Reb.	Ast.	Pts.	RPG	APG	PPG
88-89—Arkansas	32	741	148	328	.451	98	137	.715	129	49	425	4.0	1.5	13.3
89-90—Arkansas	35	1008	237	483	.491	139	183	.760	188	89	684	5.4	2.5	19.5
90-91—Arkansas	38	1121	277	586	.473	165	221	.747	201	111	786	5.3	2.9	20.7
91-92—Arkansas	22	711	173	347	.499	97	127	.764	155	70	500	7.0	3.2	22.7
Totals	127	3581	835	1744	.479	499	668	.747	673	319	2395	5.3	2.5	18.9

Three-point field goals: 1988-89, 31-for-90 (.344). 1989-90, 71-for-176 (.403). 1990-91, 67-for-189 (.354). 1991-92, 57-for-133 (.429). Totals, 226-for-588 (.384).

NBA REGULAR-SEASON RECORD

Season Team	G	Min.	FGM	FGA	Pct.	FTM	FTA	Pct.	Off.	Def.	Tot.	Ast.	St.	Blk.	TO	Pts.	RPG	APG	PPG
92-93—Milwaukee	71	1931	358	828	.432	213	297	.717	144	147	291	117	75	48	118	983	4.1	1.6	13.8
93-94—Milwaukee	76	2127	351	845	.415	231	331	.698	115	195	310	138	103	52	129	966	4.1	1.8	12.7
94-95—Milwaukee	82	2717	445	1049	.424	257	341	.754	95	227	322	134	104	63	157	1310	3.9	1.6	16.0
95-96—Mil.-Boston	79	1807	299	817	.366	224	287	.780	70	154	224	107	81	51	109	922	2.8	1.4	11.7
Totals	308	8582	1453	3539	.411	925	1256	.736	424	723	1147	496	363	214	513	4181	3.7	1.6	13.6

Three-point field goals: 1992-93, 54-for-184 (.293). 1993-94, 33-for-148 (.223). 1994-95, 163-for-418 (.390). 1995-96, 100-for-302 (.331). Totals, 350-for-1052 (.333).
Personal fouls/disqualifications: 1992-93, 222/1. 1993-94, 221/4. 1994-95, 283/6. 1995-96, 225/2. Totals, 951/13.

DeCLERCQ, ANDREW   F/C   WARRIORS

PERSONAL: Born February 1, 1973, in Detroit. ... 6-10/230. ... Name pronounced dah-CLAIR-k.
HIGH SCHOOL: Countryside (Clearwater, Fla.).
COLLEGE: Florida.
TRANSACTIONS/CAREER NOTES: Selected by Golden State Warriors in second round (34th pick overall) of 1995 NBA Draft.

COLLEGIATE RECORD

Season Team	G	Min.	FGM	FGA	Pct.	FTM	FTA	Pct.	Reb.	Ast.	Pts.	RPG	APG	PPG
91-92—Florida	33	825	117	231	.507	57	87	.655	203	26	291	6.2	0.8	8.8
92-93—Florida	28	715	118	208	.567	59	101	.584	198	15	295	7.1	0.5	10.5
93-94—Florida	37	998	129	237	.544	68	104	.654	292	54	327	7.9	1.5	8.8
94-95—Florida	30	966	138	270	.511	115	159	.723	265	42	396	8.8	1.4	13.2
Totals	128	3504	502	946	.531	299	451	.663	958	137	1309	7.5	1.1	10.2

Three-point field goals: 1993-94, 1-for-3 (.333). 1994-95, 5-for-15 (.333). Totals, 6-for-18 (.333).

NBA REGULAR-SEASON RECORD

| | | | | | | | | REBOUNDS | | | | | | | | AVERAGES | | |
Season Team	G	Min.	FGM	FGA	Pct.	FTM	FTA	Pct.	Off.	Def.	Tot.	Ast.	St.	Blk.	TO	Pts.	RPG	APG	PPG
95-96—Golden State ...	22	203	24	50	.480	11	19	.579	18	21	39	9	7	5	4	59	1.8	0.4	2.7

Three-point field goals: 1995-96, 0-for-1.
Personal fouls/disqualifications: 1995-96, 30/0.

DEHERE, TERRY   G   CLIPPERS

PERSONAL: Born September 12, 1971, in New York. ... 6-4/190. ... Full name: Lennox Dominique Dehere. ... Name pronounced da-HAIR.
HIGH SCHOOL: St. Anthony (Jersey City, N.J.).
COLLEGE: Seton Hall.
TRANSACTIONS/CAREER NOTES: Selected by Los Angeles Clippers in first round (13th pick overall) of 1993 NBA Draft.

COLLEGIATE RECORD

| | | | | | | | | | | | | AVERAGES | | |
Season Team	G	Min.	FGM	FGA	Pct.	FTM	FTA	Pct.	Reb.	Ast.	Pts.	RPG	APG	PPG
89-90—Seton Hall	28	932	134	333	.402	110	138	.797	94	60	451	3.4	2.1	16.1
90-91—Seton Hall	34	1133	213	460	.463	141	168	.839	101	76	672	3.0	2.2	19.8
91-92—Seton Hall	31	1004	196	459	.427	156	188	.830	115	85	601	3.7	2.7	19.4
92-93—Seton Hall	35	1203	242	525	.461	202	247	.818	105	93	770	3.0	2.7	22.0
Totals	128	4272	785	1777	.442	609	741	.822	415	314	2494	3.2	2.5	19.5

Three-point field goals: 1989-90, 73-for-187 (.390). 1990-91, 105-for-245 (.429). 1991-92, 53-for-165 (.321). 1992-93, 84-for-212 (.396). Totals, 315-for-809 (.389).

NBA REGULAR-SEASON RECORD

| | | | | | | | | REBOUNDS | | | | | | | | AVERAGES | | |
Season Team	G	Min.	FGM	FGA	Pct.	FTM	FTA	Pct.	Off.	Def.	Tot.	Ast.	St.	Blk.	TO	Pts.	RPG	APG	PPG
93-94—L.A. Clippers ...	64	759	129	342	.377	61	81	.753	25	43	68	78	28	3	61	342	1.1	1.2	5.3
94-95—L.A. Clippers ...	80	1774	279	685	.407	229	292	.784	35	117	152	225	45	7	157	835	1.9	2.8	10.4
95-96—L.A. Clippers ...	82	2018	315	686	.459	247	327	.755	41	102	143	350	54	16	191	1016	1.7	4.3	12.4
Totals	226	4551	723	1713	.422	537	700	.767	101	262	363	653	127	26	409	2193	1.6	2.9	9.7

Three-point field goals: 1993-94, 23-for-57 (.404). 1994-95, 48-for-163 (.294). 1995-96, 139-for-316 (.440). Totals, 210-for-536 (.392).
Personal fouls/disqualifications: 1993-94, 69/0. 1994-95, 200/0. 1995-96, 239/2. Totals, 508/2.

DEL NEGRO, VINNY   G   SPURS

PERSONAL: Born August 9, 1966, in Springfield, Mass. ... 6-4/200. ... Full name: Vincent Joseph Del Negro.
HIGH SCHOOL: Suffield (Conn.) Academy.
COLLEGE: North Carolina State.
TRANSACTIONS/CAREER NOTES: Selected by Sacramento Kings in second round (29th pick overall) of 1988 NBA Draft. ... Played in Italy (1990-91 and 1991-92). ... Signed as free agent by San Antonio Spurs (July 30, 1992).

COLLEGIATE RECORD

| | | | | | | | | | | | | AVERAGES | | |
Season Team	G	Min.	FGM	FGA	Pct.	FTM	FTA	Pct.	Reb.	Ast.	Pts.	RPG	APG	PPG
84-85—N.C. State	19	125	12	21	.571	15	23	.652	14	22	39	0.7	1.2	2.1
85-86—N.C. State	17	139	11	30	.367	7	11	.636	14	31	29	0.8	1.8	1.7
86-87—N.C. State	35	918	133	269	.494	63	71	.887	115	102	365	3.3	2.9	10.4
87-88—N.C. State	32	1093	187	363	.515	104	124	.839	158	115	509	4.9	3.6	15.9
Totals	103	2275	343	683	.502	189	229	.825	301	270	942	2.9	2.6	9.1

Three-point field goals: 1986-87, 36-for-72 (.500). 1987-88, 31-for-78 (.397). Totals, 67-for-150 (.447).

NBA REGULAR-SEASON RECORD

| | | | | | | | | REBOUNDS | | | | | | | | AVERAGES | | |
Season Team	G	Min.	FGM	FGA	Pct.	FTM	FTA	Pct.	Off.	Def.	Tot.	Ast.	St.	Blk.	TO	Pts.	RPG	APG	PPG
88-89—Sacramento	80	1556	239	503	.475	85	100	.850	48	123	171	206	65	14	77	569	2.1	2.6	7.1
89-90—Sacramento	76	1858	297	643	.462	135	155	.871	39	159	198	250	64	10	111	739	2.6	3.3	9.7
92-93—San Antonio	73	1526	218	430	.507	101	117	.863	19	144	163	291	44	1	92	543	2.2	4.0	7.4
93-94—San Antonio	77	1949	309	634	.487	140	170	.824	27	134	161	320	64	1	102	773	2.1	4.2	10.0
94-95—San Antonio	75	2360	372	766	.486	128	162	.790	28	164	192	226	61	14	56	938	2.6	3.0	12.5
95-96—San Antonio	82	2766	478	962	.497	178	214	.832	36	236	272	315	85	6	100	1191	3.3	3.8	14.5
Totals	463	12015	1913	3938	.486	767	918	.836	197	960	1157	1608	383	46	538	4753	2.5	3.5	10.3

Three-point field goals: 1988-89, 6-for-20 (.300). 1989-90, 10-for-32 (.313). 1992-93, 6-for-24 (.250). 1993-94, 15-for-43 (.349). 1994-95, 66-for-162 (.407). 1995-96, 57-for-150 (.380). Totals, 160-for-431 (.371).
Personal fouls/disqualifications: 1988-89, 160/2. 1989-90, 182/2. 1992-93, 146/0. 1993-94, 168/0. 1994-95, 179/0. 1995-96, 166/0. Totals, 1001/4.

NBA PLAYOFF RECORD

| | | | | | | | | REBOUNDS | | | | | | | | AVERAGES | | |
Season Team	G	Min.	FGM	FGA	Pct.	FTM	FTA	Pct.	Off.	Def.	Tot.	Ast.	St.	Blk.	TO	Pts.	RPG	APG	PPG
92-93—San Antonio	8	112	17	38	.447	4	4	1.000	4	13	17	24	1	1	3	40	2.4	3.0	5.0
93-94—San Antonio	4	93	12	27	.444	3	5	.600	1	6	7	18	1	0	6	29	1.8	4.5	7.3
94-95—San Antonio	15	382	51	118	.432	20	24	.833	4	28	32	37	8	2	16	131	2.1	2.5	8.7
95-96—San Antonio	10	379	57	124	.460	13	19	.684	4	22	26	29	13	3	6	143	2.6	2.9	14.3
Totals	37	966	137	307	.446	40	52	.769	15	69	84	108	23	6	31	343	2.3	2.9	9.3

Three-point field goals: 1992-93, 2-for-9 (.222). 1993-94, 2-for-4 (.500). 1994-95, 9-for-20 (.450). 1995-96, 16-for-27 (.593). Totals, 29-for-60 (.483).
Personal fouls/disqualifications: 1992-93, 13/0. 1993-94, 6/0. 1994-95, 23/0. 1995-96, 19/0. Totals, 61/0.

ITALIAN LEAGUE RECORD

Season Team	G	Min.	FGM	FGA	Pct.	FTM	FTA	Pct.	Reb.	Ast.	Pts.	AVERAGES RPG	APG	PPG
90-91—Benetton Treviso	35	1345	271	455	.596	214	263	.814	146	...	894	4.2	...	25.5
91-92—Benetton Treviso	30	1148	284	492	.577	167	183	.913	141	111	755	4.7	3.7	25.2
Totals	65	2493	555	947	.586	381	446	.854	287	...	1649	4.4	...	25.4

DEMPS, DELL   G   SPURS

PERSONAL: Born February 12, 1970, in Long Beach, Calif. ... 6-4/210.
HIGH SCHOOL: Mt. Eden (Hayward, Calif.).
COLLEGE: Pacific.
TRANSACTIONS/CAREER NOTES: Not drafted by an NBA franchise. ... Signed as free agent by Golden State Warriors (July 31, 1992). ... Waived by Warriors (October 1, 1992). ... Played in Continental Basketball Association with Yakima Sun Kings (1992-93 through 1994-95), Oklahoma City Cavalry (1992-93) and Rochester Rebels (1993-94). ... Re-signed as free agent by Warriors (September 1993). ... Waived by Warriors (November 2, 1993). ... Re-signed as free agent by Warriors (November 22, 1993). ... Waived by Warriors (December 16, 1993). ... Signed as free agent by San Antonio Spurs (October 6, 1995).

COLLEGIATE RECORD

Season Team	G	Min.	FGM	FGA	Pct.	FTM	FTA	Pct.	Reb.	Ast.	Pts.	AVERAGES RPG	APG	PPG
88-89—Pacific	28	583	67	179	.374	26	35	.743	104	69	185	3.7	2.5	6.6
89-90—Pacific	29	993	159	326	.488	94	133	.707	137	95	462	4.7	3.3	15.9
90-91—Pacific	28	977	185	407	.455	83	124	.669	155	93	526	5.5	3.3	18.8
91-92—Pacific	30	1044	187	402	.465	113	163	.693	173	93	569	5.8	3.1	19.0
Totals	115	3597	598	1314	.455	316	455	.695	569	350	1742	4.9	3.0	15.1

Three-point field goals: 1988-89, 25-for-80 (.313). 1989-90, 50-for-120 (.417). 1990-91, 73-for-175 (.417). 1991-92, 92-for-209 (.440). Totals, 240-for-584 (.411).

CBA REGULAR-SEASON RECORD

NOTES: Member of CBA championship team (1995).

Season Team	G	Min.	FGM	FGA	Pct.	FTM	FTA	Pct.	Reb.	Ast.	Pts.	AVERAGES RPG	APG	PPG
92-93—Yakima-Okla. C...............	14	128	25	44	.568	9	20	.450	11	5	63	0.8	0.4	4.5
93-94—Roch.-Yakima.................	39	1023	174	324	.537	111	166	.669	119	77	460	3.1	2.0	11.8
94-95—Yakima	39	657	109	222	.491	54	87	.621	66	53	279	1.7	1.4	7.2
Totals	92	1808	308	590	.522	174	273	.637	196	135	802	2.1	1.5	8.7

Three-point field goals: 1992-93, 4-for-10 (.400). 1993-94, 1-for-7 (.143). 1994-95, 7-for-18 (.389). Totals, 12-for-35 (.343).

NBA REGULAR-SEASON RECORD

Season Team	G	Min.	FGM	FGA	Pct.	FTM	FTA	Pct.	REBOUNDS Off.	Def.	Tot.	Ast.	St.	Blk.	TO	Pts.	AVERAGES RPG	APG	PPG
93-94—Golden State ...	2	11	2	6	.333	0	2	.000	0	0	0	1	2	0	1	4	0.0	0.5	2.0
95-96—San Antonio....	16	87	19	33	.576	14	17	.824	2	7	9	8	3	1	12	53	0.6	0.5	3.3
Totals	18	98	21	39	.538	14	19	.737	2	7	9	9	5	1	13	57	0.5	0.5	3.2

Three-point field goals: 1995-96, 1-for-2 (.500).
Personal fouls/disqualifications: 1993-94, 1/0. 1995-96, 10/0. Totals, 11/0.

DIVAC, VLADE   C   HORNETS

PERSONAL: Born February 3, 1968, in Prijepolje, Yugoslavia. ... 7-1/250. ... Name pronounced VLAH-day DEE-votz.
HIGH SCHOOL: Belgrade (Yugoslavia).
COLLEGE: Did not attend college.
TRANSACTIONS/CAREER NOTES: Selected by Los Angeles Lakers in first round (26th pick overall) of 1989 NBA Draft. ... Traded by Lakers to Charlotte Hornets for draft rights to G Kobe Bryant (July 11, 1996).
MISCELLANEOUS: Member of silver-medal-winning Yugoslavian Olympic teams (1988, 1996).

NBA REGULAR-SEASON RECORD

HONORS: NBA All-Rookie first team (1990).

Season Team	G	Min.	FGM	FGA	Pct.	FTM	FTA	Pct.	REBOUNDS Off.	Def.	Tot.	Ast.	St.	Blk.	TO	Pts.	AVERAGES RPG	APG	PPG
89-90—L.A. Lakers	82	1611	274	549	.499	153	216	.708	167	345	512	75	79	114	110	701	6.2	0.9	8.5
90-91—L.A. Lakers	82	2310	360	637	.565	196	279	.703	205	461	666	92	106	127	146	921	8.1	1.1	11.2
91-92—L.A. Lakers	36	979	157	317	.495	86	112	.768	87	160	247	60	55	35	88	405	6.9	1.7	11.3
92-93—L.A. Lakers	82	2525	397	819	.485	235	341	.689	220	509	729	232	128	140	214	1050	8.9	2.8	12.8
93-94—L.A. Lakers	79	2685	453	895	.506	208	303	.686	282	569	851	307	92	112	191	1123	10.8	3.9	14.2
94-95—L.A. Lakers	80	2807	485	957	.507	297	382	.777	261	568	829	329	109	174	205	1277	10.4	4.1	16.0
95-96—L.A. Lakers	79	2470	414	807	.513	189	295	.641	198	481	679	261	76	131	199	1020	8.7	3.3	12.9
Totals	520	15387	2540	4981	.510	1364	1928	.707	1420	3093	4513	1356	645	833	1153	6497	8.7	2.6	12.5

Three-point field goals: 1989-90, 0-for-5. 1990-91, 5-for-14 (.357). 1991-92, 5-for-19 (.263). 1992-93, 21-for-75 (.280). 1993-94, 9-for-47 (.191). 1994-95, 10-for-53 (.189). 1995-96, 3-for-18 (.167). Totals, 53-for-231 (.229).
Personal fouls/disqualifications: 1989-90, 240/2. 1990-91, 247/3. 1991-92, 114/3. 1992-93, 311/7. 1993-94, 288/5. 1994-95, 305/8. 1995-96, 274/5. Totals, 1779/33.

NBA PLAYOFF RECORD

Season Team	G	Min.	FGM	FGA	Pct.	FTM	FTA	Pct.	REBOUNDS Off.	Def.	Tot.	Ast.	St.	Blk.	TO	Pts.	AVERAGES RPG	APG	PPG
89-90—L.A. Lakers	9	175	32	44	.727	17	19	.895	16	32	48	10	8	15	13	82	5.3	1.1	9.1
90-91—L.A. Lakers	19	609	97	172	.564	57	71	.803	49	78	127	21	27	41	41	252	6.7	1.1	13.3
91-92—L.A. Lakers	4	143	15	43	.349	9	10	.900	6	16	22	15	5	3	18	39	5.5	3.8	9.8
92-93—L.A. Lakers	5	167	37	74	.500	12	22	.545	17	30	47	28	6	12	11	90	9.4	5.6	18.0

Season Team	G	Min.	FGM	FGA	Pct.	FTM	FTA	Pct.	REBOUNDS Off.	Def.	Tot.	Ast.	St.	Blk.	TO	Pts.	AVERAGES RPG	APG	PPG
94-95—L.A. Lakers	10	388	57	122	.467	40	62	.645	34	51	85	31	8	13	28	156	8.5	3.1	15.6
95-96—L.A. Lakers	4	115	15	35	.429	5	8	.625	11	19	30	8	0	5	8	36	7.5	2.0	9.0
Totals	51	1597	253	490	.516	140	192	.729	133	226	359	113	54	89	119	655	7.0	2.2	12.8

Three-point field goals: 1989-90, 1-for-2 (.500). 1990-91, 1-for-6 (.167). 1991-92, 0-for-2. 1992-93, 4-for-9 (.444). 1994-95, 2-for-5 (.222). 1995-96, 1-for-5 (.200). Totals, 9-for-33 (.273).

Personal fouls/disqualifications: 1989-90, 27/1. 1990-91, 65/2. 1991-92, 17/1. 1992-93, 22/0. 1994-95, 44/2. 1995-96, 10/0. Totals, 185/6.

DOUGLAS, SHERMAN   G   BUCKS

PERSONAL: Born September 15, 1966, in Washington, D.C. ... 6-1/198.
HIGH SCHOOL: Spingarn (Washington, D.C.).
COLLEGE: Syracuse.
TRANSACTIONS/CAREER NOTES: Selected by Miami Heat in second round (28th pick overall) of 1989 NBA Draft. ... Traded by Heat to Boston Celtics for G Brian Shaw (January 10, 1992). ... Traded by Celtics to Milwaukee Bucks for G Todd Day and C Alton Lister (November 26, 1995).

COLLEGIATE RECORD

NOTES: Shares NCAA Division I single-game record for most assists—22 (January 28, 1989, vs. Providence). ... 1986-87 minutes played totals are missing one game.

Season Team	G	Min.	FGM	FGA	Pct.	FTM	FTA	Pct.	Reb.	Ast.	Pts.	AVERAGES RPG	APG	PPG
85-86—Syracuse	27	307	57	93	.613	32	44	.727	33	57	146	1.2	2.1	5.4
86-87—Syracuse	38	1240	246	463	.531	151	203	.744	97	289	659	2.6	7.6	17.3
87-88—Syracuse	35	1195	222	428	.519	104	150	.693	76	288	562	2.2	8.2	16.1
88-89—Syracuse	38	1348	272	498	.546	110	174	.632	93	326	693	2.4	8.6	18.2
Totals	138	4090	797	1482	.538	397	571	.695	299	960	2060	2.2	7.0	14.9

Three-point field goals: 1986-87, 16-for-49 (.327). 1987-88, 14-for-53 (.264). 1988-89, 39-for-106 (.368). Totals, 69-for-208 (.332).

NBA REGULAR-SEASON RECORD

HONORS: NBA All-Rookie first team (1990).

Season Team	G	Min.	FGM	FGA	Pct.	FTM	FTA	Pct.	REBOUNDS Off.	Def.	Tot.	Ast.	St.	Blk.	TO	Pts.	AVERAGES RPG	APG	PPG
89-90—Miami	81	2470	463	938	.494	224	326	.687	70	136	206	619	145	10	246	1155	2.5	7.6	14.3
90-91—Miami	73	2562	532	1055	.504	284	414	.686	78	131	209	624	121	5	270	1352	2.9	8.5	18.5
91-92—Miami-Bos.	42	752	117	253	.462	73	107	.682	13	50	63	172	25	9	68	308	1.5	4.1	7.3
92-93—Boston	79	1932	264	530	.498	84	150	.560	65	97	162	508	49	10	161	618	2.1	6.4	7.8
93-94—Boston	78	2789	425	919	.462	177	276	.641	70	123	193	683	89	11	233	1040	2.5	8.8	13.3
94-95—Boston	65	2048	365	769	.475	204	296	.689	48	122	170	446	80	2	162	954	2.6	6.9	14.7
95-96—Bos.-Mil.	79	2335	345	685	.504	160	219	.731	55	125	180	436	63	5	194	890	2.3	5.5	11.3
Totals	497	14888	2511	5149	.488	1206	1788	.674	399	784	1183	3488	572	52	1334	6317	2.4	7.0	12.7

Three-point field goals: 1989-90, 5-for-31 (.161). 1990-91, 4-for-29 (.138). 1991-92, 1-for-10 (.100). 1992-93, 6-for-29 (.207). 1993-94, 13-for-56 (.232). 1994-95, 20-for-82 (.244). 1995-96, 40-for-110 (.364). Totals, 89-for-349 (.255).

Personal fouls/disqualifications: 1989-90, 187/0. 1990-91, 178/2. 1991-92, 78/0. 1992-93, 166/1. 1993-94, 171/2. 1994-95, 152/0. 1995-96, 163/0. Totals, 1095/5.

NBA PLAYOFF RECORD

Season Team	G	Min.	FGM	FGA	Pct.	FTM	FTA	Pct.	REBOUNDS Off.	Def.	Tot.	Ast.	St.	Blk.	TO	Pts.	AVERAGES RPG	APG	PPG
91-92—Boston	6	65	9	25	.360	1	2	.500	1	3	4	10	0	0	4	19	0.7	1.7	3.2
92-93—Boston	4	166	17	45	.378	10	15	.667	12	14	26	38	4	0	12	44	6.5	9.5	11.0
94-95—Boston	4	168	24	68	.353	8	11	.727	4	16	20	33	4	1	17	60	5.0	8.3	15.0
Totals	14	399	50	138	.362	19	28	.679	17	33	50	81	8	1	33	123	3.6	5.8	8.8

Three-point field goals: 1991-92, 0-for-2. 1992-93, 0-for-3. 1994-95, 4-for-12 (.333). Totals, 4-for-17 (.235).

Personal fouls/disqualifications: 1991-92, 8/0. 1992-93, 10/0. 1994-95, 12/0. Totals, 30/0.

DREXLER, CLYDE   G   ROCKETS

PERSONAL: Born June 22, 1962, in New Orleans. ... 6-7/222. ... Full name: Clyde Austin Drexler.
HIGH SCHOOL: Sterling (Houston).
COLLEGE: Houston.
TRANSACTIONS/CAREER NOTES: Selected after junior season by Portland Trail Blazers in first round (14th pick overall) of 1983 NBA Draft. ... Traded by Trail Blazers with F Tracy Murray to Houston Rockets for F Otis Thorpe, rights to F Marcelo Nicola and 1995 first-round draft choice (February 14, 1995).
MISCELLANEOUS: Member of NBA championship team (1995). ... Member of gold-medal-winning U.S. Olympic team (1992). ... Portland Trail Blazers all-time leading scorer with 18,040 points, all-time leading rebounder with 5,339 and all-time steals leader with 1,795 (1983-84 through 1994-95).

COLLEGIATE RECORD

Season Team	G	Min.	FGM	FGA	Pct.	FTM	FTA	Pct.	Reb.	Ast.	Pts.	AVERAGES RPG	APG	PPG
80-81—Houston	30	992	153	303	.505	50	85	.588	314	78	356	10.5	2.6	11.9
81-82—Houston	32	1077	206	362	.569	73	120	.608	336	96	485	10.5	3.0	15.2
82-83—Houston	34	1186	236	440	.536	70	95	.737	298	129	542	8.8	3.8	15.9
Totals	96	3255	595	1105	.538	193	300	.643	948	303	1383	9.9	3.2	14.4

NBA REGULAR-SEASON RECORD

HONORS: All-NBA first team (1992). ... All-NBA second team (1988, 1991). ... All-NBA third team (1990, 1995).

									REBOUNDS								AVERAGES		
Season Team	G	Min.	FGM	FGA	Pct.	FTM	FTA	Pct.	Off.	Def.	Tot.	Ast.	St.	Blk.	TO	Pts.	RPG	APG	PPG
83-84—Portland	82	1408	252	559	.451	123	169	.728	112	123	235	153	107	29	123	628	2.9	1.9	7.7
84-85—Portland	80	2555	573	1161	.494	223	294	.759	217	259	476	441	177	68	223	1377	6.0	5.5	17.2
85-86—Portland	75	2576	542	1142	.475	293	381	.769	171	250	421	600	197	46	282	1389	5.6	8.0	18.5
86-87—Portland	82	3114	707	1408	.502	357	470	.760	227	291	518	566	204	71	253	1782	6.3	6.9	21.7
87-88—Portland	81	3060	849	1679	.506	476	587	.811	261	272	533	467	203	52	236	2185	6.6	5.8	27.0
88-89—Portland	78	3064	829	1672	.496	438	548	.799	289	326	615	450	213	54	250	2123	7.9	5.8	27.2
89-90—Portland	73	2683	670	1357	.494	333	430	.774	208	299	507	432	145	51	191	1703	6.9	5.9	23.3
90-91—Portland	82	2852	645	1338	.482	416	524	.794	212	334	546	493	144	60	232	1767	6.7	6.0	21.5
91-92—Portland	76	2751	694	1476	.470	401	505	.794	166	334	500	512	138	70	240	1903	6.6	6.7	25.0
92-93—Portland	49	1671	350	816	.429	245	292	.839	126	183	309	278	95	37	115	976	6.3	5.7	19.9
93-94—Portland	68	2334	473	1105	.428	286	368	.777	154	291	445	333	98	34	167	1303	6.5	4.9	19.2
94-95—Port.-Houston.	76	2728	571	1238	.461	364	442	.824	152	328	480	362	136	45	186	1653	6.3	4.8	21.8
95-96—Houston	52	1997	331	764	.433	265	338	.784	97	276	373	302	105	24	134	1005	7.2	5.8	19.3
Totals	954	32793	7486	15715	.476	4220	5348	.789	2392	3566	5958	5389	1962	641	2632	19794	6.2	5.6	20.7

Three-point field goals: 1983-84, 1-for-4 (.250). 1984-85, 8-for-37 (.216). 1985-86, 12-for-60 (.200). 1986-87, 11-for-47 (.234). 1987-88, 11-for-52 (.212). 1988-89, 27-for-104 (.260). 1989-90, 30-for-106 (.283). 1990-91, 61-for-191 (.319). 1991-92, 114-for-338 (.337). 1992-93, 31-for-133 (.233). 1993-94, 71-for-219 (.324). 1994-95, 147-for-408 (.360). 1995-96, 78-for-235 (.332). Totals, 602-for-1934 (.311).

Personal fouls/disqualifications: 1983-84, 209/2. 1984-85, 265/3. 1985-86, 270/8. 1986-87, 281/7. 1987-88, 250/2. 1988-89, 269/2. 1989-90, 222/1. 1990-91, 226/2. 1991-92, 229/2. 1992-93, 159/1. 1993-94, 202/2. 1994-95, 206/1. 1995-96, 153/0. Totals, 2941/33.

NBA PLAYOFF RECORD

NOTES: Holds single-game playoff record for most points in an overtime period—13 (April 29, 1992, vs. Los Angeles Lakers).

									REBOUNDS								AVERAGES		
Season Team	G	Min.	FGM	FGA	Pct.	FTM	FTA	Pct.	Off.	Def.	Tot.	Ast.	St.	Blk.	TO	Pts.	RPG	APG	PPG
83-84—Portland	5	85	15	35	.429	6	7	.857	7	10	17	8	5	1	7	36	3.4	1.6	7.2
84-85—Portland	9	339	55	134	.410	38	45	.844	27	28	55	83	23	9	29	150	6.1	9.2	16.7
85-86—Portland	4	145	26	57	.456	18	23	.783	9	16	25	26	6	3	19	72	6.3	6.5	18.0
86-87—Portland	4	153	36	79	.456	23	29	.793	16	14	30	15	7	3	6	96	7.5	3.8	24.0
87-88—Portland	4	170	32	83	.386	21	29	.724	12	16	28	21	12	2	12	88	7.0	5.3	22.0
88-89—Portland	3	128	35	71	.493	13	17	.765	13	7	20	25	6	2	12	83	6.7	8.3	27.7
89-90—Portland	21	853	172	390	.441	96	124	.774	63	88	151	150	53	18	67	449	7.2	7.1	21.4
90-91—Portland	16	633	128	269	.476	76	98	.776	40	89	129	129	34	16	61	347	8.1	8.1	21.7
91-92—Portland	21	847	198	425	.466	138	171	.807	60	95	155	147	31	20	58	553	7.4	7.0	26.3
92-93—Portland	3	116	18	43	.419	16	20	.800	8	11	19	14	5	3	3	57	6.3	4.7	19.0
93-94—Portland	4	157	31	73	.425	19	23	.826	10	31	41	22	8	2	9	84	10.3	5.5	21.0
94-95—Houston	22	849	155	322	.481	110	140	.786	45	109	154	111	33	15	45	450	7.0	5.0	20.5
95-96—Houston	8	292	49	118	.415	26	34	.765	15	47	62	40	21	4	20	133	7.8	5.0	16.6
Totals	124	4767	950	2099	.453	600	760	.789	325	561	886	791	244	98	348	2598	7.1	6.4	21.0

Three-point field goals: 1983-84, 0-for-1. 1984-85, 2-for-5 (.400). 1985-86, 2-for-5 (.400). 1986-87, 1-for-4 (.250). 1987-88, 3-for-6 (.500). 1988-89, 0-for-2. 1989-90, 9-for-41 (.220). 1990-91, 15-for-56 (.268). 1991-92, 19-for-81 (.235). 1992-93, 5-for-12 (.417). 1993-94, 3-for-13 (.231). 1994-95, 30-for-99 (.303). 1995-96, 9-for-34 (.265). Totals, 98-for-361 (.271).

Personal fouls/disqualifications: 1983-84, 11/0. 1984-85, 37/0. 1985-86, 19/1. 1986-87, 16/1. 1987-88, 14/0. 1988-89, 11/0. 1989-90, 72/2. 1990-91, 56/0. 1991-92, 77/2. 1992-93, 9/0. 1993-94, 7/0. 1994-95, 56/2. 1995-96, 22/0. Totals, 419/7.

NBA ALL-STAR GAME RECORD

								REBOUNDS								
Season Team	Min.	FGM	FGA	Pct.	FTM	FTA	Pct.	Off.	Def.	Tot.	Ast.	PF	Dq.	St.	Blk.	TO	Pts.
1986 —Portland	15	5	7	.714	0	0	...	0	4	4	4	3	0	3	1	3	10
1988 —Portland	15	3	5	.600	6	6	1.000	2	3	5	0	3	0	1	0	1	12
1989 —Portland	25	7	19	.368	0	0	...	6	6	12	4	3	0	2	0	6	14
1990 —Portland	19	2	6	.333	2	2	1.000	4	0	4	2	1	0	1	1	1	7
1991 —Portland	19	4	9	.444	4	4	1.000	2	2	4	2	3	0	1	1	0	12
1992 —Portland	28	10	15	.667	0	0	...	2	7	9	6	2	0	0	2	1	22
1993 —Portland	11	1	3	.333	0	0	...	1	0	1	1	3	0	0	0	2	2
1994 —Portland	15	3	7	.429	0	0	...	0	3	3	1	1	0	1	1	1	6
1996 —Houston	19	5	8	.625	0	0	...	0	2	2	3	0	0	3	0	3	11
Totals	166	40	79	.506	12	12	1.000	17	27	44	23	19	0	12	6	18	96

Three-point field goals: 1986, 0-for-1. 1988, 0-for-1. 1990, 1-for-1. 1992, 2-for-4 (.500). 1993, 0-for-1. 1994, 0-for-2. 1996, 1-for-4 (.250). Totals, 4-for-14 (.286).

DUCKWORTH, KEVIN   C   BUCKS

PERSONAL: Born April 1, 1964, in Harvey, Ill. ... 7-0/285. ... Full name: Kevin Jerome Duckworth.
HIGH SCHOOL: Thornridge (Dolton, Ill.).
COLLEGE: Eastern Illinois.
TRANSACTIONS/CAREER NOTES: Selected by San Antonio Spurs in second round (33rd pick overall) of 1986 NBA Draft. ... Traded by Spurs to Portland Trail Blazers for F Walter Berry (December 18, 1986). ... Traded by Trail Blazers with future considerations to Washington Bullets for F Harvey Grant (June 24, 1993). ... Traded by Bullets to Milwaukee Bucks for F Bob McCann (October 18, 1995).

COLLEGIATE RECORD

												AVERAGES		
Season Team	G	Min.	FGM	FGA	Pct.	FTM	FTA	Pct.	Reb.	Ast.	Pts.	RPG	APG	PPG
82-83—Eastern Illinois	30	669	112	212	.528	64	95	.674	181	12	288	6.0	0.4	9.6
83-84—Eastern Illinois	28	642	132	221	.597	61	89	.685	191	12	325	6.8	0.4	11.6
84-85—Eastern Illinois	28	733	133	258	.516	65	99	.657	205	12	331	7.3	0.4	11.8
85-86—Eastern Illinois	32	1023	250	396	.631	125	164	.762	290	21	625	9.1	0.7	19.5
Totals	118	3067	627	1087	.577	315	447	.705	867	57	1569	7.3	0.5	13.3

NBA REGULAR-SEASON RECORD

HONORS: NBA Most Improved Player (1988).

Season Team	G	Min.	FGM	FGA	Pct.	FTM	FTA	Pct.	Off.	Def.	Tot.	Ast.	St.	Blk.	TO	Pts.	RPG	APG	PPG
86-87—S.A.-Port..........	65	875	130	273	.476	92	134	.687	76	147	223	29	21	21	78	352	3.4	0.4	5.4
87-88—Portland..........	78	2223	450	907	.496	331	430	.770	224	352	576	66	31	32	177	1231	7.4	0.8	15.8
88-89—Portland..........	79	2662	554	1161	.477	324	428	.757	246	389	635	60	56	49	200	1432	8.0	0.8	18.1
89-90—Portland..........	82	2462	548	1146	.478	231	312	.740	184	325	509	91	36	34	171	1327	6.2	1.1	16.2
90-91—Portland..........	81	2511	521	1084	.481	240	311	.772	177	354	531	89	33	34	186	1282	6.6	1.1	15.8
91-92—Portland..........	82	2222	362	786	.461	156	226	.690	151	346	497	99	38	37	143	880	6.1	1.2	10.7
92-93—Portland..........	74	1762	301	688	.438	127	174	.730	118	269	387	70	45	39	87	729	5.2	0.9	9.9
93-94—Washington	69	1485	184	441	.417	88	132	.667	103	222	325	56	37	35	101	456	4.7	0.8	6.6
94-95—Washington	40	818	118	267	.442	45	70	.643	65	130	195	20	21	24	59	283	4.9	0.5	7.1
95-96—Milwaukee	8	58	3	14	.214	3	6	.500	2	5	7	2	2	0	2	9	0.9	0.3	1.1
Totals	658	17078	3171	6767	.469	1637	2223	.736	1346	2539	3885	582	320	305	1204	7981	5.9	0.9	12.1

Three-point field goals: 1986-87, 0-for-1. 1988-89, 0-for-2. 1990-91, 0-for-2. 1991-92, 0-for-3. 1992-93, 0-for-2. 1994-95, 2-for-10 (.200). Totals, 2-for-20 (.100).

Personal fouls/disqualifications: 1986-87, 192/3. 1987-88, 280/5. 1988-89, 300/6. 1989-90, 271/2. 1990-91, 251/5. 1991-92, 264/5. 1992-93, 222/1. 1993-94, 223/2. 1994-95, 110/3. 1995-96, 19/0. Totals, 2132/32.

NBA PLAYOFF RECORD

Season Team	G	Min.	FGM	FGA	Pct.	FTM	FTA	Pct.	Off.	Def.	Tot.	Ast.	St.	Blk.	TO	Pts.	RPG	APG	PPG
86-87—Portland..........	4	53	6	12	.500	2	5	.400	3	5	8	1	4	1	6	14	2.0	0.3	3.5
87-88—Portland..........	4	151	34	70	.486	18	23	.783	20	24	44	7	1	2	21	86	11.0	1.8	21.5
88-89—Portland..........	3	83	14	35	.400	6	11	.545	8	9	17	2	1	1	5	34	5.7	0.7	11.3
89-90—Portland..........	15	453	82	187	.439	33	46	.717	28	59	87	16	5	9	33	197	5.8	1.1	13.1
90-91—Portland..........	16	511	73	182	.401	41	56	.732	40	67	107	14	8	8	39	187	6.7	0.9	11.7
91-92—Portland..........	21	647	107	216	.495	35	53	.660	40	77	117	41	11	12	45	249	5.6	2.0	11.9
92-93—Portland..........	4	58	7	21	.333	4	4	1.000	4	9	13	3	0	1	6	18	3.3	0.8	4.5
Totals	67	1956	323	723	.447	139	198	.702	143	250	393	84	30	34	155	785	5.9	1.3	11.7

Three-point field goals: 1987-88, 0-for-1.

Personal fouls/disqualifications: 1986-87, 14/0. 1987-88, 14/0. 1988-89, 17/2. 1989-90, 60/2. 1990-91, 53/1. 1991-92, 76/1. 1992-93, 12/0. Totals, 246/6.

NBA ALL-STAR GAME RECORD

Season	Team	Min.	FGM	FGA	Pct.	FTM	FTA	Pct.	Off.	Def.	Tot.	Ast.	PF	Dq.	St.	Blk.	TO	Pts.
1989	—Portland	7	2	5	.400	1	2	.500	1	0	1	0	2	0	0	0	0	5
1991	—Portland	19	2	3	.667	2	2	1.000	2	2	4	0	3	0	1	0	2	6
	Totals	26	4	8	.500	3	4	.750	3	2	5	0	5	0	1	0	2	11

D

DUDLEY, CHRIS   C   TRAIL BLAZERS

PERSONAL: Born February 22, 1965, in Stamford, Conn. ... 6-11/240. ... Full name: Christen Guilford Dudley.

HIGH SCHOOL: Torrey Pines (Encinitas, Calif.).

COLLEGE: Yale.

TRANSACTIONS/CAREER NOTES: Selected by Cleveland Cavaliers in fourth round (75th pick overall) of 1987 NBA Draft. ... Traded by Cavaliers to New Jersey Nets for 1991 and 1993 second-round draft choices (February 21, 1990). ... Signed as unrestricted free agent by Portland Trail Blazers (August 3, 1993). ... Contract disallowed by NBA (August 5, 1993); contract upheld by NBA special master (September 2, 1993).

COLLEGIATE RECORD

Season Team	G	Min.	FGM	FGA	Pct.	FTM	FTA	Pct.	Reb.	Ast.	Pts.	RPG	APG	PPG
83-84—Yale	26	498	45	97	.464	28	60	.467	132	10	118	5.1	0.4	4.5
84-85—Yale	26	795	131	294	.446	65	122	.533	266	22	327	10.2	0.8	12.6
85-86—Yale	26	756	171	317	.539	80	166	.482	256	27	422	9.8	1.0	16.2
86-87—Yale	24	749	165	290	.569	96	177	.542	320	14	426	13.3	0.6	17.8
Totals	102	2798	512	998	.513	269	525	.512	974	73	1293	9.5	0.7	12.7

HONORS: Citizenship Award (1996).

NBA REGULAR-SEASON RECORD

Season Team	G	Min.	FGM	FGA	Pct.	FTM	FTA	Pct.	Off.	Def.	Tot.	Ast.	St.	Blk.	TO	Pts.	RPG	APG	PPG
87-88—Cleveland	55	513	65	137	.474	40	71	.563	74	70	144	23	13	19	31	170	2.6	0.4	3.1
88-89—Cleveland	61	544	73	168	.435	39	107	.364	72	85	157	21	9	23	44	185	2.6	0.3	3.0
89-90—Clev.-N.J.	64	1356	146	355	.411	58	182	.319	174	249	423	39	41	72	84	350	6.6	0.6	5.5
90-91—New Jersey	61	1560	170	417	.408	94	176	.534	229	282	511	37	39	153	80	434	8.4	0.6	7.1
91-92—New Jersey	82	1902	190	472	.403	80	171	.468	343	396	739	58	38	179	79	460	9.0	0.7	5.6
92-93—New Jersey	71	1398	94	266	.353	57	110	.518	215	298	513	16	17	103	54	245	7.2	0.2	3.5
93-94—Portland	6	86	6	25	.240	2	4	.500	16	8	24	5	4	3	2	14	4.0	0.8	2.3
94-95—Portland	82	2245	181	446	.406	85	183	.464	325	439	764	34	43	126	81	447	9.3	0.4	5.5
95-96—Portland	80	1924	162	358	.453	80	157	.510	239	481	720	37	41	100	79	404	9.0	0.5	5.1
Totals	562	11528	1087	2644	.411	535	1161	.461	1687	2308	3995	270	245	778	534	2709	7.1	0.5	4.8

Three-point field goals: 1988-89, 0-for-1. 1994-95, 0-for-1. 1995-96, 0-for-1. Totals, 0-for-3.

Personal fouls/disqualifications: 1987-88, 87/2. 1988-89, 82/0. 1989-90, 164/2. 1990-91, 217/6. 1991-92, 275/5. 1992-93, 195/5. 1993-94, 18/0. 1994-95, 286/6. 1995-96, 251/4. Totals, 1575/30.

NBA PLAYOFF RECORD

Season Team	G	Min.	FGM	FGA	Pct.	FTM	FTA	Pct.	Off.	Def.	Tot.	Ast.	St.	Blk.	TO	Pts.	RPG	APG	PPG
87-88—Cleveland	4	24	2	4	.500	1	2	.500	4	2	6	2	0	0	1	5	1.5	0.5	1.3
88-89—Cleveland	1	4	0	1	.000	0	0	...	0	0	0	0	0	0	1	0	0.0	0.0	0.0

Season Team	G	Min.	FGM	FGA	Pct.	FTM	FTA	Pct.	Off.	Def.	Tot.	Ast.	St.	Blk.	TO	Pts.	RPG	APG	PPG
91-92—New Jersey.....	4	77	5	14	.357	4	8	.500	13	12	25	3	2	10	1	14	6.3	0.8	3.5
93-94—Portland.........	4	81	4	10	.400	1	2	.500	5	10	15	0	6	0	1	9	3.8	0.0	2.3
94-95—Portland.........	3	59	2	3	.667	3	8	.375	6	9	15	1	0	1	3	7	5.0	0.3	2.3
95-96—Portland.........	5	92	5	13	.385	4	6	.667	9	18	27	1	2	2	4	14	5.4	0.2	2.8
Totals	21	337	18	45	.400	13	26	.500	37	51	88	7	10	13	11	49	4.2	0.3	2.3

Personal fouls/disqualifications: 1987-88, 3/0. 1988-89, 1/0. 1991-92, 14/1. 1993-94, 16/0. 1994-95, 8/0. 1995-96, 18/0. Totals, 60/1.

DUMARS, JOE   G   PISTONS

PERSONAL: Born May 24, 1963, in Shreveport, La. ... 6-3/195. ... Full name: Joe Dumars III.
HIGH SCHOOL: Natchitoches (La.) Central.
COLLEGE: McNeese State.
TRANSACTIONS/CAREER NOTES: Selected by Detroit Pistons in first round (18th pick overall) of 1985 NBA Draft.
MISCELLANEOUS: Member of NBA championship teams (1989, 1990).

COLLEGIATE RECORD

NOTES: The Sporting News All-America second team (1985).

Season Team	G	Min.	FGM	FGA	Pct.	FTM	FTA	Pct.	Reb.	Ast.	Pts.	RPG	APG	PPG
81-82—McNeese State	29	...	206	464	.444	115	160	.719	64	80	527	2.2	2.8	18.2
82-83—McNeese State	29	...	212	487	.435	140	197	.711	128	64	569	4.4	2.2	19.6
83-84—McNeese State	31	...	276	586	.471	267	324	.824	164	80	819	5.3	2.6	26.4
84-85—McNeese State	27	...	248	501	.495	201	236	.852	132	106	697	4.9	3.9	25.8
Totals	116	...	942	2038	.462	723	917	.788	488	330	2612	4.2	2.8	22.5

Three-point field goals: 1982-83, 5-for-8 (.625).

NBA REGULAR-SEASON RECORD

HONORS: Citizenship Award (1994). ... All-NBA second team (1993). ... All-NBA third team (1990, 1991). ... NBA All-Defensive first team (1989, 1990, 1992, 1993). ... NBA All-Defensive second team (1991). ... NBA All-Rookie team (1986).

Season Team	G	Min.	FGM	FGA	Pct.	FTM	FTA	Pct.	Off.	Def.	Tot.	Ast.	St.	Blk.	TO	Pts.	RPG	APG	PPG
85-86—Detroit	82	1957	287	597	.481	190	238	.798	60	59	119	390	66	11	158	769	1.5	4.8	9.4
86-87—Detroit	79	2439	369	749	.493	184	246	.748	50	117	167	352	83	5	171	931	2.1	4.5	11.8
87-88—Detroit	82	2732	453	960	.472	251	308	.815	63	137	200	387	87	15	172	1161	2.4	4.7	14.2
88-89—Detroit	69	2408	456	903	.505	260	306	.850	57	115	172	390	63	5	178	1186	2.5	5.7	17.2
89-90—Detroit	75	2578	508	1058	.480	297	330	.900	60	152	212	368	63	2	145	1335	2.8	4.9	17.8
90-91—Detroit	80	3046	622	1292	.481	371	417	.890	62	125	187	443	89	7	189	1629	2.3	5.5	20.4
91-92—Detroit	82	3192	587	1311	.448	412	475	.867	82	106	188	375	71	12	193	1635	2.3	4.6	19.9
92-93—Detroit	77	3094	677	1454	.466	343	397	.864	63	85	148	308	78	7	138	1809	1.9	4.0	23.5
93-94—Detroit	69	2591	505	1118	.452	276	330	.836	35	116	151	261	63	4	159	1410	2.2	3.8	20.4
94-95—Detroit	67	2544	417	970	.430	277	344	.805	47	111	158	368	72	7	219	1214	2.4	5.5	18.1
95-96—Detroit	67	2193	255	598	.426	162	197	.822	28	110	138	265	43	3	97	793	2.1	4.0	11.8
Totals	829	28774	5136	11010	.466	3023	3588	.843	607	1233	1840	3907	778	78	1819	13872	2.2	4.7	16.7

Three-point field goals: 1985-86, 5-for-16 (.313). 1986-87, 9-for-22 (.409). 1987-88, 4-for-19 (.211). 1988-89, 14-for-29 (.483). 1989-90, 22-for-55 (.400). 1990-91, 14-for-45 (.311). 1991-92, 49-for-120 (.408). 1992-93, 112-for-299 (.375). 1993-94, 124-for-320 (.388). 1994-95, 103-for-338 (.305). 1995-96, 121-for-298 (.406). Totals, 577-for-1561 (.370).

Personal fouls/disqualifications: 1985-86, 200/1. 1986-87, 194/1. 1987-88, 155/1. 1988-89, 103/1. 1989-90, 129/1. 1990-91, 135/0. 1991-92, 145/0. 1992-93, 141/0. 1993-94, 118/0. 1994-95, 153/0. 1995-96, 106/0. Totals, 1579/5.

NBA PLAYOFF RECORD

NOTES: NBA Finals Most Valuable Player (1989).

Season Team	G	Min.	FGM	FGA	Pct.	FTM	FTA	Pct.	Off.	Def.	Tot.	Ast.	St.	Blk.	TO	Pts.	RPG	APG	PPG
85-86—Detroit	4	147	25	41	.610	10	15	.667	6	7	13	25	4	0	7	60	3.3	6.3	15.0
86-87—Detroit	15	473	78	145	.538	32	41	.780	8	11	19	72	12	1	27	190	1.3	4.8	12.7
87-88—Detroit	23	804	113	247	.457	56	63	.889	18	32	50	112	13	2	40	284	2.2	4.9	12.3
88-89—Detroit	17	620	106	233	.455	87	101	.861	11	33	44	96	12	1	31	300	2.6	5.6	17.6
89-90—Detroit	20	754	130	284	.458	99	113	.876	18	26	44	95	22	0	54	364	2.2	4.8	18.2
90-91—Detroit	15	588	105	245	.429	82	97	.845	21	29	50	62	16	1	17	309	3.3	4.1	20.6
91-92—Detroit	5	221	32	68	.471	15	19	.789	5	3	8	16	5	1	7	84	1.6	3.2	16.8
95-96—Detroit	3	123	16	35	.457	4	4	1.000	5	3	8	11	0	0	7	41	4.3	3.7	13.7
Totals	102	3730	605	1298	.466	385	453	.850	92	149	241	489	84	6	190	1632	2.4	4.8	16.0

Three-point field goals: 1986-87, 2-for-3 (.667). 1987-88, 2-for-6 (.333). 1988-89, 1-for-12 (.083). 1989-90, 5-for-19 (.263). 1990-91, 17-for-42 (.405). 1991-92, 5-for-10 (.500). 1995-96, 5-for-14 (.357). Totals, 37-for-106 (.349).

Personal fouls/disqualifications: 1985-86, 16/0. 1986-87, 26/0. 1987-88, 50/1. 1988-89, 31/0. 1989-90, 37/0. 1990-91, 33/1. 1991-92, 11/0. 1995-96, 5/0. Totals, 209/2.

NBA ALL-STAR GAME RECORD

Season	Team	Min.	FGM	FGA	Pct.	FTM	FTA	Pct.	Off.	Def.	Tot.	Ast.	PF	Dq.	St.	Blk.	TO	Pts.
1990	—Detroit	18	3	4	.750	1	2	.500	0	1	1	5	0	0	0	0	3	9
1991	—Detroit	15	1	4	.250	0	0	...	1	1	2	1	1	0	0	0	4	2
1992	—Detroit	17	2	7	.286	0	0	...	0	1	1	3	0	0	0	0	2	4
1993	—Detroit	17	2	8	.250	0	0	...	0	2	2	4	1	0	0	0	1	5
1995	—Detroit	21	5	8	.625	0	0	...	0	0	0	6	1	0	1	0	1	11
Totals		88	13	31	.419	1	2	.500	1	5	6	19	3	0	1	0	11	31

Three-point field goals: 1990, 2-for-2. 1991, 0-for-1. 1992, 0-for-2. 1993, 1-for-4 (.250). 1995, 1-for-2 (.500). Totals, 4-for-11 (.364).

DUMAS, RICHARD   F

PERSONAL: Born May 19, 1969, in Tulsa, Okla. ... 6-7/210. ... Full name: Richard Wayne Dumas. ... Name pronounced do-MAAS. ... Son of Richard Dumas, guard with Houston Mavericks of American Basketball Association (1968-69).
HIGH SCHOOL: Booker T. Washington (Tulsa, Okla.).
COLLEGE: Oklahoma State.
TRANSACTIONS/CAREER NOTES: Played in Israel after junior season (1990-91). ... Selected by Phoenix Suns in second round (46th pick overall) of 1991 NBA Draft. ... Suspended by NBA for failing random drug test (October 31, 1991-December 16, 1992). ... Played in Continental Basketball Association with Oklahoma City Cavalry (1991-92). ... Played in United States Basketball League with Miami Tropics (1992). ... Signed as free agent by Suns (December 16, 1992). ... Suspended by NBA for violating league drug policy (September 15, 1993). ... Reinstated by NBA (March 14, 1995). ... Waived by Suns (May 18, 1995). ... Signed as free agent by Philadelphia 76ers (September 21, 1995). ... Rights renounced by 76ers (July 11, 1996).

COLLEGIATE RECORD

Season Team	G	Min.	FGM	FGA	Pct.	FTM	FTA	Pct.	Reb.	Ast.	Pts.	RPG	APG	PPG
87-88—Oklahoma State	30	937	203	372	.546	115	154	.747	193	49	521	6.4	1.6	17.4
88-89—Oklahoma State	28	850	184	411	.448	66	107	.617	197	73	439	7.0	2.6	15.7
89-90—Oklahoma State	12	276	62	113	.549	28	44	.636	65	27	152	5.4	2.3	12.7
Totals	70	2063	449	896	.501	209	305	.685	455	149	1112	6.5	2.1	15.9

Three-point field goals: 1987-88, 0-for-2. 1988-89, 5-for-21 (.238). 1989-90, 0-for-3. Totals, 5-for-26 (.192).

ISRAELI LEAGUE RECORD

Season Team	G	Min.	FGM	FGA	Pct.	FTM	FTA	Pct.	Reb.	Ast.	Pts.	RPG	APG	PPG
90-91—Hapoel Holon	20	...	173	297	.583	72	106	.679	159	37	418	8.0	1.9	20.9

CBA REGULAR-SEASON RECORD

Season Team	G	Min.	FGM	FGA	Pct.	FTM	FTA	Pct.	Reb.	Ast.	Pts.	RPG	APG	PPG
91-92—Oklahoma City	9	349	102	180	.567	60	75	.800	78	24	264	8.7	2.7	29.3

NBA REGULAR-SEASON RECORD

HONORS: NBA All-Rookie second team (1993).

Season Team	G	Min.	FGM	FGA	Pct.	FTM	FTA	Pct.	Off.	Def.	Tot.	Ast.	St.	Blk.	TO	Pts.	RPG	APG	PPG
92-93—Phoenix	48	1320	302	576	.524	152	215	.707	100	123	223	60	85	39	92	757	4.6	1.3	15.8
93-94—Phoenix						Did not play—suspended.													
94-95—Phoenix	15	167	37	73	.507	8	16	.500	18	11	29	7	10	2	9	82	1.9	0.5	5.5
95-96—Philadelphia	39	739	95	203	.468	49	70	.700	42	57	99	44	42	6	49	241	2.5	1.1	6.2
Totals	102	2226	434	852	.509	209	301	.694	160	191	351	111	137	47	150	1080	3.4	1.1	10.6

Three-point field goals: 1992-93, 1-for-3 (.333). 1994-95, 0-for-1. 1995-96, 2-for-9 (.222). Totals, 3-for-13 (.231).
Personal fouls/disqualifications: 1992-93, 127/0. 1994-95, 21/0. 1995-96, 79/1. Totals, 228/1.

NBA PLAYOFF RECORD

Season Team	G	Min.	FGM	FGA	Pct.	FTM	FTA	Pct.	Off.	Def.	Tot.	Ast.	St.	Blk.	TO	Pts.	RPG	APG	PPG
92-93—Phoenix	23	499	107	204	.525	37	49	.755	36	29	65	24	21	13	27	251	2.8	1.0	10.9

Three-point field goals: 1992-93, 0-for-2.
Personal fouls/disqualifications: 1992-93, 52/0.

DUMAS, TONY   G   MAVERICKS

PERSONAL: Born August 25, 1972, in Chicago. ... 6-6/190.
HIGH SCHOOL: Millington (Tenn.).
COLLEGE: Missouri-Kansas City.
TRANSACTIONS/CAREER NOTES: Selected by Dallas Mavericks in first round (19th pick overall) of 1994 NBA Draft.

COLLEGIATE RECORD

Season Team	G	Min.	FGM	FGA	Pct.	FTM	FTA	Pct.	Reb.	Ast.	Pts.	RPG	APG	PPG
90-91—Missouri-K.C.	28	857	177	355	.499	89	118	.754	134	87	462	4.8	3.1	16.5
91-92—Missouri-K.C.	28	1030	200	384	.521	162	209	.775	128	72	601	4.6	2.6	21.5
92-93—Missouri-K.C.	27	1002	238	487	.489	122	170	.718	148	98	643	5.5	3.6	23.8
93-94—Missouri-K.C.	29	1113	229	544	.421	221	292	.757	166	87	753	5.7	3.0	26.0
Totals	112	4002	844	1770	.477	594	789	.753	576	344	2459	5.1	3.1	22.0

Three-point field goals: 1990-91, 19-for-68 (.279). 1991-92, 39-for-78 (.500). 1992-93, 45-for-127 (.354). 1993-94, 74-for-205 (.361). Totals, 177-for-478 (.370).

NBA REGULAR-SEASON RECORD

Season Team	G	Min.	FGM	FGA	Pct.	FTM	FTA	Pct.	Off.	Def.	Tot.	Ast.	St.	Blk.	TO	Pts.	RPG	APG	PPG
94-95—Dallas	58	613	96	250	.384	50	77	.649	32	30	62	57	13	4	50	264	1.1	1.0	4.6
95-96—Dallas	67	1284	274	655	.418	154	257	.599	58	57	115	99	42	13	77	776	1.7	1.5	11.6
Totals	125	1897	370	905	.409	204	334	.611	90	87	177	156	55	17	127	1040	1.4	1.2	8.3

Three-point field goals: 1994-95, 22-for-73 (.301). 1995-96, 74-for-207 (.357). Totals, 96-for-280 (.343).
Personal fouls/disqualifications: 1994-95, 78/0. 1995-96, 128/0. Totals, 206/0.

EACKLES, LEDELL   G

PERSONAL: Born November 24, 1966, in Baton Rouge, La. ... 6-5/231. ... Name pronounced LEE-dell ECK-els.
HIGH SCHOOL: Broadmoor (Baton Rouge, La.).
JUNIOR COLLEGE: San Jacinto (Texas).
COLLEGE: New Orleans.
TRANSACTIONS/CAREER NOTES: Selected by Washington Bullets in second round (36th pick overall) of 1988 NBA Draft. ... Played in Continental Basketball Association with Rapid City Thrillers in playoffs (1992-93). ... Rights renounced by Bullets (June 24, 1993). ... Signed as free agent by Indiana Pacers (October 8, 1993). ... Waived by Pacers (March 7, 1994). ... Signed as free agent by Miami Heat (September 30, 1994). ... Signed by Bullets for remainder of season (December 11, 1995).

COLLEGIATE RECORD

Season Team	G	Min.	FGM	FGA	Pct.	FTM	FTA	Pct.	Reb.	Ast.	Pts.	RPG	APG	PPG
84-85—San Jacinto College	29	...	...	...	...	...	...	...	156	...	552	5.4	...	19.0
85-86—San Jacinto College	37	...	417	715	.583	173	229	.755	238	105	1007	6.4	2.8	27.2
86-87—New Orleans	28	902	239	554	.431	84	116	.724	114	57	632	4.1	2.0	22.6
87-88—New Orleans	31	982	260	512	.508	186	232	.802	153	39	726	4.9	1.3	23.4
Junior college totals	66	...	...	...	...	...	...	...	394	...	1559	6.0	...	23.6
4-year-college totals	59	1884	499	1066	.468	270	348	.776	267	96	1358	4.5	1.6	23.0

Three-point field goals: 1986-87, 70-for-172 (.407). 1987-88, 20-for-84 (.238). Totals, 90-for-256 (.352).

NBA REGULAR-SEASON RECORD

Season Team	G	Min.	FGM	FGA	Pct.	FTM	FTA	Pct.	Off.	Def.	Tot.	Ast.	St.	Blk.	TO	Pts.	RPG	APG	PPG
88-89—Washington	80	1459	318	732	.434	272	346	.786	100	80	180	123	41	5	128	917	2.3	1.5	11.5
89-90—Washington	78	1696	413	940	.439	210	280	.750	74	101	175	182	50	4	143	1055	2.2	2.3	13.5
90-91—Washington	67	1616	345	762	.453	164	222	.739	47	81	128	136	47	10	115	868	1.9	2.0	13.0
91-92—Washington	65	1463	355	759	.468	139	187	.743	39	139	178	125	47	7	75	856	2.7	1.9	13.2
93-94—Indiana								Did not play.											
94-95—Miami	54	898	143	326	.439	91	126	.722	33	62	95	72	19	2	53	395	1.8	1.3	7.3
95-96—Washington	55	1238	161	377	.427	98	118	.831	44	104	148	86	28	3	57	442	2.7	1.6	8.6
Totals	399	8370	1735	3896	.445	974	1279	.762	337	567	904	724	232	31	571	4565	2.3	1.8	11.4

Three-point field goals: 1988-89, 9-for-40 (.225). 1989-90, 19-for-59 (.322). 1990-91, 14-for-59 (.237). 1991-92, 7-for-35 (.200). 1994-95, 18-for-41 (.439). 1995-96, 54-for-128 (.422). Totals, 121-for-362 (.334).
Personal fouls/disqualifications: 1988-89, 156/1. 1989-90, 157/0. 1990-91, 121/0. 1991-92, 145/1. 1994-95, 88/0. 1995-96, 84/1. Totals, 751/3.

EARL, ACIE   C   RAPTORS

PERSONAL: Born June 23, 1970, in Peoria, Ill. ... 6-10/240. ... Full name: Acie Boyd Earl. ... Name pronounced AY-see.
HIGH SCHOOL: Moline (Ill.).
COLLEGE: Iowa.
TRANSACTIONS/CAREER NOTES: Selected by Boston Celtics in first round (19th pick overall) of 1993 NBA Draft. ... Selected by Toronto Raptors from Celtics in NBA expansion draft (June 24, 1995).

COLLEGIATE RECORD

Season Team	G	Min.	FGM	FGA	Pct.	FTM	FTA	Pct.	Reb.	Ast.	Pts.	RPG	APG	PPG
88-89—Iowa					Did not play—redshirted.									
89-90—Iowa	22	352	48	109	.440	34	46	.739	78	24	131	3.5	1.1	6.0
90-91—Iowa	32	920	179	356	.503	161	242	.665	213	48	520	6.7	1.5	16.3
91-92—Iowa	30	940	212	398	.533	162	243	.667	234	27	586	7.8	0.9	19.5
92-93—Iowa	32	992	203	402	.505	136	194	.701	286	40	542	8.9	1.3	16.9
Totals	116	3204	642	1265	.508	493	725	.680	811	139	1779	7.0	1.2	15.3

Three-point field goals: 1989-90, 1-for-3 (.333). 1990-91, 1-for-1. 1992-93, 0-for-2. Totals, 2-for-6 (.333).

NBA REGULAR-SEASON RECORD

Season Team	G	Min.	FGM	FGA	Pct.	FTM	FTA	Pct.	Off.	Def.	Tot.	Ast.	St.	Blk.	TO	Pts.	RPG	APG	PPG
93-94—Boston	74	1149	151	372	.406	108	160	.675	85	162	247	12	24	53	72	410	3.3	0.2	5.5
94-95—Boston	30	208	26	68	.382	14	29	.483	19	26	45	2	6	8	14	66	1.5	0.1	2.2
95-96—Toronto	42	655	117	276	.424	82	114	.719	51	78	129	27	18	37	49	316	3.1	0.6	7.5
Totals	146	2012	294	716	.411	204	303	.673	155	266	421	41	48	98	135	792	2.9	0.3	5.4

Three-point field goals: 1993-94, 0-for-1. 1995-96, 0-for-3. Totals, 0-for-4.
Personal fouls/disqualifications: 1993-94, 178/5. 1994-95, 39/0. 1995-96, 73/0. Totals, 290/5.

NBA PLAYOFF RECORD

Season Team	G	Min.	FGM	FGA	Pct.	FTM	FTA	Pct.	Off.	Def.	Tot.	Ast.	St.	Blk.	TO	Pts.	RPG	APG	PPG
94-95—Boston	1	10	1	3	.333	0	2	.000	1	1	2	0	0	1	0	2	2.0	0.0	2.0

Personal fouls/disqualifications: 1994-95, 4/0.

EDNEY, TYUS   G   KINGS

PERSONAL: Born February 14, 1973, in Gardena, Calif. ... 5-10/152. ... Full name: Tyus Dwayne Edney. ... Name pronounced TIE-us ED-knee.
HIGH SCHOOL: Long Beach (Calif.) Poly.
COLLEGE: UCLA.
TRANSACTIONS/CAREER NOTES: Selected by Sacramento Kings in second round (47th pick overall) of 1995 NBA Draft.

E

COLLEGIATE RECORD

NOTES: Frances Pomeroy Naismith Award winner (1995). ... Member of NCAA Division I championship team (1995).

Season Team	G	Min.	FGM	FGA	Pct.	FTM	FTA	Pct.	Reb.	Ast.	Pts.	RPG	APG	PPG
												AVERAGES		
91-92—UCLA	32	586	59	125	.472	47	59	.797	67	88	179	2.1	2.8	5.6
92-93—UCLA	33	1207	142	294	.483	132	157	.841	117	186	450	3.5	5.6	13.6
93-94—UCLA	28	891	137	294	.466	132	161	.820	96	162	430	3.4	5.8	15.4
94-95—UCLA	32	976	146	294	.497	139	182	.764	99	216	456	3.1	6.8	14.3
Totals	125	3660	484	1007	.481	450	559	.805	379	652	1515	3.0	5.2	12.1

Three-point field goals: 1991-92, 14-for-41 (.341). 1992-93, 34-for-82 (.415). 1993-94, 24-for-64 (.375). 1994-95, 25-for-66 (.379). Totals, 97-for-253 (.383).

NBA REGULAR-SEASON RECORD

HONORS: NBA All-Rookie second team (1996).

Season Team	G	Min.	FGM	FGA	Pct.	FTM	FTA	Pct.	Off.	Def.	Tot.	Ast.	St.	Blk.	TO	Pts.	RPG	APG	PPG
									REBOUNDS								AVERAGES		
95-96—Sacramento	80	2481	305	740	.412	197	252	.782	63	138	201	491	89	3	192	860	2.5	6.1	10.8

Three-point field goals: 1995-96, 53-for-144 (.368).
Personal fouls/disqualifications: 1995-96, 203/2.

NBA PLAYOFF RECORD

Season Team	G	Min.	FGM	FGA	Pct.	FTM	FTA	Pct.	Off.	Def.	Tot.	Ast.	St.	Blk.	TO	Pts.	RPG	APG	PPG
									REBOUNDS								AVERAGES		
95-96—Sacramento	4	121	18	42	.429	10	12	.833	2	10	12	11	8	0	9	48	3.0	2.8	12.0

Three-point field goals: 1995-96, 2-for-8 (.250).
Personal fouls/disqualifications: 1995-96, 11/1.

EDWARDS, BLUE   G   GRIZZLIES

PERSONAL: Born October 31, 1965, in Washington, D.C. ... 6-4/228. ... Full name: Theodore Edwards.
HIGH SCHOOL: Greene Central (Snow Hill, N.C.).
JUNIOR COLLEGE: Louisburg (N.C.).
COLLEGE: East Carolina.
TRANSACTIONS/CAREER NOTES: Selected by Utah Jazz in first round (21st pick overall) of 1989 NBA Draft. ... Traded by Jazz with G Eric Murdock and 1992 first-round draft choice to Milwaukee Bucks for G Jay Humphries and F Larry Krystkowiak (June 24, 1992). ... Traded by Bucks with F Derek Strong to Boston Celtics for F Ed Pinckney and draft rights to C Andrei Fetisov (June 29, 1994). ... Traded by Celtics to Jazz for G Jay Humphries and 1995 second-round draft choice (February 3, 1995). ... Selected by Vancouver Grizzlies from Jazz in NBA expansion draft (June 24, 1995).
MISCELLANEOUS: Vancouver Grizzlies all-time leading scorer with 1,043 points (1995-96).

COLLEGIATE RECORD

Season Team	G	Min.	FGM	FGA	Pct.	FTM	FTA	Pct.	Reb.	Ast.	Pts.	RPG	APG	PPG
												AVERAGES		
84-85—Louisburg College	29	...	218	343	.636	80	124	.645	177	30	516	6.1	1.0	17.8
85-86—Louisburg College	31	...	268	407	.658	154	220	.700	187	73	690	6.0	2.4	22.3
86-87—East Carolina	28	876	169	301	.561	65	88	.739	158	52	404	5.6	1.9	14.4
87-88—East Carolina					Did not play—disciplinary reasons.									
88-89—East Carolina	29	987	297	539	.551	154	204	.755	201	92	773	6.9	3.2	26.7
Junior college totals	60	...	486	750	.648	234	344	.680	364	103	1206	6.1	1.7	20.1
4-year-college totals	57	1863	466	840	.555	219	292	.750	359	144	1177	6.3	2.5	20.6

Three-point field goals: 1986-87, 1-for-4 (.250). 1988-89, 25-for-51 (.490). Totals, 26-for-55 (.473).

NBA REGULAR-SEASON RECORD

HONORS: NBA All-Rookie second team (1990).

Season Team	G	Min.	FGM	FGA	Pct.	FTM	FTA	Pct.	Off.	Def.	Tot.	Ast.	St.	Blk.	TO	Pts.	RPG	APG	PPG
									REBOUNDS								AVERAGES		
89-90—Utah	82	1889	286	564	.507	146	203	.719	69	182	251	145	76	36	152	727	3.1	1.8	8.9
90-91—Utah	62	1611	244	464	.526	82	117	.701	51	150	201	108	57	29	105	576	3.2	1.7	9.3
91-92—Utah	81	2283	433	830	.522	113	146	.774	86	212	298	137	81	46	122	1018	3.7	1.7	12.6
92-93—Milwaukee	82	2729	554	1083	.512	237	300	.790	123	259	382	214	129	45	175	1382	4.7	2.6	16.9
93-94—Milwaukee	82	2322	382	800	.478	151	189	.799	104	225	329	171	83	27	146	953	4.0	2.1	11.6
94-95—Boston-Utah	67	1112	181	393	.461	75	90	.833	50	80	130	77	43	16	81	459	1.9	1.1	6.9
95-96—Vancouver	82	2773	401	956	.419	157	208	.755	98	248	346	212	118	46	170	1043	4.2	2.6	12.7
Totals	538	14719	2481	5090	.487	961	1253	.767	581	1356	1937	1064	587	245	951	6158	3.6	2.0	11.4

Three-point field goals: 1989-90, 9-for-30 (.300). 1990-91, 6-for-24 (.250). 1991-92, 39-for-103 (.379). 1992-93, 37-for-106 (.349). 1993-94, 38-for-106 (.358). 1994-95, 22-for-75 (.293). 1995-96, 84-for-245 (.343). Totals, 235-for-689 (.341).
Personal fouls/disqualifications: 1989-90, 280/2. 1990-91, 203/4. 1991-92, 236/1. 1992-93, 242/1. 1993-94, 235/1. 1994-95, 143/1. 1995-96, 243/1. Totals, 1582/11.

NBA PLAYOFF RECORD

Season Team	G	Min.	FGM	FGA	Pct.	FTM	FTA	Pct.	Off.	Def.	Tot.	Ast.	St.	Blk.	TO	Pts.	RPG	APG	PPG
									REBOUNDS								AVERAGES		
89-90—Utah	5	94	14	26	.538	7	8	.875	8	10	18	8	7	2	12	36	3.6	1.6	7.2
90-91—Utah	9	241	37	77	.481	16	20	.800	7	21	28	16	8	1	15	91	3.1	1.8	10.1
91-92—Utah	16	354	52	111	.468	23	32	.719	22	29	51	17	23	3	25	129	3.2	1.1	8.1
94-95—Utah	4	33	4	12	.333	0	0	...	1	5	6	3	2	0	3	9	1.5	0.8	2.3
Totals	34	722	107	226	.473	46	60	.767	38	65	103	44	40	6	55	265	3.0	1.3	7.8

Three-point field goals: 1989-90, 1-for-3 (.333). 1990-91, 1-for-2 (.500). 1991-92, 2-for-10 (.200). 1994-95, 1-for-1. Totals, 5-for-16 (.313).
Personal fouls/disqualifications: 1989-90, 16/0. 1990-91, 37/0. 1991-92, 45/0. 1994-95, 3/0. Totals, 101/0.

E

EDWARDS, DOUG   F   GRIZZLIES

PERSONAL: Born January 21, 1971, in Miami. ... 6-7/235. ... Full name: Douglas Edwards.
HIGH SCHOOL: Senior (Miami).
COLLEGE: Florida State.
TRANSACTIONS/CAREER NOTES: Selected by Atlanta Hawks in first round (15th pick overall) of 1993 NBA Draft. ... Selected by Vancouver Grizzlies from Hawks in NBA expansion draft (June 24, 1995).

COLLEGIATE RECORD

Season Team	G	Min.	FGM	FGA	Pct.	FTM	FTA	Pct.	Reb.	Ast.	Pts.	RPG	APG	PPG
89-90—Florida State						Did not play—ineligible.								
90-91—Florida State	32	1046	200	385	.519	112	158	.709	227	61	524	7.1	1.9	16.4
91-92—Florida State	30	1076	197	385	.512	106	142	.746	271	80	512	9.0	2.7	17.1
92-93—Florida State	31	1085	224	424	.528	114	158	.722	290	91	568	9.4	2.9	18.3
Totals	93	3207	621	1194	.520	332	458	.725	788	232	1604	8.5	2.5	17.2

Three-point field goals: 1990-91, 12-for-36 (.333). 1991-92, 12-for-53 (.226). 1992-93, 6-for-25 (.240). Totals, 30-for-114 (.263).

NBA REGULAR-SEASON RECORD

Season Team	G	Min.	FGM	FGA	Pct.	FTM	FTA	Pct.	Off.	Def.	Tot.	Ast.	St.	Blk.	TO	Pts.	RPG	APG	PPG
93-94—Atlanta	16	107	17	49	.347	9	16	.563	7	11	18	8	2	5	6	43	1.1	0.5	2.7
94-95—Atlanta	38	212	22	48	.458	23	32	.719	19	29	48	13	5	4	22	67	1.3	0.3	1.8
95-96—Vancouver	31	519	32	91	.352	29	38	.763	35	52	87	39	10	18	29	93	2.8	1.3	3.0
Totals	85	838	71	188	.378	61	86	.709	61	92	153	60	17	27	57	203	1.8	0.7	2.4

Three-point field goals: 1993-94, 0-for-1. 1994-95, 0-for-1. 1995-96, 0-for-4. Totals, 0-for-6.
Personal fouls/disqualifications: 1993-94, 9/0. 1994-95, 30/0. 1995-96, 51/2. Totals, 90/2.

NBA PLAYOFF RECORD

Season Team	G	Min.	FGM	FGA	Pct.	FTM	FTA	Pct.	Off.	Def.	Tot.	Ast.	St.	Blk.	TO	Pts.	RPG	APG	PPG
93-94—Atlanta	1	3	0	0	...	0	0	...	0	0	0	0	0	1	0	0	0.0	0.0	0.0

EDWARDS, JAMES   C   BULLS

PERSONAL: Born November 22, 1955, in Seattle. ... 7-1/252. ... Full name: James Franklin Edwards.
HIGH SCHOOL: Roosevelt (Seattle).
COLLEGE: Washington.
TRANSACTIONS/CAREER NOTES: Selected by Los Angeles Lakers in third round (46th pick overall) of 1977 NBA Draft. ... Traded by Lakers with G Earl Tatum and cash to Indiana Pacers for F Adrian Dantley and C/F Dave Robisch (December 13, 1977). ... Signed as veteran free agent by Cleveland Cavaliers (May 25, 1981); Pacers waived their right of first refusal in exchange for 1981 and 1982 second-round draft choices (June 8, 1981). ... Traded by Cavaliers to Phoenix Suns for F Jeff Cook, 1983 third-round draft choice and cash (February 7, 1983). ... Traded by Suns to Detroit Pistons for C Ron Moore and 1991 second-round draft choice (August 13, 1991). ... Traded by Pistons to Los Angeles Clippers for G/F Jeff Martin and 1995 second-round draft choice (August 13, 1991). ... Signed as unrestricted free agent by Lakers (August 13, 1992). ... Signed as unrestricted free agent by Portland Trail Blazers (September 19, 1994). ... Rights renounced by Trail Blazers (September 29, 1995). ... Signed as free agent by Chicago Bulls (October 26, 1995).
MISCELLANEOUS: Member of NBA championship teams (1989, 1990, 1996).

COLLEGIATE RECORD

Season Team	G	Min.	FGM	FGA	Pct.	FTM	FTA	Pct.	Reb.	Ast.	Pts.	RPG	APG	PPG
73-74—Washington	25	...	68	160	.425	34	62	.548	115	...	170	4.6	...	6.8
74-75—Washington	26	575	125	264	.473	70	129	.543	198	...	320	7.6	...	12.3
75-76—Washington	28	811	205	392	.523	83	137	.606	200	38	493	7.1	1.4	17.6
76-77—Washington	27	940	223	404	.552	119	184	.647	282	25	565	10.4	0.9	20.9
Totals	106	...	621	1220	.509	306	512	.598	795	...	1548	7.5	...	14.6

NOTES: Tied for NBA lead with 12 disqualifications (1980).

NBA REGULAR-SEASON RECORD

Season Team	G	Min.	FGM	FGA	Pct.	FTM	FTA	Pct.	Off.	Def.	Tot.	Ast.	St.	Blk.	TO	Pts.	RPG	APG	PPG
77-78—L.A.-Ind.	83	2405	495	1093	.453	272	421	.646	197	418	615	85	53	78	169	1262	7.4	1.0	15.2
78-79—Indiana	82	2546	534	1065	.501	298	441	.676	179	514	693	92	60	109	162	1366	8.5	1.1	16.7
79-80—Indiana	82	2314	528	1032	.512	231	339	.681	179	399	578	127	55	104	131	1287	7.0	1.5	15.7
80-81—Indiana	81	2375	511	1004	.509	244	347	.703	191	380	571	212	32	128	164	1266	7.0	2.6	15.6
81-82—Cleveland	77	2539	528	1033	.511	232	339	.684	189	392	581	123	24	117	162	1288	7.5	1.6	16.7
82-83—Clev.-Phoe.	31	667	128	263	.487	69	108	.639	56	99	155	40	12	19	49	325	5.0	1.3	10.5
83-84—Phoenix	72	1897	438	817	.536	183	254	.720	108	240	348	184	23	30	140	1059	4.8	2.6	14.7
84-85—Phoenix	70	1787	384	766	.501	276	370	.746	95	292	387	153	26	52	162	1044	5.5	2.2	14.9
85-86—Phoenix	52	1314	318	587	.542	212	302	.702	79	222	301	74	23	29	128	848	5.8	1.4	16.3
86-87—Phoenix	14	304	57	110	.518	54	70	.771	20	40	60	19	6	7	15	168	4.3	1.4	12.0
87-88—Phoe.-Det.	69	1705	302	643	.470	210	321	.654	119	293	412	78	16	37	130	814	6.0	1.1	11.8
88-89—Detroit	76	1254	211	422	.500	133	194	.686	68	163	231	49	11	31	72	555	3.0	0.6	7.3
89-90—Detroit	82	2283	462	928	.498	265	354	.749	112	233	345	63	23	37	133	1189	4.2	0.8	14.5
90-91—Detroit	72	1903	383	792	.484	215	295	.729	91	186	277	65	12	30	126	982	3.8	0.9	13.6
91-92—L.A. Clippers	72	1437	250	538	.465	198	271	.731	55	147	202	53	24	33	72	698	2.8	0.7	9.7
92-93—L.A. Lakers	52	617	122	270	.452	84	118	.712	30	70	100	41	10	7	51	328	1.9	0.8	6.3
93-94—L.A. Lakers	45	469	78	168	.464	54	79	.684	11	54	65	22	4	3	30	210	1.4	0.5	4.7

E

Season Team	G	Min.	FGM	FGA	Pct.	FTM	FTA	Pct.	Off.	Def.	Tot.	Ast.	St.	Blk.	TO	Pts.	RPG	APG	PPG
									REBOUNDS								**AVERAGES**		
94-95—Portland	28	266	32	83	.386	11	17	.647	10	33	43	8	5	8	14	75	1.5	0.3	2.7
95-96—Chicago	28	274	41	110	.373	16	26	.615	15	25	40	11	1	8	21	98	1.4	0.4	3.5
Totals	1168	28356	5802	11724	.495	3257	4666	.698	1804	4200	6004	1499	420	867	1931	14862	5.1	1.3	12.7

Three-point field goals: 1979-80, 0-for-1. 1980-81, 0-for-3. 1981-82, 0-for-4. 1983-84, 0-for-1. 1984-85, 0-for-3. 1987-88, 0-for-1. 1988-89, 0-for-3. 1989-90, 0-for-3. 1990-91, 1-for-2 (.500). 1991-92, 0-for-1. Totals, 1-for-21 (.048).

Personal fouls/disqualifications: 1977-78, 322/12. 1978-79, 363/16. 1979-80, 324/12. 1980-81, 304/7. 1981-82, 347/17. 1982-83, 110/5. 1983-84, 254/3. 1984-85, 237/5. 1985-86, 200/5. 1986-87, 42/1. 1987-88, 216/2. 1988-89, 226/1. 1989-90, 295/4. 1990-91, 249/4. 1991-92, 236/1. 1992-93, 122/0. 1993-94, 90/0. 1994-95, 44/0. 1995-96, 61/1. Totals, 4042/96.

NBA PLAYOFF RECORD

Season Team	G	Min.	FGM	FGA	Pct.	FTM	FTA	Pct.	Off.	Def.	Tot.	Ast.	St.	Blk.	TO	Pts.	RPG	APG	PPG
									REBOUNDS								**AVERAGES**		
80-81—Indiana	2	56	7	24	.292	0	0	...	4	10	14	5	1	1	4	14	7.0	2.5	7.0
82-83—Phoenix	3	54	11	26	.423	6	6	1.000	6	12	18	4	1	1	5	28	6.0	1.3	9.3
83-84—Phoenix	17	463	93	189	.492	48	68	.706	22	69	91	27	4	11	31	234	5.4	1.6	13.8
87-88—Detroit	22	308	56	110	.509	27	41	.659	23	45	68	11	2	10	10	139	3.1	0.5	6.3
88-89—Detroit	17	317	40	85	.471	40	51	.784	11	25	36	12	1	8	15	120	2.1	0.7	7.1
89-90—Detroit	20	536	114	231	.494	58	96	.604	24	47	71	13	5	11	31	286	3.6	0.7	14.3
90-91—Detroit	15	345	61	150	.407	38	55	.691	15	22	37	9	2	3	24	160	2.5	0.6	10.7
91-92—L.A. Clippers	5	87	10	24	.417	12	19	.632	5	8	13	3	1	1	4	32	2.6	0.6	6.4
92-93—L.A. Lakers	3	14	3	4	.750	0	0	...	0	2	2	0	0	0	1	6	0.7	0.0	2.0
94-95—Portland	1	4	0	1	.000	0	0	...	0	0	0	0	0	0	0	0	0.0	0.0	0.0
95-96—Chicago	6	28	4	9	.444	3	4	.750	0	4	4	0	0	0	1	11	0.7	0.0	1.8
Totals	111	2212	399	853	.468	232	340	.682	110	244	354	84	17	46	126	1030	3.2	0.8	9.3

Three-point field goals: 1987-88, 0-for-1. 1988-89, 0-for-1. 1989-90, 0-for-1. Totals, 0-for-3.

Personal fouls/disqualifications: 1980-81, 8/0. 1982-83, 7/0. 1983-84, 62/3. 1987-88, 55/0. 1988-89, 53/0. 1989-90, 74/0. 1990-91, 43/0. 1991-92, 11/0. 1992-93, 2/0. 1995-96, 10/0. Totals, 325/3.

EDWARDS, KEVIN   G   NETS

PERSONAL: Born October 30, 1965, in Cleveland Heights, Ohio. ... 6-3/210. ... Full name: Kevin Durell Edwards.
HIGH SCHOOL: St. Joseph Academy (Cleveland).
JUNIOR COLLEGE: Lakeland Community College (Ohio).
COLLEGE: DePaul.
TRANSACTIONS/CAREER NOTES: Selected by Miami Heat in first round (20th pick overall) of 1988 NBA Draft. ... Signed as free agent by New Jersey Nets (July 8, 1993).

COLLEGIATE RECORD

Season Team	G	Min.	FGM	FGA	Pct.	FTM	FTA	Pct.	Reb.	Ast.	Pts.	RPG	APG	PPG
												AVERAGES		
84-85—Lakeland C.C.	33	...	256	435	.589	103	144	.715	178	95	615	5.4	2.9	18.6
85-86—Lakeland C.C.	32	...	325	519	.626	121	159	.761	239	154	771	7.5	4.8	24.1
86-87—DePaul	31	1060	184	343	.536	63	78	.808	156	98	447	5.0	3.2	14.4
87-88—DePaul	30	999	220	413	.533	83	106	.783	158	117	548	5.3	3.9	18.3
Junior college totals	65	...	581	954	.609	224	303	.739	417	249	1386	6.4	3.8	21.3
4-year-college totals	61	2059	404	756	.534	146	184	.793	314	215	995	5.1	3.5	16.3

Three-point field goals: 1986-87, 16-for-36 (.444). 1987-88, 25-for-56 (.446). Totals, 41-for-92 (.446).

NBA REGULAR-SEASON RECORD

HONORS: NBA All-Rookie second team (1989).

Season Team	G	Min.	FGM	FGA	Pct.	FTM	FTA	Pct.	Off.	Def.	Tot.	Ast.	St.	Blk.	TO	Pts.	RPG	APG	PPG
									REBOUNDS								**AVERAGES**		
88-89—Miami	79	2349	470	1105	.425	144	193	.746	85	177	262	349	139	27	246	1094	3.3	4.4	13.8
89-90—Miami	78	2211	395	959	.412	139	183	.760	77	205	282	252	125	33	180	938	3.6	3.2	12.0
90-91—Miami	79	2000	380	927	.410	171	213	.803	80	125	205	240	129	46	163	955	2.6	3.0	12.1
91-92—Miami	81	1840	325	716	.454	162	191	.848	56	155	211	170	99	20	120	819	2.6	2.1	10.1
92-93—Miami	40	1134	216	462	.468	119	141	.844	48	73	121	120	68	12	75	556	3.0	3.0	13.9
93-94—New Jersey	82	2727	471	1028	.458	167	217	.770	94	187	281	232	120	34	135	1144	3.4	2.8	14.0
94-95—New Jersey	14	466	69	154	.448	40	42	.952	10	27	37	27	19	5	35	196	2.6	1.9	14.0
95-96—New Jersey	34	1007	142	390	.364	68	84	.810	14	61	75	71	54	7	68	394	2.2	2.1	11.6
Totals	487	13734	2468	5741	.430	1010	1264	.799	464	1010	1474	1461	753	184	1022	6096	3.0	3.0	12.5

Three-point field goals: 1988-89, 10-for-37 (.270). 1989-90, 9-for-30 (.300). 1990-91, 24-for-84 (.286). 1991-92, 7-for-32 (.219). 1992-93, 5-for-17 (.294). 1993-94, 35-for-99 (.354). 1994-95, 18-for-45 (.400). 1995-96, 42-for-104 (.404). Totals, 150-for-448 (.335).

Personal fouls/disqualifications: 1988-89, 154/0. 1989-90, 149/1. 1990-91, 151/2. 1991-92, 138/1. 1992-93, 69/0. 1993-94, 150/0. 1994-95, 42/0. 1995-96, 67/0. Totals, 920/4.

NBA PLAYOFF RECORD

Season Team	G	Min.	FGM	FGA	Pct.	FTM	FTA	Pct.	Off.	Def.	Tot.	Ast.	St.	Blk.	TO	Pts.	RPG	APG	PPG
									REBOUNDS								**AVERAGES**		
91-92—Miami	3	55	5	13	.385	5	8	.625	1	6	7	7	2	0	5	15	2.3	2.3	5.0
93-94—New Jersey	4	148	18	50	.360	13	14	.929	8	8	16	9	5	1	9	49	4.0	2.3	12.3
Totals	7	203	23	63	.365	18	22	.818	9	14	23	16	7	1	14	64	3.3	2.3	9.1

Three-point field goals: 1993-94, 0-for-2.

Personal fouls/disqualifications: 1991-92, 3/0. 1993-94, 9/0. Totals, 12/0.

EHLO, CRAIG   G/F   SUPERSONICS

PERSONAL: Born August 11, 1961, in Lubbock, Texas. ... 6-7/205. ... Full name: Joel Craig Ehlo. ... Name pronounced EE-low.
HIGH SCHOOL: Monterey (Lubbock, Texas).
JUNIOR COLLEGE: Odessa (Texas) Junior College.
COLLEGE: Washington State.
TRANSACTIONS/CAREER NOTES: Selected by Houston Rockets in third round (48th pick overall) of 1983 NBA Draft. ... Waived by Rockets (October 30, 1986). ... Played in Continental Basketball Association with Mississippi Jets (1986-87). ... Signed as free agent by Cleveland Cavaliers (January 13, 1987). ... Signed as free agent by Atlanta Hawks (July 2, 1993). ... Signed as free agent by Seattle SuperSonics (July 23, 1996).

COLLEGIATE RECORD

												AVERAGES		
Season Team	G	Min.	FGM	FGA	Pct.	FTM	FTA	Pct.	Reb.	Ast.	Pts.	RPG	APG	PPG
79-80—Odessa J.C.	28	...	146	300	.487	60	84	.714	142	...	352	5.1	...	12.6
80-81—Odessa J.C.	30	...	241	482	.500	139	180	.772	204	...	621	6.8	...	20.7
81-82—Wash. State	30	592	57	119	.479	39	65	.600	65	56	153	2.2	1.9	5.1
82-83—Wash. State	30	911	145	265	.547	69	109	.633	97	135	359	3.2	4.5	12.0
Junior college totals	58	...	387	782	.495	199	264	.754	346	...	973	6.0	...	16.8
4-year-college totals	60	1503	202	384	.526	108	174	.621	162	191	512	2.7	3.2	8.5

NBA REGULAR-SEASON RECORD

									REBOUNDS								AVERAGES		
Season Team	G	Min.	FGM	FGA	Pct.	FTM	FTA	Pct.	Off.	Def.	Tot.	Ast.	St.	Blk.	TO	Pts.	RPG	APG	PPG
83-84—Houston	7	63	11	27	.407	1	1	1.000	4	5	9	6	3	0	3	23	1.3	0.9	3.3
84-85—Houston	45	189	34	69	.493	19	30	.633	8	17	25	26	11	3	22	87	0.6	0.6	1.9
85-86—Houston	36	199	36	84	.429	23	29	.793	17	29	46	29	11	4	15	98	1.3	0.8	2.7
86-87—Cleveland	44	890	99	239	.414	70	99	.707	55	106	161	92	40	30	61	273	3.7	2.1	6.2
87-88—Cleveland	79	1709	226	485	.466	89	132	.674	86	188	274	206	82	30	107	563	3.5	2.6	7.1
88-89—Cleveland	82	1867	249	524	.475	71	117	.607	100	195	295	266	110	19	116	608	3.6	3.2	7.4
89-90—Cleveland	81	2894	436	940	.464	126	185	.681	147	292	439	371	126	23	161	1102	5.4	4.6	13.6
90-91—Cleveland	82	2766	344	773	.445	95	140	.679	142	246	388	376	121	34	160	832	4.7	4.6	10.1
91-92—Cleveland	63	2016	310	684	.453	87	123	.707	94	213	307	238	78	22	104	776	4.9	3.8	12.3
92-93—Cleveland	82	2559	385	785	.490	86	120	.717	113	290	403	254	104	22	124	949	4.9	3.1	11.6
93-94—Atlanta	82	2147	316	708	.446	112	154	.727	71	208	279	273	136	26	130	821	3.4	3.3	10.0
94-95—Atlanta	49	1166	191	422	.453	44	71	.620	55	92	147	113	46	6	73	477	3.0	2.3	9.7
95-96—Atlanta	79	1758	253	591	.428	81	103	.786	65	191	256	138	85	9	104	669	3.2	1.7	8.5
Totals	811	20223	2890	6331	.456	904	1304	.693	957	2072	3029	2388	953	228	1180	7278	3.7	2.9	9.0

Three-point field goals: 1984-85, 0-for-3. 1985-86, 3-for-9 (.333). 1986-87, 5-for-29 (.172). 1987-88, 22-for-64 (.344). 1988-89, 39-for-100 (.390). 1989-90, 104-for-248 (.419). 1990-91, 49-for-149 (.329). 1991-92, 69-for-167 (.413). 1992-93, 93-for-244 (.381). 1993-94, 77-for-221 (.348). 1994-95, 51-for-134 (.381). 1995-96, 82-for-221 (.371). Totals, 594-for-1589 (.374).

Personal fouls/disqualifications: 1983-84, 13/0. 1984-85, 26/0. 1985-86, 22/0. 1986-87, 80/0. 1987-88, 182/0. 1988-89, 161/0. 1989-90, 226/2. 1990-91, 209/0. 1991-92, 150/0. 1992-93, 170/0. 1993-94, 161/0. 1994-95, 86/0. 1995-96, 138/0. Totals, 1624/2.

NBA PLAYOFF RECORD

									REBOUNDS								AVERAGES		
Season Team	G	Min.	FGM	FGA	Pct.	FTM	FTA	Pct.	Off.	Def.	Tot.	Ast.	St.	Blk.	TO	Pts.	RPG	APG	PPG
84-85—Houston	3	6	1	1	1.000	2	2	1.000	0	0	0	4	0	0	4	0.0	0.0	1.3
85-86—Houston	10	38	8	16	.500	4	5	.800	1	2	3	6	4	1	3	20	0.3	0.6	2.0
87-88—Cleveland	5	128	17	40	.425	10	16	.625	3	15	18	17	5	0	12	44	3.6	3.4	8.8
88-89—Cleveland	4	97	17	39	.436	9	11	.818	2	4	6	13	3	1	5	48	1.5	3.3	12.0
89-90—Cleveland	5	196	26	62	.419	12	19	.632	7	25	32	32	6	0	12	69	6.4	6.4	13.8
91-92—Cleveland	17	552	63	152	.414	16	21	.762	22	55	77	77	21	5	18	163	4.5	4.5	9.6
92-93—Cleveland	9	289	38	91	.418	12	15	.800	10	21	31	25	12	4	17	98	3.4	2.8	10.9
93-94—Atlanta	11	317	50	118	.424	17	24	.708	11	19	30	40	11	0	13	125	2.7	3.6	11.4
94-95—Atlanta	3	49	2	12	.167	4	4	1.000	0	7	7	3	2	0	4	9	2.3	1.0	3.0
95-96—Atlanta	9	171	12	41	.293	5	7	.714	1	17	18	9	9	2	9	36	2.0	1.0	4.0
Totals	76	1843	234	572	.409	91	124	.734	57	165	222	222	77	13	93	616	2.9	2.9	8.1

Three-point field goals: 1985-86, 0-for-1. 1987-88, 0-for-8. 1988-89, 5-for-13 (.385). 1989-90, 5-for-15 (.333). 1991-92, 21-for-51 (.412). 1992-93, 10-for-26 (.385). 1993-94, 8-for-23 (.348). 1994-95, 1-for-6 (.167). 1995-96, 7-for-23 (.304). Totals, 57-for-166 (.343).

Personal fouls/disqualifications: 1984-85, 3/0. 1985-86, 4/0. 1987-88, 14/0. 1988-89, 10/0. 1989-90, 18/0. 1991-92, 40/0. 1992-93, 19/0. 1993-94, 32/0. 1995-96, 14/0. Totals, 154/0.

CBA REGULAR-SEASON RECORD

											AVERAGES		
Season Team	G	Min.	FGM	FGA	Pct.	FTM	FTA	Pct.	Reb.	Ast.	Pts.	RPG	APG	PPG
86-87—Mississippi	6	144	21	32	.656	20	30	.667	22	20	63	3.7	3.3	10.5

Three-point field goals: 1986-87, 1-for-1.

EISLEY, HOWARD   G   JAZZ

PERSONAL: Born December 4, 1972, in Detroit. ... 6-2/177. ... Full name: Howard Jonathan Eisley.
HIGH SCHOOL: Southwestern (Detroit).
COLLEGE: Boston College.
TRANSACTIONS/CAREER NOTES: Selected by Minnesota Timberwolves in second round (30th pick overall) of 1994 NBA Draft. ... Waived by Timberwolves (February 13, 1995). ... Signed by San Antonio Spurs to first of two consecutive 10-day contracts (February 26, 1995). ... Re-signed by Spurs for remainder of season (March 18, 1995). ... Waived by Spurs (April 17, 1995). ... Signed as free agent by Utah Jazz (October 5, 1995). ... Waived by Jazz (October 30, 1995). ... Played in Continental Basketball Association with Rockford Lightning (1995-96). ... Re-signed as free agent by Jazz (December 7, 1995).

E

COLLEGIATE RECORD

													AVERAGES		
Season Team	G	Min.	FGM	FGA	Pct.	FTM	FTA	Pct.	Reb.	Ast.	Pts.		RPG	APG	PPG
90-91—Boston College	30	1011	95	264	.360	81	108	.750	79	100	297		2.6	3.3	9.9
91-92—Boston College	31	1071	118	242	.488	88	118	.746	111	135	361		3.6	4.4	11.6
92-93—Boston College	31	1162	131	296	.443	121	145	.834	107	153	426		3.5	4.9	13.7
93-94—Boston College	34	1203	529	1191	.444	373	476	.784	116	156	544		3.4	4.6	16.0
Totals	126	4447	873	1993	.438	663	847	.783	413	544	1628		3.3	4.3	12.9

Three-point field goals: 1990-91, 26-for-74 (.351). 1991-92, 37-for-75 (.493). 1992-93, 43-for-104 (.413). 1993-94, 91-for-188 (.484). Totals, 197-for-441 (.447).

NBA REGULAR-SEASON RECORD

									REBOUNDS								AVERAGES		
Season Team	G	Min.	FGM	FGA	Pct.	FTM	FTA	Pct.	Off.	Def.	Tot.	Ast.	St.	Blk.	TO	Pts.	RPG	APG	PPG
94-95—Minn.-S.A.	49	552	40	122	.328	31	40	.775	12	36	48	95	18	6	50	120	1.0	1.9	2.4
95-96—Utah	65	961	104	242	.430	65	77	.844	22	56	78	146	29	3	77	287	1.2	2.2	4.4
Totals	114	1513	144	364	.396	96	117	.821	34	92	126	241	47	9	127	407	1.1	2.1	3.6

Three-point field goals: 1994-95, 9-for-37 (.243). 1995-96, 14-for-62 (.226). Totals, 23-for-99 (.232).
Personal fouls/disqualifications: 1994-95, 81/0. 1995-96, 130/0. Totals, 211/0.

NBA PLAYOFF RECORD

									REBOUNDS								AVERAGES		
Season Team	G	Min.	FGM	FGA	Pct.	FTM	FTA	Pct.	Off.	Def.	Tot.	Ast.	St.	Blk.	TO	Pts.	RPG	APG	PPG
95-96—Utah	18	202	16	42	.381	18	22	.818	4	18	22	44	3	2	11	53	1.2	2.4	2.9

Three-point field goals: 1995-96, 3-for-9 (.333).
Personal fouls/disqualifications: 1995-96, 29/0.

CBA REGULAR-SEASON RECORD

													AVERAGES		
Season Team	G	Min.	FGM	FGA	Pct.	FTM	FTA	Pct.	Reb.	Ast.	Pts.		RPG	APG	PPG
95-96—Rockford	7	168	32	58	.552	17	17	1.000	16	23	87		2.3	3.3	12.4

Three-point field goals: 1995-96, 6-for-15 (.400).

ELIE, MARIO F/G ROCKETS

PERSONAL: Born November 26, 1963, in New York. ... 6-5/210. ... Full name: Mario Antoine Elie. ... Name pronounced MARE-ee-oh ehl-LEE.
HIGH SCHOOL: Power Memorial (New York).
COLLEGE: American International (Mass.).
TRANSACTIONS/CAREER NOTES: Selected by Milwaukee Bucks in seventh round (160th pick overall) of 1985 NBA Draft. ... Waived by Bucks (July 25, 1985). ... Played in Portugal, Argentina and Ireland (1985-86 through 1988-89). ... Played in United States Basketball League with Miami Tropics (1988). ... Played in Continental Basketball Association with Albany Patroons (1989-90 and 1990-91). ... Played in World Basketball League with Youngstown Pride (1990). ... Signed as free agent by Los Angeles Lakers (October 2, 1990). ... Waived by Lakers (October 15, 1990). ... Signed by Philadelphia 76ers to 10-day contract (December 28, 1990). ... Signed by Golden State Warriors to 10-day contract (February 23, 1991). ... Re-signed by Warriors for remainder of season (March 5, 1991). ... Signed as free agent by Portland Trail Blazers (August 4, 1992); Warriors waived their right of first refusal. ... Traded by Trail Blazers to Houston Rockets for 1995 second-round draft choice (August 2, 1993).
MISCELLANEOUS: Member of NBA championship teams (1994,1995).

COLLEGIATE RECORD

													AVERAGES		
Season Team	G	Min.	FGM	FGA	Pct.	FTM	FTA	Pct.	Reb.	Ast.	Pts.		RPG	APG	PPG
81-82—American Int'l	25	754	157	268	.586	72	97	.742	207	50	386		8.3	2.0	15.4
82-83—American Int'l	31	1060	188	357	.527	116	157	.739	239	99	492		7.7	3.2	15.9
83-84—American Int'l	31	1174	225	398	.565	135	170	.794	256	59	585		8.3	1.9	18.9
84-85—American Int'l	33	1208	252	459	.549	157	202	.777	299	124	661		9.1	3.8	20.0
Totals	120	4196	822	1482	.555	480	626	.767	1001	332	2124		8.3	2.8	17.7

NOTES: CBA All-League first team (1991).

CBA REGULAR-SEASON RECORD

													AVERAGES		
Season Team	G	Min.	FGM	FGA	Pct.	FTM	FTA	Pct.	Reb.	Ast.	Pts.		RPG	APG	PPG
89-90—Albany	56	1772	367	654	.561	259	295	.878	339	193	1022		6.1	3.4	18.3
90-91—Albany	41	1451	352	658	.535	270	302	.894	235	197	1002		5.7	4.8	24.4
Totals	97	3223	719	1312	.548	529	597	.886	574	390	2024		5.9	4.0	20.9

Three-point field goals: 1989-90, 29-for-76 (.382). 1990-91, 28-for-87 (.322). Totals, 57-for-163 (.350).

NBA REGULAR-SEASON RECORD

									REBOUNDS								AVERAGES		
Season Team	G	Min.	FGM	FGA	Pct.	FTM	FTA	Pct.	Off.	Def.	Tot.	Ast.	St.	Blk.	TO	Pts.	RPG	APG	PPG
90-91—Phil.-G.S.	33	644	79	159	.497	75	89	.843	46	64	110	45	19	10	30	237	3.3	1.4	7.2
91-92—Golden State	79	1677	221	424	.521	155	182	.852	69	158	227	174	68	15	83	620	2.9	2.2	7.8
92-93—Portland	82	1757	240	524	.458	183	214	.855	59	157	216	177	74	20	89	708	2.6	2.2	8.6
93-94—Houston	67	1606	208	466	.446	154	179	.860	28	153	181	208	50	8	109	626	2.7	3.1	9.3
94-95—Houston	81	1896	243	487	.499	144	171	.842	50	146	196	189	65	12	104	710	2.4	2.3	8.8
95-96—Houston	45	1385	180	357	.504	98	115	.852	47	108	155	138	45	11	59	499	3.4	3.1	11.1
Totals	387	8965	1171	2417	.484	809	950	.852	299	786	1085	931	321	76	474	3400	2.8	2.4	8.8

Three-point field goals: 1990-91, 4-for-10 (.400). 1991-92, 23-for-71 (.329). 1992-93, 45-for-129 (.349). 1993-94, 56-for-167 (.335). 1994-95, 80-for-201 (.398). 1995-96, 41-for-127 (.323). Totals, 249-for-704 (.354).
Personal fouls/disqualifications: 1990-91, 85/1. 1991-92, 159/3. 1992-93, 145/0. 1993-94, 124/0. 1994-95, 158/0. 1995-96, 93/0. Totals, 764/4.

NBA PLAYOFF RECORD

									REBOUNDS								AVERAGES		
Season Team	G	Min.	FGM	FGA	Pct.	FTM	FTA	Pct.	Off.	Def.	Tot.	Ast.	St.	Blk.	TO	Pts.	RPG	APG	PPG
90-91—Golden State	9	197	28	56	.500	27	32	.844	17	15	32	13	5	1	10	84	3.6	1.4	9.3

E

Season Team	G	Min.	FGM	FGA	Pct.	FTM	FTA	Pct.	REBOUNDS Off.	Def.	Tot.	Ast.	St.	Blk.	TO	Pts.	AVERAGES RPG	APG	PPG
91-92—Golden State...	4	80	23	36	.639	2	3	.667	11	11	22	10	5	0	6	50	5.5	2.5	12.5
92-93—Portland.........	4	52	5	10	.500	8	9	.889	2	4	6	4	2	1	5	20	1.5	1.0	5.0
93-94—Houston.........	23	382	42	106	.396	40	47	.851	9	31	40	38	8	3	21	134	1.7	1.7	5.8
94-95—Houston.........	22	635	69	137	.504	35	44	.795	19	43	62	54	21	1	21	201	2.8	2.5	9.1
95-96—Houston.........	8	233	29	66	.439	11	12	.917	6	16	22	14	7	3	5	78	2.8	1.8	9.8
Totals	70	1579	196	411	.477	123	147	.837	64	120	184	133	48	9	68	567	2.6	1.9	8.1

Three-point field goals: 1990-91, 1-for-1. 1991-92, 2-for-2. 1992-93, 2-for-2. 1993-94, 10-for-32 (.313). 1994-95, 28-for-65 (.431). 1995-96, 9-for-24 (.375). Totals, 52-for-126 (.413).

Personal fouls/disqualifications: 1990-91, 32/0. 1991-92, 11/1. 1992-93, 1/0. 1993-94, 30/0. 1994-95, 55/0. 1995-96, 17/0. Totals, 146/1.

ELLIOTT, SEAN　　　　F　　　　SPURS

PERSONAL: Born February 2, 1968, in Tucson, Ariz. ... 6-8/220. ... Full name: Sean Michael Elliott.
HIGH SCHOOL: Cholla (Tucson, Ariz.).
COLLEGE: Arizona.
TRANSACTIONS/CAREER NOTES: Selected by San Antonio Spurs in first round (third pick overall) of 1989 NBA Draft. ... Traded by Spurs with F David Wood to Detroit Pistons for F Dennis Rodman (October 1, 1993). ... Traded by Pistons to Houston Rockets for F Robert Horry, F Matt Bullard and two future second-round draft choices (February 4, 1994); trade voided when Elliott failed physical (February 7, 1994). ... Traded by Pistons to Spurs for draft rights to C Bill Curley and 1997 second-round draft choice (July 19, 1994).

COLLEGIATE RECORD

NOTES: Wooden Award winner (1989). ... The Sporting News All-America first team (1988, 1989).

Season Team	G	Min.	FGM	FGA	Pct.	FTM	FTA	Pct.	Reb.	Ast.	Pts.	AVERAGES RPG	APG	PPG
85-86—Arizona	32	1079	187	385	.486	125	167	.749	171	70	499	5.3	2.2	15.6
86-87—Arizona	30	1046	209	410	.510	127	165	.770	181	110	578	6.0	3.7	19.3
87-88—Arizona	38	1249	263	461	.571	176	222	.793	219	137	743	5.8	3.6	19.6
88-89—Arizona	33	1125	237	494	.480	195	232	.841	237	134	735	7.2	4.1	22.3
Totals	133	4499	896	1750	.512	623	786	.793	808	451	2555	6.1	3.4	19.2

Three-point field goals: 1986-87, 33-for-89 (.371). 1987-88, 41-for-87 (.471). 1988-89, 66-for-151 (.437). Totals, 140-for-327 (.428).

NBA REGULAR-SEASON RECORD

HONORS: NBA All-Rookie second team (1990).

Season Team	G	Min.	FGM	FGA	Pct.	FTM	FTA	Pct.	REBOUNDS Off.	Def.	Tot.	Ast.	St.	Blk.	TO	Pts.	AVERAGES RPG	APG	PPG
89-90—San Antonio....	81	2032	311	647	.481	187	216	.866	127	170	297	154	45	14	112	810	3.7	1.9	10.0
90-91—San Antonio....	82	3044	478	976	.490	325	402	.808	142	314	456	238	69	33	147	1301	5.6	2.9	15.9
91-92—San Antonio....	82	3120	514	1040	.494	285	331	.861	143	296	439	214	84	29	152	1338	5.4	2.6	16.3
92-93—San Antonio....	70	2604	451	918	.491	268	337	.795	85	237	322	265	68	28	152	1207	4.6	3.8	17.2
93-94—Detroit	73	2409	360	791	.455	139	173	.803	68	195	263	197	54	27	129	885	3.6	2.7	12.1
94-95—San Antonio....	81	2858	502	1072	.468	326	404	.807	63	224	287	206	78	38	151	1466	3.5	2.5	18.1
95-96—San Antonio....	77	2901	525	1127	.466	326	423	.771	69	327	396	211	69	33	198	1537	5.1	2.7	20.0
Totals	546	18968	3141	6571	.478	1856	2286	.812	697	1763	2460	1485	467	202	1041	8544	4.5	2.7	15.6

Three-point field goals: 1989-90, 1-for-9 (.111). 1990-91, 20-for-64 (.313). 1991-92, 25-for-82 (.305). 1992-93, 37-for-104 (.356). 1993-94, 26-for-87 (.299). 1994-95, 136-for-333 (.408). 1995-96, 161-for-392 (.411). Totals, 406-for-1071 (.379).

Personal fouls/disqualifications: 1989-90, 172/0. 1990-91, 190/2. 1991-92, 149/0. 1992-93, 132/1. 1993-94, 174/3. 1994-95, 216/2. 1995-96, 178/1. Totals, 1211/9.

NBA PLAYOFF RECORD

Season Team	G	Min.	FGM	FGA	Pct.	FTM	FTA	Pct.	REBOUNDS Off.	Def.	Tot.	Ast.	St.	Blk.	TO	Pts.	AVERAGES RPG	APG	PPG
89-90—San Antonio....	10	291	53	96	.552	21	29	.724	11	30	41	18	9	6	15	127	4.1	1.8	12.7
90-91—San Antonio....	4	132	17	40	.425	25	32	.781	8	14	22	16	4	1	9	59	5.5	4.0	14.8
91-92—San Antonio....	3	137	19	40	.475	16	18	.889	4	9	13	8	3	4	6	59	4.3	2.7	19.7
92-93—San Antonio....	10	381	59	125	.472	37	40	.925	8	40	48	36	8	3	22	158	4.8	3.6	15.8
94-95—San Antonio....	15	574	87	200	.435	66	85	.776	23	49	72	40	10	7	27	260	4.8	2.7	17.3
95-96—San Antonio....	10	389	47	117	.402	51	64	.797	11	28	39	25	11	4	30	155	3.9	2.5	15.5
Totals	52	1904	282	618	.456	216	268	.806	65	170	235	143	45	25	109	818	4.5	2.8	15.7

Three-point field goals: 1989-90, 0-for-1. 1990-91, 0-for-3. 1991-92, 5-for-8 (.625). 1992-93, 3-for-14 (.214). 1994-95, 20-for-55 (.364). 1995-96, 10-for-34 (.294). Totals, 38-for-115 (.330).

Personal fouls/disqualifications: 1989-90, 37/0. 1990-91, 9/0. 1991-92, 6/0. 1992-93, 22/0. 1994-95, 38/0. 1995-96, 24/0. Totals, 136/0.

NBA ALL-STAR GAME RECORD

Season Team	Min.	FGM	FGA	Pct.	FTM	FTA	Pct.	REBOUNDS Off.	Def.	Tot.	Ast.	PF	Dq.	St.	Blk.	TO	Pts.
1993　—San Antonio	15	1	6	.167	3	4	.750	1	1	2	0	1	0	0	0	1	5
1996　—San Antonio	22	5	12	.417	1	1	1.000	2	3	5	2	4	0	0	0	2	13
Totals..........................	37	6	18	.333	4	5	.800	3	4	7	2	5	0	0	0	3	18

Three-point field goals: 1996, 2-for-6 (.333).

ELLIS, DALE　　　　G/F　　　　NUGGETS

PERSONAL: Born August 6, 1960, in Marietta, Ga. ... 6-7/215.
HIGH SCHOOL: Marietta (Ga.).
COLLEGE: Tennessee.
TRANSACTIONS/CAREER NOTES: Selected by Dallas Mavericks in first round (ninth pick overall) of 1983 NBA Draft. ... Traded by Mavericks to Seattle SuperSonics for G/F Al Wood (July 23, 1986). ... Traded by SuperSonics to Milwaukee Bucks for G/F Ricky Pierce (February 15, 1991). ... Traded by Bucks to San Antonio Spurs for draft rights to F Tracy Murray (July 1, 1992). ... Signed as free agent by Denver Nuggets (October 4, 1994).

E

COLLEGIATE RECORD

NOTES: The Sporting News All-America first team (1983).

Season Team	G	Min.	FGM	FGA	Pct.	FTM	FTA	Pct.	Reb.	Ast.	Pts.	RPG	APG	PPG
79-80—Tennessee	27	573	81	182	.445	31	40	.775	96	34	193	3.6	1.3	7.1
80-81—Tennessee	29	1057	215	360	.597	83	111	.748	185	21	513	6.4	0.7	17.7
81-82—Tennessee	30	1134	257	393	.654	121	152	.796	189	22	635	6.3	0.7	21.2
82-83—Tennessee	32	1179	279	464	.601	166	221	.751	209	32	724	6.5	1.0	22.6
Totals	118	3943	832	1399	.595	401	524	.765	679	109	2065	5.8	0.9	17.5

NBA REGULAR-SEASON RECORD

RECORDS: Holds career record for most three-point field goals made—1,269; and most three-point field goals attempted—3,147. ... Holds single-game record for most minutes played—69 (November 9, 1989, vs. Milwaukee).

HONORS: NBA Most Improved Player (1987). ... Long Distance Shootout winner (1988). ... All-NBA third team (1989).

Season Team	G	Min.	FGM	FGA	Pct.	FTM	FTA	Pct.	REBOUNDS Off.	Def.	Tot.	Ast.	St.	Blk.	TO	Pts.	AVERAGES RPG	APG	PPG
83-84—Dallas	67	1059	225	493	.456	87	121	.719	106	144	250	56	41	9	78	549	3.7	0.8	8.2
84-85—Dallas	72	1314	274	603	.454	77	104	.740	100	138	238	56	46	7	58	667	3.3	0.8	9.3
85-86—Dallas	72	1086	193	470	.411	59	82	.720	86	82	168	37	40	9	38	508	2.3	0.5	7.1
86-87—Seattle	82	3073	785	1520	.516	385	489	.787	187	260	447	238	104	32	238	2041	5.5	2.9	24.9
87-88—Seattle	75	2790	764	1519	.503	303	395	.767	167	173	340	197	74	11	172	1938	4.5	2.6	25.8
88-89—Seattle	82	3190	857	1710	.501	377	462	.816	156	186	342	164	108	22	218	2253	4.2	2.0	27.5
89-90—Seattle	55	2033	502	1011	.497	193	236	.818	90	148	238	110	59	7	119	1293	4.3	2.0	23.5
90-91—Seattle-Mil.	51	1424	340	718	.474	120	166	.723	66	107	173	95	49	8	81	857	3.4	1.9	16.8
91-92—Milwaukee	81	2191	485	1034	.469	164	212	.774	92	161	253	104	57	18	119	1272	3.1	1.3	15.7
92-93—San Antonio	82	2731	545	1092	.499	157	197	.797	81	231	312	107	78	18	111	1366	3.8	1.3	16.7
93-94—San Antonio	77	2590	478	967	.494	83	107	.776	70	185	255	80	66	11	75	1170	3.3	1.0	15.2
94-95—Denver	81	1996	351	774	.453	110	127	.866	56	166	222	57	37	9	81	918	2.7	0.7	11.3
95-96—Denver	81	2626	459	959	.479	136	179	.760	88	227	315	139	57	7	98	1204	3.9	1.7	14.9
Totals	958	28103	6258	12870	.486	2251	2877	.782	1345	2208	3553	1440	816	168	1486	16036	3.7	1.5	16.7

Three-point field goals: 1983-84, 12-for-29 (.414). 1984-85, 42-for-109 (.385). 1985-86, 63-for-173 (.364). 1986-87, 86-for-240 (.358). 1987-88, 107-for-259 (.413). 1988-89, 162-for-339 (.478). 1989-90, 96-for-256 (.375). 1990-91, 57-for-157 (.363). 1991-92, 138-for-329 (.419). 1992-93, 119-for-297 (.401). 1993-94, 131-for-332 (.395). 1994-95, 106-for-263 (.403). 1995-96, 150-for-364 (.412). Totals, 1269-for-3147 (.403).

Personal fouls/disqualifications: 1983-84, 118/0. 1984-85, 131/1. 1985-86, 78/0. 1986-87, 267/2. 1987-88, 221/1. 1988-89, 197/0. 1989-90, 124/3. 1990-91, 112/1. 1991-92, 151/0. 1992-93, 179/0. 1993-94, 141/0. 1994-95, 142/0. 1995-96, 191/1. Totals, 2052/9.

NBA PLAYOFF RECORD

Season Team	G	Min.	FGM	FGA	Pct.	FTM	FTA	Pct.	REBOUNDS Off.	Def.	Tot.	Ast.	St.	Blk.	TO	Pts.	AVERAGES RPG	APG	PPG
83-84—Dallas	8	178	26	80	.325	6	8	.750	19	23	42	4	10	2	5	59	5.3	0.5	7.4
84-85—Dallas	4	68	10	23	.435	1	2	.500	4	3	7	3	4	0	4	23	1.8	0.8	5.8
85-86—Dallas	7	67	9	22	.409	5	5	1.000	3	4	7	2	2	2	4	30	1.0	0.3	4.3
86-87—Seattle	14	530	148	304	.487	44	54	.815	37	53	90	37	10	6	33	353	6.4	2.6	25.2
87-88—Seattle	5	172	40	83	.482	21	29	.724	11	12	23	15	3	2	12	104	4.6	3.0	20.8
88-89—Seattle	8	304	72	160	.450	24	33	.727	14	18	32	10	11	1	21	183	4.0	1.3	22.9
92-93—San Antonio	10	305	51	113	.451	13	16	.813	9	26	35	11	4	0	10	125	3.5	1.1	12.5
93-94—San Antonio	4	114	17	43	.395	3	5	.600	3	7	10	1	3	0	4	42	2.5	0.3	10.5
94-95—Denver	3	73	10	28	.357	12	13	.923	6	8	14	3	2	1	2	36	4.7	1.0	12.0
Totals	63	1811	383	856	.447	129	165	.782	106	154	260	86	49	14	95	955	4.1	1.4	15.2

Three-point field goals: 1983-84, 1-for-12 (.083). 1984-85, 2-for-5 (.400). 1985-86, 7-for-12 (.583). 1986-87, 13-for-36 (.361). 1987-88, 3-for-12 (.250). 1988-89, 15-for-37 (.405). 1992-93, 10-for-32 (.313). 1993-94, 5-for-17 (.294). 1994-95, 4-for-13 (.308). Totals, 60-for-176 (.341).

Personal fouls/disqualifications: 1983-84, 17/0. 1984-85, 3/0. 1985-86, 6/0. 1986-87, 54/1. 1987-88, 17/0. 1988-89, 19/1. 1992-93, 25/0. 1993-94, 6/0. 1994-95, 6/0. Totals, 153/2.

NBA ALL-STAR GAME RECORD

Season Team	Min.	FGM	FGA	Pct.	FTM	FTA	Pct.	REBOUNDS Off.	Def.	Tot.	Ast.	PF	Dq.	St.	Blk.	TO	Pts.
1989 —Seattle	26	12	16	.750	2	2	1.000	3	3	6	2	2	0	0	0	2	27

Three-point field goals: 1989, 1-for-1.

ELLIS, LaPHONSO   F   NUGGETS

PERSONAL: Born May 5, 1970, in East St. Louis, Ill. ... 6-8/240. ... Full name: LaPhonso Darnell Ellis. ... Name pronounced la-FON-zo.

HIGH SCHOOL: Lincoln (East St. Louis, Ill.).

COLLEGE: Notre Dame.

TRANSACTIONS/CAREER NOTES: Selected by Denver Nuggets in first round (fifth pick overall) of 1992 NBA Draft.

COLLEGIATE RECORD

Season Team	G	Min.	FGM	FGA	Pct.	FTM	FTA	Pct.	Reb.	Ast.	Pts.	RPG	APG	PPG
88-89—Notre Dame	27	819	156	277	.563	52	76	.684	254	31	365	9.4	1.1	13.5
89-90—Notre Dame	22	712	114	223	.511	79	117	.675	278	33	309	12.6	1.5	14.0
90-91—Notre Dame	15	495	90	157	.573	58	81	.716	158	26	246	10.5	1.7	16.4
91-92—Notre Dame	33	1194	227	360	.631	127	194	.655	385	51	585	11.7	1.5	17.7
Totals	97	3220	587	1017	.577	316	468	.675	1075	141	1505	11.1	1.5	15.5

Three-point field goals: 1988-89, 1-for-1. 1989-90, 2-for-6 (.333). 1990-91, 8-for-17 (.471). 1991-92, 4-for-9 (.444). Totals, 15-for-33 (.455).

HONORS: NBA All-Rookie first team (1993).

NBA REGULAR-SEASON RECORD

Season Team	G	Min.	FGM	FGA	Pct.	FTM	FTA	Pct.	REBOUNDS Off.	Def.	Tot.	Ast.	St.	Blk.	TO	Pts.	AVERAGES RPG	APG	PPG
92-93—Denver	82	2749	483	958	.504	237	317	.748	274	470	744	151	72	111	153	1205	9.1	1.8	14.7
93-94—Denver	79	2699	483	963	.502	242	359	.674	220	462	682	167	63	80	172	1215	8.6	2.1	15.4

E

Season Team	G	Min.	FGM	FGA	Pct.	FTM	FTA	Pct.	REBOUNDS Off.	Def.	Tot.	Ast.	St.	Blk.	TO	Pts.	AVERAGES RPG	APG	PPG
94-95—Denver	6	58	9	25	.360	6	6	1.000	7	10	17	4	1	5	5	24	2.8	0.7	4.0
95-96—Denver	45	1269	189	432	.438	89	148	.601	93	229	322	74	36	33	83	471	7.2	1.6	10.5
Totals	212	6775	1164	2378	.489	574	830	.692	594	1171	1765	396	172	229	413	2915	8.3	1.9	13.8

Three-point field goals: 1992-93, 2-for-13 (.154). 1993-94, 7-for-23 (.304). 1995-96, 4-for-22 (.182). Totals, 13-for-58 (.224).
Personal fouls/disqualifications: 1992-93, 293/8. 1993-94, 304/6. 1994-95, 12/0. 1995-96, 163/3. Totals, 772/17.

NBA PLAYOFF RECORD

Season Team	G	Min.	FGM	FGA	Pct.	FTM	FTA	Pct.	REBOUNDS Off.	Def.	Tot.	Ast.	St.	Blk.	TO	Pts.	AVERAGES RPG	APG	PPG
93-94—Denver	12	436	68	142	.479	38	54	.704	27	70	97	26	9	11	19	177	8.1	2.2	14.8

Three-point field goals: 1993-94, 3-for-6 (.500).
Personal fouls/disqualifications: 1993-94, 46/2.

ELLIS, LeRON   C   MAGIC

PERSONAL: Born April 28, 1969, in Los Angeles. ... 6-10/240. ... Full name: LeRon Perry Ellis. ... Name pronounced luh-RON. ... Son of Leroy Ellis, center/forward with Los Angeles Lakers, Baltimore Bullets, Portland Trail Blazers and Philadelphia 76ers (1962-63 through 1975-76).
HIGH SCHOOL: Mater Dei (Santa Ana, Calif.).
COLLEGE: Kentucky, then Syracuse.
TRANSACTIONS/CAREER NOTES: Selected by Los Angeles Clippers in first round (22nd pick overall) of 1991 NBA Draft. ... Rights renounced by Clippers (July 1, 1992). ... Played in Continental Basketball Association with Columbus Horizon (1992-93). ... Played in Italy (1992-93). ... Signed as free agent by Charlotte Hornets (September 23, 1993). ... Tendered offer sheet by Minnesota Timberwolves (October 1, 1995). ... Offer matched by Hornets (October 10, 1995). ... Traded by Hornets with C Alonzo Mourning and G Pete Myers to Miami Heat for G/F Glen Rice, G Khalid Reeves, C Matt Geiger and 1996 first-round draft choice (November 3, 1995). ... Waived by Heat (December 27, 1995). ... Signed as free agent by Orlando Magic (September 3, 1996).

COLLEGIATE RECORD

Season Team	G	Min.	FGM	FGA	Pct.	FTM	FTA	Pct.	Reb.	Ast.	Pts.	AVERAGES RPG	APG	PPG
87-88—Kentucky	28	386	49	106	.462	22	42	.524	83	13	120	3.0	0.5	4.3
88-89—Kentucky	32	1006	200	385	.519	111	164	.677	177	65	511	5.5	2.0	16.0
89-90—Syracuse	32	682	79	175	.451	28	54	.519	129	24	192	4.0	0.8	6.0
90-91—Syracuse	32	929	142	280	.507	72	119	.605	246	43	356	7.7	1.3	11.1
Totals	124	3003	470	946	.497	233	379	.615	635	145	1179	5.1	1.2	9.5

Three-point field goals: 1988-89, 0-for-2. 1989-90, 6-for-15 (.400). 1990-91, 0-for-4. Totals, 6-for-21 (.286).

NBA REGULAR-SEASON RECORD

Season Team	G	Min.	FGM	FGA	Pct.	FTM	FTA	Pct.	REBOUNDS Off.	Def.	Tot.	Ast.	St.	Blk.	TO	Pts.	AVERAGES RPG	APG	PPG
91-92—L.A. Clippers	29	103	17	50	.340	9	19	.474	12	12	24	1	6	9	11	43	0.8	0.0	1.5
93-94—Charlotte	50	680	88	182	.484	45	68	.662	70	118	188	24	17	25	21	221	3.8	0.5	4.4
95-96—Miami	12	74	5	22	.227	3	6	.500	5	3	8	4	2	3	3	13	0.7	0.3	1.1
Totals	91	857	110	254	.433	57	93	.613	87	133	220	29	25	37	35	277	2.4	0.3	3.0

Personal fouls/disqualifications: 1991-92, 11/0. 1993-94, 83/1. 1995-96, 11/0. Totals, 105/1.

NBA PLAYOFF RECORD

Season Team	G	Min.	FGM	FGA	Pct.	FTM	FTA	Pct.	REBOUNDS Off.	Def.	Tot.	Ast.	St.	Blk.	TO	Pts.	AVERAGES RPG	APG	PPG
91-92—L.A. Clippers	1	2	0	0	...	0	0	...	0	0	0	0	0	0	0	0	0.0	0.0	0.0

CBA REGULAR-SEASON RECORD

Season Team	G	Min.	FGM	FGA	Pct.	FTM	FTA	Pct.	Reb.	Ast.	Pts.	AVERAGES RPG	APG	PPG
92-93—Columbus	7	214	42	85	.494	23	45	.511	57	5	107	8.1	0.7	15.3

ITALIAN LEAGUE RECORD

Season Team	G	Min.	FGM	FGA	Pct.	FTM	FTA	Pct.	Reb.	Ast.	Pts.	AVERAGES RPG	APG	PPG
92-93—Hyundai Desio	4	127	22	37	.595	15	18	.833	37	2	59	9.3	0.5	14.8

ELLISON, PERVIS   F/C   CELTICS

PERSONAL: Born April 3, 1967, in Savannah, Ga. ... 6-10/242.
HIGH SCHOOL: Savannah (Ga.).
COLLEGE: Louisville.
TRANSACTIONS/CAREER NOTES: Selected by Sacramento Kings in first round (first pick overall) of 1989 NBA Draft. ... Traded by Kings to Washington Bullets in three-way deal in which Bullets sent G Jeff Malone to Utah Jazz and Jazz sent G Bobby Hansen, F/C Eric Leckner and 1990 first- and second-round draft choices to Kings (June 25, 1990); Jazz also received 1990 second-round draft choice from Kings and Kings also received 1991 second-round draft choice from Bullets. ... Signed as unrestricted free agent by Boston Celtics (August 1, 1994).

COLLEGIATE RECORD

NOTES: The Sporting News All-America second team (1989). ... NCAA Division I Tournament Most Outstanding Player (1986). ... Member of NCAA Division I championship team (1986).

Season Team	G	Min.	FGM	FGA	Pct.	FTM	FTA	Pct.	Reb.	Ast.	Pts.	AVERAGES RPG	APG	PPG
85-86—Louisville	39	1194	210	379	.554	90	132	.682	318	78	510	8.2	2.0	13.1
86-87—Louisville	31	952	185	347	.533	100	139	.719	270	56	470	8.7	1.8	15.2

E

Season Team	G	Min.	FGM	FGA	Pct.	FTM	FTA	Pct.	Reb.	Ast.	Pts.	RPG	APG	PPG
87-88—Louisville	35	1175	235	391	.601	146	211	.692	291	108	617	8.3	3.1	17.6
88-89—Louisville	31	1014	227	369	.615	92	141	.652	270	78	546	8.7	2.5	17.6
Totals	136	4335	857	1486	.577	428	623	.687	1149	320	2143	8.4	2.4	15.8

Three-point field goals: 1987-88, 1-for-2 (.500). 1988-89, 0-for-1. Totals, 1-for-3 (.333).

NBA REGULAR-SEASON RECORD

HONORS: NBA Most Improved Player (1992).

Season Team	G	Min.	FGM	FGA	Pct.	FTM	FTA	Pct.	REBOUNDS Off.	Def.	Tot.	Ast.	St.	Blk.	TO	Pts.	AVERAGES RPG	APG	PPG
89-90—Sacramento	34	866	111	251	.442	49	78	.628	64	132	196	65	16	57	62	271	5.8	1.9	8.0
90-91—Washington	76	1942	326	636	.513	139	214	.650	224	361	585	102	49	157	146	791	7.7	1.3	10.4
91-92—Washington	66	2511	547	1014	.539	227	312	.728	217	523	740	190	62	177	196	1322	11.2	2.9	20.0
92-93—Washington	49	1701	341	655	.521	170	242	.702	138	295	433	117	45	108	110	852	8.8	2.4	17.4
93-94—Washington	47	1178	137	292	.469	70	97	.722	77	165	242	70	25	50	73	344	5.1	1.5	7.3
94-95—Boston	55	1083	152	300	.507	71	99	.717	124	185	309	34	22	54	76	375	5.6	0.6	6.8
95-96—Boston	69	1431	145	295	.492	75	117	.641	151	300	451	62	39	99	84	365	6.5	0.9	5.3
Totals	396	10712	1759	3443	.511	801	1159	.691	995	1961	2956	640	258	702	747	4320	7.5	1.6	10.9

Three-point field goals: 1989-90, 0-for-2. 1990-91, 0-for-6. 1991-92, 1-for-3 (.333). 1992-93, 0-for-4. 1993-94, 0-for-3. 1994-95, 0-for-2. Totals, 1-for-20 (.050).

Personal fouls/disqualifications: 1989-90, 132/4. 1990-91, 268/6. 1991-92, 222/2. 1992-93, 154/3. 1993-94, 140/3. 1994-95, 179/5. 1995-96, 207/2. Totals, 1302/25.

NBA PLAYOFF RECORD

Season Team	G	Min.	FGM	FGA	Pct.	FTM	FTA	Pct.	REBOUNDS Off.	Def.	Tot.	Ast.	St.	Blk.	TO	Pts.	AVERAGES RPG	APG	PPG
94-95—Boston	4	68	11	19	.579	2	2	1.000	11	6	17	2	2	5	4	24	4.3	0.5	6.0

Personal fouls/disqualifications: 1994-95, 17/1.

ESPOSITO, VINCENZO   G

PERSONAL: Born January 3, 1969, in Caserta, Italy ... 6-3/198. ... Name pronounced vin-CHEN-zoe ess-POE zee-TOE.
TRANSACTIONS/CAREER NOTES: Not drafted by an NBA franchise. ... Played in Italy (1984-85 through 1994-95). ... Signed as free agent by Toronto Raptors (May 25, 1995). ... Waived by Raptors (July 2, 1996).

ITALIAN LEAGUE RECORD

Season Team	G	Min.	FGM	FGA	Pct.	FTM	FTA	Pct.	Reb.	Ast.	Pts.	RPG	APG	PPG
84-85—Indesit Caserta	5	...	1	1	1.000	2	3	.667	0	1	4	0.0	0.2	0.8
85-86—Mobilgirgi Castera	32	...	3	6	.500	0	0	...	2	1	6	0.1	0.0	0.2
86-87—Mobilgirgi Castera	39	...	59	122	.484	35	45	.778	26	25	165	0.7	0.6	4.2
87-88—Snaidero Caserta	32	...	102	192	.531	54	62	.871	55	23	284	1.7	0.7	8.9
88-89—Snaidero Caserta	36	...	139	279	.498	78	91	.857	67	37	383	1.9	1.0	10.6
89-90—Phonola Caserta	34	...	175	339	.516	108	128	.844	68	26	498	2.0	0.8	14.6
90-91—Phonola Caserta	40	...	219	436	.502	102	122	.836	72	28	611	1.8	0.7	15.3
91-92—Phonola Caserta	29	...	132	306	.431	75	87	.862	52	30	391	1.8	1.0	13.5
92-93—Phonola Caserta	40	...	285	642	.444	178	213	.836	83	47	840	2.1	1.2	21.0
93-94—Filodoro Calze Bologna	30	...	219	557	.393	207	248	.835	55	52	719	1.8	1.7	24.0
94-95—Filodoro Calze Bologna	31	...	217	488	.445	221	238	.929	53	59	750	1.7	1.9	24.2
Totals	348	...	1551	3368	.461	1060	1237	.857	533	329	4651	1.5	0.9	13.4

NBA REGULAR-SEASON RECORD

Season Team	G	Min.	FGM	FGA	Pct.	FTM	FTA	Pct.	REBOUNDS Off.	Def.	Tot.	Ast.	St.	Blk.	TO	Pts.	AVERAGES RPG	APG	PPG
95-96—Toronto	30	282	36	100	.360	31	39	.795	4	12	16	23	7	0	39	116	0.5	0.8	3.9

Three-point field goals: 1995-96, 13-for-56 (.232).
Personal fouls/disqualifications: 1995-96, 27/0.

EWING, PATRICK   C   KNICKS

PERSONAL: Born August 5, 1962, in Kingston, Jamaica. ... 7-0/240. ... Full name: Patrick Aloysius Ewing.
HIGH SCHOOL: Cambridge (Mass.) Rindge & Latin School.
COLLEGE: Georgetown.
TRANSACTIONS/CAREER NOTES: Selected by New York Knicks in first round (first pick overall) of 1985 NBA Draft.
MISCELLANEOUS: Member of gold-medal-winning U.S. Olympic teams (1984, 1992). ... New York Knicks all-time leading scorer with 19,788 points, all-time leading rebounder with 8,679, all-time steals leader with 910 and all-time blocked shots leader with 2,327 (1985-86 through 1995-96).

COLLEGIATE RECORD

NOTES: The Sporting News College Player of the Year (1985). ... Naismith Award winner (1985). ... The Sporting News All-America first team (1985). ... The Sporting News All-America second team (1983, 1984). ... NCAA Division I Tournament Most Outstanding Player (1984). ... Member of NCAA Division I championship team (1984).

Season Team	G	Min.	FGM	FGA	Pct.	FTM	FTA	Pct.	Reb.	Ast.	Pts.	RPG	APG	PPG
81-82—Georgetown	37	1064	183	290	.631	103	167	.617	279	23	469	7.5	0.6	12.7
82-83—Georgetown	32	1024	212	372	.570	141	224	.629	325	26	565	10.2	0.8	17.7
83-84—Georgetown	37	1179	242	368	.658	124	189	.656	371	31	608	10.0	0.8	16.4
84-85—Georgetown	37	1132	220	352	.625	102	160	.638	341	48	542	9.2	1.3	14.6
Totals	143	4399	857	1382	.620	470	740	.635	1316	128	2184	9.2	0.9	15.3

E

NBA REGULAR-SEASON RECORD

HONORS: NBA Rookie of the Year (1986). ... All-NBA first team (1990). ... All-NBA second team (1988, 1989, 1991, 1992, 1993). ... NBA All-Defensive second team (1988, 1989, 1992). ... NBA All-Rookie team (1986).
NOTES: Led NBA with 332 personal fouls (1988).

Season Team	G	Min.	FGM	FGA	Pct.	FTM	FTA	Pct.	Off.	Def.	Tot.	Ast.	St.	Blk.	TO	Pts.	RPG	APG	PPG
85-86—New York	50	1771	386	814	.474	226	306	.739	124	327	451	102	54	103	172	998	9.0	2.0	20.0
86-87—New York	63	2206	530	1053	.503	296	415	.713	157	398	555	104	89	147	229	1356	8.8	1.7	21.5
87-88—New York	82	2546	656	1183	.555	341	476	.716	245	431	676	125	104	245	287	1653	8.2	1.5	20.2
88-89—New York	80	2896	727	1282	.567	361	484	.746	213	527	740	188	117	281	266	1815	9.3	2.4	22.7
89-90—New York	82	3165	922	1673	.551	502	648	.775	235	658	893	182	78	327	278	2347	10.9	2.2	28.6
90-91—New York	81	3104	845	1645	.514	464	623	.745	194	711	905	244	80	258	291	2154	11.2	3.0	26.6
91-92—New York	82	3150	796	1525	.522	377	511	.738	228	693	921	156	88	245	209	1970	11.2	1.9	24.0
92-93—New York	81	3003	779	1550	.503	400	556	.719	191	*789	980	151	74	161	265	1959	12.1	1.9	24.2
93-94—New York	79	2972	745	1503	.496	445	582	.765	219	666	885	179	90	217	260	1939	11.2	2.3	24.5
94-95—New York	79	2920	730	1452	.503	420	560	.750	157	710	867	212	68	159	256	1886	11.0	2.7	23.9
95-96—New York	76	2783	678	1456	.466	351	461	.761	157	649	806	160	68	184	221	1711	10.6	2.1	22.5
Totals	835	30516	7794	15136	.515	4183	5622	.744	2120	6559	8679	1803	910	2327	2734	19788	10.4	2.2	23.7

Three-point field goals: 1985-86, 0-for-5. 1986-87, 0-for-7. 1987-88, 0-for-3. 1988-89, 0-for-6. 1989-90, 1-for-4 (.250). 1990-91, 0-for-6. 1991-92, 1-for-6 (.167). 1992-93, 1-for-7 (.143). 1993-94, 4-for-14 (.286). 1994-95, 6-for-21 (.286). 1995-96, 4-for-28 (.143). Totals, 17-for-107 (.159).

Personal fouls/disqualifications: 1985-86, 191/7. 1986-87, 248/5. 1987-88, 332/5. 1988-89, 311/5. 1989-90, 325/7. 1990-91, 287/3. 1991-92, 277/2. 1992-93, 286/2. 1993-94, 275/3. 1994-95, 272/3. 1995-96, 247/2. Totals, 3051/44.

NBA PLAYOFF RECORD

NOTES: Holds NBA Finals single-series record for most blocked shots—30 (1994, vs. Houston). ... Shares NBA Finals single-game record for most blocked shots—8 (June 17, 1994, vs. Houston).

Season Team	G	Min.	FGM	FGA	Pct.	FTM	FTA	Pct.	Off.	Def.	Tot.	Ast.	St.	Blk.	TO	Pts.	RPG	APG	PPG
87-88—New York	4	153	28	57	.491	19	22	.864	16	35	51	10	6	13	11	75	12.8	2.5	18.8
88-89—New York	9	340	70	144	.486	39	52	.750	23	67	90	20	9	18	15	179	10.0	2.2	19.9
89-90—New York	10	395	114	219	.521	65	79	.823	21	84	105	31	13	20	27	294	10.5	3.1	29.4
90-91—New York	3	110	18	45	.400	14	18	.778	2	28	30	6	1	5	11	50	10.0	2.0	16.7
91-92—New York	12	482	109	239	.456	54	73	.740	33	100	133	27	7	31	23	272	11.1	2.3	22.7
92-93—New York	15	604	165	322	.512	51	80	.638	43	121	164	36	17	31	39	382	10.9	2.4	25.5
93-94—New York	25	1032	210	481	.437	123	163	.755	88	205	293	65	32	76	83	547	11.7	2.6	21.9
94-95—New York	11	399	80	156	.513	48	70	.686	17	89	106	27	6	25	30	209	9.6	2.5	19.0
95-96—New York	8	328	65	137	.474	41	63	.651	11	74	85	15	1	25	30	172	10.6	1.9	21.5
Totals	97	3843	859	1800	.477	454	620	.732	254	803	1057	237	92	244	269	2180	10.9	2.4	22.5

Three-point field goals: 1987-88, 0-for-1. 1989-90, 1-for-2 (.500). 1991-92, 0-for-1. 1992-93, 1-for-1. 1993-94, 4-for-11 (.364). 1994-95, 1-for-3 (.333). 1995-96, 1-for-2 (.500). Totals, 8-for-21 (.381).

Personal fouls/disqualifications: 1987-88, 17/0. 1988-89, 35/0. 1989-90, 41/0. 1990-91, 12/0. 1991-92, 49/1. 1992-93, 60/2. 1993-94, 94/1. 1994-95, 51/1. 1995-96, 22/0. Totals, 381/5.

NBA ALL-STAR GAME RECORD

Season	Team	Min.	FGM	FGA	Pct.	FTM	FTA	Pct.	Off.	Def.	Tot.	Ast.	PF	Dq.	St.	Blk.	TO	Pts.
1986	—New York									Selected, did not play—injured.								
1988	—New York	16	4	8	.500	1	1	1.000	1	5	6	0	1	0	0	1	1	9
1989	—New York	17	2	8	.250	0	4	.000	1	5	6	2	2	0	1	2	3	4
1990	—New York	27	5	9	.556	2	2	1.000	1	9	10	1	5	0	1	5	5	12
1991	—New York	30	8	10	.800	2	2	1.000	2	8	10	0	5	0	1	4	2	18
1992	—New York	17	4	7	.571	2	5	.400	2	2	4	0	3	0	2	1	2	10
1993	—New York	25	7	11	.636	1	1	1.000	3	7	10	1	4	0	2	2	4	15
1994	—New York	24	7	15	.467	6	7	.857	4	4	8	1	2	0	0	0	1	20
1995	—New York	22	4	7	.571	2	2	1.000	0	3	3	1	3	0	1	0	5	10
1996	—New York	12	3	7	.429	2	2	1.000	1	2	3	1	2	0	3	1	0	8
Totals		190	44	82	.537	18	26	.692	15	45	60	7	27	0	11	16	23	106

FERRELL, DUANE　　　　F　　　　　　　PACERS

PERSONAL: Born February 28, 1965, in Baltimore. ... 6-7/215. ... Name pronounced fur-RELL. ... Brother-in-law of Jeff Sydner, wide receiver/kick returner with Philadelphia Eagles (1992 through 1994) and New York Jets (1995).
HIGH SCHOOL: Calvert Hall (Towson, Md.).
COLLEGE: Georgia Tech.
TRANSACTIONS/CAREER NOTES: Not drafted by an NBA franchise. ... Signed as free agent by Atlanta Hawks (October 6, 1988). ... Waived by Hawks (November 2, 1989). ... Played in Continental Basketball Association with Topeka Sizzlers (1989-90). ... Signed by Hawks to first of two consecutive 10-day contracts (February 23, 1990). ... Re-signed by Hawks for remainder of season (March 15, 1990). ... Waived by Hawks (September 18, 1990). ... Re-signed as free agent by Hawks (November 2, 1990). ... Signed as free agent by Indiana Pacers (September 30, 1994).

COLLEGIATE RECORD

Season Team	G	Min.	FGM	FGA	Pct.	FTM	FTA	Pct.	Reb.	Ast.	Pts.	RPG	APG	PPG
84-85—Georgia Tech	32	802	117	232	.504	56	98	.571	131	71	290	4.1	2.2	9.1
85-86—Georgia Tech	34	1068	172	289	.595	69	91	.758	168	95	413	4.9	2.8	12.1
86-87—Georgia Tech	29	1058	201	387	.519	112	138	.812	170	79	520	5.9	2.7	17.9
87-88—Georgia Tech	32	1051	230	432	.532	131	175	.749	211	44	595	6.6	1.4	18.6
Totals	127	3979	720	1340	.537	368	502	.733	680	289	1818	5.4	2.3	14.3

Three-point field goals: 1986-87, 6-for-15 (.400). 1987-88, 4-for-14 (.286). Totals, 10-for-29 (.345).

NBA REGULAR-SEASON RECORD

Season Team	G	Min.	FGM	FGA	Pct.	FTM	FTA	Pct.	Off.	Def.	Tot.	Ast.	St.	Blk.	TO	Pts.	RPG	APG	PPG
88-89—Atlanta	41	231	35	83	.422	30	44	.682	19	22	41	10	7	6	12	100	1.0	0.2	2.4

Season Team	G	Min.	FGM	FGA	Pct.	FTM	FTA	Pct.	Off.	Def.	Tot.	Ast.	St.	Blk.	TO	Pts.	RPG	APG	PPG
89-90—Atlanta	14	29	5	14	.357	2	6	.333	3	4	7	2	1	0	2	12	0.5	0.1	0.9
90-91—Atlanta	78	1165	174	356	.489	125	156	.801	97	82	179	55	33	27	78	475	2.3	0.7	6.1
91-92—Atlanta	66	1598	331	632	.524	166	218	.761	105	105	210	92	49	17	99	839	3.2	1.4	12.7
92-93—Atlanta	82	1736	327	696	.470	176	226	.779	97	94	191	132	59	17	103	839	2.3	1.6	10.2
93-94—Atlanta	72	1155	184	379	.485	144	184	.783	62	67	129	65	44	16	64	513	1.8	0.9	7.1
94-95—Indiana	56	607	83	173	.480	64	85	.753	50	38	88	31	26	6	43	231	1.6	0.6	4.1
95-96—Indiana	54	591	80	166	.482	42	57	.737	32	61	93	30	23	3	34	202	1.7	0.6	3.7
Totals	463	7112	1219	2499	.488	749	976	.767	465	473	938	417	242	92	435	3211	2.0	0.9	6.9

Three-point field goals: 1989-90, 0-for-1. 1990-91, 2-for-3 (.667). 1991-92, 11-for-33 (.333). 1992-93, 9-for-36 (.250). 1993-94, 1-for-9 (.111). 1994-95, 1-for-6 (.167). 1995-96, 0-for-8. Totals, 24-for-96 (.250).

Personal fouls/disqualifications: 1988-89, 33/0. 1989-90, 3/0. 1990-91, 151/3. 1991-92, 134/0. 1992-93, 160/1. 1993-94, 85/0. 1994-95, 79/0. 1995-96, 83/0. Totals, 728/4.

NBA PLAYOFF RECORD

Season Team	G	Min.	FGM	FGA	Pct.	FTM	FTA	Pct.	Off.	Def.	Tot.	Ast.	St.	Blk.	TO	Pts.	RPG	APG	PPG
90-91—Atlanta	5	73	8	18	.444	8	12	.667	6	11	17	3	0	0	2	24	3.4	0.6	4.8
92-93—Atlanta	3	54	14	23	.609	4	5	.800	1	4	5	1	0	0	4	33	1.7	0.3	11.0
93-94—Atlanta	11	187	25	63	.397	27	36	.750	22	9	31	17	5	3	5	78	2.8	1.5	7.1
94-95—Indiana	10	85	8	24	.333	10	16	.625	8	3	11	13	0	2	10	27	1.1	1.3	2.7
95-96—Indiana	5	69	7	19	.368	4	8	.500	6	3	9	3	4	0	4	18	1.8	0.6	3.6
Totals	34	468	62	147	.422	53	77	.688	43	30	73	37	9	5	25	180	2.1	1.1	5.3

Three-point field goals: 1992-93, 1-for-3 (.333). 1993-94, 1-for-4 (.250). 1994-95, 1-for-2 (.500). Totals, 3-for-9 (.333).

Personal fouls/disqualifications: 1990-91, 10/0. 1992-93, 6/0. 1993-94, 24/0. 1994-95, 10/0. 1995-96, 10/0. Totals, 60/0.

CBA REGULAR-SEASON RECORD

NOTES: CBA Newcomer of the Year (1990).

Season Team	G	Min.	FGM	FGA	Pct.	FTM	FTA	Pct.	Reb.	Ast.	Pts.	RPG	APG	PPG
89-90—Topeka	40	1546	377	699	.539	212	276	.768	252	95	971	6.3	2.4	24.3

Three-point field goals: 1989-90, 5-for-16 (.313).

FERRY, DANNY   F   CAVALIERS

PERSONAL: Born October 17, 1966, in Hyattsville, Md. ... 6-10/235. ... Full name: Daniel John Willard Ferry. ... Son of Bob Ferry, center/forward with St. Louis Hawks, Detroit Pistons and Baltimore Bullets (1959-60 through 1968-69).
HIGH SCHOOL: DeMatha Catholic (Hyattsville, Md.).
COLLEGE: Duke.
TRANSACTIONS/CAREER NOTES: Selected by Los Angeles Clippers in first round (second pick overall) of 1989 NBA Draft. ... Played in Italy (1989-90). ... Draft rights traded by Clippers with G Reggie Williams to Cleveland Cavaliers for G Ron Harper, 1990 and 1992 first-round draft choices and 1991 second-round draft choice (November 16, 1989).

COLLEGIATE RECORD

NOTES: Naismith Award winner (1989). ... THE SPORTING NEWS All-America first team (1988, 1989).

Season Team	G	Min.	FGM	FGA	Pct.	FTM	FTA	Pct.	Reb.	Ast.	Pts.	RPG	APG	PPG
85-86—Duke	40	912	91	198	.460	54	86	.628	221	60	236	5.5	1.5	5.9
86-87—Duke	33	1094	172	383	.449	92	109	.844	256	141	461	7.8	4.3	14.0
87-88—Duke	35	1138	247	519	.476	135	163	.828	266	139	667	7.6	4.0	19.1
88-89—Duke	35	1163	300	575	.522	146	193	.756	260	166	791	7.4	4.7	22.6
Totals	143	4307	810	1675	.484	427	551	.775	1003	506	2155	7.0	3.5	15.1

Three-point field goals: 1986-87, 25-for-63 (.397). 1987-88, 38-for-109 (.349). 1988-89, 45-for-106 (.425). Totals, 108-for-278 (.388).

ITALIAN LEAGUE RECORD

Season Team	G	Min.	FGM	FGA	Pct.	FTM	FTA	Pct.	Reb.	Ast.	Pts.	RPG	APG	PPG
89-90—Il Messaggero Roma	30	1090	203	370	.549	125	168	.744	195	...	878	6.5	...	29.3

NBA REGULAR-SEASON RECORD

Season Team	G	Min.	FGM	FGA	Pct.	FTM	FTA	Pct.	Off.	Def.	Tot.	Ast.	St.	Blk.	TO	Pts.	RPG	APG	PPG
90-91—Cleveland	81	1661	275	643	.428	124	152	.816	99	187	286	142	43	25	120	697	3.5	1.8	8.6
91-92—Cleveland	68	937	134	328	.409	61	73	.836	53	160	213	75	22	15	46	346	3.1	1.1	5.1
92-93—Cleveland	76	1461	220	459	.479	99	113	.876	81	198	279	137	29	49	83	573	3.7	1.8	7.5
93-94—Cleveland	70	965	149	334	.446	38	43	.884	47	94	141	74	28	22	41	350	2.0	1.1	5.0
94-95—Cleveland	82	1290	223	500	.446	74	84	.881	30	113	143	96	27	22	59	614	1.7	1.2	7.5
95-96—Cleveland	82	2680	422	919	.459	103	134	.769	71	238	309	191	57	37	122	1090	3.8	2.3	13.3
Totals	459	8994	1423	3183	.447	499	599	.833	381	990	1371	715	206	170	471	3670	3.0	1.6	8.0

Three-point field goals: 1990-91, 23-for-77 (.299). 1991-92, 17-for-48 (.354). 1992-93, 34-for-82 (.415). 1993-94, 14-for-51 (.275). 1994-95, 94-for-233 (.403). 1995-96, 143-for-363 (.394). Totals, 325-for-854 (.381).

Personal fouls/disqualifications: 1990-91, 230/1. 1991-92, 135/0. 1992-93, 171/1. 1993-94, 113/0. 1994-95, 131/0. 1995-96, 233/3. Totals, 1013/5.

NBA PLAYOFF RECORD

Season Team	G	Min.	FGM	FGA	Pct.	FTM	FTA	Pct.	Off.	Def.	Tot.	Ast.	St.	Blk.	TO	Pts.	RPG	APG	PPG
91-92—Cleveland	9	55	7	15	.467	4	4	1.000	7	9	16	1	1	1	2	19	1.8	0.1	2.1
92-93—Cleveland	8	118	13	34	.382	9	10	.900	4	21	25	14	4	3	7	39	3.1	1.8	4.9
93-94—Cleveland	1	4	0	0	...	0	0	...	0	0	0	1	0	0	1	0	0.0	1.0	0.0
94-95—Cleveland	4	67	13	25	.520	4	6	.667	0	3	3	6	2	0	0	38	0.8	1.5	9.5
95-96—Cleveland	3	117	14	41	.341	0	0	...	1	14	15	9	3	2	4	29	5.0	3.0	9.7
Totals	25	361	47	115	.409	17	20	.850	12	47	59	31	10	6	14	125	2.4	1.2	5.0

Three-point field goals: 1991-92, 1-for-3 (.333). 1992-93, 4-for-9 (.444). 1994-95, 8-for-15 (.533). 1995-96, 1-for-16 (.063). Totals, 14-for-43 (.326).

Personal fouls/disqualifications: 1991-92, 7/0. 1992-93, 14/0. 1993-94, 1/0. 1994-95, 9/0. 1995-96, 13/1. Totals, 44/1.

F

FINLEY, MICHAEL F SUNS

PERSONAL: Born March 6, 1973, in Melrose Park, Ill. ... 6-7/215. ... Full name: Michael H. Finley.
HIGH SCHOOL: Proviso East (Maywood, Ill.).
COLLEGE: Wisconsin.
TRANSACTIONS/CAREER NOTES: Selected by Phoenix Suns in first round (21st pick overall) of 1995 NBA Draft.

COLLEGIATE RECORD

Season Team	G	Min.	FGM	FGA	Pct.	FTM	FTA	Pct.	Reb.	Ast.	Pts.	RPG	APG	PPG
91-92—Wisconsin	31	920	130	287	.453	95	128	.742	152	85	381	4.9	2.7	12.3
92-93—Wisconsin	28	979	223	478	.467	111	144	.771	161	86	620	5.8	3.1	22.1
93-94—Wisconsin	29	1046	208	446	.466	110	140	.786	194	92	592	6.7	3.2	20.4
94-95—Wisconsin	27	1000	178	470	.379	140	181	.773	141	108	554	5.2	4.0	20.5
Totals	115	3945	739	1681	.440	456	593	.769	648	371	2147	5.6	3.2	18.7

Three-point field goals: 1991-92, 26-for-72 (.361). 1992-93, 63-for-173 (.364). 1993-94, 66-for-182 (.363). 1994-95, 58-for-204 (.284). Totals, 213-for-631 (.338).

HONORS: NBA All-Rookie first team (1996).

NBA REGULAR-SEASON RECORD

Season Team	G	Min.	FGM	FGA	Pct.	FTM	FTA	Pct.	Off.	Def.	Tot.	Ast.	St.	Blk.	TO	Pts.	RPG	APG	PPG
95-96—Phoenix	82	3212	465	976	.476	242	323	.749	139	235	374	289	85	31	133	1233	4.6	3.5	15.0

Three-point field goals: 1995-96, 61-for-186 (.328).
Personal fouls/disqualifications: 1995-96, 199/1.

FISH, MATT C

PERSONAL: Born November 18, 1969, in Washington, Iowa. ... 6-11/235.
HIGH SCHOOL: Washington (Iowa).
COLLEGE: UNC Wilmington.
TRANSACTIONS/CAREER NOTES: Selected by Golden State Warriors in second round (50th pick overall) of 1992 NBA Draft. ... Waived by Warriors (October 15, 1992). ... Signed as free agent by Portland Trail Blazers (October 21, 1992). ... Waived by Trail Blazers (October 28, 1992). ... Played in Continental Basketball Association with Grand Rapids Hoops (1992-93), Omaha Racers (1992-93), Yakima Sun Kings (1992-93), Quad City Thunder (1993-94) and Fort Wayne Fury (1995-96). ... Signed as free agent by Los Angeles Clippers (October 5, 1994). ... Waived by Clippers (January 5, 1995). ... Signed as free agent by Detroit Pistons (November 21, 1995). ... Waived by Pistons (December 6, 1995). ... Signed by New York Knicks to 10-day contract (February 24, 1996). ... Waived by Knicks (March 5, 1996). ... Signed by Denver Nuggets to first of two consecutive 10-day contracts (March 7, 1996). ... Re-signed by Nuggets for remainder of the season (March 27, 1996). ... Rights renounced by Nuggets (July 17, 1996).

COLLEGIATE RECORD

Season Team	G	Min.	FGM	FGA	Pct.	FTM	FTA	Pct.	Reb.	Ast.	Pts.	RPG	APG	PPG
88-89—UNC Wilmington	6	50	7	12	.583	1	4	.250	7	3	15	1.2	0.5	2.5
89-90—UNC Wilmington	28	525	100	176	.568	38	77	.494	157	22	238	5.6	0.8	8.5
90-91—UNC Wilmington	28	647	114	207	.551	53	84	.631	190	25	281	6.8	0.9	10.0
91-92—UNC Wilmington	28	865	206	319	.646	82	130	.631	262	31	494	9.4	1.1	17.6
Totals	90	2087	427	714	.598	174	295	.590	616	81	1028	6.8	0.9	11.4

CBA REGULAR-SEASON RECORD

NOTES: CBA All-Rookie second team (1993). ... Member of CBA championship team (1994).

Season Team	G	Min.	FGM	FGA	Pct.	FTM	FTA	Pct.	Reb.	Ast.	Pts.	RPG	APG	PPG
92-93—G.R.-Om.-Yak.	51	1134	170	315	.540	99	160	.619	348	27	439	6.8	0.5	8.6
93-94—Quad City	56	1475	274	511	.536	126	190	.663	418	38	674	7.5	0.7	12.0
95-96—Fort Wayne	30	908	182	314	.580	92	139	.662	281	40	456	9.4	1.3	15.2
Totals	137	3517	626	1140	.549	317	489	.648	1047	105	1569	7.6	0.8	11.5

Three-point field goals: 1992-93, 0-for-1. 1993-94, 0-for-1. 1995-96, 0-for-2. Totals, 0-for-4.

NBA REGULAR-SEASON RECORD

Season Team	G	Min.	FGM	FGA	Pct.	FTM	FTA	Pct.	Off.	Def.	Tot.	Ast.	St.	Blk.	TO	Pts.	RPG	APG	PPG
94-95—L.A. Clippers	26	370	49	103	.476	25	37	.676	32	52	84	17	16	7	28	123	3.2	0.7	4.7
95-96—N.Y.-Den.	18	134	21	36	.583	10	19	.526	10	11	21	8	3	7	3	52	1.2	0.4	2.9
Totals	44	504	70	139	.504	35	56	.625	42	63	105	25	19	14	31	175	2.4	0.6	4.0

Three-point field goals: 1994-95, 0-for-1.
Personal fouls/disqualifications: 1994-95, 70/1. 1995-96, 19/0. Totals, 89/1.

F

FLEMING, VERN G

PERSONAL: Born February 4, 1962, in New York. ... 6-5/185.
HIGH SCHOOL: Mater Christi (Long Island, N.Y.).
COLLEGE: Georgia.
TRANSACTIONS/CAREER NOTES: Selected by Indiana Pacers in first round (18th pick overall) of 1984 NBA Draft. ... Signed as unrestricted free agent by New Jersey Nets (October 9, 1995). ... Rights renounced by Nets (July 16, 1996).
MISCELLANEOUS: Member of gold-medal-winning U.S. Olympic team (1984). ... Indiana Pacers all-time assists leader with 4,038 and all-time steals leader with 885 (1984-85 through 1994-95).

COLLEGIATE RECORD

													AVERAGES	
Season Team	G	Min.	FGM	FGA	Pct.	FTM	FTA	Pct.	Reb.	Ast.	Pts.	RPG	APG	PPG
80-81—Georgia	30	1082	108	225	.480	85	122	.697	80	86	301	2.7	2.9	10.0
81-82—Georgia	31	1079	117	236	.496	73	114	.640	120	107	307	3.9	3.5	9.9
82-83—Georgia	34	1130	227	424	.535	121	169	.716	158	104	575	4.6	3.1	16.9
83-84—Georgia	30	1030	248	493	.503	98	130	.754	120	103	594	4.0	3.4	19.8
Totals	125	4321	700	1378	.508	377	535	.705	478	400	1777	3.8	3.2	14.2

NBA REGULAR-SEASON RECORD

									REBOUNDS								AVERAGES		
Season Team	G	Min.	FGM	FGA	Pct.	FTM	FTA	Pct.	Off.	Def.	Tot.	Ast.	St.	Blk.	TO	Pts.	RPG	APG	PPG
84-85—Indiana	80	2486	433	922	.470	260	339	.767	148	175	323	247	99	8	197	1126	4.0	3.1	14.1
85-86—Indiana	80	2870	436	862	.506	263	353	.745	102	284	386	505	131	5	208	1136	4.8	6.3	14.2
86-87—Indiana	82	2549	370	727	.509	238	302	.788	109	225	334	473	109	18	167	980	4.1	5.8	12.0
87-88—Indiana	80	2733	442	845	.523	227	283	.802	106	258	364	568	115	11	175	1111	4.6	7.1	13.9
88-89—Indiana	76	2552	419	814	.515	243	304	.799	85	225	310	494	77	12	192	1084	4.1	6.5	14.3
89-90—Indiana	82	2876	467	919	.508	230	294	.782	118	204	322	610	92	10	206	1176	3.9	7.4	14.3
90-91—Indiana	69	1929	356	671	.531	161	221	.729	83	131	214	369	76	13	137	877	3.1	5.3	12.7
91-92—Indiana	82	1737	294	610	.482	132	179	.737	69	140	209	266	56	7	140	726	2.5	3.2	8.9
92-93—Indiana	75	1503	280	554	.505	143	197	.726	63	106	169	224	63	9	121	710	2.3	3.0	9.5
93-94—Indiana	55	1053	147	318	.462	64	87	.736	27	96	123	173	40	6	87	358	2.2	3.1	6.5
94-95—Indiana	55	686	93	188	.495	65	90	.722	20	68	88	109	27	1	43	251	1.6	2.0	4.6
95-96—New Jersey	77	1747	227	524	.433	133	177	.751	49	121	170	255	41	5	122	590	2.2	3.3	7.7
Totals	893	24721	3964	7954	.498	2159	2826	.764	979	2033	3012	4293	926	105	1795	10125	3.4	4.8	11.3

Three-point field goals: 1984-85, 0-for-4. 1985-86, 1-for-6 (.167). 1986-87, 2-for-10 (.200). 1987-88, 0-for-13. 1988-89, 3-for-23 (.130). 1989-90, 12-for-34 (.353). 1990-91, 4-for-18 (.222). 1991-92, 6-for-27 (.222). 1992-93, 7-for-36 (.194). 1993-94, 0-for-4. 1994-95, 0-for-7. 1995-96, 3-for-28 (.107). Totals, 38-for-210 (.181).

Personal fouls/disqualifications: 1984-85, 232/4. 1985-86, 230/3. 1986-87, 222/3. 1987-88, 225/0. 1988-89, 212/4. 1989-90, 213/1. 1990-91, 116/0. 1991-92, 134/0. 1992-93, 126/1. 1993-94, 98/1. 1994-95, 80/0. 1995-96, 115/0. Totals, 2003/17.

NBA PLAYOFF RECORD

									REBOUNDS								AVERAGES		
Season Team	G	Min.	FGM	FGA	Pct.	FTM	FTA	Pct.	Off.	Def.	Tot.	Ast.	St.	Blk.	TO	Pts.	RPG	APG	PPG
86-87—Indiana	4	141	13	36	.361	23	30	.767	9	17	26	24	4	1	10	49	6.5	6.0	12.3
89-90—Indiana	3	113	16	34	.471	8	9	.889	4	9	13	18	2	1	8	40	4.3	6.0	13.3
90-91—Indiana	5	115	18	40	.450	11	14	.786	10	7	17	23	1	3	8	47	3.4	4.6	9.4
91-92—Indiana	3	51	10	18	.556	1	3	.333	0	2	2	6	3	0	4	21	0.7	2.0	7.0
92-93—Indiana	3	80	12	27	.444	4	4	1.000	1	4	5	3	2	1	5	30	1.7	1.0	10.0
93-94—Indiana	16	247	39	76	.513	17	20	.850	12	9	21	38	10	1	22	95	1.3	2.4	5.9
94-95—Indiana	3	8	1	3	.333	0	3	.000	1	1	2	2	0	0	0	2	0.7	0.7	0.7
Totals	37	755	109	234	.466	64	83	.771	37	49	86	114	22	7	57	284	2.3	3.1	7.7

Three-point field goals: 1986-87, 0-for-1. 1989-90, 0-for-2. 1990-91, 0-for-1. 1992-93, 2-for-4 (.500). 1993-94, 0-for-5. 1994-95, 0-for-1. Totals, 2-for-14 (.143).

Personal fouls/disqualifications: 1986-87, 15/1. 1989-90, 6/0. 1990-91, 10/0. 1991-92, 5/0. 1992-93, 6/0. 1993-94, 27/0. Totals, 69/1.

FORD, SHERELL   F   SUPERSONICS

PERSONAL: Born August 26, 1972, in Baton Rouge, La. ... 6-7/210. ... Full name: Willard Sherell Ford. ... Name pronounced SHA-rell.

HIGH SCHOOL: Proviso East (Maywood, Ill.).

COLLEGE: Illinois-Chicago.

TRANSACTIONS/CAREER NOTES: Selected by Seattle SuperSonics in first round (26th pick overall) of 1995 NBA Draft.

COLLEGIATE RECORD

												AVERAGES		
Season Team	G	Min.	FGM	FGA	Pct.	FTM	FTA	Pct.	Reb.	Ast.	Pts.	RPG	APG	PPG
91-92—Illinois-Chicago						Did not play—ineligible.								
92-93—Illinois-Chicago	32	1044	246	516	.477	80	127	.630	270	42	601	8.4	1.3	18.8
93-94—Illinois-Chicago	29	999	279	560	.498	120	172	.698	254	32	704	8.8	1.1	24.3
94-95—Illinois-Chicago	27	969	265	562	.472	130	170	.765	283	39	707	10.5	1.4	26.2
Totals	88	3012	790	1638	.482	330	469	.704	807	113	2012	9.2	1.3	22.9

Three-point field goals: 1992-93, 29-for-94 (.309). 1993-94, 26-for-87 (.299). 1994-95, 47-for-113 (.416). Totals, 102-for-294 (.347).

NBA REGULAR-SEASON RECORD

									REBOUNDS								AVERAGES		
Season Team	G	Min.	FGM	FGA	Pct.	FTM	FTA	Pct.	Off.	Def.	Tot.	Ast.	St.	Blk.	TO	Pts.	RPG	APG	PPG
95-96—Seattle	28	139	30	80	.375	26	34	.765	12	12	24	5	8	1	6	90	0.9	0.2	3.2

Three-point field goals: 1995-96, 4-for-25 (.160).
Personal fouls/disqualifications: 1995-96, 27/0.

FOSTER, GREG   C   JAZZ

PERSONAL: Born October 3, 1968, in Oakland. ... 6-11/240. ... Full name: Gregory Clinton Foster.

HIGH SCHOOL: Skyline (Oakland).

COLLEGE: UCLA, then Texas-El Paso.

TRANSACTIONS/CAREER NOTES: Selected by Washington Bullets in second round (35th pick overall) of 1990 NBA Draft. ... Waived by Bullets (December 1, 1992). ... Signed as free agent by Atlanta Hawks (December 16, 1992). ... Waived by Hawks (November 2, 1993). ... Signed as free agent by Milwaukee Bucks (November 19, 1993). ... Waived by Bucks (December 3, 1993). ... Signed as free agent by Chicago Bulls (September 27, 1994). ... Waived by Bulls (December 12, 1994). ... Signed by Minnesota Timberwolves (December 16, 1994). ... Signed as unrestricted free agent by Utah Jazz (October 6, 1995).

Season Team	G	Min.	FGM	FGA	Pct.	FTM	FTA	Pct.	Reb.	Ast.	Pts.	RPG	APG	PPG
86-87—UCLA	31	441	44	88	.500	13	26	.500	76	25	101	2.5	0.8	3.3
87-88—UCLA	11	292	39	74	.527	16	37	.432	61	13	94	5.5	1.2	8.5
88-89—Texas-El Paso	26	728	117	242	.483	54	83	.651	189	18	288	7.3	0.7	11.1
89-90—Texas-El Paso	32	837	133	286	.465	73	90	.811	198	31	339	6.2	1.0	10.6
Totals	100	2298	333	690	.483	156	236	.661	524	87	822	5.2	0.9	8.2

Three-point field goals: 1988-89, 0-for-1. 1989-90, 0-for-2. Totals, 0-for-3.

NBA REGULAR-SEASON RECORD

| | | | | | | | | | REBOUNDS | | | | | | | AVERAGES | | |
Season Team	G	Min.	FGM	FGA	Pct.	FTM	FTA	Pct.	Off.	Def.	Tot.	Ast.	St.	Blk.	TO	Pts.	RPG	APG	PPG
90-91—Washington	54	606	97	211	.460	42	61	.689	52	99	151	37	12	22	45	236	2.8	0.7	4.4
91-92—Washington	49	548	89	193	.461	35	49	.714	43	102	145	35	6	12	36	213	3.0	0.7	4.3
92-93—Wash.-Atl.	43	298	55	120	.458	15	21	.714	32	51	83	21	3	14	25	125	1.9	0.5	2.9
93-94—Milwaukee	3	19	4	7	.571	2	2	1.000	0	3	3	0	0	1	1	10	1.0	0.0	3.3
94-95—Chi.-Min.	78	1144	150	318	.472	78	111	.703	85	174	259	39	15	28	71	385	3.3	0.5	4.9
95-96—Utah	73	803	107	244	.439	61	72	.847	53	125	178	25	7	22	58	276	2.4	0.3	3.8
Totals	300	3418	502	1093	.459	233	316	.737	265	554	819	157	43	99	236	1245	2.7	0.5	4.2

Three-point field goals: 1990-91, 0-for-5. 1991-92, 0-for-1. 1992-93, 0-for-4. 1994-95, 7-for-23 (.304). 1995-96, 1-for-8 (.125). Totals, 8-for-41 (.195).
Personal fouls/disqualifications: 1990-91, 112/1. 1991-92, 83/0. 1992-93, 58/0. 1993-94, 3/0. 1994-95, 183/0. 1995-96, 120/0. Totals, 559/1.

NBA PLAYOFF RECORD

| | | | | | | | | | REBOUNDS | | | | | | | AVERAGES | | |
Season Team	G	Min.	FGM	FGA	Pct.	FTM	FTA	Pct.	Off.	Def.	Tot.	Ast.	St.	Blk.	TO	Pts.	RPG	APG	PPG
92-93—Atlanta	1	5	1	3	.333	3	4	.750	0	1	1	0	0	0	0	5	1.0	0.0	5.0
95-96—Utah	12	76	11	22	.500	6	10	.600	6	6	12	2	1	2	5	28	1.0	0.2	2.3
Totals	13	81	12	25	.480	9	14	.643	6	7	13	2	1	2	5	33	1.0	0.2	2.5

Personal fouls/disqualifications: 1995-96, 16/0.

FOX, RICK　　　　　　　　G/F　　　　　　　　CELTICS

PERSONAL: Born July 24, 1969, in Toronto. ... 6-7/249. ... Full name: Ulrich Alexander Fox.
HIGH SCHOOL: Warsaw (Ind.) Community.
COLLEGE: North Carolina.
TRANSACTIONS/CAREER NOTES: Selected by Boston Celtics in first round (24th pick overall) of 1991 NBA Draft.

COLLEGIATE RECORD

NOTES: THE SPORTING NEWS All-America third team (1991).

Season Team	G	Min.	FGM	FGA	Pct.	FTM	FTA	Pct.	Reb.	Ast.	Pts.	RPG	APG	PPG
87-88—North Carolina	34	371	59	94	.628	15	30	.500	63	32	136	1.9	0.9	4.0
88-89—North Carolina	37	829	165	283	.583	83	105	.790	142	76	426	3.8	2.1	11.5
89-90—North Carolina	34	981	203	389	.522	75	102	.735	157	84	551	4.6	2.5	16.2
90-91—North Carolina	35	999	206	455	.453	111	138	.804	232	131	590	6.6	3.7	16.9
Totals	140	3180	633	1221	.518	284	375	.757	594	323	1703	4.2	2.3	12.2

Three-point field goals: 1987-88, 3-for-9 (.333). 1988-89, 13-for-29 (.448). 1989-90, 70-for-160 (.438). 1990-91, 67-for-196 (.342). Totals, 153-for-394 (.388).

NBA REGULAR-SEASON RECORD

HONORS: NBA All-Rookie second team (1992).

| | | | | | | | | | REBOUNDS | | | | | | | AVERAGES | | |
Season Team	G	Min.	FGM	FGA	Pct.	FTM	FTA	Pct.	Off.	Def.	Tot.	Ast.	St.	Blk.	TO	Pts.	RPG	APG	PPG
91-92—Boston	81	1535	241	525	.459	139	184	.755	73	147	220	126	78	30	123	644	2.7	1.6	8.0
92-93—Boston	71	1082	184	380	.484	81	101	.802	55	104	159	113	61	21	77	453	2.2	1.6	6.4
93-94—Boston	82	2096	340	728	.467	174	230	.757	105	250	355	217	81	52	158	887	4.3	2.6	10.8
94-95—Boston	53	1039	169	351	.481	95	123	.772	61	94	155	139	52	19	78	464	2.9	2.6	8.8
95-96—Boston	81	2588	421	928	.454	196	254	.772	158	292	450	369	113	41	216	1137	5.6	4.6	14.0
Totals	368	8340	1355	2912	.465	685	892	.768	452	887	1339	964	385	163	652	3585	3.6	2.6	9.7

Three-point field goals: 1991-92, 23-for-70 (.329). 1992-93, 4-for-23 (.174). 1993-94, 33-for-100 (.330). 1994-95, 31-for-75 (.413). 1995-96, 99-for-272 (.364). Totals, 190-for-540 (.352).
Personal fouls/disqualifications: 1991-92, 230/3. 1992-93, 133/1. 1993-94, 244/4. 1994-95, 154/1. 1995-96, 290/5. Totals, 1051/14.

NBA PLAYOFF RECORD

| | | | | | | | | | REBOUNDS | | | | | | | AVERAGES | | |
Season Team	G	Min.	FGM	FGA	Pct.	FTM	FTA	Pct.	Off.	Def.	Tot.	Ast.	St.	Blk.	TO	Pts.	RPG	APG	PPG
91-92—Boston	8	67	11	23	.478	4	4	1.000	3	3	6	4	2	2	2	29	0.8	0.5	3.6
92-93—Boston	4	71	7	25	.280	2	2	1.000	8	11	19	5	2	1	4	17	4.8	1.3	4.3
Totals	12	138	18	48	.375	6	6	1.000	11	14	25	9	4	3	6	46	2.1	0.8	3.8

Three-point field goals: 1991-92, 3-for-6 (.500). 1992-93, 1-for-3 (.333). Totals, 4-for-9 (.444).
Personal fouls/disqualifications: 1991-92, 11/0. 1992-93, 7/0. Totals, 18/0.

FG

GAMBLE, KEVIN　　　　　　　F/G　　　　　　　KINGS

PERSONAL: Born November 13, 1965, in Springfield, Ill. ... 6-6/225. ... Full name: Kevin Douglas Gamble.
HIGH SCHOOL: Lanphier (Springfield, Ill.).
JUNIOR COLLEGE: Lincoln College (Ill.).
COLLEGE: Iowa.

TRANSACTIONS/CAREER NOTES: Selected by Portland Trail Blazers in third round (63rd pick overall) of 1987 NBA Draft. ... Waived by Trail Blazers (December 9, 1987). ... Played in Continental Basketball Association with Quad City Thunder (1987-88 and 1988-89). ... Played in World Basketball League with Chicago Express (1988). ... Signed as free agent by Boston Celtics (December 15, 1988). ... Signed as free agent by Miami Heat (October 7, 1994). ... Traded by Heat with G/F Billy Owens to Sacramento Kings for F/G Walt Williams and F Tyrone Corbin (February 22, 1996).

COLLEGIATE RECORD

Season Team	G	Min.	FGM	FGA	Pct.	FTM	FTA	Pct.	Reb.	Ast.	Pts.	AVERAGES RPG	APG	PPG
83-84—Lincoln College..............	30	...	262	469	.559	115	148	.777	276	53	639	9.2	1.8	21.3
84-85—Lincoln College..............	31	...	267	461	.579	103	126	.817	301	116	637	9.7	3.7	20.5
85-86—Iowa	30	260	36	76	.474	7	10	.700	52	25	79	1.7	0.8	2.6
86-87—Iowa	35	867	162	298	.544	69	99	.697	158	53	418	4.5	1.5	11.9
Junior college totals	61		529	930	.569	218	274	.796	577	169	1276	9.5	2.8	20.9
4-year-college totals	65	1127	198	374	.529	76	109	.697	210	78	497	3.2	1.2	7.6

Three-point field goals: 1986-87, 35-for-76 (.461).

CBA REGULAR-SEASON RECORD

Season Team	G	Min.	FGM	FGA	Pct.	FTM	FTA	Pct.	Reb.	Ast.	Pts.	AVERAGES RPG	APG	PPG
87-88—Quad City......................	40	1450	330	640	.516	151	184	.821	237	149	842	5.9	3.7	21.1
88-89—Quad City......................	12	490	110	223	.493	110	129	.853	66	48	333	5.5	4.0	27.8
Totals	52	1940	440	863	.510	261	313	.834	303	197	1175	5.8	3.8	22.6

Three-point field goals: 1987-88, 31-for-75 (.413). 1988-89, 3-for-20 (.150). Totals, 34-for-95 (.358).

NBA REGULAR-SEASON RECORD

Season Team	G	Min.	FGM	FGA	Pct.	FTM	FTA	Pct.	REBOUNDS Off.	Def.	Tot.	Ast.	St.	Blk.	TO	Pts.	AVERAGES RPG	APG	PPG
87-88—Portland..........	9	19	0	3	.000	0	0	...	2	1	3	1	2	0	2	0	0.3	0.1	0.0
88-89—Boston	44	375	75	136	.551	35	55	.636	11	31	42	34	14	3	19	187	1.0	0.8	4.3
89-90—Boston	71	990	137	301	.455	85	107	.794	42	70	112	119	28	8	44	362	1.6	1.7	5.1
90-91—Boston	82	2706	548	933	.587	185	227	.815	85	182	267	256	100	34	148	1281	3.3	3.1	15.6
91-92—Boston	82	2496	480	908	.529	139	157	.885	80	206	286	219	75	37	97	1108	3.5	2.7	13.5
92-93—Boston	82	2541	459	906	.507	123	149	.826	46	200	246	226	86	37	81	1093	3.0	2.8	13.3
93-94—Boston	75	1880	368	804	.458	103	126	.817	41	118	159	149	57	22	77	864	2.1	2.0	11.5
94-95—Miami	77	1223	220	450	.489	87	111	.784	29	93	122	119	52	10	49	566	1.6	1.5	7.4
95-96—Mia.-Sac.	65	1325	152	379	.401	38	48	.792	21	92	113	100	35	8	43	386	1.7	1.5	5.9
Totals	587	13555	2439	4820	.506	795	980	.811	357	993	1350	1223	449	159	560	5847	2.3	2.1	10.0

Three-point field goals: 1987-88, 0-for-1. 1988-89, 2-for-11 (.182). 1989-90, 3-for-18 (.167). 1990-91, 0-for-7. 1991-92, 9-for-31 (.290). 1992-93, 52-for-139 (.374). 1993-94, 25-for-103 (.243). 1994-95, 39-for-98 (.398). 1995-96, 44-for-114 (.386). Totals, 174-for-522 (.333).

Personal fouls/disqualifications: 1987-88, 2/0. 1988-89, 40/0. 1989-90, 77/1. 1990-91, 237/6. 1991-92, 200/2. 1992-93, 185/1. 1993-94, 134/0. 1994-95, 130/0. 1995-96, 147/2. Totals, 1152/12.

NBA PLAYOFF RECORD

Season Team	G	Min.	FGM	FGA	Pct.	FTM	FTA	Pct.	REBOUNDS Off.	Def.	Tot.	Ast.	St.	Blk.	TO	Pts.	AVERAGES RPG	APG	PPG
88-89—Boston	1	29	4	11	.364	0	2	.000	1	0	1	2	1	0	0	8	1.0	2.0	8.0
89-90—Boston	3	8	3	5	.600	0	0	...	1	0	1	2	0	0	1	6	0.3	0.7	2.0
90-91—Boston	11	238	29	60	.483	8	12	.667	3	10	13	19	4	2	7	66	1.2	1.7	6.0
91-92—Boston	10	335	62	131	.473	12	15	.800	13	29	42	23	12	6	10	136	4.2	2.3	13.6
92-93—Boston	4	142	23	42	.548	4	4	1.000	3	6	9	10	6	1	5	55	2.3	2.5	13.8
95-96—Sacramento	2	3	0	0	...	0	0	...	0	0	0	0	0	0	0	0	0.0	0.0	0.0
Totals	31	755	121	249	.486	24	33	.727	21	45	66	56	23	9	23	271	2.1	1.8	8.7

Three-point field goals: 1988-89, 0-for-1. 1991-92, 0-for-2. 1992-93, 5-for-12 (.417). Totals, 5-for-15 (.333).

Personal fouls/disqualifications: 1988-89, 1/0. 1989-90, 1/0. 1990-91, 24/0. 1991-92, 26/0. 1992-93, 11/0. Totals, 63/0.

GARNETT, KEVIN   F   TIMBERWOLVES

PERSONAL: Born May 19, 1976, in Mauldin, S.C. ... 6-11/220.
HIGH SCHOOL: Mauldin (S.C.), then Farragut Academy (Chicago).
COLLEGE: Did not attend college.
TRANSACTIONS/CAREER NOTES: Selected out of high school by Minnesota Timberwolves in first round (fifth pick overall) of 1995 NBA Draft.

NBA REGULAR-SEASON RECORD

HONORS: NBA All-Rookie second team (1996).

Season Team	G	Min.	FGM	FGA	Pct.	FTM	FTA	Pct.	REBOUNDS Off.	Def.	Tot.	Ast.	St.	Blk.	TO	Pts.	AVERAGES RPG	APG	PPG
95-96—Minnesota.......	80	2293	361	735	.491	105	149	.705	175	326	501	145	86	131	110	835	6.3	1.8	10.4

Three-point field goals: 1995-96, 8-for-28 (.286).
Personal fouls/disqualifications: 1995-96, 189/2.

GATLING, CHRIS   F/C   MAVERICKS

PERSONAL: Born September 3, 1967, in Elizabeth City, N.J. ... 6-10/230. ... Full name: Chris Raymond Gatling.
HIGH SCHOOL: Elizabeth (N.J.).
COLLEGE: Pittsburgh, then Old Dominion.
TRANSACTIONS/CAREER NOTES: Selected by Golden State Warriors in first round (16th pick overall) of 1991 NBA Draft. ... Traded by Warriors with G Tim Hardaway to Miami Heat for F/C Kevin Willis and G Bimbo Coles (February 22, 1996). ... Rights renounced by Heat (July 17, 1996). ... Signed as free agent by Dallas Mavericks (July 16, 1996).

COLLEGIATE RECORD

Season Team	G	Min.	FGM	FGA	Pct.	FTM	FTA	Pct.	Reb.	Ast.	Pts.	AVERAGES RPG	APG	PPG
86-87—Pittsburgh						Did not play.								
87-88—Old Dominion					Did not play—transfer student.									
88-89—Old Dominion	27	839	239	388	.616	126	179	.704	244	26	604	9.0	1.0	22.4
89-90—Old Dominion	26	822	207	357	.580	120	179	.670	259	25	534	10.0	1.0	20.5
90-91—Old Dominion	32	1002	251	405	.620	171	247	.692	356	24	673	11.1	0.8	21.0
Totals	85	2663	697	1150	.606	417	605	.689	859	75	1811	10.1	0.9	21.3

Three-point field goals: 1990-91, 0-for-1.

NBA REGULAR-SEASON RECORD

Season Team	G	Min.	FGM	FGA	Pct.	FTM	FTA	Pct.	REBOUNDS Off.	Def.	Tot.	Ast.	St.	Blk.	TO	Pts.	AVERAGES RPG	APG	PPG
91-92—Golden State ...	54	612	117	206	.568	72	109	.661	75	107	182	16	31	36	44	306	3.4	0.3	5.7
92-93—Golden State ...	70	1248	249	462	.539	150	207	.725	129	191	320	40	44	53	102	648	4.6	0.6	9.3
93-94—Golden State ...	82	1296	271	461	.588	129	208	.620	143	254	397	41	40	63	84	671	4.8	0.5	8.2
94-95—Golden State ...	58	1470	324	512	*.633	148	250	.592	144	299	443	51	39	52	117	796	7.6	0.9	13.7
95-96—GS-Mia. ...	71	1427	326	567	.575	139	207	.672	129	288	417	43	36	40	95	791	5.9	0.6	11.1
Totals	335	6053	1287	2208	.583	638	981	.650	620	1139	1759	191	190	244	442	3212	5.3	0.6	9.6

Three-point field goals: 1991-92, 0-for-4. 1992-93, 0-for-6. 1993-94, 0-for-1. 1994-95, 0-for-1. 1995-96, 0-for-1. Totals, 0-for-13.
Personal fouls/disqualifications: 1991-92, 101/0. 1992-93, 197/2. 1993-94, 223/5. 1994-95, 184/4. 1995-96, 217/0. Totals, 922/11.

NBA PLAYOFF RECORD

Season Team	G	Min.	FGM	FGA	Pct.	FTM	FTA	Pct.	REBOUNDS Off.	Def.	Tot.	Ast.	St.	Blk.	TO	Pts.	AVERAGES RPG	APG	PPG
91-92—Golden State ...	4	81	18	29	.621	14	22	.636	9	16	25	0	2	10	1	50	6.3	0.0	12.5
93-94—Golden State ...	3	54	8	13	.615	10	13	.769	7	10	17	4	2	1	2	26	5.7	1.3	8.7
95-96—Miami	3	68	6	22	.273	6	12	.500	10	14	24	1	2	0	8	18	8.0	0.3	6.0
Totals	10	203	32	64	.500	30	47	.638	26	40	66	5	6	11	11	94	6.6	0.5	9.4

Personal fouls/disqualifications: 1991-92, 14/0. 1993-94, 10/0. 1995-96, 8/1. Totals, 32/1.

GATTISON, KENNY   F   JAZZ

PERSONAL: Born May 23, 1964, in Wilmington, N.C. ... 6-8/256. ... Full name: Kenneth Clay Gattison.
HIGH SCHOOL: New Hanover (Wilmington, N.C.).
COLLEGE: Old Dominion.
TRANSACTIONS/CAREER NOTES: Selected by Phoenix Suns in third round (55th pick overall) of 1986 NBA Draft. ... Played in Italy (1988-89). ... Waived by Suns (September 21, 1989). ... Signed as free agent by Charlotte Hornets (September 26, 1989). ... Waived by Hornets (October 18, 1989). ... Played in Continental Basketball Association with Quad City Thunder (1989-90). ... Signed as free agent by Hornets (December 2, 1989). ... Selected by Vancouver Grizzlies from Hornets in NBA expansion draft (June 24, 1995). ... Traded by Grizzlies with 1996 second-round draft choice to Orlando Magic for F Jeff Turner (February 22, 1996). ... Traded by Magic with G Brooks Thompson and first-round draft choice to Utah Jazz for C Felton Spencer (August 9, 1996).

COLLEGIATE RECORD

Season Team	G	Min.	FGM	FGA	Pct.	FTM	FTA	Pct.	Reb.	Ast.	Pts.	AVERAGES RPG	APG	PPG
82-83—Old Dominion	29	705	94	187	.503	55	78	.705	218	18	243	7.5	0.6	8.4
83-84—Old Dominion	31	916	127	257	.494	89	137	.650	219	16	343	7.1	0.5	11.1
84-85—Old Dominion	31	890	192	357	.538	114	187	.610	285	15	498	9.2	0.5	16.1
85-86—Old Dominion	31	1008	218	342	.637	103	153	.673	241	31	539	7.8	1.0	17.4
Totals	122	3519	631	1143	.552	361	555	.650	963	80	1623	7.9	0.7	13.3

NBA REGULAR-SEASON RECORD

Season Team	G	Min.	FGM	FGA	Pct.	FTM	FTA	Pct.	REBOUNDS Off.	Def.	Tot.	Ast.	St.	Blk.	TO	Pts.	AVERAGES RPG	APG	PPG
86-87—Phoenix	77	1104	148	311	.476	108	171	.632	87	183	270	36	24	33	88	404	3.5	0.5	5.2
87-88—Phoenix					Did not play—Injured.														
88-89—Phoenix	2	9	0	1	.000	1	2	.500	0	1	1	0	0	0	0	1	0.5	0.0	0.5
89-90—Charlotte	63	941	148	269	.550	75	110	.682	75	122	197	39	35	31	67	372	3.1	0.6	5.9
90-91—Charlotte	72	1552	243	457	.532	164	248	.661	136	243	379	44	48	67	102	650	5.3	0.6	9.0
91-92—Charlotte	82	2223	423	799	.529	196	285	.688	177	403	580	131	59	69	140	1042	7.1	1.6	12.7
92-93—Charlotte	75	1475	203	384	.529	102	169	.604	108	245	353	68	48	55	64	508	4.7	0.9	6.8
93-94—Charlotte	77	1644	233	445	.524	126	195	.646	105	253	358	95	59	46	79	592	4.6	1.2	7.7
94-95—Charlotte	21	409	47	100	.470	31	51	.608	21	54	75	7	7	15	22	125	3.6	0.8	6.0
95-96—Vancouver	25	570	91	190	.479	47	78	.603	35	79	114	14	10	11	40	229	4.6	0.6	9.2
Totals	494	9927	1536	2956	.520	850	1309	.649	744	1583	2327	444	290	327	602	3923	4.7	0.9	7.9

Three-point field goals: 1988-89, 0-for-3. 1989-90, 1-for-1. 1990-91, 0-for-2. 1991-92, 0-for-2. 1992-93, 0-for-3. 1994-95, 0-for-1. Totals, 1-for-12 (.083).
Personal fouls/disqualifications: 1986-87, 178/1. 1988-89, 2/0. 1989-90, 150/1. 1990-91, 211/3. 1991-92, 273/4. 1992-93, 237/3. 1993-94, 229/3. 1994-95, 64/1. 1995-96, 75/0. Totals, 1419/16.

NBA PLAYOFF RECORD

Season Team	G	Min.	FGM	FGA	Pct.	FTM	FTA	Pct.	REBOUNDS Off.	Def.	Tot.	Ast.	St.	Blk.	TO	Pts.	AVERAGES RPG	APG	PPG
92-93—Charlotte	9	187	22	46	.478	9	21	.429	19	20	39	11	5	1	7	53	4.3	1.2	5.9
94-95—Charlotte	4	58	5	8	.625	5	8	.625	5	7	12	2	2	0	5	15	3.0	0.5	3.8
Totals	13	245	27	54	.500	14	29	.483	24	27	51	13	7	1	12	68	3.9	1.0	5.2

Personal fouls/disqualifications: 1992-93, 18/0. 1994-95, 16/0. Totals, 34/0.

ITALIAN LEAGUE RECORD

Season Team	G	Min.	FGM	FGA	Pct.	FTM	FTA	Pct.	Reb.	Ast.	Pts.	AVERAGES RPG	APG	PPG
88-89—Jolly	21	769	147	235	.626	73	109	.670	202	...	367	9.6	...	17.5

G

Season Team	G	Min.	FGM	FGA	Pct.	FTM	FTA	Pct.	Reb.	Ast.	Pts.	AVERAGES		
												RPG	APG	PPG
89-90—Quad City	7	277	55	100	.550	51	61	.836	81	15	161	11.6	2.1	23.0

Three-point field goals: 1989-90, 0-for-1.

GEIGER, MATT　　　　　　　　C　　　　　　　　HORNETS

PERSONAL: Born September 10, 1969, in Salem, Mass. ... 7-0/245. ... Full name: Matthew Allen Geiger. ... Name pronounced GUY-gher.
HIGH SCHOOL: Countryside Senior (Clearwater, Fla.).
COLLEGE: Auburn, then Georgia Tech.
TRANSACTIONS/CAREER NOTES: Selected by Miami Heat in second round (42nd pick overall) of 1992 NBA Draft. ... Traded by Heat with G/F Glen Rice, G Khalid Reeves and 1996 first-round draft choice to Charlotte Hornets for C Alonzo Mourning, C LeRon Ellis and G Pete Myers (November 3, 1995).

COLLEGIATE RECORD

Season Team	G	Min.	FGM	FGA	Pct.	FTM	FTA	Pct.	Reb.	Ast.	Pts.	AVERAGES		
												RPG	APG	PPG
87-88—Auburn	30	597	80	156	.513	33	50	.660	124	24	193	4.1	0.8	6.4
88-89—Auburn	28	807	170	337	.504	106	154	.688	186	31	446	6.6	1.1	15.9
89-90—Georgia Tech					Did not play—transfer student.									
90-91—Georgia Tech	27	711	130	237	.549	49	73	.671	172	26	309	6.4	1.0	11.4
91-92—Georgia Tech	35	952	165	270	.611	84	119	.706	254	37	414	7.3	1.1	11.8
Totals	120	3067	545	1000	.545	272	396	.687	736	· 118	1362	6.1	1.0	11.4

Three-point field goals: 1988-89, 0-for-4. 1990-91, 0-for-3. 1991-92, 0-for-2. Totals, 0-for-9.

NBA REGULAR-SEASON RECORD

NOTES: Led NBA with 11 disqualifications (1996).

Season Team	G	Min.	FGM	FGA	Pct.	FTM	FTA	Pct.	REBOUNDS			Ast.	St.	Blk.	TO	Pts.	AVERAGES		
									Off.	Def.	Tot.						RPG	APG	PPG
92-93—Miami	48	554	76	145	.524	62	92	.674	46	74	120	14	15	18	36	214	2.5	0.3	4.5
93-94—Miami	72	1199	202	352	.574	116	149	.779	119	184	303	32	36	29	61	521	4.2	0.4	7.2
94-95—Miami	74	1712	260	485	.536	93	143	.650	146	267	413	55	41	51	113	617	5.6	0.7	8.3
95-96—Charlotte	77	2349	357	666	.536	149	205	.727	201	448	649	60	46	63	137	866	8.4	0.8	11.2
Totals	271	5814	895	1648	.543	420	589	.713	512	973	1485	161	138	161	347	2218	5.5	0.6	8.2

Three-point field goals: 1992-93, 0-for-4. 1993-94, 1-for-5 (.200). 1994-95, 4-for-10 (.400). 1995-96, 3-for-8 (.375). Totals, 8-for-27 (.296).
Personal fouls/disqualifications: 1992-93, 123/6. 1993-94, 201/2. 1994-95, 245/5. 1995-96, 290/11. Totals, 859/24.

NBA PLAYOFF RECORD

Season Team	G	Min.	FGM	FGA	Pct.	FTM	FTA	Pct.	REBOUNDS			Ast.	St.	Blk.	TO	Pts.	AVERAGES		
									Off.	Def.	Tot.						RPG	APG	PPG
93-94—Miami	2	11	0	2	.000	1	2	.500	0	4	4	0	0	0	0	1	2.0	0.0	0.5

Personal fouls/disqualifications: 1993-94, 1/0.

GILL, KENDALL　　　　　　　　G　　　　　　　　NETS

PERSONAL: Born May 25, 1968, in Chicago. ... 6-5/216. ... Full name: Kendall Cedric Gill.
HIGH SCHOOL: Rich Central (Olympia Fields, Ill.).
COLLEGE: Illinois.
TRANSACTIONS/CAREER NOTES: Selected by Charlotte Hornets in first round (fifth pick overall) of 1990 NBA Draft. ... Traded by Hornets to Seattle SuperSonics for F Eddie Johnson, G Dana Barros and option to switch 1994 first-round draft choices (September 1, 1993). ... Traded by SuperSonics to Hornets for G Hersey Hawkins and G/F David Wingate (June 27, 1995). ... Traded by Hornets with G Khalid Reeves to New Jersey Nets for G Kenny Anderson and G/F Gerald Glass (January 19, 1996).

COLLEGIATE RECORD

NOTES: THE SPORTING NEWS All-America third team (1990).

Season Team	G	Min.	FGM	FGA	Pct.	FTM	FTA	Pct.	Reb.	Ast.	Pts.	AVERAGES		
												RPG	APG	PPG
86-87—Illinois	31	345	40	83	.482	34	53	.642	42	27	114	1.4	0.9	3.7
87-88—Illinois	33	946	128	272	.471	67	89	.753	73	138	344	2.2	4.2	10.4
88-89—Illinois	24	681	143	264	.542	46	58	.793	70	91	370	2.9	3.8	15.4
89-90—Illinois	29	1000	211	422	.500	136	175	.777	143	96	581	4.9	3.3	20.0
Totals	117	2972	522	1041	.501	283	375	.755	328	352	1409	2.8	3.0	12.0

Three-point field goals: 1986-87, 0-for-1. 1987-88, 21-for-69 (.304). 1988-89, 38-for-83 (.458). 1989-90, 23-for-66 (.348). Totals, 82-for-219 (.374).

NBA REGULAR-SEASON RECORD

HONORS: NBA All-Rookie first team (1991).

Season Team	G	Min.	FGM	FGA	Pct.	FTM	FTA	Pct.	REBOUNDS			Ast.	St.	Blk.	TO	Pts.	AVERAGES		
									Off.	Def.	Tot.						RPG	APG	PPG
90-91—Charlotte	82	1944	376	836	.450	152	182	.835	105	158	263	303	104	39	163	906	3.2	3.7	11.0
91-92—Charlotte	79	2906	666	1427	.467	284	381	.745	165	237	402	329	154	46	180	1622	5.1	4.2	20.5
92-93—Charlotte	69	2430	463	1032	.449	224	290	.772	120	220	340	268	98	36	174	1167	4.9	3.9	16.9
93-94—Seattle	79	2435	429	969	.443	215	275	.782	91	177	268	275	151	32	143	1111	3.4	3.5	14.1
94-95—Seattle	73	2125	392	858	.457	155	209	.742	99	191	290	192	117	28	138	1002	4.0	2.6	13.7
95-96—Char.-N.J.	47	1683	246	524	.469	138	176	.784	72	160	232	260	64	24	131	656	4.9	5.5	14.0
Totals	429	13523	2572	5646	.456	1168	1513	.772	652	1143	1795	1627	688	205	929	6464	4.2	3.8	15.1

Three-point field goals: 1990-91, 2-for-14 (.143). 1991-92, 6-for-25 (.240). 1992-93, 17-for-62 (.274). 1993-94, 38-for-120 (.317). 1994-95, 63-for-171 (.368). 1995-96, 26-for-79 (.329). Totals, 152-for-471 (.323).
Personal fouls/disqualifications: 1990-91, 186/0. 1991-92, 237/1. 1992-93, 191/2. 1993-94, 194/1. 1994-95, 186/0. 1995-96, 131/2. Totals, 1125/6.

G

NBA PLAYOFF RECORD

								REBOUNDS								AVERAGES		
Season Team	G	Min.	FGM	FGA	Pct.	FTM	FTA	Pct.	Off.	Def.	Tot.	Ast.	St.	Blk.	TO	Pts.	RPG	APG	PPG
92-93—Charlotte........	9	353	65	162	.401	25	35	.714	26	20	46	26	21	6	19	156	5.1	2.9	17.3
93-94—Seattle	5	153	26	60	.433	13	21	.619	7	17	24	10	6	1	6	67	4.8	2.0	13.4
94-95—Seattle	4	72	9	25	.360	5	8	.625	1	3	4	10	4	1	4	25	1.0	2.5	6.3
Totals	18	578	100	247	.405	43	64	.672	34	40	74	46	31	8	29	248	4.1	2.6	13.8

Three-point field goals: 1992-93, 1-for-6 (.167). 1993-94, 2-for-9 (.222). 1994-95, 2-for-8 (.250). Totals, 5-for-23 (.217).
Personal fouls/disqualifications: 1992-93, 29/0. 1993-94, 12/0. 1994-95, 6/0. Totals, 47/0.

GILLIAM, ARMON　　　　　　　F　　　　　　　BUCKS

PERSONAL: Born May 28, 1964, in Pittsburgh. ... 6-9/250. ... Full name: Armon Louis Gilliam.
HIGH SCHOOL: Bethel Park (Pa.) Senior.
JUNIOR COLLEGE: Independence (Kan.) Junior College.
COLLEGE: UNLV.
TRANSACTIONS/CAREER NOTES: Selected by Phoenix Suns in first round (second pick overall) of 1987 NBA Draft. ... Traded by Suns to Charlotte Hornets for F Kurt Rambis and two future second-round draft choices (December 13, 1989). ... Traded by Hornets with C Dave Hoppen to Philadelphia 76ers for C Mike Gminski (January 4, 1991). ... Waived by 76ers (July 28, 1993). ... Signed as free agent by New Jersey Nets (August 11, 1993). ... Rights renounced by Nets (July 16, 1996). ... Signed as free agent by Milwaukee Bucks (August 6, 1996).

COLLEGIATE RECORD

NOTES: THE SPORTING NEWS All-America second team (1987).

											AVERAGES		
Season Team	G	Min.	FGM	FGA	Pct.	FTM	FTA	Pct.	Reb.	Ast.	Pts.	RPG	APG	PPG
82-83—Independence J.C...........	38	...	262	422	.621	117	185	.632	314	15	641	8.3	0.4	16.9
83-84—UNLV..............................						Did not play—redshirted.								
84-85—UNLV..............................	31	800	136	219	.621	98	150	.653	212	6	370	6.8	0.2	11.9
85-86—UNLV..............................	37	1243	221	418	.529	140	190	.737	315	17	582	8.5	0.5	15.7
86-87—UNLV..............................	39	1259	359	598	.600	185	254	.728	363	35	903	9.3	0.9	23.2
Junior college totals	38	...	262	422	.621	117	185	.632	314	15	641	8.3	0.4	16.9
4-year-college totals	107	3302	716	1235	.580	423	594	.712	890	58	1855	8.3	0.5	17.3

NBA REGULAR-SEASON RECORD

HONORS: NBA All-Rookie team (1988).

								REBOUNDS								AVERAGES		
Season Team	G	Min.	FGM	FGA	Pct.	FTM	FTA	Pct.	Off.	Def.	Tot.	Ast.	St.	Blk.	TO	Pts.	RPG	APG	PPG
87-88—Phoenix	55	1807	342	720	.475	131	193	.679	134	300	434	72	58	29	123	815	7.9	1.3	14.8
88-89—Phoenix	74	2120	468	930	.503	240	323	.743	165	376	541	52	54	27	140	1176	7.3	0.7	15.9
89-90—Phoe.-Char......	76	2426	484	940	.515	303	419	.723	211	388	599	99	69	51	183	1271	7.9	1.3	16.7
90-91—Char.-Phil......	75	2644	487	1001	.487	268	329	.815	220	378	598	105	69	53	174	1242	8.0	1.4	16.6
91-92—Philadelphia	81	2771	512	1001	.511	343	425	.807	234	426	660	118	51	85	166	1367	8.1	1.5	16.9
92-93—Philadelphia	80	1742	359	774	.464	274	325	.843	136	336	472	116	37	54	157	992	5.9	1.5	12.4
93-94—New Jersey	82	1969	348	682	.510	274	361	.759	197	303	500	69	38	61	106	970	6.1	0.8	11.8
94-95—New Jersey	82	2472	455	905	.503	302	392	.770	192	421	613	99	67	89	152	1212	7.5	1.2	14.8
95-96—New Jersey	78	2856	576	1216	.474	277	350	.791	241	472	713	140	73	53	177	1429	9.1	1.8	18.3
Totals	683	20807	4031	8169	.493	2412	3117	.774	1730	3400	5130	870	516	502	1378	10474	7.5	1.3	15.3

Three-point field goals: 1989-90, 0-for-2. 1990-91, 0-for-2. 1991-92, 0-for-2. 1992-93, 0-for-1. 1993-94, 0-for-1. 1994-95, 0-for-2. 1995-96, 0-for-1. Totals, 0-for-11.
Personal fouls/disqualifications: 1987-88, 143/1. 1988-89, 176/2. 1989-90, 212/4. 1990-91, 185/2. 1991-92, 176/1. 1992-93, 123/0. 1993-94, 129/0. 1994-95, 171/0. 1995-96, 180/1. Totals, 1495/11.

NBA PLAYOFF RECORD

								REBOUNDS								AVERAGES		
Season Team	G	Min.	FGM	FGA	Pct.	FTM	FTA	Pct.	Off.	Def.	Tot.	Ast.	St.	Blk.	TO	Pts.	RPG	APG	PPG
88-89—Phoenix	9	126	27	51	.529	19	22	.864	18	27	45	2	1	2	10	73	5.0	0.2	8.1
90-91—Philadelphia	8	287	48	104	.462	39	46	.848	14	38	52	10	5	6	15	135	6.5	1.3	16.9
93-94—New Jersey	4	112	15	34	.441	12	16	.750	1	24	25	1	2	7	3	42	6.3	0.3	10.5
Totals	21	525	90	189	.476	70	84	.833	33	89	122	13	8	15	28	250	5.8	0.6	11.9

Three-point field goals: 1993-94, 0-for-1.
Personal fouls/disqualifications: 1988-89, 11/0. 1990-91, 16/0. 1993-94, 7/0. Totals, 34/0.

GLASS, GERALD　　　　　G/F

PERSONAL: Born November 12, 1967, in Greenwood, Miss. ... 6-6/221. ... Full name: Gerald Damon Glass.
HIGH SCHOOL: Amanda Elzy (Greenwood, Miss.).
COLLEGE: Delta State (Miss.), then Mississippi.
TRANSACTIONS/CAREER NOTES: Selected by Minnesota Timberwolves in first round (20th pick overall) of 1990 NBA Draft. ... Traded by Timberwolves with F Mark Randall to Detroit Pistons for F/C Brad Sellers, G Lance Blanks and 2000 conditional draft choice (November 15, 1992). ... Signed as free agent by Golden State Warriors (November 1, 1993). ... Waived by Warriors (November 2, 1993). ... Signed as free agent by New Jersey Nets (October 13, 1995). ... Traded by Nets with G Kenny Anderson to Charlotte Hornets for G Khalid Reeves and G Kendall Gill (January 19, 1996). ... Waived by Hornets (February 22, 1996).

COLLEGIATE RECORD

											AVERAGES		
Season Team	G	Min.	FGM	FGA	Pct.	FTM	FTA	Pct.	Reb.	Ast.	Pts.	RPG	APG	PPG
85-86—Delta State....................	31	...	168	303	.554	52	72	.722	203	23	388	6.5	0.7	12.5
86-87—Delta State....................	33	...	360	595	.605	134	191	.702	414	98	861	12.5	3.0	26.1

G

Season Team	G	Min.	FGM	FGA	Pct.	FTM	FTA	Pct.	Reb.	Ast.	Pts.	AVERAGES		
												RPG	APG	PPG
87-88—Mississippi						Did not play—transfer student.								
88-89—Mississippi	30	1070	326	613	.532	148	201	.736	255	57	841	8.5	1.9	28.0
89-90—Mississippi	30	1108	284	580	.490	109	148	.736	229	...	723	7.6	...	24.1
Totals	124	...	1138	2091	.544	443	612	.724	1101	...	2813	8.9	...	22.7

Three-point field goals: 1986-87, 7-for-27 (.259). 1988-89, 41-for-109 (.376). 1989-90, 46-for-122 (.377). Totals, 94-for-258 (.364).

NBA REGULAR-SEASON RECORD

Season Team	G	Min.	FGM	FGA	Pct.	FTM	FTA	Pct.	REBOUNDS			Ast.	St.	Blk.	TO	Pts.	AVERAGES		
									Off.	Def.	Tot.						RPG	APG	PPG
90-91—Minnesota.......	51	606	149	340	.438	52	76	.684	54	48	102	42	28	9	41	352	2.0	0.8	6.9
91-92—Minnesota.......	75	1822	383	871	.440	77	125	.616	107	153	260	175	66	30	103	859	3.5	2.3	11.5
92-93—Minn.-Det.	60	848	142	339	.419	25	39	.641	61	81	142	77	33	18	35	316	2.4	1.3	5.3
95-96—N.J.-Char.	15	71	12	33	.364	1	1	1.000	6	2	8	4	3	1	0	26	0.5	0.3	1.7
Totals	201	3347	686	1583	.433	155	241	.643	228	284	512	298	130	58	179	1553	2.5	1.5	7.7

Three-point field goals: 1990-91, 2-for-17 (.118). 1991-92, 16-for-54 (.296). 1992-93, 7-for-33 (.212). 1995-96, 1-for-6 (.167). Totals, 26-for-110 (.236).

Personal fouls/disqualifications: 1990-91, 76/2. 1991-92, 171/0. 1992-93, 104/1. 1995-96, 10/0. Totals, 361/3.

CBA REGULAR-SEASON RECORD

Season Team	G	Min.	FGM	FGA	Pct.	FTM	FTA	Pct.	Reb.	Ast.	Pts.	AVERAGES		
												RPG	APG	PPG
93-94—La Crosse	32	847	175	339	.516	45	68	.662	120	89	398	3.8	2.8	12.4

Three-point field goals: 1993-94, 3-for-19 (.158).

ITALIAN LEAGUE RECORD

Season Team	G	Min.	FGM	FGA	Pct.	FTM	FTA	Pct.	Reb.	Ast.	Pts.	AVERAGES		
												RPG	APG	PPG
94-95—Jcoplastic Napoli	32	...	...	...	...	...	...	...	250	43	818	7.8	1.3	25.6

GOLDWIRE, ANTHONY   G   HORNETS

PERSONAL: Born September 6, 1971, in West Palm Beach, Fla. ... 6-2/182.
HIGH SCHOOL: Suncoast (Riviera Beach, Fla.).
JUNIOR COLLEGE: Pensacola (Fla.) Junior College.
COLLEGE: Houston.
TRANSACTIONS/CAREER NOTES: Selected by Phoenix Suns in second round (52nd pick overall) of 1994 NBA Draft. ... Waived by Suns (November 1, 1994). ... Played in Continental Basketball Association with Yakima Sun Kings (1994-95 and 1995-96). ... Signed by Charlotte Hornets to 10-day contract (January 22, 1996). ... Re-signed by Hornets for remainder of season (January 31, 1996).

COLLEGIATE RECORD

Season Team	G	Min.	FGM	FGA	Pct.	FTM	FTA	Pct.	Reb.	Ast.	Pts.	AVERAGES		
												RPG	APG	PPG
90-91—Pensacola J.C.................	30	...	105	234	.449	84	104	.808	91	169	305	3.0	5.6	10.2
91-92—Pensacola J.C.................	31	...	155	360	.431	128	168	.762	128	241	477	4.1	7.8	15.4
92-93—Houston	30	1110	139	313	.444	124	158	.785	92	170	427	3.1	5.7	14.2
93-94—Houston	27	995	144	366	.393	138	171	.807	100	164	463	3.7	6.1	17.1
Junior college totals	61	...	260	594	.438	212	272	.779	219	410	782	3.6	6.7	12.8
4-year-college totals	57	2105	283	679	.417	262	329	.796	192	334	890	3.4	5.9	15.6

Three-point field goals: 1992-93, 25-for-88 (.284). 1993-94, 37-for-123 (.301). Totals, 62-for-211 (.294).

CBA REGULAR-SEASON RECORD

NOTES: Member of CBA championship team (1995). ... CBA All-Rookie second team (1995).

Season Team	G	Min.	FGM	FGA	Pct.	FTM	FTA	Pct.	Reb.	Ast.	Pts.	AVERAGES		
												RPG	APG	PPG
94-95—Yakima	55	1121	150	312	.481	119	160	.744	83	217	439	1.5	3.9	8.0
95-96—Yakima	27	977	171	373	.458	139	163	.853	96	189	519	3.6	7.0	19.2
Totals	82	2098	321	685	.469	258	323	.799	179	406	958	2.2	5.0	11.7

Three-point field goals: 1994-95, 20-for-60 (.333). 1995-96, 38-for-99 (.384). Totals, 58-for-159 (.365).

NBA REGULAR-SEASON RECORD

Season Team	G	Min.	FGM	FGA	Pct.	FTM	FTA	Pct.	REBOUNDS			Ast.	St.	Blk.	TO	Pts.	AVERAGES		
									Off.	Def.	Tot.						RPG	APG	PPG
95-96—Charlotte.........	42	621	76	189	.402	46	60	.767	8	35	43	112	16	0	63	231	1.0	2.7	5.5

Three-point field goals: 1995-96, 33-for-83 (.398).
Personal fouls/disqualifications: 1995-96, 79/0.

GRAHAM, GREG   G   SUPERSONICS

PERSONAL: Born November 26, 1970, in Indianapolis. ... 6-4/182. ... Full name: Gregory Lawrence Graham.
HIGH SCHOOL: Warren Central (Indianapolis).
COLLEGE: Indiana.
TRANSACTIONS/CAREER NOTES: Selected by Charlotte Hornets in first round (17th pick overall) of 1993 NBA Draft. ... Draft rights traded by Hornets with G Dana Barros, F Sidney Green and option to switch 1994 first-round draft choices to Philadelphia 76ers for G Hersey Hawkins (September 3, 1993). ... Traded by 76ers with C Shawn Bradley and F Tim Perry to New Jersey Nets for F Derrick Coleman, F Sean Higgins and G Rex Walters (November 30, 1995). ... Traded by Nets to Seattle SuperSonics for G Vincent Askew (July 16, 1996).

G

Season Team	G	Min.	FGM	FGA	Pct.	FTM	FTA	Pct.	Reb.	Ast.	Pts.	RPG	APG	PPG
89-90—Indiana	29	609	89	189	.471	91	117	.778	76	59	281	2.6	2.0	9.7
90-91—Indiana	34	648	106	208	.510	77	111	.694	87	53	296	2.6	1.6	8.7
91-92—Indiana	34	893	132	263	.502	140	189	.741	137	90	436	4.0	2.6	12.8
92-93—Indiana	35	1116	180	327	.550	160	194	.825	112	102	577	3.2	2.9	16.5
Totals	132	3266	507	987	.514	468	611	.766	412	304	1590	3.1	2.3	12.0

Three-point field goals: 1989-90, 12-for-31 (.387). 1990-91, 7-for-29 (.241). 1991-92, 32-for-75 (.427). 1992-93, 57-for-111 (.514). Totals, 108-for-246 (.439).

NBA REGULAR-SEASON RECORD

Season Team	G	Min.	FGM	FGA	Pct.	FTM	FTA	Pct.	Off.	Def.	Tot.	Ast.	St.	Blk.	TO	Pts.	RPG	APG	PPG
93-94—Philadelphia	70	889	122	305	.400	92	110	.836	21	65	86	66	61	4	65	338	1.2	0.9	4.8
94-95—Philadelphia	50	775	95	223	.426	55	73	.753	19	43	62	66	29	6	48	251	1.2	1.3	5.0
95-96—Phil.-N.J.	53	613	78	193	.404	52	68	.765	17	40	57	52	25	1	46	240	1.1	1.0	4.5
Totals	173	2277	295	721	.409	199	251	.793	57	148	205	184	115	11	159	829	1.2	1.1	4.8

Three-point field goals: 1993-94, 2-for-25 (.080). 1994-95, 6-for-28 (.214). 1995-96, 32-for-82 (.390). Totals, 40-for-135 (.296).
Personal fouls/disqualifications: 1993-94, 54/0. 1994-95, 76/0. 1995-96, 64/0. Totals, 194/0.

GRANDISON, RONNIE   F

PERSONAL: Born July 9, 1964, in Los Angeles. ... 6-6/220. ... Full name: Ron Calvin Grandison. ... Name pronounced GRAND-uh-son.
HIGH SCHOOL: St. Bernard (Playa del Ray, Calif.).
COLLEGE: UC Irvine, then Tulane, then New Orleans.
TRANSACTIONS/CAREER NOTES: Selected by Denver Nuggets in fifth round (100th pick overall) of 1987 NBA Draft. ... Waived by Nuggets (October 29, 1987). ... Played in Continental Basketball Association with Rochester Flyers (1987-88), Omaha Racers (1991-92 and 1995-96), Rochester Renegade (1992-93 and 1993-94) and Rapid City Thrillers (1994-95). ... Signed as free agent by Boston Celtics (September 27, 1988). ... Did not play during 1989-90 season. ... Played with Athletes in Action (1990-91). ... Signed as free agent by Miami Heat (October 1, 1991). ... Waived by Heat (October 22, 1991). ... Signed as free agent by Charlotte Hornets (December 30, 1991). ... Waived by Hornets (January 7, 1992). ... Re-signed by Hornets to first of two consecutive 10-day contracts (January 10, 1992). ... Signed as free agent by Orlando Magic (October 7, 1992). ... Waived by Magic (October 22, 1992). ... Played in Italy (1992-93). ... Signed as free agent by New York Knicks (October 6, 1994). ... Waived by Knicks (December 15, 1994). ... Signed as free agent by Heat (October 5, 1995). ... Waived by Heat (January 5, 1996). ... Signed by Atlanta Hawks to first of two consecutive 10-day contracts (January 16, 1996). ... Signed by New York Knicks to first of two consecutive 10-day contracts (March 12, 1996). ... Re-signed by Knicks for remainder of season (March 29, 1996). ... Rights renounced by Knicks (July 14, 1996).

COLLEGIATE RECORD

Season Team	G	Min.	FGM	FGA	Pct.	FTM	FTA	Pct.	Reb.	Ast.	Pts.	RPG	APG	PPG
82-83—UC Irvine	28	464	66	128	.516	40	66	.606	100	13	172	3.6	0.5	6.1
83-84—UC Irvine	29	394	49	91	.538	29	50	.580	89	17	127	3.1	0.6	4.4
84-85—Tulane					Did not play—transfer student.									
85-86—New Orleans	28	934	186	363	.512	93	162	.574	271	39	465	9.7	1.4	16.6
86-87—New Orleans	30	1059	179	339	.528	155	231	.671	292	55	513	9.7	1.8	17.1
Totals	115	2851	480	921	.521	317	509	.623	752	124	1277	6.5	1.1	11.1

Three-point field goals: 1986-87, 0-for-1.

CBA REGULAR-SEASON RECORD

NOTES: CBA Most Valuable Player (1994). ... CBA All-League first team (1992, 1994). ... CBA All-Defensive team (1994).

Season Team	G	Min.	FGM	FGA	Pct.	FTM	FTA	Pct.	Reb.	Ast.	Pts.	RPG	APG	PPG
87-88—Rochester	31	1082	167	321	.520	104	148	.703	295	40	439	9.5	1.3	14.2
91-92—Omaha	43	1488	265	511	.519	242	295	.820	432	85	774	10.0	2.0	18.0
92-93—Rochester	23	907	165	309	.534	122	163	.748	243	40	457	10.6	1.7	19.9
93-94—Rochester	56	2369	322	608	.530	278	359	.774	659	83	922	11.8	1.5	16.5
94-95—Rapid City	11	418	72	119	.605	41	52	.788	116	20	185	10.5	1.8	16.8
95-96—Omaha	5	117	20	38	.526	6	7	.857	26	6	46	5.2	1.2	9.2
Totals	169	6381	1011	1906	.530	793	1024	.774	1771	274	2823	10.5	1.6	16.7

Three-point field goals: 1987-88, 1-for-4 (.250). 1991-92, 2-for-12 (.167). 1992-93, 5-for-17 (.294). 1993-94, 0-for-3. 1994-95, 0-for-1. Totals, 8-for-37 (.217).

NBA REGULAR-SEASON RECORD

Season Team	G	Min.	FGM	FGA	Pct.	FTM	FTA	Pct.	Off.	Def.	Tot.	Ast.	St.	Blk.	TO	Pts.	RPG	APG	PPG
88-89—Boston	72	528	59	142	.416	59	80	.738	47	45	92	42	18	3	36	177	1.3	0.6	2.5
91-92—Charlotte	3	25	2	4	.500	6	10	.600	3	8	11	1	1	1	3	10	3.7	0.3	3.3
94-95—New York	2	8	1	4	.250	0	0	...	3	2	5	2	0	0	0	2	2.5	1.0	1.0
95-96—Mia.-Atl.-N.Y.	28	311	22	58	.379	17	25	.680	20	35	55	13	12	2	12	65	2.0	0.5	2.3
Totals	105	872	84	208	.404	82	115	.713	73	90	163	58	31	6	51	254	1.6	0.6	2.4

Three-point field goals: 1988-89, 0-for-10. 1995-96, 4-for-14 (.286). Totals, 4-for-24 (.167).
Personal fouls/disqualifications: 1988-89, 71/0. 1991-92, 4/0. 1994-95, 2/0. 1995-96, 31/0. Totals, 108/0.

NBA PLAYOFF RECORD

Season Team	G	Min.	FGM	FGA	Pct.	FTM	FTA	Pct.	Off.	Def.	Tot.	Ast.	St.	Blk.	TO	Pts.	RPG	APG	PPG
95-96—New York	2	3	0	1	.000	0	0	...	0	0	0	0	0	0	0	0	0.0	0.0	0.0

Three-point field goals: 1995-96, 0-for-1.
Personal fouls/disqualifications: 1995-96, 1/0.

ITALIAN LEAGUE RECORD

Season Team	G	Min.	FGM	FGA	Pct.	FTM	FTA	Pct.	Reb.	Ast.	Pts.	RPG	APG	PPG
92-93—Ferrys Lliria	10	316	42	87	.483	30	37	.811	78	11	116	7.8	1.1	11.6

G

GRANT, BRIAN   F   KINGS

PERSONAL: Born March 5, 1972, in Columbus, Ohio. ... 6-9/254. ... Full name: Brian Wade Grant.
HIGH SCHOOL: Georgetown (Ohio).
COLLEGE: Xavier.
TRANSACTIONS/CAREER NOTES: Selected by Sacramento Kings in first round (eighth pick overall) of 1994 NBA Draft.

COLLEGIATE RECORD

Season Team	G	Min.	FGM	FGA	Pct.	FTM	FTA	Pct.	Reb.	Ast.	Pts.	RPG	APG	PPG
90-91—Xavier	32	932	135	236	.572	100	144	.694	273	20	370	8.5	0.6	11.6
91-92—Xavier	26	729	117	203	.576	74	127	.583	237	23	308	9.1	0.9	11.8
92-93—Xavier	30	944	223	341	.654	110	159	.692	283	46	556	9.4	1.5	18.5
93-94—Xavier	29	894	181	324	.559	122	171	.713	287	47	485	9.9	1.6	16.7
Totals	117	3499	656	1104	.594	406	601	.676	1080	136	1719	9.2	1.2	14.7

Three-point field goals: 1993-94, 1-for-3 (.333).

NBA REGULAR-SEASON RECORD

HONORS: NBA All-Rookie first team (1995).

Season Team	G	Min.	FGM	FGA	Pct.	FTM	FTA	Pct.	Off.	Def.	Tot.	Ast.	St.	Blk.	TO	Pts.	RPG	APG	PPG
94-95—Sacramento	80	2289	413	809	.511	231	363	.636	207	391	598	99	49	116	163	1058	7.5	1.2	13.2
95-96—Sacramento	78	2398	427	842	.507	262	358	.732	175	370	545	127	40	103	185	1120	7.0	1.6	14.4
Totals	158	4687	840	1651	.509	493	721	.684	382	761	1143	226	89	219	348	2178	7.2	1.4	13.8

Three-point field goals: 1994-95, 1-for-4 (.250). 1995-96, 4-for-17 (.235). Totals, 5-for-21 (.238).
Personal fouls/disqualifications: 1994-95, 276/4. 1995-96, 269/9. Totals, 545/13.

NBA PLAYOFF RECORD

Season Team	G	Min.	FGM	FGA	Pct.	FTM	FTA	Pct.	Off.	Def.	Tot.	Ast.	St.	Blk.	TO	Pts.	RPG	APG	PPG
95-96—Sacramento	4	124	16	42	.381	7	14	.500	7	13	20	4	2	7	13	39	5.0	1.0	9.8

Personal fouls/disqualifications: 1995-96, 14/1.

GRANT, GARY   G

PERSONAL: Born April 21, 1965, in Canton, Ohio. ... 6-3/185.
HIGH SCHOOL: McKinley (Canton, Ohio).
COLLEGE: Michigan.
TRANSACTIONS/CAREER NOTES: Selected by Seattle SuperSonics in first round (15th pick overall) of 1988 NBA Draft. ... Draft rights traded by SuperSonics with 1989 first-round draft choice to Los Angeles Clippers for F Michael Cage (June 28, 1988). ... Rights renounced by Clippers (September 29, 1995). ... Signed as free agent by New York Knicks (November 8, 1995). ... Rights renounced by Knicks (July 14, 1996).

COLLEGIATE RECORD

NOTES: THE SPORTING NEWS All-America second team (1988).

Season Team	G	Min.	FGM	FGA	Pct.	FTM	FTA	Pct.	Reb.	Ast.	Pts.	RPG	APG	PPG
84-85—Michigan	30	950	169	307	.550	49	60	.817	76	140	387	2.5	4.7	12.9
85-86—Michigan	33	1010	172	348	.494	58	78	.744	104	185	402	3.2	5.6	12.2
86-87—Michigan	32	...	286	533	.537	111	142	.782	159	172	716	5.0	5.4	22.4
87-88—Michigan	34	1190	269	508	.530	135	167	.808	116	234	717	3.4	6.9	21.1
Totals	129	...	896	1696	.528	353	447	.790	455	731	2222	3.5	5.7	17.2

Three-point field goals: 1986-87, 33-for-68 (.485). 1987-88, 44-for-99 (.444). Totals, 77-for-167 (.461).

NBA REGULAR-SEASON RECORD

Season Team	G	Min.	FGM	FGA	Pct.	FTM	FTA	Pct.	Off.	Def.	Tot.	Ast.	St.	Blk.	TO	Pts.	RPG	APG	PPG
88-89—L.A. Clippers	71	1924	361	830	.435	119	162	.735	80	158	238	506	144	9	258	846	3.4	7.1	11.9
89-90—L.A. Clippers	44	1529	241	517	.466	88	113	.779	59	136	195	442	108	5	206	575	4.4	10.0	13.1
90-91—L.A. Clippers	68	2105	265	587	.451	51	74	.689	69	140	209	587	103	12	210	590	3.1	8.6	8.7
91-92—L.A. Clippers	78	2049	275	595	.462	44	54	.815	34	150	184	538	138	14	187	609	2.4	6.9	7.8
92-93—L.A. Clippers	74	1624	210	476	.441	55	74	.743	27	112	139	353	106	9	129	486	1.9	4.8	6.6
93-94—L.A. Clippers	78	1533	253	563	.449	65	76	.855	42	100	142	291	119	12	136	588	1.8	3.7	7.5
94-95—L.A. Clippers	33	470	78	166	.470	45	55	.818	8	27	35	93	29	3	44	205	1.1	2.8	6.2
95-96—New York	47	596	88	181	.486	48	58	.828	12	40	52	69	39	3	45	232	1.1	1.5	4.9
Totals	493	11830	1771	3915	.452	515	666	.773	331	863	1194	2879	786	67	1215	4131	2.4	5.8	8.4

Three-point field goals: 1988-89, 5-for-22 (.227). 1989-90, 5-for-21 (.238). 1990-91, 9-for-39 (.231). 1991-92, 15-for-51 (.294). 1992-93, 11-for-42 (.262). 1993-94, 17-for-62 (.274). 1994-95, 4-for-16 (.250). 1995-96, 8-for-24 (.333). Totals, 74-for-277 (.267).
Personal fouls/disqualifications: 1988-89, 170/1. 1989-90, 120/1. 1990-91, 192/4. 1991-92, 181/4. 1992-93, 168/2. 1993-94, 139/1. 1994-95, 66/0. 1995-96, 91/0. Totals, 1127/13.

NBA PLAYOFF RECORD

Season Team	G	Min.	FGM	FGA	Pct.	FTM	FTA	Pct.	Off.	Def.	Tot.	Ast.	St.	Blk.	TO	Pts.	RPG	APG	PPG
91-92—L.A. Clippers	5	77	10	21	.476	2	2	1.000	0	4	4	18	3	2	8	22	0.8	3.6	4.4
92-93—L.A. Clippers	5	101	10	31	.323	1	2	.500	1	1	2	23	3	0	7	21	0.4	4.6	4.2
95-96—New York	1	8	2	5	.400	0	0	...	2	1	3	0	1	0	1	6	3.0	0.0	6.0
Totals	11	186	22	57	.386	3	4	.750	3	6	9	41	7	2	16	49	0.8	3.7	4.5

Three-point field goals: 1991-92, 0-for-2. 1995-96, 2-for-3 (.667). Totals, 2-for-5 (.400).
Personal fouls/disqualifications: 1991-92, 10/0. 1992-93, 13/0. Totals, 23/0.

G

GRANT, GREG   G

PERSONAL: Born August 29, 1966, in Trenton, N.J. ... 5-7/140. ... Full name: Gregory Alan Grant.
HIGH SCHOOL: Central (Trenton, N.J.).
COLLEGE: Morris Brown (Ga.), then Trenton (N.J.) State.
TRANSACTIONS/CAREER NOTES: Selected by Phoenix Suns in second round (52nd pick overall) of 1989 NBA Draft. ... Signed as unrestricted free agent by New York Knicks (October 1, 1990). ... Signed as free agent by Indiana Pacers (September 6, 1991). ... Claimed off waivers by Charlotte Hornets (October 31, 1991). ... Waived by Hornets (December 9, 1991). ... Signed as free agent by Philadelphia 76ers (December 22, 1991). ... Rights renounced by 76ers (July 28, 1993). ... Played in Continental Basketball Association with Rapid City Thrillers (1993-94), Pittsburgh Piranhas (1994-95), Mexico Aztecas (1994-95), San Diego Wildcards (1995-96) and Shreveport Storm (1995-96). ... Signed as free agent by Orlando Magic (October 7, 1994). ... Waived by Magic (November 28, 1994). ... Signed by Denver Nuggets to first of two consecutive 10-day contracts (March 14, 1995). ... Re-signed by Nuggets for remainder of season (April 5, 1995). ... Signed as free agent by 76ers (November 21, 1995). ... Waived by 76ers (December 12, 1995). ... Signed by Washington Bullets to first of two consecutive 10-day contracts (February 2, 1996). ... Re-signed by Nuggets for remainder of season (March 29, 1996). ... Rights renounced by Nuggets (July 17, 1996).

COLLEGIATE RECORD

NOTES: Outstanding Player in NCAA Division III Tournament (1989). ... Led NCAA Division III with 32.6 points per game (1989).

											AVERAGES		
Season Team	G	Min.	FGM	FGA	Pct.	FTM	FTA	Pct.	Reb.	Ast.	Pts.	RPG	APG	PPG
85-86—Morris Brown College						Statistics unavailable.								
86-87—Trenton State.................	26	...	263	543	.484	171	220	.777	104	...	740	4.0	...	28.5
87-88—Trenton State.................	27	912	302	537	.562	171	204	.838	69	...	827	2.6	...	30.6
88-89—Trenton State.................	32	1077	387	742	.522	194	239	.812	75	...	1044	2.3	...	32.6
Totals	85		952	1822	.523	536	663	.808	248	...	2611	2.9	...	30.7

Three-point field goals: 1986-87, 43-for-83 (.518). 1987-88, 52-for-105 (.495). 1988-89, 76-for-186 (.409). Totals, 171-for-374 (.457).

NBA REGULAR-SEASON RECORD

									REBOUNDS								AVERAGES		
Season Team	G	Min.	FGM	FGA	Pct.	FTM	FTA	Pct.	Off.	Def.	Tot.	Ast.	St.	Blk.	TO	Pts.	RPG	APG	PPG
89-90—Phoenix	67	678	83	216	.384	39	59	.661	16	43	59	168	36	1	77	208	0.9	2.5	3.1
90-91—New York........	22	107	10	27	.370	5	6	.833	1	9	10	20	9	0	10	26	0.5	0.9	1.2
91-92—Char.-Phil.......	68	891	99	225	.440	20	24	.833	14	55	69	217	45	2	46	225	1.0	3.2	3.3
92-93—Philadelphia ...	72	996	77	220	.350	20	31	.645	24	43	67	206	43	1	54	194	0.9	2.9	2.7
94-95—Denver...........	14	151	10	33	.303	9	12	.750	2	7	9	43	6	2	14	31	0.6	3.1	2.2
95-96—Phi.-Was.-Den.	31	527	35	99	.354	5	6	.833	7	27	34	97	22	2	30	83	1.1	3.1	2.7
Totals	274	3350	314	820	.383	98	138	.710	64	184	248	751	161	8	231	767	0.9	2.7	2.8

Three-point field goals: 1989-90, 3-for-16 (.188). 1990-91, 1-for-3 (.333). 1991-92, 7-for-18 (.389). 1992-93, 20-for-68 (.294). 1994-95, 2-for-7 (.286). 1995-96, 8-for-34 (.235). Totals, 41-for-146 (.281).
Personal fouls/disqualifications: 1989-90, 58/0. 1990-91, 12/0. 1991-92, 76/0. 1992-93, 73/0. 1994-95, 20/1. 1995-96, 43/0. Totals, 282/1.

NBA PLAYOFF RECORD

									REBOUNDS								AVERAGES		
Season Team	G	Min.	FGM	FGA	Pct.	FTM	FTA	Pct.	Off.	Def.	Tot.	Ast.	St.	Blk.	TO	Pts.	RPG	APG	PPG
89-90—Phoenix	7	47	9	20	.450	0	0	...	2	4	6	10	2	0	5	19	0.9	1.4	2.7
94-95—Denver...........	3	20	0	6	.000	2	2	1.000	3	0	3	5	1	0	0	2	1.0	1.7	0.7
Totals	10	67	9	26	.346	2	2	1.000	5	4	9	15	3	0	5	21	0.9	1.5	2.1

Three-point field goals: 1989-90, 1-for-3 (.333). 1994-95, 0-for-1. Totals, 1-for-4 (.250).
Personal fouls/disqualifications: 1989-90, 2/0. 1994-95, 5/0. Totals, 7/0.

CBA REGULAR-SEASON RECORD

											AVERAGES		
Season Team	G	Min.	FGM	FGA	Pct.	FTM	FTA	Pct.	Reb.	Ast.	Pts.	RPG	APG	PPG
93-94—Rapid City......................	41	1103	112	240	.467	57	64	.891	65	225	309	1.6	5.5	7.5
94-95—Pittsburgh-Mexico..........	33	1218	197	465	.424	114	124	*.919	76	322	556	2.3	9.8	16.8
95-96—Shreveport	21	841	101	249	.406	47	56	.839	73	229	272	3.5	10.9	13.0
Totals	95	3162	410	954	.430	218	244	.893	214	776	1137	2.3	8.2	12.0

Three-point field goals: 1993-94, 28-for-74 (.378). 1994-95, 48-for-134 (.358). 1995-96, 23-for-77 (.299). Totals, 99-for-285 (.348).

GRANT, HARVEY   F   BULLETS

PERSONAL: Born July 4, 1965, in Augusta, Ga. ... 6-9/225. ... Twin brother of Horace Grant, forward with Orlando Magic.
HIGH SCHOOL: Hancock Central (Sparta, Ga.).
JUNIOR COLLEGE: Independence (Kan.) Junior College.
COLLEGE: Clemson, then Oklahoma.
TRANSACTIONS/CAREER NOTES: Selected by Washington Bullets in first round (12th pick overall) of 1988 NBA Draft. ... Traded by Bullets to Portland Trail Blazers for C Kevin Duckworth and future considerations (June 24, 1993). ... Traded by Trail Blazers with G Rod Strickland to Bullets for F Rasheed Wallace and G Mitchell Butler (July 15, 1996).

COLLEGIATE RECORD

											AVERAGES		
Season Team	G	Min.	FGM	FGA	Pct.	FTM	FTA	Pct.	Reb.	Ast.	Pts.	RPG	APG	PPG
85-86—Independence J.C..........	33	...	340	580	.586	58	82	.707	388	71	738	11.8	2.2	22.4
83-84—Clemson					Did not play—redshirted.									
84-85—Clemson	28	418	60	121	.496	24	41	.585	126	11	144	4.5	0.4	5.1
86-87—Oklahoma	34	1165	228	427	.534	119	163	.730	338	43	575	9.9	1.3	16.9
87-88—Oklahoma	39	1339	350	640	.547	113	155	.729	365	53	816	9.4	1.4	20.9
Junior college totals	33	...	340	580	.586	58	82	.707	388	71	738	11.8	2.2	22.4
4-year-college totals	101	2922	638	1188	.537	256	359	.713	829	107	1535	8.2	1.1	15.2

Three-point field goals: 1986-87, 0-for-1. 1987-88, 3-for-14 (.214). Totals, 3-for-15 (.200).

G

NBA REGULAR-SEASON RECORD

Season Team	G	Min.	FGM	FGA	Pct.	FTM	FTA	Pct.	REBOUNDS Off.	Def.	Tot.	Ast.	St.	Blk.	TO	Pts.	AVERAGES RPG	APG	PPG
88-89—Washington	71	1193	181	390	.464	34	57	.597	75	88	163	79	35	29	28	396	2.3	1.1	5.6
89-90—Washington	81	1846	284	601	.473	96	137	.701	138	204	342	131	52	43	85	664	4.2	1.6	8.2
90-91—Washington	77	2842	609	1224	.498	185	249	.743	179	378	557	204	91	61	125	1405	7.2	2.6	18.2
91-92—Washington	64	2388	489	1022	.478	176	220	.800	157	275	432	170	74	27	109	1155	6.8	2.7	18.0
92-93—Washington	72	2667	560	1149	.487	218	300	.727	133	279	412	205	72	44	90	1339	5.7	2.8	18.6
93-94—Portland........	77	2112	356	774	.460	84	131	.641	109	242	351	107	70	49	56	798	4.6	1.4	10.4
94-95—Portland........	75	1771	286	621	.461	103	146	.705	103	181	284	82	56	53	62	683	3.8	1.1	9.1
95-96—Portland........	76	2394	314	679	.462	60	110	.545	117	244	361	111	60	43	82	709	4.8	1.5	9.3
Totals	593	17213	3079	6460	.477	956	1350	.708	1011	1891	2902	1089	510	349	637	7149	4.9	1.8	12.1

Three-point field goals: 1988-89, 0-for-1. 1989-90, 0-for-8. 1990-91, 2-for-15 (.133). 1991-92, 1-for-8 (.125). 1992-93, 1-for-10 (.100). 1993-94, 2-for-7 (.286). 1994-95, 8-for-26 (.308). 1995-96, 21-for-67 (.313). Totals, 35-for-142 (.246).

Personal fouls/disqualifications: 1988-89, 147/2. 1989-90, 194/1. 1990-91, 232/2. 1991-92, 178/1. 1992-93, 168/0. 1993-94, 179/1. 1994-95, 163/0. 1995-96, 173/1. Totals, 1434/8.

NBA PLAYOFF RECORD

Season Team	G	Min.	FGM	FGA	Pct.	FTM	FTA	Pct.	REBOUNDS Off.	Def.	Tot.	Ast.	St.	Blk.	TO	Pts.	AVERAGES RPG	APG	PPG
93-94—Portland........	4	76	17	33	.515	0	0	...	5	4	9	3	1	2	1	34	2.3	0.8	8.5
94-95—Portland........	3	115	14	28	.500	10	16	.625	3	13	16	6	3	2	4	43	5.3	2.0	14.3
95-96—Portland........	5	164	13	38	.342	0	4	.000	5	15	20	4	0	2	3	27	4.0	0.8	5.4
Totals	12	355	44	99	.444	10	20	.500	13	32	45	13	4	6	8	104	3.8	1.1	8.7

Three-point field goals: 1994-95, 5-for-9 (.556). 1995-96, 1-for-7 (.143). Totals, 6-for-16 (.375).
Personal fouls/disqualifications: 1993-94, 2/0. 1994-95, 6/0. 1995-96, 16/0. Totals, 24/0.

GRANT, HORACE   F   MAGIC

PERSONAL: Born July 4, 1965, in Augusta, Ga. ... 6-10/245. ... Full name: Horace Junior Grant. ... Twin brother of Harvey Grant, forward with Washington Bullets.
HIGH SCHOOL: Hancock Central (Sparta, Ga.).
COLLEGE: Clemson.
TRANSACTIONS/CAREER NOTES: Selected by Chicago Bulls in first round (10th pick overall) of 1987 NBA Draft. ... Signed as unrestricted free agent by Orlando Magic (July 30, 1994). ... Contract disallowed by NBA (August 2, 1994). ... Re-signed by Magic (September 19, 1994).
MISCELLANEOUS: Member of NBA championship teams (1991, 1992, 1993).

COLLEGIATE RECORD

Season Team	G	Min.	FGM	FGA	Pct.	FTM	FTA	Pct.	Reb.	Ast.	Pts.	AVERAGES RPG	APG	PPG
83-84—Clemson	28	551	64	120	.533	32	43	.744	129	49	160	4.6	1.8	5.7
84-85—Clemson	29	703	132	238	.555	65	102	.637	196	32	329	6.8	1.1	11.3
85-86—Clemson	34	1099	208	356	.584	140	193	.725	357	62	556	10.5	1.8	16.4
86-87—Clemson	31	1010	256	390	.656	138	195	.708	299	63	651	9.6	2.0	21.0
Totals	122	3363	660	1104	.598	375	533	.704	981	206	1696	8.0	1.7	13.9

Three-point field goals: 1986-87, 1-for-2 (.500).

NBA REGULAR-SEASON RECORD

HONORS: NBA All-Defensive second team (1993, 1994, 1995, 1996).

Season Team	G	Min.	FGM	FGA	Pct.	FTM	FTA	Pct.	REBOUNDS Off.	Def.	Tot.	Ast.	St.	Blk.	TO	Pts.	AVERAGES RPG	APG	PPG
87-88—Chicago	81	1827	254	507	.501	114	182	.626	155	292	447	89	51	53	86	622	5.5	1.1	7.7
88-89—Chicago	79	2809	405	781	.519	140	199	.704	240	441	681	168	86	62	128	950	8.6	2.1	12.0
89-90—Chicago	80	2753	446	853	.523	179	256	.699	236	393	629	227	92	84	110	1071	7.9	2.8	13.4
90-91—Chicago	78	2641	401	733	.547	197	277	.711	266	393	659	178	95	69	92	1000	8.4	2.3	12.8
91-92—Chicago	81	2859	457	790	.578	235	317	.741	344	463	807	217	100	131	98	1149	10.0	2.7	14.2
92-93—Chicago	77	2745	421	829	.508	174	281	.619	341	388	729	201	89	96	110	1017	9.5	2.6	13.2
93-94—Chicago	70	2570	460	878	.524	137	230	.596	306	463	769	236	74	84	109	1057	11.0	3.4	15.1
94-95—Orlando	74	2693	401	707	.567	146	211	.692	223	492	715	173	76	88	85	948	9.7	2.3	12.8
95-96—Orlando	63	2286	347	677	.513	152	207	.734	178	402	580	170	62	74	64	847	9.2	2.7	13.4
Totals	683	23183	3592	6755	.532	1474	2160	.682	2289	3727	6016	1659	725	741	882	8661	8.8	2.4	12.7

Three-point field goals: 1987-88, 0-for-2. 1988-89, 0-for-5. 1990-91, 1-for-6 (.167). 1991-92, 0-for-2. 1992-93, 1-for-5 (.200). 1993-94, 0-for-6. 1994-95, 0-for-8. 1995-96, 1-for-6 (.167). Totals, 3-for-40 (.075).

Personal fouls/disqualifications: 1987-88, 221/3. 1988-89, 251/1. 1989-90, 230/1. 1990-91, 203/2. 1991-92, 196/0. 1992-93, 218/4. 1993-94, 164/0. 1994-95, 203/2. 1995-96, 144/1. Totals, 1830/14.

NBA PLAYOFF RECORD

Season Team	G	Min.	FGM	FGA	Pct.	FTM	FTA	Pct.	REBOUNDS Off.	Def.	Tot.	Ast.	St.	Blk.	TO	Pts.	AVERAGES RPG	APG	PPG
87-88—Chicago	10	299	46	81	.568	9	15	.600	25	45	70	16	14	2	7	101	7.0	1.6	10.1
88-89—Chicago	17	625	72	139	.518	40	50	.800	53	114	167	35	11	16	31	184	9.8	2.1	10.8
89-90—Chicago	16	616	81	159	.509	33	53	.623	73	86	159	40	18	18	26	195	9.9	2.5	12.2
90-91—Chicago	17	666	91	156	.583	44	60	.733	56	82	138	38	15	6	20	226	8.1	2.2	13.3
91-92—Chicago	22	856	99	183	.541	51	76	.671	76	118	194	66	24	39	21	249	8.8	3.0	11.3
92-93—Chicago	19	651	83	152	.546	37	54	.685	61	95	156	44	23	23	17	203	8.2	2.3	10.7
93-94—Chicago	10	393	65	120	.542	31	42	.738	30	44	74	26	10	18	10	162	7.4	2.6	16.2
94-95—Orlando	21	869	121	224	.540	45	59	.763	74	145	219	39	21	24	26	287	10.4	1.9	13.7
95-96—Orlando	9	334	61	94	.649	13	15	.867	31	63	94	13	7	6	6	135	10.4	1.4	15.0
Totals	141	5309	719	1308	.550	303	424	.715	479	792	1271	317	143	152	164	1742	9.0	2.2	12.4

Three-point field goals: 1987-88, 0-for-1. 1989-90, 0-for-2. 1991-92, 0-for-2. 1993-94, 1-for-1. 1994-95, 0-for-2. Totals, 1-for-8 (.125).

Personal fouls/disqualifications: 1987-88, 35/2. 1988-89, 68/2. 1989-90, 51/1. 1990-91, 45/0. 1991-92, 68/1. 1992-93, 60/1. 1993-94, 23/0. 1994-95, 68/1. 1995-96, 23/0. Totals, 441/8.

G

NBA ALL-STAR GAME RECORD

Season Team	Min.	FGM	FGA	Pct.	FTM	FTA	Pct.	REBOUNDS Off.	Def.	Tot.	Ast.	PF	Dq.	St.	Blk.	TO	Pts.
1994 —Chicago	17	2	8	.250	0	0	...	6	2	8	2	0	0	1	0	1	4

GREEN, A.C.   F   SUNS

PERSONAL: Born October 4, 1963, in Portland, Ore. ... 6-9/225. ... Full name: A.C. Green Jr.
HIGH SCHOOL: Benson Polytechnic (Portland, Ore.).
COLLEGE: Oregon State.
TRANSACTIONS/CAREER NOTES: Selected by Los Angeles Lakers in first round (23rd pick overall) of 1985 NBA Draft. ... Signed as unrestricted free agent by Phoenix Suns (September 28, 1993).
MISCELLANEOUS: Member of NBA championship teams (1987, 1988).

COLLEGIATE RECORD

Season Team	G	Min.	FGM	FGA	Pct.	FTM	FTA	Pct.	Reb.	Ast.	Pts.	AVERAGES RPG	APG	PPG
81-82—Oregon State	30	895	99	161	.615	61	100	.610	158	32	259	5.3	1.1	8.6
82-83—Oregon State	31	1113	162	290	.559	111	161	.689	235	53	435	7.6	1.7	14.0
83-84—Oregon State	23	853	134	204	.657	141	183	.771	201	38	409	8.7	1.7	17.8
84-85—Oregon State	31	1191	217	362	.599	157	231	.680	286	62	591	9.2	2.0	19.1
Totals	115	4052	612	1017	.602	470	675	.696	880	185	1694	7.7	1.6	14.7

NBA REGULAR-SEASON RECORD

HONORS: NBA All-Defensive second team (1989).

Season Team	G	Min.	FGM	FGA	Pct.	FTM	FTA	Pct.	REBOUNDS Off.	Def.	Tot.	Ast.	St.	Blk.	TO	Pts.	AVERAGES RPG	APG	PPG
85-86—L.A. Lakers	82	1542	209	388	.539	102	167	.611	160	221	381	54	49	49	99	521	4.6	0.7	6.4
86-87—L.A. Lakers	79	2240	316	587	.538	220	282	.780	210	405	615	84	70	80	102	852	7.8	1.1	10.8
87-88—L.A. Lakers	82	2636	322	640	.503	293	379	.773	245	465	710	93	87	45	120	937	8.7	1.1	11.4
88-89—L.A. Lakers	82	2510	401	758	.529	282	359	.786	258	481	739	103	94	55	119	1088	9.0	1.3	13.3
89-90—L.A. Lakers	82	2709	385	806	.478	278	370	.751	262	450	712	90	66	50	116	1061	8.7	1.1	12.9
90-91—L.A. Lakers	82	2164	258	542	.476	223	302	.738	201	315	516	71	59	23	99	750	6.3	0.9	9.1
91-92—L.A. Lakers	82	2902	382	803	.476	340	457	.744	306	456	762	117	91	36	111	1116	9.3	1.4	13.6
92-93—L.A. Lakers	82	2819	379	706	.537	277	375	.739	287	424	711	116	88	39	116	1051	8.7	1.4	12.8
93-94—Phoenix	82	2825	465	926	.502	266	362	.735	275	478	753	137	70	38	100	1204	9.2	1.7	14.7
94-95—Phoenix	82	2687	311	617	.504	251	343	.732	194	475	669	127	55	31	114	916	8.2	1.5	11.2
95-96—Phoenix	82	2113	215	444	.484	168	237	.709	166	388	554	72	45	23	79	612	6.8	0.9	7.5
Totals	899	27147	3643	7217	.505	2700	3633	.743	2564	4558	7122	1064	774	469	1175	10108	7.9	1.2	11.2

Three-point field goals: 1985-86, 1-for-6 (.167). 1986-87, 0-for-5. 1987-88, 0-for-2. 1988-89, 4-for-17 (.235). 1989-90, 13-for-46 (.283). 1990-91, 11-for-55 (.200). 1991-92, 12-for-56 (.214). 1992-93, 16-for-46 (.348). 1993-94, 8-for-35 (.229). 1994-95, 43-for-127 (.339). 1995-96, 14-for-52 (.269). Totals, 122-for-447 (.273).
Personal fouls/disqualifications: 1985-86, 229/2. 1986-87, 171/0. 1987-88, 204/0. 1988-89, 172/0. 1989-90, 207/0. 1990-91, 117/0. 1991-92, 141/0. 1992-93, 149/0. 1993-94, 142/0. 1994-95, 146/0. 1995-96, 141/1. Totals, 1819/3.

NBA PLAYOFF RECORD

Season Team	G	Min.	FGM	FGA	Pct.	FTM	FTA	Pct.	REBOUNDS Off.	Def.	Tot.	Ast.	St.	Blk.	TO	Pts.	AVERAGES RPG	APG	PPG
85-86—L.A. Lakers	9	106	9	17	.529	4	9	.444	3	13	16	0	1	3	4	22	1.8	0.0	2.4
86-87—L.A. Lakers	18	505	71	130	.546	65	87	.747	54	88	142	11	9	8	17	207	7.9	0.6	11.5
87-88—L.A. Lakers	24	726	92	169	.544	55	73	.753	57	118	175	20	11	12	26	239	7.3	0.8	10.0
88-89—L.A. Lakers	15	502	47	114	.412	58	76	.763	38	99	137	18	16	6	23	152	9.1	1.2	10.1
89-90—L.A. Lakers	9	252	41	79	.519	24	32	.750	34	47	81	9	5	4	14	106	9.0	1.0	11.8
90-91—L.A. Lakers	19	400	41	97	.423	38	54	.704	46	56	102	9	12	3	19	124	5.4	0.5	6.5
91-92—L.A. Lakers	4	153	16	39	.410	19	23	.826	15	21	36	7	7	0	5	51	9.0	1.8	12.8
92-93—L.A. Lakers	5	220	18	42	.429	13	21	.619	26	47	73	13	7	3	9	49	14.6	2.6	9.8
93-94—Phoenix	10	350	40	83	.482	38	62	.613	29	55	84	13	10	2	7	125	8.4	1.3	12.5
94-95—Phoenix	10	368	36	78	.462	55	63	.873	38	82	120	13	6	2	10	128	12.0	1.3	12.8
95-96—Phoenix	4	87	6	17	.353	7	8	.875	6	12	18	2	1	0	2	19	4.5	0.5	4.8
Totals	127	3669	417	865	.482	376	508	.740	346	638	984	115	85	43	136	1222	7.7	0.9	9.6

Three-point field goals: 1988-89, 0-for-3. 1990-91, 4-for-8 (.500). 1992-93, 0-for-5. 1993-94, 7-for-17 (.412). 1994-95, 1-for-12 (.083). 1995-96, 0-for-3. Totals, 12-for-48 (.250).
Personal fouls/disqualifications: 1985-86, 13/0. 1986-87, 47/0. 1987-88, 61/0. 1988-89, 37/1. 1989-90, 22/0. 1990-91, 37/0. 1991-92, 10/0. 1992-93, 14/1. 1993-94, 22/0. 1994-95, 22/0. 1995-96, 7/0. Totals, 292/2.

NBA ALL-STAR GAME RECORD

Season Team	Min.	FGM	FGA	Pct.	FTM	FTA	Pct.	REBOUNDS Off.	Def.	Tot.	Ast.	PF	Dq.	St.	Blk.	TO	Pts.
1990 —L.A. Lakers	12	0	3	.000	0	0	...	0	3	3	1	1	0	0	1	1	0

G

GUGLIOTTA, TOM   F   TIMBERWOLVES

PERSONAL: Born December 19, 1969, in Huntington Station, N.Y. ... 6-10/240. ... Full name: Thomas James Gugliotta. ... Name pronounced GOOG-lee-AH-tah.
HIGH SCHOOL: Walt Whitman (Huntington Station, N.Y.).
COLLEGE: North Carolina State.
TRANSACTIONS/CAREER NOTES: Selected by Washington Bullets in first round (sixth pick overall) of 1992 NBA Draft. ... Traded by Bullets with 1996, 1998 and 2000 first-round draft choices to Golden State Warriors for F Chris Webber (November 17, 1994). ... Traded by Warriors to Minnesota Timberwolves for F Donyell Marshall (February 18, 1995).

COLLEGIATE RECORD

Season Team	G	Min.	FGM	FGA	Pct.	FTM	FTA	Pct.	Reb.	Ast.	Pts.	AVERAGES		
												RPG	APG	PPG
88-89—N.C. State	21	171	18	42	.429	19	29	.655	35	5	56	1.7	0.2	2.7
89-90—N.C. State	30	886	135	268	.504	41	61	.672	211	47	334	7.0	1.6	11.1
90-91—N.C. State	31	1123	170	340	.500	65	101	.644	281	87	471	9.1	2.8	15.2
91-92—N.C. State	30	1107	240	534	.449	102	149	.685	293	92	675	9.8	3.1	22.5
Totals	112	3287	563	1184	.476	227	340	.668	820	231	1536	7.3	2.1	13.7

Three-point field goals: 1988-89, 1-for-2 (.500). 1989-90, 23-for-47 (.489). 1990-91, 66-for-166 (.398). 1991-92, 93-for-233 (.399). Totals, 183-for-448 (.408).

NBA REGULAR-SEASON RECORD

HONORS: NBA All-Rookie first team (1993).

Season Team	G	Min.	FGM	FGA	Pct.	FTM	FTA	Pct.	REBOUNDS			Ast.	St.	Blk.	TO	Pts.	AVERAGES		
									Off.	Def.	Tot.						RPG	APG	PPG
92-93—Washington	81	2795	484	1135	.426	181	281	.644	219	562	781	306	134	35	230	1187	9.6	3.8	14.7
93-94—Washington	78	2795	540	1159	.466	213	311	.685	189	539	728	276	172	51	247	1333	9.3	3.5	17.1
94-95—Wash-GS-Minn	77	2568	371	837	.443	174	252	.690	165	407	572	279	132	62	189	976	7.4	3.6	12.7
95-96—Minnesota	78	2835	473	1004	.471	289	374	.773	176	514	690	238	139	96	234	1261	8.8	3.1	16.2
Totals	314	10993	1868	4135	.452	857	1218	.704	749	2022	2771	1099	577	244	900	4757	8.8	3.5	15.1

Three-point field goals: 1992-93, 38-for-135 (.281). 1993-94, 40-for-148 (.270). 1994-95, 60-for-186 (.323). 1995-96, 26-for-86 (.302). Totals, 164-for-555 (.295).

Personal fouls/disqualifications: 1992-93, 195/0. 1993-94, 174/0. 1994-95, 203/2. 1995-96, 265/1. Totals, 837/3.

HALEY, JACK   C   BULLS

PERSONAL: Born January 27, 1964, in Long Beach, Calif. ... 6-10/242. ... Full name: Jack Kevin Haley.
HIGH SCHOOL: Huntington Beach (Calif.).
JUNIOR COLLEGE: Golden West College (Calif.).
COLLEGE: UCLA.
TRANSACTIONS/CAREER NOTES: Selected by Chicago Bulls in fourth round (79th pick overall) of 1987 NBA Draft. ... Played in Spain (1987-88). ... Claimed off waivers by New Jersey Nets (December 20, 1989). ... Signed as unrestricted free agent by Los Angeles Lakers (October 4, 1991). ... Waived by Lakers (November 2, 1993). ... Signed as free agent by San Antonio Spurs (December 14, 1993). ... Rights renounced by Spurs (September 18, 1995). ... Re-signed as free agent by Bulls (October 6, 1995).
MISCELLANEOUS: Member of NBA championship team (1996).

COLLEGIATE RECORD

Season Team	G	Min.	FGM	FGA	Pct.	FTM	FTA	Pct.	Reb.	Ast.	Pts.	AVERAGES		
												RPG	APG	PPG
82-83—Golden West College					Did not play.									
83-84—Golden West College	24	...	53	116	.457	40	77	.519	128	15	146	5.3	0.6	6.1
84-85—UCLA	25	125	9	22	.409	7	17	.412	42	4	25	1.7	0.2	1.0
85-86—UCLA	29	709	41	108	.380	44	61	.721	183	18	126	6.3	0.6	4.3
86-87—UCLA	32	740	57	122	.467	52	84	.619	151	30	166	4.7	0.9	5.2
Junior college totals	24	...	53	116	.457	40	77	.519	128	15	146	5.3	0.6	6.1
4-year-college totals	86	1574	107	252	.425	103	162	.636	376	52	317	4.4	0.6	3.7

SPANISH LEAGUE RECORD

Season Team	G	Min.	FGM	FGA	Pct.	FTM	FTA	Pct.	Reb.	Ast.	Pts.	AVERAGES		
												RPG	APG	PPG
87-88—Grupo Ifa Espanol's	...	...	...	...	...	...	...	...	...	...	...	...	...	20.2

NBA REGULAR-SEASON RECORD

Season Team	G	Min.	FGM	FGA	Pct.	FTM	FTA	Pct.	REBOUNDS			Ast.	St.	Blk.	TO	Pts.	AVERAGES		
									Off.	Def.	Tot.						RPG	APG	PPG
88-89—Chicago	51	289	37	78	.474	36	46	.783	21	50	71	10	11	0	26	110	1.4	0.2	2.2
89-90—Chi.-N.J.	67	1084	138	347	.398	85	125	.680	115	185	300	26	18	12	72	361	4.5	0.4	5.4
90-91—New Jersey	78	1178	161	343	.469	112	140	.619	140	216	356	31	20	21	63	434	4.6	0.4	5.6
91-92—L.A. Lakers	49	394	31	84	.369	14	29	.483	31	64	95	7	7	8	25	76	1.9	0.1	1.6
92-93—L.A. Lakers					Did not play—injured.														
93-94—San Antonio	28	94	21	48	.438	17	21	.810	6	18	24	1	0	0	10	59	0.9	0.0	2.1
94-95—San Antonio	31	117	26	61	.426	21	32	.656	8	19	27	2	3	5	13	73	0.9	0.1	2.4
95-96—Chicago	1	7	2	6	.333	1	2	.500	1	1	2	0	0	0	1	5	2.0	0.0	5.0
Totals	305	3163	416	967	.430	286	436	.656	322	553	875	77	59	46	210	1118	2.9	0.3	3.7

Three-point field goals: 1989-90, 0-for-1. 1994-95, 0-for-1. Totals, 0-for-2.

Personal fouls/disqualifications: 1988-89, 56/0. 1989-90, 170/1. 1990-91, 199/0. 1991-92, 75/0. 1993-94, 18/0. 1994-95, 31/0. 1995-96, 2/0. Totals, 551/1.

NBA PLAYOFF RECORD

Season Team	G	Min.	FGM	FGA	Pct.	FTM	FTA	Pct.	REBOUNDS			Ast.	St.	Blk.	TO	Pts.	AVERAGES		
									Off.	Def.	Tot.						RPG	APG	PPG
88-89—Chicago	5	7	2	3	.667	1	2	.500	0	1	1	1	0	0	0	5	0.2	0.2	1.0
91-92—L.A. Lakers	2	12	1	4	.250	0	0	...	1	0	1	1	0	0	0	2	0.5	0.5	1.0
93-94—San Antonio	3	11	4	8	.500	5	6	.833	3	4	7	2	0	0	0	13	2.3	0.7	4.3
94-95—San Antonio	4	13	1	7	.143	1	2	.500	2	4	6	0	0	1	1	3	1.5	0.0	0.8
Totals	14	43	8	22	.364	7	10	.700	6	9	15	4	0	1	1	23	1.1	0.3	1.6

Personal fouls/disqualifications: 1988-89, 2/0. 1991-92, 3/0. 1993-94, 3/0. 1994-95, 2/0. Totals, 10/0.

GH

HAMILTON, THOMAS   C   CELTICS

PERSONAL: Born April 3, 1975, in Chicago. ... 7-2/360. ... Full name: Thomas Thaddeus Hamilton.
HIGH SCHOOL: Martin Luther King (Chicago).
COLLEGE: Pittsburgh.
TRANSACTIONS/CAREER NOTES: Not drafted by an NBA franchise. ... Signed as free agent by Boston Celtics (November 24, 1995).

COLLEGIATE RECORD

Season Team	G	Min.	FGM	FGA	Pct.	FTM	FTA	Pct.	Reb.	Ast.	Pts.	RPG	APG	PPG
94-95—Pittsburgh						Did not attend school.								

NBA REGULAR-SEASON RECORD

Season Team	G	Min.	FGM	FGA	Pct.	FTM	FTA	Pct.	Off.	Def.	Tot.	Ast.	St.	Blk.	TO	Pts.	RPG	APG	PPG
95-96—Boston	11	70	9	31	.290	7	18	.389	10	12	22	1	0	9	9	25	2.0	0.1	2.3

Personal fouls/disqualifications: 1995-96, 12/0.

HAMMINK, GEERT   F/C

PERSONAL: Born April 12, 1969, in Didam, The Netherlands. ... 7-0/262. ... Full name: Geert Hendrik Hammink. ... Name pronounced GERT HAM-ink.
HIGH SCHOOL: Thorbecke (Arnhem, The Netherlands).
COLLEGE: Louisiana State.
TRANSACTIONS/CAREER NOTES: Selected by Orlando Magic in first round (26th pick overall) of 1993 NBA Draft. ... Played in Italy (1993-94). ... Signed by Magic (April 20, 1994). ... Waived by Magic (December 8, 1995). ... Played in Continental Basketball Association with Omaha Racers (1995-96). ... Signed by Golden State Warriors to first of two consecutive 10-day contracts (March 25, 1996). ... Re-signed by Warriors for remainder of season (April 14, 1996). ... Rights renounced by Warriors (July 21, 1996).

COLLEGIATE RECORD

Season Team	G	Min.	FGM	FGA	Pct.	FTM	FTA	Pct.	Reb.	Ast.	Pts.	RPG	APG	PPG
88-89—Louisiana State	25	203	19	41	.463	11	27	.407	54	4	49	2.2	0.2	2.0
89-90—Louisiana State						Did not play—redshirted.								
90-91—Louisiana State	27	228	44	104	.423	36	44	.818	78	11	124	2.9	0.4	4.6
91-92—Louisiana State	29	235	27	67	.403	15	29	.517	79	12	69	2.7	0.4	2.4
92-93—Louisiana State	32	970	190	382	.497	108	148	.730	325	61	488	10.2	1.9	15.3
Totals	113	1636	280	594	.471	170	248	.685	536	88	730	4.7	0.8	6.5

Three-point field goals: 1990-91, 0-for-1. 1992-93, 0-for-3. Totals, 0-for-4.

ITALIAN LEAGUE RECORD

Season Team	G	Min.	FGM	FGA	Pct.	FTM	FTA	Pct.	Reb.	Ast.	Pts.	RPG	APG	PPG
93-94—S. Clear	20	613	103	210	.490	42	52	.808	150	11	248	7.5	0.6	12.4

NBA REGULAR-SEASON RECORD

Season Team	G	Min.	FGM	FGA	Pct.	FTM	FTA	Pct.	Off.	Def.	Tot.	Ast.	St.	Blk.	TO	Pts.	RPG	APG	PPG
93-94—Orlando	1	3	1	3	.333	0	0	...	1	0	1	1	0	0	0	2	1.0	1.0	2.0
94-95—Orlando	1	7	1	3	.333	2	2	1.000	0	2	2	1	0	0	0	4	2.0	1.0	4.0
95-96—Orl.-G.S.	6	17	2	4	.500	4	7	.571	2	2	4	0	0	0	2	8	0.7	0.0	1.3
Totals	8	27	4	10	.400	6	9	.667	3	4	7	2	0	0	2	14	0.9	0.3	1.8

Personal fouls/disqualifications: 1993-94, 1/0. 1994-95, 1/0. 1995-96, 2/0. Totals, 4/0.

CBA REGULAR-SEASON RECORD

Season Team	G	Min.	FGM	FGA	Pct.	FTM	FTA	Pct.	Reb.	Ast.	Pts.	RPG	APG	PPG
95-96—Omaha	29	773	143	266	.538	56	63	.889	211	35	342	7.3	1.2	11.8

HAMMONDS, TOM   F   NUGGETS

PERSONAL: Born March 27, 1967, in Fort Walton, Fla. ... 6-9/225. ... Full name: Tom Edward Hammonds.
HIGH SCHOOL: Crestview (Fla.).
COLLEGE: Georgia Tech.
TRANSACTIONS/CAREER NOTES: Selected by Washington Bullets in first round (ninth pick overall) of 1989 NBA Draft. ... Traded by Bullets to Charlotte Hornets for G Rex Chapman (February 19, 1992). ... Waived by Hornets (January 26, 1993). ... Signed as free agent by Denver Nuggets (February 5, 1993).

COLLEGIATE RECORD

Season Team	G	Min.	FGM	FGA	Pct.	FTM	FTA	Pct.	Reb.	Ast.	Pts.	RPG	APG	PPG
85-86—Georgia Tech	34	1112	168	276	.609	80	98	.816	219	37	416	6.4	1.1	12.2
86-87—Georgia Tech	29	1088	206	362	.569	59	74	.797	208	41	471	7.2	1.4	16.2
87-88—Georgia Tech	30	1076	229	403	.568	109	132	.826	216	40	567	7.2	1.3	18.9
88-89—Georgia Tech	30	1111	250	465	.538	126	163	.773	242	51	627	8.1	1.7	20.9
Totals	123	4387	853	1506	.566	374	467	.801	885	169	2081	7.2	1.4	16.9

Three-point field goals: 1988-89, 1-for-3 (.333).

H

NBA REGULAR-SEASON RECORD

Season Team	G	Min.	FGM	FGA	Pct.	FTM	FTA	Pct.	REBOUNDS Off.	Def.	Tot.	Ast.	St.	Blk.	TO	Pts.	AVERAGES RPG	APG	PPG
89-90—Washington	61	805	129	295	.437	63	98	.643	61	107	168	51	11	14	46	321	2.8	0.8	5.3
90-91—Washington	70	1023	155	336	.461	57	79	.722	58	148	206	43	15	7	54	367	2.9	0.6	5.2
91-92—Washington	37	984	195	400	.488	50	82	.610	49	136	185	36	22	13	58	440	5.0	1.0	11.9
92-93—Char.-Den.	54	713	105	221	.475	38	62	.613	38	89	127	24	18	12	34	248	2.4	0.4	4.6
93-94—Denver	74	877	115	230	.500	71	104	.683	62	137	199	34	20	12	41	301	2.7	0.5	4.1
94-95—Denver	70	956	139	260	.535	132	177	.746	55	167	222	36	11	14	56	410	3.2	0.5	5.9
95-96—Denver	71	1045	127	268	.474	88	115	.765	85	138	223	23	23	13	48	342	3.1	0.3	4.8
Totals	437	6403	965	2010	.480	499	717	.696	408	922	1330	247	120	85	337	2429	3.0	0.6	5.6

Three-point field goals: 1989-90, 0-for-1. 1990-91, 0-for-4. 1991-92, 0-for-1. 1992-93, 0-for-1. 1994-95, 0-for-1. Totals, 0-for-8.
Personal fouls/disqualifications: 1989-90, 98/0. 1990-91, 108/0. 1991-92, 118/1. 1992-93, 77/0. 1993-94, 91/0. 1994-95, 132/1. 1995-96, 137/0. Totals, 761/2.

NBA PLAYOFF RECORD

Season Team	G	Min.	FGM	FGA	Pct.	FTM	FTA	Pct.	REBOUNDS Off.	Def.	Tot.	Ast.	St.	Blk.	TO	Pts.	AVERAGES RPG	APG	PPG
93-94—Denver	8	49	2	9	.222	5	6	.833	5	8	13	2	0	0	1	9	1.6	0.3	1.1
94-95—Denver	3	44	9	14	.643	2	6	.333	3	4	7	1	0	2	4	20	2.3	0.3	6.7
Totals	11	93	11	23	.478	7	12	.583	8	12	20	3	0	2	5	29	1.8	0.3	2.6

Personal fouls/disqualifications: 1993-94, 6/0. 1994-95, 12/0. Totals, 18/0.

HANCOCK, DARRIN   G/F   HORNETS

PERSONAL: Born November 3, 1971, in Birmingham, Ala. ... 6-7/212.
HIGH SCHOOL: Griffin (Ga.).
JUNIOR COLLEGE: Garden City (Kan.) Community College.
COLLEGE: Kansas.
TRANSACTIONS/CAREER NOTES: Played in France after junior season (1993-94). ... Selected by Charlotte Hornets in second round (38th pick overall) of 1994 NBA Draft.

COLLEGIATE RECORD

Season Team	G	Min.	FGM	FGA	Pct.	FTM	FTA	Pct.	Reb.	Ast.	Pts.	AVERAGES RPG	APG	PPG
90-91—Garden City C.C.	32	...	214	377	.568	135	215	.628	288	186	570	9.0	5.8	17.8
91-92—Garden City C.C.	28	...	243	410	.593	114	180	.633	328	169	610	11.7	6.0	21.8
92-93—Kansas	34	703	103	190	.542	50	76	.658	154	46	256	4.5	1.4	7.5
Junior college totals	60	...	457	787	.581	249	395	.630	616	355	1180	10.3	5.9	19.7
4-year-college totals	34	703	103	190	.542	50	76	.658	154	46	256	4.5	1.4	7.5

Three-point field goals: 1992-93, 0-for-1.

FRENCH LEAGUE RECORD

Season Team	G	Min.	FGM	FGA	Pct.	FTM	FTA	Pct.	Reb.	Ast.	Pts.	AVERAGES RPG	APG	PPG
93-94—Maurienne	17	...	126	243	.519	33	65	.508	92	30	295	5.4	1.8	17.4

NBA REGULAR-SEASON RECORD

Season Team	G	Min.	FGM	FGA	Pct.	FTM	FTA	Pct.	REBOUNDS Off.	Def.	Tot.	Ast.	St.	Blk.	TO	Pts.	AVERAGES RPG	APG	PPG
94-95—Charlotte	46	424	68	121	.562	16	39	.410	14	39	53	30	19	4	30	153	1.2	0.7	3.3
95-96—Charlotte	63	838	112	214	.523	47	73	.644	40	58	98	47	28	5	56	272	1.6	0.7	4.3
Totals	109	1262	180	335	.537	63	112	.563	54	97	151	77	47	9	86	425	1.4	0.7	3.9

Three-point field goals: 1994-95, 1-for-3 (.333). 1995-96, 1-for-3 (.333). Totals, 2-for-6 (.333).
Personal fouls/disqualifications: 1994-95, 48/0. 1995-96, 94/2. Totals, 142/2.

NBA PLAYOFF RECORD

Season Team	G	Min.	FGM	FGA	Pct.	FTM	FTA	Pct.	REBOUNDS Off.	Def.	Tot.	Ast.	St.	Blk.	TO	Pts.	AVERAGES RPG	APG	PPG
94-95—Charlotte	3	18	2	6	.333	0	0	...	2	2	4	1	1	0	3	4	1.3	0.3	1.3

Personal fouls/disqualifications: 1994-95, 5/0.

HARDAWAY, ANFERNEE   G/F   MAGIC

PERSONAL: Born July 18, 1971, in Memphis. ... 6-7/215. ... Full name: Anfernee Deon Hardaway. ... Nickname: Penny.
HIGH SCHOOL: Treadwell (Memphis).
COLLEGE: Memphis.
TRANSACTIONS/CAREER NOTES: Selected after junior season by Golden State Warriors in first round (third pick overall) of 1993 NBA Draft. ... Draft rights traded by Warriors with 1996, 1998 and 2000 first-round draft choices to Orlando Magic for draft rights F/C Chris Webber (June 30, 1993).
MISCELLANEOUS: Member of gold-medal-winning U.S. Olympic team (1996).

NOTES: THE SPORTING NEWS All-America first team (1993).

COLLEGIATE RECORD

Season Team	G	Min.	FGM	FGA	Pct.	FTM	FTA	Pct.	Reb.	Ast.	Pts.	AVERAGES RPG	APG	PPG
90-91—Memphis						Did not play—ineligible.								
91-92—Memphis	34	1224	209	483	.433	103	158	.652	237	188	590	7.0	5.5	17.4
92-93—Memphis	32	1196	249	522	.477	158	206	.767	273	204	729	8.5	6.4	22.8
Totals	66	2420	458	1005	.456	261	364	.717	510	392	1319	7.7	5.9	20.0

Three-point field goals: 1991-92, 69-for-190 (.363). 1992-93, 73-for-220 (.332). Totals, 142-for-410 (.346).

H

NBA REGULAR-SEASON RECORD

HONORS: All-NBA first team (1995, 1996). ... NBA All-Rookie first team (1994).

Season Team	G	Min.	FGM	FGA	Pct.	FTM	FTA	Pct.	Off.	Def.	Tot.	Ast.	St.	Blk.	TO	Pts.	RPG	APG	PPG
93-94—Orlando.........	82	3015	509	1092	.466	245	330	.742	192	247	439	544	190	51	292	1313	5.4	6.6	16.0
94-95—Orlando.........	77	2901	585	1142	.512	356	463	.769	139	197	336	551	130	26	258	1613	4.4	7.2	20.9
95-96—Orlando.........	82	3015	623	1215	.513	445	580	.767	129	225	354	582	166	41	229	1780	4.3	7.1	21.7
Totals	241	8931	1717	3449	.498	1046	1373	.762	460	669	1129	1677	486	118	779	4706	4.7	7.0	19.5

Three-point field goals: 1993-94, 50-for-187 (.267). 1994-95, 87-for-249 (.349). 1995-96, 89-for-283 (.314). Totals, 226-for-719 (.314).
Personal fouls/disqualifications: 1993-94, 205/2. 1994-95, 158/1. 1995-96, 160/0. Totals, 523/3.

NBA PLAYOFF RECORD

Season Team	G	Min.	FGM	FGA	Pct.	FTM	FTA	Pct.	Off.	Def.	Tot.	Ast.	St.	Blk.	TO	Pts.	RPG	APG	PPG
93-94—Orlando.........	3	133	22	50	.440	7	10	.700	8	12	20	21	5	6	20	56	6.7	7.0	18.7
94-95—Orlando.........	21	849	144	305	.472	84	111	.757	30	49	79	162	40	15	73	412	3.8	7.7	19.6
95-96—Orlando.........	12	473	101	217	.465	58	78	.744	20	36	56	72	20	4	26	280	4.7	6.0	23.3
Totals	36	1455	267	572	.467	149	199	.749	58	97	155	255	65	25	119	748	4.3	7.1	20.8

Three-point field goals: 1993-94, 5-for-11 (.455). 1994-95, 40-for-99 (.404). 1995-96, 20-for-55 (.364). Totals, 65-for-165 (.394).
Personal fouls/disqualifications: 1993-94, 10/0. 1994-95, 70/0. 1995-96, 27/1. Totals, 107/1.

NBA ALL-STAR GAME RECORD

Season Team	Min.	FGM	FGA	Pct.	FTM	FTA	Pct.	Off.	Def.	Tot.	Ast.	PF	Dq.	St.	Blk.	TO	Pts.
1995 —Orlando	31	4	9	.444	4	6	.667	4	1	5	11	1	0	0	0	3	12
1996 —Orlando	31	6	8	.750	4	4	1.000	0	3	3	7	0	0	2	0	3	18
Totals	62	10	17	.588	8	10	.800	4	1	8	18	1	0	2	0	6	30

Three-point field goals: 1995, 0-for-2. 1996, 2-for-4 (.500). Totals, 2-for-6 (.333).

HARDAWAY, TIM   G   HEAT

PERSONAL: Born September 1, 1966, in Chicago ... 6-0/195. ... Full name: Timothy Duane Hardaway.
HIGH SCHOOL: Carver (Chicago).
COLLEGE: Texas-El Paso.
TRANSACTIONS/CAREER NOTES: Selected by Golden State Warriors in first round (14th pick overall) of 1989 NBA Draft. ... Traded by Warriors with F/C Chris Gatling to Miami Heat for F/C Kevin Willis and G Bimbo Coles (February 22, 1996).

COLLEGIATE RECORD

NOTES: Frances Pomeroy Naismith Award winner (1989).

Season Team	G	Min.	FGM	FGA	Pct.	FTM	FTA	Pct.	Reb.	Ast.	Pts.	RPG	APG	PPG
85-86—Texas-El Paso	28	435	37	71	.521	41	63	.651	35	53	115	1.3	1.9	4.1
86-87—Texas-El Paso	31	922	120	245	.490	67	101	.663	62	148	310	2.0	4.8	10.0
87-88—Texas-El Paso	32	1036	159	354	.449	98	130	.754	93	183	434	2.9	5.7	13.6
88-89—Texas-El Paso	33	1182	255	509	.501	169	228	.741	131	179	727	4.0	5.4	22.0
Totals	124	3575	571	1179	.484	375	522	.718	321	563	1586	2.6	4.5	12.8

Three-point field goals: 1986-87, 3-for-12 (.250). 1987-88, 18-for-53 (.340). 1988-89, 48-for-131 (.366). Totals, 69-for-196 (.352).

NBA REGULAR-SEASON RECORD

RECORDS: Holds single-game record for most field goals attempted, none made—17 (December 27, 1991, OT, at San Antonio).
HONORS: All-NBA second team (1992). ... All-NBA third team (1993). ... NBA All-Rookie first team (1990).

Season Team	G	Min.	FGM	FGA	Pct.	FTM	FTA	Pct.	Off.	Def.	Tot.	Ast.	St.	Blk.	TO	Pts.	RPG	APG	PPG
89-90—Golden State ...	79	2663	464	985	.471	211	276	.765	57	253	310	689	165	12	260	1162	3.9	8.7	14.7
90-91—Golden State ...	82	3215	739	1551	.476	306	381	.803	87	245	332	793	214	12	270	1881	4.0	9.7	22.9
91-92—Golden State ...	81	3332	734	1592	.461	298	389	.766	81	229	310	807	164	13	267	1893	3.8	10.0	23.4
92-93—Golden State ...	66	2609	522	1168	.447	273	367	.744	60	203	263	699	116	12	220	1419	4.0	10.6	21.5
93-94—Golden State ...								Did not play—knee injury.											
94-95—Golden State ...	62	2321	430	1007	.427	219	288	.760	46	144	190	578	88	12	214	1247	3.1	9.3	20.1
95-96—GS-Mia.	80	2534	419	992	.422	241	305	.790	35	194	229	640	132	17	235	1217	2.9	8.0	15.2
Totals	450	16674	3308	7295	.453	1548	2006	.772	366	1268	1634	4206	879	78	1466	8819	3.6	9.3	19.6

Three-point field goals: 1989-90, 23-for-84 (.274). 1990-91, 97-for-252 (.385). 1991-92, 127-for-376 (.338). 1992-93, 102-for-309 (.330). 1994-95, 168-for-444 (.378). 1995-96, 138-for-379 (.364). Totals, 655-for-1844 (.355).
Personal fouls/disqualifications: 1989-90, 232/6. 1990-91, 228/7. 1991-92, 208/1. 1992-93, 152/0. 1994-95, 155/1. 1995-96, 201/3. Totals, 1176/18.

NBA PLAYOFF RECORD

NOTES: Shares single-game playoff record for most steals—8 (May 8, 1991, vs. Los Angeles Lakers; and April 30, 1992, vs. Seattle).

Season Team	G	Min.	FGM	FGA	Pct.	FTM	FTA	Pct.	Off.	Def.	Tot.	Ast.	St.	Blk.	TO	Pts.	RPG	APG	PPG
90-91—Golden State ...	9	396	90	185	.486	30	38	.789	5	28	33	101	28	7	25	227	3.7	11.2	25.2
91-92—Golden State ...	4	176	32	80	.400	24	37	.649	6	9	15	29	13	0	14	98	3.8	7.3	24.5
95-96—Miami	3	110	20	43	.465	5	7	.714	1	4	5	17	3	0	15	53	1.7	5.7	17.7
Totals	16	682	142	308	.461	59	82	.720	12	41	53	147	44	7	54	378	3.3	9.2	23.6

Three-point field goals: 1990-91, 17-for-48 (.354). 1991-92, 10-for-29 (.345). 1995-96, 8-for-22 (.364). Totals, 35-for-99 (.354).
Personal fouls/disqualifications: 1990-91, 22/0. 1991-92, 14/0. 1995-96, 10/0. Totals, 46/0.

NBA ALL-STAR GAME RECORD

Season Team	Min.	FGM	FGA	Pct.	FTM	FTA	Pct.	Off.	Def.	Tot.	Ast.	PF	Dq.	St.	Blk.	TO	Pts.
1991 —Golden State......	12	2	7	.286	0	0	...	2	1	3	4	1	0	2	0	0	5
1992 —Golden State......	20	5	10	.500	2	2	1.000	0	0	0	7	2	0	1	0	2	14

H

Season Team	Min.	FGM	FGA	Pct.	FTM	FTA	Pct.	REBOUNDS Off.	Def.	Tot.	Ast.	PF	Dq.	St.	Blk.	TO	Pts.
1993 —Golden State......	21	3	9	.333	9	12	.750	1	5	6	4	1	0	1	0	3	16
Totals.........................	53	10	26	.385	11	14	.786	3	6	9	15	4	0	4	0	5	35

Three-point field goals: 1991, 1-for-2 (.500). 1992, 2-for-5 (.400). 1993, 1-for-3 (.333). Totals, 4-for-10 (.400).

HARPER, DEREK   G   MAVERICKS

PERSONAL: Born October 13, 1961, in Elberton, Ga. ... 6-4/206. ... Full name: Derek Ricardo Harper.
HIGH SCHOOL: North Shore (West Palm Beach, Fla.).
COLLEGE: Illinois.
TRANSACTIONS/CAREER NOTES: Selected after junior season by Dallas Mavericks in first round (11th pick overall) of 1983 NBA Draft. ... Traded by Mavericks to New York Knicks for G/F Tony Campbell and 1997 first-round draft choice (January 6, 1994). ... Rights renounced by Knicks (July 14, 1996). ... Signed as free agent by Mavericks (July 26, 1996).
MISCELLANEOUS: Dallas Mavericks all-time assists leader with 4,790 and all-time steals leader with 1,459 (1983-84 through 1993-94).

COLLEGIATE RECORD

Season Team	G	Min.	FGM	FGA	Pct.	FTM	FTA	Pct.	Reb.	Ast.	Pts.	AVERAGES RPG	APG	PPG
80-81—Illinois	29	934	104	252	.413	33	46	.717	75	156	241	2.6	5.4	8.3
81-82—Illinois	29	1059	105	230	.457	34	45	.756	133	145	244	4.6	5.0	8.4
82-83—Illinois	32	1182	198	369	.537	83	123	.675	112	118	492	3.5	3.7	15.4
Totals	90	3175	407	851	.478	150	214	.701	320	419	977	3.6	4.7	10.9

Three-point field goals: 1982-83, 13-for-24 (.542).

NBA REGULAR-SEASON RECORD

HONORS: NBA All-Defensive second team (1987, 1990).

Season Team	G	Min.	FGM	FGA	Pct.	FTM	FTA	Pct.	REBOUNDS Off.	Def.	Tot.	Ast.	St.	Blk.	TO	Pts.	AVERAGES RPG	APG	PPG
83-84—Dallas..............	82	1712	200	451	.443	66	98	.673	53	119	172	239	95	21	111	469	2.1	2.9	5.7
84-85—Dallas..............	82	2218	329	633	.520	111	154	.721	47	152	199	360	144	37	123	790	2.4	4.4	9.6
85-86—Dallas..............	79	2150	390	730	.534	171	229	.747	75	151	226	416	153	23	144	963	2.9	5.3	12.2
86-87—Dallas..............	77	2556	497	993	.501	160	234	.684	51	148	199	609	167	25	138	1230	2.6	7.9	16.0
87-88—Dallas..............	82	3032	536	1167	.459	261	344	.759	71	175	246	634	168	35	190	1393	3.0	7.7	17.0
88-89—Dallas..............	81	2968	538	1127	.477	229	284	.806	46	182	228	570	172	41	205	1404	2.8	7.0	17.3
89-90—Dallas..............	82	3007	567	1161	.488	250	315	.794	54	190	244	609	187	26	207	1473	3.0	7.4	18.0
90-91—Dallas..............	77	2879	572	1226	.467	286	391	.731	59	174	233	548	147	14	177	1519	3.0	7.1	19.7
91-92—Dallas..............	65	2252	448	1011	.443	198	261	.759	49	121	170	373	101	17	154	1152	2.6	5.7	17.7
92-93—Dallas..............	62	2108	393	939	.419	239	316	.756	42	81	123	334	80	16	136	1126	2.0	5.4	18.2
93-94—Dallas-N.Y.	82	2204	303	744	.407	112	163	.687	20	121	141	334	125	8	135	791	1.7	4.1	9.6
94-95—New York.......	80	2716	337	756	.446	139	192	.724	31	163	194	458	79	10	151	919	2.4	5.7	11.5
95-96—New York.......	82	2893	436	939	.464	156	206	.757	32	170	202	352	131	5	178	1149	2.5	4.3	14.0
Totals	1013	32695	5546	11877	.467	2378	3187	.746	630	1947	2577	5836	1749	278	2049	14378	2.5	5.8	14.2

Three-point field goals: 1983-84, 3-for-26 (.115). 1984-85, 21-for-61 (.344). 1985-86, 12-for-51 (.235). 1986-87, 76-for-212 (.358). 1987-88, 60-for-192 (.313). 1988-89, 99-for-278 (.356). 1989-90, 89-for-240 (.371). 1990-91, 89-for-246 (.362). 1991-92, 58-for-186 (.312). 1992-93, 101-for-257 (.393). 1993-94, 73-for-203 (.360). 1994-95, 106-for-292 (.363). 1995-96, 121-for-325 (.372). Totals, 908-for-2569 (.353).

Personal fouls/disqualifications: 1983-84, 143/0. 1984-85, 194/1. 1985-86, 166/1. 1986-87, 195/0. 1987-88, 164/0. 1988-89, 219/3. 1989-90, 224/1. 1990-91, 222/1. 1991-92, 150/0. 1992-93, 145/1. 1993-94, 163/0. 1994-95, 201/0. 1995-96, 201/0. Totals, 2405/8.

NBA PLAYOFF RECORD

NOTES: Shares NBA Finals single-series record for most three-point field goals made—17 (1994, vs. Houston).

Season Team	G	Min.	FGM	FGA	Pct.	FTM	FTA	Pct.	REBOUNDS Off.	Def.	Tot.	Ast.	St.	Blk.	TO	Pts.	AVERAGES RPG	APG	PPG
83-84—Dallas..............	10	226	21	54	.389	5	7	.714	8	12	20	28	11	2	6	50	2.0	2.8	5.0
84-85—Dallas..............	4	132	10	21	.476	5	7	.714	1	11	12	20	6	1	4	26	3.0	5.0	6.5
85-86—Dallas..............	10	348	57	107	.533	12	16	.750	13	6	19	76	23	0	23	134	1.9	7.6	13.4
86-87—Dallas..............	4	123	20	40	.500	24	30	.800	2	10	12	27	7	0	5	66	3.0	6.8	16.5
87-88—Dallas..............	17	602	89	202	.441	43	59	.729	11	32	43	121	32	5	32	230	2.5	7.1	13.5
89-90—Dallas..............	3	119	21	48	.438	11	16	.688	2	6	8	23	4	0	12	58	2.7	7.7	19.3
93-94—New York.......	23	750	99	231	.429	36	56	.643	13	41	54	103	42	1	41	263	2.3	4.5	11.4
94-95—New York.......	11	388	56	109	.514	18	24	.750	5	33	38	62	11	1	26	157	3.5	5.6	14.3
95-96—New York.......	8	293	29	82	.354	11	15	.733	0	17	17	38	10	1	14	80	2.1	4.8	10.0
Totals	90	2981	402	894	.450	165	230	.717	55	168	223	498	146	11	163	1064	2.5	5.5	11.8

Three-point field goals: 1983-84, 3-for-8 (.375). 1984-85, 1-for-3 (.333). 1985-86, 8-for-14 (.571). 1986-87, 2-for-9 (.222). 1987-88, 9-for-36 (.250). 1989-90, 5-for-16 (.313). 1993-94, 29-for-85 (.341). 1994-95, 27-for-47 (.574). 1995-96, 11-for-35 (.314). Totals, 95-for-253 (.375).

Personal fouls/disqualifications: 1983-84, 16/0. 1984-85, 12/0. 1985-86, 27/0. 1986-87, 7/0. 1987-88, 44/0. 1989-90, 13/0. 1993-94, 63/1. 1994-95, 29/0. 1995-96, 24/0. Totals, 235/1.

HARPER, RON   G   BULLS

PERSONAL: Born January 20, 1964, in Dayton, Ohio. ... 6-6/216. ... Full name: Ronald Harper.
HIGH SCHOOL: Kiser (Dayton, Ohio).
COLLEGE: Miami of Ohio.
TRANSACTIONS/CAREER NOTES: Selected by Cleveland Cavaliers in first round (eighth pick overall) of 1986 NBA Draft. ... Traded by Cavaliers with 1990 and 1992 first-round draft choices and 1991 second-round draft choice to Los Angeles Clippers for G Reggie Williams and draft rights to F Danny Ferry (November 16, 1989). ... Signed as unrestricted free agent by Chicago Bulls (September 15, 1994).
MISCELLANEOUS: Member of NBA championship team (1996).

H

COLLEGIATE RECORD

NOTES: THE SPORTING NEWS All-America second team (1986).

Season Team	G	Min.	FGM	FGA	Pct.	FTM	FTA	Pct.	Reb.	Ast.	Pts.	RPG	APG	PPG
82-83—Miami of Ohio	28	887	148	298	.497	64	95	.674	195	62	360	7.0	2.2	12.9
83-84—Miami of Ohio	30	989	197	367	.537	94	165	.570	229	64	488	7.6	2.1	16.3
84-85—Miami of Ohio	31	1144	312	577	.541	148	224	.661	333	79	772	10.7	2.5	24.9
85-86—Miami of Ohio	31	1144	312	572	.545	133	200	.665	362	133	757	11.7	4.3	24.4
Totals	120	4164	969	1814	.534	439	684	.642	1119	338	2377	9.3	2.8	19.8

NBA REGULAR-SEASON RECORD

HONORS: NBA All-Rookie team (1987).

Season Team	G	Min.	FGM	FGA	Pct.	FTM	FTA	Pct.	Off.	Def.	Tot.	Ast.	St.	Blk.	TO	Pts.	RPG	APG	PPG
86-87—Cleveland	82	3064	734	1614	.455	386	564	.684	169	223	392	394	209	84	*345	1874	4.8	4.8	22.9
87-88—Cleveland	57	1830	340	732	.464	196	278	.705	64	159	223	281	122	52	158	879	3.9	4.9	15.4
88-89—Cleveland	82	2851	587	1149	.511	323	430	.751	122	287	409	434	185	74	230	1526	5.0	5.3	18.6
89-90—Clev.-L.A.C.	35	1367	301	637	.473	182	231	.788	74	132	206	182	81	41	100	798	5.9	5.2	22.8
90-91—L.A. Clippers...	39	1383	285	729	.391	145	217	.668	58	130	188	209	66	35	129	763	4.8	5.4	19.6
91-92—L.A. Clippers...	82	3144	569	1292	.440	293	398	.736	120	327	447	417	152	72	252	1495	5.5	5.1	18.2
92-93—L.A. Clippers...	80	2970	542	1203	.451	307	399	.769	117	308	425	360	177	73	222	1443	5.3	4.5	18.0
93-94—L.A. Clippers...	75	2856	569	1335	.426	299	418	.715	129	331	460	344	144	54	242	1508	6.1	4.6	20.1
94-95—Chicago	77	1536	209	491	.426	81	131	.618	51	129	180	157	97	27	100	530	2.3	2.0	6.9
95-96—Chicago	80	1886	234	501	.467	98	139	.705	74	139	213	208	105	32	73	594	2.7	2.6	7.4
Totals	689	22887	4370	9683	.451	2310	3205	.721	978	2165	3143	2986	1338	544	1851	11410	4.6	4.3	16.6

Three-point field goals: 1986-87, 20-for-94 (.213). 1987-88, 3-for-20 (.150). 1988-89, 29-for-116 (.250). 1989-90, 14-for-51 (.275). 1990-91, 48-for-148 (.324). 1991-92, 64-for-211 (.303). 1992-93, 52-for-186 (.280). 1993-94, 71-for-236 (.301). 1994-95, 31-for-110 (.282). 1995-96, 28-for-104 (.269). Totals, 360-for-1276 (.282).

Personal fouls/disqualifications: 1986-87, 247/3. 1987-88, 157/3. 1988-89, 224/1. 1989-90, 105/1. 1990-91, 111/0. 1991-92, 199/0. 1992-93, 212/1. 1993-94, 167/0. 1994-95, 132/1. 1995-96, 137/0. Totals, 1691/10.

NBA PLAYOFF RECORD

Season Team	G	Min.	FGM	FGA	Pct.	FTM	FTA	Pct.	Off.	Def.	Tot.	Ast.	St.	Blk.	TO	Pts.	RPG	APG	PPG
87-88—Cleveland	4	134	30	63	.476	11	16	.688	4	16	20	15	11	4	11	71	5.0	3.8	17.8
88-89—Cleveland	5	189	39	69	.565	20	26	.769	7	14	21	20	11	4	7	98	4.2	4.0	19.6
91-92—L.A. Clippers...	5	206	39	87	.448	11	14	.786	10	22	32	23	5	4	15	90	6.4	4.6	18.0
92-93—L.A. Clippers...	5	174	37	78	.474	11	17	.647	4	16	20	16	15	10	11	90	4.0	3.2	18.0
94-95—Chicago	6	40	6	14	.429	0	0		2	4	6	4	3	1	1	12	1.0	0.7	2.0
95-96—Chicago	18	494	57	134	.425	29	42	.690	26	41	67	45	25	7	18	158	3.7	2.5	8.8
Totals	43	1237	208	445	.467	82	115	.713	53	113	166	123	70	30	63	519	3.9	2.9	12.1

Three-point field goals: 1987-88, 0-for-2. 1988-89, 0-for-2. 1991-92, 1-for-9 (.111). 1992-93, 5-for-10 (.500). 1994-95, 0-for-2. 1995-96, 15-for-47 (.319). Totals, 21-for-72 (.292).

Personal fouls/disqualifications: 1987-88, 9/0. 1988-89, 20/1. 1991-92, 13/0. 1992-93, 7/0. 1994-95, 6/0. 1995-96, 38/0. Totals, 93/1.

HARRIS, LUCIOUS   G   76ERS

PERSONAL: Born December 18, 1970, in Los Angeles. ... 6-5/205. ... Full name: Lucious H. Harris Jr. ... Name pronounced LOO-shus..
HIGH SCHOOL: Cleveland (Los Angeles).
COLLEGE: Long Beach State.
TRANSACTIONS/CAREER NOTES: Selected by Dallas Mavericks in second round (28th pick overall) of 1993 NBA Draft. ... Rights renounced by Mavericks (July 17, 1996). ... Signed as free agent by Philadelphia 76ers (July 23, 1996).

COLLEGIATE RECORD

Season Team	G	Min.	FGM	FGA	Pct.	FTM	FTA	Pct.	Reb.	Ast.	Pts.	RPG	APG	PPG
89-90—Long Beach State..........	32	945	147	342	.430	118	170	.694	152	52	457	4.8	1.6	14.3
90-91—Long Beach State..........	28	940	181	457	.396	140	200	.700	131	69	552	4.7	2.5	19.7
91-92—Long Beach State..........	30	1132	197	418	.471	127	173	.734	129	97	564	4.3	3.2	18.8
92-93—Long Beach State..........	32	1166	251	478	.525	164	212	.774	169	79	739	5.3	2.5	23.1
Totals	122	4183	776	1695	.458	549	755	.727	581	297	2312	4.8	2.4	19.0

Three-point field goals: 1989-90, 45-for-136 (.331). 1990-91, 50-for-153 (.327). 1991-92, 43-for-117 (.368). 1992-93, 73-for-177 (.412). Totals, 211-for-583 (.362).

NBA REGULAR-SEASON RECORD

Season Team	G	Min.	FGM	FGA	Pct.	FTM	FTA	Pct.	Off.	Def.	Tot.	Ast.	St.	Blk.	TO	Pts.	RPG	APG	PPG
93-94—Dallas..............	77	1165	162	385	.421	87	119	.731	45	112	157	106	49	10	78	418	2.0	1.4	5.4
94-95—Dallas..............	79	1695	280	610	.459	136	170	.800	85	135	220	132	58	14	77	751	2.8	1.7	9.5
95-96—Dallas..............	61	1016	183	397	.461	68	87	.782	41	81	122	79	35	3	46	481	2.0	1.3	7.9
Totals	217	3876	625	1392	.449	291	376	.774	171	328	499	317	142	27	201	1650	2.3	1.5	7.6

Three-point field goals: 1993-94, 7-for-33 (.212). 1994-95, 55-for-142 (.387). 1995-96, 47-for-125 (.376). Totals, 109-for-300 (.363).
Personal fouls/disqualifications: 1993-94, 117/0. 1994-95, 105/0. 1995-96, 56/0. Totals, 278/0.

HARVEY, ANTONIO   F/C   CLIPPERS

PERSONAL: Born July 6, 1970, in Pascagoula, Miss. ... 6-11/246.
HIGH SCHOOL: Pascagoula (Miss.).
JUNIOR COLLEGE: Connors State (Okla.).
COLLEGE: Southern Illinois, then Georgia, then Pfeiffer (N.C.).

H

TRANSACTIONS/CAREER NOTES: Not drafted by an NBA franchise. ... Played in United States Basketball League with Atlanta Eagles (1993). ... Signed as free agent by Los Angeles Lakers (July 15, 1993). ... Selected by Vancouver Grizzlies from Lakers in NBA expansion draft (June 24, 1995). ... Waived by Grizzlies (December 28, 1995). ... Signed as free agent by Los Angeles Clippers for remainder of season (January 3, 1996).

COLLEGIATE RECORD

NOTES: Led NCAA Division II with 5.3 blocked shots per game (1993).

												AVERAGES		
Season Team	G	Min.	FGM	FGA	Pct.	FTM	FTA	Pct.	Reb.	Ast.	Pts.	RPG	APG	PPG
88-89—Southern Illinois............	34	...	102	220	.464	31	64	.484	178	21	235	5.2	0.6	6.9
89-90—Connors State					Did not play basketball.									
90-91—Georgia.........................	29	...	87	191	.456	36	71	.507	125	21	210	4.3	0.7	7.2
91-92—Pfeiffer.........................	29	...	163	306	.533	70	101	.693	234	21	398	8.1	0.7	13.7
92-93—Pfeiffer.........................	29	...	218	415	.525	89	155	.574	294	36	530	10.1	1.2	18.3
Totals	121		570	1132	.504	226	391	.578	831	99	1373	6.9	0.8	11.3

Three-point field goals: 1990-91, 0-for-4. 1991-92, 4-for-8 (.500). 1992-93, 5-for-12 (.417). Totals, 9-for-24 (.375).

NBA REGULAR-SEASON RECORD

									REBOUNDS								AVERAGES		
Season Team	G	Min.	FGM	FGA	Pct.	FTM	FTA	Pct.	Off.	Def.	Tot.	Ast.	St.	Blk.	TO	Pts.	RPG	APG	PPG
93-94—L.A. Lakers	27	247	29	79	.367	12	26	.462	26	33	59	5	8	19	17	70	2.2	0.2	2.6
94-95—L.A. Lakers	59	572	77	176	.438	24	45	.533	39	63	102	23	15	41	25	179	1.7	0.4	3.0
95-96—Van.-LAC	55	821	83	224	.371	38	83	.458	69	131	200	15	27	47	44	204	3.6	0.3	3.7
Totals	141	1640	189	479	.395	74	154	.481	134	227	361	43	50	107	86	453	2.6	0.3	3.2

Three-point field goals: 1994-95, 1-for-1. 1995-96, 0-for-2. Totals, 1-for-3 (.333).
Personal fouls/disqualifications: 1993-94, 39/0. 1994-95, 87/0. 1995-96, 76/0. Totals, 202/0.

NBA PLAYOFF RECORD

									REBOUNDS								AVERAGES		
Season Team	G	Min.	FGM	FGA	Pct.	FTM	FTA	Pct.	Off.	Def.	Tot.	Ast.	St.	Blk.	TO	Pts.	RPG	APG	PPG
94-95—L.A. Lakers	3	4	0	0	...	0	0	...	0	1	1	0	0	0	0	0	0.3	0.0	0.0

HAWKINS, HERSEY　　　　　　　G　　　　　　　SUPERSONICS

PERSONAL: Born September 29, 1966, in Chicago. ... 6-3/190. ... Full name: Hersey R. Hawkins Jr. ... Name pronounced HER-see.
HIGH SCHOOL: Westinghouse Vocational (Chicago).
COLLEGE: Bradley.
TRANSACTIONS/CAREER NOTES: Selected by Los Angeles Clippers in first round (sixth pick overall) of 1988 NBA Draft. ... Draft rights traded by Clippers with 1989 first-round draft choice to Philadelphia 76ers for draft rights to F Charles Smith and option to switch 1994 first-round draft choices (June 28, 1988). ... Traded by 76ers to Charlotte Hornets for G Dana Barros, F Sidney Green, draft rights to G Greg Graham and option to switch 1994 first-round draft choices (September 3, 1993). ... Traded by Hornets with G/F David Wingate to Seattle SuperSonics for G Kendall Gill (June 27, 1995).
MISCELLANEOUS: Member of bronze-medal-winning U.S. Olympic team (1988).

COLLEGIATE RECORD

NOTES: THE SPORTING NEWS College Player of the Year (1988). ... THE SPORTING NEWS All-America first team (1988). ... Led NCAA Division I with 36.3 points per game (1988).

												AVERAGES		
Season Team	G	Min.	FGM	FGA	Pct.	FTM	FTA	Pct.	Reb.	Ast.	Pts.	RPG	APG	PPG
84-85—Bradley	30	1121	179	308	.581	81	105	.771	182	82	439	6.1	2.7	14.6
85-86—Bradley	35	1291	250	461	.542	156	203	.768	200	104	656	5.7	3.0	18.7
86-87—Bradley	29	1102	294	552	.533	169	213	.793	195	103	788	6.7	3.6	27.2
87-88—Bradley	31	1202	377	720	.524	284	335	.848	241	111	1125	7.8	3.6	36.3
Totals	125	4716	1100	2041	.539	690	856	.806	818	400	3008	6.5	3.2	24.1

Three-point field goals: 1986-87, 31-for-108 (.287). 1987-88, 87-for-221 (.394). Totals, 118-for-329 (.359).

NBA REGULAR-SEASON RECORD

HONORS: NBA All-Rookie first team (1989).

									REBOUNDS								AVERAGES		
Season Team	G	Min.	FGM	FGA	Pct.	FTM	FTA	Pct.	Off.	Def.	Tot.	Ast.	St.	Blk.	TO	Pts.	RPG	APG	PPG
88-89—Philadelphia	79	2577	442	971	.455	241	290	.831	51	174	225	239	120	37	158	1196	2.8	3.0	15.1
89-90—Philadelphia	82	2856	522	1136	.460	387	436	.888	85	219	304	261	130	28	185	1515	3.7	3.2	18.5
90-91—Philadelphia	80	3110	590	1251	.472	479	550	.871	48	262	310	299	178	39	213	1767	3.9	3.7	22.1
91-92—Philadelphia	81	3013	521	1127	.462	403	461	.874	53	218	271	248	157	43	189	1536	3.3	3.1	19.0
92-93—Philadelphia	81	2977	551	1172	.470	419	487	.860	91	255	346	317	137	30	180	1643	4.3	3.9	20.3
93-94—Charlotte	82	2648	395	859	.460	312	362	.862	89	288	377	216	135	22	158	1180	4.6	2.6	14.4
94-95—Charlotte	82	2731	390	809	.482	261	301	.867	60	254	314	262	122	18	150	1172	3.8	3.2	14.3
95-96—Seattle	82	2823	443	936	.473	249	285	.874	86	211	297	218	149	14	164	1281	3.6	2.7	15.6
Totals	649	22735	3854	8261	.467	2751	3172	.867	563	1881	2444	2060	1128	231	1397	11290	3.8	3.2	17.4

Three-point field goals: 1988-89, 71-for-166 (.428). 1989-90, 84-for-200 (.420). 1990-91, 108-for-270 (.400). 1991-92, 91-for-229 (.397). 1992-93, 122-for-307 (.397). 1993-94, 78-for-235 (.332). 1994-95, 131-for-298 (.440). 1995-96, 146-for-380 (.384). Totals, 831-for-2085 (.399).
Personal fouls/disqualifications: 1988-89, 184/0. 1989-90, 217/2. 1990-91, 182/0. 1991-92, 174/0. 1992-93, 189/0. 1993-94, 167/2. 1994-95, 178/1. 1995-96, 172/0. Totals, 1463/5.

NBA PLAYOFF RECORD

									REBOUNDS								AVERAGES		
Season Team	G	Min.	FGM	FGA	Pct.	FTM	FTA	Pct.	Off.	Def.	Tot.	Ast.	St.	Blk.	TO	Pts.	RPG	APG	PPG
88-89—Philadelphia	3	72	3	24	.125	2	2	1.000	1	4	5	4	3	1	3	8	1.7	1.3	2.7
89-90—Philadelphia	10	415	81	163	.497	59	63	.937	8	23	31	36	12	7	31	235	3.1	3.6	23.5

H

Season Team	G	Min.	FGM	FGA	Pct.	FTM	FTA	Pct.	Off.	Def.	Tot.	Ast.	St.	Blk.	TO	Pts.	RPG	APG	PPG
									REBOUNDS								**AVERAGES**		
90-91—Philadelphia	8	329	47	101	.465	59	63	.937	8	38	46	27	20	10	16	167	5.8	3.4	20.9
94-95—Charlotte	4	130	13	32	.406	15	17	.882	5	16	21	8	6	2	9	45	5.3	2.0	11.3
95-96—Seattle	21	713	76	168	.452	85	95	.895	17	46	63	46	27	4	33	259	3.0	2.2	12.3
Totals	46	1659	220	488	.451	220	240	.917	39	127	166	121	68	24	92	714	3.6	2.6	15.5

Three-point field goals: 1988-89, 0-for-5. 1989-90, 14-for-36 (.389). 1990-91, 14-for-26 (.538). 1994-95, 4-for-13 (.308). 1995-96, 22-for-64 (.344). Totals, 54-for-144 (.375).

Personal fouls/disqualifications: 1988-89, 6/0. 1989-90, 25/0. 1990-91, 29/1. 1994-95, 13/1. 1995-96, 55/0. Totals, 128/2.

NBA ALL-STAR GAME RECORD

Season Team	Min.	FGM	FGA	Pct.	FTM	FTA	Pct.	Off.	Def.	Tot.	Ast.	PF	Dq.	St.	Blk.	TO	Pts.
								REBOUNDS									
1991 —Philadelphia.......	14	3	5	.600	0	0	...	0	0	0	1	1	0	0	0	1	6

Three-point field goals: 1991, 0-for-1.

HEGGS, ALVIN F

PERSONAL: Born December 12, 1967, in Jacksonville. ... 6-8/225.
HIGH SCHOOL: Andrew Jackson (Jacksonville).
JUNIOR COLLEGE: Florida Community College.
COLLEGE: Texas.
TRANSACTIONS/CAREER NOTES: Not drafted by an NBA franchise. ... Played in Continental Basketball Association with Oklahoma City Cavalry (1990-91). ... Played in Argentina (1991-92 and 1992-93). ... Played in Japan (1993-94 and 1994-95). ... Signed as free agent by Houston Rockets (October 5, 1995). ... Waived by Rockets (November 20, 1995).

COLLEGIATE RECORD

Season Team	G	Min.	FGM	FGA	Pct.	FTM	FTA	Pct.	Reb.	Ast.	Pts.	RPG	APG	PPG
												AVERAGES		
86-87—Florida C.C....................						Statistics unavailable.								
87-88—Florida C.C....................						Statistics unavailable.								
88-89—Texas	29	...	166	270	.615	100	128	.781	189	23	432	6.5	0.8	14.9
89-90—Texas	34	1014	236	417	.566	96	128	.750	266	25	571	7.8	0.7	16.8
Junior college totals	...	...	...	...	...	...	...	...	...	...	...	...	...	...
4-year-college totals	63	...	402	687	.585	196	256	.766	455	48	1003	7.2	0.8	15.9

Three-point field goals: 1989-90, 0-for-1.

NBA REGULAR-SEASON RECORD

Season Team	G	Min.	FGM	FGA	Pct.	FTM	FTA	Pct.	Off.	Def.	Tot.	Ast.	St.	Blk.	TO	Pts.	RPG	APG	PPG
									REBOUNDS								**AVERAGES**		
95-96—Houston.........	4	14	3	5	.600	2	3	.667	1	1	2	0	0	0	0	8	0.5	0.0	2.0

HENDERSON, ALAN F HAWKS

PERSONAL: Born December 12, 1972, in Indianapolis. ... 6-9/235. ... Full name: Alan Lybrooks Henderson.
HIGH SCHOOL: Brebeuf Prep (Indianapolis).
COLLEGE: Indiana.
TRANSACTIONS/CAREER NOTES: Selected by Atlanta Hawks in first round (16th pick overall) of 1995 NBA Draft.

COLLEGIATE RECORD

Season Team	G	Min.	FGM	FGA	Pct.	FTM	FTA	Pct.	Reb.	Ast.	Pts.	RPG	APG	PPG
												AVERAGES		
91-92—Indiana	33	783	151	297	.508	80	121	.661	238	17	383	7.2	0.5	11.6
92-93—Indiana	30	737	130	267	.487	72	113	.637	243	27	333	8.1	0.9	11.1
93-94—Indiana	30	983	198	373	.531	136	207	.657	308	36	534	10.3	1.2	17.8
94-95—Indiana	31	1093	284	476	.597	159	251	.633	302	54	729	9.7	1.7	23.5
Totals	124	3596	763	1413	.540	447	692	.646	1091	134	1979	8.8	1.1	16.0

Three-point field goals: 1991-92, 1-for-4 (.250). 1992-93, 1-for-6 (.167). 1993-94, 2-for-6 (.333). 1994-95, 2-for-10 (.200). Totals, 6-for-26 (.231).

NBA REGULAR-SEASON RECORD

Season Team	G	Min.	FGM	FGA	Pct.	FTM	FTA	Pct.	Off.	Def.	Tot.	Ast.	St.	Blk.	TO	Pts.	RPG	APG	PPG
									REBOUNDS								**AVERAGES**		
95-96—Atlanta	79	1416	192	434	.442	119	200	.595	164	192	356	51	44	43	87	503	4.5	0.6	6.4

Three-point field goals: 1995-96, 0-for-3.
Personal fouls/disqualifications: 1995-96, 217/5.

NBA PLAYOFF RECORD

Season Team	G	Min.	FGM	FGA	Pct.	FTM	FTA	Pct.	Off.	Def.	Tot.	Ast.	St.	Blk.	TO	Pts.	RPG	APG	PPG
									REBOUNDS								**AVERAGES**		
95-96—Atlanta	10	145	23	40	.575	7	10	.700	17	10	27	7	1	4	9	53	2.7	0.7	5.3

Personal fouls/disqualifications: 1995-96, 20/0.

HERRERA, CARL F SPURS

PERSONAL: Born December 14, 1966, in Trinidad. ... 6-9/225. ... Full name: Carl Victor Herrera. ... Name pronounced HER-rare-ah.
HIGH SCHOOL: Simon Bolivar (Caracas, Venezuela).
JUNIOR COLLEGE: Jacksonville (Texas) Junior College.
COLLEGE: Houston.

H

TRANSACTIONS/CAREER NOTES: Selected after junior season by Miami Heat in second round (30th pick overall) of 1990 NBA Draft. ... Draft rights traded by Heat with draft rights to G Dave Jamerson to Houston Rockets for draft rights to F/C Alec Kessler (June 27, 1990). ... Played in Spain (1990-91). ... Signed as unrestricted free agent by San Antonio Spurs (September 29, 1995).
MISCELLANEOUS: Member of NBA championship teams (1994, 1995). ... Member of Venezuelan Olympic team (1992).

COLLEGIATE RECORD

Season Team	G	Min.	FGM	FGA	Pct.	FTM	FTA	Pct.	Reb.	Ast.	Pts.	AVERAGES RPG	APG	PPG
87-88—Jacksonville College						Statistics unavailable.								
88-89—Jacksonville College	28	...	261	459	.569	180	238	.756	...	...	713	...	...	25.5
89-90—Houston	33	1023	188	333	.565	172	214	.804	302	54	551	9.2	1.6	16.7
Junior college totals	28	...	261	459	.569	180	238	.756	...	...	713	...	...	25.5
4-year-college totals	33	1023	188	333	.565	172	214	.804	302	54	551	9.2	1.6	16.7

Three-point field goals: 1989-90, 3-for-8 (.375).

SPANISH LEAGUE RECORD

Season Team	G	Min.	FGM	FGA	Pct.	FTM	FTA	Pct.	Reb.	Ast.	Pts.	AVERAGES RPG	APG	PPG
90-91—Real Madrid...................	25	...	...	...	...	...	...	...	183	...	328	7.3	...	13.1

NBA REGULAR-SEASON RECORD

Season Team	G	Min.	FGM	FGA	Pct.	FTM	FTA	Pct.	REBOUNDS Off.	Def.	Tot.	Ast.	St.	Blk.	TO	Pts.	AVERAGES RPG	APG	PPG
91-92—Houston	43	566	83	161	.516	25	44	.568	33	66	99	27	16	25	37	191	2.3	0.6	4.4
92-93—Houston	81	1800	240	444	.541	125	176	.710	148	306	454	61	47	35	92	605	5.6	0.8	7.5
93-94—Houston	75	1292	142	310	.458	69	97	.711	101	184	285	37	32	26	69	353	3.8	0.5	4.7
94-95—Houston	61	1331	171	327	.523	73	117	.624	98	180	278	44	40	38	71	415	4.6	0.7	6.8
95-96—San Antonio ...	44	393	40	97	.412	5	17	.294	30	51	81	16	9	8	29	85	1.8	0.4	1.9
Totals	304	5382	676	1339	.505	297	451	.659	410	787	1197	185	144	132	298	1649	3.9	0.6	5.4

Three-point field goals: 1991-92, 0-for-1. 1992-93, 0-for-2. 1994-95, 0-for-2. 1995-96, 0-for-1. Totals, 0-for-6.
Personal fouls/disqualifications: 1991-92, 60/0. 1992-93, 190/1. 1993-94, 159/0. 1994-95, 136/0. 1995-96, 61/0. Totals, 606/1.

NBA PLAYOFF RECORD

Season Team	G	Min.	FGM	FGA	Pct.	FTM	FTA	Pct.	REBOUNDS Off.	Def.	Tot.	Ast.	St.	Blk.	TO	Pts.	AVERAGES RPG	APG	PPG
92-93—Houston	12	195	22	57	.386	12	20	.600	16	29	45	7	3	2	11	56	3.8	0.6	4.7
93-94—Houston	16	248	31	58	.534	13	16	.813	14	31	45	3	5	3	7	75	2.8	0.2	4.7
94-95—Houston	1	6	1	1	1.000	0	0	...	0	0	0	1	0	0	0	2	0.0	1.0	2.0
95-96—San Antonio	7	28	0	3	.000	2	2	1.000	2	2	4	1	2	1	3	2	0.6	0.1	0.3
Totals	36	477	54	119	.454	27	38	.711	32	62	94	12	10	6	21	135	2.6	0.3	3.8

Three-point field goals: 1992-93, 0-for-2.
Personal fouls/disqualifications: 1992-93, 36/1. 1993-94, 37/1. 1995-96, 7/0. Totals, 80/2.

HIGGINS, SEAN   G/F

PERSONAL: Born December 30, 1968, in Los Angeles. ... 6-9/215. ... Full name: Sean Marielle Higgins. ... Son of Earle Higgins, forward with Indiana Pacers of American Basketball Association (1970-71).
HIGH SCHOOL: Fairfax (Los Angeles).
COLLEGE: Michigan.
TRANSACTIONS/CAREER NOTES: Selected after junior season by San Antonio Spurs in second round (54th pick overall) of 1990 NBA Draft. ... Waived by Spurs (December 13, 1991). ... Signed by Orlando Magic to first of two consecutive 10-day contracts (January 10, 1992). ... Re-signed by Magic for remainder of season (January 30, 1992). ... Signed as unrestricted free agent by Los Angeles Lakers (August 13, 1992). ... Waived by Lakers (November 5, 1992). ... Signed by Golden State Warriors to 10-day contract (February 9, 1993). ... Re-signed by Warriors for remainder of season (February 19, 1993). ... Played in Greece (1993-94). ... Signed as free agent by New Jersey Nets (June 20, 1994). ... Traded by Nets with F Derrick Coleman and G Rex Walters to Philadelphia 76ers for C Shawn Bradley, F Tim Perry and G Greg Graham (November 30, 1995). ... Rights renounced by 76ers (July 11, 1996).

COLLEGIATE RECORD

NOTES: Member of NCAA Division I championship team (1989).

Season Team	G	Min.	FGM	FGA	Pct.	FTM	FTA	Pct.	Reb.	Ast.	Pts.	AVERAGES RPG	APG	PPG
87-88—Michigan	12	228	48	96	.500	11	14	.786	38	13	117	3.2	1.1	9.8
88-89—Michigan	34	782	158	312	.506	54	70	.771	107	51	421	3.1	1.5	12.4
89-90—Michigan	26	728	142	302	.470	37	46	.804	93	59	364	3.6	2.3	14.0
Totals	72	1738	348	710	.490	102	130	.785	238	123	902	3.3	1.7	12.5

Three-point field goals: 1987-88, 10-for-20 (.500). 1988-89, 51-for-110 (.464). 1989-90, 43-for-102 (.422). Totals, 104-for-232 (.448).

NBA REGULAR-SEASON RECORD

Season Team	G	Min.	FGM	FGA	Pct.	FTM	FTA	Pct.	REBOUNDS Off.	Def.	Tot.	Ast.	St.	Blk.	TO	Pts.	AVERAGES RPG	APG	PPG
90-91—San Antonio	50	464	97	212	.458	28	33	.848	18	45	63	35	8	1	49	225	1.3	0.7	4.5
91-92—S.A.-Orl...........	38	616	127	277	.458	31	36	.861	29	73	102	41	16	6	41	291	2.7	1.1	7.7
92-93—Golden State ...	29	591	96	215	.447	35	47	.745	23	45	68	66	13	5	64	240	2.3	2.3	8.3
94-95—New Jersey	57	735	105	273	.385	35	40	.875	25	52	77	29	10	9	35	268	1.4	0.5	4.7
95-96—Philadelphia ...	44	916	134	323	.415	35	37	.946	20	72	92	55	24	11	49	351	2.1	1.3	8.0
Totals	218	3322	559	1300	.430	164	193	.850	115	287	402	226	71	32	238	1375	1.8	1.0	6.3

Three-point field goals: 1990-91, 3-for-19 (.158). 1991-92, 6-for-25 (.240). 1992-93, 13-for-37 (.351). 1994-95, 23-for-78 (.295). 1995-96, 48-for-129 (.372). Totals, 93-for-288 (.323).
Personal fouls/disqualifications: 1990-91, 53/0. 1991-92, 58/0. 1992-93, 54/0. 1994-95, 93/1. 1995-96, 90/1. Totals, 348/2.

H

NBA PLAYOFF RECORD

								REBOUNDS								AVERAGES		
Season Team	G	Min.	FGM	FGA	Pct.	FTM	FTA	Pct.	Off.	Def.	Tot.	Ast.	St.	Blk.	TO	Pts.	RPG	APG	PPG
90-91—San Antonio....	3	13	0	2	.000	0	0	...	0	0	0	1	0	0	0	0	0.0	0.3	0.0

Personal fouls/disqualifications: 1990-91, 1/0.

GREEK LEAGUE RECORD

											AVERAGES		
Season Team	G	Min.	FGM	FGA	Pct.	FTM	FTA	Pct.	Reb.	Ast.	Pts.	RPG	APG	PPG
93-94—Sato Aris	15	532	117	261	.448	57	67	.851	136	28	318	9.1	1.9	21.2

HILL, GRANT — F — PISTONS

PERSONAL: Born October 5, 1972, in Dallas. ... 6-8/225. ... Full name: Grant Henry Hill. ... Son of Calvin Hill, running back with Dallas Cowboys, Washington Redskins and Cleveland Browns (1969-74 and 1976-81) and the Hawaiians of the World Football League (1975).
HIGH SCHOOL: South Lakes (Reston, Va.).
COLLEGE: Duke.
TRANSACTIONS/CAREER NOTES: Selected by Detroit Pistons in first round (third pick overall) of 1994 NBA Draft.
MISCELLANEOUS: Member of gold-medal-winning U.S. Olympic team (1996).

COLLEGIATE RECORD

NOTES: The Sporting News All-America first team (1994). ... Member of NCAA Division I championship teams (1991, 1992).

												AVERAGES		
Season Team	G	Min.	FGM	FGA	Pct.	FTM	FTA	Pct.	Reb.	Ast.	Pts.	RPG	APG	PPG
90-91—Duke	36	887	160	310	.516	81	133	.609	185	79	402	5.1	2.2	11.2
91-92—Duke	33	1000	182	298	.611	99	135	.733	187	134	463	5.7	4.1	14.0
92-93—Duke	26	822	185	320	.578	94	126	.746	166	72	468	6.4	2.8	18.0
93-94—Duke	34	1213	218	472	.462	116	165	.703	233	176	591	6.9	5.2	17.4
Totals	129	3922	745	1400	.532	390	559	.698	771	461	1924	6.0	3.6	14.9

Three-point field goals: 1990-91, 1-for-2 (.500). 1991-92, 0-for-1. 1992-93, 4-for-14 (.286). 1993-94, 39-for-100 (.390). Totals, 44-for-117 (.376).

NBA REGULAR-SEASON RECORD

HONORS: NBA co-Rookie of the Year (1995). ... All-NBA second team (1996). ... NBA All-Rookie first team (1995).

								REBOUNDS								AVERAGES		
Season Team	G	Min.	FGM	FGA	Pct.	FTM	FTA	Pct.	Off.	Def.	Tot.	Ast.	St.	Blk.	TO	Pts.	RPG	APG	PPG
94-95—Detroit	70	2678	508	1064	.477	374	511	.732	125	320	445	353	124	62	202	1394	6.4	5.0	19.9
95-96—Detroit	80	3260	564	1221	.462	485	646	.751	127	656	783	548	100	48	263	1618	9.8	6.9	20.2
Totals	150	5938	1072	2285	.469	859	1157	.742	252	976	1228	901	224	110	465	3012	8.2	6.0	20.1

Three-point field goals: 1994-95, 4-for-27 (.148). 1995-96, 5-for-26 (.192). Totals, 9-for-53 (.170).
Personal fouls/disqualifications: 1994-95, 203/1. 1995-96, 242/1. Totals, 445/2.

NBA PLAYOFF RECORD

								REBOUNDS								AVERAGES		
Season Team	G	Min.	FGM	FGA	Pct.	FTM	FTA	Pct.	Off.	Def.	Tot.	Ast.	St.	Blk.	TO	Pts.	RPG	APG	PPG
95-96—Detroit	3	115	22	39	.564	12	14	.857	4	18	22	11	3	0	8	57	7.3	3.7	19.0

Three-point field goals: 1995-96, 1-for-2 (.500).
Personal fouls/disqualifications: 1995-96, 13/0.

NBA ALL-STAR GAME RECORD

							REBOUNDS								
Season Team	Min.	FGM	FGA	Pct.	FTM	FTA	Pct.	Off.	Def.	Tot.	Ast.	PF	Dq.	St.	Blk.	TO	Pts.
1995 —Detroit	20	5	8	.625	0	4	.000	0	0	0	3	2	0	2	0	1	10
1996 —Detroit	26	6	10	.600	2	2	1.000	1	2	3	2	1	0	1	0	2	14
Totals	46	11	18	.611	2	6	.333	1	2	3	5	3	0	3	0	3	24

HILL, TYRONE — F — CAVALIERS

PERSONAL: Born March 19, 1968, in Cincinnati. ... 6-9/245.
HIGH SCHOOL: Withrow (Cincinnati).
COLLEGE: Xavier.
TRANSACTIONS/CAREER NOTES: Selected by Golden State Warriors in first round (11th pick overall) of 1990 NBA Draft. ... Traded by Warriors to Cleveland Cavaliers for 1994 first-round draft choice (July 15, 1993).

COLLEGIATE RECORD

											AVERAGES		
Season Team	G	Min.	FGM	FGA	Pct.	FTM	FTA	Pct.	Reb.	Ast.	Pts.	RPG	APG	PPG
86-87—Xavier	31	881	95	172	.552	84	125	.672	261	7	274	8.4	0.2	8.8
87-88—Xavier	30	858	172	309	.557	114	153	.745	314	21	458	10.5	0.7	15.3
88-89—Xavier	33	1094	235	388	.606	155	221	.701	403	45	625	12.2	1.4	18.9
89-90—Xavier	32	1063	250	430	.581	146	222	.658	402	49	646	12.6	1.5	20.2
Totals	126	3896	752	1299	.579	499	721	.692	1380	122	2003	11.0	1.0	15.9

Three-point field goals: 1989-90, 0-for-2.

NBA REGULAR-SEASON RECORD

NOTES: Led NBA with 315 personal fouls (1992).

								REBOUNDS								AVERAGES		
Season Team	G	Min.	FGM	FGA	Pct.	FTM	FTA	Pct.	Off.	Def.	Tot.	Ast.	St.	Blk.	TO	Pts.	RPG	APG	PPG
90-91—Golden State ...	74	1192	147	299	.492	96	152	.632	157	226	383	19	33	30	72	390	5.2	0.3	5.3

H

Season Team	G	Min.	FGM	FGA	Pct.	FTM	FTA	Pct.	REBOUNDS Off.	Def.	Tot.	Ast.	St.	Blk.	TO	Pts.	AVERAGES RPG	APG	PPG
91-92—Golden State...	82	1886	254	487	.522	163	235	.694	182	411	593	47	73	43	106	671	7.2	0.6	8.2
92-93—Golden State...	74	2070	251	494	.508	138	221	.624	255	499	754	68	41	40	92	640	10.2	0.9	8.6
93-94—Cleveland	57	1447	216	398	.543	171	256	.668	184	315	499	46	53	35	78	603	8.8	0.8	10.6
94-95—Cleveland	70	2397	350	694	.504	263	397	.662	269	496	765	55	55	41	151	963	10.9	0.8	13.8
95-96—Cleveland	44	929	130	254	.512	81	135	.600	94	150	244	33	31	20	64	341	5.5	0.8	7.8
Totals	401	9921	1348	2626	.513	912	1396	.653	1141	2097	3238	268	286	209	563	3608	8.1	0.7	9.0

Three-point field goals: 1991-92, 0-for-1. 1992-93, 0-for-4. 1993-94, 0-for-2. 1994-95, 0-for-1. Totals, 0-for-8.
Personal fouls/disqualifications: 1990-91, 264/8. 1991-92, 315/7. 1992-93, 320/8. 1993-94, 193/5. 1994-95, 245/4. 1995-96, 144/3. Totals, 1481/35.

NBA PLAYOFF RECORD

Season Team	G	Min.	FGM	FGA	Pct.	FTM	FTA	Pct.	REBOUNDS Off.	Def.	Tot.	Ast.	St.	Blk.	TO	Pts.	AVERAGES RPG	APG	PPG
90-91—Golden State...	9	80	9	14	.643	4	6	.667	7	16	23	2	3	4	2	22	2.6	0.2	2.4
91-92—Golden State...	4	47	3	7	.429	0	2	.000	3	5	8	1	2	0	3	6	2.0	0.3	1.5
93-94—Cleveland	3	123	11	27	.407	20	37	.541	14	17	31	4	1	1	8	42	10.3	1.3	14.0
94-95—Cleveland	4	139	9	29	.310	16	25	.640	8	15	23	3	7	1	10	34	5.8	0.8	8.5
95-96—Cleveland	3	53	9	12	.750	7	9	.778	7	8	15	0	0	0	3	25	5.0	0.0	8.3
Totals	23	442	41	89	.461	47	79	.595	39	61	100	10	13	6	26	129	4.3	0.4	5.6

Three-point field goals: 1990-91, 0-for-1. 1994-95, 0-for-1. Totals, 0-for-2.
Personal fouls/disqualifications: 1990-91, 25/2. 1991-92, 12/0. 1993-94, 14/1. 1994-95, 18/1. 1995-96, 11/1. Totals, 80/5.

NBA ALL-STAR GAME RECORD

Season Team	Min.	FGM	FGA	Pct.	FTM	FTA	Pct.	REBOUNDS Off.	Def.	Tot.	Ast.	PF	Dq.	St.	Blk.	TO	Pts.
1995 —Cleveland..........	6	1	1	1.000	0	0	...	2	2	4	0	1	0	0	0	0	2

HODGE, DONALD   C

PERSONAL: Born February 25, 1969, in Washington, D.C. ... 7-0/239. ... Full name: Donald Jerome Hodge.
HIGH SCHOOL: Coolidge (Washington, D.C.).
COLLEGE: Temple.
TRANSACTIONS/CAREER NOTES: Selected after junior season by Dallas Mavericks in second round (33rd pick overall) of 1991 NBA Draft. ... Waived by Mavericks (February 19, 1996). ... Signed by Charlotte Hornets to 10-day contract (February 23, 1996).

COLLEGIATE RECORD

Season Team	G	Min.	FGM	FGA	Pct.	FTM	FTA	Pct.	Reb.	Ast.	Pts.	AVERAGES RPG	APG	PPG
88-89—Temple..........................					Did not play—ineligible.									
89-90—Temple..........................	31	1118	164	303	.541	139	195	.713	253	22	467	8.2	0.7	15.1
90-91—Temple..........................	34	1187	147	275	.535	101	141	.716	234	35	395	6.9	1.0	11.6
Totals	65	2305	311	578	.538	240	336	.714	487	57	862	7.5	0.9	13.3

NBA REGULAR-SEASON RECORD

Season Team	G	Min.	FGM	FGA	Pct.	FTM	FTA	Pct.	REBOUNDS Off.	Def.	Tot.	Ast.	St.	Blk.	TO	Pts.	AVERAGES RPG	APG	PPG
91-92—Dallas.............	51	1058	163	328	.497	100	150	.667	118	157	275	39	25	23	75	426	5.4	0.8	8.4
92-93—Dallas.............	79	1267	161	400	.403	71	104	.683	93	201	294	75	33	37	90	393	3.7	0.9	5.0
93-94—Dallas.............	50	428	46	101	.455	44	52	.846	46	49	95	32	15	13	30	136	1.9	0.6	2.7
94-95—Dallas.............	54	633	83	204	.407	39	51	.765	40	82	122	41	10	14	39	209	2.3	0.8	3.9
95-96—Dal.-Char........	15	115	9	24	.375	0	0	...	9	14	23	4	1	8	2	18	1.5	0.3	1.2
Totals	249	3501	462	1057	.437	254	357	.711	306	503	809	191	84	95	236	1182	3.2	0.8	4.7

Three-point field goals: 1994-95, 4-for-14 (.286).
Personal fouls/disqualifications: 1991-92, 128/2. 1992-93, 204/2. 1993-94, 66/1. 1994-95, 107/1. 1995-96, 26/0. Totals, 531/6.

HOIBERG, FRED   G   PACERS

PERSONAL: Born October 15, 1972, in Lincoln, Neb. ... 6-4/203. ... Full name: Fredrick Kristian Hoiberg. ... Name pronounced HOY-berg. ... Nickname: The Mayor.
HIGH SCHOOL: Ames (Iowa).
COLLEGE: Iowa State.
TRANSACTIONS/CAREER NOTES: Selected by Indiana Pacers in second round (52nd pick overall) of 1995 NBA Draft.

COLLEGIATE RECORD

Season Team	G	Min.	FGM	FGA	Pct.	FTM	FTA	Pct.	Reb.	Ast.	Pts.	AVERAGES RPG	APG	PPG
91-92—Iowa State	34	1037	161	281	.573	75	93	.806	181	85	410	5.3	2.5	12.1
92-93—Iowa State	31	1018	127	231	.550	84	103	.816	194	93	360	6.3	3.0	11.6
93-94—Iowa State	27	971	177	331	.535	133	154	.864	181	97	546	6.7	3.6	20.2
94-95—Iowa State	34	1252	207	473	.438	174	202	.861	192	75	677	5.6	2.2	19.9
Totals	126	4278	672	1316	.511	466	552	.844	748	350	1993	5.9	2.8	15.8

Three-point field goals: 1991-92, 13-for-50 (.260). 1992-93, 22-for-60 (.367). 1993-94, 59-for-131 (.450). 1994-95, 89-for-216 (.412). Totals, 183-for-457 (.400).

NBA REGULAR-SEASON RECORD

Season Team	G	Min.	FGM	FGA	Pct.	FTM	FTA	Pct.	REBOUNDS Off.	Def.	Tot.	Ast.	St.	Blk.	TO	Pts.	AVERAGES RPG	APG	PPG
95-96—Indiana...........	15	85	8	19	.421	15	18	.833	4	5	9	8	6	1	7	32	0.6	0.5	2.1

Three-point field goals: 1995-96, 1-for-3 (.333).
Personal fouls/disqualifications: 1995-96, 12/0.

H

HORNACEK, JEFF G JAZZ

PERSONAL: Born May 3, 1963, in Elmhurst, Ill. ... 6-4/190. ... Full name: Jeffrey John Hornacek. ... Name pronounced HORN-a-sek.
HIGH SCHOOL: Lyons Township (La Grange, Ill.).
COLLEGE: Iowa State.
TRANSACTIONS/CAREER NOTES: Selected by Phoenix Suns in second round (46th pick overall) of 1986 NBA Draft. ... Traded by Suns with C Andrew Lang and F Tim Perry to Philadelphia 76ers for F Charles Barkley (June 17, 1992). ... Traded by 76ers with G Sean Green and 1995 or 1996 second-round draft choice to Utah Jazz for G Jeff Malone and 1994 conditional first-round draft choice (February 24, 1994).

COLLEGIATE RECORD

Season Team	G	Min.	FGM	FGA	Pct.	FTM	FTA	Pct.	Reb.	Ast.	Pts.	AVERAGES RPG	APG	PPG
81-82—Iowa State						Did not play—redshirted.								
82-83—Iowa State	27	583	57	135	.422	32	45	.711	62	82	146	2.3	3.0	5.4
83-84—Iowa State	29	1065	104	208	.500	83	105	.790	101	198	291	3.5	6.8	10.0
84-85—Iowa State	34	1224	172	330	.521	81	96	.844	122	166	425	3.6	4.9	12.5
85-86—Iowa State	33	1229	177	370	.478	97	125	.776	127	219	451	3.8	6.6	13.7
Totals	123	4101	510	1043	.489	293	371	.790	412	665	1313	3.3	5.4	10.7

NBA REGULAR-SEASON RECORD

RECORDS: Holds single-game record for most three-point field goals without a miss—8 (November 23, 1994, vs. Seattle).

Season Team	G	Min.	FGM	FGA	Pct.	FTM	FTA	Pct.	REBOUNDS Off.	Def.	Tot.	Ast.	St.	Blk.	TO	Pts.	AVERAGES RPG	APG	PPG
86-87—Phoenix	80	1561	159	350	.454	94	121	.777	41	143	184	361	70	5	153	424	2.3	4.5	5.3
87-88—Phoenix	82	2243	306	605	.506	152	185	.822	71	191	262	540	107	10	156	781	3.2	6.6	9.5
88-89—Phoenix	78	2487	440	889	.495	147	178	.826	75	191	266	465	129	8	111	1054	3.4	6.0	13.5
89-90—Phoenix	67	2278	483	901	.536	173	202	.856	86	227	313	337	117	14	125	1179	4.7	5.0	17.6
90-91—Phoenix	80	2733	544	1051	.518	201	224	.897	74	247	321	409	111	16	130	1350	4.0	5.1	16.9
91-92—Phoenix	81	2878	635	1240	.512	279	315	.886	106	301	407	411	158	31	170	1632	5.0	5.1	20.1
92-93—Philadelphia	79	2860	582	1239	.470	250	289	.865	84	258	342	548	131	21	222	1511	4.3	6.9	19.1
93-94—Phil.-Utah	80	2820	472	1004	.470	260	296	.878	60	219	279	419	127	13	171	1274	3.5	5.2	15.9
94-95—Utah	81	2696	482	937	.514	284	322	.882	53	157	210	347	129	17	145	1337	2.6	4.3	16.5
95-96—Utah	82	2588	442	880	.502	259	290	.893	62	147	209	340	106	20	127	1247	2.5	4.1	15.2
Totals	790	25344	4545	9096	.500	2099	2422	.867	712	2081	2793	4177	1185	155	1510	11789	3.5	5.3	14.9

Three-point field goals: 1986-87, 12-for-43 (.279). 1987-88, 17-for-58 (.293). 1988-89, 27-for-81 (.333). 1989-90, 40-for-98 (.408). 1990-91, 61-for-146 (.418). 1991-92, 83-for-189 (.439). 1992-93, 97-for-249 (.390). 1993-94, 70-for-208 (.337). 1994-95, 89-for-219 (.406). 1995-96, 104-for-223 (.466). Totals, 600-for-1514 (.396).
Personal fouls/disqualifications: 1986-87, 130/0. 1987-88, 151/0. 1988-89, 188/0. 1989-90, 144/2. 1990-91, 185/1. 1991-92, 218/1. 1992-93, 203/2. 1993-94, 186/0. 1994-95, 181/1. 1995-96, 171/1. Totals, 1757/8.

NBA PLAYOFF RECORD

Season Team	G	Min.	FGM	FGA	Pct.	FTM	FTA	Pct.	REBOUNDS Off.	Def.	Tot.	Ast.	St.	Blk.	TO	Pts.	AVERAGES RPG	APG	PPG
88-89—Phoenix	12	374	74	149	.497	21	25	.840	25	44	69	62	16	3	18	169	5.8	5.2	14.1
89-90—Phoenix	16	583	112	219	.511	68	73	.932	13	49	62	73	24	0	34	298	3.9	4.6	18.6
90-91—Phoenix	4	145	22	51	.431	26	28	.929	3	22	25	8	3	2	3	73	6.3	2.0	18.3
91-92—Phoenix	8	343	62	128	.484	31	34	.912	12	39	51	42	14	2	19	163	6.4	5.3	20.4
93-94—Utah	16	558	85	179	.475	62	68	.912	11	28	39	64	24	6	28	247	2.4	4.0	15.4
94-95—Utah	5	178	26	51	.510	11	14	.786	3	3	6	20	8	1	7	70	1.2	4.0	14.0
95-96—Utah	18	644	104	207	.502	73	82	.890	22	43	65	60	19	3	27	315	3.6	3.3	17.5
Totals	79	2825	485	984	.493	292	324	.901	89	228	317	329	108	17	136	1335	4.0	4.2	16.9

Three-point field goals: 1988-89, 0-for-7. 1989-90, 6-for-24 (.250). 1990-91, 3-for-6 (.500). 1991-92, 8-for-17 (.471). 1993-94, 15-for-34 (.441). 1994-95, 7-for-13 (.538). 1995-96, 34-for-58 (.586). Totals, 73-for-159 (.459).
Personal fouls/disqualifications: 1988-89, 34/0. 1989-90, 43/1. 1990-91, 13/0. 1991-92, 23/0. 1993-94, 45/0. 1994-95, 19/1. 1995-96, 41/1. Totals, 218/3.

NBA ALL-STAR GAME RECORD

Season Team	Min.	FGM	FGA	Pct.	FTM	FTA	Pct.	REBOUNDS Off.	Def.	Tot.	Ast.	PF	Dq.	St.	Blk.	TO	Pts.
1992 —Phoenix	24	5	7	.714	0	0	...	1	1	2	3	0	0	1	0	0	11

Three-point field goals: 1992, 1-for-2 (.500).

HORRY, ROBERT F SUNS

PERSONAL: Born August 25, 1970, in Andalusia, Ala. ... 6-10/220. ... Full name: Robert Keith Horry. ... Name pronounced OR-ee.
HIGH SCHOOL: Andalusia (Ala.).
COLLEGE: Alabama.
TRANSACTIONS/CAREER NOTES: Selected by Houston Rockets in first round (11th pick overall) of 1992 NBA Draft. ... Traded by Rockets with F Matt Bullard and two future second-round draft choices to Detroit Pistons for F Sean Elliott (February 4, 1994); trade voided when Elliott failed physical (February 7, 1994). ... Traded by Rockets with G Sam Cassell, F Chucky Brown and F Mark Bryant to Phoenix Suns for F Charles Barkley and 1999 second-round draft choice (August 19, 1996).
MISCELLANEOUS: Member of NBA championship teams (1994, 1995).

COLLEGIATE RECORD

Season Team	G	Min.	FGM	FGA	Pct.	FTM	FTA	Pct.	Reb.	Ast.	Pts.	AVERAGES RPG	APG	PPG
88-89—Alabama	31	590	79	185	.427	38	59	.644	156	35	200	5.0	1.1	6.5

H

Season Team	G	Min.	FGM	FGA	Pct.	FTM	FTA	Pct.	Reb.	Ast.	Pts.	AVERAGES RPG	APG	PPG
89-90—Alabama	35	1022	164	351	.467	79	104	.760	217	9	457	6.2	0.3	13.1
90-91—Alabama	32	959	133	296	.449	82	102	.804	260	56	381	8.1	1.8	11.9
91-92—Alabama	35	1185	196	417	.470	120	165	.727	296	88	554	8.5	2.5	15.8
Totals	133	3756	572	1249	.458	319	430	.742	929	188	1592	7.0	1.4	12.0

Three-point field goals: 1988-89, 4-for-13 (.308). 1989-90, 50-for-117 (.427). 1990-91, 33-for-98 (.337). 1991-92, 42-for-120 (.350). Totals, 129-for-348 (.371).

NBA REGULAR-SEASON RECORD

HONORS: NBA All-Rookie second team (1993).

Season Team	G	Min.	FGM	FGA	Pct.	FTM	FTA	Pct.	REBOUNDS Off.	Def.	Tot.	Ast.	St.	Blk.	TO	Pts.	AVERAGES RPG	APG	PPG
92-93—Houston	79	2330	323	682	.474	143	200	.715	113	279	392	191	80	83	156	801	5.0	2.4	10.1
93-94—Houston	81	2370	322	702	.459	115	157	.732	128	312	440	231	119	75	137	803	5.4	2.9	9.9
94-95—Houston	64	2074	240	537	.447	86	113	.761	81	243	324	216	94	76	122	652	5.1	3.4	10.2
95-96—Houston	71	2634	300	732	.410	111	143	.776	97	315	412	281	116	109	160	853	5.8	4.0	12.0
Totals	295	9408	1185	2653	.447	455	613	.742	419	1149	1568	919	409	343	575	3109	5.3	3.1	10.5

Three-point field goals: 1992-93, 12-for-47 (.255). 1993-94, 44-for-136 (.324). 1994-95, 86-for-227 (.379). 1995-96, 142-for-388 (.366). Totals, 284-for-798 (.356).

Personal fouls/disqualifications: 1992-93, 210/1. 1993-94, 186/0. 1994-95, 161/0. 1995-96, 197/3. Totals, 754/4.

NBA PLAYOFF RECORD

NOTES: Holds NBA Finals single-game record for most steals—7 (June 9, 1995, at Orlando).

Season Team	G	Min.	FGM	FGA	Pct.	FTM	FTA	Pct.	REBOUNDS Off.	Def.	Tot.	Ast.	St.	Blk.	TO	Pts.	AVERAGES RPG	APG	PPG
92-93—Houston	12	374	47	101	.465	20	27	.741	14	48	62	38	18	16	28	123	5.2	3.2	10.3
93-94—Houston	23	778	98	226	.434	39	51	.765	40	101	141	82	35	20	27	269	6.1	3.6	11.7
94-95—Houston	22	841	93	209	.445	58	78	.744	40	115	155	76	32	26	25	288	7.0	3.5	13.1
95-96—Houston	8	308	37	91	.407	10	23	.435	15	42	57	24	21	13	15	105	7.1	3.0	13.1
Totals	65	2301	275	627	.439	127	179	.709	109	306	415	220	106	75	95	785	6.4	3.4	12.1

Three-point field goals: 1992-93, 9-for-30 (.300). 1993-94, 34-for-89 (.382). 1994-95, 44-for-110 (.400). 1995-96, 21-for-53 (.396). Totals, 108-for-282 (.383).
Personal fouls/disqualifications: 1992-93, 30/1. 1993-94, 68/0. 1994-95, 69/2. 1995-96, 29/1. Totals, 196/4.

HOUSTON, ALLAN   G   KNICKS

PERSONAL: Born April 4, 1971, in Louisville, Ky. ... 6-6/200. ... Full name: Allan Wade Houston.
HIGH SCHOOL: Ballard (Louisville, Ky.).
COLLEGE: Tennessee.
TRANSACTIONS/CAREER NOTES: Selected by Detroit Pistons in first round (11th pick overall) of 1993 NBA Draft. ... Signed as free agent by New York Knicks (July 14, 1996).

COLLEGIATE RECORD

NOTES: The Sporting News All-America second team (1993).

Season Team	G	Min.	FGM	FGA	Pct.	FTM	FTA	Pct.	Reb.	Ast.	Pts.	AVERAGES RPG	APG	PPG
89-90—Tennessee	30	1083	203	465	.437	120	149	.805	88	127	609	2.9	4.2	20.3
90-91—Tennessee	34	1212	265	550	.482	177	205	.863	104	131	806	3.1	3.9	23.7
91-92—Tennessee	34	1236	223	492	.453	189	225	.840	180	110	717	5.3	3.2	21.1
92-93—Tennessee	30	1075	211	454	.465	165	188	.878	145	92	669	4.8	3.1	22.3
Totals	128	4606	902	1961	.460	651	767	.849	517	460	2801	4.0	3.6	21.9

Three-point field goals: 1989-90, 83-for-192 (.432). 1990-91, 99-for-231 (.429). 1991-92, 82-for-196 (.418). 1992-93, 82-for-198 (.414). Totals, 346-for-817 (.424).

NBA REGULAR-SEASON RECORD

RECORDS: Shares single-game record for most three-point field goals made in one half—7 (February 17, 1995, at Chicago).

Season Team	G	Min.	FGM	FGA	Pct.	FTM	FTA	Pct.	REBOUNDS Off.	Def.	Tot.	Ast.	St.	Blk.	TO	Pts.	AVERAGES RPG	APG	PPG
93-94—Detroit	79	1519	272	671	.405	89	108	.824	19	101	120	100	34	13	99	668	1.5	1.3	8.5
94-95—Detroit	76	1996	398	859	.463	147	171	.860	29	138	167	164	61	14	113	1101	2.2	2.2	14.5
95-96—Detroit	82	3072	564	1244	.453	298	362	.823	54	246	300	250	61	16	233	1617	3.7	3.0	19.7
Totals	237	6587	1234	2774	.445	534	641	.833	102	485	587	514	156	43	445	3386	2.5	2.2	14.3

Three-point field goals: 1993-94, 35-for-117 (.299). 1994-95, 158-for-373 (.424). 1995-96, 191-for-447 (.427). Totals, 384-for-937 (.410).
Personal fouls/disqualifications: 1993-94, 165/2. 1994-95, 182/0. 1995-96, 233/1. Totals, 580/3.

NBA PLAYOFF RECORD

Season Team	G	Min.	FGM	FGA	Pct.	FTM	FTA	Pct.	REBOUNDS Off.	Def.	Tot.	Ast.	St.	Blk.	TO	Pts.	AVERAGES RPG	APG	PPG
95-96—Detroit	3	136	25	58	.431	18	20	.900	1	7	8	6	0	1	11	75	2.7	2.0	25.0

Three-point field goals: 1995-96, 7-for-21 (.333).
Personal fouls/disqualifications: 1995-96, 11/0.

H

HOUSTON, BYRON   F   KINGS

PERSONAL: Born November 22, 1969, in Watonga, Kan. ... 6-5/250. ... Full name: Byron Dwight Houston.
HIGH SCHOOL: Star-Spencer (Oklahoma City).
COLLEGE: Oklahoma State.
TRANSACTIONS/CAREER NOTES: Selected by Chicago Bulls in first round (27th pick overall) of 1992 NBA Draft. ... Traded by Bulls to Golden State Warriors in three-way deal in which Dallas Mavericks sent F Rodney McCray to Bulls and

received conditional 1993 first-round draft choice from Warriors and two conditional second-round draft choices from Bulls (September 18, 1992). ... Traded by Warriors with G Sarunas Marciulionis to Seattle SuperSonics for G Ricky Pierce, draft rights to F Carlos Rogers and two 1995 second-round draft choices (July 18, 1994). ... Traded by SuperSonics with G Sarunas Marciulionis to Sacramento Kings for F/C Frank Brickowski (September 18, 1995).

COLLEGIATE RECORD

Season Team	G	Min.	FGM	FGA	Pct.	FTM	FTA	Pct.	Reb.	Ast.	Pts.	RPG	APG	PPG
88-89—Oklahoma State	30	842	140	240	.583	111	149	.745	251	32	391	8.4	1.1	13.0
89-90—Oklahoma State	31	1030	189	358	.528	196	268	.731	309	48	574	10.0	1.5	18.5
90-91—Oklahoma State	32	1084	250	436	.573	223	300	.743	336	67	726	10.5	2.1	22.7
91-92—Oklahoma State	34	1157	249	467	.533	168	240	.700	294	62	688	8.6	1.8	20.2
Totals	127	4113	828	1501	.552	698	957	.729	1190	209	2379	9.4	1.6	18.7

Three-point field goals: 1989-90, 0-for-6. 1990-91, 3-for-4 (.750). 1991-92, 22-for-79 (.278). Totals, 25-for-89 (.281).

NBA REGULAR-SEASON RECORD

Season Team	G	Min.	FGM	FGA	Pct.	FTM	FTA	Pct.	REBOUNDS Off.	Def.	Tot.	Ast.	St.	Blk.	TO	Pts.	RPG	APG	PPG
92-93—Golden State	79	1274	145	325	.446	129	194	.665	119	196	315	69	44	43	87	421	4.0	0.9	5.3
93-94—Golden State	71	866	81	177	.458	33	54	.611	67	127	194	32	33	31	49	196	2.7	0.5	2.8
94-95—Seattle	39	258	49	107	.458	28	38	.737	20	35	55	6	13	5	20	132	1.4	0.2	3.4
95-96—Sacramento	25	276	32	64	.500	21	26	.808	31	53	84	7	13	7	17	86	3.4	0.3	3.4
Totals	214	2674	307	673	.456	211	312	.676	237	411	648	114	103	86	173	835	3.0	0.5	3.9

Three-point field goals: 1992-93, 2-for-7 (.286). 1993-94, 1-for-7 (.143). 1994-95, 6-for-22 (.273). 1995-96, 1-for-3 (.333). Totals, 10-for-39 (.256).
Personal fouls/disqualifications: 1992-93, 253/12. 1993-94, 181/4. 1994-95, 50/0. 1995-96, 59/2. Totals, 543/18.

NBA PLAYOFF RECORD

Season Team	G	Min.	FGM	FGA	Pct.	FTM	FTA	Pct.	REBOUNDS Off.	Def.	Tot.	Ast.	St.	Blk.	TO	Pts.	RPG	APG	PPG
93-94—Golden State	3	46	6	8	.750	3	5	.600	2	3	5	3	1	2	0	15	1.7	1.0	5.0
94-95—Seattle	1	1	0	1	.000	0	0	...	0	0	0	0	0	0	0	0	0.0	0.0	0.0
Totals	4	47	6	9	.667	3	5	.600	2	3	5	3	1	2	0	15	1.3	0.8	3.8

Personal fouls/disqualifications: 1993-94, 9/0.

HOWARD, JUWAN   F   BULLETS

PERSONAL: Born February 7, 1973, in Chicago. ... 6-9/250. ... Full name: Juwan Antonio Howard.
HIGH SCHOOL: Vocational (Chicago).
COLLEGE: Michigan.
TRANSACTIONS/CAREER NOTES: Selected after junior season by Washington Bullets in first round (fifth pick overall) of 1994 NBA Draft. ... Signed as free agent by Miami Heat (July 15, 1996). ... Contract disallowed by NBA (July 31, 1996). ... Re-signed as free agent by Bullets (August 5, 1996).

COLLEGIATE RECORD

Season Team	G	Min.	FGM	FGA	Pct.	FTM	FTA	Pct.	Reb.	Ast.	Pts.	RPG	APG	PPG
91-92—Michigan	34	956	150	333	.450	77	112	.688	212	62	377	6.2	1.8	11.1
92-93—Michigan	36	1095	206	407	.506	112	160	.700	267	69	524	7.4	1.9	14.6
93-94—Michigan	30	1020	261	469	.557	102	151	.676	266	71	625	8.9	2.4	20.8
Totals	100	3071	617	1209	.510	291	423	.688	745	202	1526	7.5	2.0	15.3

Three-point field goals: 1991-92, 0-for-2. 1992-93, 0-for-2. 1993-94, 1-for-7 (.143). Totals, 1-for-11 (.091).

NBA REGULAR-SEASON RECORD

HONORS: All-NBA third team (1996). ... NBA All-Rookie second team (1995).

Season Team	G	Min.	FGM	FGA	Pct.	FTM	FTA	Pct.	REBOUNDS Off.	Def.	Tot.	Ast.	St.	Blk.	TO	Pts.	RPG	APG	PPG
94-95—Washington	65	2348	455	931	.489	194	292	.664	184	361	545	165	52	15	166	1104	8.4	2.5	17.0
95-96—Washington	81	3294	733	1500	.489	319	426	.749	188	472	660	360	67	39	303	1789	8.1	4.4	22.1
Totals	146	5642	1188	2431	.489	513	718	.714	372	833	1205	525	119	54	469	2893	8.3	3.6	19.8

Three-point field goals: 1994-95, 0-for-7. 1995-96, 4-for-13 (.308). Totals, 4-for-20 (.200).
Personal fouls/disqualifications: 1994-95, 236/2. 1995-96, 269/3. Totals, 505/5.

NBA ALL-STAR GAME RECORD

Season Team	Min.	FGM	FGA	Pct.	FTM	FTA	Pct.	REBOUNDS Off.	Def.	Tot.	Ast.	PF	Dq.	St.	Blk.	TO	Pts.
1996 —Washington	16	1	5	.200	0	0	...	4	2	6	2	3	0	1	0	0	2

HUNTER, LINDSEY   G   PISTONS

PERSONAL: Born December 3, 1970, in Utica, Miss. ... 6-2/195. ... Full name: Lindsey Benson Hunter Jr.
HIGH SCHOOL: Murrah (Jackson, Miss.).
COLLEGE: Alcorn State, then Jackson State.
TRANSACTIONS/CAREER NOTES: Selected by Detroit Pistons in first round (10th pick overall) of 1993 NBA Draft.

COLLEGIATE RECORD

Season Team	G	Min.	FGM	FGA	Pct.	FTM	FTA	Pct.	Reb.	Ast.	Pts.	RPG	APG	PPG
88-89—Alcorn State	27	624	70	178	.393	23	32	.719	67	99	167	2.5	3.7	6.2
89-90—Jackson State						Did not play—transfer student.								

H

Season Team	G	Min.	FGM	FGA	Pct.	FTM	FTA	Pct.	Reb.	Ast.	Pts.	AVERAGES RPG	APG	PPG
90-91—Jackson State	30	1042	229	560	.409	82	118	.695	100	105	626	3.3	3.5	20.9
91-92—Jackson State	28	960	249	605	.412	100	157	.637	96	121	693	3.4	4.3	24.8
92-93—Jackson State	34	1152	320	777	.412	155	201	.771	115	115	907	3.4	3.4	26.7
Totals	119	3778	868	2120	.409	360	508	.709	378	440	2393	3.2	3.7	20.1

Three-point field goals: 1988-89, 4-for-21 (.190). 1990-91, 86-for-235 (.366). 1991-92, 95-for-257 (.370). 1992-93, 112-for-328 (.341). Totals, 297-for-841 (.353).

NBA REGULAR-SEASON RECORD

HONORS: NBA All-Rookie second team (1994).

Season Team	G	Min.	FGM	FGA	Pct.	FTM	FTA	Pct.	REBOUNDS Off.	Def.	Tot.	Ast.	St.	Blk.	TO	Pts.	AVERAGES RPG	APG	PPG
93-94—Detroit	82	2172	335	893	.375	104	142	.732	47	142	189	390	121	10	184	843	2.3	4.8	10.3
94-95—Detroit	42	944	119	318	.374	40	55	.727	24	51	75	159	51	7	79	314	1.8	3.8	7.5
95-96—Detroit	80	2138	239	628	.381	84	120	.700	44	150	194	188	84	18	80	679	2.4	2.4	8.5
Totals	204	5254	693	1839	.377	228	317	.719	115	343	458	737	256	35	343	1836	2.2	3.6	9.0

Three-point field goals: 1993-94, 69-for-207 (.333). 1994-95, 36-for-108 (.333). 1995-96, 117-for-289 (.405). Totals, 222-for-604 (.368).
Personal fouls/disqualifications: 1993-94, 174/1. 1994-95, 94/1. 1995-96, 185/0. Totals, 453/2.

NBA PLAYOFF RECORD

Season Team	G	Min.	FGM	FGA	Pct.	FTM	FTA	Pct.	REBOUNDS Off.	Def.	Tot.	Ast.	St.	Blk.	TO	Pts.	AVERAGES RPG	APG	PPG
95-96—Detroit	2	36	2	8	.250	1	2	.500	1	1	2	1	1	0	0	6	1.0	0.5	3.0

Three-point field goals: 1995-96, 1-for-4 (.250).
Personal fouls/disqualifications: 1995-96, 2/0.

HURLEY, BOBBY   G   KINGS

PERSONAL: Born June 28, 1971, in Jersey City, N.J. ... 6-0/165. ... Full name: Robert Matthew Hurley.
HIGH SCHOOL: St. Anthony (Jersey City, N.J.).
COLLEGE: Duke.
TRANSACTIONS/CAREER NOTES: Selected by Sacramento Kings in first round (seventh pick overall) of 1993 NBA Draft.

COLLEGIATE RECORD

NOTES: THE SPORTING NEWS All-America first team (1993). ... THE SPORTING NEWS All-America second team (1992). ... NCAA Division I Tournament Most Outstanding Player (1992). ... Member of NCAA Division I championship teams (1991, 1992). ... Holds NCAA Division I career record for most assists—1,076.

Season Team	G	Min.	FGM	FGA	Pct.	FTM	FTA	Pct.	Reb.	Ast.	Pts.	AVERAGES RPG	APG	PPG
89-90—Duke	38	1268	92	262	.351	110	143	.769	68	288	335	1.8	7.6	8.8
90-91—Duke	39	1353	141	333	.423	83	114	.728	93	289	441	2.4	7.4	11.3
91-92—Duke	31	1043	123	284	.433	105	133	.789	61	237	410	2.0	7.6	13.2
92-93—Duke	32	1138	157	373	.421	143	178	.803	84	262	545	2.6	8.2	17.0
Totals	140	4802	513	1252	.410	441	568	.776	306	1076	1731	2.2	7.7	12.4

Three-point field goals: 1989-90, 41-for-115 (.357). 1990-91, 76-for-188 (.404). 1991-92, 59-for-140 (.421). 1992-93, 88-for-209 (.421). Totals, 264-for-652 (.405).

NBA REGULAR-SEASON RECORD

Season Team	G	Min.	FGM	FGA	Pct.	FTM	FTA	Pct.	REBOUNDS Off.	Def.	Tot.	Ast.	St.	Blk.	TO	Pts.	AVERAGES RPG	APG	PPG
93-94—Sacramento	19	499	54	146	.370	24	30	.800	6	28	34	115	13	1	48	134	1.8	6.1	7.1
94-95—Sacramento	68	1105	103	284	.363	58	76	.763	14	56	70	226	29	0	110	285	1.0	3.3	4.2
95-96—Sacramento	72	1059	65	230	.283	68	85	.800	12	63	75	216	28	3	86	220	1.0	3.0	3.1
Totals	159	2663	222	660	.336	150	191	.785	32	147	179	557	70	4	244	639	1.1	3.5	4.0

Three-point field goals: 1993-94, 2-for-16 (.125). 1994-95, 21-for-76 (.276). 1995-96, 22-for-76 (.289). Totals, 45-for-168 (.268).
Personal fouls/disqualifications: 1993-94, 28/0. 1994-95, 79/0. 1995-96, 121/0. Totals, 228/0.

NBA PLAYOFF RECORD

Season Team	G	Min.	FGM	FGA	Pct.	FTM	FTA	Pct.	REBOUNDS Off.	Def.	Tot.	Ast.	St.	Blk.	TO	Pts.	AVERAGES RPG	APG	PPG
95-96—Sacramento	1	2	0	0	...	0	0	...	0	0	0	0	0	0	0	0	0.0	0.0	0.0

JACKSON, JAREN   G/F

PERSONAL: Born October 27, 1967, in New Orleans. ... 6-6/200.
HIGH SCHOOL: Walter Cohen (New Orleans).
COLLEGE: Georgetown.
TRANSACTIONS/CAREER NOTES: Not drafted by an NBA franchise. ... Signed as free agent by New Jersey Nets (October 3, 1989). ... Waived by Nets (February 27, 1990). ... Played in Continental Basketball Association with Wichita Falls Texans (1990-91), La Crosse Catbirds (1991-92 and 1993-94), Pittsburgh Piranhas (1994-95) and Fort Wayne Fury (1995-96). ... Played in World Basketball League with Dayton Wings (1991). ... Signed by Golden State Warriors to first of two consecutive 10-day contracts (January 24, 1992). ... Signed as free agent by Los Angeles Clippers (October 7, 1992). ... Signed as free agent by Chicago Bulls (October 7, 1993). ... Waived by Bulls (October 28, 1993). ... Signed as free agent by Portland Trail Blazers (December 21, 1993). ... Waived by Trail Blazers (November 1, 1994). ... Signed as free agent by Philadelphia 76ers (November 15, 1994). ... Waived by 76ers (January 4, 1995). ... Signed by Houston Rockets to first of two consecutive 10-day contracts (February 22, 1996).

COLLEGIATE RECORD

Season Team	G	Min.	FGM	FGA	Pct.	FTM	FTA	Pct.	Reb.	Ast.	Pts.	AVERAGES RPG	APG	PPG
85-86—Georgetown	32	283	42	97	.433	18	22	.818	49	19	102	1.5	0.6	3.2

Season Team	G	Min.	FGM	FGA	Pct.	FTM	FTA	Pct.	Reb.	Ast.	Pts.	RPG	APG	PPG
86-87—Georgetown	34	387	68	148	.459	37	52	.712	69	26	193	2.0	0.8	5.7
87-88—Georgetown	30	558	100	243	.412	42	56	.750	88	46	262	2.9	1.5	8.7
88-89—Georgetown	34	923	161	357	.451	59	90	.656	176	62	417	5.2	1.8	12.3
Totals	130	2151	371	845	.439	156	220	.709	382	153	974	2.9	1.2	7.5

Three-point field goals: 1986-87, 20-for-48 (.417). 1987-88, 20-for-73 (.274). 1988-89, 36-for-87 (.414). Totals, 76-for-208 (.365).

NBA REGULAR-SEASON RECORD

Season Team	G	Min.	FGM	FGA	Pct.	FTM	FTA	Pct.	Off.	Def.	Tot.	Ast.	St.	Blk.	TO	Pts.	RPG	APG	PPG
89-90—New Jersey	28	160	25	69	.362	17	21	.810	16	8	24	13	13	1	18	67	0.9	0.5	2.4
91-92—Golden State	5	54	11	23	.478	4	6	.667	5	5	10	3	2	0	4	26	2.0	0.6	5.2
92-93—L.A. Clippers	34	350	53	128	.414	23	27	.852	19	20	39	35	19	5	17	131	1.1	1.0	3.9
93-94—Portland	29	187	34	87	.391	12	14	.857	6	11	17	27	4	2	14	80	0.6	0.9	2.8
94-95—Philadelphia	21	257	25	68	.368	16	24	.667	18	24	42	19	9	5	17	70	2.0	0.9	3.3
95-96—Houston	4	33	0	8	.000	8	10	.800	0	3	3	0	1	0	0	8	0.8	0.0	2.0
Totals	121	1041	148	383	.386	80	102	.784	64	71	135	97	48	13	70	382	1.1	0.8	3.2

Three-point field goals: 1989-90, 0-for-3. 1992-93, 2-for-5 (.400). 1993-94, 0-for-6. 1994-95, 4-for-15 (.267). 1995-96, 0-for-5. Totals, 6-for-34 (.176).
Personal fouls/disqualifications: 1989-90, 16/0. 1991-92, 7/1. 1992-93, 45/1. 1993-94, 20/0. 1994-95, 33/0. 1995-96, 5/0. Totals, 126/2.

NBA PLAYOFF RECORD

Season Team	G	Min.	FGM	FGA	Pct.	FTM	FTA	Pct.	Off.	Def.	Tot.	Ast.	St.	Blk.	TO	Pts.	RPG	APG	PPG
92-93—L.A. Clippers	4	28	5	13	.385	0	0	...	4	1	5	2	2	0	3	10	1.3	0.5	2.5
93-94—Portland	1	1	0	0	...	0	0	...	0	0	0	0	0	0	0	0	0.0	0.0	0.0
Totals	5	29	5	13	.385	0	0	...	4	1	5	2	2	0	3	10	1.0	0.4	2.0

Three-point field goals: 1992-93, 0-for-1.
Personal fouls/disqualifications: 1992-93, 6/0.

CBA REGULAR-SEASON RECORD

Season Team	G	Min.	FGM	FGA	Pct.	FTM	FTA	Pct.	Reb.	Ast.	Pts.	RPG	APG	PPG
90-91—Wichita Falls	51	1099	233	525	.444	113	165	.685	214	74	597	4.2	1.5	11.7
91-92—La Crosse	43	1596	314	674	.466	147	184	.799	215	157	785	5.0	3.7	18.3
93-94—La Crosse	14	530	114	251	.454	63	78	.808	58	35	298	4.1	2.5	21.3
94-95—Pittsburgh	22	687	118	274	.431	55	70	.786	109	101	310	5.0	4.6	14.1
95-96—Fort Wayne	24	695	135	256	.527	50	66	.758	107	57	346	4.5	2.4	14.4
Totals	154	4607	914	1980	.462	428	563	.760	703	424	2336	4.6	2.8	15.2

Three-point field goals: 1990-91, 18-for-55 (.327). 1991-92, 10-for-37 (.270). 1993-94, 7-for-24 (.292). 1994-95, 19-for-62 (.306). 1995-96, 26-for-50 (.520). Totals, 80-for-228 (.351).

JACKSON, JIM   G   MAVERICKS

PERSONAL: Born October 14, 1970, in Toledo, Ohio. ... 6-6/215. ... Full name: James Arthur Jackson.
HIGH SCHOOL: Macomber-Whitney (Toledo, Ohio).
COLLEGE: Ohio State.
TRANSACTIONS/CAREER NOTES: Selected after junior season by Dallas Mavericks in first round (fourth pick overall) of 1992 NBA Draft.

COLLEGIATE RECORD

NOTES: The Sporting News All-America first team (1992). ... The Sporting News All-America third team (1991).

Season Team	G	Min.	FGM	FGA	Pct.	FTM	FTA	Pct.	Reb.	Ast.	Pts.	RPG	APG	PPG
89-90—Ohio State	30	1035	194	389	.499	73	93	.785	166	110	482	5.5	3.7	16.1
90-91—Ohio State	31	997	228	441	.517	112	149	.752	169	133	585	5.5	4.3	18.9
91-92—Ohio State	32	1133	264	535	.493	146	180	.811	217	129	718	6.8	4.0	22.4
Totals	93	3165	686	1365	.503	331	422	.784	552	372	1785	5.9	4.0	19.2

Three-point field goals: 1989-90, 21-for-59 (.356). 1990-91, 17-for-51 (.333). 1991-92, 44-for-108 (.407). Totals, 82-for-218 (.376).

NBA REGULAR-SEASON RECORD

Season Team	G	Min.	FGM	FGA	Pct.	FTM	FTA	Pct.	Off.	Def.	Tot.	Ast.	St.	Blk.	TO	Pts.	RPG	APG	PPG
92-93—Dallas	28	938	184	466	.395	68	92	.739	42	80	122	131	40	11	115	457	4.4	4.7	16.3
93-94—Dallas	82	3066	637	1432	.445	285	347	.821	169	219	388	374	87	25	*334	1576	4.7	4.6	19.2
94-95—Dallas	51	1982	484	1026	.472	306	380	.805	120	140	260	191	28	12	160	1309	5.1	3.7	25.7
95-96—Dallas	82	2820	569	1308	.435	345	418	.825	173	237	410	235	47	22	191	1604	5.0	2.9	19.6
Totals	243	8806	1874	4232	.443	1004	1237	.812	504	676	1180	931	202	70	800	4946	4.9	3.8	20.4

Three-point field goals: 1992-93, 21-for-73 (.288). 1993-94, 17-for-60 (.283). 1994-95, 35-for-110 (.318). 1995-96, 121-for-333 (.363). Totals, 194-for-576 (.337).
Personal fouls/disqualifications: 1992-93, 80/0. 1993-94, 161/0. 1994-95, 92/0. 1995-96, 165/0. Totals, 498/0.

JACKSON, MARK   G   NUGGETS

PERSONAL: Born April 1, 1965, in Brooklyn, N.Y. ... 6-3/185. ... Full name: Mark A. Jackson.
HIGH SCHOOL: Bishop Loughlin Memorial (Brooklyn, N.Y.).
COLLEGE: St. John's.
TRANSACTIONS/CAREER NOTES: Selected by New York Knicks in first round (18th pick overall) of 1987 NBA Draft. ... Traded by Knicks with 1995 second-round draft choice to Los Angeles Clippers in three-way deal in which Clippers also received C Stanley Roberts from Orlando Magic, Knicks received G Doc Rivers, F Charles Smith and G Bo Kimble from

Clippers and Magic received 1993 first-round draft choice from Knicks and 1994 first-round draft choice from Clippers (September 22, 1992). ... Traded by Clippers with draft rights to G Greg Minor to Indiana Pacers for G Pooh Richardson, F Malik Sealy and draft rights to F Eric Piatkowski (June 30, 1994). ... Traded by Pacers with G Ricky Pierce and 1996 first-round draft choice to Denver Nuggets for G Jalen Rose, F Reggie Williams and 1996 first-round draft choice (June 13, 1996).

COLLEGIATE RECORD

NOTES: The Sporting News All-America second team (1987). ... Led NCAA Division I with 9.11 assists per game (1986).

Season Team	G	Min.	FGM	FGA	Pct.	FTM	FTA	Pct.	Reb.	Ast.	Pts.	RPG	APG	PPG
												AVERAGES		
83-84—St. John's	30	855	61	106	.575	53	77	.688	59	108	175	2.0	3.6	5.8
84-85—St. John's	35	601	57	101	.564	66	91	.725	44	109	180	1.3	3.1	5.1
85-86—St. John's	36	1340	151	316	.478	105	142	.739	125	328	407	3.5	9.1	11.3
86-87—St. John's	30	1184	196	389	.504	125	155	.806	110	193	566	3.7	6.4	18.9
Totals	131	3980	465	912	.510	349	465	.751	338	738	1328	2.6	5.6	10.1

Three-point field goals: 1986-87, 49-for-117 (.419).

NBA REGULAR-SEASON RECORD

RECORDS: Holds single-season record for most assists by a rookie—868 (1988).
HONORS: NBA Rookie of the Year (1988). ... NBA All-Rookie team (1988).

Season Team	G	Min.	FGM	FGA	Pct.	FTM	FTA	Pct.	Off.	Def.	Tot.	Ast.	St.	Blk.	TO	Pts.	RPG	APG	PPG
									REBOUNDS								AVERAGES		
87-88—New York	82	3249	438	1013	.432	206	266	.774	120	276	396	868	205	6	258	1114	4.8	10.6	13.6
88-89—New York	72	2477	479	1025	.467	180	258	.698	106	235	341	619	139	7	226	1219	4.7	8.6	16.9
89-90—New York	82	2428	327	749	.437	120	165	.727	106	212	318	604	109	4	211	809	3.9	7.4	9.9
90-91—New York	72	1595	250	508	.492	117	160	.731	62	135	197	452	60	9	135	630	2.7	6.3	8.8
91-92—New York	81	2461	367	747	.491	171	222	.770	95	210	305	694	112	13	211	916	3.8	8.6	11.3
92-93—L.A. Clippers	82	3117	459	945	.486	241	300	.803	129	259	388	724	136	12	220	1181	4.7	8.8	14.4
93-94—L.A. Clippers	79	2711	331	732	.452	167	211	.791	107	241	348	678	120	6	232	865	4.4	8.6	10.9
94-95—Indiana	82	2402	239	566	.422	119	153	.778	73	233	306	616	105	16	210	624	3.7	7.5	7.6
95-96—Indiana	81	2643	296	626	.473	150	191	.785	66	241	307	635	100	5	201	806	3.8	7.8	10.0
Totals	713	23083	3186	6911	.461	1471	1926	.764	864	2042	2906	5890	1086	78	1904	8164	4.1	8.3	11.5

Three-point field goals: 1987-88, 32-for-126 (.254). 1988-89, 81-for-240 (.338). 1989-90, 35-for-131 (.267). 1990-91, 13-for-51 (.255). 1991-92, 11-for-43 (.256). 1992-93, 22-for-82 (.268). 1993-94, 36-for-127 (.283). 1994-95, 27-for-87 (.310). 1995-96, 64-for-149 (.430). Totals, 321-for-1036 (.310).
Personal fouls/disqualifications: 1987-88, 244/2. 1988-89, 163/1. 1989-90, 121/0. 1990-91, 81/0. 1991-92, 153/0. 1992-93, 158/0. 1993-94, 115/0. 1994-95, 148/0. 1995-96, 153/0. Totals, 1336/3.

NBA PLAYOFF RECORD

Season Team	G	Min.	FGM	FGA	Pct.	FTM	FTA	Pct.	Off.	Def.	Tot.	Ast.	St.	Blk.	TO	Pts.	RPG	APG	PPG
									REBOUNDS								AVERAGES		
87-88—New York	4	171	22	60	.367	8	11	.727	6	13	19	39	10	0	14	57	4.8	9.8	14.3
88-89—New York	9	336	51	100	.510	19	28	.679	7	24	31	91	10	3	28	132	3.4	10.1	14.7
89-90—New York	9	81	13	31	.419	8	11	.727	1	4	5	21	2	0	7	34	0.6	2.3	3.8
90-91—New York	3	36	1	3	.333	0	0	...	0	0	0	8	1	1	5	2	0.0	2.7	0.7
91-92—New York	12	368	37	92	.402	22	27	.815	12	15	27	86	10	0	30	100	2.3	7.2	8.3
92-93—L.A. Clippers	5	188	28	64	.438	19	22	.864	8	21	29	38	8	1	13	76	5.8	7.6	15.2
94-95—Indiana	17	553	59	130	.454	34	46	.739	27	62	89	121	15	0	41	168	5.2	7.1	9.9
95-96—Indiana	5	186	18	51	.353	13	17	.765	3	22	25	30	6	0	13	53	5.0	6.0	10.6
Totals	64	1919	229	531	.431	123	162	.759	64	161	225	434	62	5	151	622	3.5	6.8	9.7

Three-point field goals: 1987-88, 5-for-12 (.417). 1988-89, 11-for-28 (.393). 1989-90, 0-for-2. 1991-92, 4-for-21 (.190). 1992-93, 1-for-2 (.500). 1994-95, 16-for-40 (.400). 1995-96, 4-for-18 (.222). Totals, 41-for-123 (.333).
Personal fouls/disqualifications: 1987-88, 13/0. 1988-89, 9/0. 1989-90, 5/0. 1990-91, 1/0. 1991-92, 26/0. 1992-93, 8/0. 1994-95, 34/0. 1995-96, 9/0. Totals, 105/0.

NBA ALL-STAR GAME RECORD

Season Team	Min.	FGM	FGA	Pct.	FTM	FTA	Pct.	Off.	Def.	Tot.	Ast.	PF	Dq.	St.	Blk.	TO	Pts.
								REBOUNDS									
1989 —New York	16	3	5	.600	2	4	.500	1	1	2	4	1	0	1	1	2	9

Three-point field goals: 1989, 1-for-1.

JAMES, HENRY   F

PERSONAL: Born July 29, 1965, in Centreville, Ala. ... 6-8/220. ... Full name: Henry Charles James.
HIGH SCHOOL: North Side (Fort Wayne, Ind.).
JUNIOR COLLEGE: South Plains (Texas).
COLLEGE: St. Mary's (Texas).
TRANSACTIONS/CAREER NOTES: Not drafted by an NBA franchise. ... Played in Spain (1988-89). ... Played in Continental Basketball Association with Wichita Falls Texans (1988-89, 1990-91, 1992-93 and 1993-94) and Sioux Falls Skyforce (1994-95 and 1995-96). ... Played in Belgium (1989-90). ... Signed as free agent by Cleveland Cavaliers (July 30, 1990). ... Waived by Cavaliers (November 2, 1990). ... Re-signed by Cavaliers to first of two consecutive 10-day contracts (December 31, 1990). ... Re-signed by Cavaliers for remainder of season (January 21, 1991). ... Signed as restricted free agent by Cavaliers (August 14, 1991). ... Played in Italy (1992-93). ... Signed by Sacramento Kings to first of two consecutive 10-day contracts (February 2, 1993). ... Signed by Utah Jazz to 10-day contract (April 4, 1993). ... Signed as free agent by Los Angeles Clippers (July 19, 1993). ... Waived by Clippers (January 7, 1994). ... Signed by Houston Rockets to first of two consecutive 10-day contracts (January 20, 1996).

COLLEGIATE RECORD

Season Team	G	Min.	FGM	FGA	Pct.	FTM	FTA	Pct.	Reb.	Ast.	Pts.	RPG	APG	PPG
												AVERAGES		
84-85—South Plains College	28	...	85	190	.447	21	29	.724	72	...	191	2.6	...	6.8
85-86—South Plains College	28	...	119	236	.504	72	98	.735	234	...	310	8.4	...	11.1
86-87—St. Mary's (Texas)	23	...	143	279	.513	41	57	.719	140	10	328	6.1	0.4	14.3

Season Team	G	Min.	FGM	FGA	Pct.	FTM	FTA	Pct.	Reb.	Ast.	Pts.	AVERAGES		
												RPG	APG	PPG
87-88—St. Mary's (Texas)	26	...	218	396	.551	136	158	.861	198	20	606	7.6	0.8	23.3
Junior college totals	56		204	426	.479	93	127	.732	306	...	501	5.5	...	8.9
4-year-college totals	49	...	361	675	.535	177	215	.823	338	30	934	6.9	0.6	19.1

Three-point field goals: 1986-87, 1-for-2 (.500). 1987-88, 34-for-61 (.557). Totals, 35-for-63 (.556).

CBA REGULAR-SEASON RECORD

NOTES: CBA Playoff Most Valuable Player (1996). ... CBA All-League first team (1994). ... CBA All-League second team (1993, 1996) ... Member of CBA championship team (1996).

Season Team	G	Min.	FGM	FGA	Pct.	FTM	FTA	Pct.	Reb.	Ast.	Pts.	AVERAGES		
												RPG	APG	PPG
88-89—Wichita Falls.................	12	182	40	96	.417	22	26	.846	40	5	111	3.3	0.4	9.3
90-91—Wichita Falls.................	23	826	187	400	.468	96	110	.873	179	35	501	7.8	1.5	21.8
92-93—Wichita Falls.................	36	1361	313	659	.475	176	205	.859	222	36	839	6.2	1.0	23.3
93-94—Wichita Falls.................	33	1059	266	611	.435	167	190	.879	185	33	749	5.6	1.0	22.7
94-95—Sioux Falls.................	51	1975	393	837	.470	174	193	.902	290	77	1060	5.7	1.5	20.8
95-96—Sioux Falls.................	45	1485	344	750	.459	174	190	*.916	214	66	992	4.8	1.5	22.0
Totals	200	6888	1543	3353	.460	809	914	.885	1130	252	4252	5.7	1.3	21.3

Three-point field goals: 1988-89, 9-for-23 (.391). 1990-91, 31-for-92 (.337). 1992-93, 37-for-109 (.339). 1993-94, 50-for-141 (.355). 1994-95, 100-for-249 (.402). 1995-96, 130-for-310 (.419). Totals, 357-for-924 (.387).

NBA REGULAR-SEASON RECORD

Season Team	G	Min.	FGM	FGA	Pct.	FTM	FTA	Pct.	REBOUNDS			Ast.	St.	Blk.	TO	Pts.	AVERAGES		
									Off.	Def.	Tot.						RPG	APG	PPG
90-91—Cleveland	37	505	112	254	.441	52	72	.722	26	53	79	32	15	5	37	300	2.1	0.9	8.1
91-92—Cleveland	65	866	164	403	.407	61	76	.803	35	77	112	25	16	11	43	418	1.7	0.4	6.4
92-93—Sac.-Utah........	10	88	21	51	.412	22	26	.846	7	4	11	1	3	0	7	67	1.1	0.1	6.7
93-94—L.A. Clippers....	12	75	16	42	.381	5	5	1.000	6	8	14	1	2	0	2	41	1.2	0.1	3.4
95-96—Houston........	7	58	10	24	.417	5	5	1.000	3	3	6	2	0	0	4	30	0.9	0.3	4.3
Totals	131	1592	323	774	.417	145	184	.788	77	145	222	61	36	16	93	856	1.7	0.5	6.5

Three-point field goals: 1990-91, 24-for-60 (.400). 1991-92, 29-for-90 (.322). 1992-93, 3-for-13 (.231). 1993-94, 4-for-18 (.222). 1995-96, 5-for-15 (.333). Totals, 65-for-196 (.332).
Personal fouls/disqualifications: 1990-91, 59/1. 1991-92, 94/1. 1992-93, 9/0. 1993-94, 9/0. 1995-96, 13/0. Totals, 184/2.

NBA PLAYOFF RECORD

Season Team	G	Min.	FGM	FGA	Pct.	FTM	FTA	Pct.	REBOUNDS			Ast.	St.	Blk.	TO	Pts.	AVERAGES		
									Off.	Def.	Tot.						RPG	APG	PPG
91-92—Cleveland........	8	22	1	10	.100	2	4	.500	1	1	2	2	1	0	1	4	0.3	0.3	0.5

Three-point field goals: 1991-92, 0-for-3.
Personal fouls/disqualifications: 1991-92, 2/0.

ITALIAN LEAGUE RECORD

Season Team	G	Min.	FGM	FGA	Pct.	FTM	FTA	Pct.	Reb.	Ast.	Pts.	AVERAGES		
												RPG	APG	PPG
92-93—Scavolini Pesaro............	7	160	33	74	.446	7	11	.636	18	0	87	2.6	0.0	12.4

JOHNSON, AVERY   G   SPURS

PERSONAL: Born March 25, 1965, in New Orleans. ... 5-11/180.
HIGH SCHOOL: St. Augustine (New Orleans).
JUNIOR COLLEGE: New Mexico Junior College.
COLLEGE: Cameron (Okla.), then Southern (La.).
TRANSACTIONS/CAREER NOTES: Not drafted by an NBA franchise. ... Played in United States Basketball League with Palm Beach Stingrays (1988). ... Signed as free agent by Seattle SuperSonics (August 2, 1988). ... Traded by SuperSonics to Denver Nuggets for 1997 second-round draft choice (October 24, 1990). ... Waived by Nuggets (December 24, 1990). ... Signed as free agent by San Antonio Spurs (January 17, 1991). ... Waived by Spurs (December 17, 1991). ... Signed by Houston Rockets for first of two consecutive 10-day contracts (January 10, 1992). ... Re-signed by Rockets for remainder of season (January 31, 1992). ... Signed as free agent by Spurs (November 19, 1992). ... Signed as free agent by Golden State Warriors (October 25, 1993). ... Signed as unrestricted free agent by Spurs (July 21, 1994).

COLLEGIATE RECORD

NOTES: Holds NCAA Division I career record for highest assists-per-game average—8.97. ... Shares NCAA Division I single-game record for assists—22 (January 25, 1988, vs. Texas Southern). ... Led NCAA Division I with 10.74 assists per game (1987) and 13.30 assists per game (1988).

Season Team	G	Min.	FGM	FGA	Pct.	FTM	FTA	Pct.	Reb.	Ast.	Pts.	AVERAGES		
												RPG	APG	PPG
83-84—New Mexico J.C.						Statistics unavailable.								
84-85—Cameron........................	33	...	54	106	.509	34	55	.618	31	111	142	0.9	3.4	4.3
85-86—Southern						Did not play—transfer student.								
86-87—Southern	31	1111	86	196	.439	40	65	.615	73	333	219	2.4	10.7	7.1
87-88—Southern	30	1145	138	257	.537	44	64	.688	84	399	342	2.8	13.3	11.4
Junior college totals	...	...				...	...			...	...			
4-year-college totals	94	...	278	559	.497	118	184	.641	188	843	703	2.0	9.0	7.5

Three-point field goals: 1986-87, 7-for-24 (.292). 1987-88, 22-for-47 (.468). Totals, 29-for-71 (.408).

NBA REGULAR-SEASON RECORD

Season Team	G	Min.	FGM	FGA	Pct.	FTM	FTA	Pct.	REBOUNDS			Ast.	St.	Blk.	TO	Pts.	AVERAGES		
									Off.	Def.	Tot.						RPG	APG	PPG
88-89—Seattle	43	291	29	83	.349	9	16	.563	11	13	24	73	21	3	18	68	0.6	1.7	1.6
89-90—Seattle	53	575	55	142	.387	29	40	.725	21	22	43	162	26	1	48	140	0.8	3.1	2.6

Season Team	G	Min.	FGM	FGA	Pct.	FTM	FTA	Pct.	REBOUNDS Off.	Def.	Tot.	Ast.	St.	Blk.	TO	Pts.	AVERAGES RPG	APG	PPG
90-91—Denver-S.A.	68	959	130	277	.469	59	87	.678	22	55	77	230	47	4	74	320	1.1	3.4	4.7
91-92—S.A.-Hou........	69	1235	158	330	.479	66	101	.653	13	67	80	266	61	9	110	386	1.2	3.9	5.6
92-93—San Antonio.....	75	2030	256	510	.502	144	182	.791	20	126	146	561	85	16	145	656	1.9	7.5	8.7
93-94—Golden State ...	82	2332	356	724	.492	178	253	.704	41	135	176	433	113	8	172	890	2.1	5.3	10.9
94-95—San Antonio....	82	3011	448	863	.519	202	295	.685	49	159	208	670	114	13	207	1101	2.5	8.2	13.4
95-96—San Antonio....	82	3084	438	887	.494	189	262	.721	37	169	206	789	119	21	195	1071	2.5	9.6	13.1
Totals	554	13517	1870	3816	.490	876	1236	.709	214	746	960	3184	586	75	969	4632	1.7	5.7	8.4

Three-point field goals: 1988-89, 1-for-9 (.111). 1989-90, 1-for-4 (.250). 1990-91, 1-for-9 (.111). 1991-92, 4-for-15 (.267). 1992-93, 0-for-8. 1993-94, 0-for-12. 1994-95, 3-for-22 (.136). 1995-96, 6-for-31 (.194). Totals, 16-for-110 (.145).

Personal fouls/disqualifications: 1988-89, 34/0. 1989-90, 55/0. 1990-91, 62/0. 1991-92, 89/1. 1992-93, 141/0. 1993-94, 160/0. 1994-95, 154/0. 1995-96, 179/1. Totals, 874/2.

NBA PLAYOFF RECORD

Season Team	G	Min.	FGM	FGA	Pct.	FTM	FTA	Pct.	REBOUNDS Off.	Def.	Tot.	Ast.	St.	Blk.	TO	Pts.	AVERAGES RPG	APG	PPG
88-89—Seattle	6	31	5	12	.417	1	2	.500	2	2	4	5	4	0	0	11	0.7	0.8	1.8
90-91—San Antonio	3	19	0	5	.000	2	2	1.000	0	0	0	4	1	0	0	2	0.0	1.3	0.7
92-93—San Antonio	10	314	36	70	.514	10	14	.714	8	23	31	81	10	1	23	82	3.1	8.1	8.2
93-94—Golden State ...	3	41	9	17	.529	0	0	...	0	3	3	10	4	1	3	18	1.0	3.3	6.0
94-95—San Antonio....	15	575	91	176	.517	36	58	.621	9	23	32	125	20	6	30	218	2.1	8.3	14.5
95-96—San Antonio....	10	407	52	121	.430	19	27	.704	6	30	36	94	20	1	24	123	3.6	9.4	12.3
Totals	47	1387	193	401	.481	68	103	.660	25	81	106	319	59	9	80	454	2.3	6.8	9.7

Three-point field goals: 1988-89, 0-for-4. 1990-91, 0-for-1. 1992-93, 0-for-1. 1993-94, 0-for-1. 1994-95, 0-for-1. 1995-96, 0-for-2. Totals, 0-for-10.
Personal fouls/disqualifications: 1988-89, 1/0. 1990-91, 3/0. 1992-93, 27/0. 1993-94, 2/0. 1994-95, 29/0. 1995-96, 21/0. Totals, 83/0.

JOHNSON, DARRYL   G

PERSONAL: Born October 26, 1965, in Flint, Mich. ... 6-1/185.
HIGH SCHOOL: Flint (Mich.) Central.
COLLEGE: Michigan State.
TRANSACTIONS/CAREER NOTES: Selected by Golden State Warriors in third round (58th pick overall) of 1987 NBA Draft. ... Played in Continental Basketball Association with Cedar Rapids Silver Bullets (1989-90), Rockford Lightning (1992-93 and 1993-94) and Omaha Racers (1994-95 and 1995-96). ... Played in Phillipines (1991). ... Played in Global Basketball Association with Music City Jammers (1991-92). ... Signed by Cleveland Cavaliers to first of three consecutive 10-day contracts (March 5, 1996). ... Re-signed by Cavaliers for remainder of season (March 25, 1996). ... Rights renounced by Cavaliers (August 22, 1996).

COLLEGIATE RECORD

Season Team	G	Min.	FGM	FGA	Pct.	FTM	FTA	Pct.	Reb.	Ast.	Pts.	AVERAGES RPG	APG	PPG
83-84—Michigan State	28	556	72	152	.474	23	34	.676	31	33	167	1.1	1.2	6.0
84-85—Michigan State	22	416	50	102	.490	16	22	.727	37	28	116	1.7	1.3	5.3
85-86—Michigan State	29	1038	216	371	.582	50	63	.794	96	116	482	3.3	4.0	16.6
86-87—Michigan State	28	1042	234	432	.542	111	122	.910	94	112	618	3.4	4.0	22.1
Totals	107	3052	572	1057	.541	200	241	.830	258	289	1383	2.4	2.7	12.9

Three-point field goals: 1986-87, 13-for-35 (.371).

CBA REGULAR-SEASON RECORD

NOTES: CBA All-League second team (1996).

Season Team	G	Min.	FGM	FGA	Pct.	FTM	FTA	Pct.	Reb.	Ast.	Pts.	AVERAGES RPG	APG	PPG
89-90—Cedar Rapids	56	1698	326	589	.553	103	120	.858	161	213	759	2.9	3.8	13.6
92-93—Rockford	53	917	147	288	.510	68	84	.810	80	135	369	1.5	2.5	7.0
93-94—Rockford	56	2088	356	718	.496	124	145	.855	187	358	893	3.3	6.4	15.9
94-95—Omaha.....................	52	1375	248	494	.502	86	109	.789	77	170	662	1.5	3.3	12.7
95-96—Omaha.....................	44	1566	321	597	.538	130	162	.802	147	211	874	3.3	4.8	19.9
Totals	261	7644	1398	2686	.520	511	620	.824	652	1087	3557	2.5	4.2	13.6

Three-point field goals: 1989-90, 4-for-13 (.308). 1992-93, 7-for-25 (.280). 1993-94, 57-for-129 (.442). 1994-95, 80-for-194 (.412). 1995-96, 102-for-223 (.457). Totals, 250-for-584 (.429).

NBA REGULAR-SEASON RECORD

Season Team	G	Min.	FGM	FGA	Pct.	FTM	FTA	Pct.	REBOUNDS Off.	Def.	Tot.	Ast.	St.	Blk.	TO	Pts.	AVERAGES RPG	APG	PPG
95-96—Cleveland	11	28	5	12	.417	2	2	1.000	2	0	2	1	0	0	1	12	0.2	0.1	1.1

Three-point field goals: 1995-96, 0-for-1.
Personal fouls/disqualifications: 1995-96, 3/0.

JOHNSON, EDDIE   F/G

PERSONAL: Born May 1, 1959, in Chicago. ... 6-7/215. ... Full name: Edward Arnet Johnson.
HIGH SCHOOL: Westinghouse Vocational (Chicago).
COLLEGE: Illinois.
TRANSACTIONS/CAREER NOTES: Selected by Kansas City Kings in second round (29th pick overall) of 1981 NBA Draft. ... Kings franchise moved from Kansas City to Sacramento for 1985-86 season. ... Traded by Kings to Phoenix Suns for F Ed Pinckney and 1988 second-round draft choice (June 21, 1987). ... Traded by Suns with 1991 first-round draft choice and 1993 or 1994 first-round draft choice to Seattle SuperSonics for F Xavier McDaniel (December 7, 1990). ... Traded by SuperSonics with G Dana Barros and option to switch 1994 first-round draft choices to Charlotte Hornets for G Kendall Gill (September 1, 1993). ... Played in Greece (1994-95). ... Signed as free agent by Indiana Pacers (October 3, 1995).

COLLEGIATE RECORD

Season Team	G	Min.	FGM	FGA	Pct.	FTM	FTA	Pct.	Reb.	Ast.	Pts.	RPG	APG	PPG
77-78—Illinois	27	469	100	234	.427	20	27	.741	84	16	220	3.1	0.6	8.1
78-79—Illinois	30	786	168	405	.415	26	49	.531	170	52	362	5.7	1.7	12.1
79-80—Illinois	35	1215	266	576	.462	78	119	.655	310	71	610	8.9	2.0	17.4
80-81—Illinois	29	1009	219	443	.494	62	82	.756	267	70	500	9.2	2.4	17.2
Totals	121	3479	753	1658	.454	186	277	.671	831	209	1692	6.9	1.7	14.0

HONORS: NBA Sixth Man Award (1989).

NBA REGULAR-SEASON RECORD

Season Team	G	Min.	FGM	FGA	Pct.	FTM	FTA	Pct.	Off.	Def.	Tot.	Ast.	St.	Blk.	TO	Pts.	RPG	APG	PPG
81-82—Kansas City	74	1517	295	643	.459	99	149	.664	128	194	322	109	50	14	97	690	4.4	1.5	9.3
82-83—Kansas City	82	2933	677	1370	.494	247	317	.779	191	310	501	216	70	20	181	1621	6.1	2.6	19.8
83-84—Kansas City	82	2920	753	1552	.485	268	331	.810	165	290	455	296	76	21	213	1794	5.5	3.6	21.9
84-85—Kansas City	82	3029	769	1565	.491	325	373	.871	151	256	407	273	83	22	225	1876	5.0	3.3	22.9
85-86—Sacramento	82	2514	623	1311	.475	280	343	.816	173	246	419	214	54	17	191	1530	5.1	2.6	18.7
86-87—Sacramento	81	2457	606	1309	.463	267	322	.829	146	207	353	251	42	19	163	1516	4.4	3.1	18.7
87-88—Phoenix	73	2177	533	1110	.480	204	240	.850	121	197	318	180	33	9	139	1294	4.4	2.5	17.7
88-89—Phoenix	70	2043	608	1224	.497	217	250	.868	91	215	306	162	47	7	122	1504	4.4	2.3	21.5
89-90—Phoenix	64	1811	411	907	.453	188	205	.917	69	177	246	107	32	10	108	1080	3.8	1.7	16.9
90-91—Phoe.-Sea.	81	2085	543	1122	.484	229	257	.891	107	164	271	111	58	9	122	1354	3.3	1.4	16.7
91-92—Seattle	81	2366	534	1164	.459	291	338	.861	118	174	292	161	55	11	130	1386	3.6	2.0	17.1
92-93—Seattle	82	1869	463	991	.467	234	257	.911	124	148	272	135	36	4	134	1177	3.3	1.6	14.4
93-94—Charlotte	73	1460	339	738	.459	99	127	.780	80	144	224	125	36	8	84	836	3.1	1.7	11.5
95-96—Indiana	62	1002	180	436	.413	70	79	.886	45	108	153	69	20	4	56	475	2.5	1.1	7.7
Totals	1069	30183	7334	15442	.475	3018	3588	.841	1709	2830	4539	2409	692	175	1965	18133	4.2	2.3	17.0

Three-point field goals: 1981-82, 1-for-11 (.091). 1982-83, 20-for-71 (.282). 1983-84, 20-for-64 (.313). 1984-85, 13-for-54 (.241). 1985-86, 4-for-20 (.200). 1986-87, 37-for-118 (.314). 1987-88, 24-for-94 (.255). 1988-89, 71-for-172 (.413). 1989-90, 70-for-184 (.380). 1990-91, 39-for-120 (.325). 1991-92, 27-for-107 (.252). 1992-93, 17-for-56 (.304). 1993-94, 59-for-150 (.393). 1995-96, 45-for-128 (.352). Totals, 447-for-1349 (.331).
Personal fouls/disqualifications: 1981-82, 210/6. 1982-83, 259/3. 1983-84, 266/4. 1984-85, 237/2. 1985-86, 237/0. 1986-87, 218/4. 1987-88, 190/0. 1988-89, 198/0. 1989-90, 174/4. 1990-91, 181/0. 1991-92, 199/0. 1992-93, 173/0. 1993-94, 143/2. 1995-96, 104/1. Totals, 2789/26.

NBA PLAYOFF RECORD

Season Team	G	Min.	FGM	FGA	Pct.	FTM	FTA	Pct.	Off.	Def.	Tot.	Ast.	St.	Blk.	TO	Pts.	RPG	APG	PPG
83-84—Kansas City	3	107	21	48	.438	7	7	1.000	4	6	10	12	3	1	2	51	3.3	4.0	17.0
85-86—Sacramento	3	96	24	55	.436	8	9	.889	10	11	21	4	3	1	6	56	7.0	1.3	18.7
88-89—Phoenix	12	392	85	206	.413	30	39	.769	28	59	87	25	12	2	18	213	7.3	2.1	17.8
89-90—Phoenix	16	337	72	160	.450	37	47	.787	15	42	57	17	10	4	20	196	3.6	1.1	12.3
90-91—Seattle	5	171	46	89	.517	24	29	.828	12	9	21	7	7	1	8	120	4.2	1.4	24.0
91-92—Seattle	9	247	65	137	.474	32	34	.941	8	19	27	8	3	3	15	166	3.0	0.9	18.4
92-93—Seattle	19	382	82	210	.390	29	31	.935	17	28	45	17	3	1	19	205	2.4	0.9	10.8
95-96—Indiana	1	9	0	5	.000	0	0	...	0	0	0	1	0	0	0	0	0.0	1.0	0.0
Totals	68	1741	395	910	.434	167	196	.852	94	174	268	91	41	13	88	1007	3.9	1.3	14.8

Three-point field goals: 1983-84, 2-for-5 (.400). 1985-86, 0-for-3. 1988-89, 13-for-38 (.342). 1989-90, 15-for-38 (.395). 1990-91, 4-for-15 (.267). 1991-92, 4-for-22 (.182). 1992-93, 12-for-36 (.333). 1995-96, 0-for-2. Totals, 50-for-159 (.314).
Personal fouls/disqualifications: 1983-84, 8/0. 1985-86, 7/0. 1988-89, 41/1. 1989-90, 40/0. 1990-91, 13/0. 1991-92, 19/0. 1992-93, 44/2. Totals, 172/3.

GREEK LEAGUE RECORD

Season Team	G	Min.	FGM	FGA	Pct.	FTM	FTA	Pct.	Reb.	Ast.	Pts.	RPG	APG	PPG
94-95—Olympiakos S.F.P.	25	829	188	419	.449	92	109	.844	122	48	527	4.9	1.9	21.1

JOHNSON, ERVIN   C   NUGGETS

PERSONAL: Born December 21, 1967, in New Orleans. ... 6-11/245. ... Full name: Ervin Johnson Jr.
HIGH SCHOOL: Block (Jonesville, La.).
COLLEGE: New Orleans.
TRANSACTIONS/CAREER NOTES: Selected by Seattle SuperSonics in first round (23rd pick overall) of 1993 NBA Draft. ... Rights renounced by SuperSonics (July 16, 1996). ... Signed as free agent by Denver Nuggets (July 17, 1996).

COLLEGIATE RECORD

Season Team	G	Min.	FGM	FGA	Pct.	FTM	FTA	Pct.	Reb.	Ast.	Pts.	RPG	APG	PPG
88-89—New Orleans						Did not play—redshirted.								
89-90—New Orleans	32	757	84	145	.579	32	57	.561	218	29	200	6.8	0.9	6.3
90-91—New Orleans	30	899	162	283	.572	58	108	.537	367	34	382	12.2	1.1	12.7
91-92—New Orleans	32	1073	185	317	.584	122	171	.713	356	56	492	11.1	1.8	15.4
92-93—New Orleans	29	965	208	336	.619	118	175	.674	346	16	534	11.9	0.6	18.4
Totals	123	3694	639	1081	.591	330	511	.646	1287	135	1608	10.5	1.1	13.1

NBA REGULAR-SEASON RECORD

Season Team	G	Min.	FGM	FGA	Pct.	FTM	FTA	Pct.	Off.	Def.	Tot.	Ast.	St.	Blk.	TO	Pts.	RPG	APG	PPG
93-94—Seattle	45	280	44	106	.415	29	46	.630	48	70	118	7	10	22	24	117	2.6	0.2	2.6
94-95—Seattle	64	907	85	192	.443	29	46	.630	101	188	289	16	17	67	54	199	4.5	0.3	3.1
95-96—Seattle	81	1519	180	352	.511	85	127	.669	129	304	433	48	40	129	98	446	5.3	0.6	5.5
Totals	190	2706	309	650	.475	143	219	.653	278	562	840	71	67	218	176	762	4.4	0.4	4.0

Three-point field goals: 1994-95, 0-for-1. 1995-96, 1-for-3 (.333). Totals, 1-for-4 (.250).
Personal fouls/disqualifications: 1993-94, 45/0. 1994-95, 163/1. 1995-96, 245/3. Totals, 453/4.

Season Team	G	Min.	FGM	FGA	Pct.	FTM	FTA	Pct.	Off.	Def.	Tot.	Ast.	St.	Blk.	TO	Pts.	RPG	APG	PPG
									REBOUNDS								AVERAGES		
93-94—Seattle	2	8	0	1	.000	0	0	...	0	4	4	0	0	0	1	0	2.0	0.0	0.0
94-95—Seattle	4	54	4	14	.286	6	6	1.000	8	13	21	0	1	4	1	14	5.3	0.0	3.5
95-96—Seattle	18	253	23	62	.371	9	11	.818	28	42	70	7	6	15	14	55	3.9	0.4	3.1
Totals	24	315	27	77	.351	15	17	.882	36	59	95	7	7	19	16	69	4.0	0.3	2.9

Personal fouls/disqualifications: 1993-94, 1/0. 1994-95, 16/0. 1995-96, 45/0. Totals, 62/0.

JOHNSON, KEVIN   G   SUNS

PERSONAL: Born March 4, 1966, in Sacramento. ... 6-1/190. ... Full name: Kevin Maurice Johnson.
HIGH SCHOOL: Sacramento.
COLLEGE: California.
TRANSACTIONS/CAREER NOTES: Selected by Cleveland Cavaliers in first round (seventh pick overall) of 1987 NBA Draft. ... Traded by Cavaliers with G/F Tyrone Corbin, F/C Mark West, 1988 first- and second-round draft choices and 1989 second-round draft choice to Phoenix Suns for F Larry Nance, F Mike Sanders and 1988 second-round draft choice (February 25, 1988).
MISCELLANEOUS: Phoenix Suns all-time assists leader with 5,596 (1987-88 through 1995-96).

COLLEGIATE RECORD

Season Team	G	Min.	FGM	FGA	Pct.	FTM	FTA	Pct.	Reb.	Ast.	Pts.	RPG	APG	PPG
												AVERAGES		
83-84—California	28	773	98	192	.510	75	104	.721	83	65	271	3.0	2.3	9.7
84-85—California	27	902	127	282	.450	94	142	.662	104	111	348	3.9	4.1	12.9
85-86—California	29	1024	164	335	.490	123	151	.815	104	175	451	3.6	6.0	15.6
86-87—California	34	1115	212	450	.471	113	138	.819	132	170	585	3.9	5.0	17.2
Totals	118	3814	601	1259	.477	405	535	.757	423	521	1655	3.6	4.4	14.0

Three-point field goals: 1986-87, 48-for-124 (.387).

NBA REGULAR-SEASON RECORD

HONORS: NBA Most Improved Player (1989). ... All-NBA second team (1989, 1990, 1991, 1994). ... All-NBA third team (1992).

Season Team	G	Min.	FGM	FGA	Pct.	FTM	FTA	Pct.	Off.	Def.	Tot.	Ast.	St.	Blk.	TO	Pts.	RPG	APG	PPG
									REBOUNDS								AVERAGES		
87-88—Clev.-Phoe.	80	1917	275	596	.461	177	211	.839	36	155	191	437	103	24	146	732	2.4	5.5	9.2
88-89—Phoenix	81	3179	570	1128	.505	508	576	.882	46	294	340	991	135	24	*322	1650	4.2	12.2	20.4
89-90—Phoenix	74	2782	578	1159	.499	501	598	.838	42	228	270	846	95	14	263	1665	3.6	11.4	22.5
90-91—Phoenix	77	2772	591	1145	.516	519	616	.843	54	217	271	781	163	11	269	1710	3.5	10.1	22.2
91-92—Phoenix	78	2899	539	1125	.479	448	555	.807	61	231	292	836	116	23	272	1536	3.7	10.7	19.7
92-93—Phoenix	49	1643	282	565	.499	226	276	.819	30	74	104	384	85	19	151	791	2.1	7.8	16.1
93-94—Phoenix	67	2449	477	980	.487	380	464	.819	55	112	167	637	125	10	235	1340	2.5	9.5	20.0
94-95—Phoenix	47	1352	246	523	.470	234	289	.810	32	83	115	360	47	18	105	730	2.4	7.7	15.5
95-96—Phoenix	56	2007	342	674	.507	342	398	.859	42	179	221	517	82	13	170	1047	3.9	9.2	18.7
Totals	609	21000	3900	7895	.494	3335	3983	.837	398	1573	1971	5789	951	156	1933	11201	3.2	9.5	18.4

Three-point field goals: 1987-88, 5-for-24 (.208). 1988-89, 2-for-22 (.091). 1989-90, 8-for-41 (.195). 1990-91, 9-for-44 (.205). 1991-92, 10-for-46 (.217). 1992-93, 1-for-8 (.125). 1993-94, 6-for-27 (.222). 1994-95, 4-for-26 (.154). 1995-96, 21-for-57 (.368). Totals, 66-for-295 (.224).
Personal fouls/disqualifications: 1987-88, 155/1. 1988-89, 226/1. 1989-90, 143/0. 1990-91, 174/0. 1991-92, 180/0. 1992-93, 100/0. 1993-94, 127/1. 1994-95, 88/0. 1995-96, 144/0. Totals, 1337/3.

NBA PLAYOFF RECORD

NOTES: Holds NBA Finals single-game record for most minutes played—62 (June 13, 1993, at Chicago, 3 OT).

Season Team	G	Min.	FGM	FGA	Pct.	FTM	FTA	Pct.	Off.	Def.	Tot.	Ast.	St.	Blk.	TO	Pts.	RPG	APG	PPG
									REBOUNDS								AVERAGES		
88-89—Phoenix	12	494	90	182	.495	102	110	.927	12	39	51	147	19	5	55	285	4.3	12.3	23.8
89-90—Phoenix	16	582	123	257	.479	92	112	.821	9	44	53	170	25	0	62	340	3.3	10.6	21.3
90-91—Phoenix	4	146	16	53	.302	18	30	.600	2	11	13	39	2	1	12	51	3.3	9.8	12.8
91-92—Phoenix	8	335	62	128	.484	62	72	.861	8	25	33	93	12	2	25	189	4.1	11.6	23.6
92-93—Phoenix	23	914	143	298	.480	124	156	.795	10	52	62	182	35	13	84	410	2.7	7.9	17.8
93-94—Phoenix	10	427	97	212	.458	69	81	.852	10	25	35	96	10	1	34	266	3.5	9.6	26.6
94-95—Phoenix	10	371	86	150	.573	71	84	.845	7	34	41	93	9	4	34	248	4.1	9.3	24.8
95-96—Phoenix	4	151	27	57	.474	14	17	.824	2	15	17	43	2	2	11	69	4.3	10.8	17.3
Totals	87	3420	644	1337	.482	552	662	.834	60	245	305	863	114	28	317	1858	3.5	9.9	21.4

Three-point field goals: 1988-89, 3-for-10 (.300). 1989-90, 2-for-11 (.182). 1990-91, 1-for-7 (.143). 1991-92, 3-for-6 (.500). 1992-93, 0-for-3. 1993-94, 3-for-10 (.300). 1994-95, 5-for-10 (.500). 1995-96, 1-for-4 (.250). Totals, 18-for-61 (.295).
Personal fouls/disqualifications: 1988-89, 28/0. 1989-90, 28/0. 1990-91, 9/0. 1991-92, 24/1. 1992-93, 57/1. 1993-94, 23/0. 1994-95, 25/0. 1995-96, 8/0. Totals, 202/2.

NBA ALL-STAR GAME RECORD

Season Team	Min.	FGM	FGA	Pct.	FTM	FTA	Pct.	Off.	Def.	Tot.	Ast.	PF	Dq.	St.	Blk.	TO	Pts.
								REBOUNDS									
1990 —Phoenix	14	1	1	1.000	0	0	...	0	0	0	4	2	0	0	0	3	2
1991 —Phoenix	23	2	5	.400	1	2	.500	1	1	2	7	2	0	3	1	3	5
1994 —Phoenix	14	3	6	.500	0	1	.000	0	1	1	2	1	0	1	0	2	6
Totals	51	6	12	.500	1	3	.333	1	2	3	13	5	0	4	1	8	13

RECORD AS BASEBALL PLAYER

TRANSACTIONS/CAREER NOTES: Threw right, batted both. ... Selected by Oakland Athletics organization in 23rd round of free-agent draft (June 2, 1986).

Year Team (League)	Pos.	G	AB	R	H	2B	3B	HR	RBI	Avg.	BB	SO	SB	PO	A	E	Avg.
			BATTING											FIELDING			
1986—Modesto(California)	SS	2	2	1	0	0	0	0	0	.000	0	2	0	1	2	1	.750

JOHNSON, LARRY   F   KNICKS

PERSONAL: Born March 14, 1969, in Tyler, Texas. ... 6-7/263. ... Full name: Larry Demetric Johnson.
HIGH SCHOOL: Skyline (Dallas).
JUNIOR COLLEGE: Odessa (Texas) Junior College.
COLLEGE: UNLV.
TRANSACTIONS/CAREER NOTES: Selected by Charlotte Hornets in first round (first pick overall) of 1991 NBA Draft. ... Traded by Hornets to New York Knicks for F Anthony Mason and F Brad Lohaus (July 14, 1996).
MISCELLANEOUS: Charlotte Hornets all-time leading rebounder with 3,479 (1991-92 through 1995-96).

COLLEGIATE RECORD

NOTES: THE SPORTING NEWS College Player of the Year (1991). ... Naismith Award winner (1991). ... Wooden Award winner (1991). ... THE SPORTING NEWS All-America first team (1990, 1991). ... Member of NCAA Division I championship team (1990).

Season Team	G	Min.	FGM	FGA	Pct.	FTM	FTA	Pct.	Reb.	Ast.	Pts.	RPG	APG	PPG
87-88—Odessa J.C.	35	...	324	499	.649	131	167	.784	430	...	779	12.3	...	22.3
88-89—Odessa J.C.	35	...	422	646	.653	196	258	.760	380	69	1043	10.9	2.0	29.8
89-90—UNLV	40	1259	304	487	.624	201	262	.767	457	84	822	11.4	2.1	20.6
90-91—UNLV	35	1113	308	465	.662	162	198	.818	380	104	795	10.9	3.0	22.7
Junior college totals	70	...	746	1145	.652	327	425	.769	810	...	1822	11.6	...	26.0
4-year-college totals	75	2372	612	952	.643	363	460	.789	837	188	1617	11.2	2.5	21.6

Three-point field goals: 1989-90, 13-for-38 (.342). 1990-91, 17-for-48 (.354). Totals, 30-for-86 (.349).

NBA REGULAR-SEASON RECORD

HONORS: NBA Rookie of the Year (1992). ... All-NBA second team (1993). ... NBA All-Rookie first team (1992).

Season Team	G	Min.	FGM	FGA	Pct.	FTM	FTA	Pct.	Off.	Def.	Tot.	Ast.	St.	Blk.	TO	Pts.	RPG	APG	PPG
91-92—Charlotte	82	3047	616	1258	.490	339	409	.829	323	576	899	292	81	51	160	1576	11.0	3.6	19.2
92-93—Charlotte	82	*3323	728	1385	.526	336	438	.767	281	583	864	353	53	27	227	1810	10.5	4.3	22.1
93-94—Charlotte	51	1757	346	672	.515	137	197	.695	143	305	448	184	29	14	116	834	8.8	3.6	16.4
94-95—Charlotte	81	3234	585	1219	.480	274	354	.774	190	395	585	369	78	28	207	1525	7.2	4.6	18.8
95-96—Charlotte	81	3274	583	1225	.476	427	564	.757	249	434	683	355	55	43	182	1660	8.4	4.4	20.5
Totals	377	14635	2858	5759	.496	1513	1962	.771	1186	2293	3479	1553	296	163	892	7405	9.2	4.1	19.6

Three-point field goals: 1991-92, 5-for-22 (.227). 1992-93, 18-for-71 (.254). 1993-94, 5-for-21 (.238). 1994-95, 81-for-210 (.386). 1995-96, 67-for-183 (.366). Totals, 176-for-507 (.347).
Personal fouls/disqualifications: 1991-92, 225/3. 1992-93, 187/0. 1993-94, 131/0. 1994-95, 174/2. 1995-96, 173/0. Totals, 890/5.

NBA PLAYOFF RECORD

Season Team	G	Min.	FGM	FGA	Pct.	FTM	FTA	Pct.	Off.	Def.	Tot.	Ast.	St.	Blk.	TO	Pts.	RPG	APG	PPG
92-93—Charlotte	9	348	68	122	.557	41	52	.788	19	43	62	30	5	2	19	178	6.9	3.3	19.8
94-95—Charlotte	4	172	31	65	.477	20	25	.800	10	13	23	11	4	2	6	83	5.8	2.8	20.8
Totals	13	520	99	187	.529	61	77	.792	29	56	85	41	9	4	25	261	6.5	3.2	20.1

Three-point field goals: 1992-93, 1-for-4 (.250). 1994-95, 1-for-9 (.111). Totals, 2-for-13 (.154).
Personal fouls/disqualifications: 1992-93, 27/0. 1994-95, 7/0. Totals, 34/0.

NBA ALL-STAR GAME RECORD

Season Team	Min.	FGM	FGA	Pct.	FTM	FTA	Pct.	Off.	Def.	Tot.	Ast.	PF	Dq.	St.	Blk.	TO	Pts.
1993 —Charlotte	16	2	6	.333	0	0	...	3	1	4	0	1	0	0	0	0	4
1995 —Charlotte	20	2	3	.667	2	2	1.000	1	3	4	2	0	0	0	0	1	7
Totals	36	4	9	.444	2	2	1.000	4	4	8	2	1	0	0	0	1	11

Three-point field goals: 1995, 1-for-1.

JOHNSON, MAGIC   G

PERSONAL: Born August 14, 1959, in Lansing, Mich. ... 6-9/255. ... Full name: Earvin Johnson Jr.
HIGH SCHOOL: Everett (Lansing, Mich.).
COLLEGE: Michigan State.
TRANSACTIONS/CAREER NOTES: Selected after sophomore season by Los Angeles Lakers in first round (first pick overall) of 1979 NBA Draft. ... On voluntarily retired list (November 7, 1991-January 29, 1996). ... Activated from retirement by Lakers (January 29, 1996). ... Announced retirement (May 14, 1996). ... Rights renounced by Lakers (July 16, 1996).
MISCELLANEOUS: Member of NBA championship teams (1980, 1982, 1985, 1987, 1988). ... Member of gold-medal-winning U.S. Olympic team (1992). ... Los Angeles Lakers all-time assists leader with 10,141 and all-time steals leader with 1,724 (1979-80 through 1990-91 and 1995-96).

COLLEGIATE RECORD

NOTES: THE SPORTING NEWS All-America first team (1979). ... NCAA Division I Tournament Most Outstanding Player (1979). ... Member of NCAA championship team (1979).

Season Team	G	Min.	FGM	FGA	Pct.	FTM	FTA	Pct.	Reb.	Ast.	Pts.	RPG	APG	PPG
77-78—Michigan State	30	...	175	382	.458	161	205	.785	237	222	511	7.9	7.4	17.0
78-79—Michigan State	32	1159	173	370	.468	202	240	.842	234	269	548	7.3	8.4	17.1
Totals	62	...	348	752	.463	363	445	.816	471	491	1059	7.6	7.9	17.1

NBA REGULAR-SEASON RECORD

HONORS: NBA Most Valuable Player (1987, 1989, 1990). ... IBM Award, for all-around contributions to team's success (1984). ... Citizenship Award (1992). ... All-NBA first team (1983, 1984, 1985, 1986, 1987, 1988, 1989, 1990, 1991). ... All-NBA second team (1982). ... NBA All-Rookie team (1980).
NOTES: Led NBA with 3.43 steals per game (1981) and 2.67 steals per game (1982).

Season Team	G	Min.	FGM	FGA	Pct.	FTM	FTA	Pct.	REBOUNDS Off.	Def.	Tot.	Ast.	St.	Blk.	TO	Pts.	AVERAGES RPG	APG	PPG
79-80—Los Angeles....	77	2795	503	949	.530	374	462	.810	166	430	596	563	187	41	305	1387	7.7	7.3	18.0
80-81—Los Angeles....	37	1371	312	587	.532	171	225	.760	101	219	320	317	127	27	143	798	8.6	8.6	21.6
81-82—Los Angeles....	78	2991	556	1036	.537	329	433	.760	252	499	751	743	208	34	286	1447	9.6	9.5	18.6
82-83—Los Angeles....	79	2907	511	933	.548	304	380	.800	214	469	683	*829	176	47	301	1326	8.6	*10.5	16.8
83-84—Los Angeles....	67	2567	441	780	.565	290	358	.810	99	392	491	875	150	49	306	1178	7.3	*13.1	17.6
84-85—L.A. Lakers	77	2781	504	899	.561	391	464	.843	90	386	476	968	113	25	305	1406	6.2	*12.6	18.3
85-86—L.A. Lakers	72	2578	483	918	.526	378	434	.871	85	341	426	*907	113	16	273	1354	5.9	*12.6	18.8
86-87—L.A. Lakers	80	2904	683	1308	.522	535	631	.848	122	382	504	*977	138	36	300	1909	6.3	*12.2	23.9
87-88—L.A. Lakers	72	2637	490	996	.492	417	489	.853	88	361	449	858	114	13	269	1408	6.2	11.9	19.6
88-89—L.A. Lakers	77	2886	579	1137	.509	513	563	*.911	111	496	607	988	138	22	312	1730	7.9	12.8	22.5
89-90—L.A. Lakers	79	2937	546	1138	.480	567	637	.890	128	394	522	907	132	34	289	1765	6.6	11.5	22.3
90-91—L.A. Lakers	79	2933	466	976	.477	519	573	.906	105	446	551	989	102	17	*314	1531	7.0	12.5	19.4
91-92—L.A. Lakers......						Did not play—retired.													
92-93—L.A. Lakers......						Did not play—retired.													
93-94—L.A. Lakers......						Did not play—retired.													
94-95—L.A. Lakers......						Did not play—retired.													
95-96—L.A. Lakers	32	958	137	294	.466	172	201	.856	40	143	183	220	26	13	103	468	5.7	6.9	14.6
Totals	906	33245	6211	11951	.520	4960	5850	.848	1601	4958	6559	10141	1724	374	3506	17707	7.2	11.2	19.5

Three-point field goals: 1979-80, 7-for-31 (.226). 1980-81, 3-for-17 (.176). 1981-82, 6-for-29 (.207). 1982-83, 0-for-21. 1983-84, 6-for-29 (.207). 1984-85, 7-for-37 (.189). 1985-86, 10-for-43 (.233). 1986-87, 8-for-39 (.205). 1987-88, 11-for-56 (.196). 1988-89, 59-for-188 (.314). 1989-90, 106-for-276 (.384). 1990-91, 80-for-250 (.320). 1995-96, 22-for-58 (.379). Totals, 325-for-1074 (.303).

Personal fouls/disqualifications: 1979-80, 218/1. 1980-81, 100/0. 1981-82, 223/1. 1982-83, 200/1. 1983-84, 169/1. 1984-85, 155/0. 1985-86, 133/0. 1986-87, 168/0. 1987-88, 147/0. 1988-89, 172/0. 1989-90, 167/1. 1990-91, 150/0. 1995-96, 48/0. Totals, 2050/5.

NBA PLAYOFF RECORD

NOTES: NBA Finals Most Valuable Player (1980, 1982, 1987). ... Holds career playoff records for most assists—2,346; and most steals—358. ... Holds NBA Finals single-series records for highest assists-per-game average—14.0 (1985); and highest assists-per-game average by a rookie—8.7 (1980). ... Holds NBA Finals single-game records for most points by a rookie—42 (May 16, 1980, vs. Philadelphia); most assists—21 (June 3, 1984, vs. Boston); most assists by a rookie—11 (May 7, 1980, vs. Philadelphia); and most assists in one half—14 (June 19, 1988, vs. Detroit). ... Shares NBA Finals single-game record for most assists in one quarter—8 (four times). ... Holds single-series playoff record for highest assists-per-game average—17.0 (1985). ... Holds single-game playoff record for most free throws attempted in one half—21 (May 8, 1991, vs. Golden State). ... Shares single-game playoff records for most free throws made in one half—19 (May 8, 1991, vs. Golden State); most assists—24 (May 15, 1984, vs. Phoenix); and most assists in one half—15 (May 3, 1985, vs. Portland).

Season Team	G	Min.	FGM	FGA	Pct.	FTM	FTA	Pct.	REBOUNDS Off.	Def.	Tot.	Ast.	St.	Blk.	TO	Pts.	AVERAGES RPG	APG	PPG
79-80—Los Angeles	16	658	103	199	.518	85	106	.802	52	116	168	151	49	6	65	293	10.5	9.4	18.3
80-81—Los Angeles	3	127	19	49	.388	13	20	.650	8	33	41	21	8	3	11	51	13.7	7.0	17.0
81-82—Los Angeles	14	562	83	157	.529	77	93	.828	54	104	158	130	40	3	44	243	11.3	9.3	17.4
82-83—Los Angeles	15	643	100	206	.485	68	81	.840	51	77	128	192	34	12	64	268	8.5	12.8	17.9
83-84—Los Angeles	21	837	151	274	.551	80	100	.800	26	113	139	284	42	20	79	382	6.6	13.5	18.2
84-85—L.A. Lakers	19	687	116	226	.513	100	118	.847	19	115	134	289	32	4	76	333	7.1	15.2	17.5
85-86—L.A. Lakers	14	541	110	205	.537	82	107	.766	21	79	100	211	27	1	45	302	7.1	15.1	21.6
86-87—L.A. Lakers	18	666	146	271	.539	98	118	.831	28	111	139	219	31	7	51	392	7.7	12.2	21.8
87-88—L.A. Lakers	24	965	169	329	.514	132	155	.852	32	98	130	303	34	4	83	477	5.4	12.6	19.9
88-89—L.A. Lakers	14	518	85	174	.489	78	86	.907	15	68	83	165	27	3	53	258	5.9	11.8	18.4
89-90—L.A. Lakers	9	376	76	155	.490	70	79	.886	12	45	57	115	11	1	36	227	6.3	12.8	25.2
90-91—L.A. Lakers	19	823	118	268	.440	157	178	.882	23	131	154	240	23	0	77	414	8.1	12.6	21.8
95-96—L.A. Lakers	4	135	15	39	.385	28	33	.848	8	26	34	26	0	0	12	61	8.5	6.5	15.3
Totals	190	7538	1291	2552	.506	1068	1274	.838	349	1116	1465	2346	358	64	696	3701	7.7	12.3	19.5

Three-point field goals: 1979-80, 2-for-8 (.250). 1981-82, 0-for-4. 1982-83, 0-for-11. 1983-84, 0-for-7. 1984-85, 1-for-7 (.143). 1985-86, 0-for-11. 1986-87, 2-for-10 (.200). 1987-88, 7-for-14 (.500). 1988-89, 10-for-35 (.286). 1989-90, 5-for-25 (.200). 1990-91, 21-for-71 (.296). 1995-96, 3-for-9 (.333). Totals, 51-for-212 (.241).

Personal fouls/disqualifications: 1979-80, 47/1. 1980-81, 14/1. 1981-82, 50/0. 1982-83, 49/0. 1983-84, 71/0. 1984-85, 48/0. 1985-86, 43/0. 1986-87, 37/0. 1987-88, 61/0. 1988-89, 30/1. 1989-90, 28/0. 1990-91, 43/0. 1995-96, 3/0. Totals, 524/3.

NBA ALL-STAR GAME RECORD

NOTES: NBA All-Star Game Most Valuable Player (1990, 1992). ... Holds career records for most assists—127; most three-point field goals made—10; and most three-point field goals attempted—21. ... Holds single-game record for most assists—22 (1984, OT).

Season Team	Min.	FGM	FGA	Pct.	FTM	FTA	Pct.	REBOUNDS Off.	Def.	Tot.	Ast.	PF	Dq.	St.	Blk.	TO	Pts.
1980 —Los Angeles	24	5	8	.625	2	2	1.000	2	0	2	4	3	0	3	2	2	12
1982 —Los Angeles	23	5	9	.556	6	7	.857	3	1	4	7	5	0	0	0	1	16
1983 —Los Angeles	33	7	16	.438	3	4	.750	3	2	5	16	2	0	5	0	7	17
1984 —Los Angeles	37	6	13	.462	2	2	1.000	4	5	9	22	3	0	3	2	4	15
1985 —L.A. Lakers	31	7	14	.500	7	8	.875	2	3	5	15	2	0	1	0	3	21
1986 —L.A. Lakers	28	1	3	.333	4	4	1.000	0	4	4	15	4	0	1	0	9	6
1987 —L.A. Lakers	34	4	10	.400	1	2	.500	1	6	7	13	2	0	4	0	1	9
1988 —L.A. Lakers	39	4	15	.267	9	9	1.000	1	6	7	19	5	0	0	2	8	17
1989 —L.A. Lakers					Selected, did not play—injured.												
1990 —L.A. Lakers	25	9	15	.600	0	0	...	1	5	6	4	1	0	0	1	3	22
1991 —L.A. Lakers	28	7	16	.438	0	0	...	1	3	4	3	1	0	0	0	3	16
1992 —L.A. Lakers	29	9	12	.750	4	4	1.000	3	2	5	9	0	0	2	0	7	25
Totals........................	331	64	131	.489	38	42	.905	21	36	57	127	25	0	21	7	48	176

Three-point field goals: 1980, 0-for-1. 1983, 0-for-1. 1984, 1-for-3 (.333). 1986, 0-for-1. 1988, 0-for-1. 1990, 4-for-6 (.667). 1991, 2-for-5 (.400). 1992, 3-for-3. Totals, 10-for-21 (.476).

JONES, CHARLES   F/C   ROCKETS

J

PERSONAL: Born April 3, 1957, in McGehee, Ark. ... 6-9/235. ... Brother of Caldwell Jones, forward/center with four American Basketball Association teams (1973-74 through 1975-76) and four NBA teams (1976-77 through 1989-90); brother of Major Jones, forward/center with Houston Rockets and Detroit Pistons (1979-80 through 1984-85); and brother of Wil Jones, forward with three ABA teams (1969-70 through 1975-76) and Indiana Pacers and Buffalo Braves (1976-77 and 1977-78).

HIGH SCHOOL: Delta (Rohwer, Ark.).

COLLEGE: Albany (Ga.) State.

TRANSACTIONS/CAREER NOTES: Selected by Phoenix Suns in eighth round (165th pick overall) of 1979 NBA Draft. ... Waived by Suns (October 1, 1979). ... Played in Continental Basketball Association with Maine Lumberjacks (1979-80 and 1982-83), Bay State Bombardiers (1983-84) and Tampa Bay Thrillers (1984-85). ... Signed as free agent by Portland Trail Blazers (April 14, 1980). ... Waived by Trail Blazers (July 21, 1980). ... Played in France (1980-81). ... Played in Italy (1981-82). ... Signed as free agent by New York Knicks (September 30, 1983). ... Waived by Knicks (October 24, 1983). ... Signed by Philadelphia 76ers to first of two consecutive 10-day contracts (February 1984). ... Signed as free agent by San Antonio Spurs (May 2, 1984). ... Waived by Spurs (September 11, 1984). ... Signed as free agent by Chicago Bulls (September 20, 1984). ... Waived by Bulls (November 16, 1984). ... Signed as free agent by Washington Bullets (February 14, 1985). ... Rights renounced by Bullets (June 30, 1993). ... Signed by Detroit Pistons to first of two consecutive 10-day contracts (January 21, 1994). ... Waived by Pistons (February 5, 1994). ... Re-signed by Pistons for remainder of season (February 10, 1994). ... Rights renounced by Pistons (September 6, 1994). ... Signed by Houston Rockets to 10-day contract (March 2, 1995). ... Re-signed by Rockets for remainder of season (April 22, 1995).

MISCELLANEOUS: Member of NBA championship team (1995).

COLLEGIATE RECORD

Season Team	G	Min.	FGM	FGA	Pct.	FTM	FTA	Pct.	Reb.	Ast.	Pts.	RPG	APG	PPG
75-76—Albany State	24	...	106	206	.515	16	35	.457	198	...	228	8.3	...	9.5
76-77—Albany State	27	...	136	284	.479	39	84	.464	374	...	311	13.9	...	11.5
77-78—Albany State	27	...	148	276	.536	68	100	.680	368	...	364	13.6	...	13.5
78-79—Albany State	29	...	182	352	.517	66	97	.680	438	41	430	15.1	1.4	14.8
Totals	107	...	572	1118	.512	189	316	.598	1378	...	1333	12.9	...	12.5

CBA REGULAR-SEASON RECORD

NOTES: CBA All-League second team (1984). ... CBA All-Defensive first team (1983, 1984). ... CBA All-Defensive second team (1985). ... Led CBA with 185 blocked shots (1980) and 130 blocked shots (1984). ... Led CBA with 4.7 blocked shots per game (1980), 4.0 blocked shots per game (1983) and 3.5 blocked shots per game (1984).

Season Team	G	Min.	FGM	FGA	Pct.	FTM	FTA	Pct.	Reb.	Ast.	Pts.	RPG	APG	PPG
79-80—Maine	39	1606	222	461	.482	60	94	.638	506	70	504	13.0	1.8	12.9
82-83—Maine	24	914	105	216	.486	70	89	.787	223	35	280	9.3	1.5	11.7
83-84—Bay State	37	1365	149	298	.500	94	139	.676	293	73	392	7.9	2.0	10.6
84-85—Tampa Bay	24	802	80	155	.516	38	53	.717	227	38	198	9.5	1.6	8.3
Totals	124	4687	556	1130	.492	262	375	.699	1249	216	1374	10.1	1.7	11.1

Three-point field goals: 1979-80, 0-for-2. 1982-83, 0-for-1. 1983-84, 0-for-1. 1984-85, 0-for-1. Totals, 0-for-5.

ITALIAN LEAGUE RECORD

Season Team	G	Min.	FGM	FGA	Pct.	FTM	FTA	Pct.	Reb.	Ast.	Pts.	RPG	APG	PPG
81-82—S. Benedetto	38	1458	215	398	.540	73	114	.640	429	...	503	11.3	...	13.2

NBA REGULAR-SEASON RECORD

Season Team	G	Min.	FGM	FGA	Pct.	FTM	FTA	Pct.	Off.	Def.	Tot.	Ast.	St.	Blk.	TO	Pts.	RPG	APG	PPG
83-84—Philadelphia	1	3	0	1	.000	1	4	.250	0	0	0	0	0	0	0	1	0.0	0.0	1.0
84-85—Chi.-Wash.	31	667	67	127	.528	40	58	.690	71	113	184	26	22	79	25	174	5.9	0.8	5.6
85-86—Washington	81	1609	129	254	.508	54	86	.628	122	199	321	76	57	133	71	312	4.0	0.9	3.9
86-87—Washington	79	1609	118	249	.474	48	76	.632	144	212	356	80	67	165	77	284	4.5	1.0	3.6
87-88—Washington	69	1313	72	177	.407	53	75	.707	106	219	325	59	53	113	57	197	4.7	0.9	2.9
88-89—Washington	53	1154	60	125	.480	16	25	.640	77	180	257	42	39	76	39	136	4.8	0.8	2.6
89-90—Washington	81	2240	94	185	.508	68	105	.648	145	359	504	139	50	197	76	256	6.2	1.7	3.2
90-91—Washington	62	1499	67	124	.540	29	50	.580	119	240	359	48	51	124	46	163	5.8	0.8	2.6
91-92—Washington	75	1365	33	90	.367	20	40	.500	105	212	317	62	43	92	39	86	4.2	0.8	1.1
92-93—Washington	67	1206	33	63	.524	22	38	.579	87	190	277	42	38	77	38	88	4.1	0.6	1.3
93-94—Detroit	42	877	36	78	.462	19	34	.559	89	146	235	29	14	43	12	91	5.6	0.7	2.2
94-95—Houston	3	36	1	3	.333	1	2	.500	2	5	7	0	1	0	1	3	2.3	0.0	1.0
95-96—Houston	46	297	6	19	.316	4	13	.308	28	46	74	12	5	24	3	16	1.6	0.3	0.3
Totals	690	13875	716	1495	.479	375	606	.619	1095	2121	3216	615	439	1124	483	1807	4.7	0.9	2.6

Three-point field goals: 1985-86, 0-for-2. 1986-87, 0-for-1. 1987-88, 0-for-1. 1988-89, 0-for-1. 1992-93, 0-for-1. 1993-94, 0-for-1. Totals, 0-for-7.

Personal fouls/disqualifications: 1983-84, 1/0. 1984-85, 107/3. 1985-86, 235/2. 1986-87, 252/2. 1987-88, 226/5. 1988-89, 187/4. 1989-90, 296/10. 1990-91, 199/2. 1991-92, 214/0. 1992-93, 144/1. 1993-94, 136/3. 1994-95, 8/0. 1995-96, 44/0. Totals, 2049/32.

NBA PLAYOFF RECORD

Season Team	G	Min.	FGM	FGA	Pct.	FTM	FTA	Pct.	Off.	Def.	Tot.	Ast.	St.	Blk.	TO	Pts.	RPG	APG	PPG
84-85—Washington	4	110	10	19	.526	9	16	.563	11	15	26	3	3	10	6	29	6.5	0.8	7.3
85-86—Washington	5	72	4	11	.364	4	4	1.000	6	3	9	3	2	2	5	12	1.8	0.6	2.4
86-87—Washington	3	56	3	5	.600	0	0	...	1	7	8	3	2	5	1	6	2.7	1.0	2.0
87-88—Washington	5	95	1	5	.200	1	2	.500	5	12	17	2	2	4	0	3	3.4	0.4	0.6
94-95—Houston	19	237	5	13	.385	4	12	.333	12	32	44	0	4	10	5	14	2.3	0.0	0.7
95-96—Houston	3	8	0	1	.000	0	0	...	0	1	1	0	0	0	0	0	0.3	0.0	0.0
Totals	39	578	23	54	.426	18	34	.529	35	70	105	11	13	31	17	64	2.7	0.3	1.6

Three-point field goals: 1994-95, 0-for-1.

Personal fouls/disqualifications: 1984-85, 16/0. 1985-86, 13/0. 1986-87, 9/0. 1987-88, 18/0. 1994-95, 55/0. Totals, 111/0.

J

JONES, EDDIE   G/F   LAKERS

PERSONAL: Born October 20, 1971, in Pompano Beach, Fla. ... 6-6/190. ... Full name: Eddie Charles Jones.
HIGH SCHOOL: Ely (Pompano Beach, Fla.).
COLLEGE: Temple.
TRANSACTIONS/CAREER NOTES: Selected by Los Angeles Lakers in first round (10th pick overall) of 1994 NBA Draft.

COLLEGIATE RECORD

Season Team	G	Min.	FGM	FGA	Pct.	FTM	FTA	Pct.	Reb.	Ast.	Pts.	RPG	APG	PPG
90-91—Temple						Did not play—ineligible.								
91-92—Temple	29	764	122	279	.437	41	75	.547	122	30	332	4.2	1.0	11.4
92-93—Temple	32	1169	212	463	.458	70	116	.603	225	56	543	7.0	1.8	17.0
93-94—Temple	31	1184	231	491	.470	88	133	.662	210	58	595	6.8	1.9	19.2
Totals	92	3117	565	1233	.458	199	324	.614	557	144	1470	6.1	1.6	16.0

Three-point field goals: 1991-92, 47-for-134 (.351). 1992-93, 49-for-141 (.348). 1993-94, 45-for-128 (.352). Totals, 141-for-403 (.350).

HONORS: NBA All-Rookie first team (1995).

NBA REGULAR-SEASON RECORD

Season Team	G	Min.	FGM	FGA	Pct.	FTM	FTA	Pct.	Off.	Def.	Tot.	Ast.	St.	Blk.	TO	Pts.	RPG	APG	PPG
94-95—L.A. Lakers	64	1981	342	744	.460	122	169	.722	79	170	249	128	131	41	75	897	3.9	2.0	14.0
95-96—L.A. Lakers	70	2184	337	685	.492	136	184	.739	45	188	233	246	129	45	99	893	3.3	3.5	12.8
Totals	134	4165	679	1429	.475	258	353	.731	124	358	482	374	260	86	174	1790	3.6	2.8	13.4

Three-point field goals: 1994-95, 91-for-246 (.370). 1995-96, 83-for-227 (.366). Totals, 174-for-473 (.368).
Personal fouls/disqualifications: 1994-95, 175/1. 1995-96, 162/0. Totals, 337/1.

NBA PLAYOFF RECORD

Season Team	G	Min.	FGM	FGA	Pct.	FTM	FTA	Pct.	Off.	Def.	Tot.	Ast.	St.	Blk.	TO	Pts.	RPG	APG	PPG
94-95—L.A. Lakers	10	286	30	80	.375	15	21	.714	7	25	32	20	8	9	17	87	3.2	2.0	8.7
95-96—L.A. Lakers	4	155	27	49	.551	5	8	.625	7	14	21	6	8	1	4	69	5.3	1.5	17.3
Totals	14	441	57	129	.442	20	29	.690	14	39	53	26	16	10	21	156	3.8	1.9	11.1

Three-point field goals: 1994-95, 12-for-27 (.444). 1995-96, 10-for-19 (.526). Totals, 22-for-46 (.478).
Personal fouls/disqualifications: 1994-95, 27/0. 1995-96, 16/0. Totals, 43/0.

JONES, POPEYE   F   RAPTORS

PERSONAL: Born June 17, 1970, in Dresden, Tenn. ... 6-8/250. ... Full name: Ronald Jerome Jones.
HIGH SCHOOL: Dresden (Tenn.).
COLLEGE: Murray State.
TRANSACTIONS/CAREER NOTES: Selected by Houston Rockets in second round (41st pick overall) of 1992 NBA Draft. ... Played in Italy (1992-93). ... Draft rights traded by Rockets to Dallas Mavericks for draft rights to C Eric Riley (June 30, 1993). ... Traded by Mavericks with 1997 first-round draft choice to Toronto Raptors for G Jimmy King and 1997 and 1998 second-round draft choices (July 23, 1996).

COLLEGIATE RECORD

NOTES: Led NCAA Division I with 14.4 rebounds per game (1992).

Season Team	G	Min.	FGM	FGA	Pct.	FTM	FTA	Pct.	Reb.	Ast.	Pts.	RPG	APG	PPG
88-89—Murray State	30	518	65	133	.489	43	57	.754	138	21	173	4.6	0.7	5.8
89-90—Murray State	30	1038	217	434	.500	137	181	.757	336	59	586	11.2	2.0	19.5
90-91—Murray State	33	1052	268	544	.493	123	173	.711	469	69	666	14.2	2.1	20.2
91-92—Murray State	30	994	232	475	.488	161	207	.778	431	72	632	14.4	2.4	21.1
Totals	123	3602	782	1586	.493	464	618	.751	1374	221	2057	11.2	1.8	16.7

Three-point field goals: 1989-90, 15-for-34 (.441). 1990-91, 7-for-32 (.219). 1991-92, 7-for-18 (.389). Totals, 29-for-84 (.345).

ITALIAN LEAGUE RECORD

Season Team	G	Min.	FGM	FGA	Pct.	FTM	FTA	Pct.	Reb.	Ast.	Pts.	RPG	APG	PPG
92-93—Teorematour Milan	30	1094	217	353	.615	145	189	.767	398	37	633	13.3	1.2	21.1

NBA REGULAR-SEASON RECORD

Season Team	G	Min.	FGM	FGA	Pct.	FTM	FTA	Pct.	Off.	Def.	Tot.	Ast.	St.	Blk.	TO	Pts.	RPG	APG	PPG
93-94—Dallas	81	1773	195	407	.479	78	107	.729	299	306	605	99	61	31	94	468	7.5	1.2	5.8
94-95—Dallas	80	2385	372	839	.443	80	124	.645	*329	515	844	163	35	27	124	825	10.6	2.0	10.3
95-96—Dallas	68	2322	327	733	.446	102	133	.767	260	477	737	132	54	27	109	770	10.8	1.9	11.3
Totals	229	6480	894	1979	.452	260	364	.714	888	1298	2186	394	150	85	327	2063	9.5	1.7	9.0

Three-point field goals: 1993-94, 0-for-1. 1994-95, 1-for-12 (.083). 1995-96, 14-for-39 (.359). Totals, 15-for-52 (.288).
Personal fouls/disqualifications: 1993-94, 246/2. 1994-95, 267/5. 1995-96, 262/8. Totals, 775/15.

JORDAN, MICHAEL   G   BULLS

PERSONAL: Born February 17, 1963, in Brooklyn, N.Y. ... 6-6/216. ... Full name: Michael Jeffrey Jordan.
HIGH SCHOOL: Emsley A. Laney (Wilmington, N.C.).
COLLEGE: North Carolina.
TRANSACTIONS/CAREER NOTES: Selected after junior season by Chicago Bulls in first round (third pick overall) of 1984 NBA Draft. ... On voluntarily retired list (October 6, 1993-March 18, 1995). ... Activated from retirement (March 18, 1995).

MISCELLANEOUS: Member of NBA championship teams (1991, 1992, 1993, 1996). ... Member of gold-medal-winning U.S. Olympic teams (1984, 1992). ... Chicago Bulls all-time leading scorer with 24,489 points, all-time assists leader with 4,377 and all-time steals leader with 2,025 (1984-85 through 1992-93, 1994-95 and 1995-96).

COLLEGIATE RECORD

NOTES: The Sporting News College Player of the Year (1983, 1984). ... Naismith Award winner (1984). ... Wooden Award winner (1984). ... The Sporting News All-America first team (1983, 1984). ... Member of NCAA Division I championship team (1982).

Season Team	G	Min.	FGM	FGA	Pct.	FTM	FTA	Pct.	Reb.	Ast.	Pts.	RPG	APG	PPG
81-82—North Carolina	34	1079	191	358	.534	78	108	.722	149	61	460	4.4	1.8	13.5
82-83—North Carolina	36	1113	282	527	.535	123	167	.737	197	56	721	5.5	1.6	20.0
83-84—North Carolina	31	915	247	448	.551	113	145	.779	163	64	607	5.3	2.1	19.6
Totals	101	3107	720	1333	.540	314	420	.748	509	181	1788	5.0	1.8	17.7

Three-point field goals: 1982-83, 34-for-76 (.447).

NBA REGULAR-SEASON RECORD

RECORDS: Holds career record for most seasons leading league in scoring—8; and highest points-per-game average (minimum 400 games or 10,000 points)—32.0. ... Shares career records for most seasons with 2,000 or more points—9; and most consecutive seasons leading league in scoring—7 (1986-87 through 1992-93). ... Holds single-game records for most free throws made in one half—20 (December 30, 1992, at Miami); and most free-throws attempted in one half—23 (December 30, 1992, at Miami). ... Shares single-game records for most free throws made in one quarter—14 (November 15, 1989, vs. Utah and December 30, 1992, at Miami); and most free throws attempted in one quarter—16 (December 30, 1992, at Miami).

HONORS: NBA Most Valuable Player (1988, 1991, 1992, 1996). ... NBA Defensive Player of the Year (1988). ... NBA Rookie of the Year (1985). ... IBM Award, for all-around contribution to team's success (1985, 1989). ... Slam-Dunk Championship winner (1987, 1988). ... All-NBA first team (1987, 1988, 1989, 1990, 1991, 1992, 1993, 1996). ... All-NBA second team (1985). ... NBA All-Defensive first team (1988, 1989, 1990, 1991, 1992, 1993, 1996). ... NBA All-Rookie team (1985).

NOTES: Led NBA with 3.16 steals per game (1988), 2.77 steals per game (1990) and 2.83 steals per game (1993).

Season Team	G	Min.	FGM	FGA	Pct.	FTM	FTA	Pct.	Off.	Def.	Tot.	Ast.	St.	Blk.	TO	Pts.	RPG	APG	PPG
84-85—Chicago	82	3144	837	1625	.515	630	746	.845	167	367	534	481	196	69	291	*2313	6.5	5.9	28.2
85-86—Chicago	18	451	150	328	.457	105	125	.840	23	41	64	53	37	21	45	408	3.6	2.9	22.7
86-87—Chicago	82	*3281	*1098	*2279	.482	*833	*972	.857	166	264	430	377	236	125	272	*3041	5.2	4.6	*37.1
87-88—Chicago	82	*3311	*1069	*1998	.535	*723	860	.841	139	310	449	485	*259	131	252	*2868	5.5	5.9	*35.0
88-89—Chicago	81	*3255	*966	*1795	.538	674	793	.850	149	503	652	650	234	65	290	*2633	8.0	8.0	*32.5
89-90—Chicago	82	3197	*1034	*1964	.526	593	699	.848	143	422	565	519	*227	54	247	*2753	6.9	6.3	*33.6
90-91—Chicago	82	3034	*990	*1837	.539	571	671	.851	118	374	492	453	223	83	202	*2580	6.0	5.5	*31.5
91-92—Chicago	80	3102	*943	*1818	.519	491	590	.832	91	420	511	489	182	75	200	*2404	6.4	6.1	*30.1
92-93—Chicago	78	3067	*992	*2003	.495	476	569	.837	135	387	522	428	*221	61	207	*2541	6.7	5.5	*32.6
93-94—Chicago								Did not play—retired.											
94-95—Chicago	17	668	166	404	.411	109	136	.801	25	92	117	90	30	13	35	457	6.9	5.3	26.9
95-96—Chicago	82	3090	*916	*1850	.495	548	657	.834	148	395	543	352	180	42	197	*2491	6.6	4.3	*30.4
Totals	766	29600	9161	17901	.512	5753	6818	.844	1304	3575	4879	4377	2025	739	2238	24489	6.4	5.7	32.0

Three-point field goals: 1984-85, 9-for-52 (.173). 1985-86, 3-for-18 (.167). 1986-87, 12-for-66 (.182). 1987-88, 7-for-53 (.132). 1988-89, 27-for-98 (.276). 1989-90, 92-for-245 (.376). 1990-91, 29-for-93 (.312). 1991-92, 27-for-100 (.270). 1992-93, 81-for-230 (.352). 1994-95, 16-for-32 (.500). 1995-96, 111-for-260 (.427). Totals, 414-for-1247 (.332).

Personal fouls/disqualifications: 1984-85, 285/4. 1985-86, 46/0. 1986-87, 237/0. 1987-88, 270/2. 1988-89, 247/2. 1989-90, 241/0. 1990-91, 229/1. 1991-92, 201/1. 1992-93, 188/0. 1994-95, 47/0. 1995-96, 195/0. Totals, 2186/10.

NBA PLAYOFF RECORD

NOTES: NBA Finals Most Valuable Player (1991, 1992, 1993, 1996). ... Holds NBA Finals single-series record for highest points-per-game average—41.0 (1993). ... Holds NBA Finals single-game record for most points in one half—35. ... Shares NBA Finals single-game records for most field goals made in one half—14; and most three-point field goals made in one half—6 (June 3, 1992, vs. Portland). ... Holds career playoff record for highest points-per-game average (minimum 25 games or 625 points)—33.9. ... Holds single-game playoff records for most points—63 (April 20, 1986, at Boston); most free throws made in one quarter—9; and most free throws attempted in one quarter—14 (May 21, 1991, vs. Detroit). ... Shares single-game playoff records for most field goals made—24 (May 1, 1988, vs. Cleveland); most field goals attempted in one half—25 (May 1, 1988, vs. Cleveland); and most three-point field goals made in one half—6 (June 3, 1992, vs. Portland).

Season Team	G	Min.	FGM	FGA	Pct.	FTM	FTA	Pct.	Off.	Def.	Tot.	Ast.	St.	Blk.	TO	Pts.	RPG	APG	PPG
84-85—Chicago	4	171	34	78	.436	48	58	.828	7	16	23	34	11	4	15	117	5.8	8.5	29.3
85-86—Chicago	3	135	48	95	.505	34	39	.872	5	14	19	17	7	4	14	131	6.3	5.7	43.7
86-87—Chicago	3	128	35	84	.417	35	39	.897	7	14	21	18	6	7	8	107	7.0	6.0	35.7
87-88—Chicago	10	427	138	260	.531	86	99	.869	23	48	71	47	24	11	39	363	7.1	4.7	36.3
88-89—Chicago	17	718	199	390	.510	183	229	.799	26	93	119	130	42	13	68	591	7.0	7.6	34.8
89-90—Chicago	16	674	219	426	.514	133	159	.836	24	91	115	109	45	14	56	587	7.2	6.8	36.7
90-91—Chicago	17	689	197	376	.524	125	148	.845	18	90	108	142	40	23	43	529	6.4	8.4	31.1
91-92—Chicago	22	920	290	581	.499	162	189	.857	37	100	137	127	44	16	81	759	6.2	5.8	34.5
92-93—Chicago	19	783	251	528	.475	136	169	.805	32	96	128	114	39	17	45	666	6.7	6.0	35.1
94-95—Chicago	10	420	120	248	.484	64	79	.810	20	45	65	45	23	14	41	315	6.5	4.5	31.5
95-96—Chicago	18	733	187	407	.459	153	187	.818	31	58	89	74	33	6	42	552	4.9	4.1	30.7
Totals	139	5798	1718	3473	.495	1159	1395	.831	230	665	895	857	314	129	452	4717	6.4	6.2	33.9

Three-point field goals: 1984-85, 1-for-8 (.125). 1985-86, 1-for-1. 1986-87, 2-for-5 (.400). 1987-88, 1-for-3 (.333). 1988-89, 10-for-35 (.286). 1989-90, 16-for-50 (.320). 1990-91, 10-for-26 (.385). 1991-92, 17-for-44 (.386). 1992-93, 28-for-72 (.389). 1994-95, 11-for-30 (.367). 1995-96, 25-for-62 (.403). Totals, 122-for-336 (.363).

Personal fouls/disqualifications: 1984-85, 15/0. 1985-86, 13/1. 1986-87, 11/0. 1987-88, 38/1. 1988-89, 65/1. 1989-90, 54/0. 1990-91, 53/0. 1991-92, 62/0. 1992-93, 58/0. 1994-95, 30/0. 1995-96, 49/0. Totals, 448/3.

NBA ALL-STAR GAME RECORD

NOTES: NBA All-Star Game Most Valuable Player (1988, 1996). ... Holds career record for highest points-per-game average—21.9.

Season Team	Min.	FGM	FGA	Pct.	FTM	FTA	Pct.	Off.	Def.	Tot.	Ast.	PF	Dq.	St.	Blk.	TO	Pts.
1985 —Chicago	22	2	9	.222	3	4	.750	3	3	6	2	4	0	3	1	1	7
1986 —Chicago						Selected, did not play—injured.											

Season	Team	Min.	FGM	FGA	Pct.	FTM	FTA	Pct.	REBOUNDS Off.	Def.	Tot.	Ast.	PF	Dq.	St.	Blk.	TO	Pts.
1987	—Chicago	28	5	12	.417	1	2	.500	0	0	0	4	2	0	2	0	5	11
1988	—Chicago	29	17	23	.739	6	6	1.000	3	5	8	3	5	0	4	4	2	40
1989	—Chicago	33	13	23	.565	2	4	.500	1	1	2	3	1	0	5	0	4	28
1990	—Chicago	29	8	17	.471	0	0	...	1	4	5	2	1	0	5	1	5	17
1991	—Chicago	36	10	25	.400	6	7	.857	3	2	5	5	2	0	2	0	10	26
1992	—Chicago	31	9	17	.529	0	0	...	1	0	1	5	2	0	2	0	1	18
1993	—Chicago	36	10	24	.417	9	13	.692	3	1	4	5	5	0	4	0	6	30
1996	—Chicago	22	8	11	.727	4	4	1.000	1	3	4	1	1	0	1	0	0	20
Totals		266	82	161	.509	31	40	.775	16	19	35	30	23	0	28	6	34	197

Three-point field goals: 1985, 0-for-1. 1987, 0-for-1. 1989, 0-for-1. 1990, 1-for-1. 1991, 0-for-2. 1993, 1-for-2 (.500). Totals, 2-for-8 (.250).

RECORD AS BASEBALL PLAYER

TRANSACTIONS/CAREER NOTES: Threw right, batted right. ... Signed as non-drafted free agent by Chicago White Sox organization (February 7, 1994). ... On voluntarily retired list (March 25, 1995).

Year	Team (League)	Pos.	G	BATTING AB	R	H	2B	3B	HR	RBI	Avg.	BB	SO	SB	FIELDING PO	A	E	Avg.
1994	—Birm.(South.)	OF	127	436	46	88	17	1	3	51	.202	51	114	30	213	6	†11	.952

JORDAN, REGGIE   G   TRAIL BLAZERS

PERSONAL: Born January 26, 1968, in Chicago. ... 6-4/200. ... Full name: Reginald Jordan.
HIGH SCHOOL: Proviso East (Maywood, Ill.; did not play basketball).
JUNIOR COLLEGE: Southwestern (Calif.).
COLLEGE: New Mexico State.
TRANSACTIONS/CAREER NOTES: Not drafted by an NBA franchise. ... Played in Continental Basketball Association with Grand Rapids Hoops (1991-92 through 1993-94), Yakima Sun Kings (1993-94 and 1994-95) and Sioux Falls Skyforce (1995-96). ... Signed by Los Angeles Lakers to first of two consecutive 10-day contracts (January 22, 1994). ... Re-signed by Lakers for remainder of season (February 8, 1994). ... Signed by Atlanta Hawks to first of two consecutive 10-day contracts (March 6, 1996). ... Re-signed by Hawks for remainder of season (March 26, 1996). ... Signed as free agent by Portland Trail Blazers (August 30, 1996).

COLLEGIATE RECORD

Season Team	G	Min.	FGM	FGA	Pct.	FTM	FTA	Pct.	Reb.	Ast.	Pts.	AVERAGES RPG	APG	PPG
87-88—Southwestern						Statistics unavailable.								
88-89—Southwestern	31	...	...	...	...	...	...	...	387	...	781	12.5	...	25.2
89-90—New Mexico State	31	802	137	307	.446	52	82	.634	186	60	328	6.0	1.9	10.6
90-91—New Mexico State	29	844	162	384	.422	82	136	.603	226	70	424	7.8	2.4	14.6
Junior college totals	31	...	...	...	...	...	...	...	387	...	781	12.5	...	25.2
4-year-college totals	60	1646	299	691	.433	134	218	.615	412	130	752	6.9	2.2	12.5

Three-point field goals: 1989-90, 2-for-20 (.100). 1990-91, 18-for-55 (.327). Totals, 20-for-75 (.267).

CBA REGULAR-SEASON RECORD

NOTES: CBA All-League first team (1996). ... CBA All-Defensive team (1993, 1996). ... Member of CBA championship team (1995, 1996). ... Led CBA with 2.4 steals per game (1996).

Season Team	G	Min.	FGM	FGA	Pct.	FTM	FTA	Pct.	Reb.	Ast.	Pts.	AVERAGES RPG	APG	PPG
91-92—Grand Rapids	56	1860	283	587	.482	142	222	.640	458	164	709	8.2	2.9	12.7
92-93—Grand Rapids	34	1321	232	522	.444	116	174	.667	347	126	580	10.2	3.7	17.1
93-94—Gr. Rap.-Yakima	22	843	155	321	.483	104	137	.759	202	140	414	9.2	6.4	18.8
94-95—Yakima	24	805	150	351	.427	112	161	.696	176	122	412	7.3	5.1	17.2
95-96—Sioux Falls	38	1426	292	590	.495	164	225	.729	258	249	749	6.8	6.6	19.7
Totals	174	6255	1112	2371	.469	638	919	.694	1441	801	2864	8.3	4.6	16.5

Three-point field goals: 1991-92, 1-for-10 (.100). 1992-93, 0-for-9. 1993-94, 0-for-1. 1994-95, 0-for-6. 1995-96, 1-for-8 (.125). Totals, 2-for-34 (.059).

NBA REGULAR-SEASON RECORD

Season Team	G	Min.	FGM	FGA	Pct.	FTM	FTA	Pct.	REBOUNDS Off.	Def.	Tot.	Ast.	St.	Blk.	TO	Pts.	AVERAGES RPG	APG	PPG
93-94—L.A. Lakers	23	259	44	103	.427	35	51	.686	46	21	67	26	14	5	14	125	2.9	1.1	5.4
95-96—Atlanta	24	247	36	71	.507	22	38	.579	23	29	52	29	12	7	19	94	2.2	1.2	3.9
Totals	47	506	80	174	.460	57	89	.640	69	50	119	55	26	12	33	219	2.5	1.2	4.7

Three-point field goals: 1993-94, 2-for-4 (.500).
Personal fouls/disqualifications: 1993-94, 26/0. 1995-96, 30/0. Totals, 56/0.

NBA PLAYOFF RECORD

Season Team	G	Min.	FGM	FGA	Pct.	FTM	FTA	Pct.	REBOUNDS Off.	Def.	Tot.	Ast.	St.	Blk.	TO	Pts.	AVERAGES RPG	APG	PPG
95-96—Atlanta	10	59	7	13	.538	3	7	.429	1	5	6	9	5	1	3	17	0.6	0.9	1.7

Personal fouls/disqualifications: 1995-96, 7/0.

KEEFE, ADAM   F   JAZZ

PERSONAL: Born February 22, 1970, in Irvine, Calif. ... 6-9/241. ... Full name: Adam Thomas Keefe.
HIGH SCHOOL: Woodbridge (Irvine, Calif.).
COLLEGE: Stanford.
TRANSACTIONS/CAREER NOTES: Selected by Atlanta Hawks in first round (10th pick overall) of 1992 NBA Draft. ... Traded by Hawks to Utah Jazz for F Tyrone Corbin and 1995 second-round draft choice (September 16, 1994).

COLLEGIATE RECORD

Season Team	G	Min.	FGM	FGA	Pct.	FTM	FTA	Pct.	Reb.	Ast.	Pts.	AVERAGES RPG	APG	PPG
88-89—Stanford	33	653	93	147	.633	91	132	.689	179	22	277	5.4	0.7	8.4
89-90—Stanford	30	1065	210	335	.627	179	247	.725	272	41	599	9.1	1.4	20.0
90-91—Stanford	33	1204	252	414	.609	203	267	.760	313	61	709	9.5	1.8	21.5
91-92—Stanford	29	1080	275	488	.564	179	240	.746	355	86	734	12.2	3.0	25.3
Totals	125	4002	830	1384	.600	652	886	.736	1119	210	2319	9.0	1.7	18.6

Three-point field goals: 1990-91, 2-for-4 (.500). 1991-92, 5-for-11 (.455). Totals, 7-for-15 (.467).

NBA REGULAR-SEASON RECORD

Season Team	G	Min.	FGM	FGA	Pct.	FTM	FTA	Pct.	REBOUNDS Off.	Def.	Tot.	Ast.	St.	Blk.	TO	Pts.	AVERAGES RPG	APG	PPG
92-93—Atlanta	82	1549	188	376	.500	166	237	.700	171	261	432	80	57	16	100	542	5.3	1.0	6.6
93-94—Atlanta	63	763	96	213	.451	81	111	.730	77	124	201	34	20	9	60	273	3.2	0.5	4.3
94-95—Utah	75	1270	172	298	.577	117	173	.676	135	192	327	30	36	25	62	461	4.4	0.4	6.1
95-96—Utah	82	1708	180	346	.520	139	201	.692	176	279	455	64	51	41	88	499	5.5	0.8	6.1
Totals	302	5290	636	1233	.516	503	722	.697	559	856	1415	208	164	91	310	1775	4.7	0.7	5.9

Three-point field goals: 1992-93, 0-for-1. 1995-96, 0-for-4. Totals, 0-for-5.
Personal fouls/disqualifications: 1992-93, 195/1. 1993-94, 80/0. 1994-95, 141/0. 1995-96, 174/0. Totals, 590/1.

NBA PLAYOFF RECORD

Season Team	G	Min.	FGM	FGA	Pct.	FTM	FTA	Pct.	REBOUNDS Off.	Def.	Tot.	Ast.	St.	Blk.	TO	Pts.	AVERAGES RPG	APG	PPG
92-93—Atlanta	3	53	7	13	.538	4	6	.667	4	9	13	6	1	0	3	18	4.3	2.0	6.0
93-94—Atlanta	7	62	6	10	.600	4	9	.444	3	10	13	2	1	1	4	16	1.9	0.3	2.3
94-95—Utah	4	69	7	12	.583	4	6	.667	8	9	17	2	5	1	0	18	4.3	0.5	4.5
95-96—Utah	17	178	23	34	.676	11	17	.647	9	24	33	2	3	1	8	58	1.9	0.1	3.4
Totals	31	362	43	69	.623	23	38	.605	24	52	76	12	10	3	15	110	2.5	0.4	3.5

Three-point field goals: 1995-96, 1-for-2 (.500).
Personal fouls/disqualifications: 1992-93, 7/0. 1993-94, 9/0. 1994-95, 4/0. 1995-96, 23/0. Totals, 43/0.

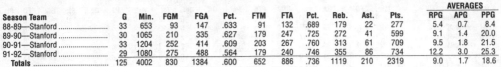

KEMP, SHAWN   F   SUPERSONICS

PERSONAL: Born November 26, 1969, in Elkhart, Ind. ... 6-10/256. ... Full name: Shawn T. Kemp.
HIGH SCHOOL: Concord (Elkhart, Ind.).
JUNIOR COLLEGE: Trinity Valley Community College (Texas).
COLLEGE: Kentucky.
TRANSACTIONS/CAREER NOTES: Selected after freshman year by Seattle SuperSonics in first round (17th pick overall) of 1989 NBA Draft.
MISCELLANEOUS: Seattle SuperSonics all-time blocked shots leader with 878 (1989-90 through 1995-96).

COLLEGIATE RECORD

Season Team	G	Min.	FGM	FGA	Pct.	FTM	FTA	Pct.	Reb.	Ast.	Pts.	AVERAGES RPG	APG	PPG
88-89—Kentucky					Did not play—left school before basketball season.									
88-89—Trinity Valley C.C.					Did not play.									

NBA REGULAR-SEASON RECORD

HONORS: All-NBA second team (1994, 1995, 1996).
NOTES: Led NBA with 13 disqualifications (1992) and 11 disqualifications (1994). ... Led NBA with 312 personal fouls (1994).

Season Team	G	Min.	FGM	FGA	Pct.	FTM	FTA	Pct.	REBOUNDS Off.	Def.	Tot.	Ast.	St.	Blk.	TO	Pts.	AVERAGES RPG	APG	PPG
89-90—Seattle	81	1120	203	424	.479	117	159	.736	146	200	346	26	47	70	107	525	4.3	0.3	6.5
90-91—Seattle	81	2442	462	909	.508	288	436	.661	267	412	679	144	77	123	202	1214	8.4	1.8	15.0
91-92—Seattle	64	1808	362	718	.504	270	361	.748	264	401	665	86	70	124	156	994	10.4	1.3	15.5
92-93—Seattle	78	2582	515	1047	.492	358	503	.712	287	546	833	155	119	146	217	1388	10.7	2.0	17.8
93-94—Seattle	79	2597	533	990	.538	364	491	.741	312	539	851	207	142	166	259	1431	10.8	2.6	18.1
94-95—Seattle	82	2679	545	997	.547	438	585	.749	318	575	893	149	102	122	259	1530	10.9	1.8	18.7
95-96—Seattle	79	2631	526	937	.561	493	664	.742	276	628	904	173	93	127	315	1550	11.4	2.2	19.6
Totals	544	15859	3146	6022	.522	2328	3199	.728	1870	3301	5171	940	650	878	1515	8632	9.5	1.7	15.9

Three-point field goals: 1989-90, 2-for-12 (.167). 1990-91, 2-for-12 (.167). 1991-92, 0-for-3. 1992-93, 0-for-4. 1993-94, 1-for-4 (.250). 1994-95, 2-for-7 (.286). 1995-96, 5-for-12 (.417). Totals, 12-for-54 (.222).
Personal fouls/disqualifications: 1989-90, 204/5. 1990-91, 319/11. 1991-92, 261/13. 1992-93, 327/13. 1993-94, 312/11. 1994-95, 337/9. 1995-96, 299/6. Totals, 2059/68.

NBA PLAYOFF RECORD

Season Team	G	Min.	FGM	FGA	Pct.	FTM	FTA	Pct.	REBOUNDS Off.	Def.	Tot.	Ast.	St.	Blk.	TO	Pts.	AVERAGES RPG	APG	PPG
90-91—Seattle	5	149	22	57	.386	22	27	.815	13	23	36	6	3	4	16	66	7.2	1.2	13.2
91-92—Seattle	9	338	48	101	.475	61	80	.763	47	63	110	4	5	14	27	157	12.2	0.4	17.4
92-93—Seattle	19	663	110	215	.512	93	115	.809	80	110	190	49	29	40	54	313	10.0	2.6	16.5
93-94—Seattle	5	206	26	70	.371	22	33	.667	20	29	49	17	10	12	14	74	9.8	3.4	14.8
94-95—Seattle	4	160	33	57	.579	32	39	.821	17	31	48	11	8	7	15	99	12.0	2.8	24.8
95-96—Seattle	20	720	147	258	.570	124	156	.795	66	142	208	30	24	40	80	418	10.4	1.5	20.9
Totals	62	2236	386	758	.509	354	450	.787	243	398	641	117	79	117	206	1127	10.3	1.9	18.2

Three-point field goals: 1990-91, 0-for-1. 1994-95, 1-for-1. 1995-96, 0-for-3. Totals, 1-for-5 (.200).
Personal fouls/disqualifications: 1990-91, 20/1. 1991-92, 41/0. 1992-93, 78/2. 1993-94, 18/0. 1994-95, 17/0. 1995-96, 84/3. Totals, 258/6.

NBA ALL-STAR GAME RECORD

Season	Team	Min.	FGM	FGA	Pct.	FTM	FTA	Pct.	REBOUNDS Off.	Def.	Tot.	Ast.	PF	Dq.	St.	Blk.	TO	Pts.
1993	—Seattle	9	0	2	.000	0	0	...	2	0	2	0	3	0	0	0	0	0
1994	—Seattle	22	3	11	.273	0	0	...	6	6	12	4	4	0	0	3	6	6
1995	—Seattle	23	4	6	.667	5	6	.833	0	2	2	2	5	0	1	0	4	13
1996	—Seattle	22	6	12	.500	1	2	.500	2	2	4	1	4	0	0	1	3	13
Totals		76	13	31	.419	6	8	.750	10	10	20	7	16	0	1	4	13	32

Three-point field goals: 1996, 0-for-2.

KEMPTON, TIM   C/F

PERSONAL: Born January 25, 1964, in Jamaica, N.Y. ... 6-10/255. ... Full name: Timothy Joseph Kempton.
HIGH SCHOOL: St. Dominic (Oyster Bay, N.Y.).
COLLEGE: Notre Dame.
TRANSACTIONS/CAREER NOTES: Selected by Los Angeles Clippers in sixth round (124th pick overall) of 1986 NBA Draft. ... Played in Italy (1987-88, 1990-91, 1991-92 and 1993-94). ... Granted free agency (July 1, 1988). ... Signed as free agent by Charlotte Hornets (August 17, 1988). ... Traded by Hornets to Denver Nuggets for 1991 second-round draft choice (September 11, 1989). ... Signed as unrestricted free agent by Phoenix Suns (August 18, 1992). ... Waived by Suns (January 21, 1994). ... Signed by Hornets to first of two consecutive 10-day contracts (February 16, 1994). ... Signed by Cleveland Cavaliers for remainder of season (April 15, 1994). ... Played in France (1994-95). ... Signed as free agent by Atlanta Hawks for remainder of season (December 14, 1995). ... Waived by Hawks (January 5, 1996).

COLLEGIATE RECORD

Season Team	G	Min.	FGM	FGA	Pct.	FTM	FTA	Pct.	Reb.	Ast.	Pts.	AVERAGES RPG	APG	PPG
82-83—Notre Dame	27	739	101	168	.601	83	113	.735	159	38	285	5.9	1.4	10.6
83-84—Notre Dame	26	775	78	165	.473	113	148	.764	165	29	269	6.3	1.1	10.3
84-85—Notre Dame	27	671	62	141	.440	68	87	.782	130	29	192	4.8	1.1	7.1
85-86—Notre Dame	27	617	69	127	.543	43	58	.741	143	61	181	5.3	2.3	6.7
Totals	107	2802	310	601	.516	307	406	.756	597	157	927	5.6	1.5	8.7

NBA REGULAR-SEASON RECORD

Season Team	G	Min.	FGM	FGA	Pct.	FTM	FTA	Pct.	REBOUNDS Off.	Def.	Tot.	Ast.	St.	Blk.	TO	Pts.	AVERAGES RPG	APG	PPG
86-87—L.A. Clippers ...	66	936	97	206	.471	95	137	.693	70	124	194	53	38	12	49	289	2.9	0.8	4.4
88-89—Charlotte	79	1341	171	335	.510	142	207	.686	91	213	304	102	41	14	121	484	3.8	1.3	6.1
89-90—Denver	71	1061	153	312	.490	77	114	.675	51	167	218	118	30	9	80	383	3.1	1.7	5.4
92-93—Phoenix	30	167	19	48	.396	18	31	.581	12	27	39	19	4	4	16	56	1.3	0.6	1.9
93-94—Char.-Clev.	13	136	15	38	.395	9	16	.563	10	14	24	9	6	2	11	39	1.8	0.7	3.0
95-96—Atlanta	3	11	0	0	...	0	0	...	2	2	2	1	0	0	1	0	0.7	0.3	0.0
Totals	262	3652	455	939	.485	341	505	.675	234	547	781	302	119	41	278	1251	3.0	1.2	4.8

Three-point field goals: 1986-87, 0-for-1. 1988-89, 0-for-1. 1989-90, 0-for-1. Totals, 0-for-3.
Personal fouls/disqualifications: 1986-87, 162/6. 1988-89, 215/3. 1989-90, 144/2. 1992-93, 30/0. 1993-94, 33/0. 1995-96, 5/0. Totals, 589/11.

NBA PLAYOFF RECORD

Season Team	G	Min.	FGM	FGA	Pct.	FTM	FTA	Pct.	REBOUNDS Off.	Def.	Tot.	Ast.	St.	Blk.	TO	Pts.	AVERAGES RPG	APG	PPG
89-90—Denver	3	32	7	9	.778	4	4	1.000	1	4	5	4	0	0	2	18	1.7	1.3	6.0
93-94—Cleveland	3	89	10	25	.400	6	6	1.000	10	6	16	8	3	0	4	26	5.3	2.7	8.7
Totals	6	121	17	34	.500	10	10	1.000	11	10	21	12	3	0	6	44	3.5	2.0	7.3

Personal fouls/disqualifications: 1989-90, 8/0. 1993-94, 9/0. Totals, 17/0.

ITALIAN LEAGUE RECORD

Season Team	G	Min.	FGM	FGA	Pct.	FTM	FTA	Pct.	Reb.	Ast.	Pts.	AVERAGES RPG	APG	PPG
87-88—Wuber	33	1229	252	462	.545	127	188	.676	298	...	631	9.0	...	19.1
90-91—Glaxo Verona	24	779	126	222	.568	136	169	.805	195	29	388	8.1	1.2	16.2
91-92—Glaxo Verona	28	1022	145	276	.525	164	196	.837	264	82	455	9.4	2.9	16.3
93-94—Teorematour Milan	7	241	43	70	.614	21	32	.656	71	20	107	10.1	2.9	15.3
Totals	92	3271	566	1030	.550	448	585	.766	828	...	1581	9.0	...	17.2

FRENCH LEAGUE RECORD

Season Team	G	Min.	FGM	FGA	Pct.	FTM	FTA	Pct.	Reb.	Ast.	Pts.	AVERAGES RPG	APG	PPG
94-95—Limoges	15	...	...	...	....	...	...	...	107	64	176	7.1	4.3	11.7

KERR, STEVE   G   BULLS

PERSONAL: Born September 27, 1965, in Beirut, Lebanon. ... 6-3/181. ... Full name: Stephen Douglas Kerr.
HIGH SCHOOL: Pacific Palisades (Calif.).
COLLEGE: Arizona.
TRANSACTIONS/CAREER NOTES: Selected by Phoenix Suns in second round (50th pick overall) of 1988 NBA Draft. ... Traded by Suns to Cleveland Cavaliers for 1993 second-round draft choice (September 5, 1989). ... Traded by Cavaliers to Orlando Magic for 1996 second-round draft choice (December 2, 1992). ... Signed as free agent by Chicago Bulls (September 29, 1993).
MISCELLANEOUS: Member of NBA championship team (1996).

COLLEGIATE RECORD

Season Team	G	Min.	FGM	FGA	Pct.	FTM	FTA	Pct.	Reb.	Ast.	Pts.	AVERAGES RPG	APG	PPG
83-84—Arizona	28	633	81	157	.516	36	52	.692	33	35	198	1.2	1.3	7.1
84-85—Arizona	31	1036	126	222	.568	57	71	.803	73	123	309	2.4	4.0	10.0
85-86—Arizona	32	1228	195	361	.540	71	79	.899	101	135	461	3.2	4.2	14.4

Season Team	G	Min.	FGM	FGA	Pct.	FTM	FTA	Pct.	Reb.	Ast.	Pts.	RPG	APG	PPG
86-87—Arizona						Did not play—knee injury.								
87-88—Arizona	38	1239	151	270	.559	61	74	.824	76	150	477	2.0	3.9	12.6
Totals	129	4136	553	1010	.548	225	276	.815	283	443	1445	2.2	3.4	11.2

Three-point field goals: 1987-88, 114-for-199 (.573).

NBA REGULAR-SEASON RECORD

RECORDS: Holds career record for highest three-point field-goal percentage (minimum 250 made)—.480. ... Holds single-season record for highest three-point field-goal percentage—.524 (1995).
NOTES: Led NBA with .507 three-point field-goal percentage (1990) and .524 three-point field-goal percentage (1995).

Season Team	G	Min.	FGM	FGA	Pct.	FTM	FTA	Pct.	Off.	Def.	Tot.	Ast.	St.	Blk.	TO	Pts.	RPG	APG	PPG
88-89—Phoenix	26	157	20	46	.435	6	9	.667	3	14	17	24	7	0	6	54	0.7	0.9	2.1
89-90—Cleveland	78	1664	192	432	.444	63	73	.863	12	86	98	248	45	7	74	520	1.3	3.2	6.7
90-91—Cleveland	57	905	99	223	.444	45	53	.849	5	32	37	131	29	4	40	271	0.6	2.3	4.8
91-92—Cleveland	48	847	121	237	.511	45	54	.833	14	64	78	110	27	10	31	319	1.6	2.3	6.6
92-93—Clev.-Orl.	52	481	53	122	.434	22	24	.917	5	40	45	70	10	1	27	134	0.9	1.3	2.6
93-94—Chicago	82	2036	287	577	.497	83	97	.856	26	105	131	210	75	3	57	709	1.6	2.6	8.6
94-95—Chicago	82	1839	261	495	.527	63	81	.778	20	99	119	151	44	3	48	674	1.5	1.8	8.2
95-96—Chicago	82	1919	244	482	.506	78	84	.929	25	85	110	192	63	2	42	688	1.3	2.3	8.4
Totals	507	9848	1277	2614	.489	405	475	.853	110	525	635	1136	300	30	325	3369	1.3	2.2	6.6

Three-point field goals: 1988-89, 8-for-17 (.471). 1989-90, 73-for-144 (.507). 1990-91, 28-for-62 (.452). 1991-92, 32-for-74 (.432). 1992-93, 6-for-26 (.231). 1993-94, 52-for-124 (.419). 1994-95, 89-for-170 (.524). 1995-96, 122-for-237 (.515). Totals, 410-for-854 (.480).
Personal fouls/disqualifications: 1988-89, 12/0. 1989-90, 59/0. 1990-91, 52/0. 1991-92, 29/0. 1992-93, 36/0. 1993-94, 97/0. 1994-95, 114/0. 1995-96, 109/0. Totals, 508/0.

NBA PLAYOFF RECORD

Season Team	G	Min.	FGM	FGA	Pct.	FTM	FTA	Pct.	Off.	Def.	Tot.	Ast.	St.	Blk.	TO	Pts.	RPG	APG	PPG
89-90—Cleveland	5	73	4	14	.286	0	0	...	1	5	6	10	4	0	2	8	1.2	2.0	1.6
91-92—Cleveland	12	149	18	41	.439	5	5	1.000	1	5	6	10	5	0	4	44	0.5	0.8	3.7
93-94—Chicago	10	186	13	36	.361	3	3	1.000	2	12	14	10	7	0	1	35	1.4	1.0	3.5
94-95—Chicago	10	193	19	40	.475	5	5	1.000	1	5	6	15	1	0	0	51	0.6	1.5	5.1
95-96—Chicago	18	357	39	87	.448	27	31	.871	3	15	18	31	14	0	13	122	1.0	1.7	6.8
Totals	55	958	93	218	.427	40	44	.909	8	42	50	76	31	0	20	260	0.9	1.4	4.7

Three-point field goals: 1989-90, 0-for-3. 1991-92, 3-for-11 (.273). 1993-94, 6-for-16 (.375). 1994-95, 8-for-19 (.421). 1995-96, 17-for-53 (.321). Totals, 34-for-102 (.333).
Personal fouls/disqualifications: 1989-90, 6/0. 1991-92, 12/0. 1993-94, 13/0. 1994-95, 14/0. 1995-96, 21/0. Totals, 66/0.

KERSEY, JEROME   F   LAKERS

PERSONAL: Born June 26, 1962, in Clarksville, Va. ... 6-7/225.
HIGH SCHOOL: Bluestone Senior (Skipwith, Va.).
COLLEGE: Longwood (Va.).
TRANSACTIONS/CAREER NOTES: Selected by Portland Trail Blazers in second round (46th pick overall) of 1984 NBA Draft. ... Selected by Toronto Raptors from Trail Blazers in NBA expansion draft (June 24, 1995). ... Rights renounced by Raptors (October 4, 1995). ... Signed as free agent by Golden State Warriors (October 18, 1995). ... Rights renounced by Warriors (July 21, 1996). ... Signed as free agent by Los Angeles Lakers (August 12, 1996).

COLLEGIATE RECORD
NOTES: Led NCAA Division II with 14.2 rebounds per game (1984).

Season Team	G	Min.	FGM	FGA	Pct.	FTM	FTA	Pct.	Reb.	Ast.	Pts.	RPG	APG	PPG
80-81—Longwood	28	...	197	313	.629	78	133	.586	249	...	472	8.9	...	16.9
81-82—Longwood	23	...	165	282	.585	62	98	.633	260	61	392	11.3	2.7	17.0
82-83—Longwood	25	...	144	257	.560	76	125	.608	270	77	364	10.8	3.1	14.6
83-84—Longwood	27	...	214	411	.521	100	165	.606	383	98	528	14.2	3.6	19.6
Totals	103	...	720	1263	.570	316	521	.607	1162	...	1756	11.3	...	17.0

NBA REGULAR-SEASON RECORD

Season Team	G	Min.	FGM	FGA	Pct.	FTM	FTA	Pct.	Off.	Def.	Tot.	Ast.	St.	Blk.	TO	Pts.	RPG	APG	PPG
84-85—Portland	77	958	178	372	.479	117	181	.646	95	111	206	63	49	29	66	473	2.7	0.8	6.1
85-86—Portland	79	1217	258	470	.549	156	229	.681	137	156	293	83	85	32	113	672	3.7	1.1	8.5
86-87—Portland	82	2088	373	733	.509	262	364	.720	201	295	496	194	122	77	149	1009	6.0	2.4	12.3
87-88—Portland	79	2888	611	1225	.499	291	396	.735	211	446	657	243	127	65	161	1516	8.3	3.1	19.2
88-89—Portland	76	2716	533	1137	.469	258	372	.694	246	383	629	243	137	84	167	1330	8.3	3.2	17.5
89-90—Portland	82	2843	519	1085	.478	269	390	.690	251	439	690	188	121	63	144	1310	8.4	2.3	16.0
90-91—Portland	73	2359	424	887	.478	232	327	.709	169	312	481	227	101	76	149	1084	6.6	3.1	14.8
91-92—Portland	77	2553	398	852	.467	174	262	.664	241	392	633	243	114	71	151	971	8.2	3.2	12.6
92-93—Portland	65	1719	281	642	.438	116	183	.634	126	280	406	121	80	41	84	686	6.2	1.9	10.6
93-94—Portland	78	1276	203	469	.433	101	135	.748	130	201	331	75	71	49	63	508	4.2	1.0	6.5
94-95—Portland	63	1143	203	489	.415	95	124	.766	93	163	256	82	52	35	64	508	4.1	1.3	8.1
95-96—Golden State	76	1620	205	500	.410	97	147	.660	154	209	363	114	91	45	75	510	4.8	1.5	6.7
Totals	907	23380	4186	8861	.472	2168	3110	.697	2054	3387	5441	1876	1150	667	1386	10577	6.0	2.1	11.7

Three-point field goals: 1984-85, 0-for-3. 1985-86, 0-for-6. 1986-87, 1-for-23 (.043). 1987-88, 3-for-15 (.200). 1988-89, 6-for-21 (.286). 1989-90, 5-for-20 (.150). 1990-91, 4-for-13 (.308). 1991-92, 1-for-8 (.125). 1992-93, 8-for-28 (.286). 1993-94, 1-for-8 (.125). 1994-95, 7-for-27 (.259). 1995-96, 3-for-17 (.176). Totals, 37-for-189 (.196).
Personal fouls/disqualifications: 1984-85, 147/1. 1985-86, 208/2. 1986-87, 328/5. 1987-88, 302/8. 1988-89, 277/6. 1989-90, 304/7. 1990-91, 251/4. 1991-92, 254/1. 1992-93, 181/2. 1993-94, 213/1. 1994-95, 173/1. 1995-96, 205/2. Totals, 2843/40.

NBA PLAYOFF RECORD

Season Team	G	Min.	FGM	FGA	Pct.	FTM	FTA	Pct.	Off.	Def.	Tot.	Ast.	St.	Blk.	TO	Pts.	RPG	APG	PPG
84-85—Portland	8	60	16	31	.516	6	8	.750	5	4	9	6	7	2	2	38	1.1	0.8	4.8
85-86—Portland	4	56	9	22	.409	4	4	1.000	7	8	15	4	1	4	6	22	3.8	1.0	5.5
86-87—Portland	4	60	10	25	.400	4	4	1.000	6	13	19	3	5	1	6	24	4.8	0.8	6.0
87-88—Portland	4	127	32	65	.492	15	21	.714	17	13	30	9	7	4	5	79	7.5	2.3	19.8
88-89—Portland	3	117	23	47	.489	15	19	.789	11	13	24	7	10	1	4	61	8.0	2.3	20.3
89-90—Portland	21	831	166	361	.460	103	144	.715	66	108	174	45	34	20	45	435	8.3	2.1	20.7
90-91—Portland	16	588	105	226	.465	76	101	.752	52	59	111	49	28	7	17	286	6.9	3.1	17.9
91-92—Portland	21	756	131	257	.510	79	114	.693	59	103	162	75	41	19	53	341	7.7	3.6	16.2
92-93—Portland	4	98	22	42	.524	12	17	.706	10	24	34	4	2	2	0	57	8.5	1.0	14.3
93-94—Portland	3	38	5	16	.313	1	5	.200	5	4	9	0	1	1	0	11	3.0	0.0	3.7
94-95—Portland	3	63	16	28	.571	6	9	.667	2	6	8	3	3	1	0	38	2.7	1.0	12.7
Totals	91	2794	535	1120	.478	321	446	.720	240	355	595	205	141	62	140	1392	6.5	2.3	15.3

Three-point field goals: 1985-86, 0-for-1. 1987-88, 0-for-1. 1988-89, 0-for-2. 1989-90, 0-for-3. 1991-92, 0-for-3. 1992-93, 1-for-1. 1994-95, 0-for-2. Totals, 1-for-13 (.077).

Personal fouls/disqualifications: 1984-85, 11/0. 1985-86, 13/0. 1986-87, 13/0. 1987-88, 17/1. 1988-89, 12/0. 1989-90, 87/2. 1990-91, 68/2. 1991-92, 85/2. 1992-93, 15/0. 1993-94, 5/0. 1994-95, 11/1. Totals, 337/8.

K

KEYS, RANDOLPH   F   BUCKS

PERSONAL: Born April 19, 1966, in Collins, Miss. ... 6-7/210.
HIGH SCHOOL: Collins (Miss.).
COLLEGE: Southern Mississippi.
TRANSACTIONS/CAREER NOTES: Selected by Cleveland Cavaliers in first round (22nd pick overall) of 1988 NBA Draft. ... Traded by Cavaliers to Charlotte Hornets for future second-round draft choice (February 22, 1990). ... Waived by Hornets (July 15, 1991). ... Played in France (1991-92). ... Played in Italy (1992-93). ... Played in Continental Basketball Association with Quad City Thunder (1993-94 and 1994-95). ... Signed by Los Angeles Lakers to first of two consecutive 10-day contracts (February 28, 1995). ... Re-signed by Lakers for remainder of season (March 14, 1995). ... Signed as free agent by Milwaukee Bucks (October 6, 1995).

COLLEGIATE RECORD

Season Team	G	Min.	FGM	FGA	Pct.	FTM	FTA	Pct.	Reb.	Ast.	Pts.	RPG	APG	PPG
84-85—Southern Miss	28	396	51	112	.455	26	36	.722	70	20	128	2.5	0.7	4.6
85-86—Southern Miss	29	923	184	366	.503	42	72	.583	164	37	410	5.7	1.3	14.1
86-87—Southern Miss	34	1142	243	525	.463	60	85	.706	268	27	558	7.9	0.8	16.4
87-88—Southern Miss	30	978	216	455	.475	78	102	.765	221	29	530	7.4	1.0	17.7
Totals	121	3439	694	1458	.476	206	295	.698	723	113	1626	6.0	0.9	13.4

Three-point field goals: 1986-87, 12-for-51 (.235). 1987-88, 20-for-58 (.345). Totals, 32-for-109 (.294).

NBA REGULAR-SEASON RECORD

Season Team	G	Min.	FGM	FGA	Pct.	FTM	FTA	Pct.	Off.	Def.	Tot.	Ast.	St.	Blk.	TO	Pts.	RPG	APG	PPG
88-89—Cleveland	42	331	74	172	.430	20	29	.690	23	33	56	19	12	6	21	169	1.3	0.5	4.0
89-90—Clev.-Char.	80	1615	293	678	.432	101	140	.721	100	153	253	88	68	8	84	701	3.2	1.1	8.8
90-91—Charlotte	44	473	59	145	.407	19	33	.576	40	60	100	18	22	15	35	140	2.3	0.4	3.2
94-95—L.A. Lakers	6	83	9	26	.346	2	2	1.000	6	11	17	2	1	2	2	20	2.8	0.3	3.3
95-96—Milwaukee	69	816	87	208	.418	36	43	.837	41	84	125	65	32	14	33	232	1.8	0.9	3.4
Totals	241	3318	522	1229	.425	178	247	.721	210	341	551	192	135	45	175	1262	2.3	0.8	5.2

Three-point field goals: 1988-89, 1-for-10 (.100). 1989-90, 14-for-43 (.326). 1990-91, 3-for-14 (.214). 1994-95, 0-for-9. 1995-96, 22-for-71 (.310). Totals, 40-for-147 (.272).

Personal fouls/disqualifications: 1988-89, 51/0. 1989-90, 224/1. 1990-91, 93/0. 1994-95, 16/0. 1995-96, 139/2. Totals, 523/3.

NBA PLAYOFF RECORD

Season Team	G	Min.	FGM	FGA	Pct.	FTM	FTA	Pct.	Off.	Def.	Tot.	Ast.	St.	Blk.	TO	Pts.	RPG	APG	PPG
88-89—Cleveland	1	12	0	3	.000	0	0	...	0	3	3	1	0	0	2	0	3.0	1.0	0.0

Three-point field goals: 1988-89, 0-for-1.

Personal fouls/disqualifications: 1988-89, 1/0.

FRENCH LEAGUE RECORD

Season Team	G	Min.	FGM	FGA	Pct.	FTM	FTA	Pct.	Reb.	Ast.	Pts.	RPG	APG	PPG
91-92—Paris Racing	15	...	...	...	...	...	...	...	96	45	260	6.4	3.0	17.3

ITALIAN LEAGUE RECORD

Season Team	G	Min.	FGM	FGA	Pct.	FTM	FTA	Pct.	Reb.	Ast.	Pts.	RPG	APG	PPG
92-93—Benetton Treviso	8	268	46	85	.541	16	20	.800	62	6	115	7.8	0.8	14.4

CBA REGULAR-SEASON RECORD

NOTES: CBA All-League second team (1995). ... CBA All-Defensive team (1995). ... Member of CBA championship team (1994).

Season Team	G	Min.	FGM	FGA	Pct.	FTM	FTA	Pct.	Reb.	Ast.	Pts.	RPG	APG	PPG
93-94—Quad City	42	1224	202	494	.409	51	69	.739	182	64	497	4.3	1.5	11.8
94-95—Quad City	44	1681	258	623	.414	91	111	.820	291	119	713	6.6	2.7	16.2
Totals	86	2905	460	1117	.412	142	180	.789	473	183	1210	5.5	2.1	14.1

Three-point field goals: 1993-94, 42-for-134 (.313). 1994-95, 106-for-288 (.368). Totals, 148-for-422 (.351).

KIDD, JASON G MAVERICKS

PERSONAL: Born March 23, 1973, in San Francisco. ... 6-4/208. ... Full name: Jason Frederick Kidd.
HIGH SCHOOL: St. Joseph of Notre Dame (Alameda, Calif.).
COLLEGE: California.
TRANSACTIONS/CAREER NOTES: Selected after sophomore season by Dallas Mavericks in first round (second pick overall) of 1994 NBA Draft.

COLLEGIATE RECORD

NOTES: THE SPORTING NEWS All-America first team (1994). ... Led NCAA Division I with 3.8 steals per game (1993). ... Led NCAA Division I with 9.1 assists per game (1994).

Season Team	G	Min.	FGM	FGA	Pct.	FTM	FTA	Pct.	Reb.	Ast.	Pts.	RPG	APG	PPG
													AVERAGES	
92-93—California	29	922	133	287	.463	88	134	.657	142	222	378	4.9	7.7	13.0
93-94—California	30	1053	166	352	.472	117	169	.692	207	272	500	6.9	9.1	16.7
Totals	59	1975	299	639	.468	205	303	.677	349	494	878	5.9	8.4	14.9

Three-point field goals: 1992-93, 24-for-84 (.286). 1993-94, 51-for-141 (.362). Totals, 75-for-225 (.333).

NBA REGULAR-SEASON RECORD

HONORS: NBA co-Rookie of the Year (1995). ... NBA All-Rookie first team (1995).

Season Team	G	Min.	FGM	FGA	Pct.	FTM	FTA	Pct.	Off.	Def.	Tot.	Ast.	St.	Blk.	TO	Pts.	RPG	APG	PPG
									REBOUNDS								AVERAGES		
94-95—Dallas	79	2668	330	857	.385	192	275	.698	152	278	430	607	151	24	250	922	5.4	7.7	11.7
95-96—Dallas	81	3034	493	1293	.381	229	331	.692	203	350	553	783	175	26	*328	1348	6.8	9.7	16.6
Totals	160	5702	823	2150	.383	421	606	.695	355	628	983	1390	326	50	578	2270	6.1	8.7	14.2

Three-point field goals: 1994-95, 70-for-257 (.272). 1995-96, 133-for-396 (.336). Totals, 203-for-653 (.311).
Personal fouls/disqualifications: 1994-95, 146/0. 1995-96, 155/0. Totals, 301/0.

NBA ALL-STAR GAME RECORD

Season Team	Min.	FGM	FGA	Pct.	FTM	FTA	Pct.	Off.	Def.	Tot.	Ast.	PF	Dq.	St.	Blk.	TO	Pts.
								REBOUNDS									
1996 —Dallas	22	3	4	.750	0	0	...	2	4	6	10	1	0	2	0	2	7

Three-point field goals: 1996, 1-for-2 (.500).

KING, CHRIS F

PERSONAL: Born July 24, 1969, in Newton Grove, N.C. ... 6-8/215. ... Full name: Christopher Donnell King.
HIGH SCHOOL: Hobbton (Newton Grove, N.C.).
COLLEGE: Wake Forest.
TRANSACTIONS/CAREER NOTES: Selected by Seattle SuperSonics in second round (45th pick overall) of 1992 NBA Draft. ... Played in Spain (1992-93). ... Waived by SuperSonics (November 1, 1994). ... Signed as free agent by Vancouver Grizzlies (October 18, 1995). ... Rights renounced by Grizzlies (July 16, 1996).

COLLEGIATE RECORD

Season Team	G	Min.	FGM	FGA	Pct.	FTM	FTA	Pct.	Reb.	Ast.	Pts.	RPG	APG	PPG
													AVERAGES	
88-89—Wake Forest	28	788	168	311	.540	68	104	.654	171	28	404	6.1	1.0	14.4
89-90—Wake Forest	28	939	189	346	.546	73	124	.589	208	27	452	7.4	1.0	16.1
90-91—Wake Forest	30	950	179	366	.489	77	121	.636	172	64	452	5.7	2.1	15.1
91-92—Wake Forest	27	845	166	329	.505	70	101	.693	139	58	413	5.1	2.1	15.3
Totals	113	3522	702	1352	.519	288	450	.640	690	177	1721	6.1	1.6	15.2

Three-point field goals: 1988-89, 0-for-2 (.500). 1989-90, 1-for-2 (.500). 1990-91, 17-for-41 (.415). 1991-92, 11-for-32 (.344). Totals, 29-for-77 (.377).

SPANISH LEAGUE RECORD

Season Team	G	Min.	FGM	FGA	Pct.	FTM	FTA	Pct.	Reb.	Ast.	Pts.	RPG	APG	PPG
													AVERAGES	
92-93—Unicaja-Mayoral	31	1012	179	371	.482	66	102	.647	158	49	459	5.1	1.6	14.8

NBA REGULAR-SEASON RECORD

Season Team	G	Min.	FGM	FGA	Pct.	FTM	FTA	Pct.	Off.	Def.	Tot.	Ast.	St.	Blk.	TO	Pts.	RPG	APG	PPG
									REBOUNDS								AVERAGES		
93-94—Seattle	15	86	19	48	.396	15	26	.577	5	10	15	11	4	0	12	55	1.0	0.7	3.7
95-96—Vancouver	80	1930	250	585	.427	90	136	.662	102	183	285	104	68	33	103	634	3.6	1.3	7.9
Totals	95	2016	269	633	.425	105	162	.648	107	193	300	115	72	33	115	689	3.2	1.2	7.3

Three-point field goals: 1993-94, 2-for-7 (.286). 1995-96, 44-for-113 (.389). Totals, 46-for-120 (.383).
Personal fouls/disqualifications: 1993-94, 12/0. 1995-96, 163/0. Totals, 175/0.

NBA PLAYOFF RECORD

Season Team	G	Min.	FGM	FGA	Pct.	FTM	FTA	Pct.	Off.	Def.	Tot.	Ast.	St.	Blk.	TO	Pts.	RPG	APG	PPG
									REBOUNDS								AVERAGES		
93-94—Seattle	2	7	0	1	.000	0	2	.000	0	0	0	0	1	0	0	0	0.0	0.0	0.0

Personal fouls/disqualifications: 1993-94, 1/0.

KING, FRANKIE G

PERSONAL: Born June 6, 1972, in Baxley, Ga. ... 6-1/185. ... Full name: Frankie Alexander King.
HIGH SCHOOL: Appling County (Baxley, Ga.).
JUNIOR COLLEGE: Brunswick (Ga.) College.
COLLEGE: Western Carolina.
TRANSACTIONS/CAREER NOTES: Selected by Los Angeles Lakers in second round (37th pick overall) of 1995 NBA Draft. ... Rights renounced by Lakers (July 17, 1996).

COLLEGIATE RECORD

Season Team	G	Min.	FGM	FGA	Pct.	FTM	FTA	Pct.	Reb.	Ast.	Pts.	RPG	APG	PPG
91-92—Brunswick College.........	34	1087	271	559	.485	148	192	.771	137	54	748	4.0	1.6	22.0
92-93—Brunswick College.........	29	1050	319	702	.454	179	225	.796	213	79	906	7.3	2.7	31.2
93-94—Western Carolina...........	28	1066	258	527	.490	207	281	.737	211	59	752	7.5	2.1	26.9
94-95—Western Carolina...........	28	1037	249	520	.479	193	232	.832	204	94	743	7.3	3.4	26.5
Junior college totals	63	2137	590	1261	.468	327	417	.784	350	133	1654	5.6	2.1	26.3
4-year-college totals	56	2103	507	1047	.484	400	513	.780	415	153	1495	7.4	2.7	26.7

Three-point field goals: 1993-94, 29-for-96 (.302). 1994-95, 52-for-134 (.388). Totals, 81-for-230 (.352).

NBA REGULAR-SEASON RECORD

Season Team	G	Min.	FGM	FGA	Pct.	FTM	FTA	Pct.	Off.	Def.	Tot.	Ast.	St.	Blk.	TO	Pts.	RPG	APG	PPG
									REBOUNDS								AVERAGES		
95-96—L.A. Lakers	6	20	3	11	.273	1	3	.333	1	1	2	2	2	0	2	7	0.3	0.3	1.2

Three-point field goals: 1995-96, 0-for-1.
Personal fouls/disqualifications: 1995-96, 4/0.

KING, JIMMY   G   MAVERICKS

PERSONAL: Born August 9, 1973, in South Bend, Ind. ... 6-5/210. ... Full name: Jimmy Hal King.
HIGH SCHOOL: Plano (Texas) East.
COLLEGE: Michigan.
TRANSACTIONS/CAREER NOTES: Selected by Toronto Raptors in second round (35th pick overall) of 1995 NBA Draft. ... Traded by Raptors with 1997 and 1998 second-round draft choices to Dallas Mavericks for F Popeye Jones and 1997 first-round draft choice (July 23, 1996).

COLLEGIATE RECORD

Season Team	G	Min.	FGM	FGA	Pct.	FTM	FTA	Pct.	Reb.	Ast.	Pts.	RPG	APG	PPG
91-92—Michigan	34	953	128	258	.496	53	72	.736	112	78	337	3.3	2.3	9.9
92-93—Michigan	36	1174	148	291	.509	57	88	.648	159	110	390	4.4	3.1	10.8
93-94—Michigan	29	931	139	284	.489	51	79	.646	109	76	358	3.8	2.6	12.3
94-95—Michigan	31	1054	168	388	.433	93	137	.679	155	90	457	5.0	2.9	14.7
Totals	130	4112	583	1221	.477	254	376	.676	535	354	1542	4.1	2.7	11.9

Three-point field goals: 1991-92, 28-for-60 (.467). 1992-93, 37-for-92 (.402). 1993-94, 29-for-87 (.333). 1994-95, 28-for-109 (.257). Totals, 122-for-348 (.351).

NBA REGULAR-SEASON RECORD

Season Team	G	Min.	FGM	FGA	Pct.	FTM	FTA	Pct.	Off.	Def.	Tot.	Ast.	St.	Blk.	TO	Pts.	RPG	APG	PPG
									REBOUNDS								AVERAGES		
95-96—Toronto	62	868	110	255	.431	54	77	.701	43	67	110	88	21	13	60	279	1.8	1.4	4.5

Three-point field goals: 1995-96, 5-for-34 (.147).
Personal fouls/disqualifications: 1995-96, 76/0.

KING, STACEY   F/C

PERSONAL: Born January 29, 1967, in Lawton, Okla. ... 6-11/250. ... Full name: Ronald Stacey King.
HIGH SCHOOL: Lawton (Okla.).
COLLEGE: Oklahoma.
TRANSACTIONS/CAREER NOTES: Selected by Chicago Bulls in first round (sixth pick overall) of 1989 NBA Draft. ... Traded by Bulls to Minnesota Timberwolves for C Luc Longley (February 23, 1994). ... Signed as free agent by Miami Heat (October 5, 1995). ... Rights renounced by Heat (July 17, 1996).
MISCELLANEOUS: Member of NBA championship teams (1991, 1992, 1993).

COLLEGIATE RECORD

NOTES: The Sporting News College Player of the Year (1989). ... The Sporting News All-America first team (1989). ... The Sporting News All-America second team (1988).

Season Team	G	Min.	FGM	FGA	Pct.	FTM	FTA	Pct.	Reb.	Ast.	Pts.	RPG	APG	PPG
85-86—Oklahoma	14	230	26	67	.388	32	43	.744	53	4	84	3.8	0.3	6.0
86-87—Oklahoma	28	441	71	162	.438	54	87	.621	108	13	196	3.9	0.5	7.0
87-88—Oklahoma	39	1212	337	621	.543	195	289	.675	332	44	869	8.5	1.1	22.3
88-89—Oklahoma	33	1142	324	618	.524	211	294	.718	332	62	859	10.1	1.9	26.0
Totals	114	3025	758	1468	.516	492	713	.690	825	123	2008	7.2	1.1	17.6

Three-point field goals: 1986-87, 0-for-1. 1987-88, 0-for-1. Totals, 0-for-2.

NBA REGULAR-SEASON RECORD

HONORS: NBA All-Rookie second team (1990).

Season Team	G	Min.	FGM	FGA	Pct.	FTM	FTA	Pct.	Off.	Def.	Tot.	Ast.	St.	Blk.	TO	Pts.	RPG	APG	PPG
									REBOUNDS								AVERAGES		
89-90—Chicago	82	1777	267	530	.504	194	267	.727	169	215	384	87	38	58	119	728	4.7	1.1	8.9
90-91—Chicago	76	1198	156	334	.467	107	152	.704	72	136	208	65	24	42	91	419	2.7	0.9	5.5
91-92—Chicago	79	1268	215	425	.506	119	158	.753	87	118	205	77	21	25	76	551	2.6	1.0	7.0
92-93—Chicago	76	1059	160	340	.471	86	122	.705	105	102	207	71	26	20	70	408	2.7	0.9	5.4
93-94—Chi.-Min.	49	1053	146	341	.428	93	136	.684	90	151	241	58	31	42	83	385	4.9	1.2	7.9
94-95—Minnesota.......	50	792	99	212	.467	68	102	.667	54	111	165	26	24	20	64	266	3.3	0.5	5.3
95-96—Miami	15	156	17	36	.472	4	8	.500	9	14	23	2	7	2	18	38	1.5	0.1	2.5
Totals	427	7303	1060	2218	.478	671	945	.710	586	847	1433	386	171	209	521	2795	3.4	0.9	6.5

Three-point field goals: 1989-90, 0-for-1. 1990-91, 0-for-2. 1991-92, 2-for-5 (.400). 1992-93, 2-for-6 (.333). 1993-94, 0-for-2. 1994-95, 0-for-1. Totals, 4-for-17 (.235).

Personal fouls/disqualifications: 1989-90, 215/0. 1990-91, 134/0. 1991-92, 129/0. 1992-93, 128/0. 1993-94, 121/1. 1994-95, 126/1. 1995-96, 39/2. Totals, 892/4.

NBA PLAYOFF RECORD

Season Team	G	Min.	FGM	FGA	Pct.	FTM	FTA	Pct.	Off.	Def.	Tot.	Ast.	St.	Blk.	TO	Pts.	RPG	APG	PPG
89-90—Chicago	16	281	37	91	.407	36	47	.766	17	34	51	9	6	8	17	110	3.2	0.6	6.9
90-91—Chicago	11	86	8	27	.296	7	11	.636	9	13	22	2	1	1	9	23	2.0	0.2	2.1
91-92—Chicago	14	111	18	40	.450	15	23	.652	7	13	20	5	5	2	10	53	1.4	0.4	3.8
92-93—Chicago	19	229	26	66	.394	25	31	.806	20	20	40	14	9	4	14	77	2.1	0.7	4.1
95-96—Miami	1	12	0	3	.000	1	2	.500	0	3	3	1	0	0	0	1	3.0	1.0	1.0
Totals	61	719	89	227	.392	84	114	.737	53	83	136	31	21	15	50	264	2.2	0.5	4.3

Three-point field goals: 1989-90, 0-for-1. 1990-91, 0-for-1. 1991-92, 2-for-2. Totals, 2-for-4 (.500).

Personal fouls/disqualifications: 1989-90, 32/0. 1990-91, 15/0. 1991-92, 12/0. 1992-93, 38/0. 1995-96, 1/0. Totals, 98/0.

KLEINE, JOE   C   SUNS

PERSONAL: Born January 4, 1962, in Colorado Springs, Colo. ... 7-0/271. ... Full name: Joseph William Kleine.
HIGH SCHOOL: Slater (Mo.).
COLLEGE: Notre Dame, then Arkansas.
TRANSACTIONS/CAREER NOTES: Selected by Sacramento Kings in first round (sixth pick overall) of 1985 NBA Draft. ... Traded by Kings with F Ed Pinckney to Boston Celtics for C/F Brad Lohaus and G Danny Ainge (February 23, 1989). ... Signed as unrestricted free agent by Phoenix Suns (August 16, 1993).
MISCELLANEOUS: Member of gold-medal-winning U.S. Olympic team (1984).

COLLEGIATE RECORD

Season Team	G	Min.	FGM	FGA	Pct.	FTM	FTA	Pct.	Reb.	Ast.	Pts.	RPG	APG	PPG
80-81—Notre Dame	29	291	32	50	.640	12	16	.750	71	11	76	2.4	0.4	2.6
81-82—Arkansas						Did not play—transfer student.								
82-83—Arkansas	30	950	165	307	.537	69	109	.633	219	18	399	7.3	0.6	13.3
83-84—Arkansas	32	1173	209	351	.595	163	211	.773	293	25	581	9.2	0.8	18.2
84-85—Arkansas	35	1289	294	484	.607	185	257	.720	294	23	773	8.4	0.7	22.1
Totals	126	3703	700	1192	.587	429	593	.723	877	77	1829	7.0	0.6	14.5

NBA REGULAR-SEASON RECORD

Season Team	G	Min.	FGM	FGA	Pct.	FTM	FTA	Pct.	Off.	Def.	Tot.	Ast.	St.	Blk.	TO	Pts.	RPG	APG	PPG
85-86—Sacramento	80	1180	160	344	.465	94	130	.723	113	260	373	46	24	34	107	414	4.7	0.6	5.2
86-87—Sacramento	79	1658	256	543	.471	110	140	.786	173	310	483	71	35	30	90	622	6.1	0.9	7.9
87-88—Sacramento	82	1999	324	686	.472	153	188	.814	179	400	579	93	28	59	107	801	7.1	1.1	9.8
88-89—Sac.-Boston	75	1411	175	432	.405	134	152	.882	124	254	378	67	33	23	104	484	5.0	0.9	6.5
89-90—Boston	81	1365	176	367	.480	83	100	.830	117	238	355	46	15	27	64	435	4.4	0.6	5.4
90-91—Boston	72	850	102	218	.468	54	69	.783	71	173	244	21	15	14	53	258	3.4	0.3	3.6
91-92—Boston	70	991	144	293	.491	34	48	.708	94	202	296	32	23	14	27	326	4.2	0.5	4.7
92-93—Boston	78	1129	108	267	.405	41	58	.707	113	233	346	39	17	17	37	257	4.4	0.5	3.3
93-94—Phoenix	74	848	125	256	.488	30	39	.769	50	143	193	45	14	19	35	285	2.6	0.6	3.9
94-95—Phoenix	75	968	119	265	.449	42	49	.857	82	177	259	39	14	18	35	280	3.5	0.5	3.7
95-96—Phoenix	56	663	71	169	.420	20	25	.800	36	96	132	44	13	6	37	164	2.4	0.8	2.9
Totals	822	13062	1760	3840	.458	795	998	.797	1152	2486	3638	543	231	261	696	4326	4.4	0.7	5.3

Three-point field goals: 1986-87, 0-for-1. 1988-89, 0-for-2. 1989-90, 0-for-4. 1990-91, 0-for-2. 1991-92, 4-for-8 (.500). 1992-93, 0-for-6. 1993-94, 5-for-11 (.455). 1994-95, 0-for-2. 1995-96, 2-for-7 (.286). Totals, 11-for-43 (.256).

Personal fouls/disqualifications: 1985-86, 224/1. 1986-87, 213/2. 1987-88, 228/1. 1988-89, 192/2. 1989-90, 170/0. 1990-91, 108/0. 1991-92, 99/0. 1992-93, 123/0. 1993-94, 118/1. 1994-95, 174/2. 1995-96, 113/0. Totals, 1762/9.

NBA PLAYOFF RECORD

Season Team	G	Min.	FGM	FGA	Pct.	FTM	FTA	Pct.	Off.	Def.	Tot.	Ast.	St.	Blk.	TO	Pts.	RPG	APG	PPG
85-86—Sacramento	3	45	5	13	.385	5	6	.833	8	6	14	1	1	1	2	15	4.7	0.3	5.0
88-89—Boston	3	65	6	11	.545	7	9	.778	4	13	17	2	0	1	6	19	5.7	0.7	6.3
89-90—Boston	5	79	13	17	.765	5	6	.833	3	11	14	2	2	3	4	31	2.8	0.4	6.2
90-91—Boston	5	31	4	9	.444	0	0	...	5	6	11	1	0	0	2	8	2.2	0.2	1.6
91-92—Boston	9	82	9	22	.409	2	2	1.000	6	16	22	1	0	1	3	20	2.4	0.1	2.2
92-93—Boston	4	29	3	5	.600	0	0	...	0	5	5	0	0	1	0	6	1.3	0.0	1.5
93-94—Phoenix	8	81	12	28	.429	4	6	.667	5	12	17	3	1	4	2	28	2.1	0.4	3.5
94-95—Phoenix	10	167	31	54	.574	0	0	...	8	23	31	8	5	3	6	63	3.1	0.8	6.3
95-96—Phoenix	2	8	0	2	.000	0	0	...	1	0	1	0	1	0	1	0	0.5	0.0	0.0
Totals	49	587	83	161	.516	23	29	.793	40	92	132	18	10	14	26	190	2.7	0.4	3.9

Three-point field goals: 1988-89, 0-for-1. 1989-90, 0-for-1. 1991-92, 0-for-1. 1994-95, 1-for-2 (.500). Totals, 1-for-5 (.200).

Personal fouls/disqualifications: 1985-86, 8/0. 1988-89, 9/0. 1989-90, 12/0. 1990-91, 7/0. 1991-92, 11/0. 1992-93, 4/0. 1993-94, 15/0. 1994-95, 35/0. 1995-96, 1/0. Totals, 102/0.

KONCAK, JON   C   MAGIC

PERSONAL: Born May 17, 1963, in Cedar Rapids, Iowa. ... 7-0/255. ... Full name: Jon Francis Koncak. ... Name pronounced CON-kack.
HIGH SCHOOL: Center (Kansas City, Mo.).
COLLEGE: Southern Methodist.
TRANSACTIONS/CAREER NOTES: Selected by Atlanta Hawks in first round (fifth pick overall) of 1985 NBA Draft. ... Signed as unrestricted free agent by Orlando Magic (October 3, 1995).
MISCELLANEOUS: Member of gold-medal-winning U.S. Olympic team (1984).

COLLEGIATE RECORD

NOTES: The Sporting News All-America second team (1985).

Season Team	G	Min.	FGM	FGA	Pct.	FTM	FTA	Pct.	Reb.	Ast.	Pts.	RPG	APG	PPG
81-82—South. Methodist...........	27	745	107	232	.461	57	92	.620	155	25	271	5.7	0.9	10.0
82-83—South. Methodist...........	30	980	176	334	.527	85	123	.691	282	38	437	9.4	1.3	14.6
83-84—South. Methodist...........	33	1162	211	340	.621	88	145	.607	378	68	510	11.5	2.1	15.5
84-85—South. Methodist...........	33	1084	219	370	.592	128	192	.667	354	42	566	10.7	1.3	17.2
Totals	123	3971	713	1276	.559	358	552	.649	1169	173	1784	9.5	1.4	14.5

NBA REGULAR-SEASON RECORD

Season Team	G	Min.	FGM	FGA	Pct.	FTM	FTA	Pct.	Off.	Def.	Tot.	Ast.	St.	Blk.	TO	Pts.	RPG	APG	PPG
85-86—Atlanta	82	1695	263	519	.507	156	257	.607	171	296	467	55	37	69	111	682	5.7	0.7	8.3
86-87—Atlanta	82	1684	169	352	.480	125	191	.654	153	340	493	31	52	76	92	463	6.0	0.4	5.6
87-88—Atlanta	49	1073	98	203	.483	83	136	.610	103	230	333	19	36	56	53	279	6.8	0.4	5.7
88-89—Atlanta	74	1531	141	269	.524	63	114	.553	147	306	453	56	54	98	60	345	6.1	0.8	4.7
89-90—Atlanta	54	977	78	127	.614	42	79	.532	58	168	226	23	38	34	47	198	4.2	0.4	3.7
90-91—Atlanta	77	1931	140	321	.436	32	54	.593	101	274	375	124	74	76	50	313	4.9	1.6	4.1
91-92—Atlanta	77	1489	111	284	.391	19	29	.655	62	199	261	132	50	67	54	241	3.4	1.7	3.1
92-93—Atlanta	78	1975	124	267	.464	24	50	.480	100	327	427	140	75	100	52	275	5.5	1.8	3.5
93-94—Atlanta	82	1823	159	369	.431	24	36	.667	83	282	365	102	63	125	44	342	4.5	1.2	4.2
94-95—Atlanta	62	943	77	187	.412	13	24	.542	23	161	184	52	36	46	20	179	3.0	0.8	2.9
95-96—Orlando	67	1288	84	175	.480	32	57	.561	63	209	272	51	27	44	41	203	4.1	0.8	3.0
Totals	784	16409	1444	3073	.470	613	1027	.597	1064	2792	3856	785	542	791	624	3520	4.9	1.0	4.5

Three-point field goals: 1985-86, 0-for-1. 1986-87, 0-for-1. 1987-88, 0-for-2. 1988-89, 0-for-3. 1989-90, 0-for-1. 1990-91, 1-for-8 (.125). 1991-92, 0-for-12. 1992-93, 3-for-8 (.375). 1993-94, 0-for-3. 1994-95, 12-for-36 (.333). 1995-96, 3-for-9 (.333). Totals, 19-for-84 (.226).
Personal fouls/disqualifications: 1985-86, 296/10. 1986-87, 262/2. 1987-88, 161/1. 1988-89, 238/4. 1989-90, 182/4. 1990-91, 265/6. 1991-92, 207/2. 1992-93, 264/6. 1993-94, 236/1. 1994-95, 137/1. 1995-96, 226/7. Totals, 2474/44.

NBA PLAYOFF RECORD

Season Team	G	Min.	FGM	FGA	Pct.	FTM	FTA	Pct.	Off.	Def.	Tot.	Ast.	St.	Blk.	TO	Pts.	RPG	APG	PPG
85-86—Atlanta	9	193	14	29	.483	26	46	.565	11	23	34	5	6	10	7	54	3.8	0.6	6.0
86-87—Atlanta	8	86	7	13	.538	6	8	.750	5	20	25	3	3	4	0	20	3.1	0.4	2.5
88-89—Atlanta	5	192	18	29	.621	28	33	.848	16	32	48	4	2	8	8	64	9.6	0.8	12.8
90-91—Atlanta	5	133	4	14	.286	2	2	1.000	4	19	23	7	2	4	3	10	4.6	1.4	2.0
92-93—Atlanta	3	89	1	10	.100	1	2	.500	8	16	24	4	3	5	2	3	8.0	1.3	1.0
93-94—Atlanta	11	195	27	66	.409	4	10	.400	5	25	30	13	6	12	6	58	2.7	1.2	5.3
95-96—Orlando	12	140	4	7	.571	3	7	.429	8	15	23	3	5	4	3	11	1.9	0.3	0.9
Totals	53	1028	75	168	.446	70	108	.648	57	150	207	39	27	47	29	220	3.9	0.7	4.2

Personal fouls/disqualifications: 1985-86, 27/2. 1986-87, 24/0. 1988-89, 23/1. 1990-91, 17/0. 1992-93, 9/0. 1993-94, 32/0. 1995-96, 39/1. Totals, 171/4.

KUKOC, TONI F/G BULLS

PERSONAL: Born September 18, 1968, in Split, Croatia. ... 6-11/232. ... Name pronounced COO-coach.
TRANSACTIONS/CAREER NOTES: Selected by Chicago Bulls in second round (29th pick overall) of 1990 NBA Draft. ... Played in Yugoslavia (1989-90 and 1990-91). ... Played in Italy (1991-92 and 1992-93). ... Signed by Bulls (July 19, 1993). ... Re-signed as unrestricted free agent by Bulls (August 12, 1994). ... Contract disallowed by NBA (August 19, 1994). ... Re-signed by Bulls (September 14, 1994).
MISCELLANEOUS: Member of NBA championship team (1996). ... Member of silver-medal-winning Yugoslavian Olympic team (1988). ... Member of silver-medal-winning Croatian Olympic team (1992). ... Member of Croatian Olympic team (1996).

ITALIAN LEAGUE RECORD

Season Team	G	Min.	FGM	FGA	Pct.	FTM	FTA	Pct.	Reb.	Ast.	Pts.	RPG	APG	PPG
91-92—Benetton Treviso	22	826	173	313	.553	59	89	.663	118	121	464	5.4	5.5	21.1
92-93—Benetton Treviso	29	1084	191	363	.526	117	150	.780	187	152	551	6.4	5.2	19.0
Totals	51	1910	364	676	.538	176	239	.736	305	273	1015	6.0	5.4	19.9

NBA REGULAR-SEASON RECORD

HONORS: NBA Sixth Man Award (1996). ... NBA All-Rookie second team (1994).

Season Team	G	Min.	FGM	FGA	Pct.	FTM	FTA	Pct.	Off.	Def.	Tot.	Ast.	St.	Blk.	TO	Pts.	RPG	APG	PPG
93-94—Chicago	75	1808	313	726	.431	156	210	.743	98	199	297	252	81	33	167	814	4.0	3.4	10.9
94-95—Chicago	81	2584	487	967	.504	235	314	.748	155	285	440	372	102	16	165	1271	5.4	4.6	15.7
95-96—Chicago	81	2103	386	787	.490	206	267	.772	115	208	323	287	64	28	114	1065	4.0	3.5	13.1
Totals	237	6495	1186	2480	.478	597	791	.755	368	692	1060	911	247	77	446	3150	4.5	3.8	13.3

Three-point field goals: 1993-94, 32-for-118 (.271). 1994-95, 62-for-198 (.313). 1995-96, 87-for-216 (.403). Totals, 181-for-532 (.340).
Personal fouls/disqualifications: 1993-94, 122/0. 1994-95, 163/1. 1995-96, 150/0. Totals, 435/1.

NBA PLAYOFF RECORD

Season Team	G	Min.	FGM	FGA	Pct.	FTM	FTA	Pct.	Off.	Def.	Tot.	Ast.	St.	Blk.	TO	Pts.	RPG	APG	PPG
93-94—Chicago	10	194	30	67	.448	25	34	.735	11	29	40	36	5	3	17	93	4.0	3.6	9.3
94-95—Chicago	10	372	53	111	.477	18	26	.692	20	48	68	57	10	2	19	138	6.8	5.7	13.8
95-96—Chicago	15	439	59	151	.391	31	37	.838	19	44	63	58	14	4	26	162	4.2	3.9	10.8
Totals	35	1005	142	329	.432	74	97	.763	50	121	171	151	29	9	62	393	4.9	4.3	11.2

Three-point field goals: 1993-94, 8-for-19 (.421). 1994-95, 14-for-32 (.438). 1995-96, 13-for-68 (.191). Totals, 35-for-119 (.294).
Personal fouls/disqualifications: 1993-94, 15/0. 1994-95, 23/0. 1995-96, 33/0. Totals, 71/0.

K

LAETTNER, CHRISTIAN　　　　F/C　　　　HAWKS

PERSONAL: Born August 17, 1969, in Angola, N.Y. ... 6-11/235. ... Full name: Christian Donald Laettner. ... Name pronounced LATE-ner.
HIGH SCHOOL: Nichols School (Buffalo).
COLLEGE: Duke.
TRANSACTIONS/CAREER NOTES: Selected by Minnesota Timberwolves in first round (third pick overall) of 1992 NBA Draft. ... Traded by Timberwolves with C Sean Rooks to Atlanta Hawks for G Spud Webb and C Andrew Lang (February 22, 1996).
MISCELLANEOUS: Member of gold-medal-winning U.S. Olympic team (1992). ... Minnesota Timberwolves all-time leading rebounder with 2,225 (1992-93 through 1995-96).

COLLEGIATE RECORD

NOTES: THE SPORTING NEWS College Player of the Year (1992). ... Naismith Award winner (1992). ... Wooden Award winner (1992). ... THE SPORTING NEWS All-America first team (1992). ... THE SPORTING NEWS All-America second team (1991). ... THE SPORTING NEWS All-America third team (1990). ... NCAA Division I Tournament Most Outstanding Player (1991). ... Member of NCAA Division I championship teams (1991, 1992). ... Holds NCAA Division I career record for most games played—148.

											AVERAGES		
Season Team	G	Min.	FGM	FGA	Pct.	FTM	FTA	Pct.	Reb.	Ast.	Pts.	RPG	APG	PPG
88-89—Duke	36	607	115	159	.723	88	121	.727	170	44	319	4.7	1.2	8.9
89-90—Duke	38	1135	194	380	.511	225	269	.836	364	84	619	9.6	2.2	16.3
90-91—Duke	39	1178	271	471	.575	211	263	.802	340	76	771	8.7	1.9	19.8
91-92—Duke	35	1128	254	442	.575	189	232	.815	275	69	751	7.9	2.0	21.5
Totals	148	4048	834	1452	.574	713	885	.806	1149	273	2460	7.8	1.8	16.6

Three-point field goals: 1988-89, 1-for-1. 1989-90, 6-for-12 (.500). 1990-91, 18-for-53 (.340). 1991-92, 54-for-97 (.557). Totals, 79-for-163 (.485).

NBA REGULAR-SEASON RECORD

HONORS: NBA All-Rookie first team (1993).

									REBOUNDS								AVERAGES		
Season Team	G	Min.	FGM	FGA	Pct.	FTM	FTA	Pct.	Off.	Def.	Tot.	Ast.	St.	Blk.	TO	Pts.	RPG	APG	PPG
92-93—Minnesota	81	2823	503	1061	.474	462	553	.835	171	537	708	223	105	83	275	1472	8.7	2.8	18.2
93-94—Minnesota	70	2428	396	883	.448	375	479	.783	160	442	602	307	87	86	259	1173	8.6	4.4	16.8
94-95—Minnesota	81	2770	450	920	.489	409	500	.818	164	449	613	234	101	87	225	1322	7.6	2.9	16.3
95-96—Minn.-Atl.	74	2495	442	907	.487	324	396	.818	184	354	538	197	71	71	187	1217	7.3	2.7	16.4
Totals	306	10516	1791	3771	.475	1570	1928	.814	679	1782	2461	961	364	327	946	5184	8.0	3.1	16.9

Three-point field goals: 1992-93, 4-for-40 (.100). 1993-94, 6-for-25 (.240). 1994-95, 13-for-40 (.325). 1995-96, 9-for-39 (.231). Totals, 32-for-144 (.222).
Personal fouls/disqualifications: 1992-93, 290/4. 1993-94, 264/6. 1994-95, 302/4. 1995-96, 276/7. Totals, 1132/21.

NBA PLAYOFF RECORD

									REBOUNDS								AVERAGES		
Season Team	G	Min.	FGM	FGA	Pct.	FTM	FTA	Pct.	Off.	Def.	Tot.	Ast.	St.	Blk.	TO	Pts.	RPG	APG	PPG
95-96—Atlanta	10	334	59	122	.484	38	54	.704	27	42	69	15	12	10	21	157	6.9	1.5	15.7

Three-point field goals: 1995-96, 1-for-3 (.333).
Personal fouls/disqualifications: 1995-96, 41/1.

LANG, ANDREW　　　　C　　　　BUCKS

PERSONAL: Born June 28, 1966, in Pine Bluff, Ark. ... 6-11/250. ... Full name: Andrew Charles Lang Jr. ... Cousin of Marvin Washington, defensive end with New York Jets.
HIGH SCHOOL: Dollarway (Pine Bluff, Ark.).
COLLEGE: Arkansas.
TRANSACTIONS/CAREER NOTES: Selected by Phoenix Suns in second round (28th pick overall) of 1988 NBA Draft. ... Traded by Suns with G Jeff Hornacek and F Tim Perry to Philadelphia 76ers for F Charles Barkley (June 17, 1992). ... Rights renounced by 76ers (August 27, 1993). ... Signed as free agent by Atlanta Hawks (September 7, 1993). ... Traded by Hawks with G Spud Webb to Minnesota Timberwolves for F Christian Laettner and C Sean Rooks (February 22, 1996). ... Traded by Timberwolves to Milwaukee Bucks for future first-round draft choice (July 11, 1996).

COLLEGIATE RECORD

											AVERAGES		
Season Team	G	Min.	FGM	FGA	Pct.	FTM	FTA	Pct.	Reb.	Ast.	Pts.	RPG	APG	PPG
84-85—Arkansas	33	467	34	84	.405	18	32	.563	67	7	86	2.0	0.2	2.6
85-86—Arkansas	26	694	88	189	.466	37	61	.607	168	13	213	6.5	0.5	8.2
86-87—Arkansas	32	722	102	204	.500	56	87	.644	240	11	260	7.5	0.3	8.1
87-88—Arkansas	30	743	126	239	.527	27	60	.450	218	10	279	7.3	0.3	9.3
Totals	121	2626	350	716	.489	138	240	.575	693	41	838	5.7	0.3	6.9

NBA REGULAR-SEASON RECORD

									REBOUNDS								AVERAGES		
Season Team	G	Min.	FGM	FGA	Pct.	FTM	FTA	Pct.	Off.	Def.	Tot.	Ast.	St.	Blk.	TO	Pts.	RPG	APG	PPG
88-89—Phoenix	62	526	60	117	.513	39	60	.650	54	93	147	9	17	48	28	159	2.4	0.1	2.6
89-90—Phoenix	74	1011	97	174	.557	64	98	.653	83	188	271	21	22	133	41	258	3.7	0.3	3.5
90-91—Phoenix	63	1152	109	189	.577	93	130	.715	113	190	303	27	17	127	45	311	4.8	0.4	4.9
91-92—Phoenix	81	1965	248	475	.522	126	164	.768	170	376	546	43	48	201	87	622	6.7	0.5	7.7
92-93—Philadelphia	73	1861	149	351	.425	87	114	.763	136	300	436	79	46	141	89	386	6.0	1.1	5.3
93-94—Atlanta	82	1608	215	458	.469	73	106	.689	126	187	313	51	38	87	81	504	3.8	0.6	6.1
94-95—Atlanta	82	2340	320	677	.473	152	188	.809	154	302	456	72	45	144	108	794	5.6	0.9	9.7
95-96—Atl.-Minn.	71	2365	353	790	.447	125	156	.801	153	302	455	65	42	126	124	832	6.4	0.9	11.7
Totals	588	12828	1551	3231	.480	759	1016	.747	989	1938	2927	367	275	1007	603	3866	5.0	0.6	6.6

Three-point field goals: 1990-91, 0-for-1. 1991-92, 0-for-1. 1992-93, 1-for-5 (.200). 1993-94, 1-for-4 (.250). 1994-95, 2-for-3 (.667). 1995-96, 1-for-5 (.200). Totals, 5-for-19 (.263).

Personal fouls/disqualifications: 1988-89, 112/1. 1989-90, 171/1. 1990-91, 168/2. 1991-92, 306/8. 1992-93, 261/4. 1993-94, 192/2. 1994-95, 271/4. 1995-96, 241/4. Totals, 1722/26.

NBA PLAYOFF RECORD

Season Team	G	Min.	FGM	FGA	Pct.	FTM	FTA	Pct.	REBOUNDS Off.	Def.	Tot.	Ast.	St.	Blk.	TO	Pts.	AVERAGES RPG	APG	PPG
88-89—Phoenix	4	8	0	2	.000	0	0	...	3	3	6	1	0	0	3	0	1.5	0.3	0.0
89-90—Phoenix	12	93	6	9	.667	4	7	.571	4	16	20	2	3	10	5	16	1.7	0.2	1.3
90-91—Phoenix	4	55	6	11	.545	14	17	.824	4	14	18	1	1	3	2	26	4.5	0.3	6.5
91-92—Phoenix	8	192	15	40	.375	15	19	.789	15	17	32	2	3	15	8	45	4.0	0.3	5.6
93-94—Atlanta	11	234	29	63	.460	17	22	.773	15	32	47	5	6	20	15	75	4.3	0.5	6.8
94-95—Atlanta	3	101	12	28	.429	7	9	.778	3	9	12	1	2	2	6	31	4.0	0.3	10.3
Totals	**42**	**683**	**68**	**153**	**.444**	**57**	**74**	**.770**	**44**	**91**	**135**	**12**	**15**	**50**	**39**	**193**	**3.2**	**0.3**	**4.6**

Three-point field goals: 1993-94, 0-for-1.

Personal fouls/disqualifications: 1988-89, 3/0. 1989-90, 17/0. 1990-91, 12/0. 1991-92, 33/2. 1993-94, 35/1. 1994-95, 12/0. Totals, 112/3.

LANG, ANTONIO F CAVALIERS

PERSONAL: Born May 15, 1972, in Mobile, Ala. ... 6-8/230. ... Full name: Antonio Maurice Lang.
HIGH SCHOOL: LeFlore (Mobile, Ala.).
COLLEGE: Duke.
TRANSACTIONS/CAREER NOTES: Selected by Phoenix Suns in second round (29th pick overall) of 1994 NBA Draft. ... Traded by Suns with G/F Dan Majerle and 1996, 1997 or 1998 first-round draft choice to Cleveland Cavaliers for F/C John Williams (October 7, 1995).

COLLEGIATE RECORD

NOTES: Member of NCAA Division I championship teams (1991, 1992).

Season Team	G	Min.	FGM	FGA	Pct.	FTM	FTA	Pct.	Reb.	Ast.	Pts.	AVERAGES RPG	APG	PPG
90-91—Duke.............................	36	426	57	94	.606	40	76	.526	82	7	154	2.3	0.2	4.3
91-92—Duke.............................	34	763	77	137	.562	65	99	.657	139	23	219	4.1	0.7	6.4
92-93—Duke.............................	31	808	80	153	.523	55	84	.655	171	25	215	5.5	0.8	6.9
93-94—Duke.............................	34	1023	153	260	.588	118	163	.724	184	35	424	5.4	1.0	12.5
Totals	**135**	**3020**	**367**	**644**	**.570**	**278**	**422**	**.659**	**576**	**90**	**1012**	**4.3**	**0.7**	**7.5**

Three-point field goals: 1992-93, 0-for-1. 1993-94, 0-for-2. Totals, 0-for-3.

NBA REGULAR-SEASON RECORD

Season Team	G	Min.	FGM	FGA	Pct.	FTM	FTA	Pct.	REBOUNDS Off.	Def.	Tot.	Ast.	St.	Blk.	TO	Pts.	AVERAGES RPG	APG	PPG
94-95—Phoenix	12	53	4	10	.400	3	4	.750	3	1	4	1	0	2	5	11	0.3	0.1	0.9
95-96—Cleveland	41	367	41	77	.532	34	47	.723	17	36	53	12	14	12	24	116	1.3	0.3	2.8
Totals	**53**	**420**	**45**	**87**	**.517**	**37**	**51**	**.725**	**20**	**37**	**57**	**13**	**14**	**14**	**29**	**127**	**1.1**	**0.2**	**2.4**

Three-point field goals: 1995-96, 0-for-2.

Personal fouls/disqualifications: 1994-95, 11/0. 1995-96, 61/0. Totals, 72/0.

NBA PLAYOFF RECORD

Season Team	G	Min.	FGM	FGA	Pct.	FTM	FTA	Pct.	REBOUNDS Off.	Def.	Tot.	Ast.	St.	Blk.	TO	Pts.	AVERAGES RPG	APG	PPG
95-96—Cleveland	1	2	0	0	...	0	0	...	0	0	0	0	0	0	0	0	0.0	0.0	0.0

LECKNER, ERIC C

PERSONAL: Born May 27, 1966, in Inglewood, Calif. ... 6-11/265. ... Full name: Eric Charles Leckner. ... Name pronounced leck-NER.
HIGH SCHOOL: Mira Costa (Manhattan Beach, Calif.).
COLLEGE: Wyoming.
TRANSACTIONS/CAREER NOTES: Selected by Utah Jazz in first round (17th pick overall) of 1988 NBA Draft. ... Traded by Jazz with G Bob Hansen and 1990 first- and second-round draft choices to Sacramento Kings in three-way deal in which Washington Bullets sent G Jeff Malone to Jazz and Kings sent F Pervis Ellison to Bullets (June 25, 1990); Jazz also received 1990 second-round draft choice from Kings and Kings also received 1991 second-round draft choice from Bullets. ... Traded by Kings to Charlotte Hornets for 1995 second-round draft choice and draft considerations (January 29, 1991). ... Played in Italy (1992-93). ... Signed as free agent by Philadelphia 76ers (August 27, 1993). ... Traded by 76ers to Detroit Pistons for 1996 second-round draft choice (July 25, 1994). ... Rights renounced by Pistons (July 15, 1996).

COLLEGIATE RECORD

Season Team	G	Min.	FGM	FGA	Pct.	FTM	FTA	Pct.	Reb.	Ast.	Pts.	AVERAGES RPG	APG	PPG
84-85—Wyoming........................	29	600	98	168	.583	48	78	.615	112	7	244	3.9	0.2	8.4
85-86—Wyoming........................	36	1113	228	392	.582	112	183	.612	207	17	568	5.8	0.5	15.8
86-87—Wyoming........................	34	1123	246	390	.631	142	201	.706	245	16	634	7.2	0.5	18.6
87-88—Wyoming........................	32	972	181	281	.644	130	172	.756	210	14	492	6.6	0.4	15.4
Totals	**131**	**3808**	**753**	**1231**	**.612**	**432**	**634**	**.681**	**774**	**54**	**1938**	**5.9**	**0.4**	**14.8**

NBA REGULAR-SEASON RECORD

Season Team	G	Min.	FGM	FGA	Pct.	FTM	FTA	Pct.	REBOUNDS Off.	Def.	Tot.	Ast.	St.	Blk.	TO	Pts.	AVERAGES RPG	APG	PPG
88-89—Utah...............	75	779	120	220	.545	79	113	.699	48	151	199	16	8	22	69	319	2.7	0.2	4.3
89-90—Utah...............	77	764	125	222	.563	81	109	.743	48	144	192	19	15	23	63	331	2.5	0.2	4.3

Season Team	G	Min.	FGM	FGA	Pct.	FTM	FTA	Pct.	Off.	Def.	Tot.	Ast.	St.	Blk.	TO	Pts.	RPG	APG	PPG
90-91—Sac.-Char.......	72	1122	131	294	.446	62	111	.559	82	213	295	39	14	22	69	324	4.1	0.5	4.5
91-92—Charlotte........	59	716	79	154	.513	38	51	.745	49	157	206	31	9	18	39	196	3.5	0.5	3.3
93-94—Philadelphia ...	71	1163	139	286	.486	84	130	.646	75	207	282	86	18	34	86	362	4.0	1.2	5.1
94-95—Detroit	57	623	87	165	.527	51	72	.708	47	127	174	14	15	15	39	225	3.1	0.2	3.9
95-96—Detroit	18	155	18	29	.621	8	13	.615	8	26	34	1	2	4	11	44	1.9	0.1	2.4
Totals	429	5322	699	1370	.510	403	599	.673	357	1025	1382	206	81	138	376	1801	3.2	0.5	4.2

Three-point field goals: 1991-92, 0-for-1. 1993-94, 0-for-2. 1994-95, 0-for-2. Totals, 0-for-5.
Personal fouls/disqualifications: 1988-89, 174/1. 1989-90, 157/0. 1990-91, 192/4. 1991-92, 114/1. 1993-94, 190/2. 1994-95, 122/1. 1995-96, 30/0. Totals, 979/9.

NBA PLAYOFF RECORD

Season Team	G	Min.	FGM	FGA	Pct.	FTM	FTA	Pct.	Off.	Def.	Tot.	Ast.	St.	Blk.	TO	Pts.	RPG	APG	PPG
88-89—Utah..............	3	10	1	4	.250	0	0	...	1	1	2	0	0	0	3	2	0.7	0.0	0.7
89-90—Utah..............	3	28	6	10	.600	5	9	.556	2	6	8	2	0	0	1	18	2.7	0.7	6.0
95-96—Detroit	1	3	0	0	...	0	0	...	0	0	0	0	0	0	0	0	0.0	0.0	0.0
Totals	7	41	7	14	.500	5	9	.556	3	7	10	2	0	0	4	20	1.4	0.3	2.9

Three-point field goals: 1989-90, 1-for-1.
Personal fouls/disqualifications: 1988-89, 2/0. 1989-90, 8/0. 1995-96, 2/0. Totals, 12/0.

ITALIAN LEAGUE RECORD

Season Team	G	Min.	FGM	FGA	Pct.	FTM	FTA	Pct.	Reb.	Ast.	Pts.	RPG	APG	PPG
92-93—Panna Firenze................	21	753	156	253	.617	84	127	.661	245	4	397	11.7	0.2	18.9

LEGLER, TIM   G   BULLETS

PERSONAL: Born December 26, 1966, in Washington, D.C. ... 6-4/200. ... Full name: Timothy Eugene Legler. ... Name pronounced LEG-ler.
HIGH SCHOOL: John Randolph Tucker (Richmond, Va.).
COLLEGE: La Salle.
TRANSACTIONS/CAREER NOTES: Not drafted by an NBA franchise. ... Played in Continental Basketball Association with Rochester Flyers (1988-89) and Omaha Racers (1989-90 through 1992-93 and 1994-95). ... Played in United States Basketball League with Philadelphia Aces (1988, 1990) and Philadelphia Spirit (1991, 1992). ... Played in World Basketball League with Youngstown Pride (1989). ... Signed by Phoenix Suns to first of two consecutive 10-day contracts (March 21, 1990). ... Signed as unrestricted free agent by Minnesota Timberwolves (July 20, 1990). ... Waived by Timberwolves (November 1, 1990). ... Signed by Denver Nuggets to first of two consecutive 10-day contracts (December 28, 1990). ... Signed as free agent by Washington Bullets (September 30, 1991). ... Waived by Bullets (October 29, 1991). ... Signed as free agent by Utah Jazz (September 28, 1992). ... Waived by Jazz (November 25, 1992). ... Signed by Dallas Mavericks to first of two consecutive 10-day contracts (March 2, 1993). ... Re-signed by Mavericks for remainder of season (March 22, 1993). ... Rights renounced by Mavericks (June 30, 1994). ... Signed by Golden State Warriors to first of two consecutive 10-day contracts (March 7, 1995). ... Re-signed by Warriors for remainder of season (March 27, 1995). ... Signed as unrestricted free agent by Bullets (September 27, 1995).

COLLEGIATE RECORD

Season Team	G	Min.	FGM	FGA	Pct.	FTM	FTA	Pct.	Reb.	Ast.	Pts.	RPG	APG	PPG
84-85—La Salle	26	494	69	147	.469	17	24	.708	72	51	155	2.8	2.0	6.0
85-86—La Salle	28	868	158	315	.502	45	54	.833	110	53	361	3.9	1.9	12.9
86-87—La Salle	33	1254	233	487	.478	93	119	.782	147	68	616	4.5	2.1	18.7
87-88—La Salle	34	1292	203	414	.490	57	71	.803	139	72	567	4.1	2.1	16.7
Totals	121	3908	663	1363	.486	212	268	.791	468	244	1699	3.9	2.0	14.0

Three-point field goals: 1986-87, 57-for-141 (.404). 1987-88, 104-for-212 (.491). Totals, 161-for-353 (.456).

CBA REGULAR-SEASON RECORD

NOTES: CBA All-League first team (1991 and 1993). ... CBA All-League second team (1995).

Season Team	G	Min.	FGM	FGA	Pct.	FTM	FTA	Pct.	Reb.	Ast.	Pts.	RPG	APG	PPG
88-89—Rochester.......................	53	1504	257	543	.473	119	151	.788	130	145	667	2.5	2.7	12.6
89-90—Omaha...........................	40	1474	337	698	.483	188	226	.832	165	178	903	4.1	4.5	22.6
90-91—Omaha...........................	45	1695	445	849	.524	198	238	.832	177	171	1137	3.9	3.8	25.3
91-92—Omaha...........................	39	1459	291	604	.482	138	158	.873	142	145	792	3.6	3.7	20.3
92-93—Omaha...........................	39	1596	384	738	.520	238	279	.853	168	167	1059	4.3	4.3	*27.2
94-95—Omaha...........................	42	1647	360	659	.546	234	264	.886	101	168	1046	2.4	4.0	24.9
Totals	258	9375	2074	4091	.507	1115	1316	.847	883	974	5604	3.4	3.8	21.7

Three-point field goals: 1988-89, 34-for-91 (.374). 1989-90, 41-for-88 (.466). 1990-91, 49-for-113 (.434). 1991-92, 72-for-155 (.465). 1992-93, 53-for-132 (.402). 1994-95, 92-for-191 (.482). Totals, 341-for-770 (.443).

NBA REGULAR-SEASON RECORD

HONORS: Long Distance Shootout winner (1996).
NOTES: Led NBA with .522 three-point field-goal percentage (1996).

Season Team	G	Min.	FGM	FGA	Pct.	FTM	FTA	Pct.	Off.	Def.	Tot.	Ast.	St.	Blk.	TO	Pts.	RPG	APG	PPG
89-90—Phoenix	11	83	11	29	.379	6	6	1.000	4	4	8	6	2	0	4	28	0.7	0.5	2.5
90-91—Denver	10	148	25	72	.347	5	6	.833	8	10	18	12	2	0	4	58	1.8	1.2	5.8
92-93—Utah-Dallas.....	33	635	105	241	.436	57	71	.803	25	34	59	46	24	6	28	289	1.8	1.4	8.8
93-94—Dallas.............	79	1322	231	528	.438	142	169	.840	36	92	128	120	52	13	60	656	1.6	1.5	8.3
94-95—Golden State ...	24	371	60	115	.522	30	34	.882	12	28	40	27	12	1	20	176	1.7	1.1	7.3
95-96—Washington	77	1775	233	460	.507	132	153	.863	29	111	140	136	45	12	45	726	1.8	1.8	9.4
Totals	234	4334	665	1445	.460	372	439	.847	114	279	393	347	137	32	161	1933	1.7	1.5	8.3

Three-point field goals: 1989-90, 0-for-1. 1990-91, 3-for-12 (.250). 1992-93, 22-for-65 (.338). 1993-94, 52-for-139 (.374). 1994-95, 26-for-50 (.520). 1995-96, 128-for-245 (.522). Totals, 231-for-512 (.451).
Personal fouls/disqualifications: 1989-90, 12/0. 1990-91, 20/0. 1992-93, 63/0. 1993-94, 133/0. 1994-95, 33/0. 1995-96, 141/0. Totals, 402/0.

LENARD, VOSHON   G   HEAT

PERSONAL: Born May 14, 1973, in Detroit. ... 6-4/205. ... Full name: Voshon Kelan Lenard.
HIGH SCHOOL: Southwestern (Detroit).
COLLEGE: Minnesota.
TRANSACTIONS/CAREER NOTES: Selected after junior season by Milwaukee Bucks in second round (46th pick overall) of 1994 NBA Draft. ... Returned to college for senior season (1994-95). ... Waived by Bucks (October 25, 1995). ... Played in Continental Basketball Association with Oklahoma City Cavalry (1995-96). ... Signed as free agent by Miami Heat for remainder of season (December 29, 1995).

COLLEGIATE RECORD

Season Team	G	Min.	FGM	FGA	Pct.	FTM	FTA	Pct.	Reb.	Ast.	Pts.	RPG	APG	PPG
91-92—Minnesota	32	868	139	330	.421	82	101	.812	118	86	411	3.7	2.7	12.8
92-93—Minnesota	31	883	192	399	.481	89	111	.802	113	82	531	3.6	2.6	17.1
93-94—Minnesota	33	1029	218	462	.472	103	122	.844	123	74	625	3.7	2.2	18.9
94-95—Minnesota	31	992	174	422	.412	107	141	.759	134	80	536	4.3	2.6	17.3
Totals	127	3772	723	1613	.448	381	475	.802	488	322	2103	3.8	2.5	16.6

Three-point field goals: 1991-92, 51-for-144 (.354). 1992-93, 58-for-158 (.367). 1993-94, 86-for-209 (.411). 1994-95, 81-for-244 (.332). Totals, 276-for-755 (.366).

CBA REGULAR-SEASON RECORD

Season Team	G	Min.	FGM	FGA	Pct.	FTM	FTA	Pct.	Reb.	Ast.	Pts.	RPG	APG	PPG
95-96—Oklahoma City	18	711	189	387	.488	75	100	.750	60	70	541	3.3	3.9	30.1

Three-point field goals: 1995-96, 88-for-203 (.433).

NBA REGULAR-SEASON RECORD

									REBOUNDS							AVERAGES		
Season Team	G	Min.	FGM	FGA	Pct.	FTM	FTA	Pct.	Off.	Def.	Tot.	Ast.	St.	Blk.	TO	Pts.	RPG	APG	PPG
95-96—Miami	30	323	53	141	.376	34	43	.791	12	40	52	31	6	1	23	176	1.7	1.0	5.9

Three-point field goals: 1995-96, 36-for-101 (.356).
Personal fouls/disqualifications: 1995-96, 31/0.

LEWIS, CEDRIC   F/C

PERSONAL: Born September 24, 1969, in Washington, D.C. ... 6-10/235.
HIGH SCHOOL: John Carroll (Bel Air, Md.).
COLLEGE: Maryland.
TRANSACTIONS/CAREER NOTES: Not drafted by an NBA franchise. ... Played in Continental Basketball Association with Albany Patroons (1991-92). ... Signed by Washington Bullets for remainder of season (April 16, 1996). ... Played in France (1992-93 and 1994-95). ... Played in Germany (1995-96).

COLLEGIATE RECORD

Season Team	G	Min.	FGM	FGA	Pct.	FTM	FTA	Pct.	Reb.	Ast.	Pts.	RPG	APG	PPG
87-88—Maryland	7	113	5	16	.313	4	13	.308	14	1	14	2.0	0.1	2.0
88-89—Maryland	27	373	35	62	.565	16	39	.410	77	5	86	2.9	0.2	3.2
89-90—Maryland	33	436	38	89	.427	25	45	.556	100	16	101	3.0	0.5	3.1
90-91—Maryland	28	961	120	249	.482	94	158	.595	233	15	334	8.3	0.5	11.9
Totals	95	1883	198	416	.476	139	255	.545	424	37	535	4.5	0.4	5.6

FRENCH LEAGUE RECORD

Season Team	G	Min.	FGM	FGA	Pct.	FTM	FTA	Pct.	Reb.	Ast.	Pts.	RPG	APG	PPG
92-93—Montpellier	1	...	...	...	....	...	...	...	9	...	13	9.0	...	13.0

GERMAN LEAGUE RECORD

Season Team	G	Min.	FGM	FGA	Pct.	FTM	FTA	Pct.	Reb.	Ast.	Pts.	RPG	APG	PPG
95-96—Scouting Bundesilga	...	...	80	140	.571	53	63	.841	218	12	213	...	...	...

NBA REGULAR-SEASON RECORD

									REBOUNDS							AVERAGES		
Season Team	G	Min.	FGM	FGA	Pct.	FTM	FTA	Pct.	Off.	Def.	Tot.	Ast.	St.	Blk.	TO	Pts.	RPG	APG	PPG
95-96—Washington	3	4	2	3	.667	0	0	...	2	0	2	0	1	0	0	4	0.7	0.0	1.3

LEWIS, MARTIN   F

PERSONAL: Born April 28, 1975, in Liberal, Kan. ... 6-5/210.
HIGH SCHOOL: Liberal (Kan.).
JUNIOR COLLEGE: Butler County (Kan.) Community College, then Seward County (Kan.) Community College.
TRANSACTIONS/CAREER NOTES: Selected after sophomore season by Golden State Warriors in second round (50th pick overall) of 1995 NBA Draft. ... Traded by Warriors with F/C Carlos Rogers, C Victor Alexander and draft rights to F Dwayne Whitfield and C Michael McDonald to Toronto Raptors for G B.J. Armstrong (September 18, 1995). ... Rights renounced by Raptors (July 24, 1996).

COLLEGIATE RECORD

Season Team	G	Min.	FGM	FGA	Pct.	FTM	FTA	Pct.	Reb.	Ast.	Pts.	RPG	APG	PPG
93-94—Butler County C.C.	33	...	212	384	.552	108	166	.651	207	88	576	6.3	2.7	17.5
94-95—Seward County C.C.	37	...	307	472	.650	202	307	.658	304	64	838	8.2	1.7	22.6
Junior college totals	70	...	519	856	.606	310	473	.655	511	152	1414	7.3	2.2	20.2

NBA REGULAR-SEASON RECORD

									REBOUNDS							AVERAGES		
Season Team	G	Min.	FGM	FGA	Pct.	FTM	FTA	Pct.	Off.	Def.	Tot.	Ast.	St.	Blk.	TO	Pts.	RPG	APG	PPG
95-96—Toronto	16	189	29	60	.483	15	25	.600	15	14	29	3	8	3	14	75	1.8	0.2	4.7

Three-point field goals: 1995-96, 2-for-7 (.286).
Personal fouls/disqualifications: 1995-96, 21/0.

LISTER, ALTON F/C CELTICS

PERSONAL: Born October 1, 1958, in Dallas. ... 7-0/245. ... Full name: Alton Lavelle Lister. ... Name pronounced AL-ton.
HIGH SCHOOL: Woodrow Wilson (Dallas).
JUNIOR COLLEGE: San Jacinto College (Texas).
COLLEGE: Arizona State.
TRANSACTIONS/CAREER NOTES: Selected by Milwaukee Bucks in first round (21st pick overall) of 1981 NBA Draft. ... Traded by Bucks with 1987 and 1989 first-round draft choices to Seattle SuperSonics for C Jack Sikma and 1987 and 1989 second-round draft choices (July 1, 1986). ... Traded by SuperSonics to Golden State Warriors for 1990 first-round draft choice (August 7, 1989). ... Waived by Warriors (March 23, 1993). ... Signed by Bucks (October 6, 1994). ... Traded by Bucks with G Todd Day to Boston Celtics for G Sherman Douglas (November 26, 1995).
MISCELLANEOUS: Member of U.S. Olympic team (1980). ... Milwaukee Bucks all-time blocked shots leader with 804 (1981-82 through 1985-86 and 1994-95 through 1995-96).

COLLEGIATE RECORD

Season Team	G	Min.	FGM	FGA	Pct.	FTM	FTA	Pct.	Reb.	Ast.	Pts.	RPG	APG	PPG
76-77—San Jacinto College........	40	...	...	...	...	...	...	...	640	...	680	16.0	...	17.0
77-78—San Jacinto College........					Did not play—redshirted.									
78-79—Arizona State	29	584	104	209	.498	47	84	.560	194	25	255	6.7	0.9	8.8
79-80—Arizona State	27	793	133	264	.504	58	104	.558	231	56	324	8.6	2.1	12.0
80-81—Arizona State	26	845	158	282	.560	85	123	.691	251	48	401	9.7	1.8	15.4
Junior college totals	40	...	...	...	...	...	...	...	640	...	680	16.0	...	17.0
4-year-college totals	82	2222	395	755	.523	190	311	.611	676	129	980	8.2	1.6	12.0

NBA REGULAR-SEASON RECORD

									REBOUNDS							AVERAGES		
Season Team	G	Min.	FGM	FGA	Pct.	FTM	FTA	Pct.	Off.	Def.	Tot.	Ast.	St.	Blk.	TO	Pts.	RPG	APG	PPG
81-82—Milwaukee	80	1186	149	287	.519	64	123	.520	108	279	387	84	18	118	129	362	4.8	1.1	4.5
82-83—Milwaukee	80	1885	272	514	.529	130	242	.537	168	400	568	111	50	177	186	674	7.1	1.4	8.4
83-84—Milwaukee	82	1955	256	512	.500	114	182	.626	156	447	603	110	41	140	153	626	7.4	1.3	7.6
84-85—Milwaukee	81	2091	322	598	.538	154	262	.588	219	428	647	127	49	167	183	798	8.0	1.6	9.9
85-86—Milwaukee	81	1812	318	577	.551	160	266	.602	199	393	592	101	49	142	161	796	7.3	1.2	9.8
86-87—Seattle	75	2288	346	687	.504	179	265	.675	223	482	705	110	32	180	169	871	9.4	1.5	11.6
87-88—Seattle	82	1812	173	343	.504	114	188	.606	200	427	627	58	27	140	90	461	7.6	0.7	5.6
88-89—Seattle	82	1806	271	543	.499	115	178	.646	207	338	545	54	28	180	117	657	6.6	0.7	8.0
89-90—Golden State ...	3	40	4	8	.500	4	7	.571	5	3	8	2	1	0	0	12	2.7	0.7	4.0
90-91—Golden State...	77	1552	188	393	.478	115	202	.569	121	362	483	93	20	90	106	491	6.3	1.2	6.4
91-92—Golden State...	26	293	44	79	.557	14	33	.424	21	71	92	14	5	16	20	102	3.5	0.5	3.9
92-93—Golden State ...	20	174	19	42	.452	7	13	.538	15	29	44	5	0	9	18	45	2.2	0.3	2.3
93-94—						Did not play.													
94-95—Milwaukee	60	776	66	134	.493	35	70	.500	67	169	236	12	16	57	38	167	3.9	0.2	2.8
95-96—Mil.-Boston	64	735	51	105	.486	41	64	.641	67	213	280	19	6	42	48	143	4.4	0.3	2.2
Totals	893	18405	2479	4822	.514	1246	2095	.595	1776	4041	5817	900	342	1458	1418	6205	6.5	1.0	6.9

Three-point field goals: 1984-85, 0-for-1. 1985-86, 0-for-2. 1986-87, 0-for-1. 1987-88, 1-for-2 (.500). 1989-90, 0-for-1. 1990-91, 0-for-1. 1994-95, 0-for-1. Totals, 1-for-9 (.111).
Personal fouls/disqualifications: 1981-82, 239/4. 1982-83, 328/18. 1983-84, 327/11. 1984-85, 287/5. 1985-86, 300/8. 1986-87, 289/11. 1987-88, 319/8. 1988-89, 310/3. 1989-90, 8/0. 1990-91, 282/4. 1991-92, 61/0. 1992-93, 40/0. 1994-95, 146/3. 1995-96, 136/1. Totals, 3072/76.

NBA PLAYOFF RECORD

									REBOUNDS							AVERAGES		
Season Team	G	Min.	FGM	FGA	Pct.	FTM	FTA	Pct.	Off.	Def.	Tot.	Ast.	St.	Blk.	TO	Pts.	RPG	APG	PPG
81-82—Milwaukee	6	112	14	24	.583	5	7	.714	6	21	27	5	2	15	9	33	4.5	0.8	5.5
82-83—Milwaukee	9	206	27	63	.429	4	5	.800	21	40	61	11	9	15	17	58	6.8	1.2	6.4
83-84—Milwaukee	16	368	39	78	.500	30	48	.625	26	70	96	10	5	24	27	108	6.0	0.6	6.8
84-85—Milwaukee	8	203	27	60	.450	15	32	.469	27	35	62	15	6	15	16	69	7.8	1.9	8.6
85-86—Milwaukee	14	335	66	103	.641	35	58	.603	37	59	96	12	7	22	21	167	6.9	0.9	11.9
86-87—Seattle	9	206	20	50	.400	14	20	.700	29	27	56	7	7	13	10	54	6.2	0.8	6.0
87-88—Seattle	5	77	12	17	.706	4	5	.800	9	20	29	5	1	5	4	28	5.8	1.0	5.6
88-89—Seattle	8	160	17	39	.436	22	26	.846	13	25	38	2	2	21	9	56	4.8	0.3	7.0
90-91—Golden State...	6	72	12	25	.480	2	5	.400	7	21	28	2	0	7	8	26	4.7	0.3	4.3
91-92—Golden State...	4	47	6	15	.400	4	5	.800	3	8	11	1	0	4	3	16	2.8	0.3	4.0
Totals	85	1786	240	474	.506	135	211	.640	178	326	504	70	39	141	124	615	5.9	0.8	7.2

Three-point field goals: 1982-83, 0-for-1. 1985-86, 0-for-1. Totals, 0-for-2.
Personal fouls/disqualifications: 1981-82, 23/0. 1982-83, 30/1. 1983-84, 63/2. 1984-85, 36/1. 1985-86, 56/3. 1986-87, 37/3. 1987-88, 17/0. 1988-89, 28/0. 1990-91, 15/0. 1991-92, 9/0. Totals, 314/10.

LOHAUS, BRAD ○ F HORNETS

PERSONAL: Born September 29, 1964, in New Ulm, Minn. ... 6-11/230. ... Full name: Brad Allen Lohaus. ... Name pronounced LOW-house.
HIGH SCHOOL: Greenway (Phoenix).
COLLEGE: Iowa.
TRANSACTIONS/CAREER NOTES: Selected by Boston Celtics in second round (45th pick overall) of 1987 NBA Draft. ... Traded by Celtics with G Danny Ainge to Sacramento Kings for C/F Joe Kleine and F Ed Pinckney (February 23, 1989). ... Selected by Minnesota Timberwolves from Kings in NBA expansion draft (June 15, 1989). ... Traded by Timberwolves to Milwaukee Bucks for C Randy Breuer and a conditional exchange of 1991 or 1992 second-round draft choices (January 4, 1990). ... Signed as free agent by Miami Heat (October 7, 1994). ... Signed as unrestricted free agent by San Antonio Spurs (September 29, 1995). ... Traded by Spurs with F J.R. Reid and 1996 first-round draft choice to New York Knicks for F Charles Smith and F Monty Williams (February 8, 1996). ... Traded by Knicks with F Anthony Mason to Charlotte Hornets for F Larry Johnson (July 14, 1996).

COLLEGIATE RECORD

Season Team	G	Min.	FGM	FGA	Pct.	FTM	FTA	Pct.	Reb.	Ast.	Pts.	AVERAGES		
												RPG	APG	PPG
82-83—Iowa	20	...	9	29	.310	7	13	.538	11	10	26	0.6	0.5	1.3
83-84—Iowa	28	626	78	193	.404	35	52	.673	146	28	191	5.2	1.0	6.8
84-85—Iowa					Did not play—redshirted.									
85-86—Iowa	32	407	44	102	.431	27	34	.794	101	13	115	3.2	0.4	3.6
86-87—Iowa	35	943	149	276	.540	72	104	.692	268	63	395	7.7	1.8	11.3
Totals	115	...	280	600	.467	141	203	.695	526	114	727	4.6	1.0	6.3

Three-point field goals: 1982-83, 1-for-1. 1986-87, 25-for-72 (.347). Totals, 26-for-73 (.356).

NBA REGULAR-SEASON RECORD

Season Team	G	Min.	FGM	FGA	Pct.	FTM	FTA	Pct.	REBOUNDS			Ast.	St.	Blk.	TO	Pts.	AVERAGES		
									Off.	Def.	Tot.						RPG	APG	PPG
87-88—Boston	70	718	122	246	.496	50	62	.806	46	92	138	49	20	41	59	297	2.0	0.7	4.2
88-89—Boston-Sac.	77	1214	210	486	.432	81	103	.786	84	172	256	66	30	56	77	502	3.3	0.9	6.5
89-90—Min.-Mil.	80	1943	305	663	.460	75	103	.728	98	300	398	168	58	88	109	732	5.0	2.1	9.2
90-91—Milwaukee	81	1219	179	415	.431	37	54	.685	59	158	217	75	50	74	60	428	2.7	0.9	5.3
91-92—Milwaukee	70	1081	162	360	.450	27	41	.659	65	184	249	74	40	71	46	408	3.6	1.1	5.8
92-93—Milwaukee	80	1766	283	614	.461	73	101	.723	59	217	276	127	47	74	93	724	3.5	1.6	9.1
93-94—Milwaukee	67	962	102	281	.363	20	29	.690	33	117	150	62	30	55	58	270	2.2	0.9	4.0
94-95—Miami	61	730	97	231	.420	10	15	.667	28	74	102	43	20	25	29	267	1.7	0.7	4.4
95-96—S.A.-N.Y.	55	598	71	175	.406	4	5	.800	7	57	64	44	10	17	20	197	1.2	0.8	3.6
Totals	641	10231	1531	3471	.441	377	513	.735	479	1371	1850	708	305	501	551	3825	2.9	1.1	6.0

Three-point field goals: 1987-88, 3-for-13 (.231). 1988-89, 1-for-11 (.091). 1989-90, 47-for-137 (.343). 1990-91, 33-for-119 (.277). 1991-92, 57-for-144 (.396). 1992-93, 85-for-230 (.370). 1993-94, 46-for-134 (.343). 1994-95, 63-for-155 (.406). 1995-96, 51-for-122 (.418). Totals, 386-for-1065 (.362).

Personal fouls/disqualifications: 1987-88, 123/1. 1988-89, 161/1. 1989-90, 211/3. 1990-91, 170/3. 1991-92, 144/5. 1992-93, 178/1. 1993-94, 142/3. 1994-95, 85/2. 1995-96, 70/0. Totals, 1284/19.

NBA PLAYOFF RECORD

Season Team	G	Min.	FGM	FGA	Pct.	FTM	FTA	Pct.	REBOUNDS			Ast.	St.	Blk.	TO	Pts.	AVERAGES		
									Off.	Def.	Tot.						RPG	APG	PPG
87-88—Boston	9	26	8	11	.727	0	0	...	1	3	4	0	0	1	1	16	0.4	0.0	1.8
89-90—Milwaukee	4	147	16	40	.400	0	0	...	4	23	27	5	8	9	9	38	6.8	1.3	9.5
90-91—Milwaukee	3	41	5	16	.313	1	2	.500	4	5	9	1	0	0	3	14	3.0	0.3	4.7
Totals	16	214	29	67	.433	1	2	.500	9	31	40	6	8	10	13	68	2.5	0.4	4.3

Three-point field goals: 1987-88, 0-for-2. 1989-90, 6-for-16 (.375). 1990-91, 3-for-8 (.375). Totals, 9-for-26 (.346).

Personal fouls/disqualifications: 1987-88, 4/0. 1989-90, 17/1. 1990-91, 6/0. Totals, 27/1.

LONG, GRANT   F   PISTONS

PERSONAL: Born March 12, 1966, in Wayne, Mich. ... 6-9/248. ... Full name: Grant Andrew Long. ... Nephew of John Long, guard with Detroit Pistons, Indiana Pacers and Atlanta Hawks (1978-79 through 1990-91); and cousin of Terry Mills, forward with Detroit Pistons.

HIGH SCHOOL: Romulus (Mich.).

COLLEGE: Eastern Michigan.

TRANSACTIONS/CAREER NOTES: Selected by Miami Heat in second round (33rd pick overall) of 1988 NBA Draft. ... Traded by Heat with G Steve Smith and conditional second-round draft choice to Atlanta Hawks for F Kevin Willis and conditional first-round draft choice (November 7, 1994). ... Traded by Hawks with G Stacey Augmon to Detroit Pistons for four conditional draft choices (July 15, 1996).

MISCELLANEOUS: Miami Heat all-time steals leader with 666 (1988-89 through 1994-95).

COLLEGIATE RECORD

Season Team	G	Min.	FGM	FGA	Pct.	FTM	FTA	Pct.	Reb.	Ast.	Pts.	AVERAGES		
												RPG	APG	PPG
84-85—Eastern Mich.	28	551	44	78	.564	28	46	.609	112	10	116	4.0	0.4	4.1
85-86—Eastern Mich.	27	803	92	175	.526	47	73	.644	178	52	231	6.6	1.9	8.6
86-87—Eastern Mich.	29	879	169	308	.549	95	131	.725	260	83	433	9.0	2.9	14.9
87-88—Eastern Mich.	30	1026	237	427	.555	215	281	.765	313	66	689	10.4	2.2	23.0
Totals	114	3259	542	988	.549	385	531	.725	863	211	1469	7.6	1.9	12.9

NBA REGULAR-SEASON RECORD

NOTES: Led NBA with 337 personal fouls (1989). ... Tied for NBA lead with 11 disqualifications (1990).

Season Team	G	Min.	FGM	FGA	Pct.	FTM	FTA	Pct.	REBOUNDS			Ast.	St.	Blk.	TO	Pts.	AVERAGES		
									Off.	Def.	Tot.						RPG	APG	PPG
88-89—Miami	82	2435	336	692	.486	304	406	.749	240	306	546	149	122	48	201	976	6.7	1.8	11.9
89-90—Miami	81	1856	257	532	.483	172	241	.714	156	246	402	96	91	38	139	686	5.0	1.2	8.5
90-91—Miami	80	2514	276	561	.492	181	230	.787	225	343	568	176	119	43	156	734	7.1	2.2	9.2
91-92—Miami	82	3063	440	890	.494	326	404	.807	259	432	691	225	139	40	185	1212	8.4	2.7	14.8
92-93—Miami	76	2728	397	847	.469	261	341	.765	197	371	568	182	104	31	133	1061	7.5	2.4	14.0
93-94—Miami	69	2201	300	672	.446	187	238	.786	190	305	495	170	89	26	125	788	7.2	2.5	11.4
94-95—Miami-Atlanta	81	2641	342	716	.478	244	325	.751	191	415	606	131	109	34	155	939	7.5	1.6	11.6
95-96—Atlanta	82	3008	395	838	.471	257	337	.763	248	540	788	183	108	34	157	1078	9.6	2.2	13.1
Totals	633	20446	2743	5748	.477	1932	2522	.766	1706	2958	4664	1312	881	294	1251	7474	7.4	2.1	11.8

Three-point field goals: 1988-89, 0-for-5. 1989-90, 0-for-3. 1990-91, 1-for-6 (.167). 1991-92, 6-for-22 (.273). 1992-93, 6-for-26 (.231). 1993-94, 1-for-6 (.167). 1994-95, 11-for-31 (.355). 1995-96, 31-for-86 (.360). Totals, 56-for-185 (.303).

Personal fouls/disqualifications: 1988-89, 337/13. 1989-90, 300/11. 1990-91, 295/10. 1991-92, 248/2. 1992-93, 264/8. 1993-94, 244/5. 1994-95, 243/3. 1995-96, 233/3. Totals, 2164/55.

NBA PLAYOFF RECORD

Season Team	G	Min.	FGM	FGA	Pct.	FTM	FTA	Pct.	REBOUNDS			Ast.	St.	Blk.	TO	Pts.	AVERAGES		
									Off.	Def.	Tot.						RPG	APG	PPG
91-92—Miami	3	120	15	36	.417	7	10	.700	7	8	15	8	5	0	5	37	5.0	2.7	12.3
93-94—Miami	4	110	14	36	.389	21	27	.778	10	8	18	7	3	2	10	49	4.5	1.8	12.3
94-95—Atlanta	3	110	14	28	.500	13	18	.722	13	21	34	4	4	1	8	41	11.3	1.3	13.7

Season Team	G	Min.	FGM	FGA	Pct.	FTM	FTA	Pct.	Off.	Def.	Tot.	Ast.	St.	Blk.	TO	Pts.	RPG	APG	PPG
95-96—Atlanta	10	362	44	111	.396	20	25	.800	30	56	86	28	7	3	19	114	8.6	2.8	11.4
Totals	20	702	87	211	.412	61	80	.763	60	93	153	47	19	6	42	241	7.7	2.4	12.1

Three-point field goals: 1991-92, 0-for-4. 1994-95, 0-for-1. 1995-96, 6-for-24 (.250). Totals, 6-for-29 (.207).
Personal fouls/disqualifications: 1991-92, 11/0. 1993-94, 16/1. 1994-95, 11/0. 1995-96, 27/1. Totals, 65/2.

LONGLEY, LUC   C   BULLS

PERSONAL: Born January 19, 1969, in Melbourne, Australia. ... 7-2/292. ... Full name: Lucien James Longley. ... Name pronounced LUKE.
HIGH SCHOOL: Scotch College (Perth, Australia).
COLLEGE: New Mexico.
TRANSACTIONS/CAREER NOTES: Selected by Minnesota Timberwolves in first round (seventh pick overall) of 1991 NBA Draft. ... Traded by Timberwolves to Chicago Bulls for F/C Stacey King (February 23, 1994).
MISCELLANEOUS: Member of NBA championship team (1996). ... Member of Australian Olympic team (1988, 1992).

COLLEGIATE RECORD

Season Team	G	Min.	FGM	FGA	Pct.	FTM	FTA	Pct.	Reb.	Ast.	Pts.	RPG	APG	PPG
87-88—New Mexico	35	424	60	120	.500	20	51	.392	94	22	140	2.7	0.6	4.0
88-89—New Mexico	33	966	174	301	.578	80	104	.769	223	78	428	6.8	2.4	13.0
89-90—New Mexico	34	1192	233	417	.559	161	196	.821	330	108	627	9.7	3.2	18.4
90-91—New Mexico	30	1067	229	349	.656	116	162	.716	275	109	574	9.2	3.6	19.1
Totals	132	3649	696	1187	.586	377	513	.735	922	317	1769	7.0	2.4	13.4

Three-point field goals: 1990-91, 0-for-2.

NBA REGULAR-SEASON RECORD

Season Team	G	Min.	FGM	FGA	Pct.	FTM	FTA	Pct.	Off.	Def.	Tot.	Ast.	St.	Blk.	TO	Pts.	RPG	APG	PPG
91-92—Minnesota	66	991	114	249	.458	53	80	.663	67	190	257	53	35	64	83	281	3.9	0.8	4.3
92-93—Minnesota	55	1045	133	292	.455	53	74	.716	71	169	240	51	47	77	88	319	4.4	0.9	5.8
93-94—Minn.-Chi.	76	1502	219	465	.471	90	125	.720	129	304	433	109	45	79	119	528	5.7	1.4	6.9
94-95—Chicago	55	1001	135	302	.447	88	107	.822	82	181	263	73	24	45	86	358	4.8	1.3	6.5
95-96—Chicago	62	1641	242	502	.482	80	103	.777	104	214	318	119	22	84	114	564	5.1	1.9	9.1
Totals	314	6180	843	1810	.466	364	489	.744	453	1058	1511	405	173	349	490	2050	4.8	1.3	6.5

Three-point field goals: 1993-94, 0-for-1. 1994-95, 0-for-2. Totals, 0-for-3.
Personal fouls/disqualifications: 1991-92, 157/0. 1992-93, 169/4. 1993-94, 216/3. 1994-95, 177/5. 1995-96, 223/4. Totals, 942/16.

NBA PLAYOFF RECORD

Season Team	G	Min.	FGM	FGA	Pct.	FTM	FTA	Pct.	Off.	Def.	Tot.	Ast.	St.	Blk.	TO	Pts.	RPG	APG	PPG
93-94—Chicago	10	170	25	50	.500	13	18	.722	13	32	45	18	6	8	21	63	4.5	1.8	6.3
94-95—Chicago	10	204	24	50	.480	8	10	.800	6	26	32	11	7	5	10	56	3.2	1.1	5.6
95-96—Chicago	18	439	61	130	.469	28	37	.757	34	48	82	28	7	25	38	150	4.6	1.6	8.3
Totals	38	813	110	230	.478	49	65	.754	53	106	159	57	20	38	69	269	4.2	1.5	7.1

Personal fouls/disqualifications: 1993-94, 38/0. 1994-95, 41/1. 1995-96, 83/4. Totals, 162/5.

LYNCH, GEORGE   F   GRIZZLIES

PERSONAL: Born September 3, 1970, in Roanoke, Va. ... 6-8/223. ... Full name: George DeWitt Lynch III.
HIGH SCHOOL: Patrick Henry (Roanoke, Va.), then Flint Hill Prep (Oakton, Va.).
COLLEGE: North Carolina.
TRANSACTIONS/CAREER NOTES: Selected by Los Angeles Lakers in first round (12th pick overall) of 1993 NBA Draft. ... Traded by Lakers with G Anthony Peeler and 1997 and 1998 second-round draft choices to Vancouver Grizzlies for 1997 and 1998 second-round draft choices (July 16, 1996).

COLLEGIATE RECORD

NOTES: Member of NCAA Division I championship team (1993).

Season Team	G	Min.	FGM	FGA	Pct.	FTM	FTA	Pct.	Reb.	Ast.	Pts.	RPG	APG	PPG
89-90—North Carolina	34	663	112	215	.521	67	101	.663	183	34	292	5.4	1.0	8.6
90-91—North Carolina	35	912	172	329	.523	85	135	.630	258	41	436	7.4	1.2	12.5
91-92—North Carolina	33	982	192	356	.539	74	114	.649	291	86	459	8.8	2.6	13.9
92-93—North Carolina	38	1148	235	469	.501	88	132	.667	365	72	560	9.6	1.9	14.7
Totals	140	3705	711	1369	.519	314	482	.651	1097	233	1747	7.8	1.7	12.5

Three-point field goals: 1989-90, 1-for-3 (.333). 1990-91, 7-for-10 (.700). 1991-92, 1-for-8 (.125). 1992-93, 2-for-11 (.182). Totals, 11-for-32 (.344).

NBA REGULAR-SEASON RECORD

Season Team	G	Min.	FGM	FGA	Pct.	FTM	FTA	Pct.	Off.	Def.	Tot.	Ast.	St.	Blk.	TO	Pts.	RPG	APG	PPG
93-94—L.A. Lakers	71	1762	291	573	.508	99	166	.596	220	190	410	96	102	27	87	681	5.8	1.4	9.6
94-95—L.A. Lakers	56	953	138	295	.468	62	86	.721	75	109	184	62	51	10	73	341	3.3	1.1	6.1
95-96—L.A. Lakers	76	1012	117	272	.430	53	80	.663	82	127	209	51	47	10	40	291	2.8	0.7	3.8
Totals	203	3727	546	1140	.479	214	332	.645	377	426	803	209	200	47	200	1313	4.0	1.0	6.5

Three-point field goals: 1993-94, 0-for-5. 1994-95, 3-for-21 (.143). 1995-96, 4-for-13 (.308). Totals, 7-for-39 (.179).
Personal fouls/disqualifications: 1993-94, 177/1. 1994-95, 86/0. 1995-96, 106/0. Totals, 369/1.

NBA PLAYOFF RECORD

Season Team	G	Min.	FGM	FGA	Pct.	FTM	FTA	Pct.	Off.	Def.	Tot.	Ast.	St.	Blk.	TO	Pts.	RPG	APG	PPG
94-95—L.A. Lakers	10	136	15	32	.469	13	20	.650	13	17	30	7	8	0	9	44	3.0	0.7	4.4
95-96—L.A. Lakers	2	15	2	4	.500	0	0	...	0	3	3	1	0	0	2	4	1.5	0.5	2.0
Totals	12	151	17	36	.472	13	20	.650	13	20	33	8	8	0	11	48	2.8	0.7	4.0

Three-point field goals: 1994-95, 1-for-5 (.200). 1995-96, 0-for-1. Totals, 1-for-6 (.167).
Personal fouls/disqualifications: 1994-95, 22/0. 1995-96, 4/0. Totals, 26/0.

MacLEAN, DON   F   76ERS

PERSONAL: Born January 16, 1970, in Palo Alto, Calif. ... 6-10/235. ... Full name: Donald James MacLean. ... Name pronounced ma-CLAYNE.
HIGH SCHOOL: Simi Valley (Calif.).
COLLEGE: UCLA.
TRANSACTIONS/CAREER NOTES: Selected by Detroit Pistons in first round (19th pick overall) of 1992 NBA Draft. ... Draft rights traded by Pistons with C William Bedford to Los Angeles Clippers for C Olden Polynice and 1996 and 1997 second-round draft choices (June 24, 1992). ... Draft rights traded by Clippers with C William Bedford to Washington Bullets for F John Williams (October 8, 1992). ... Traded by Bullets with G Doug Overton to Denver Nuggets for G Robert Pack (October 30, 1995). ... Signed as free agent by Philadelphia 76ers (July 16, 1996).

COLLEGIATE RECORD

NOTES: The Sporting News All-America second team (1992). ... Led NCAA Division I with .921 free-throw percentage (1992).

												AVERAGES		
Season Team	G	Min.	FGM	FGA	Pct.	FTM	FTA	Pct.	Reb.	Ast.	Pts.	RPG	APG	PPG
88-89—UCLA	31	999	217	391	.555	142	174	.816	231	37	577	7.5	1.2	18.6
89-90—UCLA	33	1111	238	461	.516	179	211	.848	287	35	656	8.7	1.1	19.9
90-91—UCLA	31	1008	259	470	.551	193	228	.847	226	62	714	7.3	2.0	23.0
91-92—UCLA	32	1033	229	454	.504	197	214	.921	248	66	661	7.8	2.1	20.7
Totals	127	4151	943	1776	.531	711	827	.860	992	200	2608	7.8	1.6	20.5

Three-point field goals: 1988-89, 1-for-3 (.333). 1989-90, 1-for-2 (.500). 1990-91, 3-for-13 (.231). 1991-92, 6-for-17 (.353). Totals, 11-for-35 (.314).

NBA REGULAR-SEASON RECORD

HONORS: NBA Most Improved Player (1994).

									REBOUNDS								AVERAGES		
Season Team	G	Min.	FGM	FGA	Pct.	FTM	FTA	Pct.	Off.	Def.	Tot.	Ast.	St.	Blk.	TO	Pts.	RPG	APG	PPG
92-93—Washington	62	674	157	361	.435	90	111	.811	33	89	122	39	11	4	42	407	2.0	0.6	6.6
93-94—Washington	75	2487	517	1030	.502	328	398	.824	140	327	467	160	47	22	152	1365	6.2	2.1	18.2
94-95—Washington	39	1052	158	361	.438	104	136	.765	46	119	165	51	15	3	44	430	4.2	1.3	11.0
95-96—Denver	56	1107	233	547	.426	145	198	.732	62	143	205	89	21	5	68	625	3.7	1.6	11.2
Totals	232	5320	1065	2299	.463	667	843	.791	281	678	959	339	94	34	306	2827	4.1	1.5	12.2

Three-point field goals: 1992-93, 3-for-6 (.500). 1993-94, 3-for-21 (.143). 1994-95, 10-for-40 (.250). 1995-96, 14-for-49 (.286). Totals, 30-for-116 (.259).
Personal fouls/disqualifications: 1992-93, 82/0. 1993-94, 169/0. 1994-95, 97/0. 1995-96, 105/1. Totals, 453/1.

MACK, SAM   F   ROCKETS

PERSONAL: Born May 26, 1970, in Chicago. ... 6-7/220.
HIGH SCHOOL: Thornridge (Dolton, Ill.).
JUNIOR COLLEGE: Tyler (Texas) Junior College.
COLLEGE: Iowa State, then Arizona State, then Houston.
TRANSACTIONS/CAREER NOTES: Not drafted by an NBA franchise. ... Played in United States Basketball League with New Haven Skyhawks (1992). ... Signed as free agent by San Antonio Spurs (September 25, 1992). ... Waived by Spurs (October 21, 1993). ... Played in Continental Basketball Association with Rapid City Thrillers (1993-94), Yakima Sun Kings (1993-94), Fort Wayne Fury (1993-94), Oklahoma City Cavalry (1994-95) and Rockford Lightning (1995-96). ... Signed by Houston Rockets to first of two consecutive 10-day contracts (February 12, 1996). ... Re-signed by Rockets for remainder of season (March 3, 1996).

COLLEGIATE RECORD

											AVERAGES		
Season Team	G	Min.	FGM	FGA	Pct.	FTM	FTA	Pct.	Reb.	Ast.	Pts.	RPG	APG	PPG
87-88—Iowa State						Did not play—ineligible.								
88-89—Iowa State	29	726	126	273	.462	89	124	.718	177	50	341	6.1	1.7	11.8
89-90—Arizona State						Did not play—transfer student.								
90-91—Tyler J.C.	24	...	209	378	.553	120	173	.694	226	...	591	9.4	...	24.6
91-92—Houston	31	855	178	369	.482	134	173	.775	181	43	543	5.8	1.4	17.5
Junior college totals	24	...	209	378	.553	120	173	.694	226	...	591	9.4	...	24.6
4-year-college totals	60	1581	304	642	.474	223	297	.751	358	93	884	6.0	1.6	14.7

Three-point field goals: 1988-89, 0-for-7. 1991-92, 53-for-134 (.396). Totals, 53-for-141 (.376).

NBA REGULAR-SEASON RECORD

									REBOUNDS								AVERAGES		
Season Team	G	Min.	FGM	FGA	Pct.	FTM	FTA	Pct.	Off.	Def.	Tot.	Ast.	St.	Blk.	TO	Pts.	RPG	APG	PPG
92-93—San Antonio	40	267	47	118	.398	45	58	.776	18	30	48	15	14	5	22	142	1.2	0.4	3.6
95-96—Houston	31	868	121	287	.422	39	46	.848	18	80	98	79	22	9	28	335	3.2	2.5	10.8
Totals	71	1135	168	405	.415	84	104	.808	36	110	146	94	36	14	50	477	2.1	1.3	6.7

Three-point field goals: 1992-93, 3-for-22 (.136). 1995-96, 54-for-135 (.400). Totals, 57-for-157 (.363).
Personal fouls/disqualifications: 1992-93, 44/0. 1995-96, 75/0. Totals, 119/0.

NBA PLAYOFF RECORD

									REBOUNDS								AVERAGES		
Season Team	G	Min.	FGM	FGA	Pct.	FTM	FTA	Pct.	Off.	Def.	Tot.	Ast.	St.	Blk.	TO	Pts.	RPG	APG	PPG
95-96—Houston	6	47	5	15	.333	0	3	.000	0	9	9	1	1	0	2	12	1.5	0.2	2.0

Three-point field goals: 1995-96, 2-for-9 (.222).
Personal fouls/disqualifications: 1995-96, 1/0.

NOTES: CBA All-League second team (1996).

CBA REGULAR-SEASON RECORD

											AVERAGES		
Season Team	G	Min.	FGM	FGA	Pct.	FTM	FTA	Pct.	Reb.	Ast.	Pts.	RPG	APG	PPG
93-94—R.C.-Yak.-F.W.	28	552	121	277	.437	63	77	.818	83	30	322	3.0	1.1	11.5
94-95—Oklahoma City	52	1264	284	643	.442	139	181	.768	161	98	782	3.1	1.9	15.0
95-96—Rockford	39	1411	299	655	.456	144	176	.818	169	109	808	4.3	2.8	20.7
Totals	119	3227	704	1575	.447	346	434	.797	413	237	1912	3.5	2.0	16.1

Three-point field goals: 1993-94, 17-for-61 (.279). 1994-95, 75-for-211 (.355). 1995-96, 66-for-189 (.349). Totals, 158-for-472 (.335).

M

MACON, MARK   G

PERSONAL: Born April 14, 1969, in Saginaw, Mich. ... 6-5/200. ... Full name: Mark L. Macon.
HIGH SCHOOL: Buena Vista (Saginaw, Mich.).
COLLEGE: Temple.
TRANSACTIONS/CAREER NOTES: Selected by Denver Nuggets in first round (eighth pick overall) of 1991 NBA Draft. ... Traded by Nuggets with F Marcus Liberty to Detroit Pistons for G Alvin Robertson, 1995 second-round draft choice and future considerations (November 19, 1993). ... Waived by Pistons (April 11, 1996).

COLLEGIATE RECORD

Season Team	G	Min.	FGM	FGA	Pct.	FTM	FTA	Pct.	Reb.	Ast.	Pts.	RPG	APG	PPG
87-88—Temple	34	1203	280	617	.454	74	96	.771	192	98	699	5.6	2.9	20.6
88-89—Temple	30	1137	204	501	.407	97	125	.776	168	115	548	5.6	3.8	18.3
89-90—Temple	31	1192	242	622	.389	134	168	.798	187	68	679	6.0	2.2	21.9
90-91—Temple	31	1190	254	578	.439	98	128	.766	153	71	683	4.9	2.3	22.0
Totals	126	4722	980	2318	.423	403	517	.779	700	352	2609	5.6	2.8	20.7

Three-point field goals: 1987-88, 65-for-154 (.422). 1988-89, 43-for-134 (.321). 1989-90, 61-for-185 (.330). 1990-91, 77-for-184 (.418). Totals, 246-for-657 (.374).

NBA REGULAR-SEASON RECORD

HONORS: NBA All-Rookie second team (1992).

Season Team	G	Min.	FGM	FGA	Pct.	FTM	FTA	Pct.	REBOUNDS Off.	Def.	Tot.	Ast.	St.	Blk.	TO	Pts.	RPG	APG	PPG
91-92—Denver	76	2304	333	889	.375	135	185	.730	80	140	220	168	154	14	155	805	2.9	2.2	10.6
92-93—Denver	48	1141	158	381	.415	42	60	.700	33	70	103	126	69	3	72	358	2.1	2.6	7.5
93-94—Denver-Det	42	496	69	184	.375	23	34	.676	18	23	41	51	39	1	40	163	1.0	1.2	3.9
94-95—Detroit	55	721	101	265	.381	54	68	.794	29	47	76	63	67	1	41	276	1.4	1.1	5.0
95-96—Detroit	23	287	29	67	.433	9	11	.818	10	12	22	16	15	0	9	74	1.0	0.7	3.2
Totals	244	4949	690	1786	.386	263	358	.735	170	292	462	424	344	19	317	1676	1.9	1.7	6.9

Three-point field goals: 1991-92, 4-for-30 (.133). 1992-93, 0-for-6. 1993-94, 2-for-10 (.200). 1994-95, 20-for-62 (.323). 1995-96, 7-for-15 (.467). Totals, 33-for-123 (.268).

Personal fouls/disqualifications: 1991-92, 242/4. 1992-93, 135/2. 1993-94, 73/0. 1994-95, 97/1. 1995-96, 34/0. Totals, 581/7.

MAHORN, RICK   F   PISTONS   M

PERSONAL: Born September 21, 1958, in Hartford, Conn. ... 6-10/260. ... Full name: Derrick Allen Mahorn.
HIGH SCHOOL: Weaver (Hartford, Conn.).
COLLEGE: Hampton Institute (Va.).
TRANSACTIONS/CAREER NOTES: Selected by Washington Bullets in second round (35th pick overall) of 1980 NBA Draft. ... Traded by Bullets with F Mike Gibson to Detroit Pistons for F Dan Roundfield (June 17, 1985). ... Selected by Minnesota Timberwolves from Pistons in NBA expansion draft (June 15, 1989). ... Traded by Timberwolves to Philadelphia 76ers for 1990 first-round draft choice and 1991 and 1992 second-round draft choices (October 27, 1989). ... Played in Italy (1991-92 and 1992-93). ... Signed as free agent by New Jersey Nets (November 9, 1992). ... Rights renounced by Nets (July 16, 1996). ... Signed as free agent by Pistons (August 5, 1996).
MISCELLANEOUS: Member of NBA championship team (1989).

COLLEGIATE RECORD

NOTES: Led NCAA Division II with 15.8 rebounds per game (1980).

Season Team	G	Min.	FGM	FGA	Pct.	FTM	FTA	Pct.	Reb.	Ast.	Pts.	RPG	APG	PPG
76-77—Hampton Inst.	28	...	65	159	.409	29	44	.659	168	27	159	6.0	1.0	5.7
77-78—Hampton Inst.	30	...	291	570	.511	137	202	.678	377	26	719	12.6	0.9	24.0
78-79—Hampton Inst.	30	...	274	489	.560	137	200	.685	430	21	685	14.3	0.7	22.8
79-80—Hampton Inst.	31	1123	352	621	.567	151	220	.686	490	38	855	15.8	1.2	27.6
Totals	119	...	982	1839	.534	454	666	.682	1465	112	2418	12.3	0.9	20.3

NBA REGULAR-SEASON RECORD

HONORS: NBA All-Defensive second team (1990).

Season Team	G	Min.	FGM	FGA	Pct.	FTM	FTA	Pct.	REBOUNDS Off.	Def.	Tot.	Ast.	St.	Blk.	TO	Pts.	RPG	APG	PPG
80-81—Washington	52	696	111	219	.507	27	40	.675	67	148	215	25	21	44	38	249	4.1	0.5	4.8
81-82—Washington	80	2664	414	816	.507	148	234	.632	149	555	704	150	57	138	162	976	8.8	1.9	12.2
82-83—Washington	82	3023	376	768	.490	146	254	.575	171	608	779	115	86	148	170	898	9.5	1.4	11.0
83-84—Washington	82	2701	307	605	.507	125	192	.651	169	569	738	131	62	123	142	739	9.0	1.6	9.0
84-85—Washington	77	2072	206	413	.499	71	104	.683	150	458	608	121	59	104	133	483	7.9	1.6	6.3
85-86—Detroit	80	1442	157	345	.455	81	119	.681	121	291	412	64	40	61	109	395	5.2	0.8	4.9
86-87—Detroit	63	1278	144	322	.447	96	117	.821	93	282	375	38	32	50	73	384	6.0	0.6	6.1
87-88—Detroit	67	1963	276	481	.574	164	217	.756	159	406	565	60	43	42	119	717	8.4	0.9	10.7
88-89—Detroit	72	1795	203	393	.517	116	155	.748	141	355	496	59	40	66	97	522	6.9	0.8	7.3
89-90—Philadelphia	75	2271	313	630	.497	183	256	.715	167	401	568	98	44	103	104	811	7.6	1.3	10.8
90-91—Philadelphia	80	2439	261	559	.467	189	240	.788	151	470	621	118	79	56	127	711	7.8	1.5	8.9
92-93—New Jersey	74	1077	101	214	.472	88	110	.800	93	186	279	33	19	31	58	291	3.8	0.4	3.9
93-94—New Jersey	28	226	23	47	.489	13	20	.650	16	38	54	5	3	5	7	59	1.9	0.2	2.1
94-95—New Jersey	58	630	79	151	.523	39	49	.796	45	117	162	26	11	12	34	198	2.8	0.4	3.4
95-96—New Jersey	50	450	43	122	.352	34	47	.723	31	79	110	16	14	13	30	120	2.2	0.3	2.4
Totals	1020	24727	3014	6085	.495	1520	2154	.706	1723	4963	6686	1059	610	996	1403	7553	6.6	1.0	7.4

Three-point field goals: 1981-82, 0-for-3. 1982-83, 0-for-3. 1985-86, 0-for-1. 1987-88, 1-for-2 (.500). 1988-89, 0-for-2. 1989-90, 2-for-9 (.222). 1990-91, 0-for-9. 1992-93, 1-for-3 (.333). 1993-94, 0-for-1. 1994-95, 1-for-3 (.333). 1995-96, 0-for-1. Totals, 5-for-37 (.135).

Personal fouls/disqualifications: 1980-81, 134/3. 1981-82, 349/12. 1982-83, 335/13. 1983-84, 358/14. 1984-85, 308/11. 1985-86, 261/4. 1986-87, 221/4. 1987-88, 262/4. 1988-89, 206/1. 1989-90, 251/2. 1990-91, 276/6. 1992-93, 156/0. 1993-94, 38/0. 1994-95, 93/0. 1995-96, 72/0. Totals, 3320/74.

NBA PLAYOFF RECORD

Season Team	G	Min.	FGM	FGA	Pct.	FTM	FTA	Pct.	Off.	Def.	Tot.	Ast.	St.	Blk.	TO	Pts.	RPG	APG	PPG
81-82—Washington	7	242	32	73	.438	10	14	.714	14	47	61	13	10	5	16	74	8.7	1.9	10.6
83-84—Washington	4	154	15	25	.600	8	10	.800	7	36	43	6	1	6	6	38	10.8	1.5	9.5
84-85—Washington	4	41	4	8	.500	4	4	1.000	2	5	7	0	0	3	1	12	1.8	0.0	3.0
85-86—Detroit	4	61	5	13	.385	2	2	1.000	3	9	12	0	1	0	3	12	3.0	0.0	3.0
86-87—Detroit	15	483	59	109	.541	28	35	.800	42	100	142	5	6	11	16	146	9.5	0.3	9.7
87-88—Detroit	23	409	31	90	.344	13	19	.684	19	70	89	13	5	10	16	75	3.9	0.6	3.3
88-89—Detroit	17	360	40	69	.580	17	26	.654	30	57	87	7	9	13	11	97	5.1	0.4	5.7
89-90—Philadelphia ...	10	342	37	86	.430	20	26	.769	18	52	70	10	7	8	13	94	7.0	1.0	9.4
90-91—Philadelphia ...	8	208	20	36	.556	11	14	.786	7	35	42	14	2	4	8	51	5.3	1.8	6.4
92-93—New Jersey	4	63	4	10	.400	0	0	...	4	9	13	3	0	2	1	8	3.3	0.8	2.0
93-94—New Jersey	3	19	0	1	.000	0	0	...	1	3	4	0	0	1	1	0	1.3	0.0	0.0
Totals	99	2382	247	520	.475	113	150	.753	147	423	570	71	41	63	92	607	5.8	0.7	6.1

Three-point field goals: 1983-84, 0-for-1. 1986-87, 0-for-1. 1989-90, 0-for-1. Totals, 0-for-3.

Personal fouls/disqualifications: 1981-82, 30/1. 1983-84, 19/0. 1984-85, 9/0. 1985-86, 14/0. 1986-87, 60/1. 1987-88, 64/2. 1988-89, 59/1. 1989-90, 41/1. 1990-91, 25/0. 1992-93, 9/0. 1993-94, 7/0. Totals, 337/6.

ITALIAN LEAGUE RECORD

Season Team	G	Min.	FGM	FGA	Pct.	FTM	FTA	Pct.	Reb.	Ast.	Pts.	RPG	APG	PPG
91-92—Il Messaggero Roma	28	991	172	287	.599	106	146	.726	263	23	450	9.4	0.8	16.1
92-93—Virtus Roma	3	93	9	22	.409	5	9	.556	28	4	23	9.3	1.3	7.7
Totals	31	1084	181	309	.586	111	155	.716	291	27	473	9.4	0.9	15.3

MAJERLE, DAN   G/F   HEAT

PERSONAL: Born September 9, 1965, in Traverse City, Mich. ... 6-6/220. ... Full name: Daniel Lewis Majerle. ... Name pronounced mar-LEE.

HIGH SCHOOL: Traverse City (Mich.) Senior.

COLLEGE: Central Michigan.

TRANSACTIONS/CAREER NOTES: Selected by Phoenix Suns in first round (14th pick overall) of 1988 NBA Draft. ... Traded by Suns with F Antonio Lang and 1996, 1997 or 1998 first-round draft choice to Cleveland Cavaliers for F/C John Williams (October 7, 1995). ... Rights renounced by Cavaliers (August 8, 1996). ... Signed as free agent by Miami Heat (August 22, 1996).

MISCELLANEOUS: Member of bronze-medal-winning U.S. Olympic team (1988).

COLLEGIATE RECORD

Season Team	G	Min.	FGM	FGA	Pct.	FTM	FTA	Pct.	Reb.	Ast.	Pts.	RPG	APG	PPG
83-84—Central Michigan						Did not play—back injury.								
84-85—Central Michigan	12	360	92	162	.568	39	67	.582	80	24	223	6.7	2.0	18.6
85-86—Central Michigan	27	1002	228	433	.527	122	170	.718	212	51	578	7.9	1.9	21.4
86-87—Central Michigan	23	824	191	344	.555	101	183	.552	196	53	485	8.5	2.3	21.1
87-88—Central Michigan	32	1197	279	535	.522	156	242	.645	346	81	759	10.8	2.5	23.7
Totals	94	3383	790	1474	.536	418	662	.631	834	209	2045	8.9	2.2	21.8

Three-point field goals: 1986-87, 2-for-8 (.250). 1987-88, 45-for-101 (.446). Totals, 47-for-109 (.431).

NBA REGULAR-SEASON RECORD

HONORS: NBA All-Defensive second team (1991, 1993).

Season Team	G	Min.	FGM	FGA	Pct.	FTM	FTA	Pct.	Off.	Def.	Tot.	Ast.	St.	Blk.	TO	Pts.	RPG	APG	PPG
88-89—Phoenix	54	1354	181	432	.419	78	127	.614	62	147	209	130	63	14	48	467	3.9	2.4	8.6
89-90—Phoenix	73	2244	296	698	.424	198	260	.762	144	286	430	188	100	32	82	809	5.9	2.6	11.1
90-91—Phoenix	77	2281	397	821	.484	227	298	.762	168	250	418	216	106	40	114	1051	5.4	2.8	13.6
91-92—Phoenix	82	2853	551	1153	.478	229	303	.756	148	335	483	274	131	43	101	1418	5.9	3.3	17.3
92-93—Phoenix	82	3199	509	1096	.464	203	261	.778	120	263	383	311	138	33	133	1388	4.7	3.8	16.9
93-94—Phoenix	80	3207	476	1138	.418	176	238	.740	120	229	349	275	129	43	137	1320	4.4	3.4	16.5
94-95—Phoenix	82	3091	438	1031	.425	206	282	.731	104	271	375	340	96	38	105	1281	4.6	4.1	15.6
95-96—Cleveland	82	2367	303	748	.405	120	169	.710	70	235	305	214	81	34	93	872	3.7	2.6	10.6
Totals	612	20596	3151	7117	.443	1437	1938	.741	936	2016	2952	1948	844	277	813	8606	4.8	3.2	14.1

Three-point field goals: 1988-89, 27-for-82 (.329). 1989-90, 19-for-80 (.238). 1990-91, 30-for-86 (.349). 1991-92, 87-for-228 (.382). 1992-93, 167-for-438 (.381). 1993-94, 192-for-503 (.382). 1994-95, 199-for-548 (.363). 1995-96, 146-for-414 (.353). Totals, 867-for-2379 (.364).

Personal fouls/disqualifications: 1988-89, 139/1. 1989-90, 177/5. 1990-91, 162/0. 1991-92, 158/0. 1992-93, 180/0. 1993-94, 153/0. 1994-95, 155/0. 1995-96, 131/0. Totals, 1255/6.

NBA PLAYOFF RECORD

NOTES: Shares NBA Finals single-series record for most three-point field goals made—17 (1993, vs. Chicago). ... Holds single-game playoff record for most three-point field goals made—8 (June 1, 1993, vs. Seattle).

Season Team	G	Min.	FGM	FGA	Pct.	FTM	FTA	Pct.	Off.	Def.	Tot.	Ast.	St.	Blk.	TO	Pts.	RPG	APG	PPG
88-89—Phoenix	12	352	63	144	.438	38	48	.792	22	35	57	14	13	4	15	172	4.8	1.2	14.3
89-90—Phoenix	16	479	73	150	.487	51	65	.785	30	51	81	34	20	2	18	201	5.1	2.1	12.6
90-91—Phoenix	4	110	12	32	.375	14	19	.737	6	9	15	7	5	1	2	42	3.8	1.8	10.5
91-92—Phoenix	7	266	48	111	.432	26	26	.962	13	31	44	20	10	0	9	130	6.3	2.9	18.6
92-93—Phoenix	24	1071	134	311	.431	48	69	.696	29	111	140	88	33	28	32	370	5.8	3.7	15.4
93-94—Phoenix	10	410	46	127	.362	11	16	.688	15	28	43	24	11	4	10	123	4.3	2.4	12.3
94-95—Phoenix	10	307	27	73	.370	12	17	.706	8	23	31	17	14	3	9	82	3.1	1.7	8.2
95-96—Cleveland	3	91	16	36	.444	8	9	.889	2	10	12	9	4	2	3	50	4.0	3.0	16.7
Totals	86	3086	419	984	.426	207	269	.770	125	298	423	213	110	44	98	1170	4.9	2.5	13.6

M

Three-point field goals: 1988-89, 8-for-28 (.286). 1989-90, 4-for-12 (.333). 1990-91, 4-for-11 (.364). 1991-92, 9-for-33 (.273). 1992-93, 54-for-137 (.394). 1993-94, 20-for-59 (.339). 1994-95, 16-for-44 (.364). 1995-96, 10-for-23 (.435). Totals, 125-for-347 (.360).

Personal fouls/disqualifications: 1988-89, 28/0. 1989-90, 34/0. 1990-91, 12/0. 1991-92, 11/0. 1992-93, 57/0. 1993-94, 23/0. 1994-95, 24/0. 1995-96, 6/0. Totals, 195/0.

NBA ALL-STAR GAME RECORD

Season	Team	Min.	FGM	FGA	Pct.	FTM	FTA	Pct.	Off.	Def.	Tot.	Ast.	PF	Dq.	St.	Blk.	TO	Pts.
1992	—Phoenix	12	2	5	.400	0	0	...	0	3	3	2	0	0	0	0	1	4
1993	—Phoenix	26	6	11	.545	3	4	.750	2	5	7	3	2	0	1	2	0	18
1995	—Phoenix	20	4	12	.333	0	0	...	1	4	5	3	1	0	0	0	0	10
Totals		58	12	28	.429	3	4	.750	3	12	15	8	3	0	1	2	1	32

Three-point field goals: 1992, 0-for-2. 1993, 3-for-6 (.500). 1995, 2-for-7 (.286). Totals, 5-for-15 (.333).

MALONE, JEFF   G

PERSONAL: Born June 28, 1961, in Mobile, Ala. ... 6-4/205. ... Full name: Jeffrey Nigel Malone.
HIGH SCHOOL: Southwest (Macon, Ga.).
COLLEGE: Mississippi State.
TRANSACTIONS/CAREER NOTES: Selected by Washington Bullets in first round (10th pick overall) of 1983 NBA Draft. ... Traded by Bullets to Utah Jazz in three-way deal in which Sacramento Kings sent F Pervis Ellison to Bullets and Jazz sent G Bob Hansen, F/C Eric Leckner and 1990 first- and second-round draft choices to Kings (June 25, 1990); Jazz also received 1990 second-round draft choice from Kings and Kings also received 1991 second-round draft choice from Bullets. ... Traded by Jazz with 1994 conditional first-round draft choice to Philadelphia 76ers for G Jeff Hornacek and G Sean Green (February 24, 1994). ... Waived by 76ers (January 4, 1996). ... Signed by Miami Heat to first of two consecutive 10-day contracts (February 12, 1996). ... Re-signed by Heat for remainder of season (March 3, 1996). ... Rights renounced by Heat (July 17, 1996).

COLLEGIATE RECORD

NOTES: The Sporting News All-America first team (1983).

Season Team	G	Min.	FGM	FGA	Pct.	FTM	FTA	Pct.	Reb.	Ast.	Pts.	RPG	APG	PPG
79-80—Mississippi State	27	781	139	303	.459	42	51	.824	90	39	320	3.3	1.4	11.9
80-81—Mississippi State	27	999	219	447	.490	105	128	.820	113	43	543	4.2	1.6	20.1
81-82—Mississippi State	27	1001	225	410	.549	52	70	.743	111	20	502	4.1	0.7	18.6
82-83—Mississippi State	29	1070	323	608	.531	131	159	.824	106	66	777	3.7	2.3	26.8
Totals	110	3851	906	1768	.512	330	408	.809	420	168	2142	3.8	1.5	19.5

NBA REGULAR-SEASON RECORD

HONORS: NBA All-Rookie team (1984).

Season Team	G	Min.	FGM	FGA	Pct.	FTM	FTA	Pct.	Off.	Def.	Tot.	Ast.	St.	Blk.	TO	Pts.	RPG	APG	PPG
83-84—Washington	81	1976	408	918	.444	142	172	.826	57	98	155	151	23	13	110	982	1.9	1.9	12.1
84-85—Washington	76	2613	605	1213	.499	211	250	.844	60	146	206	184	52	19	107	1436	2.7	2.4	18.9
85-86—Washington	80	2992	735	1522	.483	322	371	.868	66	222	288	191	70	12	168	1795	3.6	2.4	22.4
86-87—Washington	80	2763	689	1509	.457	376	425	.885	50	168	218	298	75	13	182	1758	2.7	3.7	22.0
87-88—Washington	80	2655	648	1360	.476	335	380	.882	44	162	206	237	51	13	172	1641	2.6	3.0	20.5
88-89—Washington	76	2418	677	1410	.480	296	340	.871	55	124	179	219	39	14	165	1651	2.4	2.9	21.7
89-90—Washington	75	2567	781	1592	.491	257	293	.877	54	152	206	243	48	6	125	1820	2.7	3.2	24.3
90-91—Utah	69	2466	525	1034	.508	231	252	.917	36	170	206	143	50	6	108	1282	3.0	2.1	18.6
91-92—Utah	81	2922	691	1353	.511	256	285	.898	49	184	233	180	56	5	140	1639	2.9	2.2	20.2
92-93—Utah	79	2558	595	1205	.494	236	277	.852	31	142	173	128	42	4	125	1429	2.2	1.6	18.1
93-94—Utah-Phil.	77	2560	525	1081	.486	205	247	.830	51	148	199	125	40	5	85	1262	2.6	1.6	16.4
94-95—Philadelphia	19	660	144	284	.507	51	59	.864	11	44	55	29	15	0	29	350	2.9	1.5	18.4
95-96—Phil.-Miami	32	510	76	193	.394	29	32	.906	8	32	40	26	16	0	22	186	1.3	0.8	5.8
Totals	905	29660	7099	14674	.484	2947	3383	.871	572	1792	2364	2154	577	100	1538	17231	2.6	2.4	19.0

Three-point field goals: 1983-84, 24-for-74 (.324). 1984-85, 15-for-72 (.208). 1985-86, 3-for-17 (.176). 1986-87, 4-for-26 (.154). 1987-88, 10-for-24 (.417). 1988-89, 1-for-19 (.053). 1989-90, 1-for-6 (.167). 1990-91, 1-for-6 (.167). 1991-92, 1-for-12 (.083). 1992-93, 3-for-9 (.333). 1993-94, 7-for-12 (.583). 1994-95, 11-for-28 (.393). 1995-96, 5-for-16 (.313). Totals, 86-for-321 (.268).

Personal fouls/disqualifications: 1983-84, 162/1. 1984-85, 176/1. 1985-86, 180/2. 1986-87, 154/0. 1987-88, 198/1. 1988-89, 155/0. 1989-90, 116/1. 1990-91, 128/0. 1991-92, 126/1. 1992-93, 117/0. 1993-94, 123/0. 1994-95, 35/0. 1995-96, 25/0. Totals, 1695/7.

NBA PLAYOFF RECORD

Season Team	G	Min.	FGM	FGA	Pct.	FTM	FTA	Pct.	Off.	Def.	Tot.	Ast.	St.	Blk.	TO	Pts.	RPG	APG	PPG
83-84—Washington	4	71	12	26	.462	0	0	...	2	3	5	2	1	0	3	24	1.3	0.5	6.0
84-85—Washington	4	126	27	56	.482	10	13	.769	3	3	6	8	5	0	4	65	1.5	2.0	16.3
85-86—Washington	5	197	42	103	.408	26	29	.897	4	12	16	17	7	3	11	110	3.2	3.4	22.0
86-87—Washington	3	105	17	46	.370	11	11	1.000	1	6	7	9	1	0	11	45	2.3	3.0	15.0
87-88—Washington	5	199	50	97	.515	28	37	.757	3	14	17	11	5	5	14	128	3.4	2.2	25.6
90-91—Utah	9	351	71	144	.493	44	48	.917	7	28	35	29	9	1	12	186	3.9	3.2	20.7
91-92—Utah	16	610	134	275	.487	62	72	.861	12	27	39	31	8	2	26	331	2.4	1.9	20.7
92-93—Utah	5	150	29	65	.446	9	13	.692	3	13	16	3	3	1	9	67	3.2	0.6	13.4
Totals	51	1809	382	812	.470	190	223	.852	35	106	141	110	39	12	90	956	2.8	2.2	18.7

Three-point field goals: 1983-84, 0-for-1. 1984-85, 1-for-3 (.333). 1985-86, 0-for-2. 1987-88, 0-for-1. 1990-91, 0-for-2. 1991-92, 1-for-3 (.333). Totals, 2-for-12 (.167).

Personal fouls/disqualifications: 1983-84, 6/0. 1984-85, 14/1. 1985-86, 13/0. 1986-87, 8/0. 1987-88, 16/0. 1990-91, 22/0. 1991-92, 33/0. 1992-93, 11/0. Totals, 123/1.

NBA ALL-STAR GAME RECORD

Season	Team	Min.	FGM	FGA	Pct.	FTM	FTA	Pct.	Off.	Def.	Tot.	Ast.	PF	Dq.	St.	Blk.	TO	Pts.
1986	—Washington	12	3	5	.600	0	0	...	0	1	1	4	0	0	1	0	0	6
1987	—Washington	13	3	5	.600	0	0	...	1	1	2	2	1	0	0	0	1	6
Totals		25	6	10	.600	0	0	...	1	2	3	6	1	0	1	0	1	12

Three-point field goals: 1987, 0-for-1.

MALONE, KARL   F   JAZZ

PERSONAL: Born July 24, 1963, in Summerfield, La. ... 6-9/256. ... Full name: Karl Malone. ... Nickname: The Mailman.
HIGH SCHOOL: Summerfield (La.).
COLLEGE: Louisiana Tech.
TRANSACTIONS/CAREER NOTES: Selected after junior season by Utah Jazz in first round (13th pick overall) of 1985 NBA Draft.
MISCELLANEOUS: Member of gold-medal-winning U.S. Olympic teams (1992, 1996). ... Utah Jazz franchise all-time leading scorer with 23,343 points and all-time leading rebounder with 9,733 (1985-86 through 1995-96).

COLLEGIATE RECORD

Season Team	G	Min.	FGM	FGA	Pct.	FTM	FTA	Pct.	Reb.	Ast.	Pts.	RPG	APG	PPG
81-82—Louisiana Tech						Did not play—redshirted.								
82-83—Louisiana Tech	28	...	217	373	.582	152	244	.623	289	10	586	10.3	0.4	20.9
83-84—Louisiana Tech	32	...	220	382	.576	161	236	.682	282	42	601	8.8	1.3	18.8
84-85—Louisiana Tech	32	...	216	399	.541	97	170	.571	288	73	529	9.0	2.3	16.5
Totals	92	...	653	1154	.566	410	650	.631	859	125	1716	9.3	1.4	18.7

NBA REGULAR-SEASON RECORD

RECORDS: Holds career record for most consecutive seasons with 2,000 or more points—9 (1987-88 through 1995-96). ... Shares career record for most seasons with 2,000 or more points—9.
HONORS: All-NBA first team (1989, 1990, 1991, 1992, 1993, 1994, 1995, 1996). ... All-NBA second team (1988). ... NBA All-Defensive second team (1988). ... NBA All-Rookie team (1986).

Season Team	G	Min.	FGM	FGA	Pct.	FTM	FTA	Pct.	Off.	Def.	Tot.	Ast.	St.	Blk.	TO	Pts.	RPG	APG	PPG
85-86—Utah	81	2475	504	1016	.496	195	405	.481	174	544	718	236	105	44	279	1203	8.9	2.9	14.9
86-87—Utah	82	2857	728	1422	.512	323	540	.598	278	577	855	158	104	60	237	1779	10.4	1.9	21.7
87-88—Utah	82	3198	858	1650	.520	552	789	.700	277	709	986	199	117	50	*325	2268	12.0	2.4	27.7
88-89—Utah	80	3126	809	1559	.519	*703	*918	.766	259	594	853	219	144	70	285	2326	10.7	2.7	29.1
89-90—Utah	82	3122	914	1627	.562	*696	*913	.762	232	679	911	226	121	50	304	2540	11.1	2.8	31.0
90-91—Utah	82	3302	847	1608	.527	*684	*888	.770	236	*731	967	270	89	79	244	2382	11.8	3.3	29.0
91-92—Utah	81	3054	798	1516	.526	*673	*865	.778	225	684	909	241	108	51	248	2272	11.2	3.0	28.0
92-93—Utah	82	3099	797	1443	.552	*619	*836	.740	227	692	919	308	124	85	240	2217	11.2	3.8	27.0
93-94—Utah	82	3329	772	1552	.497	511	736	.694	235	705	940	328	125	126	234	2063	11.5	4.0	25.2
94-95—Utah	82	3126	830	1548	.536	516	695	.742	156	*715	871	285	129	85	236	2187	10.6	3.5	26.7
95-96—Utah	82	3113	789	1520	.519	512	708	.723	175	629	804	345	138	56	199	2106	9.8	4.2	25.7
Totals	898	33801	8646	16461	.525	5984	8293	.722	2474	7259	9733	2815	1304	756	2831	23343	10.8	3.1	26.0

Three-point field goals: 1985-86, 0-for-1. 1986-87, 0-for-7. 1987-88, 0-for-5. 1988-89, 5-for-16 (.313). 1989-90, 16-for-43 (.372). 1990-91, 4-for-14 (.286). 1991-92, 3-for-17 (.176). 1992-93, 4-for-20 (.200). 1993-94, 8-for-32 (.250). 1994-95, 11-for-41 (.268). 1995-96, 16-for-40 (.400). Totals, 67-for-237 (.283).

Personal fouls/disqualifications: 1985-86, 295/2. 1986-87, 323/6. 1987-88, 296/2. 1988-89, 286/3. 1989-90, 259/1. 1990-91, 268/2. 1991-92, 226/2. 1992-93, 261/2. 1993-94, 268/2. 1994-95, 269/2. 1995-96, 245/1. Totals, 2996/25.

NBA PLAYOFF RECORD

NOTES: Shares single-game playoff record for most free throws made in one half—19 (May 9, 1991, vs. Portland).

Season Team	G	Min.	FGM	FGA	Pct.	FTM	FTA	Pct.	Off.	Def.	Tot.	Ast.	St.	Blk.	TO	Pts.	RPG	APG	PPG
85-86—Utah	4	144	38	72	.528	11	26	.423	6	24	30	4	8	0	6	87	7.5	1.0	21.8
86-87—Utah	5	200	37	88	.420	26	36	.722	15	33	48	6	11	4	17	100	9.6	1.2	20.0
87-88—Utah	11	494	123	255	.482	81	112	.723	33	97	130	17	13	7	39	327	11.8	1.5	29.7
88-89—Utah	3	136	33	66	.500	26	32	.813	22	27	49	4	3	1	13	92	16.3	1.3	30.7
89-90—Utah	5	203	46	105	.438	34	45	.756	16	35	51	11	11	5	12	126	10.2	2.2	25.2
90-91—Utah	9	383	95	209	.455	77	91	.846	23	97	120	29	9	11	26	267	13.3	3.2	29.7
91-92—Utah	16	688	148	284	.521	169	210	.805	43	138	181	42	22	19	46	465	11.3	2.6	29.1
92-93—Utah	5	216	44	97	.454	31	38	.816	12	40	52	10	6	2	20	120	10.4	2.0	24.0
93-94—Utah	16	703	158	338	.467	118	160	.738	52	146	198	54	23	13	34	434	12.4	3.4	27.1
94-95—Utah	5	216	48	103	.466	54	78	.692	15	51	66	19	7	2	14	151	13.2	3.8	30.2
95-96—Utah	18	725	188	401	.469	101	176	.574	47	139	186	79	34	10	45	477	10.3	4.4	26.5
Totals	97	4108	958	2018	.475	728	1004	.725	284	827	1111	275	147	74	272	2646	11.5	2.8	27.3

Three-point field goals: 1987-88, 0-for-1. 1989-90, 0-for-1. 1990-91, 0-for-8. 1991-92, 0-for-2. 1992-93, 1-for-2 (.500). 1993-94, 0-for-4. 1994-95, 1-for-3 (.333). 1995-96, 0-for-3. Totals, 2-for-24 (.083).

Personal fouls/disqualifications: 1985-86, 18/1. 1986-87, 20/1. 1987-88, 35/0. 1988-89, 16/1. 1989-90, 22/1. 1990-91, 35/0. 1991-92, 57/0. 1992-93, 21/0. 1993-94, 59/2. 1994-95, 18/0. 1995-96, 61/0. Totals, 362/6.

NBA ALL-STAR GAME RECORD

NOTES: NBA All-Star Game Most Valuable Player (1989). ... NBA All-Star Game co-Most Valuable Player (1993).

Season Team	Min.	FGM	FGA	Pct.	FTM	FTA	Pct.	Off.	Def.	Tot.	Ast.	PF	Dq.	St.	Blk.	TO	Pts.
1988 —Utah	33	9	19	.474	4	5	.800	4	6	10	2	4	0	2	0	3	22
1989 —Utah	26	12	17	.706	4	6	.667	4	5	9	3	3	0	2	0	2	28
1990 —Utah							Selected, did not play—injured.										
1991 —Utah	31	6	11	.545	4	6	.667	4	7	11	4	1	0	1	1	3	16
1992 —Utah	19	5	7	.714	1	2	.500	0	7	7	3	1	0	1	1	1	11
1993 —Utah	34	11	17	.647	6	9	.667	3	7	10	0	3	0	1	2	3	28
1994 —Utah	21	3	9	.333	0	0	...	3	4	7	2	2	0	1	0	1	6
1995 —Utah	16	6	6	1.000	3	4	.750	0	3	3	1	0	0	0	0	1	15
1996 —Utah	20	2	6	.333	7	8	.875	0	9	9	2	1	0	1	0	1	11
Totals	200	54	92	.587	29	40	.725	18	48	66	17	15	0	9	4	15	137

M

MANNING, DANNY   F/C   SUNS

PERSONAL: Born May 17, 1966, in Hattiesburg, Miss. ... 6-10/234. ... Full name: Daniel Ricardo Manning. ... Son of Ed Manning, forward with Baltimore Bullets, Chicago Bulls and Portland Trail Blazers of NBA (1967-68 through 1970-71) and Carolina Cougars, New York Nets and Indiana Pacers of American Basketball Association (1971-72 through 1975-76).
HIGH SCHOOL: Page (Greensboro, N.C.), then Lawrence (Kan.).
COLLEGE: Kansas.
TRANSACTIONS/CAREER NOTES: Selected by Los Angeles Clippers in first round (first pick overall) of 1988 NBA Draft. ... Traded by Clippers to Atlanta Hawks for F Dominique Wilkins and 1994 or 1995 conditional first-round draft choice (February 24, 1994). ... Signed as unrestricted free agent by Phoenix Suns (September 3, 1994).
MISCELLANEOUS: Member of bronze-medal-winning U.S. Olympic team (1988).

COLLEGIATE RECORD

NOTES: Naismith Award winner (1988). ... Wooden Award winner (1988). ... THE SPORTING NEWS All-America first team (1987, 1988). ... NCAA Division I Tournament Most Outstanding Player (1988). ... Member of NCAA Division I championship team (1988).

Season Team	G	Min.	FGM	FGA	Pct.	FTM	FTA	Pct.	Reb.	Ast.	Pts.	RPG	APG	PPG
84-85—Kansas	34	1120	209	369	.566	78	102	.765	258	108	496	7.6	3.2	14.6
85-86—Kansas	39	1256	279	465	.600	95	127	.748	245	93	653	6.3	2.4	16.7
86-87—Kansas	36	1249	347	562	.617	165	226	.730	342	64	860	9.5	1.8	23.9
87-88—Kansas	38	1336	381	653	.583	171	233	.734	342	77	942	9.0	2.0	24.8
Totals	147	4961	1216	2049	.593	509	688	.740	1187	342	2951	8.1	2.3	20.1

Three-point field goals: 1986-87, 1-for-3 (.333). 1987-88, 9-for-26 (.346). Totals, 10-for-29 (.345).

NBA REGULAR-SEASON RECORD

Season Team	G	Min.	FGM	FGA	Pct.	FTM	FTA	Pct.	Off.	Def.	Tot.	Ast.	St.	Blk.	TO	Pts.	RPG	APG	PPG
88-89—L.A. Clippers	26	950	177	358	.494	79	103	.767	70	101	171	81	44	25	93	434	6.6	3.1	16.7
89-90—L.A. Clippers	71	2269	440	826	.533	274	370	.741	142	280	422	187	91	39	188	1154	5.9	2.6	16.3
90-91—L.A. Clippers	73	2197	470	905	.519	219	306	.716	169	257	426	196	117	62	188	1159	5.8	2.7	15.9
91-92—L.A. Clippers	82	2904	650	1199	.542	279	385	.725	229	335	564	285	135	122	210	1579	6.9	3.5	19.3
92-93—L.A. Clippers	79	2761	702	1379	.509	388	484	.802	198	322	520	207	108	101	230	1800	6.6	2.6	22.8
93-94—LA Clip.-Atl.	68	2520	586	1201	.488	228	341	.669	131	334	465	261	99	82	233	1403	6.8	3.8	20.6
94-95—Phoenix	46	1510	340	622	.547	136	202	.673	97	179	276	154	41	57	121	822	6.0	3.3	17.9
95-96—Phoenix	33	816	178	388	.459	82	109	.752	30	113	143	65	38	24	77	441	4.3	2.0	13.4
Totals	478	15927	3543	6878	.515	1685	2300	.733	1066	1921	2987	1436	673	512	1340	8792	6.2	3.0	18.4

Three-point field goals: 1988-89, 1-for-5 (.200). 1989-90, 0-for-5. 1990-91, 0-for-3. 1991-92, 0-for-5. 1992-93, 8-for-30 (.267). 1993-94, 3-for-17 (.176). 1994-95, 6 for 21 (.286). 1995-96, 3-for-14 (.214). Totals, 21-for-100 (.210).
Personal fouls/disqualifications: 1988-89, 89/1. 1989-90, 261/4. 1990-91, 281/5. 1991-92, 293/5. 1992-93, 323/8. 1993-94, 260/2. 1994-95, 176/1. 1995-96, 121/2. Totals, 1804/28.

NBA PLAYOFF RECORD

Season Team	G	Min.	FGM	FGA	Pct.	FTM	FTA	Pct.	Off.	Def.	Tot.	Ast.	St.	Blk.	TO	Pts.	RPG	APG	PPG
91-92—L.A. Clippers	5	194	46	81	.568	20	31	.645	15	13	28	14	5	4	13	113	5.6	2.8	22.6
92-93—L.A. Clippers	5	171	35	85	.412	21	26	.808	12	24	36	8	7	5	13	91	7.2	1.6	18.2
93-94—Atlanta	11	426	84	172	.488	52	66	.788	28	49	77	37	15	9	26	220	7.0	3.4	20.0
95-96—Phoenix	4	90	22	48	.458	5	8	.625	4	7	11	5	4	1	6	49	2.8	1.3	12.3
Totals	25	881	187	386	.484	98	131	.748	59	93	152	64	31	19	58	473	6.1	2.6	18.9

Three-point field goals: 1991-92, 1-for-3 (.333). 1992-93, 0-for-2. 1995-96, 0-for-1. Totals, 1-for-6 (.167).
Personal fouls/disqualifications: 1991-92, 21/1. 1992-93, 19/0. 1993-94, 39/0. 1995-96, 15/1. Totals, 94/2.

NBA ALL-STAR GAME RECORD

Season Team	Min.	FGM	FGA	Pct.	FTM	FTA	Pct.	Off.	Def.	Tot.	Ast.	PF	Dq.	St.	Blk.	TO	Pts.
1993 —L.A. Clippers	18	5	5	1.000	0	0	...	1	3	4	1	1	0	0	0	0	10
1994 —L.A. Clippers	17	4	7	.571	0	0	...	0	4	4	2	4	0	0	1	0	8
Totals	35	9	12	.750	0	0	...	1	7	8	3	5	0	0	1	0	18

M

MANNING, RICH   C   GRIZZLIES

PERSONAL: Born June 23, 1970, in Tacoma, Wash. ... 6-11/260. ... Full name: Richard Alan Manning.
HIGH SCHOOL: Center (North Highlands, Calif.).
COLLEGE: Syracuse, then Washington.
TRANSACTIONS/CAREER NOTES: Selected by Atlanta Hawks in second round (40th pick overall) of 1993 NBA Draft. ... Waived by Hawks (November 2, 1993). ... Played in Continental Basketball Association with Rapid City Thrillers (1993-94) and Quad City Thunder (1994-95). ... Signed as free agent by Utah Jazz (October 3, 1994). ... Waived by Jazz (October 31, 1994). ... Signed as free agent by Vancouver Grizzlies (October 5, 1995). ... Waived by Grizzlies (November 27, 1995). ... Signed by Vancouver Grizzlies for remainder of season (January 12, 1996).

COLLEGIATE RECORD

Season Team	G	Min.	FGM	FGA	Pct.	FTM	FTA	Pct.	Reb.	Ast.	Pts.	RPG	APG	PPG
88-89—Syracuse	36	352	47	92	.511	29	38	.763	63	6	123	1.8	0.2	3.4
89-90—Syracuse	31	387	40	93	.430	17	23	.739	67	9	97	2.2	0.3	3.1
90-91—Washington					Did not play—transfer student.									
91-92—Washington	29	915	209	368	.568	68	101	.673	176	22	486	6.1	0.8	16.8
92-93—Washington	25	776	187	325	.575	72	90	.800	209	34	447	8.4	1.4	17.9
Totals	121	2430	483	878	.550	186	252	.738	515	71	1153	4.3	0.6	9.5

Three-point field goals: 1992-93, 1-for-4 (.250).

CBA REGULAR-SEASON RECORD

Season Team	G	Min.	FGM	FGA	Pct.	FTM	FTA	Pct.	Reb.	Ast.	Pts.	RPG	APG	PPG
93-94—Rapid City	45	461	102	167	.611	37	46	.804	144	10	241	3.2	0.2	5.4
94-95—Quad City	52	1371	297	553	.537	127	155	.819	303	74	721	5.8	1.4	13.9
Totals	97	1832	399	720	.554	164	201	.816	447	84	962	4.6	0.9	9.9

Three-point field goals: 1994-95, 0-for-2.

NBA REGULAR-SEASON RECORD

Season Team	G	Min.	FGM	FGA	Pct.	FTM	FTA	Pct.	Off.	Def.	Tot.	Ast.	St.	Blk.	TO	Pts.	RPG	APG	PPG
95-96—Vancouver	29	311	49	113	.434	9	14	.643	16	39	55	7	3	6	17	107	1.9	0.2	3.7

Three-point field goals: 1995-96, 0-for-1.
Personal fouls/disqualifications: 1995-96, 37/0.

MARCIULIONIS, SARUNAS   G   NUGGETS

PERSONAL: Born June 13, 1964, in Kaunas, Lithuania. ... 6-5/215. ... Full name: Raimondas Sarunas Marciulionis. ... Name pronounced sha-ROON-iss MARSH-uh-LOAN-iss.
COLLEGE: State University of Vilnius (Lithuania).
TRANSACTIONS/CAREER NOTES: Selected by Golden State Warriors in sixth round (127th pick overall) of 1987 NBA Draft; pick was disallowed by NBA officials who found Marciulionis to be eight days too old to have been eligible for the draft. ... Played in Lithuania, U.S.S.R., for Statbe and Zalgiris clubs. ... Signed as free agent by Warriors (June 23, 1989). ... Traded by Warriors with F Byron Houston to Seattle SuperSonics for G Ricky Pierce, draft rights to F Carlos Rogers and two 1995 second-round draft choices (July 18, 1994). ... Traded by SuperSonics with F Byron Houston to Sacramento Kings for F/C Frank Brickowski (September 18, 1995). ... Traded by Kings with 1996 second-round draft choice to Denver Nuggets for G Mahmoud Abdul-Rauf (June 13, 1996).
MISCELLANEOUS: Member of gold-medal-winning Soviet Olympic team (1988). ... Member of bronze-medal-winning Lithuanian Olympic teams (1992, 1996).

NBA REGULAR-SEASON RECORD

Season Team	G	Min.	FGM	FGA	Pct.	FTM	FTA	Pct.	Off.	Def.	Tot.	Ast.	St.	Blk.	TO	Pts.	RPG	APG	PPG
89-90—Golden State	75	1695	289	557	.519	317	403	.787	84	137	221	121	94	7	137	905	2.9	1.6	12.1
90-91—Golden State	50	987	183	365	.501	178	246	.724	51	67	118	85	62	4	75	545	2.4	1.7	10.9
91-92—Golden State	72	2117	491	912	.538	376	477	.788	68	140	208	243	116	10	193	1361	2.9	3.4	18.9
92-93—Golden State	30	836	178	328	.543	162	213	.761	40	57	97	105	51	2	76	521	3.2	3.5	17.4
93-94—Golden State						Did not play—knee injury.													
94-95—Seattle	66	1194	216	457	.473	145	198	.732	17	51	68	110	72	3	98	612	1.0	1.7	9.3
95-96—Sacramento	53	1039	176	389	.452	155	200	.775	20	57	77	118	52	4	96	571	1.5	2.2	10.8
Totals	346	7868	1533	3008	.510	1333	1737	.767	280	509	789	782	447	30	675	4515	2.3	2.3	13.0

Three-point field goals: 1989-90, 10-for-39 (.256). 1990-91, 1-for-6 (.167). 1991-92, 3-for-10 (.300). 1992-93, 3-for-15 (.200). 1994-95, 35-for-87 (.402). 1995-96, 64-for-157 (.408). Totals, 116-for-314 (.369).
Personal fouls/disqualifications: 1989-90, 230/5. 1990-91, 136/4. 1991-92, 237/4. 1992-93, 92/1. 1994-95, 126/1. 1995-96, 112/1. Totals, 933/16.

NBA PLAYOFF RECORD

Season Team	G	Min.	FGM	FGA	Pct.	FTM	FTA	Pct.	Off.	Def.	Tot.	Ast.	St.	Blk.	TO	Pts.	RPG	APG	PPG
90-91—Golden State	9	206	42	84	.500	35	39	.897	8	15	23	27	11	1	14	119	2.6	3.0	13.2
91-92—Golden State	4	133	25	47	.532	34	41	.829	3	6	9	20	3	1	4	85	2.3	5.0	21.3
95-96—Sacramento	4	101	8	29	.276	9	15	.600	4	3	7	14	10	0	10	29	1.8	3.5	7.3
Totals	17	440	75	160	.469	78	95	.821	15	24	39	61	24	2	28	233	2.3	3.6	13.7

Three-point field goals: 1990-91, 0-for-1. 1991-92, 1-for-2 (.500). 1995-96, 4-for-18 (.222). Totals, 5-for-21 (.238).
Personal fouls/disqualifications: 1990-91, 21/1. 1991-92, 15/0. 1995-96, 4/0. Totals, 40/1.

MARSHALL, DONNY   F   CAVALIERS

PERSONAL: Born July 17, 1972, in Detroit. ... 6-7/230. ... Full name: Donny E. Marshall.
HIGH SCHOOL: Federal Way (Wash.).
COLLEGE: Connecticut.
TRANSACTIONS/CAREER NOTES: Selected by Cleveland Cavaliers in second round (39th pick overall) of 1995 NBA Draft.

COLLEGIATE RECORD

Season Team	G	Min.	FGM	FGA	Pct.	FTM	FTA	Pct.	Reb.	Ast.	Pts.	RPG	APG	PPG
91-92—Connecticut	27	241	17	46	.370	17	24	.708	43	10	51	1.6	0.4	1.9
92-93—Connecticut	28	677	81	174	.466	54	71	.761	118	31	217	4.2	1.1	7.8
93-94—Connecticut	34	999	152	294	.517	96	124	.774	186	44	423	5.5	1.3	12.4
94-95—Connecticut	32	976	173	379	.456	136	164	.829	187	44	506	5.8	1.4	15.8
Totals	121	2893	423	893	.474	303	383	.791	534	129	1197	4.4	1.1	9.9

Three-point field goals: 1992-93, 1-for-3 (.333). 1993-94, 23-for-64 (.359). 1994-95, 24-for-92 (.261). Totals, 48-for-159 (.302).

NBA REGULAR-SEASON RECORD

Season Team	G	Min.	FGM	FGA	Pct.	FTM	FTA	Pct.	Off.	Def.	Tot.	Ast.	St.	Blk.	TO	Pts.	RPG	APG	PPG
95-96—Cleveland	34	208	24	68	.353	22	35	.629	9	17	26	7	8	2	7	77	0.8	0.2	2.3

Three-point field goals: 1995-96, 7-for-30 (.233).
Personal fouls/disqualifications: 1995-96, 26/0.

NBA PLAYOFF RECORD

Season Team	G	Min.	FGM	FGA	Pct.	FTM	FTA	Pct.	Off.	Def.	Tot.	Ast.	St.	Blk.	TO	Pts.	RPG	APG	PPG
95-96—Cleveland	1	1	0	0	...	0	0	...	0	0	0	0	0	0	0	0	0.0	0.0	0.0

MARSHALL, DONYELL   F   WARRIORS

PERSONAL: Born May 18, 1973, in Reading, Pa. ... 6-9/230. ... Full name: Donyell Lamar Marshall. ... Name pronounced don-YELL.
HIGH SCHOOL: Reading (Pa.).
COLLEGE: Connecticut.
TRANSACTIONS/CAREER NOTES: Selected after junior season by Minnesota Timberwolves in first round (fourth pick overall) of 1994 NBA Draft. ... Traded by Timberwolves to Golden State Warriors for F Tom Gugliotta (February 18, 1995).

COLLEGIATE RECORD

NOTES: THE SPORTING NEWS All-America first team (1994).

											AVERAGES		
Season Team	G	Min.	FGM	FGA	Pct.	FTM	FTA	Pct.	Reb.	Ast.	Pts.	RPG	APG	PPG
91-92—Connecticut	30	806	125	295	.424	69	93	.742	183	45	334	6.1	1.5	11.1
92-93—Connecticut	27	854	166	332	.500	107	129	.829	210	30	459	7.8	1.1	17.0
93-94—Connecticut	34	1157	306	599	.511	200	266	.752	302	56	853	8.9	1.6	25.1
Totals	91	2817	597	1226	.487	376	488	.770	695	131	1646	7.6	1.4	18.1

Three-point field goals: 1991-92, 15-for-62 (.242). 1992-93, 20-for-54 (.370). 1993-94, 41-for-132 (.311). Totals, 76-for-248 (.306).

HONORS: NBA All-Rookie second team (1995).

NBA REGULAR-SEASON RECORD

								REBOUNDS							AVERAGES		
Season Team	G	Min.	FGM	FGA	Pct.	FTM	FTA	Pct.	Off.	Def.	Tot.	Ast.	St.	Blk.	TO	Pts.	RPG	APG	PPG
94-95—Minn.-G.S.	72	2086	345	876	.394	147	222	.662	137	268	405	105	45	88	115	906	5.6	1.5	12.6
95-96—Golden State	62	934	125	314	.398	64	83	.771	65	148	213	49	22	31	48	342	3.4	0.8	5.5
Totals	134	3020	470	1190	.395	211	305	.692	202	416	618	154	67	119	163	1248	4.6	1.1	9.3

Three-point field goals: 1994-95, 69-for-243 (.284). 1995-96, 28-for-94 (.298). Totals, 97-for-337 (.288).
Personal fouls/disqualifications: 1994-95, 157/1. 1995-96, 83/0. Totals, 240/1.

MARTIN, CUONZO   G/F

PERSONAL: Born September 23, 1971, in St. Louis. ... 6-5/213. ... Full name: Cuonzo LaMar Martin.
HIGH SCHOOL: Lincoln (East St. Louis, Ill.), then New Hampton (N.H.) Prep.
COLLEGE: Purdue.
TRANSACTIONS/CAREER NOTES: Selected by Atlanta Hawks in second round (57th pick overall) of 1995 NBA Draft. ... Waived by Hawks (October 30, 1995). ... Played in Continental Basketball Association with Grand Rapids Mackers (1995-96). ... Signed by Vancouver Grizzlies to 10-day contract (April 3, 1996). ... Re-signed by Grizzlies for remainder of season (April 13, 1996). ... Rights renounced by Grizzlies (July 16, 1996).

COLLEGIATE RECORD

											AVERAGES		
Season Team	G	Min.	FGM	FGA	Pct.	FTM	FTA	Pct.	Reb.	Ast.	Pts.	RPG	APG	PPG
91-92—Purdue	33	688	62	119	.521	66	87	.759	108	50	190	3.3	1.5	5.8
92-93—Purdue	28	931	131	251	.522	71	88	.807	103	68	333	3.7	2.4	11.9
93-94—Purdue	34	1097	195	421	.463	75	102	.735	145	66	553	4.3	1.9	16.3
94-95—Purdue	32	959	192	437	.439	115	144	.799	125	70	590	3.9	2.2	18.4
Totals	127	3675	580	1228	.472	327	421	.777	481	254	1666	3.8	2.0	13.1

Three-point field goals: 1991-92, 0-for-1. 1992-93, 0-for-6. 1993-94, 88-for-196 (.449). 1994-95, 91-for-194 (.469). Totals, 179-for-397 (.451).

CBA REGULAR-SEASON RECORD

NOTES: CBA All-Rookie first team (1996).

											AVERAGES		
Season Team	G	Min.	FGM	FGA	Pct.	FTM	FTA	Pct.	Reb.	Ast.	Pts.	RPG	APG	PPG
95-96—Grand Rapids	51	1935	333	736	.452	121	145	.834	154	117	895	3.0	2.3	17.5

Three-point field goals: 1995-96, 108-for-260 (.415).

NBA REGULAR-SEASON RECORD

								REBOUNDS							AVERAGES		
Season Team	G	Min.	FGM	FGA	Pct.	FTM	FTA	Pct.	Off.	Def.	Tot.	Ast.	St.	Blk.	TO	Pts.	RPG	APG	PPG
95-96—Vancouver	4	19	3	5	.600	0	2	.000	1	1	2	2	1	0	1	9	0.5	0.5	2.3

Three-point field goals: 1995-96, 3-for-3.
Personal fouls/disqualifications: 1995-96, 1/0.

MARTIN, DARRICK   G

PERSONAL: Born March 6, 1971, in Denver. ... 5-11/170.
HIGH SCHOOL: St. Anthony (Long Beach, Calif.).
COLLEGE: UCLA.
TRANSACTIONS/CAREER NOTES: Not drafted by an NBA franchise. ... Played with Magic Johnson All-Stars (1993-94). ... Played in Continental Basketball Association with Sioux Falls Skyforce (1994-95). ... Signed by Minnesota Timberwolves to first of two consecutive 10-day contracts (February 13, 1995). ... Re-signed by Timberwolves for remainder of season (March 7, 1995). ... Signed as free agent by Vancouver Grizzlies (November 3, 1995). ... Traded by Grizzlies to Timberwolves for 1996 second-round draft choice (January 12, 1996). ... Rights renounced by Timberwolves (July 19, 1996).

COLLEGIATE RECORD

											AVERAGES		
Season Team	G	Min.	FGM	FGA	Pct.	FTM	FTA	Pct.	Reb.	Ast.	Pts.	RPG	APG	PPG
88-89—UCLA	31	929	92	203	.453	68	91	.747	59	90	265	1.9	2.9	8.5

M

Season Team	G	Min.	FGM	FGA	Pct.	FTM	FTA	Pct.	Reb.	Ast.	Pts.	RPG	APG	PPG
												AVERAGES		
89-90—UCLA	33	1069	132	283	.466	90	126	.714	71	199	374	2.2	6.0	11.3
90-91—UCLA	32	1030	129	278	.464	90	120	.750	77	217	371	2.4	6.8	11.6
91-92—UCLA	33	642	52	120	.433	68	82	.829	43	130	185	1.3	3.9	5.6
Totals	129	3670	405	884	.458	316	419	.754	250	636	1195	1.9	4.9	9.3

Three-point field goals: 1988-89, 13-for-37 (.351). 1989-90, 20-for-63 (.317). 1990-91, 23-for-79 (.291). 1991-92, 13-for-35 (.371). Totals, 69-for-214 (.322).

NOTES: CBA All-League second team (1995).

CBA REGULAR-SEASON RECORD

Season Team	G	Min.	FGM	FGA	Pct.	FTM	FTA	Pct.	Reb.	Ast.	Pts.	RPG	APG	PPG
												AVERAGES		
94-95—Sioux Falls	37	1422	285	518	.550	196	226	.867	96	289	777	2.6	7.8	21.0

Three-point field goals: 1994-95, 11-for-39 (.282).

NBA REGULAR-SEASON RECORD

Season Team	G	Min.	FGM	FGA	Pct.	FTM	FTA	Pct.	Off.	Def.	Tot.	Ast.	St.	Blk.	TO	Pts.	RPG	APG	PPG
									REBOUNDS								AVERAGES		
94-95—Minnesota	34	803	95	233	.408	57	65	.877	14	50	64	133	34	0	62	254	1.9	3.9	7.5
95-96—Minnesota	59	1149	147	362	.406	101	120	.842	16	66	82	217	53	3	107	415	1.4	3.7	7.0
Totals	93	1952	242	595	.407	158	185	.854	30	116	146	350	87	3	169	669	1.6	3.8	7.2

Three-point field goals: 1994-95, 7-for-38 (.184). 1995-96, 20-for-69 (.290). Totals, 27-for-107 (.252).
Personal fouls/disqualifications: 1994-95, 88/0. 1995-96, 123/0. Totals, 211/0.

MASHBURN, JAMAL   F   MAVERICKS

PERSONAL: Born November 29, 1972, in New York. ... 6-8/250.
HIGH SCHOOL: Cardinal Hayes (Bronx, N.Y.).
COLLEGE: Kentucky.
TRANSACTIONS/CAREER NOTES: Selected after junior season by Dallas Mavericks in first round (fourth pick overall) of 1993 NBA Draft.

COLLEGIATE RECORD

NOTES: The Sporting News All-America first team (1993).

Season Team	G	Min.	FGM	FGA	Pct.	FTM	FTA	Pct.	Reb.	Ast.	Pts.	RPG	APG	PPG
												AVERAGES		
90-91—Kentucky	28	677	137	289	.474	64	88	.727	195	42	362	7.0	1.5	12.9
91-92—Kentucky	36	1176	279	492	.567	151	213	.709	281	52	767	7.8	1.4	21.3
92-93—Kentucky	34	1109	259	526	.492	130	194	.670	284	124	714	8.4	3.6	21.0
Totals	98	2962	675	1307	.516	345	495	.697	760	218	1843	7.8	2.2	18.8

Three-point field goals: 1990-91, 23-for-82 (.280). 1991-92, 58-for-132 (.439). 1992-93, 66-for-180 (.367). Totals, 147-for-394 (.373).

NBA REGULAR-SEASON RECORD

HONORS: NBA All-Rookie first team (1994).

Season Team	G	Min.	FGM	FGA	Pct.	FTM	FTA	Pct.	Off.	Def.	Tot.	Ast.	St.	Blk.	TO	Pts.	RPG	APG	PPG
									REBOUNDS								AVERAGES		
93-94—Dallas	79	2896	561	1382	.406	306	438	.699	107	246	353	266	89	14	245	1513	4.5	3.4	19.2
94-95—Dallas	80	2980	683	1566	.436	447	605	.739	116	215	331	298	82	8	235	1926	4.1	3.7	24.1
95-96—Dallas	18	669	145	383	.379	97	133	.729	37	60	97	50	14	3	55	422	5.4	2.8	23.4
Totals	177	6545	1389	3331	.417	850	1176	.723	260	521	781	614	185	25	535	3861	4.4	3.5	21.8

Three-point field goals: 1993-94, 85-for-299 (.284). 1994-95, 113-for-344 (.328). 1995-96, 35-for-102 (.343). Totals, 233-for-745 (.313).
Personal fouls/disqualifications: 1993-94, 205/0. 1994-95, 190/0. 1995-96, 39/0. Totals, 434/0.

MASON, ANTHONY   F   HORNETS

PERSONAL: Born December 14, 1966, in Miami. ... 6-7/250. ... Full name: Anthony George Douglas Mason.
HIGH SCHOOL: Springfield Gardens (N.Y.).
COLLEGE: Tennessee State.
TRANSACTIONS/CAREER NOTES: Selected by Portland Trail Blazers in third round (53rd pick overall) of 1988 NBA Draft. ... Played in Turkey (1988-89). ... Draft rights renounced by Trail Blazers (June 30, 1989). ... Signed as free agent by New Jersey Nets (September 19, 1989). ... Waived by Nets (October 30, 1990). ... Played in Continental Basketball Association with Tulsa Fast Breakers (1990-91). ... Signed by Denver Nuggets to first of two consecutive 10-day contracts (December 28, 1990). ... Played in United States Basketball League with Long Island Surf (1991). ... Signed as free agent by New York Knicks (July 30, 1991). ... Traded by Knicks with F Brad Lohaus to Charlotte Hornets for F Larry Johnson (July 14, 1996).

COLLEGIATE RECORD

Season Team	G	Min.	FGM	FGA	Pct.	FTM	FTA	Pct.	Reb.	Ast.	Pts.	RPG	APG	PPG
												AVERAGES		
84-85—Tennessee State	28	801	100	213	.469	79	122	.648	148	46	279	5.3	1.6	10.0
85-86—Tennessee State	28	913	206	427	.482	93	130	.715	192	69	505	6.9	2.5	18.0
86-87—Tennessee State	27	951	201	449	.448	89	135	.659	262	68	508	9.7	2.5	18.8
87-88—Tennessee State	28	1064	276	608	.454	191	247	.773	292	85	783	10.4	3.0	28.0
Totals	111	3729	783	1697	.461	452	634	.713	894	268	2075	8.1	2.4	18.7

Three-point field goals: 1986-87, 17-for-49 (.347). 1987-88, 40-for-81 (.494). Totals, 57-for-130 (.438).

NBA REGULAR-SEASON RECORD

HONORS: NBA Sixth Man Award (1995).

Season Team	G	Min.	FGM	FGA	Pct.	FTM	FTA	Pct.	Off.	Def.	Tot.	Ast.	St.	Blk.	TO	Pts.	RPG	APG	PPG
89-90—New Jersey	21	108	14	40	.350	9	15	.600	11	23	34	7	2	2	11	37	1.6	0.3	1.8
90-91—Denver	3	21	2	4	.500	6	8	.750	3	2	5	0	1	0	0	10	1.7	0.0	3.3
91-92—New York	82	2198	203	399	.509	167	260	.642	216	357	573	106	46	20	101	573	7.0	1.3	7.0
92-93—New York	81	2482	316	629	.502	199	292	.682	231	409	640	170	43	19	137	831	7.9	2.1	10.3
93-94—New York	73	1903	206	433	.476	116	161	.721	158	269	427	151	31	9	107	528	5.8	2.1	7.2
94-95—New York	77	2496	287	507	.566	191	298	.641	182	468	650	240	69	21	123	765	8.4	3.1	9.9
95-96—New York	82	*3457	449	798	.563	298	414	.720	220	544	764	363	69	34	211	1196	9.3	4.4	14.6
Totals	419	12665	1477	2810	.526	986	1448	.681	1021	2072	3093	1037	261	105	690	3940	7.4	2.5	9.4

Three-point field goals: 1993-94, 0-for-1. 1994-95, 0-for-1. Totals, 0-for-2.
Personal fouls/disqualifications: 1989-90, 20/0. 1990-91, 6/0. 1991-92, 229/0. 1992-93, 240/2. 1993-94, 190/2. 1994-95, 253/3. 1995-96, 246/3. Totals, 1184/10.

NBA PLAYOFF RECORD

Season Team	G	Min.	FGM	FGA	Pct.	FTM	FTA	Pct.	Off.	Def.	Tot.	Ast.	St.	Blk.	TO	Pts.	RPG	APG	PPG
91-92—New York	12	288	19	43	.442	22	28	.786	28	48	76	10	2	8	11	60	6.3	0.8	5.0
92-93—New York	15	510	72	122	.590	43	68	.632	55	54	109	41	10	6	23	187	7.3	2.7	12.5
93-94—New York	25	660	67	137	.489	55	77	.714	53	93	146	46	15	5	36	189	5.8	1.8	7.6
94-95—New York	11	352	31	51	.608	43	69	.623	23	45	68	24	6	6	26	105	6.2	2.2	9.5
95-96—New York	8	350	41	78	.526	19	28	.679	17	45	62	26	4	1	20	101	7.8	3.3	12.6
Totals	71	2160	230	431	.534	182	270	.674	176	285	461	147	37	26	116	642	6.5	2.1	9.0

Three-point field goals: 1994-95, 0-for-1.
Personal fouls/disqualifications: 1991-92, 34/0. 1992-93, 50/2. 1993-94, 66/0. 1994-95, 28/0. 1995-96, 20/0. Totals, 198/2.

CBA REGULAR-SEASON RECORD

Season Team	G	Min.	FGM	FGA	Pct.	FTM	FTA	Pct.	Reb.	Ast.	Pts.	RPG	APG	PPG
90-91—Tulsa	26	1074	256	456	.561	266	370	.719	384	102	778	14.8	3.9	29.9

MASSENBURG, TONY   F

PERSONAL: Born July 31, 1967, in Sussex, Va. ... 6-9/245. ... Full name: Tony Arnel Massenburg.
HIGH SCHOOL: Sussex (Va.) Central.
COLLEGE: Maryland.
TRANSACTIONS/CAREER NOTES: Selected by San Antonio Spurs in second round (43rd pick overall) of 1990 NBA Draft. ... Waived by Spurs (December 2, 1991). ... Played in Italy (1991-92). ... Signed as free agent by Charlotte Hornets (December 11, 1991). ... Waived by Hornets (January 7, 1992). ... Signed by Boston Celtics to first of two consecutive 10-day contracts (January 10, 1992). ... Signed by Golden State Warriors to first of two consecutive 10-day contracts (February 13, 1992). ... Played in Spain (1992-93 and 1993-94). ... Signed as free agent by Los Angeles Clippers (June 27, 1994). ... Selected by Toronto Raptors from Clippers in NBA expansion draft (June 24, 1995). ... Traded by Raptors with F Ed Pinckney and right to swap 1996 or 1997 first-round draft choices to Philadelphia 76ers for F Sharone Wright (February 22, 1996). ... Rights renounced by 76ers (July 22, 1996).

COLLEGIATE RECORD

Season Team	G	Min.	FGM	FGA	Pct.	FTM	FTA	Pct.	Reb.	Ast.	Pts.	RPG	APG	PPG
85-86—Maryland	29	349	28	56	.500	27	48	.563	60	0	83	2.1	0.0	2.9
86-87—Maryland							Did not play.							
87-88—Maryland	23	616	93	179	.520	47	82	.573	122	10	233	5.3	0.4	10.1
88-89—Maryland	29	1001	197	358	.550	87	145	.600	226	21	481	7.8	0.7	16.6
89-90—Maryland	31	973	206	408	.505	145	201	.721	314	20	557	10.1	0.6	18.0
Totals	112	2939	524	1001	.523	306	476	.643	722	51	1354	6.4	0.5	12.1

Three-point field goals: 1988-89, 0-for-1. 1989-90, 0-for-2. Totals, 0-for-3.

NBA REGULAR-SEASON RECORD

Season Team	G	Min.	FGM	FGA	Pct.	FTM	FTA	Pct.	Off.	Def.	Tot.	Ast.	St.	Blk.	TO	Pts.	RPG	APG	PPG
90-91—San Antonio	35	161	27	60	.450	28	45	.622	23	35	58	4	4	9	13	82	1.7	0.1	2.3
91-92—SA-Cha.-B.-GS	18	90	10	25	.400	9	15	.600	7	18	25	0	1	1	9	29	1.4	0.0	1.6
94-95—L.A. Clippers	80	2127	282	601	.469	177	235	.753	160	295	455	67	48	58	118	741	5.7	0.8	9.3
95-96—Tor.-Phil.	54	1463	214	432	.495	111	157	.707	127	225	352	30	28	20	73	539	6.5	0.6	10.0
Totals	187	3841	533	1118	.477	325	452	.719	317	573	890	101	81	88	213	1391	4.8	0.5	7.4

Three-point field goals: 1994-95, 0-for-3. 1995-96, 0-for-3. Totals, 0-for-6.
Personal fouls/disqualifications: 1990-91, 26/0. 1991-92, 21/0. 1994-95, 253/2. 1995-96, 140/0. Totals, 440/2.

NBA PLAYOFF RECORD

Season Team	G	Min.	FGM	FGA	Pct.	FTM	FTA	Pct.	Off.	Def.	Tot.	Ast.	St.	Blk.	TO	Pts.	RPG	APG	PPG
90-91—San Antonio	1	1	0	0	...	0	0	...	0	0	0	0	0	0	0	0	0.0	0.0	0.0

ITALIAN LEAGUE RECORD

Season Team	G	Min.	FGM	FGA	Pct.	FTM	FTA	Pct.	Reb.	Ast.	Pts.	RPG	APG	PPG
91-92—Sid. Regg. Emilia	4	133	35	60	.583	21	33	.636	40	0	91	10.0	0.0	22.8

SPANISH LEAGUE RECORD

Season Team	G	Min.	FGM	FGA	Pct.	FTM	FTA	Pct.	Reb.	Ast.	Pts.	RPG	APG	PPG
92-93—Unicaja-Mayoral	30	1008	195	351	.556	72	106	.679	293	10	462	9.8	0.3	15.4
93-94—Barcelona	25	759	150	264	.568	88	127	.693	199	12	388	8.0	0.5	15.5
Totals	55	1767	345	615	.561	160	233	.687	492	22	850	8.9	0.4	15.5

M

MAXWELL, VERNON   G   SPURS

PERSONAL: Born September 12, 1965, in Gainesville, Fla. ... 6-4/190.
HIGH SCHOOL: Buchholz (Gainesville, Fla.).
COLLEGE: Florida.
TRANSACTIONS/CAREER NOTES: Selected by Denver Nuggets in second round (47th pick overall) of 1988 NBA Draft. ... Draft rights traded by Nuggets to San Antonio Spurs for 1989 second-round draft choice (June 28, 1988). ... Traded by Spurs to Houston Rockets for cash (February 21, 1990). ... Waived by Rockets (June 30, 1995). ... Signed as free agent by Philadelphia 76ers (September 26, 1995). ... Rights renounced by 76ers (July 11, 1996). ... Signed as free agent by Spurs (August 29, 1996).
MISCELLANEOUS: Member of NBA championship teams (1994, 1995).

COLLEGIATE RECORD

Season Team	G	Min.	FGM	FGA	Pct.	FTM	FTA	Pct.	Reb.	Ast.	Pts.	RPG	APG	PPG
84-85—Florida	30	752	163	366	.445	72	105	.686	72	40	398	2.4	1.3	13.3
85-86—Florida	33	1142	262	566	.463	124	177	.701	147	81	648	4.5	2.5	19.6
86-87—Florida	34	1086	266	548	.485	161	217	.742	125	123	738	3.7	3.6	21.7
87-88—Florida	33	1214	230	515	.447	148	207	.715	138	142	666	4.2	4.3	20.2
Totals	130	4194	921	1995	.462	505	706	.715	482	386	2450	3.7	3.0	18.8

Three-point field goals: 1986-87, 45-for-128 (.352). 1987-88, 58-for-147 (.395). Totals, 103-for-275 (.375).

NBA REGULAR-SEASON RECORD

Season Team	G	Min.	FGM	FGA	Pct.	FTM	FTA	Pct.	Off.	Def.	Tot.	Ast.	St.	Blk.	TO	Pts.	RPG	APG	PPG
88-89—San Antonio	79	2065	357	827	.432	181	243	.745	49	153	202	301	86	8	178	927	2.6	3.8	11.7
89-90—S.A.-Hou.	79	1987	275	627	.439	136	211	.645	50	178	228	296	84	10	143	714	2.9	3.7	9.0
90-91—Houston	82	2870	504	1247	.404	217	296	.733	41	197	238	303	127	15	171	1397	2.9	3.7	17.0
91-92—Houston	80	2700	502	1216	.413	206	267	.772	37	206	243	326	104	28	178	1372	3.0	4.1	17.2
92-93—Houston	71	2251	349	858	.407	164	228	.719	29	192	221	297	86	8	140	982	3.1	4.2	13.8
93-94—Houston	75	2571	380	976	.389	143	191	.749	42	187	229	380	125	20	185	1023	3.1	5.1	13.6
94-95—Houston	64	2038	306	777	.394	99	144	.688	18	146	164	274	75	13	137	854	2.6	4.3	13.3
95-96—Philadelphia	75	2467	410	1052	.390	251	332	.756	39	190	229	330	96	12	215	1217	3.1	4.4	16.2
Totals	605	18949	3083	7580	.407	1397	1912	.731	305	1449	1754	2507	783	114	1347	8486	2.9	4.1	14.0

Three-point field goals: 1988-89, 32-for-129 (.248). 1989-90, 28-for-105 (.267). 1990-91, 172-for-510 (.337). 1991-92, 162-for-473 (.342). 1992-93, 120-for-361 (.332). 1993-94, 120-for-403 (.298). 1994-95, 143-for-441 (.324). 1995-96, 146-for-460 (.317). Totals, 923-for-2882 (.320).

Personal fouls/disqualifications: 1988-89, 136/0. 1989-90, 148/0. 1990-91, 179/2. 1991-92, 200/3. 1992-93, 124/1. 1993-94, 143/0. 1994-95, 157/1. 1995-96, 182/1. Totals, 1269/8.

NBA PLAYOFF RECORD

Season Team	G	Min.	FGM	FGA	Pct.	FTM	FTA	Pct.	Off.	Def.	Tot.	Ast.	St.	Blk.	TO	Pts.	RPG	APG	PPG
89-90—Houston	4	159	30	81	.370	11	21	.524	5	7	12	17	5	0	6	79	3.0	4.3	19.8
90-91—Houston	3	113	23	56	.411	1	2	.500	1	7	8	9	2	1	7	56	2.7	3.0	18.7
92-93—Houston	9	308	47	117	.402	21	24	.875	3	19	22	32	11	2	17	126	2.4	3.6	14.0
93-94—Houston	23	880	118	314	.376	37	54	.685	12	69	81	96	20	2	49	318	3.5	4.2	13.8
94-95—Houston	1	16	1	7	.143	1	1	1.000	0	3	3	1	0	0	1	3	3.0	1.0	3.0
Totals	40	1476	219	575	.381	71	102	.696	21	105	126	155	38	5	80	582	3.2	3.9	14.6

Three-point field goals: 1989-90, 8-for-26 (.308). 1990-91, 9-for-27 (.333). 1992-93, 11-for-46 (.239). 1993-94, 45-for-138 (.326). 1994-95, 0-for-2. Totals, 73-for-239 (.305).

Personal fouls/disqualifications: 1989-90, 12/0. 1990-91, 8/0. 1992-93, 17/0. 1993-94, 55/1. 1994-95, 1/0. Totals, 93/1.

MAYBERRY, LEE   G   GRIZZLIES

PERSONAL: Born June 12, 1970, in Tulsa, Okla. ... 6-1/172. ... Full name: Orva Lee Mayberry Jr.
HIGH SCHOOL: Rogers (Tulsa, Okla.).
COLLEGE: Arkansas.
TRANSACTIONS/CAREER NOTES: Selected by Milwaukee Bucks in first round (23rd pick overall) of 1992 NBA Draft. ... Signed as free agent by Vancouver Grizzlies (July 22, 1996).

COLLEGIATE RECORD

Season Team	G	Min.	FGM	FGA	Pct.	FTM	FTA	Pct.	Reb.	Ast.	Pts.	RPG	APG	PPG
88-89—Arkansas	32	1001	157	314	.500	67	91	.736	102	135	414	3.2	4.2	12.9
89-90—Arkansas	35	1131	193	381	.507	57	72	.792	100	183	508	2.9	5.2	14.5
90-91—Arkansas	38	1216	192	397	.484	59	93	.634	129	209	500	3.4	5.5	13.2
91-92—Arkansas	34	1167	181	368	.492	93	125	.744	78	202	518	2.3	5.9	15.2
Totals	139	4515	723	1460	.495	276	381	.724	409	729	1940	2.9	5.2	14.0

Three-point field goals: 1988-89, 33-for-74 (.446). 1989-90, 65-for-129 (.504). 1990-91, 57-for-149 (.383). 1991-92, 63-for-162 (.389). Totals, 218-for-514 (.424).

NBA REGULAR-SEASON RECORD

Season Team	G	Min.	FGM	FGA	Pct.	FTM	FTA	Pct.	Off.	Def.	Tot.	Ast.	St.	Blk.	TO	Pts.	RPG	APG	PPG
92-93—Milwaukee	82	1503	171	375	.456	39	68	.574	26	92	118	273	59	7	85	424	1.4	3.3	5.2
93-94—Milwaukee	82	1472	167	402	.415	58	84	.690	26	75	101	215	46	4	97	433	1.2	2.6	5.3
94-95—Milwaukee	82	1744	172	408	.422	58	83	.699	21	61	82	276	51	4	106	474	1.0	3.4	5.8
95-96—Milwaukee	82	1705	153	364	.420	41	68	.603	21	69	90	302	64	10	89	422	1.1	3.7	5.1
Totals	328	6424	663	1549	.428	196	303	.647	94	297	391	1066	220	25	377	1753	1.2	3.3	5.3

Three-point field goals: 1992-93, 43-for-110 (.391). 1993-94, 41-for-119 (.345). 1994-95, 72-for-177 (.407). 1995-96, 75-for-189 (.397). Totals, 231-for-595 (.388).

Personal fouls/disqualifications: 1992-93, 148/1. 1993-94, 114/0. 1994-95, 123/0. 1995-96, 144/1. Totals, 529/2.

McCANN, BOB   F

PERSONAL: Born April 22, 1964, in Morristown, N.J. ... 6-7/248. ... Full name: Robert Glen McCann.
HIGH SCHOOL: Morristown (N.J.).
COLLEGE: Upsala (N.J.), then Morehead State.
TRANSACTIONS/CAREER NOTES: Selected by Milwaukee Bucks in second round (32nd pick overall) of 1987 NBA Draft. ... Played in United States Basketball League with Jersey Jammers (1987). ... Waived by Bucks (November 4, 1987). ... Played in Spain (1987-88). ... Signed as free agent by Dallas Mavericks (October 5, 1988). ... Waived by Mavericks (November 1, 1988). ... Played in Continental Basketball Association with Charleston Gunners (1988-89), Pensacola Tornados (1988-89, 1989-90 and 1990-91) and Rapid City Thrillers (1994-95). ... Re-signed by Mavericks to first of two consecutive 10-day contracts (February 12, 1990). ... Re-signed by Mavericks for remainder of season (March 5, 1990). ... Re-signed by Mavericks (October 2, 1991). ... Released by Mavericks (October 27, 1991). ... Signed by Detroit Pistons (November 2, 1991). ... Signed as free agent by Minnesota Timberwolves (August 5, 1992). ... Rights renounced by Timberwolves (July 7, 1993). ... Signed as free agent by Golden State Warriors (September 28, 1994). ... Waived by Warriors (October 24, 1994). ... Signed as free agent by Bucks (October 6, 1995). ... Traded by Bucks to Washington Bullets for C Kevin Duckworth (October 18, 1995). ... Waived by Bullets (January 5, 1996). ... Re-signed by Bullets to first of two consecutive 10-day contracts (January 10, 1996). ... Re-signed by Bullets for remainder of season (February 3, 1996).

COLLEGIATE RECORD

											AVERAGES		
Season Team	G	Min.	FGM	FGA	Pct.	FTM	FTA	Pct.	Reb.	Ast.	Pts.	RPG	APG	PPG
82-83—Upsala College	26	...	112	236	.475	34	64	.531	208	...	258	8.0	...	9.9
83-84—Morehead State	Did not play—transfer student.													
84-85—Morehead State	27	911	188	383	.491	85	152	.559	263	41	461	9.7	1.5	17.1
85-86—Morehead State	27	803	171	320	.534	113	173	.653	282	17	455	10.4	0.6	16.9
86-87—Morehead State	28	872	206	376	.548	107	170	.629	317	41	520	11.3	1.5	18.6
Totals	108	...	677	1315	.515	339	559	.606	1070	...	1694	9.9	...	15.7

Three-point field goals: 1986-87, 1-for-3 (.333).

CBA REGULAR-SEASON RECORD

											AVERAGES		
Season Team	G	Min.	FGM	FGA	Pct.	FTM	FTA	Pct.	Reb.	Ast.	Pts.	RPG	APG	PPG
88-89—Charles.-Pens.	43	1555	327	641	.510	143	213	.671	356	97	797	8.3	2.3	18.5
89-90—Pensacola	43	1879	389	742	.524	203	296	.686	374	138	982	8.7	3.2	22.8
90-91—Pensacola	8	265	54	112	.482	17	30	.567	58	6	127	7.3	0.8	15.9
94-95—Rapid City	57	2099	353	629	.561	178	290	.614	546	91	885	9.6	1.6	15.5
Totals	151	5798	1123	2124	.529	541	829	.653	1334	332	2791	8.8	2.2	18.5

Three-point field goals: 1988-89, 0-for-5. 1989-90, 1-for-7 (.143). 1990-91, 2-for-3 (.667). 1994-95, 1-for-11 (.091). Totals, 4-for-26 (.154).

NBA REGULAR-SEASON RECORD

								REBOUNDS								AVERAGES		
Season Team	G	Min.	FGM	FGA	Pct.	FTM	FTA	Pct.	Off.	Def.	Tot.	Ast.	St.	Blk.	TO	Pts.	RPG	APG	PPG
89-90—Dallas	10	62	7	21	.333	12	14	.857	4	8	12	6	2	2	6	26	1.2	0.6	2.6
91-92—Detroit	26	129	13	33	.394	4	13	.308	12	18	30	6	6	4	7	30	1.2	0.2	1.2
92-93—Minnesota	79	1536	200	410	.488	95	152	.625	92	190	282	68	51	58	79	495	3.6	0.9	6.3
95-96—Washington	62	653	76	153	.497	35	74	.473	46	97	143	24	21	15	42	188	2.3	0.4	3.0
Totals	177	2380	296	617	.480	146	253	.577	154	313	467	104	80	79	134	739	2.6	0.6	4.2

Three-point field goals: 1991-92, 0-for-1. 1992-93, 0-for-2. 1995-96, 1-for-2 (.500). Totals, 1-for-5 (.200).
Personal fouls/disqualifications: 1989-90, 7/0. 1991-92, 23/0. 1992-93, 90/2. 1995-96, 116/0. Totals, 348/2.

NBA PLAYOFF RECORD

								REBOUNDS								AVERAGES		
Season Team	G	Min.	FGM	FGA	Pct.	FTM	FTA	Pct.	Off.	Def.	Tot.	Ast.	St.	Blk.	TO	Pts.	RPG	APG	PPG
91-92—Detroit	1	13	3	6	.500	0	0	...	1	1	2	0	0	1	2	6	2.0	0.0	6.0

Personal fouls/disqualifications: 1991-92, 2/0.

McCLOUD, GEORGE   F/G   MAVERICKS

PERSONAL: Born May 27, 1967, in Daytona Beach, Fla. ... 6-8/225. ... Full name: George Aaron McCloud.
HIGH SCHOOL: Mainland (Daytona Beach, Fla.).
COLLEGE: Florida State.
TRANSACTIONS/CAREER NOTES: Selected by Indiana Pacers in first round (seventh pick overall) of 1989 NBA Draft. ... Played in Italy (1993-94). ... Played in Continental Basketball Association with Rapid City Thrillers (1994-95). ... Signed by Dallas Mavericks to first of two consecutive 10-day contracts (January 30, 1995). ... Re-signed by Mavericks for remainder of season (February 22, 1995).

COLLEGIATE RECORD

											AVERAGES		
Season Team	G	Min.	FGM	FGA	Pct.	FTM	FTA	Pct.	Reb.	Ast.	Pts.	RPG	APG	PPG
85-86—Florida State	27	283	42	87	.483	31	49	.633	49	13	115	1.8	0.5	4.3
86-87—Florida State	30	590	87	197	.442	42	68	.618	126	18	230	4.2	0.6	7.7
87-88—Florida State	30	902	193	403	.479	88	112	.786	111	48	546	3.7	1.6	18.2
88-89—Florida State	30	1067	207	462	.448	154	176	.875	109	125	683	3.6	4.2	22.8
Totals	117	2842	529	1149	.460	315	405	.778	395	204	1574	3.4	1.7	13.5

Three-point field goals: 1986-87, 14-for-47 (.298). 1987-88, 72-for-159 (.453). 1988-89, 115-for-262 (.439). Totals, 201-for-468 (.429).

NBA REGULAR-SEASON RECORD

RECORDS: Holds single-season record for most three-point field goals attempted—678 (1996). ... Holds single-game record for most three-point field goals attempted, none made—10 (March 10, 1996, vs. Toronto). ... Shares single-game records for most three-point field goals made—10 (December 16, 1995, vs. Phoenix); most three-point field goals attempted—20 (March 5, 1996, vs. New Jersey); and most three-point field goals made in one half—7 (December 16, 1995, vs. Phoenix; and February 27, 1996, vs. Philadelphia).

Season Team	G	Min.	FGM	FGA	Pct.	FTM	FTA	Pct.	Off.	Def.	Tot.	Ast.	St.	Blk.	TO	Pts.	RPG	APG	PPG
									REBOUNDS								**AVERAGES**		
89-90—Indiana	44	413	45	144	.313	15	19	.789	12	30	42	45	19	3	36	118	1.0	1.0	2.7
90-91—Indiana	74	1070	131	351	.373	38	49	.776	35	83	118	150	40	11	91	343	1.6	2.0	4.6
91-92—Indiana	51	892	128	313	.409	50	64	.781	45	87	132	116	26	11	62	338	2.6	2.3	6.6
92-93—Indiana	78	1500	216	525	.411	75	102	.735	60	145	205	192	53	11	107	565	2.6	2.5	7.2
94-95—Dallas	42	802	144	328	.439	80	96	.833	82	65	147	53	23	9	40	402	3.5	1.3	9.6
95-96—Dallas	79	2846	530	1281	.414	180	224	.804	116	263	379	212	113	38	166	1497	4.8	2.7	18.9
Totals	368	7523	1194	2942	.406	438	554	.791	350	673	1023	768	274	83	502	3263	2.8	2.1	8.9

Three-point field goals: 1989-90, 13-for-40 (.325). 1990-91, 43-for-124 (.347). 1991-92, 32-for-94 (.340). 1992-93, 58-for-181 (.320). 1994-95, 34-for-89 (.382). 1995-96, 257-for-678 (.379). Totals, 437-for-1206 (.362).
Personal fouls/disqualifications: 1989-90, 56/0. 1990-91, 141/1. 1991-92, 95/1. 1992-93, 165/0. 1994-95, 71/0. 1995-96, 212/1. Totals, 740/3.

NBA PLAYOFF RECORD

Season Team	G	Min.	FGM	FGA	Pct.	FTM	FTA	Pct.	Off.	Def.	Tot.	Ast.	St.	Blk.	TO	Pts.	RPG	APG	PPG
									REBOUNDS								**AVERAGES**		
89-90—Indiana	1	4	1	2	.500	0	0	...	1	0	1	0	0	0	1	2	1.0	0.0	2.0
91-92—Indiana	2	53	6	12	.500	8	11	.727	0	2	2	6	2	1	3	23	1.0	3.0	11.5
92-93—Indiana	4	79	8	23	.348	1	4	.250	3	8	11	14	4	1	5	19	2.8	3.5	4.8
Totals	7	136	15	37	.405	9	15	.600	4	10	14	20	6	2	9	44	2.0	2.9	6.3

Three-point field goals: 1991-92, 3-for-6 (.500). 1992-93, 2-for-12 (.167). Totals, 5-for-18 (.278).
Personal fouls/disqualifications: 1989-90, 2/0. 1991-92, 5/0. 1992-93, 14/0. Totals, 21/0.

ITALIAN LEAGUE RECORD

Season Team	G	Min.	FGM	FGA	Pct.	FTM	FTA	Pct.	Reb.	Ast.	Pts.	RPG	APG	PPG
												AVERAGES		
93-94—Scavolini Pesaro	30	1093	198	394	.503	98	124	.790	163	31	565	5.4	1.0	18.8

CBA REGULAR-SEASON RECORD

Season Team	G	Min.	FGM	FGA	Pct.	FTM	FTA	Pct.	Reb.	Ast.	Pts.	RPG	APG	PPG
												AVERAGES		
94-95—Rapid City	32	1177	225	469	.480	187	214	.874	229	109	679	7.2	3.4	21.2

Three-point field goals: 1994-95, 42-for-123 (.341).

McDANIEL, CLINT — G — KINGS

PERSONAL: Born February 26, 1972, in Tulsa, Okla. ... 6-4/180.
HIGH SCHOOL: Booker T. Washington (Tulsa, Okla.).
COLLEGE: Arkansas.
TRANSACTIONS/CAREER NOTES: Not drafted by an NBA franchise. ... Signed as free agent by Sacramento Kings (November 2, 1995).

COLLEGIATE RECORD

NOTES: Member of NCAA Division I championship team (1994).

Season Team	G	Min.	FGM	FGA	Pct.	FTM	FTA	Pct.	Reb.	Ast.	Pts.	RPG	APG	PPG
												AVERAGES		
90-91—Arkansas						Did not play—transfer student.								
91-92—Arkansas	27	264	33	97	.340	29	39	.744	29	31	106	1.1	1.1	3.9
92-93—Arkansas	30	495	76	177	.429	52	77	.675	58	48	225	1.9	1.6	7.5
93-94—Arkansas	31	669	81	199	.407	52	69	.754	87	59	252	2.8	1.9	8.1
94-95—Arkansas	37	1093	139	302	.460	91	119	.765	113	90	424	3.1	2.4	11.5
Totals	125	2521	329	775	.425	224	304	.737	287	228	1007	2.3	1.8	8.1

Three-point field goals: 1991-92, 11-for-35 (.314). 1992-93, 21-for-73 (.288). 1993-94, 38-for-108 (.352). 1994-95, 55-for-139 (.396). Totals, 125-for-355 (.352).

NBA REGULAR-SEASON RECORD

Season Team	G	Min.	FGM	FGA	Pct.	FTM	FTA	Pct.	Off.	Def.	Tot.	Ast.	St.	Blk.	TO	Pts.	RPG	APG	PPG
									REBOUNDS								**AVERAGES**		
95-96—Sacramento	12	71	8	23	.348	12	16	.750	3	7	10	7	5	0	2	30	0.8	0.6	2.5

Three-point field goals: 1995-96, 2-for-6 (.333).
Personal fouls/disqualifications: 1995-96, 10/0.

McDYESS, ANTONIO — F/C — NUGGETS

PERSONAL: Born September 7, 1974, in Quitman, Miss. ... 6-9/220. ... Full name: Antonio Keithflen McDyess. ... Name pronounced MIK-dice.
HIGH SCHOOL: Quitman (Miss.).
COLLEGE: Alabama.
TRANSACTIONS/CAREER NOTES: Selected after sophomore season by Los Angeles Clippers in first round (second pick overall) of 1995 NBA Draft. ... Draft rights traded by Clippers with G Randy Woods to Denver Nuggets for F Rodney Rogers and draft rights to G Brent Barry (June 28, 1995).

COLLEGIATE RECORD

Season Team	G	Min.	FGM	FGA	Pct.	FTM	FTA	Pct.	Reb.	Ast.	Pts.	RPG	APG	PPG
												AVERAGES		
93-94—Alabama	26	618	132	234	.564	32	60	.533	210	11	296	8.1	0.4	11.4
94-95—Alabama	33	861	185	361	.512	88	132	.667	337	21	458	10.2	0.6	13.9
Totals	59	1479	317	595	.533	120	192	.625	547	32	754	9.3	0.5	12.8

Three-point field goals: 1994-95, 0-for-1.

HONORS: NBA All-Rookie first team (1996).

| Season Team | G | Min. | FGM | FGA | Pct. | FTM | FTA | Pct. | REBOUNDS | | | Ast. | St. | Blk. | TO | Pts. | AVERAGES | | |
									Off.	Def.	Tot.						RPG	APG	PPG
95-96—Denver	76	2280	427	881	.485	166	243	.683	229	343	572	75	54	114	154	1020	7.5	1.0	13.4

Three-point field goals: 1995-96, 0-for-4.
Personal fouls/disqualifications: 1995-96, 250/4.

McILVAINE, JIM   C   SUPERSONICS

PERSONAL: Born July 30, 1972, in Racine, Wis. ... 7-1/260. ... Full name: James Michael McIlvaine. ... Name pronounced MAC-il-vain.
HIGH SCHOOL: St. Catherine (Racine, Wis.).
COLLEGE: Marquette.
TRANSACTIONS/CAREER NOTES: Selected by Washington Bullets in second round (32nd pick overall) of 1994 NBA Draft. ... Signed as free agent by Seattle SuperSonics (July 22, 1996).

COLLEGIATE RECORD

| Season Team | G | Min. | FGM | FGA | Pct. | FTM | FTA | Pct. | Reb. | Ast. | Pts. | AVERAGES | | |
												RPG	APG	PPG
90-91—Marquette	28	540	84	145	.579	55	92	.598	132	14	223	4.7	0.5	8.0
91-92—Marquette	29	696	102	187	.545	95	126	.754	134	16	299	4.6	0.6	10.3
92-93—Marquette	28	532	111	192	.578	85	119	.714	134	21	307	4.8	0.8	11.0
93-94—Marquette	33	946	170	322	.528	109	164	.665	273	43	449	8.3	1.3	13.6
Totals	118	2714	467	846	.552	344	501	.687	673	94	1278	5.7	0.8	10.8

NBA REGULAR-SEASON RECORD

| Season Team | G | Min. | FGM | FGA | Pct. | FTM | FTA | Pct. | REBOUNDS | | | Ast. | St. | Blk. | TO | Pts. | AVERAGES | | |
									Off.	Def.	Tot.						RPG	APG	PPG
94-95—Washington	55	534	34	71	.479	28	41	.683	40	65	105	10	10	60	19	96	1.9	0.2	1.7
95-96—Washington	80	1195	62	145	.428	58	105	.552	66	164	230	11	21	166	36	182	2.9	0.1	2.3
Totals	135	1729	96	216	.444	86	146	.589	106	229	335	21	31	226	55	278	2.5	0.2	2.1

Personal fouls/disqualifications: 1994-95, 95/0. 1995-96, 171/0. Totals, 266/0.

McKEY, DERRICK   F   PACERS

PERSONAL: Born October 10, 1966, in Meridian, Miss. ... 6-10/225. ... Full name: Derrick Wayne McKey.
HIGH SCHOOL: Meridian (Miss.).
COLLEGE: Alabama.
TRANSACTIONS/CAREER NOTES: Selected after junior season by Seattle SuperSonics in first round (ninth pick overall) of 1987 NBA Draft. ... Traded by SuperSonics with F Gerald Paddio to Indiana Pacers for F Detlef Schrempf (November 1, 1993).

COLLEGIATE RECORD

NOTES: THE SPORTING NEWS All-America second team (1987).

| Season Team | G | Min. | FGM | FGA | Pct. | FTM | FTA | Pct. | Reb. | Ast. | Pts. | AVERAGES | | |
												RPG	APG	PPG
84-85—Alabama	33	728	74	155	.477	20	33	.606	134	44	168	4.1	1.3	5.1
85-86—Alabama	33	1117	178	280	.636	92	117	.786	262	29	448	7.9	0.9	13.6
86-87—Alabama	33	1199	247	425	.581	100	116	.862	247	59	615	7.5	1.8	18.6
Totals	99	3044	499	860	.580	212	266	.797	643	132	1231	6.5	1.3	12.4

Three-point field goals: 1986-87, 21-for-50 (.420).

NBA REGULAR-SEASON RECORD

HONORS: NBA All-Defensive second team (1995, 1996). ... NBA All-Rookie team (1988).

| Season Team | G | Min. | FGM | FGA | Pct. | FTM | FTA | Pct. | REBOUNDS | | | Ast. | St. | Blk. | TO | Pts. | AVERAGES | | |
									Off.	Def.	Tot.						RPG	APG	PPG
87-88—Seattle	82	1706	255	519	.491	173	224	.772	115	213	328	107	70	63	108	694	4.0	1.3	8.5
88-89—Seattle	82	2804	487	970	.502	301	375	.803	167	297	464	219	105	70	188	1305	5.7	2.7	15.9
89-90—Seattle	80	2748	468	949	.493	315	403	.782	170	319	489	187	87	81	192	1254	6.1	2.3	15.7
90-91—Seattle	73	2503	438	847	.517	235	278	.845	172	251	423	169	91	56	158	1115	5.8	2.3	15.3
91-92—Seattle	52	1757	285	604	.472	188	222	.847	95	173	268	120	61	47	114	777	5.2	2.3	14.9
92-93—Seattle	77	2439	387	780	.496	220	297	.741	121	206	327	197	105	58	152	1034	4.2	2.6	13.4
93-94—Indiana	76	2613	355	710	.500	192	254	.756	129	273	402	327	111	49	228	911	5.3	4.3	12.0
94-95—Indiana	81	2805	411	833	.493	221	297	.744	125	269	394	276	125	49	168	1075	4.9	3.4	13.3
95-96—Indiana	75	2440	346	712	.486	170	221	.769	123	238	361	262	83	44	143	879	4.8	3.5	11.7
Totals	678	21815	3432	6924	.496	2015	2571	.784	1217	2239	3456	1864	838	517	1451	9044	5.1	2.7	13.3

Three-point field goals: 1987-88, 11-for-30 (.367). 1988-89, 30-for-89 (.337). 1989-90, 3-for-23 (.130). 1990-91, 4-for-19 (.211). 1991-92, 19-for-50 (.380). 1992-93, 40-for-112 (.357). 1993-94, 9-for-31 (.290). 1994-95, 32-for-89 (.360). 1995-96, 17-for-68 (.250). Totals, 165-for-511 (.323).
Personal fouls/disqualifications: 1987-88, 237/3. 1988-89, 264/4. 1989-90, 247/2. 1990-91, 220/2. 1991-92, 142/2. 1992-93, 208/5. 1993-94, 248/1. 1994-95, 260/5. 1995-96, 246/4. Totals, 2072/28.

NBA PLAYOFF RECORD

| Season Team | G | Min. | FGM | FGA | Pct. | FTM | FTA | Pct. | REBOUNDS | | | Ast. | St. | Blk. | TO | Pts. | AVERAGES | | |
									Off.	Def.	Tot.						RPG	APG	PPG
87-88—Seattle	5	109	24	38	.632	10	17	.588	7	13	20	8	3	5	5	60	4.0	1.6	12.0
88-89—Seattle	8	286	44	89	.494	17	21	.810	21	31	52	18	6	15	23	106	6.5	2.3	13.3
90-91—Seattle	4	114	16	28	.571	6	11	.545	7	16	23	8	3	0	6	38	5.8	2.0	9.5
91-92—Seattle	9	315	52	99	.525	38	45	.844	17	27	44	24	7	12	22	147	4.9	2.7	16.3

M

Season Team	G	Min.	FGM	FGA	Pct.	FTM	FTA	Pct.	Off.	Def.	Tot.	Ast.	St.	Blk.	TO	Pts.	RPG	APG	PPG
									REBOUNDS								AVERAGES		
92-93—Seattle	19	647	83	158	.525	46	69	.667	51	47	98	71	12	17	36	214	5.2	3.7	11.3
93-94—Indiana...........	16	587	58	142	.408	31	47	.660	32	66	98	67	26	9	40	155	6.1	4.2	9.7
94-95—Indiana...........	17	592	76	174	.437	54	62	.871	29	52	81	64	17	11	36	217	4.8	3.8	12.8
95-96—Indiana...........	5	180	24	57	.421	11	13	.846	8	25	33	10	7	1	14	64	6.6	2.0	12.8
Totals	83	2830	377	785	.480	213	285	.747	172	277	449	270	81	70	182	1001	5.4	3.3	12.1

Three-point field goals: 1987-88, 2-for-6 (.333). 1988-89, 1-for-9 (.111). 1990-91, 0-for-1. 1991-92, 5-for-16 (.313). 1992-93, 2-for-5 (.400). 1993-94, 8-for-24 (.333). 1994-95, 11-for-35 (.314). 1995-96, 5-for-12 (.417). Totals, 34-for-108 (.315).

Personal fouls/disqualifications: 1987-88, 12/0. 1988-89, 33/1. 1990-91, 13/0. 1991-92, 37/1. 1992-93, 51/0. 1993-94, 59/1. 1994-95, 65/2. 1995-96, 20/0. Totals, 290/5.

McKIE, AARON   G   TRAIL BLAZERS

PERSONAL: Born October 2, 1972, in Philadelphia. ... 6-5/209. ... Full name: Aaron Fitzgerald McKie. ... Name pronounced mik-KEY.
HIGH SCHOOL: Simon Gratz (Philadelphia).
COLLEGE: Temple.
TRANSACTIONS/CAREER NOTES: Selected by Portland Trail Blazers in first round (17th pick overall) of 1994 NBA Draft.

COLLEGIATE RECORD

Season Team	G	Min.	FGM	FGA	Pct.	FTM	FTA	Pct.	Reb.	Ast.	Pts.	RPG	APG	PPG
												AVERAGES		
90-91—Temple...........................						Did not play—ineligible.								
91-92—Temple...........................	28	1011	130	300	.433	86	114	.754	167	94	388	6.0	3.4	13.9
92-93—Temple...........................	33	1272	240	555	.432	123	156	.788	195	109	680	5.9	3.3	20.6
93-94—Temple...........................	31	1214	193	481	.401	137	168	.815	224	98	582	7.2	3.2	18.8
Totals	92	3497	563	1336	.421	346	438	.790	586	301	1650	6.4	3.3	17.9

Three-point field goals: 1991-92, 42-for-131 (.321). 1992-93, 77-for-196 (.393). 1993-94, 59-for-159 (.371). Totals, 178-for-486 (.366).

NBA REGULAR-SEASON RECORD

Season Team	G	Min.	FGM	FGA	Pct.	FTM	FTA	Pct.	Off.	Def.	Tot.	Ast.	St.	Blk.	TO	Pts.	RPG	APG	PPG
									REBOUNDS								AVERAGES		
94-95—Portland.........	45	827	116	261	.444	50	73	.685	35	94	129	89	36	16	39	293	2.9	2.0	6.5
95-96—Portland.........	81	2259	337	722	.467	152	199	.764	86	218	304	205	92	21	135	864	3.8	2.5	10.7
Totals	126	3086	453	983	.461	202	272	.743	121	312	433	294	128	37	174	1157	3.4	2.3	9.2

Three-point field goals: 1994-95, 11-for-28 (.393). 1995-96, 38-for-117 (.325). Totals, 49-for-145 (.338).
Personal fouls/disqualifications: 1994-95, 97/1. 1995-96, 205/5. Totals, 302/6.

NBA PLAYOFF RECORD

Season Team	G	Min.	FGM	FGA	Pct.	FTM	FTA	Pct.	Off.	Def.	Tot.	Ast.	St.	Blk.	TO	Pts.	RPG	APG	PPG
									REBOUNDS								AVERAGES		
94-95—Portland.........	3	34	8	14	.571	0	0	...	0	2	2	1	3	0	0	17	0.7	0.3	5.7
95-96—Portland.........	5	134	11	30	.367	7	9	.778	4	14	18	9	6	2	9	31	3.6	1.8	6.2
Totals	8	168	19	44	.432	7	9	.778	4	16	20	10	9	2	9	48	2.5	1.3	6.0

Three-point field goals: 1994-95, 1-for-2 (.500). 1995-96, 2-for-8 (.250). Totals, 3-for-10 (.300).
Personal fouls/disqualifications: 1994-95, 4/0. 1995-96, 13/0. Totals, 17/0.

McMILLAN, NATE   G/F   SUPERSONICS

PERSONAL: Born August 3, 1964, in Raleigh, N.C. ... 6-5/200. ... Full name: Nathaniel McMillan.
HIGH SCHOOL: Enloe (Raleigh, N.C.).
JUNIOR COLLEGE: Chowan College (N.C.).
COLLEGE: North Carolina State.
TRANSACTIONS/CAREER NOTES: Selected by Seattle SuperSonics in second round (30th pick overall) of 1986 NBA Draft.
MISCELLANEOUS: Seattle SuperSonics all-time assists leader with 4,698 and all-time steals leader with 1,472 (1986-87 through 1995-96).

COLLEGIATE RECORD

Season Team	G	Min.	FGM	FGA	Pct.	FTM	FTA	Pct.	Reb.	Ast.	Pts.	RPG	APG	PPG
												AVERAGES		
82-83—Chowan College.............	27	...	101	174	.580	64	92	.696	134	191	266	5.0	7.1	9.9
83-84—Chowan College.............	35	...	180	331	.544	100	130	.769	342	411	460	9.8	11.7	13.1
84-85—N.C. State	33	973	94	207	.454	64	95	.674	189	169	252	5.7	5.1	7.6
85-86—N.C. State	34	1208	127	262	.485	66	90	.733	155	233	320	4.6	6.9	9.4
Junior college totals	62	...	281	505	.556	164	222	.739	476	602	726	7.7	9.7	11.7
4-year-college totals	67	2181	221	469	.471	130	185	.703	344	402	572	5.1	6.0	8.5

NBA REGULAR-SEASON RECORD

RECORDS: Shares single-game record for most assists by a rookie—25 (February 23, 1987, vs. Los Angeles Clippers).
HONORS: NBA All-Defensive second team (1994, 1995).
NOTES: Led NBA with 2.96 steals per game (1994).

Season Team	G	Min.	FGM	FGA	Pct.	FTM	FTA	Pct.	Off.	Def.	Tot.	Ast.	St.	Blk.	TO	Pts.	RPG	APG	PPG
									REBOUNDS								AVERAGES		
86-87—Seattle	71	1972	143	301	.475	87	141	.617	101	230	331	583	125	45	155	373	4.7	8.2	5.3
87-88—Seattle	82	2453	235	496	.474	145	205	.707	117	221	338	702	169	47	189	624	4.1	8.6	7.6
88-89—Seattle	75	2341	199	485	.410	119	189	.630	143	245	388	696	156	42	171	532	5.2	9.3	7.1
89-90—Seattle	82	2338	207	438	.473	98	153	.641	127	276	403	598	140	37	187	523	4.9	7.3	6.4
90-91—Seattle	78	1434	132	305	.433	57	93	.613	71	180	251	371	104	20	122	338	3.2	4.8	4.3

M

Season Team	G	Min.	FGM	FGA	Pct.	FTM	FTA	Pct.	Off.	Def.	Tot.	Ast.	St.	Blk.	TO	Pts.	RPG	APG	PPG
91-92—Seattle	72	1652	177	405	.437	54	84	.643	92	160	252	359	129	29	112	435	3.5	5.0	6.0
92-93—Seattle	73	1977	213	459	.464	95	134	.709	84	222	306	384	173	33	139	546	4.2	5.3	7.5
93-94—Seattle	73	1887	177	396	.447	31	55	.564	50	233	283	387	*216	22	126	437	3.9	5.3	6.0
94-95—Seattle	80	2070	166	397	.418	34	58	.586	65	237	302	421	165	53	126	419	3.8	5.3	5.2
95-96—Seattle	55	1261	100	238	.420	29	41	.707	41	169	210	197	95	18	75	275	3.8	3.6	5.0
Totals	741	19385	1749	3920	.446	749	1153	.650	891	2173	3064	4698	1472	346	1442	4502	4.1	6.3	6.1

Three-point field goals: 1986-87, 0-for-7. 1987-88, 9-for-24 (.375). 1988-89, 15-for-70 (.214). 1989-90, 11-for-31 (.355). 1990-91, 17-for-48 (.354). 1991-92, 27-for-98 (.276). 1992-93, 25-for-65 (.385). 1993-94, 52-for-133 (.391). 1994-95, 53-for-155 (.342). 1995-96, 46-for-121 (.380). Totals, 255-for-752 (.339).

Personal fouls/disqualifications: 1986-87, 238/4. 1987-88, 238/1. 1988-89, 236/3. 1989-90, 289/7. 1990-91, 211/6. 1991-92, 218/4. 1992-93, 240/6. 1993-94, 201/1. 1994-95, 275/8. 1995-96, 143/3. Totals, 2289/43.

NBA PLAYOFF RECORD

NOTES: Shares single-game playoff record for most three-point field goals, none missed—5 (May 6, 1996, vs. Houston).

Season Team	G	Min.	FGM	FGA	Pct.	FTM	FTA	Pct.	Off.	Def.	Tot.	Ast.	St.	Blk.	TO	Pts.	RPG	APG	PPG
86-87—Seattle	14	356	27	62	.435	17	24	.708	13	41	54	112	14	10	26	71	3.9	8.0	5.1
87-88—Seattle	5	127	12	35	.343	9	14	.643	6	15	21	33	2	3	8	33	4.2	6.6	6.6
88-89—Seattle	8	200	19	40	.475	16	25	.640	9	16	25	63	10	5	19	54	3.1	7.9	6.8
90-91—Seattle	5	95	6	23	.261	2	4	.500	6	12	18	22	6	1	3	14	3.6	4.4	2.8
91-92—Seattle	9	246	35	83	.422	10	14	.714	14	19	33	63	16	3	22	86	3.7	7.0	9.6
92-93—Seattle	19	415	35	103	.340	16	30	.533	21	46	67	103	40	11	25	91	3.5	5.4	4.8
93-94—Seattle	5	109	8	25	.320	1	4	.250	6	10	16	10	6	1	5	21	3.2	2.0	4.2
94-95—Seattle	4	113	8	23	.348	2	2	1.000	7	11	18	29	10	2	7	19	4.5	7.3	4.8
95-96—Seattle	19	385	28	69	.406	9	14	.643	13	57	70	52	23	5	20	84	3.7	2.7	4.4
Totals	88	2046	178	463	.384	82	131	.626	95	227	322	487	127	41	135	473	3.7	5.5	5.4

Three-point field goals: 1987-88, 0-for-1. 1988-89, 0-for-2. 1990-91, 0-for-2. 1991-92, 6-for-26 (.231). 1992-93, 5-for-24 (.208). 1993-94, 4-for-11 (.364). 1994-95, 1-for-8 (.125). 1995-96, 19-for-40 (.475). Totals, 35-for-114 (.307).

Personal fouls/disqualifications: 1986-87, 42/1. 1987-88, 11/0. 1988-89, 21/0. 1990-91, 15/0. 1991-92, 35/1. 1992-93, 54/2. 1993-94, 18/1. 1994-95, 13/0. 1995-96, 34/0. Totals, 243/5.

MEYER, LOREN   C   MAVERICKS

PERSONAL: Born December 30, 1972, in Emmetsburg, Iowa. ... 6-10/260. ... Full name: Loren Henry Meyer.
HIGH SCHOOL: Ruthven (Iowa)-Ayrshire.
COLLEGE: Iowa State.
TRANSACTIONS/CAREER NOTES: Selected by Dallas Mavericks in first round (24th pick overall) of 1995 NBA Draft.

COLLEGIATE RECORD

Season Team	G	Min.	FGM	FGA	Pct.	FTM	FTA	Pct.	Reb.	Ast.	Pts.	RPG	APG	PPG
91-92—Iowa State	34	406	72	140	.514	28	47	.596	106	15	175	3.1	0.4	5.1
92-93—Iowa State	31	698	116	214	.542	71	100	.710	153	40	303	4.9	1.3	9.8
93-94—Iowa State	12	369	97	159	.610	73	99	.737	114	20	267	9.5	1.7	22.3
94-95—Iowa State	34	1009	198	355	.558	139	190	.732	306	50	535	9.0	1.5	15.7
Totals	111	2482	483	868	.556	311	436	.713	679	125	1280	6.1	1.1	11.5

Three-point field goals: 1991-92, 3-for-10 (.300). 1992-93, 0-for-3. 1994-95, 0-for-1. Totals, 3-for-14 (.214).

NBA REGULAR-SEASON RECORD

Season Team	G	Min.	FGM	FGA	Pct.	FTM	FTA	Pct.	Off.	Def.	Tot.	Ast.	St.	Blk.	TO	Pts.	RPG	APG	PPG
95-96—Dallas	72	1266	145	330	.439	70	102	.686	114	205	319	57	20	32	67	363	4.4	0.8	5.0

Three-point field goals: 1995-96, 3-for-11 (.273).
Personal fouls/disqualifications: 1995-96, 224/6.

MILLER, ANTHONY   F

PERSONAL: Born October 22, 1971, in Benton Harbor, Mich. ... 6-9/255.
HIGH SCHOOL: Benton Harbor (Mich.).
COLLEGE: Michigan State.
TRANSACTIONS/CAREER NOTES: Selected by Golden State Warriors in second round (39th pick overall) of 1994 NBA Draft. ... Draft rights traded by Warriors to Los Angeles Lakers for 1995 second-round draft choice (July 1, 1994). ... Rights renounced by Lakers (July 17, 1996).

COLLEGIATE RECORD

Season Team	G	Min.	FGM	FGA	Pct.	FTM	FTA	Pct.	Reb.	Ast.	Pts.	RPG	APG	PPG
90-91—Michigan State						Did not play—ineligible.								
91-92—Michigan State	30	555	83	154	.539	50	80	.625	156	24	216	5.2	0.8	7.2
92-93—Michigan State	27	474	76	124	.613	26	48	.542	139	12	179	5.1	0.4	6.6
93-94—Michigan State	32	910	162	249	.651	78	136	.574	287	30	402	9.0	0.9	12.6
Totals	89	1939	321	527	.609	154	264	.583	582	66	797	6.5	0.7	9.0

Three-point field goals: 1992-93, 1-for-1. 1993-94, 0-for-1. Totals, 1-for-2 (.500).

NBA REGULAR-SEASON RECORD

Season Team	G	Min.	FGM	FGA	Pct.	FTM	FTA	Pct.	Off.	Def.	Tot.	Ast.	St.	Blk.	TO	Pts.	RPG	APG	PPG
94-95—L.A. Lakers	46	527	70	132	.530	47	76	.618	67	85	152	35	20	7	38	189	3.3	0.8	4.1
95-96—L.A. Lakers	27	123	15	35	.429	6	10	.600	11	14	25	4	4	1	8	36	0.9	0.1	1.3
Totals	73	650	85	167	.509	53	86	.616	78	99	177	39	24	8	46	225	2.4	0.5	3.1

Three-point field goals: 1994-95, 2-for-5 (.400). 1995-96, 0-for-2. Totals, 2-for-7 (.286).
Personal fouls/disqualifications: 1994-95, 77/2. 1995-96, 19/0. Totals, 243/5.

Season Team	G	Min.	FGM	FGA	Pct.	FTM	FTA	Pct.	REBOUNDS Off.	Def.	Tot.	Ast.	St.	Blk.	TO	Pts.	AVERAGES RPG	APG	PPG
94-95—L.A. Lakers	4	15	0	2	.000	0	0	...	2	4	6	1	1	0	1	0	1.5	0.3	0.0

Personal fouls/disqualifications: 1994-95, 2/0.

MILLER, OLIVER   C

PERSONAL: Born April 6, 1970, in Fort Worth, Texas. ... 6-9/280. ... Full name: Oliver J. Miller.
HIGH SCHOOL: Southwest (Fort Worth, Texas).
COLLEGE: Arkansas.
TRANSACTIONS/CAREER NOTES: Selected by Phoenix Suns in first round (22nd pick overall) of 1992 NBA Draft. ... Signed by Detroit Pistons to offer sheet (September 6, 1994); Suns declined to match offer (September 20, 1994). ... Selected by Toronto Raptors from Pistons in NBA expansion draft (June 24, 1995). ... Rights renounced by Raptors (July 23, 1996).
MISCELLANEOUS: Toronto Raptors all-time leading rebounder with 562 and all-time blocked shots leader with 143 (1995-96).

COLLEGIATE RECORD

NOTES: Led NCAA Division I with .704 field-goal percentage (1991).

Season Team	G	Min.	FGM	FGA	Pct.	FTM	FTA	Pct.	Reb.	Ast.	Pts.	AVERAGES RPG	APG	PPG
88-89—Arkansas	30	599	88	161	.547	50	78	.641	112	41	230	3.7	1.4	7.7
89-90—Arkansas	35	757	152	238	.639	86	132	.652	219	49	390	6.3	1.4	11.1
90-91—Arkansas	38	931	254	361	.704	87	135	.644	294	103	596	7.7	2.7	15.7
91-92—Arkansas	34	956	186	309	.602	86	133	.647	261	103	458	7.7	3.0	13.5
Totals	137	3243	680	1069	.636	309	478	.646	886	296	1674	6.5	2.2	12.2

Three-point field goals: 1988-89, 4-for-12 (.333). 1989-90, 0-for-4. 1990-91, 1-for-3 (.333). 1991-92, 0-for-11. Totals, 5-for-30 (.167).

NBA REGULAR-SEASON RECORD

Season Team	G	Min.	FGM	FGA	Pct.	FTM	FTA	Pct.	REBOUNDS Off.	Def.	Tot.	Ast.	St.	Blk.	TO	Pts.	AVERAGES RPG	APG	PPG
92-93—Phoenix	56	1069	121	255	.475	71	100	.710	70	205	275	118	38	100	108	313	4.9	2.1	5.6
93-94—Phoenix	69	1786	277	455	.609	80	137	.584	140	336	476	244	83	156	164	636	6.9	3.5	9.2
94-95—Detroit	64	1558	232	418	.555	78	124	.629	162	313	475	93	60	116	115	545	7.4	1.5	8.5
95-96—Toronto	76	2516	418	795	.526	146	221	.661	177	385	562	219	108	143	202	982	7.4	2.9	12.9
Totals	265	6929	1048	1923	.545	375	582	.644	549	1239	1788	674	289	515	589	2476	6.7	2.5	9.3

Three-point field goals: 1992-93, 0-for-3. 1993-94, 2-for-9 (.222). 1994-95, 3-for-13 (.231). 1995-96, 0-for-11. Totals, 5-for-36 (.139).
Personal fouls/disqualifications: 1992-93, 145/0. 1993-94, 230/1. 1994-95, 217/1. 1995-96, 277/4. Totals, 869/6.

NBA PLAYOFF RECORD

Season Team	G	Min.	FGM	FGA	Pct.	FTM	FTA	Pct.	REBOUNDS Off.	Def.	Tot.	Ast.	St.	Blk.	TO	Pts.	AVERAGES RPG	APG	PPG
92-93—Phoenix	24	513	71	121	.587	31	55	.564	33	91	124	51	21	59	42	173	5.2	2.1	7.2
93-94—Phoenix	10	146	16	27	.593	3	7	.429	14	30	44	13	6	12	13	35	4.4	1.3	3.5
Totals	34	659	87	148	.588	34	62	.548	47	121	168	64	27	71	55	208	4.9	1.9	6.1

Three-point field goals: 1992-93, 0-for-2.
Personal fouls/disqualifications: 1992-93, 76/0. 1993-94, 22/0. Totals, 98/0.

MILLER, REGGIE   G   PACERS

PERSONAL: Born August 24, 1965, in Riverside, Calif. ... 6-7/185. ... Full name: Reginald Wayne Miller. ... Brother of Darrell Miller, outfielder/catcher with California Angels (1984-88); and brother of Cheryl Miller, member of gold-medal-winning U.S. Olympic women's basketball team (1984).
HIGH SCHOOL: Riverside (Calif.) Polytechnic.
COLLEGE: UCLA.
TRANSACTIONS/CAREER NOTES: Selected by Indiana Pacers in first round (11th pick overall) of 1987 NBA Draft.
MISCELLANEOUS: Member of gold-medal-winning U.S. Olympic team (1996). ... Indiana Pacers all-time leading scorer with 14,073 points (1987-88 through 1995-96).

COLLEGIATE RECORD

Season Team	G	Min.	FGM	FGA	Pct.	FTM	FTA	Pct.	Reb.	Ast.	Pts.	AVERAGES RPG	APG	PPG
83-84—UCLA	28	384	56	110	.509	18	28	.643	42	21	130	1.5	0.8	4.6
84-85—UCLA	33	1174	192	347	.553	119	148	.804	141	86	503	4.3	2.6	15.2
85-86—UCLA	29	1112	274	493	.556	202	229	.882	153	69	750	5.3	2.4	25.9
86-87—UCLA	32	1166	247	455	.543	149	179	.832	173	71	712	5.4	2.2	22.3
Totals	122	3836	769	1405	.547	488	584	.836	509	247	2095	4.2	2.0	17.2

Three-point field goals: 1986-87, 69-for-157 (.439).

NBA REGULAR-SEASON RECORD

HONORS: All-NBA third team (1995, 1996).

Season Team	G	Min.	FGM	FGA	Pct.	FTM	FTA	Pct.	REBOUNDS Off.	Def.	Tot.	Ast.	St.	Blk.	TO	Pts.	AVERAGES RPG	APG	PPG
87-88—Indiana...........	82	1840	306	627	.488	149	186	.801	95	95	190	132	53	19	101	822	2.3	1.6	10.0
88-89—Indiana...........	74	2536	398	831	.479	287	340	.844	73	219	292	227	93	29	143	1181	3.9	3.1	16.0
89-90—Indiana...........	82	3192	661	1287	.514	544	627	.868	95	200	295	311	110	18	222	2016	3.6	3.8	24.6
90-91—Indiana...........	82	2972	596	1164	.512	551	600	*.918	81	200	281	331	109	13	163	1855	3.4	4.0	22.6
91-92—Indiana...........	82	3120	562	1121	.501	442	515	.858	82	236	318	314	105	26	157	1695	3.9	3.8	20.7

M

Season Team	G	Min.	FGM	FGA	Pct.	FTM	FTA	Pct.	Off.	Def.	Tot.	Ast.	St.	Blk.	TO	Pts.	RPG	APG	PPG
92-93—Indiana...........	82	2954	571	1193	.479	427	485	.880	67	191	258	262	120	26	145	1736	3.1	3.2	21.2
93-94—Indiana...........	79	2638	524	1042	.503	403	444	.908	30	182	212	248	119	24	175	1574	2.7	3.1	19.9
94-95—Indiana...........	81	2665	505	1092	.462	383	427	.897	30	180	210	242	98	16	151	1588	2.6	3.0	19.6
95-96—Indiana...........	76	2621	504	1066	.473	430	498	.863	38	176	214	253	77	13	189	1606	2.8	3.3	21.1
Totals	720	24538	4627	9423	.491	3616	4122	.877	591	1679	2270	2320	884	184	1446	14073	3.2	3.2	19.5

Three-point field goals: 1987-88, 61-for-172 (.355). 1988-89, 98-for-244 (.402). 1989-90, 150-for-362 (.414). 1990-91, 112-for-322 (.348). 1991-92, 129-for-341 (.378). 1992-93, 167-for-419 (.399). 1993-94, 123-for-292 (.421). 1994-95, 195-for-470 (.415). 1995-96, 168-for-410 (.410). Totals, 1203-for-3032 (.397).

Personal fouls/disqualifications: 1987-88, 157/0. 1988-89, 170/2. 1989-90, 175/1. 1990-91, 165/1. 1991-92, 201/0. 1992-93, 182/0. 1993-94, 193/2. 1994-95, 157/0. 1995-96, 175/0. Totals, 1584/7.

NBA PLAYOFF RECORD

NOTES: Holds single-game playoff record for most three-point field goals made in one quarter—5 (June 1, 1994, at New York). ... Shares single-game playoff record for most three-point field goals made in one half—6 (June 1, 1994, at New York and April 29, 1995, vs. Atlanta).

Season Team	G	Min.	FGM	FGA	Pct.	FTM	FTA	Pct.	Off.	Def.	Tot.	Ast.	St.	Blk.	TO	Pts.	RPG	APG	PPG
89-90—Indiana...........	3	125	20	35	.571	19	21	.905	1	11	12	6	3	0	3	62	4.0	2.0	20.7
90-91—Indiana...........	5	193	34	70	.486	32	37	.865	5	11	16	14	8	2	12	108	3.2	2.8	21.6
91-92—Indiana...........	3	130	25	43	.581	24	30	.800	4	3	7	14	4	0	4	81	2.3	4.7	27.0
92-93—Indiana...........	4	175	40	75	.533	36	38	.947	4	8	12	11	3	0	10	126	3.0	2.8	31.5
93-94—Indiana...........	16	576	121	270	.448	94	112	.839	11	37	48	46	21	4	32	371	3.0	2.9	23.2
94-95—Indiana...........	17	641	138	290	.476	104	121	.860	9	52	61	36	15	4	39	434	3.6	2.1	25.5
95-96—Indiana...........	1	31	7	17	.412	13	15	.867	1	0	1	1	0	0	0	29	1.0	1.0	29.0
Totals	49	1871	385	800	.481	322	374	.861	35	122	157	128	55	10	100	1211	3.2	2.6	24.7

Three-point field goals: 1989-90, 3-for-7 (.429). 1990-91, 8-for-19 (.421). 1991-92, 7-for-11 (.636). 1992-93, 10-for-19 (.526). 1993-94, 35-for-83 (.422). 1994-95, 54-for-128 (.422). 1995-96, 2-for-6 (.333). Totals, 119-for-273 (.436).

Personal fouls/disqualifications: 1989-90, 6/0. 1990-91, 14/0. 1991-92, 12/1. 1992-93, 11/0. 1993-94, 34/0. 1994-95, 35/0. 1995-96, 1/0. Totals, 113/1.

NBA ALL-STAR GAME RECORD

Season Team	Min.	FGM	FGA	Pct.	FTM	FTA	Pct.	Off.	Def.	Tot.	Ast.	PF	Dq.	St.	Blk.	TO	Pts.
1990 —Indiana.............	14	2	3	.667	0	0	...	0	1	1	3	1	0	1	0	0	4
1995 —Indiana.............	23	3	9	.333	0	0	...	0	0	0	2	0	0	1	1	1	9
1996 —Indiana.............	18	4	8	.500	0	0	...	0	0	2	2	2	0	1	0	1	8
Totals........................	55	9	20	.450	0	0	...	0	1	3	7	3	0	3	1	2	21

Three-point field goals: 1990, 0-for-1. 1995, 3-for-6 (.500). 1996, 0-for-4. Totals, 3-for-11 (.273).

M

MILLS, CHRIS   F   CAVALIERS

PERSONAL: Born January 25, 1970, in Los Angeles. ... 6-6/216. ... Full name: Christopher Lemonte Mills.
HIGH SCHOOL: Fairfax (Los Angeles).
COLLEGE: Kentucky, then Arizona.
TRANSACTIONS/CAREER NOTES: Selected by Cleveland Cavaliers in first round (22nd pick overall) of 1993 NBA Draft.

COLLEGIATE RECORD

Season Team	G	Min.	FGM	FGA	Pct.	FTM	FTA	Pct.	Reb.	Ast.	Pts.	RPG	APG	PPG
88-89—Kentucky	32	1124	180	372	.484	82	115	.713	277	92	459	8.7	2.9	14.3
89-90—Arizona						Did not play—transfer student.								
90-91—Arizona	35	1025	206	397	.519	91	122	.746	216	66	545	6.2	1.9	15.6
91-92—Arizona	31	984	198	391	.506	80	103	.777	244	73	504	7.9	2.4	16.3
92-93—Arizona	28	870	211	406	.520	92	110	.836	222	53	570	7.9	1.9	20.4
Totals	126	4003	795	1566	.508	345	450	.767	959	284	2078	7.6	2.3	16.5

Three-point field goals: 1988-89, 17-for-54 (.315). 1990-91, 42-for-122 (.344). 1991-92, 28-for-89 (.315). 1992-93, 56-for-116 (.483). Totals, 143-for-381 (.375).

NBA REGULAR-SEASON RECORD

Season Team	G	Min.	FGM	FGA	Pct.	FTM	FTA	Pct.	Off.	Def.	Tot.	Ast.	St.	Blk.	TO	Pts.	RPG	APG	PPG
93-94—Cleveland	79	2022	284	677	.420	137	176	.778	134	267	401	128	54	50	89	743	5.1	1.6	9.4
94-95—Cleveland	80	2814	359	855	.420	174	213	.817	99	267	366	154	59	35	120	986	4.6	1.9	12.3
95-96—Cleveland	80	3060	454	971	.468	218	263	.829	112	331	443	188	73	52	121	1205	5.5	2.4	15.1
Totals	239	7896	1097	2503	.438	529	652	.811	345	865	1210	470	186	137	330	2934	5.1	2.0	12.3

Three-point field goals: 1993-94, 38-for-122 (.311). 1994-95, 94-for-240 (.392). 1995-96, 79-for-210 (.376). Totals, 211-for-572 (.369).

Personal fouls/disqualifications: 1993-94, 232/3. 1994-95, 242/2. 1995-96, 241/1. Totals, 715/6.

NBA PLAYOFF RECORD

Season Team	G	Min.	FGM	FGA	Pct.	FTM	FTA	Pct.	Off.	Def.	Tot.	Ast.	St.	Blk.	TO	Pts.	RPG	APG	PPG
93-94—Cleveland	3	112	19	38	.500	9	11	.818	10	13	23	8	7	1	5	51	7.7	2.7	17.0
94-95—Cleveland	4	139	20	37	.541	5	5	1.000	2	14	16	11	3	2	6	53	4.0	2.8	13.3
95-96—Cleveland	3	105	11	33	.333	1	1	1.000	5	11	16	5	2	2	3	23	5.3	1.7	7.7
Totals	10	356	50	108	.463	15	17	.882	17	38	55	24	12	5	14	127	5.5	2.4	12.7

Three-point field goals: 1993-94, 4-for-5 (.800). 1994-95, 8-for-14 (.571). 1995-96, 0-for-5. Totals, 12-for-24 (.500).

Personal fouls/disqualifications: 1993-94, 9/0. 1994-95, 18/1. 1995-96, 10/0. Totals, 37/1.

MILLS, TERRY   F   PISTONS

PERSONAL: Born December 21, 1967, in Romulus, Mich. ... 6-10/250. ... Full name: Terry Richard Mills. ... Nephew of John Long, guard with Detroit Pistons, Indiana Pacers and Atlanta Hawks (1978-79 through 1990-91); and cousin of Grant Long, forward with Detroit Pistons.
HIGH SCHOOL: Romulus (Mich.).
COLLEGE: Michigan.
TRANSACTIONS/CAREER NOTES: Selected by Milwaukee Bucks in first round (16th pick overall) of 1990 NBA Draft. ... Traded by Bucks to Denver Nuggets for C Danny Schayes (August 1, 1990). ... Traded by Nuggets to New Jersey Nets in three-way deal in which Nets sent F Greg Anderson to Nuggets, Nuggets sent G Walter Davis to Portland Trail Blazers and Trail Blazers sent G Drazen Petrovic to Nets (January 23, 1991); Nuggets also received 1992 first-round draft choice from Nets and 1993 second-round draft choice from Trail Blazers and Trail Blazers also received 1992 second-round draft choice from Nuggets. ... Signed as free agent by Detroit Pistons (October 1, 1992).

COLLEGIATE RECORD

NOTES: Member of NCAA Division I championship team (1989).

Season Team	G	Min.	FGM	FGA	Pct.	FTM	FTA	Pct.	Reb.	Ast.	Pts.	RPG	APG	PPG
86-87—Michigan							Did not play—ineligible.							
87-88—Michigan	34	884	181	341	.531	51	70	.729	216	56	413	6.4	1.6	12.1
88-89—Michigan	37	999	180	319	.564	70	91	.769	218	104	430	5.9	2.8	11.6
89-90—Michigan	31	961	237	405	.585	88	116	.759	247	68	562	8.0	2.2	18.1
Totals	102	2844	598	1065	.562	209	277	.755	681	228	1405	6.7	2.2	13.8

Three-point field goals: 1987-88, 0-for-2. 1988-89, 0-for-2. Totals, 0-for-4.

NBA REGULAR-SEASON RECORD

Season Team	G	Min.	FGM	FGA	Pct.	FTM	FTA	Pct.	REBOUNDS Off.	Def.	Tot.	Ast.	St.	Blk.	TO	Pts.	AVERAGES RPG	APG	PPG
90-91—Denver-N.J.	55	819	134	288	.465	47	66	.712	82	147	229	33	35	29	43	315	4.2	0.6	5.7
91-92—New Jersey	82	1714	310	670	.463	114	152	.750	187	266	453	84	48	41	82	742	5.5	1.0	9.0
92-93—Detroit	81	2183	494	1072	.461	201	254	.791	176	296	472	111	44	50	142	1199	5.8	1.4	14.8
93-94—Detroit	80	2773	588	1151	.511	181	227	.797	193	479	672	177	64	62	153	1381	8.4	2.2	17.3
94-95—Detroit	72	2514	417	933	.447	175	219	.799	124	434	558	160	68	33	144	1118	7.8	2.2	15.5
95-96—Detroit	82	1656	283	675	.419	121	157	.771	108	244	352	98	42	20	98	769	4.3	1.2	9.4
Totals	452	11659	2226	4789	.465	839	1075	.780	870	1866	2736	663	301	235	662	5524	6.1	1.5	12.2

Three-point field goals: 1990-91, 0-for-4. 1991-92, 8-for-23 (.348). 1992-93, 10-for-36 (.278). 1993-94, 24-for-73 (.329). 1994-95, 109-for-285 (.382). 1995-96, 82-for-207 (.396). Totals, 233-for-628 (.371).
Personal fouls/disqualifications: 1990-91, 100/0. 1991-92, 200/3. 1992-93, 282/6. 1993-94, 309/6. 1994-95, 253/5. 1995-96, 197/0. Totals, 1341/20.

NBA PLAYOFF RECORD

Season Team	G	Min.	FGM	FGA	Pct.	FTM	FTA	Pct.	REBOUNDS Off.	Def.	Tot.	Ast.	St.	Blk.	TO	Pts.	AVERAGES RPG	APG	PPG
91-92—New Jersey	4	77	10	27	.370	7	11	.636	9	15	24	8	1	2	7	27	6.0	2.0	6.8
95-96—Detroit	3	48	5	20	.250	5	6	.833	3	2	5	4	1	0	1	16	1.7	1.3	5.3
Totals	7	125	15	47	.319	12	17	.706	12	17	29	12	2	2	8	43	4.1	1.7	6.1

Three-point field goals: 1991-92, 0-for-1. 1995-96, 1-for-8 (.125). Totals, 1-for-9 (.111).
Personal fouls/disqualifications: 1991-92, 18/0. 1995-96, 6/0. Totals, 24/0.

MINER, HAROLD   G

PERSONAL: Born May 5, 1971, in Inglewood, Calif. ... 6-5/214. ... Full name: Harold David Miner.
HIGH SCHOOL: Inglewood (Calif.).
COLLEGE: Southern California.
TRANSACTIONS/CAREER NOTES: Selected after junior season by Miami Heat in first round (12th pick overall) of 1992 NBA Draft. ... Traded by Heat with 1995 second-round draft choice to Cleveland Cavaliers for 1995 second-round draft choice and future considerations (June 14, 1995). ... Traded by Cavaliers with 1996 second-round draft choice and cash to Toronto Raptors for C Victor Alexander (October 18, 1995); trade voided when Alexander failed physical (October 21, 1995). ... Rights renounced by Cavaliers (August 8, 1996).

COLLEGIATE RECORD

NOTES: THE SPORTING NEWS All-America second team (1992).

Season Team	G	Min.	FGM	FGA	Pct.	FTM	FTA	Pct.	Reb.	Ast.	Pts.	RPG	APG	PPG
89-90—Southern Cal	28	978	206	436	.472	106	126	.841	101	59	578	3.6	2.1	20.6
90-91—Southern Cal	29	1049	235	519	.453	152	190	.800	159	57	681	5.5	2.0	23.5
91-92—Southern Cal	30	1042	250	571	.438	232	286	.811	211	39	789	7.0	1.3	26.3
Totals	87	3069	691	1526	.453	490	602	.814	471	155	2048	5.4	1.8	23.5

Three-point field goals: 1989-90, 60-for-142 (.423). 1990-91, 59-for-175 (.337). 1991-92, 57-for-162 (.352). Totals, 176-for-479 (.367).

NBA REGULAR-SEASON RECORD

HONORS: Slam-Dunk Championship winner (1993, 1995).

Season Team	G	Min.	FGM	FGA	Pct.	FTM	FTA	Pct.	REBOUNDS Off.	Def.	Tot.	Ast.	St.	Blk.	TO	Pts.	AVERAGES RPG	APG	PPG
92-93—Miami	73	1383	292	615	.475	163	214	.762	74	73	147	73	34	8	92	750	2.0	1.0	10.3
93-94—Miami	63	1358	254	532	.477	149	180	.828	75	81	156	95	31	13	95	661	2.5	1.5	10.5
94-95—Miami	45	871	123	305	.403	69	95	.726	38	79	117	69	15	6	77	329	2.6	1.5	7.3
95-96—Cleveland	19	136	23	52	.442	13	13	1.000	4	8	12	8	0	0	14	61	0.6	0.4	3.2
Totals	200	3748	692	1504	.460	394	502	.785	191	241	432	245	80	27	278	1801	2.2	1.2	9.0

Three-point field goals: 1992-93, 3-for-9 (.333). 1993-94, 4-for-6 (.667). 1994-95, 14-for-49 (.286). 1995-96, 2-for-10 (.200). Totals, 23-for-74 (.311).
Personal fouls/disqualifications: 1992-93, 130/2. 1993-94, 132/0. 1994-95, 85/0. 1995-96, 23/1. Totals, 370/3.

NBA PLAYOFF RECORD

								REBOUNDS							AVERAGES		
Season Team	G	Min.	FGM	FGA	Pct.	FTM	FTA	Pct.	Off.	Def.	Tot.	Ast.	St.	Blk.	TO	Pts.	RPG	APG	PPG
93-94—Miami	4	57	12	26	.462	8	11	.727	3	5	8	2	1	0	2	32	2.0	0.5	8.0

Personal fouls/disqualifications: 1993-94, 4/0.

MINOR, GREG   G/F   CELTICS

PERSONAL: Born September 18, 1971, in Sandersville, Ga. ... 6-6/230. ... Full name: Greg Magado Minor.
HIGH SCHOOL: Washington County (Sandersville, Ga.).
COLLEGE: Louisville.
TRANSACTIONS/CAREER NOTES: Selected by Los Angeles Clippers in first round (25th pick overall) of 1994 NBA Draft. ... Draft rights traded by Clippers with G Mark Jackson to Indiana Pacers for G Pooh Richardson, F Malik Sealy and draft rights to F Eric Piatkowski (June 30, 1994). ... Rights renounced by Pacers (October 14, 1994). ... Signed as free agent by Boston Celtics (October 19, 1994).

COLLEGIATE RECORD

												AVERAGES		
Season Team	G	Min.	FGM	FGA	Pct.	FTM	FTA	Pct.	Reb.	Ast.	Pts.	RPG	APG	PPG
90-91—Louisville					Did not play—ineligible.									
91-92—Louisville	30	831	113	239	.473	55	75	.733	154	55	291	5.1	1.8	9.7
92-93—Louisville	31	1036	156	296	.527	84	112	.750	170	87	438	5.5	2.8	14.1
93-94—Louisville	34	1176	179	349	.513	70	96	.729	209	86	470	6.1	2.5	13.8
Totals	95	3043	448	884	.507	209	283	.739	533	228	1199	5.6	2.4	12.6

Three-point field goals: 1991-92, 10-for-43 (.233). 1992-93, 42-for-97 (.433). 1993-94, 42-for-119 (.353). Totals, 94-for-259 (.363).

NBA REGULAR-SEASON RECORD

								REBOUNDS							AVERAGES		
Season Team	G	Min.	FGM	FGA	Pct.	FTM	FTA	Pct.	Off.	Def.	Tot.	Ast.	St.	Blk.	TO	Pts.	RPG	APG	PPG
94-95—Boston	63	945	155	301	.515	65	78	.833	49	88	137	66	32	16	44	377	2.2	1.0	6.0
95-96—Boston	78	1761	320	640	.500	99	130	.762	93	164	257	146	36	11	78	746	3.3	1.9	9.6
Totals	141	2706	475	941	.505	164	208	.788	142	252	394	212	68	27	122	1123	2.8	1.5	8.0

Three-point field goals: 1994-95, 2-for-12 (.167). 1995-96, 7-for-27 (.259). Totals, 9-for-39 (.231).
Personal fouls/disqualifications: 1994-95, 89/0. 1995-96, 161/0. Totals, 250/0.

NBA PLAYOFF RECORD

								REBOUNDS							AVERAGES		
Season Team	G	Min.	FGM	FGA	Pct.	FTM	FTA	Pct.	Off.	Def.	Tot.	Ast.	St.	Blk.	TO	Pts.	RPG	APG	PPG
94-95—Boston	4	37	5	13	.385	1	1	1.000	1	0	1	2	1	1	1	11	0.3	0.5	2.8

Personal fouls/disqualifications: 1994-95, 3/0.

M

MITCHELL, SAM   F   TIMBERWOLVES

PERSONAL: Born September 2, 1963, in Columbus, Ga. ... 6-7/215. ... Full name: Samuel E. Mitchell Jr.
HIGH SCHOOL: Columbus (Ga.).
COLLEGE: Mercer (Ga.).
TRANSACTIONS/CAREER NOTES: Selected by Houston Rockets in third round (54th pick overall) of 1985 NBA Draft. ... Waived by Rockets (October 22, 1985). ... Played in Continental Basketball Association with Wisconsin Flyers (1985-86 and 1986-87) and Rapid City Thrillers (1986-87). ... Played in United States Basketball League with Tampa Bay Flash (1986). ... Signed as free agent by Rockets (October 7, 1986). ... Waived by Rockets (October 28, 1986). ... Played in France (1987-88 and 1988-89). ... Signed as free agent by Minnesota Timberwolves (July 23, 1989). ... Traded by Timberwolves with G Pooh Richardson to Indiana Pacers for F Chuck Person and G Micheal Williams (September 8, 1992). ... Signed as unrestricted free agent by Timberwolves (September 29, 1995).

COLLEGIATE RECORD

												AVERAGES		
Season Team	G	Min.	FGM	FGA	Pct.	FTM	FTA	Pct.	Reb.	Ast.	Pts.	RPG	APG	PPG
81-82—Mercer	27	...	77	155	.497	38	53	.717	100	13	192	3.7	0.5	7.1
82-83—Mercer	28	964	178	343	.519	105	134	.784	164	47	461	5.9	1.7	16.5
83-84—Mercer	26	935	219	432	.507	121	155	.781	184	46	559	7.1	1.8	21.5
84-85—Mercer	31	1157	294	570	.516	186	248	.750	255	43	774	8.2	1.4	25.0
Totals	112	...	768	1500	.512	450	590	.763	703	149	1986	6.3	1.3	17.7

CBA REGULAR-SEASON RECORD

												AVERAGES		
Season Team	G	Min.	FGM	FGA	Pct.	FTM	FTA	Pct.	Reb.	Ast.	Pts.	RPG	APG	PPG
85-86—Wisconsin	13	450	107	238	.450	55	83	.663	95	16	270	7.3	1.2	20.8
86-87—Wisc.-R.C.	42	1370	253	554	.457	154	210	.733	256	31	663	6.1	0.7	15.8
Totals	55	1820	360	792	.455	209	293	.713	351	47	933	6.4	0.9	17.0

Three-point field goals: 1985-86, 1-for-3 (.333). 1986-87, 3-for-12 (.250). Totals, 4-for-15 (.267).

NBA REGULAR-SEASON RECORD

NOTES: Led NBA with 338 personal fouls (1991).

								REBOUNDS							AVERAGES		
Season Team	G	Min.	FGM	FGA	Pct.	FTM	FTA	Pct.	Off.	Def.	Tot.	Ast.	St.	Blk.	TO	Pts.	RPG	APG	PPG
89-90—Minnesota.......	80	2414	372	834	.446	268	349	.768	180	282	462	89	66	54	96	1012	5.8	1.1	12.7
90-91—Minnesota.......	82	3121	445	1010	.441	307	396	.775	188	332	520	133	66	57	104	1197	6.3	1.6	14.6
91-92—Minnesota.......	82	2151	307	725	.423	209	266	.786	158	315	473	94	53	39	97	825	5.8	1.1	10.1
92-93—Indiana...........	81	1402	215	483	.445	150	185	.811	93	155	248	76	23	10	51	584	3.1	0.9	7.2
93-94—Indiana...........	75	1084	140	306	.458	82	110	.745	71	119	190	65	33	9	50	362	2.5	0.9	4.8

Season Team	G	Min.	FGM	FGA	Pct.	FTM	FTA	Pct.	REBOUNDS Off.	Def.	Tot.	Ast.	St.	Blk.	TO	Pts.	AVERAGES RPG	APG	PPG
94-95—Indiana	81	1377	201	413	.487	126	174	.724	95	148	243	61	43	20	54	529	3.0	0.8	6.5
95-96—Minnesota	78	2145	303	618	.490	237	291	.814	107	232	339	74	49	26	87	844	4.3	0.9	10.8
Totals	559	13694	1983	4389	.452	1379	1771	.779	892	1583	2475	592	333	215	539	5353	4.4	1.1	9.6

Three-point field goals: 1989-90, 0-for-9. 1990-91, 0-for-9. 1991-92, 2-for-11 (.182). 1992-93, 4-for-23 (.174). 1993-94, 0-for-5. 1994-95, 1-for-10 (.100). 1995-96, 1-for-18 (.056). Totals, 8-for-85 (.094).

Personal fouls/disqualifications: 1989-90, 301/7. 1990-91, 338/13. 1991-92, 230/3. 1992-93, 207/1. 1993-94, 152/1. 1994-95, 206/0. 1995-96, 220/3. Totals, 1654/28.

NBA PLAYOFF RECORD

Season Team	G	Min.	FGM	FGA	Pct.	FTM	FTA	Pct.	REBOUNDS Off.	Def.	Tot.	Ast.	St.	Blk.	TO	Pts.	AVERAGES RPG	APG	PPG
92-93—Indiana	4	25	5	8	.625	2	2	1.000	0	1	1	0	0	0	2	12	0.3	0.0	3.0
93-94—Indiana	15	99	9	26	.346	3	4	.750	5	12	17	5	2	2	4	21	1.1	0.3	1.4
94-95—Indiana	17	223	23	64	.359	22	28	.786	17	31	48	6	3	1	14	68	2.8	0.4	4.0
Totals	36	347	37	98	.378	27	34	.794	22	44	66	11	5	3	20	101	1.8	0.3	2.8

Three-point field goals: 1993-94, 0-for-1. 1994-95, 0-for-2. Totals, 0-for-3.
Personal fouls/disqualifications: 1992-93, 4/0. 1993-94, 22/0. 1994-95, 41/0. Totals, 67/0.

MOBLEY, ERIC   C   GRIZZLIES

PERSONAL: Born February 1, 1970, in Bronx, N.Y. ... 6-11/257.
HIGH SCHOOL: Salesian (New Rochelle, N.Y.).
JUNIOR COLLEGE: Allegany (Md.) Community College.
COLLEGE: Pittsburgh.
TRANSACTIONS/CAREER NOTES: Selected by Milwaukee Bucks in first round (18th pick overall) of 1994 NBA Draft. ... Traded by Bucks with G Eric Murdock to Vancouver Grizzlies for C Benoit Benjamin (November 27, 1995).

COLLEGIATE RECORD

Season Team	G	Min.	FGM	FGA	Pct.	FTM	FTA	Pct.	Reb.	Ast.	Pts.	AVERAGES RPG	APG	PPG
89-90—Allegany C.C.	23	...	...	...	...	...	...	...	242	...	378	10.5	...	16.4
90-91—Pittsburgh						Did not play—transfer student.								
91-92—Pittsburgh	33	541	99	177	.559	41	100	.410	153	19	239	4.6	0.6	7.2
92-93—Pittsburgh	28	751	117	216	.542	57	103	.553	209	50	291	7.5	1.8	10.4
93-94—Pittsburgh	27	799	155	273	.568	60	122	.492	237	55	370	8.8	2.0	13.7
Junior college totals	23	...	...	...	...	...	...	...	242	...	378	10.5	...	16.4
4-year-college totals	88	2091	371	666	.557	158	325	.486	599	124	900	6.8	1.4	10.2

NBA REGULAR-SEASON RECORD

Season Team	G	Min.	FGM	FGA	Pct.	FTM	FTA	Pct.	REBOUNDS Off.	Def.	Tot.	Ast.	St.	Blk.	TO	Pts.	AVERAGES RPG	APG	PPG
94-95—Milwaukee	46	587	78	132	.591	22	45	.489	55	98	153	21	8	27	24	180	3.3	0.5	3.9
95-96—Mil.-Van.	39	676	74	138	.536	39	87	.448	54	86	140	22	14	24	50	188	3.6	0.6	4.8
Totals	85	1263	152	270	.563	61	132	.462	109	184	293	43	22	51	74	368	3.4	0.5	4.3

Three-point field goals: 1994-95, 2-for-2. 1995-96, 1-for-2 (.500). Totals, 3-for-4 (.750).
Personal fouls/disqualifications: 1994-95, 63/0. 1995-96, 87/1. Totals, 150/1.

MONTROSS, ERIC   C   MAVERICKS

PERSONAL: Born September 23, 1971, in Indianapolis. ... 7-0/270. ... Full name: Eric Scott Montross. ... Grandson of Johnny Townsend, forward with Hammond Ciesar All-Americans (1938-39), Indianapolis Kautskys (1941-42), Toledo Jim White Chevrolets (1942-43) and Oshkosh All-Stars (1943-44) of the National Basketball League.
HIGH SCHOOL: Lawrence North (Indianapolis).
COLLEGE: North Carolina.
TRANSACTIONS/CAREER NOTES: Selected by Boston Celtics in first round (ninth pick overall) of 1994 NBA Draft. ... Traded by Celtics with 1996 first-round draft choice to Dallas Mavericks for 1996 and 1997 first-round draft choices (June 21, 1996).

COLLEGIATE RECORD

NOTES: The Sporting News All-America second team (1993, 1994). ... Member of NCAA Division I championship team (1993).

Season Team	G	Min.	FGM	FGA	Pct.	FTM	FTA	Pct.	Reb.	Ast.	Pts.	AVERAGES RPG	APG	PPG
90-91—North Carolina	35	531	81	138	.587	41	67	.612	148	11	203	4.2	0.3	5.8
91-92—North Carolina	31	784	140	244	.574	68	109	.624	218	18	348	7.0	0.6	11.2
92-93—North Carolina	38	1076	222	361	.615	156	228	.684	290	28	600	7.6	0.7	15.8
93-94—North Carolina	35	1110	183	327	.560	110	197	.558	285	29	476	8.1	0.8	13.6
Totals	139	3501	626	1070	.585	375	601	.624	941	86	1627	6.8	0.6	11.7

NBA REGULAR-SEASON RECORD

HONORS: NBA All-Rookie second team (1995).

Season Team	G	Min.	FGM	FGA	Pct.	FTM	FTA	Pct.	REBOUNDS Off.	Def.	Tot.	Ast.	St.	Blk.	TO	Pts.	AVERAGES RPG	APG	PPG
94-95—Boston	78	2315	307	575	.534	167	263	.635	196	370	566	36	29	61	112	781	7.3	0.5	10.0
95-96—Boston	61	1432	196	346	.566	50	133	.376	119	233	352	43	19	29	83	442	5.8	0.7	7.2
Totals	139	3747	503	921	.546	217	396	.548	315	603	918	79	48	90	195	1223	6.6	0.6	8.8

Three-point field goals: 1994-95, 0-for-1.
Personal fouls/disqualifications: 1994-95, 299/10. 1995-96, 181/1. Totals, 480/11.

M

NBA PLAYOFF RECORD

								REBOUNDS								AVERAGES		
Season Team	G	Min.	FGM	FGA	Pct.	FTM	FTA	Pct.	Off.	Def.	Tot.	Ast.	St.	Blk.	TO	Pts.	RPG	APG	PPG
94-95—Boston	4	62	5	11	.455	3	6	.500	7	2	9	0	0	0	8	13	2.3	0.0	3.3

Personal fouls/disqualifications: 1994-95, 13/0.

MOORE, TRACY   G   ROCKETS

PERSONAL: Born December 28, 1965, in Oklahoma City. ... 6-4/200. ... Full name: Tracy Lamont Moore.
HIGH SCHOOL: John Marshall (Oklahoma City).
COLLEGE: Tulsa.
TRANSACTIONS/CAREER NOTES: Not drafted by an NBA franchise. ... Played in Continental Basketball Association with Tulsa Fast Breakers (1988-89 and 1989-90), Quad City Thunder and Columbus Horizon (1989-90), Tulsa Zone (1990-91 and 1991-92), Fargo-Moorhead Fever (1992-93), La Crosse Catbirds (1993-94), Pittsburgh Piranhas (1994-95) and Shreveport Storm (1995-96). ... Played in World Basketball League with Youngstown Pride (1990) and Florida Jades (1991). ... Signed by Dallas Mavericks to first of two consecutive 10-day contracts (January 17, 1992). ... Re-signed by Mavericks for remainder of season (February 6, 1992). ... Waived by Mavericks (February 4, 1993). ... Signed as free agent by Detroit Pistons (September 1993). ... Waived by Pistons (December 17, 1993). ... Signed by Houston Rockets to first of two consecutive 10-day contracts (March 13, 1996). ... Re-signed by Rockets for remainder of season (April 2, 1996).

COLLEGIATE RECORD

												AVERAGES		
Season Team	G	Min.	FGM	FGA	Pct.	FTM	FTA	Pct.	Reb.	Ast.	Pts.	RPG	APG	PPG
84-85—Tulsa	31	423	75	152	.493	33	45	.733	25	26	183	0.8	0.8	5.9
85-86—Tulsa	32	1095	217	453	.479	105	139	.755	114	57	539	3.6	1.8	16.8
86-87—Tulsa	30	984	204	445	.458	88	122	.721	127	73	506	4.2	2.4	16.9
87-88—Tulsa	28	1032	211	483	.437	109	151	.722	128	67	595	4.6	2.4	21.3
Totals	121	3534	707	1533	.461	335	457	.733	394	223	1823	3.3	1.8	15.1

Three-point field goals: 1986-87, 10-for-26 (.385). 1987-88, 64-for-137 (.467). Totals, 74-for-163 (.454).

CBA REGULAR-SEASON RECORD

NOTES: CBA All-League first team (1996).

												AVERAGES		
Season Team	G	Min.	FGM	FGA	Pct.	FTM	FTA	Pct.	Reb.	Ast.	Pts.	RPG	APG	PPG
88-89—Tulsa	46	1074	235	503	.467	68	105	.648	138	55	556	3.0	1.2	12.1
89-90—Tul.-Q.C.-Col.	36	731	180	355	.507	60	75	.800	89	49	427	2.5	1.4	11.9
90-91—Tulsa	50	1583	333	665	.501	144	192	.750	250	100	848	5.0	2.0	17.0
91-92—Tulsa	27	1054	282	574	.491	241	283	.852	142	74	830	5.3	2.7	30.7
92-93—Fargo/Moor.	11	313	71	135	.526	37	47	.787	31	26	182	2.8	2.4	16.5
93-94—La Crosse	25	732	206	407	.506	106	131	.809	67	36	541	2.7	1.4	21.6
94-95—Pittsburgh	40	1298	290	597	.486	150	176	.852	112	76	825	2.8	1.9	20.6
95-96—Shreveport	49	2036	427	899	.475	285	336	.848	122	126	1266	2.5	2.6	25.8
Totals	284	8821	2024	4135	.489	1091	1345	.811	951	542	5475	3.3	1.9	19.3

Three-point field goals: 1988-89, 18-for-47 (.383). 1989-90, 7-for-19 (.368). 1990-91, 38-for-95 (.400). 1991-92, 25-for-75 (.333). 1992-93, 3-for-18 (.167). 1993-94, 23-for-56 (.411). 1994-95, 95-for-205 (.463). 1995-96, 127-for-293 (.433). Totals, 336-for-808 (.416).

NBA REGULAR-SEASON RECORD

								REBOUNDS								AVERAGES		
Season Team	G	Min.	FGM	FGA	Pct.	FTM	FTA	Pct.	Off.	Def.	Tot.	Ast.	St.	Blk.	TO	Pts.	RPG	APG	PPG
91-92—Dallas	42	782	130	325	.400	65	78	.833	31	51	82	48	32	4	44	355	2.0	1.1	8.5
92-93—Dallas	39	510	103	249	.414	53	61	.869	23	29	52	47	21	4	32	282	1.3	1.2	7.2
93-94—Detroit	3	10	2	3	.667	2	2	1.000	0	1	1	0	2	0	0	6	0.3	0.0	2.0
95-96—Houston	8	190	30	76	.395	18	19	.947	10	12	22	6	2	0	8	91	2.8	0.8	11.4
Totals	92	1492	265	653	.406	138	160	.863	64	93	157	101	57	8	84	734	1.7	1.1	8.0

Three-point field goals: 1991-92, 30-for-84 (.357). 1992-93, 23-for-67 (.343). 1995-96, 13-for-30 (.433). Totals, 66-for-181 (.365).
Personal fouls/disqualifications: 1991-92, 97/0. 1992-93, 54/0. 1995-96, 16/0. Totals, 167/0.

MORRIS, CHRIS   F   JAZZ

PERSONAL: Born January 20, 1966, in Atlanta. ... 6-8/220. ... Full name: Christopher Vernard Morris.
HIGH SCHOOL: Douglass (Atlanta).
COLLEGE: Auburn.
TRANSACTIONS/CAREER NOTES: Selected by New Jersey Nets in first round (fourth pick overall) of 1988 NBA Draft. ... Signed as unrestricted free agent by Utah Jazz (October 6, 1995).

COLLEGIATE RECORD

												AVERAGES		
Season Team	G	Min.	FGM	FGA	Pct.	FTM	FTA	Pct.	Reb.	Ast.	Pts.	RPG	APG	PPG
84-85—Auburn	34	1032	155	325	.477	44	71	.620	169	57	354	5.0	1.7	10.4
85-86—Auburn	33	1023	128	256	.500	69	103	.670	171	62	325	5.2	1.9	9.8
86-87—Auburn	31	985	170	304	.559	69	97	.711	225	80	418	7.3	2.6	13.5
87-88—Auburn	30	1018	241	501	.481	105	132	.795	295	82	620	9.8	2.7	20.7
Totals	128	4058	694	1386	.501	287	403	.712	860	281	1717	6.7	2.2	13.4

Three-point field goals: 1986-87, 9-for-27 (.333). 1987-88, 33-for-97 (.340). Totals, 42-for-124 (.339).

NBA REGULAR-SEASON RECORD

HONORS: NBA All-Rookie second team (1989).

								REBOUNDS								AVERAGES		
Season Team	G	Min.	FGM	FGA	Pct.	FTM	FTA	Pct.	Off.	Def.	Tot.	Ast.	St.	Blk.	TO	Pts.	RPG	APG	PPG
88-89—New Jersey	76	2096	414	905	.457	182	254	.717	188	209	397	119	102	60	190	1074	5.2	1.6	14.1
89-90—New Jersey	80	2449	449	1065	.422	228	316	.722	194	228	422	143	130	79	185	1187	5.3	1.8	14.8

M

Season Team	G	Min.	FGM	FGA	Pct.	FTM	FTA	Pct.	Off.	Def.	Tot.	Ast.	St.	Blk.	TO	Pts.	RPG	APG	PPG
90-91—New Jersey	79	2553	409	962	.425	179	244	.734	210	311	521	220	138	96	167	1042	6.6	2.8	13.2
91-92—New Jersey	77	2394	346	726	.477	165	231	.714	199	295	494	197	129	81	171	879	6.4	2.6	11.4
92-93—New Jersey	77	2302	436	907	.481	197	248	.794	227	227	454	106	144	52	119	1086	5.9	1.4	14.1
93-94—New Jersey	50	1349	203	454	.447	85	118	.720	91	137	228	83	55	49	52	544	4.6	1.7	10.9
94-95—New Jersey	71	2131	351	856	.410	142	195	.728	181	221	402	147	86	51	117	950	5.7	2.1	13.4
95-96—Utah	66	1424	265	606	.437	98	127	.772	100	129	229	77	63	20	71	691	3.5	1.2	10.5
Totals	576	16698	2873	6481	.443	1276	1733	.736	1390	1757	3147	1092	847	488	1072	7453	5.5	1.9	12.9

Three-point field goals: 1988-89, 64-for-175 (.366). 1989-90, 61-for-193 (.316). 1990-91, 45-for-179 (.251). 1991-92, 22-for-110 (.200). 1992-93, 17-for-76 (.224). 1993-94, 53-for-147 (.361). 1994-95, 106-for-317 (.334). 1995-96, 63-for-197 (.320). Totals, 431-for-1394 (.309).

Personal fouls/disqualifications: 1988-89, 250/4. 1989-90, 219/1. 1990-91, 248/5. 1991-92, 211/2. 1992-93, 171/2. 1993-94, 120/2. 1994-95, 155/0. 1995-96, 140/1. Totals, 1514/17.

NBA PLAYOFF RECORD

Season Team	G	Min.	FGM	FGA	Pct.	FTM	FTA	Pct.	Off.	Def.	Tot.	Ast.	St.	Blk.	TO	Pts.	RPG	APG	PPG
91-92—New Jersey	4	135	32	58	.552	7	9	.778	11	9	20	5	7	7	8	75	5.0	1.3	18.8
92-93—New Jersey	5	163	34	61	.557	11	12	.917	13	19	32	7	8	6	3	85	6.4	1.4	17.0
93-94—New Jersey	4	98	12	43	.279	10	10	1.000	11	11	22	7	5	5	6	37	5.5	1.8	9.3
95-96—Utah	18	321	45	106	.425	12	16	.750	24	46	70	19	13	8	14	112	3.9	1.1	6.2
Totals	31	717	123	268	.459	40	47	.851	59	85	144	38	33	26	31	309	4.6	1.2	10.0

Three-point field goals: 1991-92, 4-for-10 (.400). 1992-93, 6-for-16 (.375). 1993-94, 3-for-20 (.150). 1995-96, 10-for-37 (.270). Totals, 23-for-83 (.277).
Personal fouls/disqualifications: 1991-92, 11/0. 1992-93, 8/0. 1993-94, 14/0. 1995-96, 25/0. Totals, 58/0.

MOTEN, LAWRENCE   G   GRIZZLIES

PERSONAL: Born March 25, 1972, in Washington, D.C. ... 6-5/186. ... Full name: Lawrence Edward Moten III. ... Name pronounced MOE-tin.
HIGH SCHOOL: Archbishop Carroll (Washington, D.C.), then New Hampton (N.H.) Prep.
COLLEGE: Syracuse.
TRANSACTIONS/CAREER NOTES: Selected by Vancouver Grizzlies in second round (36th pick overall) of 1995 NBA Draft.

COLLEGIATE RECORD

NOTES: The Sporting News All-America second team (1995).

Season Team	G	Min.	FGM	FGA	Pct.	FTM	FTA	Pct.	Reb.	Ast.	Pts.	RPG	APG	PPG
91-92—Syracuse	32	1080	193	388	.497	152	202	.752	192	63	583	6.0	2.0	18.2
92-93—Syracuse	29	951	191	404	.473	92	141	.652	138	77	518	4.8	2.7	17.9
93-94—Syracuse	30	1043	245	489	.501	104	149	.698	135	66	644	4.5	2.2	21.5
94-95—Syracuse	30	1059	209	455	.459	113	152	.743	125	99	589	4.2	3.3	19.6
Totals	121	4133	838	1736	.483	461	644	.716	590	305	2334	4.9	2.5	19.3

Three-point field goals: 1991-92, 45-for-140 (.321). 1992-93, 44-for-131 (.336). 1993-94, 50-for-176 (.284). 1994-95, 58-for-177 (.328). Totals, 197-for-624 (.316).

NBA REGULAR-SEASON RECORD

Season Team	G	Min.	FGM	FGA	Pct.	FTM	FTA	Pct.	Off.	Def.	Tot.	Ast.	St.	Blk.	TO	Pts.	RPG	APG	PPG
95-96—Vancouver.......	44	573	112	247	.453	49	75	.653	36	25	61	50	29	8	44	291	1.4	1.1	6.6

Three-point field goals: 1995-96, 18-for-55 (.327).
Personal fouls/disqualifications: 1995-96, 54/0.

MOURNING, ALONZO   C   HEAT

PERSONAL: Born February 8, 1970, in Chesapeake, Va. ... 6-10/261.
HIGH SCHOOL: Indian River (Chesapeake, Va.).
COLLEGE: Georgetown.
TRANSACTIONS/CAREER NOTES: Selected by Charlotte Hornets in first round (second pick overall) of 1992 NBA Draft. ... Traded by Hornets with C LeRon Ellis and G Pete Myers to Miami Heat for G/F Glen Rice, G Khalid Reeves, C Matt Geiger and 1996 first-round draft choice (November 3, 1995).
MISCELLANEOUS: Charlotte Hornets all-time blocked shots leader with 684 (1992-93 through 1994-95).

COLLEGIATE RECORD

NOTES: The Sporting News All-America second team (1990, 1992). ... Holds NCAA Division I career record for most blocked shots—453. ... Led NCAA Division I with 4.97 blocked shots per game (1989). ... Led NCAA Division I in blocked shots with 169 (1989) and 160 (1992).

Season Team	G	Min.	FGM	FGA	Pct.	FTM	FTA	Pct.	Reb.	Ast.	Pts.	RPG	APG	PPG
88-89—Georgetown..................	34	962	158	262	.603	130	195	.667	248	24	447	7.3	0.7	13.1
89-90—Georgetown..................	31	937	145	276	.525	220	281	.783	265	36	510	8.5	1.2	16.5
90-91—Georgetown..................	23	682	105	201	.522	149	188	.793	176	25	363	7.7	1.1	15.8
91-92—Georgetown..................	32	1051	204	343	.595	272	359	.758	343	53	681	10.7	1.7	21.3
Totals	120	3632	612	1082	.566	771	1023	.754	1032	138	2001	8.6	1.2	16.7

Three-point field goals: 1988-89, 1-for-4 (.250). 1989-90, 0-for-2. 1990-91, 4-for-13 (.308). 1991-92, 6-for-23 (.261). Totals, 11-for-42 (.262).

HONORS: NBA All-Rookie first team (1993).

NBA REGULAR-SEASON RECORD

Season Team	G	Min.	FGM	FGA	Pct.	FTM	FTA	Pct.	Off.	Def.	Tot.	Ast.	St.	Blk.	TO	Pts.	RPG	APG	PPG
92-93—Charlotte	78	2644	572	1119	.511	495	634	.781	263	542	805	76	27	271	236	1639	10.3	1.0	21.0
93-94—Charlotte	60	2018	427	845	.505	433	568	.762	177	433	610	86	27	188	199	1287	10.2	1.4	21.5

Season Team	G	Min.	FGM	FGA	Pct.	FTM	FTA	Pct.	Off.	Def.	Tot.	Ast.	St.	Blk.	TO	Pts.	RPG	APG	PPG
94-95—Charlotte	77	2941	571	1101	.519	490	644	.761	200	561	761	111	49	225	241	1643	9.9	1.4	21.3
95-96—Miami	70	2671	563	1076	.523	488	712	.685	218	509	727	159	70	189	262	1623	10.4	2.3	23.2
Totals	285	10274	2133	4141	.515	1906	2558	.745	858	2045	2903	432	173	873	938	6192	10.2	1.5	21.7

Three-point field goals: 1992-93, 0-for-3. 1993-94, 0-for-2. 1994-95, 11-for-34 (.324). 1995-96, 9-for-30 (.300). Totals, 20-for-69 (.290).

Personal fouls/disqualifications: 1992-93, 286/6. 1993-94, 207/3. 1994-95, 275/5. 1995-96, 245/5. Totals, 1013/19.

NBA PLAYOFF RECORD

Season Team	G	Min.	FGM	FGA	Pct.	FTM	FTA	Pct.	Off.	Def.	Tot.	Ast.	St.	Blk.	TO	Pts.	RPG	APG	PPG
92-93—Charlotte	9	367	71	148	.480	72	93	.774	28	61	89	13	6	31	37	214	9.9	1.4	23.8
94-95—Charlotte	4	174	24	57	.421	36	43	.837	14	39	53	11	3	13	14	88	13.3	2.8	22.0
95-96—Miami	3	92	17	35	.486	20	28	.714	3	15	18	4	2	3	16	54	6.0	1.3	18.0
Totals	16	633	112	240	.467	128	164	.780	45	115	160	28	11	47	67	356	10.0	1.8	22.3

Three-point field goals: 1992-93, 0-for-2. 1994-95, 4-for-8 (.500). Totals, 4-for-10 (.400).

Personal fouls/disqualifications: 1992-93, 37/1. 1994-95, 17/0. 1995-96, 13/1. Totals, 67/2.

NBA ALL-STAR GAME RECORD

Season Team	Min.	FGM	FGA	Pct.	FTM	FTA	Pct.	Off.	Def.	Tot.	Ast.	PF	Dq.	St.	Blk.	TO	Pts.
1994 —Charlotte						Selected, did not play—injured.											
1995 —Charlotte	19	4	9	.444	2	3	.667	0	8	8	1	5	0	0	1	1	10
1996 —Miami	13	1	6	.167	0	0	...	0	1	1	0	2	0	0	1	2	2
Totals	32	5	15	.333	2	3	.667	0	9	9	1	7	0	0	2	3	12

Three-point field goals: 1995, 0-for-1.

MULLIN, CHRIS   F   WARRIORS

PERSONAL: Born July 30, 1963, in New York. ... 6-7/215. ... Full name: Christopher Paul Mullin.

HIGH SCHOOL: Power Memorial (New York), then Xaverian (Brooklyn, N.Y.).

COLLEGE: St. John's.

TRANSACTIONS/CAREER NOTES: Selected by Golden State Warriors in first round (seventh pick overall) of 1985 NBA Draft.

MISCELLANEOUS: Member of gold-medal-winning U.S. Olympic teams (1984, 1992). ... Golden State Warriors franchise all-time steals leader with 1,214 (1985-86 through 1995-96).

COLLEGIATE RECORD

NOTES: Wooden Award winner (1985). ... THE SPORTING NEWS All-America first team (1985). ... THE SPORTING NEWS All-America second team (1984).

Season Team	G	Min.	FGM	FGA	Pct.	FTM	FTA	Pct.	Reb.	Ast.	Pts.	RPG	APG	PPG
81-82—St. John's	30	1061	175	328	.534	148	187	.791	97	92	498	3.2	3.1	16.6
82-83—St. John's	33	1210	228	395	.577	173	197	.878	123	101	629	3.7	3.1	19.1
83-84—St. John's	27	1070	225	394	.571	169	187	.904	120	109	619	4.4	4.0	22.9
84-85—St. John's	35	1327	251	482	.521	192	233	.824	169	151	694	4.8	4.3	19.8
Totals	125	4668	879	1599	.550	682	804	.848	509	453	2440	4.1	3.6	19.5

NBA REGULAR-SEASON RECORD

HONORS: All-NBA first team (1992). ... All-NBA second team (1989, 1991). ... All-NBA third team (1990).

Season Team	G	Min.	FGM	FGA	Pct.	FTM	FTA	Pct.	Off.	Def.	Tot.	Ast.	St.	Blk.	TO	Pts.	RPG	APG	PPG
85-86—Golden State	55	1391	287	620	.463	189	211	.896	42	73	115	105	70	23	75	768	2.1	1.9	14.0
86-87—Golden State	82	2377	477	928	.514	269	326	.825	39	142	181	261	98	36	154	1242	2.2	3.2	15.1
87-88—Golden State	60	2033	470	926	.508	239	270	.885	58	147	205	290	113	32	156	1213	3.4	4.8	20.2
88-89—Golden State	82	3093	830	1630	.509	493	553	.892	152	331	483	415	176	39	296	2176	5.9	5.1	26.5
89-90—Golden State	78	2830	682	1272	.536	505	568	.889	130	333	463	319	123	45	239	1956	5.9	4.1	25.1
90-91—Golden State	82	*3315	777	1449	.536	513	580	.884	141	302	443	329	173	63	245	2107	5.4	4.0	25.7
91-92—Golden State	81	*3346	830	1584	.524	350	420	.833	127	323	450	286	173	62	202	2074	5.6	3.5	25.6
92-93—Golden State	46	1902	474	930	.510	183	226	.810	42	190	232	166	68	41	139	1191	5.0	3.6	25.9
93-94—Golden State	62	2324	410	869	.472	165	219	.753	64	281	345	315	107	53	178	1040	5.6	5.1	16.8
94-95—Golden State	25	890	170	348	.489	94	107	.879	25	90	115	125	38	19	93	476	4.6	5.0	19.0
95-96—Golden State	55	1617	269	539	.499	137	160	.856	44	115	159	194	75	32	122	734	2.9	3.5	13.3
Totals	708	25118	5676	11095	.512	3137	3640	.862	864	2327	3191	2805	1214	445	1899	14977	4.5	4.0	21.2

Three-point field goals: 1985-86, 5-for-27 (.185). 1986-87, 19-for-63 (.302). 1987-88, 34-for-97 (.351). 1988-89, 23-for-100 (.230). 1989-90, 87-for-234 (.372). 1990-91, 40-for-133 (.301). 1991-92, 64-for-175 (.366). 1992-93, 60-for-133 (.451). 1993-94, 55-for-151 (.364). 1994-95, 42-for-93 (.452). 1995-96, 59-for-150 (.393). Totals, 488-for-1356 (.360).

Personal fouls/disqualifications: 1985-86, 130/1. 1986-87, 217/1. 1987-88, 136/3. 1988-89, 178/1. 1989-90, 142/1. 1990-91, 176/2. 1991-92, 171/1. 1992-93, 76/0. 1993-94, 114/0. 1994-95, 53/0. 1995-96, 127/0. Totals, 1520/10.

NBA PLAYOFF RECORD

Season Team	G	Min.	FGM	FGA	Pct.	FTM	FTA	Pct.	Off.	Def.	Tot.	Ast.	St.	Blk.	TO	Pts.	RPG	APG	PPG
86-87—Golden State	10	262	49	98	.500	12	16	.750	2	13	15	23	9	2	16	113	1.5	2.3	11.3
88-89—Golden State	8	341	88	163	.540	58	67	.866	11	36	47	36	14	11	32	235	5.9	4.5	29.4
90-91—Golden State	8	366	69	131	.527	43	50	.860	9	49	58	23	15	12	25	190	7.3	2.9	23.8
91-92—Golden State	4	168	27	63	.429	13	14	.929	3	9	12	12	5	2	8	71	3.0	3.0	17.8
93-94—Golden State	3	135	30	51	.588	10	11	.909	4	10	14	11	0	5	7	76	4.7	3.7	25.3
Totals	33	1272	263	506	.520	136	158	.861	29	117	146	105	43	32	88	685	4.4	3.2	20.8

Three-point field goals: 1986-87, 3-for-4 (.750). 1988-89, 1-for-8 (.125). 1990-91, 9-for-13 (.692). 1991-92, 4-for-12 (.333). 1993-94, 6-for-12 (.500). Totals, 23-for-49 (.469).

Personal fouls/disqualifications: 1986-87, 31/0. 1988-89, 19/0. 1990-91, 23/0. 1991-92, 8/0. 1993-94, 4/0. Totals, 85/0.

NBA ALL-STAR GAME RECORD

Season	Team	Min.	FGM	FGA	Pct.	FTM	FTA	Pct.	REBOUNDS Off.	Def.	Tot.	Ast.	PF	Dq.	St.	Blk.	TO	Pts.
1989	—Golden State.....	14	1	4	.250	2	2	1.000	2	0	2	2	0	0	0	0	1	4
1990	—Golden State.....	16	1	5	.200	1	2	.500	1	2	3	1	0	0	2	1	1	3
1991	—Golden State.....	24	4	8	.500	4	4	1.000	0	2	2	2	2	0	2	0	2	13
1992	—Golden State.....	24	6	7	.857	0	0	...	0	1	1	3	0	0	0	0	1	13
1993	—Golden State							Selected, did not play—injured.										
Totals		78	12	24	.500	7	8	.875	3	5	8	8	2	0	4	1	5	33

Three-point field goals: 1991, 1-for-1. 1992, 1-for-1. Totals, 2-for-2.

MUNDT, TODD   C

PERSONAL: Born May 17, 1970, in Iowa City, Iowa. ... 7-0/250. ... Name pronounced MUNT.
HIGH SCHOOL: Central Merry (Jackson, Tenn.).
COLLEGE: Memphis State, then Delta (Miss.) State.
TRANSACTIONS/CAREER NOTES: Not drafted by an NBA franchise. ... Played in Continental Basketball Association with Rockford Lightning (1993-94). ... Signed as free agent by Atlanta Hawks (October 5, 1994). ... Waived by Hawks (November 1, 1994). ... Re-signed by Hawks (October 30, 1995). ... Waived by Hawks (March 9, 1996). ... Signed by Boston Celtics to first of two consecutive 10-day contracts (March 23, 1996). ... Re-signed by Celtics for remainder of season (April 12, 1996). ... Rights renounced by Celtics (July 30, 1996).

COLLEGIATE RECORD

Season Team	G	Min.	FGM	FGA	Pct.	FTM	FTA	Pct.	Reb.	Ast.	Pts.	AVERAGES RPG	APG	PPG
89-90—Memphis	28	582	80	159	.503	62	81	.765	104	28	222	3.7	1.0	7.9
90-91—Memphis	32	673	92	200	.460	34	50	.680	139	43	218	4.3	1.3	6.8
91-92—Memphis	22	268	34	80	.425	8	15	.533	48	10	76	2.2	0.5	3.5
92-93—Delta State....................	30	...	135	240	.563	87	110	.791	193	56	357	6.4	1.9	11.9
Totals	112	...	341	679	.502	191	256	.746	484	137	873	4.3	1.2	7.8

Three-point field goals: 1990-91, 0-for-1. 1992-93, 0-for-1, Totals, 0-for-2.

CBA REGULAR-SEASON RECORD

Season Team	G	Min.	FGM	FGA	Pct.	FTM	FTA	Pct.	Reb.	Ast.	Pts.	AVERAGES RPG	APG	PPG
93-94—Rockford	33	276	40	86	.465	19	27	.704	58	8	99	1.8	0.2	3.0

Three-point field goals: 1993-94, 0-for-1.

NBA REGULAR-SEASON RECORD

Season Team	G	Min.	FGM	FGA	Pct.	FTM	FTA	Pct.	REBOUNDS Off.	Def.	Tot.	Ast.	St.	Blk.	TO	Pts.	AVERAGES RPG	APG	PPG
95-96—Atl.-Bos...........	33	151	16	41	.390	5	8	.625	11	17	28	3	2	5	3	37	0.8	0.1	1.1

Personal fouls/disqualifications: 1995-96, 29/0.

MURDOCK, ERIC   G

PERSONAL: Born June 14, 1968, in Somerville, N.J. ... 6-1/200. ... Full name: Eric Lloyd Murdock.
HIGH SCHOOL: Bridgewater-Raritan (N.J.).
COLLEGE: Providence.
TRANSACTIONS/CAREER NOTES: Selected by Utah Jazz in first round (21st pick overall) of 1991 NBA Draft. ... Traded by Jazz with G Blue Edwards and 1992 first-round draft choice to Milwaukee Bucks for G Jay Humphries and F Larry Krystkowiak (June 24, 1992). ... Traded by Bucks with C Eric Mobley to Vancouver Grizzlies for C Benoit Benjamin (November 27, 1995). ... Rights renounced by Grizzlies (July 16, 1996).
MISCELLANEOUS: Vancouver Grizzlies all-time steals leader with 129 (1995-96).

NOTES: The Sporting News All-America second team (1991). ... Holds NCAA Division I career record for most steals—376.

COLLEGIATE RECORD

Season Team	G	Min.	FGM	FGA	Pct.	FTM	FTA	Pct.	Reb.	Ast.	Pts.	AVERAGES RPG	APG	PPG
87-88—Providence	28	768	114	276	.413	45	61	.738	85	85	300	3.0	3.0	10.7
88-89—Providence	29	936	164	359	.457	99	130	.762	135	135	471	4.7	4.7	16.2
89-90—Providence	28	833	147	351	.419	96	126	.762	116	116	432	4.1	4.1	15.4
90-91—Providence	32	1111	262	589	.445	238	293	.812	168	168	818	5.3	5.3	25.6
Totals	117	3648	687	1575	.436	478	610	.784	504	504	2021	4.3	4.3	17.3

Three-point field goals: 1987-88, 27-for-76 (.355). 1988-89, 44-for-126 (.349). 1989-90, 42-for-115 (.365). 1990-91, 56-for-160 (.350). Totals, 169-for-477 (.354).

NBA REGULAR-SEASON RECORD

Season Team	G	Min.	FGM	FGA	Pct.	FTM	FTA	Pct.	REBOUNDS Off.	Def.	Tot.	Ast.	St.	Blk.	TO	Pts.	AVERAGES RPG	APG	PPG
91-92—Utah...............	50	478	76	183	.415	46	61	.754	21	33	54	92	30	7	50	203	1.1	1.8	4.1
92-93—Milwaukee	79	2437	438	936	.468	231	296	.780	95	189	284	603	174	7	207	1138	3.6	7.6	14.4
93-94—Milwaukee	82	2533	477	1019	.468	234	288	.813	91	170	261	546	197	12	206	1257	3.2	6.7	15.3
94-95—Milwaukee	75	2158	338	814	.415	211	267	.790	48	166	214	482	113	12	194	977	2.9	6.4	13.0
95-96—Mil.-Van.........	73	1673	244	587	.416	114	143	.797	26	143	169	327	135	9	132	647	2.3	4.5	8.9
Totals	359	9279	1573	3539	.444	836	1055	.792	281	701	982	2050	649	47	789	4222	2.7	5.7	11.8

Three-point field goals: 1991-92, 5-for-26 (.192). 1992-93, 31-for-119 (.261). 1993-94, 69-for-168 (.411). 1994-95, 90-for-240 (.375). 1995-96, 45-for-145 (.310). Totals, 240-for-698 (.344).
Personal fouls/disqualifications: 1991-92, 52/0. 1992-93, 177/2. 1993-94, 189/2. 1994-95, 139/0. 1995-96, 140/0. Totals, 697/4.

NBA PLAYOFF RECORD

							REBOUNDS								AVERAGES		
Season Team	G	Min.	FGM	FGA	Pct.	FTM	FTA	Pct.	Off.	Def.	Tot.	Ast.	St.	Blk.	TO	Pts.	RPG	APG	PPG
91-92—Utah...............	3	11	3	5	.600	2	2	1.000	0	3	3	1	1	1	3	8	1.0	0.3	2.7

Three-point field goals: 1991-92, 0-for-1.
Personal fouls/disqualifications: 1991-92, 1/0.

MURESAN, GHEORGHE　　　C　　　BULLETS

PERSONAL: Born February 14, 1971, in Triteni, Romania. ... 7-7/303. ... Name pronounced GEORGE MUIR-ih-san.
COLLEGE: Cluj University (Romania).
TRANSACTIONS/CAREER NOTES: Played in France (1992-93). ... Selected by Washington Bullets in second round (30th pick overall) of 1993 NBA Draft.

FRENCH LEAGUE RECORD

											AVERAGES		
Season Team	G	Min.	FGM	FGA	Pct.	FTM	FTA	Pct.	Reb.	Ast.	Pts.	RPG	APG	PPG
92-93—Pau Orthez.....................	25	...	203	351	.578	62	110	.564	258	25	468	10.3	1.0	18.7

HONORS: NBA Most Improved Player (1996).

NBA REGULAR-SEASON RECORD

									REBOUNDS								AVERAGES		
Season Team	G	Min.	FGM	FGA	Pct.	FTM	FTA	Pct.	Off.	Def.	Tot.	Ast.	St.	Blk.	TO	Pts.	RPG	APG	PPG
93-94—Washington	54	650	128	235	.545	48	71	.676	66	126	192	18	28	48	54	304	3.6	0.3	5.6
94-95—Washington	73	1720	303	541	.560	124	175	.709	179	309	488	38	48	127	115	730	6.7	0.5	10.0
95-96—Washington	76	2242	466	798	*.584	172	278	.619	248	480	728	56	52	172	143	1104	9.6	0.7	14.5
Totals	203	4612	897	1574	.570	344	524	.656	493	915	1408	112	128	347	312	2138	6.9	0.6	10.5

Three-point field goals: 1995-96, 0-for-1.
Personal fouls/disqualifications: 1993-94, 120/1. 1994-95, 259/6. 1995-96, 297/8. Totals, 676/15.

MURRAY, LAMOND　　　F　　　CLIPPERS

PERSONAL: Born April 20, 1973, in Pasadena, Calif. ... 6-7/236. ... Full name: Lamond Maurice Murray. ... Cousin of Tracy Murray, forward with Washington Bullets.
HIGH SCHOOL: John Kennedy (Fremont, Calif.).
COLLEGE: California.
TRANSACTIONS/CAREER NOTES: Selected after junior season by Los Angeles Clippers in first round (seventh pick overall) of 1994 NBA Draft.

COLLEGIATE RECORD

												AVERAGES		
Season Team	G	Min.	FGM	FGA	Pct.	FTM	FTA	Pct.	Reb.	Ast.	Pts.	RPG	APG	PPG
91-92—California	28	745	152	321	.474	66	93	.710	171	56	387	6.1	2.0	13.8
92-93—California	30	897	230	445	.517	76	121	.628	189	41	572	6.3	1.4	19.1
93-94—California	30	1047	262	550	.476	159	208	.764	236	63	729	7.9	2.1	24.3
Totals	88	2689	644	1316	.489	301	422	.713	596	160	1688	6.8	1.8	19.2

Three-point field goals: 1991-92, 17-for-56 (.304). 1992-93, 36-for-99 (.364). 1993-94, 46-for-139 (.331). Totals, 99-for-294 (.337).

NBA REGULAR-SEASON RECORD

									REBOUNDS								AVERAGES		
Season Team	G	Min.	FGM	FGA	Pct.	FTM	FTA	Pct.	Off.	Def.	Tot.	Ast.	St.	Blk.	TO	Pts.	RPG	APG	PPG
94-95—L.A. Clippers ...	81	2556	439	1093	.402	199	264	.754	132	222	354	133	72	55	163	1142	4.4	1.6	14.1
95-96—L.A. Clippers ...	77	1816	257	575	.447	99	132	.750	89	157	246	84	61	25	108	650	3.2	1.1	8.4
Totals	158	4372	696	1668	.417	298	396	.753	221	379	600	217	133	80	271	1792	3.8	1.4	11.3

Three-point field goals: 1994-95, 65-for-218 (.298). 1995-96, 37-for-116 (.319). Totals, 102-for-334 (.305).
Personal fouls/disqualifications: 1994-95, 180/3. 1995-96, 151/0. Totals, 331/3.

MURRAY, TRACY　　　F　　　BULLETS

PERSONAL: Born July 25, 1971, in Los Angeles. ... 6-7/228. ... Full name: Tracy Lamonte Murray. ... Cousin of Lamond Murray, forward with Los Angeles Clippers.
HIGH SCHOOL: Glendora (Calif.).
COLLEGE: UCLA.
TRANSACTIONS/CAREER NOTES: Selected after junior season by San Antonio Spurs in first round (18th pick overall) of 1992 NBA Draft. ... Draft rights traded by Spurs to Milwaukee Bucks for G/F Dale Ellis (July 1, 1992). ... Draft rights traded by Bucks to Portland Trail Blazers for F Alaa Abdelnaby (July 1, 1992). ... Traded by Trail Blazers with G Clyde Drexler to Houston Rockets for F Otis Thorpe, rights to F Marcelo Nicola and 1995 first-round draft choice (February 14, 1995). ... Signed as free agent by Toronto Raptors (November 1, 1995). ... Signed as free agent by Washington Bullets (July 15, 1996).

COLLEGIATE RECORD

												AVERAGES		
Season Team	G	Min.	FGM	FGA	Pct.	FTM	FTA	Pct.	Reb.	Ast.	Pts.	RPG	APG	PPG
89-90—UCLA..............	33	863	146	330	.442	69	90	.767	182	41	407	5.5	1.2	12.3
90-91—UCLA..............	32	1003	247	491	.503	112	141	.794	213	43	679	6.7	1.3	21.2
91-92—UCLA..............	33	1083	240	446	.538	148	185	.800	232	59	706	7.0	1.8	21.4
Totals	98	2949	633	1267	.500	329	416	.791	627	143	1792	6.4	1.5	18.3

Three-point field goals: 1989-90, 46-for-134 (.343). 1990-91, 73-for-189 (.386). 1991-92, 78-for-156 (.500). Totals, 197-for-479 (.411).

NBA REGULAR-SEASON RECORD

									REBOUNDS								AVERAGES		
Season Team	G	Min.	FGM	FGA	Pct.	FTM	FTA	Pct.	Off.	Def.	Tot.	Ast.	St.	Blk.	TO	Pts.	RPG	APG	PPG
92-93—Portland.........	48	495	108	260	.415	35	40	.875	40	43	83	11	8	5	31	272	1.7	0.2	5.7
93-94—Portland.........	66	820	167	355	.470	50	72	.694	43	68	111	31	21	20	37	434	1.7	0.5	6.6
94-95—Port.-Hou.......	54	516	95	233	.408	33	42	.786	20	39	59	19	14	4	35	258	1.1	0.4	4.8
95-96—Toronto..........	82	2458	496	1092	.454	182	219	.831	114	238	352	131	87	40	132	1325	4.3	1.6	16.2
Totals..................	250	4289	866	1940	.446	300	373	.804	217	388	605	192	130	69	235	2289	2.4	0.8	9.2

Three-point field goals: 1992-93, 21-for-70 (.300). 1993-94, 50-for-109 (.459). 1994-95, 35-for-86 (.407). 1995-96, 151-for-358 (.422). Totals, 257-for-623 (.413).

Personal fouls/disqualifications: 1992-93, 59/0. 1993-94, 76/0. 1994-95, 73/0. 1995-96, 208/2. Totals, 416/2.

NBA PLAYOFF RECORD

									REBOUNDS								AVERAGES		
Season Team	G	Min.	FGM	FGA	Pct.	FTM	FTA	Pct.	Off.	Def.	Tot.	Ast.	St.	Blk.	TO	Pts.	RPG	APG	PPG
93-94—Portland..........	2	11	3	6	.500	0	0	...	3	0	3	1	1	0	0	6	1.5	0.5	3.0

Three-point field goals: 1993-94, 0-for-1.
Personal fouls/disqualifications: 1993-94, 3/0.

MUTOMBO, DIKEMBE   C   HAWKS

PERSONAL: Born June 25, 1966, in Kinshasa, Zaire. ... 7-2/250. ... Full name: Dikembe Mutombo Mpolondo Mukamba Jean Jacque Wamutombo. ... Name pronounced di-KEM-bay moo-TUM-bow.
HIGH SCHOOL: Institute Boboto (Kinshasa, Zaire).
COLLEGE: Georgetown.
TRANSACTIONS/CAREER NOTES: Selected by Denver Nuggets in first round (fourth pick overall) of 1991 NBA Draft. ... Rights renounced by Nuggets (July 22, 1996). ... Signed as free agent by Atlanta Hawks (July 15, 1996).
MISCELLANEOUS: Denver Nuggets all-time blocked shots leader with 1,486 (1991-92 through 1995-96).

COLLEGIATE RECORD

NOTES: The Sporting News All-America third team (1991).

M

											AVERAGES		
Season Team	G	Min.	FGM	FGA	Pct.	FTM	FTA	Pct.	Reb.	Ast.	Pts.	RPG	APG	PPG
87-88—Georgetown..................							Did not play.							
88-89—Georgetown..................	33	374	53	75	.707	23	48	.479	109	5	129	3.3	0.2	3.9
89-90—Georgetown..................	31	797	129	182	.709	73	122	.598	325	18	331	10.5	0.6	10.7
90-91—Georgetown..................	32	1090	170	290	.586	147	209	.703	389	52	487	12.2	1.6	15.2
Totals	96	2261	352	547	.644	243	379	.641	823	75	947	8.6	0.8	9.9

NBA REGULAR-SEASON RECORD

RECORDS: Holds career record for most consecutive seasons leading league in blocked shots—3 (1993-94 through 1995-96).
HONORS: NBA Defensive Player of the Year (1995). ... NBA All-Rookie first team (1992). ... NBA All-Defensive second team (1995).
NOTES: Led NBA with 4.10 blocked shots per game (1994), 3.91 blocked shots per game (1995) and 4.49 blocked shots per game (1996).

									REBOUNDS								AVERAGES		
Season Team	G	Min.	FGM	FGA	Pct.	FTM	FTA	Pct.	Off.	Def.	Tot.	Ast.	St.	Blk.	TO	Pts.	RPG	APG	PPG
91-92—Denver	71	2716	428	869	.493	321	500	.642	316	554	870	156	43	210	252	1177	12.3	2.2	16.6
92-93—Denver	82	3029	398	781	.510	335	492	.681	344	726	1070	147	43	287	216	1131	13.0	1.8	13.8
93-94—Denver	82	2853	365	642	.569	256	439	.583	286	685	971	127	59	*336	206	986	11.8	1.5	12.0
94-95—Denver	82	3100	349	628	.556	248	379	.654	319	710	*1029	113	40	*321	192	946	12.5	1.4	11.5
95-96—Denver	74	2713	284	569	.499	246	354	.695	249	622	871	108	38	*332	150	814	11.8	1.5	11.0
Totals	391	14411	1824	3489	.523	1406	2164	.650	1514	3297	4811	651	223	1486	1016	5054	12.3	1.7	12.9

Three-point field goals: 1993-94, 0-for-1. 1995-96, 0-for-1. Totals, 0-for-2.
Personal fouls/disqualifications: 1991-92, 273/1. 1992-93, 284/5. 1993-94, 262/2. 1994-95, 284/2. 1995-96, 258/4. Totals, 1361/14.

NBA PLAYOFF RECORD

									REBOUNDS								AVERAGES		
Season Team	G	Min.	FGM	FGA	Pct.	FTM	FTA	Pct.	Off.	Def.	Tot.	Ast.	St.	Blk.	TO	Pts.	RPG	APG	PPG
93-94—Denver	12	511	50	108	.463	59	98	.602	40	104	144	21	8	69	30	159	12.0	1.8	13.3
94-95—Denver	3	84	6	10	.600	6	9	.667	4	15	19	1	0	7	7	18	6.3	0.3	6.0
Totals	15	595	56	118	.475	65	107	.607	44	119	163	22	8	76	37	177	10.9	1.5	11.8

Personal fouls/disqualifications: 1993-94, 42/0. 1994-95, 15/1. Totals, 57/1.

NBA ALL-STAR GAME RECORD

							REBOUNDS								
Season Team	Min.	FGM	FGA	Pct.	FTM	FTA	Pct.	Off.	Def.	Tot.	Ast.	PF	Dq.	St.	Blk.	TO	Pts.
1992 —Denver..............	10	2	4	.500	0	0	...	1	1	2	1	0	0	1	0	2	4
1995 —Denver..............	20	6	8	.750	0	0	...	3	5	8	1	3	0	0	4	0	12
1996 —Denver..............	11	2	4	.500	0	0	...	6	3	9	0	3	0	0	0	3	4
Totals.........................	41	10	16	.625	0	0	...	10	9	19	2	6	0	1	4	5	20

MYERS, PETE   G/F   HORNETS

PERSONAL: Born September 15, 1963, in Mobile, Ala. ... 6-6/180. ... Full name: Peter E. Myers.
HIGH SCHOOL: Williamson (Mobile, Ala.).
JUNIOR COLLEGE: Faulkner State Junior College (Ala.)..
COLLEGE: Arkansas-Little Rock.
TRANSACTIONS/CAREER NOTES: Selected by Chicago Bulls in sixth round (120th pick overall) of 1986 NBA Draft. ... Waived by Bulls (November 3, 1987). ... Played in Continental Basketball Association with Rockford Lightning (1987-88).

... Signed as free agent by San Antonio Spurs (January 29, 1988). ... Traded by Spurs to Philadelphia 76ers for F Albert King (August 24, 1988). ... Waived by 76ers (December 15, 1988). ... Signed as free agent by New York Knicks (December 20, 1988). ... Claimed off waivers by New Jersey Nets (February 27, 1990). ... Waived by Nets (October 30, 1990). ... Signed as free agent by Spurs (December 10, 1990). ... Waived by Spurs (December 24, 1990). ... Signed as free agent by Washington Bullets (October 5, 1992). ... Waived by Bullets (October 26, 1992). ... Played in Italy (1991-92 and 1992-93). ... Signed as free agent by Bulls (October 7, 1993). ... Signed as unrestricted free agent by Charlotte Hornets (October 3, 1995). ... Traded by Hornets with C LeRon Ellis and C Alonzo Mourning to Miami Heat for G/F Glen Rice, G Khalid Reeves, C Matt Geiger and 1996 first-round draft choice (November 3, 1995). ... Waived by Heat (February 12, 1996). ... Signed as free agent by Hornets (February 16, 1996).

COLLEGIATE RECORD

Season Team	G	Min.	FGM	FGA	Pct.	FTM	FTA	Pct.	Reb.	Ast.	Pts.	RPG	APG	PPG
81-82—Faulkner State J.C.	26	...	109	199	.548	104	140	.743	132	...	322	5.1	...	12.4
82-83—Faulkner State J.C.	26	...	144	249	.578	106	196	.627	196	...	394	7.5	...	15.2
83-84—Ark.-Little Rock						Did not play.								
84-85—Ark.-Little Rock	30	...	162	359	.451	120	167	.719	213	...	444	7.1	...	14.8
85-86—Ark.-Little Rock	34	1142	229	429	.534	195	261	.747	270	...	653	7.9	...	19.2
Junior college totals	52	...	253	448	.565	210	309	.680	328	...	716	6.3	...	13.8
4-year-college totals	64	...	391	788	.496	315	428	.736	483	...	1097	7.5	...	17.1

NBA REGULAR-SEASON RECORD

Season Team	G	Min.	FGM	FGA	Pct.	FTM	FTA	Pct.	REBOUNDS Off.	Def.	Tot.	Ast.	St.	Blk.	TO	Pts.	AVERAGES RPG	APG	PPG
86-87—Chicago	29	155	19	52	.365	28	43	.651	8	9	17	21	14	2	10	66	0.6	0.7	2.3
87-88—San Antonio....	22	328	43	95	.453	26	39	.667	11	26	37	48	17	6	33	112	1.7	2.2	5.1
88-89—Phil.-N.Y.	33	270	31	73	.425	33	48	.688	15	18	33	48	20	2	23	95	1.0	1.5	2.9
89-90—N.Y.-N.J.	52	751	89	225	.396	66	100	.660	33	63	96	135	35	11	76	244	1.8	2.6	4.7
90-91—San Antonio....	8	103	10	23	.435	9	11	.818	2	16	18	14	3	3	14	29	2.3	1.8	3.6
93-94—Chicago	82	2030	253	556	.455	136	194	.701	54	127	181	245	78	20	136	650	2.2	3.0	7.9
94-95—Chicago	71	1270	119	287	.415	70	114	.614	57	82	139	148	58	15	88	318	2.0	2.1	4.5
95-96—Mia.-Char.	71	1092	91	247	.368	80	122	.656	35	105	140	145	34	17	81	276	2.0	2.0	3.9
Totals	368	5999	655	1558	.420	448	671	.668	215	446	661	804	259	76	461	1790	1.8	2.2	4.9

Three-point field goals: 1986-87, 0-for-6. 1987-88, 0-for-4. 1988-89, 0-for-2. 1989-90, 0-for-7. 1990-91, 0-for-1. 1993-94, 8-for-29 (.276). 1994-95, 10-for-39 (.256). 1995-96, 14-for-58 (.241). Totals, 32-for-146 (.219).

Personal fouls/disqualifications: 1986-87, 25/0. 1987-88, 30/0. 1988-89, 44/0. 1989-90, 109/0. 1990-91, 14/0. 1993-94, 195/1. 1994-95, 125/1. 1995-96, 132/1. Totals, 674/3.

NBA PLAYOFF RECORD

Season Team	G	Min.	FGM	FGA	Pct.	FTM	FTA	Pct.	REBOUNDS Off.	Def.	Tot.	Ast.	St.	Blk.	TO	Pts.	AVERAGES RPG	APG	PPG
86-87—Chicago	1	1	0	1	.000	0	0	...	0	0	0	0	0	0	0	0	0.0	0.0	0.0
88-89—New York	4	14	0	0	...	4	6	.667	1	2	3	1	0	1	0	4	0.8	0.3	1.0
93-94—Chicago	10	235	29	56	.518	12	21	.571	10	9	19	28	8	4	17	70	1.9	2.8	7.0
94-95—Chicago	9	79	5	14	.357	2	6	.333	6	4	10	8	4	1	4	13	1.1	0.9	1.4
Totals	24	329	34	71	.479	18	33	.545	17	15	32	37	12	6	21	87	1.3	1.5	3.6

Three-point field goals: 1993-94, 0-for-4. 1994-95, 1-for-2 (.500). Totals, 1-for-6 (.167).

Personal fouls/disqualifications: 1988-89, 2/0. 1993-94, 21/0. 1994-95, 10/0. Totals, 33/0.

CBA REGULAR-SEASON RECORD

NOTES: CBA All-League second team (1988).

Season Team	G	Min.	FGM	FGA	Pct.	FTM	FTA	Pct.	Reb.	Ast.	Pts.	RPG	APG	PPG
87-88—Rockford	28	1134	216	406	.532	146	199	.734	103	147	588	3.7	5.3	21.0

Three-point field goals: 1987-88, 10-for-26 (.385).

ITALIAN LEAGUE RECORD

Season Team	G	Min.	FGM	FGA	Pct.	FTM	FTA	Pct.	Reb.	Ast.	Pts.	RPG	APG	PPG
91-92—Mang. Bologna..............	28	1074	176	363	.485	175	233	.751	177	54	543	6.3	1.9	19.4
92-93—Scavolini Pesaro............	20	641	122	225	.542	112	144	.778	106	26	381	5.3	1.3	19.1
Totals	48	1715	298	588	.507	287	377	.761	283	80	924	5.9	1.7	19.3

NATHAN, HOWARD   G

PERSONAL: Born January 21, 1972, in Peoria, Ill. ... 5-11/175.
HIGH SCHOOL: Manual (Peoria, Ill.).
JUNIOR COLLEGE: Northwest Arkansas Community College.
COLLEGE: DePaul, then Northeast Louisiana..
TRANSACTIONS/CAREER NOTES: Not drafted by an NBA franchise. ... Signed as free agent by Atlanta Hawks (October 5, 1995). ... Waived by Hawks (December 14, 1995). ... Re-signed by Hawks to 10-day contract (February 22, 1996). ... Waived by Hawks from 10-day contract (March 2, 1996).

COLLEGIATE RECORD

Season Team	G	Min.	FGM	FGA	Pct.	FTM	FTA	Pct.	Reb.	Ast.	Pts.	RPG	APG	PPG
91-92—DePaul...........................	29	690	68	176	.386	61	89	.685	71	123	223	2.4	4.2	7.7
92-93—Northeast Louisiana	23	...	112	267	.419	72	95	.758	57	179	322	2.5	7.8	14.0
Totals	52	...	180	443	.406	133	184	.723	128	302	545	2.5	5.8	10.5

Three-point field goals: 1991-92, 26-for-70 (.371). 1992-93, 26-for-102 (.255). Totals, 52-for-172 (.302).

Season Team	G	Min.	FGM	FGA	Pct.	FTM	FTA	Pct.	REBOUNDS			Ast.	St.	Blk.	TO	Pts.	AVERAGES		
									Off.	Def.	Tot.						RPG	APG	PPG
95-96—Atlanta	5	15	5	9	.556	3	4	.750	0	0	0	2	3	0	8	13	0.0	0.4	2.6

Three-point field goals: 1995-96, 0-for-1.
Personal fouls/disqualifications: 1995-96, 2/0.

NEWMAN, JOHNNY   F   BUCKS

PERSONAL: Born November 28, 1963, in Danville, Va. ... 6-7/205. ... Full name: John Sylvester Newman Jr.
HIGH SCHOOL: George Washington (Danville, Va.).
COLLEGE: Richmond.
TRANSACTIONS/CAREER NOTES: Selected by Cleveland Cavaliers in second round (29th pick overall) of 1986 NBA Draft. ... Waived by Cavaliers (November 5, 1987). ... Signed as free agent by New York Knicks (November 12, 1987). ... Signed as unrestricted free agent by Charlotte Hornets (July 28, 1990). ... Traded by Hornets to New Jersey Nets for G Rumeal Robinson (December 10, 1993). ... Signed as free agent by Milwaukee Bucks (October 7, 1994).

COLLEGIATE RECORD

Season Team	G	Min.	FGM	FGA	Pct.	FTM	FTA	Pct.	Reb.	Ast.	Pts.	AVERAGES		
												RPG	APG	PPG
82-83—Richmond......................	28	763	137	259	.529	69	96	.719	87	24	343	3.1	0.9	12.3
83-84—Richmond......................	32	1189	273	517	.528	155	197	.787	196	31	701	6.1	1.0	21.9
84-85—Richmond......................	32	1128	270	490	.551	140	181	.773	166	38	680	5.2	1.2	21.3
85-86—Richmond......................	30	1123	253	489	.517	153	172	.890	219	28	659	7.3	0.9	22.0
Totals	122	4203	933	1755	.532	517	646	.800	668	121	2383	5.5	1.0	19.5

NBA REGULAR-SEASON RECORD

Season Team	G	Min.	FGM	FGA	Pct.	FTM	FTA	Pct.	REBOUNDS			Ast.	St.	Blk.	TO	Pts.	AVERAGES		
									Off.	Def.	Tot.						RPG	APG	PPG
86-87—Cleveland	59	630	113	275	.411	66	76	.868	36	34	70	27	20	7	46	293	1.2	0.5	5.0
87-88—New York	77	1589	270	620	.435	207	246	.841	87	72	159	62	72	11	103	773	2.1	0.8	10.0
88-89—New York	81	2336	455	957	.475	286	351	.815	93	113	206	162	111	23	153	1293	2.5	2.0	16.0
89-90—New York	80	2277	374	786	.476	239	299	.799	60	131	191	180	95	22	143	1032	2.4	2.3	12.9
90-91—Charlotte	81	2477	478	1017	.470	385	476	.809	94	160	254	188	100	17	189	1371	3.1	2.3	16.9
91-92—Charlotte	55	1651	295	618	.477	236	308	.766	71	108	179	146	70	14	129	839	3.3	2.7	15.3
92-93—Charlotte	64	1471	279	534	.522	194	240	.808	72	71	143	117	45	19	90	764	2.2	1.8	11.9
93-94—Char.-N.J.	81	1697	313	664	.471	182	225	.809	86	94	180	72	69	27	90	832	2.2	0.9	10.3
94-95—Milwaukee	82	1896	226	488	.463	137	171	.801	72	101	173	91	90	13	86	634	2.1	1.1	7.7
95-96—Milwaukee	82	2690	321	649	.495	186	232	.802	66	134	200	154	90	15	108	889	2.4	1.9	10.8
Totals	742	18714	3124	6608	.473	2118	2624	.807	737	1018	1755	1199	741	168	1137	8720	2.4	1.6	11.8

Three-point field goals: 1986-87, 1-for-22 (.045). 1987-88, 26-for-93 (.280). 1988-89, 97-for-287 (.338). 1989-90, 45-for-142 (.317). 1990-91, 30-for-84 (.357). 1991-92, 13-for-46 (.283). 1992-93, 12-for-45 (.267). 1993-94, 24-for-90 (.267). 1994-95, 45-for-128 (.352). 1995-96, 61-for-162 (.377). Totals, 354-for-1099 (.322).
Personal fouls/disqualifications: 1986-87, 67/0. 1987-88, 204/5. 1988-89, 259/4. 1989-90, 254/3. 1990-91, 278/7. 1991-92, 181/4. 1992-93, 154/1. 1993-94, 196/3. 1994-95, 234/3. 1995-96, 257/4. Totals, 2084/34.

NBA PLAYOFF RECORD

Season Team	G	Min.	FGM	FGA	Pct.	FTM	FTA	Pct.	REBOUNDS			Ast.	St.	Blk.	TO	Pts.	AVERAGES		
									Off.	Def.	Tot.						RPG	APG	PPG
87-88—New York	4	113	31	68	.456	14	16	.875	8	3	11	7	6	1	6	76	2.8	1.8	19.0
88-89—New York	9	258	50	107	.467	38	49	.776	13	12	25	17	8	1	18	145	2.8	1.9	16.1
89-90—New York	10	231	38	85	.447	37	49	.755	11	10	21	10	9	3	17	117	2.1	1.0	11.7
92-93—Charlotte	9	173	28	55	.509	11	16	.688	7	12	19	18	10	1	15	68	2.1	2.0	7.6
93-94—New Jersey	4	54	3	13	.231	5	7	.714	2	3	5	2	2	2	3	12	1.3	0.5	3.0
Totals	36	829	150	328	.457	105	137	.766	41	40	81	54	35	8	59	418	2.3	1.5	11.6

Three-point field goals: 1987-88, 0-for-9. 1988-89, 7-for-28 (.250). 1989-90, 4-for-10 (.400). 1992-93, 1-for-5 (.200). 1993-94, 1-for-4 (.250). Totals, 13-for-56 (.232).
Personal fouls/disqualifications: 1987-88, 16/0. 1988-89, 27/1. 1989-90, 41/1. 1992-93, 19/0. 1993-94, 11/0. Totals, 114/2.

NORMAN, KEN   F   HAWKS

PERSONAL: Born September 5, 1964, in Chicago. ... 6-8/228. ... Full name: Kenneth Darnel Norman. ... Known as Ken Colliers in high school. ... Half-brother of Bobby Duckworth, wide receiver with San Diego Chargers, Los Angeles Rams and Philadelphia Eagles (1982 through 1986).
HIGH SCHOOL: Richard T. Crane (Chicago).
JUNIOR COLLEGE: Wabash Valley (Ill.).
COLLEGE: Illinois.
TRANSACTIONS/CAREER NOTES: Selected by Los Angeles Clippers in first round (19th pick overall) of 1987 NBA Draft. ... Signed as free agent by Milwaukee Bucks (July 7, 1993). ... Traded by Bucks to Atlanta Hawks for F Roy Hinson (June 22, 1994).

COLLEGIATE RECORD

NOTES: The Sporting News All-America second team (1987).

Season Team	G	Min.	FGM	FGA	Pct.	FTM	FTA	Pct.	Reb.	Ast.	Pts.	AVERAGES		
												RPG	APG	PPG
82-83—Wabash Valley	35	...	302	499	.605	111	165	.673	362	73	715	10.3	2.1	20.4
83-84—Illinois					Did not play—redshirted.									
84-85—Illinois	29	462	86	136	.632	55	83	.663	107	26	227	3.7	0.9	7.8
85-86—Illinois	32	1015	216	337	.641	93	116	.802	226	32	525	7.1	1.0	16.4
86-87—Illinois	31	1112	256	443	.578	128	176	.727	303	68	641	9.8	2.2	20.7
Junior college totals	35	...	302	499	.605	111	165	.673	362	73	715	10.3	2.1	20.4
4-year-college totals	92	2589	558	916	.609	276	375	.736	636	126	1393	6.9	1.4	15.1

Three-point field goals: 1986-87, 1-for-4 (.250).

NBA REGULAR-SEASON RECORD

Season Team	G	Min.	FGM	FGA	Pct.	FTM	FTA	Pct.	REBOUNDS Off.	Def.	Tot.	Ast.	St.	Blk.	TO	Pts.	AVERAGES RPG	APG	PPG
87-88—L.A. Clippers...	66	1435	241	500	.482	87	170	.512	100	163	263	78	44	34	103	569	4.0	1.2	8.6
88-89—L.A. Clippers...	80	3020	638	1271	.502	170	270	.630	245	422	667	277	106	66	206	1450	8.3	3.5	18.1
89-90—L.A. Clippers...	70	2334	484	949	.510	153	242	.632	143	327	470	160	78	59	190	1128	6.7	2.3	16.1
90-91—L.A. Clippers...	70	2309	520	1037	.501	173	275	.629	177	320	497	159	63	63	139	1219	7.1	2.3	17.4
91-92—L.A. Clippers...	77	2009	402	821	.490	121	226	.535	158	290	448	125	53	66	100	929	5.8	1.6	12.1
92-93—L.A. Clippers...	76	2477	498	975	.511	131	220	.595	209	362	571	165	59	58	125	1137	7.5	2.2	15.0
93-94—Milwaukee	82	2539	412	919	.448	92	183	.503	169	331	500	222	58	46	150	979	6.1	2.7	11.9
94-95—Atlanta	74	1879	388	856	.453	64	140	.457	103	259	362	94	34	20	96	938	4.9	1.3	12.7
95-96—Atlanta	34	770	127	273	.465	17	48	.354	40	92	132	63	15	16	46	304	3.9	1.9	8.9
Totals	629	18772	3710	7601	.488	1008	1774	.568	1344	2566	3910	1343	510	428	1155	8653	6.2	2.1	13.8

Three-point field goals: 1987-88, 0-for-10. 1988-89, 4-for-21 (.190). 1989-90, 7-for-16 (.438). 1990-91, 6-for-32 (.188). 1991-92, 4-for-28 (.143). 1992-93, 10-for-38 (.263). 1993-94, 63-for-189 (.333). 1994-95, 98-for-285 (.344). 1995-96, 33-for-84 (.393). Totals, 225-for-703 (.320).

Personal fouls/disqualifications: 1987-88, 123/0. 1988-89, 223/2. 1989-90, 196/0. 1990-91, 192/0. 1991-92, 145/0. 1992-93, 156/0. 1993-94, 209/2. 1994-95, 154/0. 1995-96, 68/0. Totals, 1466/4.

NBA PLAYOFF RECORD

Season Team	G	Min.	FGM	FGA	Pct.	FTM	FTA	Pct.	REBOUNDS Off.	Def.	Tot.	Ast.	St.	Blk.	TO	Pts.	AVERAGES RPG	APG	PPG
91-92—L.A. Clippers...	5	184	27	53	.509	9	17	.529	19	30	49	15	4	3	6	63	9.8	3.0	12.6
92-93—L.A. Clippers...	5	164	25	67	.373	11	22	.500	14	27	41	12	4	0	1	64	8.2	2.4	12.8
94-95—Atlanta	3	42	7	18	.389	1	7	.143	2	7	9	3	0	1	3	16	3.0	1.0	5.3
Totals	13	390	59	138	.428	21	46	.457	35	64	99	30	8	4	10	143	7.6	2.3	11.0

Three-point field goals: 1991-92, 0-for-2. 1992-93, 3-for-8 (.375). 1994-95, 1-for-8 (.125). Totals, 4-for-18 (.222).

Personal fouls/disqualifications: 1991-92, 18/0. 1992-93, 8/0. 1994-95, 13/1. Totals, 39/1.

OAKLEY, CHARLES　　　　　F　　　　　KNICKS

PERSONAL: Born December 18, 1963, in Cleveland. ... 6-9/245.

HIGH SCHOOL: John Hay (Cleveland).

COLLEGE: Virginia Union.

TRANSACTIONS/CAREER NOTES: Selected by Cleveland Cavaliers in first round (ninth pick overall) of 1985 NBA Draft. ... Draft rights traded by Cavaliers with draft rights to G Calvin Duncan to Chicago Bulls for G Ennis Whatley and draft rights to F Keith Lee (June 18, 1985). ... Traded by Bulls with 1988 first- and third-round draft choices to New York Knicks for C Bill Cartwright and 1988 first- and third-round draft choices (June 27, 1988).

COLLEGIATE RECORD

NOTES: Led NCAA Division II with 17.3 rebounds per game (1985).

Season Team	G	Min.	FGM	FGA	Pct.	FTM	FTA	Pct.	Reb.	Ast.	Pts.	AVERAGES RPG	APG	PPG
81-82—Virginia Union	28	...	169	274	.617	106	174	.609	349	...	444	12.5	...	15.9
82-83—Virginia Union	28	...	220	378	.582	100	170	.588	365	28	540	13.0	1.0	19.3
83-84—Virginia Union	30	...	256	418	.612	139	224	.621	393	...	651	13.1	...	21.7
84-85—Virginia Union	31	...	283	453	.625	178	266	.669	535	66	744	17.3	2.1	24.0
Totals	117	...	928	1523	.609	523	834	.627	1642	...	2379	14.0	...	20.3

NBA REGULAR-SEASON RECORD

HONORS: NBA All-Defensive first team (1994). ... NBA All-Rookie team (1986).

Season Team	G	Min.	FGM	FGA	Pct.	FTM	FTA	Pct.	REBOUNDS Off.	Def.	Tot.	Ast.	St.	Blk.	TO	Pts.	AVERAGES RPG	APG	PPG
85-86—Chicago	77	1772	281	541	.519	178	269	.662	255	409	664	133	68	30	175	740	8.6	1.7	9.6
86-87—Chicago	82	2980	468	1052	.445	245	357	.686	299	*775	*1074	296	85	36	299	1192	13.1	3.6	14.5
87-88—Chicago	82	2816	375	776	.483	261	359	.727	326	*740	*1066	248	68	28	241	1014	13.0	3.0	12.4
88-89—New York	82	2604	426	835	.510	197	255	.773	343	518	861	187	104	14	248	1061	10.5	2.3	12.9
89-90—New York	61	2196	336	641	.524	217	285	.761	258	469	727	146	46	16	165	889	11.9	2.4	14.6
90-91—New York	76	2739	307	595	.516	239	305	.784	305	615	920	204	62	17	215	853	12.1	2.7	11.2
91-92—New York	82	2309	210	402	.522	86	117	.735	256	444	700	133	67	15	123	506	8.5	1.6	6.2
92-93—New York	82	2230	219	431	.508	127	176	.722	288	420	708	126	85	15	124	565	8.6	1.5	6.9
93-94—New York	82	2932	363	760	.478	243	313	.776	349	616	965	218	110	18	193	969	11.8	2.7	11.8
94-95—New York	50	1567	192	393	.489	119	150	.793	155	290	445	126	60	7	103	506	8.9	2.5	10.1
95-96—New York	53	1775	211	448	.471	175	210	.833	162	298	460	137	58	14	104	604	8.7	2.6	11.4
Totals	809	25920	3388	6874	.493	2087	2796	.746	2996	5594	8590	1954	831	210	1990	8899	10.6	2.4	11.0

Three-point field goals: 1985-86, 0-for-3. 1986-87, 11-for-30 (.367). 1987-88, 3-for-12 (.250). 1988-89, 12-for-48 (.250). 1989-90, 0-for-3. 1990-91, 0-for-2. 1991-92, 0-for-3. 1992-93, 0-for-1. 1993-94, 0-for-3. 1994-95, 3-for-12 (.250). 1995-96, 7-for-26 (.269). Totals, 36-for-143 (.252).

Personal fouls/disqualifications: 1985-86, 250/9. 1986-87, 315/4. 1987-88, 272/2. 1988-89, 270/1. 1989-90, 220/3. 1990-91, 288/4. 1991-92, 258/2. 1992-93, 289/5. 1993-94, 293/4. 1994-95, 179/3. 1995-96, 195/6. Totals, 2829/43.

NBA PLAYOFF RECORD

Season Team	G	Min.	FGM	FGA	Pct.	FTM	FTA	Pct.	REBOUNDS Off.	Def.	Tot.	Ast.	St.	Blk.	TO	Pts.	AVERAGES RPG	APG	PPG
85-86—Chicago	3	88	11	21	.524	8	13	.615	10	20	30	3	6	2	5	30	10.0	1.0	10.0
86-87—Chicago	3	129	19	50	.380	20	24	.833	17	29	46	6	4	1	8	60	15.3	2.0	20.0
87-88—Chicago	10	373	40	91	.440	21	24	.875	39	89	128	32	6	4	18	101	12.8	3.2	10.1
88-89—New York	9	299	35	73	.479	16	24	.667	43	58	101	11	12	1	22	87	11.2	1.2	9.7
89-90—New York	10	336	43	84	.512	34	52	.654	39	71	110	27	11	2	22	121	11.0	2.7	12.1
90-91—New York	3	100	10	21	.476	3	6	.500	15	16	31	3	2	1	7	23	10.3	1.0	7.7
91-92—New York	12	354	22	58	.379	20	27	.741	44	64	108	8	8	5	15	64	9.0	0.7	5.3
92-93—New York	15	507	63	131	.481	40	55	.727	71	94	165	17	16	2	36	166	11.0	1.1	11.1
93-94—New York	25	992	125	262	.477	79	102	.775	116	176	292	59	35	5	65	329	11.7	2.4	13.2

Season Team	G	Min.	FGM	FGA	Pct.	FTM	FTA	Pct.	REBOUNDS Off.	Def.	Tot.	Ast.	St.	Blk.	TO	Pts.	AVERAGES RPG	APG	PPG
94-95—New York	11	421	49	109	.450	42	51	.824	31	62	93	41	19	6	24	144	8.5	3.7	13.1
95-96—New York	8	308	39	78	.500	25	36	.694	28	41	69	14	8	0	28	105	8.6	1.8	13.1
Totals	109	3907	456	978	.466	308	414	.744	453	720	1173	221	127	29	250	1230	10.8	2.0	11.3

Three-point field goals: 1986-87, 2-for-4 (.500). 1987-88, 0-for-2. 1988-89, 1-for-2 (.500). 1989-90, 1-for-1. 1994-95, 4-for-10 (.400). 1995-96, 2-for-6 (.333). Totals, 10-for-25 (.400).

Personal fouls/disqualifications: 1985-86, 13/0. 1986-87, 13/0. 1987-88, 33/0. 1988-89, 31/1. 1989-90, 33/1. 1990-91, 13/0. 1991-92, 36/0. 1992-93, 51/1. 1993-94, 87/1. 1994-95, 42/0. 1995-96, 33/1. Totals, 385/5.

NBA ALL-STAR GAME RECORD

Season Team	Min.	FGM	FGA	Pct.	FTM	FTA	Pct.	REBOUNDS Off.	Def.	Tot.	Ast.	PF	Dq.	St.	Blk.	TO	Pts.
1994 —New York	11	1	3	.333	0	0	...	1	2	3	3	3	0	0	0	0	2

O'BANNON, ED   F   NETS

PERSONAL: Born August 14, 1972, in Los Angeles. ... 6-8/222. ... Full name: Edward Charles O'Bannon Jr.
HIGH SCHOOL: Artesia (Lakewood, Calif.).
COLLEGE: UCLA.
TRANSACTIONS/CAREER NOTES: Selected by New Jersey Nets in first round (ninth pick overall) of 1995 NBA Draft.

COLLEGIATE RECORD

NOTES: Wooden Award winner (1995). ... THE SPORTING NEWS All-America second team (1995). ... NCAA Division I Tournament Most Outstanding Player (1995). ... Member of NCAA Division I championship team (1995).

Season Team	G	Min.	FGM	FGA	Pct.	FTM	FTA	Pct.	Reb.	Ast.	Pts.	AVERAGES RPG	APG	PPG
90-91—UCLA					Did not play—knee injury.									
91-92—UCLA	23	287	32	77	.416	17	27	.630	70	12	83	3.0	0.5	3.6
92-93—UCLA	33	1099	208	386	.539	116	164	.707	230	56	550	7.0	1.7	16.7
93-94—UCLA	28	961	191	395	.484	111	149	.745	245	59	509	8.8	2.1	18.2
94-95—UCLA	33	1130	247	463	.533	124	158	.785	275	81	673	8.3	2.5	20.4
Totals	117	3477	678	1321	.513	368	498	.739	820	208	1815	7.0	1.8	15.5

Three-point field goals: 1991-92, 2-for-8 (.250). 1992-93, 18-for-40 (.450). 1993-94, 16-for-56 (.286). 1994-95, 55-for-127 (.433). Totals, 91-for-231 (.394).

NBA REGULAR-SEASON RECORD

Season Team	G	Min.	FGM	FGA	Pct.	FTM	FTA	Pct.	REBOUNDS Off.	Def.	Tot.	Ast.	St.	Blk.	TO	Pts.	AVERAGES RPG	APG	PPG
95-96—New Jersey	64	1253	156	400	.390	77	108	.713	65	103	168	63	44	11	62	399	2.6	1.0	6.2

Three-point field goals: 1995-96, 10-for-56 (.179).
Personal fouls/disqualifications: 1995-96, 95/0.

OLAJUWON, HAKEEM   C   ROCKETS

O

PERSONAL: Born January 21, 1963, in Lagos, Nigeria. ... 7-0/255. ... Full name: Hakeem Abdul Olajuwon. ... Name pronounced ah-KEEM a-LIE-shoe-on. ... Known as Akeem Olajuwon until March 9, 1991. ... Nickname: The Dream.
HIGH SCHOOL: Muslim Teachers College (Lagos, Nigeria).
COLLEGE: Houston.
TRANSACTIONS/CAREER NOTES: Selected by Houston Rockets in first round (first pick overall) of 1984 NBA Draft.
MISCELLANEOUS: Member of NBA championship teams (1994, 1995). ... Member of gold-medal-winning U.S. Olympic team (1996). ... Houston Rockets franchise all-time leading scorer with 21,840 points, all-time leading rebounder with 11,023, all-time steals leader with 1,694 and all-time blocked shots leader with 3,190 (1984-85 through 1995-96).

COLLEGIATE RECORD

NOTES: THE SPORTING NEWS All-America first team (1984). ... NCAA Division I Tournament Most Outstanding Player (1983). ... Led NCAA Division I with .675 field-goal percentage (1984). ... Led NCAA Division I with 13.5 rebounds per game (1984). ... Led NCAA Division I with 5.6 blocked shots per game (1984).

Season Team	G	Min.	FGM	FGA	Pct.	FTM	FTA	Pct.	Reb.	Ast.	Pts.	AVERAGES RPG	APG	PPG
80-81—Houston					Did not play.									
81-82—Houston	29	529	91	150	.607	58	103	.563	179	11	240	6.2	0.4	8.3
82-83—Houston	34	932	192	314	.611	88	148	.595	388	29	472	11.4	0.9	13.9
83-84—Houston	37	1260	249	369	.675	122	232	.526	500	48	620	13.5	1.3	16.8
Totals	100	2721	532	833	.639	268	483	.555	1067	88	1332	10.7	0.9	13.3

NBA REGULAR-SEASON RECORD

RECORDS: Holds career record for most blocked shots—3,190.
HONORS: NBA Most Valuable Player (1994). ... NBA Defensive Player of the Year (1993, 1994). ... IBM Award, for all-around contributions to team's success (1993). ... All-NBA first team (1987, 1988, 1989, 1993, 1994). ... All-NBA second team (1986, 1990, 1996). ... All-NBA third team (1991, 1995). ... NBA All-Defensive first team (1987, 1988, 1990, 1993, 1994). ... NBA All-Defensive second team (1985, 1991, 1996). ... NBA All-Rookie team (1985).
NOTES: Led NBA with 4.59 blocked shots per game (1990), 3.95 blocked shots per game (1991) and 4.17 blocked shots per game (1993). ... Led NBA with 344 personal fouls (1985).

Season Team	G	Min.	FGM	FGA	Pct.	FTM	FTA	Pct.	REBOUNDS Off.	Def.	Tot.	Ast.	St.	Blk.	TO	Pts.	AVERAGES RPG	APG	PPG
84-85—Houston	82	2914	677	1258	.538	338	551	.613	*440	534	974	111	99	220	234	1692	11.9	1.4	20.6
85-86—Houston	68	2467	625	1188	.526	347	538	.645	333	448	781	137	134	231	195	1597	11.5	2.0	23.5
86-87—Houston	75	2760	677	1332	.508	400	570	.702	315	543	858	220	140	254	228	1755	11.4	2.9	23.4

Season Team	G	Min.	FGM	FGA	Pct.	FTM	FTA	Pct.	Off.	Def.	Tot.	Ast.	St.	Blk.	TO	Pts.	RPG	APG	PPG
87-88—Houston	79	2825	712	1385	.514	381	548	.695	302	657	959	163	162	214	243	1805	12.1	2.1	22.8
88-89—Houston	82	3024	790	1556	.508	454	652	.696	338	*767	*1105	149	213	282	275	2034	*13.5	1.8	24.8
89-90—Houston	82	3124	806	1609	.501	382	536	.713	299	*850	*1149	234	174	*376	316	1995	*14.0	2.9	24.3
90-91—Houston	56	2062	487	959	.508	213	277	.769	219	551	770	131	121	221	174	1187	13.8	2.3	21.2
91-92—Houston	70	2636	591	1177	.502	328	428	.766	246	599	845	157	127	304	187	1510	12.1	2.2	21.6
92-93—Houston	82	3242	848	1603	.529	444	570	.779	283	785	1068	291	150	*342	262	2140	13.0	3.5	26.1
93-94—Houston	80	3277	894	*1694	.528	388	542	.716	229	726	955	287	128	297	271	2184	11.9	3.6	27.3
94-95—Houston	72	2853	798	1545	.517	406	537	.756	172	603	775	255	133	242	237	2005	10.8	3.5	27.8
95-96—Houston	72	2797	768	1494	.514	397	548	.724	176	608	784	257	113	207	247	1936	10.9	3.6	26.9
Totals	900	33981	8673	16800	.516	4478	6297	.711	3352	7671	11023	2392	1694	3190	2869	21840	12.2	2.7	24.3

Three-point field goals: 1986-87, 1-for-5 (.200). 1987-88, 0-for-4. 1988-89, 0-for-10. 1989-90, 1-for-6 (.167). 1990-91, 0-for-4. 1991-92, 0-for-1. 1992-93, 0-for-8. 1993-94, 8-for-19 (.421). 1994-95, 3-for-16 (.188). 1995-96, 3-for-14 (.214). Totals, 16-for-87 (.184).

Personal fouls/disqualifications: 1984-85, 344/10. 1985-86, 271/9. 1986-87, 294/8. 1987-88, 324/7. 1988-89, 329/10. 1989-90, 314/6. 1990-91, 221/5. 1991-92, 263/7. 1992-93, 305/5. 1993-94, 289/4. 1994-95, 250/3. 1995-96, 242/0. Totals, 3446/74.

NBA PLAYOFF RECORD

NOTES: NBA Finals Most Valuable Player (1994, 1995). ... Shares NBA Finals single game record for most blocked shots—8 (June 5, 1986, vs. Boston). ... Shares single-game playoff record for most blocked shots—10 (April 29, 1990, vs. Los Angeles Lakers).

Season Team	G	Min.	FGM	FGA	Pct.	FTM	FTA	Pct.	Off.	Def.	Tot.	Ast.	St.	Blk.	TO	Pts.	RPG	APG	PPG
84-85—Houston	5	187	42	88	.477	22	46	.478	33	32	65	7	7	13	11	106	13.0	1.4	21.2
85-86—Houston	20	766	205	387	.530	127	199	.638	101	135	236	39	40	69	43	537	11.8	2.0	26.9
86-87—Houston	10	389	110	179	.615	72	97	.742	39	74	113	25	13	43	36	292	11.3	2.5	29.2
87-88—Houston	4	162	56	98	.571	38	43	.884	20	47	67	7	9	11	9	150	16.8	1.8	37.5
88-89—Houston	4	162	42	81	.519	17	25	.680	14	38	52	12	10	11	10	101	13.0	3.0	25.3
89-90—Houston	4	161	31	70	.443	12	17	.706	15	31	46	8	10	23	11	74	11.5	2.0	18.5
90-91—Houston	3	129	26	45	.578	14	17	.824	12	32	44	6	4	8	8	66	14.7	2.0	22.0
92-93—Houston	12	518	123	238	.517	62	75	.827	52	116	168	57	21	59	45	308	14.0	4.8	25.7
93-94—Houston	23	989	267	514	.519	128	161	.795	55	199	254	98	40	92	83	664	11.0	4.3	28.9
94-95—Houston	22	929	306	576	.531	111	163	.681	44	183	227	98	26	62	69	725	10.3	4.5	33.0
95-96—Houston	8	329	75	147	.510	29	40	.725	17	56	73	31	15	17	29	179	9.1	3.9	22.4
Totals	115	4721	1283	2423	.530	632	883	.716	402	943	1345	388	195	408	354	3202	11.7	3.4	27.8

Three-point field goals: 1985-86, 0-for-1. 1986-87, 0-for-1. 1987-88, 0-for-1. 1990-91, 0-for-1. 1992-93, 0-for-1. 1993-94, 2-for-4 (.500). 1994-95, 2-for-4 (.500). 1995-96, 0-for-1. Totals, 4-for-14 (.286).

Personal fouls/disqualifications: 1984-85, 22/0. 1985-86, 87/3. 1986-87, 44/1. 1987-88, 14/0. 1988-89, 17/0. 1989-90, 19/0. 1990-91, 11/0. 1992-93, 37/0. 1993-94, 82/0. 1994-95, 95/0. 1995-96, 28/1. Totals, 456/5.

NBA ALL-STAR GAME RECORD

Season Team	Min.	FGM	FGA	Pct.	FTM	FTA	Pct.	Off.	Def.	Tot.	Ast.	PF	Dq.	St.	Blk.	TO	Pts.
1985 —Houston	15	2	2	1.000	2	6	.333	2	3	5	1	1	0	0	2	0	6
1986 —Houston	15	1	8	.125	1	2	.500	1	4	5	0	3	0	1	2	1	3
1987 —Houston	26	2	6	.333	6	8	.750	4	9	13	2	6	1	0	3	1	10
1988 —Houston	28	8	13	.615	5	7	.714	7	2	9	2	3	0	2	2	4	21
1989 —Houston	25	5	12	.417	2	3	.667	4	3	7	3	2	0	3	2	3	12
1990 —Houston	31	2	14	.143	4	10	.400	9	7	16	2	1	0	1	1	4	8
1992 —Houston	20	3	6	.500	1	2	.500	0	4	4	2	3	0	2	1	3	7
1993 —Houston	21	1	5	.200	1	2	.500	2	5	7	1	3	0	2	2	3	3
1994 —Houston	30	8	15	.533	3	6	.500	4	7	11	2	4	0	2	5	3	19
1995 —Houston	25	6	13	.462	0	2	.000	4	7	11	1	2	0	2	3	3	13
1996 —Houston	14	2	8	.250	0	0	...	1	2	3	0	2	0	0	0	0	4
Totals	250	40	102	.392	25	48	.521	38	53	91	16	30	1	15	22	25	106

Three-point field goals: 1995, 1-for-1.

O'NEAL, SHAQUILLE   C   LAKERS   0

PERSONAL: Born March 6, 1972, in Newark, N.J. ... 7-1/301. ... Full name: Shaquille Rashaun O'Neal. ... Name pronounced shuh-KEEL. ... Nickname: Shaq.
HIGH SCHOOL: Cole (San Antonio).
COLLEGE: Louisiana State.
TRANSACTIONS/CAREER NOTES: Selected after junior season by Orlando Magic in first round (first pick overall) of 1992 NBA Draft. ... Signed as free agent by Los Angeles Lakers (July 18, 1996).
MISCELLANEOUS: Member of gold-medal-winning U.S. Olympic team (1996). ... Orlando Magic all-time leading rebounder with 3,691 and all-time blocked shots leader with 824 (1992-93 through 1995-96).

COLLEGIATE RECORD

NOTES: THE SPORTING NEWS All-America first team (1991, 1992). ... Led NCAA Division I with 14.7 rebounds per game (1991). ... Led NCAA Division I with 5.2 blocked shots per game (1992).

Season Team	G	Min.	FGM	FGA	Pct.	FTM	FTA	Pct.	Reb.	Ast.	Pts.	RPG	APG	PPG
89-90—Louisiana State	32	901	180	314	.573	85	153	.556	385	61	445	12.0	1.9	13.9
90-91—Louisiana State	28	881	312	497	.628	150	235	.638	411	45	774	14.7	1.6	27.6
91-92—Louisiana State	30	959	294	478	.615	134	254	.528	421	46	722	14.0	1.5	24.1
Totals	90	2741	786	1289	.610	369	642	.575	1217	152	1941	13.5	1.7	21.6

NBA REGULAR-SEASON RECORD

HONORS: NBA Rookie of the Year (1993). ... All-NBA second team (1995). ... All-NBA third team (1994, 1996). ... NBA All-Rookie first team (1993).

Season Team	G	Min.	FGM	FGA	Pct.	FTM	FTA	Pct.	Off.	Def.	Tot.	Ast.	St.	Blk.	TO	Pts.	RPG	APG	PPG
92-93—Orlando	81	3071	733	1304	.562	427	721	.592	342	780	1122	152	60	286	*307	1893	13.9	1.9	23.4
93-94—Orlando	81	3224	*953	1591	*.599	471	850	.554	384	688	1072	195	76	231	222	2377	13.2	2.4	29.3
94-95—Orlando	79	2923	*930	*1594	.583	455	*854	.533	328	573	901	214	73	192	204	*2315	11.4	2.7	*29.3
95-96—Orlando	54	1946	592	1033	.573	249	511	.487	182	414	596	155	34	115	155	1434	11.0	2.9	26.6
Totals	295	11164	3208	5522	.581	1602	2936	.546	1236	2455	3691	716	243	824	888	8019	12.5	2.4	27.2

Three-point field goals: 1992-93, 0-for-2. 1993-94, 0-for-2. 1994-95, 0-for-5. 1995-96, 1-for-2 (.500). Totals, 1-for-11 (.091).
Personal fouls/disqualifications: 1992-93, 321/8. 1993-94, 281/3. 1994-95, 258/1. 1995-96, 193/1. Totals, 1053/13.

NBA PLAYOFF RECORD

Season Team	G	Min.	FGM	FGA	Pct.	FTM	FTA	Pct.	Off.	Def.	Tot.	Ast.	St.	Blk.	TO	Pts.	RPG	APG	PPG
93-94—Orlando	3	126	23	45	.511	16	34	.471	17	23	40	7	2	9	10	62	13.3	2.3	20.7
94-95—Orlando	21	805	195	338	.577	149	261	.571	95	155	250	70	18	40	73	539	11.9	3.3	25.7
95-96—Orlando	12	459	131	216	.606	48	122	.393	49	71	120	55	9	15	44	310	10.0	4.6	25.8
Totals	36	1390	349	599	.583	213	417	.511	161	249	410	132	29	64	127	911	11.4	3.7	25.3

Personal fouls/disqualifications: 1993-94, 13/0. 1994-95, 84/1. 1995-96, 40/0. Totals, 137/1.

NBA ALL-STAR GAME RECORD

Season Team	Min.	FGM	FGA	Pct.	FTM	FTA	Pct.	Off.	Def.	Tot.	Ast.	PF	Dq.	St.	Blk.	TO	Pts.
1993 —Orlando	25	4	9	.444	6	9	.667	3	4	7	0	3	0	0	0	0	14
1994 —Orlando	26	2	12	.167	4	11	.364	4	6	10	0	2	0	1	4	1	8
1995 —Orlando	26	9	16	.563	4	7	.571	4	3	7	1	2	0	3	2	2	22
1996 —Orlando	28	10	16	.625	5	11	.455	3	7	10	1	3	0	1	2	2	25
Totals	105	25	53	.472	19	38	.500	14	20	34	2	10	0	5	8	5	69

Three-point field goals: 1995, 0-for-1.

OSTERTAG, GREG   C   JAZZ

PERSONAL: Born March 6, 1973, in Dallas. ... 7-2/280. ... Full name: Gregory Donovan Ostertag. ... Name pronounced OH-stir-tag.
HIGH SCHOOL: Duncanville (Texas).
COLLEGE: Kansas.
TRANSACTIONS/CAREER NOTES: Selected by Utah Jazz in first round (28th pick overall) of 1995 NBA Draft.

COLLEGIATE RECORD

Season Team	G	Min.	FGM	FGA	Pct.	FTM	FTA	Pct.	Reb.	Ast.	Pts.	RPG	APG	PPG
91-92—Kansas	32	311	61	112	.545	32	49	.653	112	5	154	3.5	0.2	4.8
92-93—Kansas	29	389	61	118	.517	33	55	.600	118	11	155	4.1	0.4	5.3
93-94—Kansas	35	739	145	272	.533	70	111	.631	307	12	360	8.8	0.3	10.3
94-95—Kansas	31	603	121	203	.596	57	103	.553	233	13	299	7.5	0.4	9.6
Totals	127	2042	388	705	.550	192	318	.604	770	41	968	6.1	0.3	7.6

Three-point field goals: 1991-92, 0-for-1. 1993-94, 0-for-2. Totals, 0-for-3.

NBA REGULAR-SEASON RECORD

Season Team	G	Min.	FGM	FGA	Pct.	FTM	FTA	Pct.	Off.	Def.	Tot.	Ast.	St.	Blk.	TO	Pts.	RPG	APG	PPG
95-96—Utah	57	661	86	182	.473	36	54	.667	57	118	175	5	5	63	25	208	3.1	0.1	3.6

Personal fouls/disqualifications: 1995-96, 91/1.

NBA PLAYOFF RECORD

Season Team	G	Min.	FGM	FGA	Pct.	FTM	FTA	Pct.	Off.	Def.	Tot.	Ast.	St.	Blk.	TO	Pts.	RPG	APG	PPG
95-96—Utah	15	212	20	45	.444	13	21	.619	18	32	50	1	2	21	4	53	3.3	0.1	3.5

Personal fouls/disqualifications: 1995-96, 28/0.

O'SULLIVAN, DAN   C

PERSONAL: Born March 3, 1968, in Bronx, N.Y. ... 6-10/250. ... Full name: Daniel James O'Sullivan.
HIGH SCHOOL: Bayonne (N.J.).
COLLEGE: Fordham.
TRANSACTIONS/CAREER NOTES: Not drafted by an NBA franchise. ... Signed as free agent by New Jersey Nets (October 1, 1990). ... Waived by Nets (October 29, 1990). ... Played in Continental Basketball Association with Omaha Racers (1990-91), Rapid City Thrillers (1993-94 and 1994-95) and Shreveport Storm (1995-96). ... Signed by Utah Jazz to first of two consecutive 10-day contracts (December 28, 1990). ... Re-signed by Jazz for remainder of season (January 16, 1991). ... Waived by Jazz (April 1, 1991). ... Signed as free agent by New York Knicks (October 3, 1991). ... Waived by Knicks (October 11, 1991). ... Signed as free agent by Jazz (October 16, 1991). ... Waived by Jazz (October 28, 1991). ... Played in Global Basketball Association with Louisville Shooters (1991-92). ... Played in United States Basketball League with New Jersey Jammers (1992). ... Signed as free agent by Nets (July 30, 1992). ... Signed by Nets (January 7, 1993). ... Signed by Milwaukee Bucks to first of two consecutive 10-day contracts (February 1, 1993). ... Signed as free agent by Detroit Pistons (September 1993). ... Waived by Pistons (February 23, 1994). ... Signed as free agent by Indiana Pacers (October 6, 1994). ... Waived by Pacers (October 11, 1994). ... Signed by Toronto Raptors to 10-day contract (April 9, 1996).

COLLEGIATE RECORD

Season Team	G	Min.	FGM	FGA	Pct.	FTM	FTA	Pct.	Reb.	Ast.	Pts.	RPG	APG	PPG
86-87—Fordham	18	111	11	21	.524	6	13	.462	26	1	28	1.4	0.1	1.6
87-88—Fordham	33	942	125	220	.568	72	108	.667	190	24	322	5.8	0.7	9.8

Season Team	G	Min.	FGM	FGA	Pct.	FTM	FTA	Pct.	Reb.	Ast.	Pts.	AVERAGES RPG	APG	PPG
88-89—Fordham	29	896	108	238	.454	96	140	.686	215	41	312	7.4	1.4	10.8
89-90—Fordham	33	1062	162	331	.489	89	154	.578	249	65	413	7.5	2.0	12.5
Totals	113	3011	406	810	.501	263	415	.634	680	131	1075	6.0	1.2	9.5

Three-point field goals: 1988-89, 0-for-1. 1989-90, 0-for-1. Totals, 0-for-2.

CBA REGULAR-SEASON RECORD

Season Team	G	Min.	FGM	FGA	Pct.	FTM	FTA	Pct.	Reb.	Ast.	Pts.	AVERAGES RPG	APG	PPG
90-91—Omaha	3	48	11	17	.647	5	12	.417	16	4	27	5.3	1.3	9.0
93-94—Rapid City	2	37	4	10	.400	3	6	.500	8	1	11	4.0	0.5	5.5
94-95—Rapid City	14	282	41	65	.631	17	24	.708	95	6	99	6.8	0.4	7.1
95-96—Shreveport	23	768	160	266	.602	63	80	.788	201	38	383	8.7	1.7	16.7
Totals	42	1135	216	358	.603	88	122	.721	320	49	520	7.6	1.2	12.4

Three-point field goals: 1995-96, 0-for-5.

NBA REGULAR-SEASON RECORD

Season Team	G	Min.	FGM	FGA	Pct.	FTM	FTA	Pct.	REBOUNDS Off.	Def.	Tot.	Ast.	St.	Blk.	TO	Pts.	AVERAGES RPG	APG	PPG
90-91—Utah	21	85	7	16	.438	7	11	.636	5	12	17	4	1	1	4	21	0.8	0.2	1.0
92-93—N.J.-Mil.	6	17	3	5	.600	3	4	.750	2	4	6	1	1	0	0	9	1.0	0.2	1.5
93-94—Detroit	13	56	4	12	.333	9	12	.750	2	8	10	3	0	0	3	17	0.8	0.2	1.3
95-96—Toronto	5	139	13	35	.371	7	8	.875	13	19	32	2	2	4	5	33	6.4	0.4	6.6
Totals	45	297	27	68	.397	26	35	.743	22	43	65	10	4	5	12	80	1.4	0.2	1.8

Three-point field goals: 1995-96, 0-for-1.
Personal fouls/disqualifications: 1990-91, 18/0. 1992-93, 4/0. 1993-94, 10/0. 1995-96, 13/0. Totals, 45/0.

OUTLAW, BO   C/F   CLIPPERS

PERSONAL: Born April 13, 1971, in San Antonio. ... 6-8/210. ... Full name: Charles Outlaw.
HIGH SCHOOL: John Jay (San Antonio).
JUNIOR COLLEGE: South Plains College (Texas).
COLLEGE: Houston.
TRANSACTIONS/CAREER NOTES: Not drafted by an NBA franchise. ... Played in Continental Basketball Association with Grand Rapids Hoops (1993-94). ... Signed by Los Angeles Clippers to first of two consecutive 10-day contracts (February 14, 1994). ... Re-signed by Clippers for remainder of season (March 8, 1994).

COLLEGIATE RECORD

NOTES: Led NCAA Division I with .684 field-goal percentage (1992) and .658 field-goal percentage (1993).

Season Team	G	Min.	FGM	FGA	Pct.	FTM	FTA	Pct.	Reb.	Ast.	Pts.	AVERAGES RPG	APG	PPG
89-90—South Plains College	30	...	147	261	.563	69	136	.507	289	54	364	9.6	1.8	12.1
90-91—South Plains College	30	...	160	242	.661	70	122	.574	326	87	395	10.9	2.9	13.2
91-92—Houston	31	970	156	228	.684	57	129	.442	254	81	369	8.2	2.6	11.9
92-93—Houston	30	1055	196	298	.658	95	192	.495	301	99	487	10.0	3.3	16.2
Junior college totals	60	...	307	503	.610	139	258	.539	615	141	759	10.3	2.4	12.7
4-year-college totals	61	2025	352	526	.669	152	321	.474	555	180	856	9.1	3.0	14.0

CBA REGULAR-SEASON RECORD

NOTES: Led CBA with 3.8 blocked shots per game (1994). ... CBA All-League second team (1994). ... CBA All-Defensive team (1994). ... CBA All-Rookie first team (1994).

Season Team	G	Min.	FGM	FGA	Pct.	FTM	FTA	Pct.	Reb.	Ast.	Pts.	AVERAGES RPG	APG	PPG
93-94—Grand Rapids	32	1211	167	243	*.687	83	160	.519	349	56	417	10.9	1.8	13.0

Three-point field goals: 1993-94, 0-for-1.

NBA REGULAR-SEASON RECORD

Season Team	G	Min.	FGM	FGA	Pct.	FTM	FTA	Pct.	REBOUNDS Off.	Def.	Tot.	Ast.	St.	Blk.	TO	Pts.	AVERAGES RPG	APG	PPG
93-94—L.A. Clippers	37	871	98	167	.587	61	103	.592	81	131	212	36	36	37	31	257	5.7	1.0	6.9
94-95—L.A. Clippers	81	1655	170	325	.523	82	186	.441	121	192	313	84	90	151	78	422	3.9	1.0	5.2
95-96—L.A. Clippers	80	985	107	186	.575	72	162	.444	87	113	200	50	44	91	45	286	2.5	0.6	3.6
Totals	198	3511	375	678	.553	215	451	.477	289	436	725	170	170	279	154	965	3.7	0.9	4.9

Three-point field goals: 1993-94, 0-for-2. 1994-95, 0-for-5. 1995-96, 0-for-3. Totals, 0-for-10.
Personal fouls/disqualifications: 1993-94, 94/1. 1994-95, 227/4. 1995-96, 127/0. Totals, 448/5.

OVERTON, DOUG   G

PERSONAL: Born August 3, 1969, in Philadelphia. ... 6-3/190. ... Full name: Douglas M. Overton.
HIGH SCHOOL: Dobbins Area Vocational Technical School (Philadelphia).
COLLEGE: La Salle.
TRANSACTIONS/CAREER NOTES: Selected by Detroit Pistons in second round (40th pick overall) of 1991 NBA Draft. ... Waived by Pistons (October 29, 1991). ... Played in Continental Basketball Association with Rockford Lightning (1991-92). ... Signed as free agent by Washington Bullets (October 19, 1992). ... Traded by Bullets with F Don MacLean to Denver Nuggets for G Robert Pack (October 30, 1995). ... Rights renounced by Nuggets (July 17, 1996).

COLLEGIATE RECORD

Season Team	G	Min.	FGM	FGA	Pct.	FTM	FTA	Pct.	Reb.	Ast.	Pts.	RPG	APG	PPG
												AVERAGES		
87-88—La Salle	34	918	110	221	.498	37	44	.841	81	91	265	2.4	2.7	7.8
88-89—La Salle	32	1221	174	352	.494	47	59	.797	101	244	421	3.2	7.6	13.2
89-90—La Salle	32	1202	201	387	.519	95	119	.798	133	212	551	4.2	6.6	17.2
90-91—La Salle	25	959	199	447	.445	106	128	.828	103	124	558	4.1	5.0	22.3
Totals	123	4300	684	1407	.486	285	350	.814	418	671	1795	3.4	5.5	14.6

Three-point field goals: 1987-88, 8-for-27 (.296). 1988-89, 26-for-65 (.400). 1989-90, 54-for-124 (.435). 1990-91, 54-for-160 (.338). Totals, 142-for-376 (.378).

CBA REGULAR-SEASON RECORD

Season Team	G	Min.	FGM	FGA	Pct.	FTM	FTA	Pct.	Reb.	Ast.	Pts.	RPG	APG	PPG
												AVERAGES		
91-92—Rockford	28	1071	194	396	.490	72	85	.847	123	170	463	4.4	6.1	16.5

Three-point field goals: 1991-92, 3-for-5 (.600).

NBA REGULAR-SEASON RECORD

Season Team	G	Min.	FGM	FGA	Pct.	FTM	FTA	Pct.	Off.	Def.	Tot.	Ast.	St.	Blk.	TO	Pts.	RPG	APG	PPG
									REBOUNDS								**AVERAGES**		
92-93—Washington	45	990	152	323	.471	59	81	.728	25	81	106	157	31	6	72	366	2.4	3.5	8.1
93-94—Washington	61	749	87	216	.403	43	52	.827	19	50	69	92	21	1	54	218	1.1	1.5	3.6
94-95—Washington	82	1704	207	498	.416	109	125	.872	26	117	143	246	53	2	104	576	1.7	3.0	7.0
95-96—Denver	55	607	67	178	.376	40	55	.727	8	55	63	106	13	5	40	182	1.1	1.9	3.3
Totals	243	4050	513	1215	.422	251	313	.802	78	303	381	601	118	14	270	1342	1.6	2.5	5.5

Three-point field goals: 1992-93, 3-for-13 (.231). 1993-94, 1-for-11 (.091). 1994-95, 53-for-125 (.424). 1995-96, 8-for-26 (.308). Totals, 65-for-175 (.371).
Personal fouls/disqualifications: 1992-93, 81/0. 1993-94, 48/0. 1994-95, 126/1. 1995-96, 49/0. Totals, 304/1.

OWENS, BILLY — F/G — KINGS

PERSONAL: Born May 1, 1969, in Carlisle, Pa. ... 6-9/225. ... Full name: Billy Eugene Owens.
HIGH SCHOOL: Carlisle (Pa.).
COLLEGE: Syracuse.
TRANSACTIONS/CAREER NOTES: Selected after junior season by Sacramento Kings in first round (third pick overall) of 1991 NBA Draft. ... Traded by Kings to Golden State Warriors for G Mitch Richmond and C Les Jepsen (November 1, 1991). ... Traded by Warriors with rights to G Predrag Danilovic to Miami Heat for C Rony Seikaly (November 2, 1994). ... Traded by Heat with G/F Kevin Gamble to Sacramento Kings for F/G Walt Williams and F Tyrone Corbin (February 22, 1996).

COLLEGIATE RECORD
NOTES: The Sporting News All-America second team (1991).

Season Team	G	Min.	FGM	FGA	Pct.	FTM	FTA	Pct.	Reb.	Ast.	Pts.	RPG	APG	PPG
												AVERAGES		
88-89—Syracuse	38	1215	196	376	.521	94	145	.648	263	119	494	6.9	3.1	13.0
89-90—Syracuse	33	1188	228	469	.486	127	176	.722	276	151	602	8.4	4.6	18.2
90-91—Syracuse	32	1215	282	554	.509	157	233	.674	371	111	744	11.6	3.5	23.3
Totals	103	3618	706	1399	.505	378	554	.682	910	381	1840	8.8	3.7	17.9

Three-point field goals: 1988-89, 8-for-36 (.222). 1989-90, 19-for-60 (.317). 1990-91, 23-for-58 (.397). Totals, 50-for-154 (.325).

NBA REGULAR-SEASON RECORD
HONORS: NBA All-Rookie first team (1992).

Season Team	G	Min.	FGM	FGA	Pct.	FTM	FTA	Pct.	Off.	Def.	Tot.	Ast.	St.	Blk.	TO	Pts.	RPG	APG	PPG
									REBOUNDS								**AVERAGES**		
91-92—Golden State ...	80	2510	468	891	.525	204	312	.654	243	396	639	188	90	65	179	1141	8.0	2.4	14.3
92-93—Golden State ...	37	1201	247	493	.501	117	183	.639	108	156	264	144	35	28	106	612	7.1	3.9	16.5
93-94—Golden State ...	79	2738	492	971	.507	199	326	.610	230	410	640	326	83	60	214	1186	8.1	4.1	15.0
94-95—Miami	70	2296	403	820	.491	194	313	.620	203	299	502	246	80	30	204	1002	7.2	3.5	14.3
95-96—Mia.-Sac.	62	1982	323	673	.480	157	247	.636	143	268	411	204	49	38	164	808	6.6	3.3	13.0
Totals	328	10727	1933	3848	.502	871	1381	.631	927	1529	2456	1108	337	221	867	4749	7.5	3.4	14.5

Three-point field goals: 1991-92, 1-for-9 (.111). 1992-93, 1-for-11 (.091). 1993-94, 3-for-15 (.200). 1994-95, 2-for-22 (.091). 1995-96, 5-for-18 (.278). Totals, 12-for-75 (.160).
Personal fouls/disqualifications: 1991-92, 276/4. 1992-93, 105/1. 1993-94, 269/5. 1994-95, 205/6. 1995-96, 192/2. Totals, 1047/18.

NBA PLAYOFF RECORD

Season Team	G	Min.	FGM	FGA	Pct.	FTM	FTA	Pct.	Off.	Def.	Tot.	Ast.	St.	Blk.	TO	Pts.	RPG	APG	PPG
									REBOUNDS								**AVERAGES**		
91-92—Golden State ...	4	157	30	57	.526	17	27	.630	13	20	33	13	8	2	6	77	8.3	3.3	19.3
93-94—Golden State ...	3	127	25	50	.500	9	12	.750	12	18	30	13	4	2	7	59	10.0	4.3	19.7
95-96—Sacramento	4	131	15	34	.441	3	6	.500	5	21	26	14	4	1	11	33	6.5	3.5	8.3
Totals	11	415	70	141	.496	29	45	.644	30	59	89	40	16	5	24	169	8.1	3.6	15.4

Three-point field goals: 1993-94, 0-for-1. 1995-96, 0-for-4. Totals, 0-for-5.
Personal fouls/disqualifications: 1991-92, 14/0. 1993-94, 11/0. 1995-96, 17/1. Totals, 42/1.

PACK, ROBERT — G — NETS

PERSONAL: Born February 3, 1969, in New Orleans. ... 6-2/190. ... Full name: Robert John Pack Jr.
HIGH SCHOOL: Lawless (New Orleans).
JUNIOR COLLEGE: Tyler (Texas) Junior College.
COLLEGE: Southern California.
TRANSACTIONS/CAREER NOTES: Not drafted by an NBA franchise. ... Signed as free agent by Portland Trail Blazers

OP

(September 16, 1991). ... Traded by Trail Blazers to Denver Nuggets for 1993 second-round draft choice (October 23, 1992). ... Traded by Nuggets to Washington Bullets for G Doug Overton and F Don MacLean (October 30, 1995). ... Signed as free agent by New Jersey Nets (July 31, 1996).

COLLEGIATE RECORD

Season Team	G	Min.	FGM	FGA	Pct.	FTM	FTA	Pct.	Reb.	Ast.	Pts.	AVERAGES RPG	APG	PPG
87-88—Tyler J.C.						Statistics unavailable.								
88-89—Tyler J.C.						Statistics unavailable.								
89-90—Southern Cal	28	883	118	250	.472	84	124	.677	67	165	339	2.4	5.9	12.1
90-91—Southern Cal	29	941	145	302	.480	123	155	.794	93	154	427	3.2	5.3	14.7
Totals	57	1824	263	552	.476	207	279	.742	160	319	766	2.8	5.6	13.4

Three-point field goals: 1989-90, 19-for-57 (.333). 1990-91, 14-for-55 (.255). Totals, 33-for-112 (.295).

NBA REGULAR-SEASON RECORD

Season Team	G	Min.	FGM	FGA	Pct.	FTM	FTA	Pct.	REBOUNDS Off.	Def.	Tot.	Ast.	St.	Blk.	TO	Pts.	AVERAGES RPG	APG	PPG
91-92—Portland	72	894	115	272	.423	102	127	.803	32	65	97	140	40	4	92	332	1.3	1.9	4.6
92-93—Denver	77	1579	285	606	.470	239	311	.768	52	108	160	335	81	10	185	810	2.1	4.4	10.5
93-94—Denver	66	1382	223	503	.443	179	236	.758	25	98	123	356	81	9	204	631	1.9	5.4	9.6
94-95—Denver	42	1144	170	395	.430	137	175	.783	19	94	113	290	61	6	134	507	2.7	6.9	12.1
95-96—Washington	31	1084	190	444	.428	154	182	.846	29	103	132	242	62	1	114	560	4.3	7.8	18.1
Totals	288	6083	983	2220	.443	811	1031	.787	157	468	625	1363	325	30	729	2840	2.2	4.7	9.9

Three-point field goals: 1991-92, 0-for-10. 1992-93, 1-for-8 (.125). 1993-94, 6-for-29 (.207). 1994-95, 30-for-72 (.417). 1995-96, 26-for-98 (.265). Totals, 63-for-217 (.290).

Personal fouls/disqualifications: 1991-92, 101/0. 1992-93, 182/1. 1993-94, 147/1. 1994-95, 101/1. 1995-96, 68/0. Totals, 599/3.

NBA PLAYOFF RECORD

Season Team	G	Min.	FGM	FGA	Pct.	FTM	FTA	Pct.	REBOUNDS Off.	Def.	Tot.	Ast.	St.	Blk.	TO	Pts.	AVERAGES RPG	APG	PPG
91-92—Portland	14	52	4	18	.222	3	4	.750	2	4	6	7	5	1	3	11	0.4	0.5	0.8
93-94—Denver	12	332	48	118	.407	39	55	.709	5	23	28	51	18	6	46	141	2.3	4.3	11.8
Totals	26	384	52	136	.382	42	59	.712	7	27	34	58	23	7	49	152	1.3	2.2	5.8

Three-point field goals: 1993-94, 6-for-20 (.300).
Personal fouls/disqualifications: 1991-92, 10/0. 1993-94, 41/0. Totals, 51/0.

PARISH, ROBERT   C

PERSONAL: Born August 30, 1953, in Shreveport, La. ... 7-1/244. ... Full name: Robert Lee Parish. ... Second cousin of Larry Robinson, forward/guard with Golden State Warriors, Washington Bullets, Boston Celtics and Houston Rockets (1990-91 through 1993-94). ... Nickname: Chief.

HIGH SCHOOL: Woodlawn (Shreveport, La.).

COLLEGE: Centenary (La.).

TRANSACTIONS/CAREER NOTES: Selected by Golden State Warriors in first round (eighth pick overall) of 1976 NBA Draft. ... Traded by Warriors with 1980 first-round draft choice to Boston Celtics for two 1980 first-round draft choices (June 9, 1980). ... Signed as unrestricted free agent by Charlotte Hornets (August 4, 1994). ... Rights renounced by Hornets (July 11, 1996).

MISCELLANEOUS: Member of NBA championship teams (1981, 1984, 1986). ... Boston Celtics all-time blocked shots leader with 1,703 (1980-81 through 1993-94).

COLLEGIATE RECORD

NOTES: The Sporting News All-America first team (1976).

Season Team	G	Min.	FGM	FGA	Pct.	FTM	FTA	Pct.	Reb.	Ast.	Pts.	AVERAGES RPG	APG	PPG
72-73—Centenary	27	885	285	492	.579	50	82	.610	505	25	620	18.7	0.9	23.0
73-74—Centenary	25	841	224	428	.523	49	78	.628	382	34	497	15.3	1.4	19.9
74-75—Centenary	29	900	237	423	.560	74	112	.661	447	43	548	15.4	1.5	18.9
75-76—Centenary	27	939	288	489	.589	93	134	.694	486	48	669	18.0	1.8	24.8
Totals	108	3565	1034	1832	.564	266	406	.655	1820	150	2334	16.9	1.4	21.6

NBA REGULAR-SEASON RECORD

RECORDS: Holds career records for most games played—1,568; and most defensive rebounds—10,070. ... Shares career record for most seasons played—20.

HONORS: All-NBA second team (1982). ... All-NBA third team (1989).

Season Team	G	Min.	FGM	FGA	Pct.	FTM	FTA	Pct.	REBOUNDS Off.	Def.	Tot.	Ast.	St.	Blk.	TO	Pts.	AVERAGES RPG	APG	PPG
76-77—Golden State ...	77	1384	288	573	.503	121	171	.708	201	342	543	74	55	94	...	697	7.1	1.0	9.1
77-78—Golden State ...	82	1969	430	911	.472	165	264	.625	211	469	680	95	79	123	201	1025	8.3	1.2	12.5
78-79—Golden State ...	76	2411	554	1110	.499	196	281	.698	265	651	916	115	100	217	233	1304	12.1	1.5	17.2
79-80—Golden State ...	72	2119	510	1006	.507	203	284	.715	247	536	783	122	58	115	225	1223	10.9	1.7	17.0
80-81—Boston	82	2298	635	1166	.545	282	397	.710	245	532	777	144	81	214	191	1552	9.5	1.8	18.9
81-82—Boston	80	2534	669	1235	.542	252	355	.710	288	578	866	140	68	192	221	1590	10.8	1.8	19.9
82-83—Boston	78	2459	619	1125	.550	271	388	.698	260	567	827	141	79	148	185	1509	10.6	1.8	19.3
83-84—Boston	80	2867	623	1140	.547	274	368	.745	243	614	857	139	55	116	184	1520	10.7	1.7	19.0
84-85—Boston	79	2850	551	1016	.542	292	393	.743	263	577	840	125	56	101	186	1394	10.6	1.6	17.6
85-86—Boston	81	2567	530	966	.549	245	335	.731	246	524	770	145	65	116	187	1305	9.5	1.8	16.1
86-87—Boston	80	2995	588	1057	.556	227	309	.735	254	597	851	173	64	144	191	1403	10.6	2.2	17.5
87-88—Boston	74	2312	442	750	.589	177	241	.734	173	455	628	115	55	84	154	1061	8.5	1.6	14.3
88-89—Boston	80	2840	596	1045	.570	294	409	.719	342	654	996	175	79	116	200	1486	12.5	2.2	18.6
89-90—Boston	79	2396	505	871	.580	233	312	.747	259	537	796	103	38	69	169	1243	10.1	1.3	15.7
90-91—Boston	81	2441	485	811	.598	237	309	.767	271	585	856	66	66	103	153	1207	10.6	0.8	14.9
91-92—Boston	79	2285	468	874	.535	179	232	.772	219	486	705	70	68	97	131	1115	8.9	0.9	14.1

P

Season Team	G	Min.	FGM	FGA	Pct.	FTM	FTA	Pct.	REBOUNDS Off.	Def.	Tot.	Ast.	St.	Blk.	TO	Pts.	AVERAGES RPG	APG	PPG
92-93—Boston	79	2146	416	777	.535	162	235	.689	246	494	740	61	57	107	120	994	9.4	0.8	12.6
93-94—Boston	74	1987	356	725	.491	154	208	.740	141	401	542	82	42	96	108	866	7.3	1.1	11.7
94-95—Charlotte	81	1352	-159	372	.427	71	101	.703	93	257	350	44	27	36	66	389	4.3	0.5	4.8
95-96—Charlotte	74	1086	120	241	.498	50	71	.704	89	214	303	29	21	54	50	290	4.1	0.4	3.9
Totals	1568	45298	9544	17771	.537	4085	5663	.721	4556	10070	14626	2158	1213	2342	3155	23173	9.3	1.4	14.8

Three-point field goals: 1979-80, 0-for-1. 1980-81, 0-for-1. 1982-83, 0-for-1. 1986-87, 0-for-1. 1987-88, 0-for-1. 1990-91, 0-for-1. Totals, 0-for-6.
Personal fouls/disqualifications: 1976-77, 224/7. 1977-78, 291/10. 1978-79, 303/10. 1979-80, 248/6. 1980-81, 310/9. 1981-82, 267/5. 1982-83, 222/4. 1983-84, 266/7. 1984-85, 223/2. 1985-86, 215/3. 1986-87, 266/5. 1987-88, 198/5. 1988-89, 209/2. 1989-90, 189/2. 1990-91, 197/1. 1991-92, 172/2. 1992-93, 201/3. 1993-94, 190/3. 1994-95, 132/0. 1995-96, 80/0. Totals, 4403/86.

NBA PLAYOFF RECORD

NOTES: Holds career playoff record for most offensive rebounds—569.

Season Team	G	Min.	FGM	FGA	Pct.	FTM	FTA	Pct.	REBOUNDS Off.	Def.	Tot.	Ast.	St.	Blk.	TO	Pts.	AVERAGES RPG	APG	PPG
76-77—Golden State	10	239	52	108	.481	17	26	.654	43	60	103	11	7	11	...	121	10.3	1.1	12.1
80-81—Boston	17	492	108	219	.493	39	58	.672	50	96	146	19	21	39	44	255	8.6	1.1	15.0
81-82—Boston	12	426	102	209	.488	51	75	.680	43	92	135	18	5	48	39	255	11.3	1.5	21.3
82-83—Boston	7	249	43	89	.483	17	20	.850	21	53	74	9	5	9	17	103	10.6	1.3	14.7
83-84—Boston	23	869	139	291	.478	64	99	.646	76	172	248	27	23	41	45	342	10.8	1.2	14.9
84-85—Boston	21	803	136	276	.493	87	111	.784	57	162	219	31	21	34	50	359	10.4	1.5	17.1
85-86—Boston	18	591	106	225	.471	58	89	.652	52	106	158	25	9	30	44	270	8.8	1.4	15.0
86-87—Boston	21	734	149	263	.567	79	103	.767	59	139	198	28	18	35	38	377	9.4	1.3	18.0
87-88—Boston	17	626	100	188	.532	50	61	.820	51	117	168	21	11	19	38	250	9.9	1.2	14.7
88-89—Boston	3	112	20	44	.455	7	9	.778	6	20	26	6	4	2	6	47	8.7	2.0	15.7
89-90—Boston	5	170	31	54	.574	17	18	.944	23	27	50	13	5	7	12	79	10.0	2.6	15.8
90-91—Boston	10	296	58	97	.598	42	61	.689	33	59	92	6	8	7	16	158	9.2	0.6	15.8
91-92—Boston	10	335	50	101	.495	20	28	.714	38	59	97	14	7	15	9	120	9.7	1.4	12.0
92-93—Boston	4	146	31	57	.544	6	7	.857	13	25	38	5	1	6	6	68	9.5	1.3	17.0
94-95—Charlotte	4	71	6	11	.545	2	5	.400	4	5	9	1	0	3	1	14	2.3	0.3	3.5
Totals	182	6159	1131	2232	.507	556	770	.722	569	1192	1761	234	145	306	365	2818	9.7	1.3	15.5

Three-point field goals: 1986-87, 0-for-1.
Personal fouls/disqualifications: 1976-77, 42/1. 1980-81, 74/2. 1981-82, 47/1. 1982-83, 18/0. 1983-84, 100/6. 1984-85, 68/0. 1985-86, 47/1. 1986-87, 79/4. 1987-88, 42/0. 1988-89, 5/0. 1989-90, 21/0. 1990-91, 34/1. 1991-92, 22/0. 1992-93, 14/0. 1994-95, 2/0. Totals, 615/16.

NBA ALL-STAR GAME RECORD

Season Team	Min.	FGM	FGA	Pct.	FTM	FTA	Pct.	REBOUNDS Off.	Def.	Tot.	Ast.	PF	Dq.	St.	Blk.	TO	Pts.
1981 —Boston	25	5	18	.278	6	6	1.000	6	4	10	2	3	0	0	2	1	16
1982 —Boston	20	9	12	.750	3	4	.750	0	7	7	1	2	0	0	2	1	21
1983 —Boston	18	5	6	.833	3	4	.750	0	3	3	0	2	0	1	1	1	13
1984 —Boston	28	5	11	.455	2	4	.500	4	11	15	2	1	0	3	0	4	12
1985 —Boston	10	2	5	.400	0	0	...	3	3	6	1	0	0	0	0	0	4
1986 —Boston	7	0	0	...	0	2	.000	0	1	1	0	0	0	0	1	1	0
1987 —Boston	8	2	3	.667	0	0	...	0	3	3	0	1	0	0	1	0	4
1990 —Boston	21	7	11	.636	0	1	.000	2	2	4	2	4	0	0	1	1	14
1991 —Boston	5	1	2	.500	0	0	...	1	3	4	0	2	0	0	0	1	2
Totals	142	36	68	.529	14	21	.667	16	37	53	8	15	0	4	8	10	86

PARKS, CHEROKEE   F/C   TIMBERWOLVES

PERSONAL: Born October 11, 1972, in Huntington Beach, Calif. ... 6-11/240. ... Full name: Cherokee Bryan Parks.
HIGH SCHOOL: Marina (Huntington Beach, Calif.).
COLLEGE: Duke.
TRANSACTIONS/CAREER NOTES: Selected by Dallas Mavericks in first round (12th pick overall) of 1995 NBA Draft. ...Traded by Mavericks to Minnesota Timberwolves in exchange for Minnesota removing the 2-6 lottery protection on 1997 first-round draft choice Dallas acquired from Minnesota in 1994 trade involving C Sean Rooks (June 29, 1996).

COLLEGIATE RECORD

NOTES: Member of NCAA Division I championship team (1992).

Season Team	G	Min.	FGM	FGA	Pct.	FTM	FTA	Pct.	Reb.	Ast.	Pts.	AVERAGES RPG	APG	PPG
91-92—Duke	34	435	60	105	.571	50	69	.725	81	13	170	2.4	0.4	5.0
92-93—Duke	32	899	161	247	.652	72	100	.720	220	14	394	6.9	0.4	12.3
93-94—Duke	34	1038	186	347	.536	115	149	.772	284	31	490	8.4	0.9	14.4
94-95—Duke	31	1091	222	443	.501	114	147	.776	289	45	589	9.3	1.5	19.0
Totals	131	3463	629	1142	.551	351	465	.755	874	103	1643	6.7	0.8	12.5

Three-point field goals: 1993-94, 3-for-17 (.176). 1994-95, 31-for-85 (.365). Totals, 34-for-102 (.333).

NBA REGULAR-SEASON RECORD

Season Team	G	Min.	FGM	FGA	Pct.	FTM	FTA	Pct.	REBOUNDS Off.	Def.	Tot.	Ast.	St.	Blk.	TO	Pts.	AVERAGES RPG	APG	PPG
95-96—Dallas	64	869	101	247	.409	41	62	.661	66	150	216	29	25	32	31	250	3.4	0.5	3.9

Three-point field goals: 1995-96, 7-for-26 (.269).
Personal fouls/disqualifications: 1995-96, 100/0.

P

PAYTON, GARY　　　　　　　　G　　　　　　SUPERSONICS

PERSONAL: Born July 23, 1968, in Oakland. ... 6-4/190. ... Full name: Gary Dwayne Payton.
HIGH SCHOOL: Skyline (Oakland).
COLLEGE: Oregon State.
TRANSACTIONS/CAREER NOTES: Selected by Seattle SuperSonics in first round (second pick overall) of 1990 NBA Draft.
MISCELLANEOUS: Member of gold-medal-winning U.S. Olympic team (1996).

COLLEGIATE RECORD

NOTES: The Sporting News All-America first team (1990).

Season Team	G	Min.	FGM	FGA	Pct.	FTM	FTA	Pct.	Reb.	Ast.	Pts.	RPG	APG	PPG
86-87—Oregon State	30	1115	153	333	.459	55	82	.671	120	229	374	4.0	7.6	12.5
87-88—Oregon State	31	1178	180	368	.489	58	83	.699	103	230	449	3.3	7.4	14.5
88-89—Oregon State	30	1140	208	438	.475	105	155	.677	122	244	603	4.1	8.1	20.1
89-90—Oregon State	29	1095	288	571	.504	118	171	.690	135	235	746	4.7	8.1	25.7
Totals	120	4528	829	1710	.485	336	491	.684	480	938	2172	4.0	7.8	18.1

Three-point field goals: 1986-87, 13-for-35 (.371). 1987-88, 31-for-78 (.397). 1988-89, 82-for-213 (.385). 1989-90, 52-for-156 (.333). Totals, 178-for-482 (.369).

NBA REGULAR-SEASON RECORD

HONORS: NBA Defensive Player of the Year (1996). ... All-NBA second team (1995, 1996). ... All-NBA third team (1994). ... NBA All-Defensive first team (1994, 1995, 1996). ... NBA All-Rookie second team (1991).
NOTES: Led NBA with 2.85 steals per game (1996).

									REBOUNDS							AVERAGES		
Season Team	G	Min.	FGM	FGA	Pct.	FTM	FTA	Pct.	Off.	Def.	Tot.	Ast.	St.	Blk.	TO	Pts.	RPG	APG	PPG
90-91—Seattle	82	2244	259	575	.450	69	97	.711	108	135	243	528	165	15	180	588	3.0	6.4	7.2
91-92—Seattle	81	2549	331	734	.451	99	148	.669	123	172	295	506	147	21	174	764	3.6	6.2	9.4
92-93—Seattle	82	2548	476	963	.494	151	196	.770	95	186	281	399	177	21	148	1110	3.4	4.9	13.5
93-94—Seattle	82	2881	584	1159	.504	166	279	.595	105	164	269	494	188	19	173	1349	3.3	6.0	16.5
94-95—Seattle	82	3015	685	1345	.509	249	348	.716	108	173	281	583	204	13	201	1689	3.4	7.1	20.6
95-96—Seattle	81	3162	618	1276	.484	229	306	.748	104	235	339	608	*231	19	260	1563	4.2	7.5	19.3
Totals	490	16399	2953	6052	.488	963	1374	.701	643	1065	1708	3118	1112	108	1136	7063	3.5	6.4	14.4

Three-point field goals: 1990-91, 1-for-13 (.077). 1991-92, 3-for-23 (.130). 1992-93, 7-for-34 (.206). 1993-94, 15-for-54 (.278). 1994-95, 70-for-232 (.302). 1995-96, 98-for-299 (.328). Totals, 194-for-655 (.296).
Personal fouls/disqualifications: 1990-91, 249/3. 1991-92, 248/0. 1992-93, 250/1. 1993-94, 227/0. 1994-95, 206/1. 1995-96, 221/1. Totals, 1401/6.

NBA PLAYOFF RECORD

NOTES: Holds single-game playoff record for most three-point field goal attempts in one half—13 (May 4, 1996, vs. Houston).

									REBOUNDS							AVERAGES		
Season Team	G	Min.	FGM	FGA	Pct.	FTM	FTA	Pct.	Off.	Def.	Tot.	Ast.	St.	Blk.	TO	Pts.	RPG	APG	PPG
90-91—Seattle	5	135	11	27	.407	2	2	1.000	5	8	13	32	8	1	9	24	2.6	6.4	4.8
91-92—Seattle	8	221	27	58	.466	7	12	.583	6	15	21	38	8	2	10	61	2.6	4.8	7.6
92-93—Seattle	19	605	104	235	.443	25	37	.676	22	41	63	70	34	3	34	234	3.3	3.7	12.3
93-94—Seattle	5	181	34	69	.493	8	19	.421	6	11	17	28	8	2	8	79	3.4	5.6	15.8
94-95—Seattle	4	172	32	67	.478	5	12	.417	6	4	10	21	5	0	8	71	2.5	5.3	17.8
95-96—Seattle	21	911	162	334	.485	69	109	.633	19	89	108	143	37	7	62	434	5.1	6.8	20.7
Totals	62	2225	370	790	.468	116	191	.607	64	168	232	332	100	15	131	903	3.7	5.4	14.6

Three-point field goals: 1990-91, 0-for-1. 1991-92, 0-for-2. 1992-93, 1-for-6 (.167). 1993-94, 3-for-9 (.333). 1994-95, 2-for-10 (.200). 1995-96, 41-for-100 (.410). Totals, 47-for-128 (.367).
Personal fouls/disqualifications: 1990-91, 16/0. 1991-92, 26/1. 1992-93, 64/1. 1993-94, 15/0. 1994-95, 13/0. 1995-96, 69/0. Totals, 203/2.

NBA ALL-STAR GAME RECORD

								REBOUNDS								
Season Team	Min.	FGM	FGA	Pct.	FTM	FTA	Pct.	Off.	Def.	Tot.	Ast.	PF	Dq.	St.	Blk.	TO	Pts.
1994 —Seattle	17	3	4	.750	0	0	...	2	4	6	9	2	0	0	0	0	6
1995 —Seattle	23	3	10	.300	0	0	...	3	2	5	15	1	0	3	0	3	6
1996 —Seattle	28	6	10	.600	6	6	1.000	3	2	5	5	1	0	5	0	6	18
Totals	68	12	24	.500	6	6	1.000	8	8	16	29	4	0	8	0	9	30

Three-point field goals: 1995, 0-for-3. 1996, 0-for-1. Totals, 0-for-4.

PEELER, ANTHONY　　　　　　　G　　　　　　GRIZZLIES

PERSONAL: Born November 25, 1969, in Kansas City, Mo. ... 6-4/212. ... Full name: Anthony Eugene Peeler.
HIGH SCHOOL: Paseo (Kansas City, Mo.).
COLLEGE: Missouri.
TRANSACTIONS/CAREER NOTES: Selected by Los Angeles Lakers in first round (15th pick overall) of 1992 NBA Draft. ... Traded by Lakers with F George Lynch and 1997 and 1998 second-round draft choices to Vancouver Grizzlies for 1997 and 1998 second-round draft choices (July 16, 1996).
MISCELLANEOUS: Selected by Texas Rangers organization in 41st round of free-agent draft (June 1, 1988); did not sign.

COLLEGIATE RECORD

Season Team	G	Min.	FGM	FGA	Pct.	FTM	FTA	Pct.	Reb.	Ast.	Pts.	RPG	APG	PPG
88-89—Missouri	36	801	130	258	.504	89	118	.754	134	102	362	3.7	2.8	10.1
89-90—Missouri	31	1031	184	413	.446	130	169	.769	168	179	522	5.4	5.8	16.8
90-91—Missouri	21	725	134	282	.475	116	151	.768	131	104	408	6.2	5.0	19.4
91-92—Missouri	29	1026	218	475	.459	187	232	.806	160	112	678	5.5	3.9	23.4
Totals	117	3583	666	1428	.466	522	670	.779	593	497	1970	5.1	4.2	16.8

Three-point field goals: 1988-89, 13-for-37 (.351). 1989-90, 24-for-68 (.353). 1990-91, 24-for-58 (.414). 1991-92, 55-for-132 (.417). Totals, 116-for-295 (.393).

P

NBA REGULAR-SEASON RECORD

Season Team	G	Min.	FGM	FGA	Pct.	FTM	FTA	Pct.	REBOUNDS Off.	Def.	Tot.	Ast.	St.	Blk.	TO	Pts.	AVERAGES RPG	APG	PPG
92-93—L.A. Lakers	77	1656	297	634	.468	162	206	.786	64	115	179	166	60	14	123	802	2.3	2.2	10.4
93-94—L.A. Lakers	30	923	176	409	.430	57	71	.803	48	61	109	94	43	8	59	423	3.6	3.1	14.1
94-95—L.A. Lakers	73	1559	285	659	.432	102	128	.797	62	106	168	122	52	13	82	756	2.3	1.7	10.4
95-96—L.A. Lakers	73	1608	272	602	.452	61	86	.709	45	92	137	118	59	10	56	710	1.9	1.6	9.7
Totals	253	5746	1030	2304	.447	382	491	.778	219	374	593	500	214	45	320	2691	2.3	2.0	10.6

Three-point field goals: 1992-93, 46-for-118 (.390). 1993-94, 14-for-63 (.222). 1994-95, 84-for-216 (.389). 1995-96, 105-for-254 (.413). Totals, 249-for-651 (.382).

Personal fouls/disqualifications: 1992-93, 193/0. 1993-94, 93/0. 1994-95, 143/1. 1995-96, 139/0. Totals, 568/1.

NBA PLAYOFF RECORD

Season Team	G	Min.	FGM	FGA	Pct.	FTM	FTA	Pct.	REBOUNDS Off.	Def.	Tot.	Ast.	St.	Blk.	TO	Pts.	AVERAGES RPG	APG	PPG
94-95—L.A. Lakers	10	268	32	79	.405	17	22	.773	8	20	28	25	10	2	12	89	2.8	2.5	8.9
95-96—L.A. Lakers	3	72	9	27	.333	4	4	1.000	2	6	8	3	6	0	3	28	2.7	1.0	9.3
Totals	13	340	41	106	.387	21	26	.808	10	26	36	28	16	2	15	117	2.8	2.2	9.0

Three-point field goals: 1994-95, 8-for-31 (.258). 1995-96, 6-for-14 (.429). Totals, 14-for-45 (.311).

Personal fouls/disqualifications: 1994-95, 23/0. 1995-96, 6/0. Totals, 29/0.

PEPLOWSKI, MIKE   C   BUCKS

PERSONAL: Born October 15, 1970, in Detroit. ... 6-10/270. ... Full name: Michael Walter Peplowski.

HIGH SCHOOL: De LaSalle (Warren, Mich.).

COLLEGE: Michigan State.

TRANSACTIONS/CAREER NOTES: Selected by Sacramento Kings in second round (52nd pick overall) of 1993 NBA Draft. ... Waived by Kings (November 3, 1994). ... Signed as free agent by Detroit Pistons (December 30, 1994). ... Waived by Pistons (January 4, 1995). ... Re-signed by Pistons to 10-day contract (January 10, 1995). ... Signed as unrestricted free agent by Milwaukee Bucks (October 6, 1995). ... Waived by Bucks (November 2, 1995). ... Signed as free agent by Washington Bullets (November 9, 1995). ... Waived by Bullets (November 27, 1995). ... Signed by Bucks for remainder of season (February 27, 1996).

COLLEGIATE RECORD

Season Team	G	Min.	FGM	FGA	Pct.	FTM	FTA	Pct.	Reb.	Ast.	Pts.	AVERAGES RPG	APG	PPG
88-89—Michigan State							Did not play—knee injury.							
89-90—Michigan State	28	540	60	110	.545	27	43	.628	162	19	147	5.8	0.7	5.3
90-91—Michigan State	30	734	99	158	.627	34	50	.680	206	15	232	6.9	0.5	7.7
91-92—Michigan State	30	791	168	266	.632	64	93	.688	259	34	400	8.6	1.1	13.3
92-93—Michigan State	28	816	161	252	.639	84	126	.667	279	39	406	10.0	1.4	14.5
Totals	116	2881	488	786	.621	209	312	.670	906	107	1185	7.8	0.9	10.2

Three-point field goals: 1992-93, 0-for-1.

NBA REGULAR-SEASON RECORD

Season Team	G	Min.	FGM	FGA	Pct.	FTM	FTA	Pct.	REBOUNDS Off.	Def.	Tot.	Ast.	St.	Blk.	TO	Pts.	AVERAGES RPG	APG	PPG
93-94—Sacramento	55	667	76	141	.539	24	44	.545	49	120	169	24	17	25	34	176	3.1	0.4	3.2
94-95—Detroit	6	21	5	5	1.000	1	2	.500	1	2	3	1	1	0	2	11	0.5	0.2	1.8
95-96—Was.-Mil.	7	17	3	5	.600	1	3	.333	1	3	4	1	1	2	2	7	0.6	0.1	1.0
Totals	68	705	84	151	.556	26	49	.531	51	125	176	26	19	27	38	194	2.6	0.4	2.9

Three-point field goals: 1993-94, 0-for-1.

Personal fouls/disqualifications: 1993-94, 131/2. 1994-95, 10/0. 1995-96, 10/0. Totals, 151/2.

PERDUE, WILL   C   SPURS

PERSONAL: Born August 29, 1965, in Melbourne, Fla. ... 7-0/240. ... Full name: William Edward Perdue III.

HIGH SCHOOL: Merritt Island (Fla.).

COLLEGE: Vanderbilt.

TRANSACTIONS/CAREER NOTES: Selected by Chicago Bulls in first round (11th pick overall) of 1988 NBA Draft. ... Traded by Bulls to San Antonio Spurs for F Dennis Rodman (October 2, 1995).

MISCELLANEOUS: Member of NBA championship teams (1991, 1992, 1993).

COLLEGIATE RECORD

Season Team	G	Min.	FGM	FGA	Pct.	FTM	FTA	Pct.	Reb.	Ast.	Pts.	AVERAGES RPG	APG	PPG
83-84—Vanderbilt......................	17	111	21	45	.467	4	9	.444	38	2	46	2.2	0.1	2.7
84-85—Vanderbilt......................							Did not play—redshirted.							
85-86—Vanderbilt......................	22	181	31	53	.585	14	32	.438	61	4	76	2.8	0.2	3.5
86-87—Vanderbilt......................	34	1033	233	389	.599	126	204	.618	295	50	592	8.7	1.5	17.4
87-88—Vanderbilt......................	31	1013	234	369	.634	99	147	.673	314	81	567	10.1	2.6	18.3
Totals	104	2338	519	856	.606	243	392	.620	708	137	1281	6.8	1.3	12.3

NBA REGULAR-SEASON RECORD

Season Team	G	Min.	FGM	FGA	Pct.	FTM	FTA	Pct.	REBOUNDS Off.	Def.	Tot.	Ast.	St.	Blk.	TO	Pts.	AVERAGES RPG	APG	PPG
88-89—Chicago	30	190	29	72	.403	8	14	.571	18	27	45	11	4	6	15	66	1.5	0.4	2.2
89-90—Chicago	77	884	111	268	.414	72	104	.692	88	126	214	46	19	26	65	294	2.8	0.6	3.8
90-91—Chicago	74	972	116	235	.494	75	112	.670	122	214	336	47	23	57	75	307	4.5	0.6	4.1

P

Season Team	G	Min.	FGM	FGA	Pct.	FTM	FTA	Pct.	Off.	Def.	Tot.	Ast.	St.	Blk.	TO	Pts.	RPG	APG	PPG
91-92—Chicago	77	1007	152	278	.547	45	91	.495	108	204	312	80	16	43	72	350	4.1	1.0	4.5
92-93—Chicago	72	998	137	246	.557	67	111	.604	103	184	287	74	22	47	74	341	4.0	1.0	4.7
93-94—Chicago	43	397	47	112	.420	23	32	.719	40	86	126	34	8	11	42	117	2.9	0.8	2.7
94-95—Chicago	78	1592	254	459	.553	113	194	.582	211	311	522	90	26	56	116	621	6.7	1.2	8.0
95-96—San Antonio	80	1396	173	331	.523	67	125	.536	175	310	485	33	28	75	86	413	6.1	0.4	5.2
Totals	531	7436	1019	2001	.509	470	783	.600	865	1462	2327	415	146	321	545	2509	4.4	0.8	4.7

Three-point field goals: 1989-90, 0-for-5. 1990-91, 0-for-3. 1991-92, 1-for-2 (.500). 1992-93, 0-for-1. 1993-94, 0-for-1. 1994-95, 0-for-1. 1995-96, 0-for-1. Totals, 1-for-14 (.071).

Personal fouls/disqualifications: 1988-89, 38/0. 1989-90, 150/0. 1990-91, 147/1. 1991-92, 133/1. 1992-93, 139/2. 1993-94, 61/0. 1994-95, 220/3. 1995-96, 183/0. Totals, 1071/7.

NBA PLAYOFF RECORD

Season Team	G	Min.	FGM	FGA	Pct.	FTM	FTA	Pct.	Off.	Def.	Tot.	Ast.	St.	Blk.	TO	Pts.	RPG	APG	PPG
88-89—Chicago	3	22	6	9	.667	2	3	.667	3	3	6	2	0	0	0	14	2.0	0.7	4.7
89-90—Chicago	13	78	13	28	.464	13	18	.722	7	12	19	2	0	5	4	40	1.5	0.2	3.1
90-91—Chicago	17	198	29	53	.547	12	22	.545	32	33	65	4	2	8	14	70	3.8	0.2	4.1
91-92—Chicago	18	157	18	37	.486	9	20	.450	18	22	40	9	3	10	12	45	2.2	0.5	2.5
92-93—Chicago	13	101	10	20	.500	5	10	.500	15	15	30	5	1	2	8	25	2.3	0.4	1.9
94-95—Chicago	10	176	19	37	.514	12	21	.571	18	30	48	6	1	3	10	50	4.8	0.6	5.0
95-96—San Antonio	10	242	29	42	.690	16	20	.800	26	53	79	5	2	4	11	74	7.9	0.5	7.4
Totals	84	974	124	226	.549	69	114	.605	119	168	287	33	9	32	59	318	3.4	0.4	3.8

Three-point field goals: 1988-89, 0-for-1. 1989-90, 1-for-2 (.500). 1991-92, 0-for-1. Totals, 1-for-4 (.250).

Personal fouls/disqualifications: 1988-89, 4/0. 1989-90, 13/0. 1990-91, 41/1. 1991-92, 34/1. 1992-93, 18/0. 1994-95, 27/0. 1995-96, 24/0. Totals, 161/2.

PERKINS, SAM   F/C   SUPERSONICS

PERSONAL: Born June 14, 1961, in Brooklyn, N.Y. ... 6-9/255. ... Full name: Samuel Bruce Perkins.
HIGH SCHOOL: Shaker (Latham, N.Y.).
COLLEGE: North Carolina.
TRANSACTIONS/CAREER NOTES: Selected by Dallas Mavericks in first round (fourth pick overall) of 1984 NBA Draft. ... Signed as unrestricted free agent by Los Angeles Lakers (August 6, 1990). ... Traded by Lakers to Seattle SuperSonics for C Benoit Benjamin and G/F Doug Christie (February 22, 1993).
MISCELLANEOUS: Member of gold-medal-winning U.S. Olympic team (1984).

COLLEGIATE RECORD

NOTES: THE SPORTING NEWS All-America first team (1984). ... THE SPORTING NEWS All-America second team (1982, 1983). ... Member of NCAA Division I championship team (1982).

Season Team	G	Min.	FGM	FGA	Pct.	FTM	FTA	Pct.	Reb.	Ast.	Pts.	RPG	APG	PPG
80-81—North Carolina	37	1115	199	318	.626	152	205	.741	289	27	550	7.8	0.7	14.9
81-82—North Carolina	32	1141	174	301	.578	109	142	.768	250	35	457	7.8	1.1	14.3
82-83—North Carolina	35	1174	218	414	.527	145	177	.819	330	47	593	9.4	1.3	16.9
83-84—North Carolina	31	1029	195	331	.589	155	181	.856	298	51	545	9.6	1.6	17.6
Totals	135	4459	786	1364	.576	561	705	.796	1167	160	2145	8.6	1.2	15.9

Three-point field goals: 1982-83, 12-for-28 (.429).

NBA REGULAR-SEASON RECORD

HONORS: NBA All-Rookie team (1985).

Season Team	G	Min.	FGM	FGA	Pct.	FTM	FTA	Pct.	Off.	Def.	Tot.	Ast.	St.	Blk.	TO	Pts.	RPG	APG	PPG
84-85—Dallas	82	2317	347	736	.471	200	244	.820	189	416	605	135	63	63	102	903	7.4	1.6	11.0
85-86—Dallas	80	2626	458	910	.503	307	377	.814	195	490	685	153	75	94	145	1234	8.6	1.9	15.4
86-87—Dallas	80	2687	461	957	.482	245	296	.828	197	419	616	146	109	77	132	1186	7.7	1.8	14.8
87-88—Dallas	75	2499	394	876	.450	273	332	.822	201	400	601	118	74	54	119	1066	8.0	1.6	14.2
88-89—Dallas	78	2860	445	959	.464	274	329	.833	235	453	688	127	76	92	141	1171	8.8	1.6	15.0
89-90—Dallas	76	2668	435	883	.493	330	424	.778	209	363	572	175	88	64	148	1206	7.5	2.3	15.9
90-91—L.A. Lakers	73	2504	368	744	.495	229	279	.821	167	371	538	108	64	78	103	983	7.4	1.5	13.5
91-92—L.A. Lakers	63	2332	361	803	.450	304	372	.817	192	364	556	141	64	62	83	1041	8.8	2.2	16.5
92-93—L.A.L.-Sea.	79	2351	381	799	.477	250	305	.820	163	361	524	156	60	82	108	1036	6.6	2.0	13.1
93-94—Seattle	81	2170	341	779	.438	218	272	.801	120	246	366	111	67	31	103	999	4.5	1.4	12.3
94-95—Seattle	82	2356	346	742	.466	215	269	.799	96	302	398	135	72	45	77	1043	4.9	1.6	12.7
95-96—Seattle	82	2169	325	797	.408	191	241	.793	101	266	367	120	83	48	82	970	4.5	1.5	11.8
Totals	931	29539	4662	9985	.467	3036	3740	.812	2065	4451	6516	1625	895	790	1343	12838	7.0	1.7	13.8

Three-point field goals: 1984-85, 9-for-36 (.250). 1985-86, 11-for-33 (.333). 1986-87, 19-for-54 (.352). 1987-88, 5-for-30 (.167). 1988-89, 7-for-38 (.184). 1989-90, 6-for-28 (.214). 1990-91, 18-for-64 (.281). 1991-92, 15-for-69 (.217). 1992-93, 24-for-71 (.338). 1993-94, 99-for-270 (.367). 1994-95, 136-for-343 (.397). 1995-96, 129-for-363 (.355). Totals, 478-for-1399 (.342).

Personal fouls/disqualifications: 1984-85, 236/1. 1985-86, 212/2. 1986-87, 269/6. 1987-88, 227/2. 1988-89, 224/1. 1989-90, 225/4. 1990-91, 247/2. 1991-92, 192/1. 1992-93, 225/0. 1993-94, 197/0. 1994-95, 186/0. 1995-96, 174/1. Totals, 2614/20.

NBA PLAYOFF RECORD

Season Team	G	Min.	FGM	FGA	Pct.	FTM	FTA	Pct.	Off.	Def.	Tot.	Ast.	St.	Blk.	TO	Pts.	RPG	APG	PPG
84-85—Dallas	4	169	24	49	.490	26	34	.765	16	35	51	11	2	1	3	75	12.8	2.8	18.8
85-86—Dallas	10	347	57	133	.429	33	43	.767	30	53	83	24	9	14	16	149	8.3	2.4	14.9
86-87—Dallas	4	133	26	52	.500	16	23	.696	12	22	34	5	4	1	9	68	8.5	1.3	17.0
87-88—Dallas	17	572	88	195	.451	53	66	.803	39	73	112	31	25	17	30	230	6.6	1.8	13.5
89-90—Dallas	3	118	16	36	.444	13	17	.765	10	12	22	8	3	2	7	45	7.3	2.7	15.0

P

Season Team	G	Min.	FGM	FGA	Pct.	FTM	FTA	Pct.	Off.	Def.	Tot.	Ast.	St.	Blk.	TO	Pts.	RPG	APG	PPG
									REBOUNDS								AVERAGES		
90-91—L.A. Lakers	19	752	121	221	.548	83	109	.761	41	116	157	33	15	27	37	336	8.3	1.7	17.7
92-93—Seattle	19	626	98	225	.436	48	55	.873	33	100	133	37	19	25	21	274	7.0	1.9	14.4
93-94—Seattle	5	141	14	42	.333	15	17	.882	6	30	36	4	4	2	6	49	7.2	0.8	9.8
94-95—Seattle	4	141	21	48	.438	2	2	1.000	6	25	31	13	3	5	9	54	7.8	3.3	13.5
95-96—Seattle	21	654	90	196	.459	46	61	.754	21	69	90	35	15	6	30	258	4.3	1.7	12.3
Totals	106	3653	555	1197	.464	335	427	.785	214	535	749	201	99	100	168	1538	7.1	1.9	14.5

Three-point field goals: 1984-85, 1-for-4 (.250). 1985-86, 2-for-8 (.250). 1986-87, 0-for-4. 1987-88, 1-for-7 (.143). 1989-90, 0-for-1. 1990-91, 11-for-30 (.367). 1992-93, 30-for-79 (.380). 1993-94, 6-for-14 (.429). 1994-95, 10-for-22 (.455). 1995-96, 32-for-87 (.368). Totals, 93-for-256 (.363).

Personal fouls/disqualifications: 1984-85, 13/1. 1985-86, 32/0. 1986-87, 16/0. 1987-88, 51/1. 1989-90, 17/2. 1990-91, 69/0. 1992-93, 55/0. 1993-94, 15/0. 1994-95, 12/0. 1995-96, 44/0. Totals, 324/4.

PERRY, ELLIOT   G   SUNS

PERSONAL: Born March 28, 1969, in Memphis. ... 6-0/160. ... Full name: Elliot Lamonte Perry.
HIGH SCHOOL: Treadwell (Memphis).
COLLEGE: Memphis.
TRANSACTIONS/CAREER NOTES: Selected by Los Angeles Clippers in second round (37th pick overall) of 1991 NBA Draft. ... Waived by Clippers (November 25, 1991). ... Played in Continental Basketball Association with La Crosse Catbirds (1991-92 and 1992-93), Rochester Renegades (1992-93) and Grand Rapids Hoops (1993-94). ... Signed as free agent by Charlotte Hornets (December 9, 1991). ... Signed as free agent by Portland Trail Blazers (October 7, 1992). ... Waived by Trail Blazers (November 2, 1992). ... Re-signed by Trail Blazers (August 5, 1993). ... Waived by Trail Blazers (November 3, 1993). ... Signed by Phoenix Suns to first of two consecutive 10-day contracts (January 22, 1994). ... Re-signed by Suns for remainder of season (February 11, 1994).

COLLEGIATE RECORD

Season Team	G	Min.	FGM	FGA	Pct.	FTM	FTA	Pct.	Reb.	Ast.	Pts.	RPG	APG	PPG
												AVERAGES		
87-88—Memphis	32	968	140	336	.417	87	108	.806	113	130	420	3.5	4.1	13.1
88-89—Memphis	32	1017	202	437	.462	192	234	.821	109	118	620	3.4	3.7	19.4
89-90—Memphis	30	970	175	419	.418	137	182	.753	110	150	504	3.7	5.0	16.8
90-91—Memphis	32	1169	235	507	.464	146	184	.793	111	148	665	3.5	4.6	20.8
Totals	126	4124	752	1699	.443	562	708	.794	443	546	2209	3.5	4.3	17.5

Three-point field goals: 1987-88, 53-for-136 (.390). 1988-89, 24-for-76 (.316). 1989-90, 17-for-66 (.258). 1990-91, 49-for-136 (.360). Totals, 143-for-414 (.345).

CBA REGULAR-SEASON RECORD

Season Team	G	Min.	FGM	FGA	Pct.	FTM	FTA	Pct.	Reb.	Ast.	Pts.	RPG	APG	PPG
												AVERAGES		
91-92—La Crosse	2	59	8	18	.444	11	13	.846	2	9	27	1.0	4.5	13.5
92-93—La Crosse-Rochester	52	1682	259	543	.477	114	153	.745	136	240	633	2.6	4.6	12.2
93-94—Grand Rapids	28	933	151	283	.534	82	102	.804	99	179	387	3.5	6.4	13.8
Totals	82	2674	418	844	.495	207	268	.772	237	428	1047	2.9	5.2	12.8

Three-point field goals: 1991-92, 0-for-3. 1992-93, 1-for-13 (.077). 1993-94, 3-for-5 (.600). Totals, 4-for-21 (.191).

NBA REGULAR-SEASON RECORD

Season Team	G	Min.	FGM	FGA	Pct.	FTM	FTA	Pct.	Off.	Def.	Tot.	Ast.	St.	Blk.	TO	Pts.	RPG	APG	PPG
									REBOUNDS								AVERAGES		
91-92—LAC-Char	50	437	49	129	.380	27	41	.659	14	25	39	78	34	3	50	126	0.8	1.6	2.5
93-94—Phoenix	27	432	42	113	.372	21	28	.750	12	27	39	125	25	1	43	105	1.4	4.6	3.9
94-95—Phoenix	82	1977	306	588	.520	158	195	.810	51	100	151	394	156	4	163	795	1.8	4.8	9.7
95-96—Phoenix	81	1668	261	549	.475	151	194	.778	34	102	136	353	87	5	146	697	1.7	4.4	8.6
Totals	240	4514	658	1379	.477	357	458	.779	111	254	365	950	302	13	402	1723	1.5	4.0	7.2

Three-point field goals: 1991-92, 1-for-7 (.143). 1993-94, 0-for-3. 1994-95, 25-for-60 (.417). 1995-96, 24-for-59 (.407). Totals, 50-for-129 (.388).
Personal fouls/disqualifications: 1991-92, 36/0. 1993-94, 36/0. 1994-95, 142/0. 1995-96, 140/1. Totals, 354/1.

NBA PLAYOFF RECORD

Season Team	G	Min.	FGM	FGA	Pct.	FTM	FTA	Pct.	Off.	Def.	Tot.	Ast.	St.	Blk.	TO	Pts.	RPG	APG	PPG
									REBOUNDS								AVERAGES		
93-94—Phoenix	4	13	1	7	.143	0	0	...	0	0	0	1	1	0	1	2	0.0	0.3	0.5
94-95—Phoenix	9	106	20	42	.476	20	25	.800	3	7	10	12	5	0	9	62	1.1	1.3	6.9
95-96—Phoenix	4	51	7	14	.500	0	1	.000	0	2	2	12	2	0	0	14	0.5	3.0	3.5
Totals	17	170	28	63	.444	20	26	.769	3	9	12	25	8	0	10	78	0.7	1.5	4.6

Three-point field goals: 1994-95, 2-for-5 (.400).
Personal fouls/disqualifications: 1993-94, 2/0. 1994-95, 8/0. 1995-96, 3/0. Totals, 13/0.

P

PERRY, TIM   F

PERSONAL: Born June 4, 1965, in Freehold, N.J. ... 6-9/220. ... Full name: Timothy D. Perry.
HIGH SCHOOL: Freehold (N.J.).
COLLEGE: Temple.
TRANSACTIONS/CAREER NOTES: Selected by Phoenix Suns in first round (seventh pick overall) of 1988 NBA Draft. ... Traded by Suns with G Jeff Hornacek and C Andrew Lang to Philadelphia 76ers for F Charles Barkley (June 17, 1992). ... Traded by 76ers with C Shawn Bradley and G Greg Graham to New Jersey Nets for F Derrick Coleman, F Sean Higgins and G Rex Walters (November 30, 1995). ... Rights renounced by Nets (July 16, 1996).

COLLEGIATE RECORD

Season Team	G	Min.	FGM	FGA	Pct.	FTM	FTA	Pct.	Reb.	Ast.	Pts.	RPG	APG	PPG
												AVERAGES		
84-85—Temple	30	621	29	70	.414	10	20	.500	118	2	68	3.9	0.1	2.3
85-86—Temple	31	1101	141	249	.566	77	134	.575	293	6	359	9.5	0.2	11.6

Season Team	G	Min.	FGM	FGA	Pct.	FTM	FTA	Pct.	Reb.	Ast.	Pts.	RPG	APG	PPG
86-87—Temple	36	1271	180	350	.514	103	166	.620	310	5	463	8.6	0.1	12.9
87-88—Temple	33	1103	203	347	.585	72	113	.637	264	22	478	8.0	0.7	14.5
Totals	130	4096	553	1016	.544	262	433	.605	985	35	1368	7.6	0.3	10.5

NBA REGULAR-SEASON RECORD

Season Team	G	Min.	FGM	FGA	Pct.	FTM	FTA	Pct.	REBOUNDS Off.	Def.	Tot.	Ast.	St.	Blk.	TO	Pts.	AVERAGES RPG	APG	PPG
88-89—Phoenix	62	614	108	201	.537	40	65	.615	61	71	132	18	19	32	37	257	2.1	0.3	4.1
89-90—Phoenix	60	612	100	195	.513	53	90	.589	79	73	152	17	21	22	47	254	2.5	0.3	4.2
90-91—Phoenix	46	587	75	144	.521	43	70	.614	53	73	126	27	23	43	32	193	2.7	0.6	4.2
91-92—Phoenix	80	2483	413	789	.523	153	215	.712	204	347	551	134	44	116	141	982	6.9	1.7	12.3
92-93—Philadelphia	81	2104	287	613	.468	147	207	.710	154	255	409	126	40	91	123	731	5.0	1.6	9.0
93-94—Philadelphia	80	2336	272	625	.435	102	176	.580	117	287	404	94	60	82	80	719	5.1	1.2	9.0
94-95—Philadelphia	42	446	27	78	.346	22	40	.550	38	51	89	12	10	15	21	76	2.1	0.3	1.8
95-96—Phil.-N.J.	30	254	31	65	.477	5	9	.556	21	27	48	8	4	13	10	71	1.6	0.3	2.4
Totals	481	9436	1313	2710	.485	565	872	.648	727	1184	1911	436	221	414	491	3283	4.0	0.9	6.8

Three-point field goals: 1988-89, 1-for-4 (.250). 1989-90, 1-for-1. 1990-91, 0-for-5. 1991-92, 3-for-8 (.375). 1992-93, 10-for-49 (.204). 1993-94, 73-for-200 (.365). 1994-95, 0-for-14. 1995-96, 4-for-8 (.500). Totals, 92-for-289 (.318).

Personal fouls/disqualifications: 1988-89, 47/0. 1989-90, 76/0. 1990-91, 60/1. 1991-92, 237/2. 1992-93, 159/0. 1993-94, 154/1. 1994-95, 51/0. 1995-96, 16/0. Totals, 800/4.

NBA PLAYOFF RECORD

Season Team	G	Min.	FGM	FGA	Pct.	FTM	FTA	Pct.	REBOUNDS Off.	Def.	Tot.	Ast.	St.	Blk.	TO	Pts.	AVERAGES RPG	APG	PPG
88-89—Phoenix	4	17	2	4	.500	0	2	.000	1	1	2	0	2	1	1	4	0.5	0.0	1.0
89-90—Phoenix	11	100	13	25	.520	8	18	.444	10	11	21	2	3	6	5	34	1.9	0.2	3.1
91-92—Phoenix	8	185	38	63	.603	23	32	.719	12	27	39	11	3	6	14	99	4.9	1.4	12.4
Totals	23	302	53	92	.576	31	52	.596	23	39	62	13	8	13	20	137	2.7	0.6	6.0

Personal fouls/disqualifications: 1988-89, 1/0. 1989-90, 19/0. 1991-92, 24/1. Totals, 44/1.

PERSON, CHUCK   F   SPURS

PERSONAL: Born June 27, 1964, in Brantley, Ala. ... 6-8/230. ... Full name: Chuck Connors Person. ... Brother of Wesley Person, guard with Phoenix Suns. ... Nickname: The Rifleman.

HIGH SCHOOL: Brantley (Ala.).

COLLEGE: Auburn.

TRANSACTIONS/CAREER NOTES: Selected by Indiana Pacers in first round (fourth pick overall) of 1986 NBA Draft. ... Traded by Pacers with G Micheal Williams to Minnesota Timberwolves for G Pooh Richardson and F Sam Mitchell (September 8, 1992). ... Signed as unrestricted free agent by San Antonio Spurs (July 21, 1994).

COLLEGIATE RECORD

NOTES: The Sporting News All-America second team (1985, 1986).

Season Team	G	Min.	FGM	FGA	Pct.	FTM	FTA	Pct.	Reb.	Ast.	Pts.	AVERAGES RPG	APG	PPG
82-83—Auburn	28	636	118	218	.541	25	33	.758	128	37	261	4.6	1.3	9.3
83-84—Auburn	31	1079	255	470	.543	83	114	.728	249	38	593	8.0	1.2	19.1
84-85—Auburn	34	1240	334	614	.544	79	107	.738	303	69	747	8.9	2.0	22.0
85-86—Auburn	33	1178	310	597	.519	90	112	.804	260	30	710	7.9	0.9	21.5
Totals	126	4133	1017	1899	.536	277	366	.757	940	174	2311	7.5	1.4	18.3

NBA REGULAR-SEASON RECORD

HONORS: NBA Rookie of the Year (1987). ... NBA All-Rookie team (1987).

Season Team	G	Min.	FGM	FGA	Pct.	FTM	FTA	Pct.	REBOUNDS Off.	Def.	Tot.	Ast.	St.	Blk.	TO	Pts.	AVERAGES RPG	APG	PPG
86-87—Indiana	82	2956	635	1358	.468	222	297	.747	168	509	677	295	90	16	211	1541	8.3	3.6	18.8
87-88—Indiana	79	2807	575	1252	.459	132	197	.670	171	365	536	309	73	8	210	1341	6.8	3.9	17.0
88-89—Indiana	80	3012	711	1453	.489	243	307	.792	144	372	516	289	83	18	308	1728	6.5	3.6	21.6
89-90—Indiana	77	2714	605	1242	.487	211	270	.781	126	319	445	230	53	20	170	1515	5.8	3.0	19.7
90-91—Indiana	80	2566	620	1231	.504	165	229	.721	121	296	417	238	56	17	184	1474	5.2	3.0	18.4
91-92—Indiana	81	2923	616	1281	.480	133	197	.675	114	312	426	382	68	18	216	1497	5.3	4.7	18.5
92-93—Minnesota	78	2985	541	1248	.434	109	168	.649	98	335	433	343	67	30	219	1309	5.6	4.4	16.8
93-94—Minnesota	77	2029	356	843	.422	82	108	.759	55	198	253	185	45	12	121	894	3.3	2.4	11.6
94-95—San Antonio	81	2033	317	750	.423	66	102	.647	49	209	258	106	45	12	102	872	3.2	1.3	10.8
95-96—San Antonio	80	2131	308	705	.437	67	104	.644	76	337	413	100	49	26	91	873	5.2	1.3	10.9
Totals	795	26156	5284	11366	.465	1430	1979	.723	1122	3252	4374	2477	629	177	1832	13044	5.5	3.1	16.4

Three-point field goals: 1986-87, 49-for-138 (.355). 1987-88, 59-for-177 (.333). 1988-89, 63-for-205 (.307). 1989-90, 94-for-253 (.372). 1990-91, 86-for-203 (.340). 1991-92, 132-for-354 (.373). 1992-93, 118-for-332 (.355). 1993-94, 100-for-272 (.368). 1994-95, 172-for-445 (.387). 1995-96, 190-for-463 (.410). Totals, 1046-for-2842 (.368).

Personal fouls/disqualifications: 1986-87, 310/4. 1987-88, 266/4. 1988-89, 280/12. 1989-90, 217/1. 1990-91, 221/1. 1991-92, 247/5. 1992-93, 198/2. 1993-94, 164/0. 1994-95, 198/0. 1995-96, 197/2. Totals, 2298/31.

NBA PLAYOFF RECORD

Season Team	G	Min.	FGM	FGA	Pct.	FTM	FTA	Pct.	REBOUNDS Off.	Def.	Tot.	Ast.	St.	Blk.	TO	Pts.	AVERAGES RPG	APG	PPG
86-87—Indiana	4	159	38	74	.514	30	39	.769	6	27	33	20	5	2	15	108	8.3	5.0	27.0
89-90—Indiana	3	123	17	45	.378	5	12	.417	6	14	20	12	1	0	4	40	6.7	4.0	13.3
90-91—Indiana	5	192	48	90	.533	17	21	.810	3	25	28	16	5	0	12	130	5.6	3.2	26.0
91-92—Indiana	3	118	19	47	.404	8	12	.667	1	8	9	7	2	0	6	51	3.0	2.3	17.0
94-95—San Antonio	15	258	27	77	.351	8	11	.727	2	25	27	8	4	7	6	75	1.8	0.5	5.0

Season Team	G	Min.	FGM	FGA	Pct.	FTM	FTA	Pct.	REBOUNDS Off.	Def.	Tot.	Ast.	St.	Blk.	TO	Pts.	AVERAGES RPG	APG	PPG
95-96—San Antonio....	10	284	41	77	.532	14	17	.824	5	35	40	16	2	3	11	121	4.0	1.6	12.1
Totals	40	1134	190	410	.463	82	112	.732	23	134	157	79	19	12	54	525	3.9	2.0	13.1

Three-point field goals: 1986-87, 2-for-8 (.250). 1989-90, 1-for-10 (.100). 1990-91, 17-for-31 (.548). 1991-92, 5-for-15 (.333). 1994-95, 13-for-45 (.289). 1995-96, 25-for-47 (.532). Totals, 63-for-156 (.404).

Personal fouls/disqualifications: 1986-87, 14/0. 1989-90, 11/0. 1990-91, 15/1. 1991-92, 11/0. 1994-95, 22/0. 1995-96, 32/0. Totals, 105/1.

PERSON, WESLEY   G   SUNS

PERSONAL: Born March 28, 1971, in Crenshaw, Ala. ... 6-6/195. ... Full name: Wesley Lavon Person. ... Brother of Chuck Person, forward with San Antonio Spurs.
HIGH SCHOOL: Brantley (Ala.).
COLLEGE: Auburn.
TRANSACTIONS/CAREER NOTES: Selected by Phoenix Suns in first round (23rd pick overall) of 1994 NBA Draft.

COLLEGIATE RECORD

Season Team	G	Min.	FGM	FGA	Pct.	FTM	FTA	Pct.	Reb.	Ast.	Pts.	AVERAGES RPG	APG	PPG
90-91—Auburn	26	857	153	325	.471	52	68	.765	147	48	400	5.7	1.8	15.4
91-92—Auburn	27	955	208	411	.506	53	73	.726	183	55	538	6.8	2.0	19.9
92-93—Auburn	27	957	194	349	.556	61	79	.772	192	102	507	7.1	3.8	18.8
93-94—Auburn	28	1006	217	448	.484	94	128	.734	179	79	621	6.4	2.8	22.2
Totals	108	3775	772	1533	.504	260	348	.747	701	284	2066	6.5	2.6	19.1

Three-point field goals: 1990-91, 42-for-118 (.356). 1991-92, 69-for-141 (.489). 1992-93, 58-for-125 (.464). 1993-94, 93-for-210 (.443). Totals, 262-for-594 (.441).

HONORS: NBA All-Rookie second team (1995).

NBA REGULAR-SEASON RECORD

Season Team	G	Min.	FGM	FGA	Pct.	FTM	FTA	Pct.	REBOUNDS Off.	Def.	Tot.	Ast.	St.	Blk.	TO	Pts.	AVERAGES RPG	APG	PPG
94-95—Phoenix	78	1800	309	638	.484	80	101	.792	67	134	201	105	48	24	79	814	2.6	1.3	10.4
95-96—Phoenix	82	2609	390	877	.445	148	192	.771	56	265	321	138	55	22	89	1045	3.9	1.7	12.7
Totals	160	4409	699	1515	.461	228	293	.778	123	399	522	243	103	46	168	1859	3.3	1.5	11.6

Three-point field goals: 1994-95, 116-for-266 (.436). 1995-96, 117-for-313 (.374). Totals, 233-for-579 (.402).
Personal fouls/disqualifications: 1994-95, 149/0. 1995-96, 148/0. Totals, 297/0.

NBA PLAYOFF RECORD

Season Team	G	Min.	FGM	FGA	Pct.	FTM	FTA	Pct.	REBOUNDS Off.	Def.	Tot.	Ast.	St.	Blk.	TO	Pts.	AVERAGES RPG	APG	PPG
94-95—Phoenix	10	247	34	83	.410	11	12	.917	9	12	21	11	3	2	9	96	2.1	1.1	9.6
95-96—Phoenix	4	183	22	56	.393	4	5	.800	8	15	23	3	3	1	5	57	5.8	0.8	14.3
Totals	14	430	56	139	.403	15	17	.882	17	27	44	14	6	3	14	153	3.1	1.0	10.9

Three-point field goals: 1994-95, 17-for-45 (.378). 1995-96, 9-for-29 (.310). Totals, 26-for-74 (.351).
Personal fouls/disqualifications: 1994-95, 19/0. 1995-96, 7/0. Totals, 26/0.

PHILLS, BOBBY   G   CAVALIERS

PERSONAL: Born December 20, 1969, in Baton Rouge, La. ... 6-5/220. ... Full name: Bobby Ray Phills II.
HIGH SCHOOL: Southern University Lab (Baton Rouge, La.).
COLLEGE: Southern (La.).
TRANSACTIONS/CAREER NOTES: Selected by Milwaukee Bucks in second round (45th pick overall) of 1991 NBA Draft. ... Waived by Bucks (December 18, 1991). ... Played in Continental Basketball Association with Sioux Falls Skyforce (1991-92). ... Signed by Cleveland Cavaliers to 10-day contract (March 19, 1992). ... Re-signed by Cavaliers for remainder of season (March 29, 1992).

COLLEGIATE RECORD

NOTES: Led NCAA Division I with 4.39 three-point field-goals made per game (1991).

Season Team	G	Min.	FGM	FGA	Pct.	FTM	FTA	Pct.	Reb.	Ast.	Pts.	AVERAGES RPG	APG	PPG
87-88—Southern	23	158	26	53	.491	30	42	.714	41	8	85	1.8	0.3	3.7
88-89—Southern	31	923	166	385	.431	44	60	.733	142	55	420	4.6	1.8	13.5
89-90—Southern	31	937	232	574	.404	46	70	.657	132	89	622	4.3	2.9	20.1
90-91—Southern	28	986	260	641	.406	152	211	.720	132	52	795	4.7	1.9	28.4
Totals	113	3004	684	1653	.414	272	383	.710	447	204	1922	4.0	1.8	17.0

Three-point field goals: 1987-88, 3-for-7 (.429). 1988-89, 44-for-128 (.344). 1989-90, 112-for-300 (.373). 1990-91, 123-for-353 (.348). Totals, 282-for-788 (.358).

CBA REGULAR-SEASON RECORD

Season Team	G	Min.	FGM	FGA	Pct.	FTM	FTA	Pct.	Reb.	Ast.	Pts.	AVERAGES RPG	APG	PPG
91-92—Sioux Falls......................	34	1272	289	624	.463	177	230	.770	222	92	785	6.5	2.7	23.1

Three-point field goals: 1991-92, 30-for-106 (.283).

HONORS: NBA All-Defensive second team (1996).

NBA REGULAR-SEASON RECORD

Season Team	G	Min.	FGM	FGA	Pct.	FTM	FTA	Pct.	REBOUNDS Off.	Def.	Tot.	Ast.	St.	Blk.	TO	Pts.	AVERAGES RPG	APG	PPG
91-92—Cleveland	10	65	12	28	.429	7	11	.636	4	4	8	4	3	1	8	31	0.8	0.4	3.1

P

Season Team	G	Min.	FGM	FGA	Pct.	FTM	FTA	Pct.	Off.	Def.	Tot.	Ast.	St.	Blk.	TO	Pts.	RPG	APG	PPG
									REBOUNDS								AVERAGES		
92-93—Cleveland	31	139	38	82	.463	15	25	.600	6	11	17	10	10	2	18	93	0.5	0.3	3.0
93-94—Cleveland	72	1531	242	514	.471	113	157	.720	71	141	212	133	67	12	63	598	2.9	1.8	8.3
94-95—Cleveland	80	2500	338	816	.414	183	235	.779	90	175	265	180	115	25	113	878	3.3	2.3	11.0
95-96—Cleveland	72	2530	386	826	.467	186	240	.775	62	199	261	271	102	27	126	1051	3.6	3.8	14.6
Totals	265	6765	1016	2266.	.448	504	668	.754	233	530	763	598	297	67	328	2651	2.9	2.3	10.0

Three-point field goals: 1991-92, 0-for-2. 1992-93, 2-for-5 (.400). 1993-94, 1-for-12 (.083). 1994-95, 19-for-55 (.345). 1995-96, 93-for-211 (.441). Totals, 115-for-285 (.404).

Personal fouls/disqualifications: 1991-92, 3/0. 1992-93, 19/0. 1993-94, 135/1. 1994-95, 206/0. 1995-96, 192/3. Totals, 555/4.

NBA PLAYOFF RECORD

Season Team	G	Min.	FGM	FGA	Pct.	FTM	FTA	Pct.	Off.	Def.	Tot.	Ast.	St.	Blk.	TO	Pts.	RPG	APG	PPG
									REBOUNDS								AVERAGES		
91-92—Cleveland	5	12	4	9	.444	3	4	.750	2	4	6	5	1	0	2	11	1.2	1.0	2.2
92-93—Cleveland	2	9	1	3	.333	2	2	1.000	0	0	0	0	0	1	4	0.0	0.0	2.0
93-94—Cleveland	3	68	9	24	.375	1	2	.500	5	9	14	7	2	0	5	20	4.7	2.3	6.7
94-95—Cleveland	4	146	19	43	.442	15	20	.750	3	9	12	6	9	0	9	57	3.0	1.5	14.3
95-96—Cleveland	3	96	13	35	.371	1	4	.250	5	9	14	6	2	1	5	29	4.7	2.0	9.7
Totals	17	331	46	114	.404	22	32	.688	15	31	46	24	14	1	22	121	2.7	1.4	7.1

Three-point field goals: 1991-92, 0-for-1. 1993-94, 1-for-1. 1994-95, 4-for-7 (.571). 1995-96, 2-for-10 (.200). Totals, 7-for-19 (.368).

Personal fouls/disqualifications: 1991-92, 1/0. 1993-94, 11/0. 1994-95, 8/0. 1995-96, 4/0. Totals, 24/0.

PIATKOWSKI, ERIC   G/F   CLIPPERS

PERSONAL: Born September 30, 1970, in Steubenville, Ohio. ... 6-7/215. ... Full name: Eric Todd Piatkowski. ... Name pronounced pie-it-COW-ski. ... Son of Walt Piatkowski, forward with Denver Rockets and Floridians of ABA (1968-69 through 1971-1972).
HIGH SCHOOL: Stevens (Rapid City, S.D.).
COLLEGE: Nebraska.
TRANSACTIONS/CAREER NOTES: Selected by Indiana Pacers in first round (15th pick overall) of 1994 NBA Draft. ... Draft rights traded by Pacers with F Malik Sealy and G Pooh Richardson to Los Angeles Clippers for G Mark Jackson and draft rights to G Greg Minor (June 30, 1994).

COLLEGIATE RECORD

Season Team	G	Min.	FGM	FGA	Pct.	FTM	FTA	Pct.	Reb.	Ast.	Pts.	RPG	APG	PPG
												AVERAGES		
89-90—Nebraska							Did not play—redshirted.							
90-91—Nebraska	34	679	128	275	.465	72	86	.837	125	68	372	3.7	2.0	10.9
91-92—Nebraska	29	873	144	338	.426	79	109	.725	184	97	414	6.3	3.3	14.3
92-93—Nebraska	30	894	178	367	.485	98	129	.760	171	75	502	5.7	2.5	16.7
93-94—Nebraska	30	972	226	456	.496	131	165	.794	189	82	646	6.3	2.7	21.5
Totals	123	3418	676	1436	.471	380	489	.777	669	322	1934	5.4	2.6	15.7

Three-point field goals: 1990-91, 44-for-127 (.346). 1991-92, 47-for-136 (.346). 1992-93, 48-for-129 (.372). 1993-94, 63-for-172 (.366). Totals, 202-for-564 (.358).

NBA REGULAR-SEASON RECORD

Season Team	G	Min.	FGM	FGA	Pct.	FTM	FTA	Pct.	Off.	Def.	Tot.	Ast.	St.	Blk.	TO	Pts.	RPG	APG	PPG
									REBOUNDS								AVERAGES		
94-95—L.A. Clippers...	81	1208	201	456	.441	90	115	.783	63	70	133	77	37	15	63	566	1.6	1.0	7.0
95-96—L.A. Clippers ...	65	784	98	242	.405	67	82	.817	40	63	103	48	24	10	45	301	1.6	0.7	4.6
Totals	146	1992	299	698	.428	157	197	.797	103	133	236	125	61	25	108	867	1.6	0.9	5.9

Three-point field goals: 1994-95, 74-for-198 (.374). 1995-96, 38-for-114 (.333). Totals, 112-for-312 (.359).

Personal fouls/disqualifications: 1994-95, 150/1. 1995-96, 83/0. Totals, 233/1.

PIERCE, RICKY   G   NUGGETS

PERSONAL: Born August 19, 1959, in Dallas. ... 6-4/215. ... Full name: Ricky Charles Pierce.
HIGH SCHOOL: South Garland (Texas).
JUNIOR COLLEGE: Walla Walla (Wash.) Community College.
COLLEGE: Rice.
TRANSACTIONS/CAREER NOTES: Selected by Detroit Pistons in first round (18th pick overall) of 1982 NBA Draft. ... Traded by Pistons to San Diego Clippers for 1986 and 1987 second-round draft choices (October 17, 1983). ... Traded by Clippers with F Terry Cummings and G Craig Hodges to Milwaukee Bucks for F Marques Johnson, F/C Harvey Catchings, G/F Junior Bridgeman and cash (September 29, 1984). ... Traded by Bucks to Seattle SuperSonics for G/F Dale Ellis (February 15, 1991). ... Traded by SuperSonics with draft rights to F Carlos Rogers and two 1995 second-round draft choices to Golden State Warriors for G Sarunas Marciulionis and F Byron Houston (July 18, 1994). ... Signed as unrestricted free agent by Indiana Pacers (October 3, 1995). ... Traded by Pacers with G Mark Jackson and 1996 first-round draft choice to Denver Nuggets for G Jalen Rose, F Reggie Williams and 1996 first-round draft choice (June 13, 1996).

COLLEGIATE RECORD

Season Team	G	Min.	FGM	FGA	Pct.	FTM	FTA	Pct.	Reb.	Ast.	Pts.	RPG	APG	PPG
												AVERAGES		
78-79—Walla Walla C.C.	...	...	...	...	...	...	...	...	...	...	...	...	...	19.0
79-80—Rice	26	878	202	421	.480	94	131	.718	214	37	498	8.2	1.4	19.2
80-81—Rice	26	901	230	444	.518	84	119	.706	181	31	544	7.0	1.2	20.9
81-82—Rice	30	1104	314	614	.511	177	223	.794	226	26	805	7.5	0.9	26.8
Totals	82	2883	746	1479	.504	355	473	.751	621	94	1847	7.6	1.1	22.5

NBA REGULAR-SEASON RECORD

HONORS: NBA Sixth Man Award (1987, 1990).

P

Season Team	G	Min.	FGM	FGA	Pct.	FTM	FTA	Pct.	Off.	Def.	Tot.	Ast.	St.	Blk.	TO	Pts.	RPG	APG	PPG
82-83—Detroit	39	265	33	88	.375	18	32	.563	15	20	35	14	8	4	18	85	0.9	0.4	2.2
83-84—San Diego	69	1280	268	570	.470	149	173	.861	59	76	135	60	27	13	81	685	2.0	0.9	9.9
84-85—Milwaukee	44	882	165	307	.537	102	124	.823	49	68	117	94	34	5	63	433	2.7	2.1	9.8
85-86—Milwaukee	81	2147	429	798	.538	266	310	.858	94	137	231	177	83	6	107	1127	2.9	2.2	13.9
86-87—Milwaukee	79	2505	575	1077	.534	387	440	.880	117	149	266	144	64	24	120	1540	3.4	1.8	19.5
87-88—Milwaukee	37	965	248	486	.510	107	122	.877	30	53	83	73	21	7	57	606	2.2	2.0	16.4
88-89—Milwaukee	75	2078	527	1018	.518	255	297	.859	82	115	197	156	77	19	112	1317	2.6	2.1	17.6
89-90—Milwaukee	59	1709	503	987	.510	307	366	.839	64	103	167	133	50	7	129	1359	2.8	2.3	23.0
90-91—Mil.-Seattle	78	2167	561	1156	.485	430	471	.913	67	124	191	168	60	13	147	1598	2.4	2.2	20.5
91-92—Seattle	78	2658	620	1306	.475	417	455	.916	93	140	233	241	86	20	189	1690	3.0	3.1	21.7
92-93—Seattle	77	2218	524	1071	.489	313	352	.889	58	134	192	220	100	7	160	1403	2.5	2.9	18.2
93-94—Seattle	51	1022	272	577	.471	189	211	.896	29	54	83	91	42	5	64	739	1.6	1.8	14.5
94-95—Golden State...	27	673	111	254	.437	93	106	.877	12	52	64	40	22	2	24	338	2.4	1.5	12.5
95-96—Indiana...........	76	1404	264	590	.447	174	205	.849	40	96	136	101	57	6	93	737	1.8	1.3	9.7
Totals	870	21973	5100	10285	.496	3207	3664	.875	809	1321	2130	1712	731	138	1364	13657	2.4	2.0	15.7

Three-point field goals: 1982-83, 1-for-7 (.143). 1983-84, 0-for-9. 1984-85, 1-for-4 (.250). 1985-86, 3-for-23 (.130). 1986-87, 3-for-28 (.107). 1987-88, 3-for-14 (.214). 1988-89, 8-for-36 (.222). 1989-90, 46-for-133 (.346). 1990-91, 46-for-116 (.397). 1991-92, 33-for-123 (.268). 1992-93, 42-for-113 (.372). 1993-94, 6-for-32 (.188). 1994-95, 23-for-70 (.329). 1995-96, 35-for-104 (.337). Totals, 250-for-812 (.308).

Personal fouls/disqualifications: 1982-83, 42/0. 1983-84, 143/1. 1984-85, 117/0. 1985-86, 252/6. 1986-87, 222/0. 1987-88, 94/0. 1988-89, 193/1. 1989-90, 158/2. 1990-91, 170/1. 1991-92, 213/2. 1992-93, 167/0. 1993-94, 84/0. 1994-95, 38/0. 1995-96, 188/1. Totals, 2081/14.

NBA PLAYOFF RECORD

Season Team	G	Min.	FGM	FGA	Pct.	FTM	FTA	Pct.	Off.	Def.	Tot.	Ast.	St.	Blk.	TO	Pts.	RPG	APG	PPG
84-85—Milwaukee	8	198	36	73	.493	7	9	.778	8	10	18	15	3	1	17	79	2.3	1.9	9.9
85-86—Milwaukee	13	322	52	113	.460	40	45	.889	20	16	36	20	8	3	15	144	2.8	1.5	11.1
86-87—Milwaukee	12	317	68	142	.479	55	67	.821	12	16	28	16	10	5	19	191	2.3	1.3	15.9
87-88—Milwaukee	5	105	25	53	.472	8	9	.889	6	8	14	9	1	2	4	59	2.8	1.8	11.8
88-89—Milwaukee	9	292	77	141	.546	41	47	.872	5	20	25	25	11	2	9	201	2.8	2.8	22.3
89-90—Milwaukee	4	122	28	60	.467	28	31	.903	6	3	9	6	5	0	3	89	2.3	1.5	22.3
90-91—Seattle	5	112	19	57	.333	16	17	.941	6	8	14	4	4	1	11	57	2.8	0.8	11.4
91-92—Seattle	9	316	63	131	.481	47	54	.870	9	13	22	28	5	1	24	176	2.4	3.1	19.6
92-93—Seattle	19	578	123	270	.456	79	88	.898	17	29	46	42	12	4	28	337	2.4	2.2	17.7
93-94—Seattle	5	74	14	31	.452	12	17	.706	4	1	5	3	1	0	9	40	1.0	0.6	8.0
95-96—Indiana...........	5	133	16	47	.340	17	20	.850	3	1	4	15	8	1	12	51	0.8	3.0	10.2
Totals	94	2569	521	1118	.466	350	404	.866	96	125	221	183	68	20	151	1424	2.4	1.9	15.1

Three-point field goals: 1984-85, 0-for-2. 1985-86, 0-for-2. 1987-88, 1-for-5 (.200). 1988-89, 6-for-8 (.750). 1989-90, 5-for-10 (.500). 1990-91, 3-for-10 (.300). 1991-92, 3-for-11 (.273). 1992-93, 12-for-30 (.400). 1995-96, 2-for-8 (.250). Totals, 32-for-86 (.372).

Personal fouls/disqualifications: 1984-85, 26/0. 1985-86, 42/0. 1986-87, 39/0. 1987-88, 9/0. 1988-89, 31/1. 1989-90, 14/0. 1990-91, 12/1. 1991-92, 24/0. 1992-93, 40/0. 1993-94, 8/0. 1995-96, 13/0. Totals, 258/2.

NBA ALL-STAR GAME RECORD

Season Team	Min.	FGM	FGA	Pct.	FTM	FTA	Pct.	Off.	Def.	Tot.	Ast.	PF	Dq.	St.	Blk.	TO	Pts.
1991 —Milwaukee	19	4	8	.500	1	1	1.000	0	2	2	2	2	0	0	0	2	9

PINCKNEY, ED — F

PERSONAL: Born March 27, 1963, in Bronx, N.Y. ... 6-9/240. ... Full name: Edward Lewis Pinckney.
HIGH SCHOOL: Adlai E. Stevenson (Bronx, N.Y.).
COLLEGE: Villanova.
TRANSACTIONS/CAREER NOTES: Selected by Phoenix Suns in first round (10th pick overall) of 1985 NBA Draft. ... Traded by Suns with 1988 second-round draft choice to Sacramento Kings for F Eddie Johnson (June 21, 1987). ... Traded by Kings with C/F Joe Kleine to Boston Celtics for G Danny Ainge and C/F Brad Lohaus (February 23, 1989). ... Traded by Celtics with draft rights to C Andrei Fetisov to Milwaukee Bucks for G/F Blue Edwards and F Derek Strong (June 29, 1994). ... Selected by Toronto Raptors from Bucks in NBA expansion draft (June 24, 1995). ... Traded by Raptors with F Tony Massenburg and right to swap 1996 or 1997 first-round draft choices to Philadelphia 76ers for F Sharone Wright (February 22, 1996). ... Rights renounced by 76ers (July 15, 1996).

COLLEGIATE RECORD

NOTES: NCAA Division I Tournament Most Outstanding Player (1985). ... Member of NCAA Division I championship team (1985).

Season Team	G	Min.	FGM	FGA	Pct.	FTM	FTA	Pct.	Reb.	Ast.	Pts.	RPG	APG	PPG
81-82—Villanova.....................	32	1083	169	264	.640	115	161	.714	249	45	453	7.8	1.4	14.2
82-83—Villanova.....................	31	1029	129	227	.568	130	171	.760	301	57	388	9.7	1.8	12.5
83-84—Villanova.....................	31	1068	162	268	.604	154	222	.694	246	53	478	7.9	1.7	15.4
84-85—Villanova.....................	35	1186	177	295	.600	192	263	.730	311	71	546	8.9	2.0	15.6
Totals	129	4366	637	1054	.604	591	817	.723	1107	226	1865	8.6	1.8	14.5

NBA REGULAR-SEASON RECORD

Season Team	G	Min.	FGM	FGA	Pct.	FTM	FTA	Pct.	Off.	Def.	Tot.	Ast.	St.	Blk.	TO	Pts.	RPG	APG	PPG
85-86—Phoenix	80	1602	255	457	.558	171	254	.673	95	213	308	90	71	37	148	681	3.9	1.1	8.5
86-87—Phoenix	80	2250	290	497	.584	257	348	.739	179	401	580	116	86	54	135	837	7.3	1.5	10.5
87-88—Sacramento	79	1177	179	343	.522	133	178	.747	94	136	230	66	39	32	77	491	2.9	0.8	6.2
88-89—Sac.-Boston....	80	2012	319	622	.513	280	350	.800	166	283	449	118	83	66	119	918	5.6	1.5	11.5
89-90—Boston	77	1082	135	249	.542	92	119	.773	93	132	225	68	34	42	56	362	2.9	0.9	4.7
90-91—Boston	70	1165	131	243	.539	104	116	.897	155	186	341	45	61	43	45	366	4.9	0.6	5.2
91-92—Boston	81	1917	203	378	.537	207	255	.812	252	312	564	62	70	56	73	613	7.0	0.8	7.6

Season Team	G	Min.	FGM	FGA	Pct.	FTM	FTA	Pct.	Off.	Def.	Tot.	Ast.	St.	Blk.	TO	Pts.	RPG	APG	PPG
92-93—Boston	7	151	10	24	.417	12	13	.923	14	29	43	1	4	7	8	32	6.1	0.1	4.6
93-94—Boston	76	1524	151	289	.523	92	125	.736	160	318	478	62	58	44	62	394	6.3	0.8	5.2
94-95—Milwaukee	62	835	48	97	.495	44	62	.710	65	146	211	21	34	17	26	140	3.4	0.3	2.3
95-96—Tor.-Phil.	74	1710	171	335	.510	136	179	.760	189	269	458	72	64	28	77	478	6.2	1.0	6.5
Totals	766	15425	1892	3534	.535	1528	1999	.764	1462	2425	3887	721	604	426	826	5312	5.1	0.9	6.9

Three-point field goals: 1985-86, 0-for-2. 1986-87, 0-for-2. 1987-88, 0-for-2. 1988-89, 0-for-6. 1989-90, 0-for-1. 1990-91, 0-for-1. 1991-92, 0-for-1. 1995-96, 0-for-3. Totals, 0-for-18.

Personal fouls/disqualifications: 1985-86, 190/3. 1986-87, 196/1. 1987-88, 118/0. 1988-89, 202/2. 1989-90, 126/1. 1990-91, 147/0. 1991-92, 158/1. 1992-93, 13/0. 1993-94, 131/0. 1994-95, 64/0. 1995-96, 156/1. Totals, 1501/9.

NBA PLAYOFF RECORD

Season Team	G	Min.	FGM	FGA	Pct.	FTM	FTA	Pct.	Off.	Def.	Tot.	Ast.	St.	Blk.	TO	Pts.	RPG	APG	PPG
88-89—Boston	3	45	3	12	.250	2	2	1.000	2	3	5	1	1	1	4	8	1.7	0.3	2.7
89-90—Boston	4	25	6	7	.857	7	9	.778	2	4	6	0	0	0	2	19	1.5	0.0	4.8
90-91—Boston	11	170	16	21	.762	17	21	.810	23	17	40	2	6	2	2	49	3.6	0.2	4.5
91-92—Boston	10	314	35	58	.603	26	31	.839	36	48	84	7	12	9	13	96	8.4	0.7	9.6
Totals	28	554	60	98	.612	52	63	.825	63	72	135	10	19	12	21	172	4.8	0.4	6.1

Three-point field goals: 1991-92, 0-for-1.
Personal fouls/disqualifications: 1988-89, 7/0. 1989-90, 3/0. 1990-91, 17/0. 1991-92, 30/0. Totals, 57/0.

PIPPEN, SCOTTIE   G/F   BULLS

PERSONAL: Born September 25, 1965, in Hamburg, Ark. ... 6-7/228.
HIGH SCHOOL: Hamburg (Ark.).
COLLEGE: Central Arkansas.
TRANSACTIONS/CAREER NOTES: Selected by Seattle SuperSonics in first round (fifth pick overall) of 1987 NBA Draft. ... Draft rights traded by SuperSonics to Chicago Bulls for draft rights to F/C Olden Polynice, 1988 or 1989 second-round draft choice and option to exchange 1989 first-round draft choices (June 22, 1987).
MISCELLANEOUS: Member of NBA championship teams (1991, 1992, 1993, 1996). ... Member of gold-medal-winning U.S. Olympic teams (1992, 1996).

COLLEGIATE RECORD

Season Team	G	Min.	FGM	FGA	Pct.	FTM	FTA	Pct.	Reb.	Ast.	Pts.	RPG	APG	PPG
83-84—Central Ark.	20	...	36	79	.456	13	19	.684	59	14	85	3.0	0.7	4.3
84-85—Central Ark.	19	...	141	250	.564	69	102	.676	175	30	351	9.2	1.6	18.5
85-86—Central Ark.	29	...	229	412	.556	116	169	.686	266	102	574	9.2	3.5	19.8
86-87—Central Ark.	25	...	231	390	.592	105	146	.719	249	107	590	10.0	4.3	23.6
Totals	93	...	637	1131	.563	303	436	.695	749	253	1600	8.1	2.7	17.2

Three-point field goals: 1986-87, 23-for-40 (.575).

NBA REGULAR-SEASON RECORD

HONORS: All-NBA first team (1994, 1995, 1996). ... All-NBA second team (1992). ... All-NBA third team (1993). ... NBA All-Defensive first team (1992, 1993, 1994, 1995, 1996). ... NBA All-Defensive second team (1991).
NOTES: Led NBA with 2.94 steals per game (1995).

Season Team	G	Min.	FGM	FGA	Pct.	FTM	FTA	Pct.	Off.	Def.	Tot.	Ast.	St.	Blk.	TO	Pts.	RPG	APG	PPG
87-88—Chicago	79	1650	261	564	.463	99	172	.576	115	183	298	169	91	52	131	625	3.8	2.1	7.9
88-89—Chicago	73	2413	413	867	.476	201	301	.668	138	307	445	256	139	61	199	1048	6.1	3.5	14.4
89-90—Chicago	82	3148	562	1150	.489	199	295	.675	150	397	547	444	211	101	278	1351	6.7	5.4	16.5
90-91—Chicago	82	3014	600	1153	.520	240	340	.706	163	432	595	511	193	93	232	1461	7.3	6.2	17.8
91-92—Chicago	82	3164	687	1359	.506	330	434	.760	185	445	630	572	155	93	253	1720	7.7	7.0	21.0
92-93—Chicago	81	3123	628	1327	.473	232	350	.663	203	418	621	507	173	73	246	1510	7.7	6.3	18.6
93-94—Chicago	72	2759	627	1278	.491	270	409	.660	173	456	629	403	211	58	232	1587	8.7	5.6	22.0
94-95—Chicago	79	3014	634	1320	.480	315	440	.716	175	464	639	409	*232	89	271	1692	8.1	5.2	21.4
95-96—Chicago	77	2825	563	1216	.463	220	324	.679	152	344	496	452	133	57	207	1496	6.4	5.9	19.4
Totals	707	25110	4975	10234	.486	2106	3065	.687	1454	3446	4900	3723	1538	677	2049	12490	6.9	5.3	17.7

Three-point field goals: 1987-88, 4-for-23 (.174). 1988-89, 21-for-77 (.273). 1989-90, 28-for-112 (.250). 1990-91, 21-for-68 (.309). 1991-92, 16-for-80 (.200). 1992-93, 22-for-93 (.237). 1993-94, 63-for-197 (.320). 1994-95, 109-for-316 (.345). 1995-96, 150-for-401 (.374). Totals, 434-for-1367 (.317).
Personal fouls/disqualifications: 1987-88, 214/3. 1988-89, 261/8. 1989-90, 298/6. 1990-91, 270/3. 1991-92, 242/2. 1992-93, 219/3. 1993-94, 227/1. 1994-95, 238/4. 1995-96, 198/0. Totals, 2167/30.

NBA PLAYOFF RECORD

Season Team	G	Min.	FGM	FGA	Pct.	FTM	FTA	Pct.	Off.	Def.	Tot.	Ast.	St.	Blk.	TO	Pts.	RPG	APG	PPG
87-88—Chicago	10	294	46	99	.465	5	7	.714	24	28	52	24	8	8	26	100	5.2	2.4	10.0
88-89—Chicago	17	619	84	182	.462	32	50	.640	34	95	129	67	23	16	41	222	7.6	3.9	13.1
89-90—Chicago	15	612	104	210	.495	71	100	.710	33	75	108	83	31	19	49	289	7.2	5.5	19.3
90-91—Chicago	17	704	142	282	.504	80	101	.792	37	114	151	99	42	19	55	368	8.9	5.8	21.6
91-92—Chicago	22	899	152	325	.468	118	155	.761	59	134	193	147	41	25	70	428	8.8	6.7	19.5
92-93—Chicago	19	789	152	327	.465	74	116	.638	37	95	132	107	41	13	71	381	6.9	5.6	20.1
93-94—Chicago	10	384	85	196	.434	46	52	.885	17	66	83	46	24	7	37	228	8.3	4.6	22.8
94-95—Chicago	10	396	58	131	.443	48	71	.676	24	62	86	58	14	10	27	178	8.6	5.8	17.8
95-96—Chicago	18	742	112	287	.390	51	80	.638	62	91	153	107	47	16	41	305	8.5	5.9	16.9
Totals	138	5439	935	2039	.459	525	732	.717	327	760	1087	738	271	133	417	2499	7.9	5.3	18.1

Three-point field goals: 1987-88, 3-for-6 (.500). 1988-89, 22-for-56 (.393). 1989-90, 10-for-31 (.323). 1990-91, 4-for-17 (.235). 1991-92, 6-for-24 (.250). 1992-93, 3-for-17 (.176). 1993-94, 12-for-45 (.267). 1994-95, 14-for-38 (.368). 1995-96, 30-for-105 (.286). Totals, 104-for-339 (.307).
Personal fouls/disqualifications: 1987-88, 33/1. 1988-89, 63/2. 1989-90, 62/0. 1990-91, 58/1. 1991-92, 72/1. 1992-93, 62/0. 1993-94, 33/1. 1994-95, 40/1. 1995-96, 51/0. Totals, 474/7.

P

NBA ALL-STAR GAME RECORD

NOTES: NBA All-Star Game Most Valuable Player (1994).

Season	Team	Min.	FGM	FGA	Pct.	FTM	FTA	Pct.	Off.	Def.	Tot.	Ast.	PF	Dq.	St.	Blk.	TO	Pts.
										REBOUNDS								
1990	—Chicago	12	2	4	.500	0	0	...	0	1	1	0	1	0	1	1	1	4
1992	—Chicago	21	6	13	.462	2	3	.667	4	0	4	1	0	0	2	1	1	14
1993	—Chicago	29	4	14	.286	2	3	.667	2	3	5	4	4	0	5	2	0	10
1994	—Chicago	31	9	15	.600	6	10	.600	0	11	11	2	2	0	4	1	2	29
1995	—Chicago	30	5	15	.333	0	0	...	0	7	7	3	1	0	2	1	4	12
1996	—Chicago	25	4	7	.571	0	0	...	2	6	8	5	0	0	3	0	6	8
Totals		148	30	68	.441	10	16	.625	8	28	36	15	8	0	17	6	14	77

Three-point field goals: 1990, 0-for-1. 1993, 0-for-2. 1994, 5-for-9 (.556). 1995, 2-for-6 (.333). 1996, 0-for-1. Totals, 7-for-19 (.368).

POLYNICE, OLDEN   F/C   KINGS

PERSONAL: Born November 21, 1964, in Port-au-Prince, Haiti. ... 7-0/250. ... Name pronounced OLD-in POL-a-neece.
HIGH SCHOOL: All Hallows Institute (Bronx, N.Y.).
COLLEGE: Virginia.
TRANSACTIONS/CAREER NOTES: Played in Italy after junior season (1986-87). ... Selected by Chicago Bulls in first round (eighth pick overall) of 1987 NBA Draft. ... Draft rights traded by Bulls with 1988 or 1989 second-round draft choice and option to exchange 1989 first-round draft choices to Seattle SuperSonics for draft rights to F Scottie Pippen (June 22, 1987). ... Traded by SuperSonics with 1991 first-round draft choice and 1993 or 1994 first-round draft choice to Los Angeles Clippers for C/F Benoit Benjamin (February 20, 1991). ... Traded by Clippers with 1996 and 1997 second-round draft choices to Detroit Pistons for C William Bedford and draft rights to F Don MacLean (June 24, 1992). ... Traded by Pistons with F David Wood to Sacramento Kings for C Duane Causwell and 1994, 1995 and 1996 second-round draft choices (February 16, 1994); trade voided when Causwell failed physical (February 19, 1994). ... Traded by Pistons to Sacramento Kings for F/C Pete Chilcutt, 1994 second-round draft choice and conditional first-round draft choice (February 20, 1994).

COLLEGIATE RECORD

Season Team	G	Min.	FGM	FGA	Pct.	FTM	FTA	Pct.	Reb.	Ast.	Pts.	RPG	APG	PPG
													AVERAGES	
83-84—Virginia	33	866	98	178	.551	57	97	.588	184	20	253	5.6	0.6	7.7
84-85—Virginia	32	1095	161	267	.603	94	157	.599	243	16	416	7.6	0.5	13.0
85-86—Virginia	30	1074	183	320	.572	116	182	.637	240	16	482	8.0	0.5	16.1
Totals	95	3035	442	765	.578	267	436	.612	667	52	1151	7.0	0.5	12.1

ITALIAN LEAGUE RECORD

Season Team	G	Min.	FGM	FGA	Pct.	FTM	FTA	Pct.	Reb.	Ast.	Pts.	RPG	APG	PPG
													AVERAGES	
86-87—Rimini	30	968	214	378	.566	82	137	.599	330	...	518	11.0	...	17.3

NBA REGULAR-SEASON RECORD

Season Team	G	Min.	FGM	FGA	Pct.	FTM	FTA	Pct.	Off.	Def.	Tot.	Ast.	St.	Blk.	TO	Pts.	RPG	APG	PPG
										REBOUNDS								AVERAGES	
87-88—Seattle	82	1080	118	254	.465	101	158	.639	122	208	330	33	32	26	81	337	4.0	0.4	4.1
88-89—Seattle	80	835	91	180	.506	51	86	.593	98	108	206	21	37	30	46	233	2.6	0.3	2.9
89-90—Seattle	79	1085	156	289	.540	47	99	.475	128	172	300	15	25	21	35	360	3.8	0.2	4.6
90-91—Seattle-LAC	79	2092	316	564	.560	146	252	.579	220	333	553	42	43	32	88	778	7.0	0.5	9.8
91-92—L.A. Clippers	76	1834	244	470	.519	125	201	.622	195	341	536	46	45	20	83	613	7.1	0.6	8.1
92-93—Detroit	67	1299	210	429	.490	66	142	.465	181	237	418	29	31	21	54	486	6.2	0.4	7.3
93-94—Det.-Sac.	68	2402	346	662	.523	97	191	.508	299	510	809	41	42	67	78	789	11.9	0.6	11.6
94-95—Sacramento	81	2534	376	691	.544	124	194	.639	277	448	725	62	48	52	113	877	9.0	0.8	10.8
95-96—Sacramento	81	2441	431	818	.527	122	203	.601	257	507	764	58	52	66	127	985	9.4	0.7	12.2
Totals	693	15602	2288	4357	.525	879	1526	.576	1777	2864	4641	347	355	335	705	5458	6.7	0.5	7.9

Three-point field goals: 1987-88, 0-for-2. 1988-89, 0-for-2. 1989-90, 1-for-2 (.500). 1990-91, 0-for-1. 1991-92, 0-for-1. 1992-93, 0-for-1. 1993-94, 0-for-2. 1994-95, 1-for-1. 1995-96, 1-for-3 (.333). Totals, 3-for-15 (.200).
Personal fouls/disqualifications: 1987-88, 215/1. 1988-89, 164/0. 1989-90, 187/0. 1990-91, 192/1. 1991-92, 165/0. 1992-93, 126/0. 1993-94, 189/2. 1994-95, 238/0. 1995-96, 250/3. Totals, 1726/7.

NBA PLAYOFF RECORD

Season Team	G	Min.	FGM	FGA	Pct.	FTM	FTA	Pct.	Off.	Def.	Tot.	Ast.	St.	Blk.	TO	Pts.	RPG	APG	PPG
										REBOUNDS								AVERAGES	
87-88—Seattle	5	44	5	11	.455	0	2	.000	2	6	8	0	3	0	1	10	1.6	0	2.0
88-89—Seattle	8	162	25	41	.610	7	13	.538	27	35	62	1	6	4	5	57	7.8	0.1	7.1
91-92—L.A. Clippers	5	63	7	12	.583	2	6	.333	2	16	18	2	1	1	1	16	3.6	0.4	3.2
95-96—Sacramento	4	141	24	46	.522	6	9	.667	16	32	48	3	1	7	3	55	12.0	0.8	13.8
Totals	22	410	61	110	.555	15	30	.500	47	89	136	6	11	12	10	138	6.2	0.3	6.3

Three-point field goals: 1995-96, 1-for-1.
Personal fouls/disqualifications: 1987-88, 6/0. 1988-89, 32/1. 1991-92, 11/0. 1995-96, 15/0. Totals, 64/1.

P

PORTER, TERRY   G   TIMBERWOLVES

PERSONAL: Born April 8, 1963, in Milwaukee. ... 6-3/195.
HIGH SCHOOL: South Division (Milwaukee).
COLLEGE: Wisconsin-Stevens Point.
TRANSACTIONS/CAREER NOTES: Selected by Portland Trail Blazers in first round (24th pick overall) of 1985 NBA Draft. ... Rights renounced by Trail Blazers (September 29, 1995). ... Signed as free agent by Minnesota Timberwolves (October 14, 1995).
MISCELLANEOUS: Portland Trail Blazers all-time assists leader with 5,319 (1985-86 through 1994-95).

COLLEGIATE RECORD

Season Team	G	Min.	FGM	FGA	Pct.	FTM	FTA	Pct.	Reb.	Ast.	Pts.	AVERAGES RPG	APG	PPG
81-82—Wis.-Stevens Pt............	25	273	21	57	.368	9	13	.692	13	21	51	0.5	0.8	2.0
82-83—Wis.-Stevens Pt............	30	949	140	229	.611	62	89	.697	117	157	342	3.9	5.2	11.4
83-84—Wis.-Stevens Pt............	32	1040	244	392	.622	112	135	.830	165	133	600	5.2	4.2	18.8
84-85—Wis.-Stevens Pt............	30	1042	233	405	.575	126	151	.834	155	129	592	5.2	4.3	19.7
Totals	117	3304	638	1083	.589	309	388	.796	450	440	1585	3.8	3.8	13.5

HONORS: Citizenship Award (1993).

NBA REGULAR-SEASON RECORD

Season Team	G	Min.	FGM	FGA	Pct.	FTM	FTA	Pct.	REBOUNDS Off.	Def.	Tot.	Ast.	St.	Blk.	TO	Pts.	AVERAGES RPG	APG	PPG
85-86—Portland.........	79	1214	212	447	.474	125	155	.806	35	82	117	198	81	1	106	562	1.5	2.5	7.1
86-87—Portland.........	80	2714	376	770	.488	280	334	.838	70	267	337	715	159	9	255	1045	4.2	8.9	13.1
87-88—Portland.........	82	2991	462	890	.519	274	324	.846	65	313	378	831	150	16	244	1222	4.6	10.1	14.9
88-89—Portland.........	81	3102	540	1146	.471	272	324	.840	85	282	367	770	146	8	248	1431	4.5	9.5	17.7
89-90—Portland.........	80	2781	448	969	.462	421	472	.892	59	213	272	726	151	4	245	1406	3.4	9.1	17.6
90-91—Portland.........	81	2665	486	944	.515	279	339	.823	52	230	282	649	158	12	189	1381	3.5	8.0	17.0
91-92—Portland.........	82	2784	521	1129	.461	315	368	.856	51	204	255	477	127	12	188	1485	3.1	5.8	18.1
92-93—Portland.........	81	2883	503	1108	.454	327	388	.843	58	258	316	419	101	10	199	1476	3.9	5.2	18.2
93-94—Portland.........	77	2074	348	836	.416	204	234	.872	45	170	215	401	79	18	166	1010	2.8	5.2	13.1
94-95—Portland.........	35	770	105	267	.393	58	82	.707	18	63	81	133	30	2	58	312	2.3	3.8	8.9
95-96—Minnesota......	82	2072	269	608	.442	164	209	.785	36	176	212	452	89	15	173	773	2.6	5.5	9.4
Totals	840	26050	4270	9114	.469	2719	3229	.842	574	2258	2832	5771	1271	107	2071	12103	3.4	6.9	14.4

Three-point field goals: 1985-86, 13-for-42 (.310). 1986-87, 13-for-60 (.217). 1987-88, 24-for-69 (.348). 1988-89, 79-for-219 (.361). 1989-90, 89-for-238 (.374). 1990-91, 130-for-313 (.415). 1991-92, 128-for-324 (.395). 1992-93, 143-for-345 (.414). 1993-94, 110-for-282 (.390). 1994-95, 44-for-114 (.386). 1995-96, 71-for-226 (.314). Totals, 844-for-2232 (.378).
Personal fouls/disqualifications: 1985-86, 136/0. 1986-87, 192/0. 1987-88, 204/1. 1988-89, 187/1. 1989-90, 150/0. 1990-91, 151/2. 1991-92, 155/1. 1992-93, 122/0. 1993-94, 132/0. 1994-95, 60/0. 1995-96, 154/0. Totals, 1643/5.

NBA PLAYOFF RECORD

Season Team	G	Min.	FGM	FGA	Pct.	FTM	FTA	Pct.	REBOUNDS Off.	Def.	Tot.	Ast.	St.	Blk.	TO	Pts.	AVERAGES RPG	APG	PPG
85-86—Portland.........	4	68	12	27	.444	2	4	.500	1	4	5	12	3	2	6	27	1.3	3.0	6.8
86-87—Portland.........	4	150	24	50	.480	18	20	.900	1	18	19	40	10	2	13	68	4.8	10.0	17.0
87-88—Portland.........	4	149	29	52	.558	9	13	.692	4	10	14	28	10	0	13	68	3.5	7.0	17.0
88-89—Portland.........	3	124	26	52	.500	10	12	.833	6	10	16	25	1	1	7	66	5.3	8.3	22.0
89-90—Portland.........	21	815	127	274	.464	139	165	.842	9	52	61	155	28	3	62	433	2.9	7.4	20.6
90-91—Portland.........	16	595	102	204	.500	68	79	.861	8	36	44	105	24	1	32	289	2.8	6.6	18.1
91-92—Portland.........	21	870	147	285	.516	119	143	.832	25	72	97	141	22	3	46	450	4.6	6.7	21.4
92-93—Portland.........	4	152	27	68	.397	9	11	.818	4	16	20	8	4	0	6	66	5.0	2.0	16.5
93-94—Portland.........	4	76	12	35	.343	11	14	.786	1	11	12	9	4	0	2	41	3.0	2.3	10.3
94-95—Portland.........	3	21	7	13	.538	3	5	.600	1	1	2	4	0	0	1	19	0.7	1.3	6.3
Totals	84	3020	513	1060	.484	388	466	.833	60	230	290	527	106	12	188	1527	3.5	6.3	18.2

Three-point field goals: 1985-86, 1-for-6 (.167). 1986-87, 2-for-5 (.400). 1987-88, 1-for-3 (.333). 1988-89, 4-for-11 (.364). 1989-90, 40-for-102 (.392). 1990-91, 17-for-47 (.362). 1991-92, 37-for-78 (.474). 1992-93, 3-for-19 (.158). 1993-94, 6-for-14 (.429). 1994-95, 2-for-5 (.400). Totals, 113-for-290 (.390).
Personal fouls/disqualifications: 1985-86, 10/0. 1986-87, 14/0. 1987-88, 13/0. 1988-89, 8/0. 1989-90, 51/1. 1990-91, 32/0. 1991-92, 49/0. 1992-93, 10/0. 1993-94, 3/0. 1994-95, 6/0. Totals, 196/1.

NBA ALL-STAR GAME RECORD

Season Team	Min.	FGM	FGA	Pct.	FTM	FTA	Pct.	REBOUNDS Off.	Def.	Tot.	Ast.	PF	Dq.	St.	Blk.	TO	Pts.
1991 —Portland	15	2	6	.333	0	0	...	1	2	3	4	2	0	2	1	3	4
1993 —Portland	19	3	8	.375	0	0	...	0	0	0	3	1	0	1	0	1	7
Totals.................	34	5	14	.357	0	0	...	1	2	3	7	3	0	3	1	4	11

Three-point field goals: 1991, 0-for-2. 1993, 1-for-5 (.200). Totals, 1-for-7 (.143).

PRICE, BRENT   G   ROCKETS

PERSONAL: Born December 9, 1968, in Shawnee, Okla. ... 6-1/185. ... Full name: Hartley Brent Price. ... Brother of Mark Price, guard with Golden State Warriors.
HIGH SCHOOL: Enid (Okla.).
COLLEGE: South Carolina, then Oklahoma.
TRANSACTIONS/CAREER NOTES: Selected by Washington Bullets in second round (32nd pick overall) of 1992 NBA Draft. ... Waived by Bullets (April 19, 1995). ... Re-signed as free agent by Bullets (October 3, 1995). ... Signed as free agent by Houston Rockets (July 16, 1996).

COLLEGIATE RECORD

Season Team	G	Min.	FGM	FGA	Pct.	FTM	FTA	Pct.	Reb.	Ast.	Pts.	AVERAGES RPG	APG	PPG
87-88—South Carolina...............	29	643	98	213	.460	66	77	.857	47	78	311	1.6	2.7	10.7
88-89—South Carolina...............	30	952	144	294	.490	76	90	.844	75	128	432	2.5	4.3	14.4
89-90—Oklahoma						Did not play—transfer student.								
90-91—Oklahoma	35	1197	178	428	.416	166	198	.838	127	192	613	3.6	5.5	17.5
91-92—Oklahoma	30	1064	182	391	.465	120	152	.789	111	185	560	3.7	6.2	18.7
Totals	124	3856	602	1326	.454	428	517	.828	360	583	1916	2.9	4.7	15.5

Three-point field goals: 1987-88, 49-for-112 (.438). 1988-89, 68-for-139 (.489). 1990-91, 91-for-244 (.373). 1991-92, 76-for-194 (.392). Totals, 284-for-689 (.412).

P

NBA REGULAR-SEASON RECORD

RECORDS: Shares single-season record for most consecutive three-point field goals without a miss—13 (January 15-January 19, 1996).

Season Team	G	Min.	FGM	FGA	Pct.	FTM	FTA	Pct.	REBOUNDS Off.	Def.	Tot.	Ast.	St.	Blk.	TO	Pts.	AVERAGES RPG	APG	PPG
92-93—Washington	68	859	100	279	.358	54	68	.794	28	75	103	154	56	3	85	262	1.5	2.3	3.9
93-94—Washington	65	1035	141	326	.433	68	87	.782	31	59	90	213	55	2	119	400	1.4	3.3	6.2
95-96—Washington	81	2042	252	534	.472	167	191	.874	38	190	228	416	78	4	153	810	2.8	5.1	10.0
Totals	214	3936	493	1139	.433	289	346	.835	97	324	421	783	189	9	357	1472	2.0	3.7	6.9

Three-point field goals: 1992-93, 8-for-48 (.167). 1993-94, 50-for-150 (.333). 1995-96, 139-for-301 (.462). Totals, 197-for-499 (.395).
Personal fouls/disqualifications: 1992-93, 90/0. 1993-94, 114/1. 1995-96, 184/3. Totals, 388/4.

PRICE, MARK   G   WARRIORS

PERSONAL: Born February 15, 1964, in Bartlesville, Okla. ... 6-0/180. ... Full name: William Mark Price. ... Brother of Brent Price, guard with Houston Rockets.
HIGH SCHOOL: Enid (Okla.).
COLLEGE: Georgia Tech.
TRANSACTIONS/CAREER NOTES: Selected by Dallas Mavericks in second round (25th pick overall) of 1986 NBA Draft. ... Draft rights traded by Mavericks to Cleveland Cavaliers for 1989 second-round draft choice and cash (June 17, 1986). ... Traded by Cavaliers to Washington Bullets for 1996 first-round draft choice (September 27, 1995). ... Signed as free agent by Golden State Warriors (July 21, 1996).
MISCELLANEOUS: Cleveland Cavaliers all-time assists leader with 4,206 and all-time steals leader with 734 (1986-87 through 1994-95).

COLLEGIATE RECORD

Season Team	G	Min.	FGM	FGA	Pct.	FTM	FTA	Pct.	Reb.	Ast.	Pts.	AVERAGES RPG	APG	PPG
82-83—Georgia Tech	28	1020	201	462	.435	93	106	.877	105	91	568	3.8	3.3	20.3
83-84—Georgia Tech	29	1078	191	375	.509	70	85	.824	61	121	452	2.1	4.2	15.6
84-85—Georgia Tech	35	1302	223	462	.483	137	163	.841	71	150	583	2.0	4.3	16.7
85-86—Georgia Tech	34	1204	233	441	.528	124	145	.855	94	148	590	2.8	4.4	17.4
Totals	126	4604	848	1740	.487	424	499	.850	331	510	2193	2.6	4.0	17.4

Three-point field goals: 1982-83, 73-for-166 (.440).

NBA REGULAR-SEASON RECORD

RECORDS: Holds career record for highest free-throw percentage (minimum 1,200 made)—.907.
HONORS: Long Distance Shootout winner (1993, 1994). ... All-NBA first team (1993). ... All-NBA third team (1989, 1992, 1994).

Season Team	G	Min.	FGM	FGA	Pct.	FTM	FTA	Pct.	REBOUNDS Off.	Def.	Tot.	Ast.	St.	Blk.	TO	Pts.	AVERAGES RPG	APG	PPG
86-87—Cleveland	67	1217	173	424	.408	95	114	.833	33	84	117	202	43	4	105	464	1.7	3.0	6.9
87-88—Cleveland	80	2626	493	974	.506	221	252	.877	54	126	180	480	99	12	184	1279	2.3	6.0	16.0
88-89—Cleveland	75	2728	529	1006	.526	263	292	.901	48	178	226	631	115	7	212	1414	3.0	8.4	18.9
89-90—Cleveland	73	2706	489	1066	.459	300	338	.888	66	185	251	666	114	5	214	1430	3.4	9.1	19.6
90-91—Cleveland	16	571	97	195	.497	59	62	.952	8	37	45	166	42	2	56	271	2.8	10.4	16.9
91-92—Cleveland	72	2138	438	897	.488	270	285	*.947	38	135	173	535	94	12	159	1247	2.4	7.4	17.3
92-93—Cleveland	75	2380	477	986	.484	289	305	*.948	37	164	201	602	89	11	196	1365	2.7	8.0	18.2
93-94—Cleveland	76	2386	480	1005	.478	238	268	.888	39	189	228	589	103	11	189	1316	3.0	7.8	17.3
94-95—Cleveland	48	1375	253	612	.413	148	162	.914	25	87	112	335	35	4	142	757	2.3	7.0	15.8
95-96—Washington	7	127	18	60	.300	10	10	1.000	1	6	7	18	6	0	10	56	1.0	2.6	8.0
Totals	589	18254	3447	7225	.477	1893	2088	.907	349	1191	1540	4224	740	68	1467	9599	2.6	7.2	16.3

Three-point field goals: 1986-87, 23-for-70 (.329). 1987-88, 72-for-148 (.486). 1988-89, 93-for-211 (.441). 1989-90, 152-for-374 (.406). 1990-91, 18-for-53 (.340). 1991-92, 101-for-261 (.387). 1992-93, 122-for-293 (.416). 1993-94, 118-for-297 (.397). 1994-95, 103-for-253 (.407). 1995-96, 10-for-30 (.333). Totals, 812-for-1990 (.408).
Personal fouls/disqualifications: 1986-87, 75/1. 1987-88, 119/1. 1988-89, 98/0. 1989-90, 89/0. 1990-91, 23/0. 1991-92, 113/0. 1992-93, 105/0. 1993-94, 93/0. 1994-95, 50/0. 1995-96, 7/0. Totals, 772/2.

NBA PLAYOFF RECORD

NOTES: Holds career playoff record for highest free-throw percentage (minimum 100 made)—.944.

Season Team	G	Min.	FGM	FGA	Pct.	FTM	FTA	Pct.	REBOUNDS Off.	Def.	Tot.	Ast.	St.	Blk.	TO	Pts.	AVERAGES RPG	APG	PPG
87-88—Cleveland	5	205	38	67	.567	24	25	.960	3	15	18	38	3	0	8	105	3.6	7.6	21.0
88-89—Cleveland	4	158	22	57	.386	14	15	.933	4	9	13	22	3	0	19	64	3.3	5.5	16.0
89-90—Cleveland	5	192	32	61	.525	30	30	1.000	0	14	14	44	9	1	15	100	2.8	8.8	20.0
91-92—Cleveland	17	603	118	238	.496	66	73	.904	10	32	42	128	24	4	56	327	2.5	7.5	19.2
92-93—Cleveland	9	288	43	97	.443	23	24	.958	1	18	19	55	15	0	33	117	2.1	6.1	13.0
93-94—Cleveland	3	102	15	43	.349	13	14	.929	1	5	6	14	4	0	9	45	2.0	4.7	15.0
94-95—Cleveland	4	143	12	40	.300	32	33	.970	2	10	12	26	6	0	18	60	3.0	6.5	15.0
Totals	47	1691	280	603	.464	202	214	.944	21	103	124	327	64	5	158	818	2.6	7.0	17.4

Three-point field goals: 1987-88, 5-for-12 (.417). 1988-89, 6-for-16 (.375). 1989-90, 6-for-17 (.353). 1991-92, 25-for-69 (.362). 1992-93, 8-for-26 (.308). 1993-94, 2-for-9 (.222). 1994-95, 4-for-17 (.235). Totals, 56-for-166 (.337).
Personal fouls/disqualifications: 1987-88, 11/1. 1988-89, 3/0. 1989-90, 6/0. 1991-92, 34/0. 1992-93, 13/0. 1993-94, 6/0. 1994-95, 5/0. Totals, 81/1.

NBA ALL-STAR GAME RECORD

Season Team	Min.	FGM	FGA	Pct.	FTM	FTA	Pct.	REBOUNDS Off.	Def.	Tot.	Ast.	PF	Dq.	St.	Blk.	TO	Pts.
1989 —Cleveland..........	20	3	9	.333	2	2	1.000	1	2	3	1	2	0	2	0	2	9
1992 —Cleveland..........	15	1	5	.200	4	4	1.000	0	0	0	3	1	0	1	0	3	6
1993 —Cleveland..........	23	6	11	.545	1	2	.500	0	1	1	4	5	0	1	0	3	19
1994 —Cleveland..........	22	8	10	.800	2	2	1.000	0	2	2	5	1	0	1	1	0	20
Totals..........................	80	18	35	.514	9	10	.900	1	5	6	13	9	0	5	1	8	54

Three-point field goals: 1989, 1-for-4 (.250). 1992, 0-for-3. 1993, 6-for-9 (.667). 1994, 2-for-3 (.667). Totals, 9-for-19 (.474).

P

PRITCHARD, KEVIN   G

PERSONAL: Born July 17, 1967, in Bloomington, Ind. ... 6-3/185. ... Full name: Kevin Lee Pritchard.
HIGH SCHOOL: Thomas Edison (Tulsa, Okla.).
COLLEGE: Kansas.
TRANSACTIONS/CAREER NOTES: Selected by Golden State Warriors in second round (34th pick overall) of 1990 NBA Draft. ... Traded by Warriors to San Antonio Spurs for future considerations (May 17, 1991). ... Waived by Spurs (October 28, 1991). ... Signed as free agent by Boston Celtics (October 30, 1991). ... Waived by Celtics (November 25, 1991). ... Re-signed as free agent by Celtics (November 27, 1991). ... Waived by Celtics (January 7, 1992). ... Played in Spain (1992-93). ... Played in Italy (1993-94). ... Signed as free agent by Miami Heat (October 4, 1994). ... Waived by Heat (November 1, 1994). ... Played in Continental Basketball Association with Quad City Thunder (1994-95 and 1995-96). ... Signed by Philadelphia 76ers to 10-day contract (February 15, 1995). ... Signed by Heat to first of two consecutive 10-day contracts (March 6, 1995). ... Waived by Heat (March 19, 1995). ... Re-signed by Heat for remainder of season (March 24, 1995). ... Waived by Heat (April 18, 1995). ... Signed as free agent by Vancouver Grizzlies (May 30, 1995). ... Traded by Grizzlies with F Larry Stewart to Orlando Magic for F Anthony Avent (November 1, 1995). ... Waived by Magic (November 2, 1995). ... Signed by Washington Bullets to 10-day contract (February 22, 1996).

COLLEGIATE RECORD

NOTES: Member of NCAA Division I championship team (1988).

Season Team	G	Min.	FGM	FGA	Pct.	FTM	FTA	Pct.	Reb.	Ast.	Pts.	RPG	APG	PPG
86-87—Kansas	36	962	134	294	.456	41	54	.759	77	73	345	2.1	2.0	9.6
87-88—Kansas	37	1100	144	296	.486	88	119	.740	95	113	393	2.6	3.1	10.6
88-89—Kansas	31	944	155	306	.507	83	108	.769	76	136	448	2.5	4.4	14.5
89-90—Kansas	35	976	177	337	.525	106	130	.815	89	177	506	2.5	5.1	14.5
Totals	139	3982	610	1233	.495	318	411	.774	337	499	1692	2.4	3.6	12.2

Three-point field goals: 1986-87, 36-for-88 (.409). 1987-88, 17-for-54 (.315). 1988-89, 55-for-129 (.426). 1989-90, 46-for-108 (.426). Totals, 154-for-379 (.406).

NBA REGULAR-SEASON RECORD

Season Team	G	Min.	FGM	FGA	Pct.	FTM	FTA	Pct.	Off.	Def.	Tot.	Ast.	St.	Blk.	TO	Pts.	RPG	APG	PPG
90-91—Golden State	62	773	88	229	.384	62	77	.805	16	49	65	81	30	8	59	243	1.0	1.3	3.9
91-92—Boston	11	136	16	34	.471	14	18	.778	1	10	11	30	3	4	11	46	1.0	2.7	4.2
94-95—Phil.-Miami	19	194	13	32	.406	16	21	.762	0	12	12	34	2	1	12	44	0.6	1.8	2.3
95-96—Washington	2	22	2	3	.667	2	3	.667	0	2	2	7	2	0	0	7	1.0	3.5	3.5
Totals	94	1125	119	298	.399	94	119	.790	17	73	90	152	37	13	82	340	1.0	1.6	3.6

Three-point field goals: 1990-91, 5-for-31 (.161). 1991-92, 0-for-3. 1994-95, 2-for-8 (.250). 1995-96, 1-for-1. Totals, 8-for-43 (.186).
Personal fouls/disqualifications: 1990-91, 104/1. 1991-92, 17/0. 1994-95, 22/0. 1995-96, 3/0. Totals, 146/1.

SPANISH LEAGUE RECORD

Season Team	G	Min.	FGM	FGA	Pct.	FTM	FTA	Pct.	Reb.	Ast.	Pts.	RPG	APG	PPG
92-93—Caceres C.B.	31	1203	232	467	.497	180	215	.837	120	134	690	3.9	4.3	22.3

ITALIAN LEAGUE RECORD

Season Team	G	Min.	FGM	FGA	Pct.	FTM	FTA	Pct.	Reb.	Ast.	Pts.	RPG	APG	PPG
93-94—Pfizer Reggio Calabria	35	1171	188	349	.539	175	215	.814	113	55	575	3.2	1.6	16.4

CBA REGULAR-SEASON RECORD

NOTES: CBA All-League first team (1995).

Season Team	G	Min.	FGM	FGA	Pct.	FTM	FTA	Pct.	Reb.	Ast.	Pts.	RPG	APG	PPG
94-95—Quad City	39	1461	190	366	.519	190	224	.848	136	300	617	3.5	7.7	15.8
95-96—Quad City	20	532	55	132	.417	26	37	.703	35	82	154	1.8	4.1	7.7
Totals	59	1993	245	498	.492	216	261	.828	171	382	771	2.9	6.5	13.1

Three-point field goals: 1994-95, 47-for-96 (.490). 1995-96, 18-for-51 (.353). Totals, 65-for-147 (.443).

RADJA, DINO   F   CELTICS

PERSONAL: Born April 24, 1967, in Split, Croatia. ... 6-11/255. ... Name pronounced ROD-ja.
HIGH SCHOOL: Technical School Center (Split, Croatia).
TRANSACTIONS/CAREER NOTES: Selected by Boston Celtics in second round (40th pick overall) of 1989 NBA Draft. ... Played in Italy (1990-91 through 1992-93). ... Signed by Celtics (July 9, 1993).
MISCELLANEOUS: Member of silver-medal-winning Yugoslavian Olympic team (1988). ... Member of silver-medal-winning Croatian Olympic team (1992). ... Member of Croatian Olympic team (1996).

ITALIAN LEAGUE RECORD

Season Team	G	Min.	FGM	FGA	Pct.	FTM	FTA	Pct.	Reb.	Ast.	Pts.	RPG	APG	PPG
90-91—Il Messaggero Roma	21	767	150	253	.593	80	118	.678	213	11	380	10.1	0.5	18.1
91-92—Il Messaggero Roma	30	1045	238	369	.645	129	171	.754	297	32	606	9.9	1.1	20.2
92-93—Virtus Roma	30	1089	248	421	.589	150	195	.769	308	26	646	10.3	0.9	21.5
Totals	81	2901	636	1043	.610	359	484	.742	818	69	1632	10.1	0.9	20.1

NBA REGULAR-SEASON RECORD

HONORS: NBA All-Rookie second team (1994).

Season Team	G	Min.	FGM	FGA	Pct.	FTM	FTA	Pct.	Off.	Def.	Tot.	Ast.	St.	Blk.	TO	Pts.	RPG	APG	PPG
93-94—Boston	80	2303	491	942	.521	226	301	.751	191	386	577	114	70	67	149	1208	7.2	1.4	15.1
94-95—Boston	66	2147	450	919	.490	233	307	.759	149	424	573	111	60	86	159	1133	8.7	1.7	17.2
95-96—Boston	53	1984	426	852	.500	191	275	.695	113	409	522	83	48	81	117	1043	9.8	1.6	19.7
Totals	199	6434	1367	2713	.504	650	883	.736	453	1219	1672	308	178	234	425	3384	8.4	1.5	17.0

Three-point field goals: 1993-94, 0-for-1. 1994-95, 0-for-1. Totals, 0-for-2.
Personal fouls/disqualifications: 1993-94, 276/2. 1994-95, 232/5. 1995-96, 161/2. Totals, 669/9.

PR

NBA PLAYOFF RECORD

Season Team	G	Min.	FGM	FGA	Pct.	FTM	FTA	Pct.	REBOUNDS Off.	Def.	Tot.	Ast.	St.	Blk.	TO	Pts.	AVERAGES RPG	APG	PPG
94-95—Boston............	4	153	20	50	.400	20	28	.714	4	24	28	9	4	5	9	60	7.0	2.3	15.0

Personal fouls/disqualifications: 1994-95, 19/0.

RATLIFF, THEO   F/C   PISTONS

PERSONAL: Born April 17, 1973, in Demopolis, Ala. ... 6-10/225. ... Full name: Theo Curtis Ratliff.
HIGH SCHOOL: Demopolis (Ala.).
COLLEGE: Wyoming.
TRANSACTIONS/CAREER NOTES: Selected by Detroit Pistons in first round (18th pick overall) of 1995 NBA Draft.

COLLEGIATE RECORD

NOTES: Led NCAA Division I with 4.4 blocked shots per game (1993).

Season Team	G	Min.	FGM	FGA	Pct.	FTM	FTA	Pct.	Reb.	Ast.	Pts.	AVERAGES RPG	APG	PPG
91-92—Wyoming......................	27	298	14	32	.438	21	36	.583	54	8	49	2.0	0.3	1.8
92-93—Wyoming......................	28	824	99	184	.538	60	116	.517	173	8	258	6.2	0.3	9.2
93-94—Wyoming......................	28	892	160	281	.569	111	171	.649	217	27	431	7.8	1.0	15.4
94-95—Wyoming......................	28	912	148	272	.544	107	169	.633	211	31	404	7.5	1.1	14.4
Totals	111	2926	421	769	.547	299	492	.608	655	74	1142	5.9	0.7	10.3

Three-point field goals: 1992-93, 0-for-1. 1993-94, 0-for-1. 1994-95, 1-for-5 (.200). Totals, 1-for-7 (.143).

NBA REGULAR-SEASON RECORD

Season Team	G	Min.	FGM	FGA	Pct.	FTM	FTA	Pct.	REBOUNDS Off.	Def.	Tot.	Ast.	St.	Blk.	TO	Pts.	AVERAGES RPG	APG	PPG
95-96—Detroit	75	1305	128	230	.557	85	120	.708	110	187	297	13	16	116	56	341	4.0	0.2	4.5

Three-point field goals: 1995-96, 0-for-1.
Personal fouls/disqualifications: 1995-96, 144/1.

NBA PLAYOFF RECORD

Season Team	G	Min.	FGM	FGA	Pct.	FTM	FTA	Pct.	REBOUNDS Off.	Def.	Tot.	Ast.	St.	Blk.	TO	Pts.	AVERAGES RPG	APG	PPG
95-96—Detroit	1	4	0	0	...	0	0	...	0	0	0	0	0	0	0	0	0.0	0.0	0.0

RECASNER, ELDRIDGE   G

PERSONAL: Born December 14, 1967, in New Orleans. ... 6-3/190. ... Full name: Eldridge David Recasner. ... Name pronounced reh-CAZ-ner.
HIGH SCHOOL: Alfred Lawless (New Orleans).
COLLEGE: Washington.
TRANSACTIONS/CAREER NOTES: Not drafted by an NBA franchise. ... Played in Germany (1990-91). ... Played in Global Basketball Association with Louisville Shooters (1991-92). ... Played in Continental Basketball Association with Yakima Sun Kings (1992-93 through 1994-95). ... Signed by Denver Nuggets to 10-day contract (March 3, 1995). ... Signed as free agent by Houston Rockets (September 25, 1995). ... Rights renounced by Rockets (July 16, 1996).

COLLEGIATE RECORD

Season Team	G	Min.	FGM	FGA	Pct.	FTM	FTA	Pct.	Reb.	Ast.	Pts.	AVERAGES RPG	APG	PPG
85-86—Washington					Did not play—redshirted.									
86-87—Washington	35	1124	111	234	.474	69	99	.697	131	103	294	3.7	2.9	8.4
87-88—Washington	28	1061	173	338	.512	105	128	.820	107	78	477	3.8	2.8	17.0
88-89—Washington	28	1011	175	352	.497	106	128	.828	95	107	508	3.4	3.8	18.1
89-90—Washington	26	981	142	326	.436	99	112	.884	101	88	421	3.9	3.4	16.2
Totals	117	4177	601	1250	.481	379	467	.812	434	376	1700	3.7	3.2	14.5

Three-point field goals: 1986-87, 3-for-14 (.214). 1987-88, 36-for-67 (.537). 1988-89, 52-for-116 (.448). 1989-90, 38-for-103 (.369). Totals, 129-for-300 (.430).

CBA REGULAR-SEASON RECORD

NOTES: CBA Most Valuable Player (1995). ... CBA All-League first team (1995). ... Member of CBA championship team (1995).

Season Team	G	Min.	FGM	FGA	Pct.	FTM	FTA	Pct.	Reb.	Ast.	Pts.	AVERAGES RPG	APG	PPG
92-93—Yakima	44	1473	296	605	.489	140	158	.886	150	137	763	3.4	3.1	17.3
93-94—Yakima	25	841	171	317	.539	70	76	.921	76	70	427	3.0	2.8	17.1
94-95—Yakima	48	1779	356	640	.556	184	204	!.902	180	246	981	3.8	5.1	20.4
Totals	117	4093	823	1562	.527	394	438	.900	406	453	2171	3.5	3.9	18.6

Three-point field goals: 1992-93, 31-for-90 (.344). 1993-94, 15-for-47 (.319). 1994-95, 85-for-172 (.494). Totals, 131-for-309 (.424).

NBA REGULAR-SEASON RECORD

Season Team	G	Min.	FGM	FGA	Pct.	FTM	FTA	Pct.	REBOUNDS Off.	Def.	Tot.	Ast.	St.	Blk.	TO	Pts.	AVERAGES RPG	APG	PPG
94-95—Denver	3	13	1	6	.167	4	4	1.000	0	2	2	1	3	0	2	6	0.7	0.3	2.0
95-96—Houston	63	1275	149	359	.415	57	66	.864	31	113	144	170	23	5	61	436	2.3	2.7	6.9
Totals	66	1288	150	365	.411	61	70	.871	31	115	146	171	26	5	63	442	2.2	2.6	6.7

Three-point field goals: 1994-95, 0-for-1. 1995-96, 81-for-191 (.424). Totals, 81-for-192 (.422).
Personal fouls/disqualifications: 1995-96, 111/1.

R

NBA PLAYOFF RECORD

Season Team	G	Min.	FGM	FGA	Pct.	FTM	FTA	Pct.	REBOUNDS Off.	Def.	Tot.	Ast.	St.	Blk.	TO	Pts.	AVERAGES RPG	APG	PPG
95-96—Houston.........	1	8	0	3	.000	0	0	...	0	1	1	2	0	0	1	0	1.0	2.0	0.0

Three-point field goals: 1995-96, 0-for-1.

REEVES, BRYANT C GRIZZLIES

PERSONAL: Born June 8, 1973, in Fort Smith, Ark. ... 7-0/275. ... Nickname: Big Country.
HIGH SCHOOL: Gans (Okla.).
COLLEGE: Oklahoma State.
TRANSACTIONS/CAREER NOTES: Selected by Vancouver Grizzlies in first round (sixth pick overall) of 1995 NBA Draft.
MISCELLANEOUS: Vancouver Grizzlies all-time leading rebounder with 570 and all-time blocked shots leader with 55 (1995-96).

COLLEGIATE RECORD

Season Team	G	Min.	FGM	FGA	Pct.	FTM	FTA	Pct.	Reb.	Ast.	Pts.	AVERAGES RPG	APG	PPG
91-92—Oklahoma State..............	36	763	111	213	.521	69	109	.633	182	24	291	5.1	0.7	8.1
92-93—Oklahoma State..............	29	944	210	338	.621	145	223	.650	291	36	566	10.0	1.2	19.5
93-94—Oklahoma State..............	34	1170	264	451	.585	185	311	.595	329	52	713	9.7	1.5	21.0
94-95—Oklahoma State..............	37	1288	289	493	.586	219	310	.706	350	30	797	9.5	0.8	21.5
Totals	136	4165	874	1495	.585	618	953	.648	1152	142	2367	8.5	1.0	17.4

Three-point field goals: 1992-93, 1-for-2 (.500). 1993-94, 0-for-1. 1994-95, 0-for-5. Totals, 1-for-8 (.125).

HONORS: NBA All-Rookie second team (1996).

NBA REGULAR-SEASON RECORD

Season Team	G	Min.	FGM	FGA	Pct.	FTM	FTA	Pct.	REBOUNDS Off.	Def.	Tot.	Ast.	St.	Blk.	TO	Pts.	AVERAGES RPG	APG	PPG
95-96—Vancouver.......	77	2460	401	877	.457	219	299	.732	178	392	570	109	43	55	157	1021	7.4	1.4	13.3

Three-point field goals: 1995-96, 0-for-3.
Personal fouls/disqualifications: 1995-96, 226/2.

REEVES, KHALID G NETS

PERSONAL: Born July 15, 1972, in Queens, N.Y. ... 6-3/201. ... Name pronounced KA-lid.
HIGH SCHOOL: Christ the King (Middle Village, N.Y.).
COLLEGE: Arizona.
TRANSACTIONS/CAREER NOTES: Selected by Miami Heat in first round (12th pick overall) of 1994 NBA Draft. ... Traded by Heat with G/F Glen Rice, C Matt Geiger and 1996 first-round draft choice to Charlotte Hornets for C Alonzo Mourning, C LeRon Ellis and G Pete Myers (November 3, 1995). ... Traded by Hornets with G Kendall Gill to New Jersey Nets for G Kenny Anderson and G/F Gerald Glass (January 19, 1996).

COLLEGIATE RECORD

NOTES: THE SPORTING NEWS All-America second team (1994).

Season Team	G	Min.	FGM	FGA	Pct.	FTM	FTA	Pct.	Reb.	Ast.	Pts.	AVERAGES RPG	APG	PPG
90-91—Arizona	35	657	104	229	.454	78	113	.690	82	103	317	2.3	2.9	9.1
91-92—Arizona	30	921	148	311	.476	78	99	.788	95	110	418	3.2	3.7	13.9
92-93—Arizona	28	754	118	237	.498	80	110	.727	97	80	342	3.5	2.9	12.2
93-94—Arizona	35	1113	276	572	.483	211	264	.799	150	103	848	4.3	2.9	24.2
Totals	128	3445	646	1349	.479	447	586	.763	424	396	1925	3.3	3.1	15.0

Three-point field goals: 1990-91, 31-for-67 (.463). 1991-92, 44-for-119 (.370). 1992-93, 26-for-79 (.329). 1993-94, 85-for-224 (.379). Totals, 186-for-489 (.380).

NBA REGULAR-SEASON RECORD

Season Team	G	Min.	FGM	FGA	Pct.	FTM	FTA	Pct.	REBOUNDS Off.	Def.	Tot.	Ast.	St.	Blk.	TO	Pts.	AVERAGES RPG	APG	PPG
94-95—Miami	67	1462	206	465	.443	140	196	.714	52	134	186	288	77	10	132	619	2.8	4.3	9.2
95-96—Char.-N.J........	51	833	95	227	.419	61	82	.744	18	61	79	118	37	3	63	279	1.5	2.3	5.5
Totals	118	2295	301	692	.435	201	278	.723	70	195	265	406	114	13	195	898	2.2	3.4	7.6

Three-point field goals: 1994-95, 67-for-171 (.392). 1995-96, 28-for-91 (.308). Totals, 95-for-262 (.363).
Personal fouls/disqualifications: 1994-95, 139/1. 1995-96, 115/2. Totals, 254/3.

REID, DON F PISTONS

PERSONAL: Born December 30, 1973, in Washington, D.C. ... 6-8/250.
HIGH SCHOOL: Largo (Md.).
COLLEGE: Georgetown.
TRANSACTIONS/CAREER NOTES: Selected by Detroit Pistons in second round (58th pick overall) of 1995 NBA Draft.

COLLEGIATE RECORD

Season Team	G	Min.	FGM	FGA	Pct.	FTM	FTA	Pct.	Reb.	Ast.	Pts.	AVERAGES RPG	APG	PPG
91-92—Georgetown..................	28	215	13	30	.433	18	30	.600	59	7	44	2.1	0.3	1.6
92-93—Georgetown..................	32	279	18	43	.419	14	31	.452	68	4	50	2.1	0.1	1.6
93-94—Georgetown..................	31	713	90	140	.643	58	92	.630	182	27	238	5.9	0.9	7.7
94-95—Georgetown..................	31	731	88	148	.595	47	91	.516	178	26	223	5.7	0.8	7.2
Totals	122	1938	209	361	.579	137	244	.561	487	64	555	4.0	0.5	4.5

R

Season Team	G	Min.	FGM	FGA	Pct.	FTM	FTA	Pct.	REBOUNDS Off.	Def.	Tot.	Ast.	St.	Blk.	TO	Pts.	AVERAGES RPG	APG	PPG
95-96—Detroit	69	997	106	187	.567	51	77	.662	78	125	203	11	47	40	41	263	2.9	0.2	3.8

Personal fouls/disqualifications: 1995-96, 199/2.

NBA PLAYOFF RECORD

Season Team	G	Min.	FGM	FGA	Pct.	FTM	FTA	Pct.	REBOUNDS Off.	Def.	Tot.	Ast.	St.	Blk.	TO	Pts.	AVERAGES RPG	APG	PPG
95-96—Detroit	3	26	1	3	.333	1	3	.333	0	1	1	1	0	2	1	3	0.3	0.3	1.0

Personal fouls/disqualifications: 1995-96, 8/0.

REID, J.R.   F/C

PERSONAL: Born March 31, 1968, in Virginia Beach, Va. ... 6-9/255. ... Full name: Herman Reid Jr.
HIGH SCHOOL: Kempsville (Virginia Beach, Va.).
COLLEGE: North Carolina.
TRANSACTIONS/CAREER NOTES: Selected after junior season by Charlotte Hornets in first round (fifth pick overall) of 1989 NBA Draft. ... Traded by Hornets to San Antonio Spurs for F Sidney Green, 1993 first-round draft choice and 1996 second-round draft choice (December 9, 1992). ... Traded by Spurs with F/C Brad Lohaus and 1996 first-round draft choice to New York Knicks for F Charles Smith and F Monty Williams (February 8, 1996). ... Rights renounced by Knicks (July 14, 1996).
MISCELLANEOUS: Member of bronze-medal-winning U.S. Olympic team (1988).

COLLEGIATE RECORD

NOTES: THE SPORTING NEWS All-America second team (1988).

Season Team	G	Min.	FGM	FGA	Pct.	FTM	FTA	Pct.	Reb.	Ast.	Pts.	AVERAGES RPG	APG	PPG
86-87—North Carolina...............	36	1030	198	339	.584	132	202	.653	268	66	528	7.4	1.8	14.7
87-88—North Carolina...............	33	1042	222	366	.607	151	222	.680	293	57	595	8.9	1.7	18.0
88-89—North Carolina............	27	716	164	267	.614	101	151	.669	170	36	429	6.3	1.3	15.9
Totals	96	2788	584	972	.601	384	575	.668	731	159	1552	7.6	1.7	16.2

NBA REGULAR-SEASON RECORD

HONORS: NBA All-Rookie second team (1990).

Season Team	G	Min.	FGM	FGA	Pct.	FTM	FTA	Pct.	REBOUNDS Off.	Def.	Tot.	Ast.	St.	Blk.	TO	Pts.	AVERAGES RPG	APG	PPG
89-90—Charlotte........	82	2757	358	814	.440	192	289	.664	199	492	691	101	92	54	172	908	8.4	1.2	11.1
90-91—Charlotte........	80	2467	360	773	.466	182	259	.703	154	348	502	89	87	47	153	902	6.3	1.1	11.3
91-92—Charlotte........	51	1257	213	435	.490	134	190	.705	96	221	317	81	49	23	84	560	6.2	1.6	11.0
92-93—Char.-S.A.	83	1887	283	595	.476	214	280	.764	120	336	456	80	47	31	125	780	5.5	1.0	9.4
93-94—San Antonio....	70	1344	260	530	.491	107	153	.699	91	129	220	73	43	25	84	627	3.1	1.0	9.0
94-95—San Antonio....	81	1566	201	396	.508	160	233	.687	120	273	393	55	60	32	113	563	4.9	0.7	7.0
95-96—S.A.-N.Y.	65	1313	160	324	.494	107	142	.754	73	182	255	42	43	17	79	427	3.9	0.6	6.6
Totals	512	12591	1835	3867	.475	1096	1546	.709	853	1981	2834	521	421	229	810	4767	5.5	1.0	9.3

Three-point field goals: 1989-90, 0-for-5. 1990-91, 0-for-2. 1991-92, 0-for-3. 1992-93, 0-for-5. 1993-94, 0-for-3. 1994-95, 1-for-2 (.500). 1995-96, 0-for-1. Totals, 1-for-21 (.048).

Personal fouls/disqualifications: 1989-90, 292/7. 1990-91, 286/6. 1991-92, 159/0. 1992-93, 266/3. 1993-94, 165/0. 1994-95, 230/2. 1995-96, 187/0. Totals, 1585/18.

NBA PLAYOFF RECORD

Season Team	G	Min.	FGM	FGA	Pct.	FTM	FTA	Pct.	REBOUNDS Off.	Def.	Tot.	Ast.	St.	Blk.	TO	Pts.	AVERAGES RPG	APG	PPG
92-93—San Antonio....	10	220	29	60	.483	27	35	.771	16	34	50	15	8	8	13	85	5.0	1.5	8.5
93-94—San Antonio....	4	56	6	21	.286	3	5	.600	3	9	12	3	1	2	1	15	3.0	0.8	3.8
94-95—San Antonio....	15	209	29	59	.492	33	39	.846	14	28	42	9	7	4	15	91	2.8	0.6	6.1
95-96—New York	1	7	1	1	1.000	0	0	...	0	1	1	1	0	0	1	2	1.0	1.0	2.0
Totals	30	492	65	141	.461	63	79	.797	33	72	105	28	16	14	30	193	3.5	0.9	6.4

Three-point field goals: 1992-93, 0-for-2.
Personal fouls/disqualifications: 1992-93, 31/0. 1993-94, 10/0. 1994-95, 36/0. 1995-96, 2/0. Totals, 79/0.

RENCHER, TERRENCE   G

PERSONAL: Born February 19, 1973, in Bronx, N.Y. ... 6-3/185. ... Full name: Terrence Lamont Rencher.
HIGH SCHOOL: St. Raymond's (Bronx, N.Y.).
COLLEGE: Texas.
TRANSACTIONS/CAREER NOTES: Selected by Washington Bullets in second round (32nd pick overall) of 1995 NBA Draft. ... Draft rights traded by Bullets with G Rex Chapman to Miami Heat for draft rights to F Jeff Webster and C Ed Stokes (June 28, 1995). ... Traded by Heat to Phoenix Suns for G Tony Smith (February 22, 1996).

COLLEGIATE RECORD

Season Team	G	Min.	FGM	FGA	Pct.	FTM	FTA	Pct.	Reb.	Ast.	Pts.	AVERAGES RPG	APG	PPG
91-92—Texas	34	1147	239	516	.463	125	177	.706	146	121	648	4.3	3.6	19.1
92-93—Texas	26	966	169	448	.377	129	185	.697	130	92	496	5.0	3.5	19.1
93-94—Texas	34	1139	185	448	.413	132	187	.706	185	106	539	5.4	3.1	15.9
94-95—Texas	30	1100	233	491	.475	123	182	.676	158	121	623	5.3	4.0	20.8
Totals	124	4352	826	1903	.434	509	731	.696	619	440	2306	5.0	3.5	18.6

Three-point field goals: 1991-92, 45-for-123 (.366). 1992-93, 29-for-106 (.274). 1993-94, 37-for-143 (.259). 1994-95, 34-for-114 (.298). Totals, 145-for-486 (.298).

R

NBA REGULAR-SEASON RECORD

Season Team	G	Min.	FGM	FGA	Pct.	FTM	FTA	Pct.	REBOUNDS Off.	Def.	Tot.	Ast.	St.	Blk.	TO	Pts.	AVERAGES RPG	APG	PPG
95-96—Mia.-Phoe........	36	405	33	100	.330	31	46	.674	9	35	44	54	16	2	43	106	1.2	1.5	2.9

Three-point field goals: 1995-96, 9-for-29 (.310).
Personal fouls/disqualifications: 1995-96, 37/0.

RESPERT, SHAWN   G   BUCKS

PERSONAL: Born February 6, 1972, in Detroit. ... 6-2/195. ... Full name: Shawn Christopher Respert.
HIGH SCHOOL: Bishop Borgess (Detroit).
COLLEGE: Michigan State.
TRANSACTIONS/CAREER NOTES: Selected by Portland Trail Blazers in first round (eighth pick overall) of 1995 NBA Draft. ... Draft rights traded by Trail Blazers to Milwaukee Bucks for draft rights to F Gary Trent and conditional 1996 first-round draft choice (June 28, 1995).

COLLEGIATE RECORD

NOTES: The Sporting News College Player of the Year (1995). ... The Sporting News All-America first team (1995). ... Injured knee (1990-91); granted extra year of eligibility.

Season Team	G	Min.	FGM	FGA	Pct.	FTM	FTA	Pct.	Reb.	Ast.	Pts.	AVERAGES RPG	APG	PPG
90-91—Michigan State	1	3	0	2	.000	0	0	...	0	0	0	0.0	0.0	0.0
91-92—Michigan State	30	953	173	344	.503	68	78	.872	64	62	474	2.1	2.1	15.8
92-93—Michigan State	28	959	192	399	.481	119	139	.856	111	73	563	4.0	2.6	20.1
93-94—Michigan State	32	1076	272	562	.484	142	169	.840	127	81	778	4.0	2.5	24.3
94-95—Michigan State	28	940	229	484	.473	139	160	.869	111	85	716	4.0	3.0	25.6
Totals	119	3931	866	1791	.484	468	546	.857	413	301	2531	3.5	2.5	21.3

Three-point field goals: 1991-92, 60-for-132 (.455). 1992-93, 60-for-140 (.429). 1993-94, 92-for-205 (.449). 1994-95, 119-for-251 (.474). Totals, 331-for-728 (.455).

NBA REGULAR-SEASON RECORD

Season Team	G	Min.	FGM	FGA	Pct.	FTM	FTA	Pct.	REBOUNDS Off.	Def.	Tot.	Ast.	St.	Blk.	TO	Pts.	AVERAGES RPG	APG	PPG
95-96—Milwaukee	62	845	113	292	.387	35	42	.833	28	46	74	68	32	4	42	303	1.2	1.1	4.9

Three-point field goals: 1995-96, 42-for-122 (.344).
Personal fouls/disqualifications: 1995-96, 67/0.

REYNOLDS, JERRY   G/F

PERSONAL: Born December 23, 1962, in Brooklyn, N.Y. ... 6-8/206. ... Nickname: Ice.
HIGH SCHOOL: Alexander Hamilton (Elmsford, N.Y.).
JUNIOR COLLEGE: Madison (Wis.) Area Technical College.
COLLEGE: Louisiana State.
TRANSACTIONS/CAREER NOTES: Selected after junior season by Milwaukee Bucks in first round (22nd pick overall) of 1985 NBA Draft. ... Traded by Bucks to Seattle SuperSonics for 1990 second-round draft choice (October 4, 1988). ... Selected by Orlando Magic from SuperSonics in NBA expansion draft (June 15, 1989). ... Waived by Magic (November 22, 1993). ... Played in United States Basketball League with Atlanta Trojans (1995). ... Played in Continental Basketball Association with Connecticut Pride (1995-96). ... Signed as free agent by Bucks (December 1, 1995). ... Waived by Bucks (February 27, 1996).

COLLEGIATE RECORD

Season Team	G	Min.	FGM	FGA	Pct.	FTM	FTA	Pct.	Reb.	Ast.	Pts.	AVERAGES RPG	APG	PPG
81-82—Mad. Area Tech.						Did not play.								
82-83—Louisiana State..............	32	888	126	236	.534	88	142	.620	198	...	340	6.2	...	10.6
83-84—Louisiana State..............	29	899	162	307	.528	85	158	.538	239	...	409	8.2	...	14.1
84-85—Louisiana State..............	29	803	128	255	.502	64	107	.598	176	...	320	6.1	...	11.0
Totals	90	2590	416	798	.521	237	407	.582	613	...	1069	6.8	...	11.9

NBA REGULAR-SEASON RECORD

Season Team	G	Min.	FGM	FGA	Pct.	FTM	FTA	Pct.	REBOUNDS Off.	Def.	Tot.	Ast.	St.	Blk.	TO	Pts.	AVERAGES RPG	APG	PPG
85-86—Milwaukee	55	508	72	162	.444	58	104	.558	37	43	80	86	43	19	52	203	1.5	1.6	3.7
86-87—Milwaukee	58	963	140	356	.393	118	184	.641	72	101	173	106	50	30	82	404	3.0	1.8	7.0
87-88—Milwaukee	62	1161	188	419	.449	119	154	.773	70	90	160	104	74	32	104	498	2.6	1.7	8.0
88-89—Seattle	56	737	149	357	.417	127	167	.760	49	51	100	62	53	26	57	428	1.8	1.1	7.6
89-90—Orlando..........	67	1817	309	741	.417	239	322	.742	91	232	323	180	93	64	139	858	4.8	2.7	12.8
90-91—Orlando..........	80	1843	344	793	.434	336	419	.802	88	211	299	203	95	56	172	1034	3.7	2.5	12.9
91-92—Orlando..........	46	1159	197	518	.380	158	189	.836	47	102	149	151	63	17	96	555	3.2	3.3	12.1
92-93—Orlando—neck injury.								Did not play											
95-96—Milwaukee	19	191	21	53	.396	13	21	.619	13	20	33	12	15	6	16	56	1.7	0.6	2.9
Totals	443	8379	1420	3399	.418	1168	1560	.749	467	850	1317	904	486	250	718	4036	3.0	2.0	9.1

Three-point field goals: 1985-86, 1-for-2 (.500). 1986-87, 6-for-18 (.333). 1987-88, 3-for-7 (.429). 1988-89, 3-for-15 (.200). 1989-90, 1-for-14 (.071). 1990-91, 10-for-34 (.294). 1991-92, 3-for-24 (.125). 1995-96, 1-for-10 (.100). Totals, 28-for-124 (.226).
Personal fouls/disqualifications: 1985-86, 57/0. 1986-87, 91/0. 1987-88, 97/0. 1988-89, 58/0. 1989-90, 162/1. 1990-91, 123/0. 1991-92, 69/0. 1995-96, 20/0. Totals, 677/1.

R

NBA PLAYOFF RECORD

Season Team	G	Min.	FGM	FGA	Pct.	FTM	FTA	Pct.	REBOUNDS Off.	Def.	Tot.	Ast.	St.	Blk.	TO	Pts.	AVERAGES RPG	APG	PPG
85-86—Milwaukee	7	40	7	17	.412	6	11	.545	3	6	9	4	4	3	4	20	1.3	0.6	2.9
86-87—Milwaukee	4	5	1	3	.333	1	2	.500	1	0	1	2	3	0	0	3	0.3	0.5	0.8
87-88—Milwaukee	3	12	4	6	.667	0	0	...	0	1	1	1	0	0	1	8	0.3	0.3	2.7
88-89—Seattle	4	40	7	22	.318	7	10	.700	1	4	5	1	2	6	4	22	1.3	0.3	5.5
Totals	18	97	19	48	.396	14	23	.609	5	11	16	8	9	9	9	53	0.9	0.4	2.9

Three-point field goals: 1985-86, 0-for-1. 1986-87, 0-for-1. 1988-89, 1-for-4 (.250). Totals, 1-for-6 (.167).
Personal fouls/disqualifications: 1985-86, 5/0. 1987-88, 1/0. 1988-89, 6/0. Totals, 12/0.

CBA REGULAR-SEASON RECORD

Season Team	G	Min.	FGM	FGA	Pct.	FTM	FTA	Pct.	Reb.	Ast.	Pts.	AVERAGES RPG	APG	PPG
95-96—Connecticut	5	195	50	105	.476	41	47	.872	31	13	149	6.2	2.6	29.8

Three-point field goals: 1995-96, 8-for-19 (.421).

RICE, GLEN   G/F   HORNETS

PERSONAL: Born May 28, 1967, in Flint, Mich. ... 6-8/214. ... Full name: Glen Anthony Rice.
HIGH SCHOOL: Northwestern Community (Flint, Mich.).
COLLEGE: Michigan.
TRANSACTIONS/CAREER NOTES: Selected by Miami Heat in first round (fourth pick overall) of 1989 NBA Draft. ... Traded by Heat with G Khalid Reeves, C Matt Geiger and 1996 first-round draft choice to Charlotte Hornets for C Alonzo Mourning, C LeRon Ellis and G Pete Myers (November 3, 1995).
MISCELLANEOUS: Miami Heat all-time leading scorer with 9,248 points (1989-90 through 1994-95).

COLLEGIATE RECORD

NOTES: The Sporting News All-America second team (1989). ... NCAA Division I Tournament Most Outstanding Player (1989). ... Member of NCAA Division I championship team (1989).

Season Team	G	Min.	FGM	FGA	Pct.	FTM	FTA	Pct.	Reb.	Ast.	Pts.	AVERAGES RPG	APG	PPG
85-86—Michigan	32	520	105	191	.550	15	25	.600	97	21	225	3.0	0.7	7.0
86-87—Michigan	32	1056	226	402	.562	85	108	.787	294	76	540	9.2	2.4	16.9
87-88—Michigan	33	1155	308	539	.571	79	98	.806	236	92	728	7.2	2.8	22.1
88-89—Michigan	37	1258	363	629	.577	124	149	.832	232	85	949	6.3	2.3	25.6
Totals	134	3989	1002	1761	.569	303	380	.797	859	274	2442	6.4	2.0	18.2

Three-point field goals: 1986-87, 3-for-12 (.250). 1987-88, 33-for-77 (.429). 1988-89, 99-for-192 (.516). Totals, 135-for-281 (.480).

NBA REGULAR-SEASON RECORD

HONORS: Long Distance Shootout winner (1995). ... NBA All-Rookie second team (1990).

Season Team	G	Min.	FGM	FGA	Pct.	FTM	FTA	Pct.	REBOUNDS Off.	Def.	Tot.	Ast.	St.	Blk.	TO	Pts.	AVERAGES RPG	APG	PPG
89-90—Miami	77	2311	470	1071	.439	91	124	.734	100	252	352	138	67	27	113	1048	4.6	1.8	13.6
90-91—Miami	77	2646	550	1193	.461	171	209	.818	85	296	381	189	101	26	166	1342	4.9	2.5	17.4
91-92—Miami	79	3007	672	1432	.469	266	318	.836	84	310	394	184	90	35	145	1765	5.0	2.3	22.3
92-93—Miami	82	3082	582	1324	.440	242	295	.820	92	332	424	180	92	25	157	1554	5.2	2.2	19.0
93-94—Miami	81	2999	663	1421	.467	250	284	.880	76	358	434	184	110	32	130	1708	5.4	2.3	21.1
94-95—Miami	82	3014	667	1403	.475	312	365	.855	99	279	378	192	112	14	153	1831	4.6	2.3	22.3
95-96—Charlotte	79	3142	610	1296	.471	319	381	.837	86	292	378	232	91	19	163	1710	4.8	2.9	21.6
Totals	557	20201	4214	9140	.461	1651	1976	.836	622	2119	2741	1299	663	178	1027	10958	4.9	2.3	19.7

Three-point field goals: 1989-90, 17-for-69 (.246). 1990-91, 71-for-184 (.386). 1991-92, 155-for-396 (.391). 1992-93, 148-for-386 (.383). 1993-94, 132-for-346 (.382). 1994-95, 185-for-451 (.410). 1995-96, 171-for-403 (.424). Totals, 879-for-2235 (.393).
Personal fouls/disqualifications: 1989-90, 198/1. 1990-91, 216/0. 1991-92, 170/0. 1992-93, 201/0. 1993-94, 186/0. 1994-95, 203/1. 1995-96, 217/1. Totals, 1391/3.

NBA PLAYOFF RECORD

Season Team	G	Min.	FGM	FGA	Pct.	FTM	FTA	Pct.	REBOUNDS Off.	Def.	Tot.	Ast.	St.	Blk.	TO	Pts.	AVERAGES RPG	APG	PPG
91-92—Miami	3	119	24	64	.375	6	7	.857	3	7	10	5	2	0	6	57	3.3	1.7	19.0
93-94—Miami	5	195	26	68	.382	6	8	.750	6	30	36	10	11	2	14	65	7.2	2.0	13.0
Totals	8	314	50	132	.379	12	15	.800	9	37	46	15	13	2	20	122	5.8	1.9	15.3

Three-point field goals: 1991-92, 3-for-12 (.250). 1993-94, 7-for-23 (.304). Totals, 10-for-35 (.286).
Personal fouls/disqualifications: 1991-92, 7/0. 1993-94, 14/0. Totals, 21/0.

NBA ALL-STAR GAME RECORD

Season Team	Min.	FGM	FGA	Pct.	FTM	FTA	Pct.	REBOUNDS Off.	Def.	Tot.	Ast.	PF	Dq.	St.	Blk.	TO	Pts.
1996 —Charlotte...........	15	1	5	.200	4	4	1.000	0	0	1	2	2	0	0	0	2	7

Three-point field goals: 1996, 1-for-2 (.500).

RICHARDSON, POOH   G   CLIPPERS

PERSONAL: Born May 14, 1966, in Philadelphia. ... 6-1/180. ... Full name: Jerome Richardson Jr.
HIGH SCHOOL: Benjamin Franklin (Philadelphia).
COLLEGE: UCLA.
TRANSACTIONS/CAREER NOTES: Selected by Minnesota Timberwolves in first round (10th pick overall) of 1989 NBA Draft. ... Traded by Timberwolves with F Sam Mitchell to Indiana Pacers for F Chuck Person and G Micheal Williams (September 8, 1992). ... Traded by Pacers with F Malik Sealy and draft rights to F Eric Piatkowski to Los Angeles Clippers for G Mark Jackson and draft rights to G Greg Minor (June 30, 1994).
MISCELLANEOUS: Minnesota Timerwolves all-time assists leader with 1,973 and all-time steals leader with 383 (1989-90 through 1991-92).

R

COLLEGIATE RECORD

Season Team	G	Min.	FGM	FGA	Pct.	FTM	FTA	Pct.	Reb.	Ast.	Pts.	AVERAGES		
												RPG	APG	PPG
85-86—UCLA	29	983	128	260	.492	51	74	.689	131	179	307	4.5	6.2	10.6
86-87—UCLA	32	1112	144	273	.527	46	79	.582	163	208	336	5.1	6.5	10.5
87-88—UCLA	30	1035	142	302	.470	62	93	.667	153	210	348	5.1	7.0	11.6
88-89—UCLA	31	1167	186	335	.555	50	89	.562	118	236	470	3.8	7.6	15.2
Totals	122	4297	600	1170	.513	209	335	.624	565	833	1461	4.6	6.8	12.0

Three-point field goals: 1986-87, 2-for-8 (.250). 1987-88, 2-for-7 (.286). 1988-89, 48-for-97 (.495). Totals, 52-for-112 (.464).

NBA REGULAR-SEASON RECORD

HONORS: NBA All-Rookie first team (1990).

Season Team	G	Min.	FGM	FGA	Pct.	FTM	FTA	Pct.	REBOUNDS			Ast.	St.	Blk.	TO	Pts.	AVERAGES		
									Off.	Def.	Tot.						RPG	APG	PPG
89-90—Minnesota	82	2581	426	925	.461	63	107	.589	55	162	217	554	133	25	141	938	2.6	6.8	11.4
90-91—Minnesota	82	3154	635	1350	.470	89	165	.539	82	204	286	734	131	13	174	1401	3.5	9.0	17.1
91-92—Minnesota	82	2922	587	1261	.466	123	178	.691	91	210	301	685	119	25	204	1350	3.7	8.4	16.5
92-93—Indiana	74	2396	337	703	.479	92	124	.742	63	204	267	573	94	12	167	769	3.6	7.7	10.4
93-94—Indiana	37	1022	160	354	.452	47	77	.610	28	82	110	237	32	3	88	370	3.0	6.4	10.0
94-95—L.A. Clippers	80	2864	353	897	.394	81	125	.648	38	223	261	632	129	12	171	874	3.3	7.9	10.9
95-96—L.A. Clippers	63	2013	281	664	.423	78	105	.743	35	123	158	340	77	13	95	734	2.5	5.4	11.7
Totals	500	16952	2779	6154	.452	573	881	.650	392	1208	1600	3755	715	103	1040	6436	3.2	7.5	12.9

Three-point field goals: 1989-90, 23-for-83 (.277). 1990-91, 42-for-128 (.328). 1991-92, 53-for-155 (.342). 1992-93, 3-for-29 (.103). 1993-94, 3-for-12 (.250). 1994-95, 87-for-244 (.357). 1995-96, 94-for-245 (.384). Totals, 305-for-896 (.340).

Personal fouls/disqualifications: 1989-90, 143/0. 1990-91, 114/0. 1991-92, 152/0. 1992-93, 132/1. 1993-94, 78/0. 1994-95, 218/1. 1995-96, 134/0. Totals, 971/2.

NBA PLAYOFF RECORD

Season Team	G	Min.	FGM	FGA	Pct.	FTM	FTA	Pct.	REBOUNDS			Ast.	St.	Blk.	TO	Pts.	AVERAGES		
									Off.	Def.	Tot.						RPG	APG	PPG
92-93—Indiana	4	95	6	15	.400	4	6	.667	1	10	11	23	2	0	6	17	2.8	5.8	4.3

Three-point field goals: 1992-93, 1-for-1.
Personal fouls/disqualifications: 1992-93, 7/1.

RICHMOND, MITCH   G   KINGS

PERSONAL: Born June 30, 1965, in Fort Lauderdale. ... 6-5/215. ... Full name: Mitchell James Richmond.
HIGH SCHOOL: Boyd Anderson (Fort Lauderdale).
JUNIOR COLLEGE: Moberly (Mo.) Area Junior College.
COLLEGE: Kansas State.
TRANSACTIONS/CAREER NOTES: Selected by Golden State Warriors in first round (fifth pick overall) of 1988 NBA Draft. ... Traded by Warriors with C Les Jepsen to Sacramento Kings for F/G Billy Owens (November 1, 1991).
MISCELLANEOUS: Member of bronze-medal-winning U.S. Olympic team (1988) and gold-medal-winning U.S. Olympic team (1996).

COLLEGIATE RECORD

NOTES: The Sporting News All-America second team (1988).

Season Team	G	Min.	FGM	FGA	Pct.	FTM	FTA	Pct.	Reb.	Ast.	Pts.	AVERAGES		
												RPG	APG	PPG
84-85—Moberly Area J.C.	40	...	180	375	.480	55	85	.647	185	98	415	4.6	2.5	10.4
85-86—Moberly Area J.C.	38	...	242	506	.478	124	180	.689	251	99	608	6.6	2.6	16.0
86-87—Kansas State	30	964	201	450	.447	118	155	.761	170	80	559	5.7	2.7	18.6
87-88—Kansas State	34	1200	268	521	.514	186	240	.775	213	125	768	6.3	3.7	22.6
Junior college totals	78		422	881	.479	179	265	.675	436	197	1023	5.6	2.5	13.1
4-year-college totals	64	2164	469	971	.483	304	395	.770	383	205	1327	6.0	3.2	20.7

Three-point field goals: 1986-87, 39-for-108 (.361). 1987-88, 46-for-98 (.469). Totals, 85-for-206 (.413).

NBA REGULAR-SEASON RECORD

HONORS: NBA Rookie of the Year (1989). ... All-NBA second team (1994, 1995). ... All-NBA third team (1996). ... NBA All-Rookie first team (1989).

Season Team	G	Min.	FGM	FGA	Pct.	FTM	FTA	Pct.	REBOUNDS			Ast.	St.	Blk.	TO	Pts.	AVERAGES		
									Off.	Def.	Tot.						RPG	APG	PPG
88-89—Golden State	79	2717	649	1386	.468	410	506	.810	158	310	468	334	82	13	269	1741	5.9	4.2	22.0
89-90—Golden State	78	2799	640	1287	.497	406	469	.866	98	262	360	223	98	24	201	1720	4.6	2.9	22.1
90-91—Golden State	77	3027	703	1424	.494	394	465	.847	147	305	452	238	126	34	230	1840	5.9	3.1	23.9
91-92—Sacramento	80	3095	685	1465	.468	330	406	.813	62	257	319	411	92	34	247	1803	4.0	5.1	22.5
92-93—Sacramento	45	1728	371	782	.474	197	233	.846	18	136	154	221	53	9	130	987	3.4	4.9	21.9
93-94—Sacramento	78	2897	635	1428	.445	426	511	.834	70	216	286	313	103	17	216	1823	3.7	4.0	23.4
94-95—Sacramento	82	3172	668	1497	.446	375	446	.843	69	288	357	311	91	29	234	1867	4.4	3.8	22.8
95-96—Sacramento	81	2946	611	1368	.447	425	491	.866	54	215	269	255	125	19	220	1872	3.3	3.1	23.1
Totals	600	22381	4962	10637	.466	2963	3526	.840	676	1989	2665	2306	770	179	1747	13653	4.4	3.8	22.8

Three-point field goals: 1988-89, 33-for-90 (.367). 1989-90, 34-for-95 (.358). 1990-91, 40-for-115 (.348). 1991-92, 103-for-268 (.384). 1992-93, 48-for-130 (.369). 1993-94, 127-for-312 (.407). 1994-95, 156-for-424 (.368). 1995-96, 225-for-515 (.437). Totals, 766-for-1949 (.393).

Personal fouls/disqualifications: 1988-89, 223/5. 1989-90, 210/3. 1990-91, 207/0. 1991-92, 231/1. 1992-93, 137/3. 1993-94, 211/3. 1994-95, 227/2. 1995-96, 233/6. Totals, 1679/23.

NBA PLAYOFF RECORD

Season Team	G	Min.	FGM	FGA	Pct.	FTM	FTA	Pct.	REBOUNDS			Ast.	St.	Blk.	TO	Pts.	AVERAGES		
									Off.	Def.	Tot.						RPG	APG	PPG
88-89—Golden State	8	314	62	135	.459	34	38	.895	10	48	58	35	14	1	24	161	7.3	4.4	20.1
90-91—Golden State	9	372	85	169	.503	23	24	.958	10	37	47	22	5	6	17	201	5.2	2.4	22.3
95-96—Sacramento	4	146	24	54	.444	28	35	.800	3	14	17	12	3	0	15	84	4.3	3.0	21.0
Totals	21	832	171	358	.478	85	97	.876	23	99	122	69	22	7	56	446	5.8	3.3	21.2

Three-point field goals: 1988-89, 3-for-16 (.188). 1990-91, 8-for-24 (.333). 1995-96, 8-for-23 (.348). Totals, 19-for-63 (.302).
Personal fouls/disqualifications: 1988-89, 25/0. 1990-91, 28/1. 1995-96, 11/0. Totals, 64/1.

R

NBA ALL-STAR GAME RECORD

NOTES: NBA All-Star Game Most Valuable Player (1995).

Season Team	Min.	FGM	FGA	Pct.	FTM	FTA	Pct.	REBOUNDS Off.	Def.	Tot.	Ast.	PF	Dq.	St.	Blk.	TO	Pts.
1993 —Sacramento......								Selected, did not play—injured.									
1994 —Sacramento......	24	5	16	.313	0	0	...	0	2	2	3	0	0	0	0	0	10
1995 —Sacramento......	22	10	13	.769	0	0	...	3	1	4	2	0	0	0	0	0	23
1996 —Sacramento......	25	3	10	.300	1	2	.500	0	2	2	2	0	0	1	0	2	7
Totals..........................	71	18	39	.462	1	2	.500	3	5	8	7	0	0	1	0	2	40

Three-point field goals: 1995, 3-for-3. 1996, 0-for-3. Totals, 3-for-6 (.500).

RIDER, ISAIAH　　　　　　　　　G/F　　　　　TRAIL BLAZERS

PERSONAL: Born March 12, 1971, in Oakland. ... 6-5/222. ... Full name: Isaiah Rider Jr. ... Nickname: J.R.
HIGH SCHOOL: Encinal (Alameda, Calif.).
JUNIOR COLLEGE: Allen County (Kan.) Community College, then Antelope Valley (Calif.).
COLLEGE: UNLV.
TRANSACTIONS/CAREER NOTES: Selected by Minnesota Timberwolves in first round (fifth pick overall) of 1993 NBA Draft. ... Traded by Timberwolves to Portland Trail Blazers for F Bill Curley, G James Robinson and 1997 or 1998 first-round draft choice (July 23, 1996).

COLLEGIATE RECORD

Season Team	G	Min.	FGM	FGA	Pct.	FTM	FTA	Pct.	Reb.	Ast.	Pts.	AVERAGES RPG	APG	PPG
89-90—Allen County C.C.	30	...	340	...	...	154	...	...	...	...	929	...	...	31.0
90-91—Antelope Valley...............	24	...	319	535	.596	117	159	.736	273	92	806	11.4	3.8	33.6
91-92—UNLV	27	922	206	420	.490	65	87	.747	141	87	558	5.2	3.2	20.7
92-93—UNLV	28	992	282	548	.515	195	236	.826	250	71	814	8.9	2.5	29.1
Junior college totals	54	...	659	...	...	271	...	...	...	...	1735	...	...	32.1
4-year-college totals	55	1914	488	968	.504	260	323	.805	391	158	1372	7.1	2.9	24.9

Three-point field goals: 1991-92, 81-for-202 (.401). 1992-93, 55-for-137 (.401). Totals, 136-for-339 (.401).

NBA REGULAR-SEASON RECORD

HONORS: Slam-Dunk Championship winner (1994). ... NBA All-Rookie first team (1994).

Season Team	G	Min.	FGM	FGA	Pct.	FTM	FTA	Pct.	REBOUNDS Off.	Def.	Tot.	Ast.	St.	Blk.	TO	Pts.	AVERAGES RPG	APG	PPG
93-94—Minnesota.......	79	2415	522	1115	.468	215	265	.811	118	197	315	202	54	28	218	1313	4.0	2.6	16.6
94-95—Minnesota.......	75	2645	558	1249	.447	277	349	.817	90	159	249	245	69	23	232	1532	3.3	3.3	20.4
95-96—Minnesota.......	75	2594	560	1206	.464	248	296	.838	99	210	309	213	48	23	201	1470	4.1	2.8	19.6
Totals	229	7654	1640	3570	.459	740	900	.822	307	566	873	660	171	74	651	4315	3.8	2.9	18.8

Three-point field goals: 1993-94, 54-for-150 (.360). 1994-95, 139-for-396 (.351). 1995-96, 102-for-275 (.371). Totals, 295-for-821 (.359).
Personal fouls/disqualifications: 1993-94, 194/0. 1994-95, 194/3. 1995-96, 204/2. Totals, 592/5.

RILEY, ERIC　　　　　　　　　　C

PERSONAL: Born June 2, 1970, in Cleveland. ... 7-0/245. ... Full name: Eric Kendall Riley.
HIGH SCHOOL: St. Joseph (Cleveland).
COLLEGE: Michigan.
TRANSACTIONS/CAREER NOTES: Selected by Dallas Mavericks in second round (33rd pick overall) of 1993 NBA Draft. ... Draft rights traded by Mavericks to Houston Rockets for draft rights to F Popeye Jones (June 30, 1993). ... Waived by Rockets (December 12, 1994). ... Signed as free agent by Los Angeles Clippers (December 18, 1994). ... Signed as free agent by Minnesota Timberwolves (October 14, 1995). ... Rights renounced by Timberwolves (August 19, 1996).

COLLEGIATE RECORD

Season Team	G	Min.	FGM	FGA	Pct.	FTM	FTA	Pct.	Reb.	Ast.	Pts.	AVERAGES RPG	APG	PPG
88-89—Michigan						Did not play—redshirted.								
89-90—Michigan	31	403	34	56	.607	16	35	.457	102	15	84	3.3	0.5	2.7
90-91—Michigan	28	840	105	235	.447	87	115	.757	242	29	297	8.6	1.0	10.6
91-92—Michigan	32	480	82	139	.590	37	64	.578	139	21	201	4.3	0.7	6.3
92-93—Michigan	35	525	78	133	.586	39	53	.736	169	14	195	4.8	0.4	5.6
Totals	126	2248	299	563	.531	179	267	.670	652	79	777	5.2	0.6	6.2

Three-point field goals: 1989-90, 0-for-1. 1990-91, 0-for-1. 1992-93, 0-for-1. Totals, 0-for-3.

NBA REGULAR-SEASON RECORD

Season Team	G	Min.	FGM	FGA	Pct.	FTM	FTA	Pct.	REBOUNDS Off.	Def.	Tot.	Ast.	St.	Blk.	TO	Pts.	AVERAGES RPG	APG	PPG
93-94—Houston..........	47	219	34	70	.486	20	37	.541	24	35	59	9	5	9	15	88	1.3	0.2	1.9
94-95—L.A. Clippers...	40	434	65	145	.448	47	64	.734	45	67	112	11	17	35	31	177	2.8	0.3	4.4
95-96—Minnesota.......	25	310	35	74	.473	22	28	.786	32	44	76	5	8	16	17	92	3.0	0.2	3.7
Totals	112	963	134	289	.464	89	129	.690	101	146	247	25	30	60	63	357	2.2	0.2	3.2

Three-point field goals: 1993-94, 0-for-1. 1994-95, 0-for-1. 1995-96, 0-for-1. Totals, 0-for-3.
Personal fouls/disqualifications: 1993-94, 30/0. 1994-95, 78/1. 1995-96, 42/0. Totals, 150/1.

R

RIVERS, DOC   G

PERSONAL: Born October 13, 1961, in Chicago. ... 6-4/210. ... Full name: Glenn Anton Rivers. ... Nephew of Jim Brewer, forward with Cleveland Cavaliers, Detroit Pistons, Portland Trail Blazers and Los Angeles Lakers (1973-74 through 1981-82); cousin of Byron Irvin, guard with Portland Trail Blazers and Washington Bullets (1989-90, 1990-91 and 1992-93); and cousin of Ken Singleton, outfielder/designated hitter with New York Mets, Montreal Expos and Baltimore Orioles (1970 through 1984).
HIGH SCHOOL: Proviso East (Maywood, Ill.).
COLLEGE: Marquette.
TRANSACTIONS/CAREER NOTES: Selected after junior season by Atlanta Hawks in second round (31st pick overall) of 1983 NBA Draft. ... Traded by Hawks to Los Angeles Clippers for 1991 first-round draft choice and 1993 and 1994 second-round draft choices (June 26, 1991). ... Traded by Clippers with C/F Charles Smith and G Bo Kimble to New York Knicks in three-way deal in which Clippers received G Mark Jackson and 1995 second-round draft choice from Knicks and C Stanley Roberts from Orlando Magic and Magic received 1993 first-round draft choice from Knicks and 1994 first-round draft choice from Clippers (September 22, 1992). ... Waived by Knicks (December 15, 1994). ... Signed as free agent by San Antonio Spurs (December 26, 1994). ... Announced retirement (July 11, 1996).
MISCELLANEOUS: Atlanta Hawks franchise all-time assists leader with 3,866 (1983-84 through 1990-91).

COLLEGIATE RECORD

Season Team	G	Min.	FGM	FGA	Pct.	FTM	FTA	Pct.	Reb.	Ast.	Pts.	RPG	APG	PPG
80-81—Marquette	31	...	182	329	.553	70	119	.588	99	113	434	3.2	3.6	14.0
81-82—Marquette	29	...	173	382	.453	70	108	.648	99	170	416	3.4	5.9	14.3
82-83—Marquette	29	...	163	373	.437	58	95	.611	94	126	384	3.2	4.3	13.2
Totals	89	...	518	1084	.478	198	322	.615	292	409	1234	3.3	4.6	13.9

NBA REGULAR-SEASON RECORD

Season Team	G	Min.	FGM	FGA	Pct.	FTM	FTA	Pct.	Off.	Def.	Tot.	Ast.	St.	Blk.	TO	Pts.	RPG	APG	PPG
83-84—Atlanta	81	1938	250	541	.462	255	325	.785	72	148	220	314	127	30	174	757	2.7	3.9	9.3
84-85—Atlanta	69	2126	334	701	.476	291	378	.770	66	148	214	410	163	53	176	974	3.1	5.9	14.1
85-86—Atlanta	53	1571	220	464	.474	172	283	.608	49	113	162	443	120	13	141	612	3.1	8.4	11.5
86-87—Atlanta	82	2590	342	758	.451	365	441	.828	83	216	299	823	171	30	217	1053	3.6	10.0	12.8
87-88—Atlanta	80	2502	403	890	.453	319	421	.758	83	283	366	747	140	41	210	1134	4.6	9.3	14.2
88-89—Atlanta	76	2462	371	816	.455	247	287	.861	89	197	286	525	181	40	158	1032	3.8	6.9	13.6
89-90—Atlanta	48	1526	218	480	.454	138	170	.812	47	153	200	264	116	22	98	598	4.2	5.5	12.5
90-91—Atlanta	79	2586	444	1020	.435	221	262	.844	47	206	253	340	148	47	125	1197	3.2	4.3	15.2
91-92—L.A. Clippers	59	1657	226	533	.424	163	196	.832	23	124	147	233	111	19	92	641	2.5	3.9	10.9
92-93—New York	77	1886	216	494	.437	133	162	.821	26	166	192	405	123	9	114	604	2.5	5.3	7.8
93-94—New York	19	499	55	127	.433	14	22	.636	4	35	39	100	25	5	29	143	2.1	5.3	7.5
94-95—N.Y.-S.A.	63	989	108	302	.358	60	82	.732	15	94	109	162	65	21	60	321	1.7	2.6	5.1
95-96—San Antonio	78	1235	108	290	.372	48	64	.750	30	108	138	123	73	21	57	311	1.8	1.6	4.0
Totals	864	23567	3295	7416	.444	2426	3093	.784	634	1991	2625	4889	1563	351	1651	9377	3.0	5.7	10.9

Three-point field goals: 1983-84, 2-for-12 (.167). 1984-85, 15-for-36 (.417). 1985-86, 0-for-16. 1986-87, 4-for-21 (.190). 1987-88, 9-for-33 (.273). 1988-89, 43-for-124 (.347). 1989-90, 24-for-66 (.364). 1990-91, 88-for-262 (.336). 1991-92, 26-for-92 (.283). 1992-93, 39-for-123 (.317). 1993-94, 19-for-52 (.365). 1994-95, 45-for-127 (.354). 1995-96, 47-for-137 (.343). Totals, 361-for-1101 (.328).
Personal fouls/disqualifications: 1983-84, 286/8. 1984-85, 250/7. 1985-86, 185/2. 1986-87, 287/5. 1987-88, 272/3. 1988-89, 263/6. 1989-90, 151/2. 1990-91, 216/2. 1991-92, 166/2. 1992-93, 215/2. 1993-94, 44/0. 1994-95, 150/2. 1995-96, 175/0. Totals, 2660/41.

NBA PLAYOFF RECORD

NOTES: Shares single-game playoff record for most assists in one half—15 (May 16, 1988, vs. Boston).

Season Team	G	Min.	FGM	FGA	Pct.	FTM	FTA	Pct.	Off.	Def.	Tot.	Ast.	St.	Blk.	TO	Pts.	RPG	APG	PPG
83-84—Atlanta	5	130	16	32	.500	36	41	.878	7	3	10	16	12	4	9	68	2.0	3.2	13.6
85-86—Atlanta	9	262	40	92	.435	31	42	.738	10	32	42	78	18	0	26	114	4.7	8.7	12.7
86-87—Atlanta	8	245	18	47	.383	26	52	.500	6	21	27	90	9	3	25	62	3.4	11.3	7.8
87-88—Atlanta	12	409	71	139	.511	39	43	.907	8	51	59	115	25	2	25	188	4.9	9.6	15.7
88-89—Atlanta	5	191	22	57	.386	17	24	.708	4	20	24	34	7	2	12	67	4.8	6.8	13.4
90-91—Atlanta	5	173	30	64	.469	17	19	.895	6	14	20	15	5	2	4	78	4.0	3.0	15.6
91-92—L.A. Clippers	5	187	25	56	.446	22	27	.815	4	15	19	21	6	0	3	76	3.8	4.2	15.2
92-93—New York	15	458	48	106	.453	46	60	.767	6	33	39	86	29	1	30	153	2.6	5.7	10.2
94-95—San Antonio	15	318	37	95	.389	26	31	.839	3	26	29	24	14	9	18	117	1.9	1.6	7.8
95-96—San Antonio	2	20	1	3	.333	—	—	—	0	1	1	0	0	1	1	3	0.5	0.0	1.5
Totals	81	2393	308	691	.446	260	339	.767	54	216	270	479	125	23	153	926	3.3	5.9	11.4

Three-point field goals: 1983-84, 0-for-3. 1985-86, 3-for-6 (.500). 1987-88, 7-for-22 (.318). 1988-89, 6-for-19 (.316). 1990-91, 1-for-11 (.091). 1991-92, 4-for-8 (.500). 1992-93, 11-for-31 (.355). 1994-95, 17-for-46 (.370). 1995-96, 1-for-2 (.500). Totals, 50-for-148 (.338).
Personal fouls/disqualifications: 1983-84, 16/0. 1985-86, 38/2. 1986-87, 32/0. 1987-88, 40/1. 1988-89, 22/2. 1990-91, 14/0. 1991-92, 16/0. 1992-93, 44/0. 1994-95, 40/0. 1995-96, 3/0. Totals, 265/5.

NBA ALL-STAR GAME RECORD

Season Team	Min.	FGM	FGA	Pct.	FTM	FTA	Pct.	Off.	Def.	Tot.	Ast.	PF	Dq.	St.	Blk.	TO	Pts.
1988 —Atlanta	16	2	4	.500	5	11	.455	0	3	3	6	3	0	0	0	3	9

DID YOU KNOW...

...that Fred Roberts is the only player to have had Larry Bird and Magic Johnson as teammates in a regular-season NBA game?

R

ROBERTS, FRED   F

PERSONAL: Born August 14, 1960, in Provo, Utah. ... 6-10/218. ... Full name: Frederick Clark Roberts.
HIGH SCHOOL: Bingham (South Jordan, Utah).
COLLEGE: Brigham Young.
TRANSACTIONS/CAREER NOTES: Selected by Milwaukee Bucks in second round (27th pick overall) of 1982 NBA Draft. ... Draft rights traded by Bucks with F Mickey Johnson to New Jersey Nets for G Phil Ford and 1983 second-round draft choice (November 10, 1982). ... Played in Italy (1982-83). ... Draft rights traded by Nets with 1983 second-round draft choice and cash to San Antonio Spurs in exchange for the Spurs renouncing their rights to Coach Stan Albeck (June 7, 1983). ... Traded by Spurs to Utah Jazz for 1986 and 1988 second-round draft choices (December 18, 1984). ... Traded by Jazz to Boston Celtics for 1987 third-round draft choice (September 25, 1986). ... Selected by Miami Heat from Celtics in NBA expansion draft (June 23, 1988). ... Traded by Heat to Bucks for 1988 second-round draft choice (June 23, 1988). ... Played in Spain (1993-94). ... Played in Continental Basketball Association with Chicago Rockers (1994-95). ... Announced retirement (January 6, 1995). ... Signed by Cleveland Cavaliers to first of two consecutive 10-day contracts (February 23, 1995). ... Re-signed by Cavaliers for remainder of season (March 16, 1995). ... Signed as free agent by Los Angeles Lakers (October 3, 1995). ... Rights renounced by Lakers (July 17, 1996).

COLLEGIATE RECORD

Season Team	G	Min.	FGM	FGA	Pct.	FTM	FTA	Pct.	Reb.	Ast.	Pts.	RPG	APG	PPG
78-79—Brigham Young	28	861	158	291	.543	83	106	.783	191	63	399	6.8	2.3	14.3
79-80—Brigham Young	29	891	151	257	.588	71	98	.724	177	72	373	6.1	2.5	12.9
80-81—Brigham Young	32	1188	216	373	.579	171	220	.777	255	110	603	8.0	3.4	18.8
81-82—Brigham Young	30	1118	162	338	.479	142	178	.798	215	96	466	7.2	3.2	15.5
Totals	119	4058	687	1259	.546	467	602	.776	838	341	1841	7.0	2.9	15.5

ITALIAN LEAGUE RECORD

Season Team	G	Min.	FGM	FGA	Pct.	FTM	FTA	Pct.	Reb.	Ast.	Pts.	RPG	APG	PPG
82-83—Fort. Bologna	30	1114	233	462	.504	106	148	.716	258	...	572	8.6	...	19.1

NBA REGULAR-SEASON RECORD

Season Team	G	Min.	FGM	FGA	Pct.	FTM	FTA	Pct.	Off.	Def.	Tot.	Ast.	St.	Blk.	TO	Pts.	RPG	APG	PPG
83-84—San Antonio	79	1531	214	399	.536	144	172	.837	102	202	304	98	52	38	100	573	3.8	1.2	7.3
84-85—S.A.-Utah	74	1178	208	418	.498	150	182	.824	78	108	186	87	28	22	89	567	2.5	1.2	7.7
85-86—Utah	58	469	74	167	.443	67	87	.770	31	49	80	27	8	6	53	216	1.4	0.5	3.7
86-87—Boston	73	1079	139	270	.515	124	153	.810	54	136	190	62	22	20	89	402	2.6	0.8	5.5
87-88—Boston	74	1032	161	330	.488	128	165	.776	60	102	162	81	16	15	68	450	2.2	1.1	6.1
88-89—Milwaukee	71	1251	155	319	.486	104	129	.806	68	141	209	66	36	23	80	417	2.9	0.9	5.9
89-90—Milwaukee	82	2235	330	666	.496	195	249	.783	107	204	311	147	56	25	130	857	3.8	1.8	10.5
90-91—Milwaukee	82	2114	357	670	.533	170	209	.813	107	174	281	135	63	29	135	888	3.4	1.6	10.8
91-92—Milwaukee	80	1746	311	645	.482	128	171	.749	103	154	257	122	52	40	122	769	3.2	1.5	9.6
92-93—Milwaukee	79	1488	226	428	.528	135	169	.799	91	146	237	118	57	27	67	599	3.0	1.5	7.6
94-95—Cleveland	21	223	28	72	.389	20	26	.769	13	21	34	8	6	3	7	80	1.6	0.4	3.8
95-96—L.A. Lakers	33	317	48	97	.495	22	28	.786	18	29	47	26	16	4	24	122	1.4	0.8	3.7
Totals	806	14663	2251	4481	.502	1387	1740	.797	832	1466	2298	977	412	252	964	5940	2.9	1.2	7.4

Three-point field goals: 1983-84, 1-for-4 (.250). 1984-85, 1-for-1. 1985-86, 1-for-2 (.500). 1986-87, 0-for-3. 1987-88, 0-for-6. 1988-89, 3-for-14 (.214). 1989-90, 2-for-11 (.182). 1990-91, 4-for-25 (.160). 1991-92, 19-for-37 (.514). 1992-93, 12-for-29 (.414). 1994-95, 4-for-11 (.364). 1995-96, 4-for-14 (.286). Totals, 51-for-157 (.325).

Personal fouls/disqualifications: 1983-84, 219/4. 1984-85, 141/0. 1985-86, 72/0. 1986-87, 129/1. 1987-88, 118/0. 1988-89, 126/0. 1989-90, 210/5. 1990-91, 190/2. 1991-92, 177/0. 1992-93, 138/0. 1994-95, 26/1. 1995-96, 24/0. Totals, 1570/13.

NBA PLAYOFF RECORD

Season Team	G	Min.	FGM	FGA	Pct.	FTM	FTA	Pct.	Off.	Def.	Tot.	Ast.	St.	Blk.	TO	Pts.	RPG	APG	PPG
84-85—Utah	10	130	19	43	.442	16	20	.800	6	11	17	9	7	3	14	54	1.7	0.9	5.4
85-86—Utah	4	31	7	15	.467	8	9	.889	4	3	7	3	0	0	6	22	1.8	0.8	5.5
86-87—Boston	20	265	30	59	.508	31	44	.705	15	18	33	12	6	3	12	91	1.7	0.6	4.6
87-88—Boston	15	100	11	21	.524	7	11	.636	8	8	16	3	3	0	6	29	1.1	0.2	1.9
88-89—Milwaukee	9	345	49	100	.490	34	40	.850	11	28	39	20	5	4	13	132	4.3	2.2	14.7
89-90—Milwaukee	4	79	13	20	.650	13	16	.813	5	3	8	3	0	1	5	39	2.0	0.8	9.8
90-91—Milwaukee	3	103	16	35	.457	2	2	1.000	4	11	15	7	2	1	5	34	5.0	2.3	11.3
94-95—Cleveland	1	7	3	4	.750	0	2	.000	1	1	2	0	0	0	1	6	2.0	0.0	6.0
95-96—L.A. Lakers	1	3	0	2	.000	0	0	...	2	1	3	0	0	0	1	0	3.0	0.0	0.0
Totals	67	1063	148	299	.495	111	144	.771	56	84	140	57	23	12	63	407	2.1	0.9	6.1

Three-point field goals: 1988-89, 0-for-3. 1989-90, 0-for-1. 1990-91, 0-for-1. Totals, 0-for-5.

Personal fouls/disqualifications: 1984-85, 16/0. 1985-86, 5/0. 1986-87, 47/0. 1987-88, 20/1. 1988-89, 29/1. 1989-90, 9/0. 1990-91, 5/0. Totals, 131/2.

SPANISH LEAGUE RECORD

Season Team	G	Min.	FGM	FGA	Pct.	FTM	FTA	Pct.	Reb.	Ast.	Pts.	RPG	APG	PPG
93-94—FC Barcelona	28	903	152	309	.492	93	120	.775	162	43	426	5.8	1.5	15.2

CBA REGULAR-SEASON RECORD

Season Team	G	Min.	FGM	FGA	Pct.	FTM	FTA	Pct.	Reb.	Ast.	Pts.	RPG	APG	PPG
94-95—Chicago	8	183	33	70	.471	25	32	.781	30	6	93	3.8	0.8	11.6

Three-point field goals: 1994-95, 2-for-7 (.286).

R

ROBERTS, STANLEY   C   CLIPPERS

PERSONAL: Born February 7, 1970, in Hopkins, S.C. ... 7-0/290. ... Full name: Stanley Corvet Roberts.
HIGH SCHOOL: Lower Richland (Hopkins, S.C.).
COLLEGE: Louisiana State.
TRANSACTIONS/CAREER NOTES: Played in Spain after sophomore season (1990-91). ... Selected by Orlando Magic in first round (23rd pick overall) of 1991 NBA Draft. ... Traded by Magic to Los Angeles Clippers as part of a three-way deal in which Clippers received Roberts from Magic and G Mark Jackson and 1995 second-round draft choice from New York Knicks, the Knicks received G Doc Rivers, C/F Charles Smith and G Bo Kimble from Clippers and Magic received 1993 first-round draft choice from Knicks and 1995 first-round draft choice from Clippers (September 22, 1992).

COLLEGIATE RECORD

Season Team	G	Min.	FGM	FGA	Pct.	FTM	FTA	Pct.	Reb.	Ast.	Pts.	AVERAGES RPG	APG	PPG
88-89—Louisiana State..............						Did not play—ineligible.								
89-90—Louisiana State..............	32	859	200	347	.576	51	111	.459	315	40	451	9.8	1.3	14.1
Totals	32	859	200	347	.576	51	111	.459	315	40	451	9.8	1.3	14.1

Three-point field goals: 1989-90, 0-for-1.

SPANISH LEAGUE RECORD

Season Team	G	Min.	FGM	FGA	Pct.	FTM	FTA	Pct.	Reb.	Ast.	Pts.	AVERAGES RPG	APG	PPG
90-91—Real Madrid..................	34	992	172	286	.601	53	111	.477	296	22	397	8.7	0.6	11.7

NBA REGULAR-SEASON RECORD

HONORS: NBA All-Rookie second team (1992).
NOTES: Led NBA with 332 personal fouls and 15 disqualifications (1993).

Season Team	G	Min.	FGM	FGA	Pct.	FTM	FTA	Pct.	REBOUNDS Off.	Def.	Tot.	Ast.	St.	Blk.	TO	Pts.	AVERAGES RPG	APG	PPG
91-92—Orlando..........	55	1118	236	446	.529	101	196	.515	113	223	336	39	22	83	78	573	6.1	0.7	10.4
92-93—L.A. Clippers...	77	1816	375	711	.527	120	246	.488	181	297	478	59	34	141	121	870	6.2	0.8	11.3
93-94—L.A. Clippers...	14	350	43	100	.430	18	44	.409	27	66	93	11	6	25	24	104	6.6	0.8	7.4
94-95—L.A. Clippers ...						Did not play—Achilles' tendon injury.													
95-96—L.A. Clippers...	51	795	141	304	.464	74	133	.556	42	120	162	41	15	39	48	356	3.2	0.8	7.0
Totals	197	4079	795	1561	.509	313	619	.506	363	706	1069	150	77	288	271	1903	5.4	0.8	9.7

Three-point field goals: 1991-92, 0-for-1.
Personal fouls/disqualifications: 1991-92, 221/7. 1992-93, 332/15. 1993-94, 54/2. 1995-96, 153/3. Totals, 760/27.

NBA PLAYOFF RECORD

Season Team	G	Min.	FGM	FGA	Pct.	FTM	FTA	Pct.	REBOUNDS Off.	Def.	Tot.	Ast.	St.	Blk.	TO	Pts.	AVERAGES RPG	APG	PPG
92-93—L.A. Clippers...	5	149	26	50	.520	5	18	.278	17	24	41	1	3	3	10	57	8.2	0.2	11.4

Three-point field goals: 1992-93, 0-for-1.
Personal fouls/disqualifications: 1992-93, 24/2.

ROBERTSON, ALVIN   G

PERSONAL: Born July 22, 1962, in Barberton, Ohio. ... 6-4/208. ... Full name: Alvin Cyrrale Robertson.
HIGH SCHOOL: Barberton (Ohio).
JUNIOR COLLEGE: Crowder Junior College (Mo.).
COLLEGE: Arkansas.
TRANSACTIONS/CAREER NOTES: Selected by San Antonio Spurs in first round (seventh pick overall) of 1984 NBA Draft. ... Traded by Spurs with F/C Greg Anderson and future considerations to Milwaukee Bucks for F Terry Cummings and future considerations (May 28, 1989). ... Traded by Bucks to Detroit Pistons for F Orlando Woolridge (February 25, 1993). ... Traded by Pistons with a 1995 second-round draft choice and future considerations to Denver Nuggets for F Marcus Liberty and G Mark Macon (November 19, 1993). ... Waived by Nuggets (October 3, 1994). ... Signed as free agent by Toronto Raptors (October 5, 1995). ... Rights renounced by Raptors (July 24, 1996).
MISCELLANEOUS: Member of gold-medal-winning U.S. Olympic team (1984). ... San Antonio Spurs all-time steals leader with 1,128 (1984-85 through 1988-89). ... Toronto Raptors all-time steals leader with 166 (1995-96)

COLLEGIATE RECORD

Season Team	G	Min.	FGM	FGA	Pct.	FTM	FTA	Pct.	Reb.	Ast.	Pts.	AVERAGES RPG	APG	PPG
80-81—Crowder J.C.	34	...	269	470	.572	73	112	.652	284	206	611	8.4	6.1	18.0
81-82—Arkansas	28	495	84	159	.528	35	58	.603	62	49	203	2.2	1.8	7.3
82-83—Arkansas	28	915	161	294	.548	76	115	.661	137	101	398	4.9	3.6	14.2
83-84—Arkansas	32	1109	187	375	.499	122	182	.670	175	191	496	5.5	6.0	15.5
Junior college totals	34	...	269	470	.572	73	112	.652	284	206	611	8.4	6.1	18.0
4-year-college totals	88	2519	432	828	.522	233	355	.656	374	341	1097	4.3	3.9	12.5

NBA REGULAR-SEASON RECORD

RECORDS: Holds career record for highest steals-per-game average—2.71. ... Holds single-season record for most steals—301; and highest steals-per-game average—3.67 (1986).
HONORS: NBA Defensive Player of the Year (1986). ... NBA Most Improved Player (1986). ... All-NBA second team (1986). ... NBA All-Defensive first team (1987, 1991). ... NBA All-Defensive second team (1986, 1988, 1989, 1990).
NOTES: Led NBA with 3.67 steals per game (1986), 3.21 steals per game (1987) and 3.04 steals per game (1991).

Season Team	G	Min.	FGM	FGA	Pct.	FTM	FTA	Pct.	REBOUNDS Off.	Def.	Tot.	Ast.	St.	Blk.	TO	Pts.	AVERAGES RPG	APG	PPG
84-85—San Antonio....	79	1685	299	600	.498	124	169	.734	116	149	265	275	127	24	167	726	3.4	3.5	9.2
85-86—San Antonio....	82	2878	562	1093	.514	260	327	.795	184	332	516	448	*301	40	256	1392	6.3	5.5	17.0

R

Season Team	G	Min.	FGM	FGA	Pct.	FTM	FTA	Pct.	Off.	Def.	Tot.	Ast.	St.	Blk.	TO	Pts.	RPG	APG	PPG
									REBOUNDS								AVERAGES		
86-87—San Antonio....	81	2697	589	1264	.466	244	324	.753	186	238	424	421	*260	35	243	1435	5.2	5.2	17.7
87-88—San Antonio....	82	2978	655	1408	.465	273	365	.748	165	333	498	557	243	69	251	1610	6.1	6.8	19.6
88-89—San Antonio....	65	2287	465	962	.483	183	253	.723	157	227	384	393	197	36	231	1122	5.9	6.0	17.3
89-90—Milwaukee	81	2599	476	946	.503	197	266	.741	230	329	559	445	207	17	217	1153	6.9	5.5	14.2
90-91—Milwaukee	81	2598	438	904	.485	199	263	.757	191	268	459	444	*246	16	212	1098	5.7	5.5	13.6
91-92—Milwaukee	82	2463	396	922	.430	151	198	.763	175	175	350	360	210	32	223	1010	4.3	4.4	12.3
92-93—Mil.-Detroit	69	2006	247	539	.458	84	128	.656	107	162	269	263	155	18	133	618	3.9	3.8	9.0
93-94—Det.-Denver.....						Did not play—injured.													
95-96—Toronto	77	2478	285	607	.470	107	158	.677	110	232	342	323	166	36	183	718	4.4	4.2	9.3
Totals	779	24669	4412	9245	.477	1822	2451	.743	1621	2445	4066	3929	2112	323	2116	10882	5.2	5.0	14.0

Three-point field goals: 1984-85, 4-for-11 (.364). 1985-86, 8-for-29 (.276). 1986-87, 13-for-48 (.271). 1987-88, 27-for-95 (.284). 1988-89, 9-for-45 (.200). 1989-90, 4-for-26 (.154). 1990-91, 23-for-63 (.365). 1991-92, 67-for-210 (.319). 1992-93, 40-for-122 (.328). 1995-96, 41-for-151 (.272). Totals, 236-for-800 (.295).

Personal fouls/disqualifications: 1984-85, 217/1. 1985-86, 296/4. 1986-87, 264/2. 1987-88, 300/4. 1988-89, 259/6. 1989-90, 280/2. 1990-91, 273/5. 1991-92, 263/5. 1992-93, 218/1. 1995-96, 268/5. Totals, 2638/35.

NBA PLAYOFF RECORD

Season Team	G	Min.	FGM	FGA	Pct.	FTM	FTA	Pct.	Off.	Def.	Tot.	Ast.	St.	Blk.	TO	Pts.	RPG	APG	PPG
									REBOUNDS								AVERAGES		
85-86—San Antonio....	3	98	8	29	.276	11	13	.846	5	9	14	19	7	1	5	27	4.7	6.3	9.0
87-88—San Antonio....	3	119	30	53	.566	7	9	.778	5	9	14	28	12	1	9	70	4.7	9.3	23.3
89-90—Milwaukee	4	155	35	67	.522	24	34	.706	10	13	23	19	9	0	15	94	5.8	4.8	23.5
90-91—Milwaukee	3	118	29	49	.592	10	13	.769	7	11	18	15	8	0	10	71	6.0	5.0	23.7
Totals	13	490	102	198	.515	52	69	.754	27	42	69	81	36	2	39	262	5.3	6.2	20.2

Three-point field goals: 1987-88, 3-for-7 (.429). 1989-90, 0-for-1. 1990-91, 3-for-9 (.333). Totals, 6-for-17 (.353).
Personal fouls/disqualifications: 1985-86, 10/0. 1987-88, 15/1. 1989-90, 16/0. 1990-91, 12/0. Totals, 53/1.

NBA ALL-STAR GAME RECORD

Season Team	Min.	FGM	FGA	Pct.	FTM	FTA	Pct.	Off.	Def.	Tot.	Ast.	PF	Dq.	St.	Blk.	TO	Pts.
								REBOUNDS									
1986 —San Antonio	20	2	6	.333	0	0	...	1	8	9	5	1	0	0	0	4	4
1987 —San Antonio	16	2	5	.400	2	2	1.000	2	0	2	1	1	0	0	0	1	6
1988 —San Antonio	12	1	3	.333	0	0	...	0	0	0	1	1	0	2	0	2	2
1991 —Milwaukee	12	2	4	.500	2	2	1.000	0	2	2	0	0	0	0	0	3	6
Totals	60	7	18	.389	4	4	1.000	3	10	13	7	3	0	2	0	10	18

ROBINSON, CLIFFORD   F   TRAIL BLAZERS

PERSONAL: Born December 16, 1966, in Buffalo. ... 6-10/225. ... Full name: Clifford Ralph Robinson.
HIGH SCHOOL: Riverside (Buffalo).
COLLEGE: Connecticut.
TRANSACTIONS/CAREER NOTES: Selected by Portland Trail Blazers in second round (36th pick overall) of 1989 NBA Draft.

COLLEGIATE RECORD

Season Team	G	Min.	FGM	FGA	Pct.	FTM	FTA	Pct.	Reb.	Ast.	Pts.	RPG	APG	PPG
												AVERAGES		
85-86—Connecticut	28	442	60	164	.366	36	59	.610	88	14	156	3.1	0.5	5.6
86-87—Connecticut	16	556	107	255	.420	69	121	.570	119	32	289	7.4	2.0	18.1
87-88—Connecticut	34	1079	222	463	.479	156	238	.655	233	44	600	6.9	1.3	17.6
88-89—Connecticut	31	974	235	500	.470	145	212	.684	228	46	619	7.4	1.5	20.0
Totals	109	3051	624	1382	.452	406	630	.644	668	136	1664	6.1	1.2	15.3

Three-point field goals: 1986-87, 6-for-18 (.333). 1988-89, 4-for-12 (.333). Totals, 10-for-30 (.333).

NBA REGULAR-SEASON RECORD

HONORS: NBA Sixth Man Award (1993).

Season Team	G	Min.	FGM	FGA	Pct.	FTM	FTA	Pct.	Off.	Def.	Tot.	Ast.	St.	Blk.	TO	Pts.	RPG	APG	PPG
									REBOUNDS								AVERAGES		
89-90—Portland	82	1565	298	751	.397	138	251	.550	110	198	308	72	53	53	129	746	3.8	0.9	9.1
90-91—Portland	82	1940	373	806	.463	205	314	.653	123	226	349	151	78	76	133	957	4.3	1.8	11.7
91-92—Portland	82	2124	398	866	.466	219	330	.664	140	276	416	137	85	107	154	1016	5.1	1.7	12.4
92-93—Portland	82	2575	632	1336	.473	287	416	.690	165	377	542	182	98	163	173	1570	6.6	2.2	19.1
93-94—Portland	82	2853	641	1404	.457	352	460	.765	164	386	550	159	118	111	169	1647	6.7	1.9	20.1
94-95—Portland	75	2725	597	1302	.452	265	382	.694	152	271	423	198	79	82	158	1601	5.6	2.6	21.3
95-96—Portland	78	2980	553	1306	.423	360	542	.664	123	320	443	190	86	68	194	1644	5.7	2.4	21.1
Totals	563	16762	3492	7777	.449	1826	2695	.678	977	2054	3031	1089	597	660	1110	9181	5.4	1.9	16.3

Three-point field goals: 1989-90, 12-for-44 (.273). 1990-91, 6-for-19 (.316). 1991-92, 1-for-11 (.091). 1992-93, 19-for-77 (.247). 1993-94, 13-for-53 (.245). 1994-95, 142-for-383 (.371). 1995-96, 178-for-471 (.378). Totals, 371-for-1058 (.351).

Personal fouls/disqualifications: 1989-90, 226/4. 1990-91, 263/2. 1991-92, 274/11. 1992-93, 287/8. 1993-94, 263/0. 1994-95, 240/3. 1995-96, 248/3. Totals, 1801/31.

NBA PLAYOFF RECORD

Season Team	G	Min.	FGM	FGA	Pct.	FTM	FTA	Pct.	Off.	Def.	Tot.	Ast.	St.	Blk.	TO	Pts.	RPG	APG	PPG
									REBOUNDS								AVERAGES		
89-90—Portland	21	391	54	151	.358	29	52	.558	32	55	87	23	19	24	25	137	4.1	1.1	6.5
90-91—Portland	16	354	63	117	.538	38	69	.551	24	39	63	18	7	16	25	165	3.9	1.1	10.3
91-92—Portland	21	522	91	197	.462	44	77	.571	25	63	88	43	22	21	28	227	4.2	2.0	10.8
92-93—Portland	4	131	16	61	.262	9	22	.409	10	7	17	6	6	7	8	41	4.3	1.5	10.3
93-94—Portland	4	149	28	68	.412	7	8	.875	11	14	25	10	3	6	11	65	6.3	2.5	16.3

R

Season Team	G	Min.	FGM	FGA	Pct.	FTM	FTA	Pct.	REBOUNDS Off.	Def.	Tot.	Ast.	St.	Blk.	TO	Pts.	AVERAGES RPG	APG	PPG
94-95—Portland.........	3	119	17	47	.362	9	16	.563	7	12	19	8	2	1	8	47	6.3	2.7	15.7
95-96—Portland.........	5	181	21	61	.344	28	37	.757	4	14	18	8	7	5	16	76	3.6	1.6	15.2
Totals	74	1847	290	702	.413	246	281	.584	113	204	317	116	66	80	121	758	4.3	1.6	10.2

Three-point field goals: 1989-90, 0-for-4. 1990-91, 1-for-3 (.333). 1991-92, 1-for-6 (.167). 1992-93, 0-for-1. 1993-94, 2-for-9 (.222). 1994-95, 4-for-17 (.235). 1995-96, 6-for-23 (.261). Totals, 14-for-63 (.222).

Personal fouls/disqualifications: 1989-90, 71/1. 1990-91, 47/1. 1991-92, 84/3. 1992-93, 17/1. 1993-94, 13/0. 1994-95, 13/0. 1995-96, 19/0. Totals, 264/6.

NBA ALL-STAR GAME RECORD

Season Team	Min.	FGM	FGA	Pct.	FTM	FTA	Pct.	REBOUNDS Off.	Def.	Tot.	Ast.	PF	Dq.	St.	Blk.	TO	Pts.
1994 —Portland	18	5	8	.625	0	0	...	1	1	2	5	0	0	1	0	0	10

Three-point field goals: 1994, 0-for-1.

ROBINSON, DAVID   C   SPURS

PERSONAL: Born August 6, 1965, in Key West, Fla. ... 7-1/250. ... Full name: David Maurice Robinson. ... Nickname: The Admiral.
HIGH SCHOOL: Osbourn Park (Manassas, Va.).
COLLEGE: Navy.
TRANSACTIONS/CAREER NOTES: Selected by San Antonio Spurs in first round (first pick overall) of 1987 NBA Draft.
MISCELLANEOUS: Member of bronze-medal-winning U.S. Olympic team (1988) and gold-medal-winning U.S. Olympic teams (1992, 1996). ... San Antonio Spurs all-time leading rebounder with 6,563 and all-time blocked shots leader with 2,006 (1989-90 through 1995-96).

COLLEGIATE RECORD

NOTES: THE SPORTING NEWS College Player of the Year (1987). ... Naismith Award winner (1987). ... Wooden Award winner (1987). ... THE SPORTING NEWS All-America first team (1986, 1987). ... Holds NCAA Division I career record for highest blocked-shots-per-game average— 5.2. ... Holds NCAA Division I single-season records for highest blocked-shots-per-game average—5.91 (1986); and most blocked shots— 207 (1986). ... Shares NCAA Division I single-game record for most blocked shots—14 (January 4, 1986, vs. UNC Wilmington). ... Led NCAA Division I with 13.0 rebounds per game (1986). ... Led NCAA Division I with 5.91 blocked shots per game (1986) and 4.50 blocked shots per game (1987).

Season Team	G	Min.	FGM	FGA	Pct.	FTM	FTA	Pct.	Reb.	Ast.	Pts.	AVERAGES RPG	APG	PPG
83-84—Navy	28	...	86	138	.623	42	73	.575	111	6	214	4.0	0.2	7.6
84-85—Navy	32	...	302	469	.644	152	243	.626	370	19	756	11.6	0.6	23.6
85-86—Navy	35	...	294	484	.607	208	331	.628	455	24	796	13.0	0.7	22.7
86-87—Navy	32	...	350	592	.591	202	317	.637	378	33	903	11.8	1.0	28.2
Totals	127	...	1032	1683	.613	604	964	.627	1314	82	2669	10.3	0.6	21.0

Three-point field goals: 1986-87, 1-for-1.

NBA REGULAR-SEASON RECORD

RECORDS: Holds career record for highest blocked-shots-per-game average (minimum 400 games)—3.60.
HONORS: NBA Most Valuable Player (1995). ... NBA Defensive Player of the Year (1992). ... NBA Rookie of the Year (1990). ... IBM Award, for all-around contributions to team's success (1990, 1991, 1994, 1995, 1996). ... All-NBA first team (1991, 1992, 1995, 1996). ... All-NBA second team (1994). ... All-NBA third team (1990, 1993). ... NBA All-Defensive first team (1991, 1992, 1995, 1996). ... NBA All-Defensive second team (1990, 1993, 1994). ... NBA All-Rookie first team (1990).
NOTES: Led NBA with 4.49 blocked shots per game (1992).

Season Team	G	Min.	FGM	FGA	Pct.	FTM	FTA	Pct.	REBOUNDS Off.	Def.	Tot.	Ast.	St.	Blk.	TO	Pts.	AVERAGES RPG	APG	PPG
87-88—San Antonio						Did not play—military service.													
88-89—San Antonio						Did not play—military service.													
89-90—San Antonio	82	3002	690	1300	.531	613	837	.732	303	680	983	164	138	319	257	1993	12.0	2.0	24.3
90-91—San Antonio	82	3095	754	1366	.552	592	777	.762	335	728	*1063	208	127	*320	270	2101	*13.0	2.5	25.6
91-92—San Antonio	68	2564	592	1074	.551	393	561	.701	261	568	829	181	158	*305	155	1578	12.2	2.7	23.2
92-93—San Antonio	82	3211	676	1348	.501	561	766	.732	229	727	956	301	127	264	241	1916	11.7	3.7	23.4
93-94—San Antonio	80	3241	840	1658	.507	*693	*925	.749	241	614	855	381	139	265	253	*2383	10.7	4.8	*29.8
94-95—San Antonio	81	3074	788	1487	.530	*656	847	.775	234	640	877	236	134	262	233	2238	10.8	2.9	27.6
95-96—San Antonio	82	3019	711	1378	.516	*626	*823	.761	319	*681	*1000	247	111	271	190	2051	12.2	3.0	25.0
Totals	557	21206	5051	9611	.526	4134	5536	.747	1922	4641	6563	1718	934	2006	1626	14260	11.8	3.1	25.6

Three-point field goals: 1989-90, 0-for-2. 1990-91, 1-for-7 (.143). 1991-92, 1-for-8 (.125). 1992-93, 3-for-17 (.176). 1993-94, 10-for-29 (.345). 1994-95, 6-for-20 (.300). 1995-96, 3-for-9 (.333). Totals, 24-for-92 (.261).

Personal fouls/disqualifications: 1989-90, 259/3. 1990-91, 264/5. 1991-92, 219/5. 1992-93, 239/5. 1993-94, 228/3. 1994-95, 230/2. 1995-96, 262/1. Totals, 1701/21.

NBA PLAYOFF RECORD

Season Team	G	Min.	FGM	FGA	Pct.	FTM	FTA	Pct.	REBOUNDS Off.	Def.	Tot.	Ast.	St.	Blk.	TO	Pts.	AVERAGES RPG	APG	PPG
89-90—San Antonio	10	375	89	167	.533	65	96	.677	36	84	120	23	11	40	24	243	12.0	2.3	24.3
90-91—San Antonio	4	166	35	51	.686	33	38	.868	11	43	54	8	6	15	15	103	13.5	2.0	25.8
92-93—San Antonio	10	421	79	170	.465	73	110	.664	29	97	126	40	10	36	25	231	12.6	4.0	23.1
93-94—San Antonio	4	146	30	73	.411	20	27	.741	13	27	40	14	3	10	9	80	10.0	3.5	20.0
94-95—San Antonio	15	623	129	289	.446	121	149	.812	57	125	182	47	22	39	56	380	12.1	3.1	25.3
95-96—San Antonio	10	353	83	161	.516	70	105	.667	37	64	101	24	15	25	24	236	10.1	2.4	23.6
Totals	53	2084	445	911	.488	382	525	.728	183	440	623	156	67	165	153	1273	11.8	2.9	24.0

Three-point field goals: 1990-91, 0-for-1. 1992-93, 0-for-1. 1993-94, 0-for-1. 1994-95, 1-for-5 (.200). Totals, 1-for-8 (.125).

Personal fouls/disqualifications: 1989-90, 35/1. 1990-91, 11/0. 1992-93, 39/0. 1993-94, 14/0. 1994-95, 63/1. 1995-96, 38/2. Totals, 200/4.

R

NBA ALL-STAR GAME RECORD

Season	Team	Min.	FGM	FGA	Pct.	FTM	FTA	Pct.	REBOUNDS Off.	Def.	Tot.	Ast.	PF	Dq.	St.	Blk.	TO	Pts.
1990	—San Antonio	25	7	12	.583	1	2	.500	2	8	10	1	1	0	2	1	1	15
1991	—San Antonio	18	6	13	.462	4	5	.800	3	3	6	0	5	0	2	3	2	16
1992	—San Antonio	18	7	9	.778	5	8	.625	1	4	5	2	3	0	3	1	0	19
1993	—San Antonio	26	7	10	.700	7	12	.583	2	8	10	1	4	0	0	1	1	21
1994	—San Antonio	21	6	13	.462	7	10	.700	3	2	5	0	2	0	0	2	1	19
1995	—San Antonio	14	3	5	.600	4	6	.667	0	3	3	2	2	0	2	1	1	10
1996	—San Antonio	23	8	13	.615	2	2	1.000	6	5	11	2	4	0	2	2	1	18
Totals	....	145	44	75	.587	30	45	.667	17	33	50	8	21	0	11	11	7	118

ROBINSON, GLENN   F   BUCKS

PERSONAL: Born January 10, 1973, in Gary, Ind. ... 6-7/240. ... Full name: Glenn A. Robinson. ... Nickname: Big Dog.
HIGH SCHOOL: Roosevelt (Gary, Ind.).
COLLEGE: Purdue.
TRANSACTIONS/CAREER NOTES: Selected after junior season by Milwaukee Bucks in first round (first pick overall) of 1994 NBA Draft.

COLLEGIATE RECORD

NOTES: THE SPORTING NEWS College Player of the Year (1994). ... Naismith Award winner (1994). ... Wooden Award winner (1994). ... THE SPORTING NEWS All-America first team (1994). ... THE SPORTING NEWS All-America second team (1993). ... Led NCAA Division I with 30.3 points per game (1994).

Season Team	G	Min.	FGM	FGA	Pct.	FTM	FTA	Pct.	Reb.	Ast.	Pts.	AVERAGES RPG	APG	PPG
91-92—Purdue						Did not play—ineligible.								
92-93—Purdue	28	1010	246	519	.474	152	205	.741	258	49	676	9.2	1.8	24.1
93-94—Purdue	34	1166	368	762	.483	215	270	.796	344	66	1030	10.1	1.9	30.3
Totals	62	2176	614	1281	.479	367	475	.773	602	115	1706	9.7	1.9	27.5

Three-point field goals: 1992-93, 32-for-80 (.400). 1993-94, 79-for-208 (.380). Totals, 111-for-288 (.385).

NBA REGULAR-SEASON RECORD

HONORS: NBA All-Rookie first team (1995).

Season Team	G	Min.	FGM	FGA	Pct.	FTM	FTA	Pct.	REBOUNDS Off.	Def.	Tot.	Ast.	St.	Blk.	TO	Pts.	AVERAGES RPG	APG	PPG
94-95—Milwaukee	80	2958	636	1410	.451	397	499	.796	169	344	513	197	115	22	*313	1755	6.4	2.5	21.9
95-96—Milwaukee	82	3249	627	1382	.454	316	389	.812	136	368	504	293	95	42	282	1660	6.1	3.6	20.2
Totals	162	6207	1263	2792	.452	713	888	.803	305	712	1017	490	210	64	595	3415	6.3	3.0	21.1

Three-point field goals: 1994-95, 86-for-268 (.321). 1995-96, 90-for-263 (.342). Totals, 176-for-531 (.331).
Personal fouls/disqualifications: 1994-95, 234/2. 1995-96, 236/2. Totals, 470/4.

ROBINSON, JAMES   G   TIMBERWOLVES

PERSONAL: Born August 31, 1970, in Jackson, Miss. ... 6-2/180.
HIGH SCHOOL: Murrah (Jackson, Miss.).
COLLEGE: Alabama.
TRANSACTIONS/CAREER NOTES: Selected after junior season by Portland Trail Blazers in first round (21st pick overall) of 1993 NBA Draft. ... Traded by Trail Blazers with F Bill Curley and 1997 or 1998 first-round draft choice to Minnesota Timberwolves for G Isaiah Rider (July 23, 1996).

COLLEGIATE RECORD

Season Team	G	Min.	FGM	FGA	Pct.	FTM	FTA	Pct.	Reb.	Ast.	Pts.	AVERAGES RPG	APG	PPG
89-90—Alabama						Did not play—redshirted.								
90-91—Alabama	33	917	194	413	.470	102	146	.699	130	40	554	3.9	1.2	16.8
91-92—Alabama	34	1217	237	533	.445	104	146	.712	138	79	661	4.1	2.3	19.4
92-93—Alabama	29	1000	202	481	.420	116	170	.682	130	68	598	4.5	2.3	20.6
Totals	96	3134	633	1427	.444	322	462	.697	398	187	1813	4.1	1.9	18.9

Three-point field goals: 1990-91, 64-for-153 (.418). 1991-92, 83-for-232 (.358). 1992-93, 78-for-222 (.351). Totals, 225-for-607 (.371).

NBA REGULAR-SEASON RECORD

Season Team	G	Min.	FGM	FGA	Pct.	FTM	FTA	Pct.	REBOUNDS Off.	Def.	Tot.	Ast.	St.	Blk.	TO	Pts.	AVERAGES RPG	APG	PPG
93-94—Portland	58	673	104	285	.365	45	67	.672	34	44	78	68	30	15	52	276	1.3	1.2	4.8
94-95—Portland	71	1539	255	624	.409	65	110	.591	42	90	132	180	48	13	127	651	1.9	2.5	9.2
95-96—Portland	76	1627	229	574	.399	89	135	.659	44	113	157	150	34	16	111	649	2.1	2.0	8.5
Totals	205	3839	588	1483	.396	199	312	.638	120	247	367	398	112	44	290	1576	1.8	1.9	7.7

Three-point field goals: 1993-94, 23-for-73 (.315). 1994-95, 76-for-223 (.341). 1995-96, 102-for-284 (.359). Totals, 201-for-580 (.347).
Personal fouls/disqualifications: 1993-94, 69/0. 1994-95, 142/0. 1995-96, 146/0. Totals, 357/0.

NBA PLAYOFF RECORD

Season Team	G	Min.	FGM	FGA	Pct.	FTM	FTA	Pct.	REBOUNDS Off.	Def.	Tot.	Ast.	St.	Blk.	TO	Pts.	AVERAGES RPG	APG	PPG
93-94—Portland	4	28	4	10	.400	1	2	.500	2	1	3	6	1	1	0	10	0.8	1.5	2.5
94-95—Portland	2	4	2	3	.667	0	0	...	0	0	0	1	0	0	0	6	0.0	0.5	3.0
95-96—Portland	2	26	3	10	.300	0	0	...	0	1	1	3	1	1	3	8	0.5	1.5	4.0
Totals	8	58	9	23	.391	1	2	.500	2	2	4	10	2	2	3	24	0.5	1.3	3.0

Three-point field goals: 1993-94, 1-for-2 (.500). 1994-95, 2-for-3 (.667). 1995-96, 2-for-6 (.333). Totals, 5-for-11 (.455).
Personal fouls/disqualifications: 1993-94, 2/0. 1995-96, 4/0. Totals, 6/0.

R

ROBINSON, RUMEAL   G   LAKERS

PERSONAL: Born November 13, 1966, in Mandeville, Jamaica. ... 6-2/195. ... Full name: Rumeal James Robinson. ... Name pronounced RUE-meal.
HIGH SCHOOL: Cambridge Rindge and Latin School (Mass.).
COLLEGE: Michigan.
TRANSACTIONS/CAREER NOTES: Selected by Atlanta Hawks in first round (10th pick overall) of 1990 NBA Draft. ... Traded by Hawks to New Jersey Nets for F Roy Hinson and G Mookie Blaylock (November 3, 1992). ... Traded by Nets to Charlotte Hornets for F Johnny Newman (December 10, 1993). ... Played in Continental Basketball Association with Rapid City Thrillers (1994-95), Shreveport Crawdads (1994-95) and Connecticut Pride (1995-96). ... Signed by Portland Trail Blazers to first of two consecutive 10-day contracts (January 10, 1996). ... Re-signed by Trail Blazers for remainder of season (January 30, 1996). ... Rights renounced by Trail Blazers (July 23, 1996). ... Signed as free agent by Los Angeles Lakers (August 9, 1996).

COLLEGIATE RECORD

NOTES: The Sporting News All-America third team (1990). ... Member of NCAA Division I championship team (1989).

Season Team	G	Min.	FGM	FGA	Pct.	FTM	FTA	Pct.	Reb.	Ast.	Pts.	RPG	APG	PPG
86-87—Michigan						Did not play—ineligible.								
87-88—Michigan	33	858	115	208	.553	84	126	.667	101	158	321	3.1	4.8	9.7
88-89—Michigan	37	1110	199	357	.557	122	186	.656	125	233	550	3.4	6.3	14.9
89-90—Michigan	30	1020	201	410	.490	125	185	.676	127	184	575	4.2	6.1	19.2
Totals	100	2988	515	975	.528	331	497	.666	353	575	1446	3.5	5.8	14.5

Three-point field goals: 1987-88, 7-for-26 (.269). 1988-89, 30-for-64 (.469). 1989-90, 48-for-117 (.410). Totals, 85-for-207 (.411).

NBA REGULAR-SEASON RECORD

Season Team	G	Min.	FGM	FGA	Pct.	FTM	FTA	Pct.	Off.	Def.	Tot.	Ast.	St.	Blk.	TO	Pts.	RPG	APG	PPG
									REBOUNDS								AVERAGES		
90-91—Atlanta	47	674	108	242	.446	47	80	.588	20	51	71	132	32	8	76	265	1.5	2.8	5.6
91-92—Atlanta	81	2220	423	928	.456	175	275	.636	64	155	219	446	105	24	206	1055	2.7	5.5	13.0
92-93—New Jersey	80	1585	270	638	.423	112	195	.574	49	110	159	323	96	12	140	672	2.0	4.0	8.4
93-94—N.J.-Char.	31	396	55	152	.362	13	29	.448	6	26	32	63	18	3	43	131	1.0	2.0	4.2
95-96—Portland	43	715	92	221	.416	33	51	.647	19	59	78	142	26	5	72	247	1.8	3.3	5.7
Totals	282	5590	948	2181	.435	380	630	.603	158	401	559	1106	277	52	537	2370	2.0	3.9	8.4

Three-point field goals: 1990-91, 2-for-11 (.182). 1991-92, 34-for-104 (.327). 1992-93, 20-for-56 (.357). 1993-94, 8-for-20 (.400). 1995-96, 30-for-79 (.380). Totals, 94-for-270 (.348).
Personal fouls/disqualifications: 1990-91, 65/0. 1991-92, 178/0. 1992-93, 169/2. 1993-94, 48/0. 1995-96, 79/1. Totals, 539/3.

NBA PLAYOFF RECORD

Season Team	G	Min.	FGM	FGA	Pct.	FTM	FTA	Pct.	Off.	Def.	Tot.	Ast.	St.	Blk.	TO	Pts.	RPG	APG	PPG
									REBOUNDS								AVERAGES		
90-91—Atlanta	2	13	1	4	.250	0	0		0	1	1	1	1	0	4	2	0.5	0.5	1.0
92-93—New Jersey	5	136	21	49	.429	5	7	.714	4	8	12	35	5	0	20	49	2.4	7.0	9.8
95-96—Portland	5	43	8	19	.421	1	4	.250	0	2	2	3	3	0	3	21	0.4	0.6	4.2
Totals	12	192	30	72	.417	6	11	.545	4	11	15	39	9	0	27	72	1.3	3.3	6.0

Three-point field goals: 1992-93, 2-for-7 (.286). 1995-96, 4-for-9 (.444). Totals, 6-for-16 (.375).
Personal fouls/disqualifications: 1990-91, 1/0. 1992-93, 18/0. 1995-96, 8/0. Totals, 27/0.

CBA REGULAR-SEASON RECORD

Season Team	G	Min.	FGM	FGA	Pct.	FTM	FTA	Pct.	Reb.	Ast.	Pts.	RPG	APG	PPG
94-95—Rapid City-Shreveport	37	1228	282	589	.479	125	174	.718	89	175	749	2.4	4.7	20.2
95-96—Connecticut	14	500	109	237	.460	63	81	.778	50	59	318	3.6	4.2	22.7
Totals	51	1728	391	826	.473	188	255	.737	139	234	1067	2.7	4.6	20.9

Three-point field goals: 1994-95, 60-for-156 (.385). 1995-96, 37-for-98 (.378). Totals, 97-for-254 (.382).

RODMAN, DENNIS   F   BULLS

PERSONAL: Born May 13, 1961, in Trenton, N.J. ... 6-8/220. ... Full name: Dennis Keith Rodman. ... Nickname: Worm.
HIGH SCHOOL: South Oak Cliff (Dallas), did not play basketball.
JUNIOR COLLEGE: Cooke County (Texas) Junior College.
COLLEGE: Southeastern Oklahoma State.
TRANSACTIONS/CAREER NOTES: Selected by Detroit Pistons in second round (27th pick overall) of 1986 NBA Draft. ... Traded by Pistons to San Antonio Spurs for F Sean Elliott and F David Wood (October 1, 1993). ... Traded by Spurs to Chicago Bulls for C Will Perdue (October 2, 1995).
MISCELLANEOUS: Member of NBA championship teams (1989, 1990, 1996).

COLLEGIATE RECORD

NOTES: Led NAIA with 15.9 rebounds per game (1985) and 17.8 rebounds per game (1986).

Season Team	G	Min.	FGM	FGA	Pct.	FTM	FTA	Pct.	Reb.	Ast.	Pts.	RPG	APG	PPG
82-83—Cooke County J.C.	16	...	114	185	.616	53	91	.582	212	...	281	13.3	...	17.6
83-84—SE Oklahoma St.	30	...	303	490	.618	173	264	.655	392	23	779	13.1	0.8	26.0
84-85—SE Oklahoma St.	32	...	353	545	.648	151	267	.566	510	12	857	15.9	0.4	26.8
85-86—SE Oklahoma St.	34	...	332	515	.645	165	252	.655	605	26	829	17.8	0.8	24.4
Junior college totals	16	...	114	185	.616	53	91	.582	212	...	281	13.3	...	17.6
4-year-college totals	96	...	988	1550	.637	489	783	.625	1507	61	2465	15.7	0.6	25.7

NBA REGULAR-SEASON RECORD

HONORS: NBA Defensive Player of the Year (1990, 1991). ... IBM Award, for all-around contributions to team's success (1992). ... All-NBA third team (1992, 1995). ... NBA All-Defensive first team (1989, 1990, 1991, 1992, 1993, 1995, 1996). ... NBA All-Defensive second team (1994).

R

Season Team	G	Min.	FGM	FGA	Pct.	FTM	FTA	Pct.	REBOUNDS Off.	Def.	Tot.	Ast.	St.	Blk.	TO	Pts.	AVERAGES RPG	APG	PPG
86-87—Detroit	77	1155	213	391	.545	74	126	.587	163	169	332	56	38	48	93	500	4.3	0.7	6.5
87-88—Detroit	82	2147	398	709	.561	152	284	.535	318	397	715	110	75	45	156	953	8.7	1.3	11.6
88-89—Detroit	82	2208	316	531	*.595	97	155	.626	327	445	772	99	55	76	126	735	9.4	1.2	9.0
89-90—Detroit	82	2377	288	496	.581	142	217	.654	336	456	792	72	52	60	90	719	9.7	0.9	8.8
90-91—Detroit	82	2747	276	560	.493	111	176	.631	*361	665	1026	85	65	55	94	669	12.5	1.0	8.2
91-92—Detroit	82	3301	342	635	.539	84	140	.600	*523	*1007	*1530	191	68	70	140	800	*18.7	2.3	9.8
92-93—Detroit	62	2410	183	429	.427	87	163	.534	*367	765	*1132	102	48	45	103	468	*18.3	1.6	7.5
93-94—San Antonio	79	2989	156	292	.534	53	102	.520	*453	*914	*1367	184	52	32	138	370	*17.3	2.3	4.7
94-95—San Antonio	49	1568	137	240	.571	75	111	.676	274	549	823	97	31	23	98	349	*16.8	2.0	7.1
95-96—Chicago	64	2088	146	304	.480	56	106	.528	*356	596	952	160	36	27	138	351	*14.9	2.5	5.5
Totals	741	22990	2455	4587	.535	931	1580	.589	3478	5963	9441	1156	520	481	1176	5914	12.7	1.6	8.0

Three-point field goals: 1986-87, 0-for-1. 1987-88, 5-for-17 (.294). 1988-89, 6-for-26 (.231). 1989-90, 1-for-9 (.111). 1990-91, 6-for-30 (.200). 1991-92, 32-for-101 (.317). 1992-93, 15-for-73 (.205). 1993-94, 5-for-24 (.208). 1994-95, 0-for-2. 1995-96, 3-for-27 (.111). Totals, 73-for-310 (.235).

Personal fouls/disqualifications: 1986-87, 166/1. 1987-88, 273/5. 1988-89, 292/4. 1989-90, 276/2. 1990-91, 281/7. 1991-92, 248/0. 1992-93, 201/0. 1993-94, 229/0. 1994-95, 159/1. 1995-96, 196/1. Totals, 2321/21.

NBA PLAYOFF RECORD

NOTES: Shares NBA Finals single-game record for most offensive rebounds—11 (June 7, 1996, vs. Seattle; and June 16, 1996, vs. Seattle).

Season Team	G	Min.	FGM	FGA	Pct.	FTM	FTA	Pct.	REBOUNDS Off.	Def.	Tot.	Ast.	St.	Blk.	TO	Pts.	AVERAGES RPG	APG	PPG
86-87—Detroit	15	245	40	74	.541	18	32	.563	32	39	71	3	6	17	17	98	4.7	0.2	6.5
87-88—Detroit	23	474	71	136	.522	22	54	.407	51	85	136	21	14	14	31	164	5.9	0.9	7.1
88-89—Detroit	17	409	37	70	.529	24	35	.686	56	114	170	16	6	12	24	98	10.0	0.9	5.8
89-90—Detroit	19	560	54	95	.568	18	35	.514	55	106	161	17	9	13	31	126	8.5	0.9	6.6
90-91—Detroit	15	495	41	91	.451	10	24	.417	67	110	177	14	11	10	13	94	11.8	0.9	6.3
91-92—Detroit	5	156	16	27	.593	4	8	.500	16	35	51	9	4	2	7	36	10.2	1.8	7.2
93-94—San Antonio	3	114	12	24	.500	1	6	.167	24	24	48	2	6	4	6	25	16.0	0.7	8.3
94-95—San Antonio	14	459	52	96	.542	20	35	.571	69	138	207	18	12	0	25	124	14.8	1.3	8.9
95-96—Chicago	18	620	50	103	.485	35	59	.593	98	149	247	37	14	8	41	135	13.7	2.1	7.5
Totals	129	3532	373	716	.521	152	288	.528	468	800	1268	137	82	80	195	900	9.8	1.1	7.0

Three-point field goals: 1987-88, 0-for-2. 1988-89, 0-for-4. 1990-91, 2-for-9 (.222). 1991-92, 0-for-2. 1993-94, 0-for-5. 1994-95, 0-for-5. Totals, 2-for-27 (.074).

Personal fouls/disqualifications: 1986-87, 48/0. 1987-88, 87/1. 1988-89, 58/0. 1989-90, 62/1. 1990-91, 55/1. 1991-92, 17/0. 1993-94, 14/0. 1994-95, 51/1. 1995-96, 76/1. Totals, 468/5.

NBA ALL-STAR GAME RECORD

Season Team	Min.	FGM	FGA	Pct.	FTM	FTA	Pct.	REBOUNDS Off.	Def.	Tot.	Ast.	PF	Dq.	St.	Blk.	TO	Pts.
1990 —Detroit	11	2	4	.500	0	0	...	3	1	4	1	1	0	0	1	2	4
1992 —Detroit	25	2	7	.286	0	0	...	7	6	13	0	1	0	1	0	2	4
Totals	36	4	11	.364	0	0	...	10	7	17	1	2	0	1	1	4	8

ROE, LOU   F

PERSONAL: Born July 14, 1972, in Atlantic City, N.J. ... 6-7/220. ... Full name: Louis M. Roe.
HIGH SCHOOL: Atlantic City (N.J.).
COLLEGE: Massachusetts.
TRANSACTIONS/CAREER NOTES: Selected by Detroit Pistons in second round (30th pick overall) of 1995 NBA Draft. ... Rights renounced by Pistons (July 15, 1996).

COLLEGIATE RECORD

NOTES: The Sporting News All-America first team (1995). ... The Sporting News All-America second team (1994).

Season Team	G	Min.	FGM	FGA	Pct.	FTM	FTA	Pct.	Reb.	Ast.	Pts.	AVERAGES RPG	APG	PPG
91-92—Massachusetts	34	706	90	170	.529	86	128	.672	219	32	266	6.4	0.9	7.8
92-93—Massachusetts	31	938	154	273	.564	121	167	.725	285	40	429	9.2	1.3	13.8
93-94—Massachusetts	35	1123	218	432	.505	210	315	.667	292	61	650	8.3	1.7	18.6
94-95—Massachusetts	34	971	199	374	.532	161	228	.706	274	58	560	8.1	1.7	16.5
Totals	134	3738	661	1249	.529	578	838	.690	1070	191	1905	8.0	1.4	14.2

Three-point field goals: 1993-94, 4-for-15 (.267). 1994-95, 1-for-3 (.333). Totals, 5-for-18 (.278).

NBA REGULAR-SEASON RECORD

Season Team	G	Min.	FGM	FGA	Pct.	FTM	FTA	Pct.	REBOUNDS Off.	Def.	Tot.	Ast.	St.	Blk.	TO	Pts.	AVERAGES RPG	APG	PPG
95-96—Detroit	49	372	32	90	.356	24	32	.750	30	48	78	15	10	8	17	90	1.6	0.3	1.8

Three-point field goals: 1995-96, 2-for-9 (.222).
Personal fouls/disqualifications: 1995-96, 42/0.

NBA PLAYOFF RECORD

Season Team	G	Min.	FGM	FGA	Pct.	FTM	FTA	Pct.	REBOUNDS Off.	Def.	Tot.	Ast.	St.	Blk.	TO	Pts.	AVERAGES RPG	APG	PPG
95-96—Detroit	2	7	0	1	.000	0	0	...	1	1	2	0	1	0	0	0	1.0	0.0	0.0

Personal fouls/disqualifications: 1995-96, 1/0.

R

DID YOU KNOW...

...that rebounder-deluxe Dennis Rodman is the first player to lead the NBA
in any major statistical category with three different teams?

ROGERS, CARLOS   F/C   RAPTORS

PERSONAL: Born February 6, 1971, in Detroit. ... 6-11/220. ... Full name: Carlos Deon Rogers.
HIGH SCHOOL: Northwestern (Detroit).
COLLEGE: Arkansas-Little Rock, then Tennessee State.
TRANSACTIONS/CAREER NOTES: Selected by Seattle SuperSonics in first round (11th pick overall) of 1994 NBA Draft. ... Draft rights traded by SuperSonics with G Ricky Pierce and two 1995 second-round draft choices to Golden State Warriors for G Sarunas Marciulionis and F Byron Houston (July 18, 1994). ... Traded by Warriors with C Victor Alexander and draft rights to F Dwayne Whitfield, F Martin Lewis and C Michael McDonald to Toronto Raptors for G B.J. Armstrong (September 18, 1995).

COLLEGIATE RECORD

Season Team	G	Min.	FGM	FGA	Pct.	FTM	FTA	Pct.	Reb.	Ast.	Pts.	RPG	AVERAGES APG	PPG
89-90—Ark.-Little Rock						Did not play—ineligible.								
90-91—Ark.-Little Rock	19	393	64	126	.508	31	56	.554	132	22	159	6.9	1.2	8.4
91-92—Tennessee State						Did not play—transfer student.								
92-93—Tennessee State	29	918	239	385	.621	111	178	.624	339	30	589	11.7	1.0	20.3
93-94—Tennessee State	31	1052	288	469	.614	179	276	.649	358	47	759	11.5	1.5	24.5
Totals	79	2363	591	980	.603	321	510	.629	829	99	1507	10.5	1.3	19.1

Three-point field goals: 1992-93, 0-for-3. 1993-94, 4-for-13 (.308). Totals, 4-for-16 (.250).

NBA REGULAR-SEASON RECORD

Season Team	G	Min.	FGM	FGA	Pct.	FTM	FTA	Pct.	REBOUNDS Off.	Def.	Tot.	Ast.	St.	Blk.	TO	Pts.	RPG	AVERAGES APG	PPG
94-95—Golden State...	49	1017	180	340	.529	76	146	.521	108	170	278	37	22	52	84	438	5.7	0.8	8.9
95-96—Toronto	56	1043	178	344	.517	71	130	.546	80	90	170	35	25	48	61	430	3.0	0.6	7.7
Totals	105	2060	358	684	.523	147	276	.533	188	260	448	72	47	100	145	868	4.3	0.7	8.3

Three-point field goals: 1994-95, 2-for-14 (.143). 1995-96, 3-for-21 (.143). Totals, 5-for-35 (.143).
Personal fouls/disqualifications: 1994-95, 124/2. 1995-96, 87/0. Totals, 211/2.

ROGERS, RODNEY   F   CLIPPERS

PERSONAL: Born June 20, 1971, in Durham, N.C. ... 6-7/255. ... Full name: Rodney Ray Rogers Jr.
HIGH SCHOOL: Hillside (Durham, N.C.).
COLLEGE: Wake Forest.
TRANSACTIONS/CAREER NOTES: Selected after junior season by Denver Nuggets in first round (ninth pick overall) of 1993 NBA Draft. ... Traded by Nuggets with draft rights to G Brent Barry to Los Angeles Clippers for G Randy Woods and draft rights to F Antonio McDyess (June 28, 1995).

COLLEGIATE RECORD

NOTES: The Sporting News All-America second team (1993).

Season Team	G	Min.	FGM	FGA	Pct.	FTM	FTA	Pct.	Reb.	Ast.	Pts.	RPG	AVERAGES APG	PPG
90-91—Wake Forest	30	895	199	349	.570	81	121	.669	237	46	489	7.9	1.5	16.3
91-92—Wake Forest	29	945	245	399	.614	86	126	.683	247	81	595	8.5	2.8	20.5
92-93—Wake Forest	30	981	239	431	.555	134	187	.717	221	68	636	7.4	2.3	21.2
Totals	89	2821	683	1179	.579	301	434	.694	705	195	1720	7.9	2.2	19.3

Three-point field goals: 1990-91, 10-for-35 (.286). 1991-92, 19-for-50 (.380). 1992-93, 24-for-67 (.358). Totals, 53-for-152 (.349).

NBA REGULAR-SEASON RECORD

Season Team	G	Min.	FGM	FGA	Pct.	FTM	FTA	Pct.	REBOUNDS Off.	Def.	Tot.	Ast.	St.	Blk.	TO	Pts.	RPG	AVERAGES APG	PPG
93-94—Denver	79	1406	239	545	.439	127	189	.672	90	136	226	101	63	48	131	640	2.9	1.3	8.1
94-95—Denver	80	2142	375	769	.488	179	275	.651	132	253	385	161	95	46	173	979	4.8	2.0	12.2
95-96—L.A. Clippers...	67	1950	306	641	.477	113	180	.628	113	173	286	167	75	35	144	774	4.3	2.5	11.6
Totals	226	5498	920	1955	.471	419	644	.651	335	562	897	429	233	129	448	2393	4.0	1.9	10.6

Three-point field goals: 1993-94, 35-for-92 (.380). 1994-95, 50-for-148 (.338). 1995-96, 49-for-153 (.320). Totals, 134-for-393 (.341).
Personal fouls/disqualifications: 1993-94, 195/3. 1994-95, 281/7. 1995-96, 216/2. Totals, 692/12.

NBA PLAYOFF RECORD

Season Team	G	Min.	FGM	FGA	Pct.	FTM	FTA	Pct.	REBOUNDS Off.	Def.	Tot.	Ast.	St.	Blk.	TO	Pts.	RPG	AVERAGES APG	PPG
93-94—Denver	12	190	19	49	.388	17	27	.630	8	13	21	16	7	6	8	61	1.8	1.3	5.1
94-95—Denver	3	76	12	22	.545	1	11	.250	1	11	12	5	3	4	5	26	4.0	1.7	8.7
Totals	15	266	31	71	.437	18	31	.581	9	24	33	21	10	10	13	87	2.2	1.4	5.8

Three-point field goals: 1993-94, 6-for-19 (.316). 1994-95, 1-for-4 (.250). Totals, 7-for-23 (.304).
Personal fouls/disqualifications: 1993-94, 25/0. 1994-95, 13/1. Totals, 38/1.

ROOKS, SEAN   C   LAKERS

PERSONAL: Born September 9, 1969, in New York. ... 6-10/260. ... Full name: Sean Lester Rooks.
HIGH SCHOOL: Fontana (Calif.).
COLLEGE: Arizona.
TRANSACTIONS/CAREER NOTES: Selected by Dallas Mavericks in second round (30th pick overall) of 1992 NBA Draft. ... Traded by Mavericks to Minnesota Timberwolves for conditional 1996 first-round draft choice (November 1, 1994). ... Traded by Timberwolves with F Christian Laettner to Atlanta Hawks for G Spud Webb and C Andrew Lang (February 22, 1996). ... Signed as free agent by Los Angeles Lakers (July 16, 1996).

R

COLLEGIATE RECORD

Season Team	G	Min.	FGM	FGA	Pct.	FTM	FTA	Pct.	Reb.	Ast.	Pts.	AVERAGES RPG	APG	PPG
87-88—Arizona						Did not play—redshirted.								
88-89—Arizona	32	362	70	117	.598	40	65	.615	88	18	180	2.8	0.6	5.6
89-90—Arizona	31	684	140	263	.532	114	161	.708	151	31	394	4.9	1.0	12.7
90-91—Arizona	35	800	159	283	.562	98	149	.658	198	43	418	5.7	1.2	11.9
91-92—Arizona	31	878	181	323	.560	140	215	.651	214	54	505	6.9	1.7	16.3
Totals	129	2724	550	986	.558	392	590	.664	651	146	1497	5.0	1.1	11.6

Three-point field goals: 1990-91, 2-for-4 (.500). 1991-92, 3-for-5 (.600). Totals, 5-for-9 (.556).

NBA REGULAR-SEASON RECORD

Season Team	G	Min.	FGM	FGA	Pct.	FTM	FTA	Pct.	REBOUNDS Off.	Def.	Tot.	Ast.	St.	Blk.	TO	Pts.	AVERAGES RPG	APG	PPG
92-93—Dallas	72	2087	368	747	.493	234	389	.602	196	340	536	95	38	81	160	970	7.4	1.3	13.5
93-94—Dallas	47	1255	193	393	.491	150	210	.714	84	175	259	49	21	44	80	536	5.5	1.0	11.4
94-95—Minnesota	80	2405	289	615	.470	290	381	.761	165	321	486	97	29	71	142	868	6.1	1.2	10.9
95-96—Minn.-Atl.	65	1117	144	285	.505	135	202	.668	81	174	255	47	23	42	80	424	3.9	0.7	6.5
Totals	264	6864	994	2040	.487	809	1182	.684	526	1010	1536	288	111	238	462	2798	5.8	1.1	10.6

Three-point field goals: 1992-93, 0-for-2. 1993-94, 0-for-1. 1994-95, 0-for-5. 1995-96, 1-for-7 (.143). Totals, 1-for-15 (.067).
Personal fouls/disqualifications: 1992-93, 204/2. 1993-94, 109/0. 1994-95, 208/1. 1995-96, 141/0. Totals, 662/3.

NBA PLAYOFF RECORD

Season Team	G	Min.	FGM	FGA	Pct.	FTM	FTA	Pct.	REBOUNDS Off.	Def.	Tot.	Ast.	St.	Blk.	TO	Pts.	AVERAGES RPG	APG	PPG
95-96—Atlanta	10	140	16	28	.571	13	21	.619	13	14	27	7	4	4	9	45	2.7	0.7	4.5

Personal fouls/disqualifications: 1995-96, 35/0.

ROSE, JALEN   G   PACERS

PERSONAL: Born January 30, 1973, in Detroit. ... 6-8/210. ... Name pronounced JAY-lin. ... Son of Jimmy Walker, guard with Detroit Pistons, Houston Rockets and Kansas City Kings (1967-68 through 1975-76).
HIGH SCHOOL: Southwestern (Detroit).
COLLEGE: Michigan.
TRANSACTIONS/CAREER NOTES: Selected after junior season by Denver Nuggets in first round (13th pick overall) of 1994 NBA Draft. ... Traded by Nuggets with F Reggie Williams and 1996 first-round draft choice to Indiana Pacers for G Mark Jackson, G Ricky Pierce and 1996 first-round draft choice (June 13, 1996).

COLLEGIATE RECORD

NOTES: The Sporting News All-America first team (1994).

Season Team	G	Min.	FGM	FGA	Pct.	FTM	FTA	Pct.	Reb.	Ast.	Pts.	AVERAGES RPG	APG	PPG
91-92—Michigan	34	1126	206	424	.486	149	197	.756	146	135	597	4.3	4.0	17.6
92-93—Michigan	36	1232	203	455	.446	116	161	.721	150	140	555	4.2	3.9	15.4
93-94—Michigan	32	1152	220	477	.461	141	192	.734	181	126	636	5.7	3.9	19.9
Totals	102	3510	629	1356	.464	406	550	.738	477	401	1788	4.7	3.9	17.5

Three-point field goals: 1991-92, 36-for-111 (.324). 1992-93, 33-for-103 (.320). 1993-94, 55-for-155 (.355). Totals, 124-for-369 (.336).

NBA REGULAR-SEASON RECORD

HONORS: NBA All-Rookie second team (1995).

Season Team	G	Min.	FGM	FGA	Pct.	FTM	FTA	Pct.	REBOUNDS Off.	Def.	Tot.	Ast.	St.	Blk.	TO	Pts.	AVERAGES RPG	APG	PPG
94-95—Denver	81	1798	227	500	.454	173	234	.739	57	160	217	389	65	22	160	663	2.7	4.8	8.2
95-96—Denver	80	2134	290	604	.480	191	277	.690	46	214	260	495	53	39	234	803	3.3	6.2	10.0
Totals	161	3932	517	1104	.468	364	511	.712	103	374	477	884	118	61	394	1466	3.0	5.5	9.1

Three-point field goals: 1994-95, 36-for-114 (.316). 1995-96, 32-for-108 (.296). Totals, 68-for-222 (.306).
Personal fouls/disqualifications: 1994-95, 206/0. 1995-96, 229/3. Totals, 435/3.

NBA PLAYOFF RECORD

Season Team	G	Min.	FGM	FGA	Pct.	FTM	FTA	Pct.	REBOUNDS Off.	Def.	Tot.	Ast.	St.	Blk.	TO	Pts.	AVERAGES RPG	APG	PPG
94-95—Denver	3	99	13	28	.464	3	5	.600	4	7	11	18	3	2	9	30	3.7	6.0	10.0

Three-point field goals: 1994-95, 1-for-4 (.250).
Personal fouls/disqualifications: 1994-95, 9/0.

ROYAL, DONALD   F   MAGIC

PERSONAL: Born May 22, 1966, in New Orleans. ... 6-8/218. ... Full name: Donald Adam Royal.
HIGH SCHOOL: Augustine (New Orleans).
COLLEGE: Notre Dame.
TRANSACTIONS/CAREER NOTES: Selected by Cleveland Cavaliers in third round (52nd pick overall) of 1987 NBA Draft. ... Waived by Cavaliers (October 23, 1987). ... Played in Continental Basketball Association with Pensacola Tornados (1987-88), Cedar Rapids Silver Bullets (1988-89) and Tri-City Chinook (1991-92). ... Signed as free agent by Minnesota Timberwolves (September 12, 1989). ... Played in Israel (1990-91). ... Rights renounced by Timberwolves (August 16, 1991). ... Signed as free agent by Orlando Magic (September 26, 1991). ... Waived by Magic (October 28, 1991). ... Signed as free agent by San Antonio Spurs (December 3, 1991). ... Waived by Spurs (June 26, 1992). ... Signed as free agent by Magic (August 24, 1992).

R

COLLEGIATE RECORD

Season Team	G	Min.	FGM	FGA	Pct.	FTM	FTA	Pct.	Reb.	Ast.	Pts.	RPG	APG	PPG
83-84—Notre Dame	31	405	38	64	.594	28	45	.622	72	5	104	2.3	0.2	3.4
84-85—Notre Dame	30	848	75	151	.497	122	156	.782	164	17	272	5.5	0.6	9.1
85-86—Notre Dame	28	777	88	151	.583	121	158	.766	138	22	297	4.9	0.8	10.6
86-87—Notre Dame	28	1028	132	229	.576	178	217	.820	196	37	442	7.0	1.3	15.8
Totals	117	3058	333	595	.560	449	576	.780	570	81	1115	4.9	0.7	9.5

CBA REGULAR-SEASON RECORD

Season Team	G	Min.	FGM	FGA	Pct.	FTM	FTA	Pct.	Reb.	Ast.	Pts.	RPG	APG	PPG
87-88—Pensacola	48	904	122	234	.521	104	141	.738	158	44	348	3.3	0.9	7.3
88-89—Cedar Rapids	53	1206	216	440	.491	266	359	.741	252	98	698	4.8	1.8	13.2
91-92—Tri-City	10	368	77	138	.558	69	89	.775	66	27	223	6.6	2.7	22.3
Totals	111	2478	415	812	.511	439	589	.745	476	169	1269	4.3	1.5	11.4

Three-point field goals: 1987-88, 0-for-1. 1988-89, 0-for-2. Totals, 0-for-3.

NBA REGULAR-SEASON RECORD

Season Team	G	Min.	FGM	FGA	Pct.	FTM	FTA	Pct.	Off.	Def.	Tot.	Ast.	St.	Blk.	TO	Pts.	RPG	APG	PPG
89-90—Minnesota	66	746	117	255	.459	153	197	.777	69	68	137	43	32	8	81	387	2.1	0.7	5.9
91-92—San Antonio	60	718	80	178	.449	92	133	.692	65	59	124	34	25	7	39	252	2.1	0.6	4.2
92-93—Orlando	77	1636	194	391	.496	318	390	.815	116	179	295	80	36	25	113	706	3.8	1.0	9.2
93-94—Orlando	74	1357	174	347	.501	199	269	.740	94	154	248	61	50	16	76	547	3.4	0.8	7.4
94-95—Orlando	70	1841	206	434	.475	223	299	.746	83	196	279	198	45	16	125	635	4.0	2.8	9.1
95-96—Orlando	64	963	106	216	.491	125	164	.762	57	96	153	42	29	15	52	337	2.4	0.7	5.3
Totals	411	7261	877	1821	.482	1110	1452	.764	484	752	1236	458	217	87	486	2864	3.0	1.1	7.0

Three-point field goals: 1989-90, 0-for-1. 1992-93, 0-for-3. 1993-94, 0-for-2. 1994-95, 0-for-4. 1995-96, 0-for-2. Totals, 0-for-12.
Personal fouls/disqualifications: 1989-90, 107/0. 1991-92, 73/0. 1992-93, 179/4. 1993-94, 121/1. 1994-95, 156/0. 1995-96, 97/0. Totals, 733/5.

NBA PLAYOFF RECORD

Season Team	G	Min.	FGM	FGA	Pct.	FTM	FTA	Pct.	Off.	Def.	Tot.	Ast.	St.	Blk.	TO	Pts.	RPG	APG	PPG
91-92—San Antonio	3	57	5	9	.556	5	9	.556	5	7	12	0	2	2	6	15	4.0	0.0	5.0
93-94—Orlando	3	45	6	14	.429	9	12	.750	1	3	4	5	1	0	2	21	1.3	1.7	7.0
94-95—Orlando	18	198	11	33	.333	15	20	.750	6	13	19	9	3	0	13	37	1.1	0.5	2.1
95-96—Orlando	7	92	7	12	.583	11	16	.688	4	7	11	1	0	1	2	25	1.6	0.1	3.6
Totals	31	392	29	68	.426	40	57	.702	16	30	46	15	6	3	23	98	1.5	0.5	3.2

Personal fouls/disqualifications: 1991-92, 7/0. 1993-94, 3/0. 1994-95, 22/0. 1995-96, 7/0. Totals, 39/0.

ISRAELI LEAGUE RECORD

Season Team	G	Min.	FGM	FGA	Pct.	FTM	FTA	Pct.	Reb.	Ast.	Pts.	RPG	APG	PPG
90-91—Macabee Tel-Aviv	19	...	144	228	.632	51	70	.729	77	36	342	4.1	1.9	18.0

ROZIER, CLIFFORD   C/F   WARRIORS

PERSONAL: Born October 31, 1972, in Bradenton, Fla. ... 6-11/255. ... Full name: Clifford Glen Rozier II.
HIGH SCHOOL: Southeast (Bradenton, Fla.).
COLLEGE: North Carolina, then Louisville.
TRANSACTIONS/CAREER NOTES: Selected after junior season by Golden State Warriors in first round (16th pick overall) of 1994 NBA Draft.

COLLEGIATE RECORD

NOTES: The Sporting News All-America second team (1994).

Season Team	G	Min.	FGM	FGA	Pct.	FTM	FTA	Pct.	Reb.	Ast.	Pts.	RPG	APG	PPG
90-91—North Carolina	34	317	64	136	.471	39	69	.565	101	18	167	3.0	0.5	4.9
91-92—Louisville						Did not play—transfer student.								

Season Team	G	Min.	FGM	FGA	Pct.	FTM	FTA	Pct.	Reb.	Ast.	Pts.	RPG	APG	PPG
92-93—Louisville	31	956	192	342	.561	104	183	.568	338	62	488	10.9	2.0	15.7
93-94—Louisville	34	1104	247	400	.618	122	224	.545	377	53	616	11.1	1.6	18.1
Totals	99	2377	503	878	.573	265	476	.557	816	133	1271	8.2	1.3	12.8

Three-point field goals: 1992-93, 0-for-2. 1993-94, 0-for-1. Totals, 0-for-3.

NBA REGULAR-SEASON RECORD

Season Team	G	Min.	FGM	FGA	Pct.	FTM	FTA	Pct.	Off.	Def.	Tot.	Ast.	St.	Blk.	TO	Pts.	RPG	APG	PPG
94-95—Golden State	66	1494	189	390	.485	68	152	.447	200	286	486	45	35	39	89	448	7.4	0.7	6.8
95-96—Golden State	59	723	79	135	.585	26	55	.473	71	100	171	22	19	30	40	184	2.9	0.4	3.1
Totals	125	2217	268	525	.510	94	207	.454	271	386	657	67	54	69	129	632	5.3	0.5	5.1

Three-point field goals: 1994-95, 2-for-7 (.286). 1995-96, 0-for-2. Totals, 2-for-9 (.222).
Personal fouls/disqualifications: 1994-95, 196/2. 1995-96, 135/0. Totals, 331/2.

R

RUFFIN, TREVOR　　　　　　　G

PERSONAL: Born September 26, 1970, in Buffalo. ... 6-1/200.
HIGH SCHOOL: Bennett (Buffalo).
JUNIOR COLLEGE: Cuyahoga Community College (Ohio), then Arizona Western.
COLLEGE: Hawaii.
TRANSACTIONS/CAREER NOTES: Not drafted by an NBA franchise. ... Signed as free agent by Los Angeles Lakers (July 21, 1994). ... Waived by Lakers (November 3, 1994). ... Signed as free agent by Phoenix Suns (November 11, 1994). ... Selected by Vancouver Grizzlies from Suns in NBA expansion draft (June 24, 1995). ... Played in Greece (1994-95 and 1995-96). ... Signed as free agent by Philadelphia 76ers (December 3, 1995). ... Rights renounced by 76ers (July 11, 1996).

COLLEGIATE RECORD

Season Team	G	Min.	FGM	FGA	Pct.	FTM	FTA	Pct.	Reb.	Ast.	Pts.	RPG	APG	PPG
89-90—Cuyahoga						Statistics unavailable.								
90-91—Arizona West. College						Did not play.								
91-92—Arizona West. College						Statistics unavailable.								
92-93—Hawaii	27	...	134	322	.416	38	56	.679	69	52	342	2.6	1.9	12.7
93-94—Hawaii	30	...	213	499	.427	151	208	.726	96	93	625	3.2	3.1	20.8
4-year-college totals	57	...	347	821	.423	189	264	.716	165	145	967	2.9	2.5	17.0

Three-point field goals: 1992-93, 36-for-118 (.305). 1993-94, 86-for-215 (.400). Totals, 122-for-333 (.366).

NBA REGULAR-SEASON RECORD

Season Team	G	Min.	FGM	FGA	Pct.	FTM	FTA	Pct.	REBOUNDS Off.	Def.	Tot.	Ast.	St.	Blk.	TO	Pts.	RPG	AVERAGES APG	PPG
94-95—Phoenix	49	319	84	197	.426	27	38	.711	8	15	23	48	14	2	47	233	0.5	1.0	4.8
95-96—Philadelphia	61	1551	263	648	.406	148	182	.813	21	111	132	269	43	2	149	778	2.2	4.4	12.8
Totals	110	1870	347	845	.411	175	220	.795	29	126	155	317	57	4	196	1011	1.4	2.9	9.2

Three-point field goals: 1994-95, 38-for-99 (.384). 1995-96, 104-for-284 (.366). Totals, 142-for-383 (.371).
Personal fouls/disqualifications: 1994-95, 52/0. 1995-96, 132/0. Totals, 184/0.

NBA PLAYOFF RECORD

Season Team	G	Min.	FGM	FGA	Pct.	FTM	FTA	Pct.	REBOUNDS Off.	Def.	Tot.	Ast.	St.	Blk.	TO	Pts.	RPG	AVERAGES APG	PPG
94-95—Phoenix	5	11	4	8	.500	1	5	.200	0	3	3	2	1	0	0	10	0.6	0.4	2.0

Three-point field goals: 1994-95, 1-for-4 (.250).

GREEK LEAGUE RECORD

Season Team	G	Min.	FGM	FGA	Pct.	FTM	FTA	Pct.	Reb.	Ast.	Pts.	RPG	APG	PPG
95-96—PAOK	5	183	...	...	...	...	...	...	15	22	...	3.0	4.4	19.4

RUSCONI, STEFANO　　　　　　F/C

PERSONAL: Born February 10, 1968, in Bassano Del Grappa, Italy. ... 6-10/240. ... Name pronounced STEF-ah-no ruh-SCONE-ee.
TRANSACTIONS/CAREER NOTES: Played in Italy (1985-86 through 1994-95). ... Selected by Cleveland Cavaliers in second round (52nd pick overall) of 1990 NBA Draft. ... Rights traded by Cavaliers to Phoenix Suns for rights to Milos Babic (June 27, 1990). ... Signed by Suns (June 14, 1995). ... Waived by Suns (January 31, 1996).

ITALIAN LEAGUE RECORD

Season Team	G	Min.	FGM	FGA	Pct.	FTM	FTA	Pct.	Reb.	Ast.	Pts.	RPG	APG	PPG
85-86—Ranger Varese	4	19	0	1	.000	0	0	...	2	0	0	0.5	0.0	0.0
86-87—Ranger Varese	34	160	19	43	.442	9	17	.529	52	1	47	1.5	0.0	1.4
87-88—Ranger Varese	31	405	54	112	.482	39	75	.520	126	9	147	4.1	0.3	4.7
88-89—Ranger Varese	35	726	98	172	.570	51	87	.586	208	7	247	5.9	0.2	7.1
89-90—Ranger Varese	31	1004	158	284	.556	93	132	.705	357	15	409	11.5	0.5	13.2
90-91—Ranger Varese	28	931	174	305	.571	71	130	.546	319	13	420	11.4	0.5	15.0
91-92—Benetton Treviso	18	566	76	126	.603	24	75	.320	170	9	176	9.4	0.5	9.8
92-93—Benetton Treviso	30	945	181	291	.622	91	178	.511	262	17	453	8.7	0.6	15.1
93-94—Benetton Treviso	30	1033	204	341	.598	56	137	.409	311	24	464	10.4	0.8	15.5
94-95—Benetton Treviso	28	839	184	309	.595	99	199	.497	275	14	467	9.8	0.5	16.7
Totals	269	6628	1148	1984	.579	533	1030	.517	2082	109	2830	7.7	0.4	10.5

NBA REGULAR-SEASON RECORD

Season Team	G	Min.	FGM	FGA	Pct.	FTM	FTA	Pct.	REBOUNDS Off.	Def.	Tot.	Ast.	St.	Blk.	TO	Pts.	RPG	AVERAGES APG	PPG
95-96—Phoenix	7	30	3	9	.333	2	5	.400	3	3	6	3	0	2	3	8	0.9	0.4	1.1

Personal fouls/disqualifications: 1995-96, 10/0.

R

DID YOU KNOW...

...that Toronto's Damon Stoudamire played more minutes last season than any rookie since Kareem Abdul-Jabbar in 1969-70?

RUSSELL, BRYON　　　　　　　F　　　　　　　JAZZ

PERSONAL: Born December 31, 1970, in San Bernardino, Calif. ... 6-7/225. ... Full name: Bryon Demetrise Russell.
HIGH SCHOOL: San Bernardino (Calif.).
COLLEGE: Long Beach State.
TRANSACTIONS/CAREER NOTES: Selected by Utah Jazz in second round (45th pick overall) of 1993 NBA Draft.

COLLEGIATE RECORD

Season Team	G	Min.	FGM	FGA	Pct.	FTM	FTA	Pct.	Reb.	Ast.	Pts.	RPG	APG	PPG
89-90—Long Beach St.						Did not play—ineligible.								
90-91—Long Beach St.	28	552	83	193	.430	45	69	.652	162	41	220	5.8	1.5	7.9
91-92—Long Beach St.	26	776	126	227	.555	99	151	.656	192	30	362	7.4	1.2	13.9
92-93—Long Beach St.	32	1006	153	285	.537	104	143	.727	213	66	421	6.7	2.1	13.2
Totals	86	2334	362	705	.513	248	363	.683	567	137	1003	6.6	1.6	11.7

Three-point field goals: 1990-91, 9-for-28 (.321). 1991-92, 11-for-28 (.393). 1992-93, 11-for-34 (.324). Totals, 31-for-90 (.344).

NBA REGULAR-SEASON RECORD

Season Team	G	Min.	FGM	FGA	Pct.	FTM	FTA	Pct.	Off.	Def.	Tot.	Ast.	St.	Blk.	TO	Pts.	RPG	APG	PPG
93-94—Utah	67	1121	135	279	.484	62	101	.614	61	120	181	54	68	19	55	334	2.7	0.8	5.0
94-95—Utah	63	860	104	238	.437	62	93	.667	44	97	141	34	48	11	42	283	2.2	0.5	4.5
95-96—Utah	59	577	56	142	.394	48	67	.716	28	62	90	29	29	8	36	174	1.5	0.5	2.9
Totals	189	2558	295	659	.448	172	261	.659	133	279	412	117	145	38	133	791	2.2	0.6	4.2

Three-point field goals: 1993-94, 2-for-22 (.091). 1994-95, 13-for-44 (.295). 1995-96, 14-for-40 (.350). Totals, 29-for-106 (.274).
Personal fouls/disqualifications: 1993-94, 138/0. 1994-95, 101/0. 1995-96, 66/0. Totals, 305/0.

NBA PLAYOFF RECORD

Season Team	G	Min.	FGM	FGA	Pct.	FTM	FTA	Pct.	Off.	Def.	Tot.	Ast.	St.	Blk.	TO	Pts.	RPG	APG	PPG
93-94—Utah	6	36	4	10	.400	6	6	1.000	4	5	9	3	0	0	1	16	1.5	0.5	2.7
94-95—Utah	2	13	4	7	.571	1	2	.500	1	1	2	3	1	0	0	11	1.0	1.5	5.5
95-96—Utah	18	459	58	124	.468	31	38	.816	17	58	75	22	23	9	10	172	4.2	1.2	9.6
Totals	26	508	66	141	.468	38	46	.826	22	64	86	28	24	9	11	199	3.3	1.1	7.7

Three-point field goals: 1993-94, 2-for-3 (.667). 1994-95, 2-for-4 (.500). 1995-96, 25-for-53 (.472). Totals, 29-for-60 (.483).
Personal fouls/disqualifications: 1993-94, 3/0. 1994-95, 2/0. 1995-96, 42/0. Totals, 47/0.

SABONIS, ARVYDAS　　　　　　C　　　　　　TRAIL BLAZERS

PERSONAL: Born December 19, 1964, in Caunes, Lithuania. ... 7-3/290. ... Name pronounced uhr-VEE-dus suh-BONE-is.
TRANSACTIONS/CAREER NOTES: Selected by Atlanta Hawks in fourth round (77th pick overall) of 1985 NBA Draft. ... Declared ineligible for 1985 NBA draft. ... Selected by Portland Trail Blazers in first round (24th pick overall) of 1986 NBA Draft. ... Played in Spain (1989-90 through 1994-95). ... Signed by Trail Blazers (September 29, 1995).
MISCELLANEOUS: Member of gold-medal-winning Soviet Union Olympic team (1988). ... Member of bronze-medal-winning Lithuanian Olympic teams (1992, 1996).

SPANISH LEAGUE RECORD

Season Team	G	Min.	FGM	FGA	Pct.	FTM	FTA	Pct.	Reb.	Ast.	Pts.	RPG	APG	PPG
89-90—Forum Valladolid	35	...	324	661	.490	134	190	.705	456	65	809	13.0	1.9	23.1
90-91—Forum Valladolid	32	...	237	460	.515	102	144	.708	337	61	590	10.5	1.9	18.4
91-92—Forum Valladolid	32	...	268	498	.538	139	185	.751	425	75	696	13.3	2.3	21.8
92-93—Real Madrid	30	956	203	361	.562	87	118	.737	345	38	514	11.5	1.3	17.1
93-94—Real Madrid	27	856	181	290	.624	101	126	.802	303	54	478	11.2	2.0	17.7
94-95—Real Madrid	34	1188	300	511	.587	153	196	.781	448	82	778	13.2	2.4	22.9
Totals	190	...	1513	2781	.544	716	959	.747	2314	375	3865	12.2	2.0	20.3

HONORS: NBA All-Rookie first team (1996).

NBA REGULAR-SEASON RECORD

Season Team	G	Min.	FGM	FGA	Pct.	FTM	FTA	Pct.	Off.	Def.	Tot.	Ast.	St.	Blk.	TO	Pts.	RPG	APG	PPG
95-96—Portland	73	1735	394	723	.545	231	305	.757	147	441	588	130	64	78	154	1058	8.1	1.8	14.5

Three-point field goals: 1995-96, 39-for-104 (.375).
Personal fouls/disqualifications: 1995-96, 211/2.

NBA PLAYOFF RECORD

Season Team	G	Min.	FGM	FGA	Pct.	FTM	FTA	Pct.	Off.	Def.	Tot.	Ast.	St.	Blk.	TO	Pts.	RPG	APG	PPG
95-96—Portland	5	177	35	81	.432	43	60	.717	12	39	51	9	4	3	10	118	10.2	1.8	23.6

Three-point field goals: 1995-96, 5-for-9 (.556).
Personal fouls/disqualifications: 1995-96, 17/0.

SALLEY, JOHN　　　　　　F/C　　　　　　BULLS

PERSONAL: Born June 16, 1964, in Brooklyn, N.Y. ... 6-11/255. ... Full name: John Thomas Salley.
HIGH SCHOOL: Canarsie (Brooklyn, N.Y.).
COLLEGE: Georgia Tech.
TRANSACTIONS/CAREER NOTES: Selected by Detroit Pistons in first round (11th pick overall) of 1986 NBA Draft. ... Traded by Pistons to Miami Heat for rights to F Isaiah Morris and conditional draft choice (September 8, 1992). ... Selected by Toronto Raptors from Heat in NBA expansion draft (June 24, 1995). ... Waived by Raptors (February 2, 1996). ... Signed by Chicago Bulls to first of two consecutive 10-day contracts (March 4, 1996). ... Re-signed by Bulls for remainder of season (March 24, 1996).

MISCELLANEOUS: Member of NBA championship teams (1989, 1990, 1996).

S

COLLEGIATE RECORD

Season Team	G	Min.	FGM	FGA	Pct.	FTM	FTA	Pct.	Reb.	Ast.	Pts.	RPG	APG	PPG
82-83—Georgia Tech	27	829	104	207	.502	102	160	.638	153	36	310	5.7	1.3	11.5
83-84—Georgia Tech	29	992	126	214	.589	89	132	.674	167	73	341	5.8	2.5	11.8
84-85—Georgia Tech	35	1231	193	308	.627	105	165	.636	250	93	491	7.1	2.7	14.0
85-86—Georgia Tech	34	1145	172	284	.606	101	170	.594	228	117	445	6.7	3.4	13.1
Totals	125	4197	595	1013	.587	397	627	.633	798	319	1587	6.4	2.6	12.7

NBA REGULAR-SEASON RECORD

Season Team	G	Min.	FGM	FGA	Pct.	FTM	FTA	Pct.	Off.	Def.	Tot.	Ast.	St.	Blk.	TO	Pts.	RPG	APG	PPG
86-87—Detroit	82	1463	163	290	.562	105	171	.614	108	188	296	54	44	125	74	431	3.6	0.7	5.3
87-88—Detroit	82	2003	258	456	.566	185	261	.709	166	236	402	113	53	137	120	701	4.9	1.4	8.5
88-89—Detroit	67	1458	166	333	.499	135	195	.692	134	201	335	75	40	72	100	467	5.0	1.1	7.0
89-90—Detroit	82	1914	209	408	.512	174	244	.713	154	285	439	67	51	153	97	593	5.4	0.8	7.2
90-91—Detroit	74	1649	179	377	.475	186	256	.727	137	190	327	70	52	112	91	544	4.4	0.9	7.4
91-92—Detroit	72	1774	249	486	.512	186	260	.715	106	190	296	116	49	110	102	684	4.1	1.6	9.5
92-93—Miami	51	1422	154	307	.502	115	144	.799	113	200	313	83	32	70	101	423	6.1	1.6	8.3
93-94—Miami	76	1910	208	436	.477	164	225	.729	132	275	407	135	56	78	94	582	5.4	1.8	7.7
94-95—Miami	75	1955	197	395	.499	153	207	.739	110	226	336	123	47	85	97	547	4.5	1.6	7.3
95-96—Tor.-Chi.	42	673	63	140	.450	59	85	.694	46	94	140	54	19	27	55	185	3.3	1.3	4.4
Totals	703	16221	1846	3628	.509	1462	2048	.714	1206	2085	3291	890	443	969	931	5157	4.7	1.3	7.3

Three-point field goals: 1986-87, 0-for-1. 1988-89, 0-for-2. 1989-90, 1-for-4 (.250). 1990-91, 0-for-1. 1991-92, 0-for-3. 1993-94, 2-for-3 (.667). Totals, 3-for-14 (.214).

Personal fouls/disqualifications: 1986-87, 256/5. 1987-88, 294/4. 1988-89, 197/3. 1989-90, 282/7. 1990-91, 240/7. 1991-92, 222/1. 1992-93, 192/7. 1993-94, 260/4. 1994-95, 279/5. 1995-96, 110/3. Totals, 2332/46.

NBA PLAYOFF RECORD

Season Team	G	Min.	FGM	FGA	Pct.	FTM	FTA	Pct.	Off.	Def.	Tot.	Ast.	St.	Blk.	TO	Pts.	RPG	APG	PPG
86-87—Detroit	15	311	33	66	.500	27	42	.643	30	42	72	11	3	17	14	93	4.8	0.7	6.2
87-88—Detroit	23	623	56	104	.538	49	69	.710	64	91	155	21	15	37	23	161	6.7	0.9	7.0
88-89—Detroit	17	392	58	99	.586	36	54	.667	34	45	79	9	9	25	12	152	4.6	0.5	8.9
89-90—Detroit	20	547	58	122	.475	74	98	.755	57	60	117	20	9	33	22	190	5.9	1.0	9.5
90-91—Detroit	15	308	38	70	.543	36	60	.600	20	42	62	11	6	20	13	112	4.1	0.7	7.5
91-92—Detroit	5	149	20	44	.455	23	28	.821	10	20	30	14	3	14	9	63	6.0	2.8	12.6
93-94—Miami	5	201	22	57	.386	11	16	.688	16	24	40	8	2	5	6	55	8.0	1.6	11.0
95-96—Chicago	16	85	6	11	.545	2	7	.286	4	7	11	6	1	2	4	14	0.7	0.4	0.9
Totals	116	2616	291	573	.508	258	374	.690	235	331	566	100	48	153	103	840	4.9	0.9	7.2

Three-point field goals: 1987-88, 0-for-1. 1991-92, 0-for-1. Totals, 0-for-2.
Personal fouls/disqualifications: 1986-87, 60/1. 1987-88, 88/2. 1988-89, 58/0. 1989-90, 76/2. 1990-91, 58/1. 1991-92, 18/0. 1993-94, 21/1. 1995-96, 25/0. Totals, 404/7.

SCHAYES, DAN   C

PERSONAL: Born May 10, 1959, in Syracuse, N.Y. ... 6-11/276. ... Full name: Daniel Leslie Schayes. ... Name pronounced SHAZE. ... Son of Dolph Schayes, forward with Syracuse Nationals of National Basketball League (1948-49), Syracuse Nationals and Philadelphia 76ers of NBA (1949-50 through 1963-64), former NBA Supervisor of Referees and member of Naismith Memorial Basketball Hall of Fame.
HIGH SCHOOL: Jamesville DeWitt (DeWitt, N.Y.).
COLLEGE: Syracuse.
TRANSACTIONS/CAREER NOTES: Selected by Utah Jazz in first round (13th pick overall) of 1981 NBA Draft. ... Traded by Jazz with other considerations to Denver Nuggets for C Rich Kelley (February 7, 1983). ... Traded by Nuggets to Milwaukee Bucks for draft rights to F Terry Mills (August 1, 1990). ... Traded by Bucks to Los Angeles Lakers for 1995 conditional second-round draft choice (February 24, 1994). ... Rights renounced by Lakers (July 1, 1994). ... Signed as free agent by Phoenix Suns (October 6, 1994). ... Signed by Miami Heat for remainder of season (December 12, 1995). ... Rights renounced by Heat (July 17, 1996).

COLLEGIATE RECORD

Season Team	G	Min.	FGM	FGA	Pct.	FTM	FTA	Pct.	Reb.	Ast.	Pts.	RPG	APG	PPG
77-78—Syracuse	24	...	39	69	.565	34	45	.756	96	11	112	4.0	0.5	4.7
78-79—Syracuse	29	...	62	117	.530	55	66	.833	121	15	179	4.2	0.5	6.2
79-80—Syracuse	30	...	59	116	.509	60	78	.769	134	22	178	4.5	0.7	5.9
80-81—Syracuse	34	...	165	285	.579	166	202	.822	284	64	496	8.4	1.9	14.6
Totals	117	...	325	587	.554	315	391	.806	635	112	965	5.4	1.0	8.2

NBA REGULAR-SEASON RECORD

Season Team	G	Min.	FGM	FGA	Pct.	FTM	FTA	Pct.	Off.	Def.	Tot.	Ast.	St.	Blk.	TO	Pts.	RPG	APG	PPG
81-82—Utah	82	1623	252	524	.481	140	185	.757	131	296	427	146	46	72	151	644	5.2	1.8	7.9
82-83—Utah-Den.	82	2284	342	749	.457	228	295	.773	200	435	635	205	54	98	253	912	7.7	2.5	11.1
83-84—Denver	82	1420	183	371	.493	215	272	.790	145	288	433	91	32	60	119	581	5.3	1.1	7.1
84-85—Denver	56	542	60	129	.465	79	97	.814	48	96	144	38	20	25	44	199	2.6	0.7	3.6
85-86—Denver	80	1654	221	440	.502	216	278	.777	154	285	439	79	42	63	105	658	5.5	1.0	8.2
86-87—Denver	76	1556	210	405	.519	229	294	.779	120	260	380	85	20	74	95	649	5.0	1.1	8.5
87-88—Denver	81	2166	361	668	.540	407	487	.836	200	462	662	106	62	92	155	1129	8.2	1.3	13.9
88-89—Denver	76	1918	317	607	.522	332	402	.826	142	358	500	105	42	81	160	969	6.6	1.4	12.8
89-90—Denver	53	1194	163	330	.494	225	264	.852	117	225	342	61	41	45	72	551	6.5	1.2	10.4

Season Team	G	Min.	FGM	FGA	Pct.	FTM	FTA	Pct.	Off.	Def.	Tot.	Ast.	St.	Blk.	TO	Pts.	RPG	APG	PPG
									REBOUNDS								AVERAGES		
90-91—Milwaukee	82	2228	298	597	.499	274	328	.835	174	361	535	98	55	61	106	870	6.5	1.2	10.6
91-92—Milwaukee	43	726	83	199	.417	74	96	.771	58	110	168	34	19	19	41	240	3.9	0.8	5.6
92-93—Milwaukee	70	1124	105	263	.399	112	137	.818	72	177	249	78	36	36	65	322	3.6	1.1	4.6
93-94—Mil.-LA Lak.	36	363	28	84	.333	29	32	.906	31	48	79	13	10	10	23	85	2.2	0.4	2.4
94-95—Phoenix	69	823	126	248	.508	50	69	.725	57	151	208	89	20	37	64	303	3.0	1.3	4.4
95-96—Miami	32	399	32	94	.340	37	46	.804	29	60	89	9	11	16	23	101	2.8	0.3	3.2
Totals	1000	20020	2781	5708	.487	2647	3282	.807	1678	3612	5290	1237	510	789	1476	8213	5.3	1.2	8.2

Three-point field goals: 1981-82, 0-for-1. 1982-83, 0-for-1. 1983-84, 0-for-2. 1985-86, 0-for-1. 1987-88, 0-for-2. 1988-89, 3-for-9 (.333). 1989-90, 0-for-4. 1990-91, 0-for-5. 1992-93, 0-for-3. 1994-95, 1-for-1. Totals, 4-for-29 (.138).

Personal fouls/disqualifications: 1981-82, 292/4. 1982-83, 325/8. 1983-84, 308/5. 1984-85, 98/2. 1985-86, 298/7. 1986-87, 266/5. 1987-88, 323/9. 1988-89, 320/8. 1989-90, 200/7. 1990-91, 264/4. 1991-92, 98/0. 1992-93, 148/1. 1993-94, 45/0. 1994-95, 170/0. 1995-96, 60/0. Totals, 3215/60.

NBA PLAYOFF RECORD

Season Team	G	Min.	FGM	FGA	Pct.	FTM	FTA	Pct.	Off.	Def.	Tot.	Ast.	St.	Blk.	TO	Pts.	RPG	APG	PPG
									REBOUNDS								AVERAGES		
82-83—Denver	8	163	21	43	.488	15	15	1.000	11	29	40	14	2	5	17	57	5.0	1.8	7.1
83-84—Denver	5	81	11	18	.611	6	8	.750	3	21	24	4	4	3	7	28	4.8	0.8	5.6
84-85—Denver	9	118	11	26	.423	14	20	.700	8	22	30	12	3	4	5	36	3.3	1.3	4.0
85-86—Denver	10	295	46	86	.535	24	30	.800	34	48	82	9	4	17	21	116	8.2	0.9	11.6
86-87—Denver	3	75	12	17	.706	6	9	.667	6	11	17	2	1	2	3	30	5.7	0.7	10.0
87-88—Denver	11	314	55	88	.625	70	83	.843	30	49	79	18	3	10	24	180	7.2	1.6	16.4
88-89—Denver	2	36	1	7	.143	6	8	.750	2	9	11	1	1	1	1	8	5.5	0.5	4.0
90-91—Milwaukee	3	71	9	23	.391	10	11	.909	4	8	12	3	1	1	6	28	4.0	1.0	9.3
94-95—Phoenix	10	146	11	29	.379	7	8	.875	4	16	20	8	3	3	8	29	2.0	0.8	2.9
95-96—Miami	2	17	3	4	.750	1	2	.500	2	2	4	0	0	0	2	7	2.0	0.0	3.5
Totals	63	1316	180	341	.528	159	194	.820	104	215	319	71	24	46	94	519	5.1	1.1	8.2

Three-point field goals: 1990-91, 0-for-1. 1994-95, 0-for-1. Totals, 0-for-2.

Personal fouls/disqualifications: 1982-83, 25/0. 1983-84, 20/0. 1984-85, 22/0. 1985-86, 37/1. 1986-87, 10/0. 1987-88, 46/1. 1988-89, 4/0. 1990-91, 8/0. 1994-95, 38/0. 1995-96, 1/0. Totals, 211/2.

SCHEFFLER, STEVE   C   SUPERSONICS

PERSONAL: Born September 3, 1967, in Grand Rapids, Mich. ... 6-9/250. ... Full name: Stephen Robert Scheffler. ... Name pronounced SHEFF-ler. ... Brother of Tom Scheffler, forward with Portland Trail Blazers (1984-85).
HIGH SCHOOL: Forest Hills Northern (Grand Rapids, Mich.).
COLLEGE: Purdue.
TRANSACTIONS/CAREER NOTES: Selected by Charlotte Hornets in second round (39th pick overall) of 1990 NBA Draft. ... Waived by Hornets (May 31, 1991). ... Signed as free agent by Boston Celtics (October 2, 1991). ... Waived by Celtics (October 30, 1991). ... Played in Continental Basketball Association with Quad City Thunder (1991-92). ... Signed by Sacramento Kings to 10-day contract (February 13, 1992). ... Signed by Denver Nuggets to first of two consecutive 10-day contracts (February 27, 1992). ... Re-signed by Nuggets for remainder of season (March 17, 1992). ... Signed as free agent by Seattle SuperSonics (October 8, 1992). ... Waived by SuperSonics (November 26, 1992). ... Re-signed as free agent by SuperSonics (December 2, 1992).

COLLEGIATE RECORD

NOTES: THE SPORTING NEWS All-America second team (1990). ... Holds NCAA Division I career record for highest field-goal percentage (minimum 400 made)—.685.

Season Team	G	Min.	FGM	FGA	Pct.	FTM	FTA	Pct.	Reb.	Ast.	Pts.	RPG	APG	PPG
												AVERAGES		
86-87—Purdue	16	73	9	16	.563	6	14	.429	24	2	24	1.5	0.1	1.5
87-88—Purdue	33	548	80	113	.708	65	100	.650	144	13	225	4.4	0.4	6.8
88-89—Purdue	31	830	146	219	.667	111	143	.776	187	28	403	6.0	0.9	13.0
89-90—Purdue	30	996	173	248	.698	157	195	.805	183	36	503	6.1	1.2	16.8
Totals	110	2447	408	596	.685	339	452	.750	538	79	1155	4.9	0.7	10.5

NBA REGULAR-SEASON RECORD

Season Team	G	Min.	FGM	FGA	Pct.	FTM	FTA	Pct.	Off.	Def.	Tot.	Ast.	St.	Blk.	TO	Pts.	RPG	APG	PPG
									REBOUNDS								AVERAGES		
90-91—Charlotte	39	227	20	39	.513	19	21	.905	21	24	45	9	6	2	4	59	1.2	0.2	1.5
91-92—Sac.-Den.	11	61	6	9	.667	9	12	.750	10	4	14	0	3	1	1	21	1.3	0.0	1.9
92-93—Seattle	29	166	25	48	.521	16	24	.667	15	21	36	5	6	1	5	66	1.2	0.2	2.3
93-94—Seattle	35	152	28	46	.609	19	20	.950	11	15	26	6	7	0	8	75	0.7	0.2	2.1
94-95—Seattle	18	102	12	23	.522	15	18	.833	8	15	23	4	2	2	3	39	1.3	0.2	2.2
95-96—Seattle	35	181	24	45	.533	9	19	.474	15	18	33	2	6	2	8	58	0.9	0.1	1.7
Totals	167	889	115	210	.548	87	114	.763	80	97	177	26	30	8	29	318	1.1	0.2	1.9

Three-point field goals: 1995-96, 1-for-5 (.200).
Personal fouls/disqualifications: 1990-91, 20/0. 1991-92, 10/0. 1992-93, 37/0. 1993-94, 25/0. 1994-95, 9/0. 1995-96, 25/0. Totals, 126/0.

NBA PLAYOFF RECORD

Season Team	G	Min.	FGM	FGA	Pct.	FTM	FTA	Pct.	Off.	Def.	Tot.	Ast.	St.	Blk.	TO	Pts.	RPG	APG	PPG
									REBOUNDS								AVERAGES		
92-93—Seattle	9	22	5	10	.500	4	4	1.000	6	4	10	1	2	0	0	0	1.1	0.1	0.0
93-94—Seattle	1	9	1	1	1.000	0	2	.000	0	3	3	0	1	0	0	2	3.0	0.0	2.0
94-95—Seattle	1	1	1	1	1.000	0	0	...	0	1	1	0	0	0	0	2	1.0	0.0	2.0
95-96—Seattle	8	22	0	4	.000	0	2	.000	2	4	6	2	1	0	1	0	0.8	0.3	0.0
Totals	19	54	7	16	.438	4	8	.500	8	12	20	3	4	0	1	4	1.1	0.2	0.2

Personal fouls/disqualifications: 1992-93, 1/0. 1993-94, 1/0. 1995-96, 2/0. Totals, 4/0.

CBA REGULAR-SEASON RECORD

Season Team	G	Min.	FGM	FGA	Pct.	FTM	FTA	Pct.	Reb.	Ast.	Pts.	RPG	APG	PPG
												AVERAGES		
91-92—Quad City	41	1335	233	381	.612	144	178	.809	309	36	610	7.5	0.9	14.9

SCHINTZIUS, DWAYNE   C   PACERS

PERSONAL: Born October 14, 1968, in Brandon, Fla. ... 7-2/285. ... Full name: Dwayne Kenneth Schintzius. ... Name pronounced SHIN-sus.
HIGH SCHOOL: Brandon (Fla.).
COLLEGE: Florida.
TRANSACTIONS/CAREER NOTES: Selected by San Antonio Spurs in first round (24th pick overall) of 1990 NBA Draft. ... Traded by Spurs with 1994 second-round draft choice to Sacramento Kings for F Antoine Carr (September 23, 1991). ... Waived by Kings (July 20, 1992). ... Signed as free agent by New Jersey Nets (October 1, 1992). ... Signed as free agent by Indiana Pacers (October 18, 1995).

COLLEGIATE RECORD

Season Team	G	Min.	FGM	FGA	Pct.	FTM	FTA	Pct.	Reb.	Ast.	Pts.	RPG	APG	PPG
86-87—Florida	34	931	161	366	.440	48	65	.738	206	78	370	6.1	2.3	10.9
87-88—Florida	35	1069	224	456	.491	54	74	.730	228	79	503	6.5	2.3	14.4
88-89—Florida	30	1120	220	422	.521	99	140	.707	290	81	541	9.7	2.7	18.0
89-90—Florida	11	355	90	163	.552	30	38	.789	105	15	210	9.5	1.4	19.1
Totals	110	3475	695	1407	.494	231	317	.729	829	253	1624	7.5	2.3	14.8

Three-point field goals: 1987-88, 1-for-5 (.200). 1988-89, 2-for-6 (.333). 1989-90, 0-for-8. Totals, 3-for-19 (.158).

NBA REGULAR-SEASON RECORD

Season Team	G	Min.	FGM	FGA	Pct.	FTM	FTA	Pct.	REBOUNDS Off.	Def.	Tot.	Ast.	St.	Blk.	TO	Pts.	AVERAGES RPG	APG	PPG
90-91—San Antonio	42	398	68	155	.439	22	40	.550	28	93	121	17	2	29	34	158	2.9	0.4	3.8
91-92—Sacramento	33	400	50	117	.427	10	12	.833	43	75	118	20	6	28	19	110	3.6	0.6	3.3
92-93—New Jersey	5	35	2	7	.286	3	3	1.000	2	6	8	2	2	2	0	7	1.6	0.4	1.4
93-94—New Jersey	30	319	29	84	.345	10	17	.588	26	63	89	13	7	17	13	68	3.0	0.4	2.3
94-95—New Jersey	43	318	41	108	.380	6	11	.545	29	52	81	15	3	17	17	88	1.9	0.3	2.0
95-96—Indiana	33	297	49	110	.445	13	21	.619	23	55	78	14	9	12	19	111	2.4	0.4	3.4
Totals	186	1767	239	581	.411	64	104	.615	151	344	495	81	29	105	102	542	2.7	0.4	2.9

Three-point field goals: 1990-91, 0-for-2. 1991-92, 0-for-4. Totals, 0-for-6.
Personal fouls/disqualifications: 1990-91, 64/0. 1991-92, 67/1. 1992-93, 4/0. 1993-94, 49/1. 1994-95, 45/0. 1995-96, 53/0. Totals, 282/2.

NBA PLAYOFF RECORD

Season Team	G	Min.	FGM	FGA	Pct.	FTM	FTA	Pct.	REBOUNDS Off.	Def.	Tot.	Ast.	St.	Blk.	TO	Pts.	AVERAGES RPG	APG	PPG
92-93—New Jersey	5	106	13	29	.448	3	6	.500	6	19	25	4	1	6	3	29	5.0	0.8	5.8

Personal fouls/disqualifications: 1992-93, 12/0.

SCHREMPF, DETLEF   F   SUPERSONICS

PERSONAL: Born January 21, 1963, in Leverkusen, Germany. ... 6-10/235. ... Name pronounced SCHREMF.
HIGH SCHOOL: Centralia (Wash.).
COLLEGE: Washington.
TRANSACTIONS/CAREER NOTES: Selected by Dallas Mavericks in first round (eighth pick overall) of 1985 NBA Draft. ... Traded by Mavericks with 1990 or 1991 second-round draft choice to Indiana Pacers for C/F Herb Williams (February 21, 1989). ... Traded by Pacers to Seattle SuperSonics for F Derrick McKey and F Gerald Paddio (November 1, 1993).
MISCELLANEOUS: Member of West German Olympic team (1984). ... Member of German Olympic team (1992).

COLLEGIATE RECORD

NOTES: THE SPORTING NEWS All-America second team (1985).

Season Team	G	Min.	FGM	FGA	Pct.	FTM	FTA	Pct.	Reb.	Ast.	Pts.	RPG	APG	PPG
81-82—Washington	28	314	33	73	.452	26	47	.553	56	13	92	2.0	0.5	3.3
82-83—Washington	31	958	124	266	.466	81	113	.717	211	44	329	6.8	1.4	10.6
83-84—Washington	31	1186	195	362	.539	131	178	.736	230	93	521	7.4	3.0	16.8
84-85—Washington	32	1180	191	342	.558	125	175	.714	255	134	507	8.0	4.2	15.8
Totals	122	3638	543	1043	.521	363	513	.708	752	284	1449	6.2	2.3	11.9

NBA REGULAR-SEASON RECORD

HONORS: NBA Sixth Man Award (1991, 1992). ... All-NBA third team (1995).

Season Team	G	Min.	FGM	FGA	Pct.	FTM	FTA	Pct.	REBOUNDS Off.	Def.	Tot.	Ast.	St.	Blk.	TO	Pts.	AVERAGES RPG	APG	PPG
85-86—Dallas	64	969	142	315	.451	110	152	.724	70	128	198	88	23	10	84	397	3.1	1.4	6.2
86-87—Dallas	81	1711	265	561	.472	193	260	.742	87	216	303	161	50	16	110	756	3.7	2.0	9.3
87-88—Dallas	82	1587	246	539	.456	201	266	.756	102	177	279	159	42	32	108	698	3.4	1.9	8.5
88-89—Dallas-Ind.	69	1850	274	578	.474	273	350	.780	126	269	395	179	53	19	133	828	5.7	2.6	12.0
89-90—Indiana	78	2573	424	822	.516	402	490	.820	149	471	620	247	59	16	180	1267	7.9	3.2	16.2
90-91—Indiana	82	2632	432	831	.520	441	539	.818	178	482	660	301	58	22	175	1320	8.0	3.7	16.1
91-92—Indiana	80	2605	496	925	.536	365	441	.828	202	568	770	312	62	37	191	1380	9.6	3.9	17.3
92-93—Indiana	82	3098	517	1085	.477	525	653	.804	210	570	780	493	79	27	243	1567	9.5	6.0	19.1
93-94—Seattle	81	2728	445	903	.493	300	390	.769	144	310	454	275	73	9	173	1212	5.6	3.4	15.0
94-95—Seattle	82	2886	521	997	.523	437	521	.839	135	373	508	310	93	35	176	1572	6.2	3.8	19.2
95-96—Seattle	63	2200	360	740	.486	287	370	.776	73	255	328	276	56	8	146	1080	5.2	4.4	17.1
Totals	844	24839	4122	8296	.497	3534	4432	.797	1476	3819	5295	2801	648	231	1719	12077	6.3	3.3	14.3

Three-point field goals: 1985-86, 3-for-7 (.429). 1986-87, 33-for-69 (.478). 1987-88, 5-for-32 (.156). 1988-89, 7-for-35 (.200). 1989-90, 17-for-48 (.354). 1990-91, 15-for-40 (.375). 1991-92, 23-for-71 (.324). 1992-93, 8-for-52 (.154). 1993-94, 22-for-68 (.324). 1994-95, 93-for-181 (.514). 1995-96, 73-for-179 (.408). Totals, 299-for-782 (.382).
Personal fouls/disqualifications: 1985-86, 166/1. 1986-87, 224/2. 1987-88, 189/0. 1988-89, 220/3. 1989-90, 271/6. 1990-91, 262/3. 1991-92, 286/4. 1992-93, 305/3. 1993-94, 273/3. 1994-95, 252/0. 1995-96, 179/0. Totals, 2627/25.

NBA PLAYOFF RECORD

Season Team	G	Min.	FGM	FGA	Pct.	FTM	FTA	Pct.	REBOUNDS Off.	Def.	Tot.	Ast.	St.	Blk.	TO	Pts.	RPG	APG	PPG
85-86—Dallas............	10	120	13	28	.464	11	17	.647	7	16	23	14	2	1	10	37	2.3	1.4	3.7
86-87—Dallas............	4	97	13	35	.371	5	11	.455	4	8	12	6	3	2	6	31	3.0	1.5	7.8
87-88—Dallas............	15	274	40	86	.465	36	51	.706	25	30	55	24	8	7	21	117	3.7	1.6	7.8
89-90—Indiana..........	3	125	23	47	.489	15	16	.938	5	17	22	5	2	1	10	61	7.3	1.7	20.3
90-91—Indiana..........	5	179	27	57	.474	25	30	.833	10	26	36	11	2	0	11	79	7.2	2.2	15.8
91-92—Indiana..........	3	120	18	47	.383	25	28	.893	12	27	39	7	2	1	7	63	13.0	2.3	21.0
92-93—Indiana..........	4	165	25	64	.391	28	36	.778	3	20	23	29	1	2	17	78	5.8	7.3	19.5
93-94—Seattle	5	174	26	50	.520	39	45	.867	8	19	27	10	1	3	8	93	5.4	2.0	18.6
94-95—Seattle	4	153	23	57	.404	19	24	.792	2	17	19	12	3	2	11	75	4.8	3.0	18.8
95-96—Seattle	21	789	123	259	.475	69	92	.750	19	86	105	67	14	5	67	336	5.0	3.2	16.0
Totals	74	2196	331	730	.453	272	350	.777	95	266	361	185	38	24	168	970	4.9	2.5	13.1

Three-point field goals: 1985-86, 0-for-1. 1986-87, 0-for-3. 1987-88, 1-for-3 (.333). 1989-90, 0-for-3. 1990-91, 0-for-4. 1991-92, 2-for-4 (.500). 1992-93, 0-for-2. 1993-94, 2-for-6 (.333). 1994-95, 10-for-18 (.556). 1995-96, 21-for-57 (.368). Totals, 36-for-101 (.356).

Personal fouls/disqualifications: 1985-86, 24/0. 1986-87, 13/0. 1987-88, 29/0. 1989-90, 13/0. 1990-91, 17/0. 1991-92, 10/0. 1992-93, 14/0. 1993-94, 21/1. 1994-95, 12/0. 1995-96, 63/1. Totals, 216/2.

NBA ALL-STAR GAME RECORD

Season Team	Min.	FGM	FGA	Pct.	FTM	FTA	Pct.	REBOUNDS Off.	Def.	Tot.	Ast.	PF	Dq.	St.	Blk.	TO	Pts.
1993 —Indiana	13	1	3	.333	1	2	.500	0	3	3	0	4	0	0	0	1	3
1995 —Seattle	18	4	11	.364	0	0	...	0	4	4	5	2	0	0	0	0	9
Totals........................	31	5	14	.357	1	2	.500	0	7	7	5	6	0	0	0	1	12

Three-point field goals: 1993, 0-for-1. 1995, 1-for-4 (.250). Totals, 1-for-5 (.200).

SCOTT, BYRON   G

PERSONAL: Born March 28, 1961, in Ogden, Utah. ... 6-4/200. ... Full name: Byron Antom Scott.
HIGH SCHOOL: Morningside (Inglewood, Calif.).
COLLEGE: Arizona State.
TRANSACTIONS/CAREER NOTES: Selected by San Diego Clippers in first round (fourth pick overall) of 1983 NBA Draft. ... Draft rights traded by Clippers with C Swen Nater to Los Angeles Lakers for G Norm Nixon, G Eddie Jordan and 1986 and 1987 second-round draft choices (October 10, 1983). ... Signed as free agent by Indiana Pacers (December 6, 1993). ... Selected by Vancouver Grizzlies from Pacers in NBA expansion draft (June 24, 1995). ... Waived by Grizzlies (July 22, 1996).
MISCELLANEOUS: Member of NBA championship teams (1985, 1987, 1988).

COLLEGIATE RECORD

Season Team	G	Min.	FGM	FGA	Pct.	FTM	FTA	Pct.	Reb.	Ast.	Pts.	RPG	APG	PPG
79-80—Arizona State................	29	936	166	332	.500	63	86	.733	79	65	395	2.7	2.2	13.6
80-81—Arizona State................	28	1003	197	390	.505	70	101	.693	106	78	464	3.8	2.8	16.6
81-82—Arizona State................					Did not play—academic and personal reasons.									
82-83—Arizona State................	33	1206	283	552	.513	147	188	.782	177	140	713	5.4	4.2	21.6
Totals	90	3145	646	1274	.507	280	375	.747	362	283	1572	4.0	3.1	17.5

NBA REGULAR-SEASON RECORD

HONORS: NBA All-Rookie team (1984).
NOTES: Led NBA with .433 three-point field-goal percentage (1985).

Season Team	G	Min.	FGM	FGA	Pct.	FTM	FTA	Pct.	REBOUNDS Off.	Def.	Tot.	Ast.	St.	Blk.	TO	Pts.	RPG	APG	PPG
83-84—Los Angeles	74	1637	334	690	.484	112	139	.806	50	114	164	177	81	19	116	788	2.2	2.4	10.6
84-85—L.A. Lakers	81	2305	541	1003	.539	187	228	.820	57	153	210	244	100	17	138	1295	2.6	3.0	16.0
85-86—I A. Lakers	76	2190	507	989	.513	138	176	.784	55	134	189	164	85	15	110	1174	2.5	2.2	15.4
86-87—L.A. Lakers	82	2729	554	1134	.489	224	251	.892	63	223	286	281	125	18	144	1397	3.5	3.4	17.0
87-88—L.A. Lakers	81	3048	710	1348	.527	272	317	.858	76	257	333	335	155	27	161	1754	4.1	4.1	21.7
88-89—L.A. Lakers	74	2605	588	1198	.491	195	226	.863	72	230	302	231	114	27	157	1448	4.1	3.1	19.6
89-90—L.A. Lakers	77	2593	472	1005	.470	160	209	.766	51	191	242	274	77	31	122	1197	3.1	3.6	15.5
90-91—L.A. Lakers	82	2630	501	1051	.477	118	148	.797	54	192	246	177	95	21	85	1191	3.0	2.2	14.5
91-92—L.A. Lakers	82	2679	460	1005	.458	244	291	.838	74	236	310	226	105	28	119	1218	3.8	2.8	14.9
92-93—L.A. Lakers	58	1677	296	659	.449	156	184	.848	27	107	134	157	55	13	70	792	2.3	2.7	13.7
93-94—Indiana..........	67	1197	256	548	.467	157	195	.805	19	91	110	133	62	9	103	696	1.6	2.0	10.4
94-95—Indiana..........	80	1528	265	583	.455	193	227	.850	18	133	151	108	61	13	119	802	1.9	1.4	10.0
95-96—Vancouver......	80	1894	271	676	.401	203	243	.835	40	152	192	123	63	22	100	819	2.4	1.5	10.2
Totals	994	28712	5755	11889	.484	2359	2834	.832	656	2213	2869	2630	1178	260	1544	14571	2.9	2.6	14.7

Three-point field goals: 1983-84, 8-for-34 (.235). 1984-85, 26-for-60 (.433). 1985-86, 22-for-61 (.361). 1986-87, 65-for-149 (.436). 1987-88, 62-for-179 (.346). 1988-89, 77-for-193 (.399). 1989-90, 93-for-220 (.423). 1990-91, 71-for-219 (.324). 1991-92, 54-for-135 (.344). 1992-93, 44-for-135 (.326). 1993-94, 27-for-74 (.365). 1994-95, 79-for-203 (.389). 1995-96, 74-for-221 (.335). Totals, 702-for-1905 (.369).

Personal fouls/disqualifications: 1983-84, 174/0. 1984-85, 197/1. 1985-86, 167/0. 1986-87, 163/0. 1987-88, 204/2. 1988-89, 181/1. 1989-90, 180/2. 1990-91, 146/0. 1991-92, 140/0. 1992-93, 98/0. 1993-94, 80/0. 1994-95, 123/1. 1995-96, 126/0. Totals, 1979/7.

NBA PLAYOFF RECORD

NOTES: Shares single-game playoff record for most three-point field goals, none missed—5 (May 5, 1991, vs. Golden State).

Season Team	G	Min.	FGM	FGA	Pct.	FTM	FTA	Pct.	REBOUNDS Off.	Def.	Tot.	Ast.	St.	Blk.	TO	Pts.	RPG	APG	PPG
83-84—Los Angeles....	20	404	74	161	.460	21	35	.600	11	26	37	34	18	2	26	171	1.9	1.7	8.6
84-85—L.A. Lakers	19	585	138	267	.517	35	44	.795	16	36	52	50	41	4	24	321	2.7	2.6	16.9

Season Team	G	Min.	FGM	FGA	Pct.	FTM	FTA	Pct.	Off.	Def.	Tot.	Ast.	St.	Blk.	TO	Pts.	RPG	APG	PPG
85-86—L.A. Lakers	14	470	90	181	.497	38	42	.905	15	40	55	42	19	2	30	224	3.9	3.0	16.0
86-87—L.A. Lakers	18	608	103	210	.490	53	67	.791	20	42	62	57	19	4	25	266	3.4	3.2	14.8
87-88—L.A. Lakers	24	897	178	357	.499	90	104	.865	26	74	100	60	34	5	47	470	4.2	2.5	19.6
88-89—L.A. Lakers	11	402	79	160	.494	46	55	.836	10	35	45	25	18	2	20	219	4.1	2.3	19.9
89-90—L.A. Lakers	9	325	49	106	.462	10	13	.769	7	30	37	23	20	3	13	121	4.1	2.6	13.4
90-91—L.A. Lakers	18	678	95	186	.511	27	34	.794	13	44	57	29	23	4	17	237	3.2	1.6	13.2
91-92—L.A. Lakers	4	148	22	44	.500	24	27	.889	3	7	10	14	6	1	5	75	2.5	3.5	18.8
92-93—L.A. Lakers	5	177	21	42	.500	18	23	.783	0	11	11	9	5	0	4	68	2.2	1.8	13.6
93-94—Indiana...........	16	239	38	96	.396	40	51	.784	10	23	33	20	12	2	25	125	2.1	1.3	7.8
94-95—Indiana...........	17	298	32	94	.340	30	34	.882	5	20	25	16	10	1	22	103	1.5	0.9	6.1
Totals	175	5231	919	1904	.483	432	529	.817	136	388	524	379	225	30	258	2400	3.0	2.2	13.7

Three-point field goals: 1983-84, 2-for-10 (.200). 1984-85, 10-for-21 (.476). 1985-86, 6-for-17 (.353). 1986-87, 7-for-34 (.206). 1987-88, 24-for-55 (.436). 1988-89, 15-for-39 (.385). 1989-90, 13-for-34 (.382). 1990-91, 20-for-38 (.526). 1991-92, 7-for-12 (.583). 1992-93, 8-for-15 (.533). 1993-94, 9-for-19 (.474). 1994-95, 9-for-34 (.265). Totals, 130-for-328 (.396).

Personal fouls/disqualifications: 1983-84, 39/1. 1984-85, 47/0. 1985-86, 38/0. 1986-87, 52/0. 1987-88, 65/0. 1988-89, 31/0. 1989-90, 32/1. 1990-91, 53/0. 1991-92, 10/0. 1992-93, 11/0. 1993-94, 22/0. 1994-95, 30/0. Totals, 430/2.

SCOTT, DENNIS   G/F   MAGIC

PERSONAL: Born September 5, 1968, in Hagerstown, Md. ... 6-8/235. ... Full name: Dennis Eugene Scott.
HIGH SCHOOL: Flint Hill Prep Academy (Oakton, Va.).
COLLEGE: Georgia Tech.
TRANSACTIONS/CAREER NOTES: Selected after junior season by Orlando Magic in first round (fourth pick overall) of 1990 NBA Draft.

COLLEGIATE RECORD
NOTES: THE SPORTING NEWS College Player of the Year (1990). ... THE SPORTING NEWS All-America first team (1990).

Season Team	G	Min.	FGM	FGA	Pct.	FTM	FTA	Pct.	Reb.	Ast.	Pts.	RPG	APG	PPG
87-88—Georgia Tech	32	1113	181	411	.440	36	55	.655	161	116	496	5.0	3.6	15.5
88-89—Georgia Tech	32	1205	227	512	.443	79	97	.814	131	98	649	4.1	3.1	20.3
89-90—Georgia Tech	35	1368	336	722	.465	161	203	.793	231	71	970	6.6	2.0	27.7
Totals	99	3686	744	1645	.452	276	355	.777	523	285	2115	5.3	2.9	21.4

Three-point field goals: 1987-88, 98-for-208 (.471). 1988-89, 116-for-292 (.397). 1989-90, 137-for-331 (.414). Totals, 351-for-831 (.422).

NBA REGULAR-SEASON RECORD
RECORDS: Holds single-season record for most three-point field goals made—267 (1996). ... Shares single-game record for most three-point field goals made—11 (April 18, 1996, vs. Atlanta); and most three-point field goals made in one half—7 (April 18, 1996, vs. Atlanta).
HONORS: NBA All-Rookie first team (1991).

Season Team	G	Min.	FGM	FGA	Pct.	FTM	FTA	Pct.	Off.	Def.	Tot.	Ast.	St.	Blk.	TO	Pts.	RPG	APG	PPG
90-91—Orlando...........	82	2336	503	1183	.425	153	204	.750	62	173	235	134	62	25	127	1284	2.9	1.6	15.7
91-92—Orlando...........	18	608	133	331	.402	64	71	.901	14	52	66	35	20	9	31	359	3.7	1.9	19.9
92-93—Orlando...........	54	1759	329	763	.431	92	117	.786	38	148	186	136	57	18	104	858	3.4	2.5	15.9
93-94—Orlando...........	82	2283	384	949	.405	123	159	.774	54	164	218	216	81	32	93	1046	2.7	2.6	12.8
94-95—Orlando...........	62	1499	283	645	.439	86	114	.754	25	121	146	131	45	14	57	802	2.4	2.1	12.9
95-96—Orlando...........	82	3041	491	1117	.440	182	222	.820	63	246	309	243	90	29	122	1431	3.8	3.0	17.5
Totals	380	11526	2123	4988	.426	700	887	.789	256	904	1160	895	355	127	534	5780	3.1	2.4	15.2

Three-point field goals: 1990-91, 125-for-334 (.374). 1991-92, 29-for-89 (.326). 1992-93, 108-for-268 (.403). 1993-94, 155-for-388 (.399). 1994-95, 150-for-352 (.426). 1995-96, 267-for-628 (.425). Totals, 834-for-2059 (.405).

Personal fouls/disqualifications: 1990-91, 203/1. 1991-92, 49/1. 1992-93, 131/3. 1993-94, 161/0. 1994-95, 119/1. 1995-96, 169/1. Totals, 832/7.

NBA PLAYOFF RECORD
NOTES: Holds single-game playoff record for most three-point field goals attempted—15 (May 25, 1995, vs. Indiana).

Season Team	G	Min.	FGM	FGA	Pct.	FTM	FTA	Pct.	Off.	Def.	Tot.	Ast.	St.	Blk.	TO	Pts.	RPG	APG	PPG
93-94—Orlando...........	3	99	14	41	.341	8	10	.800	1	5	6	3	2	3	8	43	2.0	1.0	14.3
94-95—Orlando...........	21	746	109	264	.413	34	40	.850	9	54	63	45	22	5	33	308	3.0	2.1	14.7
95-96—Orlando...........	12	446	48	116	.414	14	22	.636	9	34	43	23	9	1	15	136	3.6	1.9	11.3
Totals	36	1291	171	421	.406	56	72	.778	19	93	112	71	33	9	56	487	3.1	2.0	13.5

Three-point field goals: 1993-94, 7-for-22 (.318). 1994-95, 56-for-151 (.371). 1995-96, 26-for-69 (.377). Totals, 89-for-242 (.368).
Personal fouls/disqualifications: 1993-94, 7/0. 1994-95, 62/0. 1995-96, 37/0. Totals, 106/0.

SEALY, MALIK   G   CLIPPERS

PERSONAL: Born February 1, 1970, in Bronx, N.Y. ... 6-8/190. ... Name pronounced ma-LEAK.
HIGH SCHOOL: St. Nicholas of Tolentine (Bronx, N.Y.).
COLLEGE: St. John's.
TRANSACTIONS/CAREER NOTES: Selected by Indiana Pacers in first round (14th pick overall) of 1992 NBA Draft. ... Traded by Pacers with G Pooh Richardson and draft rights to F Eric Piatkowski to Los Angeles Clippers for G Mark Jackson and draft rights to G Greg Minor (June 30, 1994).

COLLEGIATE RECORD

Season Team	G	Min.	FGM	FGA	Pct.	FTM	FTA	Pct.	Reb.	Ast.	Pts.	RPG	APG	PPG
88-89—St. John's	31	1172	163	333	.489	67	120	.558	197	67	400	6.4	2.2	12.9

Season Team	G	Min.	FGM	FGA	Pct.	FTM	FTA	Pct.	Reb.	Ast.	Pts.	RPG	APG	PPG
												AVERAGES		
89-90—St. John's	34	1304	227	432	.525	159	213	.746	233	58	615	6.9	1.7	18.1
90-91—St. John's	32	1203	263	535	.492	165	222	.743	247	54	707	7.7	1.7	22.1
91-92—St. John's	30	1162	247	523	.472	169	213	.793	203	50	679	6.8	1.7	22.6
Totals	127	4841	900	1823	.494	560	768	.729	880	229	2401	6.9	1.8	18.9

Three-point field goals: 1988-89, 7-for-33 (.212). 1989-90, 2-for-27 (.074). 1990-91, 16-for-53 (.302). 1991-92, 16-for-53 (.302). Totals, 41-for-166 (.247).

NBA REGULAR-SEASON RECORD

Season Team	G	Min.	FGM	FGA	Pct.	FTM	FTA	Pct.	REBOUNDS Off.	Def.	Tot.	Ast.	St.	Blk.	TO	Pts.	AVERAGES RPG	APG	PPG
92-93—Indiana..........	58	672	136	319	.426	51	74	.689	60	52	112	47	36	7	58	330	1.9	0.8	5.7
93-94—Indiana..........	43	623	111	274	.405	59	87	.678	43	75	118	48	31	8	51	285	2.7	1.1	6.6
94-95—L.A. Clippers...	60	1604	291	669	.435	174	223	.780	77	137	214	107	72	25	83	778	3.6	1.8	13.0
95-96—L.A. Clippers...	62	1601	272	655	.415	147	184	.799	76	164	240	116	84	28	113	712	3.9	1.9	11.5
Totals	223	4500	810	1917	.423	431	568	.759	256	428	684	318	223	68	305	2105	3.1	1.4	9.4

Three-point field goals: 1992-93, 7-for-31 (.226). 1993-94, 4-for-16 (.250). 1994-95, 22-for-73 (.301). 1995-96, 21-for-100 (.210). Totals, 54-for-220 (.245).

Personal fouls/disqualifications: 1992-93, 74/0. 1993-94, 84/0. 1994-95, 173/2. 1995-96, 150/2. Totals, 481/4.

NBA PLAYOFF RECORD

Season Team	G	Min.	FGM	FGA	Pct.	FTM	FTA	Pct.	REBOUNDS Off.	Def.	Tot.	Ast.	St.	Blk.	TO	Pts.	AVERAGES RPG	APG	PPG
92-93—Indiana..........	3	18	0	5	.000	2	2	1.000	2	0	2	0	0	0	1	2	0.7	0.0	0.7

Three-point field goals: 1992-93, 0-for-1.
Personal fouls/disqualifications: 1992-93, 1/0.

SEIKALY, RONY   C   WARRIORS

PERSONAL: Born May 10, 1965, in Beirut, Lebanon. ... 6-11/253. ... Full name: Ronald F. Seikaly. ... Name pronounced SIGH-kah-lee.
HIGH SCHOOL: American School (Athens, Greece).
COLLEGE: Syracuse.
TRANSACTIONS/CAREER NOTES: Selected by Miami Heat in first round (ninth pick overall) of 1988 NBA Draft. ... Traded by Heat to Golden State Warriors for F Billy Owens and rights to G Sasha Danilovic (November 2, 1994).
MISCELLANEOUS: Miami Heat all-time leading rebounder with 4,544 and all-time blocks leader with 610 (1988-89 through 1993-94).

COLLEGIATE RECORD

NOTES: 1986-87 minutes played totals are missing one game.

Season Team	G	Min.	FGM	FGA	Pct.	FTM	FTA	Pct.	Reb.	Ast.	Pts.	AVERAGES RPG	APG	PPG
84-85—Syracuse	31	775	96	177	.542	58	104	.558	198	13	250	6.4	0.4	8.1
85-86—Syracuse	32	875	122	223	.547	80	142	.563	250	15	324	7.8	0.5	10.1
86-87—Syracuse	38	1032	216	380	.568	141	235	.600	311	36	573	8.2	0.9	15.1
87-88—Syracuse	35	1084	218	385	.566	133	234	.568	335	22	569	9.6	0.6	16.3
Totals	136	3766	652	1165	.560	412	715	.576	1094	86	1716	8.0	0.6	12.6

Three-point field goals: 1986-87, 0-for-1.

NBA REGULAR-SEASON RECORD

HONORS: NBA Most Improved Player (1990).

Season Team	G	Min.	FGM	FGA	Pct.	FTM	FTA	Pct.	REBOUNDS Off.	Def.	Tot.	Ast.	St.	Blk.	TO	Pts.	AVERAGES RPG	APG	PPG
88-89—Miami	78	1962	333	744	.448	181	354	.511	204	345	549	55	46	96	200	848	7.0	0.7	10.9
89-90—Miami	74	2409	486	968	.502	256	431	.594	253	513	766	78	78	124	236	1228	10.4	1.1	16.6
90-91—Miami	64	2171	395	822	.481	258	417	.619	207	502	709	95	51	86	205	1050	11.1	1.5	16.4
91-92—Miami	79	2800	463	947	.489	370	505	.733	307	627	934	109	40	121	216	1296	11.8	1.4	16.4
92-93—Miami	72	2456	417	868	.480	397	540	.735	259	587	846	100	38	83	203	1232	11.8	1.4	17.1
93-94—Miami	72	2410	392	803	.488	304	422	.720	244	496	740	136	59	100	195	1088	10.3	1.9	15.1
94-95—Golden State ...	36	1035	162	314	.516	111	160	.694	77	189	266	45	20	37	104	435	7.4	1.3	12.1
95-96—Golden State ...	64	1813	285	568	.502	204	282	.723	166	333	499	71	40	69	180	776	7.8	1.1	12.1
Totals	539	17056	2933	6034	.486	2081	3111	.669	1717	3592	5309	689	372	716	1539	7953	9.8	1.3	14.8

Three-point field goals: 1988-89, 1-for-4 (.250). 1989-90, 0-for-1. 1990-91, 2-for-6 (.333). 1991-92, 0-for-3. 1992-93, 1-for-8 (.125). 1993-94, 0-for-2. 1995-96, 2-for-3 (.667). Totals, 6-for-27 (.222).

Personal fouls/disqualifications: 1988-89, 258/8. 1989-90, 258/8. 1990-91, 213/2. 1991-92, 278/2. 1992-93, 260/3. 1993-94, 279/8. 1994-95, 122/1. 1995-96, 219/5. Totals, 1887/37.

NBA PLAYOFF RECORD

Season Team	G	Min.	FGM	FGA	Pct.	FTM	FTA	Pct.	REBOUNDS Off.	Def.	Tot.	Ast.	St.	Blk.	TO	Pts.	AVERAGES RPG	APG	PPG
91-92—Miami	3	117	19	35	.543	24	32	.750	11	19	30	4	1	5	9	62	10.0	1.3	20.7
93-94—Miami	5	165	14	32	.438	13	23	.565	19	28	47	8	4	7	11	41	9.4	1.6	8.2
Totals	8	282	33	67	.493	37	55	.673	30	47	77	12	5	12	20	103	9.6	1.5	12.9

Personal fouls/disqualifications: 1991-92, 15/1. 1993-94, 22/0. Totals, 37/1.

SHAW, BRIAN G MAGIC

PERSONAL: Born March 22, 1966, in Oakland. ... 6-6/200. ... Full name: Brian K. Shaw.
HIGH SCHOOL: Bishop O'Dowd (Oakland).
COLLEGE: St. Mary's (Calif.), then UC Santa Barbara.
TRANSACTIONS/CAREER NOTES: Selected by Boston Celtics in first round (24th pick overall) of 1988 NBA Draft. ... Played in Italy (1989-90). ... Traded by Celtics to Miami Heat for G Sherman Douglas (January 10, 1992). ... Signed as unrestricted free agent by Orlando Magic (September 22, 1994).

COLLEGIATE RECORD

Season Team	G	Min.	FGM	FGA	Pct.	FTM	FTA	Pct.	Reb.	Ast.	Pts.	RPG	APG	PPG
83-84—St. Mary's (Calif.)	14	129	13	36	.361	14	19	.737	12	23	40	0.9	1.6	2.9
84-85—St. Mary's (Calif.)	27	976	99	246	.402	55	76	.724	144	142	253	5.3	5.3	9.4
85-86—UC Santa Barb..............						Did not play—transfer student.								
86-87—UC Santa Barb..............	29	1013	125	288	.434	47	66	.712	224	193	315	7.7	6.7	10.9
87-88—UC Santa Barb..............	30	1073	151	324	.466	71	96	.740	260	182	399	8.7	6.1	13.3
Totals	100	3191	388	894	.434	187	257	.728	640	540	1007	6.4	5.4	10.1

Three-point field goals: 1986-87, 18-for-42 (.429). 1987-88, 26-for-74 (.351). Totals, 44-for-116 (.379).

HONORS: NBA All-Rookie second team (1989).

NBA REGULAR-SEASON RECORD

Season Team	G	Min.	FGM	FGA	Pct.	FTM	FTA	Pct.	REBOUNDS Off.	Def.	Tot.	Ast.	St.	Blk.	TO	Pts.	RPG	APG	PPG
88-89—Boston	82	2301	297	686	.433	109	132	.826	119	257	376	472	78	27	188	703	4.6	5.8	8.6
90-91—Boston	79	2772	442	942	.469	204	249	.819	104	266	370	602	105	34	223	1091	4.7	7.6	13.8
91-92—Bos.-Miami	63	1423	209	513	.407	72	91	.791	50	154	204	250	57	22	99	495	3.2	4.0	7.9
92-93—Miami	68	1603	197	501	.393	61	78	.782	70	187	257	235	48	19	96	498	3.8	3.5	7.3
93-94—Miami	77	2037	278	667	.417	64	89	.719	104	246	350	385	71	21	173	693	4.5	5.0	9.0
94-95—Orlando	78	1836	192	494	.389	70	95	.737	52	189	241	406	73	18	184	502	3.1	5.2	6.4
95-96—Orlando	75	1679	182	486	.374	91	114	.798	58	166	224	336	58	11	173	496	3.0	4.5	6.6
Totals	522	13651	1797	4289	.419	671	848	.791	557	1465	2022	2686	490	152	1136	4478	3.9	5.1	8.6

Three-point field goals: 1988-89, 0-for-13. 1990-91, 3-for-27 (.111). 1991-92, 5-for-23 (.217). 1992-93, 43-for-130 (.331). 1993-94, 73-for-216 (.338). 1994-95, 48-for-184 (.261). 1995-96, 41-for-144 (.285). Totals, 213-for-737 (.289).
Personal fouls/disqualifications: 1988-89, 211/1. 1990-91, 206/1. 1991-92, 115/0. 1992-93, 163/2. 1993-94, 195/1. 1994-95, 184/1. 1995-96, 160/1. Totals, 1234/7.

NBA PLAYOFF RECORD

Season Team	G	Min.	FGM	FGA	Pct.	FTM	FTA	Pct.	REBOUNDS Off.	Def.	Tot.	Ast.	St.	Blk.	TO	Pts.	RPG	APG	PPG
88-89—Boston	3	124	22	43	.512	7	9	.778	2	15	17	19	3	0	6	51	5.7	6.3	17.0
90-91—Boston	11	316	47	100	.470	26	30	.867	8	30	38	51	10	1	25	121	3.5	4.6	11.0
91-92—Miami	3	85	14	30	.467	5	8	.625	2	11	13	12	2	0	7	36	4.3	4.0	12.0
93-94—Miami	5	112	16	41	.390	7	12	.583	3	17	20	9	4	1	13	39	4.0	1.8	7.8
94-95—Orlando	21	355	48	123	.390	20	32	.625	17	45	62	66	11	4	26	138	3.0	3.1	6.6
95-96—Orlando	10	217	18	52	.346	3	4	.750	6	15	21	46	5	0	19	47	2.1	4.6	4.7
Totals	53	1209	165	389	.424	68	95	.716	38	133	171	203	35	6	96	432	3.2	3.8	8.2

Three-point field goals: 1988-89, 0-for-1. 1990-91, 1-for-3 (.333). 1991-92, 3-for-5 (.600). 1993-94, 0-for-13. 1994-95, 22-for-57 (.386). 1995-96, 8-for-22 (.364). Totals, 34-for-101 (.337).
Personal fouls/disqualifications: 1988-89, 11/0. 1990-91, 34/0. 1991-92, 13/0. 1993-94, 8/0. 1994-95, 49/0. 1995-96, 27/0. Totals, 142/0.

ITALIAN LEAGUE RECORD

Season Team	G	Min.	FGM	FGA	Pct.	FTM	FTA	Pct.	Reb.	Ast.	Pts.	RPG	APG	PPG
89-90—Il Messaggero Roma......	30	1144	244	418	.584	111	139	.799	274	...	749	9.1	...	25.0

SIMMONS, LIONEL F KINGS

PERSONAL: Born November 14, 1968, in Philadelphia. ... 6-7/210. ... Full name: Lionel James Simmons. ... Name pronounced LION-el.
HIGH SCHOOL: South Philadelphia (Philadelphia).
COLLEGE: La Salle.
TRANSACTIONS/CAREER NOTES: Selected by Sacramento Kings in first round (seventh pick overall) of 1990 NBA Draft.

COLLEGIATE RECORD

NOTES: Naismith Award winner (1990). ... Wooden Award winner (1990). ... THE SPORTING NEWS All-America first team (1989). ... THE SPORTING NEWS All-America second team (1988, 1990).

Season Team	G	Min.	FGM	FGA	Pct.	FTM	FTA	Pct.	Reb.	Ast.	Pts.	RPG	APG	PPG
86-87—La Salle	33	...	263	500	.526	142	186	.763	322	59	670	9.8	1.8	20.3
87-88—La Salle	34	...	297	613	.485	196	259	.757	386	86	792	11.4	2.5	23.3
88-89—La Salle	32	1245	349	716	.487	189	266	.711	365	95	908	11.4	3.0	28.4
89-90—La Salle	32	1220	335	653	.513	146	221	.661	356	115	847	11.1	3.6	26.5
Totals	131	...	1244	2482	.501	673	932	.722	1429	355	3217	10.9	2.7	24.6

Three-point field goals: 1986-87, 2-for-6 (.333). 1987-88, 2-for-8 (.250). 1988-89, 21-for-56 (.375). 1989-90, 31-for-65 (.477). Totals, 56-for-135 (.415).

HONORS: NBA All-Rookie first team (1991).

NBA REGULAR-SEASON RECORD

Season Team	G	Min.	FGM	FGA	Pct.	FTM	FTA	Pct.	Off.	Def.	Tot.	Ast.	St.	Blk.	TO	Pts.	RPG	APG	PPG
90-91—Sacramento	79	2978	549	1301	.422	320	435	.736	193	504	697	315	113	85	230	1421	8.8	4.0	18.0
91-92—Sacramento	78	2895	527	1162	.454	281	365	.770	149	485	634	337	135	132	218	1336	8.1	4.3	17.1
92-93—Sacramento	69	2502	468	1055	.444	298	364	.819	156	339	495	312	95	38	196	1235	7.2	4.5	17.9
93-94—Sacramento	75	2702	436	996	.438	251	323	.777	168	394	562	305	104	50	183	1129	7.5	4.1	15.1
94-95—Sacramento	58	1064	131	312	.420	59	84	.702	61	135	196	89	28	23	70	327	3.4	1.5	5.6
95-96—Sacramento	54	810	86	217	.396	55	75	.733	41	104	145	83	31	20	51	246	2.7	1.5	4.6
Totals	413	12951	2197	5043	.436	1264	1646	.768	768	1961	2729	1441	506	348	948	5694	6.6	3.5	13.8

Three-point field goals: 1990-91, 3-for-11 (.273). 1991-92, 1-for-5 (.200). 1992-93, 1-for-11 (.091). 1993-94, 6-for-17 (.353). 1994-95, 6-for-16 (.375). 1995-96, 19-for-51 (.373). Totals, 36-for-111 (.324).

Personal fouls/disqualifications: 1990-91, 249/0. 1991-92, 205/0. 1992-93, 197/4. 1993-94, 189/2. 1994-95, 118/0. 1995-96, 85/0. Totals, 1043/6.

NBA PLAYOFF RECORD

Season Team	G	Min.	FGM	FGA	Pct.	FTM	FTA	Pct.	Off.	Def.	Tot.	Ast.	St.	Blk.	TO	Pts.	RPG	APG	PPG
95-96—Sacramento	4	77	15	33	.455	5	7	.714	4	8	12	8	6	2	6	38	3.0	2.0	9.5

Three-point field goals: 1995-96, 3-for-9 (.333).
Personal fouls/disqualifications: 1995-96, 12/0.

SIMPKINS, DICKEY   F   BULLS

PERSONAL: Born April 6, 1972, in Fort Washington, Md. ... 6-10/264. ... Full name: LuBara Dixon Simpkins.
HIGH SCHOOL: Friendly (Fort Washington, Md.).
COLLEGE: Providence.
TRANSACTIONS/CAREER NOTES: Selected by Chicago Bulls in first round (21st pick overall) of 1994 NBA Draft.
MISCELLANEOUS: Member of NBA championship team (1996).

COLLEGIATE RECORD

Season Team	G	Min.	FGM	FGA	Pct.	FTM	FTA	Pct.	Reb.	Ast.	Pts.	RPG	APG	PPG
90-91—Providence	32	697	90	183	.492	67	110	.609	211	33	251	6.6	1.0	7.8
91-92—Providence	30	793	89	181	.492	90	128	.703	174	37	269	5.8	1.2	9.0
92-93—Providence	33	976	122	271	.450	106	178	.596	216	41	351	6.5	1.2	10.6
93-94—Providence	30	877	129	250	.516	94	137	.686	189	38	355	6.3	1.3	11.8
Totals	125	3343	430	885	.486	357	553	.646	790	149	1226	6.3	1.2	9.8

Three-point field goals: 1990-91, 4-for-10 (.400). 1991-92, 1-for-4 (.250). 1992-93, 1-for-3 (.333). 1993-94, 3-for-9 (.333). Totals, 9-for-26 (.346).

NBA REGULAR-SEASON RECORD

Season Team	G	Min.	FGM	FGA	Pct.	FTM	FTA	Pct.	Off.	Def.	Tot.	Ast.	St.	Blk.	TO	Pts.	RPG	APG	PPG
94-95—Chicago	59	586	78	184	.424	50	72	.694	60	91	151	37	10	7	45	206	2.6	0.6	3.5
95-96—Chicago	60	685	77	160	.481	61	97	.629	66	90	156	38	9	8	56	216	2.6	0.6	3.6
Totals	119	1271	155	344	.451	111	169	.657	126	181	307	75	19	15	101	422	2.6	0.6	3.5

Three-point field goals: 1995-96, 1-for-1.
Personal fouls/disqualifications: 1994-95, 72/0. 1995-96, 78/0. Totals, 150/0.

SKILES, SCOTT   G

PERSONAL: Born March 5, 1964, in LaPorte, Ind. ... 6-1/180. ... Full name: Scott Allen Skiles.
HIGH SCHOOL: Plymouth (Ind.).
COLLEGE: Michigan State.
TRANSACTIONS/CAREER NOTES: Selected by Milwaukee Bucks in first round (22nd pick overall) of 1986 NBA Draft. ... Traded by Bucks to Indiana Pacers for second-round draft choice (June 22, 1987). ... Selected by Orlando Magic from Pacers in NBA expansion draft (June 15, 1989). ... Traded by Magic with 1996 first-round draft choice and future considerations to Washington Bullets for 1996 second-round draft choice and future considerations (July 29, 1994). ... Signed by Philadelphia 76ers for remainder of season (December 12, 1995). ... Announced retirement (January 6, 1996). ... Rights renounced by 76ers (July 11, 1996).
MISCELLANEOUS: Orlando Magic all-time assists leader with 2,776 (1989-90 through 1993-94).

COLLEGIATE RECORD

NOTES: THE SPORTING NEWS All-America first team (1986).

Season Team	G	Min.	FGM	FGA	Pct.	FTM	FTA	Pct.	Reb.	Ast.	Pts.	RPG	APG	PPG
82-83—Michigan State	30	1023	141	286	.493	69	83	.831	63	146	376	2.1	4.9	12.5
83-84—Michigan State	28	983	153	319	.480	99	119	.832	62	128	405	2.2	4.6	14.5
84-85—Michigan State	29	1107	212	420	.505	90	114	.789	93	168	514	3.2	5.8	17.7
85-86—Michigan State	31	1172	331	598	.554	188	209	.900	135	203	850	4.4	6.5	27.4
Totals	118	4285	837	1623	.516	446	525	.850	353	645	2145	3.0	5.5	18.2

Three-point field goals: 1982-83, 25-for-50 (.500).

NBA REGULAR-SEASON RECORD

RECORDS: Holds single-game record for most assists—30 (December 30, 1990, vs. Denver).
HONORS: NBA Most Improved Player (1991).

Season Team	G	Min.	FGM	FGA	Pct.	FTM	FTA	Pct.	Off.	Def.	Tot.	Ast.	St.	Blk.	TO	Pts.	RPG	APG	PPG
86-87—Milwaukee	13	205	18	62	.290	10	12	.833	6	20	26	45	5	1	21	49	2.0	3.5	3.8
87-88—Indiana............	51	760	86	209	.411	45	54	.833	11	55	66	180	22	3	76	223	1.3	3.5	4.4
88-89—Indiana............	80	1571	198	442	.448	130	144	.903	21	128	149	390	64	2	177	546	1.9	4.9	6.8
89-90—Orlando	70	1460	190	464	.409	104	119	.874	23	136	159	334	36	4	90	536	2.3	4.8	7.7

Season Team	G	Min.	FGM	FGA	Pct.	FTM	FTA	Pct.	REBOUNDS Off.	Def.	Tot.	Ast.	St.	Blk.	TO	Pts.	AVERAGES RPG	APG	PPG
90-91—Orlando	79	2714	462	1039	.445	340	377	.902	57	213	270	660	89	4	252	1357	3.4	8.4	17.2
91-92—Orlando	75	2377	359	868	.414	248	277	.895	36	166	202	544	74	5	233	1057	2.7	7.3	14.1
92-93—Orlando	78	3086	416	891	.467	289	324	.892	52	238	290	735	86	2	267	1201	3.7	9.4	15.4
93-94—Orlando	82	2303	276	644	.429	195	222	.878	42	147	189	503	47	2	193	815	2.3	6.1	9.9
94-95—Washington	62	2077	265	583	.455	179	202	.886	26	133	159	452	70	6	172	805	2.6	7.3	13.0
95-96—Philadelphia	10	236	20	57	.351	8	10	.800	1	15	16	38	7	0	16	63	1.6	3.8	6.3
Totals	600	16789	2290	5259	.435	1548	1741	.889	275	1251	1526	3881	500	29	1497	6652	2.5	6.5	11.1

Three-point field goals: 1986-87, 3-for-14 (.214). 1987-88, 6-for-20 (.300). 1988-89, 20-for-75 (.267). 1989-90, 52-for-132 (.394). 1990-91, 93-for-228 (.408). 1991-92, 91-for-250 (.364). 1992-93, 80-for-235 (.340). 1993-94, 68-for-165 (.412). 1994-95, 96-for-228 (.421). 1995-96, 15-for-34 (.441). Totals, 524-for-1381 (.379).

Personal fouls/disqualifications: 1986-87, 18/0. 1987-88, 97/0. 1988-89, 151/1. 1989-90, 126/0. 1990-91, 192/2. 1991-92, 188/0. 1992-93, 244/4. 1993-94, 171/1. 1994-95, 135/2. 1995-96, 21/0. Totals, 1343/10.

NBA PLAYOFF RECORD

Season Team	G	Min.	FGM	FGA	Pct.	FTM	FTA	Pct.	REBOUNDS Off.	Def.	Tot.	Ast.	St.	Blk.	TO	Pts.	AVERAGES RPG	APG	PPG
93-94—Orlando	2	23	4	8	.500	1	1	1.000	1	0	1	3	0	0	5	9	0.5	1.5	4.5

Three-point field goals: 1993-94, 0-for-2.
Personal fouls/disqualifications: 1993-94, 2/0.

SLATER, REGGIE   F

PERSONAL: Born August 27, 1970, in Houston. ... 6-7/215. ... Full name: Reginald Dwayne Slater.
HIGH SCHOOL: Kashmere (Houston).
COLLEGE: Wyoming.
TRANSACTIONS/CAREER NOTES: Not drafted by an NBA franchise. ... Played in Spain (1992-93). ... Signed as free agent by Denver Nuggets (August 2, 1994). ... Selected by Vancouver Grizzlies from Nuggets in NBA expansion draft (June 24, 1995). ... Signed as free agent by Portland Trail Blazers (October 1, 1995). ... Waived by Trail Blazers (December 8, 1995). ... Signed as free agent by Nuggets for remainder of season (December 26, 1995). ... Played in Continental Basketball Association with Chicago Rockers (1995-96). ... Waived by Nuggets (January 5, 1996). ... Signed by Dallas Mavericks to first of two consecutive 10-day contracts (January 10, 1996). ... Waived by Mavericks from second 10-day contract (January 27, 1996).

COLLEGIATE RECORD

Season Team	G	Min.	FGM	FGA	Pct.	FTM	FTA	Pct.	Reb.	Ast.	Pts.	AVERAGES RPG	APG	PPG
88-89—Wyoming	31	703	66	117	.564	61	102	.598	211	6	193	6.8	0.2	6.2
89-90—Wyoming	29	977	170	294	.578	145	198	.732	328	29	485	11.3	1.0	16.7
90-91—Wyoming	32	1141	224	370	.605	165	217	.760	331	39	613	10.3	1.2	19.2
91-92—Wyoming	29	1049	184	320	.575	150	210	.714	327	57	518	11.3	2.0	17.9
Totals	121	3870	644	1101	.585	521	727	.717	1197	131	1809	9.9	1.1	15.0

Three-point field goals: 1988-89, 0-for-1.

SPANISH LEAGUE RECORD

Season Team	G	Min.	FGM	FGA	Pct.	FTM	FTA	Pct.	Reb.	Ast.	Pts.	AVERAGES RPG	APG	PPG
92-93—Argal Huesca	31	1126	230	428	.537	133	197	.675	271	57	593	8.7	1.8	19.1

NBA REGULAR-SEASON RECORD

Season Team	G	Min.	FGM	FGA	Pct.	FTM	FTA	Pct.	REBOUNDS Off.	Def.	Tot.	Ast.	St.	Blk.	TO	Pts.	AVERAGES RPG	APG	PPG
94-95—Denver	25	236	40	81	.494	40	55	.727	21	36	57	12	7	3	26	120	2.3	0.5	4.8
95-96—Port.-Den.-Dal.	11	72	14	27	.519	3	7	.429	4	11	15	2	2	3	9	31	1.4	0.2	2.8
Totals	36	308	54	108	.500	43	62	.694	25	47	72	14	9	6	35	151	2.0	0.4	4.2

Personal fouls/disqualifications: 1994-95, 47/0. 1995-96, 11/0. Totals, 58/0.

CBA REGULAR-SEASON RECORD

Season Team	G	Min.	FGM	FGA	Pct.	FTM	FTA	Pct.	Reb.	Ast.	Pts.	AVERAGES RPG	APG	PPG
95-96—Chicago	5	107	29	45	.644	25	33	.758	39	7	83	7.8	1.4	16.6

SMITH, CHARLES   F   SPURS

PERSONAL: Born July 16, 1965, in Bridgeport, Conn. ... 6-10/245. ... Full name: Charles Daniel Smith.
HIGH SCHOOL: Warren Harding (Bridgeport, Conn.).
COLLEGE: Pittsburgh.
TRANSACTIONS/CAREER NOTES: Selected by Philadelphia 76ers in first round (third pick overall) of 1988 NBA Draft. ... Draft rights traded by 76ers to Los Angeles Clippers for draft rights to G Hersey Hawkins and 1989 first-round draft choice (June 28, 1988). ... Traded by Clippers with G Doc Rivers and G Bo Kimble to New York Knicks in three-way deal in which Clippers received G Mark Jackson and 1995 second-round draft choice from Knicks and C Stanley Roberts from Orlando Magic and Magic received 1993 first-round draft choice from Knicks and 1994 first-round draft choice from Clippers (September 22, 1992). ... Traded by Knicks with F Monty Williams to San Antonio Spurs for F J.R. Reid, C Brad Lohaus and 1996 first-round draft choice (February 8, 1996).
MISCELLANEOUS: Member of bronze-medal-winning U.S. Olympic team (1988).

COLLEGIATE RECORD

Season Team	G	Min.	FGM	FGA	Pct.	FTM	FTA	Pct.	Reb.	Ast.	Pts.	AVERAGES RPG	APG	PPG
84-85—Pittsburgh	29	956	151	301	.502	133	175	.760	231	15	435	8.0	0.5	15.0
85-86—Pittsburgh	29	1077	165	318	.519	131	172	.762	235	46	461	8.1	1.6	15.9
86-87—Pittsburgh	33	1050	180	327	.550	202	275	.735	282	53	562	8.5	1.6	17.0

Season Team	G	Min.	FGM	FGA	Pct.	FTM	FTA	Pct.	Reb.	Ast.	Pts.	RPG	APG	PPG
87-88—Pittsburgh	31	1020	211	378	.558	162	212	.764	239	57	587	7.7	1.8	18.9
Totals	122	4103	707	1324	.534	628	834	.753	987	171	2045	8.1	1.4	16.8

Three-point field goals: 1987-88, 3-for-11 (.273).

NBA REGULAR-SEASON RECORD

HONORS: NBA All-Rookie first team (1989).

Season Team	G	Min.	FGM	FGA	Pct.	FTM	FTA	Pct.	Off.	Def.	Tot.	Ast.	St.	Blk.	TO	Pts.	RPG	APG	PPG
88-89—L.A. Clippers	71	2161	435	878	.495	285	393	.725	173	292	465	103	68	89	146	1155	6.5	1.5	16.3
89-90—L.A. Clippers	78	2732	595	1145	.520	454	572	.794	177	347	524	114	86	119	162	1645	6.7	1.5	21.1
90-91—L.A. Clippers	74	2703	548	1168	.469	384	484	.793	216	392	608	134	81	145	165	1480	8.2	1.8	20.0
91-92—L.A. Clippers	49	1310	251	539	.466	212	270	.785	95	206	301	56	41	98	69	714	6.1	1.1	14.6
92-93—New York	81	2172	358	764	.469	287	367	.782	170	262	432	142	48	96	155	1003	5.3	1.8	12.4
93-94—New York	43	1105	176	397	.443	87	121	.719	66	99	165	50	26	45	64	447	3.8	1.2	10.4
94-95—New York	76	2150	352	747	.471	255	322	.792	144	180	324	120	49	95	147	966	4.3	1.6	12.7
95-96—N.Y.-S.A.	73	1716	244	578	.422	119	163	.730	133	229	362	65	50	80	106	609	5.0	0.9	8.3
Totals	545	16049	2959	6216	.476	2083	2692	.774	1174	2007	3181	784	449	767	1014	8019	5.8	1.4	14.7

Three-point field goals: 1988-89, 0-for-3. 1989-90, 1-for-12 (.083). 1990-91, 0-for-7. 1991-92, 0-for-6. 1992-93, 0-for-2. 1993-94, 8-for-16 (.500). 1994-95, 7-for-31 (.226). 1995-96, 2-for-15 (.133). Totals, 18-for-92 (.196).

Personal fouls/disqualifications: 1988-89, 273/6. 1989-90, 294/6. 1990-91, 267/4. 1991-92, 159/2. 1992-93, 254/4. 1993-94, 144/4. 1994-95, 286/6. 1995-96, 224/3. Totals, 1901/35.

NBA PLAYOFF RECORD

Season Team	G	Min.	FGM	FGA	Pct.	FTM	FTA	Pct.	Off.	Def.	Tot.	Ast.	St.	Blk.	TO	Pts.	RPG	APG	PPG
91-92—L.A. Clippers	5	148	22	56	.393	14	15	.933	10	18	28	9	4	12	10	58	5.6	1.8	11.6
92-93—New York	15	388	65	138	.471	37	50	.740	27	33	60	20	9	14	29	167	4.0	1.3	11.1
93-94—New York	25	612	85	177	.480	51	70	.729	34	61	95	25	12	24	32	221	3.8	1.0	8.8
94-95—New York	11	303	51	95	.537	17	30	.567	20	22	42	13	13	17	24	119	3.8	1.2	10.8
95-96—San Antonio	10	165	24	48	.500	3	8	.375	11	26	37	10	7	10	8	51	3.7	1.0	5.1
Totals	66	1616	247	514	.481	122	173	.705	102	160	262	77	45	77	103	616	4.0	1.2	9.3

Three-point field goals: 1993-94, 0-for-3. 1994-95, 0-for-2. Totals, 0-for-5.
Personal fouls/disqualifications: 1991-92, 24/2. 1992-93, 52/1. 1993-94, 92/0. 1994-95, 44/1. 1995-96, 28/0. Totals, 240/4.

SMITH, CHARLES   G

PERSONAL: Born November 29, 1967, in Washington, D.C. ... 6-1/160. ... Full name: Charles Edward Smith IV.
HIGH SCHOOL: All Saints (Washington, D.C.).
COLLEGE: Georgetown.
TRANSACTIONS/CAREER NOTES: Not drafted by an NBA franchise. ... Signed as free agent by Boston Celtics (September 27, 1989). ... Waived by Celtics (December 5, 1990). ... Played in Continental Basketball Association with Rapid City Thrillers (1990-91), Rockford Lightning (1990-91 and 1994-95), Hartford Hellcats (1994-95), Omaha Racers (1994-95) and Florida (1995-96).. ... Re-signed by Celtics to first of two consecutive 10-day contracts (March 4, 1991). ... Signed by Florida Sharks of USBL (May 4, 1995). ... Signed as free agent by Philadelphia 76ers (October 5, 1995). ... Waived by 76ers (October 13, 1995). ... Signed as free agent by Minnesota Timberwolves (December 5, 1995). ... Waived by Timberwolves (January 4, 1996).
MISCELLANEOUS: Member of bronze-medal-winning U.S. Olympic team (1988).

COLLEGIATE RECORD

NOTES: THE SPORTING NEWS All-America second team (1989).

Season Team	G	Min.	FGM	FGA	Pct.	FTM	FTA	Pct.	Reb.	Ast.	Pts.	RPG	APG	PPG
85-86—Georgetown	30	243	28	59	.475	34	45	.756	30	...	90	1.0	...	3.0
86-87—Georgetown	33	514	81	193	.420	40	62	.645	49	...	221	1.5	...	6.7
87-88—Georgetown	30	870	173	405	.427	77	100	.770	100	...	470	3.3	...	15.7
88-89—Georgetown	33	1111	222	446	.498	137	175	.783	118	...	617	3.6	...	18.7
Totals	126	2738	504	1103	.457	288	382	.754	297	...	1398	2.4	...	11.1

Three-point field goals: 1986-87, 19-for-50 (.380). 1987-88, 47-for-136 (.346). 1988-89, 36-for-89 (.404). Totals, 102-for-275 (.371).

NBA REGULAR-SEASON RECORD

Season Team	G	Min.	FGM	FGA	Pct.	FTM	FTA	Pct.	Off.	Def.	Tot.	Ast.	St.	Blk.	TO	Pts.	RPG	APG	PPG
89-90—Boston	60	519	59	133	.444	53	76	.697	14	55	69	103	35	3	36	171	1.2	1.7	2.9
90-91—Boston	5	30	3	7	.429	3	5	.600	0	2	2	6	1	0	3	9	0.4	1.2	1.8
95-96—Minnesota	8	39	3	10	.300	0	2	.000	0	5	5	6	1	0	5	6	0.6	0.8	0.8
Totals	73	588	65	150	.433	56	83	.675	14	62	76	115	37	3	44	186	1.0	1.6	2.5

Three-point field goals: 1989-90, 0-for-7. 1995-96, 0-for-3. Totals, 0-for-10.
Personal fouls/disqualifications: 1989-90, 75/0. 1990-91, 7/0. 1995-96, 7/0. Totals, 89/0.

NBA PLAYOFF RECORD

Season Team	G	Min.	FGM	FGA	Pct.	FTM	FTA	Pct.	Off.	Def.	Tot.	Ast.	St.	Blk.	TO	Pts.	RPG	APG	PPG
89-90—Boston	3	9	1	2	.500	0	0	...	1	0	1	3	1	0	0	2	0.3	1.0	0.7

CBA REGULAR-SEASON RECORD

Season Team	G	Min.	FGM	FGA	Pct.	FTM	FTA	Pct.	Reb.	Ast.	Pts.	RPG	APG	PPG
90-91—R.C.-Rock.	20	412	48	95	.505	30	39	.769	59	101	127	3.0	5.1	6.4
94-95—Rock.-Hfrd.-Omaha	49	1518	240	490	.490	140	187	.749	212	308	669	4.3	6.3	13.7
95-96—Florida	43	1234	212	422	.502	137	170	.806	145	326	589	3.4	*7.6	13.7
Totals	112	3164	500	1007	.497	307	396	.775	416	735	1385	3.7	6.6	12.4

Three-point field goals: 1990-91, 1-for-2 (.500). 1994-95, 49-for-116 (.422). 1995-96, 28-for-75 (.373). Totals, 78-for-193 (.405).

SMITH, DOUG　　　　　　　　　　　F

PERSONAL: Born September 17, 1969, in Detroit. ... 6-10/220. ... Full name: Douglas Smith.
HIGH SCHOOL: MacKenzie (Detroit).
COLLEGE: Missouri.
TRANSACTIONS/CAREER NOTES: Selected by Dallas Mavericks in first round (sixth pick overall) of 1991 NBA Draft. ... Selected by Toronto Raptors from Mavericks in NBA expansion draft (June 24, 1995). ... Signed as unrestricted free agent by Boston Celtics (October 4, 1995). ... Waived by Celtics (July 30, 1996).

COLLEGIATE RECORD

NOTES: The Sporting News All-America second team (1990, 1991).

Season Team	G	Min.	FGM	FGA	Pct.	FTM	FTA	Pct.	Reb.	Ast.	Pts.	RPG	APG	PPG
87-88—Missouri	30	792	145	288	.503	48	75	.640	197	72	338	6.6	2.4	11.3
88-89—Missouri	36	975	217	455	.477	67	91	.736	250	88	502	6.9	2.4	13.9
89-90—Missouri	32	942	260	462	.563	115	161	.714	295	64	635	9.2	2.0	19.8
90-91—Missouri	30	1051	275	553	.497	156	190	.821	311	96	709	10.4	3.2	23.6
Totals	128	3760	897	1758	.510	386	517	.747	1053	320	2184	8.2	2.5	17.1

Three-point field goals: 1988-89, 1-for-4 (.250). 1989-90, 0-for-1. 1990-91, 3-for-18 (.167). Totals, 4-for-23 (.174).

NBA REGULAR-SEASON RECORD

Season Team	G	Min.	FGM	FGA	Pct.	FTM	FTA	Pct.	Off.	Def.	Tot.	Ast.	St.	Blk.	TO	Pts.	RPG	APG	PPG
91-92—Dallas	76	1707	291	702	.415	89	121	.736	129	262	391	129	62	34	97	671	5.1	1.7	8.8
92-93—Dallas	61	1524	289	666	.434	56	74	.757	96	232	328	104	48	52	115	634	5.4	1.7	10.4
93-94—Dallas	79	1684	295	678	.435	106	127	.835	114	235	349	119	82	38	93	698	4.4	1.5	8.8
94-95—Dallas	63	826	131	314	.417	57	75	.760	43	101	144	44	29	26	37	320	2.3	0.7	5.1
95-96—Boston	17	92	14	39	.359	5	8	.625	12	10	22	4	3	0	11	33	1.3	0.2	1.9
Totals	296	5833	1020	2399	.425	313	405	.773	394	840	1234	400	224	150	353	2356	4.2	1.4	8.0

Three-point field goals: 1991-92, 0-for-11. 1992-93, 0-for-4. 1993-94, 2-for-9 (.222). 1994-95, 1-for-12 (.083). Totals, 3-for-36 (.083).
Personal fouls/disqualifications: 1991-92, 259/5. 1992-93, 280/12. 1993-94, 287/3. 1994-95, 132/1. 1995-96, 21/0. Totals, 979/21.

SMITH, JOE　　　　　　　　　F　　　　　　　WARRIORS

PERSONAL: Born July 26, 1975, in Norfolk, Va. ... 6-10/225. ... Full name: Joseph Leynard Smith.
HIGH SCHOOL: Maury (Norfolk, Va.).
COLLEGE: Maryland.
TRANSACTIONS/CAREER NOTES: Selected after sophomore season by Golden State Warriors in first round (first pick overall) of 1995 NBA Draft.

COLLEGIATE RECORD

NOTES: Naismith Award winner (1995). ... The Sporting News All-America second team (1995).

Season Team	G	Min.	FGM	FGA	Pct.	FTM	FTA	Pct.	Reb.	Ast.	Pts.	RPG	APG	PPG
93-94—Maryland	30	988	206	395	.522	168	229	.734	321	25	582	10.7	0.8	19.4
94-95—Maryland	34	1110	245	424	.578	209	282	.741	362	40	708	10.6	1.2	20.8
Totals	64	2098	451	819	.551	377	511	.738	683	65	1290	10.7	1.0	20.2

Three-point field goals: 1993-94, 2-for-5 (.400). 1994-95, 9-for-21 (.429). Totals, 11-for-26 (.423).

NBA REGULAR-SEASON RECORD

HONORS: NBA All-Rookie first team (1996).

Season Team	G	Min.	FGM	FGA	Pct.	FTM	FTA	Pct.	Off.	Def.	Tot.	Ast.	St.	Blk.	TO	Pts.	RPG	APG	PPG
95-96—Golden State	82	2821	469	1024	.458	303	392	.773	300	417	717	79	85	134	138	1251	8.7	1.0	15.3

Three-point field goals: 1995-96, 10-for-28 (.357).
Personal fouls/disqualifications: 1995-96, 224/5.

SMITH, KENNY　　　　　　　　　G

PERSONAL: Born March 8, 1965, in Queens, N.Y. ... 6-3/170. ... Full name: Kenneth Smith.
HIGH SCHOOL: Archbishop Molloy (Briarwood, N.Y.).
COLLEGE: North Carolina.
TRANSACTIONS/CAREER NOTES: Selected by Sacramento Kings in first round (sixth pick overall) of 1987 NBA Draft. ... Traded by Kings with G Mike Williams to Atlanta Hawks for F Antoine Carr, G Sedric Toney and future draft considerations (February 13, 1990). ... Traded by Hawks with G Roy Marble to Houston Rockets for C Tim McCormick and G John Lucas (September 27, 1990). ... Rights renounced by Rockets (July 16, 1996).
MISCELLANEOUS: Member of NBA championship teams (1994, 1995).

COLLEGIATE RECORD

NOTES: The Sporting News All-America first team (1987).

Season Team	G	Min.	FGM	FGA	Pct.	FTM	FTA	Pct.	Reb.	Ast.	Pts.	RPG	APG	PPG
83-84—North Carolina	23	667	83	160	.519	44	55	.800	40	114	210	1.7	5.0	9.1
84-85—North Carolina	36	1350	173	334	.518	98	114	.860	92	235	444	2.6	6.5	12.3
85-86—North Carolina	34	1109	164	318	.516	80	99	.808	75	210	408	2.2	6.2	12.0
86-87—North Carolina	34	1092	208	414	.502	71	88	.807	76	209	574	2.2	6.1	16.9
Totals	127	4218	628	1226	.512	293	356	.823	283	768	1636	2.2	6.0	12.9

Three-point field goals: 1986-87, 87-for-213 (.408).

NBA REGULAR-SEASON RECORD

HONORS: NBA All-Rookie team (1988).

Season Team	G	Min.	FGM	FGA	Pct.	FTM	FTA	Pct.	REBOUNDS Off.	Def.	Tot.	Ast.	St.	Blk.	TO	Pts.	AVERAGES RPG	APG	PPG
87-88—Sacramento	61	2170	331	694	.477	167	204	.819	40	98	138	434	92	8	184	841	2.3	7.1	13.8
88-89—Sacramento	81	3145	547	1183	.462	263	357	.737	49	177	226	621	102	7	249	1403	2.8	7.7	17.3
89-90—Sac.-Atlanta	79	2421	378	811	.466	161	196	.821	18	139	157	445	79	8	169	943	2.0	5.6	11.9
90-91—Houston	78	2699	522	1003	.520	287	340	.844	36	127	163	554	106	11	237	1380	2.1	7.1	17.7
91-92—Houston	81	2735	432	910	.475	219	253	.866	34	143	177	562	104	7	227	1137	2.2	6.9	14.0
92-93—Houston	82	2422	387	744	.520	195	222	.878	28	132	160	446	80	7	163	1065	2.0	5.4	13.0
93-94—Houston	78	2209	341	711	.480	135	155	.871	24	114	138	327	59	4	126	906	1.8	4.2	11.6
94-95—Houston	81	2030	287	593	.484	126	148	.851	27	128	155	323	71	10	123	842	1.9	4.0	10.4
95-96—Houston	68	1617	201	464	.433	87	106	.821	21	75	96	245	47	3	100	580	1.4	3.6	8.5
Totals	689	21448	3426	7113	.482	1640	1981	.828	277	1133	1410	3957	740	65	1578	9097	2.0	5.7	13.2

Three-point field goals: 1987-88, 12-for-39 (.308). 1988-89, 46-for-128 (.359). 1989-90, 26-for-83 (.313). 1990-91, 49-for-135 (.363). 1991-92, 54-for-137 (.394). 1992-93, 96-for-219 (.438). 1993-94, 89-for-220 (.405). 1994-95, 142-for-331 (.429). 1995-96, 91-for-238 (.382). Totals, 605-for-1530 (.395).

Personal fouls/disqualifications: 1987-88, 140/1. 1988-89, 173/0. 1989-90, 143/0. 1990-91, 131/0. 1991-92, 112/0. 1992-93, 110/0. 1993-94, 121/0. 1994-95, 109/1. 1995-96, 116/1. Totals, 1155/3.

NBA PLAYOFF RECORD

NOTES: Holds NBA Finals single-game records for most three-point field goals made in one game—7; and most three-point field goals made in one quarter—5 (June 7, 1995, at Orlando). ... Shares NBA Finals single-game record for most three-point field goals made in one half—6 (June 7, 1995, at Orlando). ... Shares single-game playoff records for most three-point field goals in one half—6 (April 29, 1995, at Utah and June 7, 1995, at Orlando); and most three-point field goals in one quarter—5 (June 7, 1995, at Orlando).

Season Team	G	Min.	FGM	FGA	Pct.	FTM	FTA	Pct.	REBOUNDS Off.	Def.	Tot.	Ast.	St.	Blk.	TO	Pts.	AVERAGES RPG	APG	PPG
90-91—Houston	3	113	18	38	.474	8	9	.889	4	4	8	24	4	1	6	46	2.7	8.0	15.3
92-93—Houston	12	391	63	128	.492	28	36	.778	2	22	24	50	9	1	26	177	2.0	4.2	14.8
93-94—Houston	23	696	86	189	.455	42	52	.808	5	49	54	94	22	4	33	248	2.3	4.1	10.8
94-95—Houston	22	652	78	178	.438	36	40	.900	7	42	49	99	14	3	31	238	2.2	4.5	10.8
95-96—Houston	8	191	23	53	.434	13	13	1.000	4	8	12	38	5	0	8	71	1.5	4.8	8.9
Totals	68	2043	268	586	.457	127	150	.847	22	125	147	305	54	9	104	780	2.2	4.5	11.5

Three-point field goals: 1990-91, 2-for-4 (.500). 1992-93, 23-for-46 (.500). 1993-94, 34-for-76 (.447). 1994-95, 46-for-104 (.442). 1995-96, 12-for-31 (.387). Totals, 117-for-261 (.448).

Personal fouls/disqualifications: 1990-91, 5/0. 1992-93, 18/0. 1993-94, 40/0. 1994-95, 46/0. 1995-96, 14/0. Totals, 123/0.

SMITH, MICHAEL   F   KINGS

PERSONAL: Born March 28, 1972, in Washington, D.C. ... 6-8/230. ... Full name: Michael John Smith.
HIGH SCHOOL: Dunbar (Washington, D.C.).
COLLEGE: Providence.
TRANSACTIONS/CAREER NOTES: Selected by Sacramento Kings in second round (35th pick overall) of 1994 NBA Draft.

COLLEGIATE RECORD

Season Team	G	Min.	FGM	FGA	Pct.	FTM	FTA	Pct.	Reb.	Ast.	Pts.	AVERAGES RPG	APG	PPG
90-91—Providence						Did not play—ineligible.								
91-92—Providence	31	876	108	218	.495	117	202	.579	319	41	333	10.3	1.3	10.7
92-93—Providence	33	976	125	243	.514	119	218	.546	375	38	389	11.4	1.2	11.8
93-94—Providence	30	872	144	238	.605	100	140	.714	344	25	388	11.5	0.8	12.9
Totals	94	2724	377	699	.539	336	560	.600	1038	104	1110	11.0	1.1	11.8

Three-point field goals: 1991-92, 0-for-1. 1993-94, 0-for-1. Totals, 0-for-2.

NBA REGULAR-SEASON RECORD

Season Team	G	Min.	FGM	FGA	Pct.	FTM	FTA	Pct.	REBOUNDS Off.	Def.	Tot.	Ast.	St.	Blk.	TO	Pts.	AVERAGES RPG	APG	PPG
94-95—Sacramento	82	1736	220	406	.542	127	262	.485	174	312	486	67	61	49	106	567	5.9	0.8	6.9
95-96—Sacramento	65	1384	144	238	.605	68	177	.384	143	246	389	110	47	46	72	357	6.0	1.7	5.5
Totals	147	3120	364	644	.565	195	439	.444	317	558	875	177	108	95	178	924	6.0	1.2	6.3

Three-point field goals: 1994-95, 0-for-2. 1995-96, 1-for-3. Totals, 1-for-3 (.333).
Personal fouls/disqualifications: 1994-95, 235/1. 1995-96, 166/0. Totals, 401/1.

NBA PLAYOFF RECORD

Season Team	G	Min.	FGM	FGA	Pct.	FTM	FTA	Pct.	REBOUNDS Off.	Def.	Tot.	Ast.	St.	Blk.	TO	Pts.	AVERAGES RPG	APG	PPG
95-96—Sacramento	4	87	7	12	.583	5	11	.455	7	15	22	8	1	2	2	19	5.5	2.0	4.8

Personal fouls/disqualifications: 1995-96, 14/0.

SMITH, STEVE   G   HAWKS

PERSONAL: Born March 31, 1969, in Highland Park, Mich. ... 6-8/215. ... Full name: Steven Delano Smith.
HIGH SCHOOL: Pershing (Detroit).
COLLEGE: Michigan State.
TRANSACTIONS/CAREER NOTES: Selected by Miami Heat in first round (fifth pick overall) of 1991 NBA Draft. ... Traded by Heat with F Grant Long and conditional second-round draft choice to Atlanta Hawks for F Kevin Willis and conditional first-round draft choice (November 7, 1994).

COLLEGIATE RECORD

NOTES: THE SPORTING NEWS All-America first team (1990, 1991).

Season Team	G	Min.	FGM	FGA	Pct.	FTM	FTA	Pct.	Reb.	Ast.	Pts.	RPG	APG	PPG
87-88—Michigan State	28	812	108	232	.466	69	91	.758	112	82	299	4.0	2.9	10.7
88-89—Michigan State	33	1168	217	454	.478	129	169	.763	229	112	585	6.9	3.4	17.7
89-90—Michigan State	31	1081	233	443	.526	116	167	.695	216	150	627	7.0	4.8	20.2
90-91—Michigan State	30	1134	268	566	.474	150	187	.802	183	109	752	6.1	3.6	25.1
Totals	122	4195	826	1695	.487	464	614	.756	740	453	2263	6.1	3.7	18.5

Three-point field goals: 1987-88, 14-for-30 (.467). 1988-89, 22-for-63 (.349). 1989-90, 45-for-98 (.459). 1990-91, 66-for-162 (.407). Totals, 147-for-353 (.416).

NBA REGULAR-SEASON RECORD

HONORS: NBA All-Rookie first team (1992).

Season Team	G	Min.	FGM	FGA	Pct.	FTM	FTA	Pct.	Off.	Def.	Tot.	Ast.	St.	Blk.	TO	Pts.	RPG	APG	PPG
91-92—Miami	61	1806	297	654	.454	95	127	.748	81	107	188	278	59	19	152	729	3.1	4.6	12.0
92-93—Miami	48	1610	279	619	.451	155	197	.787	56	141	197	267	50	16	129	766	4.1	5.6	16.0
93-94—Miami	78	2776	491	1076	.456	273	327	.835	156	196	352	394	84	35	202	1346	4.5	5.1	17.3
94-95—Miami-Atlanta	80	2665	428	1005	.426	312	371	.841	104	172	276	274	62	33	155	1305	3.5	3.4	16.3
95-96—Atlanta	80	2856	494	1143	.432	318	385	.826	124	202	326	224	68	17	151	1446	4.1	2.8	18.1
Totals	347	11713	1989	4497	.442	1153	1407	.819	521	818	1339	1437	323	120	789	5592	3.9	4.1	16.1

Three-point field goals: 1991-92, 40-for-125 (.320). 1992-93, 53-for-132 (.402). 1993-94, 91-for-262 (.347). 1994-95, 137-for-416 (.329). 1995-96, 140-for-423 (.331). Totals, 461-for-1358 (.339).

Personal fouls/disqualifications: 1991-92, 162/1. 1992-93, 148/3. 1993-94, 217/6. 1994-95, 225/2. 1995-96, 207/1. Totals, 959/13.

NBA PLAYOFF RECORD

Season Team	G	Min.	FGM	FGA	Pct.	FTM	FTA	Pct.	Off.	Def.	Tot.	Ast.	St.	Blk.	TO	Pts.	RPG	APG	PPG
91-92—Miami	3	100	18	34	.529	5	6	.833	3	3	6	15	4	1	3	48	2.0	5.0	16.0
93-94—Miami	5	192	33	80	.413	21	25	.840	17	13	30	11	4	2	10	96	6.0	2.2	19.2
94-95—Atlanta	3	108	17	43	.395	16	19	.842	1	7	8	6	6	1	3	57	2.7	2.0	19.0
95-96—Atlanta	10	421	75	171	.439	42	52	.808	15	26	41	32	13	13	16	217	4.1	3.2	21.7
Totals	21	821	143	328	.436	84	102	.824	36	49	85	64	27	17	32	418	4.0	3.0	19.9

Three-point field goals: 1991-92, 7-for-11 (.636). 1993-94, 9-for-22 (.409). 1994-95, 7-for-18 (.389). 1995-96, 25-for-61 (.410). Totals, 48-for-112 (.429).

Personal fouls/disqualifications: 1991-92, 2/0. 1993-94, 12/0. 1994-95, 14/0. 1995-96, 31/0. Totals, 59/0.

SMITH, TONY   G

PERSONAL: Born June 14, 1968, in Wauwatosa, Wis. ... 6-4/205. ... Full name: Charles Anton Smith.
HIGH SCHOOL: East (Wauwatosa, Wis.).
COLLEGE: Marquette.
TRANSACTIONS/CAREER NOTES: Selected by Los Angeles Lakers in second round (51st pick overall) of 1990 NBA Draft. ... Signed as unrestricted free agent by Phoenix Suns (November 1, 1995). ... Traded by Suns to Miami Heat for G Terrence Rencher (February 22, 1996). ... Rights renounced by Heat (July 17, 1996).

COLLEGIATE RECORD

Season Team	G	Min.	FGM	FGA	Pct.	FTM	FTA	Pct.	Reb.	Ast.	Pts.	RPG	APG	PPG
86-87—Marquette	29	722	86	161	.534	61	81	.753	96	62	234	3.3	2.1	8.1
87-88—Marquette	28	894	136	260	.523	88	119	.740	126	82	367	4.5	2.9	13.1
88-89—Marquette	28	943	153	275	.556	84	115	.730	109	158	398	3.9	5.6	14.2
89-90—Marquette	29	1131	240	485	.495	173	202	.856	137	167	689	4.7	5.8	23.8
Totals	114	3690	615	1181	.521	406	517	.785	468	469	1688	4.1	4.1	14.8

Three-point field goals: 1986-87, 1-for-3 (.333). 1987-88, 7-for-19 (.368). 1988-89, 8-for-12 (.667). 1989-90, 36-for-87 (.414). Totals, 52-for-121 (.430).

NBA REGULAR-SEASON RECORD

Season Team	G	Min.	FGM	FGA	Pct.	FTM	FTA	Pct.	Off.	Def.	Tot.	Ast.	St.	Blk.	TO	Pts.	RPG	APG	PPG
90-91—L.A. Lakers	64	695	97	220	.441	40	57	.702	24	47	71	135	28	12	69	234	1.1	2.1	3.7
91-92—L.A. Lakers	63	820	113	283	.399	49	75	.653	31	45	76	109	39	8	50	275	1.2	1.7	4.4
92-93—L.A. Lakers	55	752	133	275	.484	62	82	.756	46	41	87	63	50	7	40	330	1.6	1.1	6.0
93-94—L.A. Lakers	73	1617	272	617	.441	85	119	.714	106	89	195	148	59	14	76	645	2.7	2.0	8.8
94-95—L.A. Lakers	61	1024	132	309	.427	44	63	.698	43	64	107	102	46	7	50	340	1.8	1.7	5.6
95-96—Phoe.-Mia.	59	938	116	274	.423	28	46	.609	30	65	95	154	37	10	66	298	1.6	2.6	5.1
Totals	375	5846	863	1978	.436	308	442	.697	280	351	631	711	259	58	351	2122	1.7	1.9	5.7

Three-point field goals: 1990-91, 0-for-7. 1991-92, 0-for-11. 1992-93, 2-for-11 (.182). 1993-94, 16-for-50 (.320). 1994-95, 32-for-91 (.352). 1995-96, 38-for-116 (.328). Totals, 88-for-286 (.308).

Personal fouls/disqualifications: 1990-91, 80/0. 1991-92, 91/0. 1992-93, 72/1. 1993-94, 128/1. 1994-95, 111/0. 1995-96, 106/2. Totals, 588/4.

NBA PLAYOFF RECORD

Season Team	G	Min.	FGM	FGA	Pct.	FTM	FTA	Pct.	Off.	Def.	Tot.	Ast.	St.	Blk.	TO	Pts.	RPG	APG	PPG
90-91—L.A. Lakers	7	40	6	13	.462	2	3	.667	3	0	3	2	1	0	6	14	0.4	0.3	2.0
91-92—L.A. Lakers	4	40	3	10	.300	1	2	.500	1	1	2	5	4	0	3	7	0.5	1.3	1.8
92-93—L.A. Lakers	5	73	13	25	.520	6	9	.667	5	3	8	2	1	1	3	34	1.6	0.4	6.8
94-95—L.A. Lakers	6	27	3	13	.231	0	2	.000	1	2	3	3	0	0	4	9	0.5	0.5	1.5
95-96—Miami	3	61	9	19	.474	0	0	...	3	1	4	8	4	0	3	22	1.3	2.7	7.3
Totals	25	241	34	80	.425	9	16	.563	13	7	20	20	10	1	19	86	0.8	0.8	3.4

Three-point field goals: 1991-92, 0-for-2. 1992-93, 2-for-4 (.500). 1994-95, 3-for-10 (.300). 1995-96, 4-for-10 (.400). Totals, 9-for-26 (.346).

Personal fouls/disqualifications: 1990-91, 6/1. 1991-92, 5/0. 1992-93, 14/0. 1994-95, 1/0. 1995-96, 7/0. Totals, 33/1.

SMITS, RIK   C   PACERS

PERSONAL: Born August 23, 1966, in Eindhoven, Holland. ... 7-4/265.
HIGH SCHOOL: Almonta (Eindhoven, Holland).
COLLEGE: Marist (N.Y.).
TRANSACTIONS/CAREER NOTES: Selected by Indiana Pacers in first round (second pick overall) of 1988 NBA Draft.

COLLEGIATE RECORD

Season Team	G	Min.	FGM	FGA	Pct.	FTM	FTA	Pct.	Reb.	Ast.	Pts.	RPG	APG	PPG
84-85—Marist	29	776	132	233	.567	60	104	.577	162	5	324	5.6	0.2	11.2
85-86—Marist	30	870	216	347	.622	98	144	.681	242	8	530	8.1	0.3	17.7
86-87—Marist	21	634	157	258	.609	109	151	.722	171	16	423	8.1	0.8	20.1
87-88—Marist	27	861	251	403	.623	166	226	.735	236	17	668	8.7	0.6	24.7
Totals	107	3141	756	1241	.609	433	625	.693	811	46	1945	7.6	0.4	18.2

Three-point field goals: 1987-88, 0-for-2.

NBA REGULAR-SEASON RECORD

HONORS: NBA All-Rookie first team (1989).
NOTES: Led NBA with 328 personal fouls (1990) and 14 disqualifications (1989). ... Tied for NBA lead with 11 disqualifications (1990).

Season Team	G	Min.	FGM	FGA	Pct.	FTM	FTA	Pct.	Off.	Def.	Tot.	Ast.	St.	Blk.	TO	Pts.	RPG	APG	PPG
88-89—Indiana	82	2041	386	746	.517	184	255	.722	185	315	500	70	37	151	130	956	6.1	0.9	11.7
89-90—Indiana	82	2404	515	967	.533	241	297	.811	135	377	512	142	45	169	143	1271	6.2	1.7	15.5
90-91—Indiana	76	1690	342	705	.485	144	189	.762	116	241	357	84	24	111	86	828	4.7	1.1	10.9
91-92—Indiana	74	1772	436	855	.510	152	193	.788	124	293	417	116	29	100	130	1024	5.6	1.6	13.8
92-93—Indiana	81	2072	494	1017	.486	167	228	.732	126	306	432	121	27	75	147	1155	5.3	1.5	14.3
93-94—Indiana	78	2113	493	923	.534	238	300	.793	135	348	483	156	49	82	151	1224	6.2	2.0	15.7
94-95—Indiana	78	2381	558	1060	.526	284	377	.753	192	409	601	111	40	79	189	1400	7.7	1.4	17.9
95-96—Indiana	63	1901	466	894	.521	231	293	.788	119	314	433	110	21	45	160	1164	6.9	1.7	18.5
Totals	614	16374	3690	7167	.515	1641	2132	.770	1132	2603	3735	910	272	812	1136	9022	6.1	1.5	14.7

Three-point field goals: 1988-89, 0-for-1. 1989-90, 0-for-1. 1991-92, 0-for-2. 1993-94, 0-for-1. 1994-95, 0-for-2. 1995-96, 1-for-5 (.200). Totals, 1-for-12 (.083).
Personal fouls/disqualifications: 1988-89, 310/14. 1989-90, 328/11. 1990-91, 246/3. 1991-92, 231/4. 1992-93, 285/5. 1993-94, 281/11. 1994-95, 278/6. 1995-96, 226/5. Totals, 2185/59.

NBA PLAYOFF RECORD

Season Team	G	Min.	FGM	FGA	Pct.	FTM	FTA	Pct.	Off.	Def.	Tot.	Ast.	St.	Blk.	TO	Pts.	RPG	APG	PPG
89-90—Indiana	3	96	14	28	.500	9	11	.818	4	12	16	3	2	4	5	37	5.3	1.0	12.3
90-91—Indiana	5	88	21	37	.568	7	8	.875	4	14	18	2	1	7	5	49	3.6	0.4	9.8
91-92—Indiana	3	28	4	11	.364	2	2	1.000	3	3	6	0	2	1	3	10	2.0	0.3	3.3
92-93—Indiana	4	143	37	64	.578	16	22	.727	13	19	32	7	5	4	8	90	8.0	1.8	22.5
93-94—Indiana	16	450	103	218	.472	50	62	.806	23	61	84	31	10	9	43	256	5.3	1.9	16.0
94-95—Indiana	17	546	127	232	.547	86	107	.804	32	87	119	34	5	14	34	341	7.0	2.0	20.1
95-96—Indiana	5	166	42	77	.545	11	14	.786	13	24	37	8	2	2	14	95	7.4	1.6	19.0
Totals	53	1517	348	667	.522	181	226	.801	92	220	312	85	27	41	112	878	5.9	1.6	16.6

Three-point field goals: 1992-93, 0-for-1. 1994-95, 1-for-1. Totals, 1-for-2 (.500).
Personal fouls/disqualifications: 1989-90, 12/0. 1990-91, 23/1. 1991-92, 7/0. 1992-93, 18/1. 1993-94, 64/1. 1994-95, 73/2. 1995-96, 20/1. Totals, 217/6.

SNOW, ERIC   G   SUPERSONICS

PERSONAL: Born April 24, 1973, in Canton, Ohio. ... 6-3/200. ... Brother of Percy Snow, linebacker, Kansas City Chiefs and Chicago Bears (1990, 1992 and 1993).
HIGH SCHOOL: McKinley (Canton, Ohio).
COLLEGE: Michigan State.
TRANSACTIONS/CAREER NOTES: Selected by Milwaukee Bucks in second round (43rd pick overall) of 1995 NBA Draft. ... Draft rights traded by Bucks to Seattle SuperSonics for draft rights to C Aurelijius Zukauskas and 1996 second-round draft choice (June 28, 1995).

COLLEGIATE RECORD

Season Team	G	Min.	FGM	FGA	Pct.	FTM	FTA	Pct.	Reb.	Ast.	Pts.	RPG	APG	PPG
91-92—Michigan State	25	144	12	25	.480	3	15	.200	15	24	27	0.6	1.0	1.1
92-93—Michigan State	28	798	53	97	.546	15	56	.268	73	145	121	2.6	5.2	4.3
93-94—Michigan State	32	992	91	177	.514	22	49	.449	111	213	217	3.5	6.7	6.8
94-95—Michigan State	28	916	117	225	.520	62	102	.608	92	217	303	3.3	7.8	10.8
Totals	113	2850	273	524	.521	102	222	.459	291	599	668	2.6	5.3	5.9

Three-point field goals: 1991-92, 0-for-2. 1992-93, 0-for-5. 1993-94, 13-for-45 (.289). 1994-95, 7-for-24 (.292). Totals, 20-for-76 (.263).

NBA REGULAR-SEASON RECORD

Season Team	G	Min.	FGM	FGA	Pct.	FTM	FTA	Pct.	Off.	Def.	Tot.	Ast.	St.	Blk.	TO	Pts.	RPG	APG	PPG
95-96—Seattle	43	389	42	100	.420	29	49	.592	9	34	43	73	28	0	38	115	1.0	1.7	2.7

Three-point field goals: 1995-96, 2-for-10 (.200).
Personal fouls/disqualifications: 1995-96, 53/0.

NBA PLAYOFF RECORD

Season Team	G	Min.	FGM	FGA	Pct.	FTM	FTA	Pct.	Off.	Def.	Tot.	Ast.	St.	Blk.	TO	Pts.	RPG	APG	PPG
95-96—Seattle	10	24	1	7	.143	0	0	...	0	4	4	6	2	0	4	2	0.4	0.6	0.2

Three-point field goals: 1995-96, 0-for-0.
Personal fouls/disqualifications: 1995-96, 3/0.

SPENCER, ELMORE   C

PERSONAL: Born December 6, 1969, in Atlanta. ... 7-0/270.
HIGH SCHOOL: Booker T. Washington (Atlanta).
JUNIOR COLLEGE: Connors State Junior College (Okla.), then Clark County Community College (Nev.), did not play basketball.
COLLEGE: Georgia, then UNLV.
TRANSACTIONS/CAREER NOTES: Selected by Los Angeles Clippers in first round (25th pick overall) of 1992 NBA Draft. ... Traded by Clippers to Denver Nuggets for F Brian Williams (September 19, 1995). ... Waived by Nuggets (December 21, 1995). ... Signed as free agent by Portland Trail Blazers for remainder of season (January 10, 1996). ... Rights renounced by Trail Blazers (July 23, 1996).

COLLEGIATE RECORD

Season Team	G	Min.	FGM	FGA	Pct.	FTM	FTA	Pct.	Reb.	Ast.	Pts.	RPG	APG	PPG
87-88—Georgia								Did not play.						
88-89—Georgia	11	304	59	92	.641	14	28	.500	58	21	132	5.3	1.9	12.0
89-90—Connors State J.C.	...	...	...	...	...	...	...	...	...	...	...	...	...	20.0
90-91—UNLV	31	535	82	157	.522	33	70	.471	124	38	197	4.0	1.2	6.4
91-92—UNLV	28	855	174	273	.637	65	119	.546	228	47	413	8.1	1.7	14.8
Junior college totals	...	...	...	...	...	...	...	...	...	...	...	...	...	20.0
4-year-college totals	70	1694	315	522	.603	112	217	.516	410	106	742	5.9	1.5	10.6

Three-point field goals: 1988-89, 0-for-1. 1991-92, 0-for-2. Totals, 0-for-3.

NBA REGULAR-SEASON RECORD

Season Team	G	Min.	FGM	FGA	Pct.	FTM	FTA	Pct.	Off.	Def.	Tot.	Ast.	St.	Blk.	TO	Pts.	RPG	APG	PPG
92-93—L.A. Clippers	44	280	44	82	.537	16	32	.500	17	45	62	8	8	18	26	104	1.4	0.2	2.4
93-94—L.A. Clippers	76	1930	288	540	.533	97	162	.599	96	319	415	75	30	127	168	673	5.5	1.0	8.9
94-95—L.A. Clippers	19	368	52	118	.441	28	50	.560	11	54	65	25	14	23	48	132	3.4	1.3	6.9
95-96—Den.-Port.	17	58	5	13	.385	4	6	.667	3	10	13	1	0	2	6	14	0.8	0.1	0.8
Totals	156	2636	389	753	.517	145	250	.580	127	428	555	109	52	170	248	923	3.6	0.7	5.9

Three-point field goals: 1993-94, 0-for-2. 1994-95, 0-for-1. Totals, 0-for-3.
Personal fouls/disqualifications: 1992-93, 54/0. 1993-94, 208/3. 1994-95, 62/0. 1995-96, 12/1. Totals, 336/4.

NBA PLAYOFF RECORD

Season Team	G	Min.	FGM	FGA	Pct.	FTM	FTA	Pct.	Off.	Def.	Tot.	Ast.	St.	Blk.	TO	Pts.	RPG	APG	PPG
92-93—L.A. Clippers	2	4	0	2	.000	0	0	...	1	0	1	0	0	0	0	0	0.5	0.0	0.0
95-96—Portland	1	1	0	0	...	0	2	.000	0	0	0	0	0	0	0	0	0.0	0.0	0.0
Totals	3	5	0	2	.000	0	2	.000	1	0	1	0	0	0	0	0	0.3	0.0	0.0

Personal fouls/disqualifications: 1992-93, 1/0.

SPENCER, FELTON   C   MAGIC

PERSONAL: Born January 5, 1968, in Louisville, Ky. ... 7-0/265. ... Full name: Felton LaFrance Spencer.
HIGH SCHOOL: Eastern (Middletown, Ky.).
COLLEGE: Louisville.
TRANSACTIONS/CAREER NOTES: Selected by Minnesota Timberwolves in first round (sixth pick overall) of 1990 NBA Draft. ... Traded by Timberwolves to Utah Jazz for F Mike Brown (June 30, 1993). ... Traded by Jazz to Orlando Magic for G Brooks Thompson, F Kenny Gattison and undisclosed first-round draft choice (August 9, 1996).
MISCELLANEOUS: Minnesota Timberwolves all-time blocked shots leader with 266 (1990-91 through 1992-93).

COLLEGIATE RECORD

Season Team	G	Min.	FGM	FGA	Pct.	FTM	FTA	Pct.	Reb.	Ast.	Pts.	RPG	APG	PPG
86-87—Louisville	31	356	43	78	.551	32	65	.492	83	12	118	2.7	0.4	3.8
87-88—Louisville	35	532	93	157	.592	73	114	.640	146	18	259	4.2	0.5	7.4
88-89—Louisville	33	581	85	140	.607	99	135	.733	169	20	269	5.1	0.6	8.2
89-90—Louisville	35	995	188	276	.681	146	204	.716	296	45	522	8.5	1.3	14.9
Totals	134	2464	409	651	.628	350	518	.676	694	95	1168	5.2	0.7	8.7

HONORS: NBA All-Rookie second team (1991).

NBA REGULAR-SEASON RECORD

Season Team	G	Min.	FGM	FGA	Pct.	FTM	FTA	Pct.	Off.	Def.	Tot.	Ast.	St.	Blk.	TO	Pts.	RPG	APG	PPG
90-91—Minnesota	81	2099	195	381	.512	182	252	.722	272	369	641	25	48	121	77	572	7.9	0.3	7.1
91-92—Minnesota	61	1481	141	331	.426	123	178	.691	167	268	435	53	27	79	70	405	7.1	0.9	6.6
92-93—Minnesota	71	1296	105	226	.465	83	127	.654	134	190	324	17	23	66	70	293	4.6	0.2	4.1
93-94—Utah	79	2210	256	507	.505	165	272	.607	235	423	658	43	41	67	127	677	8.3	0.5	8.6
94-95—Utah	34	905	105	215	.488	107	135	.793	90	170	260	17	12	32	68	317	7.6	0.5	9.3
95-96—Utah	71	1267	146	281	.520	104	151	.689	100	206	306	11	20	54	77	396	4.3	0.2	5.6
Totals	397	9258	948	1941	.488	764	1115	.685	998	1626	2624	166	171	419	489	2660	6.6	0.4	6.7

Three-point field goals: 1990-91, 0-for-1.
Personal fouls/disqualifications: 1990-91, 337/14. 1991-92, 241/7. 1992-93, 243/10. 1993-94, 304/5. 1994-95, 131/3. 1995-96, 240/1. Totals, 1496/40.

NBA PLAYOFF RECORD

Season Team	G	Min.	FGM	FGA	Pct.	FTM	FTA	Pct.	Off.	Def.	Tot.	Ast.	St.	Blk.	TO	Pts.	RPG	APG	PPG
93-94—Utah	16	492	47	105	.448	33	50	.660	61	74	135	7	3	20	24	127	8.4	0.4	7.9
95-96—Utah	18	276	23	53	.434	5	9	.556	26	28	54	2	5	22	19	51	3.0	0.1	2.8
Totals	34	768	70	158	.443	38	59	.644	87	102	189	9	8	42	43	178	5.6	0.3	5.2

Three-point field goals: 1995-96, 0-for-1.
Personal fouls/disqualifications: 1993-94, 73/3. 1995-96, 58/0. Totals, 131/3.

PERSONAL: Born September 8, 1970, in Milwaukee. ... 6-5/190. ... Full name: Latrell Fontaine Sprewell. ... Name pronounced lah-TRELL SPREE-well.
HIGH SCHOOL: Washington (Milwaukee).
JUNIOR COLLEGE: Three Rivers Community College (Mo.).
COLLEGE: Alabama.
TRANSACTIONS/CAREER NOTES: Selected by Golden State Warriors in first round (24th pick overall) of 1992 NBA Draft.

COLLEGIATE RECORD

Season Team	G	Min.	FGM	FGA	Pct.	FTM	FTA	Pct.	Reb.	Ast.	Pts.	AVERAGES RPG	APG	PPG
88-89—Three Rivers C.C.	26	...	169	327	.517	88	133	.662	218	45	429	8.4	1.7	16.5
89-90—Three Rivers C.C.	40	...	421	827	.509	217	281	.772	365	81	1064	9.1	2.0	26.6
90-91—Alabama	33	865	116	217	.535	58	84	.690	165	62	295	5.0	1.9	8.9
91-92—Alabama	35	1266	227	460	.493	101	131	.771	183	74	623	5.2	2.1	17.8
Junior college totals	66	...	590	1154	.511	305	414	.737	583	126	1493	8.8	1.9	22.6
4-year-college totals	68	2131	343	677	.507	159	215	.740	348	136	918	5.1	2.0	13.5

Three-point field goals: 1990-91, 5-for-12 (.417). 1991-92, 68-for-171 (.398). Totals, 73-for-183 (.399).

NBA REGULAR-SEASON RECORD

HONORS: All-NBA first team (1994). ... NBA All-Defensive second team (1994). ... NBA All-Rookie second team (1993).

Season Team	G	Min.	FGM	FGA	Pct.	FTM	FTA	Pct.	REBOUNDS Off.	Def.	Tot.	Ast.	St.	Blk.	TO	Pts.	AVERAGES RPG	APG	PPG
92-93—Golden State...	77	2741	449	968	.464	211	283	.746	79	192	271	295	126	52	203	1182	3.5	3.8	15.4
93-94—Golden State...	82	*3533	613	1417	.433	353	456	.774	80	321	401	385	180	76	226	1720	4.9	4.7	21.0
94-95—Golden State...	69	2771	490	1171	.418	350	448	.781	58	198	256	279	112	46	230	1420	3.7	4.0	20.6
95-96—Golden State...	78	3064	515	1202	.428	352	446	.789	124	256	380	328	127	45	222	1473	4.9	4.2	18.9
Totals	306	12109	2067	4758	.434	1266	1633	.775	341	967	1308	1287	545	219	881	5795	4.3	4.2	18.9

Three-point field goals: 1992-93, 73-for-198 (.369). 1993-94, 141-for-391 (.361). 1994-95, 90-for-326 (.276). 1995-96, 91-for-282 (.323). Totals, 395-for-1197 (.330).
Personal fouls/disqualifications: 1992-93, 166/2. 1993-94, 158/0. 1994-95, 108/0. 1995-96, 150/1. Totals, 582/3.

NBA PLAYOFF RECORD

Season Team	G	Min.	FGM	FGA	Pct.	FTM	FTA	Pct.	REBOUNDS Off.	Def.	Tot.	Ast.	St.	Blk.	TO	Pts.	AVERAGES RPG	APG	PPG
93-94—Golden State...	3	122	26	60	.433	8	12	.667	1	8	9	21	2	3	9	68	3.0	7.0	22.7

Three-point field goals: 1993-94, 8-for-23 (.348).
Personal fouls/disqualifications: 1993-94, 15/0.

NBA ALL-STAR GAME RECORD

Season Team	Min.	FGM	FGA	Pct.	FTM	FTA	Pct.	REBOUNDS Off.	Def.	Tot.	Ast.	PF	Dq.	St.	Blk.	TO	Pts.
1994 —Golden State......	15	3	8	.375	3	7	.429	4	3	7	1	1	0	0	0	2	9
1995 —Golden State......	22	4	9	.444	1	1	1.000	2	2	4	4	0	0	3	0	1	9
Totals..........................	37	7	17	.412	4	8	.500	6	5	11	5	1	0	3	0	3	18

Three-point field goals: 1994, 0-for-2. 1995, 0-for-2. Totals, 0-for-4.

STACKHOUSE, JERRY G/F 76ERS

PERSONAL: Born November 5, 1974, in Kinston, N.C. ... 6-6/218. ... Full name: Jerry Darnell Stackhouse.
HIGH SCHOOL: Kinston (N.C.), then Oak Hill Academy (Mouth of Wilson, Va.).
COLLEGE: North Carolina.
TRANSACTIONS/CAREER NOTES: Selected after sophomore season by Philadelphia 76ers in first round (third pick overall) of 1995 NBA Draft.

COLLEGIATE RECORD

NOTES: THE SPORTING NEWS All-America second team (1995).

Season Team	G	Min.	FGM	FGA	Pct.	FTM	FTA	Pct.	Reb.	Ast.	Pts.	AVERAGES RPG	APG	PPG
93-94—North Carolina...............	35	734	138	296	.466	150	205	.732	176	69	428	5.0	2.0	12.2
94-95—North Carolina...............	34	1170	215	416	.517	185	260	.712	280	93	652	8.2	2.7	19.2
Totals	69	1904	353	712	.496	335	465	.720	456	162	1080	6.6	2.3	15.7

Three-point field goals: 1993-94, 2-for-20 (.100). 1994-95, 37-for-90 (.411). Totals, 39-for-110 (.355).

NBA REGULAR-SEASON RECORD

HONORS: NBA All-Rookie first team (1996).

Season Team	G	Min.	FGM	FGA	Pct.	FTM	FTA	Pct.	REBOUNDS Off.	Def.	Tot.	Ast.	St.	Blk.	TO	Pts.	AVERAGES RPG	APG	PPG
95-96—Philadelphia....	72	2701	452	1091	.414	387	518	.747	90	175	265	278	76	79	252	1384	3.7	3.9	19.2

Three-point field goals: 1995-96, 93-for-292 (.318).
Personal fouls/disqualifications: 1995-96, 179/0.

STARKS, JOHN G KNICKS

PERSONAL: Born August 10, 1965, in Tulsa, Okla. ... 6-5/185. ... Full name: John Levell Starks.
HIGH SCHOOL: Tulsa (Okla.) Central.
JUNIOR COLLEGE: Northern Oklahoma College, then Rogers State (Okla.), then Oklahoma Junior College.
COLLEGE: Oklahoma State.
TRANSACTIONS/CAREER NOTES: Not drafted by an NBA franchise. ... Signed as free agent by Golden State Warriors (September 29, 1988). ... Rights renounced by Warriors (June 16, 1989). ... Played in Continental Basketball Association with Cedar Rapids Silver Bullets (1989-90). ... Played in World Basketball League with Memphis Rockers (1990). ... Signed as unrestricted free agent by New York Knicks (October 1, 1990).

COLLEGIATE RECORD

Season Team	G	Min.	FGM	FGA	Pct.	FTM	FTA	Pct.	Reb.	Ast.	Pts.	RPG	APG	PPG
84-85—North. Oklahoma Coll.....	14	...	57	123	.463	41	53	.774	33	...	155	2.4	...	11.1
85-86—Rogers State College......						Statistics unavailable.								
86-87—Oklahoma J.C.						Statistics unavailable.								
87-88—Oklahoma State	30	982	154	310	.497	114	136	.838	141	137	463	4.7	4.6	15.4
Junior college totals	14	...	57	123	.463	41	53	.774	33	...	155	2.4	...	11.1
4-year-college totals	30	982	154	310	.497	114	136	.838	141	137	463	4.7	4.6	15.4

Three-point field goals: 1987-88, 41-for-108 (.380).

NBA REGULAR-SEASON RECORD

RECORDS: Shares single-game record for most three-point field goals made in one half—7 (November 22, 1993, vs. Miami).
HONORS: NBA All-Defensive second team (1993).

Season Team	G	Min.	FGM	FGA	Pct.	FTM	FTA	Pct.	Off.	Def.	Tot.	Ast.	St.	Blk.	TO	Pts.	RPG	APG	PPG
88-89—Golden State ...	36	316	51	125	.408	34	52	.654	15	26	41	27	23	3	39	146	1.1	0.8	4.1
90-91—New York	61	1173	180	410	.439	79	105	.752	30	101	131	204	59	17	74	466	2.1	3.3	7.6
91-92—New York	82	2118	405	902	.449	235	302	.778	45	146	191	276	103	18	150	1139	2.3	3.4	13.9
92-93—New York	80	2477	513	1199	.428	263	331	.795	54	150	204	404	91	12	173	1397	2.6	5.1	17.5
93-94—New York	59	2057	410	977	.420	187	248	.754	37	148	185	348	95	6	184	1120	3.1	5.9	19.0
94-95—New York	80	2725	419	1062	.395	168	228	.737	34	185	219	411	92	4	160	1223	2.7	5.1	15.3
95-96—New York	81	2491	375	846	.443	131	174	.753	31	206	237	315	103	11	156	1024	2.9	3.9	12.6
Totals	479	13357	2353	5521	.426	1097	1440	.762	246	962	1208	1985	566	71	936	6515	2.5	4.1	13.6

Three-point field goals: 1988-89, 10-for-26 (.385). 1990-91, 27-for-93 (.290). 1991-92, 94-for-270 (.348). 1992-93, 108-for-336 (.321). 1993-94, 113-for-337 (.335). 1994-95, 217-for-611 (.355). 1995-96, 143-for-396 (.361). Totals, 712-for-2069 (.344).
Personal fouls/disqualifications: 1988-89, 36/0. 1990-91, 137/1. 1991-92, 231/4. 1992-93, 234/3. 1993-94, 191/4. 1994-95, 257/3. 1995-96, 226/2. Totals, 1312/17.

NBA PLAYOFF RECORD

NOTES: Holds NBA Finals single-series record for most three-point field goals attempted—50 (1994, vs. Houston). ... Shares single-game playoff record for most three-point field goals in one half—6 (May 11, 1995, at Indiana).

Season Team	G	Min.	FGM	FGA	Pct.	FTM	FTA	Pct.	Off.	Def.	Tot.	Ast.	St.	Blk.	TO	Pts.	RPG	APG	PPG
90-91—New York	3	28	2	5	.400	2	2	1.000	1	2	3	6	0	0	6	6	1.0	2.0	2.0
91-92—New York	12	295	46	123	.374	42	52	.808	7	23	30	38	17	0	22	145	2.5	3.2	12.1
92-93—New York	15	575	88	200	.440	43	60	.717	4	48	52	96	15	3	55	247	3.5	6.4	16.5
93-94—New York	25	840	110	289	.381	97	126	.770	9	49	58	114	35	2	57	364	2.3	4.6	14.6
94-95—New York	11	380	58	129	.450	26	42	.619	2	23	25	57	13	1	26	172	2.3	5.2	15.6
95-96—New York	8	314	39	87	.448	29	39	.744	3	26	29	33	13	1	25	128	3.6	4.1	16.0
Totals	74	2432	343	833	.412	239	321	.745	26	171	197	344	93	7	191	1062	2.7	4.6	14.4

Three-point field goals: 1991-92, 11-for-46 (.239). 1992-93, 28-for-75 (.373). 1993-94, 47-for-132 (.356). 1994-95, 30-for-73 (.411). 1995-96, 21-for-45 (.467). Totals, 137-for-371 (.369).
Personal fouls/disqualifications: 1990-91, 4/0. 1991-92, 45/1. 1992-93, 57/0. 1993-94, 86/1. 1994-95, 40/0. 1995-96, 26/0. Totals, 258/2.

NBA ALL-STAR GAME RECORD

Season Team	Min.	FGM	FGA	Pct.	FTM	FTA	Pct.	Off.	Def.	Tot.	Ast.	PF	Dq.	St.	Blk.	TO	Pts.
1994 —New York...........	20	4	9	.444	0	0	...	1	2	3	3	1	0	1	0	2	9

Three-point field goals: 1994, 1-for-3 (.333).

CBA REGULAR-SEASON RECORD

Season Team	G	Min.	FGM	FGA	Pct.	FTM	FTA	Pct.	Reb.	Ast.	Pts.	RPG	APG	PPG
89-90—Cedar Rapids.................	46	1670	385	801	.481	179	240	.746	246	255	997	5.3	5.5	21.7

Three-point field goals: 1989-90, 48-for-138 (.348).

STITH, BRYANT G NUGGETS

PERSONAL: Born December 10, 1970, in Emporia, Va. ... 6-5/208. ... Full name: Bryant Lamonica Stith.
HIGH SCHOOL: Brunswick (Lawrenceville, Va.).
COLLEGE: Virginia.
TRANSACTIONS/CAREER NOTES: Selected by Denver Nuggets in first round (13th pick overall) of 1992 NBA Draft.

COLLEGIATE RECORD

Season Team	G	Min.	FGM	FGA	Pct.	FTM	FTA	Pct.	Reb.	Ast.	Pts.	RPG	APG	PPG
88-89—Virginia..........................	33	942	181	330	.548	150	195	.769	216	50	513	6.5	1.5	15.5
89-90—Virginia..........................	32	1127	217	451	.481	192	247	.777	221	53	666	6.9	1.7	20.8

Season Team	G	Min.	FGM	FGA	Pct.	FTM	FTA	Pct.	Reb.	Ast.	Pts.	AVERAGES RPG	APG	PPG
90-91—Virginia	33	1120	228	484	.471	159	201	.791	203	41	653	6.2	1.2	19.8
91-92—Virginia	33	1202	230	509	.452	189	232	.815	219	72	684	6.6	2.2	20.7
Totals	131	4391	856	1774	.483	690	875	.789	859	216	2516	6.6	1.6	19.2

Three-point field goals: 1988-89, 1-for-1. 1989-90, 40-for-102 (.392). 1990-91, 38-for-125 (.304). 1991-92, 35-for-95 (.368). Totals, 114-for-323 (.353).

NBA REGULAR-SEASON RECORD

Season Team	G	Min.	FGM	FGA	Pct.	FTM	FTA	Pct.	REBOUNDS Off.	Def.	Tot.	Ast.	St.	Blk.	TO	Pts.	AVERAGES RPG	APG	PPG
92-93—Denver	39	865	124	278	.446	99	119	.832	39	85	124	49	24	5	44	347	3.2	1.3	8.9
93-94—Denver	82	2853	365	811	.450	291	351	.829	119	230	349	199	116	16	131	1023	4.3	2.4	12.5
94-95—Denver	81	2329	312	661	.472	267	324	.824	95	173	268	153	91	18	110	911	3.3	1.9	11.2
95-96—Denver	82	2810	379	911	.416	320	379	.844	125	275	400	241	114	16	157	1119	4.9	2.9	13.6
Totals	284	8857	1180	2661	.443	977	1173	.833	378	763	1141	642	345	55	442	3400	4.0	2.3	12.0

Three-point field goals: 1992-93, 0-for-4. 1993-94, 2-for-9 (.222). 1994-95, 20-for-68 (.294). 1995-96, 41-for-148 (.277). Totals, 63-for-229 (.275).
Personal fouls/disqualifications: 1992-93, 82/0. 1993-94, 165/0. 1994-95, 142/0. 1995-96, 187/3. Totals, 576/3.

NBA PLAYOFF RECORD

Season Team	G	Min.	FGM	FGA	Pct.	FTM	FTA	Pct.	REBOUNDS Off.	Def.	Tot.	Ast.	St.	Blk.	TO	Pts.	AVERAGES RPG	APG	PPG
93-94—Denver	12	413	43	102	.422	50	60	.833	23	33	56	26	11	2	14	136	4.7	2.2	11.3
94-95—Denver	3	85	17	32	.531	15	19	.789	3	6	9	7	1	1	0	50	3.0	2.3	16.7
Totals	15	498	60	134	.448	65	79	.823	26	39	65	33	12	3	14	186	4.3	2.2	12.4

Three-point field goals: 1993-94, 0-for-1. 1994-95, 1-for-6 (.167). Totals, 1-for-7 (.143).
Personal fouls/disqualifications: 1993-94, 23/0. 1994-95, 7/0. Totals, 30/0.

STOCKTON, JOHN   G   JAZZ

PERSONAL: Born March 26, 1962, in Spokane, Wash. ... 6-1/175. ... Full name: John Houston Stockton.
HIGH SCHOOL: Gonzaga Prep School (Spokane, Wash.).
COLLEGE: Gonzaga.
TRANSACTIONS/CAREER NOTES: Selected by Utah Jazz in first round (16th pick overall) of 1984 NBA Draft.
MISCELLANEOUS: Member of gold-medal-winning U.S. Olympic teams (1992, 1996). ... Utah Jazz franchise all-time assists leader with 11,310 and all-time steals leader wiith 2,365 (1984-85 through 1995-96).

COLLEGIATE RECORD

Season Team	G	Min.	FGM	FGA	Pct.	FTM	FTA	Pct.	Reb.	Ast.	Pts.	AVERAGES RPG	APG	PPG
80-81—Gonzaga	25	235	26	45	.578	26	35	.743	11	34	78	0.4	1.4	3.1
81-82—Gonzaga	27	1054	117	203	.576	69	102	.676	67	135	303	2.5	5.0	11.2
82-83—Gonzaga	27	1036	142	274	.518	91	115	.791	87	184	375	3.2	6.8	13.9
83-84—Gonzaga	28	1053	229	397	.577	126	182	.692	66	201	584	2.4	7.2	20.9
Totals	107	3378	514	919	.559	312	434	.719	231	554	1340	2.2	5.2	12.5

NBA REGULAR-SEASON RECORD

RECORDS: Holds career records for most years leading league in assists—9; most consecutive years leading league in assists—9 (1987-88 through 1995-96); most assists—11,310; most steals—2,365; and highest assists-per-game average (minimum 400 games)—11.5. ... Holds single-season records for most assists—1,164 (1991); and highest assists-per-game average (minimum 70 games)—14.5 (1990).
HONORS: All-NBA first team (1994, 1995). ... All-NBA second team (1988, 1989, 1990, 1992, 1993, 1996). ... All-NBA third team (1991). ... NBA All-Defensive second team (1989, 1991, 1992, 1995).
NOTES: Led NBA with 3.21 steals per game (1989) and 2.98 steals per game (1992).

Season Team	G	Min.	FGM	FGA	Pct.	FTM	FTA	Pct.	REBOUNDS Off.	Def.	Tot.	Ast.	St.	Blk.	TO	Pts.	AVERAGES RPG	APG	PPG
84-85—Utah	82	1490	157	333	.471	142	193	.736	26	79	105	415	109	11	150	458	1.3	5.1	5.6
85-86—Utah	82	1935	228	466	.489	172	205	.839	33	146	179	610	157	10	168	630	2.2	7.4	7.7
86-87—Utah	82	1858	231	463	.499	179	229	.782	32	119	151	670	177	14	164	648	1.8	8.2	7.9
87-88—Utah	82	2842	454	791	.574	272	324	.840	54	183	237	*1128	242	16	262	1204	2.9	*13.8	14.7
88-89—Utah	82	3171	497	923	.538	390	452	.863	83	165	248	*1118	*263	14	308	1400	3.0	*13.6	17.1
89-90—Utah	78	2915	472	918	.514	354	432	.819	57	149	206	*1134	207	18	272	1345	2.6	*14.5	17.2
90-91—Utah	82	3103	496	978	.507	363	434	.836	46	191	237	*1164	234	16	298	1413	2.9	*14.2	17.2
91-92—Utah	82	3002	453	939	.482	308	366	.842	68	202	270	*1126	*244	22	*286	1297	3.3	*13.7	15.8
92-93—Utah	82	2863	437	899	.486	293	367	.798	64	173	237	*987	199	21	266	1239	2.9	*12.0	15.1
93-94—Utah	82	2969	458	868	.528	272	338	.805	72	186	258	*1031	199	22	266	1236	3.1	*12.6	15.1
94-95—Utah	82	2867	429	791	.542	246	306	.804	57	194	251	*1011	194	22	267	1206	3.1	*12.3	14.7
95-96—Utah	82	2915	440	818	.538	234	282	.830	54	172	226	*916	140	15	246	1209	2.8	*11.2	14.7
Totals	980	31930	4752	9187	.517	3225	3928	.821	646	1959	2605	11310	2365	201	2953	13285	2.7	11.5	13.6

Three-point field goals: 1984-85, 2-for-11 (.182). 1985-86, 2-for-15 (.133). 1986-87, 7-for-38 (.184). 1987-88, 24-for-67 (.358). 1988-89, 16-for-66 (.242). 1989-90, 47-for-113 (.416). 1990-91, 58-for-168 (.345). 1991-92, 83-for-204 (.407). 1992-93, 72-for-187 (.385). 1993-94, 48-for-149 (.322). 1994-95, 102-for-227 (.449). 1995-96, 95-for-225 (.422). Totals, 556-for-1470 (.378).
Personal fouls/disqualifications: 1984-85, 203/3. 1985-86, 227/2. 1986-87, 224/1. 1987-88, 247/5. 1988-89, 241/3. 1989-90, 233/3. 1990-91, 233/1. 1991-92, 234/3. 1992-93, 224/2. 1993-94, 236/3. 1994-95, 215/3. 1995-96, 207/1. Totals, 2724/30.

NBA PLAYOFF RECORD

NOTES: Holds single-game playoff record for most assists in one quarter—11 (May 5, 1994, vs. San Antonio). ... Shares single-game playoff record for most assists—24 (May 17, 1988, vs. Los Angeles Lakers).

Season Team	G	Min.	FGM	FGA	Pct.	FTM	FTA	Pct.	REBOUNDS Off.	Def.	Tot.	Ast.	St.	Blk.	TO	Pts.	AVERAGES RPG	APG	PPG
84-85—Utah	10	186	21	45	.467	26	35	.743	7	21	28	43	11	2	16	68	2.8	4.3	6.8
85-86—Utah	4	73	9	17	.529	8	9	.889	3	3	6	14	5	0	4	27	1.5	3.5	6.8
86-87—Utah	5	157	18	29	.621	10	13	.769	2	9	11	40	15	1	11	50	2.2	8.0	10.0

Season Team	G	Min.	FGM	FGA	Pct.	FTM	FTA	Pct.	REBOUNDS Off.	Def.	Tot.	Ast.	St.	Blk.	TO	Pts.	AVERAGES RPG	APG	PPG
87-88—Utah	11	478	68	134	.507	75	91	.824	14	31	45	163	37	3	48	215	4.1	14.8	19.5
88-89—Utah	3	139	30	59	.508	19	21	.905	2	8	10	41	11	5	11	82	3.3	13.7	27.3
89-90—Utah	5	194	29	69	.420	16	20	.800	4	12	16	75	6	0	14	75	3.2	15.0	15.0
90-91—Utah	9	373	58	108	.537	37	44	.841	10	32	42	124	20	2	32	164	4.7	13.8	18.2
91-92—Utah	16	623	77	182	.423	65	78	.833	10	37	47	217	34	5	58	237	2.9	13.6	14.8
92-93—Utah	5	193	23	51	.451	15	18	.833	5	7	12	55	12	0	15	66	2.4	11.0	13.2
93-94—Utah	16	597	88	193	.456	51	63	.810	14	38	52	157	27	8	40	231	3.3	9.8	14.4
94-95—Utah	5	193	34	74	.459	13	17	.765	6	11	17	51	7	1	14	89	3.4	10.2	17.8
95-96—Utah	18	679	70	157	.446	48	59	.814	14	44	58	195	29	7	58	199	3.2	10.8	11.1
Totals	107	3885	525	1118	.470	383	468	.818	91	253	344	1175	214	34	321	1503	3.2	11.0	14.0

Three-point field goals: 1984-85, 0-for-2. 1985-86, 1-for-1. 1986-87, 4-for-5 (.800). 1987-88, 4-for-14 (.286). 1988-89, 3-for-4 (.750). 1989-90, 1-for-13 (.077). 1990-91, 11-for-27 (.407). 1991-92, 18-for-58 (.310). 1992-93, 5-for-13 (.385). 1993-94, 4-for-24 (.167). 1994-95, 8-for-20 (.400). 1995-96, 11-for-38 (.289). Totals, 70-for-219 (.320).

Personal fouls/disqualifications: 1984-85, 30/0. 1985-86, 10/0. 1986-87, 18/0. 1987-88, 36/0. 1988-89, 15/0. 1989-90, 20/0. 1990-91, 33/0. 1991-92, 38/0. 1992-93, 16/0. 1993-94, 44/0. 1994-95, 13/0. 1995-96, 50/0. Totals, 323/0.

NBA ALL-STAR GAME RECORD

NOTES: NBA All-Star Game Co-Most Valuable Player (1993).

Season Team	Min.	FGM	FGA	Pct.	FTM	FTA	Pct.	REBOUNDS Off.	Def.	Tot.	Ast.	PF	Dq.	St.	Blk.	TO	Pts.
1989 —Utah	32	5	6	.833	0	0	...	0	2	2	17	4	0	5	0	12	11
1990 —Utah	15	1	4	.250	0	0	...	0	0	0	6	1	0	1	1	3	2
1991 —Utah	12	1	6	.167	2	4	.500	0	1	1	2	2	0	0	0	0	4
1992 —Utah	18	5	8	.625	0	0	...	0	1	1	5	2	0	3	0	3	12
1993 —Utah	31	3	6	.500	2	2	1.000	0	6	6	15	3	0	2	0	5	9
1994 —Utah	26	6	10	.600	0	0	...	1	4	5	10	2	0	1	0	4	13
1995 —Utah	14	2	6	.333	0	0	...	1	0	1	6	0	0	2	0	0	4
1996 —Utah	18	2	9	.222	0	0	...	0	1	1	3	2	0	0	1	4
Totals	166	25	55	.455	4	6	.667	2	15	17	64	16	0	14	1	28	59

Three-point field goals: 1989, 1-for-1. 1990, 0-for-1. 1992, 2-for-3 (.667). 1993, 1-for-2 (.500). 1994, 1-for-1. 1995, 0-for-3. 1996, 0-for-7. Totals, 5-for-18 (.278).

STOUDAMIRE, DAMON   G   RAPTORS

PERSONAL: Born September 3, 1973, in Portland, Ore. ... 5-10/171. ... Full name: Damon Lamon Stoudamire. ... Name pronounced DAY-min STAHD-a-mire.
HIGH SCHOOL: Woodrow Wilson (Portland, Ore.).
COLLEGE: Arizona.
TRANSACTIONS/CAREER NOTES: Selected by Toronto Raptors in first round (seventh pick overall) of 1995 NBA Draft.
MISCELLANEOUS: Toronto Raptors all-time leading scorer with 1,331 points and all-time assists leader with 653 (1995-96).

COLLEGIATE RECORD

NOTES: THE SPORTING NEWS All-America first team (1995).

Season Team	G	Min.	FGM	FGA	Pct.	FTM	FTA	Pct.	Reb.	Ast.	Pts.	AVERAGES RPG	APG	PPG
91-92—Arizona	30	540	76	167	.455	37	48	.771	65	76	217	2.2	2.5	7.2
92-93—Arizona	28	870	99	226	.438	72	91	.791	116	159	309	4.1	5.7	11.0
93-94—Arizona	35	1164	217	484	.448	112	140	.800	157	208	639	4.5	5.9	18.3
94-95—Arizona	30	1092	222	466	.476	128	155	.826	128	220	684	4.3	7.3	22.8
Totals	123	3666	614	1343	.457	349	434	.804	466	663	1849	3.8	5.4	15.0

Three-point field goals: 1991-92, 28-for-69 (.406). 1992-93, 39-for-102 (.382). 1993-94, 93-for-265 (.351). 1994-95, 112-for-241 (.465). Totals, 272-for-677 (.402).

NBA REGULAR-SEASON RECORD

RECORDS: Holds single-season record for most three-point field goals made by a rookie—133 (1995-96).
HONORS: NBA Rookie of the Year (1996). ... NBA All-Rookie first team (1996).

Season Team	G	Min.	FGM	FGA	Pct.	FTM	FTA	Pct.	REBOUNDS Off.	Def.	Tot.	Ast.	St.	Blk.	TO	Pts.	AVERAGES RPG	APG	PPG
95-96—Toronto	70	2865	481	1129	.426	236	296	.797	59	222	281	653	98	19	267	1331	4.0	9.3	19.0

Three-point field goals: 1995-96, 133-for-337 (.395).
Personal fouls/disqualifications: 1995-96, 166/0.

STRICKLAND, ROD   G   BULLETS

PERSONAL: Born July 11, 1966, in Bronx, N.Y. ... 6-3/185. ... Full name: Rodney Strickland.
HIGH SCHOOL: Harry S. Truman (Bronx, N.Y.), then Oak Hill Academy (Mouth of Wilson, Va.).
COLLEGE: DePaul.
TRANSACTIONS/CAREER NOTES: Selected after junior season by New York Knicks in first round (19th pick overall) of 1988 NBA Draft. ... Traded by Knicks to San Antonio Spurs for G Maurice Cheeks (February 21, 1990). ... Signed as free agent by Portland Trail Blazers (July 3, 1992). ... Traded by Trail Blazers with F Harvey Grant to Washington Bullets for F Rasheed Wallace and G Mitchell Butler (July 15, 1996).

COLLEGIATE RECORD

NOTES: THE SPORTING NEWS All-America first team (1988).

Season Team	G	Min.	FGM	FGA	Pct.	FTM	FTA	Pct.	Reb.	Ast.	Pts.	AVERAGES RPG	APG	PPG
85-86—DePaul	31	1063	176	354	.497	85	126	.675	84	159	437	2.7	5.1	14.1

Season Team	G	Min.	FGM	FGA	Pct.	FTM	FTA	Pct.	Reb.	Ast.	Pts.	AVERAGES		
												RPG	APG	PPG
86-87—DePaul	30	980	188	323	.582	106	175	.606	113	196	490	3.8	6.5	16.3
87-88—DePaul	26	837	207	392	.528	83	137	.606	98	202	521	3.8	7.8	20.0
Totals	87	2880	571	1069	.534	274	438	.626	295	557	1448	3.4	6.4	16.6

Three-point field goals: 1986-87, 8-for-15 (.533). 1987-88, 24-for-54 (.444). Totals, 32-for-69 (.464).

NBA REGULAR-SEASON RECORD

HONORS: NBA All-Rookie second team (1989).

Season Team	G	Min.	FGM	FGA	Pct.	FTM	FTA	Pct.	REBOUNDS			Ast.	St.	Blk.	TO	Pts.	AVERAGES		
									Off.	Def.	Tot.						RPG	APG	PPG
88-89—New York	81	1358	265	567	.467	172	231	.745	51	109	160	319	98	3	148	721	2.0	3.9	8.9
89-90—N.Y.-S.A.	82	2140	343	756	.454	174	278	.626	90	169	259	468	127	14	170	868	3.2	5.7	10.6
90-91—San Antonio	58	2076	314	651	.482	161	211	.763	57	162	219	463	117	11	156	800	3.8	8.0	13.8
91-92—San Antonio	57	2053	300	659	.455	182	265	.687	92	173	265	491	118	17	160	787	4.6	8.6	13.8
92-93—Portland	78	2474	396	816	.485	273	381	.717	120	217	337	559	131	24	199	1069	4.3	7.2	13.7
93-94—Portland	82	2889	528	1093	.483	353	471	.749	122	248	370	740	147	24	257	1411	4.5	9.0	17.2
94-95—Portland	64	2267	441	946	.466	283	380	.745	73	244	317	562	123	9	209	1211	5.0	8.8	18.9
95-96—Portland	67	2526	471	1023	.460	276	423	.652	89	208	297	640	97	16	255	1256	4.4	9.6	18.7
Totals	569	17783	3058	6511	.470	1874	2640	.710	694	1530	2224	4242	958	118	1554	8123	3.9	7.5	14.3

Three-point field goals: 1988-89, 19-for-59 (.322). 1989-90, 8-for-30 (.267). 1990-91, 11-for-33 (.333). 1991-92, 5-for-15 (.333). 1992-93, 4-for-30 (.133). 1993-94, 2-for-10 (.200). 1994-95, 46-for-123 (.374). 1995-96, 38-for-111 (.342). Totals, 133-for-411 (.324).

Personal fouls/disqualifications: 1988-89, 142/2. 1989-90, 160/3. 1990-91, 125/0. 1991-92, 122/0. 1992-93, 153/1. 1993-94, 171/0. 1994-95, 118/0. 1995-96, 135/2. Totals, 1126/8.

NBA PLAYOFF RECORD

Season Team	G	Min.	FGM	FGA	Pct.	FTM	FTA	Pct.	REBOUNDS			Ast.	St.	Blk.	TO	Pts.	AVERAGES		
									Off.	Def.	Tot.						RPG	APG	PPG
88-89—New York	9	111	22	49	.449	9	17	.529	6	7	13	25	4	1	13	54	1.4	2.8	6.0
89-90—San Antonio	10	384	54	127	.425	15	27	.556	22	31	53	112	14	0	34	123	5.3	11.2	12.3
90-91—San Antonio	4	168	29	67	.433	17	21	.810	5	16	21	35	9	0	13	75	5.3	8.8	18.8
91-92—San Antonio	2	80	13	22	.591	5	8	.625	0	7	7	19	3	2	6	31	3.5	9.5	15.5
92-93—Portland	4	156	22	52	.423	10	12	.833	9	17	26	37	5	2	7	54	6.5	9.3	13.5
93-94—Portland	4	154	36	72	.500	22	27	.815	3	13	16	39	4	2	10	94	4.0	9.8	23.5
94-95—Portland	3	126	27	65	.415	14	18	.778	1	11	12	37	3	2	10	70	4.0	12.3	23.3
95-96—Portland	5	202	37	84	.440	23	36	.639	12	19	31	42	5	0	12	103	6.2	8.4	20.6
Totals	41	1381	240	538	.446	115	166	.693	58	121	179	346	47	9	105	604	4.4	8.4	14.7

Three-point field goals: 1988-89, 1-for-1. 1989-90, 0-for-7. 1990-91, 0-for-6. 1992-93, 0-for-1. 1993-94, 0-for-1. 1994-95, 2-for-5 (.400). 1995-96, 6-for-12 (.500). Totals, 9-for-33 (.273).

Personal fouls/disqualifications: 1988-89, 21/0. 1989-90, 30/2. 1990-91, 14/0. 1991-92, 8/0. 1992-93, 10/0. 1993-94, 13/0. 1994-95, 11/0. 1995-96, 14/0. Totals, 121/2.

STRONG, DEREK   F   MAGIC

PERSONAL: Born February 9, 1968, in Los Angeles. ... 6-8/250. ... Full name: Derek Lamar Strong.
HIGH SCHOOL: Pacific Palisades (Calif.).
COLLEGE: Xavier.
TRANSACTIONS/CAREER NOTES: Selected by Philadelphia 76ers in second round (47th pick overall) of 1990 NBA Draft. ... Played in Spain (1990-91). ... Played in United States Basketball League with Miami Tropics (1991). ... Waived by 76ers (March 5, 1992). ... Signed by Washington Bullets to 10-day contract (March 13, 1992). ... Signed as free agent by Bullets (October 5, 1992). ... Waived by Bullets (October 14, 1992). ... Played in Continental Basketball Association with Quad City Thunder (1992-93). ... Signed by Milwaukee Bucks to first of two consecutive 10-day contracts (February 22, 1993). ... Re-signed by Bucks for remainder of season (March 14, 1993). ... Traded by Bucks with G/F Blue Edwards to Boston Celtics for F Ed Pinckney and draft rights to C Andrei Fetisov (June 29, 1994). ... Signed as unrestricted free agent by Los Angeles Lakers (October 26, 1995). ... Rights renounced by Lakers (July 17, 1996). ... Signed as free agent by Orlando Magic (August 26, 1996).

COLLEGIATE RECORD

Season Team	G	Min.	FGM	FGA	Pct.	FTM	FTA	Pct.	Reb.	Ast.	Pts.	AVERAGES		
												RPG	APG	PPG
86-87—Xavier					Did not play—ineligible.									
87-88—Xavier	30	668	112	197	.569	94	131	.718	213	23	318	7.1	0.8	10.6
88-89—Xavier	33	983	163	264	.617	178	218	.817	264	17	504	8.0	0.5	15.3
89-90—Xavier	33	981	146	274	.533	177	211	.839	328	31	469	9.9	0.9	14.2
Totals	96	2632	421	735	.573	449	560	.802	805	71	1291	8.4	0.7	13.4

NBA REGULAR-SEASON RECORD

Season Team	G	Min.	FGM	FGA	Pct.	FTM	FTA	Pct.	REBOUNDS			Ast.	St.	Blk.	TO	Pts.	AVERAGES		
									Off.	Def.	Tot.						RPG	APG	PPG
91-92—Washington	1	12	0	4	.000	3	4	.750	1	4	5	1	0	0	1	3	5.0	1.0	3.0
92-93—Milwaukee	23	339	42	92	.457	68	85	.800	40	75	115	14	11	1	13	156	5.0	0.6	6.8
93-94—Milwaukee	67	1131	141	341	.413	159	206	.772	109	172	281	48	38	14	61	444	4.2	0.7	6.6
94-95—Boston	70	1344	149	329	.453	141	172	.820	136	239	375	44	24	13	79	441	5.4	0.6	6.3
95-96—L.A. Lakers	63	746	72	169	.426	69	85	.812	60	118	178	32	18	12	20	214	2.8	0.5	3.4
Totals	224	3572	404	935	.432	440	552	.797	346	608	954	139	91	40	174	1258	4.3	0.6	5.6

Three-point field goals: 1992-93, 4-for-8 (.500). 1993-94, 3-for-13 (.231). 1994-95, 2-for-7 (.286). 1995-96, 1-for-9 (.111). Totals, 10-for-37 (.270).
Personal fouls/disqualifications: 1991-92, 1/0. 1992-93, 20/0. 1993-94, 69/1. 1994-95, 143/0. 1995-96, 80/1. Totals, 313/2.

NBA PLAYOFF RECORD

Season Team	G	Min.	FGM	FGA	Pct.	FTM	FTA	Pct.	REBOUNDS			Ast.	St.	Blk.	TO	Pts.	AVERAGES		
									Off.	Def.	Tot.						RPG	APG	PPG
94-95—Boston	4	81	4	12	.333	3	6	.500	13	11	24	3	3	1	5	11	6.0	0.8	2.8

Personal fouls/disqualifications: 1994-95, 7/0.

CBA REGULAR-SEASON RECORD

NOTES: CBA Most Valuable Player (1993). ... CBA Newcomer of the Year (1993). ... CBA All-League first team (1993). ... CBA All-Defensive team (1993).

Season Team	G	Min.	FGM	FGA	Pct.	FTM	FTA	Pct.	Reb.	Ast.	Pts.	RPG	APG	PPG
												AVERAGES		
92-93—Quad City	43	1513	271	487	.556	319	375	.851	485	81	861	11.3	1.9	20.0

Three-point field goals: 1992-93, 0-for-4.

SURA, BOB　　　　　　　G　　　　　　　CAVALIERS

PERSONAL: Born March 25, 1973, in Wilkes-Barre, Pa. ... 6-5/200. ... Full name: Robert Sura Jr.
HIGH SCHOOL: G.A.R. Memorial (Wilkes-Barre, Pa.).
COLLEGE: Florida State.
TRANSACTIONS/CAREER NOTES: Selected by Cleveland Cavaliers in first round (17th pick overall) of 1995 NBA Draft.

COLLEGIATE RECORD

Season Team	G	Min.	FGM	FGA	Pct.	FTM	FTA	Pct.	Reb.	Ast.	Pts.	RPG	APG	PPG
												AVERAGES		
91-92—Florida State	31	872	124	269	.461	94	150	.627	107	76	380	3.5	2.5	12.3
92-93—Florida State	34	1213	241	533	.452	120	188	.638	209	92	675	6.1	2.7	19.9
93-94—Florida State	27	932	202	431	.469	117	179	.654	213	121	573	7.9	4.5	21.2
94-95—Florida State	27	981	164	393	.417	123	179	.687	185	146	502	6.9	5.4	18.6
Totals	119	3998	731	1626	.450	454	696	.652	714	435	2130	6.0	3.7	17.9

Three-point field goals: 1991-92, 38-for-98 (.388). 1992-93, 73-for-220 (.332). 1993-94, 52-for-164 (.317). 1994-95, 51-for-158 (.323). Totals, 214-for-640 (.334).

NBA REGULAR-SEASON RECORD

Season Team	G	Min.	FGM	FGA	Pct.	FTM	FTA	Pct.	Off.	Def.	Tot.	Ast.	St.	Blk.	TO	Pts.	RPG	APG	PPG
									REBOUNDS								AVERAGES		
95-96—Cleveland	79	1150	148	360	.411	99	141	.702	34	101	135	233	56	21	115	422	1.7	2.9	5.3

Three-point field goals: 1995-96, 27-for-78 (.346).
Personal fouls/disqualifications: 1995-96, 126/1.

NBA PLAYOFF RECORD

Season Team	G	Min.	FGM	FGA	Pct.	FTM	FTA	Pct.	Off.	Def.	Tot.	Ast.	St.	Blk.	TO	Pts.	RPG	APG	PPG
									REBOUNDS								AVERAGES		
95-96—Cleveland	3	18	2	3	.667	0	0	...	0	1	1	3	1	0	4	4	0.3	1.0	1.3

Personal fouls/disqualifications: 1995-96, 4/0.

SUTTON, GREG　　　　　　　G

PERSONAL: Born December 3, 1967, in Santa Cruz, Calif. ... 6-2/170. ... Full name: Gregory Ray Sutton.
HIGH SCHOOL: Douglass (Oklahoma City).
COLLEGE: Langston (Okla.), then Oral Roberts.
TRANSACTIONS/CAREER NOTES: Selected by San Antonio Spurs in second round (49th pick overall) of 1991 NBA Draft. ... Waived by Spurs (November 3, 1992). ... Played in Continental Basketball Association with Fort Wayne Fury and Fargo/Moorhead Fever (1992-93). ... Signed as free agent by Miami Heat (October 7, 1993). ... Waived by Heat (November 2, 1993). ... Played in Greece (1993-94). ... Signed as free agent by Dallas Mavericks (October 3, 1994). ... Waived by Mavericks (October 31, 1994). ... Signed as free agent by Charlotte Hornets (November 16, 1994). ... Waived by Hornets (January 3, 1996). ... Signed by Philadelphia 76ers to first of two consecutive 10-day contracts (January 10, 1996). ... Re-signed by 76ers for remainder of season (January 30, 1996). ... Rights renounced by 76ers (July 11, 1996).

COLLEGIATE RECORD

Season Team	G	Min.	FGM	FGA	Pct.	FTM	FTA	Pct.	Reb.	Ast.	Pts.	RPG	APG	PPG
												AVERAGES		
86-87—Langston	29	...	198	487	.407	93	124	.750	90	61	536	3.1	2.1	18.5
87-88—Oral Roberts						Did not play—transfer student.								
88-89—Oral Roberts	28	936	214	564	.379	103	157	.656	121	89	614	4.3	3.2	21.9
89-90—Oral Roberts	41	...	417	976	.427	252	328	.768	205	249	1256	5.0	6.1	30.6
90-91—Oral Roberts	35	...	393	858	.458	229	280	.818	168	152	1200	4.8	4.3	34.3
Totals	133	...	1222	2885	.424	677	889	.762	584	551	3606	4.4	4.1	27.1

Three-point field goals: 1988-89, 83-for-251 (.331). 1989-90, 170-for-443 (.384). 1990-91, 185-for-463 (.400). Totals, 438-for-1157 (.379).

NBA REGULAR-SEASON RECORD

Season Team	G	Min.	FGM	FGA	Pct.	FTM	FTA	Pct.	Off.	Def.	Tot.	Ast.	St.	Blk.	TO	Pts.	RPG	APG	PPG
									REBOUNDS								AVERAGES		
91-92—San Antonio	67	601	93	240	.388	34	45	.756	6	41	47	91	26	9	70	246	0.7	1.4	3.7
94-95—Charlotte	53	690	94	230	.409	32	45	.711	8	48	56	91	33	2	51	263	1.1	1.7	5.0
95-96—Char.-Phil.	48	655	85	217	.392	35	46	.761	8	42	50	102	25	2	62	252	1.0	2.1	5.3
Totals	168	1946	272	687	.396	101	136	.743	22	131	153	284	84	13	183	761	0.9	1.7	4.5

Three-point field goals: 1991-92, 26-for-89 (.292). 1994-95, 63-for-115 (.374). 1995-96, 47-for-117 (.402). Totals, 116-for-321 (.361).
Personal fouls/disqualifications: 1991-92, 111/0. 1994-95, 114/0. 1995-96, 92/0. Totals, 317/0.

NBA PLAYOFF RECORD

Season Team	G	Min.	FGM	FGA	Pct.	FTM	FTA	Pct.	Off.	Def.	Tot.	Ast.	St.	Blk.	TO	Pts.	RPG	APG	PPG
									REBOUNDS								AVERAGES		
91-92—San Antonio	2	15	2	6	.333	3	3	1.000	0	0	0	2	1	1	0	7	0.0	1.0	3.5
94-95—Charlotte	3	23	0	7	.000	0	0	...	3	2	5	3	0	0	1	0	1.7	1.0	0.0
Totals	5	38	2	13	.154	3	3	1.000	3	2	5	5	1	1	1	7	1.0	1.0	1.4

Three-point field goals: 1991-92, 0-for-2. 1994-95, 0-for-5. Totals, 0-for-7.
Personal fouls/disqualifications: 1991-92, 3/0. 1994-95, 1/0. Totals, 4/0.

CBA REGULAR-SEASON RECORD

Season Team	G	Min.	FGM	FGA	Pct.	FTM	FTA	Pct.	Reb.	Ast.	Pts.	AVERAGES RPG	APG	PPG
92-93—Ft.Wayne-F/M	52	1962	335	768	.436	254	320	.794	184	394	989	3.5	7.6	19.0

Three-point field goals: 1992-93, 65-for-204 (.319).

GREEK LEAGUE RECORD

Season Team	G	Min.	FGM	FGA	Pct.	FTM	FTA	Pct.	Reb.	Ast.	Pts.	AVERAGES RPG	APG	PPG
93-94—Apollon Dur	18	...	122	314	.389	99	119	.832	61	37	388	3.4	2.1	21.6

SYKES, LARRY　　　　　　F

PERSONAL: Born April 11, 1973, in Toledo, Ohio. ... 6-9/255.
HIGH SCHOOL: St. Francis Desales (Toledo, Ohio).
COLLEGE: Xavier.
TRANSACTIONS/CAREER NOTES: Not drafted by an NBA franchise. ... Played in Continental Basketball Association with Rockford Lightning (1995-96). ... Signed as free agent by Boston Celtics (November 8, 1995). ... Waived by Celtics (November 24, 1995).

COLLEGIATE RECORD

Season Team	G	Min.	FGM	FGA	Pct.	FTM	FTA	Pct.	Reb.	Ast.	Pts.	AVERAGES RPG	APG	PPG
91-92—Xavier	22	133	13	25	.520	6	12	.500	22	10	32	1.0	0.5	1.5
92-93—Xavier	28	384	28	55	.509	9	22	.409	78	21	65	2.8	0.8	2.3
93-94—Xavier	28	664	96	191	.503	42	80	.525	160	26	234	5.7	0.9	8.4
94-95—Xavier	27	822	105	203	.517	65	112	.580	291	43	275	10.8	1.6	10.2
Totals	105	2003	242	474	.511	122	226	.540	551	100	606	5.2	1.0	5.8

Three-point field goals: 1994-95, 0-for-1.

CBA REGULAR-SEASON RECORD

Season Team	G	Min.	FGM	FGA	Pct.	FTM	FTA	Pct.	Reb.	Ast.	Pts.	AVERAGES RPG	APG	PPG
95-96—Rockford	38	753	113	223	.507	76	113	.673	187	32	302	4.9	0.8	7.9

Three-point field goals: 1995-96, 0-for-1.

NBA REGULAR-SEASON RECORD

Season Team	G	Min.	FGM	FGA	Pct.	FTM	FTA	Pct.	REBOUNDS Off.	Def.	Tot.	Ast.	St.	Blk.	TO	Pts.	AVERAGES RPG	APG	PPG
95-96—Boston	1	2	0	0	...	0	0	...	1	1	2	0	0	0	1	0	2.0	0.0	0.0

TABAK, ZAN　　　　　　C　　　　　　RAPTORS

PERSONAL: Born June 15, 1970, in Split, Croatia. ... 7-0/245. ... Name pronounced JEAN TAW-back.
HIGH SCHOOL: Split (Croatia).
TRANSACTIONS/CAREER NOTES: Selected by Houston Rockets in second round (51st pick overall) of 1991 NBA Draft. ... Played in Croatia (1991-92). ... Played in Italy (1992-93 and 1993-94). ... Signed by Rockets (July 20, 1994). ... Selected by Toronto Raptors from Rockets in NBA expansion draft (June 24, 1995).
MISCELLANEOUS: Member of NBA championship team (1995). ... Member of Croatian Olympic team (1996).

ITALIAN LEAGUE RECORD

Season Team	G	Min.	FGM	FGA	Pct.	FTM	FTA	Pct.	Reb.	Ast.	Pts.	AVERAGES RPG	APG	PPG
92-93—Livorno	30	1030	185	212	.873	90	129	.698	305	12	460	10.2	0.4	15.3
93-94—Milano	25	785	145	235	.617	76	116	.655	266	16	366	10.6	0.6	14.6
Totals	55	1815	330	447	.738	166	245	.678	571	28	826	10.4	0.5	15.0

NBA REGULAR-SEASON RECORD

Season Team	G	Min.	FGM	FGA	Pct.	FTM	FTA	Pct.	REBOUNDS Off.	Def.	Tot.	Ast.	St.	Blk.	TO	Pts.	AVERAGES RPG	APG	PPG
94-95—Houston	37	182	24	53	.453	27	44	.614	23	34	57	4	2	7	18	75	1.5	0.1	2.0
95-96—Toronto	67	1332	225	414	.543	64	114	.561	117	203	320	62	24	31	101	514	4.8	0.9	7.7
Totals	104	1514	249	467	.533	91	158	.576	140	237	377	66	26	38	119	589	3.6	0.6	5.7

Three-point field goals: 1994-95, 0-for-1. 1995-96, 0-for-1. Totals, 0-for-2.
Personal fouls/disqualifications: 1994-95, 37/0. 1995-96, 204/2. Totals, 241/2.

NBA PLAYOFF RECORD

Season Team	G	Min.	FGM	FGA	Pct.	FTM	FTA	Pct.	REBOUNDS Off.	Def.	Tot.	Ast.	St.	Blk.	TO	Pts.	AVERAGES RPG	APG	PPG
94-95—Houston	8	31	2	5	.400	2	2	1.000	1	0	1	1	1	3	2	6	0.1	0.1	0.8

Personal fouls/disqualifications: 1994-95, 5/0.

THOMAS, KURT　　　　　　F　　　　　　HEAT

PERSONAL: Born October 4, 1972, in Dallas. ... 6-9/230. ... Full name: Kurt Vincent Thomas.
HIGH SCHOOL: Hillcrest (Dallas).
COLLEGE: Texas Christian.
TRANSACTIONS/CAREER NOTES: Selected by Miami Heat in first round (10th pick overall) of 1995 NBA Draft.

COLLEGIATE RECORD

NOTES: Led NCAA Division I with 28.9 points per game and 14.6 rebounds per game (1995). ... One of only three players in NCAA history to lead nation in both scoring and rebounding in same season (1995).

Season Team	G	Min.	FGM	FGA	Pct.	FTM	FTA	Pct.	Reb.	Ast.	Pts.	AVERAGES RPG	APG	PPG
90-91—Texas Christian	28	42	8	18	.444	7	14	.500	13	2	23	0.5	0.1	0.8
91-92—Texas Christian	21	347	58	119	.487	34	51	.667	114	24	150	5.4	1.1	7.1
92-93—Texas Christian					Did not play—leg injury.									
93-94—Texas Christian	27	805	224	440	.509	98	152	.645	262	50	558	9.7	1.9	20.7
94-95—Texas Christian	27	872	288	526	.548	202	283	.714	393	32	781	14.6	1.2	28.9
Totals	103	2066	578	1103	.524	341	500	.682	782	108	1512	7.6	1.0	14.7

Three-point field goals: 1990-91, 0-for-2. 1993-94, 12-for-46 (.261). 1994-95, 3-for-12 (.250). Totals, 15-for-60 (.250).

NBA REGULAR-SEASON RECORD

Season Team	G	Min.	FGM	FGA	Pct.	FTM	FTA	Pct.	REBOUNDS Off.	Def.	Tot.	Ast.	St.	Blk.	TO	Pts.	AVERAGES RPG	APG	PPG
95-96—Miami	74	1655	274	547	.501	118	178	.663	122	317	439	46	47	36	98	666	5.9	0.6	9.0

Three-point field goals: 1995-96, 0-for-2.
Personal fouls/disqualifications: 1995-96, 271/7.

NBA PLAYOFF RECORD

Season Team	G	Min.	FGM	FGA	Pct.	FTM	FTA	Pct.	REBOUNDS Off.	Def.	Tot.	Ast.	St.	Blk.	TO	Pts.	AVERAGES RPG	APG	PPG
95-96—Miami	3	60	4	10	.400	4	4	1.000	4	12	16	3	2	1	5	12	5.3	1.0	4.0

Personal fouls/disqualifications: 1995-96, 13/1.

THOMPSON, BROOKS　　　G　　　　JAZZ

PERSONAL: Born July 19, 1970, in Dallas. ... 6-4/195. ... Full name: Brooks James Thompson.
HIGH SCHOOL: Littleton (Colo.).
COLLEGE: Texas A&M, then Oklahoma State.
TRANSACTIONS/CAREER NOTES: Selected by Orlando Magic in first round (27th pick overall) of 1994 NBA Draft. ... Traded by Magic with F Kenny Gattison and undisclosed first-round draft choice to Utah Jazz for C Felton Spencer (August 9, 1996).

COLLEGIATE RECORD

Season Team	G	Min.	FGM	FGA	Pct.	FTM	FTA	Pct.	Reb.	Ast.	Pts.	AVERAGES RPG	APG	PPG
89-90—Texas A&M	31	639	95	252	.377	25	39	.641	73	69	258	2.4	2.2	8.3
90-91—Texas A&M	29	1006	150	319	.470	64	86	.744	91	165	421	3.1	5.7	14.5
91-92—Oklahoma State					Did not play—transfer student.									
92-93—Oklahoma State	29	923	140	307	.456	83	110	.755	113	144	423	3.9	5.0	14.6
93-94—Oklahoma State	34	1175	179	401	.446	105	133	.789	137	195	573	4.0	5.7	16.9
Totals	123	3743	564	1279	.441	277	368	.753	414	573	1675	3.4	4.7	13.6

Three-point field goals: 1989-90, 43-for-134 (.321). 1990-91, 57-for-147 (.388). 1992-93, 60-for-161 (.373). 1993-94, 110-for-233 (.472). Totals, 270-for-675 (.400).

NBA REGULAR-SEASON RECORD

Season Team	G	Min.	FGM	FGA	Pct.	FTM	FTA	Pct.	REBOUNDS Off.	Def.	Tot.	Ast.	St.	Blk.	TO	Pts.	AVERAGES RPG	APG	PPG
94-95—Orlando	38	246	45	114	.395	8	12	.667	7	16	23	43	10	2	27	116	0.6	1.1	3.1
95-96—Orlando	33	246	48	103	.466	19	27	.704	4	20	24	31	12	0	24	140	0.7	0.9	4.2
Totals	71	492	93	217	.429	27	39	.692	11	36	47	74	22	2	51	256	0.7	1.0	3.6

Three-point field goals: 1994-95, 18-for-58 (.310). 1995-96, 25-for-64 (.391). Totals, 43-for-122 (.352).
Personal fouls/disqualifications: 1994-95, 46/1. 1995-96, 35/0. Totals, 81/1.

NBA PLAYOFF RECORD

Season Team	G	Min.	FGM	FGA	Pct.	FTM	FTA	Pct.	REBOUNDS Off.	Def.	Tot.	Ast.	St.	Blk.	TO	Pts.	AVERAGES RPG	APG	PPG
94-95—Orlando	3	11	3	4	.750	3	4	.750	1	2	3	0	1	2	12	0.7	1.0	4.0	
95-96—Orlando	5	48	10	21	.476	5	7	.714	3	2	5	7	0	1	9	26	1.0	1.4	5.2
Totals	8	59	13	25	.520	8	11	.727	4	3	7	10	0	2	11	38	0.9	1.3	4.8

Three-point field goals: 1994-95, 3-for-4 (.750). 1995-96, 1-for-6 (.167). Totals, 4-for-10 (.400).
Personal fouls/disqualifications: 1994-95, 1/0. 1995-96, 7/0. Totals, 8/0.

THOMPSON, LaSALLE　　　F/C

PERSONAL: Born June 23, 1961, in Cincinnati. ... 6-10/260. ... Full name: LaSalle Thompson III.
HIGH SCHOOL: Withrow (Cincinnati).
COLLEGE: Texas.
TRANSACTIONS/CAREER NOTES: Selected after junior season by Kansas City Kings in first round (fifth pick overall) of 1982 NBA Draft. ... Kings franchise moved from Kansas City to Sacramento for 1985-86 season. ... Traded by Kings with G/F Randy Wittman to Indiana Pacers for F Wayman Tisdale and 1990 or 1991 second-round draft choice (February 20, 1989). ... Rights renounced by Pacers (October 3, 1995). ... Signed by Philadelphia 76ers for remainder of season (January 11, 1996). ... Rights renounced by 76ers (July 11, 1996).

COLLEGIATE RECORD

NOTES: Led NCAA Division I with 13.5 rebounds per game (1982).

Season Team	G	Min.	FGM	FGA	Pct.	FTM	FTA	Pct.	Reb.	Ast.	Pts.	AVERAGES RPG	APG	PPG
79-80—Texas	30	971	153	274	.558	77	103	.748	292	13	383	9.7	0.4	12.8
80-81—Texas	30	1106	235	411	.572	107	147	.728	370	36	577	12.3	1.2	19.2
81-82—Texas	27	1042	196	371	.528	111	164	.677	365	35	503	13.5	1.3	18.6
Totals	87	3119	584	1056	.553	295	414	.713	1027	84	1463	11.8	1.0	16.8

NBA REGULAR-SEASON RECORD

NOTES: Tied for NBA lead with 11 disqualifications (1990).

									REBOUNDS								AVERAGES		
Season Team	G	Min.	FGM	FGA	Pct.	FTM	FTA	Pct.	Off.	Def.	Tot.	Ast.	St.	Blk.	TO	Pts.	RPG	APG	PPG
82-83—Kansas City.....	71	987	147	287	.512	89	137	.650	133	242	375	33	40	61	96	383	5.3	0.5	5.4
83-84—Kansas City.....	80	1915	333	637	.523	160	223	.717	260	449	709	86	71	145	168	826	8.9	1.1	10.3
84-85—Kansas City.....	82	2458	369	695	.531	227	315	.721	274	580	854	130	98	128	202	965	10.4	1.6	11.8
85-86—Sacramento ...	80	2377	411	794	.518	202	276	.732	252	518	770	168	71	109	184	1024	9.6	2.1	12.8
86-87—Sacramento ...	82	2166	362	752	.481	188	255	.737	237	450	687	122	69	126	143	912	8.4	1.5	11.1
87-88—Sacramento ...	69	1257	215	456	.472	118	164	.720	138	289	427	68	54	73	109	550	6.2	1.0	8.0
88-89—Sac.-Ind.........	76	2329	416	850	.489	227	281	.808	224	494	718	81	79	94	179	1059	9.4	1.1	13.9
89-90—Indiana...........	82	2126	223	471	.473	107	134	.799	175	455	630	106	65	71	150	554	7.7	1.3	6.8
90-91—Indiana...........	82	1946	276	565	.489	72	104	.692	154	409	563	147	63	63	168	625	6.9	1.8	7.6
91-92—Indiana...........	80	1299	168	359	.468	58	71	.817	98	283	381	102	52	34	98	394	4.8	1.3	4.9
92-93—Indiana...........	63	730	104	213	.488	29	39	.744	55	123	178	34	29	24	47	237	2.8	0.5	3.8
93-94—Indiana...........	30	282	27	77	.351	16	30	.533	26	49	75	16	10	8	23	70	2.5	0.5	2.3
94-95—Indiana...........	38	453	49	118	.415	14	16	.875	28	61	89	18	18	10	33	112	2.3	0.5	2.9
95-96—Philadelphia ...	44	773	33	83	.398	19	24	.792	62	137	199	26	19	20	37	85	4.5	0.6	1.9
Totals	959	21098	3133	6357	.493	1526	2069	.738	2116	4539	6655	1137	738	966	1637	7796	6.9	1.2	8.1

Three-point field goals: 1982-83, 0-for-1. 1985-86, 0-for-1. 1986-87, 0-for-5. 1987-88, 2-for-5 (.400). 1988-89, 0-for-1. 1989-90, 1-for-5 (.200). 1990-91, 1-for-5 (.200). 1991-92, 0-for-2. 1992-93, 0-for-1. Totals, 4-for-26 (.154).

Personal fouls/disqualifications: 1982-83, 186/1. 1983-84, 327/8. 1984-85, 328/4. 1985-86, 295/8. 1986-87, 290/6. 1987-88, 217/1. 1988-89, 285/12. 1989-90, 313/11. 1990-91, 265/4. 1991-92, 207/0. 1992-93, 137/0. 1993-94, 59/1. 1994-95, 76/0. 1995-96, 125/5. Totals, 3110/61.

NBA PLAYOFF RECORD

									REBOUNDS								AVERAGES		
Season Team	G	Min.	FGM	FGA	Pct.	FTM	FTA	Pct.	Off.	Def.	Tot.	Ast.	St.	Blk.	TO	Pts.	RPG	APG	PPG
83-84—Kansas City.....	3	93	18	40	.450	9	11	.818	11	19	30	4	3	4	5	45	10.0	1.3	15.0
85-86—Sacramento ...	3	99	11	32	.344	7	12	.583	14	21	35	2	2	6	4	29	11.7	0.7	9.7
89-90—Indiana...........	3	54	7	15	.467	4	4	1.000	6	9	15	2	0	1	7	18	5.0	0.7	6.0
90-91—Indiana...........	5	126	19	39	.487	7	7	1.000	6	25	31	8	4	7	10	45	6.2	1.6	9.0
91-92—Indiana...........	3	63	7	11	.636	2	2	1.000	2	11	13	4	1	4	3	16	4.3	1.3	5.3
92-93—Indiana...........	4	73	5	15	.333	5	6	.833	7	7	14	3	3	2	4	15	3.5	0.8	3.8
93-94—Indiana...........	7	39	4	11	.364	2	3	.667	3	7	10	5	3	1	4	10	1.4	0.7	1.4
Totals	28	547	71	163	.436	36	45	.800	49	99	148	28	16	25	37	178	5.3	1.0	6.4

Personal fouls/disqualifications: 1983-84, 14/0. 1985-86, 8/0. 1989-90, 13/0. 1990-91, 15/0. 1991-92, 11/0. 1992-93, 9/0. 1993-94, 9/0. Totals, 79/0.

THORNTON, BOB   F/C

PERSONAL: Born July 10, 1962, in Los Angeles. ... 6-10/225. ... Full name: Robert George Thornton.
HIGH SCHOOL: Mission Viejo (Calif.).
JUNIOR COLLEGE: Saddleback Community College (Calif.).
COLLEGE: UC Irvine.
TRANSACTIONS/CAREER NOTES: Selected by New York Knicks in fourth round (87th pick overall) of 1984 NBA Draft. ... Played in Spanish National League with Madrid Caja (1984-85). ... Waived by Knicks (December 16, 1987). ... Signed as free agent by Philadelphia 76ers (December 19, 1987). ... Traded by 76ers to Minnesota Timberwolves for 1991 second-round draft choice (November 10, 1990). ... Signed as free agent by Utah Jazz (April 15, 1992). ... Played in Continental Basketball Association with Sioux Falls Skyforce (1991-92) and Chicago Rockers (1995-96). ... Played in Italy (1991-92 through 94-95). ... Signed as free agent by Portland Trail Blazers (October 1, 1995). ... Waived by Trail Blazers (October 24, 1995). ... Signed by Washington Bullets to first of two consecutive 10-day contracts (March 25, 1996). ... Re-signed by Bullets for remainder of season (April 14, 1996). ... Rights renounced by Bullets (July 15, 1996).

COLLEGIATE RECORD

												AVERAGES		
Season Team	G	Min.	FGM	FGA	Pct.	FTM	FTA	Pct.	Reb.	Ast.	Pts.	RPG	APG	PPG
80-81—Saddleback C.C.	28	...	70	136	.515	31	50	.620	149	...	171	5.3	...	6.1
81-82—UC Irvine	29	452	44	88	.500	33	45	.733	93	30	121	3.2	1.0	4.2
82-83—UC Irvine	27	639	125	216	.579	75	117	.641	161	27	325	6.0	1.0	12.0
83-84—UC Irvine	29	817	151	236	.640	65	118	.551	236	27	367	8.1	0.9	12.7
Junior college totals	28		70	136	.515	31	50	.620	149	...	171	5.3	...	6.1
4-year-college totals	85	1908	320	540	.593	173	280	.618	490	84	813	5.8	1.0	9.6

NBA REGULAR-SEASON RECORD

									REBOUNDS								AVERAGES		
Season Team	G	Min.	FGM	FGA	Pct.	FTM	FTA	Pct.	Off.	Def.	Tot.	Ast.	St.	Blk.	TO	Pts.	RPG	APG	PPG
85-86—New York	71	1323	125	274	.456	86	162	.531	113	177	290	43	30	7	83	336	4.1	0.6	4.7
86-87—New York	33	282	29	67	.433	13	20	.650	18	38	56	8	4	3	24	71	1.7	0.2	2.2
87-88—N.Y.-Phil..........	48	593	65	130	.500	34	55	.618	46	66	112	15	11	3	35	164	2.3	0.3	3.4
88-89—Philadelphia	54	449	47	111	.423	32	60	.533	36	56	92	15	8	7	23	127	1.7	0.3	2.4
89-90—Philadelphia ...	56	592	48	112	.429	26	51	.510	45	88	133	17	20	12	35	123	2.4	0.3	2.2
90-91—Minnesota	12	110	4	13	.308	8	10	.800	1	14	15	1	0	3	9	16	1.3	0.1	1.3
91-92—Utah	2	6	1	7	.143	2	2	1.000	2	0	2	0	0	0	0	4	1.0	0.0	2.0
95-96—Washington	7	31	1	6	.167	1	2	.500	6	6	12	0	1	0	1	3	1.7	0.0	0.4
Totals	283	3386	320	720	.444	202	362	.558	267	445	712	99	74	35	210	844	2.5	0.3	3.0

Three-point field goals: 1986-87, 0-for-1. 1987-88, 0-for-2. 1988-89, 1-for-3 (.333). 1989-90, 1-for-3 (.333). Totals, 2-for-9 (.222).

Personal fouls/disqualifications: 1985-86, 209/5. 1986-87, 48/0. 1987-88, 103/1. 1988-89, 87/0. 1989-90, 105/1. 1990-91, 18/0. 1991-92, 1/0. 1995-96, 7/0. Totals, 578/7.

NBA PLAYOFF RECORD

									REBOUNDS								AVERAGES		
Season Team	G	Min.	FGM	FGA	Pct.	FTM	FTA	Pct.	Off.	Def.	Tot.	Ast.	St.	Blk.	TO	Pts.	RPG	APG	PPG
89-90—Philadelphia	9	89	7	18	.389	5	10	.500	11	4	15	4	2	1	2	19	1.7	0.4	2.1
91-92—Utah	7	32	2	5	.400	3	4	.750	4	5	9	1	0	0	1	7	1.3	0.1	1.0
Totals	16	121	9	23	.391	8	14	.571	15	9	24	5	2	1	3	26	1.5	0.3	1.6

Personal fouls/disqualifications: 1989-90, 22/0. 1991-92, 3/0. Totals, 25/0.

CBA REGULAR-SEASON RECORD

Season Team	G	Min.	FGM	FGA	Pct.	FTM	FTA	Pct.	Reb.	Ast.	Pts.	AVERAGES RPG	APG	PPG
91-92—Sioux Falls	13	394	64	108	.593	40	58	.690	127	22	168	9.8	1.7	12.9
95-96—Chicago	34	808	141	247	.571	68	99	.687	177	17	350	5.2	0.5	10.3
Totals	47	1202	205	355	.577	108	157	.688	304	39	518	6.5	0.8	11.0

Three-point field goals: 1995-96, 0-for-1.

ITALIAN LEAGUE RECORD

Season Team	G	Min.	FGM	FGA	Pct.	FTM	FTA	Pct.	Reb.	Ast.	Pts.	AVERAGES RPG	APG	PPG
91-92—Tic. Assic. Siena	8	233	38	78	.487	36	46	.783	63	3	112	7.9	0.4	14.0
92-93—Fernet Branca Pavia	30	1060	210	325	.646	128	168	.762	306	56	548	10.2	1.9	18.3
93-94—Tonno Auriga Trapani	11	...	...	...	...	...	...	...	83	8	200	7.6	0.7	18.2
94-95—Olitalia Sienai	27	...	...	...	...	...	...	...	233	14	408	8.6	0.5	15.1
Totals	76								685	81	1268	9.0	1.1	16.7

T

THORPE, OTIS F PISTONS

PERSONAL: Born August 5, 1962, in Boynton Beach, Fla. ... 6-10/246. ... Full name: Otis Henry Thorpe.
HIGH SCHOOL: Lake Worth (Fla.) Community.
COLLEGE: Providence.
TRANSACTIONS/CAREER NOTES: Selected by Kansas City Kings in first round (ninth pick overall) of 1984 NBA Draft. ... Kings franchise moved from Kansas City to Sacramento for 1985-86 season. ... Traded by Kings to Houston Rockets for F/G Rodney McCray and F/C Jim Petersen (October 11, 1988). ... Traded by Rockets with rights to F Marcelo Nicola and 1995 first-round draft choice to Portland Trail Blazers for G Clyde Drexler and F Tracy Murray (February 14, 1995). ... Traded by Trail Blazers to Detroit Pistons for F Bill Curley and draft rights to G Randolph Childress (September 20, 1995).
MISCELLANEOUS: Member of NBA championship team (1994).

COLLEGIATE RECORD

Season Team	G	Min.	FGM	FGA	Pct.	FTM	FTA	Pct.	Reb.	Ast.	Pts.	AVERAGES RPG	APG	PPG
80-81—Providence	26	668	100	194	.515	50	76	.658	137	11	250	5.3	0.4	9.6
81-82—Providence	27	942	153	283	.541	74	115	.643	216	36	380	8.0	1.3	14.1
82-83—Providence	31	1041	204	321	.636	91	138	.659	249	24	499	8.0	0.8	16.1
83-84—Providence	29	1051	167	288	.580	162	248	.653	300	36	496	10.3	1.2	17.1
Totals	113	3702	624	1086	.575	377	577	.653	902	107	1625	8.0	0.9	14.4

NBA REGULAR-SEASON RECORD

NOTES: Tied for NBA lead with 300 personal fouls (1996).

Season Team	G	Min.	FGM	FGA	Pct.	FTM	FTA	Pct.	REBOUNDS Off.	Def.	Tot.	Ast.	St.	Blk.	TO	Pts.	AVERAGES RPG	APG	PPG
84-85—Kansas City	82	1918	411	685	.600	230	371	.620	187	369	556	111	34	37	187	1052	6.8	1.4	12.8
85-86—Sacramento	75	1675	289	492	.587	164	248	.661	137	283	420	84	35	34	123	742	5.6	1.1	9.9
86-87—Sacramento	82	2956	567	1050	.540	413	543	.761	259	560	819	201	46	60	189	1547	10.0	2.5	18.9
87-88—Sacramento	82	3072	622	1226	.507	460	609	.755	279	558	837	266	62	56	228	1704	10.2	3.2	20.8
88-89—Houston	82	3135	521	961	.542	328	450	.729	272	515	787	202	82	37	225	1370	9.6	2.5	16.7
89-90—Houston	82	2947	547	998	.548	307	446	.688	258	476	734	261	66	24	229	1401	9.0	3.2	17.1
90-91—Houston	82	3039	549	988	.556	334	480	.696	287	559	846	197	73	20	217	1435	10.3	2.4	17.5
91-92—Houston	82	3056	558	943	.592	304	463	.657	285	577	862	250	52	37	237	1420	10.5	3.0	17.3
92-93—Houston	72	2357	385	690	.558	153	256	.598	219	370	589	181	43	19	151	923	8.2	2.5	12.8
93-94—Houston	82	2909	449	801	.561	251	382	.657	271	599	870	189	66	28	185	1149	10.6	2.3	14.0
94-95—Hou.-Port.	70	2096	385	681	.565	167	281	.594	202	356	558	112	41	28	132	937	8.0	1.6	13.4
95-96—Detroit	82	2841	452	853	.530	257	362	.710	211	477	688	158	53	39	195	1161	8.4	1.9	14.2
Totals	955	32001	5735	10368	.553	3368	4891	.689	2867	5699	8566	2212	653	419	2298	14841	9.0	2.3	15.5

Three-point field goals: 1984-85, 0-for-2. 1986-87, 0-for-3. 1987-88, 0-for-6. 1988-89, 0-for-2. 1989-90, 0-for-10. 1990-91, 3-for-7 (.429). 1991-92, 0-for-7. 1992-93, 0-for-2. 1993-94, 0-for-2. 1994-95, 0-for-7. 1995-96, 0-for-4. Totals, 3-for-52 (.058).
Personal fouls/disqualifications: 1984-85, 256/2. 1985-86, 233/3. 1986-87, 292/11. 1987-88, 264/3. 1988-89, 259/6. 1989-90, 270/5. 1990-91, 278/10. 1991-92, 307/7. 1992-93, 234/3. 1993-94, 253/1. 1994-95, 224/3. 1995-96, 300/7. Totals, 3170/61.

NBA PLAYOFF RECORD

NOTES: Holds career playoff record for highest field-goal percentage (minimum 150 made)—.585.

Season Team	G	Min.	FGM	FGA	Pct.	FTM	FTA	Pct.	REBOUNDS Off.	Def.	Tot.	Ast.	St.	Blk.	TO	Pts.	AVERAGES RPG	APG	PPG
85-86—Sacramento	3	35	3	13	.231	6	13	.462	8	4	12	0	0	1	1	12	4.0	0.0	4.0
88-89—Houston	4	152	24	37	.649	16	21	.762	6	14	20	12	5	1	15	64	5.0	3.0	16.0
89-90—Houston	4	164	27	45	.600	26	38	.684	14	19	33	7	5	0	9	80	8.3	1.8	20.0
90-91—Houston	3	116	22	38	.579	3	6	.500	7	18	25	8	2	0	6	47	8.3	2.7	15.7
92-93—Houston	12	419	73	115	.635	28	43	.651	36	67	103	31	6	1	17	174	8.6	2.6	14.5
93-94—Houston	23	854	111	194	.572	38	67	.567	68	160	228	54	13	10	37	261	9.9	2.3	11.3
94-95—Portland	3	66	12	21	.571	7	10	.700	5	8	13	2	0	0	3	31	4.3	0.7	10.3
95-96—Detroit	3	101	13	24	.542	9	12	.750	14	21	35	7	0	0	7	35	11.7	2.3	11.7
Totals	55	1907	285	487	.585	133	210	.633	158	311	469	121	31	13	95	704	8.5	2.2	12.8

Three-point field goals: 1993-94, 1-for-2 (.500).
Personal fouls/disqualifications: 1985-86, 4/0. 1988-89, 17/1. 1989-90, 12/0. 1990-91, 8/0. 1992-93, 35/0. 1993-94, 86/2. 1994-95, 12/1. 1995-96, 9/0. Totals, 183/4.

NBA ALL-STAR GAME RECORD

Season Team	Min.	FGM	FGA	Pct.	FTM	FTA	Pct.	REBOUNDS Off.	Def.	Tot.	Ast.	PF	Dq.	St.	Blk.	TO	Pts.
1992 —Houston	4	1	1	1.000	0	0	...	0	0	0	0	0	0	0	0	0	2

THREATT, SEDALE   G

PERSONAL: Born September 10, 1961, in Atlanta. ... 6-2/185. ... Full name: Sedale Eugene Threatt. ... Name pronounced suh-DALE thrEET.
HIGH SCHOOL: Therrell (Atlanta).
COLLEGE: West Virginia Tech.
TRANSACTIONS/CAREER NOTES: Selected by Philadelphia 76ers in sixth round (139th pick overall) of 1983 NBA Draft. ... Traded by 76ers to Chicago Bulls for G Steve Colter and future second-round draft choice (December 31, 1986). ... Traded by Bulls to Seattle SuperSonics for G Sam Vincent (February 25, 1988). ... Traded by SuperSonics to Los Angeles Lakers for 1994, 1995 and 1996 second-round draft choices (October 2, 1991). ... Rights renounced by Lakers (July 17, 1996).

COLLEGIATE RECORD

Season Team	G	Min.	FGM	FGA	Pct.	FTM	FTA	Pct.	Reb.	Ast.	Pts.	RPG	APG	PPG
79-80—W. Virginia Tech	28	...	204	424	.481	90	126	.714	97	109	498	3.5	3.9	17.8
80-81—W. Virginia Tech	31	...	237	524	.452	74	104	.712	122	160	548	3.9	5.2	17.7
81-82—W. Virginia Tech	34	...	299	598	.500	156	214	.729	118	199	754	3.5	5.9	22.2
82-83—W. Virginia Tech	27	951	284	510	.557	120	164	.732	104	180	688	3.9	6.7	25.5
Totals	120	...	1024	2056	.498	440	608	.724	441	648	2488	3.7	5.4	20.7

NBA REGULAR-SEASON RECORD

Season Team	G	Min.	FGM	FGA	Pct.	FTM	FTA	Pct.	Off.	Def.	Tot.	Ast.	St.	Blk.	TO	Pts.	RPG	APG	PPG
83-84—Philadelphia	45	464	62	148	.419	23	28	.821	17	23	40	41	13	2	33	148	0.9	0.9	3.3
84-85—Philadelphia	82	1304	188	416	.452	66	90	.733	21	78	99	175	80	16	99	446	1.2	2.1	5.4
85-86—Philadelphia	70	1754	310	684	.453	75	90	.833	21	100	121	193	93	5	102	696	1.7	2.8	9.9
86-87—Phil.-Chi.	68	1446	239	534	.448	95	119	.798	26	82	108	259	74	13	89	580	1.6	3.8	8.5
87-88—Chi.-Seattle	71	1055	216	425	.508	57	71	.803	23	65	88	160	60	8	63	492	1.2	2.3	6.9
88-89—Seattle	63	1220	235	476	.494	63	77	.818	31	86	117	238	83	4	77	544	1.9	3.8	8.6
89-90—Seattle	65	1481	303	599	.506	130	157	.828	43	72	115	216	65	8	77	744	1.8	3.3	11.4
90-91—Seattle	80	2066	433	835	.519	137	173	.792	25	74	99	273	113	8	138	1013	1.2	3.4	12.7
91-92—L.A. Lakers	82	3070	509	1041	.489	202	243	.831	43	210	253	593	168	16	182	1240	3.1	7.2	15.1
92-93—L.A. Lakers	82	2893	522	1028	.508	177	215	.823	47	226	273	564	142	11	173	1235	3.3	6.9	15.1
93-94—L.A. Lakers	81	2278	411	852	.482	138	155	.890	28	125	153	344	110	19	106	965	1.9	4.2	11.9
94-95—L.A. Lakers	59	1384	217	437	.497	88	111	.793	21	103	124	248	54	12	70	558	2.1	4.2	9.5
95-96—L.A. Lakers	82	1687	241	526	.458	54	71	.761	20	75	95	269	68	11	74	596	1.2	3.3	7.3
Totals	930	22102	3886	8001	.486	1305	1600	.816	366	1319	1685	3573	1123	133	1283	9257	1.8	3.8	10.0

Three-point field goals: 1983-84, 1-for-8 (.125). 1984-85, 4-for-22 (.182). 1985-86, 1-for-24 (.042). 1986-87, 7-for-32 (.219). 1987-88, 3-for-27 (.111). 1988-89, 11-for-30 (.367). 1989-90, 8-for-22 (.250). 1990-91, 10-for-35 (.286). 1991-92, 20-for-62 (.323). 1992-93, 14-for-53 (.264). 1993-94, 5-for-33 (.152). 1994-95, 36-for-95 (.379). 1995-96, 60-for-169 (.355). Totals, 180-for-622 (.289).

Personal fouls/disqualifications: 1983-84, 65/1. 1984-85, 171/2. 1985-86, 157/1. 1986-87, 164/0. 1987-88, 100/0. 1988-89, 155/0. 1989-90, 164/0. 1990-91, 191/0. 1991-92, 231/1. 1992-93, 248/1. 1993-94, 186/1. 1994-95, 139/1. 1995-96, 178/0. Totals, 2149/8.

NBA PLAYOFF RECORD

Season Team	G	Min.	FGM	FGA	Pct.	FTM	FTA	Pct.	Off.	Def.	Tot.	Ast.	St.	Blk.	TO	Pts.	RPG	APG	PPG
83-84—Philadelphia	3	6	1	3	.333	0	0	...	1	1	2	1	1	0	2	2	0.7	0.3	0.7
84-85—Philadelphia	4	28	2	7	.286	0	0	...	1	0	1	5	1	0	3	4	0.3	1.3	1.0
85-86—Philadelphia	12	312	67	143	.469	26	33	.788	6	19	25	42	23	2	15	160	2.1	3.5	13.3
86-87—Chicago	3	70	8	17	.471	4	4	1.000	2	3	5	16	1	0	2	20	1.7	5.3	6.7
87-88—Seattle	5	80	14	34	.412	4	4	1.000	2	9	11	11	1	0	5	32	2.2	2.2	6.4
88-89—Seattle	8	201	39	82	.476	17	20	.850	3	10	13	49	17	0	11	96	1.6	6.1	12.0
90-91—Seattle	5	136	30	56	.536	9	10	.900	1	7	8	17	5	0	8	73	1.6	3.4	14.6
91-92—L.A. Lakers	4	162	24	46	.522	9	12	.750	0	8	8	17	2	0	11	59	2.0	4.3	14.8
92-93—L.A. Lakers	5	205	39	89	.438	9	12	.750	3	14	17	40	13	1	12	90	3.4	8.0	18.0
94-95—L.A. Lakers	1	11	1	4	.250	0	0	...	0	0	0	2	1	0	0	2	0.0	2.0	2.0
95-96—L.A. Lakers	4	57	4	18	.222	0	0	...	1	2	3	4	2	0	3	10	0.8	1.0	2.5
Totals	54	1268	229	499	.459	78	95	.821	20	73	93	204	67	3	72	548	1.7	3.8	10.1

Three-point field goals: 1983-84, 0-for-2. 1985-86, 0-for-2. 1987-88, 0-for-1. 1988-89, 1-for-4 (.250). 1990-91, 4-for-11 (.364). 1991-92, 2-for-3 (.667). 1992-93, 3-for-13 (.231). 1994-95, 0-for-2. 1995-96, 2-for-11 (.182). Totals, 12-for-49 (.245).

Personal fouls/disqualifications: 1984-85, 2/0. 1985-86, 35/0. 1986-87, 11/0. 1987-88, 7/0. 1988-89, 22/0. 1990-91, 14/0. 1991-92, 11/0. 1992-93, 19/1. 1994-95, 2/0. 1995-96, 4/0. Totals, 127/1.

TISDALE, WAYMAN   C/F   SUNS

PERSONAL: Born June 9, 1964, in Tulsa, Okla. ... 6-9/260. ... Full name: Wayman Lawrence Tisdale.
HIGH SCHOOL: Booker T. Washington (Tulsa, Okla.).
COLLEGE: Oklahoma.
TRANSACTIONS/CAREER NOTES: Selected after junior season by Indiana Pacers in first round (second pick overall) of 1985 NBA Draft. ... Traded by Pacers with 1990 or 1991 second-round draft choice to Sacramento Kings for C LaSalle Thompson and G/F Randy Wittman (February 20, 1989). ... Rights renounced by Kings (August 19, 1994). ... Signed as free agent by Phoenix Suns (September 16, 1994).
MISCELLANEOUS: Member of gold-medal-winning U.S. Olympic team (1984).

NOTES: THE SPORTING NEWS All-America first team (1984, 1985). ... THE SPORTING NEWS All-America second team (1983).

COLLEGIATE RECORD

Season Team	G	Min.	FGM	FGA	Pct.	FTM	FTA	Pct.	Reb.	Ast.	Pts.	RPG	APG	PPG
82-83—Oklahoma	33	1138	338	583	.580	134	211	.635	341	25	810	10.3	0.8	24.5

Season Team	G	Min.	FGM	FGA	Pct.	FTM	FTA	Pct.	Reb.	Ast.	Pts.	RPG	APG	PPG
83-84—Oklahoma	34	1232	369	639	.577	181	283	.640	329	25	919	9.7	0.7	27.0
84-85—Oklahoma	37	1283	370	640	.578	192	273	.703	378	47	932	10.2	1.3	25.2
Totals	104	3653	1077	1862	.578	507	767	.661	1048	97	2661	10.1	0.9	25.6

NBA REGULAR-SEASON RECORD

Season Team	G	Min.	FGM	FGA	Pct.	FTM	FTA	Pct.	REBOUNDS Off.	Def.	Tot.	Ast.	St.	Blk.	TO	Pts.	AVERAGES RPG	APG	PPG
85-86—Indiana	81	2277	516	1002	.515	160	234	.684	191	393	584	79	32	44	188	1192	7.2	1.0	14.7
86-87—Indiana	81	2159	458	892	.513	258	364	.709	217	258	475	117	50	26	139	1174	5.9	1.4	14.5
87-88—Indiana	79	2378	511	998	.512	246	314	.783	168	323	491	103	54	34	145	1268	6.2	1.3	16.1
88-89—Ind.-Sac.	79	2434	532	1036	.514	317	410	.773	187	422	609	128	55	52	172	1381	7.7	1.6	17.5
89-90—Sacramento	79	2937	726	1383	.525	306	391	.783	185	410	595	108	54	54	153	1758	7.5	1.4	22.3
90-91—Sacramento	33	1116	262	542	.483	136	170	.800	75	178	253	66	23	28	82	660	7.7	2.0	20.0
91-92—Sacramento	72	2521	522	1043	.500	151	198	.763	135	334	469	106	55	79	124	1195	6.5	1.5	16.6
92-93—Sacramento	76	2283	544	1068	.509	175	231	.758	127	373	500	108	52	47	117	1263	6.6	1.4	16.6
93-94—Sacramento	79	2557	552	1102	.501	215	266	.808	159	401	560	139	37	52	124	1319	7.1	1.8	16.7
94-95—Phoenix	65	1276	278	574	.484	94	122	.771	83	164	247	45	29	27	64	650	3.8	0.7	10.0
95-96—Phoenix	63	1152	279	564	.495	114	149	.765	55	159	214	58	15	36	63	672	3.4	0.9	10.7
Totals	787	23090	5180	10204	.508	2172	2849	.762	1582	3415	4997	1057	456	479	1371	12532	6.3	1.3	15.9

Three-point field goals: 1985-86, 0-for-2. 1986-87, 0-for-2. 1987-88, 0-for-2. 1988-89, 0-for-4. 1989-90, 0-for-6. 1990-91, 0-for-1. 1991-92, 0-for-2. 1992-93, 0-for-2. Totals, 0-for-21.

Personal fouls/disqualifications: 1985-86, 290/3. 1986-87, 293/9. 1987-88, 274/5. 1988-89, 290/7. 1989-90, 251/3. 1990-91, 99/0. 1991-92, 248/3. 1992-93, 277/8. 1993-94, 290/4. 1994-95, 190/3. 1995-96, 188/2. Totals, 2690/47.

NBA PLAYOFF RECORD

Season Team	G	Min.	FGM	FGA	Pct.	FTM	FTA	Pct.	REBOUNDS Off.	Def.	Tot.	Ast.	St.	Blk.	TO	Pts.	AVERAGES RPG	APG	PPG
86-87—Indiana	4	108	19	31	.613	13	23	.565	5	11	16	9	1	0	5	51	4.0	2.3	12.8
94-95—Phoenix	10	170	32	71	.451	9	14	.643	6	24	30	11	0	4	6	73	3.0	1.1	7.3
95-96—Phoenix	4	67	10	30	.333	1	2	.500	3	1	4	2	1	1	1	21	1.0	0.5	5.3
Totals	18	345	61	132	.462	23	39	.590	14	36	50	22	2	5	12	145	2.8	1.2	8.1

Three-point field goals: 1994-95, 0-for-1.
Personal fouls/disqualifications: 1986-87, 17/1. 1994-95, 32/1. 1995-96, 7/0. Totals, 56/2.

TOOLSON, ANDY   G/F

PERSONAL: Born January 19, 1966, in Chicago. ... 6-6/210. ... Full name: Andrew K. Toolson.
HIGH SCHOOL: Twin Falls (Idaho).
COLLEGE: Brigham Young.
TRANSACTIONS/CAREER NOTES: Not drafted by an NBA franchise. ... Signed as free agent by Utah Jazz (October 1, 1990). ... Played in Italy (1991-92). ... Played in Continental Basketball Association with Tri-City Chinook (1992-93). ... Played in Spain (1993-94 and 1994-95). ... Signed as free agent by Jazz (June 14, 1995). ... Waived by Jazz (December 29, 1995). ... Re-signed by Jazz to 10-day contract (January 19, 1996). ... Waived by Jazz from 10-day contract (January 23, 1996).

COLLEGIATE RECORD

Season Team	G	Min.	FGM	FGA	Pct.	FTM	FTA	Pct.	Reb.	Ast.	Pts.	RPG	APG	PPG
84-85—Brigham Young	29	548	97	193	.503	53	73	.726	77	...	247	2.7	...	8.5
85-86—Brigham Young						On Mormon mission.								
86-87—Brigham Young						On Mormon mission.								
87-88—Brigham Young	32	611	64	149	.430	39	53	.736	88	41	192	2.8	1.3	6.0
88-89—Brigham Young	26	905	126	265	.475	105	126	.833	171	45	399	6.6	1.7	15.3
89-90—Brigham Young	30	1095	184	351	.524	108	141	.766	198	80	550	6.6	2.7	18.3
Totals	117	3159	471	958	.492	305	393	.776	534	...	1388	4.6	...	11.9

Three-point field goals: 1987-88, 25-for-63 (.397). 1988-89, 42-for-109 (.385). 1989-90, 74-for-151 (.490). Totals, 141-for-323 (.437).

NBA REGULAR-SEASON RECORD

Season Team	G	Min.	FGM	FGA	Pct.	FTM	FTA	Pct.	REBOUNDS Off.	Def.	Tot.	Ast.	St.	Blk.	TO	Pts.	AVERAGES RPG	APG	PPG
90-91—Utah	47	470	50	124	.403	25	33	.758	32	35	67	31	14	2	24	137	1.4	0.7	2.9
95-96—Utah	13	53	8	22	.364	3	4	.750	0	6	6	1	0	0	2	22	0.5	0.1	1.7
Totals	60	523	58	146	.397	28	37	.757	32	41	73	32	14	2	26	159	1.2	0.5	2.7

Three-point field goals: 1990-91, 12-for-32 (.375). 1995-96, 3-for-12 (.250). Totals, 15-for-44 (.341).
Personal fouls/disqualifications: 1990-91, 58/0. 1995-96, 12/0. Totals, 70/0.

NBA PLAYOFF RECORD

Season Team	G	Min.	FGM	FGA	Pct.	FTM	FTA	Pct.	REBOUNDS Off.	Def.	Tot.	Ast.	St.	Blk.	TO	Pts.	AVERAGES RPG	APG	PPG
90-91—Utah	2	4	0	2	.000	0	0	...	0	0	0	1	1	0	0	0	0.0	0.5	0.0

Three-point field goals: 1990-91, 0-for-1.

ITALIAN LEAGUE RECORD

Season Team	G	Min.	FGM	FGA	Pct.	FTM	FTA	Pct.	Reb.	Ast.	Pts.	RPG	APG	PPG
91-92—Telemarket Brescia	10	301	51	100	.510	16	22	.727	57	9	136	5.7	0.9	13.6

CBA REGULAR-SEASON RECORD

Season Team	G	Min.	FGM	FGA	Pct.	FTM	FTA	Pct.	Reb.	Ast.	Pts.	RPG	APG	PPG
92-93—Tri-City	49	1292	216	475	.455	72	87	.828	143	89	569	2.9	1.8	11.6

Three-point field goals: 1992-93, 65-for-150 (.433).

SPANISH LEAGUE RECORD

												AVERAGES		
Season Team	G	Min.	FGM	FGA	Pct.	FTM	FTA	Pct.	Reb.	Ast.	Pts.	RPG	APG	PPG
93-94—Festina Andorra.............	28	1022	210	407	.516	77	91	.846	148	27	607	5.3	1.0	21.7
94-95—Amway Zaragoza...........	38	1276	205	437	.469	96	117	.821	158	39	637	4.2	1.0	16.8
Totals	66	2298	415	844	.492	173	208	.832	306	66	1244	4.6	1.0	18.8

TOWER, KEITH   C/F

PERSONAL: Born May 15, 1970, in Libby, Mont. ... 6-11/250. ... Full name: Keith Raymond Tower.
HIGH SCHOOL: Moon (Coraopolis, Pa.).
COLLEGE: Notre Dame.
TRANSACTIONS/CAREER NOTES: Not drafted by an NBA franchise. ... Signed as free agent by Chicago Bulls (October 6, 1992). ... Waived by Bulls (October 28, 1992). ... Played in Continental Basketball Association with Columbus Horizon (1992-93). ... Signed as free agent by Orlando Magic (September 23, 1993). ... Waived by Magic (November 17, 1994). ... Signed as free agent by Los Angeles Clippers (October 4, 1995). ... Waived by Clippers (July 11, 1996).

COLLEGIATE RECORD

												AVERAGES		
Season Team	G	Min.	FGM	FGA	Pct.	FTM	FTA	Pct.	Reb.	Ast.	Pts.	RPG	APG	PPG
88-89—Notre Dame..................	29	329	28	50	.560	15	33	.455	81	8	71	2.8	0.3	2.4
89-90—Notre Dame..................	25	275	19	61	.311	15	25	.600	67	5	53	2.7	0.2	2.1
90-91—Notre Dame..................	32	971	103	222	.464	48	76	.632	223	54	254	7.0	1.7	7.9
91-92—Notre Dame..................	31	774	55	139	.396	24	44	.545	165	44	134	5.3	1.4	4.3
Totals	117	2349	205	472	.434	102	178	.573	536	111	512	4.6	0.9	4.4

Three-point field goals: 1991-92, 0-for-2.

CBA REGULAR-SEASON RECORD

												AVERAGES		
Season Team	G	Min.	FGM	FGA	Pct.	FTM	FTA	Pct.	Reb.	Ast.	Pts.	RPG	APG	PPG
92-93—Columbus......................	28	342	29	73	.397	14	22	.636	96	11	72	3.4	0.4	2.6

NBA REGULAR-SEASON RECORD

								REBOUNDS								AVERAGES		
Season Team	G	Min.	FGM	FGA	Pct.	FTM	FTA	Pct.	Off.	Def.	Tot.	Ast.	St.	Blk.	TO	Pts.	RPG	APG	PPG
93-94—Orlando...........	11	32	4	9	.444	0	0	...	0	6	6	1	0	0	0	8	0.5	0.1	0.7
94-95—Orlando...........	3	7	0	2	.000	1	2	.500	1	2	3	0	0	0	1	1	1.0	0.0	0.3
95-96—L.A. Clippers...	34	305	32	72	.444	18	26	.692	22	29	51	5	4	11	16	82	1.5	0.1	2.4
Totals	48	344	36	83	.434	19	28	.679	23	37	60	6	4	11	17	91	1.3	0.1	1.9

Three-point field goals: 1995-96, 0-for-1.
Personal fouls/disqualifications: 1993-94, 6/0. 1994-95, 1/0. 1995-96, 50/1. Totals, 57/1.

TRENT, GARY   F   TRAIL BLAZERS

PERSONAL: Born September 22, 1974, in Columbus, Ohio. ... 6-8/250. ... Full name: Gary Dajaun Trent.
HIGH SCHOOL: Hamilton Township (Columbus, Ohio).
COLLEGE: Ohio University.
TRANSACTIONS/CAREER NOTES: Selected after junior season by Milwaukee Bucks in first round (11th pick overall) of 1995 NBA Draft. ... Draft rights traded by Bucks with conditional 1996 first-round draft choice to Portland Trail Blazers for draft rights to G Shawn Respert (June 28, 1995).

COLLEGIATE RECORD

												AVERAGES		
Season Team	G	Min.	FGM	FGA	Pct.	FTM	FTA	Pct.	Reb.	Ast.	Pts.	RPG	APG	PPG
92-93—Ohio University	27	892	194	298	.651	126	101	.096	250	42	514	9.3	1.6	19.0
93-94—Ohio University..............	33	1119	309	536	.577	210	291	.722	377	65	837	11.4	2.0	25.4
94-95—Ohio University..............	33	1134	293	556	.527	163	254	.642	423	79	757	12.8	2.4	22.9
Totals	93	3145	796	1390	.573	499	726	.687	1050	186	2108	11.3	2.0	22.7

Three-point field goals: 1992-93, 0-for-1. 1993-94, 9-for-33 (.273). 1994-95, 8-for-35 (.229). Totals, 17-for-69 (.246).

NBA REGULAR-SEASON RECORD

								REBOUNDS								AVERAGES		
Season Team	G	Min.	FGM	FGA	Pct.	FTM	FTA	Pct.	Off.	Def.	Tot.	Ast.	St.	Blk.	TO	Pts.	RPG	APG	PPG
95-96—Portland..........	69	1219	220	429	.513	78	141	.553	84	154	238	50	25	11	92	518	3.4	0.7	7.5

Three-point field goals: 1995-96, 0-for-9.
Personal fouls/disqualifications: 1995-96, 116/0.

NBA PLAYOFF RECORD

								REBOUNDS								AVERAGES		
Season Team	G	Min.	FGM	FGA	Pct.	FTM	FTA	Pct.	Off.	Def.	Tot.	Ast.	St.	Blk.	TO	Pts.	RPG	APG	PPG
95-96—Portland..........	2	10	1	4	.250	0	0	...	0	1	1	0	1	0	0	2	0.5	0.0	1.0

Personal fouls/disqualifications: 1995-96, 3/0.

DID YOU KNOW...

...that Karl Malone is the only player to score more than 2,000 points
in nine consecutive NBA seasons?

TURNER, JEFF   F

PERSONAL: Born April 9, 1962, in Bangor, Me. ... 6-9/244. ... Full name: Jeffrey Steven Turner.
HIGH SCHOOL: Brandon (Fla.).
COLLEGE: Vanderbilt.
TRANSACTIONS/CAREER NOTES: Selected by New Jersey Nets in first round (17th pick overall) of 1984 NBA Draft. ... Played in Italy (1987-88 and 1988-89). ... Signed as unrestricted free agent by Orlando Magic (July 11, 1989). ... Traded by Magic to Vancouver Grizzlies for F Kenny Gattison and 1996 second-round draft choice (February 22, 1996). ... Waived by Grizzlies (March 8, 1996).
MISCELLANEOUS: Member of gold-medal-winning U.S. Olympic team (1984).

COLLEGIATE RECORD

Season Team	G	Min.	FGM	FGA	Pct.	FTM	FTA	Pct.	Reb.	Ast.	Pts.	RPG	APG	PPG
80-81—Vanderbilt	28	586	40	96	.417	20	31	.645	84	35	100	3.0	1.3	3.6
81-82—Vanderbilt	27	772	99	189	.524	52	71	.732	145	25	250	5.4	0.9	9.3
82-83—Vanderbilt	33	1008	180	366	.492	75	98	.765	182	29	435	5.5	0.9	13.2
83-84—Vanderbilt	29	953	200	375	.533	86	102	.843	213	53	486	7.3	1.8	16.8
Totals	117	3319	519	1026	.506	233	302	.772	624	142	1271	5.3	1.2	10.9

NBA REGULAR-SEASON RECORD

Season Team	G	Min.	FGM	FGA	Pct.	FTM	FTA	Pct.	REBOUNDS Off.	Def.	Tot.	Ast.	St.	Blk.	TO	Pts.	AVERAGES RPG	APG	PPG
84-85—New Jersey	72	1429	171	377	.454	79	92	.859	88	130	218	108	29	7	90	421	3.0	1.5	5.8
85-86—New Jersey	53	650	84	171	.491	58	78	.744	45	92	137	14	21	3	49	226	2.6	0.3	4.3
86-87—New Jersey	76	1003	151	325	.465	76	104	.731	80	117	197	60	33	13	81	378	2.6	0.8	5.0
89-90—Orlando	60	1105	132	308	.429	42	54	.778	52	175	227	53	23	12	61	308	3.8	0.9	5.1
90-91—Orlando	71	1683	259	532	.487	85	112	.759	108	255	363	97	29	10	126	609	5.1	1.4	8.6
91-92—Orlando	75	1591	225	499	.451	79	114	.693	62	184	246	92	24	16	106	530	3.3	1.2	7.1
92-93—Orlando	75	1479	231	437	.529	56	70	.800	74	178	252	107	19	9	66	528	3.4	1.4	7.0
93-94—Orlando	68	1536	199	426	.467	35	45	.778	79	192	271	60	23	11	75	451	4.0	0.9	6.6
94-95—Orlando	49	576	73	178	.410	26	29	.897	23	74	97	38	12	3	22	199	2.0	0.8	4.1
95-96—Orlando	13	192	18	51	.353	2	2	1.000	10	18	28	6	2	1	11	47	2.2	0.5	3.6
Totals	612	11244	1543	3304	.467	538	700	.769	621	1415	2036	635	215	85	687	3697	3.3	1.0	6.0

Three-point field goals: 1984-85, 0-for-3. 1985-86, 0-for-1. 1986-87, 0-for-1. 1989-90, 2-for-10 (.200). 1990-91, 6-for-15 (.400). 1991-92, 1-for-8 (.125). 1992-93, 10-for-17 (.588). 1993-94, 18-for-55 (.327). 1994-95, 27-for-75 (.360). 1995-96, 9-for-27 (.333). Totals, 73-for-212 (.344).

Personal fouls/disqualifications: 1984-85, 243/8. 1985-86, 125/4. 1986-87, 200/6. 1989-90, 161/4. 1990-91, 234/5. 1991-92, 229/6. 1992-93, 192/2. 1993-94, 239/1. 1994-95, 102/2. 1995-96, 33/2. Totals, 1758/40.

NBA PLAYOFF RECORD

Season Team	G	Min.	FGM	FGA	Pct.	FTM	FTA	Pct.	REBOUNDS Off.	Def.	Tot.	Ast.	St.	Blk.	TO	Pts.	AVERAGES RPG	APG	PPG
84-85—New Jersey	3	21	2	5	.400	0	0	...	2	2	4	2	0	0	0	4	1.3	0.7	1.3
85-86—New Jersey	3	18	1	3	.333	1	1	1.000	0	3	3	3	0	0	4	3	1.0	1.0	1.0
94-95—Orlando	18	179	17	40	.425	4	4	1.000	4	21	25	11	4	3	6	49	1.4	0.6	2.7
Totals	24	218	20	48	.417	5	5	1.000	6	26	32	16	4	3	10	56	1.3	0.7	2.3

Three-point field goals: 1994-95, 11-for-22 (.500).
Personal fouls/disqualifications: 1984-85, 6/0. 1985-86, 7/0. 1994-95, 44/0. Totals, 57/0.

ITALIAN LEAGUE RECORD

Season Team	G	Min.	FGM	FGA	Pct.	FTM	FTA	Pct.	Reb.	Ast.	Pts.	RPG	APG	PPG
87-88—Arexons Cantu	35	1271	216	417	.518	137	150	.913	187	...	641	5.3	...	18.3
88-89—Vis. Cantu	33	1104	186	318	.585	124	148	.838	249	...	562	7.5	...	17.0
Totals	68	2375	402	735	.547	261	298	.876	436	...	1203	6.4	...	17.7

VANDER VELDEN, LOGAN   F

PERSONAL: Born April 3, 1971, in Valders, Wis. ... 6-8/215.
HIGH SCHOOL: Valders (Wis.).
COLLEGE: Wisconsin-Green Bay.
TRANSACTIONS/CAREER NOTES: Not drafted by an NBA franchise. ... Played in Switzerland (1994-95). ... Played in Bulgaria (1994-95). ... Played in Bulgaria and Switzerland (1994-95) ... Signed as free agent by Los Angeles Clippers (October 1, 1995). ... Waived by Clippers (January 4, 1996).

COLLEGIATE RECORD

Season Team	G	Min.	FGM	FGA	Pct.	FTM	FTA	Pct.	Reb.	Ast.	Pts.	RPG	APG	PPG
90-91—Wis.-Green Bay	24	...	34	63	.540	5	12	.417	49	5	73	2.0	0.2	3.0
91-92—Wis.-Green Bay	30	...	56	102	.549	29	42	.690	77	11	141	2.6	0.4	4.7
92-93—Wis.-Green Bay	27	...	100	210	.476	45	53	.849	113	27	277	4.2	1.0	10.3
93-94—Wis.-Green Bay	31	...	127	256	.496	56	64	.875	128	37	323	4.1	1.2	10.4
Totals	112	...	317	631	.502	135	171	.789	367	80	814	3.3	0.7	7.3

Three-point field goals: 1992-93, 32-for-82 (.390). 1993-94, 13-for-38 (.342). Totals, 45-for-120 (.375).

NBA REGULAR-SEASON RECORD

Season Team	G	Min.	FGM	FGA	Pct.	FTM	FTA	Pct.	REBOUNDS Off.	Def.	Tot.	Ast.	St.	Blk.	TO	Pts.	AVERAGES RPG	APG	PPG
95-96—L.A. Clippers	15	31	3	14	.214	3	4	.750	1	5	6	1	0	0	0	9	0.4	0.1	0.6

Three-point field goals: 1995-96, 0-for-5.
Personal fouls/disqualifications: 1995-96, 4/0.

VAN EXEL, NICK   G   LAKERS

PERSONAL: Born November 27, 1971, in Kenosha, Wis. ... 6-1/183. ... Full name: Nickey Maxwell Van Exel. ... Name pronounced van EX-el.
HIGH SCHOOL: St. Joseph's (Kenosha, Wis.).
JUNIOR COLLEGE: Trinity Valley Community College (Texas).
COLLEGE: Cincinnati.
TRANSACTIONS/CAREER NOTES: Selected by Los Angeles Lakers in second round (37th pick overall) of 1993 NBA Draft.

COLLEGIATE RECORD

Season Team	G	Min.	FGM	FGA	Pct.	FTM	FTA	Pct.	Reb.	Ast.	Pts.	AVERAGES RPG	APG	PPG
89-90—Trinity Valley C.C.	31	...	200	415	.482	88	128	.688	101	166	542	3.3	5.4	17.5
90-91—Trinity Valley C.C.	27	...	190	441	.431	105	147	.714	110	185	551	4.1	6.9	20.4
91-92—Cincinnati	34	834	144	323	.446	68	101	.673	87	99	418	2.6	2.9	12.3
92-93—Cincinnati	31	1049	198	513	.386	87	120	.725	75	138	568	2.4	4.5	18.3
Junior college totals	58	...	390	856	.456	193	275	.702	211	351	1093	3.6	6.1	18.8
4-year-college totals	65	1883	342	836	.409	155	221	.701	162	237	986	2.5	3.6	15.2

Three-point field goals: 1991-92, 62-for-163 (.380). 1992-93, 85-for-248 (.343). Totals, 147-for-411 (.358).

HONORS: NBA All-Rookie second team (1994).

NBA REGULAR-SEASON RECORD

Season Team	G	Min.	FGM	FGA	Pct.	FTM	FTA	Pct.	REBOUNDS Off.	Def.	Tot.	Ast.	St.	Blk.	TO	Pts.	AVERAGES RPG	APG	PPG
93-94—L.A. Lakers	81	2700	413	1049	.394	150	192	.781	47	191	238	466	85	8	145	1099	2.9	5.8	13.6
94-95—L.A. Lakers	80	2944	465	1107	.420	235	300	.783	27	196	223	660	97	6	220	1348	2.8	8.3	16.9
95-96—L.A. Lakers	74	2513	396	950	.417	163	204	.799	29	152	181	509	70	10	156	1099	2.4	6.9	14.9
Totals	235	8157	1274	3106	.410	548	696	.787	103	539	642	1635	252	24	521	3546	2.7	7.0	15.1

Three-point field goals: 1993-94, 123-for-364 (.338). 1994-95, 183-for-511 (.358). 1995-96, 144-for-403 (.357). Totals, 450-for-1278 (.352).
Personal fouls/disqualifications: 1993-94, 154/1. 1994-95, 157/0. 1995-96, 115/0. Totals, 426/1.

NBA PLAYOFF RECORD

Season Team	G	Min.	FGM	FGA	Pct.	FTM	FTA	Pct.	REBOUNDS Off.	Def.	Tot.	Ast.	St.	Blk.	TO	Pts.	AVERAGES RPG	APG	PPG
94-95—L.A. Lakers	10	464	67	162	.414	45	59	.763	9	29	38	73	21	3	22	200	3.8	7.3	20.0
95-96—L.A. Lakers	4	137	16	54	.296	10	13	.769	4	12	16	27	2	0	11	47	4.0	6.8	11.8
Totals	14	601	83	216	.384	55	72	.764	13	41	54	100	23	3	33	247	3.9	7.1	17.6

Three-point field goals: 1994-95, 21-for-66 (.318). 1995-96, 5-for-16 (.313). Totals, 26-for-82 (.317).
Personal fouls/disqualifications: 1994-95, 33/0. 1995-96, 10/0. Totals, 43/0.

VAUGHN, DAVID   F   MAGIC

PERSONAL: Born March 23, 1973, in Tulsa, Okla. ... 6-9/240. ... Full name: David Vaughn III. ... Son of David Vaughn, center with Virginia Squires of American Basketball Association (1974-75 and 1975-76).
HIGH SCHOOL: Whites Creek (Nashville, Tenn.).
COLLEGE: Memphis.
TRANSACTIONS/CAREER NOTES: Selected after junior season by Orlando Magic in first round (25th pick overall) of 1995 NBA Draft.

COLLEGIATE RECORD

NOTES: Injured knee (1992-93); granted extra year of eligibility.

Season Team	G	Min.	FGM	FGA	Pct.	FTM	FTA	Pct.	Reb.	Ast.	Pts.	AVERAGES RPG	APG	PPG
91-92—Memphis	34	958	184	359	.513	86	113	.761	282	25	454	8.3	0.7	13.4
92-93—Memphis	1	21	4	11	.364	0	0	...	8	2	10	8.0	2.0	10.0
93-94—Memphis	28	969	172	347	.496	115	152	.757	335	30	466	12.0	1.1	16.6
94-95—Memphis	29	867	138	307	.450	94	129	.729	278	30	375	9.6	1.0	12.9
Totals	92	2815	498	1024	.486	295	394	.749	903	87	1305	9.8	0.9	14.2

Three-point field goals: 1991-92, 0-for-2. 1992-93, 2-for-3. 1993-94, 7-for-21 (.333). 1994-95, 5-for-17 (.294). Totals, 14-for-42 (.333).

NBA REGULAR-SEASON RECORD

Season Team	G	Min.	FGM	FGA	Pct.	FTM	FTA	Pct.	REBOUNDS Off.	Def.	Tot.	Ast.	St.	Blk.	TO	Pts.	AVERAGES RPG	APG	PPG
95-96—Orlando	33	266	27	80	.338	10	18	.556	33	47	80	8	6	15	18	64	2.4	0.2	1.9

Three-point field goals: 1995-96, 0-for-1.
Personal fouls/disqualifications: 1995-96, 68/2.

VAUGHT, LOY   F   CLIPPERS

PERSONAL: Born February 27, 1967, in Grand Rapids, Mich. ... 6-9/240. ... Full name: Loy Stephen Vaught. ... Name pronounced VAWT.
HIGH SCHOOL: East Kentwood (Mich.).
COLLEGE: Michigan.
TRANSACTIONS/CAREER NOTES: Selected by Los Angeles Clippers in first round (13th pick overall) of 1990 NBA Draft.

COLLEGIATE RECORD

NOTES: Member of NCAA Division I championship team (1989).

Season Team	G	Min.	FGM	FGA	Pct.	FTM	FTA	Pct.	Reb.	Ast.	Pts.	AVERAGES RPG	APG	PPG
86-87—Michigan	32	416	68	122	.557	11	22	.500	125	12	147	3.9	0.4	4.6

V

Season Team	G	Min.	FGM	FGA	Pct.	FTM	FTA	Pct.	Reb.	Ast.	Pts.	AVERAGES RPG	APG	PPG
87-88—Michigan	34	748	151	243	.621	55	76	.724	150	22	357	4.4	0.6	10.5
88-89—Michigan	37	851	201	304	.661	63	81	.778	296	36	467	8.0	1.0	12.6
89-90—Michigan	31	930	197	331	.595	86	107	.804	346	30	480	11.2	1.0	15.5
Totals	134	2945	617	1000	.617	215	286	.752	917	100	1451	6.8	0.7	10.8

Three-point field goals: 1988-89, 2-for-5 (.400). 1989-90, 0-for-1. Totals, 2-for-6 (.333).

NBA REGULAR-SEASON RECORD

Season Team	G	Min.	FGM	FGA	Pct.	FTM	FTA	Pct.	REBOUNDS Off.	Def.	Tot.	Ast.	St.	Blk.	TO	Pts.	AVERAGES RPG	APG	PPG
90-91—L.A. Clippers	73	1178	175	359	.487	49	74	.662	124	225	349	40	20	23	49	399	4.8	0.5	5.5
91-92—L.A. Clippers	79	1687	271	551	.492	55	69	.797	160	352	512	71	37	31	66	601	6.5	0.9	7.6
92-93—L.A. Clippers	79	1653	313	616	.508	116	155	.748	164	328	492	54	55	39	83	743	6.2	0.7	9.4
93-94—L.A. Clippers	75	2118	373	695	.537	131	182	.720	218	438	656	74	76	22	96	877	8.7	1.0	11.7
94-95—L.A. Clippers	80	2966	609	1185	.514	176	248	.710	261	511	772	139	104	29	166	1401	9.7	1.7	17.5
95-96—L.A. Clippers	80	2966	571	1087	.525	149	205	.727	204	604	808	112	87	40	158	1298	10.1	1.4	16.2
Totals	466	12568	2312	4493	.515	676	933	.725	1131	2458	3589	490	379	184	618	5319	7.7	1.1	11.4

Three-point field goals: 1990-91, 0-for-2. 1991-92, 4-for-5 (.800). 1992-93, 1-for-4 (.250). 1993-94, 0-for-5. 1994-95, 7-for-33 (.212). 1995-96, 7-for-19 (.368). Totals, 19-for-68 (.279).

Personal fouls/disqualifications: 1990-91, 135/2. 1991-92, 165/1. 1992-93, 172/2. 1993-94, 221/5. 1994-95, 243/4. 1995-96, 241/4. Totals, 1177/18.

NBA PLAYOFF RECORD

Season Team	G	Min.	FGM	FGA	Pct.	FTM	FTA	Pct.	REBOUNDS Off.	Def.	Tot.	Ast.	St.	Blk.	TO	Pts.	AVERAGES RPG	APG	PPG
91-92—L.A. Clippers	5	36	7	11	.636	2	2	1.000	2	10	12	4	1	1	1	17	2.4	0.8	3.4
92-93—L.A. Clippers	3	50	6	15	.400	4	5	.800	4	14	18	0	4	1	3	16	6.0	0.0	5.3
Totals	8	86	13	26	.500	6	7	.857	6	24	30	4	5	2	4	33	3.8	0.5	4.1

Three-point field goals: 1991-92, 1-for-1.
Personal fouls/disqualifications: 1991-92, 3/0. 1992-93, 7/0. Totals, 10/0.

WALLACE, RASHEED   C/F   TRAIL BLAZERS

VW

PERSONAL: Born September 17, 1974, in Philadelphia. ... 6-10/225. ... Full name: Rasheed Abdul Wallace.
HIGH SCHOOL: Simon Gratz (Philadelphia).
COLLEGE: North Carolina.
TRANSACTIONS/CAREER NOTES: Selected after sophomore season by Washington Bullets in first round (fourth pick overall) of 1995 NBA Draft. ... Traded by Bullets with G Mitchell Butler to Portland Trail Blazers for G Rod Strickland and F Harvey Grant (July 15, 1996).

COLLEGIATE RECORD

NOTES: The Sporting News All-America first team (1995).

Season Team	G	Min.	FGM	FGA	Pct.	FTM	FTA	Pct.	Reb.	Ast.	Pts.	AVERAGES RPG	APG	PPG
93-94—North Carolina	35	732	139	230	.604	55	91	.604	232	18	333	6.6	0.5	9.5
94-95—North Carolina	34	1030	238	364	.654	89	141	.631	279	35	566	8.2	1.0	16.6
Totals	69	1762	377	594	.635	144	232	.621	511	53	899	7.4	0.8	13.0

Three-point field goals: 1993-94, 0-for-1. 1994-95, 1-for-3 (.333). Totals, 1-for-4 (.250).

HONORS: NBA All-Rookie second team (1996).

NBA REGULAR-SEASON RECORD

Season Team	G	Min.	FGM	FGA	Pct.	FTM	FTA	Pct.	REBOUNDS Off.	Def.	Tot.	Ast.	St.	Blk.	TO	Pts.	AVERAGES RPG	APG	PPG
95-96—Washington	65	1788	275	565	.487	78	120	.650	93	210	303	85	42	54	103	655	4.7	1.3	10.1

Three-point field goals: 1995-96, 27-for-82 (.329).
Personal fouls/disqualifications: 1995-96, 206/4.

WALTERS, REX   G   76ERS

PERSONAL: Born March 12, 1970, in Omaha, Neb. ... 6-4/190. ... Full name: Rex Andrew Walters.
HIGH SCHOOL: Piedmont Hills (San Jose), then Independence (San Jose).
COLLEGE: Northwestern, then Kansas.
TRANSACTIONS/CAREER NOTES: Selected by New Jersey Nets in first round (16th pick overall) of 1993 NBA Draft. ... Traded by Nets with F Derrick Coleman and F Sean Higgins to Philadelphia 76ers for C Shawn Bradley, F Tim Perry and G Greg Graham (November 30, 1995).

COLLEGIATE RECORD

Season Team	G	Min.	FGM	FGA	Pct.	FTM	FTA	Pct.	Reb.	Ast.	Pts.	AVERAGES RPG	APG	PPG
88-89—Northwestern	24	165	17	45	.378	11	12	.917	17	33	50	0.7	1.4	2.1
89-90—Northwestern	28	892	181	360	.503	77	97	.794	75	125	492	2.7	4.5	17.6
90-91—Kansas						Did not play—transfer student.								
91-92—Kansas	32	918	165	314	.525	115	139	.827	105	124	513	3.3	3.9	16.0
92-93—Kansas	36	1028	179	365	.490	110	126	.873	96	154	551	2.7	4.3	15.3
Totals	120	3003	542	1084	.500	313	374	.837	293	436	1606	2.4	3.6	13.4

Three-point field goals: 1988-89, 5-for-18 (.278). 1989-90, 53-for-112 (.473). 1991-92, 68-for-168 (.405). 1992-93, 83-for-193 (.430). Totals, 209-for-491 (.426).

NBA REGULAR-SEASON RECORD

Season Team	G	Min.	FGM	FGA	Pct.	FTM	FTA	Pct.	REBOUNDS Off.	Def.	Tot.	Ast.	St.	Blk.	TO	Pts.	AVERAGES RPG	APG	PPG
93-94—New Jersey	48	386	60	115	.522	28	34	.824	6	32	38	71	15	3	30	162	0.8	1.5	3.4

Season Team	G	Min.	FGM	FGA	Pct.	FTM	FTA	Pct.	REBOUNDS Off.	Def.	Tot.	Ast.	St.	Blk.	TO	Pts.	AVERAGES RPG	APG	PPG
94-95—New Jersey	80	1435	206	469	.439	40	52	.769	18	75	93	121	37	16	71	523	1.2	1.5	6.5
95-96—N.J.-Phil.........	44	610	61	148	.412	42	52	.808	13	42	55	106	25	4	41	186	1.3	2.4	4.2
Totals	172	2431	327	732	.447	110	138	.797	37	149	186	298	77	23	142	871	1.1	1.7	5.1

Three-point field goals: 1993-94, 14-for-28 (.500). 1994-95, 71-for-196 (.362). 1995-96, 22-for-66 (.333). Totals, 107-for-290 (.369).
Personal fouls/disqualifications: 1993-94, 41/0. 1994-95, 135/0. 1995-96, 53/0. Totals, 229/0.

NBA PLAYOFF RECORD

Season Team	G	Min.	FGM	FGA	Pct.	FTM	FTA	Pct.	REBOUNDS Off.	Def.	Tot.	Ast.	St.	Blk.	TO	Pts.	AVERAGES RPG	APG	PPG
93-94—New Jersey	1	1	1	1	1.000	0	0	...	0	0	0	0	0	0	0	2	0.0	0.0	2.0

WARD, CHARLIE   G   KNICKS

PERSONAL: Born October 12, 1970, in Thomasville, Ga. ... 6-2/190. ... Full name: Charlie Ward Jr.
HIGH SCHOOL: Thomasville (Ga.) Central.
JUNIOR COLLEGE: Tallahassee (Fla.) Community College.
COLLEGE: Florida State.
TRANSACTIONS/CAREER NOTES: Selected by New York Knicks in first round (26th pick overall) of 1994 NBA Draft. ... Played in United States Basketball League with Jacksonville Hooters (1994).
MISCELLANEOUS: Heisman Trophy winner (1993). ... Named College Football Player of the Year by THE SPORTING NEWS (1993). ... Named quarterback on THE SPORTING NEWS college All-America first team (1993). ... Named quarterback on THE SPORTING NEWS college All-America second team (1992). ... Selected by Milwaukee Brewers organization in 59th round of free agent draft (June 3, 1993); did not sign. ... Selected by New York Yankees organization in 18th round of free agent draft (June 2, 1994); did not sign.

COLLEGIATE RECORD

Season Team	G	Min.	FGM	FGA	Pct.	FTM	FTA	Pct.	Reb.	Ast.	Pts.	AVERAGES RPG	APG	PPG
88-89—Tallahassee C.C.								Did not play.						
89-90—Florida State								Did not play.						
90-91—Florida State	30	715	81	178	.455	62	87	.713	89	103	239	3.0	3.4	8.0
91-92—Florida State	28	841	72	145	.497	35	66	.530	90	122	201	3.2	4.4	7.2
92-93—Florida State	17	557	49	106	.462	18	27	.667	45	93	132	2.6	5.5	7.8
93-94—Florida State	16	574	61	167	.365	25	40	.625	39	78	168	2.4	4.9	10.5
Totals	91	2687	263	596	.441	140	220	.636	263	396	740	2.9	4.4	8.1

Three-point field goals: 1990-91, 15-for-48 (.313). 1991-92, 22-for-48 (.458). 1992-93, 16-for-50 (.320). 1993-94, 21-for-83 (.253). Totals, 74-for-229 (.323).

NBA REGULAR-SEASON RECORD

Season Team	G	Min.	FGM	FGA	Pct.	FTM	FTA	Pct.	REBOUNDS Off.	Def.	Tot.	Ast.	St.	Blk.	TO	Pts.	AVERAGES RPG	APG	PPG
94-95—New York	10	44	4	19	.211	7	10	.700	1	5	6	4	2	0	8	16	0.6	0.4	1.6
95-96—New York	62	787	87	218	.399	37	54	.685	29	73	102	132	54	6	79	244	1.6	2.1	3.9
Totals	72	831	91	237	.384	44	64	.688	30	78	108	136	56	6	87	260	1.5	1.9	3.6

Three-point field goals: 1994-95, 1-for-10 (.100). 1995-96, 33-for-99 (.333). Totals, 34-for-109 (.312).
Personal fouls/disqualifications: 1994-95, 7/0. 1995-96, 98/0. Totals, 105/0.

NBA PLAYOFF RECORD

Season Team	G	Min.	FGM	FGA	Pct.	FTM	FTA	Pct.	REBOUNDS Off.	Def.	Tot.	Ast.	St.	Blk.	TO	Pts.	AVERAGES RPG	APG	PPG
95-96—New York	7	92	13	27	.481	3	7	.429	2	7	9	17	11	0	6	32	1.3	2.4	4.6

Three-point field goals: 1995-96, 3-for-12 (.250).
Personal fouls/disqualifications: 1995-96, 9/0.

W

WATSON, JAMIE   F   JAZZ

PERSONAL: Born February 23, 1972, in Elm City, N.C. ... 6-7/190. ... Full name: Jamie Lovell Watson.
HIGH SCHOOL: Wilson (N.C.) Fike.
COLLEGE: South Carolina.
TRANSACTIONS/CAREER NOTES: Selected by Utah Jazz in second round (47th pick overall) of 1994 NBA Draft.

COLLEGIATE RECORD

Season Team	G	Min.	FGM	FGA	Pct.	FTM	FTA	Pct.	Reb.	Ast.	Pts.	AVERAGES RPG	APG	PPG
90-91—South Carolina...............	33	651	81	193	.420	25	44	.568	83	77	197	2.5	2.3	6.0
91-92—South Carolina...............	28	830	92	209	.440	22	42	.524	127	81	211	4.5	2.9	7.5
92-93—South Carolina...............	27	910	159	345	.461	70	109	.642	136	72	397	5.0	2.7	14.7
93-94—South Carolina...............	27	924	185	403	.459	91	135	.674	190	66	490	7.0	2.4	18.1
Totals	115	3315	517	1150	.450	208	330	.630	536	296	1295	4.7	2.6	11.3

Three-point field goals: 1990-91, 10-for-43 (.233). 1991-92, 5-for-24 (.208). 1992-93, 9-for-49 (.184). 1993-94, 29-for-98 (.296). Totals, 53-for-214 (.248).

NBA REGULAR-SEASON RECORD

Season Team	G	Min.	FGM	FGA	Pct.	FTM	FTA	Pct.	REBOUNDS Off.	Def.	Tot.	Ast.	St.	Blk.	TO	Pts.	AVERAGES RPG	APG	PPG
94-95—Utah...............	60	673	76	152	.500	38	56	.679	16	58	74	59	35	11	51	195	1.2	1.0	3.3
95-96—Utah...............	16	217	18	43	.419	9	13	.692	5	22	27	24	8	2	17	48	1.7	1.5	3.0
Totals	76	890	94	195	.482	47	69	.681	21	80	101	83	43	13	68	243	1.3	1.1	3.2

Three-point field goals: 1994-95, 5-for-19 (.263). 1995-96, 3-for-7 (.429). Totals, 8-for-26 (.308).
Personal fouls/disqualifications: 1994-95, 86/0. 1995-96, 30/0. Totals, 116/0.

NBA PLAYOFF RECORD

								REBOUNDS							AVERAGES		
Season Team	G	Min.	FGM	FGA	Pct.	FTM	FTA	Pct.	Off.	Def.	Tot.	Ast.	St.	Blk.	TO	Pts.	RPG	APG	PPG
94-95—Utah	5	57	6	9	.667	0	0	...	1	0	1	3	2	1	6	12	0.2	0.6	2.4

Personal fouls/disqualifications: 1994-95, 12/0.

WEATHERSPOON, CLARENCE   F   76ERS

PERSONAL: Born September 8, 1970, in Crawford, Miss. ... 6-7/240.
HIGH SCHOOL: Motley (Columbus, Miss.).
COLLEGE: Southern Mississippi.
TRANSACTIONS/CAREER NOTES: Selected by Philadelphia 76ers in first round (ninth pick overall) of 1992 NBA Draft.

COLLEGIATE RECORD

											AVERAGES		
Season Team	G	Min.	FGM	FGA	Pct.	FTM	FTA	Pct.	Reb.	Ast.	Pts.	RPG	APG	PPG
88-89—Southern Miss	27	915	152	279	.545	92	156	.590	289	30	397	10.7	1.1	14.7
89-90—Southern Miss	32	1166	205	339	.605	159	230	.691	371	28	569	11.6	0.9	17.8
90-91—Southern Miss	29	1019	195	331	.589	120	161	.745	355	66	517	12.2	2.3	17.8
91-92—Southern Miss	29	1057	246	437	.563	131	194	.675	305	47	647	10.5	1.6	22.3
Totals	117	4157	798	1386	.576	502	741	.677	1320	171	2130	11.3	1.5	18.2

Three-point field goals: 1988-89, 1-for-3 (.333). 1989-90, 0-for-2. 1990-91, 7-for-14 (.500). 1991-92, 24-for-53 (.453). Totals, 32-for-72 (.444).

NBA REGULAR-SEASON RECORD

HONORS: NBA All-Rookie second team (1993).

									REBOUNDS								AVERAGES		
Season Team	G	Min.	FGM	FGA	Pct.	FTM	FTA	Pct.	Off.	Def.	Tot.	Ast.	St.	Blk.	TO	Pts.	RPG	APG	PPG
92-93—Philadelphia	82	2654	494	1053	.469	291	408	.713	179	410	589	147	85	67	176	1280	7.2	1.8	15.6
93-94—Philadelphia	82	3147	602	1246	.483	298	430	.693	254	578	832	192	100	116	195	1506	10.1	2.3	18.4
94-95—Philadelphia	76	2991	543	1238	.439	283	377	.751	144	382	526	215	115	67	191	1373	6.9	2.8	18.1
95-96—Philadelphia	78	3096	491	1015	.484	318	426	.746	237	516	753	158	112	108	179	1300	9.7	2.0	16.7
Totals	318	11888	2130	4552	.468	1190	1641	.725	814	1886	2700	712	412	358	741	5459	8.5	2.2	17.2

Three-point field goals: 1992-93, 1-for-4 (.250). 1993-94, 4-for-17 (.235). 1994-95, 4-for-21 (.190). 1995-96, 0-for-2. Totals, 9-for-44 (.205).
Personal fouls/disqualifications: 1992-93, 188/1. 1993-94, 152/0. 1994-95, 195/1. 1995-96, 214/3. Totals, 749/5.

WEBB, SPUD   G

PERSONAL: Born July 13, 1963, in Dallas. ... 5-7/133. ... Full name: Anthony Jerome Webb.
HIGH SCHOOL: Wilmer-Hutchins (Dallas).
JUNIOR COLLEGE: Midland (Texas) College.
COLLEGE: North Carolina State.
TRANSACTIONS/CAREER NOTES: Selected by Detroit Pistons in fourth round (87th pick overall) of 1985 NBA Draft. ... Played in United States Basketball League with Rhode Island Gulls (1985). ... Draft rights renounced by Pistons (September 24, 1985). ... Signed as free agent by Atlanta Hawks (September 26, 1985). ... Traded by Hawks with 1994 second-round draft choice to Sacramento Kings for G Travis Mays (July 1, 1991). ... Traded by Kings to Hawks for F Tyrone Corbin (June 29, 1995). ... Traded by Hawks with C Andrew Lang to Minnesota Timberwolves for F Christian Laettner and C Sean Rooks (February 22, 1996). ... Rights renounced by Timberwolves (July 19, 1996).

COLLEGIATE RECORD

											AVERAGES		
Season Team	G	Min.	FGM	FGA	Pct.	FTM	FTA	Pct.	Reb.	Ast.	Pts.	RPG	APG	PPG
81-82—Midland College	38	...	277	538	.515	235	301	.781	77	271	789	2.0	7.1	20.8
82-83—Midland College	35	...	196	440	.445	120	155	.774	106	355	512	3.0	10.1	14.6
83-84—N.C. State	33	980	128	279	.459	67	88	.761	59	199	323	1.8	6.0	9.8
84-85—N.C. State	33	919	140	291	.481	86	113	.761	66	174	366	2.0	5.3	11.1
Junior college totals	73	...	473	978	.484	355	456	.779	183	626	1301	2.5	8.6	17.8
4-year-college totals	66	1899	268	570	.470	153	201	.761	125	373	689	1.9	5.7	10.4

NBA REGULAR-SEASON RECORD

HONORS: Slam-Dunk Championship winner (1986).

									REBOUNDS								AVERAGES		
Season Team	G	Min.	FGM	FGA	Pct.	FTM	FTA	Pct.	Off.	Def.	Tot.	Ast.	St.	Blk.	TO	Pts.	RPG	APG	PPG
85-86—Atlanta	79	1229	199	412	.483	216	275	.785	27	96	123	337	82	5	159	616	1.6	4.3	7.8
86-87—Atlanta	33	532	71	162	.438	80	105	.762	6	54	60	167	34	2	70	223	1.8	5.1	6.8
87-88—Atlanta	82	1347	191	402	.475	107	131	.817	16	130	146	337	63	11	131	490	1.8	4.1	6.0
88-89—Atlanta	81	1219	133	290	.459	52	60	.867	21	102	123	284	70	6	83	319	1.5	3.5	3.9
89-90—Atlanta	82	2184	294	616	.477	162	186	.871	38	163	201	477	105	12	141	751	2.5	5.8	9.2
90-91—Atlanta	75	2197	359	803	.447	231	266	.868	41	133	174	417	118	6	146	1003	2.3	5.6	13.4
91-92—Sacramento	77	2724	448	1006	.445	262	305	.859	30	193	223	547	125	24	229	1231	2.9	7.1	16.0
92-93—Sacramento	69	2335	342	789	.433	279	328	.851	44	149	193	481	104	6	194	1000	2.8	7.0	14.5
93-94—Sacramento	79	2567	373	810	.461	204	251	.813	44	178	222	528	93	23	168	1005	2.8	6.7	12.7
94-95—Sacramento	76	2458	302	689	.438	226	242	*.934	29	145	174	468	75	8	185	878	2.3	6.2	11.6
95-96—Atl.-Minn.	77	1462	186	430	.433	125	145	.862	26	74	100	294	52	7	110	544	1.3	3.8	7.1
Totals	810	20254	2898	6409	.452	1944	2294	.847	322	1417	1739	4337	921	110	1616	8060	2.1	5.4	10.0

Three-point field goals: 1985-86, 2-for-11 (.182). 1986-87, 1-for-6 (.167). 1987-88, 1-for-19 (.053). 1988-89, 1-for-22 (.045). 1989-90, 1-for-19 (.053). 1990-91, 54-for-168 (.321). 1991-92, 73-for-199 (.367). 1992-93, 37-for-135 (.274). 1993-94, 55-for-164 (.335). 1994-95, 48-for-145 (.331). 1995-96, 47-for-129 (.364). Totals, 320-for-1017 (.315).
Personal fouls/disqualifications: 1985-86, 164/1. 1986-87, 65/1. 1987-88, 125/0. 1988-89, 104/0. 1989-90, 185/0. 1990-91, 180/0. 1991-92, 193/1. 1992-93, 177/0. 1993-94, 182/1. 1994-95, 148/0. 1995-96, 109/0. Totals, 1632/4.

W

NBA PLAYOFF RECORD

Season Team	G	Min.	FGM	FGA	Pct.	FTM	FTA	Pct.	REBOUNDS Off.	Def.	Tot.	Ast.	St.	Blk.	TO	Pts.	AVERAGES RPG	APG	PPG
85-86—Atlanta	9	183	42	81	.519	26	33	.788	6	25	31	65	4	1	10	110	3.4	7.2	12.2
86-87—Atlanta	8	122	9	19	.474	13	17	.765	1	7	8	38	6	0	18	31	1.0	4.8	3.9
87-88—Atlanta	12	211	35	81	.432	34	37	.919	4	16	20	56	9	0	10	106	1.7	4.7	8.8
88-89—Atlanta	5	55	3	11	.273	2	2	1.000	0	4	4	15	4	0	0	8	0.8	3.0	1.6
90-91—Atlanta	5	154	25	57	.439	11	16	.688	8	14	22	24	7	1	13	66	4.4	4.8	13.2
Totals	**39**	**725**	**114**	**249**	**.458**	**86**	**105**	**.819**	**19**	**66**	**85**	**198**	**30**	**2**	**51**	**321**	**2.2**	**5.1**	**8.2**

Three-point field goals: 1985-86, 0-for-2. 1986-87, 0-for-1. 1987-88, 2-for-8 (.250). 1990-91, 5-for-12 (.417). Totals, 7-for-23 (.304).
Personal fouls/disqualifications: 1985-86, 13/0. 1986-87, 10/0. 1987-88, 22/0. 1988-89, 6/0. 1990-91, 13/0. Totals, 64/0.

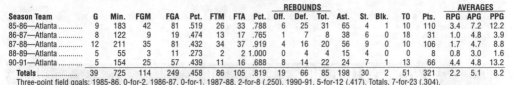

WEBBER, CHRIS   F   BULLETS

PERSONAL: Born March 1, 1973, in Detroit. ... 6-10/250. ... Full name: Mayce Edward Christopher Webber III.
HIGH SCHOOL: Detroit Country Day (Birmingham, Mich.).
COLLEGE: Michigan.
TRANSACTIONS/CAREER NOTES: Selected after sophomore season by Orlando Magic in first round (first pick overall) of 1993 NBA Draft. ... Draft rights traded by Magic to Golden State Warriors for draft rights to G Anfernee Hardaway and 1996, 1998 and 2000 first-round draft choices (June 30, 1993). ... Traded by Warriors to Washington Bullets for F Tom Gugliotta and 1996, 1998 and 2000 first-round draft choices (November 17, 1994).

COLLEGIATE RECORD

NOTES: THE SPORTING NEWS All-America first team (1993).

Season Team	G	Min.	FGM	FGA	Pct.	FTM	FTA	Pct.	Reb.	Ast.	Pts.	AVERAGES RPG	APG	PPG
91-92—Michigan	34	1088	229	412	.556	56	113	.496	340	76	528	10.0	2.2	15.5
92-93—Michigan	36	1143	281	454	.619	101	183	.552	362	90	690	10.1	2.5	19.2
Totals	**70**	**2231**	**510**	**866**	**.589**	**157**	**296**	**.530**	**702**	**166**	**1218**	**10.0**	**2.4**	**17.4**

Three-point field goals: 1991-92, 14-for-54 (.259). 1992-93, 27-for-80 (.338). Totals, 41-for-134 (.306).

NBA REGULAR-SEASON RECORD

HONORS: NBA Rookie of the Year (1994). ... NBA All-Rookie first team (1994).

Season Team	G	Min.	FGM	FGA	Pct.	FTM	FTA	Pct.	REBOUNDS Off.	Def.	Tot.	Ast.	St.	Blk.	TO	Pts.	AVERAGES RPG	APG	PPG
93-94—Golden State ...	76	2438	572	1037	.552	189	355	.532	305	389	694	272	93	164	206	1333	9.1	3.6	17.5
94-95—Washington	54	2067	464	938	.495	117	233	.502	200	318	518	256	83	85	167	1085	9.6	4.7	20.1
95-96—Washington ...	15	558	150	276	.543	41	69	.594	37	77	114	75	27	9	49	356	7.6	5.0	23.7
Totals	**145**	**5063**	**1186**	**2251**	**.527**	**347**	**657**	**.528**	**542**	**784**	**1326**	**603**	**203**	**258**	**422**	**2774**	**9.1**	**4.2**	**19.1**

Three-point field goals: 1993-94, 0-for-14. 1994-95, 40-for-145 (.276). 1995-96, 15-for-34 (.441). Totals, 55-for-193 (.285).
Personal fouls/disqualifications: 1993-94, 247/4. 1994-95, 186/2. 1995-96, 51/1. Totals, 484/7.

NBA PLAYOFF RECORD

Season Team	G	Min.	FGM	FGA	Pct.	FTM	FTA	Pct.	REBOUNDS Off.	Def.	Tot.	Ast.	St.	Blk.	TO	Pts.	AVERAGES RPG	APG	PPG
93-94—Golden State ...	3	109	22	40	.550	3	10	.300	13	13	26	27	3	9	9	47	8.7	9.0	15.7

Three-point field goals: 1993-94, 0-for-2.
Personal fouls/disqualifications: 1993-94, 11/0.

WEBSTER, JEFF   F

PERSONAL: Born February 19, 1971, in Pine Bluff, Ark. ... 6-8/232. ... Full name: Jeffrey Tyrone Webster.
HIGH SCHOOL: Carl Albert (Midwest City, Okla.).
COLLEGE: Oklahoma.
TRANSACTIONS/CAREER NOTES: Selected by Miami Heat in second round (40th pick overall) of 1994 NBA Draft. ... Played in Continental Basketball Association with Rapid City Thrillers and Tri-City Chinook (1994-95). ... Draft rights traded by Heat with draft rights to C Ed Stokes to Washington Bullets for G Rex Chapman and draft rights to G Terrence Rencher (June 28, 1995). ... Waived by Bullets (December 11, 1995).

COLLEGIATE RECORD

NOTES: Suffered stress fracture in left foot (1989-90); granted extra year of eligibility as medical hardship.

Season Team	G	Min.	FGM	FGA	Pct.	FTM	FTA	Pct.	Reb.	Ast.	Pts.	AVERAGES RPG	APG	PPG
89-90—Oklahoma	3	27	8	14	.571	1	3	.333	8	0	17	2.7	0.0	5.7
90-91—Oklahoma	35	918	253	448	.565	134	167	.802	192	8	640	5.5	0.2	18.3
91-92—Oklahoma	30	814	175	336	.521	83	104	.798	186	17	433	6.2	0.6	14.4
92-93—Oklahoma	32	942	217	442	.491	91	123	.740	186	16	528	5.8	0.5	16.5
93-94—Oklahoma	28	974	264	513	.515	132	170	.776	217	20	663	7.8	0.7	23.7
Totals	**128**	**3675**	**917**	**1753**	**.523**	**441**	**567**	**.778**	**789**	**61**	**2281**	**6.2**	**0.5**	**17.8**

Three-point field goals: 1990-91, 0-for-2. 1992-93, 3-for-9 (.333). 1993-94, 3-for-13 (.231). Totals, 6-for-24 (.250).

CBA REGULAR-SEASON RECORD

Season Team	G	Min.	FGM	FGA	Pct.	FTM	FTA	Pct.	Reb.	Ast.	Pts.	AVERAGES RPG	APG	PPG
94-95—Rapid City-Tri-City	27	275	41	90	.456	15	19	.789	45	7	97	1.7	0.3	3.6

Three-point field goals: 1994-95, 0-for-2.

NBA REGULAR-SEASON RECORD

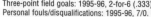

								REBOUNDS								AVERAGES		
Season Team	G	Min.	FGM	FGA	Pct.	FTM	FTA	Pct.	Off.	Def.	Tot.	Ast.	St.	Blk.	TO	Pts.	RPG	APG	PPG
95-96—Washington	11	58	8	23	.348	0	0	...	2	5	7	3	4	0	3	18	0.6	0.3	1.6

Three-point field goals: 1995-96, 2-for-6 (.333).
Personal fouls/disqualifications: 1995-96, 7/0.

WENNINGTON, BILL C BULLS

PERSONAL: Born April 26, 1963, in Montreal. ... 7-0/277. ... Full name: William Percey Wennington.
HIGH SCHOOL: Long Island Lutheran (Brookville, N.Y.).
COLLEGE: St. John's.
TRANSACTIONS/CAREER NOTES: Selected by Dallas Mavericks in first round (16th pick overall) of 1985 NBA Draft. ... Traded by Mavericks with two 1990 first-round draft choices to Sacramento Kings for F Rodney McCray and 1990 and 1991 second-round draft choices (June 26, 1990). ... Played in Italy (1991-92 and 1992-93). ... Signed as free agent by Chicago Bulls (September 29, 1993).
MISCELLANEOUS: Member of NBA championship team (1996). ... Member of Canadian Olympic teams (1984, 1992).

COLLEGIATE RECORD

												AVERAGES		
Season Team	G	Min.	FGM	FGA	Pct.	FTM	FTA	Pct.	Reb.	Ast.	Pts.	RPG	APG	PPG
81-82—St. John's	30	505	37	85	.435	23	34	.676	126	4	97	4.2	0.1	3.2
82-83—St. John's	33	656	69	114	.605	44	63	.698	146	9	182	4.4	0.3	5.5
83-84—St. John's	26	735	124	209	.593	56	83	.675	148	32	304	5.7	1.2	11.7
84-85—St. John's	35	1099	168	279	.602	102	125	.816	224	55	438	6.4	1.6	12.5
Totals	124	2995	398	687	.579	225	305	.738	644	100	1021	5.2	0.8	8.2

NBA REGULAR-SEASON RECORD

								REBOUNDS								AVERAGES		
Season Team	G	Min.	FGM	FGA	Pct.	FTM	FTA	Pct.	Off.	Def.	Tot.	Ast.	St.	Blk.	TO	Pts.	RPG	APG	PPG
85-86—Dallas..............	56	562	72	153	.471	45	62	.726	32	100	132	21	11	22	21	189	2.4	0.4	3.4
86-87—Dallas..............	58	560	56	132	.424	45	60	.750	53	76	129	24	13	10	39	157	2.2	0.4	2.7
87-88—Dallas..............	30	125	25	49	.510	12	19	.632	14	25	39	4	5	9	9	63	1.3	0.1	2.1
88-89—Dallas..............	65	1074	119	275	.433	61	82	.744	82	204	286	46	16	35	54	300	4.4	0.7	4.6
89-90—Dallas..............	60	814	105	234	.449	60	75	.800	64	134	198	41	20	21	50	270	3.3	0.7	4.5
90-91—Sacramento	77	1455	181	415	.436	74	94	.787	101	239	340	69	46	59	51	437	4.4	0.9	5.7
93-94—Chicago	76	1371	235	482	.488	72	88	.818	117	236	353	70	43	29	75	542	4.6	0.9	7.1
94-95—Chicago	73	956	156	317	.492	51	63	.810	64	126	190	40	22	17	39	363	2.6	0.5	5.0
95-96—Chicago	71	1065	169	343	.493	37	43	.860	58	116	174	46	21	16	37	376	2.5	0.6	5.3
Totals	566	7982	1118	2400	.466	457	586	.780	585	1256	1841	361	197	218	375	2697	3.3	0.6	4.8

Three-point field goals: 1985-86, 0-for-4. 1986-87, 0-for-2. 1987-88, 1-for-2 (.500). 1988-89, 1-for-9 (.111). 1989-90, 0-for-4. 1990-91, 1-for-5 (.200). 1993-94, 0-for-2. 1994-95, 0-for-4. 1995-96, 1-for-1. Totals, 4-for-33 (.121).
Personal fouls/disqualifications: 1985-86, 83/0. 1986-87, 95/0. 1987-88, 33/0. 1988-89, 211/3. 1989-90, 144/2. 1990-91, 230/4. 1993-94, 214/4. 1994-95, 198/5. 1995-96, 171/1. Totals, 1379/19.

NBA PLAYOFF RECORD

								REBOUNDS								AVERAGES		
Season Team	G	Min.	FGM	FGA	Pct.	FTM	FTA	Pct.	Off.	Def.	Tot.	Ast.	St.	Blk.	TO	Pts.	RPG	APG	PPG
85-86—Dallas..............	6	18	2	6	.333	2	2	1.000	4	1	5	0	0	0	0	7	0.8	0.0	1.2
86-87—Dallas..............	4	47	6	12	.500	3	5	.600	4	6	10	4	0	3	3	15	2.5	1.0	3.8
87-88—Dallas..............	6	14	0	4	.000	0	0	...	3	1	4	1	1	0	1	0	0.7	0.2	0.0
89-90—Dallas..............	3	25	1	5	.200	0	0	...	0	3	3	1	0	1	2	2	1.0	0.3	0.7
93-94—Chicago	7	47	3	6	.500	2	3	.667	4	3	7	4	0	1	1	8	1.0	0.6	1.1
94-95—Chicago	10	133	21	51	.412	6	6	1.000	12	16	28	3	3	3	8	48	2.8	0.3	4.8
95-96—Chicago	18	169	26	50	.520	2	4	.500	11	19	30	9	4	1	5	54	1.7	0.5	3.0
Totals	54	453	59	134	.440	15	20	.750	38	49	87	22	8	9	20	134	1.6	0.4	2.5

Three-point field goals: 1986-87, 1-for-1. 1995-96, 0-for-1. Totals, 1-for-2 (.500).
Personal fouls/disqualifications: 1985-86, 4/0. 1986-87, 9/0. 1987-88, 5/0. 1989-90, 5/0. 1993-94, 14/0. 1994-95, 32/0. 1995-96, 30/0. Totals, 99/0.

ITALIAN LEAGUE RECORD

												AVERAGES		
Season Team	G	Min.	FGM	FGA	Pct.	FTM	FTA	Pct.	Reb.	Ast.	Pts.	RPG	APG	PPG
91-92—Knorr Bologna...............	27	704	126	230	.548	48	55	.873	188	2	300	7.0	0.1	11.1
92-93—Knorr Bologna...............	29	748	140	216	.648	74	85	.871	194	5	354	6.7	0.2	12.2
Totals	56	1452	266	446	.596	122	140	.871	382	7	654	6.8	0.1	11.7

WERDANN, ROBERT C

PERSONAL: Born September 12, 1969, in Sunnyside, N.Y. ... 6-11/250. ... Name pronounced wer-DAN.
HIGH SCHOOL: Archbishop Molloy (Queens, N.Y.).
COLLEGE: St. John's.
TRANSACTIONS/CAREER NOTES: Selected by Denver Nuggets in second round (46th pick overall) of 1992 NBA Draft. ... Released by Nuggets (October 5, 1993). ... Played in Continental Basketball Association with Yakima Sun Kings (1993-94) and Harrisburg Hammerheads (1994-95). ... Played in United States Basketball League with Long Island Surf (1994). ... Signed as free agent by Los Angeles Clippers (October 5, 1994). ... Waived by Clippers (October 20, 1994). ... Signed as free agent by New Jersey Nets (October 6, 1995). ... Rights renounced by Nets (July 31, 1996).

W

COLLEGIATE RECORD

												AVERAGES		
Season Team	G	Min.	FGM	FGA	Pct.	FTM	FTA	Pct.	Reb.	Ast.	Pts.	RPG	APG	PPG
88-89—St. John's	29	774	94	190	.495	40	60	.667	191	39	228	6.6	1.3	7.9
89-90—St. John's	34	990	124	246	.504	82	123	.667	250	27	330	7.4	0.8	9.7
90-91—St. John's	32	943	128	259	.494	105	145	.724	226	45	362	7.1	1.4	11.3
91-92—St. John's	12	286	40	87	.460	36	52	.692	69	19	116	5.8	1.6	9.7
Totals	107	2993	386	782	.494	263	380	.692	736	130	1036	6.9	1.2	9.7

Three-point field goals: 1988-89, 0-for-2. 1990-91, 1-for-1. Totals, 1-for-3 (.333).

NBA REGULAR-SEASON RECORD

									REBOUNDS								AVERAGES		
Season Team	G	Min.	FGM	FGA	Pct.	FTM	FTA	Pct.	Off.	Def.	Tot.	Ast.	St.	Blk.	TO	Pts.	RPG	APG	PPG
92-93—Denver	28	149	18	59	.305	17	31	.548	23	29	52	7	6	4	12	53	1.9	0.3	1.9
95-96—New Jersey	13	93	16	32	.500	7	13	.538	5	18	23	2	5	3	6	39	1.8	0.2	3.0
Totals	41	242	34	91	.374	24	44	.545	28	47	75	9	11	7	18	92	1.8	0.2	2.2

Three-point field goals: 1992-93, 0-for-1.
Personal fouls/disqualifications: 1992-93, 38/1. 1995-96, 17/0. Totals, 55/1.

CBA REGULAR-SEASON RECORD

												AVERAGES		
Season Team	G	Min.	FGM	FGA	Pct.	FTM	FTA	Pct.	Reb.	Ast.	Pts.	RPG	APG	PPG
93-94—Yakima	17	230	34	84	.405	24	42	.571	48	12	92	2.8	0.7	5.4
94-95—Harrisburg	26	496	95	169	.562	29	44	.659	164	13	219	6.3	0.5	8.4
Totals	43	726	129	253	.510	53	86	.616	212	25	311	4.9	0.6	7.2

WESLEY, DAVID G CELTICS

PERSONAL: Born November 14, 1970, in San Antonio. ... 6-0/198. ... Full name: David Barakau Wesley.
HIGH SCHOOL: Longview (Texas).
JUNIOR COLLEGE: Temple (Texas) Junior College.
COLLEGE: Baylor.
TRANSACTIONS/CAREER NOTES: Not drafted by an NBA franchise. ... Played in Continental Basketball Association with Wichita Falls Texans (1992-93). ... Signed as free agent by New Jersey Nets (July 27, 1993). ... Signed as unrestricted free agent by Boston Celtics (July 20, 1994).

W

COLLEGIATE RECORD

												AVERAGES		
Season Team	G	Min.	FGM	FGA	Pct.	FTM	FTA	Pct.	Reb.	Ast.	Pts.	RPG	APG	PPG
88-89—Temple Junior College					Statistics unavailable.									
89-90—Baylor	18	394	61	134	.455	61	73	.836	39	37	208	2.2	2.1	11.6
90-91—Baylor	26	837	133	314	.424	125	149	.839	76	148	430	2.9	5.7	16.5
91-92—Baylor	28	1020	174	387	.450	179	219	.817	136	131	586	4.9	4.7	20.9
Junior college totals	...	...	...	...	...	...	...	...	...	...	...		...	
4-year-college totals	72	2251	368	835	.441	365	441	.828	251	316	1224	3.5	4.4	17.0

Three-point field goals: 1989-90, 25-for-56 (.446). 1990-91, 39-for-114 (.342). 1991-92, 59-for-156 (.378). Totals, 123-for-326 (.377).

CBA REGULAR-SEASON RECORD

												AVERAGES		
Season Team	G	Min.	FGM	FGA	Pct.	FTM	FTA	Pct.	Reb.	Ast.	Pts.	RPG	APG	PPG
92-93—Wichita Falls	55	1830	350	759	.461	282	360	.783	218	225	948	4.0	4.1	17.2

Three-point field goals: 1992-93, 34-for-93 (.366).

NBA REGULAR-SEASON RECORD

									REBOUNDS								AVERAGES		
Season Team	G	Min.	FGM	FGA	Pct.	FTM	FTA	Pct.	Off.	Def.	Tot.	Ast.	St.	Blk.	TO	Pts.	RPG	APG	PPG
93-94—New Jersey	60	542	64	174	.368	44	53	.830	10	34	44	123	38	4	52	183	0.7	2.1	3.1
94-95—Boston	51	1380	128	313	.409	71	94	.755	31	86	117	266	82	9	87	378	2.3	5.2	7.4
95-96—Boston	82	2104	338	736	.459	217	288	.753	68	196	264	390	100	11	159	1009	3.2	4.8	12.3
Totals	193	4026	530	1223	.433	332	435	.763	109	316	425	779	220	24	298	1570	2.2	4.0	8.1

Three-point field goals: 1993-94, 11-for-47 (.234). 1994-95, 51-for-119 (.429). 1995-96, 116-for-272 (.426). Totals, 178-for-438 (.406).
Personal fouls/disqualifications: 1993-94, 47/0. 1994-95, 144/0. 1995-96, 207/0. Totals, 398/0.

NBA PLAYOFF RECORD

									REBOUNDS								AVERAGES		
Season Team	G	Min.	FGM	FGA	Pct.	FTM	FTA	Pct.	Off.	Def.	Tot.	Ast.	St.	Blk.	TO	Pts.	RPG	APG	PPG
93-94—New Jersey	3	18	3	7	.429	2	2	1.000	0	0	0	3	2	0	4	9	0.0	1.0	3.0

Three-point field goals: 1993-94, 1-for-4 (.250).

WEST, DOUG G/F TIMBERWOLVES

PERSONAL: Born May 27, 1967, in Altoona, Pa. ... 6-6/220. ... Full name: Jeffery Douglas West.
HIGH SCHOOL: Altoona (Pa.) Area.
COLLEGE: Villanova.
TRANSACTIONS/CAREER NOTES: Selected by Minnesota Timberwolves in second round (38th pick overall) of 1989 NBA Draft.
MISCELLANEOUS: Minnesota Timberwolves all-time leading scorer with 5,528 points (1989-90 through 1995-96).

COLLEGIATE RECORD

Season Team	G	Min.	FGM	FGA	Pct.	FTM	FTA	Pct.	Reb.	Ast.	Pts.	AVERAGES RPG	APG	PPG
85-86—Villanova	37	995	158	307	.515	60	88	.682	136	16	376	3.7	0.4	10.2
86-87—Villanova	31	1022	180	376	.479	94	129	.729	151	9	470	4.9	0.3	15.2
87-88—Villanova	37	1281	215	433	.497	92	127	.724	181	82	583	4.9	2.2	15.8
88-89—Villanova	33	1137	226	488	.463	90	125	.720	162	92	608	4.9	2.8	18.4
Totals	138	4435	779	1604	.486	336	469	.716	630	199	2037	4.6	1.4	14.8

Three-point field goals: 1986-87, 16-for-43 (.372). 1987-88, 61-for-143 (.427). 1988-89, 66-for-177 (.373). Totals, 143-for-363 (.394).

NBA REGULAR-SEASON RECORD

Season Team	G	Min.	FGM	FGA	Pct.	FTM	FTA	Pct.	REBOUNDS Off.	Def.	Tot.	Ast.	St.	Blk.	TO	Pts.	AVERAGES RPG	APG	PPG
89-90—Minnesota	52	378	53	135	.393	26	32	.813	24	46	70	18	10	6	31	135	1.3	0.3	2.6
90-91—Minnesota	75	824	118	246	.480	58	84	.690	56	80	136	48	35	23	41	294	1.8	0.6	3.9
91-92—Minnesota	80	2540	463	894	.518	186	231	.805	107	150	257	281	66	26	120	1116	3.2	3.5	14.0
92-93—Minnesota	80	3104	646	1249	.517	249	296	.841	89	158	247	235	85	21	165	1543	3.1	2.9	19.3
93-94—Minnesota	72	2182	434	891	.487	187	231	.810	61	170	231	172	65	24	137	1056	3.2	2.4	14.7
94-95—Minnesota	71	2328	351	762	.461	206	246	.837	60	167	227	185	65	24	126	919	3.2	2.6	12.9
95-96—Minnesota	73	1639	175	393	.445	114	144	.792	48	113	161	119	30	17	81	465	2.2	1.6	6.4
Totals	503	12995	2240	4570	.490	1026	1264	.812	445	884	1329	1058	356	141	701	5528	2.6	2.1	11.0

Three-point field goals: 1989-90, 3-for-11 (.273). 1990-91, 0-for-1. 1991-92, 4-for-23 (.174). 1992-93, 2-for-23 (.087). 1993-94, 1-for-8 (.125). 1994-95, 11-for-61 (.180). 1995-96, 1-for-13 (.077). Totals, 22-for-140 (.157).

Personal fouls/disqualifications: 1989-90, 61/0. 1990-91, 115/0. 1991-92, 239/1. 1992-93, 279/1. 1993-94, 236/3. 1994-95, 250/4. 1995-96, 228/2. Totals, 1408/11.

WEST, MARK   C   CAVALIERS

PERSONAL: Born November 5, 1960, in Petersburg, Va. ... 6-10/246. ... Full name: Mark Andre West.
HIGH SCHOOL: Petersburg (Va.).
COLLEGE: Old Dominion.
TRANSACTIONS/CAREER NOTES: Selected by Dallas Mavericks in second round (30th pick overall) of 1983 NBA Draft. ... Waived by Mavericks (October 23, 1984). ... Signed as free agent by Milwaukee Bucks (November 6, 1984). ... Waived by Bucks (November 12, 1984). ... Signed as free agent by Cleveland Cavaliers (November 23, 1984). ... Traded by Cavaliers with G/F Tyrone Corbin, G Kevin Johnson, 1988 first- and second-round draft choices and 1989 second-round draft choice to Phoenix Suns for F Larry Nance, F Mike Sanders and 1988 first-round draft choice (February 25, 1988). ... Traded by Suns to Detroit Pistons for 1996 second-round draft choice and future considerations (August 1, 1994). ... Rights renounced by Pistons (July 15, 1996). ... Signed as free agent by Cavaliers (August 9, 1996).

COLLEGIATE RECORD

NOTES: Led NCAA Division I with 4.04 blocked shots per game (1981) and 4.1 blocked shots per game (1982).

Season Team	G	Min.	FGM	FGA	Pct.	FTM	FTA	Pct.	Reb.	Ast.	Pts.	AVERAGES RPG	APG	PPG
79-80—Old Dominion	30	679	67	141	.475	10	27	.370	212	29	144	7.1	1.0	4.8
80-81—Old Dominion	28	845	128	243	.527	48	83	.578	287	15	304	10.3	0.5	10.9
81-82—Old Dominion	30	1007	197	323	.610	78	147	.531	300	10	472	10.0	0.3	15.7
82-83—Old Dominion	29	1005	169	297	.569	80	163	.491	314	17	418	10.8	0.6	14.4
Totals	117	3536	561	1004	.559	216	420	.514	1113	71	1338	9.5	0.6	11.4

NBA REGULAR-SEASON RECORD

Season Team	G	Min.	FGM	FGA	Pct.	FTM	FTA	Pct.	REBOUNDS Off.	Def.	Tot.	Ast.	St.	Blk.	TO	Pts.	AVERAGES RPG	APG	PPG
83-84—Dallas	34	202	15	42	.357	7	22	.318	19	27	46	13	1	15	12	37	1.4	0.4	1.1
84-85—Mil.-Clev.	66	888	106	194	.546	43	87	.494	90	161	251	15	13	49	59	255	3.8	0.2	3.9
85-86—Cleveland	67	1172	113	209	.541	54	103	.524	97	225	322	20	27	62	91	280	4.8	0.3	4.2
86-87—Cleveland	78	1333	209	385	.543	89	173	.514	126	213	339	41	22	81	106	507	4.3	0.5	6.5
87-88—Clev.-Phoe.	83	2098	316	573	.551	170	285	.597	165	358	523	74	47	147	173	802	6.3	0.9	9.7
88-89—Phoenix	82	2019	243	372	.653	108	202	.535	167	384	551	39	35	187	103	594	6.7	0.5	7.2
89-90—Phoenix	82	2399	331	530	*.625	199	288	.691	212	516	728	45	36	184	126	861	8.9	0.5	10.5
90-91—Phoenix	82	1957	247	382	.647	135	206	.655	171	393	564	37	32	161	86	629	6.9	0.5	7.7
91-92—Phoenix	82	1436	196	310	.632	109	171	.637	134	238	372	22	14	81	82	501	4.5	0.3	6.1
92-93—Phoenix	82	1558	175	285	.614	86	166	.518	153	305	458	29	16	103	93	436	5.6	0.4	5.3
93-94—Phoenix	82	1236	162	286	.566	58	116	.500	112	183	295	33	31	109	74	382	3.6	0.4	4.7
94-95—Detroit	67	1543	217	390	.556	66	138	.478	160	248	408	18	27	102	85	500	6.1	0.3	7.5
95-96—Detroit	47	682	61	126	.484	28	45	.622	49	84	133	6	6	37	35	150	2.8	0.1	3.2
Totals	934	18523	2391	4084	.585	1152	2002	.575	1655	3335	4990	392	307	1318	1125	5934	5.3	0.4	6.4

Three-point field goals: 1984-85, 0-for-1. 1986-87, 0-for-2. 1987-88, 0-for-1. Totals, 0-for-4.

Personal fouls/disqualifications: 1983-84, 55/0. 1984-85, 197/7. 1985-86, 235/6. 1986-87, 229/5. 1987-88, 265/4. 1988-89, 273/4. 1989-90, 277/5. 1990-91, 266/2. 1991-92, 239/2. 1992-93, 243/3. 1993-94, 214/4. 1994-95, 247/8. 1995-96, 135/2. Totals, 2875/52.

NBA PLAYOFF RECORD

Season Team	G	Min.	FGM	FGA	Pct.	FTM	FTA	Pct.	REBOUNDS Off.	Def.	Tot.	Ast.	St.	Blk.	TO	Pts.	AVERAGES RPG	APG	PPG
83-84—Dallas	4	32	5	9	.556	2	3	.667	0	7	7	3	0	3	3	12	1.8	0.8	3.0
84-85—Cleveland	4	68	3	5	.600	2	5	.400	5	13	18	4	2	0	5	8	4.5	1.0	2.0
88-89—Phoenix	12	227	32	50	.640	10	14	.714	21	32	53	6	7	19	13	74	4.4	0.5	6.2
89-90—Phoenix	16	544	75	130	.577	27	50	.540	53	111	164	5	4	41	26	177	10.3	0.3	11.1
90-91—Phoenix	4	93	9	15	.600	5	7	.714	8	10	18	2	2	10	3	23	4.5	0.5	5.8
91-92—Phoenix	8	96	14	19	.737	4	8	.500	8	9	17	2	2	4	2	32	2.1	0.3	4.0
92-93—Phoenix	24	469	43	79	.544	28	46	.609	36	63	99	11	4	33	17	114	4.1	0.5	4.8
93-94—Phoenix	7	69	5	15	.333	7	10	.700	11	9	20	0	0	7	4	17	2.9	0.0	2.4
95-96—Detroit	3	78	11	21	.524	6	13	.462	6	10	16	1	1	1	2	28	5.3	0.3	9.3
Totals	82	1676	197	343	.574	91	156	.583	148	264	412	34	22	118	75	485	5.0	0.4	5.9

Personal fouls/disqualifications: 1983-84, 11/1. 1984-85, 19/0. 1988-89, 36/1. 1989-90, 73/0. 1990-91, 15/0. 1991-92, 21/1. 1992-93, 69/2. 1993-94, 19/0. 1995-96, 12/0. Totals, 275/8.

WHITFIELD, DWAYNE   F

PERSONAL: Born August 21, 1972, in Aberdeen, Miss. ... 6-9/240. ... Full name: Dwayne Whitfield.
HIGH SCHOOL: Aberdeen (Miss.).
COLLEGE: Jackson State.
TRANSACTIONS/CAREER NOTES: Selected by Golden State Warriors in second round (40th pick overall) of 1995 NBA Draft. ... Traded by Warriors with F/C Carlos Rogers, C Victor Alexander and draft rights to F Martin Lewis and C Michael McDonald to Toronto Raptors for G B.J. Armstrong (September 18, 1995). ... Waived by Raptors (November 2, 1995). ... Re-signed by Raptors for remainder of season (February 23, 1996). ... Rights renounced by Raptors (July 24, 1996).

COLLEGIATE RECORD

Season Team	G	Min.	FGM	FGA	Pct.	FTM	FTA	Pct.	Reb.	Ast.	Pts.	RPG	APG	PPG
91-92—Jackson State						Did not play—ineligible.								
92-93—Jackson State	12	190	29	60	.483	15	26	.577	46	2	73	3.8	0.2	6.1
93-94—Jackson State	29	702	136	237	.574	88	123	.715	195	17	360	6.7	0.6	12.4
94-95—Jackson State	26	819	194	318	.610	121	195	.621	273	15	509	10.5	0.6	19.6
Totals	67	1711	359	615	.584	224	344	.651	514	34	942	7.7	0.5	14.1

Three-point field goals: 1993-94, 0-for-1. 1994-95, 0-for-3. Totals, 0-for-4.

NBA REGULAR-SEASON RECORD

Season Team	G	Min.	FGM	FGA	Pct.	FTM	FTA	Pct.	Off.	Def.	Tot.	Ast.	St.	Blk.	TO	Pts.	RPG	APG	PPG
									REBOUNDS								**AVERAGES**		
95-96—Toronto	8	122	13	30	.433	14	22	.636	9	16	25	2	3	2	8	40	3.1	0.3	5.0

Personal fouls/disqualifications: 1995-96, 14/0.

WHITNEY, CHRIS   G   BULLETS

W

PERSONAL: Born October 5, 1971, in Hopkinsville, Ky. ... 6-0/170. ... Full name: Christopher Antoine Whitney.
HIGH SCHOOL: Christian County (Hopkinsville, Ky.).
JUNIOR COLLEGE: Lincoln Trail Community College (Ill.).
COLLEGE: Clemson.
TRANSACTIONS/CAREER NOTES: Selected by San Antonio Spurs in second round (47th pick overall) of 1993 NBA Draft. ... Waived by Spurs (February 23, 1995). ... Played in Continental Basketball Association with Rapid City Thrillers (1994-95) and Florida Beachdogs (1995-96). ... Signed by Washington Bullets to first of two consecutive 10-day contracts (March 3, 1996). ... Re-signed by Bullets for remainder of season (March 23, 1996).

COLLEGIATE RECORD

Season Team	G	Min.	FGM	FGA	Pct.	FTM	FTA	Pct.	Reb.	Ast.	Pts.	RPG	APG	PPG
89-90—Lincoln Trail C.C.	33	...	120	253	.474	74	91	.813	...	...	335	...	...	10.2
90-91—Lincoln Trail C.C.	32	...	230	447	.515	134	158	.848	154	202	653	4.8	6.3	20.4
91-92—Clemson	28	982	119	290	.410	56	73	.767	92	161	374	3.3	5.8	13.4
92-93—Clemson	30	1126	149	338	.441	85	106	.802	122	193	470	4.1	6.4	15.7
Junior college totals	65	...	350	700	.500	208	249	.835	...	...	988	...	...	15.2
4-year-college totals	58	2108	268	628	.427	141	179	.788	214	354	844	3.7	6.1	14.6

Three-point field goals: 1991-92, 80-for-191 (.419). 1992-93, 87-for-213 (.408). Totals, 167-for-404 (.413).

NBA REGULAR-SEASON RECORD

Season Team	G	Min.	FGM	FGA	Pct.	FTM	FTA	Pct.	Off.	Def.	Tot.	Ast.	St.	Blk.	TO	Pts.	RPG	APG	PPG
									REBOUNDS								**AVERAGES**		
93-94—San Antonio	40	339	25	82	.305	12	15	.800	5	24	29	53	11	1	37	72	0.7	1.3	1.8
94-95—San Antonio	25	179	14	47	.298	11	11	1.000	4	9	13	28	4	0	18	42	0.5	1.1	1.7
95-96—Washington	21	335	45	99	.455	41	44	.932	2	31	33	51	18	1	23	150	1.6	2.4	7.1
Totals	86	853	84	228	.368	64	70	.914	11	64	75	132	33	2	78	264	0.9	1.5	3.1

Three-point field goals: 1993-94, 10-for-30 (.333). 1994-95, 3-for-19 (.158). 1995-96, 19-for-44 (.432). Totals, 32-for-93 (.344).
Personal fouls/disqualifications: 1993-94, 53/0. 1994-95, 34/1. 1995-96, 46/0. Totals, 133/1.

CBA REGULAR-SEASON RECORD

Season Team	G	Min.	FGM	FGA	Pct.	FTM	FTA	Pct.	Reb.	Ast.	Pts.	RPG	APG	PPG
94-95—Rapid City	7	190	29	83	.349	23	25	.920	26	22	92	3.7	3.1	13.1
95-96—Florida	34	896	141	304	.464	91	114	.798	74	192	432	2.2	5.6	12.7
Totals	41	1086	170	387	.439	114	139	.820	100	214	524	2.4	5.2	12.8

Three-point field goals: 1994-95, 11-for-36 (.306). 1995-96, 59-for-134 (.440). Totals, 70-for-170 (.412).

WILKINS, GERALD   G   MAGIC

PERSONAL: Born September 11, 1963, in Atlanta. ... 6-6/218. ... Full name: Gerald Bernard Wilkins. ... Brother of Dominique Wilkins, forward with Atlanta Hawks, Los Angeles Clippers and Boston Celtics (1982-83 through 1994-95).
HIGH SCHOOL: Mays (Atlanta).
JUNIOR COLLEGE: Moberly (Mo.) Area Junior College
COLLEGE: UT-Chattanooga.
TRANSACTIONS/CAREER NOTES: Selected by New York Knicks in second round (47th pick overall) of 1985 NBA Draft. ... Rights renounced by Knicks (September 22, 1992). ... Signed as free agent by Cleveland Cavaliers (October 8, 1992). ... Selected by Vancouver Grizzlies from Cavaliers in NBA expansion draft (June 24, 1995). ... Rights renounced by Grizzlies (July 16, 1996). ... Signed as free agent by Orlando Magic (July 31, 1996).

COLLEGIATE RECORD

Season Team	G	Min.	FGM	FGA	Pct.	FTM	FTA	Pct.	Reb.	Ast.	Pts.	RPG	APG	PPG
81-82—Moberly Area J.C..........	39	1340	312	566	.551	97	126	.770	229	90	721	5.9	2.3	18.5
82-83—UT-Chattanooga	30	...	169	350	.483	41	62	.661	113	24	379	3.8	0.8	12.6
83-84—UT-Chattanooga	23	737	161	297	.542	73	105	.695	92	35	398	4.0	1.5	17.3
84-85—UT-Chattanooga	32	1188	276	532	.519	120	190	.632	147	81	672	4.6	2.5	21.0
Junior college totals	39	1340	312	566	.551	97	126	.770	229	90	721	5.9	2.3	18.5
4-year-college totals	85	...	606	1179	.514	234	357	.655	352	140	1449	4.1	1.6	17.0

Three-point field goals: 1982-83, 0-for-2. 1983-84, 3-for-10 (.300). Totals, 3-for-12 (.250).

NBA REGULAR-SEASON RECORD

Season Team	G	Min.	FGM	FGA	Pct.	FTM	FTA	Pct.	Off.	Def.	Tot.	Ast.	St.	Blk.	TO	Pts.	RPG	APG	PPG
85-86—New York	81	2025	437	934	.468	132	237	.557	92	116	208	161	68	9	157	1013	2.6	2.0	12.5
86-87—New York	80	2758	633	1302	.486	235	335	.702	120	174	294	354	88	18	214	1527	3.7	4.4	19.1
87-88—New York	81	2703	591	1324	.446	191	243	.786	106	164	270	326	90	22	212	1412	3.3	4.0	17.4
88-89—New York	81	2414	462	1025	.451	186	246	.756	95	149	244	274	115	22	169	1161	3.0	3.4	14.3
89-90—New York	82	2609	472	1032	.457	208	259	.803	133	238	371	330	95	21	194	1191	4.5	4.0	14.5
90-91—New York	68	2164	380	804	.473	169	206	.820	78	129	207	275	82	23	161	938	3.0	4.0	13.8
91-92—New York	82	2344	431	964	.447	116	159	.730	74	132	206	219	76	17	113	1016	2.5	2.7	12.4
92-93—Cleveland	80	2079	361	797	.453	152	181	.840	74	140	214	183	78	18	94	890	2.7	2.3	11.1
93-94—Cleveland	82	2768	446	975	.457	194	250	.776	106	197	303	255	105	38	131	1170	3.7	3.1	14.3
94-95—Cleveland							Did not play—injured.												
95-96—Vancouver.......	28	738	77	205	.376	20	23	.870	22	43	65	68	22	2	37	188	2.3	2.4	6.7
Totals	745	22602	4290	9362	.458	1603	2139	.749	900	1482	2382	2445	819	190	1482	10506	3.2	3.3	14.1

Three-point field goals: 1985-86, 7-for-25 (.280). 1986-87, 26-for-74 (.351). 1987-88, 39-for-129 (.302). 1988-89, 51-for-172 (.297). 1989-90, 39-for-125 (.312). 1990-91, 9-for-43 (.209). 1991-92, 38-for-108 (.352). 1992-93, 16-for-58 (.276). 1993-94, 84-for-212 (.396). 1995-96, 14-for-64 (.219). Totals, 323-for-1010 (.320).

Personal fouls/disqualifications: 1985-86, 155/0. 1986-87, 165/0. 1987-88, 183/1. 1988-89, 166/1. 1989-90, 188/0. 1990-91, 181/0. 1991-92, 195/4. 1992-93, 154/1. 1993-94, 186/0. 1995-96, 55/0. Totals, 1628/7.

NBA PLAYOFF RECORD

Season Team	G	Min.	FGM	FGA	Pct.	FTM	FTA	Pct.	Off.	Def.	Tot.	Ast.	St.	Blk.	TO	Pts.	RPG	APG	PPG
87-88—New York	4	149	33	69	.478	12	14	.857	1	7	8	19	4	0	11	80	2.0	4.8	20.0
88-89—New York	9	290	63	131	.481	18	23	.783	9	24	33	42	12	3	22	145	3.7	4.7	16.1
89-90—New York	10	319	63	137	.460	18	22	.818	14	22	36	52	14	1	18	146	3.6	5.2	14.6
90-91—New York	3	78	14	38	.368	2	2	1.000	2	6	8	5	5	1	8	32	2.7	1.7	10.7
91-92—New York	12	344	45	109	.413	16	23	.696	12	18	30	34	5	1	15	107	2.5	2.8	8.9
92-93—Cleveland	9	236	38	87	.437	13	17	.765	6	10	16	24	9	2	11	93	1.8	2.7	10.3
93-94—Cleveland	3	126	20	45	.444	14	16	.875	3	10	13	10	3	0	3	61	4.3	3.3	20.3
Totals	50	1542	276	616	.448	93	117	.795	47	97	144	186	52	8	88	664	2.9	3.7	13.3

Three-point field goals: 1987-88, 2-for-4 (.500). 1988-89, 1-for-10 (.100). 1989-90, 2-for-8 (.250). 1990-91, 2-for-7 (.286). 1991-92, 1-for-13 (.077). 1992-93, 4-for-12 (.333). 1993-94, 7-for-16 (.438). Totals, 19-for-70 (.271).

Personal fouls/disqualifications: 1987-88, 12/0. 1988-89, 27/1. 1989-90, 23/0. 1990-91, 11/0. 1991-92, 35/0. 1992-93, 16/0. 1993-94, 6/0. Totals, 130/1.

WILLIAMS, BRIAN   C/F   CLIPPERS

PERSONAL: Born April 6, 1969, in Fresno, Calif. ... 6-11/260. ... Full name: Brian Carson Williams.
HIGH SCHOOL: Bishop Gorman (Las Vegas), then Santa Monica (Calif.).
COLLEGE: Maryland, then Arizona.
TRANSACTIONS/CAREER NOTES: Selected after junior season by Orlando Magic in first round (10th pick overall) of 1991 NBA Draft. ... Traded by Magic to Denver Nuggets for G Todd Lichti, F/C Anthony Cook and 1994 second-round draft choice (August 19, 1993). ... Traded by Nuggets to Los Angeles Clippers for C Elmore Spencer (September 19, 1995).

COLLEGIATE RECORD

Season Team	G	Min.	FGM	FGA	Pct.	FTM	FTA	Pct.	Reb.	Ast.	Pts.	RPG	APG	PPG
87-88—Maryland	29	813	156	260	.600	51	76	.671	173	22	363	6.0	0.8	12.5
88-89—Arizona						Did not play—transfer student.								
89-90—Arizona	32	693	130	235	.553	80	110	.727	181	14	340	5.7	0.4	10.6
90-91—Arizona	35	878	195	315	.619	99	147	.673	273	21	489	7.8	0.6	14.0
Totals	96	2384	481	810	.594	230	333	.691	627	57	1192	6.5	0.6	12.4

Three-point field goals: 1989-90, 0-for-1.

NBA REGULAR-SEASON RECORD

Season Team	G	Min.	FGM	FGA	Pct.	FTM	FTA	Pct.	Off.	Def.	Tot.	Ast.	St.	Blk.	TO	Pts.	RPG	APG	PPG
91-92—Orlando	48	905	171	324	.528	95	142	.669	115	157	272	33	41	53	86	437	5.7	0.7	9.1
92-93—Orlando	21	240	40	78	.513	16	20	.800	24	32	56	5	14	17	25	96	2.7	0.2	4.6
93-94—Denver	80	1507	251	464	.541	137	211	.649	138	308	446	50	49	87	104	639	5.6	0.6	8.0
94-95—Denver	63	1261	196	333	.589	106	162	.654	98	200	298	53	38	43	114	498	4.7	0.8	7.9
95-96—L.A. Clippers ...	65	2157	416	766	.543	196	267	.734	149	343	492	122	70	55	190	1029	7.6	1.9	15.8
Totals	277	6070	1074	1965	.547	550	802	.686	524	1040	1564	263	212	255	519	2699	5.6	0.9	9.7

Three-point field goals: 1992-93, 0-for-1. 1993-94, 0-for-3. 1995-96, 1-for-6 (.167). Totals, 1-for-10 (.100).
Personal fouls/disqualifications: 1991-92, 139/2. 1992-93, 48/2. 1993-94, 221/3. 1994-95, 210/7. 1995-96, 226/5. Totals, 844/19.

NBA PLAYOFF RECORD

								REBOUNDS								AVERAGES		
Season Team	G	Min.	FGM	FGA	Pct.	FTM	FTA	Pct.	Off.	Def.	Tot.	Ast.	St.	Blk.	TO	Pts.	RPG	APG	PPG
93-94—Denver	12	289	42	76	.553	27	41	.659	33	56	89	11	4	11	17	111	7.4	0.9	9.3
94-95—Denver	3	44	10	18	.556	4	4	1.000	5	13	18	2	0	1	10	24	6.0	0.7	8.0
Totals	15	333	52	94	.553	31	45	.689	38	69	107	13	4	12	27	135	7.1	0.9	9.0

Personal fouls/disqualifications: 1993-94, 36/0. 1994-95, 15/1. Totals, 51/1.

WILLIAMS, BUCK   F   KNICKS

PERSONAL: Born March 8, 1960, in Rocky Mount, N.C. ... 6-8/225. ... Full name: Charles Linwood Williams.
HIGH SCHOOL: Rocky Mount (N.C.).
COLLEGE: Maryland.
TRANSACTIONS/CAREER NOTES: Selected after junior season by New Jersey Nets in first round (third pick overall) of 1981 NBA Draft. ... Traded by Nets to Portland Trail Blazers for C Sam Bowie and 1989 first-round draft choice (June 24, 1989). ... Rights renounced by Trail Blazers (July 23, 1996). ... Signed as free agent by New York Knicks (July 26, 1996).
MISCELLANEOUS: Member of U.S. Olympic team (1980). ... New Jersey Nets all-time leading scorer with 10,440 points and leading rebounder with 7,576 (1981-82 through 1988-89).

COLLEGIATE RECORD

											AVERAGES		
Season Team	G	Min.	FGM	FGA	Pct.	FTM	FTA	Pct.	Reb.	Ast.	Pts.	RPG	APG	PPG
78-79—Maryland	30	...	120	206	.583	60	109	.550	323	18	300	10.8	0.6	10.0
79-80—Maryland	24	...	143	236	.606	85	128	.664	242	27	371	10.1	1.1	15.5
80-81—Maryland	31	1080	183	283	.647	116	182	.637	363	31	482	11.7	1.0	15.5
Totals	85	...	446	725	.615	261	419	.623	928	76	1153	10.9	0.9	13.6

NBA REGULAR-SEASON RECORD

HONORS: NBA Rookie of the Year (1982). ... All-NBA second team (1983). ... NBA All-Defensive first team (1990, 1991). ... NBA All-Defensive second team (1988, 1992). ... NBA All-Rookie team (1982).

								REBOUNDS								AVERAGES		
Season Team	G	Min.	FGM	FGA	Pct.	FTM	FTA	Pct.	Off.	Def.	Tot.	Ast.	St.	Blk.	TO	Pts.	RPG	APG	PPG
81-82—New Jersey	82	2825	513	881	.582	242	388	.624	347	658	1005	107	84	84	235	1268	12.3	1.3	15.5
82-83—New Jersey	82	2961	536	912	.588	324	523	.620	365	662	1027	125	91	110	246	1396	12.5	1.5	17.0
83-84—New Jersey	81	3003	495	926	.535	284	498	.570	*355	645	1000	130	81	125	237	1274	12.3	1.6	15.7
84-85—New Jersey	82	*3182	577	1089	.530	336	538	.625	323	682	1005	167	63	110	238	1491	12.3	2.0	18.2
85-86—New Jersey	82	3070	500	956	.523	301	445	.676	329	657	986	131	73	96	244	1301	12.0	1.6	15.9
86-87—New Jersey	82	2976	521	936	.557	430	588	.731	322	701	1023	129	78	91	280	1472	12.5	1.6	18.0
87-88—New Jersey	70	2637	466	832	.560	346	518	.668	298	536	834	109	68	44	189	1279	11.9	1.6	18.3
88-89—New Jersey	74	2446	373	702	.531	213	320	.666	249	447	696	78	61	36	142	959	9.4	1.1	13.0
89-90—Portland	82	2801	413	754	.548	288	408	.706	250	550	800	116	69	39	168	1114	9.8	1.4	13.6
90-91—Portland	80	2582	358	595	*.602	217	308	.705	227	524	751	97	47	47	137	933	9.4	1.2	11.7
91-92—Portland	80	2519	340	563	*.604	221	293	.754	260	444	704	108	62	41	130	901	8.8	1.4	11.3
92-93—Portland	82	2498	270	528	.511	138	214	.645	232	458	690	75	81	61	101	678	8.4	0.9	8.3
93-94—Portland	81	2636	291	524	.555	201	296	.679	315	528	843	80	58	47	111	783	10.4	1.0	9.7
94-95—Portland	82	2422	309	604	.512	138	205	.673	251	418	669	78	67	69	119	757	8.2	1.0	9.2
95-96—Portland	70	1672	192	384	.500	125	187	.668	159	245	404	42	40	47	90	511	5.8	0.6	7.3
Totals	1192	40230	6154	11186	.550	3804	5729	.664	4282	8155	12437	1572	1023	1047	2667	16117	10.4	1.3	13.5

Three-point field goals: 1981-82, 0-for-1. 1982-83, 0-for-4. 1983-84, 0-for-4. 1984-85, 1-for-4 (.250). 1985-86, 0-for-2. 1986-87, 0-for-1. 1987-88, 1-for-1. 1988-89, 0-for-3. 1989-90, 0-for-1. 1991-92, 0-for-1. 1992-93, 0-for-1. 1993-94, 0-for-1. 1994-95, 1-for-2 (.500). 1995-96, 2-for-3 (.667). Totals, 5-for-29 (.172).

Personal fouls/disqualifications: 1981-82, 285/5. 1982-83, 270/4. 1983-84, 298/3. 1984-85, 293/7. 1985-86, 294/9. 1986-87, 315/8. 1987-88, 266/5. 1988-89, 223/0. 1989-90, 285/4. 1990-91, 247/2. 1991-92, 244/4. 1992-93, 270/0. 1993-94, 239/1. 1994-95, 254/2. 1995-96, 187/1. Totals, 3970/55.

NBA PLAYOFF RECORD

								REBOUNDS								AVERAGES		
Season Team	G	Min.	FGM	FGA	Pct.	FTM	FTA	Pct.	Off.	Def.	Tot.	Ast.	St.	Blk.	TO	Pts.	RPG	APG	PPG
81-82—New Jersey	2	79	14	26	.538	7	15	.467	11	10	21	3	1	2	4	35	10.5	1.5	17.5
82-83—New Jersey	2	85	11	22	.500	16	20	.800	9	14	23	4	2	2	5	38	11.5	2.0	19.0
83-84—New Jersey	11	473	63	130	.485	45	81	.556	57	98	155	16	15	17	29	171	14.1	1.5	15.5
84-85—New Jersey	3	123	26	40	.650	22	30	.733	14	18	32	1	3	5	6	74	10.7	0.3	24.7
85-86—New Jersey	3	126	21	29	.724	20	26	.769	12	19	31	2	6	1	6	62	10.3	0.7	20.7
89-90—Portland	21	776	101	199	.508	71	105	.676	67	126	193	39	13	6	41	273	9.2	1.9	13.0
90-91—Portland	16	572	65	130	.500	35	58	.603	53	90	143	14	10	4	24	165	8.9	0.9	10.3
91-92—Portland	21	758	66	130	.508	69	91	.758	61	118	179	22	27	17	45	201	8.5	1.0	9.6
92-93—Portland	4	119	11	23	.478	13	19	.684	12	17	29	1	1	3	6	35	7.3	0.3	8.8
93-94—Portland	4	125	19	28	.679	13	15	.867	14	21	35	2	4	2	8	51	8.8	0.5	12.8
94-95—Portland	3	103	9	15	.600	7	11	.636	8	11	19	1	4	2	4	25	6.3	0.3	8.3
95-96—Portland	5	133	9	23	.391	5	7	.714	13	12	25	1	1	4	5	24	5.0	0.2	4.8
Totals	95	3472	415	795	.522	323	478	.676	331	554	885	106	87	65	183	1154	9.3	1.1	12.1

Three-point field goals: 1995-96, 1-for-2 (.500).

Personal fouls/disqualifications: 1981-82, 7/0. 1982-83, 12/2. 1983-84, 44/2. 1984-85, 12/0. 1985-86, 15/1. 1989-90, 74/1. 1990-91, 55/1. 1991-92, 73/1. 1992-93, 12/1. 1993-94, 11/0. 1994-95, 14/1. 1995-96, 18/0. Totals, 347/10.

NBA ALL-STAR GAME RECORD

							REBOUNDS								
Season Team	Min.	FGM	FGA	Pct.	FTM	FTA	Pct.	Off.	Def.	Tot.	Ast.	PF	Dq.	St.	Blk.	TO	Pts.
1982 —New Jersey	22	2	7	.286	0	2	.000	1	9	10	1	3	0	0	2	3	4
1983 —New Jersey	19	3	4	.750	2	4	.500	3	4	7	1	0	0	1	0	0	8
1986 —New Jersey	20	5	8	.625	3	5	.600	3	4	7	4	0	0	0	0	1	13
Totals	61	10	19	.526	5	11	.455	7	17	24	6	3	0	1	2	4	25

W

WILLIAMS, ERIC   F   CELTICS

PERSONAL: Born July 17, 1972, in Newark, N.J. ... 6-8/220. ... Full name: Eric C. Williams.
HIGH SCHOOL: M.X. Shabazz (Newark, N.J.).
JUNIOR COLLEGE: Burlington County (N.J.) College, then Vincennes (Ind.) University.
COLLEGE: Providence.
TRANSACTIONS/CAREER NOTES: Selected by Boston Celtics in first round (14th pick overall) of 1995 NBA Draft.

COLLEGIATE RECORD

Season Team	G	Min.	FGM	FGA	Pct.	FTM	FTA	Pct.	Reb.	Ast.	Pts.	RPG	APG	PPG
90-91—Burlington County							Did not play.							
91-92—Vincennes.....................	25	...	167	271	.616	103	154	.669	189	...	437	7.6	...	17.5
92-93—Vincennes.....................	35	...	273	485	.563	182	273	.667	323	96	729	9.2	2.7	20.8
93-94—Providence	30	781	166	327	.508	138	209	.660	151	37	470	5.0	1.2	15.7
94-95—Providence	30	1041	184	445	.413	134	195	.687	201	75	531	6.7	2.5	17.7
Junior college totals	60		440	756	.582	285	427	.667	512	...	1166	8.5	...	19.4
4-year-college totals	60	1822	350	772	.453	272	404	.673	352	112	1001	5.9	1.9	16.7

Three-point field goals: 1993-94, 0-for-5. 1994-95, 29-for-78 (.372). Totals, 29-for-83 (.349).

NBA REGULAR-SEASON RECORD

									REBOUNDS								AVERAGES		
Season Team	G	Min.	FGM	FGA	Pct.	FTM	FTA	Pct.	Off.	Def.	Tot.	Ast.	St.	Blk.	TO	Pts.	RPG	APG	PPG
95-96—Boston	64	1470	241	546	.441	200	298	.671	92	125	217	70	56	11	88	685	3.4	1.1	10.7

Three-point field goals: 1995-96, 3-for-10 (.300).
Personal fouls/disqualifications: 1995-96, 147/1.

WILLIAMS, HERB   F/C   KNICKS

W

PERSONAL: Born February 16, 1958, in Columbus, Ohio. ... 6-11/260. ... Full name: Herbert L. Williams.
HIGH SCHOOL: Marion Franklin (Columbus, Ohio).
COLLEGE: Ohio State.
TRANSACTIONS/CAREER NOTES: Selected by Indiana Pacers in first round (14th pick overall) of 1981 NBA Draft. ... Traded by Pacers to Dallas Mavericks for F Detlef Schrempf and 1990 or 1991 second-round draft choice (February 21, 1989). ... Signed as free agent by New York Knicks (November 15, 1992). ... Traded by Knicks with G/F Doug Christie and cash to Toronto Raptors for G Willie Anderson and F/C Victor Alexander (February 18, 1996). ... Waived by Raptors (February 23, 1996). ... Signed by Knicks for remainder of season (February 28, 1996). ... Re-signed by Knicks (September 4, 1996).
MISCELLANEOUS: Indiana Pacers all-time leading rebounder with 4,494 and all-time blocked shots leader with 1,094 (1981-82 through 1988-89).

COLLEGIATE RECORD

Season Team	G	Min.	FGM	FGA	Pct.	FTM	FTA	Pct.	Reb.	Ast.	Pts.	RPG	APG	PPG
77-78—Ohio State	27	992	196	407	.482	60	91	.659	308	32	452	11.4	1.2	16.7
78-79—Ohio State	31	1212	253	483	.524	111	166	.669	325	27	617	10.5	0.9	19.9
79-80—Ohio State	29	1069	206	415	.496	97	147	.660	263	21	509	9.1	0.7	17.6
80-81—Ohio State	27	1020	179	368	.486	75	109	.688	215	16	433	8.0	0.6	16.0
Totals	114	4293	834	1673	.499	343	513	.669	1111	96	2011	9.7	0.8	17.6

NBA REGULAR-SEASON RECORD

									REBOUNDS								AVERAGES		
Season Team	G	Min.	FGM	FGA	Pct.	FTM	FTA	Pct.	Off.	Def.	Tot.	Ast.	St.	Blk.	TO	Pts.	RPG	APG	PPG
81-82—Indiana...........	82	2277	407	854	.477	126	188	.670	175	430	605	139	53	178	137	942	7.4	1.7	11.5
82-83—Indiana...........	78	2513	580	1163	.499	155	220	.705	151	432	583	262	54	171	229	1315	7.5	3.4	16.9
83-84—Indiana...........	69	2279	411	860	.478	207	295	.702	154	400	554	215	60	108	207	1029	8.0	3.1	14.9
84-85—Indiana...........	75	2557	575	1211	.475	224	341	.657	154	480	634	252	54	134	265	1375	8.5	3.4	18.3
85-86—Indiana...........	78	2770	627	1275	.492	294	403	.730	172	538	710	174	50	184	210	1549	9.1	2.2	19.9
86-87—Indiana...........	74	2526	451	939	.480	199	269	.740	143	400	543	174	59	93	145	1101	7.3	2.4	14.9
87-88—Indiana...........	75	1966	311	732	.425	126	171	.737	116	353	469	98	37	146	179	748	6.3	1.3	10.0
88-89—Ind.-Dallas......	76	2470	322	739	.436	133	194	.686	135	458	593	124	46	134	149	777	7.8	1.6	10.2
89-90—Dallas.............	81	2199	295	665	.444	108	159	.679	76	315	391	119	51	106	106	700	4.8	1.5	8.6
90-91—Dallas.............	60	1832	332	655	.507	83	130	.638	86	271	357	95	30	88	113	747	6.0	1.6	12.5
91-92—Dallas.............	75	2040	367	851	.431	124	171	.725	106	348	454	94	35	98	114	859	6.1	1.3	11.5
92-93—New York	55	571	72	175	.411	14	21	.667	44	102	146	19	21	28	22	158	2.7	0.3	2.9
93-94—New York	70	774	103	233	.442	27	42	.643	56	126	182	28	18	43	39	233	2.6	0.4	3.3
94-95—New York	56	743	82	180	.456	23	37	.622	23	109	132	27	13	45	40	187	2.4	0.5	3.3
95-96—Tor.-N.Y.........	44	571	62	152	.408	13	20	.650	15	75	90	27	14	33	22	138	2.0	0.6	3.1
Totals	1048	28088	4997	10684	.468	1856	2661	.697	1606	4837	6443	1847	595	1589	1917	11858	6.1	1.8	11.3

Three-point field goals: 1981-82, 2-for-7 (.286). 1982-83, 0-for-5. 1983-84, 0-for-4. 1984-85, 1-for-9 (.111). 1985-86, 1-for-12 (.083). 1986-87, 0-for-5. 1987-88, 0-for-6. 1988-89, 2-for-9 (.222). 1989-90, 0-for-4. 1991-92, 1-for-6 (.167). 1993-94, 0-for-1. 1995-96, 1-for-4 (.250). Totals, 8-for-83 (.096).
Personal fouls/disqualifications: 1981-82, 200/0. 1982-83, 230/4. 1983-84, 193/4. 1984-85, 218/1. 1985-86, 244/2. 1986-87, 255/9. 1987-88, 244/1. 1988-89, 236/5. 1989-90, 243/4. 1990-91, 197/3. 1991-92, 189/2. 1992-93, 78/0. 1993-94, 108/1. 1994-95, 108/0. 1995-96, 79/0. Totals, 2822/36.

NBA PLAYOFF RECORD

									REBOUNDS								AVERAGES		
Season Team	G	Min.	FGM	FGA	Pct.	FTM	FTA	Pct.	Off.	Def.	Tot.	Ast.	St.	Blk.	TO	Pts.	RPG	APG	PPG
86-87—Indiana...........	4	134	20	34	.588	7	13	.538	3	17	20	7	0	1	11	47	5.0	1.8	11.8
89-90—Dallas.............	3	81	14	23	.609	13	16	.813	4	9	13	5	1	2	3	41	4.3	1.7	13.7
92-93—New York	7	69	5	14	.357	4	4	1.000	5	9	14	2	1	4	2	14	2.0	0.3	2.0

Season Team	G	Min.	FGM	FGA	Pct.	FTM	FTA	Pct.	REBOUNDS Off.	Def.	Tot.	Ast.	St.	Blk.	TO	Pts.	AVERAGES RPG	APG	PPG
93-94—New York........	19	127	13	31	.419	2	3	.667	10	10	20	3	3	11	7	28	1.1	0.2	1.5
94-95—New York........	8	55	3	13	.231	2	2	1.000	3	4	7	0	5	5	1	8	0.9	0.0	1.0
95-96—New York........	5	33	3	5	.600	3	4	.750	0	0	0	0	0	2	1	9	0.0	0.0	1.8
Totals	46	499	58	120	.483	31	42	.738	25	49	74	17	10	25	25	147	1.6	0.4	3.2

Personal fouls/disqualifications: 1986-87, 12/0. 1989-90, 16/1. 1992-93, 13/0. 1993-94, 19/0. 1994-95, 13/0. 1995-96, 3/0. Totals, 76/1.

WILLIAMS, JAYSON F NETS

PERSONAL: Born February 22, 1968, in Ritter, S.C. ... 6-10/245.
HIGH SCHOOL: Christ The King (Queens, N.Y.).
COLLEGE: St. John's.
TRANSACTIONS/CAREER NOTES: Selected by Phoenix Suns in first round (21st pick overall) of 1990 NBA Draft. ... Draft rights traded by Suns to Philadelphia 76ers for 1993 first-round draft choice (October 28, 1990). ... Traded by 76ers to New Jersey Nets for 1994 and 1997 second-round draft choices (October 8, 1992).

COLLEGIATE RECORD

Season Team	G	Min.	FGM	FGA	Pct.	FTM	FTA	Pct.	Reb.	Ast.	Pts.	AVERAGES RPG	APG	PPG
86-87—St. John's						Did not play—ineligible.								
87-88—St. John's	28	662	102	199	.513	72	120	.600	143	12	276	5.1	0.4	9.9
88-89—St. John's	31	1036	236	412	.573	134	191	.702	246	18	606	7.9	0.6	19.5
89-90—St. John's	13	377	70	131	.534	49	80	.613	101	7	190	7.8	0.5	14.6
Totals	72	2075	408	742	.550	255	391	.652	490	37	1072	6.8	0.5	14.9

Three-point field goals: 1988-89, 0-for-2. 1989-90, 1-for-2 (.500). Totals, 1-for-4 (.250).

NBA REGULAR-SEASON RECORD

Season Team	G	Min.	FGM	FGA	Pct.	FTM	FTA	Pct.	REBOUNDS Off.	Def.	Tot.	Ast.	St.	Blk.	TO	Pts.	AVERAGES RPG	APG	PPG
90-91—Philadelphia....	52	508	72	161	.447	37	56	.661	41	70	111	16	9	6	40	182	2.1	0.3	3.5
91-92—Philadelphia....	50	646	75	206	.364	56	88	.636	62	83	145	12	20	20	44	206	2.9	0.2	4.1
92-93—New Jersey.....	12	139	21	46	.457	7	18	.389	22	19	41	0	4	4	8	49	3.4	0.0	4.1
93-94—New Jersey.....	70	877	125	293	.427	72	119	.605	109	154	263	26	17	36	35	322	3.8	0.4	4.6
94-95—New Jersey.....	75	982	149	323	.461	65	122	.533	179	246	425	35	26	33	59	363	5.7	0.5	4.8
95-96—New Jersey.....	80	1858	279	660	.423	161	272	.592	342	461	803	47	35	57	106	721	10.0	0.6	9.0
Totals	339	5010	721	1689	.427	398	675	.590	755	1033	1788	136	111	156	292	1843	5.3	0.4	5.4

Three-point field goals: 1990-91, 1-for-2 (.500). 1994-95, 0-for-5. 1995-96, 2-for-7 (.286). Totals, 3-for-14 (.214).
Personal fouls/disqualifications: 1990-91, 92/1. 1991-92, 110/1. 1992-93, 24/0. 1993-94, 140/1. 1994-95, 160/2. 1995-96, 238/4. Totals, 764/9.

NBA PLAYOFF RECORD

Season Team	G	Min.	FGM	FGA	Pct.	FTM	FTA	Pct.	REBOUNDS Off.	Def.	Tot.	Ast.	St.	Blk.	TO	Pts.	AVERAGES RPG	APG	PPG
90-91—Philadelphia....	4	10	4	5	.800	0	0	....	2	2	4	0	0	0	1	8	1.0	0.0	2.0
93-94—New Jersey.....	2	17	0	3	.000	1	2	.500	3	0	3	0	0	0	2	1	1.5	0.0	0.5
Totals	6	27	4	8	.500	1	2	.500	5	2	7	0	0	0	3	9	1.2	0.0	1.5

Personal fouls/disqualifications: 1990-91, 1/0. 1993-94, 5/0. Totals, 6/0.

WILLIAMS, JOHN C/F SUNS

PERSONAL: Born August 9, 1962, in Sorrento, La. ... 6-11/245. ... Nickname: Hot Rod.
HIGH SCHOOL: St. Amant (La.).
COLLEGE: Tulane.
TRANSACTIONS/CAREER NOTES: Selected by Cleveland Cavaliers in second round (45th pick overall) of 1985 NBA Draft. ... Played in United States Basketball League with Rhode Island Gulls (1985) and Staten Island Stallions (1986). ... Signed by Cavaliers (June 16, 1986). ... Traded by Cavaliers to Phoenix Suns for G/F Dan Majerle, F Antonio Lang and 1996, 1997 or 1998 first-round draft choice (October 7, 1995).
MISCELLANEOUS: Cleveland Cavaliers all-time blocked shots leader with 1,200 (1986-87 through 1994-95).

COLLEGIATE RECORD

Season Team	G	Min.	FGM	FGA	Pct.	FTM	FTA	Pct.	Reb.	Ast.	Pts.	AVERAGES RPG	APG	PPG
81-82—Tulane............................	28	932	163	279	.584	88	133	.662	202	32	414	7.2	1.1	14.8
82-83—Tulane............................	31	996	151	317	.476	83	118	.703	166	40	385	5.4	1.3	12.4
83-84—Tulane............................	28	1038	202	355	.569	140	184	.761	222	61	544	7.9	2.2	19.4
84-85—Tulane............................	28	1006	189	334	.566	120	155	.774	219	65	498	7.8	2.3	17.8
Totals	115	3972	705	1285	.549	431	590	.731	809	198	1841	7.0	1.7	16.0

HONORS: NBA All-Rookie team (1987).

NBA REGULAR-SEASON RECORD

Season Team	G	Min.	FGM	FGA	Pct.	FTM	FTA	Pct.	REBOUNDS Off.	Def.	Tot.	Ast.	St.	Blk.	TO	Pts.	AVERAGES RPG	APG	PPG
86-87—Cleveland	80	2714	435	897	.485	298	400	.745	222	407	629	154	58	167	139	1168	7.9	1.9	14.6
87-88—Cleveland	77	2106	316	663	.477	211	279	.756	159	347	506	103	61	145	104	843	6.6	1.3	10.9
88-89—Cleveland	82	2125	356	700	.509	235	314	.748	173	304	477	108	77	134	102	948	5.8	1.3	11.6
89-90—Cleveland	82	2776	528	1070	.493	325	440	.739	220	443	663	168	86	167	143	1381	8.1	2.0	16.8

W

Season Team	G	Min.	FGM	FGA	Pct.	FTM	FTA	Pct.	REBOUNDS Off.	Def.	Tot.	Ast.	St.	Blk.	TO	Pts.	AVERAGES RPG	APG	PPG
90-91—Cleveland	43	1293	199	430	.463	107	164	.652	111	179	290	100	36	69	63	505	6.7	2.3	11.7
91-92—Cleveland	80	2432	341	678	.503	270	359	.752	228	379	607	196	60	182	83	952	7.6	2.5	11.9
92-93—Cleveland	67	2055	263	560	.470	212	296	.716	127	288	415	152	48	105	116	738	6.2	2.3	11.0
93-94—Cleveland	76	2660	394	825	.478	252	346	.728	207	368	575	193	78	130	139	1040	7.6	2.5	13.7
94-95—Cleveland	74	2641	366	810	.452	196	286	.685	173	334	507	192	83	101	149	929	6.9	2.6	12.6
95-96—Phoenix	62	1652	180	397	.453	95	130	.731	129	243	372	62	46	90	62	455	6.0	1.0	7.3
Totals	723	22454	3378	7030	.481	2201	3014	.730	1749	3292	5041	1428	633	1290	1100	8959	7.0	2.0	12.4

Three-point field goals: 1986-87, 0-for-1. 1987-88, 0-for-1. 1988-89, 1-for-4 (.250). 1990-91, 0-for-1. 1991-92, 0-for-4. 1994-95, 1-for-5 (.200). 1995-96, 0-for-1. Totals, 2-for-17 (.118).

Personal fouls/disqualifications: 1986-87, 197/0. 1987-88, 203/2. 1988-89, 188/1. 1989-90, 214/2. 1990-91, 126/2. 1991-92, 191/2. 1992-93, 171/2. 1993-94, 219/3. 1994-95, 211/2. 1995-96, 170/2. Totals, 1890/18.

NBA PLAYOFF RECORD

Season Team	G	Min.	FGM	FGA	Pct.	FTM	FTA	Pct.	REBOUNDS Off.	Def.	Tot.	Ast.	St.	Blk.	TO	Pts.	AVERAGES RPG	APG	PPG
87-88—Cleveland	5	133	20	40	.500	6	13	.462	13	16	29	4	3	7	4	46	5.8	0.8	9.2
88-89—Cleveland	5	161	21	45	.467	13	18	.722	7	27	34	10	2	7	11	55	6.8	2.0	11.0
89-90—Cleveland	5	174	39	70	.557	17	22	.773	14	32	46	11	2	5	7	95	9.2	2.2	19.0
91-92—Cleveland	17	567	84	154	.545	87	109	.798	50	80	130	42	24	17	31	255	7.6	2.5	15.0
92-93—Cleveland	9	237	30	75	.400	21	28	.750	12	29	41	17	5	14	11	81	4.6	1.9	9.0
94-95—Cleveland	4	144	12	42	.286	3	8	.375	3	22	25	11	9	3	10	27	6.3	2.8	6.8
95-96—Phoenix	4	115	14	32	.438	8	12	.667	11	15	26	1	0	7	6	36	6.5	0.3	9.0
Totals	49	1531	220	458	.480	155	210	.738	110	221	331	96	45	60	80	595	6.8	2.0	12.1

Three-point field goals: 1994-95, 0-for-1.

Personal fouls/disqualifications: 1987-88, 13/0. 1988-89, 12/0. 1989-90, 23/1. 1991-92, 58/2. 1992-93, 26/1. 1994-95, 11/0. 1995-96, 17/1. Totals, 160/5.

WILLIAMS, LORENZO   C/F   BULLETS

PERSONAL: Born July 15, 1969, in Ocala, Fla. ... 6-9/230.
HIGH SCHOOL: Forest (Ocala, Fla.).
JUNIOR COLLEGE: Polk Community College (Fla.).
COLLEGE: Stetson.
TRANSACTIONS/CAREER NOTES: Not drafted by an NBA franchise. ... Played in United States Basketball League with Miami Tropics (1991) and Palm Beach Stingrays (1992). ... Played in Global Basketball Association with Fayetteville Flyers (1991-92). ... Signed as free agent by Charlotte Hornets (October 2, 1992). ... Waived by Hornets (November 12, 1992). ... Played in Continental Basketball Association with Rockford Lightning (1992-93 and 1993-94). ... Signed as free agent by Orlando Magic (December 5, 1992). ... Waived by Magic (December 10, 1992). ... Signed by Boston Celtics to first of two consecutive 10-day contracts (January 11, 1993). ... Re-signed by Celtics for remainder of season (February 1, 1993). ... Waived by Celtics (November 2, 1993). ... Signed as free agent by Magic (November 30, 1993). ... Waived by Magic (December 22, 1993). ... Signed as free agent by Hornets (January 1, 1994). ... Waived by Hornets (January 5, 1994). ... Signed by Dallas Mavericks to first of two consecutive 10-day contracts (February 14, 1994). ... Re-signed by Mavericks for remainder of season (March 8, 1994). ... Rights renounced by Mavericks (July 17, 1996). ... Signed as free agent by Washington Bullets (July 26, 1996).

COLLEGIATE RECORD

Season Team	G	Min.	FGM	FGA	Pct.	FTM	FTA	Pct.	Reb.	Ast.	Pts.	AVERAGES RPG	APG	PPG
87-88—Polk C.C.						Statistics unavailable.								
88-89—Polk C.C.						Statistics unavailable.								
89-90—Stetson	32	...	116	223	.520	18	61	.295	269	51	250	8.4	1.6	7.8
90-91—Stetson	31	...	121	224	.540	42	63	.667	312	49	284	10.1	1.6	9.2
4-year-college totals	63	...	237	447	.530	60	124	.484	581	100	534	9.2	1.6	8.5

CBA REGULAR-SEASON RECORD

Season Team	G	Min.	FGM	FGA	Pct.	FTM	FTA	Pct.	Reb.	Ast.	Pts.	AVERAGES RPG	APG	PPG
92-93—Rockford	15	561	64	130	.492	14	39	.359	163	25	143	10.9	1.7	9.5
93-94—Rockford	16	600	53	121	.438	23	46	.500	202	30	132	12.6	1.9	8.3
Totals	31	1161	117	251	.466	37	85	.435	365	55	275	11.8	1.8	8.9

Three-point field goals: 1992-93, 1-for-3 (.333). 1993-94, 3-for-10 (.300). Totals, 4-for-13 (.308).

NBA REGULAR-SEASON RECORD

Season Team	G	Min.	FGM	FGA	Pct.	FTM	FTA	Pct.	REBOUNDS Off.	Def.	Tot.	Ast.	St.	Blk.	TO	Pts.	AVERAGES RPG	APG	PPG
92-93—Cha.-Orl.-Bos.	27	179	17	36	.472	2	7	.286	17	38	55	5	5	17	8	36	2.0	0.2	1.3
93-94—Orl.-Char.-Dal.	38	716	49	110	.445	12	28	.429	95	122	217	25	18	46	22	110	5.7	0.7	2.9
94-95—Dallas	82	2383	145	304	.477	38	101	.376	291	399	690	124	52	148	105	328	8.4	1.5	4.0
95-96—Dallas	65	1806	87	214	.407	24	70	.343	234	287	521	85	48	122	78	198	8.0	1.3	3.0
Totals	212	5084	298	664	.449	76	206	.369	637	846	1483	239	123	333	213	672	7.0	1.1	3.2

Three-point field goals: 1993-94, 0-for-1. 1995-96, 0-for-1. Totals, 0-for-2.

Personal fouls/disqualifications: 1992-93, 29/0. 1993-94, 92/0. 1994-95, 306/6. 1995-96, 226/9. Totals, 653/15.

NBA PLAYOFF RECORD

Season Team	G	Min.	FGM	FGA	Pct.	FTM	FTA	Pct.	REBOUNDS Off.	Def.	Tot.	Ast.	St.	Blk.	TO	Pts.	AVERAGES RPG	APG	PPG
92-93—Boston	1	3	1	1	1.000	0	0	...	1	0	1	0	0	0	0	2	1.0	0.0	2.0

WILLIAMS, MICHEAL   G   TIMBERWOLVES

PERSONAL: Born July 23, 1966, in Dallas. ... 6-2/175. ... Full name: Micheal Douglas Williams.
HIGH SCHOOL: David Carter (Dallas).
COLLEGE: Baylor.
TRANSACTIONS/CAREER NOTES: Selected by Detroit Pistons in second round (48th pick overall) of 1988 NBA Draft. ... Traded by Pistons with draft rights to F Kenny Battle to Phoenix Suns for draft rights to F Anthony Cook (June 27, 1989). ... Waived by Suns (December 12, 1989). ... Signed as free agent by Dallas Mavericks (December 14, 1989). ... Waived by Mavericks (December 26, 1989). ... Played in Continental Basketball Association with Rapid City Thrillers (1989-90). ... Signed by Charlotte Hornets to first of two consecutive 10-day contracts (March 13, 1990). ... Re-signed by Hornets for remainder of season (April 2, 1990). ... Signed as free agent by Indiana Pacers (August 7, 1990). ... Traded by Pacers with F Chuck Person to Minnesota Timberwolves for G Pooh Richardson and F Sam Mitchell (September 8, 1992).
MISCELLANEOUS: Member of NBA championship team (1989).

COLLEGIATE RECORD

Season Team	G	Min.	FGM	FGA	Pct.	FTM	FTA	Pct.	Reb.	Ast.	Pts.	RPG	APG	PPG
84-85—Baylor	28	787	149	306	.487	111	140	.793	66	66	409	2.4	2.4	14.6
85-86—Baylor	22	...	104	225	.462	79	98	.806	63	59	287	2.9	2.7	13.0
86-87—Baylor	31	1112	188	396	.475	137	192	.714	94	157	534	3.0	5.1	17.2
87-88—Baylor	34	1262	216	428	.505	161	231	.697	108	182	625	3.2	5.4	18.4
Totals	115	...	657	1355	.485	488	661	.738	331	464	1855	2.9	4.0	16.1

Three-point field goals: 1986-87, 21-for-67 (.313). 1987-88, 32-for-85 (.376). Totals, 53-for-152 (.349).

NBA REGULAR-SEASON RECORD

RECORDS: Holds record for most consecutive free throws made—97 (March 24, 1993 through November 9, 1993).
HONORS: NBA All-Defensive second team (1992).

Season Team	G	Min.	FGM	FGA	Pct.	FTM	FTA	Pct.	Off.	Def.	Tot.	Ast.	St.	Blk.	TO	Pts.	RPG	APG	PPG
88-89—Detroit	49	358	47	129	.364	31	47	.660	9	18	27	70	13	3	42	127	0.6	1.4	2.6
89-90—Phoe.-Char.	28	329	60	119	.504	36	46	.783	12	20	32	81	22	1	33	156	1.1	2.9	5.6
90-91—Indiana	73	1706	261	523	.499	290	330	.879	49	127	176	348	150	17	150	813	2.4	4.8	11.1
91-92—Indiana	79	2750	404	824	.490	372	427	.871	73	209	282	647	233	22	240	1188	3.6	8.2	15.0
92-93—Minnesota	76	2661	353	791	.446	419	462	.907	84	189	273	661	165	23	227	1151	3.6	8.7	15.1
93-94—Minnesota	71	2206	314	687	.457	333	397	.839	67	154	221	512	118	24	203	971	3.1	7.2	13.7
94-95—Minnesota	1	28	1	4	.250	4	5	.800	0	1	1	3	2	0	3	6	1.0	3.0	6.0
95-96—Minnesota	9	189	13	40	.325	28	33	.848	3	20	23	31	5	3	23	55	2.6	3.4	6.1
Totals	386	10227	1453	3117	.466	1513	1747	.866	297	738	1035	2353	708	93	921	4467	2.7	6.1	11.6

Three-point field goals: 1988-89, 2-for-9 (.222). 1989-90, 0-for-3. 1990-91, 1-for-7 (.143). 1991-92, 8-for-33 (.242). 1992-93, 26-for-107 (.243). 1993-94, 10-for-45 (.222). 1995-96, 1-for-3 (.333). Totals, 48-for-207 (.232).
Personal fouls/disqualifications: 1988-89, 44/0. 1989-90, 39/0. 1990-91, 202/1. 1991-92, 262/7. 1992-93, 268/7. 1993-94, 193/3. 1994-95, 3/0. 1995-96, 37/0. Totals, 1048/18.

NBA PLAYOFF RECORD

Season Team	G	Min.	FGM	FGA	Pct.	FTM	FTA	Pct.	Off.	Def.	Tot.	Ast.	St.	Blk.	TO	Pts.	RPG	APG	PPG
88-89—Detroit	4	6	0	0	...	2	2	1.000	1	1	2	2	1	0	0	2	0.5	0.5	0.5
90-91—Indiana	5	183	30	65	.462	43	48	.896	7	9	16	42	14	0	12	103	3.2	8.4	20.6
91-92—Indiana	3	106	18	43	.419	11	15	.733	1	7	8	24	9	0	7	50	2.7	8.0	16.7
Totals	12	295	48	108	.444	56	65	.862	9	17	26	68	24	0	19	155	2.2	5.7	12.9

Three-point field goals: 1990-91, 0-for-1. 1991-92, 3-for-9 (.333). Totals, 3-for-10 (.300).
Personal fouls/disqualifications: 1988-89, 1/0. 1990-91, 23/2. 1991-92, 12/0. Totals, 36/2.

CBA REGULAR-SEASON RECORD

Season Team	G	Min.	FGM	FGA	Pct.	FTM	FTA	Pct.	Reb.	Ast.	Pts.	RPG	APG	PPG
89-90—Rapid City	23	817	152	272	.559	119	146	.815	94	184	423	4.1	8.0	18.4

Three-point field goals: 1989-90, 0-for-7.

WILLIAMS, MONTY   F   SPURS

PERSONAL: Born October 8, 1971, in Fredericksburg, Va. ... 6-8/225. ... Full name: Tavares Montgomery Williams.
HIGH SCHOOL: Potomac (Oxon Hill, Md.).
COLLEGE: Notre Dame.
TRANSACTIONS/CAREER NOTES: Selected by New York Knicks in first round (24th pick overall) of 1994 NBA Draft. ... Traded by Knicks with F Charles Smith to San Antonio Spurs for F J.R. Reid, C Brad Lohaus and 1996 first-round draft choice (February 8, 1996).

COLLEGIATE RECORD

Season Team	G	Min.	FGM	FGA	Pct.	FTM	FTA	Pct.	Reb.	Ast.	Pts.	RPG	APG	PPG
89-90—Notre Dame	29	588	83	172	.483	54	73	.740	108	31	222	3.7	1.1	7.7
90-91—Notre Dame						Did not play—heart problem.								
91-92—Notre Dame						Did not play—heart problem.								
92-93—Notre Dame	27	942	177	384	.461	121	153	.791	251	39	500	9.3	1.4	18.5
93-94—Notre Dame	29	1000	237	464	.511	143	205	.698	239	68	649	8.2	2.3	22.4
Totals	85	2530	497	1020	.487	318	431	.738	598	138	1371	7.0	1.6	16.1

Three-point field goals: 1989-90, 2-for-10 (.200). 1992-93, 25-for-74 (.338). 1993-94, 32-for-78 (.410). Totals, 59-for-162 (.364).

NBA REGULAR-SEASON RECORD

Season Team	G	Min.	FGM	FGA	Pct.	FTM	FTA	Pct.	Off.	Def.	Tot.	Ast.	St.	Blk.	TO	Pts.	RPG	APG	PPG
									REBOUNDS								AVERAGES		
94-95—New York	41	503	60	133	.451	17	38	.447	42	56	98	49	20	4	41	137	2.4	1.2	3.3
95-96—N.Y.-S.A.	31	184	27	68	.397	14	20	.700	20	20	40	8	6	2	18	68	1.3	0.3	2.2
Totals	72	687	87	201	.433	31	58	.534	62	76	138	57	26	6	59	205	1.9	0.8	2.8

Three-point field goals: 1994-95, 0-for-8. 1995-96, 0-for-1. Totals, 0-for-9.
Personal fouls/disqualifications: 1994-95, 87/0. 1995-96, 26/0. Totals, 113/0.

NBA PLAYOFF RECORD

Season Team	G	Min.	FGM	FGA	Pct.	FTM	FTA	Pct.	Off.	Def.	Tot.	Ast.	St.	Blk.	TO	Pts.	RPG	APG	PPG
									REBOUNDS								AVERAGES		
94-95—New York	1	4	2	2	1.000	0	0	...	0	0	0	0	0	0	0	4	0.0	0.0	4.0
95-96—San Antonio	7	29	2	9	.222	3	6	.500	3	4	7	0	0	0	4	7	1.0	0.0	1.0
Totals	8	33	4	11	.364	3	6	.500	3	4	7	0	0	0	4	11	0.9	0.0	1.4

Personal fouls/disqualifications: 1994-95, 1/0. 1995-96, 4/0. Totals, 5/0.

WILLIAMS, REGGIE   ∘   F/G   PACERS

PERSONAL: Born March 5, 1964, in Baltimore. ... 6-7/195.
HIGH SCHOOL: Dunbar (Baltimore).
COLLEGE: Georgetown.
TRANSACTIONS/CAREER NOTES: Selected by Los Angeles Clippers in first round (fourth pick overall) of 1987 NBA Draft. ... Traded by Clippers with draft rights to F Danny Ferry to Cleveland Cavaliers for G Ron Harper, 1990 and 1992 first-round draft choices and 1991 second-round draft choice (November 16, 1989). ... Waived by Cavaliers (February 26, 1990). ... Signed by San Antonio Spurs for remainder of season (March 5, 1990). ... Waived by Spurs (December 24, 1990). ... Signed as free agent by Denver Nuggets (January 4, 1991). ... Traded by Nuggets with G Jalen Rose and 1996 first-round draft choice to Indiana Pacers for G Mark Jackson, G Ricky Pierce and 1996 first-round draft choice (June 13, 1996).

COLLEGIATE RECORD

NOTES: The Sporting News All-America first team (1987). ... Member of NCAA Division I championship team (1984).

Season Team	G	Min.	FGM	FGA	Pct.	FTM	FTA	Pct.	Reb.	Ast.	Pts.	RPG	APG	PPG
												AVERAGES		
83-84—Georgetown	37	764	130	300	.433	76	99	.768	131	83	336	3.5	2.2	9.1
84-85—Georgetown	35	1043	168	332	.506	80	106	.755	200	83	416	5.7	2.4	11.9
85-86—Georgetown	32	1013	227	430	.528	109	149	.732	261	69	563	8.2	2.2	17.6
86-87—Georgetown	34	1205	284	589	.482	156	194	.804	294	92	802	8.6	2.7	23.6
Totals	138	4025	809	1651	.490	421	548	.768	886	327	2117	6.4	2.4	15.3

Three-point field goals: 1986-87, 78-for-202 (.386).

NBA REGULAR-SEASON RECORD

Season Team	G	Min.	FGM	FGA	Pct.	FTM	FTA	Pct.	Off.	Def.	Tot.	Ast.	St.	Blk.	TO	Pts.	RPG	APG	PPG
									REBOUNDS								AVERAGES		
87-88—L.A. Clippers	35	857	152	427	.356	48	66	.727	55	63	118	58	29	21	63	365	3.4	1.7	10.4
88-89—L.A. Clippers	63	1303	260	594	.438	92	122	.754	70	109	179	103	81	29	114	642	2.8	1.6	10.2
89-90—LAC-Clev.-S.A.	47	743	131	338	.388	52	68	.765	28	55	83	53	32	14	45	320	1.8	1.1	6.8
90-91—S.A.-Denver	73	1896	384	855	.449	166	197	.843	133	173	306	133	113	41	112	991	4.2	1.8	13.6
91-92—Denver	81	2623	601	1277	.471	216	269	.803	145	260	405	235	148	68	173	1474	5.0	2.9	18.2
92-93—Denver	79	2722	535	1167	.458	238	296	.804	132	296	428	295	126	76	194	1341	5.4	3.7	17.0
93-94—Denver	82	2654	418	1014	.412	165	225	.733	98	294	392	300	117	66	163	1065	4.8	3.7	13.0
94-95—Denver	74	2198	388	846	.459	132	174	.759	94	235	329	231	114	67	124	993	4.4	3.1	13.4
95-96—Denver	52	817	94	254	.370	33	39	.846	25	97	122	74	34	21	51	241	2.3	1.4	4.6
Totals	586	15813	2963	6772	.438	1142	1456	.784	780	1582	2362	1482	794	403	1039	7432	4.0	2.5	12.7

Three-point field goals: 1987-88, 13-for-58 (.224). 1988-89, 30-for-104 (.288). 1989-90, 6-for-37 (.162). 1990-91, 57-for-157 (.363). 1991-92, 56-for-156 (.359). 1992-93, 33-for-122 (.270). 1993-94, 64-for-230 (.278). 1994-95, 85-for-266 (.320). 1995-96, 20-for-89 (.225). Totals, 364-for-1219 (.299).
Personal fouls/disqualifications: 1987-88, 108/1. 1988-89, 181/1. 1989-90, 102/2. 1990-91, 253/9. 1991-92, 270/4. 1992-93, 284/6. 1993-94, 288/3. 1994-95, 264/4. 1995-96, 137/1. Totals, 1887/31.

NBA PLAYOFF RECORD

Season Team	G	Min.	FGM	FGA	Pct.	FTM	FTA	Pct.	Off.	Def.	Tot.	Ast.	St.	Blk.	TO	Pts.	RPG	APG	PPG
									REBOUNDS								AVERAGES		
89-90—San Antonio	9	49	9	27	.333	2	2	1.000	5	6	11	3	2	0	5	20	1.2	0.3	2.2
93-94—Denver	12	405	62	149	.416	27	35	.771	18	43	61	42	9	12	28	171	5.1	3.5	14.3
94-95—Denver	3	84	8	36	.222	6	6	1.000	5	11	16	12	3	1	3	26	5.3	4.0	8.7
Totals	24	538	79	212	.373	35	43	.814	28	60	88	57	14	13	36	217	3.7	2.4	9.0

Three-point field goals: 1989-90, 0-for-2. 1993-94, 20-for-50 (.400). 1994-95, 4-for-13 (.308). Totals, 24-for-65 (.369).
Personal fouls/disqualifications: 1989-90, 8/0. 1993-94, 53/1. 1994-95, 11/0. Totals, 72/1.

WILLIAMS, SCOTT   F   76ERS

PERSONAL: Born March 21, 1968, in Hacienda Heights, Calif. ... 6-10/230. ... Full name: Scott Christopher Williams.
HIGH SCHOOL: Woodrow Wilson (Los Angeles).
COLLEGE: North Carolina.
TRANSACTIONS/CAREER NOTES: Not drafted by an NBA franchise. ... Signed as free agent by Chicago Bulls (July 20, 1990). ... Signed as unrestricted free agent by Philadelphia 76ers (July 28, 1994).
MISCELLANEOUS: Member of NBA championship teams (1991, 1992, 1993).

COLLEGIATE RECORD

Season Team	G	Min.	FGM	FGA	Pct.	FTM	FTA	Pct.	Reb.	Ast.	Pts.	RPG	APG	PPG
												AVERAGES		
86-87—North Carolina	36	540	78	157	.497	43	77	.558	150	31	199	4.2	0.9	5.5

Season Team	G	Min.	FGM	FGA	Pct.	FTM	FTA	Pct.	Reb.	Ast.	Pts.	RPG	APG	PPG
												AVERAGES		
87-88—North Carolina..............	34	900	162	283	.572	107	159	.673	217	42	434	6.4	1.2	12.8
88-89—North Carolina..............	35	802	165	297	.556	68	104	.654	254	26	398	7.3	0.7	11.4
89-90—North Carolina..............	33	813	190	343	.554	96	156	.615	240	25	477	7.3	0.8	14.5
Totals	138	3055	595	1080	.551	314	496	.633	861	124	1508	6.2	0.9	10.9

Three-point field goals: 1986-87, 0-for-1. 1987-88, 3-for-7 (.429). 1988-89, 0-for-2. 1989-90, 1-for-7 (.143). Totals, 4-for-17 (.235).

NBA REGULAR-SEASON RECORD

Season Team	G	Min.	FGM	FGA	Pct.	FTM	FTA	Pct.	REBOUNDS Off.	Def.	Tot.	Ast.	St.	Blk.	TO	Pts.	AVERAGES RPG	APG	PPG
90-91—Chicago	51	337	53	104	.510	20	28	.714	42	56	98	16	12	13	23	127	1.9	0.3	2.5
91-92—Chicago	63	690	83	172	.483	48	74	.649	90	157	247	50	13	36	35	214	3.9	0.8	3.4
92-93—Chicago	71	1369	166	356	.466	90	126	.714	168	283	451	68	55	66	73	422	6.4	1.0	5.9
93-94—Chicago	38	638	114	236	.483	60	98	.612	69	112	181	39	16	21	44	289	4.8	1.0	7.6
94-95—Philadelphia	77	1781	206	434	.475	79	107	.738	173	312	485	59	71	40	84	491	6.3	0.8	6.4
95-96—Philadelphia	13	193	15	29	.517	10	12	.833	13	33	46	5	6	7	8	40	3.5	0.4	3.1
Totals	313	5008	637	1331	.479	307	445	.690	555	953	1508	237	173	183	267	1583	4.8	0.8	5.1

Three-point field goals: 1990-91, 1-for-2 (.500). 1991-92, 0-for-3. 1992-93, 0-for-7. 1993-94, 1-for-5 (.200). 1994-95, 0-for-7. 1995-96, 0-for-2. Totals, 2-for-26 (.077).

Personal fouls/disqualifications: 1990-91, 51/0. 1991-92, 122/0. 1992-93, 230/3. 1993-94, 112/1. 1994-95, 237/4. 1995-96, 27/0. Totals, 779/8.

NBA PLAYOFF RECORD

Season Team	G	Min.	FGM	FGA	Pct.	FTM	FTA	Pct.	REBOUNDS Off.	Def.	Tot.	Ast.	St.	Blk.	TO	Pts.	AVERAGES RPG	APG	PPG
90-91—Chicago	12	72	6	13	.462	11	20	.550	4	16	20	3	1	3	4	23	1.7	0.3	1.9
91-92—Chicago	22	321	34	70	.486	20	28	.714	33	62	95	7	6	18	15	88	4.3	0.3	4.0
92-93—Chicago	19	395	44	87	.506	16	29	.552	40	71	111	26	7	17	24	104	5.8	1.4	5.5
93-94—Chicago	10	151	24	57	.421	15	21	.714	15	24	39	7	7	3	9	63	3.9	0.7	6.3
Totals	63	939	108	227	.476	62	98	.633	92	173	265	43	21	41	52	278	4.2	0.7	4.4

Three-point field goals: 1990-91, 0-for-1. 1991-92, 0-for-1. 1992-93, 0-for-2. Totals, 0-for-4.

Personal fouls/disqualifications: 1990-91, 15/0. 1991-92, 65/0. 1992-93, 58/2. 1993-94, 23/0. Totals, 161/2.

WILLIAMS, WALT   F/G   RAPTORS

W

PERSONAL: Born April 16, 1970, in Washington, D.C. ... 6-8/230. ... Full name: Walter Ander Williams.
HIGH SCHOOL: Crossland (Temple Hills, Md.).
COLLEGE: Maryland.
TRANSACTIONS/CAREER NOTES: Selected by Sacramento Kings in first round (seventh pick overall) of 1992 NBA Draft. ... Traded by Kings with F Tyrone Corbin to Miami Heat for G/F Billy Owens and G/F Kevin Gamble (February 22, 1996). ... Rights renounced by Heat (July 17, 1996). ... Signed as free agent by Toronto Raptors (August 29, 1996).

COLLEGIATE RECORD

NOTES: The Sporting News All-America first team (1992).

Season Team	G	Min.	FGM	FGA	Pct.	FTM	FTA	Pct.	Reb.	Ast.	Pts.	AVERAGES RPG	APG	PPG
88-89—Maryland	26	617	75	170	.441	33	53	.623	92	66	190	3.5	2.5	7.3
89-90—Maryland	33	993	143	296	.483	104	134	.776	138	149	420	4.2	4.5	12.7
90-91—Maryland	17	537	109	243	.449	72	86	.837	86	91	318	5.1	5.4	18.7
91-92—Maryland	29	1042	256	542	.472	175	231	.758	162	104	776	5.6	3.6	26.8
Totals	105	3189	583	1251	.466	384	504	.762	478	410	1704	4.6	3.9	16.2

Three-point field goals: 1988-89, 7-for-27 (.259). 1989-90, 30-for-67 (.448). 1990-91, 28-for-95 (.295). 1991-92, 89-for-240 (.371). Totals, 154-for-429 (.359).

NBA REGULAR-SEASON RECORD

HONORS: NBA All-Rookie second team (1993).

Season Team	G	Min.	FGM	FGA	Pct.	FTM	FTA	Pct.	REBOUNDS Off.	Def.	Tot.	Ast.	St.	Blk.	TO	Pts.	AVERAGES RPG	APG	PPG
92-93—Sacramento	59	1673	358	823	.435	224	302	.742	115	150	265	178	66	29	179	1001	4.5	3.0	17.0
93-94—Sacramento	57	1356	226	580	.390	148	233	.635	71	164	235	132	52	23	145	638	4.1	2.3	11.2
94-95—Sacramento	77	2739	445	998	.446	266	364	.731	100	245	345	316	123	63	243	1259	4.5	4.1	16.4
95-96—Sac.-Mia.	73	2169	359	808	.444	163	232	.703	99	220	319	230	85	58	151	995	4.4	3.2	13.6
Totals	266	7937	1388	3209	.433	801	1131	.708	385	779	1164	856	326	173	718	3893	4.4	3.2	14.6

Three-point field goals: 1992-93, 61-for-191 (.319). 1993-94, 38-for-132 (.288). 1994-95, 103-for-296 (.348). 1995-96, 114-for-293 (.389). Totals, 316-for-912 (.346).

Personal fouls/disqualifications: 1992-93, 209/6. 1993-94, 200/6. 1994-95, 265/3. 1995-96, 238/0. Totals, 912/15.

NBA PLAYOFF RECORD

Season Team	G	Min.	FGM	FGA	Pct.	FTM	FTA	Pct.	REBOUNDS Off.	Def.	Tot.	Ast.	St.	Blk.	TO	Pts.	AVERAGES RPG	APG	PPG
95-96—Miami	3	70	6	18	.333	1	2	.500	3	9	12	5	1	1	3	14	4.0	1.7	4.7

Three-point field goals: 1995-96, 1-for-9 (.111).

Personal fouls/disqualifications: 1995-96, 4/0.

DID YOU KNOW...

...that Detroit's Grant Hill was the only player
to lead his team in points, rebounds and assists last season?

WILLIAMSON, CORLISS   F   KINGS

PERSONAL: Born December 4, 1973, in Russellville, Ark. ... 6-7/245. ... Full name: Corliss Mondari Williamson.
HIGH SCHOOL: Russellville (Ark.).
COLLEGE: Arkansas.
TRANSACTIONS/CAREER NOTES: Selected after junior season by Sacramento Kings in first round (13th pick overall) of 1995 NBA Draft.

COLLEGIATE RECORD

NOTES: THE SPORTING NEWS All-America first team (1995). ... NCAA Division I Tournament Most Outstanding Player (1994). ... Member of NCAA Division I championship team (1994).

Season Team	G	Min.	FGM	FGA	Pct.	FTM	FTA	Pct.	Reb.	Ast.	Pts.	RPG	APG	PPG
92-93—Arkansas	18	454	101	176	.574	61	98	.622	92	30	263	5.1	1.7	14.6
93-94—Arkansas	34	989	273	436	.626	149	213	.700	262	74	695	7.7	2.2	20.4
94-95—Arkansas	39	1208	283	515	.550	203	304	.668	293	89	770	7.5	2.3	19.7
Totals	91	2651	657	1127	.583	413	615	.672	647	193	1728	7.1	2.1	19.0

Three-point field goals: 1994-95, 1-for-6 (.167).

NBA REGULAR-SEASON RECORD

Season Team	G	Min.	FGM	FGA	Pct.	FTM	FTA	Pct.	Off.	Def.	Tot.	Ast.	St.	Blk.	TO	Pts.	RPG	APG	PPG
95-96—Sacramento	53	609	125	268	.466	47	84	.560	56	58	114	23	11	9	76	297	2.2	0.4	5.6

Three-point field goals: 1995-96, 0-for-3.
Personal fouls/disqualifications: 1995-96, 115/2.

NBA PLAYOFF RECORD

Season Team	G	Min.	FGM	FGA	Pct.	FTM	FTA	Pct.	Off.	Def.	Tot.	Ast.	St.	Blk.	TO	Pts.	RPG	APG	PPG
95-96—Sacramento	1	2	0	1	.000	1	1	1.000	0	0	0	0	0	0	0	1	0.0	0.0	1.0

WILLIS, KEVIN   F/C   ROCKETS

PERSONAL: Born September 6, 1962, in Los Angeles. ... 7-0/240. ... Full name: Kevin Alvin Willis.
HIGH SCHOOL: Pershing (Detroit).
JUNIOR COLLEGE: Jackson Community College (Mich.).
COLLEGE: Michigan State.
TRANSACTIONS/CAREER NOTES: Selected by Atlanta Hawks in first round (11th pick overall) of 1984 NBA Draft. ... Traded by Hawks with conditional first-round draft choice to Miami Heat for G Steve Smith, F Grant Long and conditional second-round draft choice (November 7, 1994). ... Traded by Heat with G Bimbo Coles to Golden State Warriors for G Tim Hardaway and F/C Chris Gatling (February 22, 1996). ... Rights renounced by Warriors (July 21, 1996). ... Signed as free agent by Houston Rockets (August 19, 1996).

COLLEGIATE RECORD

Season Team	G	Min.	FGM	FGA	Pct.	FTM	FTA	Pct.	Reb.	Ast.	Pts.	RPG	APG	PPG
80-81—Jackson C.C.	...	...	...	...	...	...	...	...	...	...	...	...	...	19.0
81-82—Michigan State	27	518	73	154	.474	17	30	.567	113	2	163	4.2	0.1	6.0
82-83—Michigan State	27	865	162	272	.596	36	70	.514	258	8	360	9.6	0.3	13.3
83-84—Michigan State	25	738	118	240	.492	39	59	.661	192	7	275	7.7	0.3	11.0
Junior college totals	...	...	...	...	...	...	...	...	...	...	...	...	...	...
4-year-college totals	79	2121	353	666	.530	92	159	.579	563	17	798	7.1	0.2	10.1

Three-point field goals: 1982-83, 0-for-1.

NBA REGULAR-SEASON RECORD

HONORS: All-NBA third team (1992).

Season Team	G	Min.	FGM	FGA	Pct.	FTM	FTA	Pct.	Off.	Def.	Tot.	Ast.	St.	Blk.	TO	Pts.	RPG	APG	PPG
84-85—Atlanta	82	1785	322	690	.467	119	181	.657	177	345	522	36	31	49	104	765	6.4	0.4	9.3
85-86—Atlanta	82	2300	419	811	.517	172	263	.654	243	461	704	45	66	44	177	1010	8.6	0.5	12.3
86-87—Atlanta	81	2626	538	1003	.536	227	320	.709	321	528	849	62	65	61	173	1304	10.5	0.8	16.1
87-88—Atlanta	75	2091	356	687	.518	159	245	.649	235	312	547	28	68	42	138	871	7.3	0.4	11.6
88-89—Atlanta						Did not play—injured.													
89-90—Atlanta	81	2273	418	805	.519	168	246	.683	253	392	645	57	63	47	144	1006	8.0	0.7	12.4
90-91—Atlanta	80	2373	444	881	.504	159	238	.668	259	445	704	99	60	40	153	1051	8.8	1.2	13.1
91-92—Atlanta	81	2962	591	1224	.483	292	363	.804	418	840	1258	173	72	54	197	1480	15.5	2.1	18.3
92-93—Atlanta	80	2878	616	1218	.506	196	300	.653	335	693	1028	165	68	41	213	1435	12.9	2.1	17.9
93-94—Atlanta	80	2867	627	1257	.499	268	376	.713	335	628	963	150	79	38	188	1531	12.0	1.9	19.1
94-95—Atlanta-Miami	67	2390	473	1015	.466	205	297	.690	227	505	732	86	92	36	162	1154	10.9	1.3	17.2
95-96—Mia.-GS	75	2135	325	712	.456	143	202	.708	208	430	638	53	32	41	161	794	8.5	0.7	10.6
Totals	864	26680	5129	10303	.498	2108	3031	.695	3011	5579	8590	954	664	493	1810	12401	9.9	1.1	14.4

Three-point field goals: 1984-85, 2-for-9 (.222). 1985-86, 0-for-6. 1986-87, 1-for-4 (.250). 1987-88, 0-for-2. 1989-90, 2-for-7 (.286). 1990-91, 4-for-10 (.400). 1991-92, 6-for-37 (.162). 1992-93, 7-for-29 (.241). 1993-94, 9-for-24 (.375). 1994-95, 3-for-15 (.200). 1995-96, 1-for-9 (.111). Totals, 35-for-152 (.230).

Personal fouls/disqualifications: 1984-85, 226/4. 1985-86, 294/6. 1986-87, 313/4. 1987-88, 240/2. 1989-90, 259/4. 1990-91, 235/2. 1991-92, 223/0. 1992-93, 264/1. 1993-94, 250/2. 1994-95, 215/3. 1995-96, 253/4. Totals, 2772/32.

Season Team	G	Min.	FGM	FGA	Pct.	FTM	FTA	Pct.	Off.	Def.	Tot.	Ast.	St.	Blk.	TO	Pts.	RPG	APG	PPG
										REBOUNDS							AVERAGES		
85-86—Atlanta	9	280	55	98	.561	15	23	.652	31	34	65	5	7	8	15	125	7.2	0.6	13.9
86-87—Atlanta	9	356	60	115	.522	21	31	.677	33	50	83	6	9	7	17	141	9.2	0.7	15.7
87-88—Atlanta	12	462	80	138	.580	34	50	.680	36	72	108	11	10	10	25	194	9.0	0.9	16.2
90-91—Atlanta	5	159	27	67	.403	21	30	.700	18	27	45	5	3	1	2	77	9.0	1.0	15.4
92-93—Atlanta	3	103	21	45	.467	8	14	.571	13	13	26	3	2	0	7	50	8.7	1.0	16.7
93-94—Atlanta	11	362	59	129	.457	16	21	.762	38	81	119	11	8	5	19	134	10.8	1.0	12.2
Totals	49	1722	302	592	.510	115	169	.680	169	277	446	41	39	31	85	721	9.1	0.8	14.7

Three-point field goals: 1987-88, 0-for-1. 1990-91, 2-for-3 (.667). 1992-93, 0-for-1. 1993-94, 0-for-5. Totals, 2-for-10 (.200).
Personal fouls/disqualifications: 1985-86, 38/2. 1986-87, 33/0. 1987-88, 51/1. 1990-91, 22/0. 1992-93, 13/0. 1993-94, 37/0. Totals, 194/3.

NBA ALL-STAR GAME RECORD

Season Team	Min.	FGM	FGA	Pct.	FTM	FTA	Pct.	Off.	Def.	Tot.	Ast.	PF	Dq.	St.	Blk.	TO	Pts.
									REBOUNDS								
1992 —Atlanta...............	14	4	10	.400	0	0	...	4	0	4	0	1	0	0	0	0	8

WILSON, TREVOR   F   LAKERS

PERSONAL: Born March 16, 1968, in Los Angeles. ... 6-8/215.
HIGH SCHOOL: Grover Cleveland (Reseda, Calif.).
COLLEGE: UCLA.
TRANSACTIONS/CAREER NOTES: Selected by Atlanta Hawks in second round (36th pick overall) of 1990 NBA Draft. ... Waived by Hawks (April 1, 1991). ... Played in Spain (1991-92 and 1992-93). ... Signed as free agent by Los Angeles Lakers (August 30, 1993). ... Waived by Lakers (December 7, 1993). ... Signed as free agent by Sacramento Kings (December 15, 1993). ... Waived by Kings (January 9, 1995). ... Signed as free agent by Seattle SuperSonics (October 25, 1995). ... Waived by SuperSonics (October 31, 1995). ... Signed by Philadelphia 76ers for remainder of season (December 7, 1995). ... Waived by 76ers (December 23, 1995). ... Signed as free agent by Lakers (August 15, 1996).

COLLEGIATE RECORD

Season Team	G	Min.	FGM	FGA	Pct.	FTM	FTA	Pct.	Reb.	Ast.	Pts.	RPG	APG	PPG
													AVERAGES	
86-87—UCLA.............................	32	576	65	146	.445	69	95	.726	152	44	199	4.8	1.4	6.2
87-88—UCLA	30	1010	184	353	.521	95	153	.621	281	86	463	9.4	2.9	15.488-
89—UCLA	31	1066	226	451	.501	117	203	.576	269	83	570	8.7	2.7	18.4
89-90—UCLA	33	1106	231	467	.495	103	203	.507	299	95	566	9.1	2.9	17.2
Totals	126	3758	706	1417	.498	384	654	.587	1001	308	1798	7.9	2.4	14.3

Three-point field goals: 1987-88, 0-for-3. 1988-89, 1-for-6 (.167). 1989-90, 1-for-3 (.333). Totals, 2-for-12 (.167).

NBA REGULAR-SEASON RECORD

Season Team	G	Min.	FGM	FGA	Pct.	FTM	FTA	Pct.	Off.	Def.	Tot.	Ast.	St.	Blk.	TO	Pts.	RPG	APG	PPG
										REBOUNDS							AVERAGES		
90-91—Atlanta	25	162	21	70	.300	13	26	.500	16	24	40	11	5	1	17	55	1.6	0.4	2.2
93-94—Lakers-Sac.....	57	1221	187	388	.482	92	166	.554	120	153	273	72	38	11	93	466	4.8	1.3	8.2
94-95—Sacramento	15	147	18	40	.450	11	14	.786	10	16	26	12	4	2	6	47	1.7	0.8	3.1
95-96—Philadelphia	6	79	10	20	.500	3	4	.750	7	7	14	4	3	0	1	23	2.3	0.7	3.8
Totals	103	1609	236	518	.456	119	210	.567	153	200	353	99	50	14	117	591	3.4	1.0	5.7

Three-point field goals: 1990-91, 0-for-2. 1993-94, 0-for-2. Totals, 0-for-4.
Personal fouls/disqualifications: 1990-91, 13/0. 1993-94, 123/0. 1994-95, 12/0. 1995-96, 9/0. Totals, 157/0.

SPANISH LEAGUE RECORD

Season Team	G	Min.	FGM	FGA	Pct.	FTM	FTA	Pct.	Reb.	Ast.	Pts.	RPG	APG	PPG
													AVERAGES	
91-92—C.B. OAR	...	...	...	...	...	...	...	...	...	...	...	...	...	19.0
92-93—Pescanova....................	31	1085	260	540	.481	127	193	.658	231	80	658	7.5	2.6	21.2
Totals	...	...	...	...	...	...	...	...	...	...	...	...	...	...

WINGATE, DAVID   G/F   SUPERSONICS

PERSONAL: Born December 15, 1963, in Baltimore. ... 6-5/185. ... Full name: David Grover Stacey Wingate Jr.
HIGH SCHOOL: Dunbar (Baltimore).
COLLEGE: Georgetown.
TRANSACTIONS/CAREER NOTES: Selected by Philadelphia 76ers in second round (44th pick overall) of 1986 NBA Draft. ... Traded by 76ers with G Maurice Cheeks and C Christian Welp to San Antonio Spurs for G Johnny Dawkins and F Jay Vincent (August 28, 1989). ... Waived by Spurs (June 28, 1991). ... Signed as free agent by Washington Bullets (September 30, 1991). ... Signed as free agent by Charlotte Hornets (November 18, 1992). ... Traded by Hornets with G Hersey Hawkins to Seattle SuperSonics for G Kendall Gill (June 27, 1995).

COLLEGIATE RECORD

NOTES: Member of NCAA Division I championship team (1984).

Season Team	G	Min.	FGM	FGA	Pct.	FTM	FTA	Pct.	Reb.	Ast.	Pts.	RPG	APG	PPG
													AVERAGES	
82-83—Georgetown..................	32	855	149	335	.445	87	124	.702	95	69	385	3.0	2.2	12.0
83-84—Georgetown..................	37	1005	161	370	.435	93	129	.721	135	99	415	3.6	2.7	11.2
84-85—Georgetown..................	38	1128	191	395	.484	91	132	.689	135	121	473	3.6	3.2	12.4
85-86—Georgetown..................	32	956	196	394	.497	117	155	.755	129	75	509	4.0	2.3	15.9
Totals	139	3944	697	1494	.467	388	540	.719	494	364	1782	3.6	2.6	12.8

W

NBA REGULAR-SEASON RECORD

Season Team	G	Min.	FGM	FGA	Pct.	FTM	FTA	Pct.	Off.	Def.	Tot.	Ast.	St.	Blk.	TO	Pts.	RPG	APG	PPG
86-87—Philadelphia	77	1612	259	602	.430	149	201	.741	70	86	156	155	93	19	128	680	2.0	2.0	8.8
87-88—Philadelphia	61	1419	218	545	.400	99	132	.750	44	57	101	119	47	22	104	545	1.7	2.0	8.9
88-89—Philadelphia	33	372	54	115	.470	27	34	.794	12	25	37	73	9	2	35	137	1.1	2.2	4.2
89-90—San Antonio	78	1856	220	491	.448	87	112	.777	62	133	195	208	89	18	127	527	2.5	2.7	6.8
90-91—San Antonio	25	563	53	138	.384	29	41	.707	24	51	75	46	19	5	42	136	3.0	1.8	5.4
91-92—Washington	81	2127	266	572	.465	105	146	.719	80	189	269	247	123	21	124	638	3.3	3.0	7.9
92-93—Charlotte........	72	1471	180	336	.536	79	107	.738	49	125	174	183	66	9	89	440	2.4	2.5	6.1
93-94—Charlotte........	50	1005	136	283	.481	34	51	.667	30	104	134	104	42	6	53	310	2.7	2.1	6.2
94-95—Charlotte........	52	515	50	122	.410	18	24	.750	11	49	60	56	19	6	27	122	1.2	1.1	2.3
95-96—Seattle	60	695	88	212	.415	32	41	.780	17	39	56	58	20	4	42	223	0.9	1.0	3.7
Totals	589	11635	1524	3416	.446	659	889	.741	399	858	1257	1249	527	112	771	3758	2.1	2.1	6.4

Three-point field goals: 1986-87, 13-for-52 (.250). 1987-88, 10-for-40 (.250). 1988-89, 2-for-6 (.333). 1989-90, 0-for-13. 1990-91, 1-for-9 (.111). 1991-92, 1-for-18 (.056). 1992-93, 1-for-6 (.167). 1993-94, 4-for-12 (.333). 1994-95, 4-for-22 (.182). 1995-96, 15-for-34 (.441). Totals, 51-for-212 (.241).
Personal fouls/disqualifications: 1986-87, 169/1. 1987-88, 125/0. 1988-89, 43/0. 1989-90, 154/2. 1990-91, 66/0. 1991-92, 162/1. 1992-93, 135/1. 1993-94, 85/0. 1994-95, 60/0. 1995-96, 66/0. Totals, 1065/5.

NBA PLAYOFF RECORD

Season Team	G	Min.	FGM	FGA	Pct.	FTM	FTA	Pct.	Off.	Def.	Tot.	Ast.	St.	Blk.	TO	Pts.	RPG	APG	PPG
86-87—Philadelphia	5	90	15	37	.405	9	14	.643	5	7	12	9	5	1	9	41	2.4	1.8	8.2
89-90—San Antonio	10	293	40	77	.519	9	12	.750	9	28	37	38	18	3	14	91	3.7	3.8	9.1
90-91—San Antonio	3	38	6	12	.500	2	3	.667	1	2	3	1	1	0	1	14	1.0	0.3	4.7
92-93—Charlotte........	9	117	8	22	.364	3	8	.375	4	8	12	15	4	1	1	19	1.3	1.7	2.1
94-95—Charlotte........	4	73	13	27	.481	4	6	.667	3	3	6	15	4	0	4	32	1.5	3.8	8.0
95-96—Seattle	13	68	7	16	.438	4	4	1.000	1	2	3	0	0	0	4	19	0.2	0.0	1.5
Totals	44	679	89	191	.466	31	47	.660	23	50	73	78	32	5	33	216	1.7	1.8	4.9

Three-point field goals: 1986-87, 2-for-2. 1989-90, 2-for-3 (.667). 1994-95, 2-for-6 (.333). 1995-96, 1-for-2 (.500). Totals, 7-for-13 (.538).
Personal fouls/disqualifications: 1986-87, 11/1. 1989-90, 34/1. 1990-91, 8/1. 1992-93, 9/0. 1994-95, 14/0. 1995-96, 16/0. Totals, 92/3.

WINGFIELD, DONTONIO   F   TRAIL BLAZERS

PERSONAL: Born June 23, 1974, in Albany, Ga. ... 6-8/256.
HIGH SCHOOL: Westover (Albany, Ga.).
COLLEGE: Cincinnati.
TRANSACTIONS/CAREER NOTES: Selected after freshman season by Seattle SuperSonics in second round (37th pick overall) of 1994 NBA Draft. ... Selected by Toronto Raptors from SuperSonics in NBA expansion draft (June 24, 1995). ... Signed as free agent by Portland Trail Blazers (October 5, 1995).

COLLEGIATE RECORD

Season Team	G	Min.	FGM	FGA	Pct.	FTM	FTA	Pct.	Reb.	Ast.	Pts.	RPG	APG	PPG
93-94—Cincinnati	29	834	162	384	.422	97	145	.669	260	58	465	9.0	2.0	16.0

Three-point field goals: 1993-94, 44-for-109 (.404).

NBA REGULAR-SEASON RECORD

Season Team	G	Min.	FGM	FGA	Pct.	FTM	FTA	Pct.	Off.	Def.	Tot.	Ast.	St.	Blk.	TO	Pts.	RPG	APG	PPG
94-95—Seattle	20	81	18	51	.353	8	10	.800	11	19	30	3	5	3	8	46	1.5	0.2	2.3
95-96—Portland..........	44	487	60	157	.382	26	34	.765	45	59	104	28	20	6	31	165	2.4	0.6	3.8
Totals	64	568	78	208	.375	34	44	.773	56	78	134	31	25	9	39	211	2.1	0.5	3.3

Three-point field goals: 1994-95, 2-for-12 (.167). 1995-96, 19-for-63 (.302). Totals, 21-for-75 (.280).
Personal fouls/disqualifications: 1994-95, 15/0. 1995-96, 73/1. Totals, 88/1.

NBA PLAYOFF RECORD

Season Team	G	Min.	FGM	FGA	Pct.	FTM	FTA	Pct.	Off.	Def.	Tot.	Ast.	St.	Blk.	TO	Pts.	RPG	APG	PPG
95-96—Portland..........	5	62	8	21	.381	2	6	.333	10	4	14	4	0	0	3	24	2.8	0.8	4.8

Three-point field goals: 1995-96, 6-for-10 (.600).
Personal fouls/disqualifications: 1995-96, 10/0.

WOLF, JOE   F/C   BUCKS

PERSONAL: Born December 17, 1964, in Kohler, Wis. ... 6-11/253. ... Full name: Joseph James Wolf.
HIGH SCHOOL: Kohler (Wis.).
COLLEGE: North Carolina.
TRANSACTIONS/CAREER NOTES: Selected by Los Angeles Clippers in first round (13th pick overall) of 1987 NBA Draft. ... Signed as unrestricted free agent by Denver Nuggets (October 5, 1990). ... Rights renounced by Nuggets (September 29, 1992). ... Signed as free agent by Boston Celtics (October 2, 1992). ... Waived by Celtics (November 19, 1992). ... Signed by Portland Trail Blazers (December 5, 1992). ... Played in Spain (1993-94). ... Signed as free agent by Indiana Pacers (October 1994). ... Waived by Pacers (October 31, 1994). ... Signed as free agent by Charlotte Hornets (November 3, 1994). ... Waived by Hornets (November 6, 1995). ... Signed as free agent by Orlando Magic (November 16, 1995). ... Signed as free agent by Milwaukee Bucks (September 3, 1996).

COLLEGIATE RECORD

Season Team	G	Min.	FGM	FGA	Pct.	FTM	FTA	Pct.	Reb.	Ast.	Pts.	RPG	APG	PPG
83-84—North Carolina...............	30	412	38	79	.481	25	33	.758	85	14	101	2.8	0.5	3.4
84-85—North Carolina...............	30	914	112	198	.566	50	64	.781	158	58	274	5.3	1.9	9.1

W

Season Team	G	Min.	FGM	FGA	Pct.	FTM	FTA	Pct.	Reb.	Ast.	Pts.	RPG	APG	PPG
85-86—North Carolina	34	854	149	280	.532	42	59	.712	224	72	340	6.6	2.1	10.0
86-87—North Carolina	34	1005	212	371	.571	69	87	.793	240	99	516	7.1	2.9	15.2
Totals	128	3185	511	928	.551	186	243	.765	707	243	1231	5.5	1.9	9.6

Three-point field goals: 1986-87, 23-for-40 (.575).

NBA REGULAR-SEASON RECORD

Season Team	G	Min.	FGM	FGA	Pct.	FTM	FTA	Pct.	Off.	Def.	Tot.	Ast.	St.	Blk.	TO	Pts.	RPG	APG	PPG
87-88—L.A. Clippers	42	1137	136	334	.407	45	54	.833	51	136	187	98	38	16	76	320	4.5	2.3	7.6
88-89—L.A. Clippers	66	1450	170	402	.423	44	64	.688	83	188	271	113	32	16	94	386	4.1	1.7	5.8
89-90—L.A. Clippers	77	1325	155	392	.395	55	71	.775	63	169	232	62	30	24	77	370	3.0	0.8	4.8
90-91—Denver	74	1593	234	519	.451	69	83	.831	136	264	400	107	60	31	95	539	5.4	1.4	7.3
91-92—Denver	67	1160	100	277	.361	53	66	.803	97	143	240	61	32	14	60	254	3.6	0.9	3.8
92-93—Bost.-Port.	23	165	20	44	.455	13	16	.813	14	34	48	5	7	1	7	53	2.1	0.2	2.3
94-95—Charlotte	63	583	38	81	.469	12	16	.750	34	95	129	37	9	6	22	90	2.0	0.6	1.4
95-96—Char.-Orl.	64	1065	135	263	.513	21	29	.724	49	138	187	63	15	5	42	291	2.9	1.0	4.5
Totals	476	8478	988	2312	.427	312	399	.782	527	1167	1694	546	223	113	473	2303	3.6	1.1	4.8

Three-point field goals: 1987-88, 3-for-15 (.200). 1988-89, 2-for-14 (.143). 1989-90, 5-for-25 (.200). 1990-91, 2-for-15 (.133). 1991-92, 1-for-11 (.091). 1992-93, 0-for-1. 1994-95, 2-for-6 (.333). 1995-96, 0-for-6. Totals, 15-for-93 (.161).

Personal fouls/disqualifications: 1987-88, 139/8. 1988-89, 152/1. 1989-90, 129/0. 1990-91, 244/8. 1991-92, 124/1. 1992-93, 24/0. 1994-95, 101/0. 1995-96, 163/4. Totals, 1076/22.

NBA PLAYOFF RECORD

Season Team	G	Min.	FGM	FGA	Pct.	FTM	FTA	Pct.	Off.	Def.	Tot.	Ast.	St.	Blk.	TO	Pts.	RPG	APG	PPG
92-93—Portland	2	20	1	2	.500	0	0	...	2	2	4	0	0	1	0	2	2.0	0.0	1.0
94-95—Charlotte	1	3	0	0	...	0	0	...	0	0	0	0	0	0	0	0	0.0	0.0	0.0
95-96—Orlando	11	85	8	23	.348	3	4	.750	1	5	6	2	1	0	4	20	0.5	0.2	1.8
Totals	14	108	9	25	.360	3	4	.750	3	7	10	2	1	1	4	22	0.7	0.1	1.6

Three-point field goals: 1995-96, 1-for-3 (.333).
Personal fouls/disqualifications: 1992-93, 1/0. 1995-96, 19/0. Totals, 20/0.

SPANISH LEAGUE RECORD

Season Team	G	Min.	FGM	FGA	Pct.	FTM	FTA	Pct.	Reb.	Ast.	Pts.	RPG	APG	PPG
93-94—Elmar Leon	28	...	...	...	...	...	...	...	235	48	285	8.4	1.7	10.2

W

WOOD, DAVID · F

PERSONAL: Born November 30, 1964, in Spokane, Wash. ... 6-9/230. ... Full name: David Leroy Wood.
HIGH SCHOOL: Hudson's Bay (Vancouver, Wash.).
JUNIOR COLLEGE: Skagit Valley College (Wash.).
COLLEGE: Nevada.
TRANSACTIONS/CAREER NOTES: Not drafted by an NBA franchise. ... Played in Continental Basketball Association with Rockford Lightning (1987-88 and 1988-89). ... Signed as free agent by Chicago Bulls (September 27, 1988). ... Waived by Bulls (November 17, 1988). ... Played in Italy (1988-89). ... Played in Spain (1989-90 and 1991-92). ... Signed as free agent by Houston Rockets (August 6, 1990). ... Rights renounced by Rockets (October 11, 1991). ... Re-signed as free agent by Rockets (September 25, 1992). ... Traded by Rockets to San Antonio Spurs for 1995 second-round draft choice (October 5, 1992). ... Traded by Spurs with F Sean Elliott to Detroit Pistons for F Dennis Rodman (October 1, 1993). ... Traded by Pistons with C Olden Polynice to Sacramento Kings for C Duane Causwell and 1994, 1995 and 1996 second-round draft choices (February 16, 1994); trade voided when Causwell failed physical (February 19, 1994). ... Signed as free agent by Golden State Warriors (October 6, 1994). ... Waived by Warriors (January 15, 1996). ... Signed by Phoenix Suns to 10-day contract (January 18, 1996). ... Signed by Dallas Mavericks to first of two consecutive 10-day contracts (February 1, 1996). ... Re-signed by Mavericks for remainder of season (February 23, 1996).

COLLEGIATE RECORD

Season Team	G	Min.	FGM	FGA	Pct.	FTM	FTA	Pct.	Reb.	Ast.	Pts.	RPG	APG	PPG
83-84—Skagit Valley College	29	...	112	205	.546	57	81	.704	211	...	281	7.3	...	9.7
84-85—Skagit Valley College	26	...	184	302	.609	105	146	.719	301	29	473	11.6	1.1	18.2
85-86—Nevada-Reno	28	805	97	190	.511	43	65	.662	168	41	251	6.0	1.5	9.0
86-87—Nevada-Reno	30	950	127	269	.472	77	106	.726	281	35	364	9.4	1.2	12.1
Junior college totals	55	...	296	507	.584	162	227	.714	512	...	754	9.3	...	13.7
4-year-college totals	58	1755	224	459	.488	120	171	.702	449	76	615	7.7	1.3	10.6

Three-point field goals: 1985-86, 14-for-29 (.483). 1986-87, 33-for-84 (.393). Totals, 47-for-113 (.416).

CBA REGULAR-SEASON RECORD

Season Team	G	Min.	FGM	FGA	Pct.	FTM	FTA	Pct.	Reb.	Ast.	Pts.	RPG	APG	PPG
87-88—Rockford	42	722	85	164	.518	35	43	.814	152	35	215	3.6	0.8	5.1
88-89—Rockford	52	1216	181	361	.501	105	142	.739	315	59	491	6.1	1.1	9.4
Totals	94	1938	266	525	.507	140	185	.757	467	94	706	5.0	1.0	7.5

Three-point field goals: 1987-88, 10-for-21 (.476). 1988-89, 24-for-57 (.421). Totals, 34-for-78 (.436).

ITALIAN LEAGUE RECORD

Season Team	G	Min.	FGM	FGA	Pct.	FTM	FTA	Pct.	Reb.	Ast.	Pts.	RPG	APG	PPG
88-89—Enichem Livorno	16	345	60	125	.480	35	44	.795	89	0	168	5.6	0.0	10.5

NBA REGULAR-SEASON RECORD

Season Team	G	Min.	FGM	FGA	Pct.	FTM	FTA	Pct.	REBOUNDS Off.	Def.	Tot.	Ast.	St.	Blk.	TO	Pts.	AVERAGES RPG	APG	PPG
88-89—Chicago	2	2	0	0	...	0	0	...	0	0	0	0	0	0	0	0	0.0	0.0	0.0
90-91—Houston	82	1421	148	349	.424	108	133	.812	107	139	246	94	58	16	89	432	3.0	1.1	5.3
92-93—San Antonio	64	598	52	117	.444	46	55	.836	38	59	97	34	13	12	29	155	1.5	0.5	2.4
93-94—Detroit	78	1182	119	259	.459	62	82	.756	104	135	239	51	39	19	35	322	3.1	0.7	4.1
94-95—Golden State	78	1336	153	326	.469	91	117	.778	83	158	241	65	28	13	53	428	3.1	0.8	5.5
95-96—GS-Phoe.-Dal.	62	772	75	174	.431	38	50	.760	51	103	154	34	19	10	24	208	2.5	0.5	3.4
Totals	366	5311	547	1225	.447	345	437	.789	383	594	977	278	157	70	230	1545	2.7	0.8	4.2

Three-point field goals: 1990-91, 28-for-90 (.311). 1992-93, 5-for-21 (.238). 1993-94, 22-for-49 (.449). 1994-95, 31-for-91 (.341). 1995-96, 20-for-62 (.323). Totals, 106-for-313 (.339).

Personal fouls/disqualifications: 1990-91, 236/4. 1992-93, 93/1. 1993-94, 201/3. 1994-95, 217/4. 1995-96, 150/5. Totals, 897/17.

NBA PLAYOFF RECORD

Season Team	G	Min.	FGM	FGA	Pct.	FTM	FTA	Pct.	REBOUNDS Off.	Def.	Tot.	Ast.	St.	Blk.	TO	Pts.	AVERAGES RPG	APG	PPG
90-91—Houston	3	44	2	3	.667	2	4	.500	1	4	5	3	3	0	1	7	1.7	1.0	2.3
92-93—San Antonio	5	20	2	4	.500	0	0	...	1	2	3	1	0	0	0	5	0.6	0.2	1.0
Totals	8	64	4	7	.571	2	4	.500	2	6	8	4	3	0	1	12	1.0	0.5	1.5

Three-point field goals: 1990-91, 1-for-1. 1992-93, 1-for-1. Totals, 2-for-2.

Personal fouls/disqualifications: 1990-91, 8/0. 1992-93, 7/0. Totals, 15/0.

SPANISH LEAGUE RECORD

Season Team	G	Min.	FGM	FGA	Pct.	FTM	FTA	Pct.	Reb.	Ast.	Pts.	AVERAGES RPG	APG	PPG
89-90—Barcelona	24	655	120	232	.517	61	77	.792	210	21	318	8.8	0.9	13.3
91-92—Bask. Taugres	14	389	82	154	.532	27	34	.794	73	16	205	5.2	1.1	14.6
Totals	38	1044	202	386	.523	88	111	.793	283	37	523	7.4	1.0	13.8

WOODS, RANDY   G

PERSONAL: Born September 23, 1970, in Philadelphia. ... 6-0/185. ... Full name: Randolph Woods.
HIGH SCHOOL: Ben Franklin (Philadelphia).
COLLEGE: La Salle.
TRANSACTIONS/CAREER NOTES: Selected by Los Angeles Clippers in first round (16th pick overall) of 1992 NBA Draft. ... Traded by Clippers with draft rights to F Antonio McDyess to Denver Nuggets for F Rodney Rogers and draft rights to G Brent Barry (June 28, 1995). ... Waived by Nuggets (December 21, 1995).

COLLEGIATE RECORD

Season Team	G	Min.	FGM	FGA	Pct.	FTM	FTA	Pct.	Reb.	Ast.	Pts.	AVERAGES RPG	APG	PPG
88-89—La Salle					Did not play—ineligible.									
89-90—La Salle	32	1138	146	371	.394	56	76	.737	101	111	425	3.2	3.5	13.3
90-91—La Salle	25	875	177	415	.427	105	132	.795	123	69	539	4.9	2.8	21.6
91-92—La Salle	31	1183	272	653	.417	182	224	.813	194	160	847	6.3	5.2	27.3
Totals	88	3196	595	1439	.413	343	432	.794	418	340	1811	4.8	3.9	20.6

Three-point field goals: 1989-90, 77-for-221 (.348). 1990-91, 80-for-227 (.352). 1991-92, 121-for-341 (.355). Totals, 278-for-789 (.352).

NBA REGULAR-SEASON RECORD

Season Team	G	Min.	FGM	FGA	Pct.	FTM	FTA	Pct.	REBOUNDS Off.	Def.	Tot.	Ast.	St.	Blk.	TO	Pts.	AVERAGES RPG	APG	PPG
92-93—L.A. Clippers	41	174	23	66	.348	19	26	.731	6	8	14	40	14	1	16	68	0.3	1.0	1.7
93-94—L.A. Clippers	40	352	49	133	.368	20	35	.571	13	16	29	71	24	2	34	145	0.7	1.8	3.6
94-95—L.A. Clippers	62	495	37	117	.316	28	38	.737	10	34	44	134	41	0	55	124	0.7	2.2	2.0
95-96—Denver	8	72	6	22	.273	2	2	1.000	3	3	6	12	6	1	5	19	0.8	1.5	2.4
Totals	151	1093	115	338	.340	69	101	.683	32	61	93	257	85	4	110	356	0.6	1.7	2.4

Three-point field goals: 1992-93, 3-for-14 (.214). 1993-94, 27-for-78 (.346). 1994-95, 22-for-74 (.297). 1995-96, 5-for-21 (.238). Totals, 57-for-187 (.305).

Personal fouls/disqualifications: 1992-93, 26/0. 1993-94, 40/0. 1994-95, 87/0. 1995-96, 13/0. Totals, 166/0.

WORKMAN, HAYWOODE   G   PACERS

PERSONAL: Born January 23, 1966, in Charlotte. ... 6-3/180. ... Full name: Haywoode Wilvon Workman.
HIGH SCHOOL: Myers Park (Charlotte).
COLLEGE: Winston-Salem (N.C.) State, then Oral Roberts.
TRANSACTIONS/CAREER NOTES: Selected by Atlanta Hawks in second round (49th pick overall) of 1989 NBA Draft. ... Waived by Hawks (November 2, 1989). ... Played in Continental Basketball Association with Topeka Sizzlers (1989-90). ... Signed by Hawks to first of two consecutive 10-day contracts (January 26, 1990). ... Played in World Basketball League with Illinois Express (1990). ... Signed as free agent by Washington Bullets (September 25, 1990). ... Played in Italy (1991-92 and 1992-93). ... Signed as free agent by Indiana Pacers (August 31, 1993).

COLLEGIATE RECORD

Season Team	G	Min.	FGM	FGA	Pct.	FTM	FTA	Pct.	Reb.	Ast.	Pts.	AVERAGES RPG	APG	PPG
84-85—Winst.-Salem St.	25	...	102	223	.457	53	90	.589	75	53	257	3.0	2.1	10.3
85-86—Oral Roberts					Did not play—transfer student.									

Season Team	G	Min.	FGM	FGA	Pct.	FTM	FTA	Pct.	Reb.	Ast.	Pts.	AVERAGES RPG	APG	PPG
86-87—Oral Roberts	28	1086	125	342	.366	121	152	.796	93	188	387	3.3	6.7	13.8
87-88—Oral Roberts	29	988	206	496	.415	108	143	.755	174	78	562	6.0	2.7	19.4
88-89—Oral Roberts	28	980	205	424	.484	110	135	.815	171	110	557	6.1	3.9	19.9
Totals	110	...	638	1485	.430	392	520	.754	513	429	1763	4.7	3.9	16.0

Three-point field goals: 1986-87, 16-for-56 (.286). 1987-88, 42-for-149 (.282). 1988-89, 37-for-101 (.366). Totals, 95-for-306 (.310).

CBA REGULAR-SEASON RECORD

Season Team	G	Min.	FGM	FGA	Pct.	FTM	FTA	Pct.	Reb.	Ast.	Pts.	AVERAGES RPG	APG	PPG
89-90—Topeka	46	1513	283	650	.435	179	218	.821	200	213	785	4.3	4.6	17.1

Three-point field goals: 1989-90, 40-for-154 (.260).

NBA REGULAR-SEASON RECORD

Season Team	G	Min.	FGM	FGA	Pct.	FTM	FTA	Pct.	REBOUNDS Off.	Def.	Tot.	Ast.	St.	Blk.	TO	Pts.	AVERAGES RPG	APG	PPG
89-90—Atlanta	6	16	2	3	.667	2	2	1.000	0	3	3	2	3	0	0	6	0.5	0.3	1.0
90-91—Washington	73	2034	234	515	.454	101	133	.759	51	191	242	353	87	7	135	581	3.3	4.8	8.0
93-94—Indiana	65	1714	195	460	.424	93	116	.802	32	172	204	404	85	4	151	501	3.1	6.2	7.7
94-95—Indiana	69	1028	101	269	.375	55	74	.743	21	90	111	194	59	5	73	292	1.6	2.8	4.2
95-96—Indiana	77	1164	101	259	.390	54	73	.740	27	97	124	213	65	4	93	279	1.6	2.8	3.6
Totals	290	5956	633	1506	.420	305	398	.766	131	553	684	1166	299	20	452	1659	2.4	4.0	5.7

Three-point field goals: 1990-91, 12-for-50 (.240). 1993-94, 18-for-56 (.321). 1994-95, 35-for-98 (.357). 1995-96, 23-for-71 (.324). Totals, 88-for-275 (.320).

Personal fouls/disqualifications: 1989-90, 3/0. 1990-91, 162/1. 1993-94, 152/0. 1994-95, 115/0. 1995-96, 152/0. Totals, 584/1.

NBA PLAYOFF RECORD

Season Team	G	Min.	FGM	FGA	Pct.	FTM	FTA	Pct.	REBOUNDS Off.	Def.	Tot.	Ast.	St.	Blk.	TO	Pts.	AVERAGES RPG	APG	PPG
93-94—Indiana	16	511	45	131	.344	32	38	.842	11	40	51	112	28	1	38	128	3.2	7.0	8.0
94-95—Indiana	17	275	24	67	.358	27	32	.844	5	23	28	46	11	0	16	77	1.6	2.7	4.5
95-96—Indiana	5	53	7	16	.438	2	2	1.000	1	2	3	2	2	0	2	19	0.6	0.4	3.8
Totals	38	839	76	214	.355	61	72	.847	17	65	82	160	41	1	56	224	2.2	4.2	5.9

Three-point field goals: 1993-94, 6-for-21 (.286). 1994-95, 2-for-18 (.111). 1995-96, 3-for-5 (.600). Totals, 11-for-44 (.250).

Personal fouls/disqualifications: 1993-94, 40/0. 1994-95, 45/0. 1995-96, 5/0. Totals, 90/0.

ITALIAN LEAGUE RECORD

Season Team	G	Min.	FGM	FGA	Pct.	FTM	FTA	Pct.	Reb.	Ast.	Pts.	AVERAGES RPG	APG	PPG
91-92—Scavolini Pesaro	29	970	170	354	.480	85	108	.787	130	62	470	4.5	2.1	16.2
92-93—Scavolini Pesaro	29	970	133	281	.473	111	128	.867	135	41	399	4.7	1.4	13.8
Totals	58	1940	303	635	.477	196	236	.831	265	103	869	4.6	1.8	15.0

WRIGHT, SHARONE   C/F   RAPTORS

PERSONAL: Born January 30, 1973, in Macon, Ga. ... 6-11/260. ... Full name: Sharone Addaryl Wright. ... Name pronounced sha-RON.

HIGH SCHOOL: Southwest (Macon, Ga.).

COLLEGE: Clemson.

TRANSACTIONS/CAREER NOTES: Selected after junior season by Philadelphia 76ers in first round (sixth pick overall) of 1994 NBA Draft. ... Traded by 76ers to Toronto Raptors for F Ed Pinckney, F Tony Massenburg and right to swap 1996 or 1997 first-round draft choices (February 22, 1996).

COLLEGIATE RECORD

Season Team	G	Min.	FGM	FGA	Pct.	FTM	FTA	Pct.	Reb.	Ast.	Pts.	AVERAGES RPG	APG	PPG
91-92—Clemson	28	747	137	275	.498	63	112	.563	227	11	337	8.1	0.4	12.0
92-93—Clemson	30	913	178	314	.567	93	139	.669	314	26	449	10.5	0.9	15.0
93-94—Clemson	34	1027	186	354	.525	150	233	.644	362	41	522	10.6	1.2	15.4
Totals	92	2687	501	943	.531	306	484	.632	903	78	1308	9.8	0.8	14.2

Three-point field goals: 1991-92, 0-for-2. 1992-93, 0-for-2. 1993-94, 0-for-2. Totals, 0-for-6.

NBA REGULAR-SEASON RECORD

HONORS: NBA All-Rookie second team (1995).

Season Team	G	Min.	FGM	FGA	Pct.	FTM	FTA	Pct.	REBOUNDS Off.	Def.	Tot.	Ast.	St.	Blk.	TO	Pts.	AVERAGES RPG	APG	PPG
94-95—Philadelphia	79	2044	361	776	.465	182	282	.645	191	281	472	48	37	104	151	904	6.0	0.6	11.4
95-96—Phil.-Tor.	57	1434	248	512	.484	167	259	.645	148	208	356	38	30	49	109	664	6.2	0.7	11.6
Totals	136	3478	609	1288	.473	349	541	.645	339	489	828	86	67	153	260	1568	6.1	0.6	11.5

Three-point field goals: 1994-95, 0-for-8. 1995-96, 1-for-3 (.333). Totals, 1-for-11 (.091).

Personal fouls/disqualifications: 1994-95, 246/5. 1995-96, 163/4. Totals, 409/9.

DID YOU KNOW...

...that the Toronto Raptors set an NBA record on January 9
when they failed to make a free throw (0-for-3) in a 92-91 loss to Charlotte?

ZIDEK, GEORGE   C   HORNETS

PERSONAL: Born August 2, 1973, in Zlin, Czechoslovakia. ... 7-0/266. ... Full name: Jiri Zidek. ... Name pronounced ZEE-dik.
HIGH SCHOOL: Arabska (Czechoslovakia) Secondary School.
COLLEGE: UCLA.
TRANSACTIONS/CAREER NOTES: Selected by Charlotte Hornets in first round (22nd pick overall) of 1995 NBA Draft.

COLLEGIATE RECORD

NOTES: Member of NCAA Division I championship team (1995).

												AVERAGES		
Season Team	G	Min.	FGM	FGA	Pct.	FTM	FTA	Pct.	Reb.	Ast.	Pts.	RPG	APG	PPG
91-92—UCLA	17	66	8	21	.381	2	4	.500	19	2	18	1.1	0.1	1.1
92-93—UCLA	26	233	22	52	.423	19	25	.760	43	8	63	1.7	0.3	2.4
93-94—UCLA	28	688	120	232	.517	71	93	.763	197	15	311	7.0	0.5	11.1
94-95—UCLA	33	771	140	253	.553	68	93	.731	178	15	350	5.4	0.5	10.6
Totals	104	1758	290	558	.520	160	215	.744	437	40	742	4.2	0.4	7.1

Three-point field goals: 1991-92, 0-for-1. 1993-94, 0-for-2. 1994-95, 2-for-5 (.400). Totals, 2-for-8 (.250).

NBA REGULAR-SEASON RECORD

								REBOUNDS								AVERAGES		
Season Team	G	Min.	FGM	FGA	Pct.	FTM	FTA	Pct.	Off.	Def.	Tot.	Ast.	St.	Blk.	TO	Pts.	RPG	APG	PPG
95-96—Charlotte	71	888	105	248	.423	71	93	.763	69	114	183	16	9	7	38	281	2.6	0.2	4.0

Personal fouls/disqualifications: 1995-96, 170/2.

Z

INDIVIDUAL CAREER HIGHS

REGULAR SEASON

Player	FGM	FGA	FTM	FTA	Reb.	Ast.	Stl.	Blk. Sh.	Pts.
Abdul-Rauf, Mahmoud	17	32	10	13	9	20	5	2	51
Adams, Michael	17	34	17	19	11	19	9	2	54
Addison, Rafael	10	20	7	8	11	8	4	3	25
Alexander, Cory	5	8	4	4	4	9	3	1	14
Alexander, Victor	12	18	8	10	17	5	4	3	29
Allen, Jerome	2	8	4	6	3	4	3	1	9
Alston, Derrick	13	17	4	7	12	3	4	3	30
Amaechi, John	5	9	4	6	6	1	2	2	11
Amaya, Ashraf	8	16	7	9	16	4	2	1	18
Anderson, Greg	13	19	11	16	22	6	5	6	31
Anderson, Kenny	17	33	20	23	13	18	6	2	45
Anderson, Nick	17	31	14	15	15	12	8	4	50
Anderson, Willie	18	26	12	14	12	12	6	4	36
Anthony, Greg	11	20	14	16	10	15	6	2	32
Armstrong, B.J.	12	24	13	15	7	14	4	2	35
Armstrong, Darrell	3	8	2	2	1	2	2	0	8
Askew, Vincent	8	16	13	16	9	9	4	2	21
Askins, Keith	8	15	6	6	16	7	4	5	21
Augmon, Stacey	14	23	13	16	12	7	7	4	36
Avent, Anthony	12	18	8	12	17	7	4	5	28
Baker, Vin	16	31	12	16	21	12	4	6	41
Bardo, Stephen	3	7	4	4	6	5	2	2	8
Barkley, Charles	18	30	22	27	26	14	7	7	47
Barros, Dana	21	26	11	12	13	19	6	1	50
Barry, Brent	9	18	9	11	6	11	6	2	30
Barry, Jon	8	17	11	13	8	10	5	2	23
Beck, Corey	2	4	1	2	3	2	1	0	5
Benjamin, Benoit	15	23	12	15	23	9	4	10	34
Bennett, Elmer	3	7	3	4	1	4	2	1	6
Bennett, Mario	5	10	4	6	8	1	2	3	12
Benoit, David	10	17	13	18	17	5	3	5	24
Best, Travis	6	8	6	7	6	7	3	1	13
Blaylock, Mookie	12	25	8	11	13	23	8	3	35
Blount, Corie	7	13	6	6	15	6	4	3	17
Bogues, Muggsy	11	20	9	9	10	19	7	2	24
Bonner, Anthony	10	19	7	11	17	8	6	4	23
Booker, Melvin	3	10	4	5	2	4	2	1	9
Bowie, Anthony	13	22	8	8	10	10	4	3	31
Boyce, Donnie	3	6	1	2	3	1	1	1	8
Bradley, Shawn	13	23	9	11	22	7	4	12	32
Bragg, Marques	5	11	3	4	7	1	2	2	13
Brandon, Terrell	12	24	14	14	10	15	6	5	32
Breaux, Tim	7	12	6	8	11	4	2	1	17
Brickowski, Frank	14	28	15	20	17	10	6	4	34
Brooks, Scott	9	15	9	10	6	13	5	2	23
Brown, Chucky	12	17	10	10	14	5	4	3	30
Brown, P.J.	13	18	8	10	17	8	5	5	30
Brown, Dee	15	26	14	15	10	18	7	4	41
Brown, Mike	8	16	10	12	16	6	3	4	24
Brown, Randy	10	15	6	8	10	8	7	4	27
Bryant, Mark	12	19	8	13	15	4	3	4	30
Buechler, Jud	8	16	5	9	9	4	4	3	19
Bullard, Matt	11	15	5	5	9	6	3	2	28
Burrell, Scott	10	19	7	9	11	7	5	2	26
Burrough, Junior	6	12	4	6	6	2	2	2	13
Butler, Mitchell	10	17	10	12	12	6	4	3	26
Caffey, Jason	5	11	6	10	8	2	2	1	13
Cage, Michael	12	19	15	19	30	6	7	6	29
Caldwell, Adrian	4	8	3	4	12	2	3	3	11
Campbell, Elden	12	26	9	14	18	9	4	9	32
Carr, Antoine	18	29	14	18	14	8	4	7	41
Carr, Chris	6	11	5	5	7	5	1	1	15
Cassell, Sam	11	23	11	12	9	16	5	2	33
Causwell, Duane	10	17	8	12	16	5	5	9	22
Ceballos, Cedric	21	31	16	19	17	7	6	3	50
Chapman, Rex	17	32	13	13	11	11	5	3	39
Cheaney, Calbert	14	26	9	11	11	9	5	2	32
Chilcutt, Pete	9	16	5	7	15	6	5	3	25
Childress, Randolph	5	8	5	6	3	5	1	1	18
Childs, Chris	10	23	13	14	11	17	5	1	30
Christie, Doug	11	21	10	14	13	8	5	3	33
Churchwell, Robert	3	7	0	0	3	1	0	0	6
Claxton, Charles	1	1	0	2	1	0	0	1	2
Coker, John	2	2	0	0	1	1	0	1	4

Player	FGM	FGA	FTM	FTA	Reb.	Ast.	Stl.	Blk. Sh.	Pts.
Coleman, Derrick	15	28	18	20	24	11	6	9	42
Coles, Bimbo	10	20	12	13	9	15	7	2	26
Conlon, Marty	10	16	8	13	13	8	3	3	22
Cook, Anthony	7	15	7	10	18	2	4	5	14
Corbin, Tyrone	15	27	9	11	19	10	8	5	36
Courtney, Joe	4	10	5	6	9	2	2	2	13
Crotty, John	7	12	9	10	6	11	4	1	19
Cummings, Terry	19	32	14	20	24	10	6	5	52
Curley, Bill	6	11	4	4	10	3	2	3	15
Curry, Michael	5	11	6	8	6	3	2	1	17
Curry, Dell	14	26	9	12	11	10	7	3	33
Cvetkovic, Rastko	1	3	0	2	2	1	1	1	2
Danilovic, Sasha	9	15	10	14	4	4	2	2	30
Dare, Yinka	4	9	6	8	9	0	1	4	12
Davis, Antonio	9	14	10	16	16	4	4	6	26
Davis, Dale	11	15	11	18	22	6	5	7	28
Davis, Hubert	12	19	9	9	7	8	3	2	32
Davis, Mark	4	9	7	8	9	4	4	2	12
Davis, Terry	13	21	9	15	21	4	3	3	35
Day, Todd	13	25	14	18	11	6	7	4	41
DeClercq, Andrew	4	12	3	3	8	2	2	1	10
Dehere, Terry	10	18	12	14	6	12	5	2	31
Del Negro, Vinny	13	20	12	15	10	13	5	2	31
Demps, Dell	6	8	8	9	3	4	2	1	15
Divac, Vlade	15	26	12	15	24	13	6	8	33
Donaldson, James	12	19	13	17	27	7	3	7	29
Douglas, Sherman	15	26	13	17	10	22	6	2	42
Drexler, Clyde	20	33	15	19	18	16	10	5	50
Duckworth, Kevin	14	27	14	16	18	5	4	7	32
Dudley, Chris	7	16	9	18	21	4	4	7	20
Dumars, Joe	19	33	18	19	10	15	5	2	45
Dumas, Richard	14	28	12	12	12	5	6	3	32
Dumas, Tony	15	23	11	16	6	7	4	2	39
Eackles, Ledell	17	33	12	14	9	9	3	3	40
Earl, Acie	13	30	14	19	12	4	3	4	40
Edney, Tyus	8	17	6	9	8	14	4	1	20
Edwards, Doug	4	7	4	6	7	4	2	2	11
Edwards, James	16	29	18	19	18	7	3	6	39
Edwards, Kevin	14	26	13	15	12	12	6	4	34
Edwards, Blue	14	23	9	11	13	11	6	4	36
Ehlo, Craig	12	25	8	11	14	12	7	4	31
Eisley, Howard	6	10	7	8	5	7	2	1	15
Elie, Mario	10	17	11	12	15	9	6	2	27
Elliott, Sean	16	26	14	16	17	12	6	4	41
Ellis, Dale	20	39	17	19	12	9	5	2	53
Ellis, LaPhonso	12	21	11	11	19	7	4	6	29
Ellis, LeRon	7	9	5	8	11	3	2	3	15
Ellison, Pervis	14	28	12	14	22	7	5	8	31
Esposito, Vincenzo	5	14	7	8	4	3	1	0	18
Ewing, Patrick	22	37	18	23	26	11	5	9	51
Ferrell, Duane	11	22	10	11	10	7	4	2	27
Ferry, Danny	12	21	9	10	16	7	4	4	32
Finley, Michael	12	19	11	12	10	10	5	3	27
Fish, Matt	5	8	4	6	9	4	3	2	10
Fleming, Vern	15	25	14	18	13	18	5	2	31
Ford, Sherell	3	7	5	7	4	1	2	1	9
Foster, Greg	8	12	7	8	11	4	2	3	17
Fox, Rick	14	23	17	18	16	10	5	4	33
Gamble, Kevin	16	25	9	12	12	10	5	3	37
Garnett, Kevin	14	21	5	8	19	7	5	7	33
Gatling, Chris	13	26	9	14	18	4	4	4	29
Gattison, Kenny	14	21	10	11	18	5	5	6	29
Geiger, Matt	13	19	11	12	21	5	4	4	28
Gill, Kendall	15	27	11	13	13	12	7	4	34
Gilliam, Armon	18	26	12	15	21	9	6	6	41
Glass, Gerald	14	27	6	7	13	7	5	2	32
Goldwire, Anthony	7	16	5	6	5	15	2	0	20
Graham, Greg	8	14	10	10	7	6	5	2	20
Grandison, Ronnie	5	9	9	10	8	5	3	1	15
Grant, Brian	14	22	14	17	16	5	4	6	32
Grant, Gary	13	23	9	10	11	21	8	3	31
Grant, Greg	7	14	5	6	7	14	6	1	15
Grant, Harvey	16	26	11	13	16	8	6	5	41
Grant, Horace	15	22	13	14	23	10	5	7	31
Green, A.C.	14	23	17	21	20	6	6	5	35
Gugliotta, Tom	17	28	14	16	20	11	8	5	39
Haley, Jack	8	16	7	11	18	3	3	3	19
Hamilton, Thomas	6	9	2	4	6	1	0	2	13
Hammink, Geert	1	3	2	4	2	1	0	0	4
Hammonds, Tom	14	24	10	10	17	5	3	3	31
Hancock, Darrin	7	12	6	8	6	4	3	1	16
Hardaway, Anfernee	17	27	15	20	13	19	7	4	42

Player	FGM	FGA	FTM	FTA	Reb.	Ast.	Stl.	Blk. Sh.	Pts.
Hardaway, Tim	17	33	15	19	11	22	8	3	43
Harper, Derek	16	29	14	16	11	18	8	4	42
Harper, Ron	19	31	16	20	16	15	10	5	40
Harris, Lucious	11	23	10	10	9	6	5	2	31
Harvey, Antonio	8	15	4	8	11	3	3	3	18
Haskin, Scott	4	6	3	4	7	2	2	4	8
Hawkins, Hersey	14	25	15	17	14	11	9	3	43
Heggs, Alvin	3	3	1	2	1	0	0	0	7
Henderson, Alan	7	11	7	9	13	4	3	4	16
Herrera, Carl	9	13	10	13	15	4	4	3	22
Higgins, Sean	13	19	8	8	11	6	3	2	29
Hill, Grant	13	27	16	19	17	13	6	3	35
Hill, Tyrone	12	20	11	16	20	5	5	3	29
Hodge, Donald	9	15	7	9	14	5	3	3	24
Hoiberg, Fred	1	4	6	6	3	2	3	1	8
Hornacek, Jeff	14	27	14	14	14	18	7	2	40
Horry, Robert	16	26	9	10	15	10	6	6	40
Houston, Allan	15	30	14	15	11	8	4	2	38
Houston, Byron	7	12	10	10	12	5	4	4	18
Howard, Juwan	19	29	14	17	15	9	4	2	42
Hunter, Lindsey	12	26	9	11	10	15	5	2	29
Hurley, Bobby	6	15	6	6	5	17	3	2	17
Jackson, Jim	17	36	16	18	14	11	7	3	50
Jackson, Jaren	6	12	7	8	6	5	3	3	14
Jackson, Mark	14	27	12	15	13	19	8	2	34
James, Henry	10	16	6	8	8	5	3	2	25
Johnson, Avery	12	19	12	13	10	18	6	2	29
Johnson, Darryl	1	3	2	2	1	1	0	0	2
Johnson, Magic	18	36	19	22	18	24	9	5	46
Johnson, Eddie	18	32	16	18	15	10	5	3	45
Johnson, Ervin	10	16	7	9	14	3	3	6	28
Johnson, Kevin	17	29	23	24	13	25	10	3	44
Johnson, Larry	16	27	18	19	23	14	5	3	44
Jones, Charles	7	13	6	9	16	7	5	10	17
Jones, Eddie	12	24	9	10	10	11	6	4	31
Jones, Popeye	11	19	6	8	28	7	4	5	25
Jordan, Michael	27	49	26	27	18	17	10	6	69
Jordan, Reggie	9	14	9	10	9	5	4	1	28
Keefe, Adam	12	14	9	12	17	4	4	3	30
Kemp, Shawn	13	23	20	22	22	12	6	10	42
Kempton, Tim	8	13	9	11	10	7	4	2	21
Kerr, Steve	9	16	7	9	6	11	6	2	24
Kersey, Jerome	15	26	15	16	20	10	6	5	36
Keys, Randolph	11	20	5	8	9	5	5	3	22
Kidd, Jason	14	29	14	16	16	25	6	2	38
King, Chris	8	18	7	12	14	4	4	3	21
King, Frankie	1	4	1	2	1	1	2	0	3
King, Jimmy	7	14	6	9	7	8	2	2	14
King, Stacey	10	19	10	14	16	7	3	7	24
Kleine, Joe	10	17	8	10	20	8	3	3	23
Koncak, Jon	9	19	9	16	20	7	5	6	25
Kukoc, Toni	13	21	11	13	13	11	5	3	34
Laettner, Christian	12	25	18	21	19	9	6	5	35
Lang, Andrew	14	20	9	9	20	4	4	8	29
Lang, Antonio	6	7	3	5	6	2	2	2	14
Leckner, Eric	8	15	7	10	17	6	3	4	21
Legler, Tim	10	15	10	12	7	7	4	2	25
Lenard, Voshon	6	12	6	8	6	6	1	1	20
Lewis, Cedric	1	1	0	0	1	0	1	0	2
Lewis, Martin	7	13	5	6	5	1	2	2	17
Lister, Alton	13	17	8	12	21	6	5	9	30
Lohaus, Brad	15	24	7	10	16	7	4	5	34
Long, Grant	13	23	12	15	21	9	7	6	33
Longley, Luc	9	16	7	9	19	8	5	7	21
Lynch, George	12	19	7	10	18	6	7	2	30
Mack, Sam	10	20	12	13	8	8	3	2	38
MacLean, Don	14	27	12	15	15	7	3	2	38
Macon, Mark	10	19	9	14	10	9	7	3	23
Mahorn, Rick	12	23	14	15	20	7	5	8	34
Majerle, Dan	15	27	14	15	15	13	6	4	37
Malone, Jeff	19	35	14	15	11	10	5	2	48
Malone, Karl	22	34	20	28	23	10	7	5	61
Manning, Danny	21	32	15	19	18	11	7	6	43
Manning, Rich	6	9	3	4	5	1	1	5	13
Marciulionis, Sarunas	13	21	13	18	9	10	6	3	35
Marshall, Donny	3	6	4	6	3	2	3	1	9
Marshall, Donyell	12	26	10	11	13	5	3	5	30
Martin, Cuonzo	1	3	0	2	1	1	1	0	3
Martin, Darrick	9	14	11	12	6	13	3	1	24
Mashburn, Jamal	19	37	13	18	13	9	5	2	50
Mason, Anthony	11	20	9	12	20	11	5	4	30
Massenburg, Tony	11	18	10	14	16	3	4	3	26

Player	FGM	FGA	FTM	FTA	Reb.	Ast.	Stl.	Blk. Sh.	Pts.
Maxwell, Vernon	15	33	19	22	11	14	6	3	51
Mayberry, Lee	7	15	7	8	6	10	3	2	22
McCann, Bob	8	16	5	9	10	4	3	4	18
McCloud, George	14	28	7	9	12	9	7	2	37
McDaniel, Clint	2	5	8	8	3	2	2	0	8
McDyess, Antonio	14	22	10	11	16	3	3	5	32
McIlvaine, Jim	5	7	6	8	11	3	3	9	12
McKey, Derrick	15	25	15	15	17	11	5	6	34
McKie, Aaron	10	18	7	8	10	11	5	3	24
McMillan, Nate	9	15	10	13	14	25	8	4	24
Meyer, Loren	6	12	5	8	13	5	2	2	14
Miller, Anthony	6	9	7	9	15	4	4	2	18
Miller, Oliver	15	25	8	10	19	11	6	9	35
Miller, Reggie	16	29	21	23	10	11	6	3	57
Mills, Chris	11	21	8	12	14	7	4	4	30
Mills, Terry	16	28	11	13	19	7	3	4	41
Miner, Harold	10	20	9	13	10	8	3	2	28
Minor, Greg	13	20	7	9	9	7	3	2	31
Mitchell, Sam	14	24	13	14	17	7	6	5	37
Mobley, Eric	7	10	4	8	12	5	2	5	14
Montross, Eric	13	17	9	13	16	3	3	4	28
Moore, Tracy	8	18	6	8	6	5	3	1	20
Morris, Chris	14	25	11	14	18	10	7	5	33
Moten, Lawrence	8	12	6	8	5	3	4	2	21
Mourning, Alonzo	19	34	16	20	22	7	4	9	50
Mullin, Chris	19	32	17	19	18	14	7	4	47
Mundt, Todd	3	5	2	2	5	1	1	1	8
Murdock, Eric	12	23	12	14	15	17	9	3	32
Muresan, Gheorghe	14	19	10	15	21	5	5	9	31
Murray, Lamond	12	25	9	10	13	7	4	5	30
Murray, Tracy	15	25	8	11	12	5	5	3	40
Mutombo, Dikembe	12	22	15	21	31	7	5	12	39
Myers, Pete	10	17	9	10	10	11	5	2	26
Nathan, Howard	3	4	2	3	0	2	3	0	6
Newman, Johnny	14	25	18	22	11	8	7	3	41
Norman, Ken	18	31	12	15	20	12	5	7	38
Oakley, Charles	14	27	13	15	35	15	5	3	35
O'Bannon, Ed	8	15	6	9	11	5	4	2	19
Olajuwon, Hakeem	21	37	17	20	25	12	8	12	52
O'Neal, Shaquille	22	40	15	22	28	8	5	15	53
Ostertag, Greg	7	11	4	4	9	1	1	5	14
O'Sullivan, Dan	6	12	4	5	10	1	2	2	15
Outlaw, Charles	8	11	5	12	14	6	4	9	19
Overton, Doug	11	17	8	9	8	18	6	1	30
Owens, Billy	15	27	9	14	22	11	6	4	34
Pack, Robert	13	27	14	16	10	19	6	2	35
Parish, Robert	16	31	13	18	32	10	6	11	40
Parks, Cherokee	9	17	5	6	10	3	3	5	25
Payton, Gary	15	28	11	13	11	17	8	3	38
Peeler, Anthony	12	24	13	13	9	8	6	2	28
Peplowski, Mike	7	13	4	6	11	3	2	2	14
Perdue, Will	8	14	9	14	17	5	3	5	19
Perkins, Sam	19	29	14	16	20	10	7	5	45
Perry, Elliot	14	22	9	10	7	17	6	1	35
Perry, Tim	12	27	12	12	16	7	4	7	31
Person, Chuck	19	32	12	13	18	11	6	3	47
Person, Wesley	11	23	11	11	11	6	4	3	29
Phills, Bobby	13	24	10	11	11	11	5	3	43
Piatkowski, Eric	8	14	7	7	8	6	2	2	23
Pierce, Ricky	17	28	16	17	12	9	6	3	45
Pinckney, Ed	11	17	12	15	22	8	7	5	27
Pippen, Scottie	18	34	12	21	18	15	9	5	43
Polynice, Olden	13	22	9	13	25	5	4	6	30
Porter, Terry	15	26	14	16	13	19	8	3	40
Price, Brent	10	18	9	12	9	14	5	2	30
Price, Mark	14	24	18	20	11	20	6	2	39
Pritchard, Kevin	7	14	7	10	4	8	2	2	15
Radja, Dino	15	31	12	18	18	5	4	6	36
Ratliff, Theo	7	11	7	7	15	2	3	5	21
Recasner, Eldridge	7	14	7	7	11	10	3	1	21
Reeves, Bryant	13	21	12	14	18	5	4	7	28
Reeves, Khalid	9	20	12	13	10	14	4	2	32
Reid, Don	6	10	5	5	9	1	4	3	12
Reid, J.R.	12	22	11	16	20	6	5	4	29
Rencher, Terrence	3	8	5	7	4	5	2	1	8
Respert, Shawn	8	11	4	4	6	6	4	1	20
Reynolds, Jerry	13	25	14	17	14	11	7	5	34
Rice, Glen	20	36	15	15	17	9	6	3	56
Richardson, Pooh	16	27	12	14	10	17	8	4	35
Richmond, Mitch	18	34	16	19	12	12	7	3	47
Rider, Isaiah	15	28	14	16	15	9	3	3	42

Player	FGM	FGA	FTM	FTA	Reb.	Ast.	Stl.	Blk. Sh.	Pts.
Riley, Eric	6	11	6	6	10	2	3	3	14
Rivers, Doc	14	24	17	17	14	21	9	3	37
Roberts, Fred	14	20	13	14	15	9	6	4	34
Roberts, Stanley	12	19	8	14	16	4	3	7	27
Robertson, Alvin	17	29	14	15	16	17	10	5	41
Robinson, Clifford	18	30	15	19	16	9	6	7	41
Robinson, David	26	41	18	25	24	11	6	12	71
Robinson, Glenn	17	33	17	20	17	10	5	3	39
Robinson, James	12	22	6	9	7	11	4	2	30
Robinson, Rumeal	12	23	11	15	12	15	7	3	31
Rodman, Dennis	15	21	9	12	34	10	4	5	34
Roe, Lou	5	10	4	4	9	3	1	2	14
Rogers, Carlos	12	20	8	12	17	7	3	7	28
Rogers, Rodney	12	22	9	13	21	8	5	5	31
Rooks, Sean	12	21	10	14	18	6	5	5	28
Rose, Jalen	8	19	9	10	10	16	4	6	21
Royal, Donald	9	16	11	14	14	8	3	2	28
Rozier, Clifford	11	18	7	11	21	6	3	4	26
Ruffin, Trevor	11	20	10	12	8	11	4	1	32
Rusconi, Stefano	3	5	1	3	2	2	0	2	7
Russell, Bryon	7	11	8	8	9	4	5	2	19
Sabonis, Arvydas	11	20	8	10	17	5	3	5	26
Salley, John	10	18	11	12	17	8	5	8	28
Schayes, Danny	12	23	18	18	24	11	4	7	37
Scheffler, Steve	5	6	4	6	6	2	2	1	11
Schintzius, Dwayne	8	14	4	8	12	5	2	4	17
Schrempf, Detlef	13	25	22	23	23	14	4	3	36
Scott, Byron	15	27	13	16	11	11	7	3	38
Scott, Dennis	16	33	10	12	11	8	5	5	41
Sealy, Malik	14	25	11	13	13	8	6	4	34
Seikaly, Rony	15	24	16	26	34	6	4	8	40
Shaw, Brian	14	24	10	12	15	17	7	3	32
Simmons, Lionel	16	31	14	16	19	13	6	7	42
Simpkins, Dickey	6	11	7	8	10	4	2	2	16
Slater, Reggie	5	10	8	10	6	3	3	2	16
Smith, Tony	11	23	9	12	10	9	5	2	25
Smith, Charles	17	28	18	21	17	6	5	8	52
Smith, Charles E.	5	12	6	8	7	9	5	1	12
Smith, Doug	13	23	10	12	14	8	4	5	36
Smith, Joe	13	21	11	14	20	4	4	6	30
Smith, Kenny	16	24	13	15	8	17	7	2	41
Smith, Michael	8	15	6	10	13	7	4	4	18
Smith, Steve	13	25	14	15	11	15	4	4	37
Smits, Rik	20	29	13	16	16	8	4	8	44
Snow, Eric	4	7	3	4	5	13	3	0	9
Spencer, Elmore	11	15	6	9	14	5	3	8	28
Spencer, Felton	9	19	10	12	19	4	3	7	23
Sprewell, Latrell	16	31	17	19	13	11	8	5	41
Stackhouse, Jerry	13	27	18	19	15	10	3	5	34
Starks, John	15	36	12	15	9	14	7	3	39
Stewart, Larry	12	19	10	13	16	11	5	4	32
Stith, Bryant	14	21	15	15	12	8	5	3	33
Stockton, John	14	22	15	16	9	28	9	2	34
Stoudamire, Damon	14	27	14	15	12	19	5	2	30
Strickland, Rod	15	25	16	18	11	20	6	2	36
Strong, Derek	10	17	11	12	16	4	3	2	25
Sura, Bob	7	13	8	10	8	10	4	3	19
Sutton, Greg	7	13	5	6	5	7	3	1	17
Sykes, Larry	0	0	0	0	2	0	0	0	0
Tabak, Zan	12	16	5	7	16	5	3	2	26
Tarpley, Roy	15	25	11	13	25	7	5	6	35
Thomas, Kurt	11	24	8	10	15	5	4	4	29
Thompson, Brooks	7	13	5	6	4	4	2	1	21
Thompson, LaSalle	13	20	13	14	22	8	5	7	31
Thornton, Bob	7	13	6	8	14	5	3	4	17
Thorpe, Otis	15	27	14	19	26	11	6	3	40
Threatt, Sedale	16	29	12	14	11	15	7	3	42
Tisdale, Wayman	19	28	13	17	18	7	4	4	40
Toolson, Andy	4	10	4	4	5	4	2	1	13
Tower, Keith	8	9	3	4	6	1	1	2	19
Trent, Gary	9	18	7	10	11	5	2	2	21
Tucker, Anthony	8	13	6	8	11	7	3	1	18
Turner, Jeff	10	19	8	9	13	6	3	4	28
Tyler, B.J.	6	10	4	4	5	10	4	1	16
Vander Velden, Logan	1	2	2	2	2	1	0	0	2
Van Exel, Nick	12	24	12	13	10	17	5	2	40
Vaughn, David	4	7	2	4	6	1	1	3	10
Vaught, Loy	14	25	12	13	21	7	6	4	33
Wallace, Rasheed	9	22	7	10	14	4	3	5	22
Walters, Rex	10	16	6	8	6	12	5	2	23
Ward, Charlie	6	10	4	6	6	7	4	1	15
Watson, Jamie	6	8	4	4	5	4	4	1	14

Player	FGM	FGA	FTM	FTA	Reb.	Ast.	Stl.	Blk. Sh.	Pts.
Weatherspoon, Clarence	14	26	12	19	23	13	7	7	35
Webb, Spud	14	26	13	14	9	17	6	2	34
Webber, Chris	18	29	7	12	20	12	5	6	40
Webster, Jeff	5	8	0	0	2	1	2	0	12
Wennington, Bill	9	21	8	8	14	5	3	4	21
Werdann, Robert	4	7	4	4	7	2	2	2	10
Wesley, David	11	19	13	13	9	14	7	1	37
West, Doug	16	26	10	12	11	9	4	3	39
West, Mark	11	17	12	14	24	5	3	9	27
Whitfield, Dwayne	4	9	8	10	12	2	1	1	16
Whitney, Chris	5	10	6	6	5	10	3	1	19
Wilkins, Gerald	18	30	13	14	14	13	7	4	43
Williams, Brian	16	23	9	13	18	6	4	5	35
Williams, Buck	14	22	18	19	27	7	5	7	35
Williams, Eric	12	18	8	12	9	4	4	2	31
Williams, Herb	17	32	17	20	29	8	5	9	40
Williams, Jayson	16	25	7	12	25	4	3	3	35
Williams, John	13	23	13	15	18	7	6	9	33
Williams, Lorenzo	9	12	5	7	20	6	4	6	19
Williams, Micheal	12	22	16	19	13	18	8	4	33
Williams, Reggie	15	27	11	13	13	12	7	5	35
Williams, Scott	9	18	9	12	20	4	4	4	22
Williams, Monty	6	10	4	4	8	5	3	1	14
Williams, Walt	13	29	14	17	15	9	5	4	40
Williamson, Corliss	10	17	6	9	8	4	2	2	26
Willis, Kevin	16	31	12	16	33	8	5	4	39
Wilson, Trevor	9	15	7	8	14	5	2	1	25
Wingate, David	11	24	11	13	13	15	7	3	28
Wingfield, Dontonio	5	14	4	4	8	5	3	1	17
Wolf, Joe	9	17	6	7	16	7	4	4	23
Wood, David	10	14	9	10	12	6	4	2	27
Woods, Randy	7	12	4	6	4	11	5	1	20
Workman, Haywoode	8	15	9	12	9	15	6	2	21
Wright, Sharone	11	21	13	17	15	4	3	7	30
Zidek, George	7	16	7	8	9	2	2	1	21

PLAYOFFS

Player	FGM	FGA	FTM	FTA	Reb.	Ast.	Stl.	Blk. Sh.	Pts.
Abdul-Rauf, Mahmoud	9	21	6	6	4	6	1	1	23
Adams, Michael	8	19	7	8	12	9	4	1	25
Addison, Rafael	3	9	3	3	4	2	1	0	9
Alexander, Cory	3	6	2	2	3	3	1	0	8
Alexander, Victor	2	4	1	1	4	1	2	0	4
Amaechi, John	0	1	0	0	0	0	0	0	0
Anderson, Greg	8	14	3	4	10	2	2	2	18
Anderson, Kenny	6	15	9	13	5	11	3	0	21
Anderson, Nick	9	18	8	10	11	7	6	2	24
Anderson, Willie	18	25	7	9	10	7	4	2	38
Anthony, Greg	5	13	4	7	6	8	4	1	16
Armstrong, B.J.	10	17	10	10	6	10	4	1	23
Askew, Vincent	5	8	5	8	6	5	2	3	12
Askins, Keith	4	7	3	3	5	2	1	0	13
Augmon, Stacey	7	14	9	11	8	6	3	2	23
Avent, Anthony	3	7	7	8	7	1	0	1	13
Barkley, Charles	23	31	19	22	24	12	7	6	56
Barros, Dana	5	9	3	4	3	4	3	0	12
Benjamin, Benoit	6	13	14	14	9	1	2	6	26
Bennett, Mario	1	3	0	0	3	0	0	0	2
Benoit, David	8	16	5	6	11	3	2	3	20
Best, Travis	4	7	5	6	5	3	2	0	10
Blaylock, Mookie	8	21	9	9	10	18	8	3	29
Blount, Corie	0	2	0	0	2	0	0	0	0
Bogues, Muggsy	6	14	4	6	9	15	5	0	16
Bonner, Anthony	3	4	3	4	9	1	1	1	7
Bowie, Anthony	5	8	2	2	4	3	1	1	14
Boyce, Donnie	0	2	0	0	0	0	0	0	0
Brandon, Terrell	8	17	7	8	6	12	2	2	21
Brickowski, Frank	10	18	6	10	12	5	3	2	23
Brooks, Scott	3	8	2	4	2	7	2	0	10
Brown, Chucky	6	11	4	6	8	2	3	2	16
Brown, P.J.	2	4	6	6	4	1	0	1	10
Brown, Dee	9	17	8	10	9	10	2	2	22
Brown, Mike	6	10	6	7	12	2	1	1	15
Brown, Randy	3	5	2	2	5	2	2	1	9
Bryant, Mark	8	16	5	5	7	1	2	3	21
Buechler, Jud	4	7	2	2	4	2	2	2	8
Bullard, Matt	3	9	4	4	5	4	1	2	12
Cage, Michael	7	10	5	7	14	2	3	5	16
Caldwell, Adrian	1	1	0	0	1	0	0	0	2
Campbell, Elden	12	22	7	11	18	3	3	5	29

Player	FGM	FGA	FTM	FTA	Reb.	Ast.	Stl.	Blk. Sh.	Pts.
Carr, Antoine	10	16	6	9	12	5	2	7	21
Carr, Chris	6	9	3	3	4	3	2	1	17
Cassell, Sam	10	20	12	12	6	12	3	2	31
Causwell, Duane	1	2	3	4	3	1	0	0	3
Ceballos, Cedric	10	20	8	10	12	6	4	3	25
Chapman, Rex	5	10	0	0	4	2	2	0	11
Chilcutt, Pete	5	10	5	6	9	3	2	1	13
Christie, Doug	2	5	0	0	2	4	1	1	5
Coleman, Derrick	13	26	21	25	21	9	3	9	33
Coles, Bimbo	7	13	5	7	6	7	4	1	18
Conlon, Marty	0	1	2	2	1	0	0	0	2
Corbin, Tyrone	11	16	8	8	14	4	5	2	28
Crotty, John	2	3	2	3	1	4	1	1	6
Cummings, Terry	16	26	13	16	18	6	3	3	41
Curry, Michael	1	3	0	0	2	1	1	1	2
Curry, Dell	12	17	4	4	7	5	6	1	27
Danilovic, Sasha	5	9	3	3	1	2	1	0	15
Davis, Antonio	7	9	8	10	10	2	2	4	17
Davis, Dale	8	11	5	9	18	3	4	4	16
Davis, Hubert	5	10	6	7	4	4	3	2	15
Davis, Mike	0	0	0	0	0	0	0	0	0
Del Negro, Vinny	13	19	5	5	7	8	3	1	29
Divac, Vlade	12	22	9	15	15	6	3	5	30
Donaldson, James	8	12	9	10	20	3	2	3	18
Douglas, Sherman	9	22	6	7	9	15	2	1	21
Drexler, Clyde	15	30	13	15	15	15	6	4	42
Duckworth, Kevin	14	22	9	11	16	5	3	2	33
Dudley, Chris	2	5	3	6	10	2	3	4	6
Dumars, Joe	15	26	13	17	7	11	4	1	35
Dumas, Richard	12	20	6	8	12	4	3	3	25
Earl, Acie	1	3	0	2	2	0	0	1	2
Edney, Tyus	7	13	5	6	6	5	3	0	17
Edwards, Doug	0	0	0	0	0	0	0	1	0
Edwards, James	13	23	9	10	9	4	2	3	32
Edwards, Kevin	6	15	5	5	5	3	3	1	16
Edwards, Blue	7	13	8	8	10	3	4	2	22
Ehlo, Craig	9	19	5	7	10	13	4	2	25
Eisley, Howard	6	6	4	4	4	5	1	1	14
Elie, Mario	11	16	10	10	9	8	4	1	22
Elliott, Sean	9	21	14	16	11	8	3	2	26
Ellis, Dale	18	30	8	11	14	6	4	2	43
Ellis, LaPhonso	10	20	9	10	17	4	2	3	27
Ellis, LeRon	0	0	0	0	0	0	0	0	0
Ellison, Pervis	5	8	2	2	10	1	1	3	10
Ewing, Patrick	18	34	17	18	22	10	7	8	45
Ferroll, Duane	8	11	11	12	9	4	2	1	23
Ferry, Danny	7	17	3	4	6	4	2	2	20
Finley, Michael	0	0	0	0	0	0	0	0	0
Fleming, Vern	9	14	9	11	11	8	3	1	19
Foster, Greg	4	6	3	4	4	1	1	1	10
Fox, Rick	4	10	2	2	6	2	1	2	10
Gamble, Kevin	10	21	4	4	8	6	3	2	22
Gatling, Chris	7	9	6	9	12	2	2	3	16
Gattison, Kenny	4	7	3	6	7	5	3	1	9
Geiger, Matt	0	2	1	2	4	0	0	0	1
Gill, Kendall	12	24	6	9	10	6	6	2	30
Gilliam, Armon	8	16	9	10	15	3	2	4	25
Grandison, Ronnie	0	1	0	0	0	0	0	0	0
Grant, Brian	6	13	5	6	7	2	1	3	13
Grant, Gary	3	10	2	2	3	8	2	1	6
Grant, Greg	4	7	2	2	3	3	1	0	9
Grant, Harvey	7	12	6	8	7	4	1	2	21
Grant, Horace	14	17	8	9	20	7	6	5	29
Green, A.C.	9	16	10	15	20	7	3	3	25
Haley, Jack	2	4	2	2	3	1	0	1	5
Hammonds, Tom	5	9	2	4	5	2	0	1	10
Hancock, Darrin	2	4	0	0	3	1	1	0	4
Hardaway, Anfernee	15	27	10	12	11	15	5	3	38
Hardaway, Tim	15	29	8	15	8	20	8	2	33
Harper, Derek	12	21	9	12	8	16	7	1	35
Harper, Ron	12	25	7	10	12	7	6	4	31
Harvey, Antonio	0	0	0	0	1	0	0	0	0
Hawkins, Hersey	14	26	15	15	10	8	6	4	39
Henderson, Alan	8	10	4	5	8	2	1	2	17
Herrera, Carl	6	10	6	6	7	2	3	1	12
Higgins, Sean	0	1	0	0	0	1	0	0	0
Hill, Grant	10	18	9	11	11	5	2	0	21
Hill, Tyrone	5	12	10	14	13	2	4	1	16
Hornacek, Jeff	13	22	14	14	11	12	5	2	36
Horry, Robert	10	18	7	11	17	8	7	5	24
Houston, Allan	11	25	9	10	5	4	0	1	33

Player	FGM	FGA	FTM	FTA	Reb.	Ast.	Stl.	Blk. Sh.	Pts.
Houston, Byron	3	3	2	2	2	2	1	2	8
Hunter, Lindsey	1	6	1	2	2	1	1	0	3
Hurley, Bobby	0	0	0	0	0	0	0	0	0
Jackson, Jaren	3	5	0	0	3	1	1	0	6
Jackson, Mark	11	24	9	11	8	16	5	1	28
James, Henry	1	4	2	4	1	1	1	0	4
Johnson, Avery	10	18	8	12	8	18	6	2	24
Johnson, Magic	15	26	20	22	18	24	7	3	44
Johnson, Eddie	13	27	10	10	11	6	3	3	35
Johnson, Ervin	6	9	2	2	10	2	2	3	12
Johnson, Kevin	18	31	21	22	9	19	5	2	46
Johnson, Larry	11	18	9	12	13	6	2	1	31
Jones, Charles	5	9	4	6	9	2	2	4	11
Jones, Eddie	9	18	5	6	11	5	5	2	20
Jordan, Michael	24	45	23	28	19	14	6	5	63
Jordan, Reggie	1	3	1	2	1	3	2	1	3
Keefe, Adam	8	11	4	7	8	4	3	1	18
Kemp, Shawn	13	24	14	16	20	6	6	7	33
Kempton, Tim	5	13	6	6	9	4	2	0	16
Kerr, Steve	5	8	6	6	4	6	3	0	14
Kersey, Jerome	14	23	12	15	16	8	6	4	34
Keys, Randolph	0	3	0	0	3	1	0	0	0
King, Chris	0	1	0	2	0	0	1	0	0
King, Stacey	9	15	7	8	9	3	2	3	21
Kleine, Joe	6	12	6	7	11	3	2	1	15
Koncak, Jon	5	10	11	11	13	4	3	4	19
Kukoc, Toni	9	17	7	8	11	11	4	1	22
Laettner, Christian	11	20	10	11	11	3	3	3	26
Lang, Andrew	7	12	8	11	10	2	2	5	20
Lang, Antonio	0	0	0	0	0	0	0	0	0
Leckner, Eric	3	7	3	4	6	2	0	0	8
Lister, Alton	9	14	9	13	17	3	3	8	22
Lohaus, Brad	6	14	1	2	8	2	4	3	15
Long, Grant	10	16	12	14	14	6	2	1	24
Longley, Luc	8	13	5	7	9	4	2	4	19
Lynch, George	6	11	3	4	8	3	2	0	13
Mack, Sam	4	8	0	2	4	1	1	0	9
Mahorn, Rick	8	14	8	8	18	4	3	4	17
Majerle, Dan	12	24	10	12	12	9	5	5	34
Malone, Jeff	15	24	14	15	8	8	4	2	35
Malone, Karl	17	31	22	24	22	8	6	5	44
Manning, Danny	14	25	9	13	12	8	3	3	35
Marciulionis, Sarunas	8	14	15	15	4	9	3	1	27
Marshall, Donny	0	0	0	0	0	0	0	0	0
Mason, Anthony	11	15	8	12	14	7	5	2	25
Massenburg, Tony	0	0	0	0	0	0	0	0	0
Maxwell, Vernon	14	25	7	8	9	9	3	2	34
McCann, Bob	3	6	0	0	2	0	0	1	6
McCloud, George	5	8	4	7	5	6	2	1	17
McKey, Derrick	12	19	8	11	13	8	4	5	27
McKie, Aaron	6	11	7	9	10	4	2	2	16
McMillan, Nate	7	17	7	8	8	16	6	4	17
Miller, Anthony	0	2	0	0	4	1	1	0	0
Miller, Oliver	7	12	5	10	14	5	2	7	17
Miller, Reggie	14	26	17	19	11	6	4	2	39
Mills, Chris	10	17	5	6	10	5	5	2	25
Mills, Terry	4	11	4	6	7	4	1	1	10
Miner, Harold	7	13	4	6	3	1	1	0	15
Minor, Greg	5	10	1	1	1	2	1	1	11
Mitchell, Sam	4	8	4	6	5	2	1	1	11
Montross, Eric	2	4	2	2	5	0	0	0	6
Morris, Chris	12	20	6	6	12	4	4	4	28
Mourning, Alonzo	13	26	15	18	20	4	2	7	34
Mullin, Chris	16	30	16	19	11	7	4	5	41
Murdock, Eric	2	3	2	2	2	1	1	1	6
Murray, Tracy	2	4	0	0	2	1	1	0	4
Mutombo, Dikembe	9	13	13	18	17	5	3	8	23
Myers, Pete	7	8	4	6	4	6	2	2	15
Newman, Johnny	14	25	10	14	6	6	3	2	34
Norman, Ken	6	15	8	12	14	6	2	1	16
Oakley, Charles	10	20	10	12	24	8	5	2	26
Olajuwon, Hakeem	20	34	18	20	26	10	6	10	49
O'Neal, Shaquille	18	28	13	20	22	9	4	5	41
Ostertag, Greg	6	7	4	6	8	1	1	5	12
Owens, Billy	13	23	8	10	17	6	3	1	27
Pack, Robert	8	15	11	12	4	8	6	1	23
Parish, Robert	14	25	11	15	19	6	5	7	33
Payton, Gary	12	22	12	16	10	12	4	2	31
Peeler, Anthony	6	11	6	6	6	5	2	1	16
Perdue, Will	8	10	6	9	12	4	1	4	17
Perkins, Sam	13	22	11	13	19	5	4	5	29
Perry, Elliot	5	9	9	9	5	6	2	0	14

Player	FGM	FGA	FTM	FTA	Reb.	Ast.	Stl.	Blk. Sh.	Pts.
Perry, Tim	12	17	7	9	10	3	2	3	31
Person, Chuck	16	27	12	15	17	7	3	2	40
Person, Wesley	9	19	4	4	9	2	2	1	23
Phills, Bobby	8	15	9	10	7	4	4	1	21
Pierce, Ricky	13	24	14	17	7	7	3	3	35
Pinckney, Ed	6	9	8	8	14	2	4	2	17
Pippen, Scottie	13	35	11	14	18	13	6	5	32
Polynice, Olden	8	16	5	5	16	2	2	3	18
Porter, Terry	13	19	15	16	8	15	5	2	41
Price, Mark	11	19	16	16	6	18	6	1	35
Radja, Dino	7	16	7	10	8	3	1	3	18
Rasmussen, Blair	13	23	6	8	13	4	2	3	28
Ratliff, Theo	0	0	0	0	0	0	0	0	0
Recasner, Eldridge	0	3	0	0	1	2	0	0	0
Reid, Don	1	3	1	3	1	1	0	2	3
Reid, J.R.	6	14	10	11	12	5	3	2	17
Reynolds, Jerry	4	10	5	6	4	2	3	3	14
Rice, Glen	10	26	4	5	10	3	3	1	25
Richardson, Pooh	2	7	2	4	4	9	1	0	7
Richmond, Mitch	13	29	9	12	13	8	4	2	37
Rinaldi, Rich	1	2	0	0	0	1	0	0	2
Rivers, Doc	14	19	15	16	13	22	6	2	34
Roberts, Fred	12	19	9	11	7	5	2	1	33
Roberts, Stanley	10	16	3	8	13	1	2	2	20
Robertson, Alvin	15	23	10	11	8	12	6	1	38
Robinson, Clifford	12	21	7	14	10	6	3	6	28
Robinson, David	14	27	18	23	22	11	4	8	40
Robinson, James	2	7	1	2	2	2	1	1	6
Robinson, Rumeal	7	12	3	4	3	9	2	0	14
Rodman, Dennis	10	16	6	10	22	5	4	4	23
Roe, Lou	0	1	0	0	2	0	1	0	0
Rogers, Rodney	8	12	5	7	9	3	2	2	18
Rooks, Sean	4	8	4	4	5	2	2	1	10
Rose, Jalen	7	11	2	3	6	10	2	1	15
Royal, Donald	4	8	6	8	8	3	1	2	14
Ruffin, Trevor	2	4	1	2	1	1	1	0	4
Russell, Bryon	8	14	5	7	10	5	4	2	24
Sabonis, Arvydas	10	22	16	20	13	4	2	1	27
Salley, John	10	17	9	12	13	4	3	6	23
Schayes, Danny	11	16	13	15	14	5	2	5	33
Scheffler, Steve	2	3	4	4	4	1	1	0	6
Schintzius, Dwayne	5	8	2	2	6	2	1	3	10
Schrempf, Detlef	10	22	13	18	16	9	3	3	29
Scott, Byron	14	24	10	12	11	7	7	2	35
Scott, Dennis	9	18	4	6	7	5	4	2	25
Sealy, Malik	0	4	2	2	1	0	0	0	2
Seikaly, Rony	9	15	14	16	20	4	2	5	26
Shaw, Brian	9	21	7	8	8	11	3	1	22
Simmons, Lionel	9	20	4	5	6	3	2	1	24
Smith, Tony	5	10	4	5	3	3	2	1	15
Smith, Charles	10	16	8	9	9	4	6	5	24
Smith, Charles E.	1	1	0	0	1	3	1	0	2
Smith, Kenny	13	16	8	8	7	12	3	2	32
Smith, Michael	2	5	3	6	9	3	1	2	7
Smith, Steve	12	31	10	12	9	9	3	3	35
Smits, Rik	13	21	10	15	14	7	4	4	34
Snow, Eric	1	2	0	0	2	2	1	0	2
Spencer, Elmore	0	1	0	2	1	0	0	0	0
Spencer, Felton	6	11	5	6	15	1	2	4	15
Sprewell, Latrell	10	24	4	6	5	10	1	2	27
Starks, John	11	21	11	14	7	12	5	1	30
Stith, Bryant	7	13	14	14	8	5	2	2	22
Stockton, John	13	21	16	19	9	24	6	3	34
Strickland, Rod	12	23	10	11	9	17	4	2	30
Strong, Derek	2	5	2	2	8	1	1	1	6
Sura, Bob	2	3	0	0	1	2	1	0	4
Sutton, Greg	1	5	3	3	2	2	1	1	5
Tabak, Zan	1	2	2	2	1	1	1	1	2
Tarpley, Roy	12	24	9	15	20	6	4	5	27
Thomas, Kurt	2	5	2	2	8	2	1	1	6
Thompson, Brooks	7	10	2	3	3	3	0	1	17
Thompson, LaSalle	9	19	5	6	17	3	3	4	23
Thornton, Bob	3	4	2	4	7	2	1	1	6
Thorpe, Otis	12	17	11	14	17	6	4	2	28
Threatt, Sedale	17	24	6	9	7	10	6	2	35
Tisdale, Wayman	10	14	5	8	6	6	1	2	21
Toolson, Andy	0	1	0	0	0	1	1	0	0
Tower, Keith	0	0	0	0	0	0	0	0	0
Trent, Gary	1	3	0	0	1	0	1	0	2
Turner, Jeff	4	8	2	2	7	3	2	2	11
Van Exel, Nick	13	23	9	13	7	12	4	1	34
Vaught, Loy	4	7	3	3	8	2	3	1	8

INDIVIDUAL CAREER HIGHS

Player	FGM	FGA	FTM	FTA	Reb.	Ast.	Stl.	Blk. Sh.	Pts.
Walters, Rex	1	1	0	0	0	0	0	0	2
Ward, Charlie	5	6	2	4	3	4	4	0	12
Watson, Jamie	3	3	0	0	1	1	1	1	6
Webb, Spud	10	19	13	16	7	18	3	1	21
Webber, Chris	8	14	2	4	10	13	2	4	17
Wennington, Bill	5	11	4	4	5	3	2	1	14
Wesley, David	3	4	2	2	0	2	2	0	9
West, Mark	10	17	6	10	21	2	3	7	24
Wilkins, Gerald	16	22	8	9	11	10	4	1	34
Williams, Brian	7	11	7	10	19	2	1	4	19
Williams, Buck	12	17	11	16	18	5	4	4	28
Williams, Herb	9	12	6	8	8	4	2	3	19
Williams, Jayson	3	4	1	2	3	0	0	0	6
Williams, John	10	17	10	12	13	5	6	4	23
Williams, Lorenzo	1	1	0	0	1	0	0	0	2
Williams, Micheal	8	16	12	14	6	11	5	0	24
Williams, Reggie	11	16	6	9	11	8	3	3	31
Williams, Scott	8	14	5	6	14	4	3	3	21
Williams, Monty	2	4	1	2	2	0	0	0	4
Williams, Walt	5	11	1	2	8	2	1	1	12
Williamson, Corliss	0	1	1	1	0	0	0	0	1
Willis, Kevin	12	24	8	11	16	3	4	4	27
Wingate, David	6	14	5	6	8	6	4	1	16
Wingfield, Dontonio	3	8	1	2	5	3	0	0	9
Wolf, Joe	2	5	2	2	2	1	1	1	5
Wood, David	2	2	1	2	3	2	2	0	5
Workman, Haywoode	5	14	6	6	7	11	7	1	15

PROMISING NEWCOMERS

ABDUR-RAHIM, SHAREEF F GRIZZLIES

PERSONAL: Born December 11, 1976, in Marietta, Ga. ... 6-9/225. ... Full name: Julius Shareef Abdur-Rahim
HIGH SCHOOL: Wheeler (Marietta, Ga.).
COLLEGE: California.
TRANSACTIONS/CAREER NOTES: Selected after freshman season by Vancouver Grizzlies in first round (third pick overall) of 1996 NBA Draft.

COLLEGIATE RECORD

Season Team	G	Min.	FGM	FGA	Pct.	FTM	FTA	Pct.	Reb.	Ast.	Pts.	AVERAGES RPG	APG	PPG
95-96—California	28	972	206	398	.518	170	249	.683	236	29	590	8.4	1.0	21.1

Three-point field goals: 1995-96, 8-for-21 (.381).

ALLEN, RAY G BUCKS

PERSONAL: Born July 20, 1975, in Merced, Calif. ... 6-5/205. ... Full name: Walter Ray Allen.
HIGH SCHOOL: Hillcrest (Dalzell, S.C.).
COLLEGE: Connecticut.
TRANSACTIONS/CAREER NOTES: Selected after junior season by Minnesota Timberwolves in first round (fifth pick overall) of 1996 NBA Draft. ... Draft rights traded by Timberwolves with undisclosed first-round draft choice to Milwaukee Bucks for draft rights to G Stephon Marbury (June 26, 1996).

NOTES: THE SPORTING NEWS All-America first team (1996).

COLLEGIATE RECORD

Season Team	G	Min.	FGM	FGA	Pct.	FTM	FTA	Pct.	Reb.	Ast.	Pts.	AVERAGES RPG	APG	PPG
93-94—Connecticut	34	735	158	310	.510	80	101	.792	155	53	429	4.6	1.6	12.6
94-95—Connecticut	32	1051	255	521	.489	80	110	.727	218	75	675	6.8	2.3	21.1
95-96—Connecticut	35	1098	292	618	.473	119	147	.810	228	117	818	6.5	3.3	23.4
Totals	101	2884	705	1449	.487	279	358	.779	601	245	1922	6.0	2.4	19.0

Three-point field goals: 1993-94, 33-for-82 (.402). 1994-95, 85-for-191 (.445). 1995-96, 115-for-247 (.466). Totals, 233-for-520 (.448).

ANDERSON, SHANDON F/G JAZZ

PERSONAL: Born December 31, 1973, in Atlanta. ... 6-6/208. ... Full name: Shandon Rodriguez Anderson. ... Brother of Willie Anderson, guard with three NBA teams (1988-89 through 1995-96).
HIGH SCHOOL: Crim (Atlanta).
COLLEGE: Georgia.
TRANSACTIONS/CAREER NOTES: Selected by Utah Jazz in second round (54th pick overall) of 1996 NBA Draft.

COLLEGIATE RECORD

Season Team	G	Min.	FGM	FGA	Pct.	FTM	FTA	Pct.	Reb.	Ast.	Pts.	AVERAGES RPG	APG	PPG
92-93—Georgia	29	554	99	201	.493	64	105	.610	103	44	271	3.6	1.5	9.3
93-94—Georgia	30	859	157	324	.485	93	141	.660	168	114	413	5.6	3.8	13.8
94-95—Georgia	28	827	149	315	.473	59	95	.621	145	83	371	5.2	3.0	13.3
95-96—Georgia	31	891	176	327	.538	94	143	.657	171	83	462	5.5	2.7	14.9
Totals	118	3131	581	1167	.498	310	484	.640	587	324	1517	5.0	2.7	12.9

Three-point field goals: 1992-93, 9-for-26 (.346). 1993-94, 6-for-34 (.176). 1994-95, 17-for-53 (.321). 1995-96, 16-for-52 (.300). Totals, 40-for-165 (.291).

BARRY, DREW G SUPERSONICS

PERSONAL: Born February 17, 1973, in Oakland. ... 6-5/191. ... Full name: Drew William Barry. ... Son of Rick Barry, forward with San Francisco/Golden State Warriors and Houston Rockets of NBA (1965-66, 1966-67 and 1972-73 through 1979-80), Oakland Oaks, Washington Capitols and New York Nets of American Basketball Association (1968-69 through 1971-72), and member of Naismith Memorial Basketball Hall of Fame; brother of Brent Barry, guard with Los Angeles Clippers; and brother of Jon Barry, guard with Atlanta Hawks.
HIGH SCHOOL: De La Salle Catholic (Concord, Calif.).
COLLEGE: Georgia Tech.
TRANSACTIONS/CAREER NOTES: Selected by Seattle SuperSonics in second round (57th pick overall) of 1996 NBA draft.

COLLEGIATE RECORD

Season Team	G	Min.	FGM	FGA	Pct.	FTM	FTA	Pct.	Reb.	Ast.	Pts.	AVERAGES RPG	APG	PPG
92-93—Georgia Tech	30	806	80	171	.468	33	41	.805	102	164	218	3.4	5.5	7.3
93-94—Georgia Tech	24	787	61	145	.421	45	58	.776	82	141	194	3.4	5.9	8.1
94-95—Georgia Tech	27	966	119	232	.513	73	97	.753	131	181	361	4.9	6.7	13.4
95-96—Georgia Tech	36	1315	149	367	.406	105	133	.789	167	238	480	4.6	6.6	13.3
Totals	117	3874	409	915	.447	256	329	.778	482	724	1253	4.1	6.2	10.7

Three-point field goals: 1992-93, 25-for-78 (.321). 1993-94, 27-for-81 (.333). 1994-95, 50-for-117 (.427). 1995-96, 77-for-209 (.368). Totals, 179-for-485 (.369).

BELL, TERRELL   C   ROCKETS

PERSONAL: Born December 15, 1973, in Athens, Ga. ... 6-10/240. ... Full name: Johneirio Terrell Bell.
HIGH SCHOOL: Cedar Shoals (Athens, Ga).
COLLEGE: Georgia.
TRANSACTIONS/CAREER NOTES: Selected by Houston Rockets in second round (50th pick overall) of 1996 NBA Draft.

COLLEGIATE RECORD

Season Team	G	Min.	FGM	FGA	Pct.	FTM	FTA	Pct.	Reb.	Ast.	Pts.	AVERAGES RPG	APG	PPG
92-93—Georgia	16	59	7	15	.467	7	12	.583	20	0	21	1.3	0.0	1.3
93-94—Georgia	27	362	38	71	.535	18	42	.429	103	4	94	3.8	0.1	3.5
94-95—Georgia	28	364	39	75	.520	25	43	.581	89	7	104	3.2	0.3	3.7
95-96—Georgia	31	729	70	140	.500	54	92	.587	195	23	194	6.3	0.7	6.3
Totals	102	1514	154	301	.512	104	189	.550	407	34	413	4.0	0.3	4.0

Three-point field goals: 1994-95, 1-for-2 (.500). 1995-96, 0-for-1. Totals, 1-for-3 (.333).

BLAIR, JOSEPH   F   SUPERSONICS

PERSONAL: Born June 12, 1974, in Akron, Ohio. ... 6-10/251. ... Full name: Joseph J. Blair.
HIGH SCHOOL: C.E. King (Houston).
COLLEGE: Arizona.
TRANSACTIONS/CAREER NOTES: Selected by Seattle SuperSonics in second round (35th pick overall) of 1996 NBA Draft.

COLLEGIATE RECORD

Season Team	G	Min.	FGM	FGA	Pct.	FTM	FTA	Pct.	Reb.	Ast.	Pts.	AVERAGES RPG	APG	PPG
92-93—Arizona	28	453	86	132	.652	28	47	.596	107	12	200	3.8	0.4	7.1
93-94—Arizona	34	967	153	252	.607	37	85	.435	246	21	343	7.2	0.6	10.1
94-95—Arizona	28	723	142	254	.559	53	114	.465	195	25	337	7.0	0.9	12.0
95-96—Arizona	14	427	89	129	.690	28	70	.400	124	30	206	8.9	2.1	14.7
Totals	104	2570	470	767	.613	146	316	.462	672	88	1086	6.5	0.8	10.4

Three-point field goals: 1993-94, 0-for-1.

BROWN, MARCUS   G   TRAIL BLAZERS

PERSONAL: Born April 3, 1974, in West Memphis, Ark. ... 6-3/185. ... Full name: Marcus James Brown.
HIGH SCHOOL: West Memphis (Ark.).
COLLEGE: Murray State.
TRANSACTIONS/CAREER NOTES: Selected by Portland Trail Blazers in second round (46th pick overall) of 1996 NBA Draft.

COLLEGIATE RECORD

Season Team	G	Min.	FGM	FGA	Pct.	FTM	FTA	Pct.	Reb.	Ast.	Pts.	AVERAGES RPG	APG	PPG
92-93—Murray State	30	591	81	166	.488	86	109	.789	84	33	266	2.8	1.1	8.9
93-94—Murray State	29	747	182	362	.503	125	149	.839	111	79	526	3.8	2.7	18.1
94-95—Murray State	30	973	219	429	.510	189	211	.896	147	63	671	4.9	2.1	22.4
95-96—Murray State	29	1080	254	536	.474	185	220	.841	139	119	767	4.8	4.1	26.4
Totals	118	3391	736	1493	.493	585	689	.849	481	294	2230	4.1	2.5	18.9

Three-point field goals: 1992-93, 18-for-50 (.360). 1993-94, 37-for-121 (.306). 1994-95, 44-for-119 (.370). 1995-96, 74-for-175 (.423). Totals, 173-for-465 (.372).

BRYANT, KOBE   G   LAKERS

PERSONAL: Born August 23, 1978, in Philadelphia. ... 6-6/200. ... Full name: Kobe B. Bryant. ... Son of Joe "Jelly Bean" Bryant, forward with Philadelphia 76ers, San Diego Clippers and Houston Rockets of NBA (1975-76 through 1982-83).
HIGH SCHOOL: Lower Merion (Pa.).
COLLEGE: Did not attend college.
TRANSACTIONS/CAREER NOTES: Selected out of high school by Charlotte Hornets in first round (13th pick overall) of 1996 NBA Draft. ... Draft rights traded by Hornets to Los Angeles Lakers for C Vlade Divac (July 11, 1996).

CAMBY, MARCUS   C/F   RAPTORS

PERSONAL: Born March 22, 1974, in Hartford. ... 6-11/220. ... Full name: Marcus D. Camby.
HIGH SCHOOL: Hartford Public (Conn.).
COLLEGE: Massachusetts.
TRANSACTIONS/CAREER NOTES: Selected after junior season by Toronto Raptors in first round (second pick overall) of 1996 NBA Draft.

COLLEGIATE RECORD

NOTES: THE SPORTING NEWS College Player of the Year (1996). ... Naismith Award winner (1996). ... Wooden Award winner (1996). ... THE SPORTING NEWS All-America first team (1996).

Season Team	G	Min.	FGM	FGA	Pct.	FTM	FTA	Pct.	Reb.	Ast.	Pts.	AVERAGES RPG	APG	PPG
93-94—Massachusetts	29	634	117	237	.494	62	104	.596	185	36	296	6.4	1.2	10.2
94-95—Massachusetts	30	679	166	302	.550	83	129	.643	186	37	416	6.2	1.2	13.9
95-96—Massachusetts	33	1011	256	537	.477	163	233	.700	271	58	675	8.2	1.8	20.5
Totals	92	2324	539	1076	.501	308	466	.661	642	131	1387	7.0	1.4	15.1

Three-point field goals: 1993-94, 0-for-4. 1994-95, 1-for-1. 1995-96, 0-for-8. Totals, 1-for-13 (.077).

DAMPIER, ERICK　　　　C/F　　　　PACERS

PERSONAL: Born July 14, 1974, in Jackson, Miss. ... 6-11/265. ... Full name: Erick Trevez Dampier.
HIGH SCHOOL: Lawrence County (Monticello, Miss.).
COLLEGE: Mississippi State.
TRANSACTIONS/CAREER NOTES: Selected after junior season by Indiana Pacers in first round (10th pick overall) of 1996 NBA Draft.

COLLEGIATE RECORD

Season Team	G	Min.	FGM	FGA	Pct.	FTM	FTA	Pct.	Reb.	Ast.	Pts.	AVERAGES RPG	APG	PPG
93-94—Mississippi State	29	678	133	226	.589	78	159	.491	251	23	344	8.7	0.8	11.9
94-95—Mississippi State	30	853	153	239	.640	87	146	.596	291	28	393	9.7	0.9	13.1
95-96—Mississippi State	34	1112	195	354	.551	104	170	.612	317	77	494	9.3	2.3	14.5
Totals	93	2643	481	819	.587	269	475	.566	859	128	1231	9.2	1.4	13.2

DAVIS, BEN　　　　F　　　　SUNS

PERSONAL: Born December 26, 1972, in Vero Beach, Fla. ... 6-9/240. ... Full name: Ben Jerome Davis.
HIGH SCHOOL: Oak Hill Academy (Mouth of Wilson, Va.).
JUNIOR COLLEGE: Hutchinson (Kan.) Community College.
COLLEGE: Kansas, then Florida, then Arizona.
TRANSACTIONS/CAREER NOTES: Selected by Phoenix Suns in second round (43rd pick overall) of 1996 NBA Draft.

COLLEGIATE RECORD

Season Team	G	Min.	FGM	FGA	Pct.	FTM	FTA	Pct.	Reb.	Ast.	Pts.	AVERAGES RPG	APG	PPG
91-92—Kansas	32	564	82	173	.474	48	92	.522	145	15	212	4.5	0.5	6.6
92-93—Florida					Did not play—transfer student.									
93-94—Hutchinson C.C.	39	...	303	516	.587	167	241	.693	470	55	776	12.1	1.4	19.9
94-95—Arizona	21	440	85	158	.538	38	60	.633	124	8	208	5.9	0.4	9.9
95-96—Arizona	33	1039	171	313	.546	127	184	.690	313	23	469	9.5	0.7	14.2
Junior college totals	39	...	303	516	.587	167	241	.693	470	55	776	12.1	1.4	19.9
4-year-college totals	86	2043	338	644	.525	213	336	.634	582	46	889	6.8	0.5	10.3

Three-point field goals: 1993-94, 1-for-1.

DELK, TONY　　　　G　　　　HORNETS

PERSONAL: Born January 28, 1974, in Covington, Tenn. ... 6-2/193. ... Full name: Tony Lorenzo Delk.
HIGH SCHOOL: Haywood (Brownsville, Tenn.).
COLLEGE: Kentucky.
TRANSACTIONS/CAREER NOTES: Selected by Charlotte Hornets in first round (16th pick overall) of 1996 NBA Draft.

COLLEGIATE RECORD
NOTES: The Sporting News All-America second team (1996). ... NCAA Division I Tournament Most Outstanding Player (1996). ... Member of NCAA Division I championship team (1996).

Season Team	G	Min.	FGM	FGA	Pct.	FTM	FTA	Pct.	Reb.	Ast.	Pts.	AVERAGES RPG	APG	PPG
92-93—Kentucky	30	287	47	104	.452	24	33	.727	57	22	136	1.9	0.7	4.5
93-94—Kentucky	34	957	200	440	.455	69	108	.639	153	59	564	4.5	1.7	16.6
94-95—Kentucky	33	960	207	433	.478	60	89	.674	110	65	551	3.3	2.0	16.7
95-96—Kentucky	36	947	229	464	.494	88	110	.800	150	64	639	4.2	1.8	17.8
Totals	133	2891	683	1441	.474	241	340	.709	470	210	1890	3.5	1.6	14.2

Three-point field goals: 1992-93, 18-for-51 (.353). 1993-94, 95-for-254 (.374). 1994-95, 77-for-197 (.391). 1995-96, 93-for-210 (.443). Totals, 283-for-712 (.397).

EVANS, BRIAN　　　　F　　　　MAGIC

PERSONAL: Born September 13, 1973, in Rockford, Ill. ... 6-8/220. ... Full name: Brian Keith Evans.
HIGH SCHOOL: South (Terre Haute, Ind.).
COLLEGE: Indiana.
TRANSACTIONS/CAREER NOTES: Selected by Orlando Magic in first round (27th pick overall) of 1996 NBA Draft.

COLLEGIATE RECORD

Season Team	G	Min.	FGM	FGA	Pct.	FTM	FTA	Pct.	Reb.	Ast.	Pts.	AVERAGES RPG	APG	PPG
91-92—Indiana					Did not play—redshirted.									
92-93—Indiana	35	615	62	146	.425	37	54	.685	138	46	184	3.9	1.3	5.3

Season Team	G	Min.	FGM	FGA	Pct.	FTM	FTA	Pct.	Reb.	Ast.	Pts.	AVERAGES		
												RPG	APG	PPG
93-94—Indiana	27	791	116	259	.448	46	58	.793	183	59	321	6.8	2.2	11.9
94-95—Indiana	31	1051	177	383	.462	126	161	.783	208	101	538	6.7	3.3	17.4
95-96—Indiana	31	1156	212	474	.447	172	203	.847	221	126	658	7.1	4.1	21.2
Totals	124	3613	567	1262	.449	381	476	.800	750	332	1701	6.0	2.7	13.7

Three-point field goals: 1992-93, 23-for-65 (.354). 1993-94, 43-for-94 (.457). 1994-95, 58-for-139 (.417). 1995-96, 62-for-158 (.392). Totals, 186-for-456 (.408).

FEICK, JAMIE   C   76ERS

PERSONAL: Born July 3, 1974, in Lexington, Ohio. ... 6-9/255.
HIGH SCHOOL: Lexington (Lexington, Ohio).
COLLEGE: Michigan State.
TRANSACTIONS/CAREER NOTES: Selected by Philadelphia 76ers in second round (48th pick overall) of 1996 NBA Draft.

COLLEGIATE RECORD

Season Team	G	Min.	FGM	FGA	Pct.	FTM	FTA	Pct.	Reb.	Ast.	Pts.	AVERAGES		
												RPG	APG	PPG
92-93—Michigan State	14	55	2	15	.133	1	4	.250	20	1	5	1.4	0.1	0.4
93-94—Michigan State	32	506	38	69	.551	20	41	.488	104	23	96	3.3	0.7	3.0
94-95—Michigan State	28	875	111	180	.617	54	93	.581	281	29	276	10.0	1.0	9.9
95-96—Michigan State	32	986	116	268	.433	71	115	.617	303	75	323	9.5	2.3	10.1
Totals	106	2422	267	532	.502	146	253	.577	708	128	700	6.7	1.2	6.6

Three-point field goals: 1992-93, 0-for-1. 1993-94, 0-for-2. 1995-96, 20-for-65 (.308). Totals, 20-for-68 (.294).

FISHER, DEREK   G   LAKERS

PERSONAL: Born August 9, 1974, in Little Rock, Ark. ... 6-1/200. ... Full name: Derek Lamar Fisher.
HIGH SCHOOL: Parkview (Little Rock, Ark.).
COLLEGE: Arkansas-Little Rock.
TRANSACTIONS/CAREER NOTES: Selected by Los Angeles Lakers in first round (24th pick overall) of 1996 NBA Draft.

COLLEGIATE RECORD

Season Team	G	Min.	FGM	FGA	Pct.	FTM	FTA	Pct.	Reb.	Ast.	Pts.	AVERAGES		
												RPG	APG	PPG
92-93—Ark.-Little Rock	27	749	57	138	.413	71	92	.772	89	92	194	3.3	3.4	7.2
93-94—Ark.-Little Rock	28	888	94	212	.443	72	93	.774	109	102	283	3.9	3.6	10.1
94-95—Ark.-Little Rock	27	938	153	386	.396	130	180	.722	135	124	479	5.0	4.6	17.7
95-96—Ark.-Little Rock	30	1041	128	313	.409	126	169	.746	155	154	437	5.2	5.1	14.6
Totals	112	3616	432	1049	.412	399	534	.747	488	472	1393	4.4	4.2	12.4

Three-point field goals: 1992-93, 9-for-31 (.290). 1993-94, 23-for-55 (.418). 1994-95, 43-for-113 (.381). 1995-96, 50-for-130 (.385). Totals, 125-for-329 (.380).

FULLER, TODD   C   WARRIORS

PERSONAL: Born July 25, 1974, in Fayettville, N.C. ... 6-11/255. ... Full name: Todd Douglas Fuller.
HIGH SCHOOL: Charlotte Christian.
COLLEGE: North Carolina State.
TRANSACTIONS/CAREER NOTES: Selected by Golden State Warriors in first round (11th pick overall) of 1996 NBA Draft.

COLLEGIATE RECORD

Season Team	G	Min.	FGM	FGA	Pct.	FTM	FTA	Pct.	Reb.	Ast.	Pts.	AVERAGES		
												RPG	APG	PPG
92-93—N.C. State	27	413	53	116	.457	34	44	.773	97	6	141	3.6	0.2	5.2
93-94—N.C. State	30	875	144	299	.482	67	89	.753	253	33	355	8.4	1.1	11.8
94-95—N.C. State	27	816	164	316	.519	116	138	.841	229	35	440	8.5	1.3	16.3
95-96—N.C. State	31	1044	225	445	.506	183	229	.799	308	39	649	9.9	1.3	20.9
Totals	115	3248	586	1176	.498	400	500	.800	887	113	1585	7.7	1.0	13.8

Three-point field goals: 1992-93, 1-for-2 (.500). 1993-94, 0-for-4. 1994-95, 0-for-6. 1995-96, 16-for-43 (.372). Totals, 17-for-55 (.309).

GEARY, REGGIE   G   CAVALIERS

PERSONAL: Born August 31, 1973, in Trenton, N.J. ... 6-2/187. ... Full name: Reggie Elliot Geary.
HIGH SCHOOL: Mater Dei (Santa Ana, Calif.).
COLLEGE: Arizona.
TRANSACTIONS/CAREER NOTES: Selected by Cleveland Cavaliers in second round (56th pick overall) of 1996 NBA Draft.

COLLEGIATE RECORD

Season Team	G	Min.	FGM	FGA	Pct.	FTM	FTA	Pct.	Reb.	Ast.	Pts.	AVERAGES		
												RPG	APG	PPG
92-93—Arizona	28	582	44	104	.423	22	48	.458	52	94	117	1.9	3.4	4.2
93-94—Arizona	35	1026	94	209	.450	45	75	.600	131	122	260	3.7	3.5	7.4
94-95—Arizona	31	853	69	167	.413	19	44	.432	96	113	193	3.1	3.6	6.2
95-96—Arizona	33	1090	108	250	.432	63	86	.733	119	231	324	3.6	7.0	9.8
Totals	127	3551	315	730	.432	149	253	.589	398	560	894	3.1	4.4	7.0

Three-point field goals: 1992-93, 7-for-31 (.226). 1993-94, 27-for-89 (.303). 1994-95, 36-for-94 (.383). 1995-96, 45-for-117 (.385). Totals, 115-for-331 (.347).

HAMER, STEVE C CELTICS

PERSONAL: Born November 13, 1973, in Memphis. ... 7-0/245. ... Full name: Stevie Ray Hamer.
HIGH SCHOOL: Middleton (Tenn.).
COLLEGE: Tennessee.
TRANSACTIONS/CAREER NOTES: Selected by Boston Celtics in second round (38th pick overall) of 1996 NBA Draft.

COLLEGIATE RECORD

Season Team	G	Min.	FGM	FGA	Pct.	FTM	FTA	Pct.	Reb.	Ast.	Pts.	RPG	APG	PPG
92-93—Tennessee	26	553	74	136	.544	33	52	.635	119	7	181	4.6	0.3	7.0
93-94—Tennessee	24	620	119	206	.578	93	116	.802	139	20	334	5.8	0.8	13.9
94-95—Tennessee	25	773	138	261	.529	98	153	.641	220	14	374	8.8	0.6	15.0
95-96—Tennessee	29	956	187	325	.575	155	252	.615	272	30	529	9.4	1.0	18.2
Totals	104	2902	518	928	.558	379	573	.661	750	71	1418	7.2	0.7	13.6

Three-point field goals: 1993-94, 3-for-11 (.273).

HARRINGTON, OTHELLA F ROCKETS

PERSONAL: Born January 31, 1974, in Jackson, Miss. ... 6-9/235.
HIGH SCHOOL: Murrah (Jackson, Miss.).
COLLEGE: Georgetown.
TRANSACTIONS/CAREER NOTES: Selected by Houston Rockets in second round (30th pick overall) of 1996 NBA Draft.

COLLEGIATE RECORD

Season Team	G	Min.	FGM	FGA	Pct.	FTM	FTA	Pct.	Reb.	Ast.	Pts.	RPG	APG	PPG
92-93—Georgetown	33	1075	205	358	.573	144	193	.746	291	32	554	8.8	1.0	16.8
93-94—Georgetown	31	897	152	276	.551	151	206	.733	248	36	455	8.0	1.2	14.7
94-95—Georgetown	31	767	132	236	.559	115	163	.706	187	25	379	6.0	0.8	12.2
95-96—Georgetown	37	983	161	288	.559	129	174	.741	257	44	451	6.9	1.2	12.2
Totals	132	3722	650	1158	.561	539	736	.732	983	137	1839	7.4	1.0	13.9

HARVEY, SHAWN G MAVERICKS

PERSONAL: Born December 31, 1973, in Philadelphia. ... 6-4/180.
HIGH SCHOOL: West Philadelphia.
JUNIOR COLLEGE: Essex Community College (Newark, N.J.).
COLLEGE: West Virginia State.
TRANSACTIONS/CAREER NOTES: Selected by Dallas Mavericks in second round (34th pick overall) of 1996 NBA Draft.

COLLEGIATE RECORD

Season Team	G	Min.	FGM	FGA	Pct.	FTM	FTA	Pct.	Reb.	Ast.	Pts.	RPG	APG	PPG
91-92—Essex C.C.	27	...	239	495	.483	82	109	.752	247	82	605	9.1	3.0	22.4
93-94—West Virginia State	26	...	226	509	.444	107	144	.743	142	68	601	5.5	2.6	23.1
94-95—West Virginia State	26	...	232	484	.479	130	163	.798	174	108	658	6.7	4.2	25.3
95-96—West Virginia State	26	947	256	578	.443	135	182	.742	256	120	716	9.8	4.6	27.5
Junior college totals	27	...	239	495	.483	82	109	.752	247	82	605	9.1	3.0	22.4
4-year-college totals	78		714	1571	.454	372	489	.761	572	296	1975	7.3	3.8	25.3

Three-point field goals: 1993-94, 42-for-129 (.326). 1994-95, 64-for-178 (.360). 1995-96, 69-for-214 (.322). Totals, 175-for-521 (.336).

HENDERSON, RONNIE G BULLETS

PERSONAL: Born March 29, 1974, in Gulfport, Miss. ... 6-4/206.
HIGH SCHOOL: Murrah (Jackson, Miss).
COLLEGE: Louisiana State.
TRANSACTIONS/CAREER NOTES: Selected after junior season by Washington Bullets in second round (55th pick overall) of 1996 NBA Draft.

COLLEGIATE RECORD

Season Team	G	Min.	FGM	FGA	Pct.	FTM	FTA	Pct.	Reb.	Ast.	Pts.	RPG	APG	PPG
93-94—Louisiana State	27	678	144	381	.378	69	97	.711	96	31	429	3.6	1.1	15.9
94-95—Louisiana State	27	977	219	511	.429	124	169	.734	142	59	630	5.3	2.2	23.3
95-96—Louisiana State	23	717	183	397	.461	87	127	.685	107	32	502	4.7	1.4	21.8
Totals	77	2372	546	1289	.424	280	393	.712	345	122	1561	4.5	1.6	20.3

Three-point field goals: 1993-94, 72-for-228 (.316). 1994-95, 68-for-212 (.321). 1995-96, 49-for-146 (.336). Totals, 189-for-586 (.323).

DID YOU KNOW...

...that Georgetown coach John Thompson was an expansion draft pick of the Chicago Bulls in 1966?

HENDRICKSON, MARK   F   76ERS

PERSONAL: Born June 23, 1974, in Mount Vernon, Wash. ... 6-9/220. ... Full name: Mark Allan Hendrickson.
HIGH SCHOOL: Mount Vernon (Wash.).
COLLEGE: Washington State.
TRANSACTIONS/CAREER NOTES: Selected by Philadelphia 76ers in second round (31st pick overall) of 1996 NBA Draft.

COLLEGIATE RECORD

Season Team	G	Min.	FGM	FGA	Pct.	FTM	FTA	Pct.	Reb.	Ast.	Pts.	RPG	APG	PPG
												AVERAGES		
92-93—Wash. State	27	927	119	214	.556	89	125	.712	217	50	339	8.0	1.9	12.6
93-94—Wash. State	28	889	96	198	.485	90	126	.714	222	46	294	7.9	1.6	10.5
94-95—Wash. State	30	991	183	292	.627	104	131	.794	269	38	484	9.0	1.3	16.1
95-96—Wash. State	23	763	127	222	.572	117	165	.709	219	37	379	9.5	1.6	16.5
Totals	108	3570	525	926	.567	400	547	.731	927	171	1496	8.6	1.6	13.9

Three-point field goals: 1992-93, 12-for-23 (.522). 1993-94, 12-for-35 (.343). 1994-95, 14-for-34 (.412). 1995-96, 8-for-31 (.258). Totals, 46-for-123 (.374).

ILGAUSKAS, ZYDRUNAS   C   CAVALIERS

PERSONAL: Born June 5, 1975, in Kaunas, Lithuania. ... 7-3/238. ... Name pronounced ZHEE-drew-nus ill-GAUS-kus.
TRANSACTIONS/CAREER NOTES: Played in Lithuania (1994-95). ... Selected by Cleveland Cavaliers in first round (20th pick overall) of 1996 NBA Draft.

LITHUANIAN LEAGUE RECORD

Season Team	G	Min.	FGM	FGA	Pct.	FTM	FTA	Pct.	Reb.	Ast.	Pts.	RPG	APG	PPG
												AVERAGES		
94-95—Atletas	36	...	303	504	.601	123	180	.683	460	26	731	12.8	0.7	20.3

IVERSON, ALLEN   G   76ERS

PERSONAL: Born June 7, 1975, in Hampton, Va. ... 6-0/165.
HIGH SCHOOL: Bethel (Hampton, Va.).
COLLEGE: Georgetown.
TRANSACTIONS/CAREER NOTES: Selected after sophomore season by Philadelphia 76ers in first round (first pick overall) of 1996 NBA Draft.

NOTES: The Sporting News All-America first-team (1996).

COLLEGIATE RECORD

Season Team	G	Min.	FGM	FGA	Pct.	FTM	FTA	Pct.	Reb.	Ast.	Pts.	RPG	APG	PPG
												AVERAGES		
94-95—Georgetown	30	966	203	520	.390	172	250	.688	99	134	613	3.3	4.5	20.4
95-96—Georgetown	37	1213	312	650	.480	215	317	.678	141	173	926	3.8	4.7	25.0
Totals	67	2179	515	1170	.440	387	567	.683	240	307	1539	3.6	4.6	23.0

Three-point field goals: 1994-95, 35-for-151 (.232). 1995-96, 87-for-238 (.366). Totals, 122-for-389 (.314).

JONES, DONTAE'   F   KNICKS

PERSONAL: Born June 2, 1975, in Nashville. ... 6-7/220. ... Full name: Dontae' Antijuaine Jones.
HIGH SCHOOL: Stratford (Nashville).
JUNIOR COLLEGE: Northeast Mississippi Community College (Booneville, Miss.).
COLLEGE: Mississippi State.
TRANSACTIONS/CAREER NOTES: Selected after junior season by New York Knicks in first round (21st pick overall) of 1996 NBA Draft.

COLLEGIATE RECORD

Season Team	G	Min.	FGM	FGA	Pct.	FTM	FTA	Pct.	Reb.	Ast.	Pts.	RPG	APG	PPG
												AVERAGES		
93-94—Northeast Miss. C.C.	29	841	291	574	.507	115	191	.602	326	34	731	11.2	1.2	25.2
94-95—Northeast Miss. C.C.	32	1024	352	711	.495	184	287	.641	425	77	917	13.3	2.4	28.7
95-96—Mississippi State	33	1007	198	418	.474	64	86	.744	225	63	484	6.8	1.9	14.7
Junior college totals	61	1865	643	1285	.500	299	478	.626	751	111	1648	12.3	1.8	27.0
4-year-college totals	33	1007	198	418	.474	64	86	.744	225	63	484	6.8	1.9	14.7

Three-point field goals: 1995-96, 24-for-81 (.296).

KITTLES, KERRY   G   NETS

PERSONAL: Born June 12, 1974, in Dayton, Ohio. ... 6-5/179.
HIGH SCHOOL: St. Augustine, (New Orleans).
COLLEGE: Villanova.
TRANSACTIONS/CAREER NOTES: Selected by New Jersey Nets in first round (eighth pick overall) of 1996 NBA Draft.

COLLEGIATE RECORD

NOTES: The Sporting News All-America first team (1996).

Season Team	G	Min.	FGM	FGA	Pct.	FTM	FTA	Pct.	Reb.	Ast.	Pts.	AVERAGES RPG	APG	PPG
92-93—Villanova	27	875	108	224	.482	37	55	.673	94	79	294	3.5	2.9	10.9
93-94—Villanova	32	1258	233	516	.452	91	129	.705	207	109	630	6.5	3.4	19.7
94-95—Villanova	33	1218	264	504	.524	92	120	.767	201	115	706	6.1	3.5	21.4
95-96—Villanova	30	1059	216	475	.455	103	145	.710	213	105	613	7.1	3.5	20.4
Totals	122	4410	821	1719	.478	323	449	.719	715	408	2243	5.9	3.3	18.4

Three-point field goals: 1992-93, 41-for-95 (.432). 1993-94, 73-for-209 (.349). 1994-95, 86-for-209 (.411). 1995-96, 78-for-193 (.404). Totals, 278-for-706 (.394).

KNIGHT, TRAVIS   C   LAKERS

PERSONAL: Born September 13, 1974, in Salt Lake City. ... 7-0/235. ... Full name: Travis James Knight.
HIGH SCHOOL: Alta (Sandy, Utah).
COLLEGE: Connecticut.
TRANSACTIONS/CAREER NOTES: Selected by Chicago Bulls in first round (29th pick overall) of 1996 NBA Draft. ... Draft rights renounced by Bulls (July 12, 1996). ... Signed as free agent by Los Angeles Lakers (July 31, 1996).

COLLEGIATE RECORD

Season Team	G	Min.	FGM	FGA	Pct.	FTM	FTA	Pct.	Reb.	Ast.	Pts.	AVERAGES RPG	APG	PPG
92-93—Connecticut	24	278	29	63	.460	11	27	.407	61	9	69	2.5	0.4	2.9
93-94—Connecticut	33	390	36	82	.439	9	18	.500	97	24	81	2.9	0.7	2.5
94-95—Connecticut	33	768	129	231	.558	41	63	.651	272	38	299	8.2	1.2	9.1
95-96—Connecticut	34	854	126	242	.521	59	85	.694	317	71	311	9.3	2.1	9.1
Totals	124	2290	320	618	.518	120	193	.622	747	142	760	6.0	1.1	6.1

Three-point field goals: 1992-93, 0-for-5.

LAUDERDALE, PRIEST   C   HAWKS

PERSONAL: Born August 31, 1973, in Chicago. ... 7-4/343.
HIGH SCHOOL: Carver (Chicago).
COLLEGE: Central State (Ohio).
TRANSACTIONS/CAREER NOTES: Selected by Atlanta Hawks in first round (28th pick overall) of 1996 NBA Draft. ... Played in Greece (1995-96).

COLLEGIATE RECORD

Season Team	G	Min.	FGM	FGA	Pct.	FTM	FTA	Pct.	Reb.	Ast.	Pts.	AVERAGES RPG	APG	PPG
93-94—Central State	13	...	121	177	.684	19	47	.404	132	16	261	10.2	1.2	20.1

Three-point field goals: 1993-94, 0-for-2.

GREEK LEAGUE RECORD

Season Team	G	Min.	FGM	FGA	Pct.	FTM	FTA	Pct.	Reb.	Ast.	Pts.	AVERAGES RPG	APG	PPG
95-96—Peristeri Nikas	23	...	160	226	.708	51	98	.520	258	32	371	11.2	1.4	16.1

LIVINGSTON, RANDY   G   ROCKETS

PERSONAL: Born April 2, 1975, in New Orleans. ... 6-4/209. ... Full name: Randy Anthony Livingston.
HIGH SCHOOL: Newman (New Orleans).
COLLEGE: Louisiana State.
TRANSACTIONS/CAREER NOTES: Selected after sophomore season by Houston Rockets in second round (42nd pick overall) of 1996 NBA Draft.

COLLEGIATE RECORD

Season Team	G	Min.	FGM	FGA	Pct.	FTM	FTA	Pct.	Reb.	Ast.	Pts.	AVERAGES RPG	APG	PPG
94-95—Louisiana State	16	550	81	185	.438	42	62	.677	64	151	224	4.0	9.4	14.0
95-96—Louisiana State	13	318	24	83	.289	30	38	.789	30	69	79	2.3	5.3	6.1
Totals	29	868	105	268	.392	72	100	.720	94	220	303	3.2	7.6	10.4

Three-point field goals: 1994-95, 20-for-65 (.308). 1995-96, 1-for-20 (.050). Totals, 21-for-85 (.247).

MANN, MARCUS   F   WARRIORS

PERSONAL: Born December 19, 1973, in Carthage, Miss. ... 6-8/245. ... Full name: Marcus Lashuan Mann.
HIGH SCHOOL: South Leake (Walnut Grove, Miss.).
JUNIOR COLLEGE: East Central Community College (Miss.).
COLLEGE: Mississippi Valley State.
TRANSACTIONS/CAREER NOTES: Selected by Golden State Warriors in second round (40th pick overall) of 1996 NBA Draft.

COLLEGIATE RECORD

NOTES: Led NCAA Division I with 13.8 rebounds per game (1996).

Season Team	G	Min.	FGM	FGA	Pct.	FTM	FTA	Pct.	Reb.	Ast.	Pts.	RPG	APG	PPG
													AVERAGES	
92-93—East Central C.C.	30	...	259	446	.581	96	151	.636	360	55	610	12.0	1.8	20.3
93-94—East Central C.C.	26	...	225	357	.630	104	152	.684	286	46	578	11.0	1.8	22.2
94-95—Miss. Valley St.	27	807	192	349	.550	68	114	.597	317	24	452	11.7	0.9	16.7
95-96—Miss. Valley St.	28	970	241	390	.618	122	192	.635	387	44	602	13.8	1.6	21.5
Junior college totals	56	...	484	803	.603	200	303	.660	646	101	1188	11.5	1.8	21.2
4-year-college totals	55	1777	433	739	.586	190	306	.621	704	68	1054	12.8	1.2	19.2

Three-point field goals: 1995-96, 1-for-2 (.500).

MARBURY, STEPHON　　　　　　G　　　　　　TIMBERWOLVES

PERSONAL: Born February 20, 1977, in Brooklyn, N.Y. ... 6-2/180.
HIGH SCHOOL: Abraham Lincoln (Brooklyn, N.Y.).
COLLEGE: Georgia Tech.
TRANSACTIONS/CAREER NOTES: Selected after freshman season by Milwaukee Bucks in first round (fourth pick overall) of 1996 NBA Draft. ... Draft rights traded by Bucks to Minnesota Timberwolves for draft rights to G Ray Allen (June 26, 1996).

COLLEGIATE RECORD

Season Team	G	Min.	FGM	FGA	Pct.	FTM	FTA	Pct.	Reb.	Ast.	Pts.	RPG	APG	PPG
													AVERAGES	
95-96—Georgia Tech	36	1345	235	514	.457	121	164	.738	113	161	679	3.1	4.5	18.9

Three-point field goals: 1995-96, 88-for-238 (.370).

McCARTY, WALTER　　　　　　F　　　　　　KNICKS

PERSONAL: Born February 1, 1974, in Evansville, Ind. ... 6-10/230. ... Full name: Walter Lee McCarty.
HIGH SCHOOL: Harrison (Evansville, Ind.).
COLLEGE: Kenutcky.
TRANSACTIONS/CAREER NOTES: Selected by New York Knicks in first round (19th pick overall) of 1996 NBA Draft.

COLLEGIATE RECORD
NOTES: Member of NCAA Division I championship team (1996).

Season Team	G	Min.	FGM	FGA	Pct.	FTM	FTA	Pct.	Reb.	Ast.	Pts.	RPG	APG	PPG
													AVERAGES	
92-93—Kentucky					Did not play—ineligible									
93-94—Kentucky	34	484	72	153	.471	31	56	.554	131	39	194	3.9	1.1	5.7
94-95—Kentucky	33	744	128	251	.510	61	84	.726	185	50	345	5.6	1.5	10.5
95-96—Kentucky	36	888	152	280	.543	75	104	.721	206	92	407	5.7	2.6	11.3
Totals	103	2116	352	684	.515	167	244	.684	522	181	946	5.1	1.8	9.2

Three-point field goals: 1993-94, 19-for-50 (.380). 1994-95, 28-for-77 (.364). 1995-96, 28-for-60 (.467). Totals, 75-for-187 (.401).

McCASKILL, AMAL　　　　　　F/C　　　　　　MAGIC

PERSONAL: Born October 28, 1973, in Maywood, Ill. ... 6-11/235. ... Full name: Amal Omari McCaskill.
HIGH SCHOOL: St. Joseph (Westchester, Ill).
COLLEGE: Marquette.
TRANSACTIONS/CAREER NOTES: Selected by Orlando Magic in second round (49th pick overall) of 1996 NBA Draft.

COLLEGIATE RECORD

Season Team	G	Min.	FGM	FGA	Pct.	FTM	FTA	Pct.	Reb.	Ast.	Pts.	RPG	APG	PPG
													AVERAGES	
91-92—Marquette.....................	15	120	9	25	.360	8	15	.533	47	5	26	3.1	0.3	1.7
92-93—Marquette.....................					Did not play—redshirted.									
93-94—Marquette.....................	33	363	62	91	.681	47	74	.635	108	17	171	3.3	0.5	5.2
94-95—Marquette.....................	33	924	134	262	.511	85	129	.659	279	26	354	8.5	0.8	10.7
95-96—Marquette.....................	30	796	123	224	.549	63	97	.649	266	38	310	8.9	1.3	10.3
Totals	111	2203	328	602	.545	203	315	.644	700	86	861	6.3	0.8	7.8

Three-point field goals: 1994-95, 1-for-3 (.333). 1995-96, 1-for-2 (.500). Totals, 2-for-5 (.400).

McINNIS, JEFF　　　　　　G　　　　　　NUGGETS

PERSONAL: Born October 22, 1974, in Charlotte. ... 6-4/190. ... Full name: Jeff Lemans McInnis.
HIGH SCHOOL: West Charlotte (Charlotte), then Oak Hill Academy (Mouth of Wilson, Va).
COLLEGE: North Carolina.
TRANSACTIONS/CAREER NOTES: Selected after junior season by Denver Nuggets in second round (37th pick overall) of 1996 NBA Draft.

COLLEGIATE RECORD

Season Team	G	Min.	FGM	FGA	Pct.	FTM	FTA	Pct.	Reb.	Ast.	Pts.	RPG	APG	PPG
													AVERAGES	
93-94—North Carolina...............	35	512	70	153	.458	30	47	.638	58	85	197	1.7	2.4	5.6
94-95—North Carolina...............	34	981	155	316	.491	66	99	.667	138	180	420	4.1	5.3	12.4
95-96—North Carolina...............	31	1067	178	409	.435	88	110	.800	81	170	511	2.6	5.5	16.5
Totals	100	2560	403	878	.459	184	256	.719	277	435	1128	2.8	4.4	11.3

Three-point field goals: 1993-94, 27-for-65 (.415). 1994-95, 44-for-112 (.393). 1995-96, 67-for-171 (.392). Totals, 138-for-348 (.397).

MILLARD, RUSS   F   SUNS

PERSONAL: Born March 1, 1973, in Cedar Rapids, Iowa. ... 6-8/240. ... Full name: Russ Dwayne Millard.
HIGH SCHOOL: Washington (Cedar Rapids, Iowa).
COLLEGE: Iowa.
TRANSACTIONS/CAREER NOTES: Selected by Phoenix Suns in second round (39th pick overall) of 1996 NBA Draft.

COLLEGIATE RECORD

Season Team	G	Min.	FGM	FGA	Pct.	FTM	FTA	Pct.	Reb.	Ast.	Pts.	AVERAGES RPG	APG	PPG
91-92—Iowa						Did not play—redshirted.								
92-93—Iowa	17	256	28	62	.452	29	43	.674	64	8	88	3.8	0.5	5.2
93-94—Iowa	27	604	108	213	.507	71	97	.732	142	36	302	5.3	1.3	11.2
94-95—Iowa	12	168	24	47	.511	10	17	.588	39	11	62	3.3	0.9	5.2
95-96—Iowa	32	861	151	248	.609	115	144	.799	225	29	439	7.0	0.9	13.7
Totals	88	1889	311	570	.546	225	301	.748	470	84	891	5.3	1.0	10.1

Three-point field goals: 1992-93, 3-for-8 (.375). 1993-94, 15-for-49 (.306). 1994-95, 4-for-13 (.308). 1995-96, 22-for-50 (.440). Totals, 44-for-120 (.367).

MINOR, RYAN   F   76ERS

PERSONAL: Born January 5, 1974, in Canton, Ohio. ... 6-7/220. ... Full name: Ryan Dale Minor.
HIGH SCHOOL: Hammon (Hammon, Okla.).
COLLEGE: Oklahoma.
TRANSACTIONS/CAREER NOTES: Selected by Philadelphia 76ers in second round (32nd pick overall) of 1996 NBA Draft.

COLLEGIATE RECORD

Season Team	G	Min.	FGM	FGA	Pct.	FTM	FTA	Pct.	Reb.	Ast.	Pts.	AVERAGES RPG	APG	PPG
92-93—Oklahoma	31	427	52	120	.433	32	48	.667	85	32	145	2.7	1.0	4.7
93-94—Oklahoma	25	761	148	297	.498	85	110	.773	184	45	406	7.4	1.8	16.2
94-95—Oklahoma	32	1168	260	535	.486	167	203	.823	269	68	756	8.4	2.1	23.6
95-96—Oklahoma	30	1112	217	521	.417	143	174	.822	229	79	639	7.6	2.6	21.3
Totals	118	3468	677	1473	.460	427	535	.798	767	224	1946	6.5	1.9	16.5

Three-point field goals: 1992-93, 9-for-21 (.429). 1993-94, 30-for-78 (.385). 1994-95, 69-for-176 (.392). 1995-96, 62-for-191 (.325). Totals, 170-for-466 (.365).

MUURSEPP, MARTIN   F   HEAT

PERSONAL: Born September 26, 1974, in Estonia. ... 6-9/235.
TRANSACTIONS/CAREER NOTES: Selected by Utah Jazz in first round (25th pick overall) of 1996 NBA Draft. ... Draft rights traded by Jazz to Miami Heat for future first-round draft choice (June 26, 1996). ... Played in Sweden (1991-92 and 1992-93) ... Played in Israel (1993-94 and 1994-95). ... Played in Estonia (1995-96).

NASH, STEVE   G   SUNS

PERSONAL: Born February 7, 1974, in Johannesburg, South Africa. ... 6-3/195. ... Full name: Stephen John Nash.
HIGH SCHOOL: St. Michael's Victoria (British, Columbia).
COLLEGE: Santa Clara.
TRANSACTIONS/CAREER NOTES: Selected by Phoenix Suns in first round (15th pick overall) of 1996 NBA Draft.

COLLEGIATE RECORD

Season Team	G	Min.	FGM	FGA	Pct.	FTM	FTA	Pct.	Reb.	Ast.	Pts.	AVERAGES RPG	APG	PPG
92-93—Santa Clara	31	743	78	184	.424	47	57	.825	79	67	252	2.5	2.2	8.1
93-94—Santa Clara	26	778	122	295	.414	69	83	.831	65	95	380	2.5	3.7	14.6
94-95—Santa Clara	27	902	164	369	.444	153	174	.879	102	174	565	3.8	6.4	20.9
95-96—Santa Clara	29	979	164	381	.430	101	113	.894	102	174	492	3.5	6.0	17.0
Totals	113	3402	528	1229	.430	370	427	.867	348	510	1689	3.1	4.5	14.9

Three-point field goals: 1992-93, 49-for-120 (.408). 1993-94, 67-for-168 (.399). 1994-95, 84-for-185 (.454). 1995-96, 63-for-183 (.344). Totals, 263-for-656 (.401).

DID YOU KNOW...

...that in 1984, the year the Chicago Bulls drafted Michael Jordan in the first round, they drafted track star Carl Lewis in the last round?

NORDGAARD, JEFF   F   BUCKS

PERSONAL: Born February 23, 1973, in Dawson, Minn. ... 6-7/226. ... Full name: Jeff Wallace Nordgaard.
HIGH SCHOOL: Dawson-Boyd (Dawson, Minn.).
COLLEGE: Wisconsin-Green Bay.
TRANSACTIONS/CAREER NOTES: Selected by Milwaukee Bucks in second round (53rd pick overall) of 1996 NBA Draft.

COLLEGIATE RECORD

Season Team	G	Min.	FGM	FGA	Pct.	FTM	FTA	Pct.	Reb.	Ast.	Pts.	AVERAGES RPG	APG	PPG
92-93—Wis.-Green Bay	27	271	75	148	.507	13	28	.464	77	29	166	2.9	1.1	6.1
93-94—Wis.-Green Bay	34	1028	207	351	.590	116	151	.768	217	71	531	6.4	2.1	15.6
94-95—Wis.-Green Bay	30	1070	214	391	.547	130	165	.788	224	69	559	7.5	2.3	18.6
95-96—Wis.-Green Bay	29	1154	277	500	.554	93	131	.710	183	68	655	6.3	2.3	22.6
Totals	120	3523	773	1390	.556	352	475	.741	701	237	1911	5.8	2.0	15.9

Three-point field goals: 1992-93, 3-for-6 (.500). 1993-94, 1-for-6 (.167). 1994-95, 1-for-6 (.167). 1995-96, 8-for-25 (.320). Totals, 13-for-43 (.302).

NORRIS, MOOCHIE   G   BUCKS

PERSONAL: Born July 27, 1973, in Washington, D.C. ... 6-1/175. ... Full name: Martyn Norris.
HIGH SCHOOL: Cardoza (Washington, D.C.).
JUNIOR COLLEGE: Odessa (Texas).
COLLEGE: Auburn, then West Florida.
TRANSACTIONS/CAREER NOTES: Selected by Milwaukee Bucks in second round (33rd pick overall) of 1996 NBA Draft.

COLLEGIATE RECORD

Season Team	G	Min.	FGM	FGA	Pct.	FTM	FTA	Pct.	Reb.	Ast.	Pts.	AVERAGES RPG	APG	PPG
92-93—Odessa J.C.	32	...	160	290	.552	121	171	.708	91	225	459	2.8	7.0	14.3
93-94—Odessa J.C.	27	...	147	264	.557	83	120	.692	104	214	401	3.9	7.9	14.9
94-95—Auburn	29	1019	124	312	.397	58	83	.699	116	143	363	4.0	4.9	12.5
95-96—West Florida	16	615	121	265	.457	86	113	.761	92	143	378	5.8	8.9	23.6
Junior college totals	59	...	307	554	.554	204	291	.701	195	439	860	3.3	7.4	14.6
4-year-college totals	45	1634	245	577	.425	144	196	.735	208	286	741	4.6	6.4	16.5

Three-point field goals:1994-95, 57-for-161 (.354). 1995-96, 50-for-118 (.424). Totals, 107-for-279 (.384).

O'NEAL, JERMAINE   F/C   TRAIL BLAZERS

PERSONAL: Born October 13, 1978. ... 6-11/226.
HIGH SCHOOL: Eau Claire (Columbia, S.C.).
COLLEGE: Did not attend college.
TRANSACTIONS/CAREER NOTES: Selected out of high school by Portland Trail Blazers in first round (17th pick overall) of 1996 NBA Draft.

POPE, MARK   F   PACERS

PERSONAL: Born September 11, 1972, in Omaha, Neb. ... 6-10/235. ... Full name: Mark Edward Pope.
HIGH SCHOOL: Newport (Bellevue, Wash.).
COLLEGE: Washington, then Kentucky.
TRANSACTIONS/CAREER NOTES: Selected by Indiana Pacers in second round (52nd pick overall) of 1996 NBA Draft.

COLLEGIATE RECORD
NOTES: Member of NCAA Division I championship team (1996).

Season Team	G	Min.	FGM	FGA	Pct.	FTM	FTA	Pct.	Reb.	Ast.	Pts.	AVERAGES RPG	APG	PPG
91-92—Washington	29	872	110	190	.579	74	92	.804	234	58	300	8.1	2.0	10.3
92-93—Washington	27	868	106	201	.527	112	130	.862	217	34	329	8.0	1.3	12.2
93-94—Kentucky						Did not play-transfer student.								
94-95—Kentucky	33	728	89	173	.514	72	99	.727	207	29	271	6.3	0.9	8.2
95-96—Kentucky	36	716	94	195	.482	71	104	.683	187	37	275	5.2	1.0	7.6
Totals	125	3184	399	759	.527	329	425	.774	845	158	1175	6.8	1.3	9.4

Three-point field goals: 1991-92, 21-for-44 (.477). 1992-93, 5-for-20 (.250). 1994-95, 21-for-44 (.477). 1995-96, 16-for-45 (.356). Totals, 63-for-153 (.412).

POTAPENKO, VITALY   C/F   CAVALIERS

PERSONAL: Born March 21, 1975, in Kiev, Ukraine. ... 6-10/280. ... Full name: Vitaly Nikolaevich Potapenko. ... Name pronounced VEE-tal-lee poe-TAH-pen-koe.
COLLEGE: Wright State.
TRANSACTIONS/CAREER NOTES: Selected after junior season by Cleveland Cavaliers in first round (12th pick overall) of 1996 NBA Draft.

Season Team	G	Min.	FGM	FGA	Pct.	FTM	FTA	Pct.	Reb.	Ast.	Pts.	AVERAGES RPG	APG	PPG
94-95—Wright State	30	900	212	352	.602	151	206	.733	193	41	575	6.4	1.4	19.2
95-96—Wright State	25	807	197	322	.612	139	195	.713	182	36	534	7.3	1.4	21.4
Totals	55	1707	409	674	.607	290	401	.723	375	77	1109	6.8	1.4	20.2

Three-point field goals: 1995-96, 1-for-6 (.167).

RENTZIAS, EFTHIMIOS   C   NUGGETS

PERSONAL: Born January 11, 1976, in Trikala, Greece. ... 6-11/243. ... Name pronounced Ah-thee-ME-os Ren-SEE-us.
TRANSACTIONS/CAREER NOTES: Selected by Denver Nuggets in first round (23rd pick overall) of 1996 NBA Draft.

GREEK LEAGUE RECORD

Season Team	G	Min.	FGM	FGA	Pct.	FTM	FTA	Pct.	Reb.	Ast.	Pts.	AVERAGES RPG	APG	PPG
94-95—PAOK	32	...	44	84	.524	22	32	.688	109	7	110	3.4	0.2	3.4
95-96—PAOK	35	...	111	199	.558	58	82	.707	191	14	274	5.5	0.4	7.8
Totals	67	...	155	283	.548	80	114	.702	300	21	384	4.5	0.3	5.7

RILEY, RON   G/F   PISTONS

PERSONAL: Born December 27, 1973, in Las Vegas. ... 6-5/205.
HIGH SCHOOL: Clark (Las Vegas).
COLLEGE: Arizona State.
TRANSACTIONS/CAREER NOTES: Selected by Seattle SuperSonics in second round (47th pick overall) of 1996 NBA Draft. ... Draft rights traded by SuperSonics to Detroit Pistons for 1997 second-round draft choice (June 28, 1996).

COLLEGIATE RECORD

Season Team	G	Min.	FGM	FGA	Pct.	FTM	FTA	Pct.	Reb.	Ast.	Pts.	AVERAGES RPG	APG	PPG
92-93—Arizona State	28	696	134	377	.355	31	47	.660	98	51	365	3.5	1.8	13.0
93-94—Arizona State	28	908	139	383	.363	61	91	.670	139	71	398	5.0	2.5	14.2
94-95—Arizona State	33	997	192	437	.439	64	86	.744	176	48	528	5.3	1.5	16.0
95-96—Arizona State	27	900	186	478	.389	113	157	.720	166	69	543	6.1	2.6	20.1
Totals	116	3501	651	1675	.389	269	381	.706	579	239	1834	5.0	2.1	15.8

Three-point field goals: 1992-93, 66-for-217 (.304). 1993-94, 59-for-194 (.304). 1994-95, 80-for-222 (.360). 1995-96, 58-for-198 (.293). Totals, 263-for-831 (.316).

ROBINSON, CHRIS   G   GRIZZLIES

PERSONAL: Born April 2, 1974, in Columbus, Ga. ... 6-5/205. ... Full name: Christopher Sean Robinson.
HIGH SCHOOL: Southwest (Macon, Ga).
COLLEGE: Western Kentucky.
TRANSACTIONS/CAREER NOTES: Selected by Vancouver Grizzlies in second round (51st pick overall) of 1996 NBA Draft.

COLLEGIATE RECORD

Season Team	G	Min.	FGM	FGA	Pct.	FTM	FTA	Pct.	Reb.	Ast.	Pts.	AVERAGES RPG	APG	PPG
92-93—Western Ky.	32	574	89	175	.509	41	64	.641	110	37	235	3.4	1.2	7.3
93-94—Western Ky.	31	954	187	391	.478	49	68	.721	178	63	457	5.7	2.0	14.7
94-95—Western Ky.	31	951	203	448	.453	86	121	.711	207	68	527	6.7	2.2	17.0
95-96—Western Ky.	26	860	163	358	.455	81	120	.675	161	61	437	6.2	2.3	16.8
Totals	120	3339	642	1372	.468	257	373	.689	656	229	1656	5.5	1.9	13.8

Three-point field goals: 1992-93, 16-for-52 (.308). 1993-94, 34-for-93 (.366). 1994-95, 35-for-110 (.318). 1995-96, 30-for-101 (.297). Totals, 115-for-356 (.323).

ROBINSON, DARNELL   C   MAVERICKS

PERSONAL: Born May 30, 1974, in Oakland. ... 6-11/270. ... Full name: Darnell Lamont Robinson.
HIGH SCHOOL: Emery (Oakland).
COLLEGE: Arkansas.
TRANSACTIONS/CAREER NOTES: Selected after junior season by Dallas Mavericks in second round (58th pick overall) of 1996 NBA Draft.

COLLEGIATE RECORD

NOTES: Member of NCAA Division I championship team (1994).

Season Team	G	Min.	FGM	FGA	Pct.	FTM	FTA	Pct.	Reb.	Ast.	Pts.	AVERAGES RPG	APG	PPG
93-94—Arkansas	27	479	84	184	.457	30	52	.577	127	50	205	4.7	1.9	7.6
94-95—Arkansas	37	528	97	236	.411	28	63	.444	140	35	236	3.8	0.9	6.4
95-96—Arkansas	20	499	102	223	.457	42	79	.532	140	18	253	7.0	0.9	12.7
Totals	84	1506	283	643	.440	100	194	.515	407	103	694	4.8	1.2	8.3

Three-point field goals: 1993-94, 7-for-23 (.304). 1994-95, 14-for-40 (.350). 1995-96, 7-for-22 (.318). Totals, 28-for-85 (.329).

ROGERS, ROY   F   GRIZZLIES

PERSONAL: Born August 19, 1973, in Linden, Ala. ... 6-10/235. ... Full name: Roy Rogers Jr.
HIGH SCHOOL: Linden (Linden, Ala.).
COLLEGE: Alabama.
TRANSACTIONS/CAREER NOTES: Selected by Vancouver Grizzlies in first round (22nd pick overall) of 1996 NBA Draft.

COLLEGIATE RECORD

Season Team	G	Min.	FGM	FGA	Pct.	FTM	FTA	Pct.	Reb.	Ast.	Pts.	RPG	APG	PPG
91-92—Alabama					Did not play—redshirted.									
92-93—Alabama	14	155	16	31	.516	3	6	.500	32	4	35	2.3	0.3	2.5
93-94—Alabama	23	275	27	55	.491	15	22	.682	63	2	69	2.7	0.1	3.0
94-95—Alabama	33	479	47	93	.505	21	38	.553	120	19	115	3.6	0.6	3.5
95-96—Alabama	32	1173	186	355	.524	61	98	.622	299	30	433	9.3	0.9	13.5
Totals	102	2082	276	534	.517	100	164	.610	514	55	652	5.0	0.5	6.4

ROSE, MALIK   F   HORNETS

PERSONAL: Born November 23, 1974, in Philadelphia. ... 6-7/250. ... Full name: Malik Jabari Rose.
HIGH SCHOOL: Overbrook (Philadelphia).
COLLEGE: Drexel.
TRANSACTIONS/CAREER NOTES: Selected by Charlotte Hornets in second round (44th pick overall) of 1996 NBA Draft.

COLLEGIATE RECORD

Season Team	G	Min.	FGM	FGA	Pct.	FTM	FTA	Pct.	Reb.	Ast.	Pts.	RPG	APG	PPG
92-93—Drexel	29	820	144	287	.502	107	190	.563	330	10	395	11.4	0.3	13.6
93-94—Drexel	30	875	154	296	.520	110	202	.545	371	20	418	12.4	0.7	13.9
94-95—Drexel	30	984	216	384	.563	152	213	.714	404	36	584	13.5	1.2	19.5
95-96—Drexel	31	972	219	368	.595	182	255	.714	409	53	627	13.2	1.7	20.2
Totals	120	3651	733	1335	.549	551	860	.641	1514	119	2024	12.6	1.0	16.9

Three-point field goals: 1994-95, 0-for-3. 1995-96, 7-for-21 (.333). Totals, 7-for-24 (.292).

SASSER, JASON   F   TRAIL BLAZERS

PERSONAL: Born January 13, 1974, in Denton, Texas. ... 6-7/225. ... Full name: Jason Jermane Sasser.
HIGH SCHOOL: Kimball (Dallas).
COLLEGE: Texas Tech.
TRANSACTIONS/CAREER NOTES: Selected by Sacramento Kings in second round (41st pick overall) of 1996 NBA Draft.
... Draft rights traded by Kings to Portland Trail Blazers for undisclosed future considerations (June 27, 1996).

COLLEGIATE RECORD

Season Team	G	Min.	FGM	FGA	Pct.	FTM	FTA	Pct.	Reb.	Ast.	Pts.	RPG	APG	PPG
92-93—Texas Tech	30	729	118	272	.434	66	105	.629	154	48	319	5.1	1.6	10.6
93-94—Texas Tech	28	1032	205	425	.482	149	210	.710	264	81	576	9.4	2.9	20.6
94-95—Texas Tech	30	1024	211	414	.510	169	213	.793	235	88	602	7.8	2.9	20.1
95-96—Texas Tech	31	1071	202	441	.458	170	234	.727	242	90	605	7.8	2.9	19.5
Totals	119	3856	736	1552	.474	554	762	.727	895	307	2102	7.5	2.6	17.7

Three-point field goals: 1992-93, 17-for-54 (.315). 1993-94, 17-for-70 (.243). 1994-95, 11-for-42 (.262). 1995-96, 31-for-101 (.307). Totals, 76-for-267 (.285).

SHEFFER, DORON   G   CLIPPERS

PERSONAL: Born March 12, 1972, in Petch-Tikra, Israel. ... 6-5/197.
COLLEGE: Connecticut.
TRANSACTIONS/CAREER NOTES: Played in Israel (1991-92 and 1992-93). ... Selected by Los Angeles Clippers in second round (36th pick overall) of 1996 NBA Draft. ... Signed to play with Maccabi Tel Aviv (Israel) during 1996-97 season.

COLLEGIATE RECORD

Season Team	G	Min.	FGM	FGA	Pct.	FTM	FTA	Pct.	Reb.	Ast.	Pts.	RPG	APG	PPG
93-94—Connecticut	34	1036	141	279	.505	72	89	.809	128	164	404	3.8	4.8	11.9
94-95—Connecticut	33	951	121	302	.401	85	113	.752	155	183	365	4.7	5.5	11.1
95-96—Connecticut	35	1006	182	423	.430	101	119	.849	169	212	560	4.8	6.1	16.0
Totals	102	2993	444	1004	.442	258	321	.804	452	559	1329	4.4	5.5	13.0

Three-point field goals: 1993-94, 50-for-123 (.407). 1994-95, 38-for-104 (.365). 1995-96, 95-for-234 (.406). Totals, 183-461 (.397).

DID YOU KNOW...

...that in the 12 years of the NBA draft lottery, Utah is the only team not to make a lottery selection?

STOJAKOVIC, PREDRAG   F/G   KINGS

PERSONAL: Born June 9, 1977, in Belgrade, Yugoslavia. ... 6-9/229.
TRANSACTIONS/CAREER NOTES: Selected by Sacramento Kings in first round (14th pick overall) of 1996 NBA Draft.

GREEK LEAGUE RECORD

Season Team	G	Min.	FGM	FGA	Pct.	FTM	FTA	Pct.	Reb.	Ast.	Pts.	RPG	APG	PPG
95-96—PAOK	31	...	185	343	.539	115	145	.793	159	47	523	5.1	1.5	16.9

VOGEL, JOE   F/C   SUPERSONICS

PERSONAL: Born September 15, 1973, in North Platte, Neb. ... 6-11/255.
HIGH SCHOOL: North Platte (Neb.).
COLLEGE: Colorado State.
TRANSACTIONS/CAREER NOTES: Selected by Seattle SuperSonics in second round (45th pick overall) of 1996 NBA Draft.

COLLEGIATE RECORD

Season Team	G	Min.	FGM	FGA	Pct.	FTM	FTA	Pct.	Reb.	Ast.	Pts.	RPG	APG	PPG
92-93—Colorado State	29	274	53	120	.442	25	41	.610	60	...	133	2.1	...	4.6
93-94—Colorado State	28	650	99	222	.446	32	58	.552	110	...	239	2.1	...	4.6
94-95—Colorado State	31	721	113	251	.450	71	101	.770	165	...	301	5.3	...	9.7
95-96—Colorado State	27	754	111	227	.489	60	83	.743	179	...	285	6.6	...	10.6
Totals	115	2399	376	820	.459	188	283	.664	514	...	958	4.5		8.3

Three-point field goals: 1992-93, 2-for-5 (.400). 1993-94, 9-for-28 (.321). 1994-95, 4-for-9 (.444). 1995-96, 3-for-6 (.500). Totals, 18-for-48 (.375).

WALKER, ANTOINE   F   CELTICS

PERSONAL: Born August 12, 1976, in Chicago. ... 6-8/224. ... Full name: Antoine Devon Walker.
HIGH SCHOOL: Mt. Carmel (Chicago).
COLLEGE: Kentucky.
TRANSACTIONS/CAREER NOTES: Selected after sophomore season by Boston Celtics in first round (sixth pick overall) of 1996 NBA Draft.

COLLEGIATE RECORD

NOTES: Member of NCAA Division I championship team (1996).

Season Team	G	Min.	FGM	FGA	Pct.	FTM	FTA	Pct.	Reb.	Ast.	Pts.	RPG	APG	PPG
94-95—Kentucky	33	479	95	227	.419	52	73	.712	148	47	259	4.5	1.4	7.8
95-96—Kentucky	36	971	228	492	.463	82	130	.631	302	104	547	8.4	2.9	15.2
Totals	69	1450	323	719	.449	134	203	.660	450	151	806	6.5	2.2	11.7

Three-point field goals: 1994-95, 17-for-55 (.309). 1995-96, 9-for-48 (.188). Totals, 26-for-103 (.252).

WALKER, SAMAKI   F   MAVERICKS

PERSONAL: Born February 25, 1976, in Columbus, Ohio. ... 6-9/240. ... Full name: Samaki Ijuma Walker.
HIGH SCHOOL: Whitehall (Columbus, Ohio).
COLLEGE: Louisville.
TRANSACTIONS/CAREER NOTES: Selected after sophomore season by Dallas Mavericks in first round (ninth pick overall) of 1996 NBA Draft.

COLLEGIATE RECORD

Season Team	G	Min.	FGM	FGA	Pct.	FTM	FTA	Pct.	Reb.	Ast.	Pts.	RPG	APG	PPG
94-95—Louisville	29	841	153	279	.548	88	164	.537	210	37	396	7.2	1.3	13.7
95-96—Louisville	21	634	124	207	.599	70	114	.614	157	23	318	7.5	1.1	15.1
Totals	50	1475	277	486	.570	158	278	.568	367	60	714	7.3	1.2	14.3

Three-point field goals: 1994-95, 2-for-6 (.333). 1995-96, 0-for-1. Totals, 2-for-7 (.286).

WALLACE, JOHN   F   KNICKS

PERSONAL: Born February 9, 1974, in Rochester, N.Y. ... 6-8/225.
HIGH SCHOOL: Greece-Athena (Rochester, N.Y.).
COLLEGE: Syracuse.
TRANSACTIONS/CAREER NOTES: Selected by New York Knicks in first round (18th pick overall) of 1996 NBA Draft.

COLLEGIATE RECORD

NOTES: THE SPORTING NEWS All-America second team (1996).

Season Team	G	Min.	FGM	FGA	Pct.	FTM	FTA	Pct.	Reb.	Ast.	Pts.	RPG	APG	PPG
92-93—Syracuse	29	839	130	247	.526	61	85	.718	221	38	321	7.6	1.3	11.1
93-94—Syracuse	30	979	164	290	.566	121	159	.761	270	50	449	9.0	1.7	15.0
94-95—Syracuse	30	990	197	335	.588	106	156	.679	245	77	504	8.2	2.6	16.8
95-96—Syracuse	38	1379	293	599	.489	222	291	.763	329	90	845	8.7	2.4	22.2
Totals	127	4187	784	1471	.533	510	691	.738	1065	255	2119	8.4	2.0	16.7

Three-point field goals: 1992-93, 0-for-1. 1993-94, 0-for-2. 1994-95, 4-for-14 (.286). 1995-96, 37-for-88 (.420). Totals, 41-for-105 (.390).

WILLIAMS, JEROME   F   PISTONS

PERSONAL: Born May 10, 1973, in Washington, D.C. ... 6-9/206.
HIGH SCHOOL: Magruder (Germantown, Md.).
JUNIOR COLLEGE: Montgomery College (Md.).
COLLEGE: Georgetown.
TRANSACTIONS/CAREER NOTES: Selected by Detroit Pistons in first round (26th pick overall) of 1996 NBA Draft.

COLLEGIATE RECORD

Season Team	G	Min.	FGM	FGA	Pct.	FTM	FTA	Pct.	Reb.	Ast.	Pts.	RPG	APG	PPG
92-93—Montgomery College......						Statistics unavailable.								
93-94—Montgomery College......						Statistics unavailable.								
94-95—Georgetown...................	31	939	126	252	.500	83	132	.629	310	45	337	10.0	1.5	10.9
95-96—Georgetown...................	37	1016	147	250	.588	85	133	.639	324	51	380	8.8	1.4	10.3
Totals	68	1955	273	502	.544	168	265	.634	634	96	717	9.3	1.4	10.5

Three-point field goals: 1994-95, 2-for-11 (.182). 1995-96, 1-for-7 (.143). Totals, 3-for-18 (.167).

WRIGHT, LORENZEN   F   CLIPPERS

PERSONAL: Born November 4, 1975, in Memphis. ... 6-11/225. ... Full name: Lorenzen Vern-Gagne Wright.
HIGH SCHOOL: Booker T. Washington (Memphis).
COLLEGE: Memphis.
TRANSACTIONS/CAREER NOTES: Selected after sophomore season by Los Angeles Clippers in first round (seventh pick overall) of 1996 NBA Draft.

COLLEGIATE RECORD

Season Team	G	Min.	FGM	FGA	Pct.	FTM	FTA	Pct.	Reb.	Ast.	Pts.	RPG	APG	PPG
94-95—Memphis	34	1170	198	353	.561	107	171	.626	345	50	503	10.1	1.5	14.8
95-96—Memphis	30	1056	207	382	.542	109	169	.645	313	35	523	10.4	1.2	17.4
Totals	64	2226	405	735	.551	216	340	.635	658	85	1026	10.3	1.3	16.0

Three-point field goals: 1994-95, 0-for-1. 1995-96, 0-for-1. Totals, 0-for-2.

PROMISING NEWCOMERS

HEAD COACHES

ADELMAN, RICK   WARRIORS

PERSONAL: Born June 16, 1946, in Lynwood, Calif. ... 6-2/180. ... Full name: Richard Leonard Adelman. ... Name pronounced ADD-el-mun.
HIGH SCHOOL: St. Pius X (Downey, Calif.).
COLLEGE: Loyola Marymount.
TRANSACTIONS/CAREER NOTES: Selected by San Diego Rockets in seventh round (79th pick overall) of 1968 NBA Draft. ... Selected by Portland Trail Blazers from Rockets in NBA expansion draft (May 11, 1970). ... Traded by Trail Blazers to Chicago Bulls for cash and 1974 second-round draft choice (September 14, 1973). ... Traded by Bulls to New Orleans Jazz for F/C John Block (November 11, 1974). ... Traded by Jazz with F Ollie Johnson to Kansas City/Omaha Kings for F Nate Williams (February 1, 1975). ... Kings franchise moved from Kansas City/Omaha to Kansas City for 1975-76 season. ... Released by Kings (October 21, 1975).

COLLEGIATE RECORD

Season Team	G	Min.	FGM	FGA	Pct.	FTM	FTA	Pct.	Reb.	Ast.	Pts.	RPG	APG	PPG
64-65—Loyola (Calif.)‡						Freshman team statistics unavailable.								
65-66—Loyola (Calif.)	26	...	149	376	.396	129	152	.849	113	...	427	4.3	...	16.4
66-67—Loyola (Calif.)	25	...	151	349	.433	171	214	.799	124	...	473	5.0	...	18.9
67-68—Loyola (Calif.)	25	...	177	420	.421	171	216	.792	127	...	525	5.1	...	21.0
Varsity totals	76	...	477	1145	.417	471	582	.809	364	...	1425	4.8	...	18.8

NBA REGULAR-SEASON RECORD

Season Team	G	Min.	FGM	FGA	Pct.	FTM	FTA	Pct.	Reb.	Ast.	PF	Dq.	Pts.	RPG	APG	PPG
68-69—San Diego	77	1448	177	449	.394	131	204	.642	216	238	158	1	485	2.8	3.1	6.3
69-70—San Diego	35	717	96	247	.389	68	91	.747	81	113	90	0	260	2.3	3.2	7.4
70-71—Portland	81	2303	378	895	.422	267	369	.724	282	380	214	2	1023	3.5	4.7	12.6
71-72—Portland	80	2445	329	753	.437	151	201	.751	229	413	209	2	808	2.9	5.2	10.1
72-73—Portland	76	1822	214	525	.408	73	102	.716	157	294	155	2	591	2.1	3.9	7.8

									REBOUNDS							AVERAGES		
Season Team	G	Min.	FGM	FGA	Pct.	FTM	FTA	Pct.	Off.	Def.	Tot.	Ast.	St.	Blk.	TO	Pts.	RPG	APG	PPG
73-74—Chicago	55	618	64	170	.376	54	76	.711	16	53	69	56	36	1	...	182	1.3	1.0	3.3
74-75—Ch-NO-KC/O	58	1074	123	291	.423	73	103	.709	25	70	95	112	70	8	...	319	1.6	1.9	5.5
Totals	462	10427	1381	3330	.415	817	1146	.713	...	...	1129	1606	106	9	...	3668	2.4	3.5	7.9

Personal fouls/disqualifications: 1973-74, 63/0. 1974-75, 101/1. Totals, 990/8.

NBA PLAYOFF RECORD

Season Team	G	Min.	FGM	FGA	Pct.	FTM	FTA	Pct.	Reb.	Ast.	PF	Dq.	Pts.	RPG	APG	PPG
68-69—San Diego	6	187	24	53	.453	22	37	.595	15	29	18	0	70	2.5	4.8	11.7

									REBOUNDS							AVERAGES		
Season Team	G	Min.	FGM	FGA	Pct.	FTM	FTA	Pct.	Off.	Def.	Tot.	Ast.	St.	Blk.	TO	Pts.	RPG	APG	PPG
73-74—Chicago	9	108	16	34	.471	7	11	.636	1	9	10	7	7	0	...	39	1.1	0.8	4.3
74-75—K.C./Omaha	6	34	3	9	.333	6	8	.750	1	1	2	3	1	0	...	12	0.3	0.5	2.0
Totals	21	329	43	96	.448	35	56	.625	...	...	27	39	8	0	...	121	1.3	1.9	5.8

Personal fouls/disqualifications: 1973-74, 5/0. 1974-75, 9/0. Totals, 32/0.

HEAD COACHING RECORD
BACKGROUND: Head coach, Chemeketa Community College, Ore. (1977-78 through 1982-83; record: 141-39, .783). ... Assistant coach, Portland Trail Blazers (1983-84 to February 18, 1989).

NBA COACHING RECORD

	REGULAR SEASON				PLAYOFFS		
Season Team	W	L	Pct.	Finish	W	L	Pct.
88-89 —Portland	14	21	.400	5th/Pacific Division	0	3	.000
89-90 —Portland	59	23	.720	2nd/Pacific Division	12	9	.571
90-91 —Portland	63	19	.768	1st/Pacific Division	9	7	.563
91-92 —Portland	57	25	.695	1st/Pacific Division	13	8	.619
92-93 —Portland	51	31	.622	3rd/Pacific Division	1	3	.250
93-94 —Portland	47	35	.573	4th/Pacific Division	1	3	.250
95-96 —Golden State	36	46	.439	6th/Pacific Division	—	—	—
Totals (7 years)	327	200	.620	**Totals (6 years)**	36	33	.522

NOTES:
1989—Replaced Mike Schuler as Portland head coach (February 18), with record of 25-22. Lost to Los Angeles Lakers in Western Conference first round.
1990—Defeated Dallas, 3-0, in Western Conference first round; defeated San Antonio, 4-3, in Western Conference semifinals; defeated Phoenix, 4-2, in Western Conference finals; lost to Detroit, 4-1, in NBA Finals.
1991—Defeated Seattle, 3-2, in Western Conference first round; defeated Utah, 4-1, in Western Conference semifinals; lost to Los Angeles Lakers, 4-2, in Western Conference finals.
1992—Defeated Los Angeles Lakers, 3-1, in Western Conference first round; defeated Phoenix, 4-1, in Western Conference semifinals; defeated Utah, 4-2, in Western Conference finals; lost to Chicago, 4-2, in NBA Finals.
1993—Lost to San Antonio in Western Conference first round.
1994—Lost to Houston in Western Conference first round.

BICKERSTAFF, BERNIE — NUGGETS

PERSONAL: Born February 11, 1944, in Benham, Ky. ... 6-3/185. ... Full name: Bernard Tyrone Bickerstaff.
HIGH SCHOOL: East Benham (Benham, Ky.).
COLLEGE: Rio Grande (Ohio), then San Diego.

COLLEGIATE RECORD

Season Team	G	Min.	FGM	FGA	Pct.	FTM	FTA	Pct.	Reb.	Ast.	Pts.	RPG	APG	PPG
64-65—San Diego	26	...	78	211	.370	46	91	.506	135	...	202	5.2	...	7.8
65-66—San Diego	28	...	88	249	.353	82	116	.707	201	...	248	7.2	...	8.9
Totals	54	...	166	460	.361	128	207	.618	336	...	450	6.2	...	8.3

HEAD COACHING RECORD

BACKGROUND: Assistant coach, University of San Diego (1967-68 and 1968-69). ... Assistant coach, Capital Bullets of NBA (1973-74). ... Assistant coach, Washington Bullets (1974-75 through 1984-85). ... Vice president/general manager, Denver Nuggets (July 1990 through 1995-96). ... President, Nuggets (1996-97 season).

COLLEGIATE COACHING RECORD

Season Team	W	L	Pct.	Finish
69-70 —San Diego	14	12	.538	Division II Independent
70-71 —San Diego	10	14	.417	Division II Independent
71-72 —San Diego	12	14	.462	Division II Independent
72-73 —San Diego	19	9	.679	Division II Independent
Totals (4 years)	55	49	.529	

NBA COACHING RECORD

	REGULAR SEASON				PLAYOFFS		
Season Team	W	L	Pct.	Finish	W	L	Pct.
85-86 —Seattle	31	51	.378	5th/Pacific Division			
86-87 —Seattle	39	43	.476	4th/Pacific Division	7	7	.500
87-88 —Seattle	44	38	.537	3rd/Pacific Division	2	3	.400
88-89 —Seattle	47	35	.573	3rd/Pacific Division	3	5	.375
89-90 —Seattle	41	41	.500	4th/Pacific Division	—	—	—
94-95 —Denver	20	12	.625	4th/Midwest Division	0	3	.000
95-96 —Denver	35	47	.427	4th/Midwest Division	—	—	—
Totals (7 years)	257	267	.490	Totals (4 years)	12	18	.400

NOTES:
1987—Defeated Dallas, 3-1, in Western Conference first round; defeated Houston, 4-2, in Western Conference semifinals; lost to Los Angeles Lakers, 4-0, in Western Conference finals.
1988—Lost to Denver in Western Conference first round.
1989—Defeated Houston, 3-1, in Western Conference first round; lost to Los Angeles Lakers, 4-0, in Western Conference semifinals.
1995—Replaced Dan Issel (18-16) and Gene Littles (interim head coach, 3-13) as Denver head coach (February 20), with record of 21-29 and club in fourth place. Lost to San Antonio in Western Conference first round.

BROWN, LARRY — PACERS

PERSONAL: Born September 14, 1940, in Brooklyn, N.Y. ... 5-9/160. ... Full name: Lawrence Harvey Brown.
HIGH SCHOOL: Long Beach (N.Y.).
COLLEGE: North Carolina.
TRANSACTIONS/CAREER NOTES: Signed by New Orleans Buccaneers of American Basketball Association (1967). ... Traded by Buccaneers with F/G Doug Moe to Oakland Oaks for F Steve Jones, F Ron Franz and G Barry Leibowitz (June 18, 1968). ... Oaks franchise moved from Oakland to Washington and renamed Capitols for 1969-70 season. ... Capitols franchise moved from Washington to Virginia and renamed Squires for 1970-71 season. ... Contract sold by Squires to Denver Rockets (January 23, 1971).
MISCELLANEOUS: Member of gold-medal-winning U.S. Olympic team (1964).

COLLEGIATE RECORD

Season Team	G	Min.	FGM	FGA	Pct.	FTM	FTA	Pct.	Reb.	Ast.	Pts.	RPG	APG	PPG
59-60—North Carolina‡	15	...	88	...	...	100	143	.699	...	...	276	...	...	18.4
60-61—North Carolina	18	...	28	54	.519	25	34	.735	28	...	81	1.6	...	4.5
61-62—North Carolina	17	...	90	204	.441	101	127	.795	52	...	281	3.1	...	16.5
62-63—North Carolina	21	...	102	231	.442	95	122	.779	50	...	299	2.4	...	14.2
Varsity totals	56	...	220	489	.450	221	283	.781	130	...	661	2.3	...	11.8

AMATEUR PLAYING RECORD

Season Team	G	Min.	FGM	FGA	Pct.	FTM	FTA	Pct.	Reb.	Ast.	Pts.	RPG	APG	PPG
63-64—Akron (Ohio)	33	...	149	...	...	31	...	...	...	...	329	...	...	10.0
64-65—Akron (Ohio)	32	...	144	297	.485	139	167	.832	90	...	427	2.8	...	13.3
Totals	65	...	293	...	...	170	...	...	...	...	756	...	...	11.6

ABA REGULAR-SEASON RECORD

NOTES: ABA All-Star second team (1968). ... Member of ABA championship team (1969). ... Holds single-game record for most assists—23 (February 20, 1972, vs. Pittsburgh).

Season Team	G	Min.	2-POINT FGM	FGA	Pct.	3-POINT FGM	FGA	Pct.	FTM	FTA	Pct.	Reb.	Ast.	Pts.	AVERAGES RPG	APG	PPG
67-68—New Orleans	78	2807	311	812	.383	19	89	.213	366	450	.813	249	*506	1045	3.2	6.5	13.4
68-69—Oakland	77	2381	300	671	.447	8	35	.229	301	379	.794	235	*544	925	3.1	7.1	12.0
69-70—Washington	82	2766	366	815	.449	10	39	.256	362	439	.825	246	*580	1124	3.0	7.1	13.7
70-71—Virginia-Denver	63	1343	121	319	.379	6	21	.286	186	225	.827	109	330	446	1.7	5.2	7.1
71-72—Denver	76	2012	238	531	.448	5	25	.200	198	244	.811	166	549	689	2.2	7.2	9.1
Totals	376	11309	1336	3148	.424	48	209	.230	1413	1737	.813	1005	2509	4229	2.7	6.7	11.2

ABA PLAYOFF RECORD

Season Team	G	Min.	2-POINT FGM	FGA	Pct.	3-POINT FGM	FGA	Pct.	FTM	FTA	Pct.	Reb.	Ast.	Pts.	AVERAGES RPG	APG	PPG
67-68—New Orleans	17	696	86	194	.443	4	18	.222	100	122	.820	59	129	284	3.5	7.6	16.7
68-69—Oakland	16	534	74	170	.435	0	3	.000	76	90	.844	52	87	224	3.3	5.4	14.0
69-70—Washington	7	269	32	68	.471	1	5	.200	30	34	.882	35	68	97	5.0	9.7	13.9
71-72—Denver	7	211	21	47	.447	0	3	.000	23	24	.958	10	36	65	1.4	5.1	9.3
Totals	47	1710	213	479	.445	5	29	.172	229	270	.848	156	320	670	3.3	6.8	14.3

ABA ALL-STAR GAME RECORD

NOTES: ABA All-Star Game Most Valuable Player (1968).

Season Team	Min.	2-POINT FGM	FGA	Pct.	3-POINT FGM	FGA	Pct.	FTM	FTA	Pct.	Reb.	Ast.	Pts.
1968—New Orleans	22	5	7	.714	2	2	1.000	1	1	1.000	3	5	17
1969—Oakland	25	1	6	.167	0	1	.000	3	5	.600	0	7	5
1970—Washington	15	0	2	.000	0	0	...	3	3	1.000	3	3	3
Totals	62	6	15	.400	2	3	.667	7	9	.778	6	15	25

HEAD COACHING RECORD

BACKGROUND: Assistant coach, University of North Carolina (1965-66 and 1966-67).
HONORS: ABA Coach of the Year (1973, 1975, 1976).

ABA COACHING RECORD

Season Team	REGULAR SEASON W	L	Pct.	Finish	PLAYOFFS W	L	Pct.
72-73 —Carolina	57	27	.679	1st/Eastern Division	7	5	.583
73-74 —Carolina	47	37	.560	3rd/Eastern Division	0	4	.000
74-75 —Denver	65	19	.774	1st/Western Division	7	6	.538
75-76 —Denver	60	24	.714	1st	6	7	.462
Totals (4 years)	229	107	.682	Totals (4 years)	20	22	.476

NBA COACHING RECORD

Season Team	REGULAR SEASON W	L	Pct.	Finish	PLAYOFFS W	L	Pct.
76-77 —Denver	50	32	.610	1st/Midwest Division	2	4	.500
77-78 —Denver	48	34	.585	1st/Midwest Division	6	7	.462
78-79 —Denver	28	25	.528		—	—	—
81-82 —New Jersey	44	38	.537	3rd/Atlantic Division	0	2	.000
82-83 —New Jersey	47	29	.618		—	—	—
88-89 —San Antonio	21	61	.256	5th/Midwest Division	—	—	—
89-90 —San Antonio	56	26	.683	1st/Midwest Division	6	4	.600
90-91 —San Antonio	55	27	.671	1st/Midwest Division	1	3	.250
91-92 —San Antonio	21	17	.553		—	—	—
—Los Angeles Clippers	23	12	.657	5th/Pacific Division	2	3	.400
92-93 —Los Angeles Clippers	41	41	.500	4th/Pacific Division	2	3	.400
93-94 —Indiana	47	35	.573	T3rd/Central Division	10	6	.625
94-95 —Indiana	52	30	.634	1st/Central Division	10	7	.588
95-96 —Indiana	52	30	.634	2nd/Central Division	2	3	.400
Totals (13 years)	585	437	.572	Totals (10 years)	41	42	.494

COLLEGIATE COACHING RECORD

Season Team	W	L	Pct.	Finish
79-80 —UCLA	22	10	.688	4th/Pacific-10 Conference
80-81 —UCLA	20	7	.741	3rd/Pacific-10 Conference
83-84 —Kansas	22	10	.688	2nd/Big Eight Conference
84-85 —Kansas	26	8	.765	2nd/Big Eight Conference
85-86 —Kansas	35	4	.897	1st/Big Eight Conference
86-87 —Kansas	25	11	.694	T2nd/Big Eight Conference
87-88 —Kansas	27	11	.711	3rd/Big Eight Conference
Totals (7 years)	177	61	.744	

NOTES:
1973—Defeated New York, 4-1, in Eastern Division semifinals; lost to Kentucky, 4-3, in Eastern Division finals.
1974—Lost to Kentucky in Eastern Division semifinals.
1975—Defeated Utah, 4-2, in Western Division semifinals; lost to Indiana, 4-3, in Western Division finals.
1976—Defeated Kentucky, 4-3, in semifinals; lost to New York, 4-2, in ABA Finals.
1977—Lost to Portland in Western Conference semifinals.
1978—Defeated Milwaukee, 4-3, in Western Conference semifinals; lost to Seattle, 4-2, in Western Conference finals.
1979—Resigned as Denver head coach (February 1); replaced by Donnie Walsh with club in second place.
1980—Defeated Old Dominion, 87-74, in NCAA Tournament first round; defeated DePaul, 77-71, in second round; defeated Ohio State, 72-68, in regional semifinals; defeated Clemson, 85-74, in regional finals; defeated Purdue, 67-62, in semifinals; lost to Louisville, 59-54, in championship game.

1981—Lost to Brigham Young, 78-55, in NCAA Tournament second round.
1982—Lost to Washington in Eastern Conference first round.
1983—Resigned as New Jersey head coach (April 7); replaced by Bill Blair with club in third place.
1984—Defeated Alcorn State, 57-56, in NCAA Tournament first round; lost to Wake Forest, 69-59, in second round.
1985—Defeated Ohio University, 49-38, in NCAA Tournament first round; lost to Auburn, 66-64, in second round.
1986—Defeated North Carolina A&T, 71-46, in NCAA Tournament first round; defeated Temple, 65-43, in second round; defeated Michigan State, 96-86 (OT), in regional semifinals; defeated North Carolina State, 75-67, in regional finals; lost to Duke, 71-67, in semifinals.
1987—Defeated Houston, 66-55, in NCAA Tournament first round; defeated Southwest Missouri State, 67-63, in second round; lost to Georgetown, 70-57, in regional semifinals.
1988—Defeated Xavier, 85-72, in NCAA Tournament first round; defeated Murray State, 61-58, in second round; defeated Vanderbilt, 77-64, in regional semifinals; defeated Kansas State, 71-58, in regional finals; defeated Duke, 66-59, in semifinals; defeated Oklahoma, 83-79, in championship game.
1990—Defeated Denver, 3-0, in Western Conference first round; lost to Portland, 4-3, in Western Conference semifinals.
1991—Lost to Golden State in Western Conference first round.
1992—Replaced as San Antonio head coach by Bob Bass with club in second place (January 21); replaced Mike Schuler (21-24) and Mack Calvin (interim head coach, 1-1) as Los Angeles Clippers head coach (February 6), with record of 22-25 and club in sixth place. Lost to Utah in Western Conference first round.
1993—Lost to Houston in Western Conference first round.
1994—Defeated Orlando, 3-0, in Eastern Conference first round; defeated Atlanta, 4-2, in Eastern Conference semifinals; lost to New York, 4-3, in Eastern Conference finals.
1995—Defeated Atlanta, 3-0, in Eastern Confrence first round; defeated New York, 4-3, Eastern Conference semifinals; lost to Orlando, 4-3, in Eastern Conference finals.
1996—Lost to Atlanta in Eastern Conference first round.

CALIPARI, JOHN — NETS

PERSONAL: Born February 10, 1959, in Moon, Pa. ... 5-11/165.
HIGH SCHOOL: Moon (Pa.).
COLLEGE: UNC Wilmington, then Clarion (Pa.) University.

COLLEGIATE RECORD

												AVERAGES		
Season Team	**G**	**Min.**	**FGM**	**FGA**	**Pct.**	**FTM**	**FTA**	**Pct.**	**Reb.**	**Ast.**	**Pts.**	**RPG**	**APG**	**PPG**
78-79—UNC Wilmington	25	...	4	17	.235	21	25	.840	7	22	29	0.3	0.9	1.2
79-80—UNC Wilmington	9	...	0	2	.000	6	7	.857	3	4	6	0.3	0.4	0.7
80-81—Clarion University	19	...	21	46	.457	16	26	.615	18	49	58	0.9	2.6	3.1
81-82—Clarion University	27	...	53	137	.387	38	53	.717	26	143	144	1.0	5.3	5.3
Totals	80	...	78	202	.386	81	111	.730	54	218	237	0.7	2.7	3.0

HEAD COACHING RECORD

BACKGROUND: Assistant coach, University of Kansas (1982-83 through 1984-85). ... Assistant coach, University of Pittsburgh (1985-86 through 1987-88).
HONORS: The Sporting News Coach of the Year (1996).

COLLEGIATE COACHING RECORD

Season Team	**W**	**L**	**Pct.**	**Finish**
88-89 —Massachusetts	10	18	.357	8th/Atlantic-10 Conference
89-90 —Massachusetts	17	14	.548	6th/Atlantic-10 Conference
90-91 —Massachusetts	20	13	.606	T3rd/Atlantic-10 Conference
91-92 —Massachusetts	30	5	.857	1st/Atlantic-10 Conference
92-93 —Massachusetts	24	7	.774	1st/Atlantic-10 Conference
93-94 —Massachusetts	28	7	.800	1st/Atlantic-10 Conference
94-95 —Massachusetts	29	5	.853	1st/Atlantic-10 Conference
95-96 —Massachusetts	35	2	.946	1st/Atlantic-10 Conference
Totals (8 years)	193	71	.731	

NOTES:
1990—Lost to Maryland, 91-81, in NIT first round.
1991—Defeated La Salle, 93-90, in NIT first round; defeated Fordham, 78-74, in second round; defeated Siena, 82-80 (OT), in third round; lost to Stanford, 73-71, in semifinals; lost to Colorado, 98-91, in third-place consolation game.
1992—Defeated Fordham, 85-58, in NCAA Tournament first round; defeated Syracuse, 77-71 (OT), in second round; lost to Kentucky, 87-77, in regional semifinals.
1993—Defeated Pennsylvania, 54-50, in NCAA Tournament first round; lost to Virginia, 71-56, in second round.
1994—Defeated Southwest Texas, 78-60, in NCAA Tournament first round; lost to Maryland, 95-87, in second round.
1995—Defeated St. Peter's, 68-51, in NCAA Tournament first round; defeated Stanford, 75-53, in second round; defeated Stanford, 75-53, in regional semifinals; lost to Oklahoma State, 68-54, in regional finals.
1996—Defeated Central Florida, 92-70, in NCAA Tournament first round; defeated Stanford, 79-74, in second round; defeated Arkansas, 79-63, in regional semifinals; defeated Georgetown, 86-62, in regional final; lost to Kentucky, 81-74, in semifinals.

DID YOU KNOW...

...that three times in his career, Bill Fitch has coached a rookie All-Star in his first season with a club? In 1970-71, it was John Johnson in Cleveland, in 1979-80, Larry Bird in Boston, in 1983-84, Ralph Sampson in Houston.

CARLESIMO, P.J.

PERSONAL: Born May 30, 1949, in Scranton, Pa. ... 6-1/185. ... Full name: Peter J. Carlesimo. ... Name pronounced car-LES-i-moe.
HIGH SCHOOL: Scranton (Pa.) Prep.
COLLEGE: Fordham.

COLLEGIATE RECORD

Season Team	G	Min.	FGM	FGA	Pct.	FTM	FTA	Pct.	Reb.	Ast.	Pts.	RPG	APG	PPG
67-68—Fordham‡	13	...	53	89	.596	32	47	.681	92	...	138	7.1	...	10.6
68-69—Fordham	1	...	0	0	...	0	0	...	0	...	0	0.0	...	0.0
69-70—Fordham	2	...	2	3	.667	1	2	.500	0	0	5	0.0	0.0	2.5
70-71—Fordham	9	...	1	2	.500	0	0	...	0	6	2	0.0	0.7	0.2
Varsity totals	12	...	3	5	.600	1	2	.500	0	...	7	0.0	...	0.6

COLLEGIATE COACHING RECORD
BACKGROUND: Assistant coach, Fordham University (1971-72 through 1974-75).

Season Team	W	L	Pct.	Finish
75-76 —New Hampshire College	14	13	.519	1st/Mayflower Conference
76-77 —Wagner	3	21	.125	Independent
77-78 —Wagner	7	19	.368	Independent
78-79 —Wagner	21	7	.750	Independent
79-80 —Wagner	14	13	.519	Independent
80-81 —Wagner	16	11	.593	Independent
81-82 —Wagner	4	22	.154	Independent
82-83 —Seton Hall	6	23	.207	9th/Big East Conference
83-84 —Seton Hall	9	19	.321	9th/Big East Conference
84-85 —Seton Hall	10	18	.357	9th/Big East Conference
85-86 —Seton Hall	14	18	.438	T8th/Big East Conference
86-87 —Seton Hall	15	14	.517	7th/Big East Conference
87-88 —Seton Hall	22	13	.629	T5th/Big East Conference
88-89 —Seton Hall	31	7	.816	2nd/Big East Conference
89-90 —Seton Hall	12	16	.429	T7th/Big East Conference
90-91 —Seton Hall	25	9	.735	T3rd/Big East Conference
91-92 —Seton Hall	23	9	.719	T1st/Big East Conference
92-93 —Seton Hall	28	7	.800	1st/Big East Conference
93-94 —Seton Hall	17	13	.567	7th/Big East Conference
Totals (19 years)	291	272	.517	

NBA COACHING RECORD

	REGULAR SEASON				PLAYOFFS		
Season Team	W	L	Pct.	Finish	W	L	Pct.
94-95 —Portland	44	38	.537	4th/Pacific Division	0	3	.000
95-96 —Portland	44	38	.537	3rd/Pacific Division	2	3	.400
Totals (2 years)	88	76	.537	Totals (2 years)	2	6	.250

NOTES:
1979—Lost to Old Dominion, 83-81, in NIT first round.
1987—Lost to Niagara, 74-65, in NIT first round.
1988—Defeated Texas-El Paso, 80-64, in NCAA Tournament first round; lost to Arizona, 84-55, in second round.
1989—Defeated Southwest Missouri, 60-51, in NCAA Tournament first round; defeated Evansville, 87-73, in second round; defeated Indiana, 78-65, in regional semifinals; defeated UNLV, 84-61, in regional finals; defeated Duke, 95-78, in semifinals; lost to Michigan, 80-79 (OT), in championship game.
1991—Defeated Pepperdine, 71-51, in NCAA Tournament first round; defeated Creighton, 81-69, in second round; defeated Arizona, 81-77, in regional semifinals; lost to UNLV, 77-65, in regional finals.
1992—Defeated La Salle, 78-76, in NCAA Tournament first round; defeated Missouri, 88-71, in second round; lost to Duke, 81-69, in regional semifinals.
1993—Defeated Tennessee State, 81-59, in NCAA Tournament first round; lost to Western Kentucky, 72-68, in second round.
1994—Lost to Michigan State, 84-73, in NCAA Tournament first round.
1995—Lost to Phoenix in Western Conference first round.
1996—Lost to Utah in Western Conference first round.

CARR, M.L.

PERSONAL: Born January 9, 1951, in Wallace, N.C. ... 6-6/205. ... Full name: Michael Leon Carr.
HIGH SCHOOL: Wallace Rose Hill (Teachey, N.C.).
COLLEGE: Guilford College (N.C.).
TRANSACTIONS/CAREER NOTES: Selected by Kentucky Colonels in third round of 1973 American Basketball Association draft. ... Selected by Kansas City/Omaha Kings in fifth round (76th pick overall) of 1973 NBA Draft. ... Waived by Colonels (September 15, 1973). ... Played in Eastern Basketball Association with Hamilton (1973-74) and Scranton (1974-75). ... Waived by Kings (September 30, 1974). ... Signed as free agent by Boston Celtics (October 10, 1974). ... Waived by Celtics (October 15, 1974). ... Played in Israel (1974-75). ... Signed as free agent by Spirits of St. Louis of ABA (July 31, 1975). ... Signed as free agent by Detroit Pistons (June 12, 1976). ... Signed as veteran free agent by Celtics (July 24, 1979); Pistons received C/F Bob McAdoo and Celtics received two 1980 first-round draft choices to complete compensation (September 6, 1979).
MISCELLANEOUS: Member of NBA championship teams (1981, 1984).

HEAD COACHES

COLLEGIATE RECORD

NOTES: Member of NAIA championship team (1973).

												AVERAGES		
Season Team	G	Min.	FGM	FGA	Pct.	FTM	FTA	Pct.	Reb.	Ast.	Pts.	RPG	APG	PPG
69-70—Guilford College	36	...	249	411	.606	84	144	.583	383	...	582	10.6	...	16.2
70-71—Guilford College	28	...	203	347	.585	102	151	.676	292	...	508	10.4	...	18.1
71-72—Guilford College	13	...	122	204	.598	33	67	.493	164	...	277	12.6	...	21.3
72-73—Guilford College	34	...	278	526	.529	70	106	.660	426	...	626	12.5	...	18.4
Totals	111	...	852	1488	.573	289	468	.618	1265	...	1993	11.4	...	18.0

ABA REGULAR-SEASON RECORD

NOTES: ABA All-Rookie team (1976).

			2-POINT			3-POINT								AVERAGES		
Season Team	G	Min.	FGM	FGA	Pct.	FGM	FGA	Pct.	FTM	FTA	Pct.	Reb.	Ast.	Pts.	RPG	APG	PPG
75-76—St. Louis	74	2174	371	762	.487	9	24	.375	137	206	.665	459	224	906	6.2	3.0	12.2

NBA REGULAR-SEASON RECORD

HONORS: NBA All-Defensive second team (1979).

									REBOUNDS								AVERAGES		
Season Team	G	Min.	FGM	FGA	Pct.	FTM	FTA	Pct.	Off.	Def.	Tot.	Ast.	St.	Blk.	TO	Pts.	RPG	APG	PPG
76-77—Detroit	82	2643	443	931	.476	205	279	.735	211	420	631	181	165	58	...	1091	7.7	2.2	13.3
77-78—Detroit	79	2556	390	857	.455	200	271	.738	202	355	557	185	147	27	210	980	7.1	2.3	12.4
78-79—Detroit	80	3207	587	1143	.514	323	435	.743	219	370	589	262	197	46	255	1497	7.4	3.3	18.7
79-80—Boston	82	1994	362	763	.474	178	241	.739	106	224	330	156	120	36	143	914	4.0	1.9	11.1
80-81—Boston	41	655	97	216	.449	53	67	.791	26	57	83	56	30	18	47	248	2.0	1.4	6.0
81-82—Boston	56	1296	184	409	.450	82	116	.707	56	94	150	128	67	21	63	455	2.7	2.3	8.1
82-83—Boston	77	883	135	315	.429	60	81	.741	51	86	137	71	48	10	79	333	1.8	0.9	4.3
83-84—Boston	60	585	70	171	.409	42	48	.875	26	49	75	49	17	4	46	185	1.3	0.8	3.1
84-85—Boston	47	397	62	149	.416	17	17	1.000	21	22	43	24	21	6	24	150	0.9	0.5	3.2
Totals	604	14216	2330	4954	.470	1160	1555	.746	918	1677	2595	1112	812	226	867	5853	4.3	1.8	9.7

Three-point field goals: 1979-80, 12-for-41 (.293). 1980-81, 1-for-14 (.071). 1981-82, 5-for-17 (.294). 1982-83, 3-for-19 (.158). 1983-84, 3-for-15 (.200). 1984-85, 9-for-23 (.391). Totals, 33-for-129 (.256).

Personal fouls/disqualifications: 1976-77, 287/8. 1977-78, 243/4. 1978-79, 279/2. 1979-80, 214/1. 1980-81, 74/0. 1981-82, 136/2. 1982-83, 140/0. 1983-84, 67/0. 1984-85, 44/0. Totals, 1484/17.

NBA PLAYOFF RECORD

									REBOUNDS								AVERAGES		
Season Team	G	Min.	FGM	FGA	Pct.	FTM	FTA	Pct.	Off.	Def.	Tot.	Ast.	St.	Blk.	TO	Pts.	RPG	APG	PPG
76-77—Detroit	3	112	12	31	.387	4	7	.571	9	8	17	6	1	3	...	28	5.7	2.0	9.3
79-80—Boston	9	172	32	80	.400	16	24	.667	14	19	33	11	6	1	7	82	3.7	1.2	9.1
80-81—Boston	17	288	42	101	.416	18	24	.750	8	17	25	14	10	6	8	102	1.5	0.8	6.0
81-82—Boston	12	305	37	105	.352	15	23	.652	21	22	43	28	11	0	21	89	3.6	2.3	7.4
82-83—Boston	3	22	2	8	.250	2	2	1.000	1	0	1	0	2	0	0	6	0.0	0.0	2.0
83-84—Boston	16	82	13	32	.406	10	11	.909	5	3	8	4	7	0	3	38	0.5	0.3	2.4
84-85—Boston	7	24	4	15	.267	0	0	...	1	1	2	1	1	0	1	9	0.3	0.1	1.3
Totals	67	1005	142	372	.382	65	91	.714	59	70	129	64	38	10	40	354	1.9	1.0	5.3

Three-point field goals: 1979-80, 2-for-5 (.400). 1980-81, 0-for-4. 1981-82, 0-for-4. 1982-83, 0-for-1. 1983-84, 2-for-6 (.333). 1984-85, 1-for-2 (.500). Totals, 5-for-22 (.227).

Personal fouls/disqualifications: 1976-77, 9/0. 1979-80, 20/0. 1980-81, 32/0. 1981-82, 30/0. 1982-83, 3/0. 1983-84, 13/0. 1984-85, 4/0. Totals, 111/0.

HEAD COACHING RECORD

BACKGROUND: Scout, Boston Celtics (1985-86 through 1990-91). ... Community relations director, Celtics (1991-92 through 1993-94). ... Vice president/director of basketball operations, Celtics (June 14, 1994 to present).

NBA COACHING RECORD

	REGULAR SEASON				PLAYOFFS		
Season Team	W	L	Pct.	Finish	W	L	Pct.
1995-96—Boston	33	49	.402	5th/Atlantic Division	—	—	—

CLEAMONS, JIM — MAVERICKS

PERSONAL: Born September 13, 1949, in Lincolnton, N.C. ... 6-3/185. ... Full name: James Mitchell Cleamons.

HIGH SCHOOL: Linden McKinley (Columbus, Ohio).

COLLEGE: Ohio State

TRANSACTIONS/CAREER NOTES: Selected by Los Angeles Lakers in first round (13th pick overall) of 1971 NBA Draft. ... Traded by Lakers to Cleveland Cavaliers for future draft choice (August 31, 1972). ... Signed as free agent by New York Knicks (October 10, 1977); Cavaliers received G Walt Frazier as compensation. ... Traded by Knicks to Washington Bullets for 1981 third-round draft choice (December 4, 1979). ... Selected by Dallas Mavericks from Knicks in NBA expansion draft (May 28, 1980).

MISCELLANEOUS: Member of NBA championship team (1972).

COLLEGIATE RECORD

												AVERAGES		
Season Team	G	Min.	FGM	FGA	Pct.	FTM	FTA	Pct.	Reb.	Ast.	Pts.	RPG	APG	PPG
68-69—Ohio State	24	915	137	270	.507	125	163	.767	178	...	399	7.4	...	16.6
69-70—Ohio State	24	930	211	353	.598	96	124	.774	193	...	518	8.0	...	21.6
70-71—Ohio State	24	879	157	308	.510	104	140	.743	151	...	418	6.3	...	17.4
Totals	72	2724	505	931	.542	325	427	.761	522	...	1335	7.3	...	18.5

NBA REGULAR-SEASON RECORD

HONORS: NBA All-Defensive second team (1976).

														AVERAGES		
Season Team	G	Min.	FGM	FGA	Pct.	FTM	FTA	Pct.	Reb.	Ast.	PF	Dq.	Pts.	RPG	APG	PPG
71-72 —Los Angeles	38	201	35	100	.350	28	36	.778	39	35	21	0	98	1.0	0.9	2.6
72-73 —Cleveland	80	1392	192	423	.454	75	101	.743	167	205	108	0	459	2.1	2.6	5.7

									REBOUNDS							AVERAGES		
Season Team	G	Min.	FGM	FGA	Pct.	FTM	FTA	Pct.	Off.	Def.	Tot.	Ast.	St.	Blk.	TO	Pts.	RPG	APG	PPG
73-74—Cleveland	81	1642	236	545	.433	93	133	.699	63	167	230	227	61	17	...	565	2.8	2.8	7.0
74-75—Cleveland	74	2691	369	768	.480	144	181	.796	97	232	329	381	84	21	...	882	4.4	5.1	11.9
75-76—Cleveland	82	2835	413	887	.466	174	218	.798	124	230	354	428	124	20	...	1000	4.3	5.2	12.2
76-77—Cleveland	60	2045	257	592	.434	112	148	.757	99	174	273	308	66	23	...	626	4.6	5.1	10.4
77-78—New York	79	2009	215	448	.480	81	103	.786	69	143	212	283	68	17	113	511	2.7	3.6	6.5
78-79—New York	79	2390	311	657	.473	130	171	.760	65	160	225	376	73	11	142	752	2.8	4.8	9.5
79-80—N.Y.-Wash.	79	1789	214	450	.476	84	113	.743	53	99	152	288	57	11	109	519	1.9	3.6	6.6
Totals	652	16994	2242	4870	.460	921	1204	.765	...	...	1981	2531	533	120	364	5412	3.0	3.9	8.3

Personal fouls/disqualifications: 1973-74, 152/1. 1974-75, 194/0. 1975-76, 214/2. 1976-77, 126/0. 1977-78, 142/1. 1978-79, 147/1. 1979-80, 133/0. Totals, 1237/5.

NBA PLAYOFF RECORD

														AVERAGES		
Season Team	G	Min.	FGM	FGA	Pct.	FTM	FTA	Pct.	Reb.	Ast.	PF	Dq.	Pts.	RPG	APG	PPG
71-72 —Los Angeles	6	17	4	7	.571	0	0	...	4	4	3	0	8	0.7	0.7	1.3

									REBOUNDS							AVERAGES		
Season Team	G	Min.	FGM	FGA	Pct.	FTM	FTA	Pct.	Off.	Def.	Tot.	Ast.	St.	Blk.	TO	Pts.	RPG	APG	PPG
75-76—Cleveland	13	503	73	184	.397	33	40	.825	23	48	71	61	8	3	...	179	5.5	4.7	13.8
77-78—New York	6	127	14	36	.389	6	6	1.000	5	8	13	23	3	0	...	34	2.2	3.8	5.7
79-80—Washington	2	20	0	3	.000	0	0	...	0	1	1	1	1	0	...	0	0.5	0.5	0.0
Totals	27	667	91	230	.396	39	46	.848	...	...	89	89	12	3	9	221	3.3	3.3	8.2

Personal fouls/disqualifications: 1975-76, 34/0. 1977-78, 13/0. Totals, 50/0.

HEAD COACHING RECORD

BACKGROUND: Assistant coach, Furman University (1982-83). ... Assistant coach, Ohio State University (1983-84 through 1986-87). ... Assistant coach, Chicago Bulls (1989-90 through 1995-96).

COLLEGIATE COACHING RECORD

Season Team	W	L	Pct.	Finish
87-88 —Youngstown State	7	21	.250	6th/Ohio Valley Conference
88-89 —Youngstown State	5	23	.179	Independent
Totals (2 years)	12	44	.214	

COLLINS, DOUG — PISTONS

PERSONAL: Born July 28, 1951, in Christopher, Ill. ... 6-6/180. ... Full name: Paul Douglas Collins.
HIGH SCHOOL: Benton, Ill.
COLLEGE: Illinois State.
TRANSACTIONS/CAREER NOTES: Selected by Philadelphia 76ers in first round (first pick overall) of 1973 NBA Draft.
MISCELLANEOUS: Member of silver-medal-winning U.S. Olympic team (1972).

COLLEGIATE RECORD

NOTES: The Sporting News All-America second team (1973).

												AVERAGES		
Season Team	G	Min.	FGM	FGA	Pct.	FTM	FTA	Pct.	Reb.	Ast.	Pts.	RPG	APG	PPG
69-70—Illinois State‡	21	...	173	376	.460	95	113	.841	196	...	441	9.3	...	21.0
70-71—Illinois State	26	...	273	609	.448	197	235	.838	166	...	743	6.4	...	28.6
71-72—Illinois State	26	...	352	704	.500	143	177	.808	133	...	847	5.1	...	32.6
72-73—Illinois State	25	...	269	565	.476	112	137	.818	126	...	650	5.0	...	26.0
Varsity totals	77	...	894	1878	.476	452	549	.823	425	...	2240	5.5	...	29.1

NBA REGULAR-SEASON RECORD

									REBOUNDS							AVERAGES		
Season Team	G	Min.	FGM	FGA	Pct.	FTM	FTA	Pct.	Off.	Def.	Tot.	Ast.	St.	Blk.	TO	Pts.	RPG	APG	PPG
73-74—Philadelphia	25	436	72	194	.371	55	72	.764	7	39	46	40	13	2	...	199	1.8	1.6	8.0
74-75—Philadelphia	81	2820	561	1150	.488	331	392	.844	104	211	315	213	108	17	...	1453	3.9	2.6	17.9
75-76—Philadelphia	77	2995	614	1196	.513	372	445	.836	126	181	307	191	110	24	...	1600	4.0	2.5	20.8
76-77—Philadelphia	58	2037	426	823	.518	210	250	.840	64	131	195	271	70	15	...	1062	3.4	4.7	18.3
77-78—Philadelphia	79	2770	643	1223	.526	267	329	.812	87	143	230	320	129	25	250	1553	2.9	4.1	19.7
78-79—Philadelphia	47	1595	358	717	.499	201	247	.814	36	87	123	191	52	20	131	917	2.6	4.1	19.5
79-80—Philadelphia	36	963	191	410	.466	113	124	.911	29	65	94	100	30	7	82	495	2.6	2.8	13.8
80-81—Philadelphia	12	329	62	126	.492	24	29	.828	6	23	29	42	7	4	22	148	2.4	3.5	12.3
Totals	415	13945	2927	5839	.501	1573	1888	.833	459	880	1339	1368	519	114	485	7427	3.2	3.3	17.9

Three-point field goals: 1979-80, 0-for-1.
Personal fouls/disqualifications: 1973-74, 65/1. 1974-75, 291/6. 1975-76, 249/2. 1976-77, 174/2. 1977-78, 228/2. 1978-79, 139/1. 1979-80, 76/0. 1980-81, 23/0. Totals, 1245/14.

NBA PLAYOFF RECORD

									REBOUNDS							AVERAGES		
Season Team	G	Min.	FGM	FGA	Pct.	FTM	FTA	Pct.	Off.	Def.	Tot.	Ast.	St.	Blk.	TO	Pts.	RPG	APG	PPG
75-76—Philadelphia	3	117	23	53	.434	12	14	.857	13	8	21	10	3	1	...	58	7.0	3.3	19.3

Season Team	G	Min.	FGM	FGA	Pct.	FTM	FTA	Pct.	Off.	Def.	Tot.	Ast.	St.	Blk.	TO	Pts.	RPG	APG	PPG
									REBOUNDS								AVERAGES		
76-77—Philadelphia ..	19	759	177	318	.557	71	96	.740	30	49	79	74	28	3	...	425	4.2	3.9	22.4
77-78—Philadelphia ..	10	342	82	165	.497	40	49	.816	8	23	31	27	3	0	...	204	3.1	2.7	20.4
Totals	32	1218	282	536	.526	123	159	.774	51	80	131	111	34	4	34	687	4.1	3.5	21.5

Personal fouls/disqualifications: 1975-76, 9/0. 1976-77, 57/0. 1977-78, 29/0. Totals, 95/0.

NBA ALL-STAR GAME RECORD

Season Team	Min.	FGM	FGA	Pct.	FTM	FTA	Pct.	Off.	Def.	Tot.	Ast.	PF	Dq.	St.	Blk.	TO	Pts.
								REBOUNDS									
1977 —Philadelphia......	20	5	10	.500	2	2	1.000	2	4	6	3	3	0	3	0	...	12
1978 —Philadelphia......	21	3	6	.500	2	2	1.000	1	1	2	6	2	0	1	0	...	8
1979 —Philadelphia......	27	3	8	.375	8	11	.727	4	1	5	8	3	0	2	0	...	14
1980 —Philadelphia								Selected, did not play—injured.									
Totals........................	68	11	24	.458	12	15	.800	7	6	13	17	8	0	6	0	...	34

HEAD COACHING RECORD

BACKGROUND: Assistant coach, University of Pennsylvania (1981-82). ... Assistant coach, Arizona State (1982-83 and 1983-84). ... Broadcaster, CBS Sports (1984-85 and 1985-86). ... Broadcaster, Turner Sports (1989-90 through 1994-95).

NBA COACHING RECORD

Season Team	REGULAR SEASON				PLAYOFFS		
	W	L	Pct.	Finish	W	L	Pct.
86-87 —Chicago	40	42	.488	5th/Central Division	0	3	.000
87-88 —Chicago	50	32	.610	2nd/Central Division	4	6	.400
88-89 —Chicago	47	35	.573	5th/Central Division	9	8	.529
95-96 —Detroit	46	36	.561	4th/Central Division	0	3	.000
Totals (4 years)..	183	145	.558	Totals (4 years).......	13	20	.394

NOTES:
1987—Lost to Boston in Eastern Conference first round.
1988—Defeated Cleveland, 3-2, in Eastern Conference first round; lost to Detroit, 4-1, in Eastern Conference semifinals.
1989—Defeated Cleveland, 3-2, in Eastern Conference first round; defeated New York, 4-2, in Eastern Conference semifinals.; lost to Detroit, 4-2, in Eastern Conference finals.
1996—Lost to Orlando in Eastern Conference first round.

COWENS, DAVE　　　　　　　　　　　HORNETS

PERSONAL: Born October 25, 1948, in Newport, Ky. ... 6-9/230. ... Full name: David William Cowens.
HIGH SCHOOL: Newport (Ky.) Central Catholic.
COLLEGE: Florida State.
TRANSACTIONS/CAREER NOTES: Selected by Boston Celtics in first round (fourth pick overall) of 1970 NBA Draft. ... Traded by Celtics to Milwaukee Bucks for G Quinn Buckner (September 9, 1982).
CAREER HONORS: Elected to Naismith Memorial Basketball Hall of Fame (1990).
MISCELLANEOUS: Member of NBA championship teams (1974, 1976).

COLLEGIATE RECORD

NOTES: THE SPORTING NEWS All-America second team (1970).

Season Team	G	Min.	FGM	FGA	Pct.	FTM	FTA	Pct.	Reb.	Ast.	Pts.	RPG	APG	PPG
												AVERAGES		
66-67—Florida State‡................	18	...	105	208	.505	49	90	.544	357	...	259	19.8	...	14.4
67-68—Florida State	27	...	206	383	.538	96	131	.733	456	...	508	16.9	...	18.8
68-69—Florida State	25	...	202	384	.526	104	164	.634	437	...	508	17.5	...	20.3
69-70—Florida State	26	...	174	355	.490	115	169	.680	447	...	463	17.2	...	17.8
Varsity totals.........................	78	...	582	1122	.519	315	464	.679	1340	...	1479	17.2	...	19.0

NBA REGULAR-SEASON RECORD

HONORS: NBA Most Valuable Player (1973). ... NBA co-Rookie of the Year (1971). ... All-NBA second team (1973, 1975, 1976). ... NBA All-Defensive first team (1976). ... NBA All-Defensive second team (1975, 1980). ... NBA All-Rookie team (1971).

Season Team	G	Min.	FGM	FGA	Pct.	FTM	FTA	Pct.	Reb.	Ast.	PF	Dq.	Pts.	RPG	APG	PPG
														AVERAGES		
70-71—Boston	81	3076	550	1302	.422	273	373	.732	1216	228	*350	15	1373	15.0	2.8	17.0
71-72—Boston	79	3186	657	1357	.484	175	243	.720	1203	245	*314	10	1489	15.2	3.1	18.8
72-73—Boston	82	3425	740	1637	.452	204	262	.779	1329	333	311	7	1684	16.2	4.1	20.5

Season Team	G	Min.	FGM	FGA	Pct.	FTM	FTA	Pct.	Off.	Def.	Tot.	Ast.	St.	Blk.	TO	Pts.	RPG	APG	PPG
									REBOUNDS								AVERAGES		
73-74—Boston	80	3352	645	1475	.437	228	274	.832	264	993	1257	354	95	101	...	1518	15.7	4.4	19.0
74-75—Boston	65	2632	569	1199	.475	191	244	.783	229	729	958	296	87	73	...	1329	14.7	4.6	20.4
75-76—Boston	78	3101	611	1305	.468	257	340	.756	335	911	1246	325	94	71	...	1479	16.0	4.2	19.0
76-77—Boston	50	1888	328	756	.434	162	198	.818	147	550	697	248	46	49	...	818	13.9	5.0	16.4
77-78—Boston	77	3215	598	1220	.490	239	284	.842	248	830	1078	351	102	67	217	1435	14.0	4.6	18.6
78-79—Boston	68	2517	488	1010	.483	151	187	.807	152	500	652	242	76	51	174	1127	9.6	3.6	16.6
79-80—Boston	66	2159	422	932	.453	95	122	.779	126	408	534	206	69	61	108	940	8.1	3.1	14.2
80-81—									Did not play—retired.										
81-82—									Did not play—retired.										
82-83—Milwaukee......	40	1014	136	306	.444	52	63	.825	73	201	274	82	30	15	44	324	6.9	2.1	8.1
Totals	766	29565	5744	12499	.460	2027	2590	.783	...	...	10444	2910	599	488	543	13516	13.6	3.8	17.6

Three-point field goals: 1979-80, 1-for-12 (.083). 1982-83, 0-for-2. Totals, 1-for-14 (.071).
Personal fouls/disqualifications: 1973-74, 294/7. 1974-75, 243/7. 1975-76, 314/10. 1976-77, 181/7. 1977-78, 297/5. 1978-79, 263/16. 1979-80, 216/2. 1982-83, 137/4. Totals, 2920/90.

NBA PLAYOFF RECORD

NOTES: Shares single-game playoff record for most defensive rebounds—20 (April 22, 1975, vs. Houston; and May 1, 1977, vs. Philadelphia).

Season Team	G	Min.	FGM	FGA	Pct.	FTM	FTA	Pct.	Reb.	Ast.	PF	Dq.	Pts.	RPG	APG	PPG
														AVERAGES		
71-72—Boston	11	441	71	156	.455	28	47	.596	152	33	50	2	170	13.8	3.0	15.5
72-73—Boston	13	598	129	273	.473	27	41	.659	216	48	54	2	285	16.6	3.7	21.9

Season Team	G	Min.	FGM	FGA	Pct.	FTM	FTA	Pct.	Off.	Def.	Tot.	Ast.	St.	Blk.	TO	Pts.	RPG	APG	PPG
									REBOUNDS								**AVERAGES**		
73-74—Boston	18	772	161	370	.435	47	59	.797	60	180	240	66	21	17	...	369	13.3	3.7	20.5
74-75—Boston	11	479	101	236	.428	23	26	.885	49	132	181	46	18	6	...	225	16.5	4.2	20.5
75-76—Boston	18	798	156	341	.457	66	87	.759	87	209	296	83	22	13	...	378	16.4	4.6	21.0
76-77—Boston	9	379	66	148	.446	17	22	.773	29	105	134	36	8	13	...	149	14.9	4.0	16.6
79-80—Boston	9	301	49	103	.476	10	11	.909	18	48	66	21	9	7	8	108	7.3	2.3	12.0
Totals	89	3768	733	1627	.451	218	293	.744	...	...	1285	333	78	56	8	1684	14.4	3.7	18.9

Three-point field goals: 1979-80, 0-for-2.

Personal fouls/disqualifications: 1973-74, 85/2. 1974-75, 50/2. 1975-76, 85/4. 1976-77, 37/3. 1979-80, 37/0. Totals, 398/15.

NBA ALL-STAR GAME RECORD

NOTES: NBA All-Star Game Most Valuable Player (1973).

Season Team	Min.	FGM	FGA	Pct.	FTM	FTA	Pct.	Reb	Ast.	PF	Dq.	Pts.
1972 —Boston	32	5	12	.417	4	5	.800	20	1	4	0	14
1973 —Boston	30	7	15	.467	1	1	1.000	13	1	2	0	15

Season Team	Min.	FGM	FGA	Pct.	FTM	FTA	Pct.	Off.	Def.	Tot.	Ast.	PF	Dq.	St.	Blk.	TO	Pts.
								REBOUNDS									
1974 —Boston	26	5	10	.500	1	3	.333	6	6	12	1	3	0	0	1	...	11
1975 —Boston	15	3	7	.429	0	0		0	6	6	3	4	0	1	0	...	6
1976 —Boston	23	6	13	.462	4	5	.800	8	8	16	1	3	0	1	0	...	16
1977 —Boston							Selected, did not play—injured.										
1978 —Boston	28	7	9	.778	0	0		6	8	14	5	5	0	2	0	2	14
Totals	154	33	66	.500	10	14	.714	...	...	81	12	21	0	4	1	2	76

HEAD COACHING RECORD

BACKGROUND: Assistant coach, University of Kansas (1982-83 through 1984-85). ... Assistant coach, University of Pittsburgh (1985-86 through 1987-88). ... Assistant coach, San Antonio Spurs (1994-95 and 1995-96).

NBA COACHING RECORD

Season Team		REGULAR SEASON				PLAYOFFS		
	W	L	Pct.	Finish		W	L	Pct.
78-79 —Boston	27	41	.397	5th/Atlantic Division		—	—	—

CBA COACHING RECORD

Season Team		REGULAR SEASON				PLAYOFFS		
	W	L	Pct.	Finish		W	L	Pct.
84-85 —Bay State	20	28	.417	6th/Atlantic Division		—	—	—

NOTES:
1978—Replaced Satch Sanders as Boston head coach (November), with record of 2-12.

DAVIS, JOHNNY — 76ERS

PERSONAL: Born October 21, 1955, in Detroit. ... 6-2/180. ... Full name: Johnny Reginald Davis.

HIGH SCHOOL: Murray-Wright (Detroit).

COLLEGE: Dayton.

TRANSACTIONS/CAREER NOTES: Selected after junior season by Portland Trail Blazers in second round (22nd pick overall) of 1978 NBA Draft. ... Traded by Trail Blazers with 1978 first-round draft choice to Indiana Pacers for 1978 first-round draft choice (June 8, 1978). ... Traded by Pacers to Atlanta Hawks for 1983 second-round draft choice and cash (December 31, 1982). ... Traded by Hawks to Cleveland Cavaliers for G Stewart Granger and F John Garris (August 8, 1984). ... Traded by Cavaliers to Hawks for F/G Eddie Johnson (February 10, 1986). ... Waived by Hawks (October 30, 1986).

MISCELLANEOUS: Member of NBA championship team (1977).

COLLEGIATE RECORD

Season Team	G	Min.	FGM	FGA	Pct.	FTM	FTA	Pct.	Reb.	Ast.	Pts.	RPG	APG	PPG
												AVERAGES		
73-74—Dayton	29	...	173	407	.425	69	105	.657	106	...	415	3.7	...	14.3
74-75—Dayton	26	1002	228	477	.478	125	158	.791	93	...	581	3.6	...	22.3
75-76—Dayton	26	1007	206	453	.455	154	193	.798	85	...	566	3.3	...	21.8
Totals	81	...	607	1337	.454	348	456	.763	284	...	1562	3.5	...	19.3

NBA REGULAR-SEASON RECORD

Season Team	G	Min.	FGM	FGA	Pct.	FTM	FTA	Pct.	Off.	Def.	Tot.	Ast.	St.	Blk.	TO	Pts.	RPG	APG	PPG
									REBOUNDS								**AVERAGES**		
76-77—Portland	79	1451	234	531	.441	166	209	.794	62	64	126	148	41	11	...	634	1.6	1.9	8.0
77-78—Portland	82	2188	343	756	.454	188	227	.828	65	108	173	217	81	14	151	874	2.1	2.6	10.7
78-79—Indiana	79	2971	565	1240	.456	314	396	.793	70	121	191	453	95	22	214	1444	2.4	5.7	18.3
79-80—Indiana	82	2912	496	1159	.428	304	352	.864	102	124	226	440	110	23	202	1300	2.8	5.4	15.9
80-81—Indiana	76	2536	426	917	.465	238	299	.796	56	114	170	480	95	14	167	1094	2.2	6.3	14.4
81-82—Indiana	82	2664	538	1153	.467	315	394	.800	72	106	178	346	76	11	186	1396	2.2	4.2	17.0
82-83—Atlanta	53	1456	258	567	.455	164	206	.796	37	91	128	315	43	7	114	685	2.4	5.9	12.9

Season Team	G	Min.	FGM	FGA	Pct.	FTM	FTA	Pct.	Off.	Def.	Tot.	Ast.	St.	Blk.	TO	Pts.	RPG	APG	PPG
									REBOUNDS								**AVERAGES**		
83-84—Atlanta	75	2079	354	800	.443	217	256	.848	53	86	139	326	62	6	134	925	1.9	4.3	12.3
84-85—Cleveland	76	1920	337	791	.426	255	300	.850	35	84	119	426	43	4	152	941	1.6	5.6	12.4
85-86—Clev.-Atla.	66	1014	148	344	.430	118	138	.855	8	47	55	217	37	4	78	417	0.8	3.3	6.3
Totals	750	21191	3699	8258	.448	2279	2777	.821	560	945	1505	3368	683	116	1398	9710	2.0	4.5	12.9

Three-point field goals: 1979-80, 4-for-42 (.095). 1980-81, 4-for-33 (.121). 1981-82, 5-for-27 (.185). 1982-83, 5-for-18 (.278). 1983-84, 0-for-8. 1984-85, 12-for-46 (.261). 1985-86, 3-for-13 (.231). Totals, 33-for-187 (.176).

Personal fouls/disqualifications: 1976-77, 128/1. 1977-78, 173/0. 1978-79, 177/1. 1979-80, 178/0. 1980-81, 179/2. 1981-82, 176/1. 1982-83, 100/0. 1983-84, 146/0. 1984-85, 136/1. 1985-86, 76/0. Totals, 1469/6.

NBA PLAYOFF RECORD

Season Team	G	Min.	FGM	FGA	Pct.	FTM	FTA	Pct.	Off.	Def.	Tot.	Ast.	St.	Blk.	TO	Pts.	RPG	APG	PPG
									REBOUNDS								**AVERAGES**		
76-77—Portland	16	436	65	133	.489	38	53	.717	10	23	33	52	28	3	...	168	2.1	3.3	10.5
77-78—Portland	6	201	35	76	.461	16	23	.696	7	10	17	13	1	2	...	86	2.8	2.2	14.3
80-81—Indiana	2	74	14	35	.400	12	13	.923	2	6	8	11	2	0	...	40	4.0	5.5	20.0
82-83—Atlanta	3	113	21	52	.404	9	10	.900	1	4	5	27	0	0	...	51	1.7	9.0	17.0
83-84—Atlanta	5	131	22	55	.400	6	6	1.000	2	8	10	24	1	0	...	50	2.0	4.8	10.0
84-85—Cleveland	3	50	12	16	.750	4	5	.800	1	5	6	15	5	0	...	28	2.0	5.0	9.3
85-86—Atlanta	8	65	9	25	.360	4	4	1.000	2	4	6	15	2	0	...	22	0.8	1.9	2.8
Totals	43	1070	178	392	.454	89	114	.781	25	60	85	157	39	5	28	445	2.0	3.7	10.3

Three-point field goals: 1980-81, 0-for-1. 1982-83, 0-for-1. 1984-85, 0-for-1. Totals, 0-for-3.

Personal fouls/disqualifications: 1976-77, 32/0. 1977-78, 15/0. 1980-81, 6/0. 1982-83, 6/0. 1983-84, 10/0. 1984-85, 5/0. 1985-86, 6/0. Totals, 80/0.

HEAD COACHING RECORD

BACKGROUND: Director of community relations, Atlanta Hawks (1987-88 through 1989-90). ... Assistant coach, Hawks (1990-91 through 1992-93). ... Assistant coach, Los Angeles Clippers (1993-94). ... Assistant coach, Portland Trail Blazers (1994-95 and 1995-96).

FITCH, BILL   CLIPPERS

PERSONAL: Born May 19, 1934, in Davenport, Iowa. ... 6-2/205. ... Full name: Billy Charles Fitch.
HIGH SCHOOL: Cedar Rapids (Iowa).
COLLEGE: Coe College (Iowa).

COLLEGIATE RECORD

Season Team	G	Min.	FGM	FGA	Pct.	FTM	FTA	Pct.	Reb.	Ast.	Pts.	RPG	APG	PPG
													AVERAGES	
50-51—Coe College						Statistics unavailable.								
51-52—Coe College	20	...	63	...	...	50	...	...	...	...	176	...	...	8.8
52-53—Coe College	19	...	83	...	...	72	...	...	...	...	238	...	...	12.5
53-54—Coe College	22	...	123	...	...	92	...	...	...	...	338	...	...	15.4
Totals	61	...	269	...	...	214	...	...	...	...	752	...	...	12.3

HEAD COACHING RECORD

BACKGROUND: Head baseball coach and assistant basketball coach, Creighton University (1956-57 and 1957-58).
HONORS: NBA Coach of the Year (1976, 1980).

COLLEGIATE COACHING RECORD

Season Team	W	L	Pct.	Finish
58-59 —Coe College	11	9	.550	6th/Midwest Collegiate Athletic Conference
59-60 —Coe College	12	9	.571	T5th/Midwest Collegiate Athletic Conference
60-61 —Coe College	10	12	.455	T4th/Midwest Collegiate Athletic Conference
61-62 —Coe College	11	10	.524	T6th/Midwest Collegiate Athletic Conference
62-63 —North Dakota	14	13	.519	3rd/North Central Intercollegiate Athletic Conference
63-64 —North Dakota	10	16	.385	T3rd/North Central Intercollegiate Athletic Conference
64-65 —North Dakota	26	5	.839	1st/North Central Intercollegiate Athletic Conference
65-66 —North Dakota	24	5	.828	1st/North Central Intercollegiate Athletic Conference
66-67 —North Dakota	20	6	.769	1st/North Central Intercollegiate Athletic Conference
67-68 —Bowling Green	18	7	.720	1st/Mid-American Conference
68-69 —Minnesota	12	12	.500	T5th/Big Ten Conference
69-70 —Minnesota	13	11	.542	5th/Big Ten Conference
Totals (12 years)..	181	115	.611	

NBA COACHING RECORD

Season Team	W	L	Pct.	Finish	W	L	Pct.
	REGULAR SEASON				**PLAYOFFS**		
70-71 —Cleveland...	15	67	.183	4th/Central Division	—	—	—
71-72 —Cleveland...	23	59	.280	4th/Central Division	—	—	—
72-73 —Cleveland...	32	50	.390	4th/Central Division	—	—	—
73-74 —Cleveland...	29	53	.354	4th/Central Division	—	—	—
74-75 —Cleveland...	40	42	.488	3rd/Central Division	—	—	—
75-76 —Cleveland...	49	33	.598	1st/Central Division	6	7	.462
76-77 —Cleveland...	43	39	.524	4th/Central Division	1	2	.538
77-78 —Cleveland...	43	39	.524	3rd/Central Division	0	2	.000
78-79 —Cleveland...	30	52	.366	T4th/Central Division	—	—	—
79-80 —Boston...	61	21	.744	1st/Atlantic Division	5	4	.556
80-81 —Boston...	62	20	.756	T1st/Atlantic Division	12	5	.706
81-82 —Boston...	63	19	.768	1st/Atlantic Division	7	5	.583
82-83 —Boston...	56	26	.683	2nd/Atlantic Division	2	5	.286
83-84 —Houston..	29	53	.354	6th/Midwest Division	—	—	—
84-85 —Houston..	48	34	.585	2nd/Midwest Division	2	3	.400

Season	Team	REGULAR SEASON				PLAYOFFS		
		W	L	Pct.	Finish	W	L	Pct.
85-86	—Houston	51	31	.622	1st/Midwest Division	13	7	.650
86-87	—Houston	42	40	.512	3rd/Midwest Division	5	5	.500
87-88	—Houston	46	36	.561	4th/Midwest Division	1	3	.250
89-90	—New Jersey	17	65	.207	6th/Atlantic Division	—	—	—
90-91	—New Jersey	26	56	.317	5th/Atlantic Division	—	—	—
91-92	—New Jersey	40	42	.489	3rd/Atlantic Division	1	3	.250
94-95	—L.A. Clippers	17	65	.207	7th/Pacific Division	—	—	—
95-96	—L.A. Clippers	29	53	.354	7th/Pacific Division	—	—	—
	Totals (23 years)	891	995	.472	Totals (12 years).....	55	51	.519

NOTES:
1965—Defeated Minnesota-Duluth, 67-57, in College Division Tournament first round; defeated Moorhead (Minn.) State in second round; defeated Seattle Pacific, 97-83, in national quarterfinals; lost to Southern Illinois, 97-64, in national semifinals; defeated St. Michael's (Vt.), 94-86, in national third-place game.
1966—Defeated Northern Colorado, 84-71, in College Division Tournament regional semifinals; defeated Valparaiso, 112-82, in regional finals; defeated Abilene Christian, 63-62, in national quarterfinals; lost to Southern Illinois, 69-61, in national semifinals; lost to Akron, 76-71, in national third-place game.
1967—Lost to Louisiana Tech, 86-77, in College Division Tournament regional semifinals; defeated Parsons (Ia.), 107-56, in regional third-place game.
1968—Lost to Marquette, 72-71, in NCAA Tournament first round.
1976—Defeated Washington, 4-3, in Eastern Conference semifinals; lost to Boston, 4-2, in Eastern Conference finals.
1977—Lost to Washington in Eastern Conference first round.
1978—Lost to New York in Eastern Conference first round.
1980—Defeated Houston, 4-0, in Eastern Conference semifinals; lost to Philadelphia, 4-1, in Eastern Conference finals.
1981—Defeated Chicago, 4-0, in Eastern Conference semifinals; defeated Philadelphia, 4-3, in Eastern Conference finals; defeated Houston, 4-2, in NBA Finals.
1982—Defeated Washington, 4-1, in Eastern Conference semifinals; lost to Philadelphia, 4-3, in Eastern Conference finals.
1983—Defeated Atlanta, 2-1, in Eastern Conference first round; lost to Milwaukee, 4-0, in Eastern Conference semifinals.
1985—Lost to Utah in Western Conference first round.
1986—Defeated Sacramento, 3-0, in Western Conference first round; defeated Denver, 4-2, in Western Conference semifinals; defeated Los Angeles Lakers, 4-1, in Western Conference finals; lost to Boston, 4-2, in NBA Finals.
1987—Defeated Portland, 3-1, in Western Conference first round; lost to Seattle, 4-2, in Western Conference semifinals.
1988—Lost to Dallas in Western Conference first round.
1992—Lost to Cleveland in Eastern Conference first round.

FITZSIMMONS, COTTON — SUNS

PERSONAL: Born October 7, 1931, in Hannibal, Mo. ... 5-7/160. ... Full name: Lowell Fitzsimmons. ... Father of Gary Fitzsimmons, director of player personnel with Cleveland Cavaliers.
HIGH SCHOOL: Bowling Green (Mo.).
COLLEGE: Hannibal (Mo.)-LaGrange, then Midwestern State (Texas).

COLLEGIATE RECORD

Season Team	G	Min.	FGM	FGA	Pct.	FTM	FTA	Pct.	Reb.	Ast.	Pts.	AVERAGES		
												RPG	APG	PPG
52-53—Hann.-LaGrange‡	33	...	...	...	...	128	173	.740	...	...	838	...	...	25.4
53-54—Midwestern St.	27	...	53	161	.329	128	173	.740	...	...	234	...	...	8.7
54-55—Midwestern St.	27	...	118	258	.457	162	210	.771	...	...	398	...	...	14.7
55-56—Midwestern St.	28	...	148	319	.464	164	223	.735	...	...	460	...	...	16.4
Varsity totals	82	...	319	738	.432	454	606	.749	...	...	1092	...	...	13.3

HEAD COACHING RECORD

BACKGROUND: Assistant coach, Kansas State University (1967-68). ... Director of player personnel, Golden State Warriors (1976-77). ... Director of player personnel, Phoenix Suns (1987-88). ... Head coach/director of player personnel, Suns (1988-89 through 1991-92).
HONORS: NBA Coach of the Year (1979, 1989).

COLLEGE COACHING RECORD

Season	Team	W	L	Pct.	
58-59	—Moberly J.C. (Mo.)	16	15	.516	
59-60	—Moberly J.C. (Mo.)	19	8	.704	
60-61	—Moberly J.C. (Mo.)	26	5	.839	
61-62	—Moberly J.C. (Mo.)	26	9	.743	
62-63	—Moberly J.C. (Mo.)	26	6	.813	
63-64	—Moberly J.C. (Mo.)	24	5	.828	
64-65	—Moberly J.C. (Mo.)	25	5	.833	
65-66	—Moberly J.C. (Mo.)	29	5	.853	
66-67	—Moberly J.C. (Mo.)	31	2	.939	
68-69	—Kansas State	14	12	.538	T2nd/Big Eight Conference
69-70	—Kansas State	20	8	.714	1st/Big Eight Conference
	Junior college totals (9 years)	222	60	.787	
	4-year college totals (2 years)	34	20	.630	

NBA COACHING RECORD

Season	Team	REGULAR SEASON				PLAYOFFS		
		W	L	Pct.	Finish	W	L	Pct.
70-71	—Phoenix	48	34	.585	3rd/Midwest Division	—	—	—
71-72	—Phoenix	49	33	.598	3rd/Midwest Division	—	—	—

Season	Team	REGULAR SEASON				PLAYOFFS		
		W	L	Pct.	Finish	W	L	Pct.
72-73	—Atlanta	46	36	.561	2nd/Central Division	2	4	.333
73-74	—Atlanta	35	47	.427	2nd/Central Division	—	—	—
74-75	—Atlanta	31	51	.378	4th/Central Division	—	—	—
75-76	—Atlanta	28	46	.378		—	—	—
77-78	—Buffalo	27	55	.329	4th/Atlantic Division	—	—	—
78-79	—Kansas City	48	34	.585	1st/Midwest Division	1	4	.200
79-80	—Kansas City	47	35	.573	2nd/Midwest Division	1	2	.333
80-81	—Kansas City	40	42	.488	T2nd/Midwest Division	7	8	.467
81-82	—Kansas City	30	52	.366	4th/Midwest Division	—	—	—
82-83	—Kansas City	45	37	.549	T2nd/Midwest Division	—	—	—
83-84	—Kansas City	38	44	.463	T3rd/Midwest Division	0	3	.000
84-85	—San Antonio	41	41	.500	T4th/Midwest Division	2	3	.400
85-86	—San Antonio	35	47	.427	6th/Midwest Division	0	3	.000
88-89	—Phoenix	55	27	.671	2nd/Pacific Division	7	5	.583
89-90	—Phoenix	54	28	.659	3rd/Pacific Division	9	7	.563
90-91	—Phoenix	55	27	.671	3rd/Pacific Division	1	3	.250
91-92	—Phoenix	53	29	.646	3rd/Pacific Division	4	4	.500
95-96	—Phoenix	27	22	.551	4th/Pacific Division	1	3	.250
Totals (20 years)		832	767	.520	**Totals (12 years)**	35	49	.417

NOTES:
1966—Won National Junior College Athletic Association national tournament.
1967—Won National Junior College Athletic Association national tournament.
1970—Lost to New Mexico, 70-66, in NCAA Tournament regional semifinal.
1973—Lost to Boston in Eastern Conference semifinals.
1976—Replaced as Atlanta head coach by Gene Tormohlen with club in fifth place (March).
1979—Lost to Phoenix in Western Conference semifinals.
1980—Lost to Phoenix in Western Conference first round.
1981—Defeated Portland, 2-1, in Western Conference first round; defeated Phoenix, 4-3, in Western Conference semifinals; lost to Houston, 4-1, in Western Conference finals.
1984—Lost to Los Angeles Lakers in Western Conference first round.
1985—Lost to Denver in Western Conference first round.
1986—Lost to Los Angeles Lakers in Western Conference first round.
1989—Defeated Denver, 3-0, in Western Conference first round; defeated Golden State, 4-1, in Western Conference semifinals; lost to Los Angeles Lakers, 4-0, in Western Conference finals.
1990—Defeated Utah, 3-2, in Western Conference first round; defeated Los Angeles Lakers, 4-1, in Western Conference semifinals; lost to Portland, 4-2, in Western Conference finals.
1991—Lost to Utah in Western Conference first round.
1992—Defeated San Antonio, 3-0, in Western Conference first round; lost to Portland, 4-1, in Western Conference semifinals.
1996—Replaced Paul Westphal as Phoenix head coach (January 16) with record of 14-19 and club in sixth place. Lost to San Antonio in Western Conference first round.

FORD, CHRIS — BUCKS

PERSONAL: Born January 11, 1949, in Atlantic City, N.J. ... 6-5/190. ... Full name: Christopher Joseph Ford.
HIGH SCHOOL: Holy Spirit (Absecon, N.J.).
COLLEGE: Villanova.
TRANSACTIONS/CAREER NOTES: Selected by Detroit Pistons in second round (17th pick overall) of 1972 NBA Draft. ... Traded by Pistons with 1981 second-round draft choice to Boston Celtics for G Earl Tatum (October 19, 1978).
MISCELLANEOUS: Member of NBA championship team (1981).

COLLEGIATE RECORD

Season Team	G	Min.	FGM	FGA	Pct.	FTM	FTA	Pct.	Reb.	Ast.	Pts.	RPG	APG	PPG
68-69—Villanova‡	18	...	118	...	...	87	...	...	...	...	323	...	...	17.9
69-70—Villanova	29	...	188	396	.475	89	124	.718	168	88	465	5.8	3.0	16.0
70-71—Villanova	34	...	180	400	.450	108	176	.614	200	238	468	5.9	7.0	13.8
71-72—Villanova	28	...	206	399	.516	88	146	.603	180	145	500	6.4	5.2	17.9
Varsity totals	91	...	574	1195	.480	285	446	.639	548	471	1433	6.0	5.2	15.7

NBA REGULAR-SEASON RECORD

Season Team	G	Min.	FGM	FGA	Pct.	FTM	FTA	Pct.	REBOUNDS Off.	Def.	Tot.	Ast.	St.	Blk.	TO	Pts.	RPG	APG	PPG
72-73—Detroit	74	1537	208	434	.479	60	93	.645	...	...	266	194	...	...	...	476	3.6	2.6	6.4
73-74—Detroit	82	2059	264	595	.444	57	77	.740	109	195	304	279	148	14	...	585	3.7	3.4	7.1
74-75—Detroit	80	1962	206	435	.474	63	95	.663	93	176	269	230	113	26	...	475	3.4	2.9	5.9
75-76—Detroit	82	2198	301	707	.426	83	115	.722	80	211	291	272	178	24	...	685	3.5	3.3	8.4
76-77—Detroit	82	2539	437	918	.476	131	170	.771	96	174	270	337	179	26	...	1005	3.3	4.1	12.3
77-78—Detroit	82	2582	374	800	.468	113	154	.734	117	151	268	381	166	17	232	861	3.3	4.6	10.5
78-79—Detroit-Bos	81	2737	538	1142	.471	172	227	.758	124	150	274	374	115	25	210	1248	3.4	4.6	15.4
79-80—Boston	73	2115	330	709	.465	86	114	.754	77	104	181	215	111	27	105	816	2.5	2.9	11.2
80-81—Boston	82	2723	314	707	.444	64	87	.736	72	91	163	295	100	23	127	728	2.0	3.6	8.9
81-82—Boston	76	1591	188	450	.418	39	56	.696	52	56	108	142	42	10	52	435	1.4	1.9	5.7
Totals	794	22043	3160	6874	.460	868	1188	.731	...	...	2394	2719	1152	192	726	7314	3.0	3.4	9.2

Three-point field goals: 1979-80, 70-for-164 (.427). 1980-81, 36-for-109 (.330). 1981-82, 20-for-63 (.317). Totals, 126-for-336 (.375).
Personal fouls/disqualifications: 1972-73, 133/1. 1973-74, 159/1. 1974-75, 187/0. 1975-76, 222/0. 1976-77, 192/1. 1977-78, 182/2. 1978-79, 209/3. 1979-80, 178/0. 1980-81, 212/2. 1981-82, 143/0. Totals, 1817/10.

NBA PLAYOFF RECORD

Season Team	G	Min.	FGM	FGA	Pct.	FTM	FTA	Pct.	Off.	Def.	Tot.	Ast.	St.	Blk.	TO	Pts.	RPG	APG	PPG
73-74—Detroit..........	5	94	8	17	.471	4	6	.667	4	11	15	7	2	2	...	20	3.0	1.4	4.0
74-75—Detroit..........	3	82	6	11	.545	0	0	...	2	11	13	10	1	0	...	12	4.3	3.3	4.0
75-76—Detroit..........	9	276	33	81	.407	12	15	.800	6	30	36	40	11	5	...	78	4.0	4.4	8.7
76-77—Detroit..........	3	101	18	44	.409	5	9	.556	8	11	19	12	7	0	...	41	6.3	4.0	13.7
79-80—Boston	9	279	34	79	.430	12	15	.800	9	16	25	21	14	6	13	82	2.8	2.3	9.1
80-81—Boston	17	507	66	146	.452	15	25	.600	13	32	45	46	14	1	19	154	2.6	2.7	9.1
81-82—Boston	12	138	20	42	.476	5	7	.714	6	9	15	15	1	3	3	47	1.3	1.3	3.9
Totals	58	1477	185	420	.440	53	77	.688	48	120	168	151	50	17	35	434	2.9	2.6	7.5

Three-point field goals: 1979-80, 2-for-13 (.154). 1980-81, 7-for-25 (.280). 1981-82, 2-for-7 (.286). Totals, 11-for-45 (.244).

Personal fouls/disqualifications: 1973-74, 10/0. 1974-75, 8/0. 1975-76, 33/1. 1976-77, 11/0. 1979-80, 35/1. 1980-81, 47/0. 1981-82, 15/0. Totals, 159/2.

HEAD COACHING RECORD

BACKGROUND: Broadcaster, Boston Celtics (1982-83). ... Assistant coach, Celtics (1983-84 through 1989-90).

NBA COACHING RECORD

Season Team	W	L	Pct.	Finish	W	L	Pct.
		REGULAR SEASON				PLAYOFFS	
90-91 —Boston.............................	56	26	.683	1st/Atlantic Division	5	6	.455
91-92 —Boston.............................	51	31	.622	T1st/Atlantic Division	6	4	.600
92-93 —Boston.............................	48	34	.585	2nd/Atlantic Division	1	3	.250
93-94 —Boston.............................	32	50	.390	5th/Atlantic Division	—	—	—
94-95 —Boston.............................	35	47	.427	3rd/Atlantic Division	1	3	250
Totals (5 years).............................	222	188	.541	Totals (4 years).......	13	16	.448

NOTES:

1991—Defeated Indiana, 3-2, in Eastern Conference first round; lost to Detroit, 4-2, in Eastern Conference semifinals.

1992—Defeated Indiana, 3-0, in Eastern Conference first round; lost to Cleveland, 4-3, in Eastern Conference semifinals.

1993—Lost to Charlotte in Eastern Conference first round.

1995—Lost to Orlando in Eastern Conference first round.

FRATELLO, MIKE   CAVALIERS

PERSONAL: Born February 24, 1947, in Hackensack, N.J. ... 5-7/150. ... Full name: Michael Robert Fratello.
HIGH SCHOOL: Hackensack (N.J.).
COLLEGE: Montclair (N.J.) State College, then graduate work at Rhode Island.

HEAD COACHING RECORD

BACKGROUND: Football and basketball coach, Hackensack (N.J.) High (1969-70). ... Assistant coach/freshman coach, University of Rhode Island (1970-71 and 1971-72). ... Assistant coach, James Madison University (1972-73 through 1974-75). ... Assistant coach, Villanova University (1975-76 through 1977-78). ... Assistant coach, Atlanta Hawks (1978-79 through 1981-82). ... Assistant coach, New York Knicks (1982-83). ... Vice president/head coach, Hawks (1986-87 through 1989-90). ... Broadcaster, NBC television (1990-91 through 1992-93).
HONORS: NBA Coach of the Year (1986).

NBA COACHING RECORD

Season Team	W	L	Pct.	Finish	W	L	Pct.
		REGULAR SEASON				PLAYOFFS	
80-81 —Atlanta...	0	3	.000	4th/Central Division	—	—	—
83-84 —Atlanta...	40	42	.488	3rd/Central Division	2	3	.400
84-85 —Atlanta...	34	48	.415	5th/Central Division	—	—	—
85-86 —Atlanta...	50	32	.610	2nd/Central Division	4	5	.444
86-87 —Atlanta...	57	25	.695	1st/Central Division	4	5	.444
87-88 —Atlanta...	50	32	.610	T2nd/Central Division	6	6	.500
88-89 —Atlanta...	52	30	.634	3rd/Central Division	2	3	.400
89-90 —Atlanta...	41	41	.500	6th/Central Division	—	—	—
93-94 —Cleveland..	47	35	.573	T3rd/Central Division	0	3	.000
94-95 —Cleveland..	43	39	.524	4th/Central Division	1	3	.250
95-96 —Cleveland..	47	35	.573	3rd/Central Division	0	3	.000
Totals (11 years)...	461	362	.560	Totals (8 years).......	19	31	.380

NOTES:

1981—Replaced Hubie Brown as Atlanta head coach (March 26), with record of 31-48 and club in fourth place. Served as interim co-head coach with Brendan Suhr for remainder of season.

1984—Lost to Milwaukee in Eastern Conference first round.

1986—Defeated Detroit, 3-1, in Eastern Conference first round; lost to Boston, 4-1, in Eastern Conference semifinals.

1987—Defeated Indiana, 3-1, in Eastern Conference first round; lost to Detroit, 4-1, in Eastern Conference semifinals.

1988—Defeated Milwaukee, 3-2, in Eastern Conference first round; lost to Boston, 4-3, in Eastern Conference semifinals.

1989—Lost to Milwaukee in Eastern Conference first round.

1994—Lost to Chicago in Eastern Conference first round.

1995—Lost to New York in Eastern Conference first round.

1996—Lost to New York in Eastern Conference first round.

HEAD COACHES

HARRIS, DEL

PERSONAL: Born June 18, 1937, in Plainfield, Ind. ... 6-4/205. ... Full name: Delmer W. Harris.
HIGH SCHOOL: Plainfield (Ind.).
COLLEGE: Milligan College (Tenn.).

COLLEGIATE RECORD

NOTES: Field-goal attempts for five games and rebounds for 13 games are unavailable.

Season Team	G	Min.	FGM	FGA	Pct.	FTM	FTA	Pct.	Reb.	Ast.	Pts.	AVERAGES RPG	APG	PPG
55-56—Milligan College	24	...	101	232	.435	89	126	.706	122	...	291	5.1	...	12.1
56-57—Milligan College	24	...	162	375	.432	141	197	.716	165	...	465	6.9	...	19.4
57-58—Milligan College	22	...	167	378	.442	119	149	.799	240	...	453	10.9	...	20.6
58-59—Milligan College	21	...	136	306	.444	158	202	.782	338	...	430	16.1	...	20.5
Totals	91	...	566	1291	.438	507	674	.752	865	...	1639	9.5	...	18.0

HEAD COACHING RECORD

BACKGROUND: Head coach, Superior League, Puerto Rico (1969 through 1975). ... Assistant coach, Utah Stars of ABA (1975-76). ... Assistant coach, Houston Rockets (1976-77 through 1978-79). ... Scout, Milwaukee Bucks (1983 through 1986). ... Assistant coach, Bucks (1986-87). ... Vice president, Bucks (1987 through 1992). ... Consultant, Sacramento Kings (1993-94).
HONORS: NBA Coach of the Year (1995).

COLLEGIATE COACHING RECORD

Season Team	W	L	Pct.	Finish
65-66 —Earlham College	14	8	.636	Hoosier Collegiate Conference
66-67 —Earlham College	15	9	.625	4th/Hoosier Collegiate Conference
67-68 —Earlham College	25	3	.893	1st/Hoosier Collegiate Conference
68-69 —Earlham College	18	8	.692	2nd/Hoosier Collegiate Conference
69-70 —Earlham College	22	8	.733	1st/Hoosier Collegiate Conference
70-71 —Earlham College	24	5	.828	1st/Hoosier Collegiate Conference
71-72 —Earlham College	21	9	.700	1st/Hoosier Collegiate Conference
72-73 —Earlham College	17	11	.607	3rd/Hoosier Collegiate Conference
73-74 —Earlham College	19	9	.679	3rd/Hoosier Collegiate Conference
Totals (9 years)	175	70	.714	

NBA COACHING RECORD

Season Team	REGULAR SEASON W	L	Pct.	Finish	PLAYOFFS W	L	Pct.
79-80 —Houston	41	41	.500	T2nd/Central Division	2	5	.286
80-81 —Houston	40	42	.488	T2nd/Midwest Division	12	9	.571
81-82 —Houston	46	36	.561	T2nd/Midwest Division	1	2	.333
82-83 —Houston	14	68	.171	6th/Midwest Division	—	—	—
87-88 —Milwaukee	42	40	.512	T4th/Central Division	2	3	.400
88-89 —Milwaukee	49	33	.598	4th/Central Division	3	6	.333
89-90 —Milwaukee	44	38	.537	3rd/Central Division	1	3	.250
90-91 —Milwaukee	48	34	.585	3rd/Central Division	0	3	.000
91-92 —Milwaukee	8	9	.471	—	—	—	—
94-95 —L.A. Lakers	48	34	.585	3rd/Pacific Division	5	5	.500
95-96 —L.A. Lakers	53	29	.646	2nd/Pacific Division	1	3	.250
Totals (11 years)	433	404	.517	Totals (9 years)	27	39	.409

NOTES:
1968—Posted 1-1 record in NAIA District Tournament.
1969—Posted 0-1 record in NAIA District Tournament.
1970—Posted 1-1 record in NAIA District Tournament.
1971—Posted 2-0 record in NAIA District Tournament; posted 1-1 record in NAIA National Tournament.
1972—Posted 1-1 record in NAIA District Tournament.
1973—Posted 2-1 record in NAIA District Tournament.
1980—Defeated San Antonio, 2-1, in Eastern Conference first round; lost to Boston, 4-0, in Eastern Conference semifinals.
1981—Defeated Los Angeles Lakers, 2-1, in Western Conference first round; defeated San Antonio, 4-3, in Western Conference semifinals; defeated Kansas City, 4-1, in Western Conference finals; lost to Boston, 4-2, in NBA Finals.
1982—Lost to Seattle in Western Conference first round.
1988—Lost to Atlanta in Eastern Conference first round.
1989—Defeated Atlanta, 3-2, in Eastern Conference first round; lost to Detroit, 4-0, in Eastern Conference semifinals.
1990—Lost to Chicago in Eastern Conference first round.
1991—Lost to Philadelphia in Eastern Conference first round. Replaced as Milwaukee head coach by Frank Hamblen (December 4) with club in third place.
1995—Defeated Seattle, 3-1, in Western Conference first round; lost to San Antonio, 4-2, in Western Conference semifinals.
1996—Lost to Houston in Western Conference first round.

DID YOU KNOW...

...that the Indiana Pacers were the only team to beat Chicago
twice in the Bulls' 72-win 1995-96 season?

HILL, BOB — SPURS

PERSONAL: Born November 24, 1948, in Columbus, Ohio. ... 6-5/200. ... Full name: Robert W. Hill.
HIGH SCHOOL: Worthington (Ohio).
COLLEGE: Bowling Green State.

COLLEGIATE RECORD

Season Team	G	Min.	FGM	FGA	Pct.	FTM	FTA	Pct.	Reb.	Ast.	Pts.	RPG	APG	PPG
67-68—Bowling Green‡	14	...	108	215	.502	41	57	.719	127	...	257	9.1	...	18.4
68-69—Bowling Green	20	...	22	54	.407	12	22	.545	21	...	56	1.1	...	2.8
69-70—Bowling Green	16	...	5	23	.217	6	12	.500	14	...	16	0.9	...	1.0
70-71—Bowling Green	21	...	22	49	.449	9	16	.563	31	...	53	1.5	...	2.5
Varsity totals	57	...	49	126	.389	27	50	.540	66	...	125	1.2	...	2.2

HEAD COACHING RECORD

BACKGROUND: Assistant coach, Bowling Green State University (1971-72 through 1974-75). ... Assistant coach, University of Pittsburgh (1975-76 and 1976-77). ... Assistant coach, University of Kansas (1977-78 through 1984-85). ... Assistant coach, New York Knicks (1985-86). ... Scout, Charlotte Hornets (1987-88). ... Broadcaster, New Jersey Nets (1987-88). ... Head coach, Vitrus Knorr of Italian League (1988-89). ... Assistant coach, Indiana Pacers (1989-90 to December 20, 1990). ... Assistant coach, Orlando Magic (1993-94).

NBA COACHING RECORD

Season Team	REGULAR SEASON				PLAYOFFS		
	W	L	Pct.	Finish	W	L	Pct.
86-87 —New York	20	46	.303	T4th/Atlantic Division	—	—	—
90-91 —Indiana	32	25	.561	5th/Central Division	2	3	.400
91-92 —Indiana	40	42	.488	4th/Central Division	0	3	.000
92-93 —Indiana	41	41	.500	5th/Central Division	1	3	.250
94-95 —San Antonio	62	20	.756	1st/Midwest Division	9	6	.600
95-96 —San Antonio	59	23	.720	1st/Midwest Division	5	5	.500
Totals (6 years)	254	197	.563	**Totals (5 years)** 17	20	.459	

CBA COACHING RECORD

Season Team	REGULAR SEASON				PLAYOFFS		
	W	L	Pct.	Finish	W	L	Pct.
87-88 —Topeka	5	12	.294	5th/Eastern Division	—	—	—

NOTES:
1986—Replaced Hubie Brown as New York head coach, with record of 4-12 and club in fourth place.
1988—Replaced John Killilea (13-17) and John Darr (interim head coach, 3-4) as Topeka head coach (February), with record of 16-21 and club in third place.
1990—Replaced Dick Versace as Indiana head coach (December 20), with record of 9-16 and club in sixth place.
1991—Lost to Boston in Eastern Conference first round.
1992—Lost to Boston in Eastern Conference first round.
1993—Lost to New York in Eastern Conference first round.
1995—Defeated Denver, 3-0, in Western Conference first round; defeated L.A. Lakers, 4-2, in Western Conference semifinals; lost to Houston, 4-2, in Western Conference finals.
1996—Defeated Phoenix, 3-1, in Western Conference first round; lost to Utah, 4-2, in Western Conference semifinals.

RECORD AS BASEBALL PLAYER

TRANSACTIONS/CAREER NOTES: Selected by San Diego Padres organization in 14th round of free-agent draft (June 8, 1971). ... Released by Padres organization (July 27, 1971).

Year Team (League)	W	L	Pct.	ERA	G	GS	CG	ShO	Sv.	IP	H	R	ER	BB	SO
1971—Tri-City (Northwest)	0	0	.000	12.00	2	0	0	0	0	3	5	4	4	2	1

HILL, BRIAN — MAGIC

PERSONAL: Born September 19, 1947, in East Orange, N.J. ... 5-9/175. ... Full name: Brian Alfred Hill. ... Brother of Fred Hill, head baseball coach with Rutgers University.
HIGH SCHOOL: Our Lady of the Valley (East Orange, N.J.).
COLLEGE: Kennedy (Neb.).

HEAD COACHING RECORD

BACKGROUND: Assistant coach, Piscataway (N.J.) Township High School (1969-70 and 1970-71). ... Assistant coach, Clifford J. Scott High School, N.J. (1971-72). ... Assistant coach, Montclair (N.J.) State University (1972-73 and 1973-74). ... Assistant coach, Lehigh University (1974-75). ... Assistant coach, Penn State University (1983-84 through 1985-86). ... Assistant coach, Atlanta Hawks (1986-87 through 1989-90). ... Assistant coach, Orlando Magic (1990-91 through 1992-93).

COLLEGIATE COACHING RECORD

Season Team	W	L	Pct.	Finish
75-76 —Lehigh	9	15	.375	6th/East Coast Conference Western section
76-77 —Lehigh	12	15	.444	3rd/East Coast Conference Western section
77-78 —Lehigh	8	18	.308	4th/East Coast Conference Western section
78-79 —Lehigh	8	18	.308	5th/East Coast Conference Western section
79-80 —Lehigh	5	20	.200	5th/East Coast Conference Western section
80-81 —Lehigh	14	12	.538	4th/East Coast Conference Western section
81-82 —Lehigh	9	17	.346	6th/East Coast Conference Western section
82-83 —Lehigh	10	16	.384	5th/East Coast Conference Western section
Totals (8 years)	75	131	.364	

NBA COACHING RECORD

Season Team	REGULAR SEASON W	L	Pct.	Finish	PLAYOFFS W	L	Pct.
93-94 —Orlando	50	32	.610	2nd/Atlantic Division	0	3	.000
94-95 —Orlando	57	25	.695	1st/Atlantic Division	11	10	.524
95-96 —Orlando	60	22	.732	1st/Atlantic Division	7	5	.583
Totals (3 years)	167	79	.679	Totals (3 years)	18	18	.500

NOTES:
1994—Lost to Indiana in Eastern Conference first round.
1995—Defeated Boston, 3-1, in Eastern Conference first round; defeated Chicago, 4-2, in Eastern Conference semifinals; defeated Indiana, 4-3, in Eastern Conference finals; lost to Houston, 4-0, in NBA Finals.
1996—Defeated Detroit, 3-0, in Eastern Conference first round; defeated Atlanta, 4-1, in Eastern Conference semifinals; lost to Chicago, 4-0, in Eastern Conference finals.

JACKSON, PHIL   BULLS

PERSONAL: Born September 17, 1945, in Deer Lodge, Mont. ... 6-8/230. ... Full name: Philip D. Jackson.
HIGH SCHOOL: Williston (N.D.).
COLLEGE: North Dakota.
TRANSACTIONS/CAREER NOTES: Selected by New York Knicks in second round (17th pick overall) of 1967 NBA Draft. ... Traded by Knicks with future draft choice to New Jersey Nets for future draft choices (June 8, 1978). ... Waived by Nets (October 11, 1978). ... Re-signed as free agent by Nets (November 10, 1978). ... Waived by Nets (October 12, 1979). ... Re-signed as free agent by Nets (February 15, 1980).
MISCELLANEOUS: Member of NBA championship team (1973).

COLLEGIATE RECORD

Season Team	G	Min.	FGM	FGA	Pct.	FTM	FTA	Pct.	Reb.	Ast.	Pts.	AVERAGES RPG	APG	PPG
63-64—North Dakota‡	...	...	...	...	...	...	...	...	...	...	...	...	...	24.3
64-65—North Dakota	31	...	129	307	.420	107	156	.686	361	...	365	11.6	...	11.8
65-66—North Dakota	29	...	238	439	.542	155	203	.764	374	...	631	12.9	...	21.8
66-67—North Dakota	26	...	252	468	.538	208	278	.748	374	...	712	14.4	...	27.4
Varsity totals	86	...	619	1214	.510	470	637	.738	1109	...	1708	12.9	...	19.9

NBA REGULAR-SEASON RECORD

HONORS: NBA All-Rookie team (1968).
NOTES: Led NBA with 330 personal fouls (1975).

Season Team	G	Min.	FGM	FGA	Pct.	FTM	FTA	Pct.	Reb.	Ast.	PF	Dq.	Pts.	AVERAGES RPG	APG	PPG
67-68 —New York	75	1093	182	455	.400	99	168	.589	338	55	212	3	463	4.5	0.7	6.2
68-69 —New York	47	924	126	294	.429	80	119	.672	246	43	168	6	332	5.2	0.9	7.1
69-70 —New York						Did not play—injured.										
70-71 —New York	71	771	118	263	.449	95	133	.714	238	31	169	4	331	3.4	0.4	4.7
71-72 —New York	80	1273	205	466	.440	167	228	.732	326	72	224	4	577	4.1	0.9	7.2
72-73 —New York	80	1393	245	553	.443	154	195	.790	344	94	218	2	644	4.3	1.2	8.1

Season Team	G	Min.	FGM	FGA	Pct.	FTM	FTA	Pct.	REBOUNDS Off.	Def.	Tot.	Ast.	St.	Blk.	TO	Pts.	AVERAGES RPG	APG	PPG
73-74—New York	82	2050	361	757	.477	191	246	.776	123	355	478	134	42	67	...	913	5.8	1.6	11.1
74-75—New York	78	2285	324	712	.455	193	253	.763	137	463	600	136	84	53	...	841	7.7	1.7	10.8
75-76—New York	80	1461	185	387	.478	110	150	.733	80	263	343	105	41	20	...	480	4.3	1.3	6.0
76-77—N.Y. Knicks	76	1033	102	232	.440	51	71	.718	75	154	229	85	33	18	...	255	3.0	1.1	3.4
77-78—New York	63	654	55	115	.478	43	56	.768	29	81	110	46	31	15	47	153	1.7	0.7	2.4
78-79—New Jersey	59	1070	144	303	.475	86	105	.819	59	119	178	85	45	22	78	374	3.0	1.4	6.3
79-80—New Jersey	16	194	29	46	.630	7	10	.700	12	12	24	12	5	4	9	65	1.5	0.8	4.1
Totals	807	14201	2076	4583	.453	1276	1734	.736	...	...	3454	898	281	199	134	5428	4.3	1.1	6.7

Three-point field goals: 1979-80, 0-for-2.
Personal fouls/disqualifications: 1973-74, 277/7. 1974-75, 330/10. 1975-76, 275/3. 1976-77, 184/4. 1977-78, 106/0. 1978-79, 168/7. 1979-80, 35/1. Totals, 2366/51.

NBA PLAYOFF RECORD

Season Team	G	Min.	FGM	FGA	Pct.	FTM	FTA	Pct.	Reb.	Ast.	PF	Dq.	Pts.	AVERAGES RPG	APG	PPG
67-68 — New York	6	90	10	35	.286	4	5	.800	25	2	23	0	24	4.2	0.3	4.0
68-69 —New York						Did not play—injured.										
70-71 —New York	5	30	4	14	.286	1	1	1.000	10	2	8	0	9	2.0	0.4	1.8
71-72 —New York	16	320	57	120	.475	42	57	.737	82	15	51	1	156	5.1	0.9	9.8
72-73 —New York	17	338	60	120	.500	28	38	.737	72	24	59	3	148	4.2	1.4	8.7

Season Team	G	Min.	FGM	FGA	Pct.	FTM	FTA	Pct.	REBOUNDS Off.	Def.	Tot.	Ast.	St.	Blk.	TO	Pts.	AVERAGES RPG	APG	PPG
73-74—New York	12	297	54	116	.466	27	30	.900	15	42	57	15	10	5	...	135	4.8	1.3	11.3
74-75—New York	3	78	10	21	.476	7	8	.875	5	20	25	2	4	3	...	27	8.3	0.7	9.0
77-78—New York	6	50	4	8	.500	4	6	.667	4	6	10	3	3	0	4	12	1.7	0.5	2.0
78-79—New Jersey	2	20	1	3	.333	2	2	1.000	2	1	3	0	1	0	0	4	1.5	0.0	2.0
Totals	67	1223	200	437	.458	115	147	.782	...	...	284	63	18	8	4	515	4.2	0.9	7.7

Personal fouls/disqualifications: 1973-74, 40/0. 1974-75, 15/0. 1977-78, 11/0. 1978-79, 1/0. Totals, 208/4.

HEAD COACHING RECORD

BACKGROUND: Player/assistant coach, New Jersey Nets (1978-79 and 1979-80). ... Assistant coach, Nets (1980-81). ... Broadcaster, Nets (1981-82). ... Assistant coach, Chicago Bulls (1987-88 and 1988-89).
HONORS: NBA Coach of the Year (1996). ... CBA Coach of the Year (1985).
RECORDS: Holds NBA playoff record for highest winning percentage (minimum 25 games)—.723.

CBA COACHING RECORD

Season Team		REGULAR SEASON				PLAYOFFS		
	W	L	Pct.	Finish		W	L	Pct.
82-83 —Albany	8	11	.421	4th/Eastern Division		—	—	—
83-84 —Albany	25	19	.568	2nd/Eastern Division		9	5	.643
84-85 —Albany	34	14	.708	1st/Eastern Division		5	5	.500
85-86 —Albany	24	24	.500	4th/Eastern Division		3	4	.429
86-87 —Albany	26	22	.542	T2nd/Eastern Division		4	4	.500
Totals (5 years)	117	90	.565		Totals (4 years)	21	18	.538

NBA COACHING RECORD

Season Team		REGULAR SEASON				PLAYOFFS		
	W	L	Pct.	Finish		W	L	Pct.
89-90 —Chicago	55	27	.671	2nd/Central Division		10	6	.625
90-91 —Chicago	61	21	.744	1st/Central Division		15	2	.882
91-92 —Chicago	67	15	.817	1st/Central Division		15	7	.682
92-93 —Chicago	57	25	.695	1st/Central Division		15	4	.789
93-94 —Chicago	55	27	.671	2nd/Central Division		6	4	.600
94-95 —Chicago	47	35	.573	2nd/Central Division		5	5	.500
95-96 —Chicago	72	10	.878	1st/Central Division		15	3	.833
Totals (7 years)	414	160	.721		Totals (7 years)	81	31	.723

NOTES:
1983—Replaced Dean Meminger (8-15) and player/interim coach Sam Worthen (0-2) as Albany Patroons head coach (January 29), with record of 8-17.
1984—Defeated Bay State, 3-2, in Eastern semifinals; defeated Puerto Rico, 3-1, in Eastern finals; defeated Wyoming, 3-2, in CBA Championship Series.
1985—Defeated Toronto, 3-2, in Eastern semifinals; lost to Tampa Bay, 3-2, in Eastern finals.
1986—Lost to Tampa Bay in Eastern semifinals.
1987—Defeated Mississippi, 4-0, in Eastern semifinals; lost to Rapid City, 4-0, in Eastern finals.
1990—Defeated Milwaukee, 3-1, in Eastern Conference first round; defeated Philadelphia, 4-1, in Eastern Conference semifinals; lost to Detroit, 4-3, in Eastern Conference finals.
1991—Defeated New York, 3-0, in Eastern Conference first round; defeated Philadelphia, 4-1, in Eastern Conference semifinals; defeated Detroit, 4-0, in Eastern Conference finals; defeated Los Angeles Lakers, 4-1, in NBA Finals.
1992—Defeated Miami, 3-0, in Eastern Conference first round; defeated New York, 4-3, in Eastern Conference semifinals; defeated Cleveland, 4-2, in Eastern Conference finals; defeated Portland, 4-2, in NBA Finals.
1993—Defeated Atlanta, 3-0, in Eastern Conference first round; defeated Cleveland, 4-0, in Eastern Conference semifinals; defeated New York, 4-2, in Eastern Conference finals; defeated Phoenix, 4-2, in NBA Finals.
1994—Defeated Cleveland, 3-0, in Eastern Conference first round; lost to New York, 4-3, in Eastern Conference semifinals.
1995—Defeated Charlotte, 3-1, in Eastern Conference first round; lost to Orlando, 4-2, in Eastern Conference semifinals.
1996—Defeated Miami, 3-0, in Eastern Conference first round; defeated New York, 4-1, in Eastern Conference semifinals; defeated Orlando, 4-0, in Eastern Conference finals; defeated Seattle, 4-2, in NBA Finals.

KARL, GEORGE   SUPERSONICS

PERSONAL: Born May 12, 1951, in Penn Hills, Pa. ... 6-2/190. ... Full name: George Matthew Karl.
HIGH SCHOOL: Penn Hills (Pa.).
COLLEGE: North Carolina.
TRANSACTIONS/CAREER NOTES: Signed as free agent by San Antonio Spurs of American Basketball Association (1973). ... Spurs franchise became part of NBA for 1976-77 season.

COLLEGIATE RECORD

Season Team	G	Min.	FGM	FGA	Pct.	FTM	FTA	Pct.	Reb.	Ast.	Pts.	AVERAGES		
												RPG	APG	PPG
69-70—North Carolina‡	6	...	56	97	.577	20	23	.870	29	...	132	4.8	...	22.0
70-71—North Carolina	32	...	150	286	.524	92	115	.800	104	78	392	3.3	2.4	12.3
71-72—North Carolina	29	...	125	241	.519	89	113	.788	72	124	339	2.5	4.3	11.7
72-73—North Carolina	33	...	219	437	.501	124	163	.761	103	192	562	3.1	5.8	17.0
Varsity totals	94	...	494	964	.512	305	391	.780	279	394	1293	3.0	4.2	13.8

ABA REGULAR-SEASON RECORD

Season Team	G	Min.	2-POINT			3-POINT			FTM	FTA	Pct.	Reb.	Ast.	Pts.	AVERAGES		
			FGM	FGA	Pct.	FGM	FGA	Pct.							RPG	APG	PPG
73-74—San Antonio	74	1339	228	480	.475	8	22	.364	94	113	.832	126	160	574	1.7	2.2	7.8
74-75—San Antonio	82	1629	257	511	.503	4	23	.174	137	177	.774	155	334	663	1.9	4.1	8.1
75-76—San Antonio	75	1200	150	325	.462	0	9	.000	81	106	.764	66	250	381	0.9	3.3	5.1
Totals	231	4168	635	1316	.483	12	54	.222	312	396	.788	347	744	1618	1.5	3.2	7.0

ABA PLAYOFF RECORD

Season Team	G	Min.	2-POINT			3-POINT			FTM	FTA	Pct.	Reb.	Ast.	Pts.	AVERAGES		
			FGM	FGA	Pct.	FGM	FGA	Pct.							RPG	APG	PPG
73-74—San Antonio	7	141	13	27	.481	0	1	.000	2	5	.400	15	23	28	2.1	3.3	4.0
74-75—San Antonio	4	40	1	7	.143	0	1	.000	3	4	.750	3	5	5	0.8	1.3	1.3
75-76—San Antonio	6	64	10	21	.476	0	1	.000	6	9	.667	4	17	26	0.7	2.8	4.3
Totals	17	245	24	55	.436	0	3	.000	11	18	.611	22	45	59	1.3	2.6	3.5

NBA REGULAR-SEASON RECORD

Season Team	G	Min.	FGM	FGA	Pct.	FTM	FTA	Pct.	Off.	Def.	Tot.	Ast.	St.	Blk.	TO	Pts.	RPG	APG	PPG
									REBOUNDS								AVERAGES		
76-77—San Antonio ..	29	251	25	73	.342	29	42	.690	4	13	17	46	10	0	...	79	0.6	1.6	2.7
77-78—San Antonio ..	4	30	2	6	.333	2	2	1.000	0	5	5	5	1	0	4	6	1.3	1.3	1.5
Totals	33	281	27	79	.342	31	44	.705	4	18	22	51	11	0	4	85	0.7	1.5	2.6

Personal fouls/disqualifications: 1976-77, 36/0. 1977-78, 6/0. Totals, 42/0.

NBA PLAYOFF RECORD

Season Team	G	Min.	FGM	FGA	Pct.	FTM	FTA	Pct.	Off.	Def.	Tot.	Ast.	St.	Blk.	TO	Pts.	RPG	APG	PPG
									REBOUNDS								AVERAGES		
76-77—San Antonio ..	1	1	0	0	...	0	0	...	0	0	0	0	0	0	...	0	0.0	0.0	0.0

COMBINED ABA AND NBA REGULAR-SEASON RECORDS

	G	Min.	FGM	FGA	Pct.	FTM	FTA	Pct.	Off.	Def.	Tot.	Ast.	Stl.	Blk.	TO	Pts.	RPG	APG	PPG
									REBOUNDS								AVERAGES		
Totals	264	4449	674	1449	.465	343	440	.780	105	264	369	795	232	20	...	1703	1.4	3.0	6.5

Three-point field goals: 12-for-54 (.222).
Personal fouls/disqualifications: 559.

HEAD COACHING RECORD

BACKGROUND: Assistant coach, San Antonio Spurs (1978-79 and 1979-80). ... Director of player acquisition, Cleveland Cavaliers (1983-84). ... Head coach, Real Madrid of Spanish League (1989-90 and 1991-January 1992).

HONORS: CBA Coach of the Year (1981, 1983, 1991).

CBA COACHING RECORD

Season Team	W	L	Pct.	Finish	W	L	Pct.
	REGULAR SEASON				PLAYOFFS		
80-81 —Montana	27	15	.643	1st/Western Division	5	5	.500
81-82 —Montana	30	16	.652	2nd/Western Division	2	3	.400
82-83 —Montana	33	11	.750	1st/Western Division	6	5	.545
88-89 —Albany	36	18	.667	1st/Eastern Division	2	4	.333
90-91 —Albany	50	6	.893	1st/Eastern Division	5	6	.455
Totals (5 years).................................	176	66	.727	Totals (5 years).......	20	23	.465

NBA COACHING RECORD

Season Team	W	L	Pct.	Finish	W	L	Pct.
	REGULAR SEASON				PLAYOFFS		
84-85 —Cleveland.................................	36	46	.439	4th/Central Division	1	3	.250
85-86 —Cleveland.................................	25	42	.373		—	—	—
86-87 —Golden State.................................	42	40	.512	3rd/Pacific Division	4	6	.400
87-88 —Golden State.................................	16	48	.250		—	—	—
91-92 —Seattle.................................	27	15	.643	4th/Pacific Division	4	5	.444
92-93 —Seattle.................................	55	27	.671	2nd/Pacific Division	10	9	.526
93-94 —Seattle.................................	63	19	.768	1st/Pacific Division	2	3	.400
94-95 —Seattle.................................	57	25	.695	2nd/Pacific Division	1	3	.250
95-96 —Seattle.................................	64	18	.780	1st/Pacific Division	13	8	.619
Totals (9 years).................................	385	280	.579	Totals (7 years).......	35	37	.486

NOTES:
1981—Defeated Alberta, 2-0, in Western semifinals; defeated Billings, 3-1, in Western finals; lost to Rochester, 4-0, in CBA Championship Series.
1982—Lost to Billings in Western finals.
1983—Defeated Wyoming, 3-1, in Western finals; lost to Detroit, 4-3, in CBA Championship Series.
1985—Lost to Boston in Eastern Conference first round.
1986—Replaced as Cleveland head coach by Gene Littles (March 16).
1987—Defeated Utah, 3-2, in Western Conference first round; lost to Los Angeles Lakers, 4-1, in Western Conference semifinals.
1988—Resigned as Golden State head coach (March 23).
1989—Lost to Wichita Falls in Eastern semifinals.
1991—Defeated Grand Rapids, 3-2, in National Conference first round; lost to Wichita Falls, 4-2, in National Conference finals.
1992—Replaced K.C. Jones (18-18) and Bob Kloppenburg (2-2) as Seattle head coach (January 23), with record of 20-20 and club in fifth place. Defeated Golden State, 3-1, in Western Conference first round; lost to Utah, 4-1, in Western Conference semifinals.
1993—Defeated Utah, 3-2, in Western Conference first round; defeated Houston, 4-3, in Western Conference semifinals; lost to Phoenix, 4-3, in Western Conference finals.
1994—Lost to Denver in Western Conference first round.
1995—Lost to Los Angeles Lakers in Western Conference first round.
1996—Defeated Sacramento, 3-1, in Western Conference first round; defeated Houston, 4-0, in Western Conference semifinals; defeated Utah, 4-3, in Western Conference finals; lost to Chicago, 4-2, in NBA Finals.

LYNAM, JIM — BULLETS

PERSONAL: Born September 15, 1941, in Philadelphia. ... 5-8/160. ... Full name: James Francis Lynam.
HIGH SCHOOL: West Catholic (Philadelphia).
COLLEGE: St. Joseph's (Pa.).

COLLEGIATE RECORD

Season Team	G	Min.	FGM	FGA	Pct.	FTM	FTA	Pct.	Reb.	Ast.	Pts.	RPG	APG	PPG
												AVERAGES		
59-60—St. Joseph's‡..................	14	...	88	...	...	94	...	...	43	...	270	3.1	...	19.3
60-61—St. Joseph's	30	...	110	260	.423	118	143	.825	71	...	338	2.4	...	11.3

Season Team	G	Min.	FGM	FGA	Pct.	FTM	FTA	Pct.	Reb.	Ast.	Pts.	AVERAGES		
												RPG	APG	PPG
61-62—St. Joseph's	27	...	98	228	.430	111	140	.793	49	...	307	1.8	...	11.4
62-63—St. Joseph's	26	...	139	281	.495	89	131	.679	95	...	367	3.7	...	14.1
Varsity totals	83	...	347	769	.451	318	414	.768	215	...	1012	2.6	...	12.2

HEAD COACHING RECORD

BACKGROUND: Assistant coach, St. Joseph's (1970-71 through 1972-73). ... Assistant coach, Portland Trail Blazers (1981-82). ... Assistant coach, Philadelphia 76ers (1985-86 through 1987-88). ... General manager, 76ers (1992-93 and 1993-94).

COLLEGIATE COACHING RECORD

Season Team	W	L	Pct.	Finish
68-69 —Fairfield	10	16	.385	Independent
69-70 —Fairfield	13	13	.500	Independent
73-74 —American	16	10	.615	T3rd/Middle Atlantic Conference (East)
74-75 —American	16	10	.615	T1st/East Coast Conference (East)
75-76 —American	9	16	.360	T5th/East Coast Conference (East)
76-77 —American	13	13	.500	T4th/East Coast Conference (East)
77-78 —American	16	12	.571	T3rd/East Coast Conference (East)
78-79 —St. Joseph's	19	11	.633	2nd/East Coast Conference (East)
79-80 —St. Joseph's	21	9	.700	1st/East Coast Conference (East)
80-81 —St. Joseph's	25	8	.758	1st/East Coast Conference
Totals (10 years)	158	118	.572	

NBA COACHING RECORD

Season Team	REGULAR SEASON				PLAYOFFS		
	W	L	Pct.	Finish	W	L	Pct.
83-84 —San Diego	30	52	.366	6th/Pacific Division	—	—	—
84-85 —L.A. Clippers	22	39	.361		—	—	—
87-88 —Philadelphia	16	23	.410	2nd/Atlantic Division	—	—	—
88-89 —Philadelphia	46	36	.561	2nd/Atlantic Division	0	3	.000
89-90 —Philadelphia	53	29	.646	1st/Atlantic Division	4	6	.400
90-91 —Philadelphia	44	38	.537	2nd/Atlantic Division	4	4	.500
91-92 —Philadelphia	35	47	.427	3rd/Atlantic Division	—	—	—
94-95 —Washington	21	61	.256	7th/Atlantic Division	—	—	—
95-96 —Washington	39	43	.476	5th/Atlantic Division	—	—	—
Totals (9 years)	306	368	.454	**Totals (3 years)**	8	13	.381

NOTES:
1979—Lost to Ohio State, 80-66, in NIT first round.
1980—Lost to Texas, 70-61, in NIT first round.
1981—Defeated Creighton, 59-57, in NCAA Tournament first round; defeated DePaul, 49-48, in NCAA Tournament second round; defeated Boston College, 42-41, in NCAA regional semifinals; lost to Indiana, 78-46, in regional finals.
1985—Replaced as Los Angeles Clippers head coach by Don Chaney (March 4).
1988—Replaced Matt Guokas as Philadelphia head coach (February 8), with record of 20-23.
1989—Lost to New York in Eastern Conference first round.
1990—Defeated Cleveland, 3-2, in Eastern Conference first round; lost to Chicago, 4-1, in Eastern Conference semifinals.
1991—Defeated Milwaukee, 3-0, in Eastern Conference first round; lost to Chicago, 4-1, in Eastern Conference semifinals.

RILEY, PAT — HEAT

PERSONAL: Born March 20, 1945, in Rome, N.Y. ... 6-4/205. ... Full name: Patrick James Riley. ... Son of Leon Riley, outfielder/catcher with Philadelphia Phillies (1944) and minor league manager; and brother of Lee Riley, defensive back with Detroit Lions, Philadelphia Eagles and New York Giants (1955-1960) and New York Titans of American Football League (1961, 1962).

HIGH SCHOOL: Linton (Schenectady, N.Y.).

COLLEGE: Kentucky.

TRANSACTIONS/CAREER NOTES: Selected by San Diego Rockets in first round (seventh pick overall) of 1967 NBA Draft. ... Selected by Portland Trail Blazers from Rockets in NBA expansion draft (May 11, 1970). ... Contract sold by Trail Blazers to Los Angeles Lakers (October 9, 1970). ... Traded by Lakers to Phoenix Suns for draft rights to G John Roche and 1976 second-round draft choice (November 3, 1975).

MISCELLANEOUS: Member of NBA championship team (1972). ... Selected by Dallas Cowboys in 11th round of 1967 National Football League draft.

COLLEGIATE RECORD

Season Team	G	Min.	FGM	FGA	Pct.	FTM	FTA	Pct.	Reb.	Ast.	Pts.	AVERAGES		
												RPG	APG	PPG
63-64—Kentucky‡	16	...	120	259	.463	93	146	.637	235	...	333	14.7	...	20.8
64-65—Kentucky	25	825	160	370	.432	55	89	.618	212	27	375	8.5	1.1	15.0
65-66—Kentucky	29	1078	265	514	.516	107	153	.699	259	64	637	8.9	2.2	22.0
66-67—Kentucky	26	953	165	373	.442	122	156	.782	201	68	452	7.7	2.6	17.4
Varsity totals	80	2856	590	1257	.469	284	398	.714	672	159	1464	8.4	2.0	18.3

NBA REGULAR-SEASON RECORD

Season Team	G	Min.	FGM	FGA	Pct.	FTM	FTA	Pct.	Reb.	Ast.	PF	Dq.	Pts.	AVERAGES		
														RPG	APG	PPG
67-68—San Diego	80	1263	250	660	.379	128	202	.634	177	138	205	1	628	2.2	1.7	7.9
68-69—San Diego	56	1027	202	498	.406	90	134	.672	112	136	146	1	494	2.0	2.4	8.8
69-70—San Diego	36	474	75	180	.417	40	55	.727	57	85	68	0	190	1.6	2.4	5.3
70-71—Los Angeles	54	506	105	254	.413	56	87	.644	54	72	84	0	266	1.0	1.3	4.9

Season Team	G	Min.	FGM	FGA	Pct.	FTM	FTA	Pct.	Reb.	Ast.	PF	Dq.	Pts.	RPG	APG	PPG
71-72 —Los Angeles	67	926	197	441	.447	55	74	.743	127	75	110	0	449	1.9	1.1	6.7
72-73 —Los Angeles	55	801	167	390	.428	65	82	.793	65	81	126	0	399	1.2	1.5	7.3

Season Team	G	Min.	FGM	FGA	Pct.	FTM	FTA	Pct.	REBOUNDS Off.	Def.	Tot.	Ast.	St.	Blk.	TO	Pts.	AVERAGES RPG	APG	PPG
73-74—Los Angeles ..	72	1361	287	667	.430	110	144	.764	38	90	128	148	54	3	...	684	1.8	2.1	9.5
74-75—Los Angeles ..	46	1016	219	523	.419	69	93	.742	25	60	85	121	36	4	...	507	1.8	2.6	11.0
75-76—L.A.-Phoe......	62	813	117	301	.389	55	77	.714	16	34	50	57	22	6	...	289	0.8	0.9	4.7
Totals	528	8187	1619	3914	.414	668	948	.705	...	...	855	913	112	13	...	3906	1.6	1.7	7.4

Personal fouls/disqualifications: 1973-74, 173/1. 1974-75, 128/0. 1975-76, 112/0. Totals, 1152/3.

NBA PLAYOFF RECORD

Season Team	G	Min.	FGM	FGA	Pct.	FTM	FTA	Pct.	Reb.	Ast.	PF	Dq.	Pts.	RPG	APG	PPG
68-69 —San Diego	5	76	16	37	.432	5	6	.833	11	2	13	0	37	2.2	0.4	7.4
70-71 —Los Angeles	7	135	29	69	.420	8	11	.727	15	14	12	0	66	2.1	2.0	9.4
71-72 —Los Angeles	15	244	33	99	.333	12	16	.750	29	14	37	0	78	1.9	0.9	5.2
72-73 —Los Angeles	7	53	9	27	.333	0	0	...	5	7	10	0	18	0.7	1.0	2.6

Season Team	G	Min.	FGM	FGA	Pct.	FTM	FTA	Pct.	REBOUNDS Off.	Def.	Tot.	Ast.	St.	Blk.	TO	Pts.	AVERAGES RPG	APG	PPG
73-74—Los Angeles ..	5	106	18	50	.360	3	4	.750	3	3	6	10	4	0	...	39	1.2	2.0	7.8
75-76—Phoenix.........	5	27	6	15	.400	1	1	1.000	0	0	0	5	0	0	...	13	0.0	1.0	2.6
Totals	44	641	111	297	.374	29	38	.763	...	...	66	52	4	0	...	251	1.5	1.2	5.7

Personal fouls/disqualifications: 1973-74, 11/0. 1975-76, 3/0. Totals, 86/0.

HEAD COACHING RECORD

BACKGROUND: Broadcaster, Los Angeles Lakers (1977-79). ... Assistant coach, Lakers (1979-80 to November 19, 1981). ... Broadcaster, NBC television (1990-91). ... President, Miami Heat (1995-96 to present).

HONORS: NBA Coach of the Year (1990, 1993).

RECORDS: Holds NBA career record for most playoff wins—137.

NBA COACHING RECORD

Season Team	REGULAR SEASON W	L	Pct.	Finish	PLAYOFFS W	L	Pct.
81-82 —Los Angeles...............	50	21	.704	1st/Pacific Division	12	2	.857
82-83 —Los Angeles...............	58	24	.707	1st/Pacific Division	8	7	.533
83-84 —Los Angeles...............	54	28	.659	1st/Pacific Division	14	7	.667
84-85 —Los Angeles Lakers.....	62	20	.756	1st/Pacific Division	15	4	.789
85-86 —Los Angeles Lakers.....	62	20	.756	1st/Pacific Division	8	6	571
86-87 —Los Angeles Lakers.....	65	17	.793	1st/Pacific Division	15	3	.833
87-88 —Los Angeles Lakers.....	62	20	.756	1st/Pacific Division	15	9	.625
88-89 —Los Angeles Lakers.....	57	25	.695	1st/Pacific Division	11	4	.733
89-90 —Los Angeles Lakers.....	63	19	.768	1st/Pacific Division	4	5	.444
91-92 —New York....................	51	31	.622	T1st/Atlantic Division	6	6	.500
92-93 —New York....................	60	22	.732	1st/Atlantic Division	9	6	.600
93-94 —New York....................	57	25	.695	1st/Atlantic Division	14	11	.560
94-95 —New York....................	55	27	.671	2nd/Atlantic Division	6	5	.545
95-96 —Miami.........................	42	40	.512	3rd/Atlantic Division	0	3	.000
Totals (14 years)................	**798**	**339**	**.702**	**Totals (14 years)**.....	**137**	**78**	**.637**

NOTES:

1981—Replaced Paul Westhead as Los Angeles head coach (November 19), with record of 7-4 and club in second place.

1982—Defeated Phoenix, 4-0, in Western Conference semifinals; defeated San Antonio, 4-0, in Western Conference finals; defeated Philadelphia, 4-2, in World Championship Series.

1983—Defeated Portland, 4-1, in Western Conference semifinals; defeated San Antonio, 4-2, in Western Conference finals; lost to Philadelphia, 4-0, in World Championship Series.

1984—Defeated Kansas City, 3-0, in Western Conference first round; defeated Dallas, 4-1, in Western Conference semifinals; defeated Phoenix, 4-2, in Western Conference finals; lost to Boston, 4-3, in World Championship Series.

1985—Defeated Phoenix, 3-0, in Western Conference first round; defeated Portland, 4-1, in Western Conference semifinals; defeated Denver, 4-1, in Western Conference finals; defeated Boston, 4-2, in World Championship Series.

1986—Defeated San Antonio, 3-0, in Western Conference first round; defeated Dallas, 4-2, in Western Conference semifinals; lost to Houston, 4-1, in Western Conference finals.

1987—Defeated Denver, 3-0, in Western Conference first round; defeated Golden State, 4-1, in Western Conference semifinals; defeated Seattle, 4-0, in Western Conference finals; defeated Boston, 4-2, in NBA Finals.

1988—Defeated San Antonio, 3-0, in Western Conference first round; defeated Utah, 4-3, in Western Conference semifinals; defeated Dallas, 4-3, in Western Conference finals; defeated Detroit, 4-3, in NBA Finals.

1989—Defeated Portland, 3-0, in Western Conference first round; defeated Seattle, 4-0, in Western Conference semifinals; defeated Phoenix, 4-0, in Western Conference finals; lost to Detroit, 4-0, in NBA Finals.

1990—Defeated Houston, 3-1, in Western Conference first round; lost to Phoenix, 4-1, in Western Conference semifinals.

1992—Defeated Detroit, 3-2, in Eastern Conference first round; lost to Chicago, 4-3, in Eastern Conference semifinals.

1993—Defeated Indiana, 3-1, in Eastern Conference first round; defeated Charlotte, 4-1, in Eastern Conference semifinals; lost to Chicago, 4-2, in Eastern Conference finals.

1994—Defeated New Jersey, 3-1, in Eastern Conference first round; defeated Chicago, 4-3, in Eastern Conference semifinals; defeated Indiana, 4-3, in Eastern Conference finals; lost to Houston, 4-3, in NBA Finals.

1995—Defeated Cleveland, 3-1, in Eastern Conference first round; lost to Indiana, 4-3, in Eastern Conference semifinals.

1996—Lost to Chicago in Eastern Conference first round.

SAUNDERS, FLIP — TIMBERWOLVES

PERSONAL: Born February 23, 1955, in Cleveland. ... 5-11/175. ... Full name: Philip D. Saunders.
HIGH SCHOOL: Cuyahoga Heights (Ohio).
COLLEGE: Minnesota.

COLLEGIATE RECORD

Season Team	G	Min.	FGM	FGA	Pct.	FTM	FTA	Pct.	Reb.	Ast.	Pts.	RPG	APG	PPG
73-74—Minnesota	24	...	93	209	.445	53	61	.869	93	...	239	3.9	...	9.9
74-75—Minnesota	26	...	67	154	.435	54	74	.730	74	...	188	2.8	...	7.2
75-76—Minnesota	26	...	99	209	.474	47	55	.854	95	...	245	3.8	...	9.4
76-77—Minnesota	27	...	77	172	.448	16	20	.800	103	107	170	3.8	4.0	6.3
Varsity totals	103	...	336	744	.452	170	210	.810	365	...	842	3.5	...	8.2

HEAD COACHING RECORD

BACKGROUND: Assistant coach, University of Minnesota (1982-83 through 1985-86). ... Assistant coach, University of Tulsa (1986-87 and 1987-88). ... General manager, Minnesota Timberwolves (1994-95 and 1995-96)
HONORS: CBA Coach of the Year (1990, 1992).

COLLEGIATE COACHING RECORD

Season Team	W	L	Pct.
77-78 —Golden Valley Lutheran College	19	5	.792
78-79 —Golden Valley Lutheran College	21	4	.840
79-80 —Golden Valley Lutheran College	23	2	.920
80-81 —Golden Valley Lutheran College	28	2	.933
Totals (4 years)	91	13	.875

CBA COACHING RECORD

Season Team	REGULAR SEASON				PLAYOFFS		
	W	L	Pct.	Finish	W	L	Pct.
88-89 —Rapid City	38	16	.704	1st/Western Division	6	5	.545
89-90 —La Crosse	42	14	.750	1st/Central Division	11	4	.733
90-91 —La Crosse	32	24	.571	2nd/Central Division	2	3	.400
91-92 —La Crosse	40	16	.714	2nd/Midwest Division	10	6	.625
92-93 —La Crosse	32	24	.571	3rd/Mideast Division	2	3	.400
93-94 —La Crosse	35	21	.625	1st/Mideast Division	3	3	.500
94-95 —Sioux Falls	34	22	.607	2nd/Western Division	1	2	.333
Totals (7 years)	253	137	.649	**Totals (7 years)**	35	26	.574

NBA COACHING RECORD

Season Team	REGULAR SEASON				PLAYOFFS		
	W	L	Pct.	Finish	W	L	Pct.
95-96 —Minnesota	20	42	.323	T5th/Midwest Division	—	—	—

NOTES:
1989—Defeated Cedar Rapids, 4-1, in Western semifinals; lost to Rockford, 4-2, in Western finals.
1990—Defeated Quad City, 3-0, in American semifinals; defeated Albany, 4-3, in American finals; defeated Rapid City, 4-1, in CBA Championship Series.
1991—Lost to Quad City, 3-2, in American first round.
1992—Defeated Grand Rapids, 3-1, in American second round; defeated Quad City, 3-2, in American finals; defeated Rapid City, 4-3, in CBA Championship Series.
1993—Lost to Rockford, 3-2, in American first round.
1994—Defeated Rockford, 3-0, in American first round; lost to Quad City, 3-0, in American finals.
1995—Lost to Omaha, 2-1, in National first round. Replaced Bill Blair as Minnesota head coach (December 18), with record of 6-14 and club in sixth place.

SLOAN, JERRY — JAZZ

PERSONAL: Born March 28, 1942, in McLeansboro, Ill. ... 6-5/200. ... Full name: Gerald Eugene Sloan.
HIGH SCHOOL: McLeansboro (Ill.).
COLLEGE: Illinois, then Evansville.
TRANSACTIONS/CAREER NOTES: Selected by Baltimore Bullets in third round of 1964 NBA Draft. ... Selected by Bullets in second round of 1965 NBA Draft. ... Selected by Chicago Bulls from Bullets in NBA expansion draft (April 30, 1966).

COLLEGIATE RECORD

NOTES: Left Illinois before 1961 basketball season. ... Outstanding Player in NCAA College Division Tournament (1964, 1965). ... THE SPORTING NEWS All-America second team (1965).

Season Team	G	Min.	FGM	FGA	Pct.	FTM	FTA	Pct.	Reb.	Ast.	Pts.	RPG	APG	PPG
61-62—Evansville						Did not play—transfer student.								
62-63—Evansville	27	...	152	446	.341	103	151	.682	293	...	407	10.9	...	15.1
63-64—Evansville	29	...	160	385	.416	84	114	.737	335	...	404	11.6	...	13.9
64-65—Evansville	29	...	207	458	.452	95	126	.754	425	...	509	14.7	...	17.6
Totals	85	...	519	1289	.403	282	391	.721	1053	...	1320	12.4	...	15.5

NBA REGULAR-SEASON RECORD

HONORS: NBA All-Defensive first team (1969, 1972, 1974, 1975). ... NBA All-Defensive second team (1970, 1971).

HEAD COACHES

Season Team	G	Min.	FGM	FGA	Pct.	FTM	FTA	Pct.	Reb.	Ast.	PF	Dq.	Pts.	RPG	APG	PPG
65-66 —Baltimore	59	952	120	289	.415	98	139	.705	230	110	176	7	338	3.9	1.9	5.7
66-67 —Chicago	80	2942	525	1214	.432	340	427	.796	726	170	293	7	1390	9.1	2.1	17.4
67-68 —Chicago	77	2454	369	959	.385	280	386	.725	591	229	291	11	1027	7.7	3.0	13.3
68-69 —Chicago	78	2939	488	1179	.414	333	447	.745	619	276	313	6	1309	7.9	3.5	16.8
69-70 —Chicago	53	1822	310	737	.421	207	318	.651	372	165	179	3	827	7.0	3.1	15.6
70-71 —Chicago	80	3140	592	1342	.441	278	389	.715	701	281	289	5	1462	8.8	3.5	18.3
71-72 —Chicago	82	3035	535	1206	.444	258	391	.660	691	211	309	8	1328	8.4	2.6	16.2
72-73 —Chicago	69	2412	301	733	.411	94	133	.707	475	151	235	5	696	6.9	2.2	10.1

									REBOUNDS						AVERAGES		
Season Team	G	Min.	FGM	FGA	Pct.	FTM	FTA	Pct.	Off.	Def.	Tot.	Ast.	St.	Blk.	TO	Pts.	RPG	APG	PPG
73-74—Chicago	77	2860	412	921	.447	194	273	.711	150	406	556	149	183	10	...	1018	7.2	1.9	13.2
74-75—Chicago	8	2577	380	865	.439	193	258	.748	177	361	538	161	171	17	...	953	6.9	2.1	12.2
75-76—Chicago	22	617	84	210	.400	55	78	.705	40	76	116	22	27	5	...	223	5.3	1.0	10.1
Totals	755	25750	4116	9655	.426	2330	3239	.719	...	...	5615	1925	381	32	...	10571	7.4	2.5	14.0

Personal fouls/disqualifications: 1973-74, 273/3. 1974-75, 265/5. 1975-76, 77/1. Totals, 2700/61.

NBA PLAYOFF RECORD

														AVERAGES		
Season Team	G	Min.	FGM	FGA	Pct.	FTM	FTA	Pct.	Reb.	Ast.	PF	Dq.	Pts.	RPG	APG	PPG
65-66 —Baltimore	2	34	5	12	.417	3	4	.750	16	6	6	1	13	8.0	3.0	6.5
66-67 —Chicago	3	71	12	31	.387	6	9	.667	10	1	7	0	30	3.3	0.3	10.0
67-68 —Chicago	5	137	12	37	.324	19	25	.760	32	12	19	0	43	6.4	2.4	8.6
69-70 —Chicago	5	190	29	74	.392	16	25	.640	39	11	18	0	74	7.8	2.2	14.8
70-71 —Chicago	7	284	51	117	.436	17	23	.739	63	17	25	1	119	9.0	2.4	17.0
71-72 —Chicago	4	170	26	64	.406	11	19	.579	35	10	18	1	63	8.8	2.5	15.8
72-73 —Chicago	7	292	45	103	.437	14	19	.737	59	14	31	1	104	8.4	2.0	14.9

									REBOUNDS								AVERAGES		
Season Team	G	Min.	FGM	FGA	Pct.	FTM	FTA	Pct.	Off.	Def.	Tot.	Ast.	St.	Blk.	TO	Pts.	RPG	APG	PPG
73-74—Chicago	6	240	39	88	.443	22	29	.759	18	44	62	12	7	1	...	100	10.3	2.0	16.7
74-75—Chicago	13	470	75	163	.460	20	36	.556	24	72	96	26	20	0	...	170	7.4	2.0	13.1
Totals	52	1888	294	689	.427	128	189	.677	...	...	412	109	27	1	...	716	7.9	2.1	13.8

Personal fouls/disqualifications: 1973-74, 17/0. 1974-75, 46/0. Totals, 187/4.

NBA ALL-STAR GAME RECORD

Season Team	Min.	FGM	FGA	Pct.	FTM	FTA	Pct.	Reb	Ast.	PF	Dq.	Pts.
1967 —Chicago	22	4	9	.444	0	0	...	4	4	5	0	8
1969 —Chicago	18	2	8	.250	0	1	.000	3	0	5	0	4
Totals	40	6	17	.353	0	1	.000	7	4	10	0	12

HEAD COACHING RECORD

BACKGROUND: Scout, Chicago Bulls (1976-77). ... Assistant coach, Bulls (1977-78 and 1978-79). ... Scout, Utah Jazz (1983-84). ... Head coach, Evansville Thunder of CBA (1984-November 19, 1984; no record). ... Assistant coach, Jazz (November 19, 1984-December 9, 1988).

NBA COACHING RECORD

		REGULAR SEASON				PLAYOFFS		
Season Team	W	L	Pct.	Finish	W	L	Pct.
79-80 —Chicago	30	52	.366	4th/Midwest Division	—	—	—
80-81 —Chicago	45	37	.549	2nd/Central Division	2	4	.333
81-82 —Chicago	19	32	.373		—	—	—
88-89 —Utah	40	25	.615	1st/Midwest Division	0	3	.000
89-90 —Utah	55	27	.671	2nd/Midwest Division	2	3	.400
90-91 —Utah	54	28	.659	2nd/Midwest Division	4	5	.444
91-92 —Utah	55	27	.671	1st/Midwest Division	9	7	.563
92-93 —Utah	47	35	.573	3rd/Midwest Division	2	3	.400
93-94 —Utah	53	29	.646	3rd/Midwest Division	8	8	.500
94-95 —Utah	60	22	.732	2nd/Midwest Division	2	3	.400
95-96 —Utah	55	27	.671	2nd/Midwest Division	10	8	.556
Totals (11 years)	513	341	.601	Totals (9 years)	39	44	.470

NOTES:
1981—Defeated New York, 2-0, in Eastern Conference first round; lost to Boston, 4-0, in Eastern Conference semifinals.
1982—Replaced as Chicago head coach by Rod Thorn (February 17).
1988—Replaced retiring Utah head coach Frank Layden (December 9), with record of 11-6.
1989—Lost to Golden State in Western Conference first round.
1990—Lost to Phoenix in Western Conference first round.
1991—Defeated Phoenix, 3-1, in Western Conference first round; lost to Portland, 4-1, in Western Conference semifinals.
1992—Defeated Los Angeles Clippers, 3-2, in Western Conference first round; defeated Seattle, 4-1, in Western Conference semifinals; lost to Portland, 4-2, in Western Conference finals.
1993—Lost to Seattle in Western Conference first round.
1994—Defeated San Antonio, 3-1, in Western Conference first round; defeated Denver, 4-3, in Western Conference semifinals; lost to Houston, 4-1, in Western Conference finals.
1995—Lost to Houston in Western Conference first round.
1996—Defeated Portland, 3-2, in Western Conference first round; Defeated San Antonio, 4-2, in Western Conference semifinals; lost to Seattle, 4-3, in Western Conference finals.

ST. JEAN, GARRY — KINGS

PERSONAL: Born February 10, 1950, in Chicopee, Mass. ... 6-4/210. ... Full name: Garry St. Jean. ... Name pronounced Saint Jean.
HIGH SCHOOL: Chicopee (Mass.).
COLLEGE: Springfield (Mass.) College.

Season Team	G	Min.	FGM	FGA	Pct.	FTM	FTA	Pct.	Reb.	Ast.	Pts.	RPG	APG	PPG
												AVERAGES		
69-70—Springfield (Mass.)‡	...	...	...	...	...	...	...	...	...	...	...	...	...	13.1

HEAD COACHING RECORD

BACKGROUND: Head coach, Chicopee High School, Mass. (1973-80; record: 122-65, .652). ... Assistant coach, Milwaukee Bucks (1980-81 through 1984-85). ... Assistant coach, New Jersey Nets (1985-86). ... Assistant coach/assistant director of player personnel, Nets (1986-87 and 1987-88). ... Assistant coach, Golden State Warriors (1988-89 through 1991-92).

NBA COACHING RECORD

	REGULAR SEASON				PLAYOFFS		
Season Team	W	L	Pct.	Finish	W	L	Pct.
92-93 —Sacramento	25	57	.305	7th/Pacific Division	—	—	—
93-94 —Sacramento	28	54	.341	6th/Pacific Division	—	—	—
94-95 —Sacramento	39	43	.476	5th/Pacific Division	—	—	—
95-96 —Sacramento	39	43	.476	5th/Pacific Division	1	3	.250
Totals (4 years)	**131**	**197**	**.399**	**Totals (1 year)**	**1**	**3**	**.250**

NOTES:
1996—Lost to Seattle in Western Conference first round.

TOMJANOVICH, RUDY — ROCKETS

PERSONAL: Born November 24, 1948, in Hamtramck, Mich. ... 6-8/220. ... Full name: Rudolph Tomjanovich. ... Name pronounced Tom-JOHN-a-vitch.
HIGH SCHOOL: Hamtramck (Mich.).
COLLEGE: Michigan.
TRANSACTIONS/CAREER NOTES: Selected by San Diego Rockets in first round (second pick overall) of 1970 NBA Draft. ... Rockets franchise moved from San Diego to Houston for 1971-72 season.

COLLEGIATE RECORD

NOTES: THE SPORTING NEWS All-America first team (1970). ... THE SPORTING NEWS All-America second team (1969).

Season Team	G	Min.	FGM	FGA	Pct.	FTM	FTA	Pct.	Reb.	Ast.	Pts.	RPG	APG	PPG
												AVERAGES		
66-67—Michigan‡	3	...	28	...	...	6	15	.400	...	...	62	...	...	20.7
67-68—Michigan	24	...	210	446	.471	49	78	.628	323	...	469	13.5	...	19.5
68-69—Michigan	24	...	269	541	.497	79	131	.603	340	...	617	14.2	...	25.7
69-70—Michigan	24	...	286	604	.474	150	200	.750	376	...	722	15.7	...	30.1
Varsity totals	**72**	...	**765**	**1591**	**.481**	**278**	**409**	**.680**	**1039**	...	**1808**	**14.4**	...	**25.1**

NBA REGULAR-SEASON RECORD

Season Team	G	Min.	FGM	FGA	Pct.	FTM	FTA	Pct.	Reb.	Ast.	PF	Dq.	Pts.	RPG	APG	PPG
														AVERAGES		
70-71 —San Diego	77	1062	168	439	.383	73	112	.652	381	73	124	0	409	4.9	0.9	5.3
71-72 —Houston	78	2689	500	1010	.495	172	238	.723	923	117	193	2	1172	11.8	1.5	15.0
72-73 —Houston	81	2972	655	1371	.478	250	335	.746	938	178	225	1	1560	11.6	2.2	19.3

Season Team	G	Min.	FGM	FGA	Pct.	FTM	FTA	Pct.	REBOUNDS			Ast.	St.	Blk.	TO	Pts.	AVERAGES		
									Off.	Def.	Tot.						RPG	APG	PPG
73-74—Houston	80	3227	788	1470	.536	385	454	.848	230	487	717	250	89	66	...	1961	9.0	3.1	24.5
74-75—Houston	81	3134	694	1323	.525	289	366	.790	184	429	613	236	76	24	...	1677	7.6	2.9	20.7
75-76—Houston	79	2912	622	1202	.517	221	288	.767	167	499	666	188	42	19	...	1465	8.4	2.4	18.5
76-77—Houston	81	3130	733	1437	.510	287	342	.839	172	512	684	172	57	27	...	1753	8.4	2.1	21.6
77-78—Houston	23	849	217	447	.485	61	81	.753	40	98	138	32	15	5	38	495	6.0	1.4	21.5
78-79—Houston	74	2641	620	1200	.517	168	221	.760	170	402	572	137	44	18	138	1408	7.7	1.9	19.0
79-80—Houston	62	1834	370	778	.476	118	147	.803	132	226	358	109	32	10	98	880	5.8	1.8	14.2
80-81—Houston	52	1264	263	563	.467	65	82	.793	78	130	208	81	19	6	58	603	4.0	1.6	11.6
Totals	**768**	**25714**	**5630**	**11240**	**.501**	**2089**	**2666**	**.784**			**6198**	**1573**	**374**	**175**	**332**	**13383**	**8.1**	**2.0**	**17.4**

Three-point field goals: 1979-80, 22-for-79 (.278). 1980-81, 12-for-51 (.235). Totals, 34-for-130 (.262).
Personal fouls/disqualifications: 1973-74, 230/0. 1974-75, 230/1. 1975-76, 206/1. 1976-77, 198/1. 1977-78, 63/0. 1978-79, 186/0. 1979-80, 161/2. 1980-81, 121/0. Totals, 1937/8.

NBA PLAYOFF RECORD

Season Team	G	Min.	FGM	FGA	Pct.	FTM	FTA	Pct.	REBOUNDS			Ast.	St.	Blk.	TO	Pts.	AVERAGES		
									Off.	Def.	Tot.						RPG	APG	PPG
74-75—Houston	8	304	72	128	.563	40	48	.833	22	42	64	23	1	4	...	184	8.0	2.9	23.0
76-77—Houston	12	457	107	212	.505	29	37	.784	24	41	65	24	7	3	...	243	5.4	2.0	20.3
78-79—Houston	2	64	9	23	.391	2	5	.400	7	7	14	2	1	1	1	20	7.0	1.0	10.0
79-80—Houston	7	185	24	64	.375	9	13	.692	12	28	40	10	2	0	14	58	5.7	1.4	8.3
80-81—Houston	8	31	1	9	.111	4	6	.667	2	4	6	0	0	0	2	6	0.8	0.0	0.8
Totals	**37**	**1041**	**213**	**436**	**.489**	**84**	**109**	**.771**	**67**	**122**	**189**	**59**	**11**	**8**	**17**	**511**	**5.1**	**1.6**	**13.8**

Three-point field goals: 1979-80, 1-for-7 (.143). 1980-81, 0-for-3. Totals, 1-for-10 (.100).
Personal fouls/disqualifications: 1974-75, 17/0. 1976-77, 36/0. 1978-79, 1/0. 1979-80, 21/1. 1980-81, 3/0. Totals, 78/1.

HEAD COACHES

NBA ALL-STAR GAME RECORD

Season	Team	Min.	FGM	FGA	Pct.	FTM	FTA	Pct.	Off.	Def.	Tot.	Ast.	PF	Dq.	St.	Blk.	TO	Pts.
1974	—Houston	17	2	5	.400	0	0	...	2	3	5	0	1	0	0	0	...	4
1975	—Houston	14	0	3	.000	0	0	...	1	2	3	0	3	0	0	0	...	0
1976	—Houston	12	1	2	.500	0	0	...	1	2	3	0	2	0	0	0	...	2
1977	—Houston	22	3	9	.333	0	0	...	2	8	10	1	1	0	1	1	...	6
1979	—Houston	24	6	13	.462	0	0	...	4	2	6	1	2	0	0	0	0	12
	Totals	89	12	32	.375	0	0		10	17	27	2	9	0	1	1	0	24

HEAD COACHING RECORD

BACKGROUND: Scout, Houston Rockets (1981-82 and 1982-83). ... Assistant coach, Rockets (1983-84 to February 18, 1992).

NBA COACHING RECORD

		REGULAR SEASON				PLAYOFFS		
Season	Team	W	L	Pct.	Finish	W	L	Pct.
91-92	—Houston	16	14	.533	3rd/Midwest Division	—	—	—
92-93	—Houston	55	27	.671	1st/Midwest Division	6	6	.500
93-94	—Houston	58	24	.707	1st/Midwest Division	15	8	.652
94-95	—Houston	47	35	.573	3rd/Midwest Division	15	7	.682
95-96	—Houston	48	34	.585	2nd/Midwest Division	3	5	.375
	Totals (5 years)	224	134	.626	Totals (4 years)	39	26	.600

NOTES:

1992—Replaced Don Chaney as Houston head coach (February 18), with record of 26-26 and club in third place.

1993—Defeated L.A. Clippers, 3-2, in Western Conference first round; lost to Seattle, 4-3, in Western Conference semifinals.

1994—Defeated Portland, 3-1, in Western Conference first round; defeated Phoenix, 4-3, in Western Conference semifinals; defeated Utah, 4-1, in Western Conference finals; defeated New York, 4-3, in NBA Finals.

1995—Defeated Utah, 3-2, in Western Conference first round, defeated Phoenix, 4-3, in Western Conference semifinals; defeated San Antonio, 4-2, in Western Conference finals; defeated Orlando, 4-0, in NBA Finals.

1996—Defeated L.A. Lakers, 3-1, in Western Conference first round; lost to Seattle, 4-0, in Western Conference semifinals.

VAN GUNDY, JEFF — KNICKS

PERSONAL: Born January 19, 1962, in Hemet, Calif. ... 5-9/150. ... Brother of Stan Van Gundy, assistant coach, Miami Heat.
HIGH SCHOOL: Brockport (N.Y.).
JUNIOR COLLEGE: Menlo Junior College (Palo Alto, Calif.).
COLLEGE: SUNY-Brockport (N.Y.), then Nazareth (Rochester, N.Y.).

COLLEGIATE RECORD

												AVERAGES		
Season Team	G	Min.	FGM	FGA	Pct.	FTM	FTA	Pct.	Reb.	Ast.	Pts.	RPG	APG	PPG
81-82—Menlo Junior College						Statistics unavailable.								
82-83—SUNY-Brockport						Statistics unavailable.								
83-84—Nazareth	28	...	84	146	.575	41	48	.854	42	118	209	1.5	4.2	7.5
84-85—Nazareth	26	...	88	156	.564	91	104	.875	64	133	267	2.5	5.1	10.3
Varsity totals	54	...	172	302	.570	132	152	.868	106	251	476	2.0	4.6	8.8

HEAD COACHING RECORD

BACKGROUND: Head coach, McQuaid Jesuit (Rochester, N.Y.) High School (1985-86). ... Graduate assistant, Providence College (1986-87). ... Assistant coach, Providence (1987-88). ... Assistant coach, Rutgers University (1988-89). ... Assistant coach, New York Knicks (1989-90 to March 8, 1996).

NBA COACHING RECORD

		REGULAR SEASON				PLAYOFFS		
Season	Team	W	L	Pct.	Finish	W	L	Pct.
95-96	—New York	13	9	.591	2nd/Atlantic Division	4	4	.500

NOTES:

1996—Replaced Don Nelson as New York Knicks head coach (March 8), with record of 34-26 and club in second place. Defeated Cleveland, 3-0, in Eastern Conference first round; lost to Chicago, 4-1, in Eastern Conference semifinals.

WALKER, DARRELL — RAPTORS

PERSONAL: Born March 9, 1961, in Chicago. ... 6-4/180. ... Full name: Darrell Walker.
HIGH SCHOOL: Corliss (Chicago).
JUNIOR COLLEGE: Westark Community College (Ark.).
COLLEGE: Arkansas.
TRANSACTIONS/CAREER NOTES: Selected by New York Knicks in first round (12th pick overall) of 1983 NBA Draft. ... Traded by Knicks to Denver Nuggets for 1987 first-round draft choice (October 2, 1986). ... Traded by Nuggets with F Mark Alarie to Washington Bullets for G Michael Adams and F Jay Vincent (November 2, 1987). ... Traded by Bullets to Detroit Pistons for draft considerations (September 5, 1991). ... Waived by Pistons (November 25, 1992). ... Signed by Chicago Bulls to first of two 10-day contracts (January 28, 1993). ... Re-signed by Bulls for remainder of season (February 17, 1993).
MISCELLANEOUS: Member of NBA championship team (1993).

COLLEGIATE RECORD

												AVERAGES		
Season Team	G	Min.	FGM	FGA	Pct.	FTM	FTA	Pct.	Reb.	Ast.	Pts.	RPG	APG	PPG
79-80—Westark C.C.	37	1332	255	472	.540	117	178	.657	259	...	627	7.0	...	16.9
80-81—Arkansas	31	926	137	269	.509	75	125	.600	139	103	349	4.5	3.3	11.3

Season Team	G	Min.	FGM	FGA	Pct.	FTM	FTA	Pct.	Reb.	Ast.	Pts.	RPG	APG	PPG
81-82—Arkansas	29	1039	162	316	.513	106	161	.658	152	47	430	5.2	1.6	14.8
82-83—Arkansas	30	1105	197	374	.527	152	238	.639	172	98	546	5.7	3.3	18.2
Junior college totals..............	37	1332	255	472	.540	117	178	.657	259	...	627	7.0	...	16.9
4-year-college totals	90	3070	496	959	.517	333	524	.635	463	248	1325	5.1	2.8	14.7

HONORS: NBA All-Rookie team (1984).

NBA REGULAR-SEASON RECORD

Season Team	G	Min.	FGM	FGA	Pct.	FTM	FTA	Pct.	REBOUNDS Off.	Def.	Tot.	Ast.	St.	Blk.	TO	Pts.	RPG	APG	PPG
83-84—New York	82	1324	216	518	.417	208	263	.791	74	93	167	284	127	15	194	644	2.0	3.5	7.9
84-85—New York	82	2489	430	989	.435	243	347	.700	128	150	278	408	167	21	204	1103	3.4	5.0	13.5
85-86—New York	81	2023	324	753	.430	190	277	.686	100	120	220	337	146	36	192	838	2.7	4.2	10.3
86-87—Denver	81	2020	358	742	.482	272	365	.745	157	170	327	282	120	37	187	988	4.0	3.5	12.2
87-88—Washington ..	52	940	114	291	.392	82	105	.781	43	84	127	100	62	10	69	310	2.4	1.9	6.0
88-89—Washington ..	79	2565	286	681	.420	142	184	.772	135	372	507	496	155	23	184	714	6.4	6.3	9.0
89-90—Washington ..	81	2883	316	696	.454	138	201	.687	173	541	714	652	139	30	173	772	8.8	8.0	9.5
90-91—Washington ..	71	2305	230	535	.430	93	154	.604	140	358	498	459	78	33	154	553	7.0	6.5	7.8
91-92—Detroit..........	74	1541	161	381	.423	65	105	.619	85	153	238	205	63	18	79	387	3.2	2.8	5.2
92-93—Det.-Chi.	37	511	34	96	.354	12	26	.462	22	36	58	53	33	2	25	80	1.6	1.4	2.2
Totals	720	18601	2469	5682	.435	1445	2027	.713	1057	2077	3134	3276	1090	225	1461	6389	4.4	4.6	8.9

Three-point field goals: 1983-84, 4-for-15 (.267). 1984-85, 0-for-17. 1985-86, 0-for-10. 1986-87, 0-for-4. 1987-88, 0-for-6. 1988-89, 0-for-9. 1989-90, 2-for-21 (.095). 1990-91, 0-for-9. 1991-92, 0-for-10. 1992-93, 0-for-1. Totals, 6-for-102 (.059).
Personal fouls/disqualifications: 1983-84, 202/1. 1984-85, 244/2. 1985-86, 216/1. 1986-87, 229/0. 1987-88, 105/2. 1988-89, 215/2. 1989-90, 220/1. 1990-91, 199/2. 1991-92, 134/0. 1992-93, 63/0. Totals, 1827/11.

NBA PLAYOFF RECORD

Season Team	G	Min.	FGM	FGA	Pct.	FTM	FTA	Pct.	REBOUNDS Off.	Def.	Tot.	Ast.	St.	Blk.	TO	Pts.	RPG	APG	PPG
83-84—New York	12	195	27	73	.370	28	46	.609	20	15	35	20	24	2	32	82	2.9	1.7	6.8
86-87—Denver	3	68	11	34	.324	4	7	.571	3	7	10	5	2	0	4	26	3.3	1.7	8.7
87-88—Washington ..	5	155	22	54	.407	11	16	.688	9	15	24	14	7	4	9	55	4.8	2.8	11.0
91-92—Detroit..........	5	68	3	9	.333	4	4	1.000	5	7	12	4	1	0	5	10	2.4	0.8	2.0
92-93—Chicago..........	9	22	1	4	.250	2	3	.667	0	1	1	5	0	0	1	4	0.1	0.6	0.4
Totals	34	508	64	174	.368	49	76	.645	37	45	82	48	34	6	51	177	2.4	1.4	5.2

Three-point field goals: 1987-88, 0-for-1.
Personal fouls/disqualifications: 1983-84, 29/0. 1986-87, 4/0. 1987-88, 18/0. 1991-92, 7/0. Totals, 58/0.

HEAD COACHING RECORD

BACKGROUND: Field representative, NBA Players Association (1993-94 and 1994-95). ... Assistant coach, Toronto Raptors (1995-96).

WILKENS, LENNY
HAWKS

PERSONAL: Born October 28, 1937, in Brooklyn, N.Y. ... 6-1/180. ... Full name: Leonard Randolph Wilkens.
HIGH SCHOOL: Boys (Brooklyn, N.Y.).
COLLEGE: Providence.
TRANSACTIONS/CAREER NOTES: Selected by St. Louis Hawks in first round of 1960 NBA Draft. ... Hawks franchise moved from St. Louis to Atlanta for 1968-69 season. ... Traded by Hawks to Seattle SuperSonics for G Walt Hazzard (October 12, 1968). ... Player/head coach, SuperSonics (1969-70 through 1971-72). ... Traded by SuperSonics with F Barry Clemens to Cleveland Cavaliers for G Butch Beard (August 23, 1972). ... Playing rights transferred from Cavaliers to Portland Trail Blazers for cash (October 7, 1974).
CAREER HONORS: Elected to Naismith Memorial Basketball Hall of Fame (1988).

COLLEGIATE RECORD

NOTES: THE SPORTING NEWS All-America second team (1960).

Season Team	G	Min.	FGM	FGA	Pct.	FTM	FTA	Pct.	Reb.	Ast.	Pts.	RPG	APG	PPG
56-57—Providence‡	23	...	...	...	...	...	...	...	...	...	488	...	...	21.2
57-58—Providence	24	...	137	316	.434	84	130	.646	190	...	358	7.9	...	14.9
58-59—Providence	27	...	167	390	.428	89	144	.618	188	...	423	7.0	...	15.7
59-60—Providence	29	...	157	362	.434	98	140	.700	205	...	412	7.1	...	14.2
Varsity totals...........................	80	...	461	1068	.432	271	414	.655	583	...	1193	7.3	...	14.9

NBA REGULAR-SEASON RECORD

Season Team	G	Min.	FGM	FGA	Pct.	FTM	FTA	Pct.	Reb.	Ast.	PF	Dq.	Pts.	RPG	APG	PPG
60-61 —St. Louis	75	1898	333	783	.425	214	300	.713	335	212	215	5	880	4.5	2.8	11.7
61-62 —St. Louis	20	870	140	364	.385	84	110	.764	131	116	63	0	364	6.6	5.8	18.2
62-63 —St. Louis	75	2569	333	834	.399	222	319	.696	403	381	256	6	888	5.4	5.1	11.8
63-64 —St. Louis	78	2526	334	808	.413	270	365	.740	335	359	287	7	938	4.3	4.6	12.0
64-65 —St. Louis	78	2854	434	1048	.414	416	558	.746	365	431	283	7	1284	4.7	5.5	16.5
65-66 —St. Louis	69	2692	411	954	.431	422	532	.793	322	429	248	4	1244	4.7	6.2	18.0
66-67 —St. Louis	78	2974	448	1036	.432	459	583	.787	412	442	280	6	1355	5.3	5.7	17.4
67-68 —St. Louis	82	3169	546	1246	.438	546	711	.768	438	679	255	7	1638	5.3	8.3	20.0
68-69 —Seattle	82	3463	644	1462	.441	547	710	.770	511	674	294	8	1835	6.2	8.2	22.4
69-70 —Seattle	75	2802	448	1066	.420	438	556	.788	378	*683	212	5	1334	5.0	9.1	17.8
70-71 —Seattle	71	2641	471	1125	.419	461	574	.803	319	654	201	3	1403	4.5	9.2	19.8
71-72 —Seattle	80	2989	479	1027	.466	480	620	.774	338	*766	209	4	1438	4.2	9.6	18.0
72-73 —Cleveland	75	2973	572	1275	.449	394	476	.828	346	628	221	2	1538	4.6	8.4	20.5

Season Team	G	Min.	FGM	FGA	Pct.	FTM	FTA	Pct.	REBOUNDS Off.	Def.	Tot.	Ast.	St.	Blk.	TO	Pts.	AVERAGES RPG	APG	PPG
73-74—Cleveland	74	2483	462	994	.465	289	361	.801	80	197	277	522	97	17	...	1213	3.7	7.1	16.4
74-75—Portland	65	1161	134	305	.439	152	198	.768	38	82	120	235	77	9	...	420	1.8	3.6	6.5
Totals	1077	38064	6189	14327	.432	5394	6973	.774	...	...	5030	7211	174	26	...	17772	4.7	6.7	16.5

Personal fouls/disqualifications: 1973-74, 165/2. 1974-75, 96/1. Totals, 3285/63.

NBA PLAYOFF RECORD

Season Team	G	Min.	FGM	FGA	Pct.	FTM	FTA	Pct.	Reb.	Ast.	PF	Dq.	Pts.	AVERAGES RPG	APG	PPG
60-61 —St. Louis..................	12	437	63	166	.380	44	58	.759	72	42	51	4	170	6.0	3.5	14.2
62-63 —St. Louis..................	11	400	57	154	.370	37	49	.755	69	69	51	2	151	6.3	6.3	13.7
63-64 —St. Louis..................	12	413	64	143	.448	44	58	.759	60	64	42	0	172	5.0	5.3	14.3
64-65 —St. Louis..................	4	147	20	57	.351	24	29	.828	12	15	14	0	64	3.0	3.8	16.0
65-66 —St. Louis..................	10	391	57	143	.399	57	83	.687	54	70	43	0	171	5.4	7.0	17.1
66-67 —St. Louis..................	9	378	58	145	.400	77	90	.856	68	65	34	0	193	7.6	7.2	21.4
67-68 —St. Louis..................	6	237	40	91	.440	30	40	.750	38	47	23	1	110	6.3	7.8	18.3
Totals.................................	64	2403	359	899	.399	313	407	.769	373	372	258	7	1031	5.8	5.8	16.1

NBA ALL-STAR GAME RECORD

NOTES: NBA All-Star Game Most Valuable Player (1971).

Season Team	Min.	FGM	FGA	Pct.	FTM	FTA	Pct.	Reb	Ast.	PF	Dq.	Pts.
1963 —St. Louis..................	25	2	7	.286	0	1	.000	2	3	0	0	4
1964 —St. Louis..................	14	1	5	.200	1	1	1.000	0	0	3	0	3
1965 —St. Louis..................	20	2	6	.333	4	4	1.000	3	3	3	0	8
1967 —St. Louis..................	16	2	6	.333	2	3	.667	2	6	2	0	6
1968 —St. Louis..................	22	4	10	.400	6	8	.750	3	3	1	0	14
1969 —Seattle....................	24	3	15	.200	4	5	.800	7	5	3	0	10
1970 —Seattle....................	17	5	7	.714	2	3	.667	2	4	1	0	12
1971 —Seattle....................	20	8	11	.727	5	5	1.000	1	1	1	0	21
1973 —Cleveland................	24	3	8	.375	1	2	.500	2	1	1	0	7
Totals	182	30	75	.400	25	32	.781	22	26	15	0	85

HEAD COACHING RECORD

BACKGROUND: Player/head coach, Seattle SuperSonics (1969-70 through 1971-72). ... Player/head coach, Portland Trail Blazers (1974-75). ... Director of player personnel, SuperSonics (May 13-November 1977). ... Head coach/director of player personnel, SuperSonics (November 1977 through 1984-85). ... Vice president/general manager, SuperSonics (1985-86). ... Assistant coach, U.S. Olympic team (1992).

HONORS: NBA Coach of the Year (1994).

RECORDS: Holds NBA career record for most wins—1,014.

NBA COACHING RECORD

Season Team	REGULAR SEASON W	L	Pct.	Finish	PLAYOFFS W	L	Pct.
69-70 —Seattle.................................	36	46	.439	5th/Western Division	—	—	—
70-71 —Seattle.................................	38	44	.463	4th/Pacific Division	—	—	—
71-72 —Seattle.................................	47	35	.573	3rd/Pacific Division	—	—	—
74-75 —Portland...............................	38	44	.463	3rd/Pacific Division	—	—	—
75-76 —Portland...............................	37	45	.451	5th/Pacific Division	—	—	—
77-78 —Seattle.................................	42	18	.700	3rd/Pacific Division	13	9	.591
78-79 —Seattle.................................	52	30	.634	1st/Pacific Division	12	5	.706
79-80 —Seattle.................................	56	26	.683	2nd/Pacific Division	7	8	.467
80-81 —Seattle.................................	34	48	.415	6th/Pacific Division	—	—	—
81-82 —Seattle.................................	52	30	.634	2nd/Pacific Division	3	5	.375
82-83 —Seattle.................................	48	34	.585	3rd/Pacific Division	0	2	.000
83-84 —Seattle.................................	42	40	.512	3rd/Pacific Division	2	3	.400
84-85 —Seattle.................................	31	51	.378	4th/Pacific Division	—	—	—
86-87 —Cleveland.............................	31	51	.378	6th/Central Division	—	—	—
87-88 —Cleveland.............................	42	40	.512	T4th/Central Division	2	3	.400
88-89 —Cleveland.............................	57	25	.695	2nd/Central Division	2	3	.400
89-90 —Cleveland.............................	42	40	.512	T4th/Central Division	2	3	.400
90-91 —Cleveland.............................	33	49	.402	6th/Central Division	—	—	—
91-92 —Cleveland.............................	57	25	.695	2nd/Central Division	9	8	.529
92-93 —Cleveland.............................	54	28	.659	2nd/Central Division	3	6	.333
93-94 —Atlanta.................................	57	25	.695	1st/Central Division	5	6	.455
94-95 —Atlanta.................................	42	40	.512	5th/Central Division	0	3	.000
95-96 —Atlanta.................................	46	36	.561	4th/Central Division	4	6	.400
Totals (23 years)...	1,014	850	.544	Totals (14 years).....	64	70	.478

OLYMPIC RECORD

Season Team	REGULAR SEASON W	L	Pct.	Finish	PLAYOFFS W	L	Pct.
1996 —Team USA................	8	0	1.000	Gold medal	—	—	—

NOTES:

1977—Replaced Bob Hopkins as Seattle head coach (November), with record of 5-17.

1978—Defeated Los Angeles Lakers, 2-1, in Western Conference first round; defeated Portland, 4-2, in Western Conference semifinals; defeated Denver, 4-2, in Western Conference finals; lost to Washington, 4-3, in World Championship Series.

1979—Defeated Los Angeles Lakers, 4-1, in Western Conference semifinals; defeated Phoenix, 4-3, in Western Conference finals; defeated Washington, 4-1, in World Championship Series.

1980—Defeated Portland, 2-1, in Western Conference first round; defeated Milwaukee, 4-3, in Western Conference semifinals; lost to Los Angeles Lakers, 4-1, in Western Conference finals.

1982—Defeated Houston, 2-1, in Western Conference first round; lost to San Antonio, 4-1, in Western Conference semifinals.
1983—Lost to Portland in Western Conference first round.
1984—Lost to Dallas in Western Conference first round.
1988—Lost to Chicago in Eastern Conference first round.
1989—Lost to Chicago in Eastern Conference first round.
1990—Lost to Philadelphia in Eastern Conference first round.
1992—Defeated New Jersey, 3-1, in Eastern Conference first round; defeated Boston, 4-3, in Eastern Conference semifinals; lost to Chicago, 4-2, in Eastern Conference finals.
1993—Defeated New Jersey, 3-2, in Eastern Conference first round; lost to Chicago, 4-0, in Eastern Conference semifinals.
1994—Defeated Miami, 3-2, in Eastern Conference first round; lost to Indiana, 4-2, in Eastern Conference semifinals.
1995—Lost to Indiana in Eastern Conference first round.
1996—Defeated Indiana, 3-2, in Eastern Conference first round; lost to Orlando, 4-1, in Eastern Conference semifinals.
Team USA defeated Argentina, 96-68; Angola, 87-54; Lithuania, 104-82; China, 133-70; and Croatia, 102-71, in preliminary round. Defeated Brazil, 98-75, in medal round quarterfinals; defeated Australia, 101-73, in semifinals; defeated Yugoslavia, 95-69, in gold-medal game.

WINTERS, BRIAN — GRIZZLIES

PERSONAL: Born March 1, 1952, in Rockaway, N.Y. ... 6-4/185. ... Full name: Brian Joseph Winters.
HIGH SCHOOL: Archbishop Molloy (Queens, N.Y.).
COLLEGE: South Carolina.
TRANSACTIONS/CAREER NOTES: Selected by Los Angeles Lakers in first round (12th pick overall) of 1974 NBA Draft. ... Traded by Lakers with C Elmore Smith, F/C Dave Meyers and F/G Junior Bridgeman to Milwaukee Bucks for C Kareem Abdul-Jabbar and C Walt Wesley (June 16, 1975).

COLLEGIATE RECORD

Season Team	G	Min.	FGM	FGA	Pct.	FTM	FTA	Pct.	Reb.	Ast.	Pts.	RPG	APG	PPG
70-71—South Carolina‡	16	...	138	299	.462	92	108	.852	156	69	368	9.8	4.3	23.0
71-72—South Carolina	29	692	90	175	.514	60	71	.845	82	55	240	2.8	1.9	8.3
72-73—South Carolina	26	834	120	258	.465	59	81	.728	164	69	299	6.3	2.7	11.5
73-74—South Carolina	27	1016	229	446	.513	82	100	.820	85	68	540	3.1	2.5	20.0
Varsity totals	82	2542	439	879	.499	201	252	.798	331	192	1079	4.0	2.3	13.2

NBA REGULAR-SEASON RECORD

HONORS: NBA All-Rookie team (1975).

Season Team	G	Min.	FGM	FGA	Pct.	FTM	FTA	Pct.	Off.	Def.	Tot.	Ast.	St.	Blk.	TO	Pts.	RPG	APG	PPG
74-75—Los Angeles	68	1516	359	810	.443	76	92	.826	39	99	138	195	74	18	...	794	2.0	2.9	11.7
75-76—Milwaukee	78	2795	618	1333	.464	180	217	.830	66	183	249	366	124	25	...	1416	3.2	4.7	18.2
76-77—Milwaukee	78	2717	652	1308	.498	205	242	.847	64	167	231	337	114	29	...	1509	3.0	4.3	19.3
77-78—Milwaukee	80	2751	674	1457	.463	246	293	.840	87	163	250	393	124	27	236	1594	3.1	4.9	19.9
78-79—Milwaukee	79	2575	662	1343	.493	237	277	.856	48	129	177	383	83	40	257	1561	2.2	4.8	19.8
79-80—Milwaukee	80	2623	535	1116	.479	184	214	.860	48	175	223	362	101	28	186	1292	2.8	4.5	16.2
80-81—Milwaukee	69	1771	331	697	.475	119	137	.869	32	108	140	185	70	10	136	799	2.0	2.7	11.6
81-82—Milwaukee	61	1829	404	806	.501	123	156	.788	51	119	170	253	57	9	118	967	2.8	4.1	15.9
82-83—Milwaukee	57	1361	255	587	.434	73	85	.859	35	75	110	156	45	4	81	605	1.9	2.7	10.6
Totals	650	19938	4490	9457	.475	1443	1713	.842	470	1218	1688	2630	792	190	1014	10537	2.6	4.0	16.2

Three-point field goals: 1979-80, 38-for-102 (.373). 1980-81, 18-for-51 (.353). 1981-82, 36-for-93 (.387). 1982-83, 22-for-68 (.324). Totals, 114-for-314 (.363).
Personal fouls/disqualifications: 1974-75, 168/1. 1975-76, 240/0. 1976-77, 228/1. 1977-78, 239/4. 1978-79, 243/1. 1979-80, 208/0. 1980-81, 185/2. 1981-82, 187/1. 1982-83, 132/2. Totals, 1830/12.

NBA PLAYOFF RECORD

Season Team	G	Min.	FGM	FGA	Pct.	FTM	FTA	Pct.	Off.	Def.	Tot.	Ast.	St.	Blk.	TO	Pts.	RPG	APG	PPG
75-76—Milwaukee	3	126	39	62	.629	4	5	.800	3	4	7	15	5	2	...	82	2.3	5.0	27.3
77-78—Milwaukee	9	305	82	165	.497	20	27	.741	26	4	30	58	12	8	...	184	3.3	6.4	20.4
79-80—Milwaukee	7	268	46	100	.460	10	10	1.000	4	17	21	37	11	0	...	111	3.0	5.3	15.9
80-81—Milwaukee	7	181	28	61	.459	12	16	.750	4	19	23	22	10	1	...	70	3.3	3.1	10.0
81-82—Milwaukee	6	232	38	77	.494	20	24	.833	4	11	15	28	8	1	...	101	2.5	4.7	16.8
82-83—Milwaukee	9	240	36	84	.429	14	17	.824	7	15	22	32	6	4	...	89	2.4	3.6	9.9
Totals	41	1352	269	549	.490	80	99	.808	48	70	118	192	52	16	123	637	2.9	4.7	15.5

Three-point field goals: 1979-80, 9-for-21 (.429). 1980-81, 2-for-6 (.333). 1981-82, 5-for-10 (.500). 1982-83, 3-for-11 (.273). Totals, 19-for-48 (.396).
Personal fouls/disqualifications: 1975-76, 11/1. 1977-78, 20/0. 1979-80, 25/1. 1980-81, 22/1. 1981-82, 23/0. 1982-83, 22/0. Totals, 123/3.

NBA ALL-STAR GAME RECORD

Season Team	Min.	FGM	FGA	Pct.	FTM	FTA	Pct.	Off.	Def.	Tot.	Ast.	PF	Dq.	St.	Blk.	TO	Pts.
1977 —Milwaukee	16	1	5	.200	0	0	...	0	2	2	1	2	0	1	0	...	2
1979 —Milwaukee	14	4	7	.571	0	0	...	2	2	4	1	2	0	0	0	...	8
Totals	30	5	12	.417	0	0	...	2	4	6	2	4	0	1	0	...	10

BACKGROUND: Assistant coach, Princeton (1984-85 and 1985-86). ... Assistant coach, Cleveland Cavaliers (1986-87 through 1992-93). ... Assistant coach, Atlanta Hawks (1993-94 and 1994-95).

NBA COACHING RECORD

	REGULAR SEASON				PLAYOFFS		
Season Team	W	L	Pct.	Finish	W	L	Pct.
1995-96—Vancouver	15	67	.183	7th/Midwest Division	—	—	—

ABDUL-JABBAR, KAREEM   C

PERSONAL: Born April 16, 1947, in New York. ... 7-2/267. ... Full name: Kareem Abdul-Jabbar. ... Formerly known as Lew Alcindor.
HIGH SCHOOL: Power Memorial (New York).
COLLEGE: UCLA.
TRANSACTIONS/CAREER NOTES: Selected by Milwaukee Bucks in first round (first pick overall) of 1969 NBA Draft. ... Traded by Bucks with C Walt Wesley to Los Angeles Lakers for C Elmore Smith, G/F Brian Winters, F Dave Meyers and F/G Junior Bridgeman (June 16, 1975).
CAREER HONORS: Elected to Naismith Memorial Basketball Hall of Fame (1995). ... NBA 35th Anniversary All-Time Team (1980).
MISCELLANEOUS: Member of NBA championship teams (1971, 1980, 1982, 1985, 1987, 1988). ... Milwaukee Bucks all-time leading scorer with 14,211 points and all-time leading rebounder with 7,161 (1969-70 through 1974-75). ... Los Angeles Lakers all-time blocked shots leader with 2,694 (1975-76 through 1988-89).

COLLEGIATE RECORD

NOTES: THE SPORTING NEWS College Player of the Year (1967, 1969). ... Naismith Award winner (1969). ... THE SPORTING NEWS All-America first team (1967, 1968, 1969). ... NCAA Tournament Most Outstanding Player (1967, 1968, 1969). ... Member of NCAA championship teams (1967, 1968, 1969). ... Led NCAA Division I with .667 field-goal percentage (1967) and .635 field-goal percentage (1969).

Season Team	G	Min.	FGM	FGA	Pct.	FTM	FTA	Pct.	Reb.	Ast.	Pts.	AVERAGES RPG	APG	PPG
65-66—UCLA‡	21	...	295	432	.683	106	179	.592	452	...	696	21.5	...	33.1
66-67—UCLA	30	...	346	519	.667	178	274	.650	466	...	870	15.5	...	29.0
67-68—UCLA	28	...	294	480	.613	146	237	.616	461	...	734	16.5	...	26.2
68-69—UCLA	30	...	303	477	.635	115	188	.612	440	...	721	14.7	...	24.0
Varsity totals	88	...	943	1476	.639	439	699	.628	1367	...	2325	15.5	...	26.4

NBA REGULAR-SEASON RECORD

RECORDS: Holds career records for most minutes played—57,446; most points—38,387; most field goals made—15,837; most field goals attempted—28,307. ... Shares career records for most seasons played—20; and most seasons with 2,000 or more points—9. ... Holds single-season record for most defensive rebounds—1,111 (1976). ... Holds single-game record for most defensive rebounds—29 (December 14, 1975, vs. Detroit).
HONORS: NBA Most Valuable Player (1971, 1972, 1974, 1976, 1977, 1980). ... NBA Rookie of the Year (1970). ... All-NBA first team (1971, 1972, 1973, 1974, 1976, 1977, 1980, 1981, 1984, 1986). ... All-NBA second team (1970, 1978, 1979, 1983, 1985). ... NBA All-Defensive first team (1974, 1975, 1979, 1980, 1981). ... NBA All-Defensive second team (1970, 1971, 1976, 1977, 1978, 1984). ... NBA All-Rookie team (1970).
NOTES: Led NBA with 3.26 blocked shots per game (1975), 4.12 blocked shots per game (1976), 3.95 blocked shots per game (1979) and 3.41 blocked shots per game (1980).

Season Team	G	Min.	FGM	FGA	Pct.	FTM	FTA	Pct.	Reb.	Ast.	PF	Dq.	Pts.	AVERAGES RPG	APG	PPG
69-70—Milwaukee	82	3534	*938	1810	.518	485	743	.653	1190	337	283	8	*2361	14.5	4.1	28.8
70-71—Milwaukee	82	3288	*1063	1843	.577	470	681	.690	1311	272	264	4	*2596	16.0	3.3	*31.7
71-72—Milwaukee	81	3583	*1159	*2019	.574	504	732	.689	1346	370	235	1	*2822	16.6	4.6	*34.8
72-73—Milwaukee	76	3254	982	1772	.554	328	460	.713	1224	379	208	0	2292	16.1	5.0	30.2

Season Team	G	Min.	FGM	FGA	Pct.	FTM	FTA	Pct.	REBOUNDS Off.	Def.	Tot.	Ast.	St.	Blk.	TO	Pts.	AVERAGES RPG	APG	PPG
73-74—Milwaukee	81	3548	*948	1759	.539	295	420	.702	287	891	1178	386	112	283	...	2191	14.5	4.8	27.0
74-75—Milwaukee	65	2747	812	1584	.513	325	426	.763	194	718	912	264	65	212	...	1949	14.0	4.1	30.0
75-76—Los Angeles	82	*3379	914	1728	.529	447	636	.703	272	*1111	*1383	413	119	*338	...	2275	*16.9	5.0	27.7
76-77—Los Angeles	82	3016	*888	1533	*.579	376	536	.702	266	*824	*1090	319	101	*261	...	2152	13.3	3.9	26.2
77-78—Los Angeles	62	2265	663	1205	.550	274	350	.783	186	615	801	269	103	185	208	1600	12.9	4.3	25.8
78-79—Los Angeles	80	3157	777	1347	.577	349	474	.736	207	818	1025	431	76	*316	282	1903	12.8	5.4	23.8
79-80—Los Angeles	82	3143	835	1383	.604	364	476	.765	190	696	886	371	81	*280	297	2034	10.8	4.5	24.8
80-81—Los Angeles	80	2976	836	1457	.574	423	552	.766	197	624	821	272	59	228	249	2095	10.3	3.4	26.2
81-82—Los Angeles	76	2677	753	1301	.579	312	442	.706	172	487	659	225	63	207	230	1818	8.7	3.0	23.9
82-83—Los Angeles	79	2554	722	1228	.588	278	371	.749	167	425	592	200	61	170	200	1722	7.5	2.5	21.8
83-84—Los Angeles	80	2622	716	1238	.578	285	394	.723	169	418	587	211	55	143	221	1717	7.3	2.6	21.5
84-85—L.A. Lakers	79	2630	723	1207	.599	289	395	.732	162	460	622	249	63	162	197	1735	7.9	3.2	22.0
85-86—L.A. Lakers	79	2629	755	1338	.564	336	439	.765	133	345	478	280	67	130	203	1846	6.1	3.5	23.4
86-87—L.A. Lakers	78	2441	560	993	.564	245	343	.714	152	371	523	203	49	97	186	1366	6.7	2.6	17.5
87-88—L.A. Lakers	80	2308	480	903	.532	205	269	.762	118	360	478	135	48	92	159	1165	6.0	1.7	14.6
88-89—L.A. Lakers	74	1695	313	659	.475	122	165	.739	103	231	334	74	38	85	95	748	4.5	1.0	10.1
Totals	1560	57446	15837	28307	.559	6712	9304	.721	...	...17440	5660	1160	3189	2527	38387	11.2	3.6	24.6

Three-point field goals: 1979-80, 0-for-1. 1980-81, 0-for-1. 1981-82, 0-for-3. 1982-83, 0-for-2. 1983-84, 0-for-1. 1984-85, 0-for-1. 1985-86, 0-for-2. 1986-87, 1-for-3 (.333). 1987-88, 0-for-1. 1988-89, 0-for-3. Totals, 1-for-18 (.056).
Personal fouls/disqualifications: 1973-74, 238/2. 1974-75, 205/2. 1975-76, 292/6. 1976-77, 262/4. 1977-78, 182/1. 1978-79, 230/3. 1979-80, 216/2. 1980-81, 244/4. 1981-82, 224/0. 1982-83, 220/1. 1983-84, 211/1. 1984-85, 238/3. 1985-86, 248/2. 1986-87, 245/2. 1987-88, 216/1. 1988-89, 196/1. Totals, 4657/48.

NBA PLAYOFF RECORD

NOTES: NBA Finals Most Valuable Player (1971, 1985). ... Holds career playoff records for most seasons played—18; most games played—237; most minutes played—8,851; most field goals made—2,356; most field goals attempted—4,422; most points—5,762; most blocked shots—476; and most personal fouls—797.

Season Team	G	Min.	FGM	FGA	Pct.	FTM	FTA	Pct.	Reb.	Ast.	PF	Dq.	Pts.	AVERAGES RPG	APG	PPG
69-70—Milwaukee	10	435	139	245	.567	74	101	.733	168	41	25	1	352	16.8	4.1	35.2
70-71—Milwaukee	14	577	152	295	.515	68	101	.673	238	35	45	0	372	17.0	2.5	26.6

Season Team	G	Min.	FGM	FGA	Pct.	FTM	FTA	Pct.	Reb.	Ast.	PF	Dq.	Pts.	RPG	APG	PPG
71-72—Milwaukee	11	510	139	318	.437	38	54	.704	200	56	35	0	316	18.2	5.1	28.7
72-73—Milwaukee	6	276	59	138	.428	19	35	.543	97	17	26	0	137	16.2	2.8	22.8

Season Team	G	Min.	FGM	FGA	Pct.	FTM	FTA	Pct.	REBOUNDS Off.	Def.	Tot.	Ast.	St.	Blk.	TO	Pts.	AVERAGES RPG	APG	PPG
73-74—Milwaukee	16	758	224	402	.557	67	91	.736	67	186	253	78	20	39	...	515	15.8	4.9	32.2
76-77—Los Angeles	11	467	147	242	.607	87	120	.725	51	144	195	45	19	38	...	381	17.7	4.1	34.6
77-78—Los Angeles	3	134	38	73	.521	5	9	.556	14	27	41	11	2	12	14	81	13.7	3.7	27.0
78-79—Los Angeles	8	367	88	152	.579	52	62	.839	18	83	101	38	8	33	29	228	12.6	4.8	28.5
79-80—Los Angeles	15	618	198	346	.572	83	105	.790	51	130	181	46	17	58	55	479	12.1	3.1	31.9
80-81—Los Angeles	3	134	30	65	.462	20	28	.714	13	37	50	12	3	8	11	80	16.7	4.0	26.7
81-82—Los Angeles	14	493	115	221	.520	55	87	.632	33	86	119	51	14	45	41	285	8.5	3.6	20.4
82-83—Los Angeles	15	588	163	287	.568	80	106	.755	25	90	115	42	17	55	50	406	7.7	2.8	27.1
83-84—Los Angeles	21	767	206	371	.555	90	120	.750	56	117	173	79	23	45	45	502	8.2	3.8	23.9
84-85—L.A. Lakers	19	610	168	300	.560	80	103	.777	50	104	154	76	23	36	52	416	8.1	4.0	21.9
85-86—L.A. Lakers	14	489	157	282	.557	48	61	.787	26	57	83	49	15	24	42	362	5.9	3.5	25.9
86-87—L.A. Lakers	18	559	124	234	.530	97	122	.795	39	84	123	36	8	35	40	345	6.8	2.0	19.2
87-88—L.A. Lakers	24	718	141	304	.464	56	71	.789	49	82	131	36	15	37	46	338	5.5	1.5	14.1
88-89—L.A. Lakers	15	351	68	147	.463	31	43	.721	13	46	59	19	5	11	22	167	3.9	1.3	11.1
Totals	237	8851	2356	4422	.533	1050	1419	.740	...	...	2481	767	189	476	447	5762	10.5	3.2	24.3

Three-point field goals: 1982-83, 0-for-1. 1986-87, 0-for-1. 1987-88, 0-for-2. 1988-89, 0-for-1. Totals, 0-for-5.

Personal fouls/disqualifications: 1973-74, 41/0. 1976-77, 42/0. 1977-78, 14/1. 1978-79, 26/0. 1979-80, 51/0. 1980-81, 14/0. 1981-82, 45/0. 1982-83, 61/1. 1983-84, 71/2. 1984-85, 67/1. 1985-86, 54/0. 1986-87, 56/0. 1987-88, 81/1. 1988-89, 43/0. Totals, 797/7.

NBA ALL-STAR GAME RECORD

NOTES: Holds career records for most games played—18; most minutes played—449; most field goals made—105; most field goals attempted—213; most points—251; most blocked shots—31; and most personal fouls—57. ... Holds single-game record for most blocked shots—6 (1980, OT).

Season Team	Min.	FGM	FGA	Pct.	FTM	FTA	Pct.	Reb.	Ast.	PF	Dq.	Pts.
1970 —Milwaukee	18	4	8	.500	2	2	1.000	11	4	6	1	10
1971 —Milwaukee	30	8	16	.500	3	4	.750	14	1	2	0	19
1972 —Milwaukee	19	5	10	.500	2	2	1.000	7	2	0	0	12
1973 —Milwaukee					Selected, did not play.							

Season Team	Min.	FGM	FGA	Pct.	FTM	FTA	Pct.	REBOUNDS Off.	Def.	Tot.	Ast.	PF	Dq.	St.	Blk.	TO	Pts.
1974 —Milwaukee	23	7	11	.636	0	0		1	7	8	6	2	0	1	1	...	14
1975 —Milwaukee	19	3	10	.300	1	2	.500	5	5	10	3	2	0	0	1	...	7
1976 —Los Angeles	36	9	16	.563	4	4	1.000	2	13	15	3	3	0	0	3	...	22
1977 —Los Angeles	23	8	14	.571	5	6	.833	1	3	4	2	1	0	0	1	...	21
1979 —Los Angeles	28	5	12	.417	1	2	.500	1	7	8	3	4	0	1	1	3	11
1980 —Los Angeles	30	6	17	.353	5	6	.833	5	11	16	9	5	0	0	6	9	17
1981 —Los Angeles	23	6	9	.667	3	3	1.000	2	4	6	4	3	0	0	4	3	15
1982 —Los Angeles	22	1	10	.100	0	0		1	2	3	1	3	0	0	2	1	2
1983 —Los Angeles	32	9	12	.750	2	3	.667	2	4	6	5	1	0	1	4	1	20
1984 —Los Angeles	37	11	19	.579	3	4	.750	5	8	13	2	5	0	0	1	4	25
1985 —L.A. Lakers	23	5	10	.500	1	2	.500	0	6	6	1	5	0	1	1	1	11
1986 —L.A. Lakers	32	9	15	.600	3	4	.750	2	5	7	2	4	0	2	2	5	21
1987 —L.A. Lakers	27	4	9	.444	2	2	1.000	2	6	8	3	5	0	0	2	1	10
1988 —L.A. Lakers	14	4	9	.444	2	2	1.000	2	2	4	0	3	0	0	0	0	10
1989 —L.A. Lakers	13	1	6	.167	2	2	1.000	0	3	3	0	3	0	0	2	0	4
Totals	449	105	213	.493	41	50	.820	...	...	149	51	57	1	6	31	28	251

Three-point field goals: 1989, 0-for-1.

AGUIRRE, MARK   F

PERSONAL: Born December 10, 1959, in Chicago. ... 6-6/232. ... Full name: Mark Anthony Aguirre. ... Name pronounced a-GWIRE.

HIGH SCHOOL: Austin (Chicago), then Westinghouse Vocational (Chicago).

COLLEGE: DePaul.

TRANSACTIONS/CAREER NOTES: Selected after junior season by Dallas Mavericks in first round (first pick overall) of 1981 NBA Draft. ... Traded by Mavericks to Detroit Pistons for F Adrian Dantley and 1991 first-round draft choice (February 15, 1989). ... Waived by Pistons (October 7, 1993). ... Signed as free agent by Los Angeles Clippers (October 25, 1993). ... Waived by Clippers (February 1, 1994).

MISCELLANEOUS: Member of NBA championship teams (1989, 1990). ... Member of U.S. Olympic team (1980).

COLLEGIATE RECORD

NOTES: The Sporting News College Player of the Year (1981). ... The Sporting News All-America first team (1980, 1981). ... Naismith Award winner (1980).

Season Team	G	Min.	FGM	FGA	Pct.	FTM	FTA	Pct.	Reb.	Ast.	Pts.	RPG	APG	PPG
78-79—DePaul	32	...	302	581	.520	163	213	.765	244	86	767	7.6	2.7	24.0
79-80—DePaul	28	...	281	520	.540	187	244	.766	213	77	749	7.6	2.8	26.8
80-81—DePaul	29	1069	280	481	.582	106	137	.774	249	131	666	8.6	4.5	23.0
Totals	89	...	863	1582	.546	456	594	.768	706	294	2182	7.9	3.3	24.5

NBA REGULAR-SEASON RECORD

Season Team	G	Min.	FGM	FGA	Pct.	FTM	FTA	Pct.	REBOUNDS Off.	Def.	Tot.	Ast.	St.	Blk.	TO	Pts.	AVERAGES RPG	APG	PPG
81-82—Dallas	51	1468	381	820	.465	168	247	.680	89	160	249	164	37	22	135	955	4.9	3.2	18.7
82-83—Dallas	81	2784	767	1589	.483	429	589	.728	191	317	508	332	80	26	261	1979	6.3	4.1	24.4

Season Team	G	Min.	FGM	FGA	Pct.	FTM	FTA	Pct.	REBOUNDS Off.	Def.	Tot.	Ast.	St.	Blk.	TO	Pts.	AVERAGES RPG	APG	PPG
83-84—Dallas	79	2900	*925	*1765	.524	465	621	.749	161	308	469	358	80	22	285	2330	5.9	4.5	29.5
84-85—Dallas	80	2699	794	1569	.506	440	580	.759	188	289	477	249	60	24	253	2055	6.0	3.1	25.7
85-86—Dallas	74	2501	668	1327	.503	318	451	.705	177	268	445	339	62	14	252	1670	6.0	4.6	22.6
86-87—Dallas	80	2663	787	1590	.495	429	557	.770	181	246	427	254	84	30	217	2056	5.3	3.2	25.7
87-88—Dallas	77	2610	746	1571	.475	388	504	.770	182	252	434	278	70	57	203	1932	5.6	3.6	25.1
88-89—Dallas-Det.	80	2597	586	1270	.461	288	393	.733	146	240	386	278	45	36	208	1511	4.8	3.5	18.9
89-90—Detroit	78	2005	438	898	.488	192	254	.756	117	188	305	145	34	19	121	1099	3.9	1.9	14.1
90-91—Detroit	78	2006	420	909	.462	240	317	.757	134	240	374	139	47	20	128	1104	4.8	1.8	14.2
91-92—Detroit	75	1582	339	787	.431	158	230	.687	67	169	236	126	51	11	105	851	3.1	1.7	11.3
92-93—Detroit	51	1056	187	422	.443	99	129	.767	43	109	152	105	16	7	68	503	3.0	2.1	9.9
93-94—L.A. Clippers	39	859	163	348	.468	50	72	.694	28	88	116	104	21	8	70	413	3.0	2.7	10.6
Totals	923	27730	7201	14865	.484	3664	4944	.741	1704	2874	4578	2871	687	296	2306	18458	5.0	3.1	20.0

Three-point field goals: 1981-82, 25-for-71 (.352). 1982-83, 16-for-76 (.211). 1983-84, 15-for-56 (.268). 1984-85, 27-for-85 (.318). 1985-86, 16-for-56 (.286). 1986-87, 53-for-150 (.353). 1987-88, 52-for-172 (.302). 1988-89, 51-for-174 (.293). 1989-90, 31-for-93 (.333). 1990-91, 24-for-78 (.308). 1991-92, 15-for-71 (.211). 1992-93, 30-for-83 (.361). 1993-94, 37-for-93 (.398). Totals, 392-for-1258 (.312).

Personal fouls/disqualifications: 1981-82, 152/0. 1982-83, 247/5. 1983-84, 246/5. 1984-85, 250/3. 1985-86, 229/6. 1986-87, 243/4. 1987-88, 223/1. 1988-89, 229/2. 1989-90, 201/2. 1990-91, 209/2. 1991-92, 171/0. 1992-93, 101/1. 1993-94, 98/2. Totals, 2599/33.

NBA PLAYOFF RECORD

Season Team	G	Min.	FGM	FGA	Pct.	FTM	FTA	Pct.	REBOUNDS Off.	Def.	Tot.	Ast.	St.	Blk.	TO	Pts.	AVERAGES RPG	APG	PPG
83-84—Dallas	10	350	88	184	.478	44	57	.772	21	55	76	32	5	5	27	220	7.6	3.2	22.0
84-85—Dallas	4	164	44	89	.494	27	32	.844	16	14	30	16	3	0	15	116	7.5	4.0	29.0
85-86—Dallas	10	345	105	214	.491	35	55	.636	21	50	71	54	9	0	23	247	7.1	5.4	24.7
86-87—Dallas	4	130	31	62	.500	23	30	.767	11	13	24	8	8	0	9	85	6.0	2.0	21.3
87-88—Dallas	17	558	147	294	.500	60	86	.698	34	66	100	56	14	9	41	367	5.9	3.3	21.6
88-89—Detroit	17	462	89	182	.489	28	38	.737	26	49	75	28	8	3	20	214	4.4	1.6	12.6
89-90—Detroit	20	439	86	184	.467	39	52	.750	31	60	91	27	10	3	30	219	4.6	1.4	11.0
90-91—Detroit	15	397	90	178	.506	42	51	.824	17	44	61	29	12	1	20	234	4.1	1.9	15.6
91-92—Detroit	5	113	16	48	.333	12	16	.750	4	5	9	12	2	1	13	45	1.8	2.4	9.0
Totals	102	2958	696	1435	.485	310	417	.743	181	356	537	262	71	22	198	1747	5.3	2.6	17.1

Three-point field goals: 1983-84, 0-for-5. 1984-85, 1-for-2 (.500). 1985-86, 2-for-6 (.333). 1986-87, 0-for-4. 1987-88, 13-for-34 (.382). 1988-89, 8-for-29 (.276). 1989-90, 8-for-24 (.333). 1990-91, 12-for-33 (.364). 1991-92, 1-for-5 (.200). Totals, 45-for-142 (.317).

Personal fouls/disqualifications: 1983-84, 34/2. 1984-85, 16/1. 1985-86, 28/1. 1986-87, 15/1. 1987-88, 49/0. 1988-89, 38/0. 1989-90, 51/0. 1990-91, 41/0. 1991-92, 9/0. Totals, 281/5.

NBA ALL-STAR GAME RECORD

Season Team	Min.	FGM	FGA	Pct.	FTM	FTA	Pct.	REBOUNDS Off.	Def.	Tot.	Ast.	PF	Dq.	St.	Blk.	TO	Pts.
1984 —Dallas	13	5	8	.625	3	4	.750	1	0	1	2	1	0	1	1	2	13
1987 —Dallas	17	3	6	.500	2	3	.667	1	1	2	1	1	0	0	0	2	9
1988 —Dallas	12	5	10	.500	3	3	1.000	0	1	1	1	3	0	1	0	3	14
Totals	42	13	24	.542	8	10	.800	2	2	4	4	5	0	2	1	7	36

Three-point field goals: 1987, 1-for-2 (.500). 1988, 1-for-3 (.333). Totals, 2-for-5 (.400).

ARCHIBALD, NATE   G

PERSONAL: Born September 2, 1948, in New York. ... 6-1/160. ... Full name: Nathaniel Archibald. ... Nickname: Tiny.
HIGH SCHOOL: DeWitt Clinton (Bronx, N.Y.).
JUNIOR COLLEGE: Arizona Western College.
COLLEGE: Texas-El Paso.
TRANSACTIONS/CAREER NOTES: Selected by Cincinnati Royals in second round (19th pick overall) of 1970 NBA Draft. ... Royals franchise moved from Cincinnati to Kansas City/Omaha and renamed Kings for 1972-73 season. ... Kings franchise moved from Kansas City/Omaha to Kansas City for 1975-76 season. ... Traded by Kings to New York Nets for G Brian Taylor, C Jim Eakins and 1977 and 1978 first-round draft choices (September 10, 1976). ... Nets franchise moved from New York to New Jersey for 1977-78 season. ... Traded by Nets to Buffalo Braves for C George Johnson and 1979 first-round draft choice (September 1, 1977). ... Braves franchise moved from Buffalo to San Diego and renamed Clippers for 1978-79 season. ... Traded by Clippers with F Marvin Barnes, F/G Billy Knight and 1981 and 1983 second-round draft choices to Boston Celtics for F Kermit Washington, C Kevin Kunnert, F Sidney Wicks and draft rights to G Freeman Williams (August 4, 1978). ... Waived by Celtics (July 22, 1983). ... Signed as free agent by Milwaukee Bucks (August 1, 1983).
CAREER HONORS: Elected to Naismith Memorial Basketball Hall of Fame (1990).
MISCELLANEOUS: Member of NBA championship team (1981).

COLLEGIATE RECORD

Season Team	G	Min.	FGM	FGA	Pct.	FTM	FTA	Pct.	Reb.	Ast.	Pts.	AVERAGES RPG	APG	PPG
66-67—Arizona Western College	27	...	303	...	...	190	...	...	...	...	796	...	...	29.5
67-68—Texas-El Paso	23	...	131	281	.466	102	140	.729	81	...	364	3.5	...	15.8
68-69—Texas-El Paso	25	...	199	374	.532	161	194	.830	69	...	559	2.8	...	22.4
69-70—Texas-El Paso	25	...	180	351	.513	176	225	.782	66	...	536	2.6	...	21.4
Junior college totals	27	...	303	...	...	190	...	...	...	...	796	...	...	29.5
4-year-college totals	73	...	510	1006	.507	439	559	.785	216	...	1459	3.0	...	20.0

NBA REGULAR-SEASON RECORD

HONORS: All-NBA first team (1973, 1975, 1976). ... All-NBA second team (1972, 1981).

Season Team	G	Min.	FGM	FGA	Pct.	FTM	FTA	Pct.	Reb.	Ast.	PF	Dq.	Pts.	AVERAGES RPG	APG	PPG
70-71—Cincinnati	82	2867	486	1095	.444	336	444	.757	242	450	218	2	1308	3.0	5.5	16.0
71-72—Cincinnati	76	3272	734	1511	.486	*677	*824	.822	222	701	198	3	2145	2.9	9.2	28.2
72-73—K.C./Omaha	80	*3681	*1028	*2106	.488	*663	*783	.847	223	*910	207	2	*2719	2.8	*11.4	*34.0

Season Team	G	Min.	FGM	FGA	Pct.	FTM	FTA	Pct.	Off.	Def.	Tot.	Ast.	St.	Blk.	TO	Pts.	RPG	APG	PPG
73-74—K.C./Omaha	35	1272	222	492	.451	173	211	.820	21	64	85	266	56	7	...	617	2.4	7.6	17.6
74-75—K.C./Omaha	82	3244	759	1664	.456	*652	748	.872	48	174	222	557	119	7	...	2170	2.7	6.8	26.5
75-76—Kansas City.....	78	3184	717	1583	.453	501	625	.802	67	146	213	615	126	15	...	1935	2.7	7.9	24.8
76-77—N.Y. Nets....	34	1277	250	560	.446	197	251	.785	22	58	80	254	59	11	...	697	2.4	7.5	20.5
77-78—Buffalo								Did not play—torn Achilles' tendon.											
78-79—Boston	69	1662	259	573	.452	242	307	.788	25	78	103	324	55	6	197	760	1.5	4.7	11.0
79-80—Boston	80	2864	383	794	.482	361	435	.830	59	138	197	671	106	10	242	1131	2.5	8.4	14.1
80-81—Boston	80	2820	382	766	.499	342	419	.816	36	140	176	618	75	18	265	1106	2.2	7.7	13.8
81-82—Boston	68	2167	308	652	.472	236	316	.747	25	91	116	541	52	3	178	858	1.7	8.0	12.6
82-83—Boston	66	1811	235	553	.425	220	296	.743	25	66	91	409	38	4	163	695	1.4	6.2	10.5
83-84—Milwaukee	46	1038	136	279	.487	64	101	.634	16	60	76	160	33	0	78	340	1.7	3.5	7.4
Totals	876	31159	5899	12628	.467	4664	5760	.810	...	...	2046	6476	719	81	1123	16481	2.3	7.4	18.8

Three-point field goals: 1979-80, 4-for-18 (.222). 1980-81, 0-for-9. 1981-82, 6-for-16 (.375). 1982-83, 5-for-24 (.208). 1983-84, 4-for-18 (.222). Totals, 19-for-85 (.224).

Personal fouls/disqualifications: 1973-74, 76/0. 1974-75, 187/0. 1975-76, 169/0. 1976-77, 77/1. 1978-79, 132/2. 1979-80, 218/2. 1980-81, 201/1. 1981-82, 131/1. 1982-83, 110/1. 1983-84, 78/0. Totals, 2002/15.

NBA PLAYOFF RECORD

Season Team	G	Min.	FGM	FGA	Pct.	FTM	FTA	Pct.	Off.	Def.	Tot.	Ast.	St.	Blk.	TO	Pts.	RPG	APG	PPG
74-75—K.C./Omaha	6	242	43	118	.364	35	43	.814	2	9	11	32	4	0	...	121	1.8	5.3	20.2
79-80—Boston	9	332	45	89	.506	37	42	.881	3	8	11	71	10	0	38	128	1.2	7.9	14.2
80-81—Boston	17	630	95	211	.450	76	94	.809	6	22	28	107	13	0	50	266	1.6	6.3	15.6
81-82—Boston	8	277	30	70	.429	25	28	.893	1	16	17	52	5	2	23	85	2.1	6.5	10.6
82-83—Boston	7	161	22	68	.324	22	29	.759	3	7	10	44	2	0	11	67	1.4	6.3	9.6
Totals	47	1642	235	556	.423	195	236	.826	15	62	77	306	34	2	122	667	1.6	6.5	14.2

Three-point field goals: 1979-80, 1-for-2 (.500). 1980-81, 0-for-5. 1981-82, 0-for-4. 1982-83, 1-for-6 (.167). Totals, 2-for-17 (.118).

Personal fouls/disqualifications: 1974-75, 18/0. 1979-80, 28/1. 1980-81, 39/0. 1981-82, 21/0. 1982-83, 12/0. Totals, 118/1.

NBA ALL-STAR GAME RECORD

NOTES: NBA All-Star Game Most Valuable Player (1981).

Season Team	Min.	FGM	FGA	Pct.	FTM	FTA	Pct.	Reb	Ast.	PF	Dq.	Pts.
1973 —Kansas City/Omaha	27	6	12	.500	5	5	1.000	1	5	1	0	17

Season Team	Min.	FGM	FGA	Pct.	FTM	FTA	Pct.	Off.	Def.	Tot.	Ast.	PF	Dq.	St.	Blk.	TO	Pts.
1975 —K.C./Omaha	36	10	15	.667	7	8	.875	1	1	2	6	2	0	3	1	...	27
1976 —Kansas City	30	5	13	.385	3	3	1.000	2	3	5	7	0	0	2	0	...	13
1980 —Boston..............	21	0	8	.000	2	3	.667	1	2	3	6	1	0	2	0	2	2
1981 —Boston..............	25	4	7	.571	1	3	.333	0	5	5	9	3	0	3	0	2	9
1982 —Boston..............	23	2	5	.400	2	2	1.000	1	1	2	7	3	0	1	0	2	6
Totals..................	162	27	60	.450	20	24	.833	...	...	18	40	10	0	11	1	6	74

ARIZIN, PAUL   F

PERSONAL: Born April 9, 1928, in Philadelphia. ... 6-4/200. ... Full name: Paul Joseph Arizin.
HIGH SCHOOL: La Salle (Philadelphia).
COLLEGE: Villanova.
TRANSACTIONS/CAREER NOTES: Selected by Philadelphia Warriors in first round of 1950 NBA Draft. ... Played in Eastern Basketball League with Camden Bullets (1962-63 through 1964-65).
CAREER HONORS: Elected to Naismith Memorial Basketball Hall of Fame (1977). ... NBA 25th Anniversary All-Time Team (1970).
MISCELLANEOUS: Member of NBA championship team (1956).

COLLEGIATE RECORD

NOTES: THE SPORTING NEWS College Player of the Year (1950). ... THE SPORTING NEWS All-America first team (1950). ... Led NCAA Division I with 25.3 points per game (1950).

Season Team	G	Min.	FGM	FGA	Pct.	FTM	FTA	Pct.	Reb.	Ast.	Pts.	RPG	APG	PPG
46-47—Villanova........................						Did not play.								
47-48—Villanova........................	24	...	101	...	...	65	...	...	...	...	267	...	...	11.1
48-49—Villanova........................	27	...	210	...	...	174	233	.747	...	...	594	...	...	22.0
49-50—Villanova........................	29	...	260	527	.493	215	277	.776	...	...	735	...	...	25.3
Totals	80	...	571	...	...	454	...	...	...	...	1596	...	...	20.0

NBA REGULAR-SEASON RECORD

HONORS: All-NBA first team (1952, 1956, 1957). ... All-NBA second team (1959).

Season Team	G	Min.	FGM	FGA	Pct.	FTM	FTA	Pct.	Reb.	Ast.	PF	Dq.	Pts.	RPG	APG	PPG
50-51 —Philadelphia	65	...	352	864	.407	417	526	.793	640	138	284	18	1121	9.8	2.1	17.2
51-52 —Philadelphia	66	*2939	*548	1222	*.448	*578	707	.818	745	170	250	5	*1674	11.3	2.6	*25.4
52-53 —Philadelphia					Did not play—in military service.											
53-54 —Philadelphia					Did not play—in military service.											
54-55 —Philadelphia	72	*2953	*529	*1325	.399	454	585	.776	675	210	270	5	1512	9.4	2.9	21.0
55-56 —Philadelphia	72	2724	617	1378	.448	507	626	.810	539	189	282	11	1741	7.5	2.6	24.2
56-57 —Philadelphia	71	2767	613	1451	.422	591	*713	.829	561	150	274	13	*1817	7.9	2.1	*25.6
57-58 —Philadelphia	68	2377	483	1229	.393	440	544	.809	503	135	235	7	1406	7.4	2.0	20.7
58-59 —Philadelphia	70	2799	632	1466	.431	587	722	.813	637	119	264	7	1851	9.1	1.7	26.4
59-60 —Philadelphia	72	2618	593	1400	.424	420	526	.798	621	165	263	6	1606	8.6	2.3	22.3
60-61 —Philadelphia	79	2935	650	1529	.425	532	639	.833	681	188	*335	11	1832	8.6	2.4	23.2

Season Team	G	Min.	FGM	FGA	Pct.	FTM	FTA	Pct.	Reb.	Ast.	PF	Dq.	Pts.	AVERAGES RPG	APG	PPG
61-62 —Philadelphia	78	2785	611	1490	.410	484	601	.805	527	201	307	18	1706	6.8	2.6	21.9
Totals	713	...	5628	13354	.421	5010	6189	.810	6129	1665	2764	101	16266	8.6	2.3	22.8

NBA PLAYOFF RECORD

Season Team	G	Min.	FGM	FGA	Pct.	FTM	FTA	Pct.	Reb.	Ast.	PF	Dq.	Pts.	AVERAGES RPG	APG	PPG
50-51 —Philadelphia	2		14	27	.519	13	16	.813	20	3	10	1	41	10.0	1.5	20.5
51-52 —Philadelphia	3	120	24	53	.453	29	33	.879	38	8	17	2	77	12.7	2.7	25.7
55-56 —Philadelphia	10	409	103	229	.450	83	99	.838	84	29	31	1	289	8.4	2.9	28.9
56-57 —Philadelphia	2	22	3	8	.375	3	5	.600	8	1	3	0	9	4.0	0.5	4.5
57-58 —Philadelphia	8	309	66	169	.391	56	72	.778	62	16	26	1	188	7.8	2.0	23.5
59-60 —Philadelphia	9	371	84	195	.431	69	79	.873	86	33	29	0	237	9.6	3.7	26.3
60-61 —Philadelphia	3	125	22	67	.328	23	33	.697	26	12	17	2	67	8.7	4.0	22.3
61-62 —Philadelphia	12	459	95	253	.376	88	102	.863	80	26	44	1	278	6.7	2.2	23.2
Totals	49	...	411	1001	.411	364	439	.829	404	128	177	8	1186	8.2	2.6	24.2

NBA ALL-STAR GAME RECORD

NOTES: NBA All-Star Game Most Valuable Player (1952).

Season Team	Min.	FGM	FGA	Pct.	FTM	FTA	Pct.	Reb	Ast.	PF	Dq.	Pts.
1951 —Philadelphia	...	7	12	.583	1	2	.500	7	0	2	0	15
1952 —Philadelphia	32	9	13	.692	8	8	1.000	6	0	1	0	26
1955 —Philadelphia	23	4	9	.444	1	2	.500	2	2	5	0	9
1956 —Philadelphia	28	5	13	.385	3	5	.600	7	1	6	1	13
1957 —Philadelphia	26	6	13	.462	1	2	.500	5	0	2	0	13
1958 —Philadelphia	29	11	17	.647	2	2	1.000	8	2	3	0	24
1959 —Philadelphia	30	4	15	.267	8	9	.889	8	0	2	0	16
1960 —Philadelphia				Selected, did not play—injured.								
1961 —Philadelphia	17	6	12	.500	5	6	.833	2	1	4	0	17
1962 —Philadelphia	21	2	12	.167	0	0	...	2	0	4	0	4
Totals	...	54	116	.466	29	36	.806	47	6	29	1	137

EBL REGULAR-SEASON RECORD

NOTES: Eastern Basketball League Most Valuable Player (1963). ... EBL All-Star first team (1963, 1964). ... EBL All-Star second team (1965).

Season Team	G	Min.	FGM	FGA	Pct.	FTM	FTA	Pct.	Reb.	Ast.	PF	Dq.	Pts.	AVERAGES RPG	APG	PPG
62-63 —Camden	28	...	264	...	...	196	249	.787	203	42	...	...	724	7.3	1.5	25.9
63-64 —Camden	27	...	261	...	...	174	218	.798	226	52	...	...	696	8.4	1.9	25.8
64-65 —Camden	28	...	226	...	...	196	244	.803	164	50	...	...	657	5.9	1.8	23.5
Totals	83	...	751	...	...	566	711	.796	593	144	...	...	2077	7.1	1.7	25.0

BARRY, RICK   F

PERSONAL: Born March 28, 1944, in Elizabeth, N.J. ... 6-7/220. ... Full name: Richard Francis Dennis Barry III. ... Father of Jon Barry, guard with Atlanta Hawks; father of Brent Barry, guard with Los Angeles Clippers; and father of Drew Barry, guard with Seattle SuperSonics.

HIGH SCHOOL: Roselle Park (N.J.).

COLLEGE: Miami (Fla.).

TRANSACTIONS/CAREER NOTES: Selected by San Francisco Warriors in first round of 1965 NBA Draft. ... Signed as free agent by Oakland Oaks of American Basketball Association (1967); court order required him to sit out option season with Warriors (1967-68). ... Oaks franchise moved to Washington and renamed Capitols for 1969-70 season. ... Capitols franchise moved from Washington to Virginia and renamed Squires for 1970-71 season. ... Traded by Squires to New York Nets for first-round draft choice and cash (August 1970). ... Returned to NBA with Golden State Warriors for 1972-73 season. ... Signed as veteran free agent by Houston Rockets (June 17, 1978); Warriors waived their right of first refusal in exchange for G John Lucas and cash.

CAREER HONORS: Elected to Naismith Memorial Basketball Hall of Fame (1986).

MISCELLANEOUS: Member of NBA championship team (1975).

COLLEGIATE RECORD

NOTES: The Sporting News All-America second team (1965). ... Led NCAA Division I with 37.4 points per game (1965).

Season Team	G	Min.	FGM	FGA	Pct.	FTM	FTA	Pct.	Reb.	Ast.	Pts.	AVERAGES RPG	APG	PPG
61-62—Miami (Fla.)‡	17	...	208	...	...	73	...	...	...	...	489	...	...	28.8
62-63—Miami (Fla.)	24	...	162	341	.475	131	158	.829	351	...	455	14.6	...	19.0
63-64—Miami (Fla.)	27	...	314	572	.549	242	287	.843	448	...	870	16.6	...	32.2
64-65—Miami (Fla.)	26	...	340	651	.522	293	341	.859	475	...	973	18.3	...	37.4
Varsity totals	77	...	816	1564	.522	666	786	.847	1274	...	2298	16.5	...	29.8

NBA REGULAR-SEASON RECORD

RECORDS: Shares single-game record for most free throws made in one quarter—14 (December 6, 1966, vs. New York).

HONORS: NBA Rookie of the Year (1966). ... All-NBA first team (1966, 1967, 1974, 1975, 1976). ... All-NBA second team (1973). ... NBA All-Rookie team (1966).

NOTES: Led NBA with 2.85 steals per game (1975).

Season Team	G	Min.	FGM	FGA	Pct.	FTM	FTA	Pct.	Reb.	Ast.	PF	Dq.	Pts.	AVERAGES RPG	APG	PPG
65-66 —San Fran.	80	2990	745	1698	.439	569	660	.862	850	173	297	2	2059	10.6	2.2	25.7
66-67 —San Fran.	78	3175	*1011	*2240	.451	*753	852	.884	714	282	258	1	*2775	9.2	3.6	*35.6
72-73 —Golden State	82	3075	737	1630	.452	358	397	*.902	728	399	245	2	1832	8.9	4.9	22.3

Season Team	G	Min.	FGM	FGA	Pct.	FTM	FTA	Pct.	REBOUNDS Off.	Def.	Tot.	Ast.	St.	Blk.	TO	Pts.	AVERAGES RPG	APG	PPG
73-74—Golden State...	80	2918	796	1746	.456	417	464	.899	103	437	540	484	169	40	...	2009	6.8	6.1	25.1
74-75—Golden State...	80	3235	1028	*2217	.464	394	436	*.904	92	364	456	492	*228	33	...	2450	5.7	6.2	30.6
75-76—Golden State...	81	3122	707	1624	.435	287	311	*.923	74	422	496	496	202	27	...	1701	6.1	6.1	21.0
76-77—Golden State...	79	2904	682	1551	.440	359	392	.916	73	349	422	475	172	58	...	1723	5.3	6.0	21.8
77-78—Golden State...	82	3024	760	1686	.451	378	409	*.924	75	374	449	446	158	45	224	1898	5.5	5.4	23.1
78-79—Houston.........	80	2566	461	1000	.461	160	169	*.947	40	237	277	502	95	38	198	1082	3.5	6.3	13.5
79-80—Houston.........	72	1816	325	771	.422	143	153	*.935	53	183	236	268	80	28	152	866	3.3	3.7	12.0
Totals	794	28825	7252	16163	.449	3818	4243	.900	...	...	5168	4017	1104	269	574	18395	6.5	5.1	23.2

Three-point field goals: 1979-80, 73-for-221 (.330).
Personal fouls/disqualifications: 1973-74, 265/4. 1974-75, 225/0. 1975-76, 215/1. 1976-77, 194/2. 1977-78, 188/1. 1978-79, 195/0. 1979-80, 182/0. Totals, 2264/13.

NBA PLAYOFF RECORD

NOTES: NBA Finals Most Valuable Player (1975). ... Holds NBA Finals single-game records for most field goals attempted—48 (April 18, 1967, vs. Philadelphia); and most field goals attempted in one quarter—17 (April 14, 1967, vs. Philadelphia). ... Shares NBA Finals single-game records for most field goals made—22 (April 18, 1967, vs. Philadelphia); and most free throws made in one half—12 (April 24, 1967, vs. Philadelphia). ... Holds single-game playoff record for most field goals attempted in one quarter—17 (April 14, 1967, vs. Philadelphia). ... Shares single-game playoff record for most steals—8 (April 14, 1975, vs. Seattle).

Season Team	G	Min.	FGM	FGA	Pct.	FTM	FTA	Pct.	Reb.	Ast.	PF	Dq.	Pts.	AVERAGES RPG	APG	PPG
66-67 —San Fran.	15	614	197	489	.403	127	157	.809	113	58	49	0	521	7.5	3.9	34.7
72-73 —Golden State	11	292	65	164	.396	50	55	.909	54	24	41	1	180	4.9	2.2	16.4

Season Team	G	Min.	FGM	FGA	Pct.	FTM	FTA	Pct.	REBOUNDS Off.	Def.	Tot.	Ast.	St.	Blk.	TO	Pts.	AVERAGES RPG	APG	PPG
74-75—Golden State...	17	726	189	426	.444	101	110	.918	22	72	94	103	50	15	...	479	5.5	6.1	28.2
75-76—Golden State...	13	532	126	289	.436	60	68	.882	20	64	84	84	38	14	...	312	6.5	6.5	24.0
76-77—Golden State...	10	415	122	262	.466	40	44	.909	25	34	59	47	17	7	...	284	5.9	4.7	28.4
78-79—Houston.........	2	65	8	25	.320	8	8	1.000	2	6	8	9	0	2	2	24	4.0	4.5	12.0
79-80—Houston.........	6	79	12	33	.364	6	6	1.000	0	6	6	15	1	1	10	33	1.0	2.5	5.5
Totals	74	2723	719	1688	.426	392	448	.875	...	...	418	340	106	39	12	1833	5.6	4.6	24.8

Three-point field goals: 1979-80, 3-for-12 (.250).
Personal fouls/disqualifications: 1974-75, 51/1. 1975-76, 40/1. 1976-77, 32/0. 1978-79, 8/0. 1979-80, 11/0. Totals, 232/3.

NBA ALL-STAR GAME RECORD

NOTES: NBA All-Star Game Most Valuable Player (1967). ... Holds single-game records for most field goals attempted—27 (1967); and most steals—8 (1975).

Season Team	Min.	FGM	FGA	Pct.	FTM	FTA	Pct.	Reb.	Ast.	PF	Dq.	Pts.
1966 —San Francisco.............	17	4	10	.400	2	4	.500	2	2	6	1	10
1967 —San Francisco.............	34	16	27	.593	6	8	.750	6	3	5	0	38
1973 —Golden State..............						Selected, did not play—injured.						

Season Team	Min.	FGM	FGA	Pct.	FTM	FTA	Pct.	REBOUNDS Off.	Def.	Tot.	Ast.	PF	Dq.	St.	Blk.	TO	Pts.
1974 —Golden State......	19	3	6	.500	2	2	1.000	1	3	4	3	3	0	1	0	...	8
1975 —Golden State......	38	11	20	.550	0	0	...	1	4	5	8	4	0	8	1	...	22
1976 —Golden State......	28	6	15	.400	5	5	1.000	2	2	4	2	5	0	2	0	...	17
1977 —Golden State......	29	7	16	.438	4	4	1.000	1	3	4	8	1	0	2	0	...	18
1978 —Golden State......	30	7	17	.412	1	1	1.000	2	2	4	5	6	1	3	0	5	15
Totals..........................	195	54	111	.486	20	24	.833	...	...	29	31	30	2	16	1	5	128

ABA REGULAR-SEASON RECORD

NOTES: ABA All-Star first team (1969, 1970, 1971, 1972).

Season Team	G	Min.	2-POINT FGM	FGA	Pct.	3-POINT FGM	FGA	Pct.	FTM	FTA	Pct.	Reb.	Ast.	Pts.	AVERAGES RPG	APG	PPG
67-68—					Did not play—sat out option year.												
68-69—Oakland	35	1361	389	757	.514	3	10	.300	403	454	*.888	329	136	*1190	9.4	3.9	*34.0
69-70—Washington	52	1849	509	907	.561	8	39	.205	400	463	.864	363	178	1442	7.0	3.4	27.7
70-71—New York	59	2502	613	1262	.486	19	86	.221	451	507	*.890	401	294	1734	6.8	5.0	29.4
71-72—New York	80	3616	829	1732	.479	73	237	.308	*641	730	*.878	602	327	2518	7.5	4.1	31.5
Totals	226	9328	2340	4658	.502	103	372	.277	1895	2154	.880	1695	935	6884	7.5	4.1	30.5

ABA PLAYOFF RECORD

Season Team	G	Min.	2-POINT FGM	FGA	Pct.	3-POINT FGM	FGA	Pct.	FTM	FTA	Pct.	Reb.	Ast.	Pts.	AVERAGES RPG	APG	PPG
69-70—Washington	7	302	105	194	.541	3	9	.333	62	68	.912	70	23	281	10.0	3.3	40.1
70-71—New York	6	287	46	108	.426	14	27	.519	48	59	.814	70	24	202	11.7	4.0	33.7
71-72—New York	18	749	180	368	.489	23	61	.377	125	146	.856	117	69	554	6.5	3.8	30.8
Totals	31	1338	331	670	.494	40	97	.412	235	273	.861	257	116	1037	8.3	3.7	33.5

ABA ALL-STAR GAME RECORD

Season Team	Min.	2-POINT FGM	FGA	Pct.	3-POINT FGM	FGA	Pct.	FTM	FTA	Pct.	Reb.	Ast.	Pts.
1968—Oakland	12	3	9	.333	0	0	...	4	5	.800	3	1	10
1969—Washington	27	7	12	.583	0	0	...	2	2	1.000	7	7	16
1970—New York	17	4	6	.667	0	0	...	6	6	1.000	2	2	14
1971—New York.........................	26	2	10	.200	0	0	...	0	1	.000	12	8	4
Totals	82	16	37	.432	0	0	...	12	14	.857	24	18	44

COMBINED ABA AND NBA REGULAR-SEASON RECORDS

	G	Min.	FGM	FGA	Pct.	FTM	FTA	Pct.	REBOUNDS Off.	Def.	Tot.	Ast.	Stl.	Blk.	TO	Pts.	AVERAGES RPG	APG	PPG
Totals	1020	38153	9695	21193	.457	5713	6397	.893	...	...	6863	4952	...	...	...	25279	6.7	4.9	24.8

Three-point field goals: 176-for-593 (.297).
Personal fouls/disqualifications: 3028.

BAYLOR, ELGIN   F

PERSONAL: Born September 16, 1934, in Washington, D.C. ... 6-5/225. ... Full name: Elgin Gay Baylor.
HIGH SCHOOL: Phelps Vocational (Washington, D.C.), then Spingarn (Washington, D.C.).
COLLEGE: The College of Idaho, then Seattle.
TRANSACTIONS/CAREER NOTES: Selected after junior season by Minneapolis Lakers in first round (first pick overall) of 1958 NBA Draft. ... Lakers franchise moved to Los Angeles for 1960-61 season.
CAREER HONORS: Elected to Naismith Memorial Basketball Hall of Fame (1976). ... NBA 35th Anniversary All-Time Team (1980).
MISCELLANEOUS: Los Angeles Lakers franchise all-time leading rebounder with 11,463 (1958-59 through 1971-72).

COLLEGIATE RECORD

NOTES: The Sporting News All-America first team (1958). ... NCAA University Division Tournament Most Valuable Player (1958). ... Led NCAA Division I with .235 rebound average (1957), when championship was determined by highest individual recoveries as percentage of total recoveries by both teams in all games. ... Played for Westside Ford (AAU team in Seattle) averaging 34 points per game (1955-56).

Season Team	G	Min.	FGM	FGA	Pct.	FTM	FTA	Pct.	Reb.	Ast.	Pts.	AVERAGES RPG	APG	PPG
54-55—The College of Idaho	26	...	332	651	.510	150	232	.647	492	...	814	18.9	...	31.3
55-56—Seattle					Did not play—transfer student.									
56-57—Seattle	25	...	271	555	.488	201	251	.801	508	...	743	20.3	...	29.7
57-58—Seattle	29	...	353	697	.506	237	308	.769	559	...	943	19.3	...	32.5
Totals	80	...	956	1903	.502	588	791	.743	1559	...	2500	19.5	...	31.3

NBA REGULAR-SEASON RECORD

HONORS: NBA Rookie of the Year (1959). ... All-NBA first team (1959, 1960, 1961, 1962, 1963, 1964, 1965, 1967, 1968, 1969).

Season Team	G	Min.	FGM	FGA	Pct.	FTM	FTA	Pct.	Reb.	Ast.	PF	Dq.	Pts.	AVERAGES RPG	APG	PPG
58-59—Minneapolis	70	2855	605	1482	.408	532	685	.777	1050	287	270	4	1742	15.0	4.1	24.9
59-60—Minneapolis	70	2873	755	1781	.424	564	770	.732	1150	243	234	2	2074	16.4	3.5	29.6
60-61—Los Angeles	73	3133	931	2166	.430	676	863	.783	1447	371	279	3	2538	19.8	5.1	34.8
61-62—Los Angeles	48	2129	680	1588	.428	476	631	.754	892	222	155	1	1836	18.6	4.6	38.3
62-63—Los Angeles	80	3370	1029	2273	.453	661	790	.837	1146	386	226	1	2719	14.3	4.8	34.0
63-64—Los Angeles	78	3164	756	1778	.425	471	586	.804	936	347	235	1	1983	12.0	4.4	25.4
64-65—Los Angeles	74	3056	763	1903	.401	483	610	.792	950	280	235	0	2009	12.8	3.8	27.1
65-66—Los Angeles	65	1975	415	1034	.401	249	337	.739	621	224	157	0	1079	9.6	3.4	16.6
66-67—Los Angeles	70	2706	711	1658	.429	440	541	.813	898	215	211	1	1862	12.8	3.1	26.6
67-68—Los Angeles	77	3029	757	1709	.443	488	621	.786	941	355	232	0	2002	12.2	4.6	26.0
68-69—Los Angeles	76	3064	730	1632	.447	421	567	.743	805	408	204	0	1881	10.6	5.4	24.8
69-70—Los Angeles	54	2213	511	1051	.486	276	357	.773	559	292	132	1	1298	10.4	5.4	24.0
70-71—Los Angeles	2	57	8	19	.421	4	6	.667	11	2	6	0	20	5.5	1.0	10.0
71-72—Los Angeles	9	239	42	97	.433	22	27	.815	57	18	20	0	106	6.3	2.0	11.8
Totals....................................	846	33863	8693	20171	.431	5763	7391	.780	11463	3650	2596	14	23149	13.5	4.3	27.4

NBA PLAYOFF RECORD

NOTES: Holds NBA Finals single-game records for most points—61; and most field goals attempted in one half—25 (April 14, 1962, vs. Boston). ... Shares NBA Finals single-game record for most field goals made—22 (April 14, 1962, vs. Boston). ... Shares single-game playoff record for most field goals attempted in one half—25 (April 14, 1962, vs. Boston).

Season Team	G	Min.	FGM	FGA	Pct.	FTM	FTA	Pct.	Reb.	Ast.	PF	Dq.	Pts.	AVERAGES RPG	APG	PPG
58-59—Minneapolis	13	556	122	303	.403	87	113	.770	156	43	52	0	331	12.0	3.3	25.5
59-60—Minneapolis	9	408	111	234	.474	79	94	.840	127	31	38	0	301	14.1	3.4	33.4
60-61—Los Angeles	12	540	170	362	.470	117	142	.824	183	55	44	1	457	15.3	4.6	38.1
61-62—Los Angeles	13	571	186	425	.438	130	168	.774	230	47	45	1	502	17.7	3.6	38.6
62-63—Los Angeles	13	562	160	362	.442	104	126	.825	177	58	48	0	424	13.6	4.5	32.6
63-64—Los Angeles	5	221	45	119	.378	31	40	.775	58	28	17	0	121	11.6	5.6	24.2
64-65—Los Angeles	1	5	0	2	.000	0	0	...	0	1	0	0	0	0.0	1.0	0.0
65-66—Los Angeles	14	586	145	328	.442	85	105	.810	197	52	38	0	375	14.1	3.7	26.8
66-67—Los Angeles	3	121	28	76	.368	15	20	.750	39	9	6	0	71	13.0	3.0	23.7
67-68—Los Angeles	15	633	176	376	.468	76	112	.679	218	60	41	0	428	14.5	4.0	28.5
68-69—Los Angeles	18	640	107	278	.385	63	97	.649	166	74	56	0	277	9.2	4.1	15.4
69-70—Los Angeles	18	667	138	296	.466	60	81	.741	173	83	50	1	336	9.6	4.6	18.7
Totals....................................	134	5510	1388	3161	.439	847	1098	.771	1724	541	435	3	3623	12.9	4.0	27.0

NBA ALL-STAR GAME RECORD

NOTES: NBA All-Star Game co-Most Valuable Player (1959). ... Holds career record for most free throws made—78. ... Shares career record for most free throws attempted—98. ... Shares single-game record for most free throws made—12 (1962).

Season Team	Min.	FGM	FGA	Pct.	FTM	FTA	Pct.	Reb.	Ast.	PF	Dq.	Pts.
1959 —Minneapolis...............	32	10	20	.500	4	5	.800	11	1	3	0	24
1960 —Minneapolis...............	28	10	18	.556	5	7	.714	13	3	4	0	25
1961 —Los Angeles	27	3	11	.273	9	10	.900	10	4	5	0	15
1962 —Los Angeles	37	10	23	.435	12	14	.857	9	4	2	0	32
1963 —Los Angeles	36	4	15	.267	9	13	.692	14	7	0	0	17

Season	Team	Min.	FGM	FGA	Pct.	FTM	FTA	Pct.	Reb	Ast.	PF	Dq.	Pts.
1964	—Los Angeles	29	5	15	.333	5	11	.455	8	5	1	0	15
1965	—Los Angeles	27	5	13	.385	8	8	1.000	7	0	4	0	18
1967	—Los Angeles	20	8	14	.571	4	4	1.000	5	5	2	0	20
1968	—Los Angeles	27	8	13	.615	6	7	.857	6	1	5	0	22
1969	—Los Angeles	32	5	13	.385	11	12	.917	9	5	2	0	21
1970	—Los Angeles	26	2	9	.222	5	7	.714	7	3	3	0	9
Totals		321	70	164	.427	78	98	.796	99	38	31	0	218

NBA COACHING RECORD

BACKGROUND: Assistant coach, New Orleans Jazz (1974-75 and 1975-76). ... Vice president of basketball operations, Los Angeles Clippers (1986 to present).

		REGULAR SEASON				PLAYOFFS		
Season	Team	W	L	Pct.	Finish	W	L	Pct.
74-75	—New Orleans	0	1	.000		—	—	—
76-77	—New Orleans	21	35	.375	5th/Central Division	—	—	—
77-78	—New Orleans	39	43	.476	5th/Central Division	—	—	—
78-79	—New Orleans	26	56	.317	6th/Central Division	—	—	—
Totals (4 years)		86	135	.389				

NOTES:
1974—Replaced Scotty Robertson as New Orleans head coach (November), with record of 1-14; replaced as New Orleans head coach by Bill van Breda Kolff (November).
1976—Replaced Bill van Breda Kolff as New Orleans head coach (December), with record of 14-12.

BELLAMY, WALT   C

PERSONAL: Born July 24, 1939, in New Bern, N.C. ... 6-11/245. ... Full name: Walter Jones Bellamy. ... Nickname: Bells.
HIGH SCHOOL: J.T. Barber (New Bern, N.C.).
COLLEGE: Indiana.
TRANSACTIONS/CAREER NOTES: Selected by Chicago Packers in first round (first pick overall) of 1961 NBA Draft. ... Packers franchise renamed Zephyrs for 1962-63 season. ... Zephyrs franchise moved to Baltimore and renamed Bullets for 1963-64 season. ... Traded by Bullets to New York Knicks for F John Green, G John Egan, F/C Jim Barnes and cash (November 2, 1965). ... Traded by Knicks with G Howard Komives to Detroit Pistons for F Dave DeBusschere (December 19, 1968). ... Traded by Pistons to Atlanta Hawks for future considerations (February 1, 1970); Pistons received G John Arthurs from Milwaukee Bucks as part of deal. ... Selected by New Orleans Jazz from Hawks in NBA expansion draft (May 20, 1974). ... Waived by Jazz (October 18, 1974).
CAREER HONORS: Elected to Naismith Memorial Basketball Hall of Fame (1993).
MISCELLANEOUS: Member of gold-medal-winning U.S. Olympic Team (1960).

COLLEGIATE RECORD

NOTES: THE SPORTING NEWS All-America second team (1961).

Season Team	G	Min.	FGM	FGA	Pct.	FTM	FTA	Pct.	Reb.	Ast.	Pts.	RPG	APG	PPG
57-58—Indiana‡				Freshman team did not play intercollegiate schedule.										
58-59—Indiana	22	...	148	289	.512	86	141	.610	335	...	382	15.2	...	17.4
59-60—Indiana	24	...	212	396	.535	113	161	.702	324	...	537	13.5	...	22.4
60-61—Indiana	24	...	195	389	.501	132	204	.647	428	...	522	17.8	...	21.8
Varsity totals	70	...	555	1074	.517	331	506	.654	1087	...	1441	15.5	...	20.6

NBA REGULAR-SEASON RECORD

RECORDS: Holds single-season record for most games played—88 (1969).
HONORS: NBA Rookie of the Year (1962).

														AVERAGES		
Season Team	G	Min.	FGM	FGA	Pct.	FTM	FTA	Pct.	Reb.	Ast.	PF	Dq.	Pts.	RPG	APG	PPG
61-62 —Chicago	79	3344	973	1875	*.519	549	853	.644	1500	210	281	6	2495	19.0	2.7	31.6
62-63 —Chicago	80	3306	840	1595	.527	553	821	.674	1309	233	283	7	2233	16.4	2.9	27.9
63-64 —Baltimore	80	3394	811	1582	.513	537	825	.651	1361	126	300	7	2159	17.0	1.6	27.0
64-65 —Baltimore	80	3301	733	1441	.509	515	752	.685	1166	191	260	2	1981	14.6	2.4	24.8
65-66 —Balt.-N.Y.	80	3352	695	1373	.506	430	689	.624	1254	235	294	9	1820	15.7	2.9	22.8
66-67 —New York	79	3010	565	1084	.521	369	580	.636	1064	206	275	5	1499	13.5	2.6	19.0
67-68 —New York	82	2695	511	944	.541	350	529	.662	961	164	259	3	1372	11.7	2.0	16.7
68-69 —N.Y.-Detroit	88	3159	563	1103	.510	401	618	.649	1101	176	320	5	1527	12.5	2.0	17.4
69-70 —Detroit-Atl.	79	2028	351	671	.523	215	373	.576	707	143	260	5	917	8.9	1.8	11.6
70-71 —Atlanta	82	2908	433	879	.493	336	556	.604	1060	230	271	4	1202	12.9	2.8	14.7
71-72 —Atlanta	82	3187	593	1089	.545	340	581	.585	1049	262	255	2	1526	12.8	3.2	18.6
72-73 —Atlanta	74	2802	455	901	.505	283	526	.538	964	179	244	1	1193	13.0	2.4	16.1

									REBOUNDS							AVERAGES		
Season Team	G	Min.	FGM	FGA	Pct.	FTM	FTA	Pct.	Off.	Def.	Tot.	Ast.	St.	Blk.	TO	Pts.	RPG	APG	PPG
73-74—Atlanta	77	2440	389	801	.486	233	383	.608	264	476	740	189	52	48	...	1011	9.6	2.5	13.1
74-75—New Orleans	1	14	2	2	1.000	2	2	1.000	0	5	5	0	0	0	...	6	5.0	0.0	6.0
Totals	1043	38940	7914	15340	.516	5113	8088	.632	...	...	14241	2544	52	48	...	20941	13.7	2.4	20.1

Personal fouls/disqualifications: 1973-74, 232/2. 1974-75, 2/0. Totals, 3536/58.

NBA PLAYOFF RECORD

													AVERAGES		
Season Team	G	Min.	FGM	FGA	Pct.	FTM	FTA	Pct.	Reb.	Ast.	PF	Dq.	Pts.	RPG	APG	PPG
64-65 —Baltimore	10	427	74	158	.468	61	92	.663	151	34	38	0	209	15.1	3.4	20.9
66-67 —New York	4	157	28	54	.519	17	29	.586	66	12	15	0	73	16.5	3.0	18.3

Season	Team	G	Min.	FGM	FGA	Pct.	FTM	FTA	Pct.	Reb.	Ast.	PF	Dq.	Pts.	RPG	APG	PPG
67-68	—New York	6	277	45	107	.421	30	48	.625	96	21	22	0	120	16.0	3.5	20.0
69-70	—Atlanta	9	368	59	126	.468	33	46	.717	140	35	32	0	151	15.6	3.9	16.8
70-71	—Atlanta	5	216	41	69	.594	22	29	.759	72	10	16	0	104	14.4	2.0	20.8
71-72	—Atlanta	6	247	42	86	.488	27	43	.628	82	11	20	0	111	13.7	1.8	18.5
72-73	—Atlanta	6	247	34	86	.395	14	31	.452	73	13	17	0	82	12.2	2.2	13.7
	Totals	46	1939	323	686	.471	204	318	.642	680	136	160	0	850	14.8	3.0	18.5

NBA ALL-STAR GAME RECORD

Season	Team	Min.	FGM	FGA	Pct.	FTM	FTA	Pct.	Reb	Ast.	PF	Dq.	Pts.
1962	—Chicago	29	10	18	.556	3	8	.375	17	1	6	1	23
1963	—Chicago	14	1	4	.250	0	2	.000	1	2	3	0	2
1964	—Baltimore	23	4	11	.364	3	5	.600	7	0	3	0	11
1965	—Baltimore	17	4	5	.800	4	4	1.000	5	1	3	0	12
	Totals	83	19	38	.500	10	19	.526	30	4	15	1	48

BING, DAVE   G

PERSONAL: Born November 24, 1943, in Washington, D.C. ... 6-3/185. ... Full name: David Bing.
HIGH SCHOOL: Spingarn (Washington, D.C.).
COLLEGE: Syracuse.
TRANSACTIONS/CAREER NOTES: Selected by Detroit Pistons in first round (second pick overall) of 1966 NBA Draft. ... Traded by Pistons with 1977 first-round draft choice to Washington Bullets for G Kevin Porter (August 28, 1975). ... Waived by Bullets (September 20, 1977). ... Signed as free agent by Boston Celtics (September 28, 1977).
CAREER HONORS: Elected to Naismith Memorial Basketball Hall of Fame (1989).

COLLEGIATE RECORD

NOTES: The Sporting News All-America first team (1966).

Season	Team	G	Min.	FGM	FGA	Pct.	FTM	FTA	Pct.	Reb.	Ast.	Pts.	RPG	APG	PPG
62-63	—Syracuse‡	17	...	170	341	.499	97	131	.740	192	...	437	11.3	...	25.7
63-64	—Syracuse	25	...	215	460	.467	126	172	.733	206	...	556	8.2	...	22.2
64-65	—Syracuse	23	...	206	444	.464	121	162	.747	277	...	533	12.0	...	23.2
65-66	—Syracuse	28	...	308	569	.541	178	222	.802	303	...	794	10.8	...	28.4
	Varsity totals	76	...	729	1473	.495	425	556	.764	786	...	1883	10.3	...	24.8

NBA REGULAR-SEASON RECORD

HONORS: NBA Rookie of the Year (1967). ... All-NBA first team (1968, 1971). ... All-NBA second team (1974). ... NBA All-Rookie team (1967).

Season	Team	G	Min.	FGM	FGA	Pct.	FTM	FTA	Pct.	Reb.	Ast.	PF	Dq.	Pts.	RPG	APG	PPG
66-67	—Detroit	80	2762	664	1522	.436	273	370	.738	359	330	217	2	1601	4.5	4.1	20.0
67-68	—Detroit	79	3209	*835	*1893	.441	472	668	.707	373	509	254	2	*2142	4.7	6.4	*27.1
68-69	—Detroit	77	3039	678	1594	.425	444	623	.713	382	546	256	3	1800	5.0	7.1	23.4
69-70	—Detroit	70	2334	575	1295	.444	454	580	.783	299	418	196	0	1604	4.3	6.0	22.9
70-71	—Detroit	82	3065	799	1710	.467	*615	*772	.797	364	408	228	4	2213	4.4	5.0	27.0
71-72	—Detroit	45	1936	369	891	.414	278	354	.785	186	317	138	3	1016	4.1	7.0	22.6
72-73	—Detroit	82	3361	692	1545	.448	456	560	.814	298	637	229	1	1840	3.6	7.8	22.4

Season	Team	G	Min.	FGM	FGA	Pct.	FTM	FTA	Pct.	Off.	Def.	Tot.	Ast.	St.	Blk.	TO	Pts.	RPG	APG	PPG
73-74	—Detroit	81	3124	582	1336	.436	356	438	.813	160	173	281	555	109	17	...	1520	3.5	6.9	18.8
74-75	—Detroit	79	3222	578	1333	.434	343	424	.809	86	200	286	610	116	26	...	1499	3.6	7.7	19.0
75-76	—Washington	82	2945	497	1113	.447	332	422	.787	94	143	237	492	118	23	...	1326	2.9	6.0	16.2
76-77	—Washington	64	1516	271	597	.454	136	176	.773	54	89	143	275	61	5	...	678	2.2	4.3	10.6
77-78	—Boston	80	2256	422	940	.449	244	296	.824	76	136	212	300	79	18	216	1088	2.7	3.8	13.6
	Totals	901	32769	6962	15769	.441	4403	5683	.775	...	...	3420	5397	483	89	216	18327	3.8	6.0	20.3

Personal fouls/disqualifications: 1973-74, 216/1. 1974-75, 222/3. 1975-76, 262/0. 1976-77, 150/1. 1977-78, 247/2. Totals, 2615/22.

NBA PLAYOFF RECORD

Season	Team	G	Min.	FGM	FGA	Pct.	FTM	FTA	Pct.	Off.	Def.	Tot.	Ast.	St.	Blk.	TO	Pts.	RPG	APG	PPG
67-68	—Detroit	6	254	68	166	.410	33	45	.733	...	...	24	29	...	...	...	169	4.0	4.8	28.2
73-74	—Detroit	7	312	55	131	.420	22	30	.733	6	20	26	42	3	1	...	132	3.7	6.0	18.9
74-75	—Detroit	3	134	20	47	.426	8	13	.615	3	8	11	29	5	0	...	48	3.7	9.7	16.0
75-76	—Washington	7	209	34	76	.447	28	35	.800	6	12	18	28	7	2	...	96	2.6	4.0	13.7
76-77	—Washington	8	55	14	32	.438	4	4	1.000	3	3	6	5	0	1	...	32	0.8	0.6	4.0
	Totals	31	964	191	452	.423	95	127	.748	...	...	85	133	15	4	...	477	2.7	4.3	15.4

Personal fouls/disqualifications: 1967-68, 21/0. 1973-74, 20/0. 1974-75, 12/0. 1975-76, 18/0. 1976-77, 5/0. Totals, 76/0.

NBA ALL-STAR GAME RECORD

NOTES: NBA All-Star Game Most Valuable Player (1976).

Season	Team	Min.	FGM	FGA	Pct.	FTM	FTA	Pct.	Reb	Ast.	PF	Dq.	Pts.
1968	—Detroit	20	4	7	.571	1	1	1.000	2	4	3	0	9
1969	—Detroit	13	1	3	.333	1	1	1.000	0	3	0	0	3
1971	—Detroit	19	2	7	.286	0	0	...	2	2	1	0	4
1973	—Detroit	19	0	4	.000	2	2	1.000	3	0	1	0	2

Season	Team	Min.	FGM	FGA	Pct.	FTM	FTA	Pct.	Off.	Def.	Tot.	Ast.	PF	Dq.	St.	Blk.	TO	Pts.
1974	—Detroit	16	2	9	.222	1	1	1.000	1	5	6	2	1	0	0	0	...	5
1975	—Detroit	12	0	2	.000	2	2	1.000	0	0	0	1	0	0	0	0	...	2
1976	—Washington	26	7	11	.636	2	2	1.000	1	2	3	4	1	0	0	0	...	16
	Totals	125	16	43	.372	9	9	1.000	...	...	16	16	7	0	0	0	...	41

BIRD, LARRY　　　　　　　　　F　　　　　　　　　CELTICS

PERSONAL: Born December 7, 1956, in West Baden, Ind. ... 6-9/220. ... Full name: Larry Joe Bird.
HIGH SCHOOL: Springs Valley (French Lick, Ind.).
COLLEGE: Indiana, then Northwood Institute (Ind.), then Indiana State.
TRANSACTIONS/CAREER NOTES: Selected after junior season by Boston Celtics in first round (sixth pick overall) of 1978 NBA Draft.
MISCELLANEOUS: Member of NBA championship teams (1981, 1984, 1986). ... Member of gold-medal-winning U.S. Olympic team (1992). ... Boston Celtics all-time steals leader with 1,556 (1979-80 through 1991-92).

COLLEGIATE RECORD

NOTES: The Sporting News College Player of the Year (1979). ... Naismith Award winner (1979). ... Wooden Award winner (1979). ... The Sporting News All-America first team (1978, 1979).

Season Team	G	Min.	FGM	FGA	Pct.	FTM	FTA	Pct.	Reb.	Ast.	Pts.	RPG	APG	PPG
74-75—Indiana						Did not play.								
75-76—Indiana State						Did not play—transfer student.								
76-77—Indiana State	28	1033	375	689	.544	168	200	.840	373	122	918	13.3	4.4	32.8
77-78—Indiana State	32	...	403	769	.524	153	193	.793	369	125	959	11.5	3.9	30.0
78-79—Indiana State	34	...	376	707	.532	221	266	.831	505	187	973	14.9	5.5	28.6
Totals	94	...	1154	2165	.533	542	659	.822	1247	434	2850	13.3	4.6	30.3

NBA REGULAR-SEASON RECORD

HONORS: NBA Most Valuable Player (1984, 1985, 1986). ... NBA Rookie of the Year (1980). ... All-NBA first team (1980, 1981, 1982, 1983, 1984, 1985, 1986, 1987, 1988). ... All-NBA second team (1990). ... NBA All-Defensive second team (1982, 1983, 1984). ... NBA All-Rookie team (1980). ... Long Distance Shootout winner (1986, 1987, 1988).

									REBOUNDS								AVERAGES		
Season Team	G	Min.	FGM	FGA	Pct.	FTM	FTA	Pct.	Off.	Def.	Tot.	Ast.	St.	Blk.	TO	Pts.	RPG	APG	PPG
79-80—Boston	82	2955	693	1463	.474	301	360	.836	216	636	852	370	143	53	263	1745	10.4	4.5	21.3
80-81—Boston	82	3239	719	1503	.478	283	328	.863	191	704	895	451	161	63	289	1741	10.9	5.5	21.2
81-82—Boston	77	2923	711	1414	.503	328	380	.863	200	637	837	447	143	66	254	1761	10.9	5.8	22.9
82-83—Boston	79	2982	747	1481	.504	351	418	.840	193	677	870	458	148	71	240	1867	11.0	5.8	23.6
83-84—Boston	79	3028	758	1542	.492	374	421 *.888		181	615	796	520	144	69	237	1908	10.1	6.6	24.2
84-85—Boston	80	3161	918	1760	.522	403	457	.882	164	678	842	531	129	98	248	2295	10.5	6.6	28.7
85-86—Boston	82	3113	796	1606	.496	441	492 *.896		190	615	805	557	166	51	266	2115	9.8	6.8	25.8
86-87—Boston	74	3005	786	1497	.525	414	455 *.910		124	558	682	566	135	70	240	2076	9.2	7.6	28.1
87-88—Boston	76	2965	881	1672	.527	415	453	.916	108	595	703	467	125	57	213	2275	9.3	6.1	29.9
88-89—Boston	6	189	49	104	.471	18	19	.947	1	36	37	29	6	5	11	116	6.2	4.8	19.3
89-90—Boston	75	2944	718	1517	.473	319	343 *.930		90	622	712	562	106	61	243	1820	9.5	7.5	24.3
90-91—Boston	60	2277	462	1017	.454	163	183	.891	53	456	509	431	108	58	187	1164	8.5	7.2	19.4
91-92—Boston	45	1662	353	758	.466	150	162	.926	46	388	434	306	42	33	125	908	9.6	6.8	20.2
Totals	897	34443	8591	17334	.496	3960	4471	.886	1757	7217	8974	5695	1556	755	2816	21791	10.0	6.3	24.3

Three-point field goals: 1979-80, 58-for-143 (.406). 1980-81, 20-for-74 (.270). 1981-82, 11-for-52 (.212). 1982-83, 22-for-77 (.286). 1983-84, 18-for-73 (.247). 1984-85, 56-for-131 (.427). 1985-86, 82-for-194 (.423). 1986-87, 90-for-225 (.400). 1987-88, 98-for-237 (.414). 1989-90, 65-for-195 (.333). 1990-91, 77-for-198 (.389). 1991-92, 52-for-128 (.406). Totals, 649-for-1727 (.376).

Personal fouls/disqualifications: 1979-80, 279/4. 1980-81, 239/2. 1981-82, 244/0. 1982-83, 197/0. 1983-84, 197/0. 1984-85, 208/0. 1985-86, 182/0. 1986-87, 185/3. 1987-88, 157/0. 1988-89, 18/0. 1989-90, 173/2. 1990-91, 118/0. 1991-92, 82/0. Totals, 2279/11.

NBA PLAYOFF RECORD

NOTES: NBA Finals Most Valuable Player (1984, 1986). ... Holds career playoff record for most defensive rebounds—1,323.

									REBOUNDS								AVERAGES		
Season Team	G	Min.	FGM	FGA	Pct.	FTM	FTA	Pct.	Off.	Def.	Tot.	Ast.	St.	Blk.	TO	Pts.	RPG	APG	PPG
79-80—Boston	9	372	83	177	.469	22	25	.880	22	79	101	42	14	8	33	192	11.2	4.7	21.3
80-81—Boston	17	750	147	313	.470	76	85	.894	49	189	238	103	39	17	62	373	14.0	6.1	21.9
81-82—Boston	12	490	88	206	.427	37	45	.822	33	117	150	67	23	17	38	214	12.5	5.6	17.8
82-83—Boston	6	240	49	116	.422	24	29	.828	20	55	75	41	13	3	19	123	12.5	6.8	20.5
83-84—Boston	23	961	229	437	.524	167	190	.879	62	190	252	136	54	27	87	632	11.0	5.9	27.5
84-85—Boston	20	815	196	425	.461	121	136	.890	53	129	182	115	34	19	57	520	9.1	5.8	26.0
85-86—Boston	18	770	171	331	.517	101	109	.927	34	134	168	148	37	11	47	466	9.3	8.2	25.9
86-87—Boston	23	1015	216	454	.476	176	193	.912	41	190	231	165	27	19	71	622	10.0	7.2	27.0
87-88—Boston	17	763	152	338	.450	101	113	.894	29	121	150	115	36	14	49	417	8.8	6.8	24.5
89-90—Boston	5	207	44	99	.444	29	32	.906	7	39	46	44	5	5	18	122	9.2	8.8	24.4
90-91—Boston	10	396	62	152	.408	44	51	.863	8	64	72	65	13	3	19	171	7.2	6.5	17.1
91-92—Boston	4	107	21	42	.500	3	4	.750	2	16	18	21	1	2	6	45	4.5	5.3	11.3
Totals	164	6886	1458	3090	.472	901	1012	.890	360	1323	1683	1062	296	145	506	3897	10.3	6.5	23.8

Three-point field goals: 1979-80, 4-for-15 (.267). 1980-81, 3-for-8 (.375). 1981-82, 1-for-6 (.167). 1982-83, 1-for-4 (.250). 1983-84, 7-for-17 (.412). 1984-85, 7-for-25 (.280). 1985-86, 23-for-56 (.411). 1986-87, 14-for-41 (.341). 1987-88, 12-for-32 (.375). 1989-90, 5-for-19 (.263). 1990-91, 3-for-21 (.143). 1991-92, 0-for-5. Totals, 80-for-249 (.321).

Personal fouls/disqualifications: 1979-80, 30/0. 1980-81, 53/0. 1981-82, 43/0. 1982-83, 15/0. 1983-84, 71/0. 1984-85, 54/0. 1985-86, 55/0. 1986-87, 55/1. 1987-88, 45/0. 1989-90, 10/0. 1990-91, 28/0. 1991-92, 7/0. Totals, 466/1.

NBA ALL-STAR GAME RECORD

NOTES: NBA All-Star Game Most Valuable Player (1982).

								REBOUNDS								
Season Team	Min.	FGM	FGA	Pct.	FTM	FTA	Pct.	Off.	Def.	Tot.	Ast.	PF	Dq.	St.	Blk.	TO	Pts.
1980 —Boston	23	3	6	.500	0	0	...	3	3	6	7	1	0	1	0	3	7
1981 —Boston	18	1	5	.200	0	0	...	1	3	4	3	1	0	1	0	2	2
1982 —Boston	28	7	12	.583	5	8	.625	0	12	12	5	3	0	1	1	4	19
1983 —Boston	29	7	14	.500	0	0	...	3	10	13	7	4	0	2	0	5	14
1984 —Boston	33	6	18	.333	4	4	1.000	1	6	7	3	1	0	2	0	2	16
1985 —Boston	31	8	16	.500	5	6	.833	5	3	8	2	3	0	0	1	4	21
1986 —Boston	35	8	18	.444	5	6	.833	2	6	8	5	5	0	7	0	4	23

ALL-TIME GREAT PLAYERS

Season Team	Min.	FGM	FGA	Pct.	FTM	FTA	Pct.	Off.	Def.	Tot.	Ast.	PF	Dq.	St.	Blk.	TO	Pts.
								REBOUNDS									
1987 —Boston	35	7	18	.389	4	4	1.000	2	4	6	5	5	0	2	0	2	18
1988 —Boston	32	2	8	.250	2	2	1.000	0	7	7	1	4	0	4	1	2	6
1990 —Boston	23	3	8	.375	2	2	1.000	2	6	8	3	1	0	3	0	3	8
1991 —Boston							Selected, did not play—injured.										
1992 —Boston							Selected, did not play—injured.										
Totals	287	52	123	.423	27	32	.844	19	60	79	41	28	0	23	3	31	134

Three-point field goals: 1980, 1-for-2 (.500). 1983, 0-for-1. 1985, 0-for-1. 1986, 2-for-4 (.500). 1987, 0-for-3. 1988, 0-for-1. 1990, 0-for-1. Totals, 3-for-13 (.231).

BLACKMAN, ROLANDO   G

PERSONAL: Born February 26, 1959, in Panama City, Panama. ... 6-6/206. ... Full name: Rolando Antonio Blackman. ... Name pronounced roll-ON-doe.
HIGH SCHOOL: William E. Grady Vocational Technical School (Brooklyn, N.Y.).
COLLEGE: Kansas State.
TRANSACTIONS/CAREER NOTES: Selected by Dallas Mavericks in first round (ninth pick overall) of 1981 NBA Draft. ... Traded by Mavericks to New York Knicks for 1995 first-round draft choice (June 24, 1992). ... Waived by Knicks (July 4, 1994).
MISCELLANEOUS: Member of U.S. Olympic team (1980). ... Dallas Mavericks all-time leading scorer with 16,643 points (1981-82 through 1991-92).

COLLEGIATE RECORD

NOTES: THE SPORTING NEWS All-America first team (1981).

Season Team	G	Min.	FGM	FGA	Pct.	FTM	FTA	Pct.	Reb.	Ast.	Pts.	RPG	APG	PPG
												AVERAGES		
77-78—Kansas State	29	...	127	269	.472	61	93	.656	187	45	315	6.4	1.6	10.9
78-79—Kansas State	28	...	200	392	.510	83	113	.735	110	79	483	3.9	2.8	17.3
79-80—Kansas State	31	...	226	419	.539	100	145	.690	145	97	552	4.7	3.1	17.8
80-81—Kansas State	33	...	202	380	.532	90	115	.783	165	102	494	5.0	3.1	15.0
Totals	121	...	755	1460	.517	334	466	.717	607	323	1844	5.0	2.7	15.2

NBA REGULAR-SEASON RECORD

Season Team	G	Min.	FGM	FGA	Pct.	FTM	FTA	Pct.	Off.	Def.	Tot.	Ast.	St.	Blk.	TO	Pts.	RPG	APG	PPG
									REBOUNDS								**AVERAGES**		
81-82—Dallas	82	1979	439	855	.513	212	276	.768	97	157	254	105	46	30	113	1091	3.1	1.3	13.3
82-83—Dallas	75	2349	513	1042	.492	297	381	.780	108	185	293	185	37	29	118	1326	3.9	2.5	17.7
83-84—Dallas	81	3025	721	1320	.546	372	458	.812	124	249	373	288	56	37	169	1815	4.6	3.6	22.4
84-85—Dallas	81	2834	625	1230	.508	342	413	.828	107	193	300	289	61	16	162	1544	3.7	3.6	19.7
85-86—Dallas	82	2787	677	1318	.514	404	483	.836	88	203	291	271	79	25	189	1762	3.5	3.3	21.5
86-87—Dallas	80	2758	626	1264	.495	419	474	.884	96	182	278	266	64	21	174	1676	3.5	3.3	21.0
87-88—Dallas	71	2580	497	1050	.473	331	379	.873	82	164	246	262	64	18	144	1325	3.5	3.7	18.7
88-89—Dallas	78	2946	594	1249	.476	316	370	.854	70	203	273	288	65	20	165	1534	3.5	3.7	19.7
89-90—Dallas	80	2934	626	1256	.498	287	340	.844	88	192	280	289	77	21	174	1552	3.5	3.6	19.4
90-91—Dallas	80	2965	634	1316	.482	282	346	.815	63	193	256	301	69	19	159	1560	3.2	3.8	19.9
91-92—Dallas	75	2527	535	1161	.461	239	266	.899	78	161	239	204	50	22	153	1374	3.2	2.7	18.3
92-93—New York	60	1434	239	539	.443	71	90	.789	23	79	102	157	22	10	65	580	1.7	2.6	9.7
93-94—New York	55	969	161	369	.436	48	53	.906	23	76	99	76	25	6	44	400	1.7	1.4	7.3
Totals	980	32087	6887	13969	.493	3620	4309	.840	1047	2231	3278	2981	715	274	1829	17623	3.3	3.0	18.0

Three-point field goals: 1981-82, 1-for-4 (.250). 1982-83, 3-for-15 (.200). 1983-84, 1-for-11 (.091). 1984-85, 6-for-20 (.300). 1985-86, 4-for-29 (.138). 1986-87, 5-for-15 (.333). 1987-88, 0-for-5. 1988-89, 30-for-85 (.353). 1989-90, 13-for-43 (.302). 1990-91, 40-for-114 (.351). 1991-92, 65-for-169 (.385). 1992-93, 31-for-73 (.425). 1993-94, 30-for-84 (.357). Totals, 229-for-667 (.343).

Personal fouls/disqualifications: 1981-82, 122/0. 1982-83, 116/0. 1983-84, 127/0. 1984-85, 96/0. 1985-86, 138/0. 1986-87, 142/0. 1987-88, 112/0. 1988-89, 137/0. 1989-90, 128/0. 1990-91, 153/0. 1991-92, 134/0. 1992-93, 129/1. 1993-94, 100/0. Totals, 1634/1.

NBA PLAYOFF RECORD

Season Team	G	Min.	FGM	FGA	Pct.	FTM	FTA	Pct.	Off.	Def.	Tot.	Ast.	St.	Blk.	TO	Pts.	RPG	APG	PPG
									REBOUNDS								**AVERAGES**		
83-84—Dallas	10	397	93	175	.531	53	63	.841	15	26	41	40	6	4	24	239	4.1	4.0	23.9
84-85—Dallas	4	169	47	92	.511	36	38	.947	11	15	26	19	2	2	14	131	6.5	4.8	32.8
85-86—Dallas	10	371	83	167	.497	42	53	.792	15	20	35	32	8	1	20	208	3.5	3.2	20.8
86-87—Dallas	4	153	36	73	.493	22	24	.917	4	10	14	17	2	0	8	94	3.5	4.3	23.5
87-88—Dallas	17	672	126	261	.483	55	62	.887	26	29	55	77	15	3	25	307	3.2	4.5	18.1
89-90—Dallas	3	127	24	54	.444	10	10	1.000	2	7	9	13	6	2	13	60	3.0	4.3	20.0
92-93—New York	15	214	22	64	.344	15	18	.833	4	13	17	16	3	2	21	63	1.1	1.1	4.2
93-94—New York	6	34	3	11	.273	0	0	...	1	2	3	3	0	0	1	8	0.5	0.5	1.3
Totals	69	2137	434	897	.484	233	268	.869	78	122	200	217	42	14	126	1110	2.9	3.1	16.1

Three-point field goals: 1984-85, 1-for-2 (.500). 1985-86, 0-for-1. 1986-87, 0-for-1. 1987-88, 0-for-3. 1989-90, 2-for-5 (.400). 1992-93, 4-for-15 (.267). 1993-94, 2-for-4 (.500). Totals, 9-for-31 (.290).

Personal fouls/disqualifications: 1983-84, 15/0. 1984-85, 8/0. 1985-86, 26/1. 1986-87, 7/0. 1987-88, 28/0. 1989-90, 7/0. 1992-93, 22/0. 1993-94, 6/0. Totals, 119/1.

NBA ALL-STAR GAME RECORD

Season Team	Min.	FGM	FGA	Pct.	FTM	FTA	Pct.	Off.	Def.	Tot.	Ast.	PF	Dq.	St.	Blk.	TO	Pts.
								REBOUNDS									
1985 —Dallas	23	7	14	.500	1	2	.500	1	2	3	2	1	0	1	1	0	15
1986 —Dallas	22	6	11	.545	0	0	...	1	3	4	8	1	0	2	1	1	12
1987 —Dallas	22	9	15	.600	11	13	.846	1	3	4	1	2	0	0	0	2	29
1990 —Dallas	21	7	9	.778	1	1	1.000	1	1	2	2	1	0	2	0	2	15
Totals	88	29	49	.592	13	16	.813	4	9	13	13	5	0	5	2	5	71

ALL-TIME GREAT PLAYERS

BOONE, RON   G

PERSONAL: Born September 6, 1946, in Oklahoma City. ... 6-2/200. ... Full name: Ronald Bruce Boone.
HIGH SCHOOL: Tech (Omaha, Neb.).
JUNIOR COLLEGE: Iowa Western Community College.
COLLEGE: Idaho State.
TRANSACTIONS/CAREER NOTES: Selected by Phoenix Suns in 11th round (147th pick overall) of 1968 NBA Draft. ... Selected by Dallas Chaparrals in eighth round of 1968 ABA Draft. ... Traded by Chaparrals with G Glen Combs to Utah Stars for G Donnie Freeman and C Wayne Hightower (January 8, 1971). ... Contract sold by Stars to Spirits of St. Louis (December 2, 1975). ... Selected by Kansas City Kings of NBA from Spirits in ABA dispersal draft (August 5, 1976). ... Traded by Kings with 1979 second-round draft choice to Denver Nuggets for F Darnell Hillman and draft rights to G Mike Evans (June 26, 1978). ... Traded by Nuggets with two 1979 second-round draft choices to Los Angeles Lakers for G Charlie Scott (June 26, 1978). ... Traded by Lakers to Utah Jazz for 1981 third-round draft choice (October 25, 1979). ... Waived by Jazz (January 26, 1981).
MISCELLANEOUS: Set professional basketball record by playing in most consecutive games—1,041.

COLLEGIATE RECORD

Season Team	G	Min.	FGM	FGA	Pct.	FTM	FTA	Pct.	Reb.	Ast.	Pts.	RPG	APG	PPG
64-65—Iowa Western C.C..........	9	...	...	...	...	...	...	...	...	...	227	...	...	25.2
65-66—Idaho State....................	10	...	46	119	.387	17	26	.654	95	...	109	9.5	...	10.9
66-67—Idaho State....................	25	...	199	416	.478	160	215	.744	128	...	558	5.1	...	22.3
67-68—Idaho State....................	26	...	223	519	.430	108	159	.679	110	...	554	4.2	...	21.3
Junior college totals	9	...	...	...	...	...	...	...	...	...	227	...	...	25.2
4-year-college totals	61	...	468	1054	.444	285	400	.713	333	...	1221	5.5	...	20.0

ABA REGULAR-SEASON RECORD

NOTES: ABA All-Star first team (1975). ... ABA All-Star second team (1974). ... ABA All-Rookie team (1969). ... Member of ABA championship team (1971).

			2-POINT			3-POINT								AVERAGES		
Season Team	G	Min.	FGM	FGA	Pct.	FGM	FGA	Pct.	FTM	FTA	Pct.	Reb.	Ast.	Pts.	RPG	APG	PPG
68-69—Dallas....................	78	2682	518	1182	.438	2	15	.133	436	537	.812	394	279	1478	5.1	3.6	18.9
69-70—Dallas....................	84	2340	406	925	.439	17	55	.309	300	382	.785	366	272	1163	4.4	3.2	13.8
70-71—Dallas-Utah..............	86	2476	561	1257	.446	49	138	.355	278	357	.779	564	256	1547	6.6	3.0	18.0
71-72—Utah	84	2040	391	897	.436	13	65	.200	271	341	.795	393	233	1092	4.7	2.8	13.0
72-73—Utah	84	2585	556	1096	.507	10	40	.250	415	479	.866	423	353	1557	5.0	4.2	18.5
73-74—Utah	84	3098	581	1162	.500	6	26	.231	300	343	.875	435	417	1480	5.2	5.0	17.6
74-75—Utah	84	3414	862	1743	.495	10	33	.303	363	422	.860	406	372	2117	4.8	4.4	25.2
75-76—Utah-St. Louis	78	2961	697	1424	.489	16	43	.372	277	318	.871	319	387	1719	4.1	5.0	22.0
Totals	662	21596	4572	9686	.472	123	415	.296	2640	3179	.830	3300	2569	12153	5.0	3.9	18.4

ABA PLAYOFF RECORD

			2-POINT			3-POINT								AVERAGES		
Season Team	G	Min.	FGM	FGA	Pct.	FGM	FGA	Pct.	FTM	FTA	Pct.	Reb.	Ast.	Pts.	RPG	APG	PPG
68-69—Dallas....................	7	196	38	81	.469	0	4	.000	21	25	.840	22	27	97	3.1	3.9	13.9
69-70—Dallas....................	6	193	43	89	.483	3	8	.375	15	21	.714	27	27	110	4.5	4.5	18.3
70-71—Utah	18	569	104	229	.454	9	27	.333	74	86	.860	110	94	309	6.1	5.2	17.2
71-72—Utah	11	209	49	100	.490	1	5	.200	25	29	.862	24	26	126	2.2	2.4	11.5
72-73—Utah	10	360	68	132	.515	0	3	.000	33	34	.971	43	47	169	4.3	4.7	16.9
73-74—Utah	18	747	137	282	.486	0	7	.000	34	37	.919	108	109	308	6.0	6.1	17.1
74-75—Utah	6	219	54	127	.425	0	0	...	34	38	.895	24	41	142	4.0	6.8	23.7
Totals	76	2493	493	1040	.474	13	54	.241	236	270	.874	358	371	1261	4.7	4.9	16.6

ABA ALL-STAR GAME RECORD

		2-POINT			3-POINT								
Season Team	Min.	FGM	FGA	Pct.	FGM	FGA	Pct.	FTM	FTA	Pct.	Reb.	Ast.	Pts.
1971—Utah.............................	4	2	4	.500	0	0	...	2	3	.667	2	0	6
1974—Utah.............................	24	6	11	.545	1	2	.500	0	0	...	3	5	15
1975—Utah.............................	23	4	8	.500	0	0	...	2	2	1.000	2	2	10
1976—St. Louis......................	16	5	11	.455	0	0	...	0	0	...	3	2	10
Totals	67	17	34	.500	1	2	.500	4	5	.800	10	9	41

NBA REGULAR-SEASON RECORD

								REBOUNDS								AVERAGES		
Season Team	G	Min.	FGM	FGA	Pct.	FTM	FTA	Pct.	Off.	Def.	Tot.	Ast.	St.	Blk.	TO	Pts.	RPG	APG	PPG
76-77—Kansas City.....	82	3021	747	1577	.474	324	384	.844	128	193	321	338	119	19	...	1818	3.9	4.1	22.2
77-78—Kansas City.....	82	2653	563	1271	.443	322	377	.854	112	157	269	311	105	11	303	1448	3.3	3.8	17.7
78-79—Los Angeles	82	1583	259	569	.455	90	104	.865	53	92	145	154	66	11	147	608	1.8	1.9	7.4
79-80—L.A.-Utah	81	2392	405	915	.443	175	196	.893	54	173	227	309	97	3	197	1004	2.8	3.8	12.4
80-81—Utah................	52	1146	160	371	.431	75	94	.798	17	67	84	161	33	8	111	406	1.6	3.1	7.8
Totals	379	10795	2134	4703	.454	986	1155	.854	364	682	1046	1273	420	52	758	5284	2.8	3.4	13.9

Three-point field goals: 1979-80, 19-for-50 (.380). 1980-81, 11-for-39 (.282). Totals, 30-for-89 (.337).
Personal fouls/disqualifications: 1976-77, 258/1. 1977-78, 233/3. 1978-79, 171/1. 1979-80, 232/3. 1980-81, 126/0. Totals, 1020/8.

NBA PLAYOFF RECORD

								REBOUNDS								AVERAGES		
Season Team	G	Min.	FGM	FGA	Pct.	FTM	FTA	Pct.	Off.	Def.	Tot.	Ast.	St.	Blk.	TO	Pts.	RPG	APG	PPG
78-79—Los Angeles....	8	226	37	77	.481	20	21	.952	7	8	15	14	9	0	14	94	1.9	1.8	11.8

Personal fouls/disqualifications: 1978-79, 28/0.

COMBINED ABA AND NBA REGULAR-SEASON RECORDS

								REBOUNDS								AVERAGES		
	G	Min.	FGM	FGA	Pct.	FTM	FTA	Pct.	Off.	Def.	Tot.	Ast.	Stl.	Blk.	TO	Pts.	RPG	APG	PPG
Totals	1041	32391	6829	14804	.461	3626	4334	.837	...	...	4346	3842	...	...	...	17437	4.2	3.7	16.8

Three-point field goals: 153-for-504 (.304).

BRIAN, FRANK   G

PERSONAL: Born May 1, 1923, in Zachary, La. ... 6-1/180. ... Full name: Frank Sands Brian. ... Nickname: Flash.
HIGH SCHOOL: Zachary (La.).
COLLEGE: Louisiana State.
TRANSACTIONS/CAREER NOTES: Signed by Anderson of National Basketball League (1947). ... Selected by Chicago from Anderson in NBL dispersal draft (April 25, 1950). ... Traded by Chicago to Tri-Cities, 1950. ... Traded by Tri-Cities to Fort Wayne for C/F Howie Schultz, F/C/G Dick Mehen and cash, May 31, 1951.
MISCELLANEOUS: Member of NBL championship team (1949).

COLLEGIATE RECORD

Season Team	G	Min.	FGM	FGA	Pct.	FTM	FTA	Pct.	Reb.	Ast.	Pts.	RPG	APG	PPG
42-43—Louisiana State..............	15	...	77	...	...	56	...	...	...	...	210	...	...	14.0
43-44—Louisiana State..............						Did not play—military service.								
44-45—Louisiana State..............						Did not play—military service.								
45-46—Louisiana State..............						Did not play—military service.								
46-47—Louisiana State..............	21	...	127	...	...	86	...	...	...	...	340	...	...	16.2
Totals	36	...	204	...	...	142	...	...	...	...	550	...	...	15.3

NBL AND NBA REGULAR-SEASON RECORD

HONORS: All-NBA second team (1950, 1951). ... All-NBL first team (1949). ... All-NBL second team (1948).

Season Team	G	Min.	FGM	FGA	Pct.	FTM	FTA	Pct.	Reb.	Ast.	PF	Dq.	Pts.	RPG	APG	PPG
47-48 —And. (NBL)	59	...	248	...	...	155	210	.738	...	...	148	...	651	...	...	11.0
48-49 —And. (NBL)	64	...	216	...	...	201	256	.785	...	...	144	...	633	...	...	9.9
49-50 —Anderson	64	...	368	1156	.318	402	488	*.824	...	189	192	...	1138	...	3.0	17.8
50-51 —Tri-Cities	68	...	363	1127	.322	418	508	.823	244	266	215	4	1144	3.6	3.9	16.8
51-52 —Fort Wayne	66	2672	342	972	.352	367	433	.848	232	233	220	6	1051	3.5	3.5	15.9
52-53 —Fort Wayne	68	1910	245	699	.351	236	297	.795	133	142	142	8	726	2.0	2.1	10.7
53-54 —Fort Wayne	64	973	132	352	.375	137	182	.753	79	92	100	2	401	1.2	1.4	6.3
54-55 —Fort Wayne	71	1381	237	623	.380	217	255	.851	127	142	133	0	691	1.8	2.0	9.7
55-56 —Fort Wayne	37	680	78	263	.297	72	88	.818	88	74	62	0	228	2.4	2.0	6.2
Totals.................................	561	...	2229	...	...	2205	2717	.812	...	...	1419	...	6663	...	...	11.9

NBL AND NBA PLAYOFF RECORD

Season Team	G	Min.	FGM	FGA	Pct.	FTM	FTA	Pct.	Reb.	Ast.	PF	Dq.	Pts.	RPG	APG	PPG
47-48 —And. (NBL)	6	...	18	...	...	11	16	.688	...	...	...	...	47	...	...	7.8
48-49 —And. (NBL)	7	...	26	...	...	27	32	.844	...	...	...	...	79	...	...	11.3
49-50 —Anderson	8	...	26	96	.271	43	48	.896	...	19	24	...	95	...	2.4	11.9
51-52 —Fort Wayne	2	81	6	24	.250	5	6	.833	6	9	10	0	17	3.0	4.5	8.5
52-53 —Fort Wayne	8	146	13	42	.310	19	25	.760	9	11	23	1	45	1.1	1.4	5.6
53-54 —Fort Wayne	4	106	15	36	.417	11	16	.688	12	10	7	0	41	3.0	2.5	10.3
54-55 —Fort Wayne	11	269	48	120	.400	31	38	.816	22	27	26	0	127	2.0	2.5	11.5
55-56 —Fort Wayne	10	166	26	68	.382	17	21	.810	12	17	15	0	69	1.2	1.7	6.9
Totals.................................	56	...	178	...	...	164	202	.812	...	...	...	...	520	...	...	9.3

NBA ALL-STAR GAME RECORD

Season Team	Min.	FGM	FGA	Pct.	FTM	FTA	Pct.	Reb	Ast.	PF	Dq.	Pts.
1951 —Tri-Cities......................	...	5	14	.357	4	5	.800	6	3	2	...	14
1952 —Fort Wayne.................	25	4	10	.400	5	6	.833	7	4	2	...	13
Totals	...	9	24	.375	9	11	.818	13	7	4	...	27

BRIDGES, BILL   F

PERSONAL: Born April 4, 1939, in Hobbs, N.M. ... 6-6/235. ... Full name: William C. Bridges.
HIGH SCHOOL: Hobbs (N.M.).
COLLEGE: Kansas.
TRANSACTIONS/CAREER NOTES: Selected by Chicago Packers in third round (32nd pick overall) of 1961 NBA Draft. ... Played in American Basketball League with Kansas City Steers (1961-62 and 1962-63). ... Draft rights traded by Packers with G Ralph Davis to St. Louis Hawks for G Al Ferrari and F Shellie McMillion (June 14, 1962). ... Hawks franchise moved to Atlanta for 1968-69 season. ... Traded by Hawks to Philadelphia 76ers for F/C Jim Washington (November 19, 1971). ... Traded by 76ers with C/F Mel Counts to Los Angeles Lakers for F/C Leroy Ellis and F John Q. Trapp (November 2, 1972). ... Waived by Lakers (December 6, 1974). ... Signed as free agent by Golden State Warriors (March 1, 1975).
MISCELLANEOUS: Member of NBA championship team (1975).

COLLEGIATE RECORD

Season Team	G	Min.	FGM	FGA	Pct.	FTM	FTA	Pct.	Reb.	Ast.	Pts.	RPG	APG	PPG
57-58—Kansas‡						Freshman team did not play intercollegiate schedule.								
58-59—Kansas	25	...	117	307	.381	74	129	.574	343	...	308	13.7	...	12.3
59-60—Kansas	28	...	112	293	.382	94	142	.662	385	...	318	13.8	...	11.4
60-61—Kansas	25	...	146	334	.437	110	155	.710	353	...	402	14.1	...	16.1
Varsity totals	78	...	375	934	.401	278	426	.653	1081	...	1028	13.9	...	13.2

ABL REGULAR-SEASON RECORD

ABL: ABL All-Star first team (1962). ... Holds single-game record for most points—55 (December 9, 1962, vs. Oakland).

Season Team	G	Min.	FGM	FGA	Pct.	FTM	FTA	Pct.	Reb.	Ast.	Pts.	AVERAGES RPG	APG	PPG
61-62—Kansas City	79	3259	638	1400	.456	412	587	.702	*1059	181	1697	13.4	2.3	21.5
62-63—Kansas City	29	1185	312	606	.515	225	289	.779	*437	87	*849	15.1	3.0	29.3
Totals	108	4444	950	2006	.474	637	876	.727	1496	268	2546	13.9	2.5	23.6

NBA REGULAR-SEASON RECORD

HONORS: NBA All-Defensive second team (1969, 1970).

Season Team	G	Min.	FGM	FGA	Pct.	FTM	FTA	Pct.	Reb.	Ast.	PF	Dq.	Pts.	AVERAGES RPG	APG	PPG
62-63—St. Louis	27	374	66	160	.413	32	51	.627	144	23	58	0	164	5.3	0.9	6.1
63-64—St. Louis	80	1949	268	675	.397	146	224	.652	680	181	269	6	682	8.5	2.3	8.5
64-65—St. Louis	79	2362	362	938	.386	186	275	.676	853	187	276	3	910	10.8	2.4	11.5
65-66—St. Louis	78	2677	377	927	.407	257	364	.706	951	208	333	11	1011	12.2	2.7	13.0
66-67—St. Louis	79	3130	503	1106	.455	367	523	.702	1190	222	325	12	1373	15.1	2.8	17.4
67-68—St. Louis	82	3197	466	1009	.462	347	484	.717	1102	253	*366	12	1279	13.4	3.1	15.6
68-69—Atlanta	80	2930	351	775	.453	239	353	.677	1132	298	290	3	941	14.2	3.7	11.8
69-70—Atlanta	82	3269	443	932	.475	331	451	.734	1181	345	292	6	1217	14.4	4.2	14.8
70-71—Atlanta	82	3140	382	834	.458	211	330	.639	1233	240	317	7	975	15.0	2.9	11.9
71-72—Atl.-Phil.	78	2756	379	779	.487	222	316	.703	1051	198	269	6	980	13.5	2.5	12.6
72-73—Phil.-L.A.	82	2867	333	722	.461	179	255	.702	904	219	296	3	845	11.0	2.7	10.3

Season Team	G	Min.	FGM	FGA	Pct.	FTM	FTA	Pct.	REBOUNDS Off.	Def.	Tot.	Ast.	St.	Blk.	TO	Pts.	AVERAGES RPG	APG	PPG
73-74—Los Angeles	65	1812	216	513	.421	116	164	.707	193	306	499	148	58	31	...	548	7.7	2.3	8.4
74-75—L.A.-G.S.	32	415	35	93	.376	17	34	.500	64	70	134	31	11	5	...	87	4.2	1.0	2.7
Totals	926	30878	4181	9463	.442	2650	3824	.693	...	...	11054	2553	69	36	...	11012	11.9	2.8	11.9

Personal fouls/disqualifications: 1973-74, 219/3. 1974-75, 65/1. Totals, 3375/73.

NBA PLAYOFF RECORD

Season Team	G	Min.	FGM	FGA	Pct.	FTM	FTA	Pct.	Reb.	Ast.	PF	Dq.	Pts.	AVERAGES RPG	APG	PPG
62-63—St. Louis	11	204	41	96	.427	20	27	.741	86	9	31	0	102	7.8	0.8	9.3
63-64—St. Louis	12	240	26	83	.313	12	19	.632	84	24	40	0	64	7.0	2.0	5.3
64-65—St. Louis	4	145	21	59	.356	10	15	.667	67	9	19	1	52	16.8	2.3	13.0
65-66—St. Louis	10	421	86	170	.506	31	43	.721	149	28	47	2	203	14.9	2.8	20.3
66-67—St. Louis	9	369	48	128	.375	45	67	.672	169	22	36	2	141	18.8	2.4	15.7
67-68—St. Louis	6	216	38	75	.507	18	25	.720	77	14	23	0	94	12.8	2.3	15.7
68-69—Atlanta	11	442	69	156	.442	34	48	.708	178	37	48	2	172	16.2	3.4	15.6
69-70—Atlanta	9	381	44	110	.400	16	27	.593	154	29	37	1	104	17.1	3.2	11.6
70-71—Atlanta	5	229	23	58	.397	3	9	.333	104	5	17	0	49	20.8	1.0	9.8
72-73—Los Angeles	17	582	57	136	.419	38	49	.776	158	29	68	2	152	9.3	1.7	8.9

Season Team	G	Min.	FGM	FGA	Pct.	FTM	FTA	Pct.	REBOUNDS Off.	Def.	Tot.	Ast.	St.	Blk.	TO	Pts.	AVERAGES RPG	APG	PPG
73-74—Los Angeles	5	144	12	41	.293	6	13	.462	14	16	30	6	7	0	...	30	6.0	1.2	6.0
74-75—Golden State	14	148	10	23	.435	2	7	.286	13	36	49	7	9	4	...	22	3.5	0.5	1.6
Totals	113	3521	475	1135	.419	235	349	.673	...	...	1305	219	16	4	...	1185	11.5	1.9	10.5

Personal fouls/disqualifications: 1973-74, 19/0. 1974-75, 23/0. Totals, 408/10.

NBA ALL-STAR GAME RECORD

Season Team	Min.	FGM	FGA	Pct.	FTM	FTA	Pct.	Reb	Ast.	PF	Dq.	Pts.
1967—St. Louis	17	4	5	.800	0	2	.000	3	3	1	0	8
1968—St. Louis	21	7	9	.778	1	4	.250	7	1	4	0	15
1970—Atlanta	15	2	2	1.000	1	5	.200	4	2	1	0	5
Totals	53	13	16	.813	2	11	.182	14	6	6	0	28

CERVI, AL   G

PERSONAL: Born February 12, 1917, in Buffalo. ... 5-11/185. ... Full name: Alfred Nicholas Cervi. ... Nickname: Digger.
HIGH SCHOOL: East (Buffalo).
COLLEGE: Did not attend college.
TRANSACTIONS/CAREER NOTES: Played with independent teams (1935-36, 1936-37 and 1938-39 through 1944-45 seasons). ... Syracuse Nationals franchise became part of NBA for 1949-50 season.
CAREER HONORS: Elected to Naismith Memorial Basketball Hall of Fame (1984).
MISCELLANEOUS: Member of NBL championship team (1946).

NBL AND NBA REGULAR-SEASON RECORD

HONORS: All-NBA second team (1950). ... All-NBL first team (1947, 1948, 1949). ... All-NBL second team (1946).

Season Team	G	Min.	FGM	FGA	Pct.	FTM	FTA	Pct.	Reb.	Ast.	PF	Dq.	Pts.	AVERAGES RPG	APG	PPG
37-38—Buff. (NBL)	9	...	19	...	...	6	...	...	...	...	...	...	44	...	...	4.9
45-46—Roc. (NBL)	28	...	112	...	...	76	108	.704	...	...	21	...	300	...	...	10.7
46-47—Roc. (NBL)	44	...	228	...	...	176	236	.746	...	...	127	...	*632	...	...	14.4
47-48—Roc. (NBL)	49	...	234	...	...	187	242	.773	...	...	118	...	655	...	...	13.4
48-49—Syr. (NBL)	57	...	204	...	...	287	382	.751	...	...	170	...	695	...	...	12.2
49-50—Syracuse	56	...	143	431	.332	287	346	.829	...	264	223	...	573	...	4.7	10.2
50-51—Syracuse	53	...	132	346	.382	194	237	.819	152	208	180	9	458	2.9	3.9	8.6
51-52—Syracuse	55	850	99	280	.354	219	248	.883	87	148	176	7	417	1.6	2.7	7.6
52-53—Syracuse	38	301	31	71	.437	81	100	.810	22	28	90	2	143	0.6	0.7	3.8
Totals	389	...	1202	...	...	1513	...	...	...	...	...	...	3917	...	...	10.1

NBL AND NBA PLAYOFF RECORD

Season Team	G	Min.	FGM	FGA	Pct.	FTM	FTA	Pct.	Reb.	Ast.	PF	Dq.	Pts.	AVERAGES RPG	APG	PPG
45-46 —Roc. (NBL)	7	...	23	...	...	24	30	.800	...	...	21	...	70	...	...	10.0
46-47 —Roc. (NBL)	11	...	49	...	...	50	68	.735	...	...	41	...	148	...	...	13.5
47-48 —Roc. (NBL)	6	...	18	...	...	14	19	.737	13	...	...	...	50	2.2	...	8.3
48-49 —Syr. (NBL)	6	...	12	...	...	22	30	.733	...	...	23	...	46	...	...	7.7
49-50 —Syracuse	11	...	23	68	.338	38	46	.826	...	52	36	...	84	...	4.7	7.6
50-51 —Syracuse	7	...	17	56	.304	44	50	.880	33	38	31	1	78	4.7	5.4	11.1
51-52 —Syracuse	7	88	7	30	.233	22	23	.957	10	15	23	1	36	1.4	2.1	5.1
52-53 —Syracuse	2	...	3	5	.600	12	15	.800	0	1	12	1	18	0.0	0.5	9.0
Totals	57	...	152	...	...	226	281	.804	...	...	...	...	530	...	...	9.3

HONORS: NBL Coach of the Year (1949).

HEAD COACHING RECORD

NBL AND NBA COACHING RECORD

Season Team	REGULAR SEASON W	L	Pct.	Finish	PLAYOFFS W	L	Pct.
48-49 —Syracuse (NBL)	40	23	.635	2nd/Eastern Division	3	3	.500
49-50 —Syracuse	51	13	.797	1st/Eastern Division	6	5	.545
50-51 —Syracuse	32	34	.485	4th/Eastern Division	4	3	.571
51-52 —Syracuse	40	26	.606	1st/Eastern Division	3	4	.429
52-53 —Syracuse	47	24	.662	2nd/Eastern Division	0	2	.000
53-54 —Syracuse	42	30	.583	3rd/Eastern Division	9	4	.692
54-55 —Syracuse	43	29	.597	1st/Eastern Division	7	4	.636
55-56 —Syracuse	35	37	.493	3rd/Eastern Division	5	4	.555
56-57 —Syracuse	4	8	.333		—	—	—
58-59 —Philadelphia	32	40	.444	4th/Eastern Division	—	—	—
Totals (10 years)	366	264	.581	Totals (8 years)	37	29	.561

NOTES:

1949—Defeated Hammond, 2-0, in Eastern Division first round; lost to Anderson, 3-1, in Eastern Division finals.

1950—Defeated Philadelphia, 2-0, in Eastern Division semifinals; defeated New York, 2-1, in Eastern Division finals; lost to Minneapolis, 4-2, in World Championship Series.

1951—Defeated Philadelphia, 2-0, in Eastern Division semifinals; lost to New York, 3-2, in Eastern Division finals.

1952—Defeated Philadelphia, 2-1, in Eastern Division semifinals; lost to New York, 3-1, in Eastern Division finals.

1953—Lost to Boston in Eastern Division semifinals.

1954—Defeated Boston, 96-95 (OT); defeated New York, 75-68; defeated New York, 103-99; and defeated Boston, 98-85, in Eastern Division round robin; defeated Boston, 2-0, in Eastern Division finals; lost to Minneapolis, 4-3, in World Championship Series.

1955—Defeated Boston, 3-1, in Eastern Division finals; defeated Fort Wayne, 4-3, in World Championship Series.

1956—Defeated New York, 82-77, in Eastern Division third-place game; Defeated Boston, 2-1, in Eastern Division semifinals; lost to Philadelphia, 3-2, in Eastern Division finals. Replaced as Syracuse head coach by Paul Seymour (November).

CHAMBERLAIN, WILT   C

PERSONAL: Born August 21, 1936, in Philadelphia. ... 7-1/275. ... Full name: Wilton Norman Chamberlain. ... Nickname: Wilt the Stilt and The Big Dipper.
HIGH SCHOOL: Overbrook (Philadelphia).
COLLEGE: Kansas.
TRANSACTIONS/CAREER NOTES: Played with Harlem Globetrotters during 1958-59 season. ... Selected by Philadelphia Warriors in 1959 NBA Draft (territorial pick). ... Warriors franchise moved from Philadelphia to San Francisco for 1962-63 season. ... Traded by Warriors to Philadelphia 76ers for G Paul Neumann, C/F Connie Dierking, F Lee Shaffer and cash (January 15, 1965). ... Traded by 76ers to Los Angeles Lakers for F Jerry Chambers, G Archie Clark and C Darrall Imhoff (July 9, 1968).
CAREER HONORS: Elected to Naismith Memorial Basketball Hall of Fame (1978). ... NBA 35th Anniversary All-Time Team (1980).
MISCELLANEOUS: Member of NBA championship teams (1967, 1972). ... Golden State Warriors franchise all-time leading scorer with 17,783 points (1959-60 through 1964-65).

COLLEGIATE RECORD

NOTES: THE SPORTING NEWS All-America first team (1958).

Season Team	G	Min.	FGM	FGA	Pct.	FTM	FTA	Pct.	Reb.	Ast.	Pts.	AVERAGES RPG	APG	PPG
55-56 —Kansas‡					Freshman team did not play intercollegiate schedule.									
56-57 —Kansas	27	...	275	588	.468	250	399	.627	510	...	800	18.9	...	29.6
57-58 —Kansas	21	...	228	482	.473	177	291	.608	367	...	633	17.5	...	30.1
Varsity totals	48	...	503	1070	.470	427	690	.619	877	...	1433	18.3	...	29.9

NBA REGULAR-SEASON RECORD

RECORDS: Holds career records for most games with 50 or more points—118; most seasons leading league in field-goal percentage—9; most free throws attempted—11,862; most rebounds—23,924; and highest rebounds-per-game average (minimum 400 games)—22.9. ... Shares career records for most consecutive seasons leading league in scoring—7 (1959-60 through 1965-66). ... Holds single-season records for most games with 50 or more points—45 (1962); most minutes played—3,882 (1962); most points—4,029 (1962); highest points-per-game average—50.4 (1962); most points by a rookie—2,707 (1960); most field goals made—1,597 (1962); most consecutive field goals made—35 (February 17 through February 28, 1967); most field goals attempted—3,159 (1962); highest field-goal percentage—.727 (1973); most free throws attempted—1,363 (1962); most rebounds—2,149 (1961); most rebounds by a rookie—1,941 (1960); and highest rebounds-per-game average—27.2 (1961). ... Holds single-game records for most points—100; most points in one half—59; most field goals made—36; most field goals made in one half—22; most field goals attempted—63; most field goals attempted in one half—37; and most field goals attempted in one quarter—21 (March 2, 1962, vs. New York at Hershey, Pa.). ... Holds single-game records for most points by a rookie—58 (January 25, 1960, vs. Detroit); highest field-goal percentage (minimum 15 made)—1.000 (January 20, 1967, vs. Los Angeles, 15-for-15; February 24, 1967, vs. Baltimore, 18-for-18; and March 19, 1967, vs. Baltimore, 16-for-16); most rebounds—55 (November 24, 1960, vs. Boston); and most rebounds by a rookie—45 (February 6, 1960, vs. Syracuse). ... Shares single-game record for most free throws made—28 (March 2, 1962, vs. New York at Hershey, Pa.).

HONORS: NBA Most Valuable Player (1960, 1966, 1967, 1968). ... NBA Rookie of the Year (1960). ... All-NBA first team (1960, 1961, 1962, 1964, 1966, 1967, 1968). ... All-NBA second team (1963, 1965, 1972). ... NBA All-Defensive first team (1972, 1973).

Season Team	G	Min.	FGM	FGA	Pct.	FTM	FTA	Pct.	Reb.	Ast.	PF	Dq.	Pts.	RPG	APG	PPG
59-60 —Philadelphia	72	†3338	*1065	*2311	.461	577	*991	.582	*1941	168	150	0	*2707	*27.0	2.3	*37.6
60-61 —Philadelphia	79	*3773	*1251	*2457	*.509	531	*1054	.504	*2149	148	130	0	*3033	*27.2	1.9	*38.4
61-62 —Philadelphia	80	*3882	*1597	*3159	.506	*835	*1363	.613	*2052	192	123	0	*4029	*25.7	2.4	*50.4
62-63 —San Fran.	80	*3806	*1463	*2770	*.528	660	*1113	.593	*1946	275	136	0	*3586	*24.3	3.4	*44.8
63-64 —San Fran.	80	*3689	*1204	*2298	.524	540	*1016	.532	1787	403	182	0	*2948	22.3	5.0	*36.9
64-65 —S.F.-Phil.	73	3301	*1063	*2083	*.510	408	*880	.464	1673	250	146	0	*2534	22.9	3.4	*34.7
65-66 —Philadelphia	79	*3737	*1074	*1990	*.540	501	976	.513	*1943	414	171	0	*2649	*24.6	5.2	*33.5
66-67 —Philadelphia	81	*3682	785	1150	*.683	386	*875	.441	*1957	630	143	0	1956	24.2	7.8	24.1
67-68 —Philadelphia	82	*3836	819	1377	*.595	354	*932	.380	*1952	*702	160	0	1992	*23.8	8.6	24.3
68-69 —Los Angeles	81	3669	641	1099	*.583	382	*857	.446	*1712	366	142	0	1664	*21.1	4.5	20.5
69-70 —Los Angeles	12	505	129	227	.568	70	157	.446	221	49	31	0	328	18.4	4.1	27.3
70-71 —Los Angeles	82	3630	668	1226	.545	360	669	.538	*1493	352	174	0	1696	*18.2	4.3	20.7
71-72 —Los Angeles	82	3469	496	764	*.649	221	524	.422	*1572	329	196	0	1213	*19.2	4.0	14.8
72-73 —Los Angeles	82	3542	426	586	*.727	232	455	.510	*1526	365	191	0	1084	*18.6	4.5	13.2
Totals	1045	47859	12681	23497	.540	6057	11862	.511	23924	4643	2075	0	31419	22.9	4.4	30.1

NBA PLAYOFF RECORD

NOTES: NBA Finals Most Valuable Player (1972). ... Holds career playoff record for most free throws attempted—1,627. ... Holds NBA Finals single-game record for most rebounds in one half—26 (April 16, 1967, vs. San Francisco). ... Shares NBA Finals single-game record for most free throws attempted in one quarter—11 (April 16, 1967, vs. San Francisco). ... Holds single-series playoff record for highest rebounds-per-game average—32.0 (1967). ... Holds single-game playoff records for most rebounds—41 (April 5, 1967, vs. Boston); most rebounds in one half—26 (April 16, 1967, vs. San Francisco); and most points by a rookie—53 (March 14, 1960, vs. Syracuse). ... Shares single-game play-off records for most field-goals made—24 (March 14, 1960, vs. Syracuse); most field goals attempted—48 (March 22, 1962, vs. Syracuse); and most field goals attempted in one half—25 (March 22, 1962, vs. Syracuse).

Season Team	G	Min.	FGM	FGA	Pct.	FTM	FTA	Pct.	Reb.	Ast.	PF	Dq.	Pts.	RPG	APG	PPG
59-60 —Philadelphia	9	415	125	252	.496	49	110	.445	232	19	17	0	299	25.8	2.1	33.2
60-61 —Philadelphia	3	144	45	96	.469	21	38	.553	69	6	10	0	111	23.0	2.0	37.0
61-62 —Philadelphia	12	576	162	347	.467	96	151	.636	319	37	27	0	420	26.6	3.1	35.0
63-64 —San Fran.	12	558	175	322	.543	66	139	.475	302	39	27	0	416	25.2	3.3	34.7
64-65 —Philadelphia	11	536	123	232	.530	76	136	.559	299	48	29	0	322	27.2	4.4	29.3
65-66 —Philadelphia	5	240	56	110	.509	28	68	.412	151	15	10	0	140	30.2	3.0	28.0
66-67 —Philadelphia	15	718	132	228	.579	62	160	.388	437	135	37	0	326	29.1	9.0	21.7
67-68 —Philadelphia	13	631	124	232	.534	60	158	.380	321	85	29	0	308	24.7	6.5	23.7
68-69 —Los Angeles	18	832	96	176	.545	58	148	.392	444	46	56	0	250	24.7	2.6	13.9
69-70 —Los Angeles	18	851	158	288	.549	82	202	.406	399	81	42	0	398	22.2	4.5	22.1
70-71 —Los Angeles	12	554	85	187	.455	50	97	.515	242	53	33	0	220	20.2	4.4	18.3
71-72 —Los Angeles	15	703	80	142	.563	60	122	.492	315	49	47	0	220	21.0	3.3	14.7
72-73 —Los Angeles	17	801	64	116	.552	49	98	.500	383	60	48	0	177	22.5	3.5	10.4
Totals	160	7559	1425	2728	.522	757	1627	.465	3913	673	412	0	3607	24.5	4.2	22.5

NBA ALL-STAR GAME RECORD

NOTES: NBA All-Star Game Most Valuable Player (1960). ... Holds career record for most rebounds—197. ... Holds single-game records for most points—42 (1962); most free throws attempted—16 (1962); and most field goals made in one half—10 (1962). ... Shares single-game records for most points in one half—23 (1962); most field goals made—17 (1962); and most rebounds in one half—16 (1960).

Season Team	Min.	FGM	FGA	Pct.	FTM	FTA	Pct.	Reb	Ast.	PF	Dq.	Pts.
1960 —Philadelphia	30	9	20	.450	5	7	.714	25	2	1	0	23
1961 —Philadelphia	38	2	8	.250	8	15	.533	18	5	1	0	12
1962 —Philadelphia	37	17	23	.739	8	16	.500	24	1	4	0	42
1963 —San Francisco	35	7	11	.636	3	7	.429	19	1	2	0	17
1964 —San Francisco	37	4	14	.286	11	14	.786	20	1	2	0	19
1965 —San Francisco	31	9	15	.600	2	8	.250	16	1	4	0	20
1966 —Philadelphia	25	8	11	.727	5	9	.556	9	3	2	0	21
1967 —Philadelphia	39	6	7	.857	2	5	.400	22	4	1	0	14
1968 —Philadelphia	25	3	4	.750	1	4	.250	7	6	2	0	7
1969 —Los Angeles	27	2	3	.667	0	1	.000	12	2	2	0	4
1971 —Los Angeles	18	1	1	1.000	0	0	...	8	5	0	0	2
1972 —Los Angeles	24	3	3	1.000	2	8	.250	10	3	2	0	8
1973 —Los Angeles	22	1	2	.500	0	0	...	7	3	0	0	2
Totals	388	72	122	.590	47	94	.500	197	36	23	0	191

ABA COACHING RECORD

	REGULAR SEASON				PLAYOFFS		
Season Team	W	L	Pct.	Finish	W	L	Pct.
73-74 —San Diego	37	47	.440	T4th/Western Division	2	4	.333

NOTES:
1974—Lost to Utah in Western Division semifinals.

DID YOU KNOW...

... that Elgin Baylor retired from the Lakers on the same day (November 5, 1971) the team began its NBA-record 33-game winning streak?

CHAMBERS, TOM   F

PERSONAL: Born June 21, 1959, in Ogden, Utah. ... 6-10/230. ... Full name: Thomas Doane Chambers.
HIGH SCHOOL: Fairview (Boulder, Colo.).
COLLEGE: Utah.
TRANSACTIONS/CAREER NOTES: Selected by San Diego Clippers in first round (eighth pick overall) of 1981 NBA Draft. ... Traded by Clippers with F Al Wood, 1987 second-round draft choice and future third-round draft choice to Seattle SuperSonics for C James Donaldson, F Greg Kelser, G Mark Radford, 1984 first-round draft choice and 1985 second-round draft choice (August 18, 1983). ... Signed as unrestricted free agent by Phoenix Suns (July 5, 1988). ... Signed as unrestricted free agent by Utah Jazz (August 12, 1993).

COLLEGIATE RECORD

Season Team	G	Min.	FGM	FGA	Pct.	FTM	FTA	Pct.	Reb.	Ast.	Pts.	RPG	APG	PPG
77-78—Utah	28	355	69	139	.496	40	64	.625	104	7	178	3.7	0.3	6.4
78-79—Utah	30	853	206	379	.544	69	127	.543	266	28	481	8.9	0.9	16.0
79-80—Utah	28	792	195	359	.543	92	129	.713	244	23	482	8.7	0.8	17.2
80-81—Utah	30	959	221	372	.594	115	155	.742	262	24	557	8.7	0.8	18.6
Totals	116	2959	691	1249	.553	316	475	.665	876	82	1698	7.6	0.7	14.6

HONORS: All-NBA second team (1989, 1990).

NBA REGULAR-SEASON RECORD

Season Team	G	Min.	FGM	FGA	Pct.	FTM	FTA	Pct.	Off.	Def.	Tot.	Ast.	St.	Blk.	TO	Pts.	RPG	APG	PPG
81-82—San Diego	81	2682	554	1056	.525	284	458	.620	211	350	561	146	58	46	220	1392	6.9	1.8	17.2
82-83—San Diego	79	2665	519	1099	.472	353	488	.723	218	301	519	192	79	57	234	1391	6.6	2.4	17.6
83-84—Seattle	82	2570	554	1110	.499	375	469	.800	219	313	532	133	47	51	192	1483	6.5	1.6	18.1
84-85—Seattle	81	2923	629	1302	.483	475	571	.832	164	415	579	209	70	57	260	1739	7.1	2.6	21.5
85-86—Seattle	66	2019	432	928	.466	346	414	.836	126	305	431	132	55	37	194	1223	6.5	2.0	18.5
86-87—Seattle	82	3018	660	1446	.456	535	630	.849	163	382	545	245	81	50	268	1909	6.6	3.0	23.3
87-88—Seattle	82	2680	611	1364	.448	419	519	.807	135	355	490	212	87	53	209	1674	6.0	2.6	20.4
88-89—Phoenix	81	3002	774	1643	.471	509	598	.851	143	541	684	231	87	55	231	2085	8.4	2.9	25.7
89-90—Phoenix	81	3046	810	1617	.501	557	647	.861	121	450	571	190	88	47	218	2201	7.0	2.3	27.2
90-91—Phoenix	76	2475	556	1271	.437	379	459	.826	104	386	490	194	65	52	177	1511	6.4	2.6	19.9
91-92—Phoenix	69	1948	426	989	.431	258	311	.830	86	315	401	142	57	37	103	1128	5.8	2.1	16.3
92-93—Phoenix	73	1723	320	716	.447	241	288	.837	96	249	345	101	43	23	92	892	4.7	1.4	12.2
93-94—Utah	80	1838	329	748	.440	221	281	.786	87	239	326	79	40	32	89	893	4.1	1.0	11.2
94-95—Utah	81	1240	195	427	.457	109	135	.807	66	147	213	73	25	30	52	503	2.6	0.9	6.2
Totals	1094	33829	7369	15716	.469	5061	6268	.807	1939	4748	6687	2279	882	627	2539	20024	6.1	2.1	18.3

Three-point field goals: 1981-82, 0-for-2. 1982-83, 0-for-8. 1983-84, 0-for-12. 1984-85, 6-for-22 (.273). 1985-86, 13-for-48 (.271). 1986-87, 54-for-145 (.372). 1987-88, 33-for-109 (.303). 1988-89, 21-for-86 (.326). 1989-90, 24-for-86 (.279). 1990-91, 20-for-73 (.274). 1991-92, 18-for-49 (.367). 1992-93, 11-for-28 (.393). 1993-94, 14-for-45 (.311). 1994-95, 4-for-24 (.167). Totals, 225-for-737 (.305).

Personal fouls/disqualifications: 1981-82, 341/17. 1982-83, 333/15. 1983-84, 309/8. 1984-85, 312/4. 1985-86, 248/6. 1986-87, 307/9. 1987-88, 297/4. 1988-89, 271/2. 1989-90, 260/1. 1990-91, 235/3. 1991-92, 196/1. 1992-93, 212/2. 1993-94, 232/2. 1994-95, 173/1. Totals, 3726/75.

NBA PLAYOFF RECORD

Season Team	G	Min.	FGM	FGA	Pct.	FTM	FTA	Pct.	Off.	Def.	Tot.	Ast.	St.	Blk.	TO	Pts.	RPG	APG	PPG
83-84—Seattle	5	191	28	59	.475	12	18	.667	4	29	33	8	5	3	9	68	6.6	1.6	13.6
86-87—Seattle	14	498	118	263	.449	80	99	.808	32	58	90	32	12	13	34	322	6.4	2.3	23.0
87-88—Seattle	5	168	50	91	.549	29	35	.829	8	23	31	11	3	1	13	129	6.2	2.2	25.8
88-89—Phoenix	12	495	118	257	.459	67	78	.859	22	109	131	46	13	15	39	312	10.9	3.8	26.0
89-90—Phoenix	16	612	117	275	.425	116	132	.879	20	87	107	31	7	7	49	355	6.7	1.9	22.2
90-91—Phoenix	4	142	27	66	.409	14	19	.737	2	21	23	10	7	5	12	68	5.8	2.5	17.0
91-92—Phoenix	7	194	39	85	.459	27	32	.844	8	23	31	19	2	5	15	109	4.4	2.7	15.6
92-93—Phoenix	24	376	64	165	.388	44	54	.815	23	42	65	12	6	10	26	174	2.7	0.5	7.3
93-94—Utah	16	325	35	97	.361	23	29	.793	16	29	45	12	5	9	8	93	2.8	0.8	5.8
94-95—Utah	5	60	11	22	.500	9	13	.692	3	10	13	2	2	0	3	32	2.6	0.4	6.4
Totals	108	3061	607	1380	.440	421	509	.827	138	431	569	183	62	68	208	1662	5.3	1.7	15.4

Three-point field goals: 1983-84, 0-for-1. 1986-87, 6-for-17 (.353). 1987-88, 0-for-2. 1988-89, 9-for-22 (.409). 1989-90, 5-for-19 (.263). 1990-91, 0-for-5. 1991-92, 4-for-7 (.571). 1992-93, 2-for-5 (.400). 1993-94, 0-for-7. 1994-95, 1-for-3 (.333). Totals, 27-for-88 (.307).

Personal fouls/disqualifications: 1983-84, 23/0. 1986-87, 51/0. 1987-88, 24/1. 1988-89, 44/0. 1989-90, 54/0. 1990-91, 12/1. 1991-92, 25/1. 1992-93, 58/0. 1993-94, 50/1. 1994-95, 18/1. Totals, 359/5.

NBA ALL-STAR GAME RECORD

NOTES: NBA All-Star Game Most Valuable Player (1987).

Season Team	Min.	FGM	FGA	Pct.	FTM	FTA	Pct.	Off.	Def.	Tot.	Ast.	PF	Dq.	St.	Blk.	TO	Pts.
1987 —Seattle	29	13	25	.520	6	9	.667	3	1	4	2	5	0	4	0	3	34
1989 —Phoenix	16	4	8	.500	6	6	1.000	2	3	5	1	3	0	0	0	2	14
1990 —Phoenix	21	8	12	.667	5	7	.714	2	1	3	1	0	0	1	0	3	21
1991 —Phoenix	18	4	11	.364	0	0		2	2	4	1	3	0	1	0	4	8
Totals	84	29	56	.518	17	22	.773	9	7	16	5	11	0	6	0	12	77

Three-point field goals: 1987, 2-for-3 (.667). 1990, 0-for-1. 1991, 0-for-1. Totals, 2-for-5 (.400).

DID YOU KNOW...

...that Don Chaney is the only Boston Celtic to play with both Bill Russell and Larry Bird?

CHEEKS, MAURICE   G

PERSONAL: Born September 8, 1956, in Chicago. ... 6-1/180. ... Full name: Maurice Edward Cheeks.
HIGH SCHOOL: Du Sable (Chicago).
COLLEGE: West Texas State.
TRANSACTIONS/CAREER NOTES: Selected by Philadelphia 76ers in second round (36th pick overall) of 1978 NBA Draft. ... Traded by 76ers with C Christian Welp and G David Wingate to San Antonio Spurs for G Johnny Dawkins and F Jay Vincent (August 28, 1989). ... Traded by Spurs to New York Knicks for G Rod Strickland (February 21, 1990). ... Traded by Knicks to Atlanta Hawks for C Tim McCormick (October 3, 1991). ... Signed as free agent by New Jersey Nets (January 7, 1993). ... Assistant coach, 76ers (1994-95 to present).
MISCELLANEOUS: Member of NBA championship team (1983). ... Philadelphia 76ers franchise all-time assists leader with 6,212 and all-time steals leader with 1,942 (1978-79 through 1988-89).

COLLEGIATE RECORD

Season Team	G	Min.	FGM	FGA	Pct.	FTM	FTA	Pct.	Reb.	Ast.	Pts.	RPG	APG	PPG
74-75—West Texas State...........	26	...	35	75	.467	31	53	.585	56	...	101	2.2	...	3.9
75-76—West Texas State...........	23	767	102	170	.600	52	84	.619	91	...	256	4.0	...	11.1
76-77—West Texas State...........	30	1095	149	246	.606	119	169	.704	119	212	417	4.0	7.1	13.9
77-78—West Texas State...........	27	941	174	319	.545	105	147	.714	152	153	453	5.6	5.7	16.8
Totals	106	...	460	810	.568	307	453	.678	418	...	1227	3.9	...	11.6

NBA REGULAR-SEASON RECORD

HONORS: NBA All-Defensive first team (1983, 1984, 1985, 1986). ... NBA All-Defensive second team (1987).

Season Team	G	Min.	FGM	FGA	Pct.	FTM	FTA	Pct.	Off.	Def.	Tot.	Ast.	St.	Blk.	TO	Pts.	RPG	APG	PPG
78-79—Philadelphia	82	2409	292	572	.510	101	140	.721	63	191	254	431	174	12	193	685	3.1	5.3	8.4
79-80—Philadelphia	79	2623	357	661	.540	180	231	.779	75	199	274	556	183	32	216	898	3.5	7.0	11.4
80-81—Philadelphia	81	2415	310	581	.534	140	178	.787	67	178	245	560	193	39	174	763	3.0	6.9	9.4
81-82—Philadelphia	79	2498	352	676	.521	171	220	.777	51	197	248	667	209	33	184	881	3.1	8.4	11.2
82-83—Philadelphia	79	2465	404	745	.542	181	240	.754	53	156	209	543	184	31	179	990	2.6	6.9	12.5
83-84—Philadelphia	75	2494	386	702	.550	170	232	.733	44	161	205	478	171	20	182	950	2.7	6.4	12.7
84-85—Philadelphia	78	2616	422	741	.570	175	199	.879	54	163	217	497	169	24	155	1025	2.8	6.4	13.1
85-86—Philadelphia	82	*3270	490	913	.537	282	335	.842	55	180	235	753	207	27	238	1266	2.9	9.2	15.4
86-87—Philadelphia	68	2624	415	788	.527	227	292	.777	47	168	215	538	180	15	173	1061	3.2	7.9	15.6
87-88—Philadelphia	79	2871	428	865	.495	227	275	.825	59	194	253	635	167	22	160	1086	3.2	8.0	13.7
88-89—Philadelphia	71	2298	336	696	.483	151	195	.774	39	144	183	554	105	17	116	824	2.6	7.8	11.6
89-90—S.A.-N.Y.	81	2519	307	609	.504	171	202	.847	50	190	240	453	124	10	121	789	3.0	5.6	9.7
90-91—New York	76	2147	241	483	.499	105	129	.814	22	151	173	435	128	10	108	592	2.3	5.7	7.8
91-92—Atlanta	56	1086	115	249	.462	26	43	.605	29	66	95	185	83	0	36	259	1.7	3.3	4.6
92-93—New Jersey	35	510	51	93	.548	24	27	.889	5	37	42	107	33	2	33	126	1.2	3.1	3.6
Totals	1101	34845	4906	9374	.523	2331	2938	.793	713	2375	3088	7392	2310	294	2268	12195	2.8	6.7	11.1

Three-point field goals: 1979-80, 4-for-9 (.444). 1980-81, 3-for-8 (.375). 1981-82, 6-for-22 (.273). 1982-83, 1-for-6 (.167). 1983-84, 8-for-20 (.400). 1984-85, 6-for-26 (.231). 1985-86, 4-for-17 (.235). 1986-87, 4-for-17 (.235). 1987-88, 3-for-22 (.136). 1988-89, 1-for 13 (.077). 1989-90, 4-for-16 (.250). 1990-91, 5-for-20 (.250). 1991-92, 3-for-6 (.500). 1992-93, 0-for-2. Totals, 52-for-204 (.255).
Personal fouls/disqualifications: 1978-79, 198/2. 1979-80, 197/1. 1980-81, 231/1. 1981-82, 247/0. 1982-83, 182/0. 1983-84, 196/1. 1984-85, 184/0. 1985-86, 160/0. 1986-87, 109/0. 1987-88, 116/0. 1988-89, 114/0. 1989-90, 78/0. 1990-91, 138/0. 1991-92, 73/0. 1992-93, 35/0. Totals, 2258/5.

NBA PLAYOFF RECORD

NOTES: Shares single-game playoff record for most steals—8 (April 11, 1979, vs. New Jersey).

Season Team	G	Min.	FGM	FGA	Pct.	FTM	FTA	Pct.	Off.	Def.	Tot.	Ast.	St.	Blk.	TO	Pts.	RPG	APG	PPG
78-79—Philadelphia	9	330	66	121	.545	37	56	.661	13	22	35	63	37	4	29	169	3.9	7.0	18.8
79-80—Philadelphia	18	675	89	174	.512	29	41	.707	22	52	74	111	45	4	45	208	4.1	6.2	11.6
80-81—Philadelphia	16	513	68	125	.544	32	42	.762	4	47	51	116	40	12	36	168	3.2	7.3	10.5
81-82—Philadelphia	21	765	125	265	.472	50	65	.769	15	47	62	172	48	6	49	301	3.0	8.2	14.3
82-83—Philadelphia	13	483	83	165	.503	45	64	.703	11	28	39	91	26	2	34	212	3.0	7.0	16.3
83-84—Philadelphia	5	171	35	67	.522	13	15	.867	2	10	12	19	13	0	10	83	2.4	3.8	16.6
84-85—Philadelphia	13	483	81	153	.529	36	42	.857	12	34	46	67	31	5	34	198	3.5	5.2	15.2
85-86—Philadelphia	12	519	94	182	.516	62	73	.849	13	43	56	85	13	3	32	250	4.7	7.1	20.8
86-87—Philadelphia	5	210	35	66	.530	18	21	.857	1	12	13	44	9	4	12	88	2.6	8.8	17.6
88-89—Philadelphia	3	128	21	41	.512	11	13	.846	3	8	11	39	7	1	3	53	3.7	13.0	17.7
89-90—New York	10	388	50	104	.481	28	31	.903	12	27	39	85	17	2	19	128	3.9	8.5	12.8
90-91—New York	3	101	14	23	.609	1	2	.500	3	6	9	16	3	1	8	30	3.0	5.3	10.0
92-93—New Jersey	5	82	11	23	.478	0	1	1.000	3	3	6	14	6	1	7	22	1.2	2.8	4.4
Totals	133	4848	772	1509	.512	362	466	.777	114	339	453	922	295	45	318	1910	3.4	6.9	14.4

Three-point field goals: 1979-80, 1-for-6 (.167). 1980-81, 0-for-3. 1981-82, 1-for-9 (.111). 1982-83, 1-for-2 (.500). 1983-84, 0-for-1. 1984-85, 0-for-5. 1985-86, 0-for-7. 1986-87, 0-for-1. 1988-89, 0-for-1. 1989-90, 0-for-4. 1990-91, 1-for-3 (.333). Totals, 4-for-41 (.098).
Personal fouls/disqualifications: 1978-79, 29/0. 1979-80, 43/0. 1980-81, 55/1. 1981-82, 58/0. 1982-83, 23/0. 1983-84, 18/0. 1984-85, 29/0. 1985-86, 18/0. 1986-87, 14/0. 1988-89, 4/0. 1989-90, 21/0. 1990-91, 9/0. 1992-93, 3/0. Totals, 324/1.

NBA ALL-STAR GAME RECORD

Season Team	Min.	FGM	FGA	Pct.	FTM	FTA	Pct.	Off.	Def.	Tot.	Ast.	PF	Dq.	St.	Blk.	TO	Pts.
1983 —Philadelphia.......	18	3	8	.375	0	0	...	0	1	1	1	0	0	0	0	0	6
1986 —Philadelphia.......	14	3	6	.500	0	0	...	0	0	0	2	0	0	2	0	3	6
1987 —Philadelphia.......	8	1	2	.500	2	2	1.000	0	0	0	0	1	0	1	0	1	4
1988 —Philadelphia.......	4	0	0	...	0	0	...	0	2	2	1	1	0	0	0	0	0
Totals............................	44	7	16	.438	2	2	1.000	0	3	3	4	2	0	3	0	4	16

ALL-TIME GREAT PLAYERS

COSTELLO, LARRY   G

See All-Time Great Coaches, page 405.

COUSY, BOB   G

PERSONAL: Born August 9, 1928, in New York. ... 6-1/175. ... Full name: Robert Joseph Cousy. ... Nickname: Houdini of the Hardwood.
HIGH SCHOOL: Andrew Jackson (Queens, N.Y.).
COLLEGE: Holy Cross.
TRANSACTIONS/CAREER NOTES: Selected by Tri-Cities Blackhawks in first round of 1950 NBA Draft. ... Traded by Blackhawks to Chicago Stags for F/G Gene Vance (1950). ... NBA rights drawn out of a hat by Boston Celtics in dispersal of Stags franchise (1950). ... Traded by Celtics to Cincinnati Royals for F Bill Dinwiddie (November 18, 1969).
CAREER HONORS: Elected to Naismith Memorial Basketball Hall of Fame (1970). ... NBA 25th Anniversary All-Time Team (1970) and 35th Anniversary All-Time Team (1980).
MISCELLANEOUS: Member of NBA championship teams (1957, 1959, 1960, 1961, 1962, 1963). ... Commissioner of American Soccer League (1975 through mid-1980 season). ... Boston Celtics all-time assists leader with 6,945 (1950-51 through 1962-63).

COLLEGIATE RECORD

NOTES: The Sporting News All-America first team (1950). ... The Sporting News All-America second team (1949). ... Member of NCAA championship team (1947).

Season Team	G	Min.	FGM	FGA	Pct.	FTM	FTA	Pct.	Reb.	Ast.	Pts.	RPG	APG	PPG
46-47—Holy Cross	30	...	91	...	...	45	...	...	...	...	227	...	...	7.6
47-48—Holy Cross	30	...	207	...	...	72	108	.667	...	...	486	...	...	16.2
48-49—Holy Cross	27	...	195	...	...	90	134	.672	...	...	480	...	...	17.8
49-50—Holy Cross	30	...	216	659	.328	150	199	.754	...	...	582	...	...	19.4
Totals	117		709			357					1775			15.2

NBA REGULAR-SEASON RECORD

RECORDS: Holds single-game record for most assists in one half—19 (February 27, 1959, vs. Minneapolis).
HONORS: NBA Most Valuable Player (1957). ... All-NBA first team (1952, 1953, 1954, 1955, 1956, 1957, 1958, 1959, 1960, 1961). ... All-NBA second team (1962, 1963).

Season Team	G	Min.	FGM	FGA	Pct.	FTM	FTA	Pct.	Reb.	Ast.	PF	Dq.	Pts.	RPG	APG	PPG
50-51 —Boston	69	...	401	1138	.352	276	365	.756	474	341	185	2	1078	6.9	4.9	15.6
51-52 —Boston	66	2681	512	1388	.369	409	506	.808	421	441	190	5	1433	6.4	6.7	21.7
52-53 —Boston	71	2945	464	*1320	.352	479	587	.816	449	*547	227	4	1407	6.3	*7.7	19.8
53-54 —Boston	72	2857	486	1262	.385	411	522	.787	394	*518	201	3	1383	5.5	*7.2	19.2
54-55 —Boston	71	2747	522	1316	.397	460	570	.807	424	*557	165	1	1504	6.0	*7.8	21.2
55-56 —Boston	72	2767	440	1223	.360	476	564	.844	492	*642	206	2	1356	6.8	*8.9	18.8
56-57 —Boston	64	2364	478	1264	.378	363	442	.821	309	*478	134	0	1319	4.8	*7.5	20.6
57-58 —Boston	65	2222	445	1262	.353	277	326	.850	322	*463	136	1	1167	5.0	*7.1	18.0
58-59 —Boston	65	2403	484	1260	.384	329	385	.855	359	*557	135	0	1297	5.5	*8.6	20.0
59-60 —Boston	75	2588	568	1481	.384	319	403	.792	352	*715	146	2	1455	4.7	*9.5	19.4
60-61 —Boston	76	2468	513	1382	.371	352	452	.779	331	587	196	0	1378	4.4	7.7	18.1
61-62 —Boston	75	2114	462	1181	.391	251	333	.754	261	584	135	0	1175	3.5	7.8	15.7
62-63 —Boston	76	1975	392	988	.397	219	298	.735	193	515	175	0	1003	2.5	6.8	13.2
69-70 —Cincinnati	7	34	1	3	.333	3	3	1.000	5	10	11	0	5	0.7	1.4	0.7
Totals	924	...	6168	16468	.375	4624	5756	.803	4786	6955	2242	20	16960	5.2	7.5	18.4

NBA PLAYOFF RECORD

NOTES: Shares NBA Finals single-game record for most assists in one quarter—8 (April 9, 1957, vs. St. Louis). ... Holds single-game playoff records for most free throws made—30; and most free throws attempted—32 (March 21, 1953, vs. Syracuse).

Season Team	G	Min.	FGM	FGA	Pct.	FTM	FTA	Pct.	Reb.	Ast.	PF	Dq.	Pts.	RPG	APG	PPG
50-51 —Boston	2	...	9	42	.214	10	12	.833	15	12	8	...	28	7.5	6.0	14.0
51-52 —Boston	3	138	26	65	.400	41	44	.932	12	19	13	1	93	4.0	6.3	31.0
52-53 —Boston	6	270	46	120	.383	61	73	.836	25	37	21	0	153	4.2	6.2	25.5
53-54 —Boston	6	259	33	116	.284	60	75	.800	32	38	20	0	126	5.3	6.3	21.0
54-55 —Boston	7	299	53	139	.381	46	48	.958	43	65	26	0	152	6.1	9.3	21.7
55-56 —Boston	3	124	28	56	.500	23	25	.920	24	26	4	0	79	8.0	8.7	26.3
56-57 —Boston	10	440	67	207	.324	68	91	.747	61	93	27	0	202	6.1	9.3	20.2
57-58 —Boston	11	457	67	196	.342	64	75	.853	71	82	20	0	198	6.5	7.5	18.0
58-59 —Boston	11	460	72	221	.326	70	94	.745	76	119	28	0	214	6.9	10.8	19.5
59-60 —Boston	13	468	80	262	.305	39	51	.765	48	116	27	0	199	3.7	8.9	15.3
60-61 —Boston	10	337	50	147	.340	67	88	.761	43	91	33	1	167	4.3	9.1	16.7
61-62 —Boston	14	474	86	241	.357	52	76	.684	64	123	43	0	224	4.6	8.8	16.0
62-63 —Boston	13	393	72	204	.353	39	47	.830	32	116	44	2	183	2.5	8.9	14.1
Totals	109	...	689	2016	.342	640	799	.801	546	937	314	...	2018	5.0	8.6	18.5

NBA ALL-STAR GAME RECORD

NOTES: NBA All-Star Game Most Valuable Player (1954, 1957).

Season Team	Min.	FGM	FGA	Pct.	FTM	FTA	Pct.	Reb	Ast.	PF	Dq.	Pts.
1951 —Boston	...	2	12	.167	4	5	.800	9	8	3	0	8
1952 —Boston	33	4	14	.286	1	2	.500	4	13	3	0	9
1953 —Boston	36	4	11	.364	7	7	1.000	5	3	1	0	15
1954 —Boston	34	6	15	.400	8	8	1.000	11	4	1	0	20
1955 —Boston	35	7	14	.500	6	7	.857	9	5	1	0	20

Season	Team	Min.	FGM	FGA	Pct.	FTM	FTA	Pct.	Reb	Ast.	PF	Dq.	Pts.
1956	—Boston	24	2	8	.250	3	4	.750	7	2	6	1	7
1957	—Boston	28	4	14	.286	2	2	1.000	5	7	0	0	10
1958	—Boston	31	8	20	.400	4	6	.667	5	10	0	0	20
1959	—Boston	32	4	8	.500	5	6	.833	5	4	0	0	13
1960	—Boston	26	1	7	.143	0	0	...	5	8	2	0	2
1961	—Boston	33	2	11	.182	0	0	...	3	8	6	1	4
1962	—Boston	31	4	13	.308	3	4	.750	6	8	2	0	11
1963	—Boston	25	4	11	.364	0	0	...	4	6	2	0	8
	Totals	...	52	158	.329	43	51	.843	78	86	27	2	147

COLLEGIATE COACHING RECORD

Season	Team	W	L	Pct.
63-64	—Boston College	10	11	.476
64-65	—Boston College	22	7	.759
65-66	—Boston College	21	5	.808
66-67	—Boston College	23	3	.885
67-68	—Boston College	17	8	.680
68-69	—Boston College	24	4	.857
	Totals (6 years)	117	38	.755

NBA COACHING RECORD

Season	Team	REGULAR SEASON				PLAYOFFS		
		W	L	Pct.	Finish	W	L	Pct.
69-70	—Cincinnati	36	46	.439	5th/Eastern Division	—	—	—
70-71	—Cincinnati	33	49	.402	3rd/Central Division	—	—	—
71-72	—Cincinnati	30	52	.366	3rd/Central Division	—	—	—
72-73	—Kansas City/Omaha	36	46	.439	4th/Midwest Division	—	—	—
73-74	—Kansas City/Omaha	6	16	.273		—	—	—
	Totals (5 years)	141	209	.403		—	—	—

NOTES:
1965—Lost to St. John's, 114-92, in NIT first round.
1966—Defeated Louisville, 96-90 (3 OT), in NIT first round; lost to Villanova, 86-85, in quarterfinals.
1967—Defeated Connecticut, 48-42, in NCAA Tournament first round; defeated St. John's, 63-62, in regional semifinal; lost to North Carolina, 96-80, in regional final.
1968—Lost to St. Bonaventure, 102-93, in NCAA Tournament first round.
1969—Defeated Kansas, 78-62, in NIT first round; defeated Louisville, 88-83, in quarterfinals; defeated Army, 73-61, in semifinals; lost to Temple 89-76, in championship game.
1973—Replaced as Kansas City/Omaha head coach by Draff Young (November).

COWENS, DAVE   C

See Head Coaches, page 282.

CUNNINGHAM, BILLY   F

See All-Time Great Coaches, page 406.

DANIELS, MEL   C

PERSONAL: Born July 20, 1944, in Detroit. ... 6-9/225. ... Full name: Melvin Joe Daniels.
HIGH SCHOOL: Pershing (Detroit).
JUNIOR COLLEGE: Burlington (Iowa) Junior College.
COLLEGE: New Mexico.
TRANSACTIONS/CAREER NOTES: Selected by Minnesota Muskies in first round of 1967 ABA draft. ... Traded by Muskies to Indiana Pacers for 1969 first-round draft choice, G James Dawson, F Ron Kozlicki and cash (May 1968). ... Traded by Pacers with G Freddie Lewis to Memphis Sounds for F Charlie Edge and cash (July 26, 1974). ... Memphis franchise transferred to Baltimore and renamed Claws for 1975-76 season. ... Baltimore franchise folded prior to 1975-76 season. ... Signed as free agent by New York Nets of NBA (October 19, 1976). ... Waived by Nets (December 13, 1976).

COLLEGIATE RECORD

Season Team	G	Min.	FGM	FGA	Pct.	FTM	FTA	Pct.	Reb.	Ast.	Pts.	RPG	APG	PPG
												AVERAGES		
63-64—Burlington County J.C.	34	...	334	...	...	100	...	...	...	...	768	...	...	22.6
64-65—New Mexico	27	...	178	366	.486	111	182	.610	302	...	467	11.2	...	17.3
65-66—New Mexico	23	...	191	394	.485	107	145	.738	238	...	489	10.3	...	21.3
66-67—New Mexico	27	...	225	468	.481	131	191	.686	313	...	581	11.6	...	21.5
Totals	111	...	928	...	...	449	...	...	...	...	2305	...	...	20.8

ABA REGULAR-SEASON RECORD

NOTES: ABA Most Valuable Player (1969, 1971). ... ABA Rookie of the Year (1968). ... All-ABA first team (1968, 1969, 1970, 1971). ... All-ABA second team (1973). ... ABA All-Rookie team (1968). ... Member of ABA championship teams (1970, 1972, 1973).

Season Team	G	Min.	2-POINT			3-POINT			FTM	FTA	Pct.	Reb.	Ast.	Pts.	AVERAGES		
			FGM	FGA	Pct.	FGM	FGA	Pct.							RPG	APG	PPG
67-68—Minnesota	78	2938	669	1640	.408	1	5	.200	390	678	.575	1213	109	1729	*15.6	1.4	22.2
68-69—Indiana	76	2934	712	1496	.476	0	4	.000	400	662	.604	1256	116	1824	*16.5	1.5	24.0

Season Team	G	Min.	2-POINT			3-POINT			FTM	FTA	Pct.	Reb.	Ast.	Pts.	AVERAGES		
			FGM	FGA	Pct.	FGM	FGA	Pct.							RPG	APG	PPG
69-70—Indiana	83	3039	613	1295	.473	0	2	.000	330	489	.675	1462	131	1556	17.6	1.6	18.7
70-71—Indiana	82	3170	698	1357	.514	1	13	.077	326	480	.679	1475	178	1723	*18.0	2.2	21.0
71-72—Indiana	79	2971	598	1184	.505	0	6	.000	317	451	.703	1297	176	1513	16.4	2.2	19.2
72-73—Indiana	81	3103	587	1217	.482	1	4	.250	322	446	.722	1247	177	1497	15.4	2.2	18.5
73-74—Indiana	78	2539	492	1117	.440	0	0	...	217	287	.756	906	120	1201	11.6	1.5	15.4
74-75—Memphis	71	1646	290	644	.450	0	0	...	116	183	.634	638	125	696	9.0	1.8	9.8
Totals	628	22340	4659	9950	.468	3	34	.088	2418	3676	.658	9494	1132	11739	15.1	1.8	18.7

ABA PLAYOFF RECORD

Season Team	G	Min.	2-POINT			3-POINT			FTM	FTA	Pct.	Reb.	Ast.	Pts.	AVERAGES		
			FGM	FGA	Pct.	FGM	FGA	Pct.							RPG	APG	PPG
67-68—Minnesota	10	409	98	226	.434	0	0	...	54	94	.574	161	19	253	16.1	1.9	25.3
68-69—Indiana	17	570	127	300	.423	0	1	.000	79	130	.608	237	22	333	13.9	1.3	19.6
69-70—Indiana	15	533	108	242	.446	0	1	.000	74	111	.667	265	15	290	17.7	1.0	19.3
70-71—Indiana	11	457	94	194	.485	0	0	...	47	63	.746	211	16	235	19.2	1.5	21.4
71-72—Indiana	20	744	121	249	.486	0	3	.000	64	85	.753	302	28	306	15.1	1.4	15.3
72-73—Indiana	18	636	112	238	.471	0	0	...	62	81	.765	248	40	286	13.8	2.2	15.9
73-74—Indiana	14	498	69	172	.401	0	0	...	33	43	.767	160	27	171	11.4	1.9	12.2
74-75—Indiana	4	54	11	22	.500	0	0	...	5	9	.556	24	1	27	6.0	0.3	6.8
Totals	109	3901	740	1643	.450	0	5	.000	418	616	.679	1608	168	1901	14.8	1.5	17.4

ABA ALL-STAR GAME RECORD

NOTES: ABA All-Star Game Most Valuable Player (1971).

Season Team	Min.	2-POINT			3-POINT			FTM	FTA	Pct.	Reb.	Ast.	Pts.
		FGM	FGA	Pct.	FGM	FGA	Pct.						
1968—Minnesota	29	9	18	.500	0	0	...	4	11	.364	15	0	22
1969—Indiana	31	5	16	.313	0	0	...	7	10	.700	10	2	17
1970—Indiana	26	6	14	.429	0	0	...	1	3	.333	12	1	13
1971—Indiana	30	12	19	.632	0	0	...	5	7	.714	13	3	29
1972—Indiana	26	8	14	.571	0	0	...	5	8	.625	9	1	21
1973—Indiana	33	8	19	.421	0	0	...	9	12	.750	11	1	25
1974—Indiana	20	2	11	.182	0	0	...	1	2	.500	7	0	5
Totals	195	50	111	.450	0	0	...	32	53	.604	77	8	132

NBA REGULAR-SEASON RECORD

Season Team	G	Min.	FGM	FGA	Pct.	FTM	FTA	Pct.	REBOUNDS			Ast.	St.	Blk.	TO	Pts.	AVERAGES		
									Off.	Def.	Tot.						RPG	APG	PPG
76-77—N.Y. Nets	11	126	13	35	.371	13	23	.565	10	24	34	6	3	11		39	3.1	0.5	3.5

Personal fouls/disqualifications: 1976-77, 29/0.

COMBINED ABA AND NBA REGULAR-SEASON RECORDS

	G	Min.	FGM	FGA	Pct.	FTM	FTA	Pct.	REBOUNDS			Ast.	Stl.	Blk.	TO	Pts.	AVERAGES		
									Off.	Def.	Tot.						RPG	APG	PPG
Totals	639	22466	4675	10019	.467	2431	3699	.657	...	...	9528	1138	...	...	...	11778	14.9	1.8	18.4

Three-point field goals: 3-for-34 (.088).
Personal fouls/disqualifications: 2309.

HEAD COACHING RECORD

BACKGROUND: Assistant coach, Indiana State (1978-79 through 1981-82). ... Assistant coach, Indiana Pacers (1984-85 through 1988-89 and 1991-92 and 1992-93). ... Scout, Pacers (1984-85 to 1995-96). ... Director of player personnel (1996 to present).
HONORS: USBL Coach of the Year (1993).

NBA COACHING RECORD

Season Team	REGULAR SEASON				PLAYOFFS		
	W	L	Pct.	Finish	W	L	Pct.
88-89 —Indiana	0	2	.000	—	—	—	—

NOTES:
1988—Replaced Jack Ramsay as Indiana head coach (November 17), with record of 0-7 and club in sixth place. Replaced as Indiana interim coach by George Irvine (November 21).

DANTLEY, ADRIAN   F/G

PERSONAL: Born February 28, 1956, in Washington, D.C. ... 6-5/210. ... Full name: Adrian Delano Dantley.
HIGH SCHOOL: DeMatha Catholic (Hyattsville, Md.).
COLLEGE: Notre Dame.
TRANSACTIONS/CAREER NOTES: Selected after junior season by Buffalo Braves in first round (sixth pick overall) of 1976 NBA Draft. ... Traded by Braves with F Mike Bantom to Indiana Pacers for G/F Billy Knight (September 1, 1977). ... Traded by Pacers with C/F Dave Robisch to Los Angeles Lakers for C James Edwards, G Earl Tatum and cash (December 13, 1977). ... Traded by Lakers to Utah Jazz for F Spencer Haywood (September 13, 1979). ... Traded by Jazz with 1987 and 1990 second-round draft choices to Detroit Pistons for F Kelly Tripucka and F/C Kent Benson (August 21, 1986). ... Traded by Pistons with 1991 first-round draft choice to Dallas Mavericks for F Mark Aguirre (February 15, 1989). ... Waived by Mavericks (April 2, 1990). ... Signed as free agent by Milwaukee Bucks (April 2, 1991). ... Played in Italy (1991-92).
MISCELLANEOUS: Member of gold-medal-winning U.S. Olympic team (1976).

COLLEGIATE RECORD

NOTES: THE SPORTING NEWS All-America first team (1975, 1976).

Season Team	G	Min.	FGM	FGA	Pct.	FTM	FTA	Pct.	Reb.	Ast.	Pts.	RPG	APG	PPG
73-74—Notre Dame	28	795	189	339	.558	133	161	.826	255	40	511	9.1	1.4	18.3
74-75—Notre Dame	29	1091	315	581	.542	253	314	.806	296	47	883	10.2	1.6	30.4
75-76—Notre Dame	29	1056	300	510	.588	229	294	.779	292	49	829	10.1	1.7	28.6
Totals	86	2942	804	1430	.562	615	769	.800	843	136	2223	9.8	1.6	25.8

NBA REGULAR-SEASON RECORD

RECORDS: Shares single-game records for most free throws made—28 (January 4, 1984, vs. Houston); and most free throws made in one quarter—14 (December 10, 1986, vs. Sacramento).

HONORS: NBA Rookie of the Year (1977). ... All-NBA second team (1981, 1984). ... NBA All-Rookie team (1977). ... NBA Comeback Player of the Year (1984).

Season Team	G	Min.	FGM	FGA	Pct.	FTM	FTA	Pct.	REBOUNDS Off.	Def.	Tot.	Ast.	St.	Blk.	TO	Pts.	AVERAGES RPG	APG	PPG
76-77—Buffalo	77	2816	544	1046	.520	476	582	.818	251	336	587	144	91	15	...	1564	7.6	1.9	20.3
77-78—Ind.-L.A.	79	2933	578	1128	.512	*541	680	.796	265	355	620	253	118	24	228	1697	7.8	3.2	21.5
78-79—Los Angeles	60	1775	374	733	.510	292	342	.854	131	211	342	138	63	12	155	1040	5.7	2.3	17.3
79-80—Utah	68	2674	730	1267	.576	443	526	.842	183	333	516	191	96	14	233	1903	7.6	2.8	28.0
80-81—Utah	80	*3417	*909	1627	.559	*632	784	.806	192	317	509	322	109	18	282	*2452	6.4	4.0	*30.7
81-82—Utah	81	3222	904	1586	.570	*648	818	.792	231	283	514	324	95	14	†299	2457	6.3	4.0	30.3
82-83—Utah	22	887	233	402	.580	210	248	.847	58	82	140	105	20	0	81	676	6.4	4.8	30.7
83-84—Utah	79	2984	802	1438	.558	*813	*946	.859	179	269	448	310	61	4	263	*2418	5.7	3.9	*30.6
84-85—Utah	55	1971	512	964	.531	438	545	.804	148	175	323	186	57	8	171	1462	5.9	3.4	26.6
85-86—Utah	76	2744	818	1453	.563	*630	796	.791	178	217	395	264	64	4	231	2267	5.2	3.5	29.8
86-87—Detroit	81	2736	601	1126	.534	539	664	.812	104	228	332	162	63	7	181	1742	4.1	2.0	21.5
87-88—Detroit	69	2144	444	863	.514	492	572	.860	84	143	227	171	39	10	135	1380	3.3	2.5	20.0
88-89—Detroit-Dal.	73	2422	470	954	.493	460	568	.810	117	200	317	171	43	13	163	1400	4.3	2.3	19.2
89-90—Dallas	45	1300	231	484	.477	200	254	.787	78	94	172	80	20	7	75	662	3.8	1.8	14.7
90-91—Milwaukee	10	126	19	50	.380	18	26	.692	8	5	13	9	5	0	6	57	1.3	0.9	5.7
Totals	955	34151	8169	15121	.540	6832	8351	.818	2207	3248	5455	2830	944	150	2503	23177	5.7	3.0	24.3

Three-point field goals: 1979-80, 0-for-2. 1980-81, 2-for-7 (.286). 1981-82, 1-for-3 (.333). 1983-84, 1-for-4 (.250). 1985-86, 1-for-11 (.091). 1986-87, 1-for-6 (.167). 1987-88, 0-for-2. 1988-89, 0-for-1. 1989-90, 0-for-2. 1990-91, 1-for-3 (.333). Totals, 7-for-41 (.171).

Personal fouls/disqualifications: 1976-77, 215/2. 1977-78, 233/2. 1978-79, 162/0. 1979-80, 211/2. 1980-81, 245/1. 1981-82, 252/1. 1982-83, 62/2. 1983-84, 201/0. 1984-85, 133/0. 1985-86, 206/2. 1986-87, 193/1. 1987-88, 144/0. 1988-89, 186/1. 1989-90, 99/0. 1990-91, 8/0. Totals, 2550/14.

NBA PLAYOFF RECORD

Season Team	G	Min.	FGM	FGA	Pct.	FTM	FTA	Pct.	REBOUNDS Off.	Def.	Tot.	Ast.	St.	Blk.	TO	Pts.	AVERAGES RPG	APG	PPG
77-78—Los Angeles	3	104	20	35	.571	11	17	.647	9	16	25	11	5	3	6	51	8.3	3.7	17.0
78-79—Los Angeles	8	236	50	89	.562	41	52	.788	10	23	33	11	6	1	19	141	4.1	1.4	17.6
83-84—Utah	11	454	117	232	.504	120	139	.863	37	46	83	46	10	1	38	354	7.5	4.2	32.2
84-85—Utah	10	398	79	151	.523	95	122	.779	25	50	75	20	16	0	36	253	7.5	2.0	25.3
85-86—Utah							Did not play—injured.												
86-87—Detroit	15	500	111	206	.539	86	111	.775	29	39	68	35	13	0	33	308	4.5	2.3	20.5
87-88—Detroit	23	804	153	292	.524	140	178	.787	37	70	107	46	19	1	51	446	4.7	2.0	19.4
90-91—Milwaukee	3	19	1	7	.143	3	4	.750	2	2	4	0	0	0	2	5	1.3	0.0	1.7
Totals	73	2515	531	1012	.525	496	623	.796	149	246	395	169	69	6	185	1558	5.4	2.3	21.3

Three-point field goals: 1984-85, 0-for-1. 1987-88, 0-for-2. Totals, 0-for-3.

Personal fouls/disqualifications: 1977-78, 9/0. 1978-79, 24/0. 1983-84, 30/0. 1984-85, 39/1. 1986-87, 36/0. 1987-88, 50/0. Totals, 188/1.

NBA ALL-STAR GAME RECORD

Season Team	Min.	FGM	FGA	Pct.	FTM	FTA	Pct.	REBOUNDS Off.	Def.	Tot.	Ast.	PF	Dq.	St.	Blk.	TO	Pts.
1980 —Utah	30	8	15	.533	7	8	.875	4	1	5	2	1	0	2	0	2	23
1981 —Utah	21	3	9	.333	2	2	1.000	2	3	5	0	1	0	1	0	0	8
1982 —Utah	21	6	8	.750	0	1	.000	1	1	2	0	2	0	0	0	1	12
1984 —Utah	18	1	8	.125	0	0	...	0	2	2	1	4	0	1	0	1	2
1985 —Utah	23	2	6	.333	6	6	1.000	0	2	2	1	4	0	1	0	2	10
1986 —Utah	17	3	8	.375	2	2	1.000	1	6	7	3	1	0	1	0	0	8
Totals	130	23	54	.426	17	19	.895	8	15	23	7	13	0	6	0	6	63

ITALIAN LEAGUE RECORD

Season Team	G	Min.	FGM	FGA	Pct.	FTM	FTA	Pct.	Reb.	Ast.	Pts.	RPG	APG	PPG
91-92—Breeze Milan	27	906	253	427	.593	179	221	.810	152	10	721	5.6	0.4	26.7

DAVIES, BOB   G

PERSONAL: Born January 15, 1920, in Harrisburg, Pa. ... Died April 22, 1990. ... 6-1/175. ... Full name: Robert Edris Davies. ... Nickname: The Harrisburg Houdini.

HIGH SCHOOL: John Harris (Harrisburg, Pa.).

COLLEGE: Franklin & Marshall (Pa.), then Seton Hall.

TRANSACTIONS/CAREER NOTES: Played with Great Lakes (Ill.) Naval Training Station during 1942-43 season (led team in scoring—269 points, 114 field goals and 41 free throws). ... In military service during 1942-43, 1943-44 and 1944-45 seasons. ... Played in American Basketball League with Brooklyn Indians (1943-44) and New York Gothams (1944-45). ... Signed as free agent by Rochester Royals of National Basketball League (1945). ... Royals franchise transferred to Basketball Association of America for 1948-49 season.

CAREER HONORS: Elected to Naismith Memorial Basketball Hall of Fame (1969). ... NBA 25th Anniversary All-Time Team (1970).

MISCELLANEOUS: Member of NBA championship team (1951). ... Member of NBL championship team (1946).

ALL-TIME GREAT PLAYERS

COLLEGIATE RECORD

Season Team	G	Min.	FGM	FGA	Pct.	FTM	FTA	Pct.	Reb.	Ast.	Pts.	AVERAGES RPG	APG	PPG
37-38—Frank. & Marsh.‡					Freshman team statistics unavailable.									
38-39—Seton Hall‡					Freshman team statistics unavailable.									
39-40—Seton Hall...	18	...	78	...	...	56	...	...	...	...	212	...	...	11.8
40-41—Seton Hall...	22	...	91	...	...	42	...	...	...	...	224	...	...	10.2
41-42—Seton Hall...	19	...	81	...	...	63	...	...	...	...	225	...	...	11.8
Varsity totals	59	...	250	...	...	161	...	...	...	...	661	...	...	11.2

ABL REGULAR-SEASON RECORD

Season Team	G	Min.	FGM	FGA	Pct.	FTM	FTA	Pct.	Reb.	Ast.	Pts.	AVERAGES RPG	APG	PPG
43-44—Brooklyn...	4	...	8	...	...	8	...	...	...	...	24	...	...	6.0
44-45—New York...	5	...	21	...	...	21	...	...	...	...	63	...	...	12.6
Totals	9	...	29	...	...	29	...	...	...	...	87	...	...	9.7

NBL AND NBA REGULAR-SEASON RECORD

HONORS: All-NBA first team (1950, 1951, 1952). ... All-NBA second team (1953). ... All-BAA first team (1949). ... NBL Most Valuable Player (1947). ... All-NBL first team (1947). ... All-NBL second team (1948).

Season Team	G	Min.	FGM	FGA	Pct.	FTM	FTA	Pct.	Reb.	Ast.	PF	Dq.	Pts.	AVERAGES RPG	APG	PPG
45-46—Roc. (NBL)	27	...	86	...	...	70	103	.680	...	...	85	...	242	...	...	9.0
46-47—Roc. (NBL)	32	...	166	...	...	130	166	.783	...	...	90	...	462	...	...	14.4
47-48—Roc. (NBL)	48	...	176	...	...	120	160	.750	...	...	111	...	472	...	...	9.8
48-49—Rochester (BAA)	60	...	317	871	.364	270	348	.776	...	*321	197	...	904	...	*5.4	15.1
49-50—Rochester	64	...	317	887	.357	261	347	.752	...	294	187	...	895	...	4.6	14.0
50-51—Rochester	63	...	326	877	.372	303	381	.795	197	287	208	7	955	3.1	4.6	15.2
51-52—Rochester	65	2394	379	990	.383	294	379	.776	189	390	269	10	1052	2.9	6.0	16.2
52-53—Rochester	66	2216	339	880	.385	351	466	.753	195	280	261	7	1029	3.0	4.2	15.6
53-54—Rochester	72	2137	288	777	.371	311	433	.718	194	323	224	4	887	2.7	4.5	12.3
54-55—Rochester	72	1870	326	785	.415	220	293	.751	205	355	220	2	872	2.8	4.9	12.1
Totals.........	569	...	2720	...	...	2330	3076	.757	...	...	1852	...	7770	...	...	13.7

NBL AND NBA PLAYOFF RECORD

Season Team	G	Min.	FGM	FGA	Pct.	FTM	FTA	Pct.	Reb.	Ast.	PF	Dq.	Pts.	AVERAGES RPG	APG	PPG
45-46—Roc. (NBL)	7	...	28	...	...	30	41	.732	...	...	17	...	86	...	...	12.3
46-47—Roc. (NBL)	11	...	54	...	...	43	63	.683	...	...	30	...	151	...	...	13.7
47-48—Roc. (NBL)	11	...	56	...	...	49	64	.766	...	...	24	...	161	...	...	14.6
48-49—Rochester (BAA)	4	...	19	51	.373	10	13	.769	...	13	11	...	48	...	3.3	12.0
49-50—Rochester	2	...	4	17	.235	7	8	.875	...	9	11	...	15	...	4.5	7.5
50-51—Rochester	14	...	79	234	.338	64	80	.800	43	75	45	1	222	3.1	5.4	15.9
51-52—Rochester	6	233	37	92	.402	45	55	.818	13	28	18	0	119	2.2	4.7	19.8
52-53—Rochester	3	91	6	29	.207	14	20	.700	4	14	11	0	26	1.3	4.7	8.7
53-54—Rochester	6	172	17	52	.327	17	23	.739	12	14	16	0	51	2.0	2.3	8.5
54-55—Rochester	3	75	11	33	.333	3	4	.750	6	9	11	0	25	2.0	3.0	8.3
Totals.........	67	...	311	...	...	282	371	.760	...	...	194	...	904	...	...	13.5

NBA ALL-STAR GAME RECORD

Season Team	Min.	FGM	FGA	Pct.	FTM	FTA	Pct.	Reb	Ast.	PF	Dq.	Pts.
1951 —Rochester...	...	4	6	.667	5	5	1.000	5	5	3	0	13
1952 —Rochester...	27	4	11	.364	0	0	...	0	5	4	0	8
1953 —Rochester...	17	3	7	.429	3	6	.500	3	2	2	0	9
1954 —Rochester...	31	8	16	.500	2	3	.667	5	5	4	0	18
Totals	...	19	40	.475	10	14	.714	13	17	13	0	48

COLLEGIATE COACHING RECORD

Season Team	W	L	Pct.
46-47 —Seton Hall...	24	3	.889
55-56 —Gettysburg...	11	17	.393
56-57 —Gettysburg...	7	18	.280
Totals (3 years).........	42	38	.525

DAVIS, WALTER   G

PERSONAL: Born September 9, 1954, in Pineville, N.C. ... 6-6/200. ... Full name: Walter Paul Davis. ... Uncle of Hubert Davis, guard with Toronto Raptors.

HIGH SCHOOL: South Mecklenburg (Charlotte).

COLLEGE: North Carolina.

TRANSACTIONS/CAREER NOTES: Selected by Phoenix Suns in first round (fifth pick overall) of 1977 NBA Draft. ... Signed as unrestricted free agent by Denver Nuggets (July 6, 1988). ... Traded by Nuggets to Portland Trail Blazers in three-way deal in which Trail Blazers sent G Drazen Petrovic to New Jersey Nets, Nets sent F Greg Anderson to Nuggets, and Nuggets sent F Terry Mills to Nets (January 23, 1991); Nuggets also received 1992 first-round draft choice from Nets and 1993 second-round draft choice from Trail Blazers and Trail Blazers also received 1992 second-round draft choice from Nuggets. ... Waived by Trail Blazers (October 29, 1991). ... Signed as free agent by Nuggets (November 1, 1991).

MISCELLANEOUS: Member of gold-medal-winning U.S. Olympic team (1976). ... Phoenix Suns all-time leading scorer with 15,666 points (1977-78 through 1987-88).

COLLEGIATE RECORD

Season Team	G	Min.	FGM	FGA	Pct.	FTM	FTA	Pct.	Reb.	Ast.	Pts.	AVERAGES		
												RPG	APG	PPG
73-74—North Carolina	27	...	161	322	.500	65	82	.793	126	72	387	4.7	2.7	14.3
74-75—North Carolina	31	...	200	396	.505	98	130	.754	195	137	498	6.3	4.4	16.1
75-76—North Carolina	29	...	190	351	.541	101	130	.777	166	96	481	5.7	3.3	16.6
76-77—North Carolina	32	...	203	351	.578	91	117	.778	183	104	497	5.7	3.3	15.5
Totals	119	...	754	1420	.531	355	459	.773	670	409	1863	5.6	3.4	15.7

NBA REGULAR-SEASON RECORD

HONORS: NBA Rookie of the Year (1978). ... All-NBA second team (1978, 1979). ... NBA All-Rookie team (1978).

Season Team	G	Min.	FGM	FGA	Pct.	FTM	FTA	Pct.	REBOUNDS			Ast.	St.	Blk.	TO	Pts.	AVERAGES		
									Off.	Def.	Tot.						RPG	APG	PPG
77-78—Phoenix	81	2590	786	1494	.526	387	466	.830	158	326	484	273	113	20	283	1959	6.0	3.4	24.2
78-79—Phoenix	79	2437	764	1362	.561	340	409	.831	111	262	373	339	147	26	293	1868	4.7	4.3	23.6
79-80—Phoenix	75	2309	657	1166	.563	299	365	.819	75	197	272	337	114	19	242	1613	3.6	4.5	21.5
80-81—Phoenix	78	2182	593	1101	.539	209	250	.836	63	137	200	302	97	12	222	1402	2.6	3.9	18.0
81-82—Phoenix	55	1182	350	669	.523	91	111	.820	21	82	103	162	46	3	112	794	1.9	2.9	14.4
82-83—Phoenix	80	2491	665	1289	.516	184	225	.818	63	134	197	397	117	12	188	1521	2.5	5.0	19.0
83-84—Phoenix	78	2546	652	1274	.512	233	270	.863	38	164	202	429	107	12	213	1557	2.6	5.5	20.0
84-85—Phoenix	23	570	139	309	.450	64	73	.877	6	29	35	98	18	0	50	345	1.5	4.3	15.0
85-86—Phoenix	70	2239	624	1287	.485	257	305	.843	54	149	203	361	99	3	219	1523	2.9	5.2	21.8
86-87—Phoenix	79	2646	779	1515	.514	288	334	.862	90	154	244	364	96	5	226	1867	3.1	4.6	23.6
87-88—Phoenix	68	1951	488	1031	.473	205	231	.887	32	127	159	278	86	3	126	1217	2.3	4.1	17.9
88-89—Denver	81	1857	536	1076	.498	175	199	.879	41	110	151	190	72	5	132	1267	1.9	2.3	15.6
89-90—Denver	69	1635	497	1033	.481	207	227	.912	46	133	179	155	59	9	102	1207	2.6	2.2	17.5
90-91—Den.-Port.	71	1483	403	862	.468	107	117	.915	71	110	181	125	80	3	88	924	2.5	1.8	13.0
91-92—Denver	46	741	185	403	.459	82	94	.872	20	50	70	68	29	1	45	457	1.5	1.5	9.9
Totals	1033	28859	8118	15871	.511	3128	3676	.851	889	2164	3053	3878	1280	133	2541	19521	3.0	3.8	18.9

Three-point field goals: 1979-80, 0-for-4. 1980-81, 7-for-17 (.412). 1981-82, 3-for-16 (.188). 1982-83, 7-for-23 (.304). 1983-84, 20-for-87 (.230). 1984-85, 3-for-10 (.300). 1985-86, 18-for-76 (.237). 1986-87, 21-for-81 (.259). 1987-88, 36-for-96 (.375). 1988-89, 20-for-69 (.290). 1989-90, 6-for-46 (.130). 1990-91, 11-for-36 (.306). 1991-92, 5-for-16 (.313). Totals, 157-for-577 (.272).

Personal fouls/disqualifications: 1977-78, 242/2. 1978-79, 250/5. 1979-80, 202/2. 1980-81, 192/3. 1981-82, 104/1. 1982-83, 186/2. 1983-84, 202/0. 1984-85, 42/0. 1985-86, 153/1. 1986-87, 184/1. 1987-88, 131/0. 1988-89, 187/1. 1989-90, 160/1. 1990-91, 150/2. 1991-92, 69/0. Totals, 2454/21.

NBA PLAYOFF RECORD

Season Team	G	Min.	FGM	FGA	Pct.	FTM	FTA	Pct.	REBOUNDS			Ast.	St.	Blk.	TO	Pts.	AVERAGES		
									Off.	Def.	Tot.						RPG	APG	PPG
77-78—Phoenix	2	66	19	40	.475	12	16	.750	4	13	17	8	3	0	6	50	8.5	4.0	25.0
78-79—Phoenix	15	490	127	244	.521	78	96	.813	24	45	69	79	26	5	66	332	4.6	5.3	22.1
79-80—Phoenix	8	245	69	137	.504	28	38	.737	9	14	23	35	4	1	20	166	2.9	4.4	20.8
80-81—Phoenix	7	199	51	106	.481	10	17	.588	7	12	19	22	7	1	17	112	2.7	3.1	16.0
81-82—Phoenix	7	173	52	116	.448	22	24	.917	5	17	22	30	5	1	12	127	3.1	4.3	18.1
82-83—Phoenix	3	113	30	69	.435	17	21	.810	5	10	15	13	6	5	5	78	5.0	4.3	26.0
83-84—Phoenix	17	623	175	327	.535	70	78	.897	15	31	46	109	29	3	43	423	2.7	6.4	24.9
88-89—Denver	3	94	31	60	.517	15	15	1.000	2	3	5	4	3	0	8	77	1.7	1.3	25.7
89-90—Denver	3	70	18	45	.400	6	6	1.000	4	5	9	6	1	0	5	42	3.0	2.0	14.0
90-91—Portland	13	111	19	48	.396	5	6	.833	7	8	15	6	4	0	7	43	1.2	0.5	3.3
Totals	78	2184	591	1192	.496	263	317	.830	82	158	240	312	88	16	189	1450	3.1	4.0	18.6

Three-point field goals: 1979-80, 0-for-3. 1980-81, 0-for-1. 1981-82, 1-for-3 (.333). 1982-83, 1-for-2 (.500). 1983-84, 3-for-11 (.273). 1988-89, 0-for-4. 1989-90, 0-for-1. 1990-91, 0-for-1. Totals, 5-for-26 (.192).

Personal fouls/disqualifications: 1977-78, 8/0. 1978-79, 41/0. 1979-80, 20/0. 1980-81, 17/0. 1981-82, 19/0. 1982-83, 6/0. 1983-84, 55/0. 1988-89, 11/0. 1989-90, 4/0. 1990-91, 5/0. Totals, 186/0.

NBA ALL-STAR GAME RECORD

Season Team	Min.	FGM	FGA	Pct.	FTM	FTA	Pct.	REBOUNDS			Ast.	PF	Dq.	St.	Blk.	TO	Pts.
								Off.	Def.	Tot.							
1978 —Phoenix	15	3	6	.500	4	4	1.000	0	1	1	6	1	0	1	0	0	10
1979 —Phoenix	19	4	9	.444	0	0	...	1	3	4	4	0	0	1	0	2	8
1980 —Phoenix	23	5	10	.500	2	2	1.000	2	2	4	2	2	0	4	0	3	12
1981 —Phoenix	22	5	9	.556	2	2	1.000	1	6	7	1	2	0	0	0	1	12
1984 —Phoenix	15	5	9	.556	0	0	...	0	2	2	1	0	0	1	0	0	10
1987 —Phoenix	15	3	12	.250	0	0	...	2	0	2	1	0	0	0	0	1	7
Totals	109	25	55	.455	8	8	1.000	6	14	20	15	5	0	7	0	6	59

Three-point field goals: 1987, 1-for-1.

DeBUSSCHERE, DAVE   F

PERSONAL: Born October 16, 1940, in Detroit. ... 6-6/235. ... Full name: David Albert DeBusschere.
HIGH SCHOOL: Austin Catholic (Detroit).
COLLEGE: Detroit.
TRANSACTIONS/CAREER NOTES: Selected by Detroit Pistons in 1962 NBA Draft (territorial pick). ... Traded by Pistons to New York Knicks for C Walt Bellamy and G Howard Komives (December 19, 1968).
CAREER HONORS: Elected to Naismith Memorial Basketball Hall of Fame (1982).
MISCELLANEOUS: Member of NBA championship teams (1970, 1973).

COLLEGIATE RECORD

Season Team	G	Min.	FGM	FGA	Pct.	FTM	FTA	Pct.	Reb.	Ast.	Pts.	AVERAGES		
												RPG	APG	PPG
58-59—Detroit‡	15	...	144	306	.471	68	101	.673	305	...	356	20.3	...	23.7
59-60—Detroit	27	...	288	665	.433	115	196	.587	540	...	691	20.0	...	25.6
60-61—Detroit	27	...	256	636	.403	86	155	.555	514	...	598	19.0	...	22.1
61-62—Detroit	26	...	267	616	.433	162	242	.669	498	...	696	19.2	...	26.8
Varsity totals	80	...	811	1917	.423	363	593	.612	1552	...	1985	19.4	...	24.8

NBA REGULAR-SEASON RECORD

HONORS: All-NBA second team (1969). ... NBA All-Defensive first team (1969, 1970, 1971, 1972, 1973, 1974). ... NBA All-Rookie team (1963).

Season Team	G	Min.	FGM	FGA	Pct.	FTM	FTA	Pct.	Reb.	Ast.	PF	Dq.	Pts.	RPG	APG	PPG
62-63 —Detroit	80	2352	406	944	.430	206	287	.718	694	207	247	2	1018	8.7	2.6	12.7
63-64 —Detroit	15	304	52	133	.391	25	43	.581	105	23	32	1	129	7.0	1.5	8.6
64-65 —Detroit	79	2769	508	1196	.425	306	437	.700	874	253	242	5	1322	11.1	3.2	16.7
65-66 —Detroit	79	2696	524	1284	.408	249	378	.659	916	209	252	5	1297	11.6	2.6	16.4
66-67 —Detroit	78	2897	531	1278	.416	361	512	.705	924	216	297	7	1423	11.8	2.8	18.2
67-68 —Detroit	80	3125	573	1295	.442	289	435	.664	1081	181	304	3	1435	13.5	2.3	17.9
68-69 —Detroit-N.Y.	76	2943	506	1140	.444	229	328	.698	888	191	290	6	1241	11.7	2.5	16.3
69-70 —New York	79	2627	488	1082	.451	176	256	.688	790	194	244	2	1152	10.0	2.5	14.6
70-71 —New York	81	2891	523	1243	.421	217	312	.696	901	220	237	2	1263	11.1	2.7	15.6
71-72 —New York	80	3072	520	1218	.427	193	265	.728	901	291	219	1	1233	11.3	3.6	15.4
72-73 —New York	77	2827	532	1224	.435	194	260	.746	787	259	215	1	1258	10.2	3.4	16.3

										REBOUNDS						AVERAGES		
Season Team	G	Min.	FGM	FGA	Pct.	FTM	FTA	Pct.	Off.	Def.	Tot.	Ast.	St.	Blk.	TO	Pts.	RPG	APG	PPG
73-74—New York	71	2699	559	1212	.461	164	217	.756	134	623	757	253	67	39	...	1282	10.7	3.6	18.1
Totals	875	31202	5722	13249	.432	2609	3730	.699	...	...	9618	2497	67	39	...	14053	11.0	2.9	16.1

Personal fouls/disqualifications: 1973-74, 222/2.

NBA PLAYOFF RECORD

Season Team	G	Min.	FGM	FGA	Pct.	FTM	FTA	Pct.	Reb.	Ast.	PF	Dq.	Pts.	RPG	APG	PPG
62-63 —Detroit	4	159	25	59	.424	30	44	.682	63	6	14	1	80	15.8	1.5	20.0
67-68 —Detroit	6	263	45	106	.425	26	45	.578	97	13	23	0	116	16.2	2.2	19.3
68-69 —New York	10	419	61	174	.351	41	50	.820	148	33	43	0	163	14.8	3.3	16.3
69-70 —New York	19	701	130	309	.421	45	68	.662	220	46	63	1	305	11.6	2.4	16.1
70-71 —New York	12	488	84	202	.416	29	44	.659	156	22	40	1	197	13.0	1.8	16.4
71-72 —New York	16	616	109	242	.450	48	64	.750	193	37	51	2	266	12.1	2.3	16.6
72-73 —New York	17	632	117	265	.442	31	40	.775	179	58	57	0	265	10.5	3.4	15.6

									REBOUNDS							AVERAGES		
Season Team	G	Min.	FGM	FGA	Pct.	FTM	FTA	Pct.	Off.	Def.	Tot.	Ast.	St.	Blk.	TO	Pts.	RPG	APG	PPG
73-74—New York	12	404	63	166	.380	18	29	.621	25	74	99	38	7	4	...	144	8.3	3.2	12.0
Totals	96	3682	634	1523	.416	268	384	.698	...	...	1155	253	...	...	...	1536	12.0	2.6	16.0

Personal fouls/disqualifications: 1973-74, 36/0.

NBA ALL-STAR GAME RECORD

NOTES: Holds single-game record for most field goals made in one quarter—8 (1967).

Season Team	Min.	FGM	FGA	Pct.	FTM	FTA	Pct.	Reb	Ast.	PF	Dq.	Pts.
1966 —Detroit	22	1	14	.071	2	2	1.000	6	1	1	0	4
1967 —Detroit	25	11	17	.647	0	0	...	6	0	1	0	22
1968 —Detroit	12	0	3	.000	0	0	...	4	0	1	0	0
1970 —New York	14	5	10	.500	0	0	...	7	2	1	0	10
1971 —New York	19	4	7	.571	0	0	...	7	3	3	0	8
1972 —New York	26	4	8	.500	0	0	...	11	0	2	0	8
1973 —New York	25	4	8	.500	1	2	.500	7	2	1	0	9

							REBOUNDS								
Season Team	Min.	FGM	FGA	Pct.	FTM	FTA	Pct.	Off.	Def.	Tot.	Ast.	PF	Dq.	St.	Blk.	TO	Pts.
1974 —New York	24	8	14	.571	0	0	...	2	1	3	3	2	0	1	0	...	16
Totals	167	37	81	.457	3	4	.750	...	...	51	11	12	0	1	0	...	77

NBA COACHING RECORD

BACKGROUND: Player/head coach, Detroit Pistons (November 1964 to March 1967).
MISCELLANEOUS: Youngest coach in NBA history.

		REGULAR SEASON				PLAYOFFS		
Season Team	W	L	Pct.	Finish		W	L	Pct.
64-65 —Detroit	29	40	.420	4th/Western Division		—	—	—
65-66 —Detroit	22	58	.275	5th/Western Division		—	—	—
66-67 —Detroit	28	45	.384			—	—	—
Totals (3 years)	79	143	.356					

NOTES:

1964—Replaced Charles Wolf as Detroit head coach (November), with record of 2-9.

1967—Replaced as Detroit head coach by Donnis Butcher (March).

RECORD AS BASEBALL PLAYER

TRANSACTIONS/CAREER NOTES: Signed by Chicago White Sox (April 1, 1962). ... On disabled list (June 4-20, 1964). ... On restricted list (September 7, 1965-December 19, 1968). ... Released by White Sox organization (December 23, 1968).

Year Team (League)	W	L	Pct.	ERA	G	GS	CG	ShO	Sv.	IP	H	R	ER	BB	SO
1962—Chicago (A.L.)	0	0	...	2.00	12	0	0	0	...	18	5	7	4	23	8
Savannah (S. Atl.)	10	1	.909	2.49	15	14	7	2	...	94	62	35	26	53	93
1963—Chicago (A.L.)	3	4	.429	3.11	24	10	1	1	...	84	80	35	29	34	53
1964—Indianapolis (PCL)	15	8	.652	3.93	32	30	10	2	...	174	173	88	76	66	126
1965—Indianapolis (PCL)	15	12	.556	3.65	35	*34	10	1	...	*244	*255	120	99	66	176
Major league totals (2 years)	3	4	.429	2.91	36	10	1	1	...	102	85	42	33	66	126

ENGLISH, ALEX　　　　　　　　　F

PERSONAL: Born January 5, 1954, in Columbia, S.C. ... 6-7/190. ... Full name: Alexander English.
HIGH SCHOOL: Dreher (Columbia, S.C.).
COLLEGE: South Carolina.
TRANSACTIONS/CAREER NOTES: Selected by Milwaukee Bucks in second round (23rd pick overall) of 1976 NBA Draft. ... Signed as veteran free agent by Indiana Pacers (June 8, 1978); Bucks waived their right of first refusal in exchange for 1979 first-round draft choice (October 3, 1978). ... Traded by Pacers with 1980 first-round draft choice to Denver Nuggets for F George McGinnis (February 1, 1980). ... Signed as unrestricted free agent by Dallas Mavericks (August 15, 1990). ... Played in Italy (1991-92).
MISCELLANEOUS: Denver Nuggets all-time leading scorer with 21,645 points and all-time assists leader with 3,679 (1979-80 through 1989-90).

COLLEGIATE RECORD

Season Team	G	Min.	FGM	FGA	Pct.	FTM	FTA	Pct.	Reb.	Ast.	Pts.	AVERAGES RPG	APG	PPG
72-73—South Carolina	29	1037	189	368	.514	44	70	.629	306	25	422	10.6	0.9	14.6
73-74—South Carolina	27	1007	209	395	.529	75	112	.670	237	28	493	8.8	1.0	18.3
74-75—South Carolina	28	1024	199	359	.554	49	77	.636	244	30	447	8.7	1.1	16.0
75-76—South Carolina	27	1045	258	468	.551	94	134	.702	277	27	610	10.3	1.0	22.6
Totals	111	4113	855	1590	.538	262	393	.667	1064	110	1972	9.6	1.0	17.8

NBA REGULAR-SEASON RECORD

HONORS: All-NBA second team (1982, 1983, 1986).

Season Team	G	Min.	FGM	FGA	Pct.	FTM	FTA	Pct.	REBOUNDS Off.	Def.	Tot.	Ast.	St.	Blk.	TO	Pts.	AVERAGES RPG	APG	PPG
76-77—Milwaukee	60	648	132	277	.477	46	60	.767	68	100	168	25	17	18	...	310	2.8	0.4	5.2
77-78—Milwaukee	82	1552	343	633	.542	104	143	.727	144	251	395	129	41	55	137	790	4.8	1.6	9.6
78-79—Indiana	81	2696	563	1102	.511	173	230	.752	253	402	655	271	70	78	196	1299	8.1	3.3	16.0
79-80—Ind.-Denver	78	2401	553	1113	.497	210	266	.789	269	336	605	224	73	62	214	1318	7.8	2.9	16.9
80-81—Denver	81	3093	768	1555	.494	390	459	.850	273	373	646	290	106	100	241	1929	8.0	3.6	23.8
81-82—Denver	82	3015	855	1553	.551	372	443	.840	210	348	558	433	87	120	261	2082	6.8	5.3	25.4
82-83—Denver	82	2988	*959	*1857	.516	406	490	.829	263	338	601	397	116	126	263	*2326	7.3	4.8	*28.4
83-84—Denver	82	2870	907	1714	.529	352	427	.824	216	248	464	406	83	95	222	2167	5.7	5.0	26.4
84-85—Denver	81	2924	*939	1812	.518	383	462	.829	203	255	458	344	101	46	251	2262	5.7	4.2	27.9
85-86—Denver	81	3024	*951	1888	.504	511	593	.862	192	213	405	320	73	29	249	*2414	5.0	4.0	29.8
86-87—Denver	82	3085	965	1920	.503	411	487	.844	146	198	344	422	73	21	214	2345	4.2	5.1	28.6
87-88—Denver	80	2818	843	1704	.495	314	379	.829	166	207	373	377	70	23	181	2000	4.7	4.7	25.0
88-89—Denver	82	2990	924	1881	.491	325	379	.858	148	178	326	383	66	12	198	2175	4.0	4.7	26.5
89-90—Denver	80	2211	635	1293	.491	161	183	.880	119	167	286	225	51	23	93	1433	3.6	2.8	17.9
90-91—Dallas	79	1748	322	734	.439	119	140	.850	108	146	254	105	40	25	101	763	3.2	1.3	9.7
Totals	1193	38063	10659	21036	.507	4277	5141	.832	2778	3760	6538	4351	1067	833	2821	25613	5.5	3.6	21.5

Three-point field goals: 1979-80, 2-for-6 (.333). 1980-81, 3-for-5 (.600). 1981-82, 0-for-5. 1982-83, 2-for-12 (.167). 1983-84, 1-for-7 (.143). 1984-85, 1-for-5 (.200). 1985-86, 1-for-5 (.200). 1986-87, 4-for-15 (.267). 1987-88, 0-for-6. 1988-89, 2-for-8 (.250). 1989-90, 2-for-5 (.400). 1990-91, 0-for-1. Totals, 18-for-83 (.217).
Personal fouls/disqualifications: 1976-77, 78/0. 1977-78, 178/1. 1978-79, 214/3. 1979-80, 206/0. 1980-81, 255/2. 1981-82, 261/2. 1982-83, 235/1. 1983-84, 252/3. 1984-85, 259/1. 1985-86, 235/1. 1986-87, 216/0. 1987-88, 193/1. 1988-89, 174/0. 1989-90, 130/0. 1990-91, 141/0. Totals, 3027/15.

NBA PLAYOFF RECORD

Season Team	G	Min.	FGM	FGA	Pct.	FTM	FTA	Pct.	REBOUNDS Off.	Def.	Tot.	Ast.	St.	Blk.	TO	Pts.	AVERAGES RPG	APG	PPG
77-78—Milwaukee	9	208	48	78	.615	25	32	.781	16	26	42	13	6	7	12	121	4.7	1.4	13.4
81-82—Denver	3	118	26	55	.473	6	7	.857	8	15	23	17	3	3	4	58	7.7	5.7	19.3
82-83—Denver	7	270	67	150	.447	47	53	.887	20	24	44	42	4	7	21	181	6.3	6.0	25.9
83-84—Denver	5	203	60	102	.588	25	28	.893	16	24	40	28	3	2	7	145	8.0	5.6	29.0
84-85—Denver	14	536	163	304	.536	97	109	.890	36	56	92	63	17	5	30	423	6.6	4.5	30.2
85-86—Denver	10	394	106	229	.463	61	71	.859	18	17	35	52	4	4	28	273	3.5	5.2	27.3
86-87—Denver	3	76	25	49	.510	6	7	.857	10	4	14	10	0	0	8	56	4.7	3.3	18.7
87-88—Denver	11	438	116	255	.455	35	43	.814	31	28	59	48	7	3	16	267	5.4	4.4	24.3
88-89—Denver	3	108	32	62	.516	14	16	.875	8	5	13	11	1	0	14	78	4.3	3.7	26.0
89-90—Denver	3	76	25	44	.568	9	11	.818	3	6	9	9	2	1	2	59	3.0	3.0	19.7
Totals	68	2427	668	1328	.503	325	377	.862	166	205	371	293	47	32	142	1661	5.5	4.3	24.4

Three-point field goals: 1982-83, 0-for-2. 1983-84, 0-for-1. 1984-85, 0-for-1. 1985-86, 0-for-1. 1987-88, 0-for-3. Totals, 0-for-8.
Personal fouls/disqualifications: 1977-78, 20/0. 1981-82, 6/0. 1982-83, 21/0. 1983-84, 17/0. 1984-85, 40/1. 1985-86, 29/0. 1986-87, 9/1. 1987-88, 34/0. 1988-89, 6/0. 1989-90, 6/0. Totals, 188/2.

NBA ALL-STAR GAME RECORD

Season Team	Min.	FGM	FGA	Pct.	FTM	FTA	Pct.	REBOUNDS Off.	Def.	Tot.	Ast.	PF	Dq.	St.	Blk.	TO	Pts.
1982 —Denver	12	2	6	.333	0	0	...	2	3	5	1	2	0	1	0	1	4
1983 —Denver	23	7	14	.500	0	1	.000	2	2	4	0	2	0	1	2	2	14
1984 —Denver	19	6	8	.750	1	1	1.000	0	0	0	2	2	0	1	1	3	13
1985 —Denver	14	0	3	.000	0	0	...	1	1	2	1	1	0	0	0	2	0
1986 —Denver	16	8	12	.667	0	0	...	1	0	1	2	0	0	0	1	1	16
1987 —Denver	13	0	6	.000	0	0	...	0	0	0	1	1	0	0	0	0	0
1988 —Denver	22	5	10	.500	0	0	...	2	1	3	4	0	0	1	0	0	10
1989 —Denver	29	8	13	.615	0	0	...	1	2	3	4	0	0	2	0	3	16
Totals	148	36	72	.500	1	2	.500	9	9	18	15	8	0	6	4	14	73

ITALIAN LEAGUE RECORD

Season Team	G	Min.	FGM	FGA	Pct.	FTM	FTA	Pct.	Reb.	Ast.	Pts.	AVERAGES RPG	APG	PPG
91-92—Depi Napoli	18	566	103	214	.481	44	55	.800	86	5	251	4.8	0.3	13.9

ALL-TIME GREAT PLAYERS

ERVING, JULIUS   F

PERSONAL: Born February 22, 1950, in Roosevelt, N.Y. ... 6-7/210. ... Full name: Julius Winfield Erving II. ... Cousin of Mark Williams, linebacker with Jacksonville Jaguars. ... Nickname: Dr. J.
HIGH SCHOOL: Roosevelt (N.Y.).
COLLEGE: Massachusetts.
TRANSACTIONS/CAREER NOTES: Signed as free agent after junior season by Virginia Squires of American Basketball Association (April 6, 1971). ... Selected by Milwaukee Bucks in first round (12th pick overall) of 1972 NBA draft. ... Traded by Squires with C Willie Sojourner to New York Nets for F George Carter, draft rights to F/C Kermit Washington and cash (August 1, 1973). ... Nets franchise became part of NBA for 1976-77 season. ... Contract sold by Nets to Philadelphia 76ers (October 20, 1976).
CAREER HONORS: Elected to Naismith Memorial Basketball Hall of Fame (1993). ... NBA 35th Anniversary All-Time Team (1980).
MISCELLANEOUS: Member of NBA championship team (1983). ... Philadelphia 76ers franchise all-time blocked shots leader with 1,293 (1976-77 through 1986-87).

COLLEGIATE RECORD

Season Team	G	Min.	FGM	FGA	Pct.	FTM	FTA	Pct.	Reb.	Ast.	Pts.	RPG	APG	PPG
68-69—Massachusetts‡	15	...	112	216	.519	49	81	.605	214	...	273	14.3	...	18.2
69-70—Massachusetts	25	969	238	468	.509	167	230	.726	522	89	643	20.9	3.6	25.7
70-71—Massachusetts	27	1029	286	609	.470	155	206	.752	527	99	727	19.5	3.7	26.9
Varsity totals	52	1998	524	1077	.487	322	436	.739	1049	188	1370	20.2	3.6	26.3

ABA REGULAR-SEASON RECORD

NOTES: ABA Most Valuable Player (1974, 1976). ... ABA co-Most Valuable Player (1975). ... ABA All-Star first team (1973, 1974, 1975, 1976). ... ABA All-Star second team (1972). ... ABA All-Defensive team (1976). ... ABA All-Rookie team (1972). ... Member of ABA championship teams (1974, 1976). ... Holds career record for highest points-per-game average (minimum 250 games)—28.7.

Season Team	G	Min.	2-POINT FGM	2-POINT FGA	2-POINT Pct.	3-POINT FGM	3-POINT FGA	3-POINT Pct.	FTM	FTA	Pct.	Reb.	Ast.	Pts.	RPG	APG	PPG
71-72—Virginia	84	3513	907	1810	.501	3	16	.188	467	627	.745	1319	335	2290	15.7	4.0	27.3
72-73—Virginia	71	2993	889	1780	.499	5	24	.208	475	612	.776	867	298	*2268	12.2	4.2	*31.9
73-74—New York	84	3398	897	1742	.515	17	43	.395	454	593	.766	899	434	*2299	10.7	5.2	*27.4
74-75—New York	84	3402	885	1719	.515	29	87	.333	486	608	.799	914	462	2343	10.9	5.5	27.9
75-76—New York	84	3244	915	1770	.517	34	103	.330	530	662	.801	925	423	*2462	11.0	5.0	*29.3
Totals	407	16550	4493	8821	.509	88	273	.322	2412	3102	.778	4924	1952	11662	12.1	4.8	28.7

ABA PLAYOFF RECORD

NOTES: ABA Playoff Most Valuable Player (1974, 1976).

Season Team	G	Min.	2-POINT FGM	2-POINT FGA	2-POINT Pct.	3-POINT FGM	3-POINT FGA	3-POINT Pct.	FTM	FTA	Pct.	Reb.	Ast.	Pts.	RPG	APG	PPG
71-72—Virginia	11	504	146	280	.521	1	4	.250	71	85	.835	224	72	366	20.4	6.5	33.3
72-73—Virginia	5	219	59	109	.541	0	3	.000	30	40	.750	45	16	148	9.0	3.2	29.6
73-74—New York	14	579	156	294	.531	5	11	.455	63	85	.741	135	67	390	9.6	4.8	27.9
74-75—New York	5	211	55	113	.487	0	8	.000	27	32	.844	49	28	137	9.8	5.6	27.4
75-76—New York	13	551	156	286	.545	4	14	.286	127	158	.804	164	64	451	12.6	4.9	34.7
Totals	48	2064	572	1082	.529	10	40	.250	318	400	.795	617	247	1492	12.9	5.1	31.1

ABA ALL-STAR GAME RECORD

Season Team	Min.	2-POINT FGM	2-POINT FGA	2-POINT Pct.	3-POINT FGM	3-POINT FGA	3-POINT Pct.	FTM	FTA	Pct.	Reb.	Ast.	Pts.
1972—Virginia	25	9	15	.600	0	0	...	2	2	1.000	6	3	20
1973—Virginia	30	8	16	.500	0	0	...	6	8	.750	5	1	22
1974—New York	27	6	15	.400	0	0	...	2	2	1.000	11	8	14
1975—New York	27	5	11	.455	1	1	1.000	8	10	.800	7	7	21
1976—New York	25	9	12	.750	0	1	.000	5	7	.714	7	5	23
Totals	134	37	69	.536	1	2	.500	23	29	.793	36	24	100

NBA REGULAR-SEASON RECORD

HONORS: NBA Most Valuable Player (1981). ... All-NBA first team (1978, 1980, 1981, 1982, 1983). ... All-NBA second team (1977, 1984).

Season Team	G	Min.	FGM	FGA	Pct.	FTM	FTA	Pct.	REBOUNDS Off.	REBOUNDS Def.	REBOUNDS Tot.	Ast.	St.	Blk.	TO	Pts.	RPG	APG	PPG
76-77—Philadelphia	82	2940	685	1373	.499	400	515	.777	192	503	695	306	159	113	...	1770	8.5	3.7	21.6
77-78—Philadelphia	74	2429	611	1217	.502	306	362	.845	179	302	481	279	135	97	238	1528	6.5	3.8	20.6
78-79—Philadelphia	78	2802	715	1455	.491	373	501	.745	198	366	564	357	133	100	315	1803	7.2	4.6	23.1
79-80—Philadelphia	78	2812	838	1614	.519	420	534	.787	215	361	576	355	170	140	284	2100	7.4	4.6	26.9
80-81—Philadelphia	82	2874	794	1524	.521	422	536	.787	244	413	657	364	173	147	266	2014	8.0	4.4	24.6
81-82—Philadelphia	81	2789	780	1428	.546	411	539	.763	220	337	557	319	161	141	214	1974	6.9	3.9	24.4
82-83—Philadelphia	72	2421	605	1170	.517	330	435	.759	173	318	491	263	112	131	196	1542	6.8	3.7	21.4
83-84—Philadelphia	77	2683	678	1324	.512	364	483	.754	190	342	532	309	141	139	230	1727	6.9	4.0	22.4
84-85—Philadelphia	78	2535	610	1236	.494	338	442	.765	172	242	414	233	135	109	208	1561	5.3	3.0	20.0
85-86—Philadelphia	74	2474	521	1085	.480	289	368	.785	169	201	370	248	113	82	214	1340	5.0	3.4	18.1
86-87—Philadelphia	60	1918	400	850	.471	191	235	.813	115	149	264	191	76	94	158	1005	4.4	3.2	16.8
Totals	836	28677	7237	14276	.507	3844	4950	.777	2067	3534	5601	3224	1508	1293	2323	18364	6.7	3.9	22.0

Three-point field goals: 1979-80, 4-for-20 (.200). 1980-81, 4-for-18 (.222). 1981-82, 3-for-11 (.273). 1982-83, 2-for-7 (.286). 1983-84, 7-for-21 (.333). 1984-85, 3-for-14 (.214). 1985-86, 9-for-32 (.281). 1986-87, 14-for-53 (.264). Totals, 46-for-176 (.261).
Personal fouls/disqualifications: 1976-77, 251/1. 1977-78, 207/0. 1978-79, 207/0. 1979-80, 208/0. 1980-81, 233/0. 1981-82, 229/1. 1982-83, 202/1. 1983-84, 217/3. 1984-85, 199/0. 1985-86, 196/3. 1986-87, 137/0. Totals, 2286/9.

NBA PLAYOFF RECORD

Season Team	G	Min.	FGM	FGA	Pct.	FTM	FTA	Pct.	REBOUNDS Off.	Def.	Tot.	Ast.	St.	Blk.	TO	Pts.	AVERAGES RPG	APG	PPG
76-77—Philadelphia....	19	758	204	390	.523	110	134	.821	41	81	122	85	41	23	...	518	6.4	4.5	27.3
77-78—Philadelphia....	10	358	88	180	.489	42	56	.750	40	57	97	40	15	18	35	218	9.7	4.0	21.8
78-79—Philadelphia....	9	372	89	172	.517	51	67	.761	29	41	70	53	18	17	38	229	7.8	5.9	25.4
79-80—Philadelphia....	18	694	165	338	.488	108	136	.794	31	105	136	79	36	37	56	440	7.6	4.4	24.4
80-81—Philadelphia....	16	592	143	301	.475	81	107	.757	52	62	114	54	22	41	55	367	7.1	3.4	22.9
81-82—Philadelphia....	21	780	168	324	.519	124	165	.752	57	99	156	99	37	37	67	461	7.4	4.7	22.0
82-83—Philadelphia....	13	493	95	211	.450	49	68	.721	32	67	99	44	15	27	39	239	7.6	3.4	18.4
83-84—Philadelphia....	5	194	36	76	.474	19	22	.864	9	23	32	25	8	6	21	91	6.4	5.0	18.2
84-85—Philadelphia....	13	434	84	187	.449	54	63	.857	29	44	73	48	25	11	37	222	5.6	3.7	17.1
85-86—Philadelphia....	12	433	81	180	.450	48	65	.738	26	44	70	50	11	16	39	212	5.8	4.2	17.7
86-87—Philadelphia....	5	180	34	82	.415	21	25	.840	14	11	25	17	7	6	9	91	5.0	3.4	18.2
Totals	141	5288	1187	2441	.486	707	908	.779	360	634	994	594	235	239	396	3088	7.0	4.2	21.9

Three-point field goals: 1979-80, 2-for-9 (.222). 1980-81, 0-for-1. 1981-82, 1-for-6 (.167). 1982-83, 0-for-1. 1983-84, 0-for-1. 1984-85, 0-for-1. 1985-86, 2-for-11 (.182). 1986-87, 2-for-6 (.333). Totals, 7-for-36 (.194).

Personal fouls/disqualifications: 1976-77, 45/0. 1977-78, 30/0. 1978-79, 22/0. 1979-80, 56/0. 1980-81, 54/0. 1981-82, 55/0. 1982-83, 42/1. 1983-84, 14/0. 1984-85, 34/0. 1985-86, 32/0. 1986-87, 19/0. Totals, 403/1.

NBA ALL-STAR GAME RECORD

NOTES: NBA All-Star Game Most Valuable Player (1977, 1983). ... Holds single-game record for most free throws attempted in one quarter—11 (1978). ... Shares single-game record for most free throws made in one quarter—9 (1978).

Season Team	Min.	FGM	FGA	Pct.	FTM	FTA	Pct.	REBOUNDS Off.	Def.	Tot.	Ast.	PF	Dq.	St.	Blk.	TO	Pts.
1977 —Philadelphia......	30	12	20	.600	6	6	1.000	5	7	12	3	2	0	4	1	...	30
1978 —Philadelphia......	27	3	14	.214	10	12	.833	2	6	8	3	1	0	0	1	2	16
1979 —Philadelphia......	39	10	22	.455	9	12	.750	6	2	8	5	4	0	2	0	1	29
1980 —Philadelphia......	20	4	12	.333	3	4	.750	2	3	5	2	5	0	2	1	2	11
1981 —Philadelphia......	29	6	15	.400	6	7	.857	3	0	3	2	2	0	2	1	2	18
1982 —Philadelphia......	32	7	16	.438	2	4	.500	3	5	8	2	4	0	1	2	4	16
1983 —Philadelphia......	28	11	19	.579	3	3	1.000	3	3	6	3	1	0	1	2	2	25
1984 —Philadelphia......	36	14	22	.636	6	8	.750	4	4	8	5	4	0	2	2	1	34
1985 —Philadelphia......	23	5	15	.333	2	2	1.000	2	2	4	3	3	0	1	0	1	12
1986 —Philadelphia......	19	4	10	.400	0	2	.000	1	3	4	2	2	0	2	0	2	8
1987 —Philadelphia......	33	9	13	.692	3	3	1.000	3	1	4	5	3	0	1	1	2	22
Totals.........................	316	85	178	.478	50	63	.794	34	36	70	35	31	0	18	11	19	221

Three-point field goals: 1987, 1-for-1.

COMBINED ABA AND NBA REGULAR-SEASON RECORDS

	G	Min.	FGM	FGA	Pct.	FTM	FTA	Pct.	REBOUNDS Off.	Def.	Tot.	Ast.	Stl.	Blk.	TO	Pts.	AVERAGES RPG	APG	PPG
Totals	1243	45227	11818	23370	.506	6256	8052	.777	...	...	10525	5176	...	...	...	30026	8.5	4.2	24.2

Three-point field goals: 134-for-449 (.298).
Personal fouls/disqualifications: 3494.

FLOYD, SLEEPY   G

PERSONAL: Born March 6, 1960, in Gastonia, N.C. ... 6-3/185. ... Full name: Eric Augustus Floyd.
HIGH SCHOOL: Hunter Huss (Gastonia, N.C.).
COLLEGE: Georgetown.
TRANSACTIONS/CAREER NOTES: Selected by New Jersey Nets in first round (13th pick overall) of 1982 NBA Draft. ... Traded by Nets with F Mickey Johnson to Golden State Warriors for G Micheal Ray Richardson (February 6, 1983). ... Traded by Warriors with C Joe Barry Carroll to Houston Rockets for C Ralph Sampson and G Steve Harris (December 12, 1987). ... Waived by Rockets (August 2, 1993). ... Signed as free agent by San Antonio Spurs (August 13, 1993). ... Signed as free agent by Nets (October 6, 1994).

COLLEGIATE RECORD

NOTES: THE SPORTING NEWS All-America second team (1982).

Season Team	G	Min.	FGM	FGA	Pct.	FTM	FTA	Pct.	Reb.	Ast.	Pts.	AVERAGES RPG	APG	PPG
78-79—Georgetown....................	29	975	177	388	.456	126	155	.813	119	78	480	4.1	2.7	16.6
79-80—Georgetown....................	32	1052	246	444	.554	106	140	.757	98	95	598	3.1	3.0	18.7
80-81—Georgetown....................	32	1115	237	508	.467	133	165	.806	133	83	607	4.2	2.6	19.0
81-82—Georgetown....................	37	1200	249	494	.504	121	168	.720	127	99	619	3.4	2.7	16.7
Totals	130	4342	909	1834	.496	486	628	.774	477	355	2304	3.7	2.7	17.7

NBA REGULAR-SEASON RECORD

Season Team	G	Min.	FGM	FGA	Pct.	FTM	FTA	Pct.	REBOUNDS Off.	Def.	Tot.	Ast.	St.	Blk.	TO	Pts.	AVERAGES RPG	APG	PPG
82-83—N.J.-G.S.........	76	1248	226	527	.429	150	180	.833	56	81	137	138	58	17	106	612	1.8	1.8	8.1
83-84—Golden State ...	77	2555	484	1045	.463	315	386	.816	87	184	271	269	103	31	196	1291	3.5	3.5	16.8
84-85—Golden State ...	82	2873	610	1372	.445	336	415	.810	62	140	202	406	134	41	251	1598	2.5	5.0	19.5
85-86—Golden State ...	82	2764	510	1007	.506	351	441	.796	76	221	297	746	157	16	290	1410	3.6	9.1	17.2
86-87—Golden State ...	82	3064	503	1030	.488	462	537	.860	56	212	268	848	146	18	280	1541	3.3	10.3	18.8
87-88—G.S.-Hou.........	77	2514	420	969	.433	301	354	.850	77	219	296	544	95	12	223	1155	3.8	7.1	15.0
88-89—Houston	82	2788	396	893	.443	261	309	.845	48	258	306	709	124	11	253	1162	3.7	8.6	14.2
89-90—Houston	82	2630	362	803	.451	187	232	.806	46	152	198	600	94	11	204	1000	2.4	7.3	12.2
90-91—Houston	82	1850	386	939	.411	185	246	.752	52	107	159	317	95	17	140	1005	1.9	3.9	12.3
91-92—Houston	82	1662	286	704	.406	135	170	.794	34	116	150	239	57	21	128	744	1.8	2.9	9.1
92-93—Houston	52	867	124	305	.407	81	102	.794	14	72	86	132	32	6	68	345	1.7	2.5	6.6

Season Team	G	Min.	FGM	FGA	Pct.	FTM	FTA	Pct.	REBOUNDS Off.	Def.	Tot.	Ast.	St.	Blk.	TO	Pts.	AVERAGES RPG	APG	PPG
93-94—San Antonio....	53	737	70	209	.335	52	78	.667	10	60	70	101	12	8	61	200	1.3	1.9	3.8
94-95—New Jersey.....	48	831	71	212	.335	30	43	.698	8	46	54	126	13	6	51	197	1.1	2.6	4.1
Totals	957	26383	4448	10015	.444	2846	3493	.815	626	1868	2494	5175	1120	215	2251	12260	2.6	5.4	12.8

Three-point field goals: 1982-83, 10-for-25 (.400). 1983-84, 8-for-45 (.178). 1984-85, 42-for-143 (.294). 1985-86, 39-for-119 (.328). 1986-87, 73-for-190 (.384). 1987-88, 14-for-72 (.194). 1988-89, 109-for-292 (.373). 1989-90, 89-for-234 (.380). 1990-91, 48-for-176 (.273). 1991-92, 37-for-123 (.301). 1992-93, 16-for-56 (.286). 1993-94, 8-for-36 (.222). 1994-95, 25-for-88 (.284). Totals, 518-for-1599 (.324).

Personal fouls/disqualifications: 1982-83, 134/3. 1983-84, 216/0. 1984-85, 226/1. 1985-86, 199/2. 1986-87, 191/1. 1987-88, 190/1. 1988-89, 196/1. 1989-90, 159/0. 1990-91, 122/0. 1991-92, 128/0. 1992-93, 59/0. 1993-94, 71/0. 1994-95, 73/0. Totals, 1972/9.

NBA PLAYOFF RECORD

NOTES: Holds single-game playoff records for most points in one half—39; most points in one quarter—29; and most field goals in one quarter—12 (May 10, 1987, vs. Los Angeles Lakers). ... Shares single-game playoff record for most field goals made in one half—15 (May 10, 1987, vs. Los Angeles Lakers).

Season Team	G	Min.	FGM	FGA	Pct.	FTM	FTA	Pct.	REBOUNDS Off.	Def.	Tot.	Ast.	St.	Blk.	TO	Pts.	AVERAGES RPG	APG	PPG
86-87—Golden State........	10	414	77	152	.507	47	51	.922	9	21	30	102	18	2	35	214	3.0	10.2	21.4
87-88—Houston..........	4	154	26	61	.426	19	22	.864	3	4	7	34	8	0	12	75	1.8	8.5	18.8
88-89—Houston..........	4	160	22	46	.478	10	14	.714	3	15	18	26	8	1	10	62	4.5	6.5	15.5
89-90—Houston..........	4	172	30	64	.469	11	17	.647	7	8	15	41	5	1	15	74	3.8	10.3	18.5
90-91—Houston..........	3	41	8	24	.333	0	0	...	0	2	2	7	2	1	7	16	0.7	2.3	5.3
92-93—Houston..........	7	60	6	19	.316	7	10	.700	1	3	4	8	2	0	9	20	0.6	1.1	2.9
93-94—San Antonio.......	4	37	2	8	.250	2	4	.500	0	1	1	1	0	0	4	6	0.3	0.3	1.5
Totals	36	1038	171	374	.457	96	118	.814	23	54	77	219	43	5	92	467	2.1	6.1	13.0

Three-point field goals: 1986-87, 13-for-28 (.464). 1987-88, 4-for-8 (.500). 1988-89, 8-for-15 (.533). 1989-90, 3-for-12 (.250). 1990-91, 0-for-4. 1992-93, 1-for-3 (.333). Totals, 29-for-70 (.414).

Personal fouls/disqualifications: 1986-87, 24/0. 1987-88, 10/0. 1988-89, 10/0. 1989-90, 5/0. 1990-91, 4/0. 1992-93, 2/0. 1993-94, 3/0. Totals, 58/0.

NBA ALL-STAR GAME RECORD

Season Team	Min.	FGM	FGA	Pct.	FTM	FTA	Pct.	REBOUNDS Off.	Def.	Tot.	Ast.	PF	Dq.	St.	Blk.	TO	Pts.
1987 —Golden State......	19	4	7	.571	5	7	.714	2	3	5	1	2	0	1	0	2	14

Three-point field goals: 1987, 1-for-3 (.333).

FOUST, LARRY   C/F

PERSONAL: Born June 24, 1928, in Painesville, Ohio. ... Died October 27, 1984. ... 6-9/250. ... Full name: Lawrence Michael Foust.

HIGH SCHOOL: South Catholic (Philadelphia).

COLLEGE: La Salle.

TRANSACTIONS/CAREER NOTES: Selected by Chicago Stags in first round of 1950 NBA Draft. ... Draft rights selected by Fort Wayne Pistons in dispersal of Stags franchise (1950). ... Pistons franchise moved from Fort Wayne to Detroit for 1957-58 season. ... Traded by Pistons with cash to Minneapolis Lakers for C Walt Dukes (September 12, 1957). ... Traded by Lakers to St. Louis Hawks for C Charlie Share, draft rights to G Nick Mantis, G Willie Merriweather and cash (February 1, 1960).

COLLEGIATE RECORD

NOTES: The Sporting News All-America fifth team (1950).

Season Team	G	Min.	FGM	FGA	Pct.	FTM	FTA	Pct.	Reb.	Ast.	Pts.	AVERAGES RPG	APG	PPG
46-47—La Salle	26	...	103	...	...	49	...	...	...	...	255	...	...	9.8
47-48—La Salle	24	...	157	...	...	87	...	...	...	...	401	...	...	16.7
48-49—La Salle	28	...	177	...	...	99	164	.604	...	...	453	...	...	16.2
49-50—La Salle	25	...	136	...	...	83	122	.680	...	...	355	...	...	14.2
Totals	103	...	573	...	...	318	...	...	...	...	1464	...	...	14.2

NBA REGULAR-SEASON RECORD

HONORS: All-NBA first team (1955). ... All-NBA second team (1952).

Season Team	G	Min.	FGM	FGA	Pct.	FTM	FTA	Pct.	Reb.	Ast.	PF	Dq.	Pts.	AVERAGES RPG	APG	PPG
50-51 —Fort Wayne	68	...	327	944	.346	261	396	.659	681	90	247	6	915	10.0	1.3	13.5
51-52 —Fort Wayne	66	2615	390	989	.394	267	394	.678	/d880	200	245	10	1047	13.3	3.0	15.9
52-53 —Fort Wayne	67	2303	311	865	.360	336	465	.723	769	151	267	16	958	11.5	2.3	14.3
53-54 —Fort Wayne	72	2693	376	919	.409	338	475	.712	967	161	258	4	1090	13.4	2.2	15.1
54-55 —Fort Wayne	70	2264	398	818	*.487	393	513	.766	700	118	264	9	1189	10.0	1.7	17.0
55-56 —Fort Wayne	72	2024	367	821	.447	432	555	.778	648	127	263	7	1166	9.0	1.8	16.2
56-57 —Fort Wayne	61	1533	243	617	.394	273	380	.718	555	71	221	7	759	9.1	1.2	12.4
57-58 —Minneapolis	72	2200	391	982	.398	428	566	.756	876	108	299	11	1210	12.2	1.5	16.8
58-59 —Minneapolis	72	1933	301	771	.390	280	366	.765	627	91	233	5	882	8.7	1.3	12.3
59-60 —Minn.-St.L.	72	1964	312	766	.407	253	320	.791	621	96	241	7	877	8.6	1.3	12.2
60-61 —St. Louis	68	1208	194	489	.397	164	208	.788	389	77	165	0	552	5.7	1.1	8.1
61-62 —St. Louis	57	1153	204	433	.471	145	178	.815	328	78	186	2	553	5.8	1.4	9.7
Totals	817	...	3814	9414	.405	3570	4816	.741	8041	1368	2889	84	11198	9.8	1.7	13.7

NBA PLAYOFF RECORD

Season Team	G	Min.	FGM	FGA	Pct.	FTM	FTA	Pct.	Reb.	Ast.	PF	Dq.	Pts.	AVERAGES RPG	APG	PPG
50-51 —Fort Wayne	3	...	14	45	.311	8	10	.800	37	5	5	...	36	12.3	1.7	12.0
51-52 —Fort Wayne	2	77	12	23	.522	6	7	.857	30	5	8	1	30	15.0	2.5	15.0
52-53 —Fort Wayne	8	332	48	121	.397	57	68	.838	111	6	34	2	153	13.9	0.8	19.1
53-54 —Fort Wayne	4	129	11	41	.268	19	25	.760	38	7	21	2	41	9.5	1.8	10.3

Season Team	G	Min.	FGM	FGA	Pct.	FTM	FTA	Pct.	Reb.	Ast.	PF	Dq.	Pts.	AVERAGES RPG	APG	PPG
54-55 —Fort Wayne	11	331	60	152	.395	52	73	.712	107	26	43	0	172	9.7	2.4	15.6
55-56 —Fort Wayne	10	289	49	130	.377	70	89	.787	127	14	38	2	168	12.7	1.4	16.8
56-57 —Fort Wayne	2	64	13	23	.565	19	23	.826	25	6	10	0	45	12.5	3.0	22.5
58-59 —Minneapolis	13	404	56	134	.418	41	50	.820	136	12	47	2	153	10.5	0.9	11.8
59-60 —St. Louis	12	205	29	74	.392	20	25	.800	68	11	36	0	78	5.7	0.9	6.5
60-61 —St. Louis	8	89	9	20	.450	8	14	.571	28	2	13	0	26	3.5	0.3	3.3
Totals	73	...	301	763	.394	300	384	.781	707	94	255	...	902	9.7	1.3	12.4

NBA ALL-STAR GAME RECORD

Season Team	Min.	FGM	FGA	Pct.	FTM	FTA	Pct.	Reb	Ast.	PF	Dq.	Pts.
1951 —Fort Wayne	...	1	6	.167	0	0	...	5	2	3	0	2
1952 —Fort Wayne					Selected. did not play—injured.							
1953 —Fort Wayne	18	5	7	.714	0	0	...	6	0	4	0	10
1954 —Fort Wayne	27	1	9	.111	1	1	1.000	15	0	1	0	3
1955 —Fort Wayne	24	3	10	.300	1	1	1.000	7	1	1	0	7
1956 —Fort Wayne	20	3	9	.333	3	4	.750	4	0	1	0	9
1958 —Minneapolis	13	1	4	.250	8	8	1.000	3	0	3	0	10
1959 —Minneapolis	16	3	9	.333	2	2	1.000	9	0	3	0	8
Totals	...	17	54	.315	15	16	.938	49	3	16	0	49

FRAZIER, WALT   G

PERSONAL: Born March 29, 1945, in Atlanta. ... 6-4/205. ... Full name: Walter Frazier Jr. ... Nickname: Clyde.
HIGH SCHOOL: David Howard (Atlanta).
COLLEGE: Southern Illinois.
TRANSACTIONS/CAREER NOTES: Selected by New York Knicks in first round (fifth pick overall) of 1967 NBA Draft. ... Acquired by Cleveland Cavaliers as compensation for Knicks signing veteran free agent G Jim Cleamons (October 7, 1977). ... Waived by Cavaliers (October 19, 1979).
CAREER HONORS: Elected to Naismith Memorial Basketball Hall of Fame (1986).
MISCELLANEOUS: Member of NBA championship teams (1970, 1973). ... New York Knicks all-time assists leader with 4,791 (1967-68 through 1976-77).

COLLEGIATE RECORD

NOTES: THE SPORTING NEWS All-America second team (1967).

Season Team	G	Min.	FGM	FGA	Pct.	FTM	FTA	Pct.	Reb.	Ast.	Pts.	AVERAGES RPG	APG	PPG
63-64—Southern Illinois‡	14	...	133	225	.591	52	85	.612	129	...	318	9.2	...	22.7
64-65—Southern Illinois	24	...	161	353	.456	88	111	.793	221	...	410	9.2	...	17.1
65-66—Southern Illinois					Did not play—ineligible.									
66-67—Southern Illinois	26	...	192	397	.484	90	126	.714	310	...	474	11.9	...	18.2
Varsity totals	50	...	353	750	.471	178	237	.751	531	...	884	10.6	...	17.7

NBA REGULAR-SEASON RECORD

HONORS: All-NBA first team (1970, 1972, 1974, 1975). ... All-NBA second team (1971, 1973). ... NBA All-Defensive first team (1969, 1970, 1971, 1972, 1973, 1974, 1975). ... NBA All-Rookie team (1968).

Season Team	G	Min.	FGM	FGA	Pct.	FTM	FTA	Pct.	Reb.	Ast.	PF	Dq.	Pts.	AVERAGES RPG	APG	PPG
67-68 —New York	74	1588	256	568	.451	154	235	.655	313	305	199	2	666	4.2	4.1	9.0
68-69 —New York	80	2949	531	1052	.505	341	457	.746	499	635	245	2	1403	6.2	7.9	17.5
69-70 —New York	77	3040	600	1158	.518	409	547	.748	465	629	203	1	1609	6.0	8.2	20.9
70-71 —New York	80	3455	651	1317	.494	434	557	.779	544	536	240	1	1736	6.8	6.7	21.7
71-72 —New York	77	3126	669	1307	.512	450	557	.808	513	446	185	0	1788	6.7	5.8	23.2
72-73 —New York	78	3181	681	1389	.490	286	350	.817	570	461	186	0	1648	7.3	5.9	21.1

Season Team	G	Min.	FGM	FGA	Pct.	FTM	FTA	Pct.	REBOUNDS Off.	Def.	Tot.	Ast.	St.	Blk.	TO	Pts.	AVERAGES RPG	APG	PPG
73-74—New York	80	3338	674	1429	.472	295	352	.838	120	416	536	551	161	15	...	1643	6.7	6.9	20.5
74-75—New York	78	3204	672	1391	.483	331	400	.828	90	375	465	474	190	14	...	1675	6.0	6.1	21.5
75-76—New York	59	2427	470	969	.485	186	226	.823	79	321	400	351	106	9	...	1126	6.8	5.9	19.1
76-77—N.Y. Knicks	76	2687	532	1089	.489	259	336	.771	52	241	293	403	132	9	...	1323	3.9	5.3	17.4
77-78—Cleveland	51	1664	336	714	.471	153	180	.850	54	155	209	209	77	9	113	825	4.1	4.1	16.2
78-79—Cleveland	12	279	54	122	.443	21	27	.778	7	13	20	32	13	2	22	129	1.7	2.7	10.8
79-80—Cleveland	3	27	4	11	.364	2	2	1.000	1	2	3	8	2	1	4	10	1.0	2.7	3.3
Totals	825	30965	6130	12516	.490	3321	4226	.786	...	...	4830	5040	681	59	139	15581	5.9	6.1	18.9

Three-point field goals: 1979-80, 0-for-1.
Personal fouls/disqualifications: 1973-74, 212/2. 1974-75, 205/2. 1975-76, 163/1. 1976-77, 194/0. 1977-78, 124/1. 1978-79, 22/0. 1979-80, 2/0. Totals, 2180/12.

NBA PLAYOFF RECORD

Season Team	G	Min.	FGM	FGA	Pct.	FTM	FTA	Pct.	Reb.	Ast.	PF	Dq.	Pts.	AVERAGES RPG	APG	PPG
67-68 —New York	4	119	12	33	.364	14	18	.778	22	25	12	0	38	5.5	6.3	9.5
68-69 —New York	10	415	89	177	.503	34	57	.597	74	91	30	0	212	7.4	9.1	21.2
69-70 —New York	19	834	118	247	.478	68	89	.764	149	156	53	0	304	7.8	8.2	16.0
70-71 —New York	12	501	108	204	.529	55	75	.733	70	54	45	0	271	5.8	4.5	22.6
71-72 —New York	16	704	148	276	.536	92	125	.736	112	98	48	0	388	7.0	6.1	24.3
72-73 —New York	17	765	150	292	.514	73	94	.777	124	106	52	1	373	7.3	6.2	21.9

Season Team	G	Min.	FGM	FGA	Pct.	FTM	FTA	Pct.	REBOUNDS Off.	Def.	Tot.	Ast.	St.	Blk.	TO	Pts.	AVERAGES RPG	APG	PPG
73-74—New York	12	491	113	225	.502	44	49	.898	21	74	95	48	21	4	...	270	7.9	4.0	22.5
74-75—New York	3	124	29	46	.630	13	16	.813	3	17	20	21	11	0	...	71	6.7	7.0	23.7
Totals	93	3953	767	1500	.511	393	523	.751	...	...	666	599	32	4	...	1927	7.2	6.4	20.7

Personal fouls/disqualifications: 1973-74, 41/1. 1974-75, 4/0. Totals, 285/2.

NBA ALL-STAR GAME RECORD

NOTES: NBA All-Star Game Most Valuable Player (1975).

Season Team	Min.	FGM	FGA	Pct.	FTM	FTA	Pct.	Reb	Ast.	PF	Dq.	Pts.
1970 —New York	24	3	7	.429	1	2	.500	3	4	2	0	7
1971 —New York	26	3	9	.333	0	0	...	6	5	2	0	6
1972 —New York	25	7	11	.636	1	2	.500	3	5	2	0	15
1973 —New York	26	5	15	.333	0	0	...	6	2	1	0	10

Season Team	Min.	FGM	FGA	Pct.	FTM	FTA	Pct.	REBOUNDS Off.	Def.	Tot.	Ast.	PF	Dq.	St.	Blk.	TO	Pts.
1974 —New York	28	5	12	.417	2	2	1.000	1	1	2	5	1	0	3	0	...	12
1975 —New York	35	10	17	.588	10	11	.909	0	5	5	2	2	0	4	0	...	30
1976 —New York	19	2	7	.286	4	4	1.000	0	2	2	3	0	0	2	0	...	8
Totals	183	35	78	.449	18	21	.857	...	...	27	26	10	0	9	0	...	88

FREE, WORLD B.   G

PERSONAL: Born December 9, 1953, in Atlanta. ... 6-3/190. ... Formerly known as Lloyd Free.
HIGH SCHOOL: Canarsie (Brooklyn, N.Y.).
COLLEGE: Guilford (N.C.).
TRANSACTIONS/CAREER NOTES: Selected after junior season by Philadelphia 76ers in second round (23rd pick overall) of 1975 NBA Draft. ... Traded by 76ers to San Diego Clippers for 1984 first-round draft choice (October 12, 1978). ... Traded by Clippers to Golden State Warriors for G Phil Smith and 1984 first-round draft choice (August 28, 1980). ... Traded by Warriors to Cleveland Cavaliers for G Ron Brewer (December 15, 1982). ... Signed as veteran free agent by 76ers (December 30, 1986); Cavaliers waived their right of first refusal in exchange for 1990 second-round draft choice. ... Waived by 76ers (March 4, 1987). ... Played in United States Basketball League with Miami Tropics (1987). ... Signed as free agent by Houston Rockets (October 1, 1987).

COLLEGIATE RECORD

NOTES: Most Valuable Player in NAIA tournament (1973). ... Member of NAIA championship team (1973).

Season Team	G	Min.	FGM	FGA	Pct.	FTM	FTA	Pct.	Reb.	Ast.	Pts.	AVERAGES RPG	APG	PPG
72-73—Guilford (N.C.)	33	...	272	572	.476	153	217	.705	191	...	697	5.8	...	21.1
73-74—Guilford (N.C.)	24	...	216	456	.474	165	225	.733	200	...	597	8.3	...	24.9
74-75—Guilford (N.C.)	28	...	247	486	.508	218	291	.749	163	...	712	5.8	...	25.4
Totals	85	...	735	1514	.485	536	733	.731	554	...	2006	6.5	...	23.6

NBA REGULAR-SEASON RECORD

HONORS: All-NBA second team (1979).

Season Team	G	Min.	FGM	FGA	Pct.	FTM	FTA	Pct.	REBOUNDS Off.	Def.	Tot.	Ast.	St.	Blk.	TO	Pts.	AVERAGES RPG	APG	PPG
75-76—Philadelphia	71	1121	239	533	.448	112	186	.602	64	61	125	104	37	6	...	590	1.8	1.5	8.3
76-77—Philadelphia	78	2253	467	1022	.457	334	464	.720	97	140	237	266	75	25	...	1268	3.0	3.4	16.3
77-78—Philadelphia	76	2050	390	857	.455	411	562	.731	92	120	212	306	68	41	200	1191	2.8	4.0	15.7
78-79—San Diego	78	2954	795	1653	.481	*654	*865	.756	127	174	301	340	111	35	297	2244	3.9	4.4	28.8
79-80—San Diego	68	2585	737	1556	.474	*572	760	.753	129	109	238	283	81	32	228	2055	3.5	4.2	30.2
80-81—Golden State	65	2370	516	1157	.446	528	649	.814	48	111	159	361	85	11	195	1565	2.4	5.6	24.1
81-82—Golden State	78	2796	650	1452	.448	479	647	.740	118	130	248	419	71	8	208	1789	3.2	5.4	22.9
82-83—G.S.-Clev.	73	2638	649	1423	.456	430	583	.738	92	109	201	290	97	15	209	1743	2.8	4.0	23.9
83-84—Cleveland	75	2375	626	1407	.445	395	504	.784	89	128	217	226	94	8	154	1669	2.9	3.0	22.3
84-85—Cleveland	71	2249	609	1328	.459	308	411	.749	61	150	211	320	75	16	139	1597	3.0	4.5	22.5
85-86—Cleveland	75	2535	652	1433	.455	379	486	.780	72	146	218	314	91	19	172	1754	2.9	4.2	23.4
86-87—Philadelphia	20	285	39	123	.317	36	47	.766	5	14	19	30	5	4	18	116	1.0	1.5	5.8
87-88—Houston	58	682	143	350	.409	80	100	.800	14	30	44	60	20	3	49	374	0.8	1.0	6.4
Totals	886	26893	6512	14294	.456	4718	6264	.753	1008	1422	2430	3319	910	223	1869	17955	2.7	3.7	20.3

Three-point field goals: 1979-80, 9-for-25 (.360). 1980-81, 5-for-31 (.161). 1981-82, 10-for-56 (.179). 1982-83, 15-for-45 (.333). 1983-84, 22-for-69 (.319). 1984-85, 71-for-193 (.368). 1985-86, 71-for-169 (.420). 1986-87, 2-for-9 (.222). 1987-88, 8-for-35 (.229). Totals, 213-for-632 (.337).

Personal fouls/disqualifications: 1975-76, 107/0. 1976-77, 207/2. 1977-78, 199/0. 1978-79, 253/8. 1979-80, 195/0. 1980-81, 183/1. 1981-82, 222/1. 1982-83, 241/4. 1983-84, 214/2. 1984-85, 163/0. 1985-86, 186/1. 1986-87, 26/0. 1987-88, 74/2. Totals, 2270/21.

NBA PLAYOFF RECORD

Season Team	G	Min.	FGM	FGA	Pct.	FTM	FTA	Pct.	REBOUNDS Off.	Def.	Tot.	Ast.	St.	Blk.	TO	Pts.	AVERAGES RPG	APG	PPG
75-76—Philadelphia	3	62	11	28	.393	10	13	.769	1	0	1	5	3	0	...	32	0.3	1.7	10.7
76-77—Philadelphia	15	281	63	170	.371	53	77	.688	10	22	32	29	12	8	...	179	2.1	1.9	11.9
77-78—Philadelphia	10	268	51	124	.411	59	81	.728	10	21	31	37	4	6	26	161	3.1	3.7	16.1
84-85—Cleveland	4	150	41	93	.441	23	25	.920	4	6	10	31	6	0	6	105	2.5	7.8	26.3
87-88—Houston	2	12	0	2	.000	0	0	...	1	1	2	1	0	0	3	0	1.0	0.5	0.0
Totals	34	773	166	417	.398	145	196	.740	26	50	76	103	25	14	35	477	2.2	3.0	14.0

Three-point field goals: 1984-85, 0-for-4. 1987-88, 0-for-1. Totals, 0-for-5.

Personal fouls/disqualifications: 1975-76, 6/0. 1976-77, 33/0. 1977-78, 26/0. 1984-85, 12/0. 1987-88, 2/0. Totals, 79/0.

NBA ALL-STAR GAME RECORD

Season Team	Min.	FGM	FGA	Pct.	FTM	FTA	Pct.	REBOUNDS Off.	Def.	Tot.	Ast.	PF	Dq.	St.	Blk.	TO	Pts.
1980 —San Diego	21	7	13	.538	0	1	.000	1	2	3	5	1	0	0	1	5	14

FULKS, JOE   F/C

PERSONAL: Born October 26, 1921, in Birmingham, Ky. ... Died March 21, 1976. ... 6-5/190. ... Full name: Joseph Franklin Fulks. ... Nickname: Jumpin' Joe.
HIGH SCHOOL: Birmingham (Ky.), then Kuttawa (Ky.).
COLLEGE: Murray State.
TRANSACTIONS/CAREER NOTES: In military service (1943-44 through 1945-46 seasons). ... Signed by Philadelphia Warriors of Basketball Association of America (1946).
CAREER HONORS: Elected to Naismith Memorial Basketball Hall of Fame (1977). ... NBA 25th Anniversary All-Time Team (1970).
MISCELLANEOUS: Member of BAA championship team (1947).

COLLEGIATE RECORD

NOTES: Elected to NAIA Basketball Hall of Fame (1952).

Season Team	G	Min.	FGM	FGA	Pct.	FTM	FTA	Pct.	Reb.	Ast.	Pts.	RPG	APG	PPG
41-42—Murray State	22	...	117	...	...	50	76	.658	...	...	284	...	...	12.9
42-43—Murray State	25	...	135	...	...	67	100	.670	...	...	337	...	...	13.5
Totals	47	...	252	...	...	117	176	.665	...	...	621	...	...	13.2

NBA REGULAR-SEASON RECORD

HONORS: All-NBA second team (1951). ... All-BAA first team (1947, 1948, 1949).

Season Team	G	Min.	FGM	FGA	Pct.	FTM	FTA	Pct.	Reb.	Ast.	PF	Dq.	Pts.	RPG	APG	PPG
46-47 —Philadelphia (BAA)	60	...	*475	*1557	.305	*439	*601	.730	...	25	199	...	*1389	...	0.4	*23.2
47-48 —Philadelphia (BAA)	43	...	326	*1258	.259	*297	390	.762	...	26	162	...	949	...	0.6	*22.1
48-49 —Philadelphia (BAA)	60	...	529	*1689	.313	502	638	.787	...	74	262	...	1560	...	1.2	26.0
49-50 —Philadelphia	68	...	336	1209	.278	293	421	.696	...	56	240	...	965	...	0.8	14.2
50-51 —Philadelphia	66	...	429	1358	.316	378	442	*.855	523	117	247	8	1236	7.9	1.8	18.7
51-52 —Philadelphia	61	1904	336	1078	.312	250	303	.825	368	123	255	13	922	6.0	2.0	15.1
52-53 —Philadelphia	70	2085	332	960	.346	168	231	.727	387	138	319	20	832	5.5	2.0	11.9
53-54 —Philadelphia	61	501	61	229	.266	28	49	.571	101	28	90	0	150	1.7	0.5	2.5
Totals	489	...	2824	9338	.302	2355	3075	.766	...	587	1774	...	8003	...	1.2	16.4

NBA PLAYOFF RECORD

Season Team	G	Min.	FGM	FGA	Pct.	FTM	FTA	Pct.	Reb.	Ast.	PF	Dq.	Pts.	RPG	APG	PPG
46-47 —Philadelphia (BAA)	10	...	74	257	.288	74	94	.787	...	3	32	...	222	...	0.3	22.2
47-48 —Philadelphia (BAA)	13	...	92	380	.242	98	121	.810	...	3	55	...	282	...	0.2	21.7
48-49 —Philadelphia (BAA)	1	...	0	0	...	0	0	...	...	0	1	0	0	...	0.0	0.0
49-50 —Philadelphia	2	...	5	26	.192	5	10	.500	...	2	10	...	15	...	1.0	7.5
50-51 —Philadelphia	2	...	16	49	.327	20	27	.741	16	1	9	0	52	8.0	0.5	26.0
51-52 —Philadelphia	3	70	5	33	.152	7	9	.778	12	2	13	1	17	4.0	0.7	5.7
Totals	31	...	192	745	.258	204	261	.782	...	11	120	...	588	...	0.4	19.0

NBA ALL-STAR GAME RECORD

Season Team	Min.	FGM	FGA	Pct.	FTM	FTA	Pct.	Reb	Ast.	PF	Dq.	Pts.
1951 —Philadelphia	...	6	15	.400	7	9	.778	7	3	5	0	19
1952 —Philadelphia	9	3	7	.429	0	1	.000	5	2	2	0	6
Totals	...	9	22	.409	7	10	.700	12	5	7	0	25

GALLATIN, HARRY   F/C

PERSONAL: Born April 26, 1927, in Roxana, Ill. ... 6-6/215. ... Full name: Harry Junior Gallatin. ... Nickname: The Horse.
HIGH SCHOOL: Roxana (Ill.).
COLLEGE: Northeast Missouri State Teachers College.
TRANSACTIONS/CAREER NOTES: Selected by New York Knicks in first round of 1948 BAA Draft. ... Knicks franchise became part of NBA for 1949-50 season. ... Traded by Knicks with G Dick Atha and C/F Nat Clifton to Detroit Pistons for F Mel Hutchins and first-round draft choice (April 3, 1957).
CAREER HONORS: Elected to Naismith Memorial Basketball Hall of Fame (1990).

COLLEGIATE RECORD

NOTES: Elected to NAIA Basketball Hall of Fame (1957).

Season Team	G	Min.	FGM	FGA	Pct.	FTM	FTA	Pct.	Reb.	Ast.	Pts.	RPG	APG	PPG
46-47—NE Missouri St.	31	...	149	...	...	53	89	.596	...	...	351	...	...	11.3
47-48—NE Missouri St.	31	...	178	465	.383	109	162	.673	...	...	465	...	...	15.0
Totals	62	...	327	...	...	162	251	.645	...	...	816	...	...	13.2

NBA REGULAR-SEASON RECORD

HONORS: All-NBA first team (1954). ... All-NBA second team (1955).

Season Team	G	Min.	FGM	FGA	Pct.	FTM	FTA	Pct.	Reb.	Ast.	PF	Dq.	Pts.	RPG	APG	PPG
48-49 —New York (BAA)	52	...	157	479	.328	120	169	.710	...	63	127	...	434	...	1.2	8.3
49-50 —New York	68	...	263	664	.396	277	366	.757	...	56	215	...	803	...	0.8	11.8
50-51 —New York	66	...	293	705	.416	259	354	.732	800	180	244	4	845	12.1	2.7	12.8
51-52 —New York	66	1931	233	527	.442	275	341	.806	661	115	223	5	741	10.0	1.7	11.2
52-53 —New York	70	2333	282	635	.444	301	430	.700	916	126	224	6	865	13.1	1.8	12.4

Season Team	G	Min.	FGM	FGA	Pct.	FTM	FTA	Pct.	Reb.	Ast.	PF	Dq.	Pts.	AVERAGES RPG	APG	PPG
53-54 —New York	72	2690	258	639	.404	433	552	.784	*1098	153	208	2	949	*15.3	2.1	13.2
54-55 —New York	72	2548	330	859	.384	393	483	.814	995	176	206	5	1053	13.8	2.4	14.6
55-56 —New York	72	2378	322	834	.386	358	455	.787	740	168	220	6	1002	10.3	2.3	13.9
56-57 —New York	72	1943	332	817	.406	415	519	.800	725	85	202	1	1079	10.1	1.2	15.0
57-58 —Detroit	72	1990	340	898	.379	392	498	.787	749	86	217	5	1072	10.4	1.2	14.9
Totals	682	...	2810	7057	.398	3223	4167	.773	...	1208	2086	...	8843	...	1.8	13.0

NBA PLAYOFF RECORD

Season Team	G	Min.	FGM	FGA	Pct.	FTM	FTA	Pct.	Reb.	Ast.	PF	Dq.	Pts.	AVERAGES RPG	APG	PPG
48-49 —New York (BAA)	6	...	20	56	.357	32	39	.821	...	10	31	...	72	...	1.7	12.0
49-50 —New York	5	...	20	52	.385	25	32	.781	...	6	23	...	65	...	1.2	13.0
50-51 —New York	14	...	49	140	.350	67	87	.770	163	26	57	3	165	11.6	1.9	11.8
51-52 —New York	14	471	50	122	.410	51	66	.773	134	19	45	1	151	9.6	1.4	10.8
52-53 —New York	11	303	36	86	.419	44	59	.746	120	15	29	0	116	10.9	1.4	10.5
53-54 —New York	4	151	16	35	.457	22	31	.710	61	6	12	0	54	15.3	1.5	13.5
54-55 —New York	3	108	19	42	.452	17	22	.773	44	7	11	0	55	14.7	2.3	18.3
57-58 —Detroit	7	182	32	87	.368	26	37	.703	70	11	27	1	90	10.0	1.6	12.9
Totals	64	...	242	620	.390	284	373	.761	100	...	235	...	768	...	1.6	12.0

NBA ALL-STAR GAME RECORD

Season Team	Min.	FGM	FGA	Pct.	FTM	FTA	Pct.	Reb	Ast.	PF	Dq.	Pts.
1951 —New York	...	2	4	.500	1	1	1.000	5	2	4	0	5
1952 —New York	22	3	5	.600	1	4	.250	9	3	3	0	7
1953 —New York	19	1	4	.250	1	2	.500	3	2	1	0	3
1954 —New York	28	0	2	.000	5	6	.833	18	3	0	0	5
1955 —New York	36	4	7	.571	5	5	1.000	14	3	2	0	13
1956 —New York	30	5	12	.417	6	7	.857	5	2	4	0	16
1957 —New York	24	4	7	.571	0	2	.000	11	1	3	0	8
Totals	...	19	41	.463	19	27	.704	65	16	17	0	57

HEAD COACHING RECORD

HONORS: NBA Coach of the Year (1963).

COLLEGIATE COACHING RECORD

Season Team	W	L	Pct.	Finish
58-59 —Southern Illinois-Carbondale	17	10	.630	2nd/Interstate Intercollegiate Athletic Conference
59-60 —Southern Illinois-Carbondale	20	9	.690	T1st/Interstate Intercollegiate Athletic Conference
60-61 —Southern Illinois-Carbondale	21	6	.778	1st/Interstate Intercollegiate Athletic Conference
61-62 —Southern Illinois-Carbondale	21	10	.677	1st/Interstate Intercollegiate Athletic Conference
67-68 —Southern Ill.-Edwardsville	5	5	.500	
68-69 —Southern Ill.-Edwardsville	7	10	.412	
69-70 —Southern Ill.-Edwardsville	7	16	.304	
Totals (7 years)	98	66	.598	

NBA COACHING RECORD

Season Team	REGULAR SEASON W	L	Pct.	Finish	PLAYOFFS W	L	Pct.
62-63 —St. Louis	48	32	.600	2nd/Western Division	6	5	.545
63-64 —St. Louis	46	34	.575	2nd/Western Division	6	6	.500
64-65 —St. Louis	17	16	.515		—	—	—
—New York	19	23	.452	4th/Eastern Division	—	—	—
65-66 —New York	6	15	.286		—	—	—
Totals (4 years)	136	120	.531	Totals (2 years)	12	11	.522

NOTES:

1959—Defeated Wittenberg, 90-80, in NCAA College Division Tournament regional semifinal; lost to Belmont Academy, 79-70, in regional final.

1960—Defeated McKendree, 97-71, in NCAA College Division Tournament regional; lost to Oklahoma Baptist, 75-71, in semifinal.

1961—Defeated Trinity (Tex.), 96-84, in NCAA College Division Tournament regional semifinal; lost to Southeast Missouri, 87-84, in regional final.

1962—Defeated Union, 78-56, in NCAA College Division Tournament regional semifinal; defeated Evansville, 88-83, in regional final; defeated Northeastern, 73-57, in quarterfinal; lost to Mount St. Mary's, 58-57, in semifinals; defeated Nebraska Wesleyan 98-81, in third-place game.

1963—Defeated Detroit, 3-1, in Western Division semifinals; lost to Los Angeles, 4-3, in Western Division finals.

1964—Defeated Los Angeles, 3-2, in Western Division semifinals; lost to San Francisco, 4-3, in Western Division finals. Replaced as St. Louis head coach by Richie Guerin (November).

1965—Replaced Eddie Donovan as New York head coach (January), with record of 12-26. Replaced as New York head coach by Dick McGuire (November 29).

RECORD AS BASEBALL PLAYER

TRANSACTIONS/CAREER NOTES: Signed by Erwin (Tenn.) of Appalachian League (January 1945). ... On military service list (July 1945-February 24, 1949). ... Placed on suspended list (July 13, 1950). ... Released (September 29, 1950).

Year Team (League)	W	L	Pct.	ERA	G	GS	CG	ShO	Sv.	IP	H	R	ER	BB	SO
1949—Decatur (Three I)	7	9	.438	4.28	32	...	10	1	...	166	171	88	79	85	78

GERVIN, GEORGE G/F

PERSONAL: Born April 27, 1952, in Detroit. ... 6-7/185. ... Full name: George Gervin. ... Nickname: Iceman. ... Brother of Derrick Gervin, guard with New Jersey Nets (1989-90 and 1990-91).
HIGH SCHOOL: Martin Luther King (Detroit).
COLLEGE: Long Beach State, then Eastern Michigan.
TRANSACTIONS/CAREER NOTES: Selected after sophomore season by Virginia Squires in first round of 1973 ABA special circumstance draft. ... Selected by Phoenix Suns in third round (40th pick overall) of 1974 NBA Draft. ... Contract sold by Squires to San Antonio Spurs (January 30, 1974). ... Spurs franchise became part of NBA for 1976-77 season. ... Traded by Spurs to Chicago Bulls for F David Greenwood (October 24, 1985). ... Played in Italy (1986-87). ... Played with Quad City Thunder of Continental Basketball Association (1989-90).
CAREER HONORS: Elected to Naismith Memorial Basketball Hall of Fame (1996).
MISCELLANEOUS: San Antonio Spurs all-time leading scorer with 19,383 points (1976-77 through 1984-85).

COLLEGIATE RECORD

NOTES: Left Long Beach State before the start of 1969-70 season.

Season Team	G	Min.	FGM	FGA	Pct.	FTM	FTA	Pct.	Reb.	Ast.	Pts.	RPG	APG	PPG
70-71—Eastern Mich.	9	300	65	123	.528	28	39	.718	104	29	158	11.6	3.2	17.6
71-72—Eastern Mich.	30	1098	339	571	.594	208	265	.785	458	103	886	15.3	3.4	29.5
Totals	39	1398	404	694	.582	236	304	.776	562	132	1044	14.4	3.4	26.8

ABA REGULAR-SEASON RECORD

NOTES: ABA All-Star second team (1975, 1976). ... ABA All-Rookie team (1973).

Season Team	G	Min.	2-POINT			3-POINT			FTM	FTA	Pct.	Reb.	Ast.	Pts.	AVERAGES		
			FGM	FGA	Pct.	FGM	FGA	Pct.							RPG	APG	PPG
72-73—Virginia	30	689	155	315	.492	6	26	.231	96	118	.814	128	34	424	4.3	1.1	14.1
73-74—Virginia-San Antonio	74	2511	664	1370	.485	8	56	.143	378	464	.815	624	142	1730	8.4	1.9	23.4
74-75—San Antonio	84	3113	767	1600	.479	17	55	.309	380	458	.830	697	207	1965	8.3	2.5	23.4
75-76—San Antonio	81	2748	692	1359	.509	14	55	.255	342	399	.857	546	201	1768	6.7	2.5	21.8
Totals	269	9061	2278	4644	.491	45	192	.234	1196	1439	.831	1995	584	5887	7.4	2.2	21.9

ABA PLAYOFF RECORD

Season Team	G	Min.	2-POINT			3-POINT			FTM	FTA	Pct.	Reb.	Ast.	Pts.	AVERAGES		
			FGM	FGA	Pct.	FGM	FGA	Pct.							RPG	APG	PPG
72-73—Virginia	5	200	33	72	.458	1	5	.200	23	34	.676	38	8	93	7.6	1.6	18.6
73-74—San Antonio	7	226	56	114	.491	1	1	1.000	29	31	.935	52	19	144	7.4	2.7	20.6
74-75—San Antonio	6	276	76	159	.478	3	12	.250	43	52	.827	84	8	204	14.0	1.3	34.0
75-76—San Antonio	7	288	67	125	.536	0	3	.000	56	69	.812	64	19	190	9.1	2.7	27.1
Totals	25	990	232	470	.494	5	21	.238	151	186	.812	238	54	631	9.5	2.2	25.2

ABA ALL-STAR GAME RECORD

Season Team	Min.	2-POINT			3-POINT			FTM	FTA	Pct.	Reb.	Ast.	Pts.
		FGM	FGA	Pct.	FGM	FGA	Pct.						
1974—Virginia	21	3	8	.375	0	1	.000	3	4	.750	5	3	9
1975—San Antonio	30	8	14	.571	0	1	.000	7	8	.875	6	3	23
1976—San Antonio	16	3	13	.231	0	0	...	1	2	.500	6	1	8
Totals	67	14	35	.400	0	2	.000	11	14	.786	17	7	40

NBA REGULAR-SEASON RECORD

RECORDS: Holds single-game record for most points in one quarter—33 (April 9, 1978, vs. New Orleans).
HONORS: All-NBA first team (1978, 1979, 1980, 1981, 1982). ... All-NBA second team (1977, 1983).

Season Team	G	Min.	FGM	FGA	Pct.	FTM	FTA	Pct.	REBOUNDS			Ast.	St.	Blk.	TO	Pts.	AVERAGES		
									Off.	Def.	Tot.						RPG	APG	PPG
76-77—San Antonio	82	2705	726	1335	.544	443	532	.833	134	320	454	238	105	104	...	1895	5.5	2.9	23.1
77-78—San Antonio	82	2857	*864	1611	.536	504	607	.830	118	302	420	302	136	110	306	*2232	5.1	3.7	*27.2
78-79—San Antonio	80	2888	*947	*1749	.541	471	570	.826	142	258	400	219	137	91	286	*2365	5.0	2.7	*29.6
79-80—San Antonio	78	2934	*1024	*1940	.528	505	593	.852	154	249	403	202	110	79	254	*2585	5.2	2.6	*33.1
80-81—San Antonio	82	2765	850	1729	.492	512	620	.826	126	293	419	260	94	56	251	2221	5.1	3.2	27.1
81-82—San Antonio	79	2817	*993	*1987	.500	555	642	.864	138	254	392	187	77	45	210	*2551	5.0	2.4	*32.3
82-83—San Antonio	78	2830	757	1553	.487	517	606	.853	111	246	357	264	88	67	247	2043	4.6	3.4	26.2
83-84—San Antonio	76	2584	765	1561	.490	427	507	.842	106	207	313	220	79	47	224	1967	4.1	2.9	25.9
84-85—San Antonio	72	2091	600	1182	.508	324	384	.844	79	155	234	178	66	48	198	1524	3.3	2.5	21.2
85-86—Chicago	82	2065	519	1100	.472	283	322	.879	78	137	215	144	49	23	161	1325	2.6	1.8	16.2
Totals	791	26536	8045	15747	.511	4541	5383	.844	1186	2421	3607	2214	941	670	2137	20708	4.6	2.8	26.2

Three-point field goals: 1979-80, 32-for-102 (.314). 1980-81, 9-for-35 (.257). 1981-82, 10-for-36 (.278). 1982-83, 12-for-33 (.364). 1983-84, 10-for-24 (.417). 1984-85, 0-for-10. 1985-86, 4-for-19 (.211). Totals, 77-for-259 (.297).

Personal fouls/disqualifications: 1976-77, 286/12. 1977-78, 255/3. 1978-79, 275/5. 1979-80, 208/0. 1980-81, 212/4. 1981-82, 215/2. 1982-83, 243/5. 1983-84, 219/3. 1984-85, 208/2. 1985-86, 210/4. Totals, 2331/40.

NBA PLAYOFF RECORD

Season Team	G	Min.	FGM	FGA	Pct.	FTM	FTA	Pct.	REBOUNDS			Ast.	St.	Blk.	TO	Pts.	AVERAGES		
									Off.	Def.	Tot.						RPG	APG	PPG
76-77—San Antonio	2	62	19	44	.432	12	15	.800	5	6	11	3	1	2	...	50	5.5	1.5	25.0
77-78—San Antonio	6	227	78	142	.549	43	56	.768	11	23	34	19	6	16	19	199	5.7	3.2	33.2
78-79—San Antonio	14	513	158	295	.536	84	104	.808	33	49	82	35	27	14	40	400	5.9	2.5	28.6
79-80—San Antonio	3	122	37	74	.500	26	30	.867	9	11	20	12	5	3	9	100	6.7	4.0	33.3
80-81—San Antonio	7	274	77	154	.500	36	45	.800	9	26	35	24	5	5	20	190	5.0	3.4	27.1
81-82—San Antonio	9	373	103	228	.452	59	71	.831	19	47	66	41	10	4	31	265	7.3	4.6	29.4
82-83—San Antonio	11	437	108	208	.519	61	69	.884	21	53	74	37	12	4	46	277	6.7	3.4	25.2

Season Team	G	Min.	FGM	FGA	Pct.	FTM	FTA	Pct.	REBOUNDS Off.	Def.	Tot.	Ast.	St.	Blk.	TO	Pts.	AVERAGES RPG	APG	PPG
84-85—San Antonio....	5	183	42	79	.532	27	34	.794	3	15	18	14	3	3	20	111	3.6	2.8	22.2
85-86—Chicago	2	11	0	1	.000	0	0	...	0	1	1	1	0	0	2	0	0.5	0.5	0.0
Totals	59	2202	622	1225	.508	348	424	.821	110	231	341	186	69	51	187	1592	5.8	3.2	27.0

Three-point field goals: 1979-80, 0-for-2. 1980-81, 0-for-3. 1981-82, 0-for-3. 1982-83, 0-for-2. 1984-85, 0-for-3. Totals, 0-for-13.
Personal fouls/disqualifications: 1976-77, 9/1. 1977-78, 23/0. 1978-79, 51/1. 1979-80, 8/0. 1980-81, 19/1. 1981-82, 36/1. 1982-83, 39/1. 1984-85, 19/0. 1985-86, 3/0. Totals, 207/5.

NBA ALL-STAR GAME RECORD

NOTES: NBA All-Star Game Most Valuable Player (1980).

Season Team	Min.	FGM	FGA	Pct.	FTM	FTA	Pct.	REBOUNDS Off.	Def.	Tot.	Ast.	PF	Dq.	St.	Blk.	TO	Pts.
1977 —San Antonio	12	0	6	.000	0	0	...	0	1	1	0	1	0	0	1	...	0
1978 —San Antonio	18	4	11	.364	1	3	.333	1	1	2	1	2	0	2	1	2	9
1979 —San Antonio	34	8	16	.500	10	11	.909	2	4	6	2	4	0	1	1	3	26
1980 —San Antonio	40	14	26	.538	6	9	.667	4	6	10	3	2	0	3	0	3	34
1981 —San Antonio	24	5	9	.556	1	2	.500	1	2	3	0	3	0	2	1	2	11
1982 —San Antonio	27	5	14	.357	2	2	1.000	1	5	6	1	3	0	3	3	0	12
1983 —San Antonio	14	3	8	.375	2	2	1.000	0	0	0	3	3	0	2	0	0	9
1984 —San Antonio	21	5	6	.833	3	3	1.000	0	2	2	1	5	0	0	1	6	13
1985 —San Antonio	25	10	12	.833	3	4	.750	0	3	3	1	2	0	3	1	4	23
Totals..............................	215	54	108	.500	28	36	.778	9	24	33	12	25	0	16	9	20	137

COMBINED ABA AND NBA REGULAR-SEASON RECORDS

	G	Min.	FGM	FGA	Pct.	FTM	FTA	Pct.	REBOUNDS Off.	Def.	Tot.	Ast.	Stl.	Blk.	TO	Pts.	AVERAGES RPG	APG	PPG
Totals	1060	35597	10368	20583	.504	5737	6822	.841	...	...	5602	2798	...	...	...	26595	5.3	2.6	25.1

Three-point field goals: 122-for-451 (.271).
Personal fouls/disqualifications: 3250.

ITALIAN LEAGUE RECORD

Season Team	G	Min.	FGM	FGA	Pct.	FTM	FTA	Pct.	Reb.	Ast.	Pts.	AVERAGES RPG	APG	PPG
86-87—Banco Roma..................	27	893	263	525	.501	159	190	.837	134	9	704	5.0	0.3	26.1

CBA REGULAR-SEASON RECORD

Season Team	G	Min.	FGM	FGA	Pct.	FTM	FTA	Pct.	Reb.	Ast.	Pts.	AVERAGES RPG	APG	PPG
89-90—Quad City......................	14	391	115	235	.489	54	73	.740	91	20	284	6.5	1.4	20.3

GILMORE, ARTIS   C

PERSONAL: Born September 21, 1949, in Chipley, Fla. ... 7-2/265. ... Full name: Artis Gilmore.
HIGH SCHOOL: Roulhac (Chipley, Fla.), then Carver (Dothan, Ala.).
JUNIOR COLLEGE: Gardner-Webb Junior College (N.C.).
COLLEGE: Jacksonville.
TRANSACTIONS/CAREER NOTES: Selected by Chicago Bulls in seventh round (117th pick overall) of 1971 NBA Draft. ... Selected by Kentucky Colonels in first round of 1971 ABA draft. ... Selected by Bulls from Colonels in ABA dispersal draft (August 5, 1976). ... Traded by Bulls to San Antonio Spurs for C Dave Corzine, F Mark Olberding and cash (July 22, 1982). ... Traded by Spurs to Bulls for 1988 second-round draft choice (June 22, 1987). ... Waived by Bulls (December 26, 1987). ... Signed as free agent by Boston Celtics (January 8, 1988). ... Played in Italy (1988-89).
MISCELLANEOUS: Chicago Bulls all-time blocked shots leader with 1,017 (1976-77 through 1981-82 and 1987-88).

COLLEGIATE RECORD

NOTES: THE SPORTING NEWS All-America first team (1971). ... THE SPORTING NEWS All-America second team (1970). ... Holds NCAA career record for average rebounds per game—22.7. ... Led NCAA Division I with 22.2 rebounds per game (1970) and 23.2 rebounds per game (1971).

Season Team	G	Min.	FGM	FGA	Pct.	FTM	FTA	Pct.	Reb.	Ast.	Pts.	AVERAGES RPG	APG	PPG
67-68—Gardner-Webb J.C.........	31	...	296	...	...	121	...	...	...	...	713	...	...	23.0
68-69—Gardner-Webb J.C.........	36	...	326	...	...	140	...	...	...	...	792	...	...	22.0
69-70—Jacksonville....................	28	...	307	529	.580	128	202	.634	621	51	742	22.2	1.8	26.5
70-71—Jacksonville....................	26	...	229	405	.565	112	188	.596	603	42	570	23.2	1.6	21.9
Junior college totals	67	...	622	...	...	261	...	...	...	...	1505	...	...	22.5
4-year-college totals	54	...	536	934	.574	240	390	.615	1224	93	1312	22.7	1.7	24.3

ABA REGULAR-SEASON RECORD

NOTES: ABA Most Valuable Player (1972). ... ABA Rookie of the Year (1972). ... ABA All-Star first team (1972, 1973, 1974, 1975, 1976). ... ABA All-Defensive team (1973, 1974, 1975, 1976). ... ABA All-Rookie Team (1972). ... Member of ABA championship team (1975). ... Holds single-game record for most rebounds—40 (February 3, 1974, vs. New York). ... Holds single-season record for most blocked shots—422 (1972). ... Led ABA with 341 personal fouls (1972).

Season Team	G	Min.	2-POINT FGM	FGA	Pct.	3-POINT FGM	FGA	Pct.	FTM	FTA	Pct.	Reb.	Ast.	Pts.	AVERAGES RPG	APG	PPG
71-72—Kentucky..................	84	*3666	806	1348	*.598	0	0	...	391	605	.646	*1491	230	2003	*17.8	2.7	23.8
72-73—Kentucky..................	84	3502	686	1226	*.560	1	2	.500	368	572	.643	*1476	295	1743	*17.6	3.5	20.8
73-74—Kentucky..................	84	*3502	621	1257	.494	0	3	.000	326	489	.667	*1538	329	1568	*18.3	3.9	18.7
74-75—Kentucky..................	84	*3493	783	1349	.580	1	2	.500	412	592	.696	*1361	208	1981	16.2	2.5	23.6
75-76—Kentucky..................	84	3286	773	1401	.552	0	0	...	521	*764	.682	*1303	211	2067	*15.5	2.5	24.6
Totals	420	17449	3669	6581	.558	2	7	.286	2018	3022	.668	7169	1273	9362	17.1	3.0	22.3

ABA PLAYOFF RECORD

NOTES: ABA Playoff Most Valuable Player (1975).

Season Team	G	Min.	2-POINT			3-POINT			FTM	FTA	Pct.	Reb.	Ast.	Pts.	AVERAGES		
			FGM	FGA	Pct.	FGM	FGA	Pct.							RPG	APG	PPG
71-72—Kentucky	6	285	52	90	.578	0	1	.000	27	38	.711	106	25	131	17.7	4.2	21.8
72-73—Kentucky	19	780	142	261	.544	0	0	...	77	123	.626	260	75	361	13.7	3.9	19.0
73-74—Kentucky	8	344	71	127	.559	0	0	...	38	66	.576	149	28	180	18.6	3.5	22.5
74-75—Kentucky	15	679	132	245	.539	0	0	...	98	127	.772	264	38	362	17.6	2.5	24.1
75-76—Kentucky	10	390	93	153	.608	0	0	...	56	74	.757	152	19	242	15.2	1.9	24.2
Totals	58	2478	490	876	.559	0	1	.000	296	428	.692	931	185	1276	16.1	3.2	22.0

ABA ALL-STAR GAME RECORD

NOTES: ABA All-Star Game Most Valuable Player (1974).

Season Team	Min.	2-POINT			3-POINT			FTM	FTA	Pct.	Reb.	Ast.	Pts.
		FGM	FGA	Pct.	FGM	FGA	Pct.						
1972—Kentucky	27	4	5	.800	0	0	...	6	10	.600	10	2	14
1973—Kentucky	31	3	8	.375	0	0	...	4	8	.500	16	0	10
1974—Kentucky	27	8	12	.667	0	0	...	2	3	.667	13	1	18
1975—Kentucky	28	4	8	.500	0	0	...	3	7	.429	13	2	11
1976—Kentucky	27	5	7	.714	0	0	...	4	6	.667	7	1	14
Totals	140	24	40	.600	0	0	...	19	34	.559	59	6	67

NBA REGULAR-SEASON RECORD

RECORDS: Holds career record for highest field-goal percentage (minimum 2,000 made)—.599.
HONORS: NBA All-Defensive second team (1978).

Season Team	G	Min.	FGM	FGA	Pct.	FTM	FTA	Pct.	REBOUNDS			Ast.	St.	Blk.	TO	Pts.	AVERAGES		
									Off.	Def.	Tot.						RPG	APG	PPG
76-77—Chicago	82	2877	570	1091	.522	387	586	.660	313	757	1070	199	44	203	...	1527	13.0	2.4	18.6
77-78—Chicago	82	3067	704	1260	.559	471	*669	.704	318	753	1071	263	42	181	*366	1879	13.1	3.2	22.9
78-79—Chicago	82	3265	753	1310	.575	434	587	.739	293	750	1043	274	50	156	310	1940	12.7	3.3	23.7
79-80—Chicago	48	1568	305	513	.595	245	344	.712	108	324	432	133	29	59	133	855	9.0	2.8	17.8
80-81—Chicago	82	2832	547	816	*.670	375	532	.705	220	608	828	172	47	198	236	1469	10.1	2.1	17.9
81-82—Chicago	82	2796	546	837	*.652	424	552	.768	224	611	835	136	49	220	227	1517	10.2	1.7	18.5
82-83—San Antonio	82	2797	556	888	*.626	367	496	.740	299	685	984	126	40	192	254	1479	12.0	1.5	18.0
83-84—San Antonio	64	2034	351	556	*.631	280	390	.718	213	449	662	70	36	132	149	982	10.3	1.1	15.3
84-85—San Antonio	81	2756	532	854	.623	484	646	.749	231	615	846	131	40	173	241	1548	10.4	1.6	19.1
85-86—San Antonio	71	2395	423	684	.618	338	482	.701	166	434	600	102	39	108	186	1184	8.5	1.4	16.7
86-87—San Antonio	82	2405	346	580	.597	242	356	.680	185	394	579	150	39	95	178	934	7.1	1.8	11.4
87-88—Chi.-Boston	71	893	99	181	.547	67	128	.523	69	142	211	21	15	30	67	265	3.0	0.3	3.7
Totals	909	29685	5732	9570	.599	4114	5768	.713	2639	6522	9161	1777	470	1747	2347	15579	10.1	2.0	17.1

Three-point field goals: 1981-82, 1-for-1. 1982-83, 0-for-6. 1983-84, 0-for-3. 1984-85, 0-for-2. 1985-86, 0-for-1. Totals, 1-for-13 (.077).
Personal fouls/disqualifications: 1976-77, 266/4. 1977-78, 261/4. 1978-79, 280/2. 1979-80, 167/5. 1980-81, 295/2. 1981-82, 287/4. 1982-83, 273/4. 1983-84, 229/4. 1984-85, 306/4. 1985-86, 239/3. 1986-87, 235/2. 1987-88, 148/0. Totals, 2986/38.

NBA PLAYOFF RECORD

Season Team	G	Min.	FGM	FGA	Pct.	FTM	FTA	Pct.	REBOUNDS			Ast.	St.	Blk.	TO	Pts.	AVERAGES		
									Off.	Def.	Tot.						RPG	APG	PPG
76-77—Chicago	3	126	19	40	.475	18	23	.783	15	24	39	6	3	8	...	56	13.0	2.0	18.7
80-81—Chicago	6	247	35	59	.593	38	55	.691	24	43	67	12	6	17	17	108	11.2	2.0	18.0
82-83—San Antonio	11	401	76	132	.576	32	46	.696	37	105	142	18	9	34	27	184	12.9	1.6	16.7
84-85—San Antonio	5	185	29	52	.558	31	45	.689	10	40	50	7	2	7	23	89	10.0	1.4	17.8
85-86—San Antonio	3	107	16	24	.667	8	14	.571	7	11	18	3	7	1	10	40	6.0	1.0	13.3
87-88—Boston	14	86	4	8	.500	7	14	.500	4	16	20	1	0	4	4	15	1.4	0.1	1.1
Totals	42	1152	179	315	.568	134	197	.680	97	239	336	47	27	71	81	492	8.0	1.1	11.7

Personal fouls/disqualifications: 1976-77, 9/0. 1980-81, 15/0. 1982-83, 46/1. 1984-85, 18/0. 1985-86, 11/0. 1987-88, 14/0. Totals, 113/1.

NBA ALL-STAR GAME RECORD

Season	Team	Min.	FGM	FGA	Pct.	FTM	FTA	Pct.	REBOUNDS			Ast.	PF	Dq.	St.	Blk.	TO	Pts.
									Off.	Def.	Tot.							
1978	—Chicago	13	2	4	.500	6	8	.750	0	2	2	0	1	0	1	2	1	10
1979	—Chicago	15	3	4	.750	2	2	1.000	1	0	1	2	1	0	0	0	1	8
1981	—Chicago	22	5	7	.714	1	2	.500	1	5	6	2	4	0	0	1	0	11
1982	—Chicago	16	3	6	.500	1	1	1.000	1	2	3	2	4	0	0	1	2	7
1983	—San Antonio	16	2	4	.500	2	2	.500	1	4	5	1	4	0	1	0	1	5
1986	—San Antonio	13	3	4	.750	4	4	1.000	1	1	2	1	4	0	2	0	0	10
Totals		95	18	29	.621	15	19	.789	5	14	19	8	18	0	4	4	5	51

COMBINED ABA AND NBA REGULAR-SEASON RECORDS

	G	Min.	FGM	FGA	Pct.	FTM	FTA	Pct.	REBOUNDS			Ast.	Stl.	Blk.	TO	Pts.	AVERAGES		
									Off.	Def.	Tot.						RPG	APG	PPG
Totals	1329	33356	9403	16158	.582	6132	8790	.698	...	...	16330	3050	...	...	...	24041	12.3	2.3	18.1

Three-point field goals: 3-for-20 (.150).
Personal fouls/disqualifications: 4529.

ITALIAN LEAGUE RECORD

Season Team	G	Min.	FGM	FGA	Pct.	FTM	FTA	Pct.	Reb.	Ast.	Pts.	AVERAGES		
												RPG	APG	PPG
88-89—Bologna Arimo	35	1101	166	270	.615	97	147	.660	386	21	429	11.0	0.6	12.3

GOODRICH, GAIL — G

PERSONAL: Born April 23, 1943, in Los Angeles. ... 6-1/175. ... Full name: Gail Charles Goodrich Jr.
HIGH SCHOOL: Los Angeles Polytechnic.
COLLEGE: UCLA.
TRANSACTIONS/CAREER NOTES: Selected by Los Angeles Lakers in 1965 NBA Draft (territorial pick). ... Selected by Phoenix Suns from Lakers in NBA expansion draft (May 6, 1968). ... Traded by Suns to Lakers for F Mel Counts (May 20, 1970). ... Signed as veteran free agent by New Orleans Jazz (July 19, 1976); Lakers received 1977 and 1979 first-round draft choices and 1980 second-round draft choice as compensation; Jazz received 1977 second-round draft choice to complete transaction (October 6, 1976).
CAREER HONORS: Elected to Naismith Memorial Basketball Hall of Fame (1996).
MISCELLANEOUS: Member of NBA championship team (1972).

COLLEGIATE RECORD

NOTES: The Sporting News All-America first team (1965). ... Member of NCAA Division I championship teams (1964, 1965).

Season Team	G	Min.	FGM	FGA	Pct.	FTM	FTA	Pct.	Reb.	Ast.	Pts.	RPG	APG	PPG
61-62—UCLA‡	20	...	189	385	.491	110	155	.710	122	...	488	6.1	...	24.4
62-63—UCLA	29	...	117	280	.418	66	103	.641	101	...	300	3.5	...	10.3
63-64—UCLA	30	...	243	530	.459	160	225	.711	156	...	646	5.2	...	21.5
64-65—UCLA	30	...	277	528	.525	190	265	.717	158	...	744	5.3	...	24.8
Varsity totals	89	...	637	1338	.476	416	593	.702	415	...	1690	4.7	...	19.0

NBA REGULAR-SEASON RECORD

HONORS: All-NBA first team (1974).

Season Team	G	Min.	FGM	FGA	Pct.	FTM	FTA	Pct.	Reb.	Ast.	PF	Dq.	Pts.	RPG	APG	PPG
65-66 —Los Angeles	65	1008	203	503	.404	103	149	.691	130	103	103	1	509	2.0	1.6	7.8
66-67 —Los Angeles	77	1780	352	776	.454	337	337	.751	251	210	194	3	957	3.3	2.7	12.4
67-68 —Los Angeles	79	2057	395	812	.486	302	392	.770	199	205	228	2	1092	2.5	2.6	13.8
68-69 —Phoenix	81	3236	718	1746	.411	495	663	.747	437	518	253	3	1931	5.4	6.4	23.8
69-70 —Phoenix	81	3234	568	1251	.454	488	604	.808	340	605	251	3	1624	4.2	7.5	20.0
70-71 —Los Angeles	79	2808	558	1174	.475	264	343	.770	260	380	258	3	1380	3.3	4.8	17.5
71-72 —Los Angeles	82	3040	826	1695	.487	475	559	.850	295	365	210	0	2127	3.6	4.5	25.9
72-73 —Los Angeles	76	2697	750	1615	.464	314	374	.840	263	332	193	1	1814	3.5	4.4	23.9

Season Team	G	Min.	FGM	FGA	Pct.	FTM	FTA	Pct.	Off.	Def.	Tot.	Ast.	St.	Blk.	TO	Pts.	RPG	APG	PPG
73-74—Los Angeles	82	3061	784	1773	.442	*508	*588	.864	95	155	250	427	126	12	...	2076	3.0	5.2	25.3
74-75—Los Angeles	72	2668	656	1429	.459	318	378	.841	96	123	219	420	102	6	...	1630	3.0	5.8	22.6
75-76—Los Angeles	75	2646	583	1321	.441	293	346	.847	94	120	214	421	123	17	...	1459	2.9	5.6	19.5
76-77—New Orleans	27	609	136	305	.446	68	85	.800	25	36	61	74	22	2	...	340	2.3	2.7	12.6
77-78—New Orleans	81	2553	520	1050	.495	264	332	.795	75	102	177	388	82	22	205	1304	2.2	4.8	16.1
78-79—New Orleans	74	2130	382	850	.449	174	204	.853	68	115	183	357	90	13	185	938	2.5	4.8	12.7
Totals	1031	33527	7431	16300	.456	4319	5354	.807	...	...	3279	4805	545	72	390	19181	3.2	4.7	18.6

Personal fouls/disqualifications: 1973-74, 227/3. 1974-75, 214/1. 1975-76, 238/3. 1976-77, 43/0. 1977-78, 186/0. 1978-79, 177/1. Totals, 2775/24.

NBA PLAYOFF RECORD

Season Team	G	Min.	FGM	FGA	Pct.	FTM	FTA	Pct.	Reb.	Ast.	PF	Dq.	Pts.	RPG	APG	PPG
65-66 —Los Angeles	11	290	43	92	.467	29	43	.674	42	33	35	0	115	3.8	3.0	10.5
66-67 —Los Angeles	3	81	11	31	.355	11	18	.611	9	10	5	0	33	3.0	3.3	11.0
67-68 —Los Angeles	10	100	23	47	.489	14	18	.778	14	14	10	0	60	1.4	1.4	6.0
69-70 —Phoenix	7	265	56	118	.475	30	35	.857	32	38	21	0	142	4.6	5.4	20.3
70-71 —Los Angeles	12	518	105	247	.425	95	113	.841	38	91	38	0	305	3.2	7.6	25.4
71-72 —Los Angeles	15	575	130	292	.445	97	108	.898	38	50	50	0	357	2.5	3.3	23.8
72-73 —Los Angeles	17	604	139	310	.448	62	79	.785	61	67	53	1	340	3.6	3.9	20.0

Season Team	G	Min.	FGM	FGA	Pct.	FTM	FTA	Pct.	Off.	Def.	Tot.	Ast.	St.	Blk.	TO	Pts.	RPG	APG	PPG
73-74—Los Angeles	5	189	35	90	.389	28	33	.848	7	9	16	30	7	1	...	98	3.2	6.0	19.6
Totals	80	2622	542	1227	.442	366	447	.819	...	...	250	333	7	1	...	1450	3.1	4.2	18.1

Personal fouls/disqualifications: 1973-74, 7/0.

NBA ALL-STAR GAME RECORD

Season Team	Min.	FGM	FGA	Pct.	FTM	FTA	Pct.	Reb	Ast.	PF	Dq.	Pts.
1969 —Phoenix	6	2	4	.500	1	2	.500	1	1	1	0	5
1972 —Los Angeles	14	2	7	.286	0	0	...	1	2	2	0	4
1973 —Los Angeles	16	1	7	.143	0	0	...	2	1	2	0	2

Season Team	Min.	FGM	FGA	Pct.	FTM	FTA	Pct.	Off.	Def.	Tot.	Ast.	PF	Dq.	St.	Blk.	TO	Pts.
1974 —Los Angeles	26	9	16	.563	0	0	...	1	3	4	6	2	0	1	0	...	18
1975 —Los Angeles	15	2	4	.500	0	0	...	0	1	1	4	1	0	0	0	...	4
Totals	77	16	38	.421	1	2	.500	...	...	9	14	8	0	1	0	...	33

DID YOU KNOW...

...that John Havlicek is the only Boston Celtic to score 40 points in an NBA finals game?

GREER, HAL   G

PERSONAL: Born June 26, 1936, in Huntington, W.Va. ... 6-2/175. ... Full name: Harold Everett Greer.
HIGH SCHOOL: Douglass (Huntington, W.Va.).
COLLEGE: Marshall.
TRANSACTIONS/CAREER NOTES: Selected by Syracuse Nationals in second round (14th pick overall) of 1958 NBA Draft. ... Nationals franchise moved from Syracuse to Philadelphia and renamed 76ers for 1963-64 season.
CAREER HONORS: Elected to Naismith Memorial Basketball Hall of Fame (1981).
MISCELLANEOUS: Member of NBA championship team (1967). ... Philadelphia 76ers franchise all-time leading scorer with 21,586 points (1958-59 through 1972-73).

COLLEGIATE RECORD

Season Team	G	Min.	FGM	FGA	Pct.	FTM	FTA	Pct.	Reb.	Ast.	Pts.	RPG	APG	PPG
54-55—Marshall‡	...	...	...	...	...	...	...	...	...	...	...	...	...	18.0
55-56—Marshall	23	...	128	213	.601	101	145	.697	153	...	357	6.7	...	15.5
56-57—Marshall	24	...	167	329	.508	119	156	.763	332	...	453	13.8	...	18.9
57-58—Marshall	24	...	236	432	.546	95	114	.833	280	...	567	11.7	...	23.6
Varsity totals	71	...	531	974	.545	315	415	.759	765	...	1377	10.8	...	19.4

NBA REGULAR-SEASON RECORD

HONORS: All-NBA second team (1963, 1964, 1965, 1966, 1967, 1968, 1969).

Season Team	G	Min.	FGM	FGA	Pct.	FTM	FTA	Pct.	Reb.	Ast.	PF	Dq.	Pts.	RPG	APG	PPG
58-59 —Syracuse	68	1625	308	679	.454	137	176	.778	196	101	189	1	753	2.9	1.5	11.1
59-60 —Syracuse	70	1979	388	815	.476	148	189	.783	303	188	208	4	924	4.3	2.7	13.2
60-61 —Syracuse	79	2763	623	1381	.451	305	394	.774	455	302	242	0	1551	5.8	3.8	19.6
61-62 —Syracuse	71	2705	644	1442	.447	331	404	.819	524	313	252	2	1619	7.4	4.4	22.8
62-63 —Syracuse	80	2631	600	1293	.464	362	434	.834	457	275	286	4	1562	5.7	3.4	19.5
63-64 —Philadelphia	80	3157	715	1611	.444	435	525	.829	484	374	291	6	1865	6.1	4.7	23.3
64-65 —Philadelphia	70	2600	539	1245	.433	335	413	.811	355	313	254	7	1413	5.1	4.5	20.2
65-66 —Philadelphia	80	3326	703	1580	.445	413	514	.804	473	384	315	6	1819	5.9	4.8	22.7
66-67 —Philadelphia	80	3086	699	1524	.459	367	466	.788	422	303	302	5	1765	5.3	3.8	22.1
67-68 —Philadelphia	82	3263	777	1626	.478	422	549	.769	444	372	289	6	1976	5.4	4.5	24.1
68-69 —Philadelphia	82	3311	732	1595	.459	432	543	.796	435	414	294	8	1896	5.3	5.0	23.1
69-70 —Philadelphia	80	3024	705	1551	.455	352	432	.815	376	405	300	8	1762	4.7	5.1	22.0
70-71 —Philadelphia	81	3060	591	1371	.431	326	405	.805	364	369	289	4	1508	4.5	4.6	18.6
71-72 —Philadelphia	81	2410	389	866	.449	181	234	.774	271	316	268	10	959	3.3	3.9	11.8
72-73 —Philadelphia	38	848	91	232	.392	32	39	.821	106	111	76	1	214	2.8	2.9	5.6
Totals	1122	39788	8504	18811	.452	4578	5717	.801	5665	4540	3855	72	21586	5.0	4.0	19.2

NBA PLAYOFF RECORD

Season Team	G	Min.	FGM	FGA	Pct.	FTM	FTA	Pct.	Reb.	Ast.	PF	Dq.	Pts.	RPG	APG	PPG
58-59 —Syracuse	9	277	39	93	.419	26	32	.813	47	20	35	2	104	5.2	2.2	11.6
59-60 —Syracuse	3	84	22	43	.512	3	4	.750	14	10	5	0	47	4.7	3.3	15.7
60-61 —Syracuse	8	232	41	106	.387	33	40	.825	33	19	32	1	115	4.1	2.4	14.4
61-62 —Syracuse	1	5	0	0	...	0	0	...	0	0	1	0	0	0.0	0.0	0.0
62-63 —Syracuse	5	214	44	87	.506	29	35	.829	27	21	21	1	117	5.4	4.2	23.4
63-64 —Philadelphia	5	211	37	95	.389	33	39	.846	28	30	19	1	107	5.6	6.0	21.4
64-65 —Philadelphia	11	505	101	222	.455	69	87	.793	81	55	45	2	271	7.4	5.0	24.6
65-66 —Philadelphia	5	226	32	91	.352	18	23	.783	36	21	21	0	82	7.2	4.2	16.4
66-67 —Philadelphia	15	688	161	375	.429	94	118	.797	88	79	55	1	416	5.9	5.3	27.7
67-68 —Philadelphia	13	553	120	278	.432	95	111	.856	79	55	49	1	335	6.1	4.2	25.8
68-69 —Philadelphia	5	204	26	81	.321	28	36	.778	30	23	23	0	80	6.0	4.6	16.0
69-70 —Philadelphia	5	178	33	74	.446	11	13	.846	17	27	16	0	77	3.4	5.4	15.4
70-71 —Philadelphia	7	265	49	112	.438	27	36	.750	25	33	35	4	125	3.6	4.7	17.9
Totals	92	3642	705	1657	.425	466	574	.812	505	393	357	13	1876	5.5	4.3	20.4

NBA ALL-STAR GAME RECORD

NOTES: NBA All-Star Game Most Valuable Player (1968). ... Holds single-game record for most points in one quarter—19 (1968).

Season Team	Min.	FGM	FGA	Pct.	FTM	FTA	Pct.	Reb	Ast.	PF	Dq.	Pts.
1961 —Syracuse	18	7	11	.636	0	0	...	6	2	2	0	14
1962 —Syracuse	24	3	14	.214	2	7	.286	10	9	3	0	8
1963 —Syracuse	15	3	7	.429	0	0	...	3	2	4	0	6
1964 —Philadelphia	20	5	10	.500	3	4	.750	3	4	1	0	13
1965 —Philadelphia	21	5	11	.455	3	4	.750	4	1	2	0	13
1966 —Philadelphia	23	4	13	.308	1	1	1.000	5	1	4	0	9
1967 —Philadelphia	31	5	16	.313	7	8	.875	4	1	5	0	17
1968 —Philadelphia	17	8	8	1.000	5	7	.714	3	3	2	0	21
1969 —Philadelphia	17	0	1	.000	4	5	.800	3	2	2	0	4
1970 —Philadelphia	21	7	11	.636	1	1	1.000	4	3	4	0	15
Totals	207	47	102	.461	26	37	.703	45	28	29	0	120

CBA COACHING RECORD

Season Team	REGULAR SEASON				PLAYOFFS		
	W	L	Pct.	Finish	W	L	Pct.
80-81 —Philadelphia	17	23	.425	3rd/Eastern Division	3	3	.500

NOTES:
1981—Defeated Atlantic City, 2-1, in Eastern Division semifinals; lost to Rochester, 2-1, in Eastern Division finals.

ALL-TIME GREAT PLAYERS

GUERIN, RICHIE   G

PERSONAL: Born May 29, 1932, in New York. ... 6-4/210. ... Full name: Richard V. Guerin.
HIGH SCHOOL: Mt. St. Michael Academy (Bronx, N.Y.).
COLLEGE: Iona.
TRANSACTIONS/CAREER NOTES: Selected by New York Knicks in second round of 1954 NBA Draft. ... In military service during 1954-55 and 1955-56 seasons; played with Quantico Marines and Marine All-Star teams. ... Traded by Knicks to St. Louis Hawks for cash and second-round draft choice (October 18, 1963). ... Selected by Seattle SuperSonics from Hawks in NBA expansion draft (1967). ... Traded by SuperSonics to Atlanta Hawks for Dick Smith (November 15, 1968).

COLLEGIATE RECORD

Season Team	G	Min.	FGM	FGA	Pct.	FTM	FTA	Pct.	Reb.	Ast.	Pts.	RPG	APG	PPG
50-51—Iona‡						Freshman team statistics unavailable.								
51-52—Iona	27	...	159	...	...	146	...	...	...	...	464	...	...	17.2
52-53—Iona	21	...	139	283	.491	114	172	.663	...	...	392	...	...	18.7
53-54—Iona	21	...	171	405	.422	177	249	.711	...	...	519	...	...	24.7
Varsity totals	69	...	469	...	...	437	...	...	...	...	1375	...	...	19.9

NBA REGULAR-SEASON RECORD

HONORS: All-NBA second team (1959, 1960, 1962).

Season Team	G	Min.	FGM	FGA	Pct.	FTM	FTA	Pct.	Reb.	Ast.	PF	Dq.	Pts.	RPG	APG	PPG
56-57—New York	72	1793	257	699	.368	181	292	.620	334	182	186	3	695	4.6	2.5	9.7
57-58—New York	63	2368	344	973	.354	353	511	.691	489	317	202	3	1041	7.8	5.0	16.5
58-59—New York	71	2558	443	1046	.424	405	505	.802	518	364	255	1	1291	7.3	5.1	18.2
59-60—New York	74	2429	579	1379	.420	457	591	.773	505	468	242	3	1615	6.8	6.3	21.8
60-61—New York	79	3023	612	1545	.396	496	626	.792	628	503	310	3	1720	7.9	6.4	21.8
61-62—New York	78	3348	839	1897	.442	625	762	.820	501	539	299	3	2303	6.4	6.9	29.5
62-63—New York	79	2712	596	1380	.432	509	600	.848	331	348	228	2	1701	4.2	4.4	21.5
63-64—N.Y.-St.L.	80	2366	351	846	.415	347	424	.818	256	375	276	4	1049	3.2	4.7	13.1
64-65—St. Louis	57	1678	295	662	.446	231	301	.767	149	271	193	1	821	2.6	4.8	14.4
65-66—St. Louis	80	2363	414	998	.415	362	446	.812	314	388	256	4	1190	3.9	4.9	14.9
66-67—St. Louis	80	2275	394	904	.436	304	416	.731	192	345	247	2	1092	2.4	4.3	13.7
67-68—					Did not play—retired.											
68-69—Atlanta	27	472	47	111	.423	57	74	.770	59	99	66	0	151	2.2	3.7	5.6
69-70—Atlanta	8	64	3	11	.273	1	1	1.000	2	12	9	0	7	0.3	1.5	0.9
Totals	848	27449	5174	12451	.416	4328	5549	.780	4278	4211	2769	29	14676	5.0	5.0	17.3

NBA PLAYOFF RECORD

Season Team	G	Min.	FGM	FGA	Pct.	FTM	FTA	Pct.	Reb.	Ast.	PF	Dq.	Pts.	RPG	APG	PPG
58-59—New York	2	77	9	35	.257	12	14	.857	18	15	11	1	30	9.0	7.5	15.0
63-64—St. Louis	12	428	75	169	.444	67	85	.788	50	49	54	1	217	4.2	4.1	18.1
64-65—St. Louis	4	125	25	65	.385	19	25	.760	8	21	14	0	69	2.0	5.3	17.3
65-66—St. Louis	10	399	72	159	.453	62	76	.816	37	79	41	0	206	3.7	7.9	20.6
66-67—St. Louis	9	228	36	86	.419	24	30	.800	23	39	23	0	96	2.6	4.3	10.7
68-69—Atlanta	3	32	1	4	.250	1	2	.500	5	7	8	0	3	1.7	2.3	1.0
69-70—Atlanta	2	56	13	21	.619	7	7	1.000	8	4	6	0	33	4.0	2.0	16.5
Totals	42	1345	231	539	.429	192	239	.803	149	214	157	2	654	3.5	5.1	15.6

NBA ALL-STAR GAME RECORD

Season Team	Min.	FGM	FGA	Pct.	FTM	FTA	Pct.	Reb	Ast.	PF	Dq.	Pts.
1958 —New York	22	2	10	.200	3	4	.750	8	7	3	0	7
1959 —New York	22	1	7	.143	3	5	.600	3	3	1	0	5
1960 —New York	22	5	11	.455	2	2	1.000	4	4	4	0	12
1961 —New York	15	3	8	.375	5	6	.833	0	2	1	0	11
1962 —New York	27	10	17	.588	3	6	.500	3	1	6	1	23
1963 —New York	14	2	3	.667	1	3	.333	1	1	2	0	5
Totals	122	23	56	.411	17	26	.654	19	18	17	1	63

NBA COACHING RECORD

HONORS: NBA Coach of the Year (1968).

	REGULAR SEASON				PLAYOFFS		
Season Team	W	L	Pct.	Finish	W	L	Pct.
64-65—St. Louis	28	19	.596	2nd/Western Division	1	3	.250
65-66—St. Louis	36	44	.450	3rd/Western Division	6	4	.600
66-67—St. Louis	39	42	.481	2nd/Western Division	5	4	.556
67-68—St. Louis	56	26	.683	1st/Western Division	2	4	.333
68-69—Atlanta	48	34	.585	2nd/Western Division	5	6	.455
69-70—Atlanta	48	34	.585	1st/Western Division	4	5	.444
70-71—Atlanta	36	46	.439	2nd/Central Division	1	4	.200
71-72—Atlanta	36	46	.439	2nd/Central Division	2	4	.333
Totals (8 years)	327	291	.529	Totals (8 years)	26	34	.433

NOTES:
1964—Replaced Harry Gallatin as St. Louis head coach (November), with record of 17-16.
1965—Lost to Baltimore in Western Division semifinals.
1966—Defeated Baltimore, 3-0, in Western Division semifinals; lost to Los Angeles, 4-3, in Western Division finals.
1967—Defeated Chicago, 3-0, in Western Division semifinals; lost to San Francisco, 4-2, in Western Division finals.
1968—Lost to San Francisco in Western Division semifinals. Hawks franchise moved to Atlanta for 1968-69 season.
1969—Defeated San Diego, 4-2, in Western Division semifinals; lost to Los Angeles, 4-1, in Western Division finals.
1970—Defeated Chicago, 4-1, in Western Division semifinals; lost to Los Angeles, 4-0, in Western Division finals.
1971—Lost to New York in Eastern Conference semifinals.
1972—Lost to Boston in Eastern Conference semifinals.

HAGAN, CLIFF   F

PERSONAL: Born December 9, 1931, in Owensboro, Ky. ... 6-4/215. ... Full name: Clifford Oldham Hagan. ... Nickname: Li'l Abner.
HIGH SCHOOL: Owensboro (Ky.).
COLLEGE: Kentucky.
TRANSACTIONS/CAREER NOTES: Selected by Boston Celtics in third round of 1953 NBA Draft. ... In military service during 1954-55 and 1955-56 seasons; played at Andrews Air Force Base. ... Draft rights traded by Celtics with C/F Ed Macauley to St. Louis Hawks for draft rights to C Bill Russell (April 29, 1956). ... Signed as player/head coach by Dallas Chaparrals of American Basketball Association (June 1967).
CAREER HONORS: Elected to Naismith Memorial Basketball Hall of Fame (1977).
MISCELLANEOUS: Member of NBA championship team (1958).

COLLEGIATE RECORD

NOTES: Member of NCAA championship team (1951).

Season Team	G	Min.	FGM	FGA	Pct.	FTM	FTA	Pct.	Reb.	Ast.	Pts.	RPG	APG	PPG
49-50—Kentucky‡	12	...	114	244	.467	42	58	.724	...	...	270	...	...	22.5
50-51—Kentucky‡	20	...	69	188	.367	45	61	.738	169	...	183	8.5	...	9.2
51-52—Kentucky	32	...	264	633	.417	164	235	.698	528	...	692	16.5	...	21.6
52-53—Kentucky					Did not play—team suspended for season.									
53-54—Kentucky	25	...	234	514	.455	132	191	.691	338	...	600	13.5	...	24.0
Varsity totals	77	...	567	1335	.425	341	487	.700	1035	...	1475	13.4	...	19.2

NBA REGULAR-SEASON RECORD

HONORS: All-NBA second team (1958, 1959).

Season Team	G	Min.	FGM	FGA	Pct.	FTM	FTA	Pct.	Reb.	Ast.	PF	Dq.	Pts.	RPG	APG	PPG
56-57 —St. Louis	67	971	134	371	.361	100	145	.690	247	86	165	3	368	3.7	1.3	5.5
57-58 —St. Louis	70	2190	503	1135	.443	385	501	.768	707	175	267	9	1391	10.1	2.5	19.9
58-59 —St. Louis	72	2702	646	1417	.456	415	536	.774	783	245	275	10	1707	10.9	3.4	23.7
59-60 —St. Louis	75	2798	719	1549	.464	421	524	.803	803	299	270	4	1859	10.7	4.0	24.8
60-61 —St. Louis	77	2701	661	1490	.444	383	467	.820	715	381	286	9	1705	9.3	4.9	22.1
61-62 —St. Louis	77	2784	701	1490	.470	362	439	.825	633	370	282	8	1764	8.2	4.8	22.9
62-63 —St. Louis	79	1716	491	1055	.465	244	305	.800	341	193	211	2	1226	4.3	2.4	15.5
63-64 —St. Louis	77	2279	572	1280	.447	269	331	.813	377	193	273	4	1413	4.9	2.5	18.4
64-65 —St. Louis	77	1739	393	901	.436	214	268	.799	276	136	182	0	1000	3.6	1.8	13.0
65-66 —St. Louis	74	1851	419	942	.445	176	206	.854	234	164	177	1	1014	3.2	2.2	13.7
Totals	745	21731	5239	11630	.450	2969	3722	.798	5116	2242	2388	50	13447	6.9	3.0	18.0

NBA PLAYOFF RECORD

Season Team	G	Min.	FGM	FGA	Pct.	FTM	FTA	Pct.	Reb.	Ast.	PF	Dq.	Pts.	RPG	APG	PPG
56-57 —St. Louis	10	319	62	143	.434	46	63	.730	112	28	47	3	170	11.2	2.8	17.0
57-58 —St. Louis	11	418	111	221	.502	83	99	.838	115	37	48	3	305	10.5	3.4	27.7
58-59 —St. Louis	6	259	63	123	.512	45	54	.833	72	16	21	0	171	12.0	2.7	28.5
59-60 —St. Louis	14	544	125	296	.422	89	109	.817	138	54	54	1	339	9.9	3.9	24.2
60-61 —St. Louis	12	455	104	235	.443	56	69	.812	118	54	45	1	264	9.8	4.5	22.0
62-63 —St. Louis	11	255	83	179	.464	37	53	.698	55	34	42	4	203	5.0	3.1	18.5
63-64 —St. Louis	12	392	75	175	.429	45	54	.833	74	57	34	0	195	6.2	4.8	16.3
64-65 —St. Louis	4	123	34	75	.453	6	12	.500	26	7	14	0	74	6.5	1.8	18.5
65-66 —St. Louis	10	200	44	97	.454	25	27	.926	34	18	15	0	113	3.4	1.8	11.3
Totals	90	2965	701	1544	.454	432	540	.800	744	305	320	12	1834	8.3	3.4	20.4

NBA ALL-STAR GAME RECORD

Season Team	Min.	FGM	FGA	Pct.	FTM	FTA	Pct.	Reb	Ast.	PF	Dq.	Pts.
1958 —St. Louis				Selected, did not play—injured.								
1959 —St. Louis	22	6	12	.500	3	3	1.000	8	3	5	0	15
1960 —St. Louis	21	1	9	.111	0	0	...	3	2	1	0	2
1961 —St. Louis	13	0	2	.000	2	2	1.000	2	0	1	0	2
1962 —St. Louis	9	1	3	.333	0	0	...	2	1	1	0	2
Totals	65	8	26	.308	5	5	1.000	15	6	8	0	21

ABA REGULAR-SEASON RECORD

Season Team	G	Min.	2-POINT FGM	2-POINT FGA	2-POINT Pct.	3-POINT FGM	3-POINT FGA	3-POINT Pct.	FTM	FTA	Pct.	Reb.	Ast.	Pts.	RPG	APG	PPG
67-68—Dallas	56	1737	371	756	.491	0	3	.000	277	351	.789	334	276	1019	6.0	4.9	18.2
68-69—Dallas	35	579	132	258	.512	0	1	.000	123	144	.854	102	122	387	2.9	3.5	11.1
69-70—Dallas	3	27	8	12	.667	0	1	.000	1	2	.500	3	6	17	1.0	2.0	5.7
Totals	94	2343	511	1026	.498	0	5	.000	401	497	.807	439	404	1423	4.7	4.3	15.1

ABA PLAYOFF RECORD

Season Team	G	Min.	2-POINT FGM	2-POINT FGA	2-POINT Pct.	3-POINT FGM	3-POINT FGA	3-POINT Pct.	FTM	FTA	Pct.	Reb.	Ast.	Pts.	RPG	APG	PPG
67-68—Dallas	3	70	14	37	.378	0	0	...	9	13	.692	13	9	37	4.3	3.0	12.3
68-69—Dallas	2	45	5	14	.357	0	0	...	8	10	.800	6	14	18	3.0	7.0	9.0
Totals	5	115	19	51	.373	0	0	...	17	23	.739	19	23	55	3.8	4.6	11.0

ABA ALL-STAR GAME RECORD

Season Team	Min.	2-POINT FGM	FGA	Pct.	3-POINT FGM	FGA	Pct.	FTM	FTA	Pct.	Reb.	Ast.	Pts.
1968—Dallas	24	4	11	.364	0	0	...	2	2	1.000	0	5	10

COMBINED ABA AND NBA REGULAR-SEASON RECORDS

	G	Min.	FGM	FGA	Pct.	FTM	FTA	Pct.	REBOUNDS Off.	Def.	Tot.	Ast.	Stl.	Blk.	TO	Pts.	AVERAGES RPG	APG	PPG
Totals	839	24074	5750	12661	.454	3370	4219	.799	...	...	5555	2646	...	...	...	14870	6.6	3.2	17.7

Three-point field goals: 0-for-5.
Personal fouls/disqualifications: 2678/58.

ABA COACHING RECORD

BACKGROUND: Player/head coach, Dallas Chaparrals of American Basketball Association (1967-68 to January 1970).

Season Team	REGULAR SEASON W	L	Pct.	Finish	PLAYOFFS W	L	Pct.
67-68 —Dallas	46	32	.590	2nd/Western Division	4	4	.500
68-69 —Dallas	41	37	.526	4th/Western Division	3	4	.426
69-70 —Dallas	22	21	.512		—	—	—
Totals (3 years)	109	90	.548	Totals (2 years)	7	8	.467

NOTES:

1968—Defeated Houston, 3-0, in Western Division semifinals; lost to New Orleans, 4-1, in Western Division finals.
1969—Lost to New Orleans in Western Division semifinals.
1970—Replaced as Dallas head coach by Max Williams (January).

HAVLICEK, JOHN   F/G

PERSONAL: Born April 8, 1940, in Martins Ferry, Ohio. ... 6-5/205. ... Full name: John J. Havlicek. ... Nickname: Hondo.
HIGH SCHOOL: Bridgeport (Ohio).
COLLEGE: Ohio State.
TRANSACTIONS/CAREER NOTES: Selected by Boston Celtics in first round of 1962 NBA Draft.
CAREER HONORS: Elected to Naismith Memorial Basketball Hall of Fame (1983). ... NBA 35th Anniversary All-Time Team (1980).
MISCELLANEOUS: Member of NBA championship teams (1963, 1964, 1965, 1966, 1968, 1969, 1974, 1976). ... Selected as wide receiver by Cleveland Browns in seventh round of 1962 National Football League draft. ... Boston Celtics all-time leading scorer with 26,395 points (1962-63 through 1977-78).

COLLEGIATE RECORD

NOTES: The Sporting News All-America second team (1962). ... Member of NCAA championship team (1960).

Season Team	G	Min.	FGM	FGA	Pct.	FTM	FTA	Pct.	Reb.	Ast.	Pts.	AVERAGES RPG	APG	PPG
58-59—Ohio State‡					Freshman team did not play intercollegiate schedule.									
59-60—Ohio State	28	...	144	312	.462	53	74	.716	205	...	341	7.3	...	12.2
60-61—Ohio State	28	...	173	321	.539	61	87	.701	244	...	407	8.7	...	14.5
61-62—Ohio State	28	...	196	377	.520	83	109	.761	271	...	475	9.7	...	17.0
Varsity totals	84	...	513	1010	.508	197	270	.730	720	...	1223	8.6	...	14.6

NBA REGULAR-SEASON RECORD

HONORS: All-NBA first team (1971, 1972, 1973, 1974). ... All-NBA second team (1964, 1966, 1968, 1969, 1970, 1975, 1976). ... NBA All-Defensive first team (1972, 1973, 1974, 1975, 1976). ... NBA All-Defensive second team (1969, 1970, 1971).

Season Team	G	Min.	FGM	FGA	Pct.	FTM	FTA	Pct.	Reb.	Ast.	PF	Dq.	Pts.	AVERAGES RPG	APG	PPG
62-63 —Boston	80	2200	483	1085	.445	174	239	.728	534	179	189	2	1140	6.7	2.2	14.3
63-64 —Boston	80	2587	640	1535	.417	315	422	.746	428	238	227	1	1595	5.4	3.0	19.9
64-65 —Boston	75	2169	570	1420	.401	235	316	.744	371	199	200	2	1375	4.9	2.7	18.3
65-66 —Boston	71	2175	530	1328	.399	274	349	.785	423	210	158	1	1334	6.0	3.0	18.8
66-67 —Boston	81	2602	684	1540	.444	365	441	.828	532	278	210	0	1733	6.6	3.4	21.4
67-68 —Boston	82	2921	666	1551	.429	368	453	.812	546	384	237	2	1700	6.7	4.7	20.7
68-69 —Boston	82	3174	692	1709	.405	387	496	.780	570	441	247	0	1771	7.0	5.4	21.6
69-70 —Boston	81	3369	736	1585	.464	488	578	.844	635	550	211	1	1960	7.8	6.8	24.2
70-71 —Boston	81	*3678	892	1982	.450	554	677	.818	730	607	200	0	2338	9.0	7.5	28.9
71-72 —Boston	82	*3698	897	1957	.458	458	549	.834	672	614	183	1	2252	8.2	7.5	27.5
72-73 —Boston	80	3367	766	1704	.450	370	431	.858	567	529	195	1	1902	7.1	6.6	23.8

Season Team	G	Min.	FGM	FGA	Pct.	FTM	FTA	Pct.	REBOUNDS Off.	Def.	Tot.	Ast.	St.	Blk.	TO	Pts.	AVERAGES RPG	APG	PPG
73-74—Boston	76	3091	685	1502	.456	346	416	.832	138	349	487	447	95	32	...	1716	6.4	5.9	22.6
74-75—Boston	82	3132	642	1411	.455	289	332	.870	154	330	484	432	110	16	...	1573	5.9	5.3	19.2
75-76—Boston	76	2598	504	1121	.450	281	333	.844	116	198	314	278	97	29	...	1289	4.1	3.7	17.0
76-77—Boston	79	2913	580	1283	.452	235	288	.816	109	273	382	400	84	18	...	1395	4.8	5.1	17.7
77-78—Boston	82	2797	546	1217	.449	230	269	.855	93	239	332	328	90	22	204	1322	4.0	4.0	16.1
Totals	1270	46471	10513	23930	.439	5369	6589	.815	...	8007	6114	476	117	204	26395	6.3	4.8	20.8

Personal fouls/disqualifications: 1973-74, 196/1. 1974-75, 231/2. 1975-76, 204/1. 1976-77, 208/4. 1977-78, 185/2. Totals, 3281/21.

NBA PLAYOFF RECORD

NOTES: NBA Finals Most Valuable Player (1974). ... Shares NBA Finals single-game record for most points in an overtime period—9 (May 10, 1974, vs. Milwaukee). ... Shares single-game playoff record for most field goals made—24 (April 1, 1973, vs. Atlanta).

Season Team	G	Min.	FGM	FGA	Pct.	FTM	FTA	Pct.	Reb.	Ast.	PF	Dq.	Pts.	AVERAGES		
														RPG	APG	PPG
62-63 —Boston	11	254	56	125	.448	18	27	.667	53	17	28	1	130	4.8	1.5	11.8
63-64 —Boston	10	289	61	159	.384	35	44	.795	43	32	26	0	157	4.3	3.2	15.7
64-65 —Boston	12	405	88	250	.352	46	55	.836	88	29	44	1	222	7.3	2.4	18.5
65-66 —Boston	17	719	153	374	.409	95	113	.841	154	70	69	2	401	9.1	4.1	23.6
66-67 —Boston	9	330	95	212	.448	57	71	.803	73	28	30	0	247	8.1	3.1	27.4
67-68 —Boston	19	862	184	407	.452	125	151	.828	164	142	67	1	493	8.6	7.5	25.9
68-69 —Boston	18	850	170	382	.445	118	138	.855	179	100	58	2	458	9.9	5.6	25.4
71-72 —Boston	11	517	108	235	.460	85	99	.859	92	70	35	1	301	8.4	6.4	27.4
72-73 —Boston	12	479	112	235	.477	61	74	.824	62	65	24	0	285	5.2	5.4	23.8

Season Team	G	Min.	FGM	FGA	Pct.	FTM	FTA	Pct.	REBOUNDS			Ast.	St.	Blk.	TO	Pts.	AVERAGES		
									Off.	Def.	Tot.						RPG	APG	PPG
73-74—Boston	18	811	199	411	.484	89	101	.881	28	88	116	108	24	6	...	487	6.4	6.0	27.1
74-75—Boston	11	464	83	192	.432	66	76	.868	18	39	57	51	16	1	...	232	5.2	4.6	21.1
75-76—Boston	15	505	80	180	.444	38	47	.809	18	38	56	51	12	5	...	198	3.7	3.4	13.2
76-77—Boston	9	375	62	167	.371	41	50	.820	15	34	49	62	8	4	...	165	5.4	6.9	18.3
Totals	172	6860	1451	3329	.436	874	1046	.836	...	...	1186	825	60	16	...	3776	6.9	4.8	22.0

Personal fouls/disqualifications: 1973-74, 43/0. 1974-75, 38/1. 1975-76, 22/0. 1976-77, 33/0. Totals, 517/9.

NBA ALL-STAR GAME RECORD

Season Team	Min.	FGM	FGA	Pct.	FTM	FTA	Pct.	Reb	Ast.	PF	Dq.	Pts.
1966 —Boston	25	6	16	.375	6	6	1.000	6	1	2	0	18
1967 —Boston	17	7	14	.500	0	0	...	2	1	1	0	14
1968 —Boston	22	9	15	.600	8	11	.727	5	4	0	0	26
1969 —Boston	31	6	14	.429	2	2	1.000	7	2	2	0	14
1970 —Boston	29	7	15	.467	3	3	1.000	5	7	2	0	17
1971 —Boston	24	6	12	.500	0	2	.000	3	2	3	0	12
1972 —Boston	24	5	13	.385	5	5	1.000	3	2	2	0	15
1973 —Boston	22	6	10	.600	2	5	.400	3	5	1	0	14

Season Team	Min.	FGM	FGA	Pct.	FTM	FTA	Pct.	REBOUNDS			Ast.	PF	Dq.	St.	Blk.	TO	Pts.
								Off.	Def.	Tot.							
1974 —Boston	18	5	10	.500	0	2	.000	0	0	0	2	2	0	1	0	...	10
1975 —Boston	31	7	12	.583	2	2	1.000	1	5	6	1	2	0	2	0	...	16
1976 —Boston	21	3	10	.300	3	3	1.000	1	1	2	2	0	0	1	0	...	9
1977 —Boston	17	2	5	.400	0	0	...	0	1	1	1	1	0	0	0	...	4
1978 —Boston	22	5	8	.625	0	0	...	0	3	3	1	2	0	0	0	4	10
Totals	303	74	154	.481	31	41	.756	...	...	46	31	20	0	4	0	-4	179

HAWKINS, CONNIE   F/C

PERSONAL: Born July 17, 1942, in Brooklyn, N.Y. ... 6-8/215. ... Full name: Cornelius L. Hawkins.
HIGH SCHOOL: Boys (Brooklyn, N.Y.).
COLLEGE: Iowa.
TRANSACTIONS/CAREER NOTES: Signed after freshman season by Pittsburgh Rens of American Basketball League (1961). ... ABL ceased operations (December 31, 1962). ... Played with Harlem Globetrotters (1963-64 through 1966-67) ... Signed by Pittsburgh Pipers of the American Basketball Association (1967). ... Pipers franchise transferred to Minnesota (1968). ... Signed as free agent by Phoenix Suns of NBA (June 20, 1969). ... Traded by Suns to Los Angeles Lakers for Keith Erickson and second-round draft choice (October 30, 1973). ... Traded by Lakers to Atlanta Hawks for draft choices (August 8, 1975). ... Waived by Hawks (1976).

COLLEGIATE RECORD

Season Team	G	Min.	FGM	FGA	Pct.	FTM	FTA	Pct.	Reb.	Ast.	Pts.	AVERAGES		
												RPG	APG	PPG
60-61—Iowa					Freshman team did not play intercollegiate schedule.									

ABL REGULAR-SEASON RECORD

ABL: ABL Most Valuable Player (1962). ... ABL All-Star first team (1962).

Season Team	G	Min.	FGM	FGA	Pct.	FTM	FTA	Pct.	Reb.	Ast.	Pts.	AVERAGES		
												RPG	APG	PPG
61-62—Pittsburgh	78	3349	760	1490	.510	622	787	.790	1038	183	2145	13.3	2.3	*27.5
62-63—Pittsburgh	16	668	160	326	.491	127	165	.770	205	42	447	12.8	2.6	27.9
Totals	94	4017	920	1816	.507	749	952	.787	1243	225	2592	13.2	2.4	27.6

ABL PLAYOFF RECORD

Season Team	G	Min.	FGM	FGA	Pct.	FTM	FTA	Pct.	Reb.	Ast.	Pts.	AVERAGES		
												RPG	APG	PPG
61-62—Pittsburgh	1	53	14	23	.609	13	14	.929	17	4	41	17.0	4.0	41.0

ABA REGULAR-SEASON RECORD

NOTES: ABA Most Valuable Player (1968). ... ABA All-Star first team (1968 and 1969). ... Member of ABA championship team (1968). ... Led ABA in scoring with 26.79 average (1968).

Season Team	G	Min.	2-POINT			3-POINT			FTM	FTA	Pct.	Reb.	Ast.	Pts.	AVERAGES		
			FGM	FGA	Pct.	FGM	FGA	Pct.							RPG	APG	PPG
67-68—Pittsburgh	70	3146	633	1214	.521	2	9	.222	603	789	.764	945	320	1875	13.5	4.6	*26.8
68-69—Minnesota	47	1852	493	949	.520	3	22	.136	425	554	.767	534	184	1420	11.4	3.9	30.2
Totals	117	4998	1126	2163	.521	5	31	.161	1028	1343	.765	1479	504	3295	12.6	4.3	28.2

ABA PLAYOFF RECORD

Season Team	G	Min.	2-POINT FGM	FGA	Pct.	3-POINT FGM	FGA	Pct.	FTM	FTA	Pct.	Reb.	Ast.	Pts.	AVERAGES RPG	APG	PPG
67-68—Pittsburgh	14	616	145	244	.594	0	0	...	129	177	.729	172	64	419	12.3	4.6	29.9
68-69—Minnesota	7	320	61	164	.372	4	8	.500	40	62	.645	86	27	174	12.3	3.9	24.9
Totals	21	936	206	408	.505	...	4	...	169	239	.707	258	91	593	12.3	4.3	28.2

HONORS: All-NBA first team (1970).

NBA REGULAR-SEASON RECORD

Season Team	G	Min.	FGM	FGA	Pct.	FTM	FTA	Pct.	Reb.	Ast.	PF	Dq.	Pts.	AVERAGES RPG	APG	PPG
69-70 —Phoenix	81	3312	709	1447	.490	577	741	.779	846	391	287	4	1995	10.4	4.8	24.6
70-71 —Phoenix	71	2662	512	1181	.434	457	560	.816	643	322	197	2	1481	9.1	4.5	20.9
71-72 —Phoenix	76	2798	571	1244	.459	456	565	.807	633	296	235	2	1598	8.3	3.9	21.0
72-73 —Phoenix	75	2768	441	920	.479	322	404	.797	641	304	229	5	1204	8.5	4.1	16.1

Season Team	G	Min.	FGM	FGA	Pct.	FTM	FTA	Pct.	REBOUNDS Off.	Def.	Tot.	Ast.	St.	Blk.	TO	Pts.	AVERAGES RPG	APG	PPG
73-74—Pho-Lakers	79	2761	404	807	.501	191	251	.761	176	389	565	407	113	81	...	999	7.2	5.2	12.6
74-75—Los Angeles	43	1026	139	324	.429	68	99	.687	54	144	198	120	51	23	...	346	4.6	2.8	8.0
75-76—Atlanta	74	1907	237	530	.447	136	191	.712	102	343	445	212	80	46	...	610	6.0	2.9	8.2
Totals	499	17234	3013	6453	.467	2207	2811	.785	...	...	3971	2052	...	...	...	8233	8.0	4.1	16.5

Personal fouls/disqualifications: 1973-74, 223/1. 1974-75, 116/1. 1975-76, 172/2. Totals, 1459/17.

NBA PLAYOFF RECORD

Season Team	G	Min.	FGM	FGA	Pct.	FTM	FTA	Pct.	Reb.	Ast.	PF	Dq.	Pts.	AVERAGES RPG	APG	PPG
69-70 —Phoenix	7	328	62	150	.413	54	66	.818	97	41	22	0	178	13.9	5.9	25.4

Season Team	G	Min.	FGM	FGA	Pct.	FTM	FTA	Pct.	REBOUNDS Off.	Def.	Tot.	Ast.	St.	Blk.	TO	Pts.	AVERAGES RPG	APG	PPG
73-74—Los Angeles	5	172	21	60	.350	12	15	.800	14	26	40	16	7	1	...	54	8.0	3.2	10.8
Totals	12	500	83	210	.395	66	81	.815	...	...	137	57	7	1	...	232	11.4	4.8	19.3

Personal fouls/disqualifications: 1973-74, 13/0.

NBA ALL-STAR GAME RECORD

Season Team	Min.	FGM	FGA	Pct.	FTM	FTA	Pct.	Reb	Ast.	PF	Dq.	Pts.
1970 —Phoenix	19	2	4	.500	6	6	1.000	4	2	3	...	10
1971 —Phoenix	1	0	0	...	0	0	...	0	0	0	...	0
1972 —Phoenix	14	5	7	.714	3	4	.750	4	0	1	0	13
1973 —Phoenix	11	1	5	.200	0	0	...	2	3	1	0	2
Totals	45	8	16	.500	9	10	.900	10	5	5	...	25

COMBINED ABA AND NBA REGULAR-SEASON RECORDS

	G	Min.	FGM	FGA	Pct.	FTM	FTA	Pct.	REBOUNDS Off.	Def.	Tot.	Ast.	Stl.	Blk.	TO	Pts.	AVERAGES RPG	APG	PPG
Totals	616	22232	4144	8647	.479	3235	4154	.779	...	...	5450	2556	...	...	...	11528	8.8	4.1	18.7

Three-point field goals: 5-for-31 (.161).
Personal fouls/disqualifications: 1873/22.

HAYES, ELVIN   F/C

PERSONAL: Born November 17, 1945, in Rayville, La. ... 6-9/235. ... Full name: Elvin Ernest Hayes.
HIGH SCHOOL: Eula D. Britton (Rayville, La.).
COLLEGE: Houston.
TRANSACTIONS/CAREER NOTES: Selected by San Diego Rockets in first round (first pick overall) of 1968 NBA Draft. ... Rockets franchise moved from San Diego to Houston for 1971-72 season. ... Traded by Rockets to Baltimore Bullets for F Jack Marin and future considerations (June 23, 1972). ... Bullets franchise moved from Baltimore to Washington and renamed Capital Bullets for 1973-74 season. ... Bullets franchise renamed Washington Bullets for 1974-75 season. ... Traded by Bullets to Rockets for 1981 and 1983 second-round draft choices (June 8, 1981).
CAREER HONORS: Elected to Naismith Memorial Basketball Hall of Fame (1989).
MISCELLANEOUS: Member of NBA championship team (1978). ... Washington Bullets franchise all-time leading scorer with 15,551 points and all-time blocked shots leader with 1,558 (1973-74 through 1980-81).

COLLEGIATE RECORD

NOTES: The Sporting News College Player of the Year (1968). ... The Sporting News All-America first team (1967, 1968). ... The Sporting News All-America second team (1966).

Season Team	G	Min.	FGM	FGA	Pct.	FTM	FTA	Pct.	Reb.	Ast.	Pts.	AVERAGES RPG	APG	PPG
64-65—Houston‡	21	...	217	478	.454	93	176	.528	500	43	527	23.8	2.0	25.1
65-66—Houston	29	946	323	570	.567	143	257	.556	490	6	789	16.9	0.2	27.2
66-67—Houston	31	1119	373	750	.497	135	227	.595	488	33	881	15.7	1.1	28.4
67-68—Houston	33	1270	519	945	.549	176	285	.618	624	59	1214	18.9	1.8	36.8
Varsity totals	93	3335	1215	2265	.536	454	769	.590	1602	98	2884	17.2	1.1	31.0

NBA REGULAR-SEASON RECORD

RECORDS: Holds single-season record for most minutes played by a rookie—3,695 (1969).
HONORS: All-NBA first team (1975, 1977, 1979). ... All-NBA second team (1973, 1974, 1976). ... NBA All-Defensive second team (1974, 1975). ... NBA All-Rookie team (1969).

Season Team	G	Min.	FGM	FGA	Pct.	FTM	FTA	Pct.	Reb.	Ast.	PF	Dq.	Pts.	RPG	APG	PPG
68-69—San Diego	82	*3695	*930	*2082	.447	467	746	.626	1406	113	266	2	*2327	17.1	1.4	*28.4
69-70—San Diego	82	*3665	914	*2020	.452	428	622	.688	*1386	162	270	5	2256	16.9	2.0	27.5
70-71—San Diego	82	3633	948	*2215	.428	454	676	.672	1362	186	225	1	2350	16.6	2.3	28.7
71-72—Houston	82	3461	832	1918	.434	399	615	.649	1197	270	233	1	2063	14.6	3.3	25.2
72-73—Baltimore	81	3347	713	1607	.444	291	434	.671	1177	127	232	3	1717	14.5	1.6	21.2

Season Team	G	Min.	FGM	FGA	Pct.	FTM	FTA	Pct.	Off.	Def.	Tot.	Ast.	St.	Blk.	TO	Pts.	RPG	APG	PPG
73-74—Capital	81	*3602	689	1627	.423	357	495	.721	*354	*1109	*1463	163	86	240	...	1735	18.1	2.0	21.4
74-75—Washington	82	3465	739	1668	.443	409	534	.766	221	783	1004	206	158	187	...	1887	12.2	2.5	23.0
75-76—Washington	80	2975	649	1381	.470	287	457	.628	210	668	878	121	104	202	...	1585	11.0	1.5	19.8
76-77—Washington	82	*3364	760	1516	.501	422	614	.687	289	740	1029	158	87	220	...	1942	12.5	1.9	23.7
77-78—Washington	81	3246	636	1409	.451	326	514	.634	335	740	1075	149	96	159	229	1598	13.3	1.8	19.7
78-79—Washington	82	3105	720	1477	.487	349	534	.654	312	682	994	143	75	190	235	1789	12.1	1.7	21.8
79-80—Washington	81	3183	761	1677	.454	334	478	.699	269	627	896	129	62	189	215	1859	11.1	1.6	23.0
80-81—Washington	81	2931	584	1296	.451	271	439	.617	235	554	789	98	68	171	189	1439	9.7	1.2	17.8
81-82—Houston	82	3032	519	1100	.472	280	422	.664	267	480	747	144	62	104	208	1318	9.1	1.8	16.1
82-83—Houston	81	2302	424	890	.476	196	287	.683	199	417	616	158	50	81	200	1046	7.6	2.0	12.9
83-84—Houston	81	994	158	389	.406	86	132	.652	87	173	260	71	16	28	82	402	3.2	0.9	5.0
Totals	1303	50000	10976	24272	.452	5356	7999	.670	...	16279	2398	864	1771	1358		27313	12.5	1.8	21.0

Three-point field goals: 1979-80, 3-for-13 (.231). 1980-81, 0-for-10. 1981-82, 0-for-5. 1982-83, 2-for-4 (.500). 1983-84, 0-for-2. Totals, 5-for-34 (.147).
Personal fouls/disqualifications: 1973-74, 252/1. 1974-75, 238/0. 1975-76, 293/5. 1976-77, 312/1. 1977-78, 313/7. 1978-79, 308/5. 1979-80, 309/9. 1980-81, 300/6. 1981-82, 287/4. 1982-83, 232/2. 1983-84, 123/1. Totals, 4193/53.

NBA PLAYOFF RECORD

NOTES: Shares NBA Finals single-game record for most offensive rebounds—11 (May 27, 1979, vs. Seattle).

Season Team	G	Min.	FGM	FGA	Pct.	FTM	FTA	Pct.	Reb.	Ast.	PF	Dq.	Pts.	RPG	APG	PPG
68-69—San Diego	6	278	60	114	.526	35	53	.660	83	5	21	0	155	13.8	0.8	25.8
72-73—Baltimore	5	228	53	105	.505	23	33	.697	57	5	16	0	129	11.4	1.0	25.8

Season Team	G	Min.	FGM	FGA	Pct.	FTM	FTA	Pct.	Off.	Def.	Tot.	Ast.	St.	Blk.	TO	Pts.	RPG	APG	PPG
73-74—Capital	7	323	76	143	.531	29	41	.707	31	80	111	21	5	15	...	181	15.9	3.0	25.9
74-75—Washington	17	751	174	372	.468	86	127	.677	46	140	186	37	26	39	...	434	10.9	2.2	25.5
75-76—Washington	7	305	54	122	.443	32	55	.582	16	72	88	10	5	28	...	140	12.6	1.4	20.0
76-77—Washington	9	405	74	173	.428	41	59	.695	29	93	122	17	10	22	...	189	13.6	1.9	21.0
77-78—Washington	21	868	189	385	.491	79	133	.594	103	176	279	43	32	52	58	457	13.3	2.0	21.8
78-79—Washington	19	786	170	396	.429	87	130	.669	94	172	266	38	17	52	56	427	14.0	2.0	22.5
79-80—Washington	2	92	16	41	.390	8	10	.800	10	12	22	6	0	4	4	40	11.0	3.0	20.0
81-82—Houston	3	124	17	50	.340	8	15	.533	7	23	30	3	2	10	6	42	10.0	1.0	14.0
Totals	96	4160	883	1901	.464	428	656	.652	...	1244	185	77	222	124	2194	13.0	1.9	22.9

Personal fouls/disqualifications: 1973-74, 23/0. 1974-75, 70/3. 1975-76, 24/0. 1976-77, 39/0. 1977-78, 86/2. 1978-79, 79/3. 1979-80, 8/0. 1981-82, 12/0. Totals, 378/8.

NBA ALL-STAR GAME RECORD

Season Team	Min.	FGM	FGA	Pct.	FTM	FTA	Pct.	Reb	Ast	PF	Dq.	Pts.
1969 —San Diego	21	4	9	.444	3	3	1.000	5	0	4	0	11
1970 —San Diego	35	9	21	.429	6	12	.500	15	1	1	0	24
1971 —San Diego	19	4	13	.308	2	3	.667	4	2	1	0	10
1972 —Houston	11	1	6	.167	2	2	1.000	2	0	2	0	4
1973 —Baltimore	16	4	13	.308	2	2	1.000	12	0	0	0	10

Season Team	Min.	FGM	FGA	Pct.	FTM	FTA	Pct.	Off.	Def.	Tot.	Ast.	PF	Dq.	St.	Blk.	TO	Pts.
1974 —Capital	35	5	13	.385	2	3	.667	4	11	15	6	4	0	0	1	...	12
1975 —Washington	17	2	6	.333	0	0	...	0	5	5	2	1	0	1	0	...	4
1976 —Washington	31	6	14	.429	0	2	.000	3	7	10	1	5	0	1	0	...	12
1977 —Washington	11	6	6	1.000	0	0	...	0	2	2	1	5	0	0	0	...	12
1978 —Washington	11	1	7	.143	0	0	...	3	1	4	0	4	0	1	0	1	2
1979 —Washington	28	5	11	.455	3	5	.600	4	9	13	0	5	0	1	1		13
1980 —Washington	29	5	10	.500	2	2	1.000	2	3	5	4	5	0	1	4		12
Totals	264	52	129	.403	22	34	.647	...	...	92	17	37	0	5	6	5	126

HAYWOOD, SPENCER   F/C

PERSONAL: Born April 22, 1949, in Silver City, Miss. ... 6-9/225. ... Full name: Spencer Haywood.
HIGH SCHOOL: Pershing (Detroit).
JUNIOR COLLEGE: Trinidad State Junior College (Colo.).
COLLEGE: Detroit.
TRANSACTIONS/CAREER NOTES: Signed as free agent after sophomore season by Denver Rockets of American Basketball Association (August 16, 1969). ... Selected by Buffalo Braves in second round (30th pick overall) of 1971 NBA Draft. ... Terminated contract with Rockets and signed by Seattle SuperSonics (1971). ... Traded by SuperSonics to New York Knicks for cash and the option of F Eugene Short or future draft choice (October 24, 1975). ... Traded by Knicks to New Orleans Jazz for C Joe C. Meriweather (January 5, 1979). ... Jazz franchise moved from New Orleans to Utah for 1979-80 season. ... Traded by Jazz to Los Angeles Lakers for F Adrian Dantley (September 13, 1979). ... Waived by Lakers (August 19, 1980). ... Played in Italy (1980-81 and 1981-82). ... Signed as free agent by Washington Bullets (October 24, 1981). ... Waived by Bullets (March 9, 1983).
MISCELLANEOUS: Member of NBA championship team (1980). ... Member of gold-medal-winning U.S. Olympic team (1968).

COLLEGIATE RECORD

NOTES: THE SPORTING NEWS All-America first team (1969). ... Led NCAA Division I with 22.1 rebounds per game (1969).

Season Team	G	Min.	FGM	FGA	Pct.	FTM	FTA	Pct.	Reb.	Ast.	Pts.	AVERAGES RPG	APG	PPG
67-68—Trinidad State J.C.	30	...	358	675	.530	129	195	.662	663	...	845	22.1	...	28.2
68-69—Detroit	24	...	288	508	.567	195	254	.768	530	...	771	22.1	...	32.1
Junior college totals	30	...	358	675	.530	129	195	.662	663	...	845	22.1	...	28.2
4-year-college totals	24	...	288	508	.567	195	254	.768	530	...	771	22.1	...	32.1

NOTES: ABA Most Valuable Player (1970). ... ABA Rookie of the Year (1970). ... ABA All-Star first team (1970). ... ABA All-Rookie team (1970). ... Holds single-season records for most minutes played—3,808; most field goals made—986; most rebounds—1,637; and highest rebounds-per-game average—19.5 (1970).

ABA REGULAR-SEASON RECORD

Season Team	G	Min.	2-POINT FGM	FGA	Pct.	3-POINT FGM	FGA	Pct.	FTM	FTA	Pct.	Reb.	Ast.	Pts.	AVERAGES RPG	APG	PPG
69-70—Denver	84	*3808	*986	1987	.496	0	11	.000	547	705	.776	*1637	190	*2519	19.5	2.3	*30.0

ABA PLAYOFF RECORD

Season Team	G	Min.	2-POINT FGM	FGA	Pct.	3-POINT FGM	FGA	Pct.	FTM	FTA	Pct.	Reb.	Ast.	Pts.	AVERAGES RPG	APG	PPG
69-70—Denver	12	568	185	362	.511	1	5	.200	69	83	.831	237	39	440	19.8	3.3	36.7

ABA ALL-STAR GAME RECORD

NOTES: ABA All-Star Game Most Valuable Player (1970).

Season Team	Min.	2-POINT FGM	FGA	Pct.	3-POINT FGM	FGA	Pct.	FTM	FTA	Pct.	Reb.	Ast.	Pts.
1970—Denver	39	10	19	.526	0	0	...	3	4	.750	19	2	23

NBA REGULAR-SEASON RECORD

HONORS: All-NBA first team (1972, 1973). ... All-NBA second team (1974, 1975).

Season Team	G	Min.	FGM	FGA	Pct.	FTM	FTA	Pct.	Reb.	Ast.	PF	Dq.	Pts.	AVERAGES RPG	APG	PPG
70-71—Seattle	33	1162	260	579	.449	160	218	.734	396	48	84	1	680	12.0	1.5	20.6
71-72—Seattle	73	3167	717	1557	.461	480	586	.819	926	148	208	0	1914	12.7	2.0	26.2
72-73—Seattle	77	3259	889	1868	.476	473	564	.839	995	196	213	2	2251	12.9	2.5	29.2

Season Team	G	Min.	FGM	FGA	Pct.	FTM	FTA	Pct.	REBOUNDS Off.	Def.	Tot.	Ast.	St.	Blk.	TO	Pts.	AVERAGES RPG	APG	PPG
73-74—Seattle	75	3039	694	1520	.457	373	458	.814	318	689	1007	240	65	106	...	1761	13.4	3.2	23.5
74-75—Seattle	68	2529	608	1325	.459	309	381	.811	198	432	630	137	54	108	...	1525	9.3	2.0	22.4
75-76—New York	78	2892	605	1360	.445	339	448	.757	234	644	878	92	53	80	...	1549	11.3	1.2	19.9
76-77—N.Y. Knicks	31	1021	202	449	.450	109	131	.832	77	203	280	50	14	29	...	513	9.0	1.6	16.5
77-78—New York	67	1765	412	852	.484	96	135	.711	141	301	442	126	37	72	140	920	6.6	1.9	13.7
78-79—N.Y.-N.O.	68	2361	595	1205	.494	231	292	.791	172	361	533	127	40	82	200	1421	7.8	1.9	20.9
79-80—Los Angeles	76	1544	288	591	.487	159	206	.772	132	214	346	93	35	57	134	736	4.6	1.2	9.7
81-82—Washington	76	2086	395	829	.476	219	260	.842	144	278	422	64	45	68	175	1009	5.6	0.8	13.3
82-83—Washington	38	775	125	312	.401	63	87	.724	77	106	183	30	12	27	67	313	4.8	0.8	8.2
Totals	760	25600	5790	12447	.465	3011	3766	.800	...	...	7038	1351	355	629	716	14592	9.3	1.8	19.2

Three-point field goals: 1979-80, 1-for-4 (.250). 1981-82, 0-for-3. 1982-83, 0-for-1. Totals, 1-for-8 (.125).

Personal fouls/disqualifications: 1973-74, 198/2. 1974-75, 173/1. 1975-76, 255/1. 1976-77, 72/0. 1977-78, 188/1. 1978-79, 236/8. 1979-80, 197/2. 1981-82, 249/6. 1982-83, 94/2. Totals, 2167/26.

NBA PLAYOFF RECORD

Season Team	G	Min.	FGM	FGA	Pct.	FTM	FTA	Pct.	REBOUNDS Off.	Def.	Tot.	Ast.	St.	Blk.	TO	Pts.	AVERAGES RPG	APG	PPG
74-75—Seattle	9	337	47	131	.359	47	61	.771	20	61	81	18	7	11	...	141	9.0	2.0	15.7
77-78—New York	6	177	43	85	.506	11	11	1.000	19	23	42	12	5	10	97	7.0	2.0	16.2
79-80—Los Angeles	11	145	25	53	.472	13	16	.813	14	12	26	4	0	6	20	63	2.4	0.4	5.7
81-82—Washington	7	231	57	115	.496	26	35	.743	16	23	39	7	4	14	15	140	5.6	1.0	20.0
Totals	33	890	172	384	.448	97	123	.789	69	119	188	41	13	36	45	441	5.7	1.2	13.4

Three-point field goals: 1979-80, 0-for-1.

Personal fouls/disqualifications: 1974-75, 29/0. 1977-78, 24/1. 1979-80, 17/0. 1981-82, 28/0. Totals, 98/1.

NBA ALL-STAR GAME RECORD

Season Team	Min.	FGM	FGA	Pct.	FTM	FTA	Pct.	Reb	Ast.	PF	Dq.	Pts.
1972 —Seattle	25	4	10	.400	3	4	.750	7	1	2	0	11
1973 —Seattle	22	5	10	.500	2	2	1.000	10	0	5	0	12

Season Team	Min.	FGM	FGA	Pct.	FTM	FTA	Pct.	REBOUNDS Off.	Def.	Tot.	Ast.	PF	Dq.	St.	Blk.	TO	Pts.
1974 —Seattle	33	10	17	.588	3	3	1.000	2	9	11	5	5	0	0	3	...	23
1975 —Seattle	17	1	9	.111	0	0	...	1	2	3	0	1	0	0	0	...	2
Totals	97	20	46	.435	8	9	.889			31	6	13	0	0	3	...	48

COMBINED ABA AND NBA REGULAR-SEASON RECORDS

	G	Min.	FGM	FGA	Pct.	FTM	FTA	Pct.	REBOUNDS Off.	Def.	Tot.	Ast.	Stl.	Blk.	TO	Pts.	AVERAGES RPG	APG	PPG
Totals	844	29408	6776	14445	.470	3558	4471	.796	...	...	8675	1541	...	...	...	17111	10.3	1.8	20.3

Three-point field goals: 1-for-19 (.053).

Personal fouls/disqualifications: 2388/27.

ITALIAN LEAGUE RECORD

Season Team	G	Min.	FGM	FGA	Pct.	FTM	FTA	Pct.	Reb.	Ast.	Pts.	AVERAGES RPG	APG	PPG
80-81—Venezia	34	...	334	601	.556	132	179	.737	354	...	800	10.4	...	23.5
81-82—Carrera	5	175	63	100	.630	24	32	.750	37	...	150	7.4	...	30.0
Totals	39	...	397	701	.566	156	211	.739	391	...	950	10.0	...	24.4

HEINSOHN, TOM   F

See All-Time Great Coaches, page 410.

HOWELL, BAILEY   F

PERSONAL: Born January 20, 1937, in Middleton, Tenn. ... 6-7/220. ... Full name: Bailey E. Howell.
HIGH SCHOOL: Middleton (Tenn.).
COLLEGE: Mississippi State.
TRANSACTIONS/CAREER NOTES: Selected by Detroit Pistons in first round of 1959 NBA Draft. ... Traded by Pistons with C/F Bob Ferry, G Don Ohl, G Wally Jones and F Les Hunter to Baltimore Bullets for F/G Terry Dischinger, F Don Kojis and G Rod Thorn (June 18, 1964). ... Traded by Bullets to Boston Celtics for F/C Mel Counts (September 1, 1966). ... Selected by Buffalo Braves from Celtics in NBA expansion draft (May 11, 1970). ... Traded by Braves to Philadelphia 76ers for C Bob Kauffman and cash or future draft choice (May 11, 1970).
MISCELLANEOUS: Member of NBA championship teams (1968, 1969).

COLLEGIATE RECORD

NOTES: THE SPORTING NEWS All-America first team (1959). ... Led NCAA major college division with .568 field-goal percentage (1957).

Season Team	G	Min.	FGM	FGA	Pct.	FTM	FTA	Pct.	Reb.	Ast.	Pts.	RPG	APG	PPG
55-56—Mississippi State‡					Freshman team statistics unavailable.									
56-57—Mississippi State	25	...	217	382	.568	213	285	.747	492	...	647	19.7	...	25.9
57-58—Mississippi State	25	...	226	439	.515	243	315	.771	406	...	695	16.2	...	27.8
58-59—Mississippi State	25	...	231	464	.498	226	292	.774	379	...	688	15.2	...	27.5
Varsity totals	75	...	674	1285	.525	682	892	.765	1277	...	2030	17.0	...	27.1

NBA REGULAR-SEASON RECORD

HONORS: All-NBA second team (1963).

Season Team	G	Min.	FGM	FGA	Pct.	FTM	FTA	Pct.	Reb.	Ast.	PF	Dq.	Pts.	RPG	APG	PPG
59-60 —Detroit	75	2346	510	1119	.456	312	422	.739	790	63	282	13	1332	10.5	0.8	17.8
60-61 —Detroit	77	2952	607	1293	.469	601	798	.753	1111	196	297	10	1815	14.4	2.5	23.6
61-62 —Detroit	79	2857	553	1193	.464	470	612	.768	996	186	317	10	1576	12.6	2.4	19.9
62-63 —Detroit	79	2971	637	1235	.516	519	650	.798	910	232	300	9	1793	11.5	2.9	22.7
63-64 —Detroit	77	2700	598	1267	.472	470	581	.809	776	205	290	9	1666	10.1	2.7	21.6
64-65 —Baltimore	80	2975	515	1040	.495	504	629	.801	869	208	*345	10	1534	10.9	2.6	19.2
65-66 —Baltimore	78	2328	481	986	.488	402	551	.730	773	155	306	12	1364	9.9	2.0	17.5
66-67 —Boston	81	2503	636	1242	.512	349	471	.741	677	103	296	4	1621	8.4	1.3	20.0
67-68 —Boston	82	2801	643	1336	.481	335	461	.727	805	133	285	4	1621	9.8	1.6	19.8
68-69 —Boston	78	2527	612	1257	.487	313	426	.735	685	137	285	3	1537	8.8	1.8	19.7
69-70 —Boston	82	2078	399	931	.429	235	308	.763	550	120	261	4	1033	6.7	1.5	12.6
70-71 —Philadelphia	82	1589	324	686	.472	230	315	.730	441	115	234	2	878	5.4	1.4	10.7
Totals	950	30627	6515	13585	.480	4740	6224	.762	9383	1853	3498	90	17770	9.9	2.0	18.7

NBA PLAYOFF RECORD

Season Team	G	Min.	FGM	FGA	Pct.	FTM	FTA	Pct.	Reb.	Ast.	PF	Dq.	Pts.	RPG	APG	PPG
59-60 —Detroit	2	72	14	41	.341	6	8	.750	17	3	8	0	34	8.5	1.5	17.0
60-61 —Detroit	5	144	20	57	.351	16	23	.696	46	22	22	1	56	9.2	4.4	11.2
61-62 —Detroit	10	378	69	163	.423	62	75	.827	96	23	48	3	200	9.6	2.3	20.0
62-63 —Detroit	4	163	24	64	.375	23	27	.852	42	11	19	1	71	10.5	2.8	17.8
64-65 —Baltimore	9	350	67	130	.515	53	70	.757	105	19	38	3	187	11.7	2.1	20.8
65-66 —Baltimore	3	94	23	50	.460	8	11	.727	30	2	13	1	54	10.0	0.7	18.0
66-67 —Boston	9	241	59	122	.464	20	30	.667	66	5	35	2	138	7.3	0.6	15.3
67-68 —Boston	19	597	135	264	.511	74	107	.692	146	22	84	6	344	7.7	1.2	18.1
68-69 —Boston	18	551	112	229	.489	46	64	.719	118	19	84	3	270	6.6	1.1	15.0
70-71 —Philadelphia	7	122	19	45	.422	9	18	.500	31	4	25	1	47	4.4	0.6	6.7
Totals	86	2712	542	1165	.465	317	433	.732	697	130	376	21	1401	8.1	1.5	16.3

NBA ALL-STAR GAME RECORD

Season Team	Min.	FGM	FGA	Pct.	FTM	FTA	Pct.	Reb	Ast.	PF	Dq.	Pts.
1961 —Detroit	16	5	10	.500	3	4	.750	3	3	4	0	13
1962 —Detroit	8	1	2	.500	0	0	...	0	1	1	0	2
1963 —Detroit	11	2	3	.667	0	0	...	1	1	2	0	4
1964 —Detroit	6	1	3	.333	0	0	...	2	0	0	0	2
1966 —Baltimore	26	3	11	.273	1	2	.500	2	2	4	0	7
1967 —Boston	14	1	4	.250	2	2	1.000	2	1	1	0	4
Totals	81	13	33	.394	6	8	.750	10	8	12	0	32

DID YOU KNOW...

...that Cleveland set an NBA record last season for fewest points allowed per game (88.5)?

HUDSON, LOU   F/G

PERSONAL: Born July 11, 1944, in Greensboro, N.C. ... 6-5/210. ... Full name: Louis Clyde Hudson. ... Nickname: Sweet Lou.
HIGH SCHOOL: Dudley Senior (Greensboro, N.C.).
COLLEGE: Minnesota.
TRANSACTIONS/CAREER NOTES: Selected by St. Louis Hawks in first round (fourth pick overall) of 1966 NBA Draft. ... Hawks franchise moved from St. Louis to Atlanta for 1968-69 season. ... Traded by Hawks to Los Angeles Lakers for F Ollie Johnson (September 30, 1977).

COLLEGIATE RECORD

Season Team	G	Min.	FGM	FGA	Pct.	FTM	FTA	Pct.	Reb.	Ast.	Pts.	AVERAGES RPG	APG	PPG
62-63—Minnesota‡					Freshman team did not play intercollegiate schedule.									
63-64—Minnesota	24	...	191	435	.439	53	85	.624	191	...	435	8.0	...	18.1
64-65—Minnesota	24	...	231	463	.499	96	123	.780	247	...	558	10.3	...	23.3
65-66—Minnesota	17	...	143	303	.472	50	77	.649	138	...	336	8.1	...	19.8
Varsity totals	65	...	565	1201	.470	199	285	.698	576	...	1329	8.9	...	20.4

NBA REGULAR-SEASON RECORD

HONORS: All-NBA second team (1970). ... NBA All-Rookie team (1967).

Season Team	G	Min.	FGM	FGA	Pct.	FTM	FTA	Pct.	Reb.	Ast.	PF	Dq.	Pts.	AVERAGES RPG	APG	PPG
66-67—St. Louis	80	2446	620	1328	.467	231	327	.706	435	95	277	3	1471	5.4	1.2	18.4
67-68—St. Louis	46	966	227	500	.454	120	164	.732	193	65	113	2	574	4.2	1.4	12.5
68-69—Atlanta	81	2869	716	1455	.492	338	435	.777	533	216	248	0	1770	6.6	2.7	21.9
69-70—Atlanta	80	3091	830	1564	.531	371	450	.824	373	276	225	1	2031	4.7	3.5	25.4
70-71—Atlanta	76	3113	829	1713	.484	381	502	.759	386	257	186	0	2039	5.1	3.4	26.8
71-72—Atlanta	77	3042	775	1540	.503	349	430	.812	385	309	225	0	1899	5.0	4.0	24.7
72-73—Atlanta	75	3027	816	1710	.477	397	481	.825	467	258	197	1	2029	6.2	3.4	27.1

Season Team	G	Min.	FGM	FGA	Pct.	FTM	FTA	Pct.	REBOUNDS Off.	Def.	Tot.	Ast.	St.	Blk.	TO	Pts.	AVERAGES RPG	APG	PPG
73-74—Atlanta	65	2588	678	1356	.500	295	353	.836	126	224	350	213	160	29	...	1651	5.4	3.3	25.4
74-75—Atlanta	11	380	97	225	.431	48	57	.842	14	33	47	40	13	2	...	242	4.3	3.6	22.0
75-76—Atlanta	81	2558	569	1205	.472	237	291	.814	104	196	300	214	124	17	...	1375	3.7	2.6	17.0
76-77—Atlanta	58	1745	413	905	.456	142	169	.840	48	81	129	155	67	19	...	968	2.2	2.7	16.7
77-78—Los Angeles	82	2283	493	992	.497	137	177	.774	80	108	188	193	94	14	150	1123	2.3	2.4	13.7
78-79—Los Angeles	78	1686	329	636	.517	110	124	.887	64	76	140	141	58	17	99	768	1.8	1.8	9.8
Totals	890	29794	7392	15129	.489	3156	3960	.797	...	...	3926	2432	516	98	249	17940	4.4	2.7	20.2

Personal fouls/disqualifications: 1973-74, 205/3. 1974-75, 33/1. 1975-76, 241/3. 1976-77, 160/2. 1977-78, 196/0. 1978-79, 133/1. Totals, 2439/17.

NBA PLAYOFF RECORD

Season Team	G	Min.	FGM	FGA	Pct.	FTM	FTA	Pct.	Reb.	Ast.	PF	Dq.	Pts.	AVERAGES RPG	APG	PPG
66-67—St. Louis	9	317	77	179	.430	49	68	.721	48	15	35	1	203	5.3	1.7	22.6
67-68—St. Louis	6	181	44	99	.444	42	47	.894	43	14	21	0	130	7.2	2.3	21.7
68-69—Atlanta	11	424	101	216	.468	40	52	.769	59	32	43	1	242	5.4	2.9	22.0
69-70—Atlanta	9	360	78	187	.417	41	50	.820	40	33	34	2	197	4.4	3.7	21.9
70-71—Atlanta	5	213	49	108	.454	29	39	.744	35	15	19	0	127	7.0	3.0	25.4
71-72—Atlanta	6	266	63	139	.453	24	29	.828	33	21	13	0	150	5.5	3.5	25.0
72-73—Atlanta	6	255	76	166	.458	26	29	.897	47	17	16	0	178	7.8	2.8	29.7

Season Team	G	Min.	FGM	FGA	Pct.	FTM	FTA	Pct.	REBOUNDS Off.	Def.	Tot.	Ast.	St.	Blk.	TO	Pts.	AVERAGES RPG	APG	PPG
77-78—Los Angeles	3	93	14	38	.368	7	8	.875	7	2	9	9	5	0	5	35	3.0	3.0	11.7
78-79—Los Angeles	6	90	17	32	.531	4	4	1.000	1	3	4	8	1	0	5	38	0.7	1.3	6.3
Totals	61	2199	519	1164	.446	262	326	.804	...	...	318	164	6	0	10	1300	5.2	2.7	21.3

Personal fouls/disqualifications: 1977-78, 9/0. 1978-79, 6/0. Totals, 196/4.

NBA ALL-STAR GAME RECORD

Season Team	Min.	FGM	FGA	Pct.	FTM	FTA	Pct.	Reb	Ast.	PF	Dq.	Pts.
1969 —Atlanta	20	6	13	.462	1	1	1.000	1	1	0	0	13
1970 —Atlanta	18	5	12	.417	5	5	1.000	1	0	1	0	15
1971 —Atlanta	17	6	13	.462	2	3	.667	3	1	3	0	14
1972 —Atlanta	18	2	7	.286	2	2	1.000	3	3	3	0	6
1973 —Atlanta	9	2	8	.250	2	2	1.000	2	0	2	0	6

Season Team	Min.	FGM	FGA	Pct.	FTM	FTA	Pct.	REBOUNDS Off.	Def.	Tot.	Ast.	PF	Dq.	St.	Blk.	TO	Pts.
1974 —Atlanta	17	5	8	.625	2	2	1.000	1	2	3	1	2	0	0	1	...	12
Totals	99	26	61	.426	14	15	.933	...	...	13	6	11	0	0	1	...	66

DID YOU KNOW...

...that Boston swept its season series against Philadelphia (4-0) for the first time since 1972-73?

ISSEL, DAN F/C

PERSONAL: Born October 25, 1948, in Batavia, Ill. ... 6-9/240. ... Full name: Daniel Paul Issel.
HIGH SCHOOL: Batavia (Ill.).
COLLEGE: Kentucky.
TRANSACTIONS/CAREER NOTES: Selected by Detroit Pistons in eighth round (122nd pick overall) of 1970 NBA Draft. ... Selected by Kentucky Colonels in first round of 1970 ABA draft. ... Traded by Colonels to Baltimore Claws for C Tom Owens and cash (September 19, 1975). ... Traded by Claws to Denver Nuggets for C Dave Robisch and cash (October 8, 1975). ... Nuggets franchise became part of NBA for 1976-77 season.
MISCELLANEOUS: Denver Nuggets all-time leading rebounder with 5,707 (1976-77 through 1984-85).

COLLEGIATE RECORD

NOTES: THE SPORTING NEWS All-America first team (1970). ... THE SPORTING NEWS All-America second team (1969).

Season Team	G	Min.	FGM	FGA	Pct.	FTM	FTA	Pct.	Reb.	Ast.	Pts.	AVERAGES RPG	APG	PPG
66-67—Kentucky‡	20	...	168	332	.506	80	111	.721	355	...	416	17.8	...	20.8
67-68—Kentucky	27	836	171	390	.438	102	154	.662	328	10	444	12.1	0.4	16.4
68-69—Kentucky	28	1063	285	534	.534	176	232	.759	381	49	746	13.6	1.8	26.6
69-70—Kentucky	28	1044	369	667	.553	210	275	.764	369	39	948	13.2	1.4	33.9
Varsity totals	83	2943	825	1591	.519	488	661	.738	1078	98	2138	13.0	1.2	25.8

ABA REGULAR-SEASON RECORD

NOTES: ABA co-Rookie of the Year (1971). ... ABA All-Star first team (1972). ... ABA All-Star second team (1971, 1973, 1974, 1976). ... ABA All-Rookie team (1971). ... Member of ABA championship team (1975). ... Holds single-season record for most points—2,538 (1972).

Season Team	G	Min.	2-POINT FGM	FGA	Pct.	3-POINT FGM	FGA	Pct.	FTM	FTA	Pct.	Reb.	Ast.	Pts.	AVERAGES RPG	APG	PPG
70-71—Kentucky	83	3274	938	1989	.472	0	5	.000	604	748	.807	1093	162	*2480	13.2	2.0	*29.9
71-72—Kentucky	83	3570	969	1990	.487	3	11	.273	591	*753	.785	931	195	*2538	11.2	2.3	30.6
72-73—Kentucky	84	*3531	899	1742	.516	3	15	.200	485	635	.764	922	220	*2292	11.0	2.6	27.3
73-74—Kentucky	83	3347	826	1709	.483	3	17	.176	457	581	.787	847	137	2118	10.2	1.7	25.5
74-75—Kentucky	83	2864	614	1298	.473	0	5	.000	237	321	.738	710	188	1465	8.6	2.3	17.7
75-76—Denver	84	2858	751	1468	.512	1	4	.250	425	521	.816	923	201	1930	11.0	2.4	23.0
Totals	500	19444	4997	10196	.490	10	57	.175	2799	3559	.786	5426	1103	12823	10.9	2.2	25.6

ABA PLAYOFF RECORD

Season Team	G	Min.	2-POINT FGM	FGA	Pct.	3-POINT FGM	FGA	Pct.	FTM	FTA	Pct.	Reb.	Ast.	Pts.	AVERAGES RPG	APG	PPG
70-71—Kentucky	19	670	207	408	.507	0	0	...	123	141	.872	221	28	536	11.6	1.5	28.2
71-72—Kentucky	6	269	47	113	.416	0	1	.000	38	50	.760	54	5	132	9.0	0.8	22.0
72-73—Kentucky	19	821	197	392	.503	1	6	.167	124	156	.795	225	28	521	11.8	1.5	27.4
73-74—Kentucky	8	311	60	135	.444	0	0	...	28	33	.848	87	14	148	10.9	1.8	18.5
74-75—Kentucky	15	578	122	261	.467	0	0	...	60	74	.811	119	29	304	7.9	1.9	20.3
75-76—Denver	13	470	111	226	.491	0	1	.000	44	56	.786	156	32	266	12.0	2.5	20.5
Totals	80	3119	744	1535	.485	1	8	.125	417	510	.818	862	136	1907	10.8	1.7	23.8

ABA ALL-STAR GAME RECORD

NOTES: ABA All-Star Game Most Valuable Player (1972).

Season Team	Min.	2-POINT FGM	FGA	Pct.	3-POINT FGM	FGA	Pct.	FTM	FTA	Pct.	Reb.	Ast.	Pts.
1971—Kentucky	34	8	15	.533	0	0	...	5	8	.625	11	0	21
1972—Kentucky	23	9	13	.692	0	0	...	3	4	.750	9	5	21
1973—Kentucky	29	6	14	.429	0	0	...	2	2	1.000	7	4	14
1974—Kentucky	26	10	15	.667	0	0	...	1	1	1.000	4	1	21
1975—Kentucky	20	3	6	.500	0	0	...	1	2	.500	7	1	7
1976—Denver	31	6	16	.375	0	0	...	7	9	.778	9	5	19
Totals	163	42	79	.532	0	0	...	19	26	.731	47	16	103

NBA REGULAR-SEASON RECORD

Season Team	G	Min.	FGM	FGA	Pct.	FTM	FTA	Pct.	REBOUNDS Off.	Def.	Tot.	Ast.	St.	Blk.	TO	Pts.	AVERAGES RPG	APG	PPG
76-77—Denver	79	2507	660	1282	.515	445	558	.798	211	485	696	177	91	29	...	1765	8.8	2.2	22.3
77-78—Denver	82	2851	659	1287	.512	428	547	.782	253	577	830	304	100	41	259	1746	10.1	3.7	21.3
78-79—Denver	81	2742	532	1030	.517	316	419	.754	240	498	738	255	61	46	171	1380	9.1	3.1	17.0
79-80—Denver	82	2938	715	1416	.505	517	667	.775	236	483	719	198	88	54	163	1951	8.8	2.4	23.8
80-81—Denver	80	2641	614	1220	.503	519	684	.759	229	447	676	158	83	53	130	1749	8.5	2.0	21.9
81-82—Denver	81	2472	651	1236	.527	546	655	.834	174	434	608	179	82	55	169	1852	7.5	2.2	22.9
82-83—Denver	80	2431	661	1296	.510	400	479	.835	151	445	596	223	83	43	174	1726	7.5	2.8	21.6
83-84—Denver	76	2076	569	1153	.494	364	428	.850	112	401	513	173	60	44	122	1506	6.8	2.3	19.8
84-85—Denver	77	1684	363	791	.459	257	319	.806	80	251	331	137	65	31	93	984	4.3	1.8	12.8
Totals	718	22342	5424	10711	.506	3792	4756	.797	1686	4021	5707	1804	698	396	1281	14659	7.9	2.5	20.4

Three-point field goals: 1979-80, 4-for-12 (.333). 1980-81, 2-for-12 (.167). 1981-82, 4-for-6 (.667). 1982-83, 4-for-19 (.211). 1983-84, 4-for-19 (.211). 1984-85, 1-for-7 (.143). Totals, 19-for-75 (.253).
Personal fouls/disqualifications: 1976-77, 246/7. 1977-78, 279/5. 1978-79, 233/6. 1979-80, 190/1. 1980-81, 249/6. 1981-82, 245/4. 1982-83, 227/0. 1983-84, 182/2. 1984-85, 171/1. Totals, 2022/32.

NBA PLAYOFF RECORD

Season Team	G	Min.	FGM	FGA	Pct.	FTM	FTA	Pct.	REBOUNDS Off.	Def.	Tot.	Ast.	St.	Blk.	TO	Pts.	AVERAGES RPG	APG	PPG
76-77—Denver	6	222	49	96	.510	34	45	.756	18	40	58	17	5	4	...	132	9.7	2.8	22.0
77-78—Denver	13	460	103	212	.486	56	65	.862	41	93	134	53	7	3	39	262	10.3	4.1	20.2

Season Team	G	Min.	FGM	FGA	Pct.	FTM	FTA	Pct.	Off.	Def.	Tot.	Ast.	St.	Blk.	TO	Pts.	RPG	APG	PPG
78-79—Denver...........	3	109	24	45	.533	25	31	.806	7	21	28	10	0	0	9	73	9.3	3.3	24.3
81-82—Denver...........	3	103	32	60	.533	12	12	1.000	8	13	21	5	3	1	7	76	7.0	1.7	25.3
82-83—Denver...........	8	227	69	136	.507	25	29	.862	13	45	58	25	9	5	10	163	7.3	3.1	20.4
83-84—Denver...........	5	153	52	102	.510	32	39	.821	10	30	40	8	6	6	15	137	8.0	1.6	27.4
84-85—Denver...........	15	325	73	159	.459	39	48	.813	14	40	54	27	12	5	13	186	3.6	1.8	12.4
Totals	53	1599	402	810	.496	223	269	.829	111	282	393	145	42	24	93	1029	7.4	2.7	19.4

Three-point field goals: 1982-83, 0-for-1. 1983-84, 1-for-2 (.500). 1984-85, 1-for-1. Totals, 2-for-4 (.500).

Personal fouls/disqualifications: 1976-77, 20/0. 1977-78, 43/1. 1978-79, 15/0. 1981-82, 10/0. 1982-83, 18/0. 1983-84, 15/0. 1984-85, 36/0. Totals, 157/1.

NBA ALL-STAR GAME RECORD

Season Team	Min.	FGM	FGA	Pct.	FTM	FTA	Pct.	Off.	Def.	Tot.	Ast.	PF	Dq.	St.	Blk.	TO	Pts.
1977 —Denver..............	10	0	3	.000	0	0	...	1	0	1	0	0	0	0	0	...	0

COMBINED ABA AND NBA REGULAR-SEASON RECORDS

	G	Min.	FGM	FGA	Pct.	FTM	FTA	Pct.	Off.	Def.	Tot.	Ast.	Stl.	Blk.	TO	Pts.	RPG	APG	PPG
Totals	1218	41786	10431	20964	.498	6591	8315	.793	...	...	11133	2907	...	...	...	27482	9.1	2.4	22.6

Three-point field goals: 29-for-132 (.220)

Personal fouls/disqualifications: 3504.

NBA COACHING RECORD

		REGULAR SEASON				PLAYOFFS		
Season Team	W	L	Pct.	Finish		W	L	Pct.
92-93 —Denver....................	36	46	.439	4th/Midwest Division		—	—	—
93-94 —Denver....................	42	40	.512	4th/Midwest Division		6	6	.500
94-95 —Denver....................	18	16	.529			—	—	—
Totals (3 years)................	96	102	.484	Totals (1 year)........		6	6	.500

NOTES:

1994—Defeated Seattle, 3-2, in Western Conference first round; lost to Utah, 4-3, in Western Conference semifinals.

1995—Resigned as Denver head coach (January 15); replaced by Gene Littles with club in fourth place.

JEANNETTE, BUDDY   G

PERSONAL: Born September 15, 1917, in New Kensington, Pa. ... 5-11/175. ... Full name: Harry Edward Jeannette.

HIGH SCHOOL: New Kensington (Pa.).

COLLEGE: Washington & Jefferson (Pa.).

TRANSACTIONS/CAREER NOTES: Warren Penns franchise transferred to Cleveland and renamed White Horses (February 10, 1939). ... Played in New York-Penn League with Elmira in 1939 and New York State League with Saratoga in 1942.

CAREER HONORS: Elected to Naismith Memorial Basketball Basketball Hall of Fame (1994).

MISCELLANEOUS: Member of BAA championship team (1948). ... Member of NBL championship teams (1943, 1944, 1945).

COLLEGIATE RECORD

												AVERAGES		
Season Team	G	Min.	FGM	FGA	Pct.	FTM	FTA	Pct.	Reb.	Ast.	Pts.	RPG	APG	PPG
34-35—Wash. & Jeff.	14	...	62	...	...	35	...	...	...	...	159	...	...	11.4
35-36—Wash. & Jeff.	20	...	92	...	...	42	...	...	...	...	226	...	...	11.3
36-37—Wash. & Jeff.	18	...	92	...	...	56	...	...	...	...	240	...	...	13.3
37-38—Wash. & Jeff.	20	...	...	...	...	...	...	...	...	...	240	...	...	12.0
Totals	72	...	...	...	...	...	...	...	...	...	865	...	...	12.0

NBL AND NBA REGULAR-SEASON RECORD

HONORS: All-BAA second team (1948). ... All-NBL first team (1941, 1944, 1945, 1946). ... All-NBL second team (1943).

														AVERAGES		
Season Team	G	Min.	FGM	FGA	Pct.	FTM	FTA	Pct.	Reb.	Ast.	PF	Dq.	Pts.	RPG	APG	PPG
38-39—W-CI (NBL)	26	...	54	...	...	65	...	...	...	...	57	...	173	...	...	6.7
39-40—Det. (NBL)	25	...	45	...	...	52	80	.650	...	...	62	...	142	...	...	5.7
40-41—Det. (NBL)	23	...	75	...	...	54	86	.628	...	...	56	...	204	...	...	8.9
42-43—Shb. (NBL)	4	...	24	...	...	14	17	.824	...	...	8	...	62	...	...	15.5
43-44—F.W. (NBL)	22	...	68	...	...	48	65	.738	...	...	46	...	184	...	...	8.4
44-45—F.W. (NBL)	27	...	85	...	...	82	111	*.739	...	...	67	...	252	...	...	9.3
45-46—F.W. (NBL)	34	...	99	...	...	105	136	.772	...	...	184	...	303	...	...	8.9
47-48—Baltimore (BAA)................	46	...	150	430	.349	191	252	.758	...	70	147	...	491	...	1.5	10.7
48-49—Baltimore (BAA)................	56	...	73	199	.367	167	213	.784	...	124	157	...	313	...	2.2	5.6
49-50—Baltimore	37	...	42	148	.284	109	133	.820	...	93	82	...	193	...	2.5	5.2
Totals...................................	300	...	715	...	...	887	...	...	...	...	866	...	2317	...	...	7.7

NBL AND NBA PLAYOFF RECORD

														AVERAGES		
Season Team	G	Min.	FGM	FGA	Pct.	FTM	FTA	Pct.	Reb.	Ast.	PF	Dq.	Pts.	RPG	APG	PPG
39-40—Det. (NBL)	3	...	6	...	...	8	...	...	...	...	...	...	20	...	...	6.7
40-41—Det. (NBL)	3	...	8	...	...	5	...	...	...	...	...	...	21	...	...	7.0
42-43—Shb. (NBL)	5	...	16	...	...	17	...	...	...	...	...	...	49	...	...	9.8
43-44—F.W. (NBL)	5	...	12	...	...	10	...	...	...	...	...	...	34	...	...	6.8
44-45—F.W. (NBL)	7	...	22	...	...	23	...	...	...	...	...	...	67	...	...	9.6

Season Team	G	Min.	FGM	FGA	Pct.	FTM	FTA	Pct.	Reb.	Ast.	PF	Dq.	Pts.	RPG	APG	PPG
45-46 —F.W. (NBL)	4	...	7	...	...	5	6	.833	...	...	...	...	19	...	...	4.8
47-48 —Baltimore (BAA)	11	...	30	61	.492	37	42	.881	...	12	45	...	97	...	1.1	8.8
48-49 —Baltimore (BAA)	3	...	2	13	.154	4	4	1.000	...	5	11	...	8	...	1.7	2.7
Totals	41	...	103	...	...	109	...	...	...	...	...	...	315	...	...	7.7

ABL REGULAR-SEASON RECORD

Season Team	G	Min.	FGM	FGA	Pct.	FTM	FTA	Pct.	Reb.	Ast.	Pts.	RPG	APG	PPG
46-47—Baltimore	29	...	113	...	...	118	...	...	...	...	344	...	...	11.9

HEAD COACHING RECORD

BACKGROUND: Player/head coach, Baltimore Bullets of ABL (1946-47). ... Assistant coach, Pittsburgh Condors of ABA (1970-71).

ABL COACHING RECORD

Season Team	REGULAR SEASON				PLAYOFFS		
	W	L	Pct.	Finish	W	L	Pct.
46-47 —Baltimore	31	3	.912	1st/Southern Division	2	1	.667

COLLEGIATE COACHING RECORD

Season Team	W	L	Pct.
52-53 —Georgetown	13	7	.650
53-54 —Georgetown	11	18	.379
54-55 —Georgetown	12	13	.480
55-56 —Georgetown	13	11	.542
Totals (4 years)	49	49	.500

NBA COACHING RECORD

Season Team	REGULAR SEASON				PLAYOFFS		
	W	L	Pct.	Finish	W	L	Pct.
47-48 —Baltimore (BAA)	28	20	.583	2nd/Western Division	9	3	.750
48-49 —Baltimore (BAA)	29	31	.483	3rd/Eastern Division	1	2	.333
49-50 —Baltimore	25	43	.368	5th/Eastern Division	—	—	—
50-51 —Baltimore	14	23	.378				
64-65 —Baltimore	37	43	.463	3rd/Western Division	5	5	.500
66-67 —Baltimore	3	13	.188				
Totals (6 years)	136	173	.440	Totals (3 years)	15	10	.600

EBL COACHING RECORD

Season Team	REGULAR SEASON				PLAYOFFS		
	W	L	Pct.	Finish	W	L	Pct.
59-60 —Baltimore	20	8	.714	2nd	2	2	.500
60-61 —Baltimore	19	9	.679	1st	2	0	1.000
Totals (2 years)	39	17	.696	Totals (2 years)	4	2	.667

ABA COACHING RECORD

Season Team	REGULAR SEASON				PLAYOFFS		
	W	L	Pct.	Finish	W	L	Pct.
69-70 —Pittsburgh	15	30	.333	5th/Eastern Division	—	—	—

NOTES:

1948—Defeated Chicago, 75-72, in Western Division tie-breaker; defeated New York, 2-1, in quarterfinals; defeated Chicago, 2-0, in semifinals; defeated Philadelphia, 4-2, in World Championship Series.

1949—Lost to New York in Eastern Division semifinals.

1951—Replaced as Baltimore head coach by Walt Budko (January).

1960—Defeated Allentown, 103-89, in semifinal; lost to Easton, 2-1, in EBL Finals.

1961—Defeated Scranton, 132-107, in semifinal; defeated Allentown, 119-104, in EBL Final.

1965—Defeated St. Louis, 3-1, in Western Division semifinals; lost to Los Angeles, 4-2, in Western Division finals.

1966—Replaced Michael Farmer as Baltimore head coach, with record of 1-8 (November). Replaced as Baltimore head coach by Gene Shue (December).

JOHNSON, DENNIS   G

PERSONAL: Born September 18, 1954, in San Pedro, Calif. ... 6-4/202. ... Full name: Dennis Wayne Johnson. ... Nickname: D.J.

HIGH SCHOOL: Dominquez (Compton, Calif.).

JUNIOR COLLEGE: Los Angeles Harbor Junior College.

COLLEGE: Pepperdine.

TRANSACTIONS/CAREER NOTES: Selected after junior season by Seattle SuperSonics in second round (29th pick overall) of 1976 NBA Draft. ... Traded by SuperSonics to Phoenix Suns for G Paul Westphal (June 4, 1980). ... Traded by Suns with 1983 first- and third-round draft choices to Boston Celtics for F/C Rick Robey and two 1983 second-round draft choices (June 27, 1983).

MISCELLANEOUS: Member of NBA championship teams (1979, 1984, 1986).

COLLEGIATE RECORD

Season Team	G	Min.	FGM	FGA	Pct.	FTM	FTA	Pct.	Reb.	Ast.	Pts.	RPG	APG	PPG
73-74—Los Angeles Harbor J.C.	...	699	103	191	.539	45	82	.549	230	...	251	...	...	...
74-75—Los Angeles Harbor J.C.	28	967	...	...	...	...	...	...	336	...	511	12.0	...	18.3
75-76—Pepperdine	27	930	181	378	.479	63	112	.563	156	88	425	5.8	3.3	15.7
Junior college totals	...	1666	...	...	...	...	...	...	566	...	762	...	...	...
4-year-college totals	27	930	181	378	.479	63	112	.563	156	88	425	5.8	3.3	15.7

NBA REGULAR-SEASON RECORD

HONORS: All-NBA first team (1981). ... All-NBA second team (1980). ... NBA All-Defensive first team (1979, 1980, 1981, 1982, 1983, 1987). ... NBA All-Defensive second team (1984, 1985, 1986).

Season Team	G	Min.	FGM	FGA	Pct.	FTM	FTA	Pct.	Off.	Def.	Tot.	Ast.	St.	Blk.	TO	Pts.	RPG	APG	PPG
76-77—Seattle	81	1667	285	566	.504	179	287	.624	161	141	302	123	123	57	...	749	3.7	1.5	9.2
77-78—Seattle	81	2209	367	881	.417	297	406	.732	152	142	294	230	118	51	164	1031	3.6	2.8	12.7
78-79—Seattle	80	2717	482	1110	.434	306	392	.781	146	228	374	280	100	97	191	1270	4.7	3.5	15.9
79-80—Seattle	81	2937	574	1361	.422	380	487	.780	173	241	414	332	144	82	227	1540	5.1	4.1	19.0
80-81—Phoenix	79	2615	532	1220	.436	411	501	.820	160	203	363	291	136	61	208	1486	4.6	3.7	18.8
81-82—Phoenix	80	2937	577	1228	.470	399	495	.806	142	268	410	369	105	55	233	1561	5.1	4.6	19.5
82-83—Phoenix	77	2551	398	861	.462	292	369	.791	92	243	335	388	97	39	204	1093	4.4	5.0	14.2
83-84—Boston	80	2665	384	878	.437	281	330	.852	87	193	280	338	93	57	172	1053	3.5	4.2	13.2
84-85—Boston	80	2976	493	1066	.462	261	306	.853	91	226	317	543	96	39	212	1254	4.0	6.8	15.7
85-86—Boston	78	2732	482	1060	.455	243	297	.818	69	199	268	456	110	35	173	1213	3.4	5.8	15.6
86-87—Boston	79	2933	423	953	.444	209	251	.833	45	216	261	594	87	38	177	1062	3.3	7.5	13.4
87-88—Boston	77	2670	352	803	.438	255	298	.856	62	178	240	598	93	29	195	971	3.1	7.8	12.6
88-89—Boston	72	2309	277	638	.434	160	195	.821	31	159	190	472	94	21	175	721	2.6	6.6	10.0
89-90—Boston	75	2036	206	475	.434	118	140	.843	48	153	201	485	81	14	117	531	2.7	6.5	7.1
Totals	1100	35954	5832	13100	.445	3791	4754	.797	1459	2790	4249	5499	1477	675	2448	15535	3.9	5.0	14.1

Three-point field goals: 1979-80, 12-for-58 (.207). 1980-81, 11-for-51 (.216). 1981-82, 8-for-42 (.190). 1982-83, 5-for-31 (.161). 1983-84, 4-for-32 (.125). 1984-85, 7-for-26 (.269). 1985-86, 6-for-42 (.143). 1986-87, 7-for-62 (.113). 1987-88, 12-for-46 (.261). 1988-89, 7-for-50 (.140). 1989-90, 1-for-24 (.042). Totals, 80-for-464 (.172).

Personal fouls/disqualifications: 1976-77, 221/3. 1977-78, 213/2. 1978-79, 209/2. 1979-80, 267/6. 1980-81, 244/2. 1981-82, 253/6. 1982-83, 204/1. 1983-84, 251/6. 1984-85, 224/2. 1985-86, 206/3. 1986-87, 201/0. 1987-88, 204/0. 1988-89, 211/3. 1989-90, 179/2. Totals, 3087/38.

NBA PLAYOFF RECORD

NOTES: NBA Finals Most Valuable Player (1979). ... Shares NBA Finals single-game record for most free throws made in one half—12 (June 12, 1984, vs. Los Angeles).

Season Team	G	Min.	FGM	FGA	Pct.	FTM	FTA	Pct.	Off.	Def.	Tot.	Ast.	St.	Blk.	TO	Pts.	RPG	APG	PPG
77-78—Seattle	22	827	121	294	.412	112	159	.704	47	54	101	72	23	23	56	354	4.6	3.3	16.1
78-79—Seattle	17	681	136	302	.450	84	109	.771	44	60	104	69	28	26	51	356	6.1	4.1	20.9
79-80—Seattle	15	582	100	244	.410	52	62	.839	25	39	64	57	27	10	43	257	4.3	3.8	17.1
80-81—Phoenix	7	267	52	110	.473	32	42	.762	7	26	33	20	9	9	19	137	4.7	2.9	19.6
81-82—Phoenix	7	271	63	132	.477	30	39	.769	13	18	31	32	15	4	25	156	4.4	4.6	22.3
82-83—Phoenix	3	108	22	48	.458	10	12	.833	6	17	23	17	5	2	8	54	7.7	5.7	18.0
83-84—Boston	22	808	129	319	.404	104	120	.867	30	49	79	97	25	7	53	365	3.6	4.4	16.6
84-85—Boston	21	848	142	319	.445	80	93	.860	24	60	84	154	31	9	72	364	4.0	7.3	17.3
85-86—Boston	18	715	109	245	.445	67	84	.798	23	53	76	107	39	5	51	291	4.2	5.9	16.2
86-87—Boston	23	964	168	361	.465	96	113	.850	24	67	91	205	16	8	44	435	4.0	8.9	18.9
87-88—Boston	17	702	91	210	.433	82	103	.796	15	62	77	139	24	8	45	270	4.5	8.2	15.9
88-89—Boston	3	59	4	15	.267	0	0	...	2	2	4	9	3	0	3	8	1.3	3.0	2.7
89-90—Boston	5	162	30	62	.484	7	7	1.000	2	12	14	28	2	2	10	69	2.8	5.6	13.8
Totals	180	6994	1167	2661	.439	756	943	.802	262	519	781	1006	247	113	480	3116	4.3	5.6	17.3

Three-point field goals: 1979-80, 5-for-15 (.333). 1980-81, 1-for-5 (.200). 1981-82, 0-for-4. 1982-83, 0-for-1. 1983-84, 3-for-7 (.429). 1984-85, 0-for-14. 1985-86, 6-for-16 (.375). 1986-87, 3-for-26 (.115). 1987-88, 6-for-16 (.375). 1989-90, 2-for-6 (.333). Totals, 26-for-110 (.236).

Personal fouls/disqualifications: 1977-78, 63/0. 1978-79, 63/0. 1979-80, 48/2. 1980-81, 18/0. 1981-82, 28/2. 1982-83, 9/0. 1983-84, 75/1. 1984-85, 66/0. 1985-86, 58/2. 1986-87, 71/0. 1987-88, 51/0. 1988-89, 8/0. 1989-90, 17/1. Totals, 575/8.

NBA ALL-STAR GAME RECORD

Season	Team	Min.	FGM	FGA	Pct.	FTM	FTA	Pct.	Off.	Def.	Tot.	Ast.	PF	Dq.	St.	Blk.	TO	Pts.
1979	—Seattle	27	5	7	.714	2	2	1.000	1	0	1	3	3	0	0	1	1	12
1980	—Seattle	20	7	13	.538	5	6	.833	2	2	4	1	3	0	2	1	2	19
1981	—Phoenix	24	5	8	.625	9	10	.900	1	1	2	1	1	0	3	0	2	19
1982	—Phoenix	15	0	2	.000	1	2	.500	2	3	5	1	1	0	0	2	3	1
1985	—Boston	12	3	7	.429	2	2	1.000	1	5	6	3	2	0	0	0	1	8
Totals	....	98	20	37	.541	19	22	.864	7	11	18	9	10	0	5	4	9	59

JOHNSON, GUS   F

PERSONAL: Born December 13, 1938, in Akron, Ohio. ... Died April 29, 1987. ... 6-6/235. ... Full name: Gus Johnson Jr. ... Nickname: Honeycomb.
HIGH SCHOOL: Central Hower (Akron, Ohio).
JUNIOR COLLEGE: Boise (Idaho) Junior College.
COLLEGE: Akron, then Idaho.
TRANSACTIONS/CAREER NOTES: Selected by Baltimore Bullets in second round (11th pick overall) of 1963 NBA Draft. ... Traded by Bullets to Phoenix Suns for second-round draft choice (April 10, 1972). ... Waived by Suns (December 1, 1972). ... Signed as free agent by Indiana Pacers of American Basketball Association (December 15, 1972).

COLLEGIATE RECORD

NOTES: Left Akron before start of 1959-60 basketball season.

Season Team	G	Min.	FGM	FGA	Pct.	FTM	FTA	Pct.	Reb.	Ast.	Pts.	RPG	APG	PPG
62-63—Idaho	23	...	188	438	.429	62	105	.590	466	...	438	20.3	...	19.0

NBA REGULAR-SEASON RECORD

HONORS: All-NBA second team (1965, 1966, 1970, 1971). ... NBA All-Defensive first team (1970, 1971). ... NBA All-Rookie team (1964).

Season Team	G	Min.	FGM	FGA	Pct.	FTM	FTA	Pct.	Reb.	Ast.	PF	Dq.	Pts.	RPG	APG	PPG
63-64 —Baltimore	78	2847	571	1329	.430	210	319	.658	1064	169	321	†11	1352	13.6	2.2	17.3
64-65 —Baltimore	76	2899	577	1379	.418	261	386	.676	988	270	258	4	1415	13.0	3.6	18.6
65-66 —Baltimore	41	1284	273	661	.413	131	178	.736	546	114	136	3	677	13.3	2.8	16.5
66-67 —Baltimore	73	2626	620	1377	.450	271	383	.708	855	194	281	7	1511	11.7	2.7	20.7
67-68 —Baltimore	60	2271	482	1033	.467	180	270	.667	782	159	223	7	1144	13.0	2.7	19.1
68-69 —Baltimore	49	1671	359	782	.459	160	223	.717	568	97	176	1	878	11.6	2.0	17.9
69-70 —Baltimore	78	2919	578	1282	.451	197	272	.724	1086	264	269	6	1353	13.9	3.4	17.3
70-71 —Baltimore	66	2538	494	1090	.453	214	290	.738	1128	192	227	4	1202	17.1	2.9	18.2
71-72 —Baltimore	39	668	103	269	.383	43	63	.683	226	51	91	0	249	5.8	1.3	6.4
72-73 —Phoenix	21	417	69	181	.381	25	36	.694	136	31	55	0	163	6.5	1.5	7.8
Totals	581	20140	4126	9383	.440	1692	2420	.699	7379	1541	2037	43	9944	12.7	2.7	17.1

NBA PLAYOFF RECORD

Season Team	G	Min.	FGM	FGA	Pct.	FTM	FTA	Pct.	Reb.	Ast.	PF	Dq.	Pts.	RPG	APG	PPG
64-65 —Baltimore	10	377	62	173	.358	34	46	.739	111	34	38	1	158	11.1	3.4	15.8
65-66 —Baltimore	1	8	1	4	.250	0	0	...	0	0	1	0	2	0.0	0.0	2.0
69-70 —Baltimore	7	298	51	111	.459	27	34	.794	80	9	20	0	129	11.4	1.3	18.4
70-71 —Baltimore	11	365	54	128	.422	35	47	.745	114	30	34	0	143	10.4	2.7	13.0
71-72 —Baltimore	5	77	9	30	.300	2	2	1.000	25	3	17	0	20	5.0	0.6	4.0
Totals	34	1125	177	446	.397	98	129	.760	330	76	110	1	452	9.7	2.2	13.3

NBA ALL-STAR GAME RECORD

Season Team	Min.	FGM	FGA	Pct.	FTM	FTA	Pct.	Reb	Ast.	PF	Dq.	Pts.
1965 —Baltimore	25	7	13	.538	11	13	.846	8	2	2	0	25
1968 —Baltimore	16	3	9	.333	1	2	.500	6	1	2	0	7
1969 —Baltimore	18	4	10	.400	5	8	.625	10	0	3	0	13
1970 —Baltimore	17	5	12	.417	0	0	...	7	1	2	0	10
1971 —Baltimore	23	5	12	.417	2	2	1.000	4	2	3	0	12
Totals	99	24	56	.429	19	25	.760	35	6	12	0	67

ABA REGULAR-SEASON RECORD

NOTES: Member of ABA championship team (1973).

Season Team	G	Min.	2-POINT			3-POINT			FTM	FTA	Pct.	Reb.	Ast.	Pts.	AVERAGES		
			FGM	FGA	Pct.	FGM	FGA	Pct.							RPG	APG	PPG
72-73—Indiana	50	753	128	278	.460	4	21	.190	31	42	.738	245	62	299	4.9	1.2	6.0

ABA PLAYOFF RECORD

Season Team	G	Min.	2-POINT			3-POINT			FTM	FTA	Pct.	Reb.	Ast.	Pts.	AVERAGES		
			FGM	FGA	Pct.	FGM	FGA	Pct.							RPG	APG	PPG
72-73—Indiana	17	184	15	56	.268	0	3	.000	12	16	.750	69	15	42	4.1	0.9	2.5

COMBINED ABA AND NBA REGULAR-SEASON RECORDS

	G	Min.	FGM	FGA	Pct.	FTM	FTA	Pct.	REBOUNDS			Ast.	Stl.	Blk.	TO	Pts.	AVERAGES		
									Off.	Def.	Tot.						RPG	APG	PPG
Totals	631	20893	4258	9682	.440	1723	2462	.700	...	...	7624	1603	...	...	...	10243	12.1	2.5	16.2

Three-point field goals: 4-for-21 (.190).
Personal fouls/disqualifications: 2150.

JOHNSTON, NEIL   C

PERSONAL: Born February 4, 1929, in Chillicothe, Ohio. ... Died September 27, 1978. ... 6-8/210. ... Full name: Donald Neil Johnston. ... Nickname: Gabby.
HIGH SCHOOL: Chillicothe (Ohio).
COLLEGE: Ohio State.
TRANSACTIONS/CAREER NOTES: Signed as free agent by Philadelphia Warriors (1951). ... Signed as player/head coach by Pittsburgh Rens of American Basketball League (1961).
CAREER HONORS: Elected to Naismith Memorial Basketball Hall of Fame (1989).
MISCELLANEOUS: Member of NBA championship team (1956).

COLLEGIATE RECORD

NOTES: Signed pro baseball contract in 1948 and became ineligible for his final two years at Ohio State.

Season Team	G	Min.	FGM	FGA	Pct.	FTM	FTA	Pct.	Reb.	Ast.	Pts.	RPG	APG	PPG
46-47 —Ohio State	7	...	5	...	...	3	8	.375	...	...	13	...	...	1.9
47-48 —Ohio State	20	...	67	219	.306	46	87	.529	...	...	180	...	...	9.0
Totals	27	...	72	...	...	49	95	.516	...	...	193	...	...	7.1

NBA REGULAR-SEASON RECORD

HONORS: All-NBA first team (1953, 1954, 1955, 1956). ... All-NBA second team (1957).

Season Team	G	Min.	FGM	FGA	Pct.	FTM	FTA	Pct.	Reb.	Ast.	PF	Dq.	Pts.	RPG	APG	PPG
51-52 —Philadelphia	64	993	141	299	.472	100	151	.662	342	39	154	5	382	5.3	0.6	6.0
52-53 —Philadelphia	70	*3166	*504	1114	*.452	*556	*794	.700	976	197	248	6	*1564	13.9	2.8	*22.3
53-54 —Philadelphia	72	*3296	*591	*1317	.449	*577	*772	.747	797	203	259	7	*1759	11.1	2.8	*24.4
54-55 —Philadelphia	72	2917	521	1184	.440	*589	*769	.766	*1085	215	255	4	*1631	*15.1	3.0	*22.7
55-56 —Philadelphia	70	2594	499	1092	*.457	549	685	.801	872	225	251	8	1547	12.5	3.2	22.1

Season Team	G	Min.	FGM	FGA	Pct.	FTM	FTA	Pct.	Reb.	Ast.	PF	Dq.	Pts.	AVERAGES RPG	APG	PPG
56-57 —Philadelphia	69	2531	520	1163	*.447	535	648	.826	855	203	231	2	1575	12.4	2.9	22.8
57-58 —Philadelphia	71	2408	473	1102	.429	442	540	.819	790	166	233	4	1388	11.1	2.3	19.5
58-59 —Philadelphia	28	393	54	164	.329	69	88	.784	139	21	50	0	177	5.0	0.8	6.3
Totals	516	18298	3303	7435	.444	3417	4447	.768	5856	1269	1681	36	10023	11.3	2.5	19.4

NBA PLAYOFF RECORD

Season Team	G	Min.	FGM	FGA	Pct.	FTM	FTA	Pct.	Reb.	Ast.	PF	Dq.	Pts.	AVERAGES RPG	APG	PPG
51-52 —Philadelphia	3	32	5	10	.500	6	8	.750	10	1	8	0	16	3.3	0.3	5.3
55-56 —Philadelphia	10	397	69	169	.408	65	92	.707	143	51	41	0	203	14.3	5.1	20.3
56-57 —Philadelphia	2	84	17	53	.321	4	6	.667	35	9	9	0	38	17.5	4.5	19.0
57-58 —Philadelphia	8	189	30	78	.385	27	33	.818	69	14	18	0	87	8.6	1.8	10.9
Totals	23	702	121	310	.390	102	139	.734	257	75	76	0	344	11.2	3.3	15.0

NBA ALL-STAR GAME RECORD

Season Team	Min.	FGM	FGA	Pct.	FTM	FTA	Pct.	Reb	Ast.	PF	Dq.	Pts.
1953 —Philadelphia	27	5	13	.385	1	2	.500	12	0	2	0	11
1954 —Philadelphia	20	2	9	.222	2	4	.500	7	2	1	0	6
1955 —Philadelphia	15	1	7	.143	1	1	1.000	6	1	0	0	3
1956 —Philadelphia	25	5	9	.556	7	11	.636	10	1	3	0	17
1957 —Philadelphia	23	8	12	.667	3	3	1.000	9	1	2	0	19
1958 —Philadelphia	22	6	13	.462	2	2	1.000	8	1	5	0	14
Totals	132	27	63	.429	16	23	.696	52	6	13	0	70

ABL REGULAR-SEASON RECORD

Season Team	G	Min.	FGM	FGA	Pct.	FTM	FTA	Pct.	Reb.	Ast.	Pts.	AVERAGES RPG	APG	PPG
61-62—Pittsburgh	5	106	15	37	.405	24	16	1.500	18	10	49	3.6	2.0	9.8

HEAD COACHING RECORD

BACKGROUND: Player/head coach, Pittsburgh Rens of American Basketball League (1961-62).

NBA COACHING RECORD

Season Team	REGULAR SEASON W	L	Pct.	Finish		PLAYOFFS W	L	Pct.
59-60 —Philadelphia	49	26	.653	2nd/Eastern Division		4	5	.444
60-61 —Philadelphia	46	33	.582	2nd/Eastern Division		0	3	.000
Totals (2 years)	95	59	.617		Totals (2 years)	4	8	.333

ABL COACHING RECORD

Season Team	W	L	Pct.	Finish		W	L	Pct.
61-62 —Pittsburgh	41	40	.506	2nd/Eastern Division		0	1	.000
62-63 —Pittsburgh	12	10	.545	3rd		—	—	—
Totals (2 years)	53	50	.515		Totals (1 year)	0	1	.000

EBL COACHING RECORD

Season Team	W	L	Pct.	Finish		W	L	Pct.
64-65 —Wilmington	12	16	.429	5th		—	—	—
65-66 —Wilmington	20	8	.714	1st/Eastern Division		4	2	.667
Totals (2 years)	32	24	.571		Totals (1 year)	4	2	.667

NOTES:
1960—Defeated Syracuse, 2-1, in Eastern Division semifinals; lost to Boston, 4-2, in Eastern Division finals.
1961—Lost to Syracuse in Eastern Division semifinals.
1962—ABL disbanded (December 31).
1966—Defeated Trenton, 2-1, in Eastern Finals; defeated Wilkes-Barre, 2-1, in EBL Finals.

RECORD AS BASEBALL PLAYER

TRANSACTION/CAREER NOTES: Signed by Philadelphia Phillies organization (August 1948). ... Released by Phillies organization (June 1, 1952).

Year Team (League)	G	W	L	Pct.	ERA	Sv.	IP	H	R	ER	BB	SO
1949—Terre Haute (Three I)	29	10	12	.455	3.14	...	166	159	85	58	73	129
1950—Terre Haute (Three I)	28	11	12	.478	2.89	...	168	132	78	54	102	126
1951—Wilmington (Inter-State)	27	3	9	.250	5.40	...	115	126	76	69	79	104

JONES, BOBBY   F

PERSONAL: Born December 18, 1951, in Charlotte. ... 6-9/210. ... Full name: Robert Clyde Jones.
HIGH SCHOOL: South Mecklenburg (Charlotte).
COLLEGE: North Carolina
TRANSACTIONS/CAREER NOTES: Selected by Carolina Cougars in second round of 1973 ABA special circumstance draft. ... Cougars franchise moved to St. Louis and renamed Spirits of St. Louis for 1974-75 season. ... Draft rights traded by Spirits of St. Louis to Denver Nuggets for draft rights to Marvin Barnes (1974). ... Nuggets franchise became part of NBA for 1976-77 season. ... Traded by Nuggets with Ralph Simpson to Philadelphia 76ers for F George McGinnis (August 16, 1978).
MISCELLANEOUS: Member of NBA championship team (1983). ... Member of silver-medal-winning U.S. Olympic team (1972).

DID YOU KNOW...
...that Muggsy Bogues is the all-time leader in assists-to-turnover ratio?

COLLEGIATE RECORD

Season Team	G	Min.	FGM	FGA	Pct.	FTM	FTA	Pct.	Reb.	Ast.	Pts.	AVERAGES		
												RPG	APG	PPG
70-71—North Carolina	16	...	136	237	.574	86	113	.761	236	...	358	14.8	...	22.4
71-72—North Carolina	31	...	127	190	.668	62	95	.653	195	75	316	6.3	2.4	10.2
72-73—North Carolina	33	...	206	343	.601	84	128	.656	348	130	496	10.5	3.9	15.0
73-74—North Carolina	28	...	189	326	.580	74	120	.617	274	80	452	9.8	2.9	16.1
Totals	108	...	658	1096	.600	306	456	.671	1053	...	1622	9.8	...	15.0

ABA REGULAR-SEASON RECORD

NOTES: ABA All-Star second team (1976). ... ABA All-Defensive Team (1975 and 1976). ... ABA All-Rookie team (1975). ... Holds ABA single-season record for highest field-goal percentage—.605 (1975).

Season Team	G	Min.	2-POINT			3-POINT			FTM	FTA	Pct.	Reb.	Ast.	Pts.	AVERAGES		
			FGM	FGA	Pct.	FGM	FGA	Pct.							RPG	APG	PPG
74-75—Denver	84	2706	529	875	*.605	0	1	.000	187	269	.695	692	303	1245	8.2	3.6	14.8
75-76—Denver	83	2845	510	878	*.581	0	0	...	215	308	.698	791	331	1235	9.5	4.0	14.9
Totals	167	5551	1039	1753	.593	0	1	.000	402	577	.697	1483	634	2480	8.9	3.8	14.9

ABA PLAYOFF RECORD

Season Team	G	Min.	2-POINT			3-POINT			FTM	FTA	Pct.	Reb.	Ast.	Pts.	AVERAGES		
			FGM	FGA	Pct.	FGM	FGA	Pct.							RPG	APG	PPG
74-75—Denver	13	428	69	128	.539	0	1	.000	31	40	.775	111	38	169	8.5	2.9	13.0
75-76—Denver	13	433	74	127	.583	0	0	...	30	41	.732	112	59	178	8.6	4.5	13.7
Totals	26	861	143	255	.561	0	1	.000	61	81	.753	223	97	347	8.6	3.7	13.3

ABA ALL-STAR GAME RECORD

Season Team	Min.	2-POINT			3-POINT			FTM	FTA	Pct.	Reb.	Ast.	Pts.
		FGM	FGA	Pct.	FGM	FGA	Pct.						
1976—Denver	29	8	12	.667	0	0	...	8	11	.727	10	3	24

NBA REGULAR-SEASON RECORD

HONORS: NBA Sixth Man Award (1983). ... NBA All-Defensive first team (1977, 1978, 1979, 1980, 1981, 1982, 1983, 1984) ... NBA All-Defensive second team (1985).

Season Team	G	Min.	FGM	FGA	Pct.	FTM	FTA	Pct.	REBOUNDS			Ast.	St.	Blk.	TO	Pts.	AVERAGES		
									Off.	Def.	Tot.						RPG	APG	PPG
76-77—Denver	82	2419	501	879	.570	236	329	.717	174	504	678	264	186	162	...	1238	8.3	3.2	15.1
77-78—Denver	75	2440	440	761	*.578	208	277	.751	164	472	636	252	137	126	194	1088	8.5	3.4	14.5
78-79—Philadelphia	80	2304	378	704	.537	209	277	.755	199	332	531	201	107	96	165	965	6.6	2.5	12.1
79-80—Philadelphia	81	2125	398	748	.532	257	329	.781	152	298	450	146	102	118	146	1053	5.6	1.8	13.0
80-81—Philadelphia	81	2046	407	755	.539	282	347	.813	142	293	435	226	95	74	149	1096	5.4	2.8	13.5
81-82—Philadelphia	76	2181	416	737	.564	263	333	.790	109	284	393	189	99	112	145	1095	5.2	2.5	14.4
82-83—Philadelphia	74	1749	250	460	.543	165	208	.793	102	242	344	142	85	91	109	665	4.6	1.9	9.0
83-84—Philadelphia	75	1761	226	432	.523	167	213	.784	92	231	323	187	107	103	101	619	4.3	2.5	8.3
84-85—Philadelphia	80	1633	207	385	.538	186	216	.861	105	192	297	155	84	50	118	600	3.7	1.9	7.5
85-86—Philadelphia	70	1519	189	338	.559	114	145	.786	49	120	169	126	48	50	90	492	2.4	1.8	7.0
Totals	774	20177	3412	6199	.550	2087	2674	.780	1288	2968	4256	1888	1050	982	1217	8911	5.5	2.4	11.5

Three-point field goals: 1979-80, 0-for-3. 1980-81, 0-for-3. 1981-82, 0-for-3. 1982-83, 0-for-1. 1983-84, 0-for-1. 1984-85, 0-for-4. 1985 86, 0-for-1. Totals, 0-for-16.

Personal fouls/disqualifications: 1976-77, 238/3. 1977-78, 221/2. 1978-79, 245/2. 1979-80, 223/3. 1980-81, 226/2. 1981-82, 211/3. 1982-83, 199/4. 1983-84, 199/1. 1984-85, 183/2. 1985-86, 159/0. Totals, 2104/22.

NBA PLAYOFF RECORD

Season Team	G	Min.	FGM	FGA	Pct.	FTM	FTA	Pct.	REBOUNDS			Ast.	St.	Blk.	TO	Pts.	AVERAGES		
									Off.	Def.	Tot.						RPG	APG	PPG
76-77—Denver	6	187	31	64	.484	10	17	.588	11	24	35	21	17	14	...	72	5.8	3.5	12.0
77-78—Denver	13	390	66	116	.569	34	46	.739	36	66	102	35	16	9	24	166	7.8	2.7	12.8
78-79—Philadelphia	9	260	48	87	.552	22	26	.846	12	31	43	19	5	4	15	118	4.8	2.1	13.1
79-80—Philadelphia	18	470	90	172	.523	53	62	.855	29	57	86	31	21	32	23	233	4.8	1.7	12.9
80-81—Philadelphia	16	443	81	160	.506	73	88	.830	35	53	88	33	18	21	32	235	5.5	2.1	14.7
01-02—Philadelphia	21	589	94	174	.540	68	81	.840	37	62	99	52	15	22	33	256	4.7	2.5	12.2
82-83—Philadelphia	12	324	43	78	.551	17	20	.850	19	39	58	34	15	18	18	103	4.8	2.8	8.6
83-84—Philadelphia	5	130	15	31	.484	18	19	.947	9	14	23	9	3	7	8	48	4.6	1.8	9.6
84-85—Philadelphia	13	309	46	78	.590	14	20	.700	22	26	48	16	12	15	19	106	3.7	1.2	8.2
85-86—Philadelphia	12	329	39	74	.527	38	50	.760	9	23	32	34	10	14	15	116	2.7	2.8	9.7
Totals	125	3431	553	1034	.535	347	429	.809	219	395	614	284	132	156	187	1453	4.9	2.3	11.6

Three-point field goals: 1979-80, 0-for-1. 1982-83, 0-for-1. 1985-86, 0-for-1. Totals, 0-for-3.

Personal fouls/disqualifications: 1976-77, 25/1. 1977-78, 42/1. 1978-79, 30/0. 1979-80, 56/1. 1980-81, 60/1. 1981-82, 69/0. 1982-83, 29/0. 1983-84, 12/0. 1984-85, 38/0. 1985-86, 39/0. Totals, 400/4.

NBA ALL-STAR GAME RECORD

Season	Team	Min.	FGM	FGA	Pct.	FTM	FTA	Pct.	REBOUNDS			Ast.	PF	Dq.	St.	Blk.	TO	Pts.
									Off.	Def.	Tot.							
1977	—Denver	14	1	4	.250	0	0	...	0	0	0	3	0	0	1	...		2
1978	—Denver	18	1	3	.333	0	0	...	1	5	6	2	4	0	1	1		2
1981	—Philadelphia	16	5	11	.455	1	1	1.000	1	3	4	2	0	1	1	0		11
1982	—Philadelphia	14	2	5	.400	1	2	.500	1	3	4	1	2	0	1	0	0	5
Totals		62	9	23	.391	2	3	.667	3	11	14	6	8	0	2	3	1	20

COMBINED ABA AND NBA REGULAR-SEASON RECORDS

	G	Min.	FGM	FGA	Pct.	FTM	FTA	Pct.	REBOUNDS			Ast.	Stl.	Blk.	TO	Pts.	AVERAGES		
									Off.	Def.	Tot.						RPG	APG	PPG
Totals	941	25728	4451	7953	.560	2489	3251	.766	1759	3980	5739	2522	1387	1319	1683	11391	6.1	2.7	12.1

Three-point field goals: 0-for-17.
Personal fouls/disqualifications: 2620

ALL-TIME GREAT PLAYERS

JONES, SAM G

PERSONAL: Born June 24, 1933, in Wilmington, N.C. ... 6-4/205. ... Full name: Samuel Jones.
HIGH SCHOOL: Laurinburg Institute (N.C.).
COLLEGE: North Carolina Central.
TRANSACTIONS/CAREER NOTES: Selected by Boston Celtics in first round (eighth pick overall) of 1957 NBA Draft.
CAREER HONORS: Elected to Naismith Memorial Basketball Hall of Fame (1983). ... NBA 25th Anniversary All-Time Team (1970).
MISCELLANEOUS: Member of NBA championship teams (1959, 1960, 1961, 1962, 1963, 1964, 1965, 1966, 1968, 1969).

COLLEGIATE RECORD

NOTES: Elected to NAIA Basketball Hall of Fame (1962).

Season Team	G	Min.	FGM	FGA	Pct.	FTM	FTA	Pct.	Reb.	Ast.	Pts.	RPG	APG	PPG
51-52—North Carolina Central....	22	...	126	263	.479	48	78	.615	150	...	300	6.8	...	13.6
52-53—North Carolina Central....	24	...	169	370	.457	115	180	.639	248	...	453	10.3	...	18.9
53-54—North Carolina Central....	27	...	208	432	.481	98	137	.715	223	...	514	8.3	...	19.0
54-55—						Did not play—in military service.								
55-56—						Did not play—in military service.								
56-57—North Carolina Central....	27	...	174	398	.437	155	202	.767	288	...	503	10.7	...	18.6
Totals	100	...	677	1463	.463	416	597	.697	909	...	1770	9.1	...	17.7

NBA REGULAR-SEASON RECORD

HONORS: All-NBA second team (1965, 1966, 1967).

Season Team	G	Min.	FGM	FGA	Pct.	FTM	FTA	Pct.	Reb.	Ast.	PF	Dq.	Pts.	RPG	APG	PPG
57-58 —Boston	56	594	100	233	.429	60	84	.714	160	37	42	0	260	2.9	0.7	4.6
58-59 —Boston	71	1466	305	703	.434	151	196	.770	428	101	102	0	761	6.0	1.4	10.7
59-60 —Boston	74	1512	355	782	.454	168	220	.764	375	125	101	1	878	5.1	1.7	11.9
60-61 —Boston	78	2028	480	1069	.449	211	268	.787	421	217	148	1	1171	5.4	2.8	15.0
61-62 —Boston	78	2388	596	1284	.464	243	297	.818	458	232	149	0	1435	5.9	3.0	18.4
62-63 —Boston	76	2323	621	1305	.476	257	324	.793	396	241	162	1	1499	5.2	3.2	19.7
63-64 —Boston	76	2381	612	1359	.450	249	318	.783	349	202	192	1	1473	4.6	2.7	19.4
64-65 —Boston	80	2885	821	1818	.452	428	522	.820	411	223	176	0	2070	5.1	2.8	25.9
65-66 —Boston	67	2155	626	1335	.469	325	407	.799	347	216	170	0	1577	5.2	3.2	23.5
66-67 —Boston	72	2325	638	1406	.454	318	371	.857	338	217	191	1	1594	4.7	3.0	22.1
67-68 —Boston	73	2408	621	1348	.461	311	376	.827	357	216	181	0	1553	4.9	3.0	21.3
68-69 —Boston	70	1820	496	1103	.450	148	189	.783	265	182	121	0	1140	3.8	2.6	16.3
Totals	871	24285	6271	13745	.456	2869	3572	.803	4305	2209	1735	5	15411	4.9	2.5	17.7

NBA PLAYOFF RECORD

Season Team	G	Min.	FGM	FGA	Pct.	FTM	FTA	Pct.	Reb.	Ast.	PF	Dq.	Pts.	RPG	APG	PPG
57-58 —Boston	8	75	10	22	.455	11	16	.688	24	4	7	0	31	3.0	0.5	3.9
58-59 —Boston	11	192	40	108	.370	33	39	.846	63	17	14	0	113	5.7	1.5	10.3
59-60 —Boston	13	197	45	117	.385	17	21	.810	41	18	15	0	107	3.2	1.4	8.2
60-61 —Boston	10	258	50	112	.446	31	35	.886	54	22	22	0	131	5.4	2.2	13.1
61-62 —Boston	14	504	123	277	.444	42	60	.700	99	44	30	0	288	7.1	3.1	20.6
62-63 —Boston	13	450	120	248	.484	69	83	.831	81	32	42	1	309	6.2	2.5	23.8
63-64 —Boston	10	356	91	180	.506	50	68	.735	47	23	24	0	232	4.7	2.3	23.2
64-65 —Boston	12	495	135	294	.459	73	84	.869	55	30	39	1	343	4.6	2.5	28.6
65-66 —Boston	17	602	154	343	.449	114	136	.838	86	53	65	1	422	5.1	3.1	24.8
66-67 —Boston	9	326	95	207	.459	50	58	.862	46	28	30	1	240	5.1	3.1	26.7
67-68 —Boston	19	685	162	367	.441	66	84	.786	64	50	58	0	390	3.4	2.6	20.5
68-69 —Boston	18	514	124	296	.419	55	69	.797	58	37	45	1	303	3.2	2.1	16.8
Totals	154	4654	1149	2571	.447	611	753	.811	718	358	391	5	2909	4.7	2.3	18.9

NBA ALL-STAR GAME RECORD

Season Team	Min.	FGM	FGA	Pct.	FTM	FTA	Pct.	Reb	Ast.	PF	Dq.	Pts.
1962 —Boston	14	1	8	.125	0	1	.000	1	0	1	0	2
1964 —Boston	27	8	20	.400	0	0		4	3	2	0	16
1965 —Boston	24	2	12	.167	2	2	1.000	5	3	2	0	6
1966 —Boston	22	5	11	.455	2	2	1.000	2	5	0	0	12
1968 —Boston	15	2	5	.400	1	1	1.000	2	4	1	0	5
Totals	102	18	56	.321	5	6	.833	14	15	6	0	41

HEAD COACHING RECORD

BACKGROUND: Athletic director/head coach, Federal City College, Washington, D.C. (1969-1973). ... Assistant coach, New Orleans Jazz (1974-75).

COLLEGIATE COACHING RECORD

Season Team	W	L	Pct.	Finish
69-70 —Federal City College	5	8	.385	
70-71 —Federal City College	12	9	.571	
71-72 —Federal City College	11	9	.550	
72-73 —Federal City College	11	13	.458	
73-74 —North Carolina Central	5	16	.238	7th/Mid-Eastern Athletic Conference
Totals (5 years)	44	55	.444	

KERR, RED   C

PERSONAL: Born August 17, 1932, in Chicago. ... 6-9/230. ... Full name: John G. Kerr.
HIGH SCHOOL: Tilden Technical School (Chicago).
COLLEGE: Illinois.
TRANSACTIONS/CAREER NOTES: Selected by Syracuse Nationals in first round (sixth pick overall) of 1954 NBA Draft. ... Nationals franchise moved from Syracuse to Philadelphia and renamed 76ers for 1963-64 season. ... Traded by 76ers to Baltimore Bullets for G Wally Jones (September 22, 1965). ... Selected by Chicago Bulls from Bullets in NBA expansion draft (April 30, 1966).
MISCELLANEOUS: Member of NBA championship team (1955).

COLLEGIATE RECORD

Season Team	G	Min.	FGM	FGA	Pct.	FTM	FTA	Pct.	Reb.	Ast.	Pts.	RPG	APG	PPG
50-51—Illinois‡						Freshman team did not play intercollegiate schedule.								
51-52—Illinois	26	...	143	365	.392	71	124	.573	...	...	357	...	...	13.7
52-53—Illinois	22	...	153	397	.385	80	123	.650	...	...	386	...	...	17.5
53-54—Illinois	22	...	210	520	.404	136	214	.636	...	...	556	...	...	25.3
Varsity totals	70	...	506	1282	.395	287	461	.623	...	...	1299	...	...	18.6

NBA REGULAR-SEASON RECORD

Season Team	G	Min.	FGM	FGA	Pct.	FTM	FTA	Pct.	Reb.	Ast.	PF	Dq.	Pts.	RPG	APG	PPG
54-55—Syracuse	72	1529	301	718	.419	152	223	.682	474	80	165	2	754	6.6	1.1	10.5
55-56—Syracuse	72	2114	377	935	.403	207	316	.655	607	84	168	3	961	8.4	1.2	13.3
56-57—Syracuse	72	2191	333	827	.403	225	313	.719	807	90	190	3	891	11.2	1.3	12.4
57-58—Syracuse	72	2384	407	1020	.399	280	422	.664	963	88	197	4	1094	13.4	1.2	15.2
58-59—Syracuse	72	2671	502	1139	.441	281	367	.766	1008	142	183	1	1285	14.0	2.0	17.8
59-60—Syracuse	75	2372	436	1111	.392	233	310	.752	913	167	207	4	1105	12.2	2.2	14.7
60-61—Syracuse	79	2676	419	1056	.397	218	299	.729	951	199	230	4	1056	12.0	2.5	13.4
61-62—Syracuse	80	2768	541	1220	.443	222	302	.735	1176	243	272	7	1304	14.7	3.0	16.3
62-63—Syracuse	80	2561	507	1069	.474	241	320	.753	1039	214	208	3	1255	13.0	2.7	15.7
63-64—Philadelphia	80	2938	536	1250	.429	268	357	.751	1017	275	187	2	1340	12.7	3.4	16.8
64-65—Philadelphia	80	1810	264	714	.370	126	181	.696	551	197	132	1	654	6.9	2.5	8.2
65-66—Baltimore	71	1770	286	692	.413	209	272	.768	586	225	148	0	781	8.3	3.2	11.0
Totals	905	27784	4909	11751	.418	2662	3682	.723	10092	2004	2287	34	12480	11.2	2.2	13.8

NBA PLAYOFF RECORD

Season Team	G	Min.	FGM	FGA	Pct.	FTM	FTA	Pct.	Reb.	Ast.	PF	Dq.	Pts.	RPG	APG	PPG
54-55—Syracuse	11	363	59	151	.391	34	61	.557	118	13	27	0	152	10.7	1.2	13.8
55-56—Syracuse	8	213	37	77	.481	15	33	.455	68	10	23	0	89	8.5	1.3	11.1
56-57—Syracuse	5	162	28	65	.431	20	29	.690	69	6	7	0	76	13.8	1.2	15.2
57-58—Syracuse	3	116	18	55	.327	14	18	.778	61	3	5	0	50	20.3	1.0	16.7
58-59—Syracuse	9	312	50	142	.352	30	33	.909	108	24	20	0	130	12.0	2.7	14.4
59-60—Syracuse	3	104	15	51	.294	11	12	.917	25	9	9	0	41	8.3	3.0	13.7
60-61—Syracuse	8	210	30	88	.341	16	23	.696	99	20	18	0	76	12.4	2.5	9.5
61-62—Syracuse	5	193	41	109	.376	6	8	.750	80	10	15	0	88	16.0	2.0	17.6
62-63—Syracuse	5	187	26	60	.433	16	21	.762	75	9	12	0	68	15.0	1.8	13.6
63-64—Philadelphia	5	185	40	83	.482	15	20	.750	69	16	12	0	95	13.8	3.2	19.0
64-65—Philadelphia	11	181	24	67	.358	15	21	.714	38	28	20	0	63	3.5	2.5	5.7
65-66—Baltimore	3	49	2	11	.182	1	2	.500	17	4	5	0	5	5.7	1.3	1.7
Totals	76	2275	370	959	.386	193	281	.687	827	152	173	0	933	10.9	2.0	12.3

NBA ALL-STAR GAME RECORD

Season Team	Min.	FGM	FGA	Pct.	FTM	FTA	Pct.	Reb	Ast.	PF	Dq.	Pts.
1956 —Syracuse	16	2	4	.500	0	1	.000	8	0	2	0	4
1959 —Syracuse	21	3	14	.214	1	2	.500	9	2	0	0	7
1963 —Syracuse	11	0	4	.000	2	2	1.000	2	1	3	0	2
Totals	48	5	22	.227	3	5	.600	19	3	5	0	13

NBA COACHING RECORD

HONORS: NBA Coach of the Year (1967).

		REGULAR SEASON				PLAYOFFS		
Season Team	W	L	Pct.	Finish		W	L	Pct.
66-67 —Chicago	33	48	.407	4th/Western Division		0	3	.000
67-68 —Chicago	29	53	.354	4th/Western Division		1	4	.200
68-69 —Phoenix	16	66	.195	7th/Western Division		—	—	—
69-70 —Phoenix	15	23	.395			—	—	—
Totals (4 years)	93	190	.329		Totals (2 years)	1	7	.125

NOTES:
1967—Lost to St. Louis in Western Division semifinals.
1968—Lost to Los Angeles in Western Division semifinals.
1970—Resigned as Phoenix head coach (January 2); replaced by Jerry Colangelo.

ALL-TIME GREAT PLAYERS

KING, BERNARD   F

PERSONAL: Born December 4, 1956, in Brooklyn, N.Y. ... 6-7/205. ... Brother of Albert King, guard/forward with New Jersey Nets, Philadelphia 76ers, San Antonio Spurs and Washington Bullets (1981-82 through 1988-89 and 1991-92).
HIGH SCHOOL: Fort Hamilton (Brooklyn, N.Y.).
COLLEGE: Tennessee.
TRANSACTIONS/CAREER NOTES: Selected after junior season by New Jersey Nets in first round (seventh pick overall) of 1977 NBA Draft. ... Traded by Nets with C/F John Gianelli and G Jim Boylan to Utah Jazz for C Rich Kelley (October 2, 1979). ... Traded by Jazz to Golden State Warriors for C/F Wayne Cooper and 1981 second-round draft choice (September 11, 1980). ... Signed as veteran free agent by New York Knicks (September 28, 1982); Warriors matched offer and traded King to Knicks for G Micheal Ray Richardson and 1984 fifth-round draft choice (October 22, 1982). ... Rights renounced by Knicks (1987). ... Signed as free agent by Washington Bullets (October 16, 1987). ... Waived by Bullets (January 22, 1993). ... Signed as free agent by New Jersey Nets (February 6, 1993).

COLLEGIATE RECORD

NOTES: The Sporting News All-America second team (1977). ... Led NCAA Division I with .622 field-goal percentage (1975).

Season Team	G	Min.	FGM	FGA	Pct.	FTM	FTA	Pct.	Reb.	Ast.	Pts.	RPG	APG	PPG
74-75—Tennessee	25	...	273	439	.622	115	147	.782	308	39	661	12.3	1.6	26.4
75-76—Tennessee	25	...	260	454	.573	109	163	.669	325	40	629	13.0	1.6	25.2
76-77—Tennessee	26	...	278	481	.578	116	163	.712	371	82	672	14.3	3.2	25.8
Totals	76	...	811	1374	.590	340	473	.719	1004	161	1962	13.2	2.1	25.8

NBA REGULAR-SEASON RECORD

HONORS: NBA Comeback Player of the Year (1981). ... All-NBA first team (1984, 1985). ... All-NBA second team (1982). ... All-NBA third team (1991). ... NBA All-Rookie team (1978).

Season Team	G	Min.	FGM	FGA	Pct.	FTM	FTA	Pct.	Off.	Def.	Tot.	Ast.	St.	Blk.	TO	Pts.	RPG	APG	PPG
77-78—New Jersey	79	3092	798	1665	.479	313	462	.677	265	486	751	193	122	36	311	1909	9.5	2.4	24.2
78-79—New Jersey	82	2859	710	1359	.522	349	619	.564	251	418	669	295	118	39	323	1769	8.2	3.6	21.6
79-80—Utah	19	419	71	137	.518	34	63	.540	24	64	88	52	7	4	50	176	4.6	2.7	9.3
80-81—Golden State	81	2914	731	1244	.588	307	437	.703	178	373	551	287	72	34	265	1771	6.8	3.5	21.9
81-82—Golden State	79	2861	740	1307	.566	352	499	.705	140	329	469	282	78	23	267	1833	5.9	3.6	23.2
82-83—New York	68	2207	603	1142	.528	280	388	.722	99	227	326	195	90	13	197	1486	4.8	2.9	21.9
83-84—New York	77	2667	795	1391	.572	437	561	.779	123	271	394	164	75	17	197	2027	5.1	2.1	26.3
84-85—New York	55	2063	691	1303	.530	426	552	.772	114	203	317	204	71	15	204	1809	5.8	3.7	*32.9
85-86—New York						Did not play—injured.													
86-87—New York	6	214	52	105	.495	32	43	.744	13	19	32	19	2	0	15	136	5.3	3.2	22.7
87-88—Washington	69	2044	470	938	.501	247	324	.762	86	194	280	192	49	10	211	1188	4.1	2.8	17.2
88-89—Washington	81	2559	654	1371	.477	361	441	.819	133	251	384	294	64	13	227	1674	4.7	3.6	20.7
89-90—Washington	82	2687	711	1459	.487	412	513	.803	129	275	404	376	51	7	248	1837	4.9	4.6	22.4
90-91—Washington	64	2401	713	1511	.472	383	485	.790	114	205	319	292	56	16	255	1817	5.0	4.6	28.4
91-92—Washington						Did not play—injured.													
92-93—New Jersey	32	430	91	177	.514	39	57	.684	35	41	76	18	11	3	21	223	2.4	0.6	7.0
Totals	874	29417	7830	15109	.518	3972	5444	.730	1704	3356	5060	2863	866	230	2791	19655	5.8	3.3	22.5

Three-point field goals: 1980-81, 2-for-6 (.333). 1981-82, 1-for-5 (.200). 1982-83, 0-for-6. 1983-84, 0-for-4. 1984-85, 1-for-10 (.100). 1987-88, 1-for-6 (.167). 1988-89, 5-for-30 (.167). 1989-90, 3-for-23 (.130). 1990-91, 8-for-37 (.216). 1992-93, 2-for-7 (.286). Totals, 23-for-134 (.172).
Personal fouls/disqualifications: 1977-78, 302/5. 1978-79, 326/10. 1979-80, 66/3. 1980-81, 304/5. 1981-82, 285/6. 1982-83, 233/5. 1983-84, 273/2. 1984-85, 191/3. 1986-87, 14/0. 1987-88, 202/3. 1988-89, 219/1. 1989-90, 230/1. 1990-91, 377/1. 1992-93, 53/0. Totals, 2885/45.

NBA PLAYOFF RECORD

Season Team	G	Min.	FGM	FGA	Pct.	FTM	FTA	Pct.	Off.	Def.	Tot.	Ast.	St.	Blk.	TO	Pts.	RPG	APG	PPG
78-79—New Jersey	2	81	21	42	.500	10	24	.417	5	6	11	7	4	0	6	52	5.5	3.5	26.0
82-83—New York	6	184	56	97	.577	28	35	.800	8	16	24	13	2	0	10	141	4.0	2.2	23.5
83-84—New York	12	477	162	282	.574	93	123	.756	28	46	74	36	14	6	31	417	6.2	3.0	34.8
87-88—Washington	5	168	26	53	.491	17	21	.810	3	8	11	9	3	0	14	69	2.2	1.8	13.8
92-93—New Jersey	3	24	4	7	.571	0	0	...	1	0	1	0	1	0	1	8	0.3	0.0	2.7
Totals	28	934	269	481	.559	148	203	.729	45	76	121	65	24	6	62	687	4.3	2.3	24.5

Three-point field goals: 1982-83, 1-for-3 (.333). 1983-84, 0-for-1. Totals, 1-for-4 (.250).
Personal fouls/disqualifications: 1978-79, 10/0. 1982-83, 16/0. 1983-84, 48/0. 1987-88, 17/0. 1992-93, 3/0. Totals, 94/0.

NBA ALL-STAR GAME RECORD

Season Team	Min.	FGM	FGA	Pct.	FTM	FTA	Pct.	Off.	Def.	Tot.	Ast.	PF	Dq.	St.	Blk.	TO	Pts.
1982 —Golden State	14	2	7	.286	2	2	1.000	0	4	4	1	2	0	3	1	2	6
1984 —New York	22	8	13	.615	2	5	.400	2	1	3	4	2	0	0	0	0	18
1985 —New York	22	6	10	.600	1	2	.500	4	3	7	1	5	0	0	1	1	13
1991 —Washington	26	2	8	.250	4	4	1.000	2	1	3	3	1	0	0	1	1	8
Totals	84	18	38	.474	9	13	.692	8	9	17	9	10	0	3	2	4	45

DID YOU KNOW...

...that with five more assists Charles Barkley will become the fourth player in NBA history to collect 20,000 points, 10,000 rebounds and 3,500 assists?
Kareem Abdul-Jabbar, Wilt Chamberlain and Elgin Baylor are the other three players.

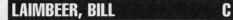

LAIMBEER, BILL   C

PERSONAL: Born May 19, 1957, in Boston. ... 6-11/260. ... Full name: William Laimbeer Jr. ... Name pronounced lam-BEER.
HIGH SCHOOL: Palos Verdes (Calif.).
JUNIOR COLLEGE: Owens Technical (Ohio).
COLLEGE: Notre Dame.
TRANSACTIONS/CAREER NOTES: Selected by Cleveland Cavaliers in third round (65th pick overall) of 1979 NBA Draft. ... Played in Italy (1979-80). ... Traded by Cavaliers with F Kenny Carr to Detroit Pistons for F Phil Hubbard, C Paul Mokeski and 1982 first- and second-round draft choices (February 16, 1982). ... Announced retirement (December 1, 1993).
MISCELLANEOUS: Member of NBA championship teams (1989, 1990). ... Detroit Pistons all-time leading rebounder with 9,430 (1981-82 through 1993-94).

COLLEGIATE RECORD

Season Team	G	Min.	FGM	FGA	Pct.	FTM	FTA	Pct.	Reb.	Ast.	Pts.	RPG	APG	PPG
76-77—Owens Tech..............							Did not play.							
75-76—Notre Dame..............	10	190	32	65	.492	18	23	.783	79	10	82	7.9	1.0	8.2
77-78—Notre Dame..............	29	654	97	175	.554	42	62	.677	190	31	236	6.6	1.1	8.1
78-79—Notre Dame..............	30	614	78	145	.538	35	50	.700	164	30	191	5.5	1.0	6.4
Totals	69	1458	207	385	.538	95	135	.704	433	71	509	6.3	1.0	7.4

ITALIAN LEAGUE RECORD

Season Team	G	Min.	FGM	FGA	Pct.	FTM	FTA	Pct.	Reb.	Ast.	Pts.	RPG	APG	PPG
79-80—Brescia	29	...	258	465	.555	97	124	.782	363	...	613	12.5	...	21.1

NBA REGULAR-SEASON RECORD

Season Team	G	Min.	FGM	FGA	Pct.	FTM	FTA	Pct.	Off.	Def.	Tot.	Ast.	St.	Blk.	TO	Pts.	RPG	APG	PPG
80-81—Cleveland	81	2460	337	670	.503	117	153	.765	266	427	693	216	56	78	132	791	8.6	2.7	9.8
81-82—Clev.-Det........	80	1829	265	536	.494	184	232	.793	234	383	617	100	39	64	121	718	7.7	1.3	9.0
82-83—Detroit	82	2871	436	877	.497	245	310	.790	282	711	993	263	51	118	176	1119	12.1	3.2	13.6
83-84—Detroit	82	2864	553	1044	.530	316	365	.866	329	674*1003		149	49	84	151	1422	12.2	1.8	17.3
84-85—Detroit	82	2892	595	1177	.506	244	306	.797	295	718	1013	154	69	71	129	1468	12.4	1.9	17.5
85-86—Detroit	82	2891	545	1107	.492	266	319	.834	305	*770*1075		146	59	65	133	1360	*13.1	1.8	16.6
86-87—Detroit	82	2854	506	1010	.501	245	274	.894	243	712	955	151	72	69	120	1263	11.6	1.8	15.4
87-88—Detroit	82	2897	455	923	.493	187	214	.874	165	667	832	199	66	78	136	1110	10.1	2.4	13.5
88-89—Detroit	81	2640	449	900	.499	178	212	.840	138	638	776	177	51	100	129	1106	9.6	2.2	13.7
89-90—Detroit	81	2675	380	785	.484	164	192	.854	166	614	780	171	57	84	98	981	9.6	2.1	12.1
90-91—Detroit	82	2668	372	778	.478	123	147	.837	173	564	737	157	38	56	98	904	9.0	1.9	11.0
91-92—Detroit	81	2234	342	727	.470	67	75	.893	104	347	451	160	51	54	102	783	5.6	2.0	9.7
92-93—Detroit	79	1933	292	574	.509	93	104	.894	110	309	419	127	46	40	59	687	5.3	1.6	8.7
93-94—Detroit	11	248	47	90	.522	11	13	.846	9	47	56	14	6	4	10	108	5.1	1.3	9.8
Totals	1068	33956	5574	11198	.498	2440	2916	.837	2819	7581	10400	2184	710	965	1594	13790	9.7	2.0	12.9

Three-point field goals: 1981-82, 4-for-13 (.308). 1982-83, 2-for-13 (.154). 1983-84, 0-for-11. 1984-85, 4-for-18 (.222). 1985-86, 4-for-14 (.286). 1986-87, 6-for-21 (.286). 1987-88, 13-for-39 (.333). 1988-89, 30-for-86 (.349). 1989-90, 57-for-158 (.361). 1990-91, 37-for-125 (.296). 1991-92, 32-for-85 (.376). 1992-93, 10-for-27 (.370). 1993-94, 3-for-9 (.333). Totals, 202-for-619 (.326).

Personal fouls/disqualifications: 1980-81, 332/14. 1981-82, 296/5. 1982-83, 320/9. 1983-84, 273/4. 1984-85, 308/4. 1985-86, 291/4. 1986-87, 283/4. 1987-88, 284/6. 1988-89, 259/2. 1989-90, 278/4. 1990-91, 242/3. 1991-92, 225/0. 1992-93, 212/4. 1993-94, 30/0. Totals, 3633/63.

NBA PLAYOFF RECORD

NOTES: Shares NBA Finals single-game record for most points in an overtime period—9 (June 7, 1990, vs. Portland).

Season Team	G	Min.	FGM	FGA	Pct.	FTM	FTA	Pct.	Off.	Def.	Tot.	Ast.	St.	Blk.	TO	Pts.	RPG	APG	PPG
83-84—Detroit	5	165	29	51	.569	18	20	.900	14	48	62	12	4	3	12	76	12.4	2.4	15.2
84-85—Detroit	9	325	48	107	.449	36	51	.706	36	60	96	15	7	7	16	132	10.7	1.7	14.7
85-86—Detroit	4	168	34	68	.500	21	23	.913	20	36	56	1	2	3	8	90	14.0	0.3	22.5
86-87—Detroit	15	543	84	163	.515	15	24	.625	30	126	156	37	15	12	20	184	10.4	2.5	12.3
87-88—Detroit	23	779	114	250	.456	40	45	.889	43	178	221	44	18	19	30	273	9.6	1.9	11.9
88-89—Detroit	17	497	66	142	.465	25	31	.806	26	114	140	31	6	8	19	172	8.2	1.8	10.1
89-90—Detroit	20	667	91	199	.457	25	29	.862	41	170	211	28	23	18	16	222	10.6	1.4	11.1
90-91—Detroit	15	446	66	148	.446	27	31	.871	42	80	122	19	5	12	17	164	8.1	1.3	10.9
91-92—Detroit	5	145	17	46	.370	5	5	1.000	5	28	33	8	4	1	5	41	6.6	1.6	8.2
Totals	113	3735	549	1174	.468	212	259	.819	257	840	1097	195	84	83	143	1354	9.7	1.7	12.0

Three-point field goals: 1984-85, 0-for-2. 1985-86, 1-for-1. 1986-87, 1-for-5 (.200). 1987-88, 5-for-17 (.294). 1988-89, 15-for-42 (.357). 1989-90, 15-for-43 (.349). 1990-91, 5-for-17 (.294). 1991-92, 2-for-10 (.200). Totals, 44-for-137 (.321).

Personal fouls/disqualifications: 1983-84, 23/2. 1984-85, 32/1. 1985-86, 19/1. 1986-87, 53/2. 1987-88, 77/2. 1988-89, 55/1. 1989-90, 77/3. 1990-91, 54/0. 1991-92, 18/1. Totals, 408/13.

NBA ALL-STAR GAME RECORD

Season Team	Min.	FGM	FGA	Pct.	FTM	FTA	Pct.	Off.	Def.	Tot.	Ast.	PF	Dq.	St.	Blk.	TO	Pts.
1983 —Detroit	6	1	1	1.000	0	0	...	1	0	1	0	1	0	0	0	1	2
1984 —Detroit	17	6	8	.750	1	1	1.000	1	4	5	0	3	0	1	2	0	13
1985 —Detroit	11	2	4	.500	1	2	.500	1	2	3	1	1	0	0	0	0	5
1987 —Detroit	11	4	7	.571	0	0	...	0	2	2	1	2	0	1	0	0	8
Totals	45	13	20	.650	2	3	.667	3	8	11	2	7	0	2	2	1	28

LANIER, BOB   C

PERSONAL: Born September 10, 1948, in Buffalo. ... 6-11/265. ... Full name: Robert Jerry Lanier Jr.
HIGH SCHOOL: Bennett (Buffalo).
COLLEGE: St. Bonaventure.
TRANSACTIONS/CAREER NOTES: Selected by Detroit Pistons in first round (first pick overall) of 1970 NBA Draft. ... Traded by Pistons to Milwaukee Bucks for C Kent Benson and 1980 first-round draft choice (February 4, 1980).
CAREER HONORS: Elected to Naismith Memorial Basketball Hall of Fame (1991).

COLLEGIATE RECORD

NOTES: THE SPORTING NEWS All-America first team (1970).

Season Team	G	Min.	FGM	FGA	Pct.	FTM	FTA	Pct.	Reb.	Ast.	Pts.	RPG	APG	PPG
66-67—St. Bonaventure‡	15	...	...	...	...	...	...	...	...	...	450	...	...	30.0
67-68—St. Bonaventure	25	...	272	466	.584	112	175	.640	390	...	656	15.6	...	26.2
68-69—St. Bonaventure	24	...	270	460	.587	114	181	.630	374	...	654	15.6	...	27.3
69-70—St. Bonaventure	26	...	308	549	.561	141	194	.727	416	...	757	16.0	...	29.1
Varsity totals	75	...	850	1475	.576	367	550	.667	1180	...	2067	15.7	...	27.6

NBA REGULAR-SEASON RECORD

HONORS: NBA All-Rookie team (1971).

Season Team	G	Min.	FGM	FGA	Pct.	FTM	FTA	Pct.	Reb.	Ast.	PF	Dq.	Pts.	RPG	APG	PPG
70-71—Detroit	82	2017	504	1108	.455	273	376	.726	665	146	272	4	1281	8.1	1.8	15.6
71-72—Detroit	80	3092	834	1690	.494	388	505	.768	1132	248	297	6	2056	14.2	3.1	25.7
72-73—Detroit	81	3150	810	1654	.490	307	397	.773	1205	260	278	4	1927	14.9	3.2	23.8

									REBOUNDS						AVERAGES		
Season Team	G	Min.	FGM	FGA	Pct.	FTM	FTA	Pct.	Off.	Def.	Tot.	Ast.	St.	Blk.	TO	Pts.	RPG	APG	PPG
---	---	---	---	---	---	---	---	---	---	---	---	---	---	---	---	---	---	---	---
73-74—Detroit	81	3047	748	1483	.504	326	409	.797	269	805	1074	343	110	247	...	1822	13.3	4.2	22.5
74-75—Detroit	76	2987	731	1433	.510	361	450	.802	225	689	914	350	75	172	...	1823	12.0	4.6	24.0
75-76—Detroit	64	2363	541	1017	.532	284	370	.768	217	529	746	217	79	86	...	1366	11.7	3.4	21.3
76-77—Detroit	64	2446	678	1269	.534	260	318	.818	200	545	745	214	70	126	...	1616	11.6	3.3	25.3
77-78—Detroit	63	2311	622	1159	.537	298	386	.772	197	518	715	216	82	93	225	1542	11.3	3.4	24.5
78-79—Detroit	53	1835	489	950	.515	275	367	.749	164	330	494	140	50	75	175	1253	9.3	2.6	23.6
79-80—Detroit-Mil.	63	2131	466	867	.537	277	354	.782	152	400	552	184	74	89	162	1210	8.8	2.9	19.2
80-81—Milwaukee	67	1753	376	716	.525	208	277	.751	128	285	413	179	73	81	139	961	6.2	2.7	14.3
81-82—Milwaukee	74	1986	407	729	.558	182	242	.752	92	296	388	219	72	56	166	996	5.2	3.0	13.5
82-83—Milwaukee	39	978	163	332	.491	91	133	.684	58	142	200	105	34	24	82	417	5.1	2.7	10.7
83-84—Milwaukee	72	2007	392	685	.572	194	274	.708	141	314	455	186	58	51	163	978	6.3	2.6	13.6
Totals	959	32103	7761	15092	.514	3724	4858	.767	...	...	9698	3007	777	1100	1112	19248	10.1	3.1	20.1

Three-point field goals: 1979-80, 1-for-6 (.167). 1980-81, 1-for-1. 1981-82, 0-for-2. 1982-83, 0-for-1. 1983-84, 0-for-3. Totals, 2-for-13 (.154).
Personal fouls/disqualifications: 1973-74, 273/7. 1974-75, 237/1. 1975-76, 203/2. 1976-77, 174/0. 1977-78, 185/2. 1978-79, 181/5. 1979-80, 200/3. 1980-81, 184/0. 1981-82, 211/3. 1982-83, 125/2. 1983-84, 228/8. Totals, 3048/47.

NBA PLAYOFF RECORD

									REBOUNDS								AVERAGES		
Season Team	G	Min.	FGM	FGA	Pct.	FTM	FTA	Pct.	Off.	Def.	Tot.	Ast.	St.	Blk.	TO	Pts.	RPG	APG	PPG
73-74—Detroit	7	303	77	152	.507	30	38	.789	26	81	107	21	4	14	...	184	15.3	3.0	26.3
74-75—Detroit	3	128	26	51	.510	9	12	.750	5	27	32	19	4	12	...	61	10.7	6.3	20.3
75-76—Detroit	9	359	95	172	.552	45	50	.900	39	75	114	30	8	21	...	235	12.7	3.3	26.1
76-77—Detroit	3	118	34	54	.630	16	19	.842	13	37	50	6	3	7	...	84	16.7	2.0	28.0
79-80—Milwaukee	7	256	52	101	.515	31	42	.738	17	48	65	31	7	8	17	135	9.3	4.4	19.3
80-81—Milwaukee	7	236	50	85	.588	23	32	.719	12	40	52	28	12	8	15	123	7.4	4.0	17.6
81-82—Milwaukee	6	212	41	80	.513	14	25	.560	18	27	45	22	8	5	14	96	7.5	3.7	16.0
82-83—Milwaukee	9	250	51	89	.573	21	35	.600	17	46	63	23	5	14	21	123	7.0	2.6	13.7
83-84—Milwaukee	16	499	82	171	.480	39	44	.886	32	85	117	55	11	10	38	203	7.3	3.4	12.7
Totals	67	2361	508	955	.532	228	297	.768	179	466	645	235	62	99	105	1244	9.6	3.5	18.6

Three-point field goals: 1981-82, 0-for-1.
Personal fouls/disqualifications: 1973-74, 28/1. 1974-75, 10/0. 1975-76, 34/1. 1976-77, 10/0. 1979-80, 23/0. 1980-81, 18/0. 1981-82, 21/2. 1982-83, 32/2. 1983-84, 57/1. Totals, 233/7.

NBA ALL-STAR GAME RECORD

NOTES: NBA All-Star Game Most Valuable Player (1974).

Season Team	Min.	FGM	FGA	Pct.	FTM	FTA	Pct.	Reb	Ast.	PF	Dq.	Pts.
1972 —Detroit	5	0	2	.000	2	3	.667	3	0	0	0	2
1973 —Detroit	12	5	9	.556	0	0	...	6	0	1	0	10

								REBOUNDS								
Season Team	Min.	FGM	FGA	Pct.	FTM	FTA	Pct.	Off.	Def.	Tot.	Ast.	PF	Dq.	St.	Blk.	TO	Pts.
1974 —Detroit	26	11	15	.733	2	2	1.000	2	8	10	2	1	0	0	2	...	24
1975 —Detroit	12	1	4	.250	0	0	...	2	5	7	2	3	0	2	0	...	2
1977 —Detroit	20	7	8	.875	3	3	1.000	5	5	10	4	3	0	1	1	...	17
1978 —Detroit	4	0	0	...	1	2	.500	2	0	2	0	0	0	0	0	1	1
1979 —Detroit	31	5	10	.500	0	0	...	1	3	4	4	4	0	1	1	0	10
1982 —Milwaukee	11	3	7	.429	2	2	1.000	2	1	3	0	3	0	0	1	1	8
Totals	121	32	55	.582	10	12	.833		...	45	12	15	0	4	5	2	74

NBA COACHING RECORD

BACKGROUND: Assistant coach, Golden State Warriors (beginning of 1994-95 season-February 13, 1995).

Season Team		REGULAR SEASON					PLAYOFFS		
	W	L	Pct.	Finish			W	L	Pct.
94-95 —Golden State	12	25	.324	6th/Pacific Division			—	—	—

NOTES:
1995—Replaced Don Nelson as Golden State head coach (February 13), with record of 14-31 and club in sixth place.

LUCAS, JERRY   F/C

PERSONAL: Born March 30, 1940, in Middletown, Ohio. ... 6-8/235. ... Full name: Jerry Ray Lucas. ... Nickname: Luke.
HIGH SCHOOL: Middletown (Ohio).
COLLEGE: Ohio State.
TRANSACTIONS/CAREER NOTES: Selected by Cincinnati Royals in 1962 NBA Draft (territorial pick). ... Signed by Cleveland Pipers of American Basketball League (1962); Pipers dropped out of ABL prior to 1962-63 season. ... Did not play pro basketball (1962-63). ... Traded by Royals to San Francisco Warriors for G Jim King and F Bill Turner (October 25, 1969). ... Traded by Warriors to New York Knicks for F Cazzie Russell (May 7, 1971).
CAREER HONORS: Elected to Naismith Memorial Basketball Hall of Fame (1979).
MISCELLANEOUS: Member of NBA championship team (1973). ... Member of gold-medal-winning U.S. Olympic team (1960).

COLLEGIATE RECORD

NOTES: THE SPORTING NEWS College Player of the Year (1961, 1962). ... THE SPORTING NEWS All-America first team (1960, 1961, 1962). ... Member of NCAA championship team (1960). ... Led NCAA Division I with .637 field-goal percentage (1960), .623 field-goal percentage (1961) and .611 field-goal percentage (1962). ... Led NCAA Division I with .198 rebound average (1960-61) and .211 rebound average (1961-62), when championship was determined by highest individual recoveries as percentage of total recoveries by both teams in all games.

Season Team	G	Min.	FGM	FGA	Pct.	FTM	FTA	Pct.	Reb.	Ast.	Pts.	AVERAGES		
												RPG	APG	PPG
58-59—Ohio State‡					Freshman team did not play intercollegiate schedule.									
59-60—Ohio State	27	...	283	444	.637	144	187	.770	442	...	710	16.4	...	26.3
60-61—Ohio State	27	...	256	411	.623	159	208	.764	470	...	671	17.4	...	24.9
61-62—Ohio State	28	...	237	388	.611	135	169	.799	499	...	609	17.8	...	21.8
Varsity totals	82	...	776	1243	.624	438	564	.777	1411	...	1990	17.2	...	24.3

NBA REGULAR-SEASON RECORD

HONORS: NBA Rookie of the Year (1964). ... All-NBA first team (1965, 1966, 1968). ... All-NBA second team (1964, 1967). ... NBA All-Rookie team (1964).

Season Team	G	Min.	FGM	FGA	Pct.	FTM	FTA	Pct.	Reb.	Ast.	PF	Dq.	Pts.	AVERAGES		
														RPG	APG	PPG
63-64—Cincinnati	79	3273	545	1035 *.527		310	398	.779	1375	204	300	6	1400	17.4	2.6	17.7
64-65—Cincinnati	66	2864	558	1121	.498	298	366	.814	1321	157	214	1	1414	20.0	2.4	21.4
65-66—Cincinnati	79	3517	690	1523	.453	317	403	.787	1668	213	274	5	1697	21.1	2.7	21.5
66-67—Cincinnati	81	3558	577	1257	.459	284	359	.791	1547	268	280	2	1438	19.1	3.3	17.8
67-68—Cincinnati	82	3619	707	1361	.519	346	445	.778	1560	251	243	3	1760	19.0	3.1	21.5
68-69—Cincinnati	74	3075	555	1007	.551	247	327	.755	1360	306	206	0	1357	18.4	4.1	18.3
69-70—Cin.-S.F.	67	2420	405	799	.507	200	255	.784	951	173	166	2	1010	14.2	2.6	15.1
70-71—San Fran.	80	3251	623	1250	.498	289	367	.787	1265	293	197	0	1535	15.8	3.7	19.2
71-72—New York	77	2926	543	1060	.512	197	249	.791	1011	318	218	1	1283	13.1	4.1	16.7
72-73—New York	71	2001	312	608	.513	80	100	.800	510	317	157	0	704	7.2	4.5	9.9

Season Team	G	Min.	FGM	FGA	Pct.	FTM	FTA	Pct.	REBOUNDS			Ast.	St.	Blk.	TO	Pts.	AVERAGES		
									Off.	Def.	Tot.						RPG	APG	PPG
73-74—New York	73	1627	194	420	.462	67	96	.698	62	312	374	230	28	24	...	455	5.1	3.2	6.2
Totals	829	32131	5709	11441	.499	2635	3365	.783	...	...	12942	2730	28	24	...	14053	15.6	3.3	17.0

Personal fouls/disqualifications: 1973-74, 134/0.

NBA PLAYOFF RECORD

Season Team	G	Min.	FGM	FGA	Pct.	FTM	FTA	Pct.	Reb.	Ast.	PF	Dq.	Pts.	AVERAGES		
														RPG	APG	PPG
63-64—Cincinnati	10	370	48	123	.390	26	37	.703	125	34	37	1	122	12.5	3.4	12.2
64-65—Cincinnati	4	195	38	75	.507	17	22	.773	84	9	12	0	93	21.0	2.3	23.3
65-66—Cincinnati	5	231	40	85	.471	27	35	.771	101	14	14	0	107	20.2	2.8	21.4
66-67—Cincinnati	4	183	24	55	.436	2	2	1.000	77	8	15	0	50	19.3	2.0	12.5
70-71—San Fran.	5	171	39	77	.507	11	16	.688	50	16	14	0	89	10.0	3.2	17.8
71-72—New York	16	737	119	238	.500	59	71	.831	173	85	49	1	297	10.8	5.3	18.6
72-73—New York	17	368	54	112	.482	20	23	.870	85	39	47	0	128	5.0	2.3	7.5

Season Team	G	Min.	FGM	FGA	Pct.	FTM	FTA	Pct.	REBOUNDS			Ast.	St.	Blk.	TO	Pts.	AVERAGES		
									Off.	Def.	Tot.						RPG	APG	PPG
73-74—New York	11	115	5	21	.238	0	0	...	6	16	22	9	4	0	...	10	2.0	0.8	0.9
Totals	72	2370	367	786	.467	162	206	.786	...	...	717	214	4	0	...	896	10.0	3.0	12.4

Personal fouls/disqualifications: 1973-74, 9/0.

NBA ALL-STAR GAME RECORD

NOTES: NBA All-Star Game Most Valuable Player (1965).

Season Team	Min.	FGM	FGA	Pct.	FTM	FTA	Pct.	Reb	Ast.	PF	Dq.	Pts.
1964 —Cincinnati	36	3	6	.500	5	6	.833	8	0	5	0	11
1965 —Cincinnati	35	12	19	.632	1	1	1.000	10	1	2	0	25
1966 —Cincinnati	23	4	11	.364	2	2	1.000	19	0	2	0	10
1967 —Cincinnati	22	3	5	.600	1	1	1.000	7	2	3	0	7
1968 —Cincinnati	21	6	9	.667	4	4	1.000	5	4	3	0	16
1969 —Cincinnati	17	2	5	.400	4	5	.800	6	1	3	0	8
1971 —San Francisco	29	5	9	.556	2	2	1.000	9	4	2	0	12
Totals	183	35	64	.547	19	21	.905	64	12	20	0	89

ALL-TIME GREAT PLAYERS

MACAULEY, ED   C/F

PERSONAL: Born March 22, 1928, in St. Louis. ... 6-8/190. ... Full name: Charles Edward Macauley Jr. ... Nickname: Easy Ed.

HIGH SCHOOL: St. Louis University High School (St. Louis).

COLLEGE: St. Louis.

TRANSACTIONS/CAREER NOTES: Selected by St. Louis Bombers in 1949 Basketball Association of America Draft (territorial pick). ... Selected by Boston Celtics in NBA dispersal draft (April 25, 1950). ... Traded by Celtics with draft rights to F/G Cliff Hagan to St. Louis Hawks for draft rights to C Bill Russell (April 29, 1956).

CAREER HONORS: Elected to Naismith Memorial Basketball Hall of Fame (1960).

MISCELLANEOUS: Member of NBA championship team (1958).

COLLEGIATE RECORD

NOTES: THE SPORTING NEWS All-America first team (1949). ... Led NCAA Division I with .524 field-goal percentage (1949).

Season Team	G	Min.	FGM	FGA	Pct.	FTM	FTA	Pct.	Reb.	Ast.	Pts.	RPG	APG	PPG
45-46—St. Louis	23	...	94	...	...	71	...	...	...	...	259	...	...	11.3
46-47—St. Louis	28	...	141	...	...	104	...	...	...	...	386	...	...	13.8
47-48—St. Louis	27	...	132	324	.407	104	159	.654	...	...	368	...	...	13.6
48-49—St. Louis	26	...	144	275	.524	116	153	.758	...	...	404	...	...	15.5
Totals	104	...	511	...	...	395	...	...	...	...	1417	...	...	13.6

NBA REGULAR-SEASON RECORD

HONORS: All-NBA first team (1951, 1952, 1953). ... All-NBA second team (1954).

Season Team	G	Min.	FGM	FGA	Pct.	FTM	FTA	Pct.	Reb.	Ast.	PF	Dq.	Pts.	RPG	APG	PPG
49-50—St. Louis	67	...	351	882	.398	379	528	.718	...	200	221	...	1081	...	3.0	16.1
50-51—Boston	68	...	459	985	.466	466	614	.759	616	252	205	4	1384	9.1	3.7	20.4
51-52—Boston	66	2631	384	888	.432	496	621	.799	529	232	174	0	1264	8.0	3.5	19.2
52-53—Boston	69	2902	451	997	.452	500	667	.750	629	280	188	0	1402	9.1	4.1	20.3
53-54—Boston	71	2792	462	950*	.486	420	554	.758	571	271	168	1	1344	8.0	3.8	18.9
54-55—Boston	71	2706	403	951	.424	442	558	.792	600	275	171	0	1248	8.5	3.9	17.6
55-56—Boston	71	2354	420	995	.422	400	504	.794	422	211	158	2	1240	5.9	3.0	17.5
56-57—St. Louis	72	2582	414	987	.419	359	479	.749	440	202	206	2	1187	6.1	2.8	16.5
57-58—St. Louis	72	1908	376	879	.428	267	369	.724	478	143	156	2	1019	6.6	2.0	14.2
58-59—St. Louis	14	196	22	75	.293	21	35	.600	40	13	20	1	65	2.9	0.9	4.6
Totals	641	...	3742	8589	.436	3750	4929	.761	...	2079	1667	...	11234	...	3.2	17.5

NBA PLAYOFF RECORD

Season Team	G	Min.	FGM	FGA	Pct.	FTM	FTA	Pct.	Reb.	Ast.	PF	Dq.	Pts.	RPG	APG	PPG
50-51—Boston	2	...	17	36	.472	10	16	.625	18	8	4	0	44	9.0	4.0	22.0
51-52—Boston	3	129	27	49	.551	16	19	.842	33	11	11	1	70	11.0	3.7	23.3
52-53—Boston	6	278	31	71	.437	39	54	.722	58	21	23	2	101	9.7	3.5	16.8
53-54—Boston	5	127	8	22	.364	9	13	.692	21	21	14	0	25	4.2	4.2	5.0
54-55—Boston	7	283	43	93	.462	41	54	.759	52	32	21	0	127	7.4	4.6	18.1
55-56—Boston	3	73	12	30	.400	7	11	.636	15	5	6	0	31	5.0	1.7	10.3
56-57—St. Louis	10	297	44	109	.404	54	74	.730	62	22	39	3	142	6.2	2.2	14.2
57-58—St. Louis	11	227	36	89	.405	36	50	.720	62	18	23	0	108	5.6	1.6	9.8
Totals	47	...	218	499	.437	212	291	.729	321	138	141	6	648	6.8	2.9	13.8

NBA ALL-STAR GAME RECORD

NOTES: NBA All-Star Game Most Valuable Player (1951).

Season Team	Min.	FGM	FGA	Pct.	FTM	FTA	Pct.	Reb	Ast.	PF	Dq.	Pts.
1951 —Boston	...	7	12	.583	6	7	.857	6	1	3	0	20
1952 —Boston	28	3	7	.429	9	9	1.000	7	3	2	0	15
1953 —Boston	35	5	12	.417	8	8	1.000	7	3	2	0	18
1954 —Boston	25	4	11	.364	5	6	.833	1	3	2	0	13
1955 —Boston	27	1	5	.200	4	5	.800	4	2	1	0	6
1956 —Boston	20	1	9	.111	2	4	.500	2	3	3	0	4
1957 —St. Louis	19	3	6	.500	1	2	.500	5	3	0	0	7
Totals	...	24	62	.387	35	41	.854	32	18	13	0	83

NBA COACHING RECORD

	REGULAR SEASON				PLAYOFFS		
Season Team	W	L	Pct.	Finish	W	L	Pct.
58-59 —St. Louis	43	19	.694	1st/Western Division	2	4	.333
59-60 —St. Louis	46	29	.613	1st/Western Division	7	7	.500
Totals (2 years)	89	48	.650	Totals (2 years)	9	11	.450

NOTES:

1958—Replaced Andy Phillip as St. Louis head coach (November), with record of 6-4.

1959—Lost to Minneapolis in Western Division finals.

1960—Defeated Minneapolis, 4-3, in Western Division finals; lost to Boston, 4-3, in World Championship Series.

DID YOU KNOW...

...that in 1972-73, Nate Archibald led the NBA in both scoring and assists?

MALONE, MOSES   C

PERSONAL: Born March 23, 1955, in Petersburg, Va. ... 6-10/260. ... Full name: Moses Eugene Malone.
HIGH SCHOOL: Petersburg (Va.).
COLLEGE: Did not attend college.
TRANSACTIONS/CAREER NOTES: Selected out of high school by Utah Stars in third round of 1974 American Basketball Association Draft. ... Contract sold by Stars to Spirits of St. Louis (December 2, 1975). ... Selected by Portland Trail Blazers of NBA from Spirits in ABA dispersal draft (August 5, 1976). ... Traded by Trail Blazers to Buffalo Braves for 1978 first-round draft choice (October 18, 1976). ... Traded by Braves to Houston Rockets for 1977 and 1978 first-round draft choices (October 24, 1976). ... Signed as veteran free agent by Philadelphia 76ers (September 2, 1982); Rockets matched offer and traded Malone to 76ers for F/C Caldwell Jones and 1983 first-round draft choice (September 15, 1982). ... Traded by 76ers with F Terry Catledge and 1986 and 1988 first-round draft choices to Washington Bullets for C/F Jeff Ruland and F Cliff Robinson (June 16, 1986). ... Signed as unrestricted free agent by Atlanta Hawks (August 16, 1988). ... Signed as unrestricted free agent by Milwaukee Bucks (July 10, 1991). ... Signed as free agent by 76ers (August 12, 1993). ... Waived by 76ers (June 17, 1994). ... Signed as free agent by San Antonio Spurs (August 10, 1994).
MISCELLANEOUS: Member of NBA championship team (1983).

ABA REGULAR-SEASON RECORD

NOTES: ABA All-Rookie team (1975).

			2-POINT			3-POINT									AVERAGES		
Season Team	G	Min.	FGM	FGA	Pct.	FGM	FGA	Pct.	FTM	FTA	Pct.	Reb.	Ast.	Pts.	RPG	APG	PPG
74-75—Utah	83	3205	591	1034	.572	0	1	.000	375	591	.635	1209	82	1557	14.6	1.0	18.8
75-76—St. Louis	43	1168	251	488	.514	0	2	.000	112	183	.612	413	58	614	9.6	1.3	14.3
Totals	126	4373	842	1522	.553	0	3	.000	487	774	.629	1622	140	2171	12.9	1.1	17.2

ABA PLAYOFF RECORD

			2-POINT			3-POINT									AVERAGES		
Season Team	G	Min.	FGM	FGA	Pct.	FGM	FGA	Pct.	FTM	FTA	Pct.	Reb.	Ast.	Pts.	RPG	APG	PPG
74-75—Utah	6	235	51	80	.638	0	0	...	34	51	.667	105	9	136	17.5	1.5	22.7

ABA ALL-STAR GAME RECORD

		2-POINT			3-POINT							
Season Team	Min.	FGM	FGA	Pct.	FGM	FGA	Pct.	FTM	FTA	Pct.	Reb.	Ast.	Pts.
1975—Utah	20	2	3	.667	0	0	...	2	5	.400	10	0	6

NBA REGULAR-SEASON RECORD

RECORDS: Holds career records for most consecutive games without a disqualification—1,212 (January 7, 1978 through 1994-95 season); most free throws made—8,531; most offensive rebounds—6,731; and most turnovers—3,804. ... Holds single-season record for most offensive rebounds—587 (1979). ... Holds single-game record for most offensive rebounds—21 (February 11, 1982, vs. Seattle).
HONORS: NBA Most Valuable Player (1979, 1982, 1983). ... All-NBA first team (1979, 1982, 1983, 1985). ... All-NBA second team (1980, 1981, 1984, 1987). ... NBA All-Defensive first team (1983). ... NBA All-Defensive second team (1979).

								REBOUNDS								AVERAGES		
Season Team	G	Min.	FGM	FGA	Pct.	FTM	FTA	Pct.	Off.	Def.	Tot.	Ast.	St.	Blk.	TO	Pts.	RPG	APG	PPG
76-77—Buff.-Hou.	82	2506	389	810	.480	305	440	.693	*437	635	1072	89	67	181	...	1083	13.1	1.1	13.2
77-78—Houston	59	2107	413	828	.499	318	443	.718	*380	506	886	31	48	76	220	1144	15.0	0.5	19.4
78-79—Houston	82	*3390	716	1325	.540	599	811	.739	*587	*857	*1444	147	79	119	326	2031	*17.6	1.8	24.8
79-80—Houston	82	3140	778	1549	.502	*783	.719	*573	617	1190	147	80	107	300	2119	14.5	1.8	25.8
80-81—Houston	80	3245	806	1545	.522	609	*804	.757	*474	706	*1180	141	83	150	*308	2222	*14.8	1.8	27.8
81-82—Houston	81	*3398	945	1822	.519	630	*827	.762	*558	630	*1188	142	76	125	294	2520	*14.7	1.8	31.1
82-83—Philadelphia	78	2922	654	1305	.501	*600	*788	.761	*445	*749	*1194	101	89	157	264	1908	*15.3	1.3	24.5
83-84—Philadelphia	71	2613	532	1101	.483	545	727	.750	352	598	950	96	71	110	250	1609	*13.4	1.4	22.7
84-85—Philadelphia	79	2957	602	1284	.469	*737	*904	.815	385	646	*1031	130	67	123	286	1941	*13.1	1.6	24.6
85-86—Philadelphia	74	2706	571	1246	.458	*617	*784	.787	339	533	872	90	67	71	261	1759	11.8	1.2	23.8
86-87—Washington	73	2488	595	1311	.454	570	692	.824	340	484	824	120	59	92	202	1760	11.3	1.6	24.1
87-88—Washington	79	2692	531	1090	.487	543	689	.788	372	512	884	112	59	72	249	1607	11.2	1.4	20.3
88-89—Atlanta	81	2878	538	1096	.491	561	711	.789	386	570	956	112	70	100	245	1637	11.8	1.4	20.2
89-90—Atlanta	81	2735	517	1077	.480	493	631	.781	*364	448	812	130	47	84	232	1528	10.0	1.6	18.9
90-91—Atlanta	82	1912	280	598	.468	309	372	.831	271	396	667	68	30	74	137	869	8.1	0.8	10.6
91-92—Milwaukee	82	2511	440	929	.474	396	504	.786	320	424	744	93	74	64	150	1279	9.1	1.1	15.6
92-93—Milwaukee	11	104	13	42	.310	24	31	.774	22	24	46	7	1	8	10	50	4.2	0.6	4.5
93-94—Philadelphia	55	618	102	232	.440	90	117	.769	106	120	226	34	11	17	59	294	4.1	0.6	5.3
94-95—San Antonio	17	149	13	35	.371	22	32	.688	20	26	46	6	2	3	11	49	2.7	0.4	2.9
Totals	1329	45071	9435	19225	.491	8531	11090	.769	6731	9481	16212	1796	1089	1733	3804	27409	12.2	1.4	20.6

Three-point field goals: 1979-80, 0-for-6. 1980-81, 1-for-3 (.333). 1981-82, 0-for-6. 1982-83, 0-for-1. 1983-84, 0-for-4. 1984-85, 0-for-2. 1985-86, 0-for-1. 1986-87, 0-for-11. 1987-88, 2-for-7 (.286). 1988-89, 0-for-12. 1989-90, 1-for-9 (.111). 1990-91, 0-for-7. 1991-92, 3-for-8 (.375). 1993-94, 0-for-1. 1994-95, 1-for-2 (.500). Totals, 8-for-80 (.100).

Personal fouls/disqualifications: 1976-77, 275/3. 1977-78, 179/2. 1978-79, 223/0. 1979-80, 210/0. 1980-81, 223/0. 1981-82, 208/0. 1982-83, 206/0. 1983-84, 188/0. 1984-85, 216/0. 1985-86, 194/0. 1986-87, 139/0. 1987-88, 160/0. 1988-89, 154/0. 1989-90, 158/0. 1990-91, 134/0. 1991-92, 136/0. 1992-93, 6/0. 1993-94, 52/0. 1994-95, 15/0. Totals, 3076/5.

NBA PLAYOFF RECORD

NOTES: NBA Finals Most Valuable Player (1983). ... Holds single-game playoff record for most offensive rebounds—15 (April 21, 1977, vs. Washington).

								REBOUNDS								AVERAGES		
Season Team	G	Min.	FGM	FGA	Pct.	FTM	FTA	Pct.	Off.	Def.	Tot.	Ast.	St.	Blk.	TO	Pts.	RPG	APG	PPG
76-77—Houston	12	518	81	162	.500	63	91	.692	84	119	203	7	13	21	...	225	16.9	0.6	18.8
78-79—Houston	2	78	18	41	.439	13	18	.722	25	16	41	2	1	8	8	49	20.5	1.0	24.5
79-80—Houston	7	275	74	138	.536	33	43	.767	42	55	97	7	4	16	22	181	13.9	1.0	25.9
80-81—Houston	21	955	207	432	.479	148	208	.712	125	180	305	35	13	34	59	562	14.5	1.7	26.8
81-82—Houston	3	136	29	67	.433	14	15	.933	28	23	51	10	2	2	6	72	17.0	3.3	24.0
82-83—Philadelphia	13	524	126	235	.536	86	120	.717	70	136	206	20	19	25	40	338	15.8	1.5	26.0

Season Team	G	Min.	FGM	FGA	Pct.	FTM	FTA	Pct.	REBOUNDS Off.	Def.	Tot.	Ast.	St.	Blk.	TO	Pts.	AVERAGES RPG	APG	PPG
83-84—Philadelphia	5	212	38	83	.458	31	32	.969	20	49	69	7	3	11	21	107	13.8	1.4	21.4
84-85—Philadelphia	13	505	90	212	.425	82	103	.796	36	102	138	24	17	22	23	262	10.6	1.8	20.2
86-87—Washington	3	114	21	47	.447	20	21	.952	15	23	38	5	0	3	8	62	12.7	1.7	20.7
87-88—Washington	5	198	30	65	.462	33	40	.825	22	34	56	7	3	4	15	93	11.2	1.4	18.6
88-89—Atlanta	5	197	32	64	.500	40	51	.784	27	33	60	9	7	4	11	105	12.0	1.8	21.0
90-91—Atlanta	5	84	4	20	.200	13	14	.929	16	15	31	3	2	1	2	21	6.2	0.6	4.2
Totals	94	3796	750	1566	.479	576	756	.762	510	785	1295	136	84	151	215	2077	13.8	1.4	22.1

Three-point field goals: 1979-80, 0-for-1. 1980-81, 0-for-2. 1982-83, 0-for-1. 1984-85, 0-for-1. 1987-88, 0-for-1. 1988-89, 1-for-1. Totals, 1-for-7 (.143).
Personal fouls/disqualifications: 1976-77, 42/0. 1978-79, 5/0. 1979-80, 18/0. 1980-81, 54/0. 1981-82, 8/0. 1982-83, 40/0. 1983-84, 15/0. 1984-85, 39/0. 1986-87, 5/0. 1987-88, 9/0. 1988-89, 5/0. 1990-91, 4/0. Totals, 244/0.

NBA ALL-STAR GAME RECORD

Season Team	Min.	FGM	FGA	Pct.	FTM	FTA	Pct.	REBOUNDS Off.	Def.	Tot.	Ast.	PF	Dq.	St.	Blk.	TO	Pts.
1978 —Houston	14	1	1	1.000	2	4	.500	1	3	4	1	1	0	1	0	0	4
1979 —Houston	17	2	2	1.000	4	5	.800	2	5	7	1	0	0	1	0	1	8
1980 —Houston	31	7	12	.583	6	12	.500	6	6	12	2	4	0	1	2	5	20
1981 —Houston	22	3	8	.375	2	4	.500	2	4	6	3	3	0	1	0	1	8
1982 —Houston	20	5	11	.455	2	6	.333	5	6	11	0	2	0	1	1	3	12
1983 —Philadelphia......	24	3	8	.375	4	6	.667	2	6	8	3	1	0	0	1	1	10
1984 —Philadelphia							Selected, did not play—injured.										
1985 —Philadelphia......	33	2	10	.200	3	6	.500	5	7	12	1	4	0	0	0	3	7
1986 —Philadelphia......	34	5	12	.417	6	9	.667	5	8	13	0	4	0	1	0	1	16
1987 —Washington......	35	11	19	.579	5	6	.833	7	11	18	2	4	0	2	1	1	27
1988 —Washington......	22	2	6	.333	3	6	.500	5	4	9	2	2	0	0	2	7	
1989 —Atlanta.............	19	3	9	.333	3	3	1.000	4	4	8	0	1	0	1	1	1	9
Totals	271	44	98	.449	40	67	.597	44	64	108	15	26	0	9	6	19	128

COMBINED ABA AND NBA REGULAR-SEASON RECORDS

	G	Min.	FGM	FGA	Pct.	FTM	FTA	Pct.	REBOUNDS Off.	Def.	Tot.	Ast.	Stl.	Blk.	TO	Pts.	AVERAGES RPG	APG	PPG
Totals	1455	49444	10277	20750	.495	9018	11864	.760	7382	10452	17834	1936	1199	1889	4264	29580	12.3	1.3	20.3

Three-point field goals: 8-for-83 (.096).

MARAVICH, PETE G

PERSONAL: Born June 22, 1947, in Aliquippa, Pa. ... Died January 5, 1988. ... 6-5/200. ... Full name: Peter Press Maravich. ... Nickname: Pistol Pete. ... Son of Press Maravich, former college coach; and guard with Youngstown Bears of National Basketball League (1945-46) and Pittsburgh Ironmen of Basketball Association of America (1946-47).
HIGH SCHOOL: Daniels (Clemson, S.C.), then Needham Broughton (Raleigh, N.C.), then Edwards Military Institute (Salemburg, N.C.).
COLLEGE: Louisiana State.
TRANSACTIONS/CAREER NOTES: Selected by Atlanta Hawks in first round (third pick overall) of 1970 NBA Draft. ... Traded by Hawks to New Orleans Jazz for G Dean Meminger, C/F Bob Kauffman, 1974 and 1975 first-round draft choices and 1975 and 1976 second-round draft choices (May 3, 1974). ... Jazz franchise moved from New Orleans to Utah for 1979-80 season. ... Waived by Jazz (January 17, 1980). ... Signed as free agent by Boston Celtics (January 22, 1980).
CAREER HONORS: Elected to Naismith Memorial Basketball Hall of Fame (1986).

COLLEGIATE RECORD

NOTES: THE SPORTING NEWS College Player of the Year (1970). ... Naismith Award winner (1970). ... THE SPORTING NEWS All-America first team (1968, 1969, 1970). ... Holds NCAA career records for most points—3667; highest points-per-game average—44.2; most field goals made—1387; most field goals attempted—3166; most free throws made (three-year career)—893; most free throws attempted (three-year career)—1152; and most games scoring at least 50 points—28. ... Holds NCAA single-season records for most points—1381; highest points-per-game average—44.5; most field goals made—522; most field goals attempted—1168; and most games scoring at least 50 points—10 (1970). ... Holds NCAA single-game record for most free throws made—30 (December 22, 1969, vs. Oregon State in 31 attempts). ... Led NCAA Division I with 43.8 points per game (1968), 44.2 points per game (1969) and 44.5 points per game (1970).

Season Team	G	Min.	FGM	FGA	Pct.	FTM	FTA	Pct.	Reb.	Ast.	Pts.	AVERAGES RPG	APG	PPG
66-67—Louisiana State‡............	17	...	273	604	.452	195	234	.833	176	124	741	10.4	7.3	43.6
67-68—Louisiana State..............	26	...	432	1022	.423	274	338	.811	195	105	1138	7.5	4.0	43.8
68-69—Louisiana State..............	26	...	433	976	.444	282	378	.746	169	128	1148	6.5	4.9	44.2
69-70—Louisiana State..............	31	...	522	1168	.447	337	436	.773	164	192	1381	5.3	6.2	44.5
Varsity totals	83	...	1387	3166	.438	893	1152	.775	528	425	3667	6.4	5.1	44.2

NBA REGULAR-SEASON RECORD

RECORDS: Shares single-game records for most free throws made in one quarter—14 (November 28, 1973, vs. Buffalo); and most free throws attempted in one quarter—16 (January 2, 1973, vs. Chicago).
HONORS: All-NBA first team (1976, 1977). ... All-NBA second team (1973, 1978). ... NBA All-Rookie team (1971).

Season Team	G	Min.	FGM	FGA	Pct.	FTM	FTA	Pct.	Reb.	Ast.	PF	Dq.	Pts.	AVERAGES RPG	APG	PPG
70-71 —Atlanta	81	2926	738	1613	.458	404	505	.800	298	355	238	1	1880	3.7	4.4	23.2
71-72 —Atlanta	66	2302	460	1077	.427	355	438	.811	256	393	207	0	1275	3.9	6.0	19.3
72-73 —Atlanta	79	3089	789	1788	.441	485	606	.800	346	546	245	1	2063	4.4	6.9	26.1

Season Team	G	Min.	FGM	FGA	Pct.	FTM	FTA	Pct.	REBOUNDS Off.	Def.	Tot.	Ast.	St.	Blk.	TO	Pts.	AVERAGES RPG	APG	PPG
73-74—Atlanta	76	2903	819	*1791	.457	469	568	.826	98	276	374	396	111	13	...	2107	4.9	5.2	27.7

Season Team	G	Min.	FGM	FGA	Pct.	FTM	FTA	Pct.	Off.	Def.	Tot.	Ast.	St.	Blk.	TO	Pts.	RPG	APG	PPG
74-75—New Orleans ...	79	2853	655	1562	.419	390	481	.811	93	329	422	488	120	18	...	1700	5.3	6.2	21.5
75-76—New Orleans ...	62	2373	604	1316	.459	396	488	.811	46	254	300	332	87	23	...	1604	4.8	5.4	25.9
76-77—New Orleans ...	73	3041	886	*2047	.433	*501	600	.835	90	284	374	392	84	22	...	*2273	5.1	5.4	*31.1
77-78—New Orleans ...	50	2041	556	1253	.444	240	276	.870	49	129	178	335	101	8	248	1352	3.6	6.7	27.0
78-79—New Orleans ...	49	1824	436	1035	.421	233	277	.841	33	88	121	243	60	18	200	1105	2.5	5.0	22.6
79-80—Utah-Boston ..	43	964	244	543	.449	91	105	.867	17	61	78	83	24	6	82	589	1.8	1.9	13.7
Totals	658	24316	6187	14025	.441	3564	4344	.820	...	...	2747	3563	587	108	530	15948	4.2	5.4	24.2

Three-point field goals: 1979-80, 10-for-15 (.667).
Personal fouls/disqualifications: 1973-74, 261/4. 1974-75, 227/4. 1975-76, 197/3. 1976-77, 191/1. 1977-78, 116/1. 1978-79, 104/2. 1979-80, 79/1. Totals, 1865/18.

NBA PLAYOFF RECORD

Season Team	G	Min.	FGM	FGA	Pct.	FTM	FTA	Pct.	Reb.	Ast.	PF	Dq.	Pts.	RPG	APG	PPG
70-71 —Atlanta	5	199	46	122	.377	18	26	.692	26	24	14	0	110	5.2	4.8	22.0
71-72 —Atlanta	6	219	54	121	.446	58	71	.817	32	28	24	0	166	5.3	4.7	27.7
72-73 —Atlanta	6	234	65	155	.419	27	34	.794	29	40	24	1	157	4.8	6.7	26.2

Season Team	G	Min.	FGM	FGA	Pct.	FTM	FTA	Pct.	Off.	Def.	Tot.	Ast.	St.	Blk.	TO	Pts.	RPG	APG	PPG
79-80—Boston	9	104	25	51	.490	2	3	.667	0	8	8	6	3	0	9	54	0.9	0.7	6.0
Totals	26	756	190	449	.423	105	134	.784	...	...	95	98	3	0	9	487	3.7	3.8	18.7

Three-point field goals: 1979-80, 2-for-6 (.333).
Personal fouls/disqualifications: 1979-80, 12/0.

NBA ALL-STAR GAME RECORD

Season Team	Min.	FGM	FGA	Pct.	FTM	FTA	Pct.	Reb	Ast.	PF	Dq.	Pts.
1973 —Atlanta......................	22	4	8	.500	0	0	...	3	5	4	0	8

Season Team	Min.	FGM	FGA	Pct.	FTM	FTA	Pct.	Off.	Def.	Tot.	Ast.	PF	Dq.	St.	Blk.	TO	Pts.
1974 —Atlanta..............	22	4	15	.267	7	9	.778	1	2	3	4	2	0	0	0	...	15
1977 —New Orleans......	21	5	13	.385	0	0	...	0	0	0	4	1	0	4	0	...	10
1978 —New Orleans							Selected, did not play—injured.										
1979 —New Orleans......	14	5	8	.625	0	0	...	0	2	2	2	1	0	0	0	4	10
Totals..........................	79	18	44	.409	7	9	.778	...	...	8	15	8	0	4	0	4	43

MARTIN, SLATER   G

PERSONAL: Born October 22, 1925, in Houston. ... 5-10/170. ... Full name: Slater Nelson Martin Jr. ... Nickname: Dugie.
HIGH SCHOOL: Jefferson Davis (Houston).
COLLEGE: Texas.
TRANSACTIONS/CAREER NOTES: Selected by Minneapolis Lakers in 1949 Basketball Association of America Draft. ... Traded by Lakers with F Jerry Bird and player to be named later to New York Knicks for C Walter Dukes and draft rights to F/C Burdette Haldorson (October 26, 1956). ... Traded by Knicks to St. Louis Hawks for F Willie Naulls (December 10, 1956).
CAREER HONORS: Elected to Naismith Memorial Basketball Hall of Fame (1981).
MISCELLANEOUS: Member of NBA championship teams (1950, 1952, 1953, 1954, 1958).

COLLEGIATE RECORD

NOTES: The Sporting News All-America fifth team (1949).

Season Team	G	Min.	FGM	FGA	Pct.	FTM	FTA	Pct.	Reb.	Ast.	Pts.	RPG	APG	PPG
43-44—Texas............................	14	...	75	...	...	34	...	...	...	...	184	...	...	13.1
44-45—						Did not play—in military service.								
45-46—						Did not play—in military service.								
46-47—Texas............................	27	...	109	...	...	37	...	...	...	...	255	...	...	9.4
47-48—Texas............................	25	...	126	...	...	65	85	.765	...	...	317	...	...	12.7
48-49—Texas............................	24	...	165	...	...	54	...	...	...	...	384	...	...	16.0
Totals	90	...	475	...	...	190	...	...	...	...	1140	...	...	12.7

NBA REGULAR-SEASON RECORD

HONORS: All-NBA second team (1954, 1956, 1957, 1958, 1959).

Season Team	G	Min.	FGM	FGA	Pct.	FTM	FTA	Pct.	Reb.	Ast.	PF	Dq.	Pts.	RPG	APG	PPG
49-50 —Minneapolis	67	...	106	302	.351	59	93	.634	...	148	162	...	271	...	2.2	4.0
50-51 —Minneapolis	68	...	227	627	.362	121	177	.684	246	235	199	3	575	3.6	3.5	8.5
51-52 —Minneapolis	66	2480	237	632	.375	142	190	.747	228	249	226	9	616	3.5	3.8	9.3
52-53 —Minneapolis	70	2556	260	634	.410	224	287	.780	186	250	246	4	744	2.7	3.6	10.6
53-54 —Minneapolis	69	2472	254	654	.388	176	243	.724	166	253	198	3	684	2.4	3.7	9.9
54-55 —Minneapolis	72	2784	350	919	.381	276	359	.769	260	427	221	7	976	3.6	5.9	13.6
55-56 —Minneapolis	72	*2838	309	863	.358	329	395	.833	260	445	202	2	947	3.6	6.2	13.2
56-57 —N.Y.-St.L.	66	2401	244	736	.332	230	291	.790	288	269	193	1	718	4.4	4.1	10.9
57-58 —St. Louis	60	2098	258	768	.336	206	276	.746	228	218	187	0	722	3.8	3.6	12.0
58-59 —St. Louis	71	2504	245	706	.347	197	254	.776	253	336	230	8	687	3.6	4.7	9.7
59-60 —St. Louis	64	1756	142	383	.371	113	155	.729	187	330	174	2	397	2.9	5.2	6.2
Totals....................	745	...	2632	7224	.364	2073	2720	.762	...	3160	2238	...	7337	...	4.2	9.8

NBA PLAYOFF RECORD

														AVERAGES		
Season Team	G	Min.	FGM	FGA	Pct.	FTM	FTA	Pct.	Reb.	Ast.	PF	Dq.	Pts.	RPG	APG	PPG
49-50 —Minneapolis	12	...	21	50	.420	14	24	.583	...	25	35	...	56	...	2.1	4.7
50-51 —Minneapolis	7	...	18	51	.353	14	27	.519	42	25	20	...	50	6.0	3.6	7.1
51-52 —Minneapolis	13	523	38	110	.345	41	56	.732	37	56	64	4	117	2.8	4.3	9.0
52-53 —Minneapolis	12	453	41	103	.398	39	51	.765	31	43	49	1	121	2.6	3.6	10.1
53-54 —Minneapolis	13	533	37	112	.330	52	70	.743	29	60	52	1	126	2.2	4.6	9.7
54-55 —Minneapolis	7	315	28	94	.298	40	49	.816	28	31	23	0	96	4.0	4.4	13.7
55-56 —Minneapolis	3	121	17	37	.459	20	24	.833	7	15	9	0	54	2.3	5.0	18.0
56-57 —St. Louis	10	439	55	155	.355	56	74	.757	42	49	39	2	166	4.2	4.9	16.6
57-58 —St. Louis	11	416	44	137	.321	39	63	.619	48	40	40	1	127	4.4	3.6	11.5
58-59 —St. Louis	1	18	4	5	.800	0	0	...	3	2	2	0	8	3.0	2.0	8.0
59-60 —St. Louis	3	58	1	13	.077	1	4	.250	3	8	9	0	3	1.0	2.7	1.0
Totals	92	...	304	867	.351	316	442	.715	...	354	342	...	924	...	3.8	10.0

NBA ALL-STAR GAME RECORD

Season Team	Min.	FGM	FGA	Pct.	FTM	FTA	Pct.	Reb	Ast.	PF	Dq.	Pts.
1953 —Minneapolis	26	2	10	.200	1	1	1.000	2	1	2	0	5
1954 —Minneapolis	23	1	5	.200	0	0	...	0	3	3	0	2
1955 —Minneapolis	23	2	5	.400	1	2	.500	2	5	3	0	5
1956 —Minneapolis	29	3	7	.429	3	3	1.000	1	7	5	0	9
1957 —St. Louis	31	4	11	.364	0	0	...	2	3	1	0	8
1958 —St. Louis	26	2	9	.222	2	4	.500	2	8	3	0	6
1959 —St. Louis	22	2	6	.333	1	2	.500	6	1	2	0	5
Totals	180	16	53	.302	8	12	.667	15	28	19	0	40

NBA COACHING RECORD

BACKGROUND: Player/head coach, St. Louis Hawks (1957). ... Head coach/general manager, Houston Mavericks of ABA (1967-68).

		REGULAR SEASON				PLAYOFFS		
Season Team	W	L	Pct.	Finish		W	L	Pct.
56-57 —St. Louis	5	3	.625			—	—	—

ABA COACHING RECORD

		REGULAR SEASON				PLAYOFFS		
Season Team	W	L	Pct.	Finish		W	L	Pct.
67-68 —Houston	29	49	.372	4th/Western Division		0	3	.000
68-69 —Houston	3	9	.250			—	—	—
Totals (2 years)	32	58	.356	Totals (1 year)		0	3	.000>

NOTES:

1957—Replaced Red Holzman as St. Louis head coach (January), with record of 14-19; replaced as St. Louis head coach by Alex Hannum (January).

1968—Lost to Dallas in Western Division semifinals. Replaced as Houston head coach by Jim Weaver (November).

McADOO, BOB   C/F

PERSONAL: Born September 25, 1951, in Greensboro, N.C. ... 6-9/225. ... Full name: Robert Allen McAdoo Jr.
HIGH SCHOOL: Ben Smith (Greensboro, N.C.).
JUNIOR COLLEGE: Vincennes (Ind.).
COLLEGE: North Carolina.
TRANSACTIONS/CAREER NOTES: Selected after junior season by Buffalo Braves in first round (second pick overall) of 1972 NBA Draft. ... Traded by Braves with C/F Tom McMillen to New York Knicks for C/F John Gianelli and cash (December 9, 1976). ... Traded by Knicks to Boston Celtics for three 1979 first-round draft choices and player to be named later (February 12, 1979); Knicks acquired C Tom Barker to complete deal (February 14, 1979). ... Acquired by Detroit Pistons for two 1980 first-round draft choices to complete compensation for Celtics signing of veteran free agent F/G M.L. Carr (September 6, 1979). ... Waived by Pistons (March 11, 1981). ... Signed as free agent by New Jersey Nets (March 13, 1981). ... Traded by Nets to Los Angeles Lakers for 1983 second-round draft choice and cash (December 24, 1981). ... Signed as veteran free agent by Philadelphia 76ers (January 31, 1986); Lakers waived their right of first refusal. ... Played in Italy (1986-87 through 1992-93). ... Assistant coach, Miami Heat (September 20, 1995 to present).
MISCELLANEOUS: Member of NBA championship teams (1982, 1985). ... Los Angeles Clippers franchise all-time leading rebounder with 4,229 (1972-73 through 1976-77).

COLLEGIATE RECORD

NOTES: The Sporting News All-America first team (1972).

												AVERAGES		
Season Team	G	Min.	FGM	FGA	Pct.	FTM	FTA	Pct.	Reb.	Ast.	Pts.	RPG	APG	PPG
69-70—Vincennes	32	...	258	...	...	101	134	.754	320	...	617	10.0	...	19.3
70-71—Vincennes	27	...	273	...	...	129	164	.787	297	...	675	11.0	...	25.0
71-72—North Carolina	31	...	243	471	.516	118	167	.707	312	72	604	10.1	2.3	19.5
Junior college totals	59	...	531	...	...	230	298	.772	617	...	1292	10.5	...	21.9
4-year-college totals	31	...	243	471	.516	118	167	.707	312	72	604	10.1	2.3	19.5

NBA REGULAR-SEASON RECORD

HONORS: NBA Most Valuable Player (1975). ... NBA Rookie of the Year (1973). ... All-NBA first team (1975). ... All-NBA second team (1974). ... NBA All-Rookie team (1973).

														AVERAGES		
Season Team	G	Min.	FGM	FGA	Pct.	FTM	FTA	Pct.	Reb.	Ast.	PF	Dq.	Pts.	RPG	APG	PPG
72-73—Buffalo	80	2562	585	1293	.452	271	350	.774	728	139	256	6	1441	9.1	1.7	18.0

Season Team	G	Min.	FGM	FGA	Pct.	FTM	FTA	Pct.	REBOUNDS Off.	Def.	Tot.	Ast.	St.	Blk.	TO	Pts.	AVERAGES RPG	APG	PPG
73-74—Buffalo	74	3185	901	1647	*.547	459	579	.793	281	836	1117	170	88	246	...	*2261	15.1	2.3	*30.6
74-75—Buffalo	82	*3539	*1095	2138	.512	641	*796	.805	307	848	*1155	179	92	174	...	*2831	14.1	2.2	*34.5
75-76—Buffalo	78	3328	*934	*1918	.487	*559	*734	.762	241	724	965	315	93	160	...	*2427	12.4	4.0	*31.1
76-77—Buff-Knicks	72	2798	740	1445	.512	381	516	.738	199	727	926	205	77	99	...	1861	12.9	2.8	25.8
77-78—New York	79	3182	814	1564	.520	469	645	.727	236	774	1010	298	105	126	346	2097	12.8	3.8	26.5
78-79—N.Y.-Boston	60	2231	596	1127	.529	295	450	.656	130	390	520	168	74	67	217	1487	8.7	2.8	24.8
79-80—Detroit	58	2097	492	1025	.480	235	322	.730	100	367	467	200	73	65	238	1222	8.1	3.4	21.1
80-81—Detroit-N.J.	16	321	68	157	.433	29	41	.707	17	50	67	30	17	13	32	165	4.2	1.9	10.3
81-82—Los Angeles	41	746	151	330	.458	90	126	.714	45	114	159	32	22	36	51	392	3.9	0.8	9.6
82-83—Los Angeles	47	1019	292	562	.520	119	163	.730	76	171	247	39	40	40	68	703	5.3	0.8	15.0
83-84—Los Angeles	70	1456	352	748	.471	212	264	.803	82	207	289	74	42	50	127	916	4.1	1.1	13.1
84-85—L.A. Lakers	66	1254	284	546	.520	122	162	.753	79	216	295	67	18	53	95	690	4.5	1.0	10.5
85-86—Philadelphia	29	609	116	251	.462	62	81	.765	25	78	103	35	10	18	49	294	3.6	1.2	10.1
Totals	852	28327	7420	14751	.503	3944	5229	.754	...	...	8048	1951	751	1147	1223	18787	9.4	2.3	22.1

Three-point field goals: 1979-80, 3-for-24 (.125). 1980-81, 0-for-1. 1981-82, 0-for-5. 1982-83, 0-for-1. 1983-84, 0-for-5. 1984-85, 0-for-1. Totals, 3-for-37 (.081).

Personal fouls/disqualifications: 1973-74, 252/3. 1974-75, 278/3. 1975-76, 298/5. 1976-77, 262/3. 1977-78, 297/6. 1978-79, 189/3. 1979-80, 178/3. 1980-81, 38/0. 1981-82, 109/1. 1982-83, 153/2. 1983-84, 170/0. 1985-86, 64/0. Totals, 2726/35.

NBA PLAYOFF RECORD

Season Team	G	Min.	FGM	FGA	Pct.	FTM	FTA	Pct.	REBOUNDS Off.	Def.	Tot.	Ast.	St.	Blk.	TO	Pts.	AVERAGES RPG	APG	PPG
73-74—Buffalo	6	271	76	159	.478	38	47	.809	14	68	82	9	6	13	...	190	13.7	1.5	31.7
74-75—Buffalo	7	327	104	216	.481	54	73	.740	25	69	94	10	6	19	...	262	13.4	1.4	37.4
75-76—Buffalo	9	406	97	215	.451	58	82	.707	31	97	128	29	7	18	...	252	14.2	3.2	28.0
77-78—New York	6	238	61	126	.484	21	35	.600	11	47	58	23	7	12	23	143	9.7	3.8	23.8
81-82—Los Angeles	14	388	101	179	.564	32	47	.681	21	74	95	22	10	21	35	234	6.8	1.6	16.7
82-83—Los Angeles	8	166	37	84	.440	11	14	.786	15	31	46	5	11	10	14	87	5.8	0.6	10.9
83-84—Los Angeles	20	447	111	215	.516	57	81	.704	30	78	108	12	12	27	39	279	5.4	0.6	14.0
84-85—L.A. Lakers	19	398	91	193	.472	35	47	.745	25	61	86	15	9	26	32	217	4.5	0.8	11.4
85-86—Philadelphia	5	73	20	36	.556	14	16	.875	8	6	14	2	4	5	2	54	2.8	0.4	10.8
Totals	94	2714	698	1423	.491	320	442	.724	180	531	711	127	72	151	145	1718	7.6	1.4	18.3

Three-point field goals: 1982-83, 2-for-6 (.333). 1983-84, 0-for-1. 1984-85, 0-for-1. Totals, 2-for-8 (.250).

Personal fouls/disqualifications: 1973-74, 25/1. 1974-75, 29/1. 1975-76, 37/3. 1977-78, 19/0. 1981-82, 43/2. 1982-83, 23/0. 1983-84, 63/0. 1984-85, 66/2. 1985-86, 13/0. Totals, 318/9.

NBA ALL-STAR GAME RECORD

Season Team	Min.	FGM	FGA	Pct.	FTM	FTA	Pct.	REBOUNDS Off.	Def.	Tot.	Ast.	PF	Dq.	St.	Blk.	TO	Pts.
1974 —Buffalo	13	3	4	.750	5	8	.625	1	2	3	1	4	0	0	1	...	11
1975 —Buffalo	26	4	9	.444	3	3	1.000	4	2	6	2	4	0	0	0	...	11
1976 —Buffalo	29	10	14	.714	2	4	.500	2	5	7	1	5	0	0	0	...	22
1977 —N.Y. Knicks	38	13	23	.565	4	4	1.000	3	7	10	2	3	0	3	1	...	30
1978 —New York	20	7	14	.500	0	0	...	3	1	4	0	2	0	1	0	3	14
Totals	126	37	64	.578	14	19	.737	13	17	30	6	18	0	4	2	3	88

ITALIAN LEAGUE RECORD

Season Team	G	Min.	FGM	FGA	Pct.	FTM	FTA	Pct.	Reb.	Ast.	Pts.	AVERAGES RPG	APG	PPG
86-87—Tracer Milan	38	1320	387	730	.530	205	268	.765	388	54	991	10.2	1.4	26.1
87-88—Tracer Milan	39	1398	422	730	.578	236	293	.805	333	71	1097	8.5	1.8	28.1
88-89—Philips Milano	38	1195	334	610	.548	161	200	.805	299	60	861	7.9	1.6	22.7
89-90—Philips Milano	33	1014	329	587	.560	178	215	.828	248	41	851	7.5	1.2	25.8
90-91—Filanto	23	858	278	490	.567	179	225	.796	219	28	759	9.5	1.2	33.0
91-92—Filanto Forli	20	700	199	399	.499	129	159	.811	188	20	538	9.4	1.0	26.9
92-93—Teamsystem Fabriano	2	58	14	27	.519	12	17	.706	13	2	44	6.5	1.0	22.0
Totals	193	6543	1963	3573	.549	1100	1377	.799	1688	276	5141	8.7	1.4	26.6

McGINNIS, GEORGE　　F

PERSONAL: Born August 12, 1950, in Indianapolis. ... 6-8/235. ... Full name: George F. McGinnis.
HIGH SCHOOL: George Washington (Indianapolis).
COLLEGE: Indiana.
TRANSACTIONS/CAREER NOTES: Signed as free agent after sophomore season by Indiana Pacers of American Basketball Association in lieu of 1972 first-round draft choice (1971). ... Selected by Philadelphia 76ers in second round (22nd pick overall) of 1973 NBA Draft. ... Invoked proviso to buy his way out of contract with Pacers. ... Signed by 76ers (July 10, 1975) after Commissioner Larry O'Brien revoked contract McGinnis had signed with New York Knicks (May 30, 1975). ... Traded by 76ers to Denver Nuggets for F Bobby Jones and G Ralph Simpson (August 16, 1978). ... Traded by Nuggets to Pacers for F Alex English and 1980 first-round draft choice (February 1, 1980). ... Waived by Pacers (October 27, 1982).

COLLEGIATE RECORD

Season Team	G	Min.	FGM	FGA	Pct.	FTM	FTA	Pct.	Reb.	Ast.	Pts.	AVERAGES RPG	APG	PPG
69-70—Indiana‡						Did not play—ineligible.								
70-71—Indiana	24	...	283	615	.460	153	249	.614	352	66	719	14.7	2.8	30.0
Varsity totals	24	...	283	615	.460	153	249	.614	352	66	719	14.7	2.8	30.0

ABA REGULAR-SEASON RECORD

NOTES: ABA co-Most Valuable Player (1975). ... ABA All-Star first team (1974, 1975). ... ABA All-Star second team (1973). ... ABA All-Rookie team (1972). ... Member of ABA championship teams (1972, 1973).

Season Team	G	Min.	2-POINT			3-POINT			FTM	FTA	Pct.	Reb.	Ast.	Pts.	AVERAGES		
			FGM	FGA	Pct.	FGM	FGA	Pct.							RPG	APG	PPG
71-72—Indiana	73	2179	459	961	.478	6	38	.158	298	462	.645	,711	137	1234	9.7	1.9	16.9
72-73—Indiana	82	3347	860	1723	.499	8	32	.250	517	*778	.665	1022	205	2261	12.5	2.5	27.6
73-74—Indiana	80	3266	784	1652	.475	5	34	.147	488	*715	.683	1197	267	2071	15.0	3.3	25.9
74-75—Indiana	79	3193	811	1759	.461	62	175	.354	*545	*753	.724	1126	495	*2353	14.3	6.3	*29.8
Totals	314	11985	2914	6095	.478	81	279	.290	1848	2708	.682	4056	1104	7919	12.9	3.5	25.2

ABA PLAYOFF RECORD

NOTES: ABA Playoff Most Valuable Player (1973).

Season Team	G	Min.	2-POINT			3-POINT			FTM	FTA	Pct.	Reb.	Ast.	Pts.	AVERAGES		
			FGM	FGA	Pct.	FGM	FGA	Pct.							RPG	APG	PPG
71-72—Indiana	20	633	102	246	.415	4	15	.267	94	150	.627	227	52	310	11.4	2.6	15.5
72-73—Indiana	18	731	161	352	.457	0	5	.000	109	149	.732	222	39	431	12.3	2.2	23.9
73-74—Indiana	14	585	117	254	.461	2	7	.286	96	129	.744	166	47	336	11.9	3.4	24.0
74-75—Indiana	18	731	190	382	.497	23	73	.315	132	192	.688	286	148	581	15.9	8.2	32.3
Totals	70	2680	570	1234	.462	29	100	.290	431	620	.695	901	286	1658	12.9	4.1	23.7

ABA ALL-STAR GAME RECORD

Season Team	Min.	2-POINT			3-POINT			FTM	FTA	Pct.	Reb.	Ast.	Pts.
		FGM	FGA	Pct.	FGM	FGA	Pct.						
1972—Indiana	34	10	14	.714	0	1	.000	3	6	.500	15	2	23
1973—Indiana	30	7	21	.333	0	0	...	0	0	...	11	1	14
1974—Indiana	32	6	13	.462	0	1	.000	6	11	.545	12	5	18
Totals	96	23	48	.479	0	2	.000	9	17	.529	38	8	55

NBA REGULAR-SEASON RECORD

HONORS: All-NBA first team (1976). ... All-NBA second team (1977).
NOTES: Tied for NBA lead with 12 disqualifications (1980).

Season Team	G	Min.	FGM	FGA	Pct.	FTM	FTA	Pct.	REBOUNDS			Ast.	St.	Blk.	TO	Pts.	AVERAGES		
									Off.	Def.	Tot.						RPG	APG	PPG
75-76—Philadelphia	77	2946	647	1552	.417	475	642	.740	260	707	967	359	198	41	...	1769	12.6	4.7	23.0
76-77—Philadelphia	79	2769	659	1439	.458	372	546	.681	324	587	911	302	163	37	...	1690	11.5	3.8	21.4
77-78—Philadelphia	78	2533	588	1270	.463	411	574	.716	282	528	810	294	137	27	312	1587	10.4	3.8	20.3
78-79—Denver	76	2552	603	1273	.474	509	765	.665	256	608	864	283	129	52	*346	1715	11.4	3.7	22.6
79-80—Denver-Ind.	73	2208	400	886	.451	270	488	.553	222	477	699	333	101	23	281	1072	9.6	4.6	14.7
80-81—Indiana	69	1845	348	768	.453	207	385	.538	164	364	528	210	99	28	221	903	7.7	3.0	13.1
81-82—Indiana	76	1341	141	378	.373	72	159	.453	93	305	398	204	96	28	131	354	5.2	2.7	4.7
Totals	528	16194	3386	7566	.448	2316	3559	.651	1601	3576	5177	1985	923	236	1291	9090	9.8	3.8	17.2

Three-point field goals: 1979-80, 2-for-15 (.133). 1980-81, 0-for-7. 1981-82, 0-for-3. Totals, 2-for-25 (.080).
Personal fouls/disqualifications: 1975-76, 334/13. 1976-77, 299/4. 1977-78, 287/6. 1978-79, 321/16. 1979-80, 303/12. 1980-81, 242/3. 1981-82, 98/4. Totals, 1884/58.

NBA PLAYOFF RECORD

Season Team	G	Min.	FGM	FGA	Pct.	FTM	FTA	Pct.	REBOUNDS			Ast.	St.	Blk.	TO	Pts.	AVERAGES		
									Off.	Def.	Tot.						RPG	APG	PPG
75-76—Philadelphia	3	120	29	61	.475	11	18	.611	9	32	41	12	1	4	...	69	13.7	4.0	23.0
76-77—Philadelphia	19	603	102	273	.374	65	114	.570	62	136	198	69	23	6	...	269	10.4	3.6	14.2
77-78—Philadelphia	10	273	53	125	.424	41	49	.837	24	54	78	30	15	1	38	147	7.8	3.0	14.7
80-81—Indiana	2	39	3	15	.200	4	8	.500	2	8	10	7	2	0	5	10	5.0	3.5	5.0
Totals	34	1035	187	474	.395	121	189	.640	97	230	327	118	41	11	43	495	9.6	3.5	14.6

Personal fouls/disqualifications: 1975-76, 14/1. 1976-77, 83/2. 1977-78, 40/1. 1980-81, 6/0. Totals, 143/4.

NBA ALL-STAR GAME RECORD

Season Team	Min.	FGM	FGA	Pct.	FTM	FTA	Pct.	REBOUNDS			Ast.	PF	Dq.	St.	Blk.	TO	Pts.
								Off.	Def.	Tot.							
1976—Philadelphia	19	4	9	.444	2	4	.500	1	6	7	2	2	0	0	0	...	10
1977—Philadelphia	26	2	9	.222	0	2	.000	5	2	7	2	3	0	4	0	...	4
1979—Denver	25	5	12	.417	6	11	.545	2	4	6	3	4	0	5	0	0	16
Totals	70	11	30	.367	8	17	.471	8	12	20	7	9	0	9	0	0	30

COMBINED ABA AND NBA REGULAR-SEASON RECORDS

	G	Min.	FGM	FGA	Pct.	FTM	FTA	Pct.	REBOUNDS			Ast.	Stl.	Blk.	TO	Pts.	AVERAGES		
									Off.	Def.	Tot.						RPG	APG	PPG
Totals	842	28179	6381	13940	.458	4164	6267	.664	...	...	9233	3089	1448	332	...	17009	11.0	3.7	20.2

Three-point field goals: 83-for-304 (.273).
Personal fouls/disqualifications: 3220.

McGUIRE, DICK   G

PERSONAL: Born January 25, 1926, in Huntington, N.Y. ... 6-0/180. ... Full name: Richard Joseph McGuire. ... Brother of Al McGuire, guard with New York Knicks (1951-52 through 1953-54) and Baltimore Bullets (1954-55); and head coach, Belmont Abbey (1957-58 through 1963-64) and Marquette University (1964-65 through 1976-77). ... Nickname: Tricky Dick.
HIGH SCHOOL: LaSalle Academy (New York).
COLLEGE: St. John's and Dartmouth.
TRANSACTIONS/CAREER NOTES: Selected by New York Knicks in first round of 1949 Basketball Association of America Draft. ... Traded by Knicks to Detroit Pistons for 1958 first-round draft choice (April 3, 1957).
CAREER HONORS: Elected to Naismith Memorial Basketball Hall of Fame (1993).

COLLEGIATE RECORD

NOTES: THE SPORTING NEWS All-America second team (1944).

Season Team	G	Min.	FGM	FGA	Pct.	FTM	FTA	Pct.	Reb.	Ast.	Pts.	AVERAGES		
												RPG	APG	PPG
43-44—St. John's	16	...	43	...	...	20	...	...	...	...	106	...	...	6.6
44-45—						Did not play—in military service.								
45-46—						Did not play—in military service.								
46-47—St. John's	21	...	63	...	...	37	...	...	...	...	163	...	...	7.8
47-48—St. John's	22	...	75	...	...	72	115	.626	...	...	222	...	...	10.1
48-49—St. John's	25	...	121	...	...	72	125	.576	...	...	314	...	...	12.6
Totals	84	...	302	...	...	201	...	...	...	...	805	...	...	9.6

NBA REGULAR-SEASON RECORD

HONORS: All-NBA second team (1951).

Season Team	G	Min.	FGM	FGA	Pct.	FTM	FTA	Pct.	Reb.	Ast.	PF	Dq.	Pts.	AVERAGES		
														RPG	APG	PPG
49-50 —New York	68	...	190	563	.337	204	313	.652	...	*386	160	...	584	...	5.7	8.6
50-51 —New York	64	...	179	482	.371	179	276	.649	334	400	154	2	537	5.2	†6.3	8.4
51-52 —New York	64	2018	204	474	.430	183	290	.631	332	388	181	4	591	5.2	6.1	9.2
52-53 —New York	61	1783	142	373	.381	153	269	.569	280	296	172	3	437	4.6	4.9	7.2
53-54 —New York	68	2343	201	493	.408	220	345	.638	310	354	199	3	622	4.6	5.2	9.1
54-55 —New York	71	2310	226	581	.389	195	303	.644	322	542	143	0	647	4.5	7.6	9.1
55-56 —New York	62	1685	152	438	.347	121	193	.627	220	362	146	0	425	3.5	5.8	6.9
56-57 —New York	72	1191	140	366	.383	105	163	.644	146	222	103	0	385	2.0	3.1	5.3
57-58 —Detroit	69	2311	203	544	.373	150	225	.667	291	454	178	0	556	4.2	6.6	8.1
58-59 —Detroit	71	2063	232	543	.427	191	258	.740	285	443	147	1	655	4.0	6.2	9.2
59-60 —Detroit	68	1466	179	402	.445	124	201	.617	264	358	112	0	482	3.9	5.3	7.1
Totals	738	...	2048	5259	.389	1825	2836	.644	...	4205	1695	...	5921	...	5.7	8.0

NBA PLAYOFF RECORD

Season Team	G	Min.	FGM	FGA	Pct.	FTM	FTA	Pct.	Reb.	Ast.	PF	Dq.	Pts.	AVERAGES		
														RPG	APG	PPG
49-50 —New York	5	...	22	52	.423	19	26	.731	...	27	21	...	63	...	5.4	12.6
50-51 —New York	14	...	25	80	.313	24	53	.453	83	78	50	1	74	5.9	5.6	5.3
51-52 —New York	14	546	48	107	.449	49	86	.570	71	90	46	1	145	5.1	6.4	10.4
52-53 —New York	11	360	24	59	.407	35	55	.636	63	70	25	0	83	5.7	6.4	7.5
53-54 —New York	4	68	4	16	.250	3	5	.600	4	5	12	0	11	1.0	1.3	2.8
54-55 —New York	3	75	6	19	.316	8	12	.667	9	12	7	0	20	3.0	4.0	6.7
57-58 —Detroit	7	236	25	60	.417	17	24	.708	33	40	13	0	67	4.7	5.7	9.6
58-59 —Detroit	3	109	20	32	.625	7	11	.636	17	19	10	0	47	5.7	6.3	15.7
59-60 —Detroit	2	42	5	12	.417	1	3	.333	4	9	3	0	11	2.0	4.5	5.5
Totals	63	...	179	437	.410	163	275	.593	...	350	187	...	521	...	5.6	8.3

NBA ALL-STAR GAME RECORD

Season Team	Min.	FGM	FGA	Pct.	FTM	FTA	Pct.	Reb	Ast.	PF	Dq.	Pts.
1951 —New York	...	3	4	.750	0	0	...	5	10	2	0	6
1952 —New York	18	0	0	...	1	3	.333	1	4	0	0	1
1954 —New York	24	2	5	.400	0	0	...	4	2	1	0	4
1955 —New York	25	1	2	.500	1	2	.500	3	6	1	0	3
1956 —New York	29	2	9	.222	2	5	.400	0	3	1	0	6
1958 —Detroit	31	2	4	.500	0	0	...	7	10	4	0	4
1959 —Detroit	24	2	7	.286	1	2	.500	3	3	2	0	5
Totals	...	12	31	.387	5	12	.417	23	38	11	0	29

NBA COACHING RECORD

BACKGROUND: Player/head coach, Detroit Pistons (December 28, 1959-remainder of season).

Season Team	REGULAR SEASON				PLAYOFFS		
	W	L	Pct.	Finish	W	L	Pct.
59-60 —Detroit	17	24	.415	2nd/Western Division	0	2	.000
60-61 —Detroit	34	45	.430	3rd/Western Division	2	3	.400
61-62 —Detroit	37	43	.463	3rd/Western Division	5	5	.500
62-63 —Detroit	34	46	.425	3rd/Western Division	1	3	.250
65-66 —New York	24	35	.407	4th/Eastern Division	—	—	—
66-67 —New York	36	45	.444	4th/Eastern Division	1	3	.250
67-68 —New York	15	22	.405		—	—	—
Totals (7 years)	197	260	.431	Totals (5 years)	9	16	.360

NOTES:
1959—Replaced Detroit head coach Red Rocha (December 28), with record of 13-21.
1960—Lost to Minneapolis in Western Division semifinals.
1961—Lost to Los Angeles in Western Division semifinals.
1962—Defeated Cincinnati, 3-1, in Western Division semifinals; lost to Los Angeles, 4-2, in Western Division finals.
1963—Lost to St. Louis in Western Division semifinals.
1965—Replaced Harry Gallatin as New York head coach (November 29), with record of 6-15 and in fourth place.
1967—Lost to Boston in Eastern Division semifinals. Replaced as New York head coach by Red Holzman (December).

McHALE, KEVIN F/C

PERSONAL: Born December 19, 1957, in Hibbing, Minn. ... 6-10/225. ... Full name: Kevin Edward McHale.
HIGH SCHOOL: Hibbing (Minn.).
COLLEGE: Minnesota.
TRANSACTIONS/CAREER NOTES: Selected by Boston Celtics in first round (third pick overall) of 1980 NBA Draft. ... Assistant general manager, Minnesota Timberwolves (1994-95). ... Vice president of basketball operations, Timberwolves (May 1995 to present).
MISCELLANEOUS: Member of NBA championship teams (1981, 1984, 1986).

COLLEGIATE RECORD

Season Team	G	Min.	FGM	FGA	Pct.	FTM	FTA	Pct.	Reb.	Ast.	Pts.	RPG	APG	PPG
76-77—Minnesota	27	...	133	241	.552	58	77	.753	218	36	324	8.1	1.3	12.0
77-78—Minnesota	26	...	143	242	.591	54	77	.701	192	27	340	7.4	1.0	13.1
78-79—Minnesota	27	...	202	391	.517	79	96	.823	259	33	483	9.6	1.2	17.9
79-80—Minnesota	32	...	236	416	.567	85	107	.794	281	28	557	8.8	0.9	17.4
Totals	112		714	1290	.553	276	357	.773	950	124	1704	8.5	1.1	15.2

NBA REGULAR-SEASON RECORD

HONORS: NBA Sixth Man Award (1984, 1985). ... All-NBA first team (1987). ... NBA All-Defensive first team (1986, 1987, 1988). ... NBA All-Defensive second team (1983, 1989, 1990). ... NBA All-Rookie team (1981).

									REBOUNDS								AVERAGES		
Season Team	G	Min.	FGM	FGA	Pct.	FTM	FTA	Pct.	Off.	Def.	Tot.	Ast.	St.	Blk.	TO	Pts.	RPG	APG	PPG
80-81—Boston	82	1645	355	666	.533	108	159	.679	155	204	359	55	27	151	110	818	4.4	0.7	10.0
81-82—Boston	82	2332	465	875	.531	187	248	.754	191	365	556	91	30	185	137	1117	6.8	1.1	13.6
82-83—Boston	82	2345	483	893	.541	193	269	.717	215	338	553	104	34	192	159	1159	6.7	1.3	14.1
83-84—Boston	82	2577	587	1055	.556	336	439	.765	208	402	610	104	23	126	150	1511	7.4	1.3	18.4
84-85—Boston	79	2653	605	1062	.570	355	467	.760	229	483	712	141	28	120	157	1565	9.0	1.8	19.8
85-86—Boston	68	2397	561	978	.574	326	420	.776	171	380	551	181	29	134	149	1448	8.1	2.7	21.3
86-87—Boston	77	3060	790	1307	*.604	428	512	.836	247	516	763	198	38	172	197	2008	9.9	2.6	26.1
87-88—Boston	64	2390	550	911	*.604	346	434	.797	159	377	536	171	27	92	141	1446	8.4	2.7	22.6
88-89—Boston	78	2876	661	1211	.546	436	533	.818	223	414	637	172	26	97	196	1758	8.2	2.2	22.5
89-90—Boston	82	2722	648	1181	.549	393	440	.893	201	476	677	172	30	157	183	1712	8.3	2.1	20.9
90-91—Boston	68	2067	504	912	.553	228	275	.829	145	335	480	126	25	146	140	1251	7.1	1.9	18.4
91-92—Boston	56	1398	323	634	.509	134	163	.822	119	211	330	82	11	59	82	780	5.9	1.5	13.9
92-93—Boston	71	1656	298	649	.459	164	195	.841	95	263	358	73	16	59	92	762	5.0	1.0	10.7
Totals	971	30118	6830	12334	.554	3634	4554	.798	2358	4764	7122	1670	344	1690	1893	17335	7.3	1.7	17.9

Three-point field goals: 1980-81, 0-for-2. 1982-83, 0-for-1. 1983-84, 1-for-3 (.333). 1984-85, 0-for-6. 1986-87, 0-for-4. 1988-89, 0-for-4. 1989-90, 23-for-69 (.333). 1990-91, 15-for-37 (.405). 1991-92, 0-for-13. 1992-93, 2-for-18 (.111). Totals, 41-for-157 (.261).

Personal fouls/disqualifications: 1980-81, 260/3. 1981-82, 264/1. 1982-83, 241/3. 1983-84, 243/5. 1984-85, 234/3. 1985-86, 192/2. 1986-87, 240/1. 1987-88, 179/1. 1988-89, 223/2. 1989-90, 250/3. 1990-91, 194/2. 1991-92, 112/1. 1992-93, 126/0. Totals, 2758/27.

NBA PLAYOFF RECORD

									REBOUNDS								AVERAGES		
Season Team	G	Min.	FGM	FGA	Pct.	FTM	FTA	Pct.	Off.	Def.	Tot.	Ast.	St.	Blk.	TO	Pts.	RPG	APG	PPG
80-81—Boston	17	296	61	113	.540	23	36	.639	29	30	59	14	4	25	15	145	3.5	0.8	8.5
81-82—Boston	12	344	77	134	.575	40	53	.755	41	44	85	11	5	27	16	194	7.1	0.9	16.2
82-83—Boston	7	177	34	62	.548	10	18	.556	15	27	42	5	3	7	10	78	6.0	0.7	11.1
83-84—Boston	23	702	123	244	.504	94	121	.777	62	81	143	27	3	35	38	340	6.2	1.2	14.8
84-85—Boston	21	837	172	303	.568	121	150	.807	74	134	208	32	13	46	60	465	9.9	1.5	22.1
85-86—Boston	18	715	168	290	.579	112	141	.794	51	104	155	48	8	43	48	448	8.6	2.7	24.9
86-87—Boston	21	827	174	298	.584	96	126	.762	66	128	194	39	7	30	54	444	9.2	1.9	21.1
87-88—Boston	17	716	158	262	.603	115	137	.839	55	81	136	40	7	30	39	432	8.0	2.4	25.4
88-89—Boston	3	115	20	41	.488	17	23	.739	7	17	24	9	1	2	4	57	8.0	3.0	19.0
89-90—Boston	5	192	42	69	.609	25	29	.862	8	31	39	13	2	10	14	110	7.8	2.6	22.0
90-91—Boston	11	376	78	148	.527	66	80	.825	18	54	72	20	5	14	14	228	6.5	1.8	20.7
91-92—Boston	10	306	65	126	.516	35	44	.795	21	46	67	13	5	5	9	165	6.7	1.3	16.5
92-93—Boston	4	113	32	55	.582	12	14	.857	9	20	29	3	2	7	5	76	7.3	0.8	19.0
Totals	169	5716	1204	2145	.561	766	972	.788	456	797	1253	274	65	281	326	3182	7.4	1.6	18.8

Three-point field goals: 1982-83, 0-for-1. 1983-84, 0-for-3. 1985-86, 0-for-1. 1987-88, 1-for-1. 1989-90, 1-for-3 (.333). 1990-91, 6-for-11 (.545). 1991-92, 0-for-1. Totals, 8-for-21 (.381).

Personal fouls/disqualifications: 1980-81, 51/1. 1981-82, 44/0. 1982-83, 16/0. 1983-84, 75/1. 1984-85, 73/3. 1985-86, 64/0. 1986-87, 71/2. 1987-88, 65/1. 1988-89, 13/0. 1989-90, 17/0. 1990-91, 42/0. 1991-92, 34/0. 1992-93, 6/0. Totals, 571/8.

NBA ALL-STAR GAME RECORD

								REBOUNDS								
Season	Team	Min.	FGM	FGA	Pct.	FTM	FTA	Pct.	Off.	Def.	Tot.	Ast.	PF	Dq.	St.	Blk.	TO	Pts.
1984	—Boston	11	3	7	.429	4	6	.667	2	3	5	0	1	0	0	0	2	10
1986	—Boston	20	3	8	.375	2	2	1.000	3	7	10	2	4	0	4	0	0	8
1987	—Boston	30	7	11	.636	2	2	1.000	4	3	7	2	5	0	4	0	0	16
1988	—Boston	14	0	1	.000	2	2	1.000	0	1	1	1	2	0	2	2	2	2
1989	—Boston	16	5	7	.714	0	0	...	1	2	3	0	3	0	2	2	1	10
1990	—Boston	20	6	11	.545	0	0		2	6	8	1	4	0	0	0	0	13
1991	—Boston	14	0	3	.000	2	2	1.000	1	2	3	2	2	0	1	0	0	2
Totals		125	24	48	.500	12	14	.857	13	24	37	8	21	0	1	12	5	61

Three-point field goals: 1990, 1-for-1. 1991, 0-for-1. Totals, 1-for-2 (.500).

MIKAN, GEORGE   C

PERSONAL: Born June 18, 1924, in Joliet, Ill. ... 6-10/245. ... Full name: George Lawrence Mikan Jr. ... Brother of Ed Mikan, forward/center with Chicago Stags of Basketball Association of America (1948-49) and six NBA teams (1949-50 through 1953-54); and father of Larry Mikan, forward with Cleveland Cavaliers (1970-71).
HIGH SCHOOL: Joliet (Ill.) Catholic, then Quigley Prep (Chicago).
COLLEGE: DePaul.
TRANSACTIONS/CAREER NOTES: Signed by Chicago Gears of National Basketball League (March 16, 1946). ... Gears dropped out of NBL and entered Professional Basketball League of America for 1947-48 season. ... PBLA disbanded (November 13, 1947); Chicago was refused a franchise in the NBL and Mikan was awarded to Minneapolis Lakers at NBL meeting (November 17, 1947). Mikan scored 193 points in the eight PBLA games played by Gears before the league folded and led the league in total points and scoring average. ... Signed by Minneapolis Lakers of NBL (November 1947). ... Lakers franchise transferred to Basketball Association of America for 1948-49 season. ... Lakers franchise became part of NBA upon merger of BAA and NBL for 1949-50 season.
CAREER HONORS: Elected to Naismith Memorial Basketball Hall of Fame (1959). ... NBA 25th Anniversary All-Time Team (1970) and 35th Anniversary All-Time Team (1980).
MISCELLANEOUS: Member of NBA championship teams (1950, 1952, 1953, 1954). ... Member of BAA championship team (1949). ... Member of NBL championship teams (1947, 1948).

COLLEGIATE RECORD

NOTES: THE SPORTING NEWS All-America first team (1944, 1945).

Season Team	G	Min.	FGM	FGA	Pct.	FTM	FTA	Pct.	Reb.	Ast.	Pts.	RPG	APG	PPG
41-42—DePaul‡						Freshman team statistics unavailable.								
42-43—DePaul	24	...	97	...		77	111	.694	...	...	271	...	...	11.3
43-44—DePaul	26	...	188	...		110	169	.651	...	...	486	...	...	18.7
44-45—DePaul	24	...	218	...		122	199	.613	...	...	558	...	...	23.3
45-46—DePaul	24	...	206	...		143	186	.769	...	...	555	...	...	23.1
Varsity totals	98	...	709	...		452	665	.680	...	...	1870	...	...	19.1

NBL AND NBA REGULAR-SEASON RECORD

HONORS: All-NBA first team (1950, 1951, 1952, 1953, 1954). ... NBL Most Valuable Player (1948). ... All-NBL first team (1947, 1948). ... All-BAA first team (1949).

Season Team	G	Min.	FGM	FGA	Pct.	FTM	FTA	Pct.	Reb.	Ast.	PF	Dq.	Pts.	RPG	APG	PPG
46-47 —Chi. (NBL)	25	...	147	...		119	164	.726	...	...	90	...	413	...	...	*16.5
47-48 —Minn. (NBL)	56	...	*406	...		*383	*509	.752	...	...	210	...	*1195	...	...	*21.3
48-49 —Minneapolis (BAA)	60	...	*583	1403	.416	*532	*689	.772	...	218	260	...	*1698	...	3.6	*28.3
49-50 —Minneapolis	68	...	*649	*1595	.407	*567	*728	.779	...	197	*297	...	*1865	...	2.9	*27.4
50-51 —Minneapolis	68	...	*678	*1584	.428	*576	*717	.803	958	208	*308	14	*1932	14.1	3.1	*28.4
51-52 —Minneapolis	64	2572	545	*1414	.385	433	555	.780	866	194	*286	14	*1523	*13.5	3.0	*23.8
52-53 —Minneapolis	70	2651	500	1252	.399	442	567	.780	*1007	201	290	12	1442	*14.4	2.9	20.6
53-54 —Minneapolis	72	2362	441	1160	.380	424	546	.777	1028	174	268	4	1306	14.3	2.4	18.1
54-55 —						Did not play—retired.										
55-56 —Minneapolis	37	765	148	375	.395	94	122	.771	308	53	153	6	390	8.3	1.4	10.5
Totals	520	...	4097	...		3570	4597	.777	...	...	2162	...	11764	...	...	22.6

NBL AND NBA PLAYOFF RECORD

Season Team	G	Min.	FGM	FGA	Pct.	FTM	FTA	Pct.	Reb.	Ast.	PF	Dq.	Pts.	RPG	APG	PPG
46-47 —Chi. (NBL)	11	...	72	...		73	104	.702	...	...	48	...	217	...	...	19.7
47-48 —Minn. (NBL)	10	...	88	...		68	97	.701	...	...	37	...	244	...	...	24.4
48-49 —Minneapolis (BAA)	10	...	103	227	.454	97	121	.802	...	21	44	...	303	...	2.1	30.3
49-50 —Minneapolis	12	...	121	316	.383	134	170	.788	...	36	47	...	376	...	3.0	31.3
50-51 —Minneapolis	7	...	62	152	.408	44	55	.800	74	9	25	1	168	10.6	1.3	24.0
51-52 —Minneapolis	13	553	99	261	.379	109	138	.790	207	36	63	3	307	15.9	2.8	23.6
52-53 —Minneapolis	12	463	78	213	.366	82	112	.732	185	23	56	5	238	15.4	1.9	19.8
53-54 —Minneapolis	13	424	87	190	.458	78	96	.813	171	25	56	1	252	13.2	1.9	19.4
55-56 —Minneapolis	3	60	13	35	.371	10	13	.769	28	5	14	0	36	9.3	1.7	12.0
Totals	91	...	723	...		695	906	.767	...	...	390	...	2141	...	...	23.5

NBA ALL-STAR GAME RECORD

NOTES: NBA All-Star Game Most Valuable Player (1953).

Season Team	Min.	FGM	FGA	Pct.	FTM	FTA	Pct.	Reb	Ast.	PF	Dq.	Pts.
1951 —Minneapolis	...	4	17	.235	4	6	.667	11	3	2	0	12
1952 —Minneapolis	29	9	19	.474	8	9	.889	15	1	5	0	26
1953 —Minneapolis	40	9	26	.346	4	4	1.000	16	2	2	0	22
1954 —Minneapolis	31	6	18	.333	6	8	.750	9	1	5	0	18
Totals	...	28	80	.350	22	27	.815	51	7	14	0	78

NBA COACHING RECORD

	REGULAR SEASON				PLAYOFFS		
Season Team	W	L	Pct.		W	L	Pct.
57-58 —Minneapolis	9	30	.231		—	—	—

NOTES:
1958—Resigned as Minneapolis head coach and replaced by John Kundla (January).

MIKKELSEN, VERN F/C

PERSONAL: Born October 21, 1928, in Fresno, Calif. ... 6-7/230. ... Full name: Arild Verner Agerskov Mikkelsen.
HIGH SCHOOL: Askov (Minn.).
COLLEGE: Hamline University (Minn.).
TRANSACTIONS/CAREER NOTES: Selected by Minneapolis Lakers in first round of 1949 NBA Draft.
CAREER HONORS: Elected to Naismith Memorial Basketball Hall of Fame (1995).
MISCELLANEOUS: Member of NBA championship teams (1950, 1952, 1953, 1954).

COLLEGIATE RECORD

NOTES: THE SPORTING NEWS All-America fourth team (1949). ... Inducted into NAIA Basketball Hall of Fame (1956). ... Led NCAA Division II with .538 field-goal percentage (1949).

Season Team	G	Min.	FGM	FGA	Pct.	FTM	FTA	Pct.	Reb.	Ast.	Pts.	RPG	APG	PPG
45-46—Hamline University	17	...	49	...	...	25	...	...	...	...	123	...	...	7.2
46-47—Hamline University	26	...	102	...	...	52	...	...	...	...	256	...	...	9.8
47-48—Hamline University	31	...	199	...	...	119	...	...	...	...	517	...	...	16.7
48-49—Hamline University	30	...	203	377	.538	113	177	.638	...	...	519	...	...	17.3
Totals	104	...	553	...	...	309	...	...	...	...	1415	...	...	13.6

NBA REGULAR-SEASON RECORD

RECORDS: Holds career record for most disqualifications—127.
HONORS: All-NBA second team (1951, 1952, 1953, 1955).

Season Team	G	Min.	FGM	FGA	Pct.	FTM	FTA	Pct.	Reb.	Ast.	PF	Dq.	Pts.	RPG	APG	PPG
49-50—Minneapolis	68	...	288	722	.399	215	286	.752	...	123	222	...	791	...	1.8	11.6
50-51—Minneapolis	64	...	359	893	.402	186	275	.676	655	181	260	13	904	10.2	2.8	14.1
51-52—Minneapolis	66	2345	363	866	.419	283	372	.761	681	180	282	16	1009	10.3	2.7	15.3
52-53—Minneapolis	70	2465	378	868	.435	291	387	.752	654	148	289	14	1047	9.3	2.1	15.0
53-54—Minneapolis	72	2247	288	771	.374	221	298	.742	615	119	264	7	797	8.5	1.7	11.1
54-55—Minneapolis	71	2559	440	1043	.422	447	598	.748	722	145	*319	14	1327	10.2	2.0	18.7
55-56—Minneapolis	72	2100	317	821	.386	328	408	.804	608	173	*319	†17	962	8.4	2.4	13.4
56-57—Minneapolis	72	2198	322	854	.377	342	424	.807	630	121	*312	*18	986	8.8	1.7	13.7
57-58—Minneapolis	72	2390	439	1070	.410	370	471	.786	805	166	299	*20	1248	11.2	2.3	17.3
58-59—Minneapolis	72	2139	353	904	.390	286	355	.806	570	159	246	8	992	7.9	2.2	13.8
Totals................................	699	...	3547	8812	.403	2969	3874	.766	...	1515	2812	...	10063	...	2.2	14.4

NBA PLAYOFF RECORD

Season Team	G	Min.	FGM	FGA	Pct.	FTM	FTA	Pct.	Reb.	Ast.	PF	Dq.	Pts.	RPG	APG	PPG
49-50—Minneapolis	12	...	55	149	.369	46	60	.767	...	18	52	...	156	...	1.5	13.0
50-51—Minneapolis	7	...	39	96	.406	31	47	.660	67	17	35	3	109	9.6	2.4	15.6
51-52—Minneapolis	13	496	60	139	.432	53	64	.828	110	20	66	4	173	8.5	1.5	13.3
52-53—Minneapolis	12	400	44	133	.331	56	66	.848	104	24	59	3	144	8.7	2.0	12.0
53-54—Minneapolis	13	375	51	111	.459	31	36	.861	73	17	52	1	133	5.6	1.3	10.2
54-55—Minneapolis	7	209	30	85	.353	36	46	.783	78	13	36	4	96	11.1	1.9	13.7
55-56—Minneapolis	3	90	11	26	.423	18	20	.900	17	2	14	2	40	5.7	0.7	13.3
56-57—Minneapolis	5	162	33	83	.398	22	34	.647	43	17	29	4	88	8.6	3.4	17.6
58-59—Minneapolis	13	371	73	177	.412	56	73	.767	93	24	54	3	202	7.2	1.8	15.5
Totals................................	85	...	396	999	.396	349	446	.783	...	152	397	...	1141	...	1.8	13.4

NBA ALL-STAR GAME RECORD

Season Team	Min.	FGM	FGA	Pct.	FTM	FTA	Pct.	Reb	Ast.	PF	Dq.	Pts.
1951 —Minneapolis................	...	4	11	.364	3	4	.750	9	1	3	0	11
1952 —Minneapolis	23	5	8	.625	2	2	1.000	10	0	2	0	12
1953 —Minneapolis	19	3	13	.231	0	0	...	6	3	3	0	6
1955 —Minneapolis	25	7	15	.467	2	3	.667	9	1	5	0	16
1956 —Minneapolis	22	5	13	.385	6	7	.857	9	2	4	0	16
1957 —Minneapolis	21	3	10	.300	0	4	.000	9	1	3	0	6
Totals	...	27	70	.386	13	20	.650	52	8	20	0	67

ABA COACHING RECORD

BACKGROUND: General manager, Minnesota Pipers of ABA (1968-69).

		REGULAR SEASON				PLAYOFFS		
Season Team	W	L	Pct.	Finish		W	L	Pct.
68-69 —Minnesota	6	7	.462			—	—	—

NOTES:
1969—Replaced Jim Harding as Minnesota head coach (January), with record of 20-12; later replaced by Gus Young.

MONCRIEF, SIDNEY G

PERSONAL: Born September 21, 1957, in Little Rock, Ark. ... 6-3/183. ... Full name: Sidney A. Moncrief. ... Nickname: The Squid.
HIGH SCHOOL: Hall (Little Rock, Ark.).
COLLEGE: Arkansas.
TRANSACTIONS/CAREER NOTES: Selected by Milwaukee Bucks in first round (fifth pick overall) of 1979 NBA Draft. ... Signed as unrestricted free agent by Atlanta Hawks (October 4, 1990). ... Rights renounced by Hawks (September 29, 1991).

COLLEGIATE RECORD

NOTES: THE SPORTING NEWS All-America second team (1979). ... Led NCAA Division I with .665 field-goal percentage (1976).

Season Team	G	Min.	FGM	FGA	Pct.	FTM	FTA	Pct.	Reb.	Ast.	Pts.	AVERAGES RPG	APG	PPG
75-76—Arkansas	28	...	149	224	.665	56	77	.727	213	59	354	7.6	2.1	12.6
76-77—Arkansas	28	997	157	242	.649	117	171	.684	235	41	431	8.4	1.5	15.4
77-78—Arkansas	36	1293	209	354	.590	203	256	.793	278	60	621	7.7	1.7	17.3
78-79—Arkansas	30	1157	224	400	.560	212	248	.855	289	80	660	9.6	2.7	22.0
Totals	122	...	739	1220	.606	588	752	.782	1015	240	2066	8.3	2.0	16.9

NBA REGULAR-SEASON RECORD

HONORS: NBA Defensive Player of the Year (1983, 1984). ... All-NBA first team (1983). ... All-NBA second team (1982, 1984, 1985, 1986). ... NBA All-Defensive first team (1983, 1984, 1985, 1986). ... NBA All-Defensive second team (1982).

Season Team	G	Min.	FGM	FGA	Pct.	FTM	FTA	Pct.	REBOUNDS Off.	Def.	Tot.	Ast.	St.	Blk.	TO	Pts.	AVERAGES RPG	APG	PPG
79-80—Milwaukee	77	1557	211	451	.468	232	292	.795	154	184	338	133	72	16	117	654	4.4	1.7	8.5
80-81—Milwaukee	80	2417	400	739	.541	320	398	.804	186	220	406	264	90	37	145	1122	5.1	3.3	14.0
81-82—Milwaukee	80	2980	556	1063	.523	468	573	.817	221	313	534	382	138	22	208	1581	6.7	4.8	19.8
82-83—Milwaukee	76	2710	606	1156	.524	499	604	.826	192	245	437	300	113	23	197	1712	5.8	3.9	22.5
83-84—Milwaukee	79	3075	560	1125	.498	529	624	.848	215	313	528	358	108	27	217	1654	6.7	4.5	20.9
84-85—Milwaukee	73	2734	561	1162	.483	454	548	.828	149	242	391	382	117	39	184	1585	5.4	5.2	21.7
85-86—Milwaukee	73	2567	470	962	.489	498	580	.859	115	219	334	357	103	18	174	1471	4.6	4.9	20.2
86-87—Milwaukee	39	992	158	324	.488	136	162	.840	57	70	127	121	27	10	63	460	3.3	3.1	11.8
87-88—Milwaukee	56	1428	217	444	.489	164	196	.837	58	122	180	204	41	12	86	603	3.2	3.6	10.8
88-89—Milwaukee	62	1594	261	532	.491	205	237	.865	46	126	172	188	65	13	94	752	2.8	3.0	12.1
89-90—								Did not play—retired.										
90-91—Atlanta	72	1096	117	240	.488	82	105	.781	31	97	128	104	50	9	66	337	1.8	1.4	4.7
Totals	767	23150	4117	8198	.502	3587	4319	.831	1424	2151	3575	2793	924	226	1551	11931	4.7	3.6	15.6

Three-point field goals: 1979-80, 0-for-1. 1980-81, 2-for-9 (.222). 1981-82, 1-for-14 (.071). 1982-83, 1-for-10 (.100). 1983-84, 5-for-18 (.278). 1984-85, 9-for-33 (.273). 1985-86, 33-for-103 (.320). 1986-87, 8-for-31 (.258). 1987-88, 5-for-31 (.161). 1988-89, 25-for-73 (.342). 1990-91, 21-for-64 (.328). Totals, 110-for-387 (.284).

Personal fouls/disqualifications: 1979-80, 106/0. 1980-81, 156/1. 1981-82, 206/3. 1982-83, 180/1. 1983-84, 204/2. 1984-85, 197/1. 1985-86, 178/1. 1986-87, 73/0. 1987-88, 109/0. 1988-89, 114/1. 1990-91, 112/0. Totals, 1635/10.

NBA PLAYOFF RECORD

Season Team	G	Min.	FGM	FGA	Pct.	FTM	FTA	Pct.	REBOUNDS Off.	Def.	Tot.	Ast.	St.	Blk.	TO	Pts.	AVERAGES RPG	APG	PPG
79-80—Milwaukee	7	182	30	51	.588	27	31	.871	17	14	31	11	5	1	14	87	4.4	1.6	12.4
80-81—Milwaukee	7	277	30	69	.435	38	51	.745	19	28	47	20	12	3	21	98	6.7	2.9	14.0
81-82—Milwaukee	6	252	31	74	.419	30	38	.789	15	15	30	24	9	2	12	92	5.0	4.0	15.3
82-83—Milwaukee	9	377	62	142	.437	46	61	.754	28	32	60	33	18	3	27	170	6.7	3.7	18.9
83-84—Milwaukee	16	618	99	191	.518	106	134	.791	44	67	111	68	28	9	61	305	6.9	4.3	19.1
84-85—Milwaukee	8	319	55	99	.556	70	75	.933	10	24	34	40	5	4	20	184	4.3	5.0	23.0
85-86—Milwaukee	9	327	52	122	.426	44	63	.698	15	26	41	44	5	5	21	152	4.6	4.9	16.9
86-87—Milwaukee	12	426	78	165	.473	73	90	.811	21	33	54	36	13	6	24	233	4.5	3.0	19.4
87-88—Milwaukee	5	173	24	50	.480	26	27	.963	6	13	19	26	3	1	11	75	3.8	5.2	15.0
88-89—Milwaukee	9	184	19	48	.396	15	16	.938	8	18	26	13	5	2	11	55	2.9	1.4	6.1
90-91—Atlanta	5	91	11	22	.500	13	16	.813	6	10	16	2	3	0	3	36	3.2	0.4	7.2
Totals	93	3226	491	1033	.475	488	602	.811	189	280	469	317	106	36	225	1487	5.0	3.4	16.0

Three-point field goals: 1981-82, 0-for-1. 1982-83, 0-for-1. 1983-84, 1-for-4 (.250). 1984-85, 4-for-10 (.400). 1985-86, 4-for-14 (.286). 1986-87, 4-for-14 (.286). 1987-88, 1-for-1. 1988-89, 2-for-7 (.286). 1990-91, 1-for-6 (.167). Totals, 17-for-58 (.293).

Personal fouls/disqualifications: 1979-80, 14/0. 1980-81, 24/0. 1981-82, 22/1. 1982-83, 25/1. 1983-84, 54/1. 1984-85, 26/0. 1985-86, 30/0. 1986-87, 43/0. 1987-88, 14/0. 1988-89, 17/0. 1990-91, 16/0. Totals, 285/3.

NBA ALL-STAR GAME RECORD

Season Team	Min.	FGM	FGA	Pct.	FTM	FTA	Pct.	REBOUNDS Off.	Def.	Tot.	Ast.	PF	Dq.	St.	Blk.	TO	Pts.
1982 —Milwaukee	22	3	11	.273	0	2	.000	3	1	4	1	2	0	1	0	1	6
1983 —Milwaukee	23	8	14	.571	4	5	.800	3	2	5	4	1	0	6	1	1	20
1984 —Milwaukee	26	3	6	.500	2	2	1.000	1	4	5	2	3	0	5	0	4	8
1985 —Milwaukee	22	1	5	.200	6	6	1.000	2	3	5	4	1	0	0	0	2	8
1986 —Milwaukee	26	4	11	.364	7	7	1.000	3	0	3	1	0	0	0	1	0	16
Totals	119	19	47	.404	19	22	.864	12	10	22	12	7	0	12	2	8	58

Three-point field goals: 1986, 1-for-1.

MONROE, EARL   G

PERSONAL: Born November 21, 1944, in Philadelphia. ... 6-3/190. ... Full name: Vernon Earl Monroe. ... Nickname: The Pearl.

HIGH SCHOOL: John Bartram (Philadelphia).

COLLEGE: Winston-Salem (N.C.) State.

TRANSACTIONS/CAREER NOTES: Selected by Baltimore Bullets in first round (second pick overall) of 1967 NBA Draft. ... Traded by Bullets to New York Knicks for F Dave Stallworth, G Mike Riordan and cash (November 10, 1971).

CAREER HONORS: Elected to Naismith Memorial Basketball Hall of Fame (1989).

MISCELLANEOUS: Member of NBA championship team (1973).

COLLEGIATE RECORD

NOTES: THE SPORTING NEWS All-America first team (1966). ... Holds NCAA Division II single-season record for most points—1329 (1967). ... Inducted into NAIA Basketball Hall of Fame (1975). ... NCAA College Division and NAIA Leading Scorer (1967). ... Outstanding Player in NCAA College Division Tournament (1967). ... Member of NCAA College Division tournament championship team (1967). ... Led NCAA Division II with 41.5 points per game (1967).

Season Team	G	Min.	FGM	FGA	Pct.	FTM	FTA	Pct.	Reb.	Ast.	Pts.	AVERAGES RPG	APG	PPG
63-64—Winst.-Salem State	23	...	71	...	...	21	...	...	...	...	163	...	...	7.1
64-65—Winst.-Salem State	30	...	286	...	...	125	176	.710	211	...	697	7.0	...	23.2
65-66—Winst.-Salem State	25	...	292	519	.563	162	187	.866	167	...	746	6.7	...	29.8
66-67—Winst.-Salem State	32	...	509	839	.607	311	391	.795	218	...	1329	6.8	...	41.5
Totals	110	...	1158	...	...	619	...	...	...	...	2935	...	...	26.7

NBA REGULAR-SEASON RECORD

HONORS: NBA Rookie of the Year (1968). ... All-NBA first team (1969). ... NBA All-Rookie team (1968).

Season Team	G	Min.	FGM	FGA	Pct.	FTM	FTA	Pct.	Reb.	Ast.	PF	Dq.	Pts.	AVERAGES RPG	APG	PPG
67-68 —Baltimore	82	3012	742	1637	.453	507	649	.781	465	349	282	3	1991	5.7	4.3	24.3
68-69 —Baltimore	80	3075	809	1837	.440	447	582	.768	280	392	261	1	2065	3.5	4.9	25.8
69-70 —Baltimore	82	3051	695	1557	.446	532	641	.830	257	402	258	3	1922	3.1	4.9	23.4
70-71 —Baltimore	81	2843	663	1501	.442	406	506	.802	213	354	220	3	1732	2.6	4.4	21.4
71-72 —Balt.-N.Y.	63	1337	287	662	.434	175	224	.781	100	142	139	1	749	1.6	2.3	11.9
72-73 —New York	75	2370	496	1016	.488	171	208	.822	245	288	195	1	1163	3.3	3.8	15.5

Season Team	G	Min.	FGM	FGA	Pct.	FTM	FTA	Pct.	REBOUNDS Off.	Def.	Tot.	Ast.	St.	Blk.	TO	Pts.	AVERAGES RPG	APG	PPG
73-74—New York	41	1194	240	513	.468	93	113	.823	22	99	121	110	34	19	...	573	3.0	2.7	14.0
74-75—New York	78	2814	668	1462	.457	297	359	.827	56	271	327	270	108	29	...	1633	4.2	3.5	20.9
75-76—New York	76	2889	647	1354	.478	280	356	.787	48	225	273	304	111	22	...	1574	3.6	4.0	20.7
76-77—N.Y. Knicks	77	2656	613	1185	.517	307	366	.839	45	178	223	366	91	23	...	1533	2.9	4.8	19.9
77-78—New York	76	2369	556	1123	.495	242	291	.832	47	135	182	361	60	19	179	1354	2.4	4.8	17.8
78-79—New York	64	1393	329	699	.471	129	154	.838	26	48	74	189	48	6	98	787	1.2	3.0	12.3
79-80—New York	51	633	161	352	.457	56	64	.875	16	20	36	67	21	3	28	378	0.7	1.3	7.4
Totals	926	29636	6906	14898	.464	3642	4513	.807	...	2796	3594	473	121	305		17454	3.0	3.9	18.8

Personal fouls/disqualifications: 1973-74, 97/0. 1974-75, 200/0. 1975-76, 209/1. 1976-77, 197/0. 1977-78, 189/0. 1978-79, 123/0. 1979-80, 46/0. Totals, 2416/13.

NBA PLAYOFF RECORD

Season Team	G	Min.	FGM	FGA	Pct.	FTM	FTA	Pct.	Reb.	Ast.	PF	Dq.	Pts.	AVERAGES RPG	APG	PPG
68-69 —Baltimore	4	171	44	114	.386	25	31	.806	21	16	10	0	113	5.3	4.0	28.3
69-70 —Baltimore	7	299	74	154	.481	48	60	.800	23	28	23	0	196	3.3	4.0	28.0
70-71 —Baltimore	18	671	145	356	.407	107	135	.793	64	74	56	0	397	3.6	4.1	22.1
71-72 —New York	16	429	76	185	.411	45	57	.789	45	47	41	0	197	2.8	2.9	12.3
72-73 —New York	16	504	111	211	.526	36	48	.750	51	51	39	0	258	3.2	3.2	16.1

Season Team	G	Min.	FGM	FGA	Pct.	FTM	FTA	Pct.	REBOUNDS Off.	Def.	Tot.	Ast.	St.	Blk.	TO	Pts.	AVERAGES RPG	APG	PPG
73-74—New York	12	407	81	165	.491	47	55	.855	8	40	48	25	8	9	...	209	4.0	2.1	17.4
74-75—New York	3	89	12	45	.267	8	22	.818	1	8	9	6	4	2	...	42	3.0	2.0	14.0
77-78—New York	6	145	24	62	.387	11	18	.611	1	4	5	17	6	0	6	59	0.8	2.8	9.8
Totals	82	2715	567	1292	.439	337	426	.791	...	...	266	264	18	11	6	1471	3.2	3.2	17.9

Personal fouls/disqualifications: 1973-74, 26/0. 1974-75, 6/0. 1977-78, 15/0. Totals, 216/0.

NBA ALL-STAR GAME RECORD

Season Team	Min.	FGM	FGA	Pct.	FTM	FTA	Pct.	Reb	Ast.	PF	Dq.	Pts.
1969 —Baltimore	27	6	15	.400	9	12	.750	4	4	4	0	21
1971 —Baltimore	18	3	9	.333	0	0	...	5	2	3	0	6

Season Team	Min.	FGM	FGA	Pct.	FTM	FTA	Pct.	REBOUNDS Off.	Def.	Tot.	Ast.	PF	Dq.	St.	Blk.	TO	Pts.
1975 —New York	25	3	8	.375	3	5	.600	0	3	3	2	2	0	1	0	...	9
1977 —N.Y. Knicks	15	2	7	.286	0	0	...	0	0	0	3	1	0	0	0	...	4
Totals	85	14	39	.359	12	17	.706	...	...	12	11	10	0	1		...	40

MURPHY, CALVIN   G

PERSONAL: Born May 9, 1948, in Norwalk, Conn. ... 5-9/165. ... Full name: Calvin Jerome Murphy.
HIGH SCHOOL: Norwalk (Conn.).
COLLEGE: Niagara.
TRANSACTIONS/CAREER NOTES: Selected by San Diego Rockets in second round (18th pick overall) of 1970 NBA Draft. ... Rockets franchise moved from San Diego to Houston for 1971-72 season.
CAREER HONORS: Elected to Naismith Memorial Basketball Hall of Fame (1992).
MISCELLANEOUS: Houston Rockets franchise all-time assists leader with 4,402 (1970-71 through 1982-83).

COLLEGIATE RECORD

NOTES: THE SPORTING NEWS All-America second team (1969, 1970).

Season Team	G	Min.	FGM	FGA	Pct.	FTM	FTA	Pct.	Reb.	Ast.	Pts.	AVERAGES RPG	APG	PPG
66-67—Niagara‡	19	...	364	719	.506	201	239	.841	102	...	929	5.4	...	48.9
67-68—Niagara	24	...	337	772	.437	242	288	.840	118	...	916	4.9	...	38.2
68-69—Niagara	24	...	294	700	.420	190	230	.826	87	...	778	3.6	...	32.4
69-70—Niagara	29	...	316	692	.457	222	252	.881	103	...	854	3.6	...	29.4
Varsity totals	77	...	947	2164	.438	654	770	.849	308	...	2548	4.0	...	33.1

NBA REGULAR-SEASON RECORD

RECORDS: Holds single-season record for highest free-throw percentage—.958 (1981).
HONORS: NBA All-Rookie team (1971).

Season Team	G	Min.	FGM	FGA	Pct.	FTM	FTA	Pct.	Reb.	Ast.	PF	Dq.	Pts.	AVERAGES RPG	APG	PPG
70-71—San Diego	82	2020	471	1029	.458	356	434	.820	245	329	263	4	1298	3.0	4.0	15.8
71-72—Houston	82	2538	571	1255	.455	349	392	.890	258	393	298	6	1491	3.1	4.8	18.2
72-73—Houston	77	1697	381	820	.465	239	269	.888	149	262	211	3	1001	1.9	3.4	13.0

Season Team	G	Min.	FGM	FGA	Pct.	FTM	FTA	Pct.	REBOUNDS Off.	Def.	Tot.	Ast.	St.	Blk.	TO	Pts.	AVERAGES RPG	APG	PPG
73-74—Houston	81	2922	671	1285	.522	310	357	.868	51	137	188	603	157	4	...	1652	2.3	7.4	20.4
74-75—Houston	78	2513	557	1152	.484	341	386	.883	52	121	173	381	128	4	...	1455	2.2	4.9	18.7
75-76—Houston	82	2995	675	1369	.493	372	410	.907	52	157	209	596	151	6	...	1722	2.5	7.3	21.0
76-77—Houston	82	2764	596	1216	.490	272	307	.886	54	118	172	386	144	8	...	1464	2.1	4.7	17.9
77-78—Houston	76	2900	852	*1737	.491	245	267	.918	57	107	164	259	112	3	173	1949	2.2	3.4	25.6
78-79—Houston	82	2941	707	1424	.496	246	265	.928	78	95	173	351	117	6	187	1660	2.1	4.3	20.2
79-80—Houston	76	2676	624	1267	.493	271	302	.897	68	82	150	299	143	9	162	1520	2.0	3.9	20.0
80-81—Houston	76	2014	528	1074	.492	206	215	*.958	33	54	87	222	111	6	129	1266	1.1	2.9	16.7
81-82—Houston	64	1204	277	648	.427	100	110	.909	20	41	61	163	43	1	82	655 ·	1.0	2.5	10.2
82-83—Houston	64	1423	337	754	.447	138	150	*.920	34	40	74	158	59	4	89	816	1.2	2.5	12.8
Totals	1002	30607	7247	15030	.482	3445	3864	.892	...		2103	4402	1165	51	822	17949	2.1	4.4	17.9

Three-point field goals: 1979-80, 1-for-25 (.040). 1980-81, 4-for-17 (.235). 1981-82, 1-for-16 (.063). 1982-83, 4-for-14 (.286). Totals, 10-for-75 (.139).
Personal fouls/disqualifications: 1973-74, 310/8. 1974-75, 281/8. 1975-76, 294/3. 1976-77, 281/6. 1977-78, 241/4. 1978-79, 288/5. 1979-80, 269/3. 1980-81, 209/0. 1981-82, 142/0. 1982-83, 163/3. Totals, 3250/53.

NBA PLAYOFF RECORD

Season Team	G	Min.	FGM	FGA	Pct.	FTM	FTA	Pct.	REBOUNDS Off.	Def.	Tot.	Ast.	St.	Blk.	TO	Pts.	AVERAGES RPG	APG	PPG
74-75—Houston	8	305	72	156	.462	51	57	.895	9	10	19	45	14	1	...	195	2.4	5.6	24.4
76-77—Houston	12	420	102	213	.479	28	30	.933	7	12	19	75	19	2	...	232	1.6	6.3	19.3
78-79—Houston	2	73	9	31	.290	8	9	.889	2	1	3	6	8	1	2	26	1.5	3.0	13.0
79-80—Houston	7	265	58	108	.537	13	13	1.000	4	6	10	26	11	0	16	131	1.4	3.7	18.7
80-81—Houston	19	540	142	287	.495	58	60	.967	7	17	24	57	26	0	42	344	1.3	3.0	18.1
81-82—Houston	3	57	5	22	.227	7	8	.875	2	1	3	4	1	0	4	17	1.0	1.3	5.7
Totals	51	1660	388	817	.475	165	177	.932	31	47	78	213	79	4	64	945	1.5	4.2	18.5

Three-point field goals: 1979-80, 2-for-4 (.500). 1980-81, 2-for-7 (.286). 1981-82, 0-for-3. Totals, 4-for-14 (.286).
Personal fouls/disqualifications: 1974-75, 36/2. 1976-77, 47/1. 1978-79, 9/0. 1979-80, 29/1. 1980-81, 69/0. 1981-82, 7/0. Totals, 197/4.

NBA ALL-STAR GAME RECORD

Season Team	Min.	FGM	FGA	Pct.	FTM	FTA	Pct.	REBOUNDS Off.	Def.	Tot.	Ast.	PF	Dq.	St.	Blk.	TO	Pts.
1979 —Houston	15	3	5	.600	0	0	...	0	1	1	5	4	0	2	0	4	6

NIXON, NORM G

PERSONAL: Born October 10, 1955, in Macon, Ga. ... 6-2/175. ... Full name: Norman Ellard Nixon.
HIGH SCHOOL: Southwest (Macon, Ga.).
COLLEGE: Duquesne.
TRANSACTIONS/CAREER NOTES: Selected by Los Angeles Lakers in first round (22nd pick overall) of 1977 NBA Draft. ... Traded by Lakers with G Eddie Jordan and 1986 and 1987 second-round draft choices to San Diego Clippers for C Swen Nater and draft rights to G Byron Scott (October 10, 1983). ... Played in Italy (1988-89).
MISCELLANEOUS: Member of NBA championship teams (1980, 1982).

COLLEGIATE RECORD

Season Team	G	Min.	FGM	FGA	Pct.	FTM	FTA	Pct.	Reb.	Ast.	Pts.	AVERAGES RPG	APG	PPG
73-74—Duquesne	24	...	113	257	.440	31	45	.689	99	144	257	4.1	6.0	10.7
74-75—Duquesne	25	...	147	282	.521	69	92	.750	88	105	363	3.5	4.2	14.5
75-76—Duquesne	25	...	214	434	.493	96	127	.756	105	150	524	4.2	6.0	21.0
76-77—Duquesne	30	1106	279	539	.518	103	138	.746	119	178	661	4.0	5.9	22.0
Totals	104	...	753	1512	.498	299	402	.744	411	577	1805	4.0	5.5	17.4

NBA REGULAR-SEASON RECORD

HONORS: NBA All-Rookie Team (1978).

Season Team	G	Min.	FGM	FGA	Pct.	FTM	FTA	Pct.	REBOUNDS Off.	Def.	Tot.	Ast.	St.	Blk.	TO	Pts.	AVERAGES RPG	APG	PPG
77-78—Los Angeles	81	2779	496	998	.497	115	161	.714	41	198	239	553	138	7	251	1107	3.0	6.8	13.7
78-79—Los Angeles	82	3145	623	1149	.542	158	204	.775	48	183	231	737	201	17	231	1404	2.8	9.0	17.1
79-80—Los Angeles	82	*3226	624	1209	.516	197	253	.779	52	177	229	642	147	14	288	1446	2.8	7.8	17.6
80-81—Los Angeles	79	2962	576	1210	.476	196	252	.778	64	168	232	696	146	11	285	1350	2.9	8.8	17.1
81-82—Los Angeles	82	3024	628	1274	.493	181	224	.808	38	138	176	652	132	7	238	1440	2.1	8.0	17.6
82-83—Los Angeles	79	2711	533	1123	.475	125	168	.744	61	144	205	566	104	4	237	1191	2.6	7.2	15.1
83-84—San Diego	82	3053	587	1270	.462	206	271	.760	56	147	203	914	94	4	257	1391	2.5	11.1	17.0
84-85—L.A. Clippers	81	2894	596	1281	.465	170	218	.780	55	163	218	711	95	4	273	1395	2.7	8.8	17.2
85-86—L.A. Clippers	67	2138	403	921	.438	131	162	.809	45	135	180	576	84	3	190	979	2.7	8.6	14.6
87-88—L.A. Clippers	...						Did not play—Achilles' tendon injury.												
88-89—L.A. Clippers	53	1318	153	370	.414	48	65	.738	13	65	78	339	46	0	118	362	1.5	6.4	6.8
Totals	768	27250	5219	10805	.483	1527	1978	.772	473	1518	1991	6386	1187	71	2368	12065	2.6	8.3	15.7

Three-point field goals: 1979-80, 1-for-8 (.125). 1980-81, 2-for-12 (.167). 1981-82, 3-for-12 (.250). 1982-83, 0-for-13. 1983-84, 11-for-46 (.239). 1984-85, 33-for-99 (.333). 1985-86, 42-for-121 (.347). 1988-89, 8-for-29 (.276). Totals, 100-for-340 (.294).
Personal fouls/disqualifications: 1977-78, 259/3. 1978-79, 250/6. 1979-80, 241/1. 1980-81, 226/2. 1981-82, 264/3. 1982-83, 176/1. 1983-84, 180/1. 1984-85, 175/2. 1985-86, 143/0. 1988-89, 69/0. Totals, 1983/19.

NBA PLAYOFF RECORD

Season Team	G	Min.	FGM	FGA	Pct.	FTM	FTA	Pct.	REBOUNDS Off.	Def.	Tot.	Ast.	St.	Blk.	TO	Pts.	AVERAGES RPG	APG	PPG
77-78—Los Angeles	3	92	11	24	.458	2	3	.667	4	5	9	16	4	1	5	24	3.0	5.3	8.0

Season Team	G	Min.	FGM	FGA	Pct.	FTM	FTA	Pct.	REBOUNDS Off.	Def.	Tot.	Ast.	St.	Blk.	TO	Pts.	AVERAGES RPG	APG	PPG
78-79—Los Angeles....	8	327	56	119	.471	11	15	.733	6	22	28	94	11	0	24	123	3.5	11.8	15.4
79-80—Los Angeles....	16	648	114	239	.477	41	51	.804	13	43	56	125	32	3	49	270	3.5	7.8	16.9
80-81—Los Angeles....	3	133	25	49	.510	8	10	.800	1	10	11	26	1	1	5	58	3.7	8.7	19.3
81-82—Los Angeles....	14	549	121	253	.478	43	57	.754	13	30	43	114	23	2	34	286	3.1	8.1	20.4
82-83—Los Angeles....	14	538	113	237	.477	37	50	.740	13	35	48	89	18	1	34	266	3.4	6.4	19.0
Totals..................	58	2287	440	921	.478	142	186	.763	50	145	195	464	89	8	151	1027	3.4	8.0	17.7

Three-point field goals: 1979-80, 1-for-5 (.200). 1981-82, 1-for-3 (.333). 1982-83, 3-for-7 (.429). Totals, 5-for-15 (.333).
Personal fouls/disqualifications: 1977-78, 13/0. 1978-79, 37/1. 1979-80, 59/0. 1980-81, 9/0. 1981-82, 43/0. 1982-83, 40/0. Totals, 201/1.

NBA ALL-STAR GAME RECORD

Season Team	Min.	FGM	FGA	Pct.	FTM	FTA	Pct.	REBOUNDS Off.	Def.	Tot.	Ast.	PF	Dq.	St.	Blk.	TO	Pts.
1982 —Los Angeles	19	7	14	.500	0	0	...	0	0	0	2	0	0	1	0	0	14
1985 —L.A. Clippers......	19	5	7	.714	1	2	.500	0	2	2	8	0	0	1	0	1	11
1987 —L.A. Clippers							Did not play—Achilles' tendon injury.										
Totals..............	38	12	21	.571	1	2	.500	0	2	2	10	0	0	2	0	1	25

ITALIAN LEAGUE RECORD

Season Team	G	Min.	FGM	FGA	Pct.	FTM	FTA	Pct.	Reb.	Ast.	Pts.	AVERAGES RPG	APG	PPG
88-89—Scavolini Pesaro............	7	217	37	75	.493	4	7	.571	15	19	87	2.1	2.7	12.4

PETTIT, BOB — F/C

PERSONAL: Born December 12, 1932, in Baton Rouge, La. ... 6-9/215. ... Full name: Robert Lee Pettit Jr.
HIGH SCHOOL: Baton Rouge (La.).
COLLEGE: Louisiana State.
TRANSACTIONS/CAREER NOTES: Selected by Milwaukee Hawks in first round of 1954 NBA Draft. ... Hawks franchise moved from Milwaukee to St. Louis for 1955-56 season.
CAREER HONORS: Elected to Naismith Memorial Basketball Hall of Fame (1970). ... NBA 25th Anniversary All-Time Team (1970) and 35th Anniversary All-Time Team (1980).
MISCELLANEOUS: Member of NBA championship team (1958). ... Atlanta Hawks franchise all-time leading rebounder with 12,849 (1954-55 through 1964-65).

COLLEGIATE RECORD

Season Team	G	Min.	FGM	FGA	Pct.	FTM	FTA	Pct.	Reb.	Ast.	Pts.	AVERAGES RPG	APG	PPG
50-51—Louisiana State‡............	10	...	...	...	...	...	...	...	...	...	270	...	...	27.0
51-52—Louisiana State...............	23	...	237	549	.432	115	192	.599	315	...	589	13.7	...	25.6
52-53—Louisiana State...............	21	...	193	394	.490	133	215	.619	263	...	519	12.5	...	24.7
53-54—Louisiana State...............	25	...	281	573	.490	223	308	.724	432	...	785	17.3	...	31.4
Varsity totals	69	...	711	1516	.469	471	715	.659	1010	...	1893	14.6	...	27.4

NBA REGULAR-SEASON RECORD

HONORS: NBA Most Valuable Player (1956, 1959). ... NBA Rookie of the Year (1955). ... All-NBA first team (1955, 1956, 1957, 1958, 1959, 1960, 1961, 1962, 1963, 1964). ... All-NBA second team (1965).

Season Team	G	Min.	FGM	FGA	Pct.	FTM	FTA	Pct.	Reb.	Ast.	PF	Dq.	Pts.	AVERAGES RPG	APG	PPG
54-55 —Milwaukee	72	2659	520	1279	.407	426	567	.751	994	229	258	5	1466	13.8	3.2	20.4
55-56 —St. Louis	72	2794	*646	*1507	.429	*557	*757	.736	*1164	189	202	1	*1849	16.2	2.6	*25.7
56-57 —St. Louis	71	2491	*613	*1477	.415	529	684	.773	1037	133	181	1	1755	14.6	1.9	24.7
57-58 —St. Louis	70	2528	581	1418	.410	557	744	.749	1216	157	222	6	1719	17.4	2.2	24.6
58-59 —St. Louis	72	2873	*719	1640	.438	*667	*879	.759	1182	221	200	3	*2105	16.4	3.1	*29.2
59-60 —St. Louis	72	2896	669	1526	.438	544	722	.753	1221	257	204	0	1882	17.0	3.6	26.1
60-61 —St. Louis	76	3027	769	1720	.447	582	804	.724	1540	262	217	1	2120	20.3	3.4	27.9
61-62 —St. Louis	78	3282	867	1928	.450	695	901	.771	1459	289	296	4	2429	18.7	3.7	31.1
62-63 —St. Louis	79	3090	778	1746	.446	*685	885	.774	1191	245	282	8	2241	15.1	3.1	28.4
63-64 —St. Louis	80	3296	791	1708	.463	608	771	.789	1224	259	300	3	2190	15.3	3.2	27.4
64-65 —St. Louis	50	1754	396	923	.429	332	405	.820	621	128	167	0	1124	12.4	2.6	22.5
Totals.............................	792	30690	7349	16872	.436	6182	8119	.761	12849	2369	2529	32	20880	16.2	3.0	26.4

NBA PLAYOFF RECORD

NOTES: Holds NBA Finals single-game records for most free throws made—19; and most free throws attempted—24 (April 9, 1958, vs. Boston). ... Shares NBA Finals single-game record for most free throws attempted in one quarter—11 (April 9, 1958, vs. Boston).

Season Team	G	Min.	FGM	FGA	Pct.	FTM	FTA	Pct.	Reb.	Ast.	PF	Dq.	Pts.	AVERAGES RPG	APG	PPG
55-56 —St. Louis	8	274	47	128	.367	59	70	.843	84	18	20	0	153	10.5	2.3	19.1
56-57 —St. Louis	10	430	98	237	.414	102	133	.767	168	25	33	0	298	16.8	2.5	29.8
57-58 —St. Louis	11	430	90	230	.391	86	118	.729	181	20	31	0	266	16.5	1.8	24.2
58-59 —St. Louis	6	257	58	137	.423	51	65	.785	75	14	20	0	167	12.5	2.3	27.8
59-60 —St. Louis	14	576	129	292	.442	107	142	.754	221	52	43	1	365	15.8	3.7	26.1
60-61 —St. Louis	12	526	117	284	.412	109	144	.757	211	38	42	0	343	17.6	3.2	28.6
62-63 —St. Louis	11	463	119	259	.459	112	144	.778	166	33	34	0	350	15.1	3.0	31.8
63-64 —St. Louis	12	494	93	226	.412	66	79	.835	174	33	44	0	252	14.5	2.8	21.0
64-65 —St. Louis	4	95	15	41	.366	16	20	.800	24	8	10	0	46	6.0	2.0	11.5
Totals.............................	88	3545	766	1834	.418	708	915	.774	1304	241	277	1	2240	14.8	2.7	25.5

NBA ALL-STAR GAME RECORD

NOTES: NBA All-Star Game Most Valuable Player (1956, 1958, 1962). ... NBA All-Star Game co-Most Valuable Player (1959). ... Holds single-game records for most rebounds—27; and most rebounds in one quarter—10 (1962). ... Shares single-game record for most rebounds in one half—16 (1962).

Season	Team	Min.	FGM	FGA	Pct.	FTM	FTA	Pct.	Reb	Ast.	PF	Dq.	Pts.
1955	—Milwaukee	27	3	14	.214	2	4	.500	9	2	0	0	8
1956	—St. Louis	31	7	17	.412	6	7	.857	24	7	4	0	20
1957	—St. Louis	31	8	18	.444	5	6	.833	11	2	2	0	21
1958	—St. Louis	38	10	21	.476	8	10	.800	26	1	1	0	28
1959	—St. Louis	34	8	21	.381	9	9	1.000	16	5	1	0	25
1960	—St. Louis	28	4	15	.267	3	6	.500	14	2	2	0	11
1961	—St. Louis	32	13	22	.591	3	7	.429	9	0	2	0	29
1962	—St. Louis	37	10	20	.500	5	5	1.000	27	2	5	0	25
1963	—St. Louis	32	7	16	.438	11	12	.917	13	0	1	0	25
1964	—St. Louis	36	6	15	.400	7	9	.778	17	2	3	0	19
1965	—St. Louis	34	5	14	.357	3	5	.600	12	0	4	0	13
Totals		360	81	193	.420	62	80	.775	178	23	25	0	224

NBA COACHING RECORD

		REGULAR SEASON					PLAYOFFS		
Season	Team	W	L	Pct.	Finish	W	L	Pct.
61-62	—St. Louis	4	2	.667	4th/Western Division	—	—	—

NOTES:
1962—Replaced Paul Seymour (5-9) and Andrew Levane (20-40) as St. Louis head coach (March), with record of 25-49.

POLLARD, JIM   F

PERSONAL: Born July 9, 1922, in Oakland. ... 6-5/185. ... Full name: James Clifford Pollard. ... Died January 22, 1993. ... Nickname: The Kangaroo Kid.
HIGH SCHOOL: Oakland Technical.
COLLEGE: Stanford.
TRANSACTIONS/CAREER NOTES: Signed by Minneapolis Lakers of National Basketball League (1947). ... Lakers franchise transferred to Basketball Association of America for 1948-49 season.
CAREER HONORS: Elected to Naismith Memorial Basketball Hall of Fame (1977).
MISCELLANEOUS: Member of NBA championship teams (1950, 1952, 1953, 1954). ... Member of BAA championship team (1949). ... Member of NBL championship team (1948).

COLLEGIATE RECORD

NOTES: Member of NCAA Division I championship team (1942). ... In military service during 1942-43, 1943-44 and 1944-45 seasons; played with Alameda, Calif. Coast Guard team.

Season Team	G	Min.	FGM	FGA	Pct.	FTM	FTA	Pct.	Reb.	Ast.	Pts.	RPG	APG	PPG
40-41—Stanford‡						Freshman team statistics unavailable.								
41-42—Stanford	23	...	103	...	...	35	48	.729	...	...	241	...	...	10.5
Varsity totals	23	...	103	...	...	35	48	.729	...	...	241	...	...	10.5

ABL REGULAR-SEASON RECORD

| | | | | | | | | | | | | AVERAGES | | |
Season Team	G	Min.	FGM	FGA	Pct.	FTM	FTA	Pct.	Reb.	Ast.	Pts.	RPG	APG	PPG
45-46—San Diego Dons	15	...	84	...	...	55	...	...	...	...	*223	...	...	14.9
46-47—Oakland Bittners	20	...	113	...	...	53	...	...	...	...	*279	...	...	14.0
Totals	35	...	197	...	...	108	...	...	...	...	502	...	...	14.3

NBL AND NBA REGULAR-SEASON RECORD

HONORS: All-NBA first team (1950). ... All-NBA second team (1952, 1954). ... All-BAA first team (1949).

| | | | | | | | | | | | | | AVERAGES | | |
Season Team	G	Min.	FGM	FGA	Pct.	FTM	FTA	Pct.	Reb.	Ast.	PF	Dq.	Pts.	RPG	APG	PPG
47-48—Minn. (NBL)	59	...	310	...	...	140	207	.676	...	...	147	...	760	...	...	12.9
48-49—Minneapolis (BAA)	53	...	314	792	.396	156	227	.687	...	142	144	...	784	...	2.7	14.8
49-50—Minneapolis	66	...	394	1140	.346	185	242	.764	...	252	143	...	973	...	3.8	14.7
50-51—Minneapolis	54	...	256	728	.352	117.	156	.750	484	184	157	4	629	9.0	3.4	11.6
51-52—Minneapolis	65	2545	411	1155	.356	183	260	.704	593	234	199	4	1005	9.1	3.6	15.5
52-53—Minneapolis	66	2403	333	933	.357	193	251	.769	452	231	194	3	859	6.8	3.5	13.0
53-54—Minneapolis	71	2483	326	882	.370	179	230	.778	500	214	161	0	831	7.0	3.0	11.7
54-55—Minneapolis	63	1960	265	749	.354	151	186	.812	458	160	147	3	681	7.3	2.5	10.8
Totals	497	...	2609	...	...	1304	1759	.741	...	...	1292	...	6522	...	...	13.1

NBL AND NBA PLAYOFF RECORD

| | | | | | | | | | | | | | AVERAGES | | |
Season Team	G	Min.	FGM	FGA	Pct.	FTM	FTA	Pct.	Reb.	Ast.	PF	Dq.	Pts.	RPG	APG	PPG
47-48—Minn. (NBL)	10	...	48	...	...	27	41	.659	...	...	...	...	123	...	...	12.3
48-49—Minneapolis (BAA)	10	...	43	147	.293	44	62	.710	...	39	31	...	130	...	3.9	13.0
49-50—Minneapolis	12	...	50	175	.286	44	62	.710	...	56	36	...	144	...	4.7	12.0
50-51—Minneapolis	7	...	35	108	.324	25	30	.833	62	27	27	1	95	8.9	3.9	13.6
51-52—Minneapolis	11	469	70	173	.405	37	50	.740	71	33	34	1	177	6.5	3.0	16.1
52-53—Minneapolis	12	455	62	167	.371	48	62	.774	86	49	37	2	172	7.2	4.1	14.3
53-54—Minneapolis	13	543	56	155	.361	48	60	.800	110	41	27	0	160	8.5	3.2	12.3
54-55—Minneapolis	7	257	33	104	.317	33	46	.717	78	14	13	0	99	11.1	2.0	14.1
Totals	82	...	397	...	...	306	413	.741	...	...	...	...	1100	...	...	13.4

NBA ALL-STAR GAME RECORD

Season	Team	Min.	FGM	FGA	Pct.	FTM	FTA	Pct.	Reb.	Ast.	PF	Dq.	Pts.
1951	—Minneapolis	...	2	11	.182	0	0	...	4	5	1	0	4
1952	—Minneapolis	29	2	17	.118	0	0	...	11	5	3	0	4
1954	—Minneapolis	41	10	22	.455	3	5	.600	3	3	3	0	23
1955	—Minneapolis	27	7	19	.368	3	3	1.000	4	0	1	0	17
	Totals	...	21	69	.304	6	8	.750	22	13	8	0	48

COLLEGIATE COACHING RECORD

Season	Team	W	L	Pct.
55-56	—LaSalle	15	10	.600
56-57	—LaSalle	17	9	.654
57-58	—LaSalle	16	9	.640
	Totals (3 years)	48	28	.632

NBA COACHING RECORD

Season	Team	REGULAR SEASON				PLAYOFFS		
		W	L	Pct.	Finish	W	L	Pct.
59-60	—Minneapolis	14	25	.359	3rd/Western Division	5	4	.556
61-62	—Chicago	18	62	.225	5th/Western Division	—	—	—
	Totals (2 years)	32	87	.269	Totals (1 year)	5	4	.556

ABA COACHING RECORD

Season	Team	REGULAR SEASON				PLAYOFFS		
		W	L	Pct.	Finish	W	L	Pct.
67-68	—Minnesota	50	28	.641	2nd/Eastern Division	4	6	.400
68-69	—Miami	43	35	.551	2nd/Eastern Division	5	7	.417
69-70	—Miami	5	15	.250		—	—	—
	Totals (3 years)	98	78	.557	Totals (2 years)	9	13	.409

NOTES:

1960—Replaced John Castellani as Minneapolis head coach (January 2), with 11-25 record. Defeated Detroit, 2-0, in Western Division semifinals; lost to St. Louis, 4-3, in Western Division finals.

1968—Defeated Kentucky, 3-2, in Eastern Division semifinals; lost to Pittsburgh, 4-1, in Eastern Division finals. Minnesota Muskies franchise moved to Miami and renamed the Floridians for 1968-69 season.

1969—Defeated Minnesota, 4-3, in Eastern Division semifinals; lost to Indiana, 4-1, in Eastern Division finals. Replaced as Miami head coach by Hal Blitman (November).

REED, WILLIS   C/F

PERSONAL: Born June 25, 1942, in Hico, La. ... 6-10/240. ... Full name: Willis Reed Jr.
HIGH SCHOOL: West Side (Lillie, La.).
COLLEGE: Grambling State.
TRANSACTIONS/CAREER NOTES: Selected by New York Knicks in second round (10th pick overall) of 1964 NBA Draft.
CAREER HONORS: Elected to Naismith Memorial Basketball Hall of Fame (1981).
MISCELLANEOUS: Member of NBA championship teams (1970, 1973).

COLLEGIATE RECORD

NOTES: Member of NAIA championship team (1961). ... Elected to NAIA Basketball Hall of Fame (1970).

Season Team	G	Min.	FGM	FGA	Pct.	FTM	FTA	Pct.	Reb.	Ast.	Pts.	RPG	APG	PPG
60-61—Grambling State	35	...	146	239	.611	86	122	.705	312	...	378	8.9	...	10.8
61-62—Grambling State	26	...	189	323	.585	80	102	.784	380	...	458	14.6	...	17.6
62-63—Grambling State	33	...	282	489	.577	135	177	.763	563	...	699	17.1	...	21.2
63-64—Grambling State	28	...	301	486	.619	143	199	.719	596	...	745	21.3	...	26.6
Totals	122	...	918	1537	.597	444	600	.740	1851	...	2280	15.2	...	18.7

NBA REGULAR-SEASON RECORD

HONORS: NBA Most Valuable Player (1970). ... NBA Rookie of the Year (1965). ... All-NBA first team (1970). ... All-NBA second team (1967, 1968, 1969, 1971). ... NBA All-Defensive first team (1970). ... NBA All-Rookie team (1965).

Season Team	G	Min.	FGM	FGA	Pct.	FTM	FTA	Pct.	Reb.	Ast.	PF	Dq.	Pts.	RPG	APG	PPG
64-65—New York	80	3042	629	1457	.432	302	407	.742	1175	133	339	14	1560	14.7	1.7	19.5
65-66—New York	76	2537	438	1009	.434	302	399	.757	883	91	323	13	1178	11.6	1.2	15.5
66-67—New York	78	2824	635	1298	.489	358	487	.735	1136	126	293	9	1628	14.6	1.6	20.9
67-68—New York	81	2879	659	1346	.490	367	509	.721	1073	159	343	12	1685	13.2	2.0	20.8
68-69—New York	82	3108	704	1351	.521	325	435	.747	1191	190	314	7	1733	14.5	2.3	21.1
69-70—New York	81	3089	702	1385	.507	351	464	.756	1126	161	287	2	1755	13.9	2.0	21.7
70-71—New York	73	2855	614	1330	.462	299	381	.785	1003	148	228	1	1527	13.7	2.0	20.9
71-72—New York	11	363	60	137	.438	27	39	.692	96	22	30	0	147	8.7	2.0	13.4
72-73—New York	69	1876	334	705	.474	92	124	.742	590	126	205	0	760	8.6	1.8	11.0

Season Team	G	Min.	FGM	FGA	Pct.	FTM	FTA	Pct.	REBOUNDS			Ast.	St.	Blk.	TO	Pts.	RPG	APG	PPG
									Off.	Def.	Tot.								
73-74—New York	19	500	84	184	.457	42	53	.792	47	94	141	30	12	21	...	210	7.4	1.6	11.1
Totals	650	23073	4859	10202	.476	2465	3298	.747	...	...	8414	1186	12	21	...	12183	12.9	1.8	18.7

Personal fouls/disqualifications: 1973-74, 49/0.

NBA PLAYOFF RECORD

NOTES: NBA Finals Most Valuable Player (1970, 1973).

Season Team	G	Min.	FGM	FGA	Pct.	FTM	FTA	Pct.	Reb.	Ast.	PF	Dq.	Pts.	AVERAGES RPG	APG	PPG
66-67 —New York	4	148	43	80	.538	24	25	.960	55	7	19	1	110	13.8	1.8	27.5
67-68 —New York	6	210	53	98	.541	22	30	.733	62	11	24	1	128	10.3	1.8	21.3
68-69 —New York	10	429	101	198	.510	55	70	.786	141	19	40	1	257	14.1	1.9	25.7
69-70 —New York	18	732	178	378	.471	70	95	.737	248	51	60	0	426	13.8	2.8	23.7
70-71 —New York	12	504	81	196	.413	26	39	.667	144	27	41	0	188	12.0	2.3	15.7
72-73 —New York	17	486	97	208	.466	18	21	.857	129	30	65	1	212	7.6	1.8	12.5

Season Team	G	Min.	FGM	FGA	Pct.	FTM	FTA	Pct.	REBOUNDS Off.	Def.	Tot.	Ast.	St.	Blk.	TO	Pts.	AVERAGES RPG	APG	PPG
73-74—New York	11	132	17	45	.378	3	5	.600	4	18	22	4	2	0	...	37	2.0	0.4	3.4
Totals	78	2641	570	1203	.474	218	285	.765	...	...	801	149	2	0	...	1358	10.3	1.9	17.4

Personal fouls/disqualifications: 1973-74, 26/0.

NOTES: NBA All-Star Game Most Valuable Player (1970).

NBA ALL-STAR GAME RECORD

Season Team	Min.	FGM	FGA	Pct.	FTM	FTA	Pct.	Reb.	Ast.	PF	Dq.	Pts.
1965 —New York	25	3	11	.273	1	2	.500	5	1	2	0	7
1966 —New York	23	7	11	.636	2	2	1.000	8	1	3	0	16
1967 —New York	17	2	6	.333	0	0	...	9	1	0	0	4
1968 —New York	25	7	14	.500	2	3	.667	8	1	4	0	16
1969 —New York	14	5	8	.625	0	0	...	4	2	2	0	10
1970 —New York	30	9	18	.500	3	3	1.000	11	0	6	1	21
1971 —New York	27	5	16	.313	4	6	.667	13	1	3	0	14
Totals	161	38	84	.452	12	16	.750	58	7	20	1	88

HEAD COACHING RECORD

BACKGROUND: Volunteer assistant, St. John's University (1980-81). ... Assistant coach, Atlanta Hawks (1985-86 and 1986-87). ... Assistant coach, Sacramento Kings (1987-88). ... General manager/vice president of basketball operations, New Jersey Nets (1988-89 to 1995-96). ... Senior vice president/Player development and scouting (1996-97 season).

NBA COACHING RECORD

Season Team	REGULAR SEASON W	L	Pct.	Finish	PLAYOFFS W	L	Pct.
77-78 —New York	43	39	.524	2nd/Atlantic Division	2	4	.333
78-79 —New York	6	8	.429		—	—	—
87-88 —New Jersey	7	21	.250	5th/Atlantic Division	—	—	—
88-89 —New Jersey	26	56	.317	5th/Atlantic Division	—	—	—
Totals (4 years)	82	124	.398	Totals (1 year)	2	4	.333

COLLEGIATE COACHING RECORD

Season Team	W	L	Pct.	Finish
81-82 —Creighton	7	20	.259	8th/Missouri Valley Conference
82-83 —Creighton	8	19	.296	10th/Missouri Valley Conference
83-84 —Creighton	17	14	.548	4th/Missouri Valley Conference
84-85 —Creighton	20	11	.645	4th/Missouri Valley Conference
Totals (4 years)	52	64	.448	

NOTES:

1978—Defeated Cleveland, 2-0, in Eastern Conference first round; lost to Philadelphia, 4-0, in Eastern Conference semifinals. Replaced as New York head coach by Red Holzman (November).

1984—Lost to Nebraska, 56-54, in NIT first round.

1988—Replaced interim head coach Bob MacKinnon as New Jersey head coach (February 29), with record of 12-42.

ROBERTSON, OSCAR   G

PERSONAL: Born November 24, 1938, in Charlotte, Tenn. ... 6-5/220. ... Full name: Oscar Palmer Robertson. ... Nickname: Big O.

HIGH SCHOOL: Crispus Attucks (Indianapolis).

COLLEGE: Cincinnati.

TRANSACTIONS/CAREER NOTES: Selected by Cincinnati Royals in 1960 NBA Draft (territorial pick). ... Traded by Royals to Milwaukee Bucks for G Flynn Robinson and F Charlie Paulk (April 21, 1970).

CAREER HONORS: Elected to Naismith Memorial Basketball Hall of Fame (1979). ... NBA 35th Anniversary All-Time Team (1980).

MISCELLANEOUS: Member of NBA championship team (1971). ... Member of gold-medal-winning U.S. Olympic team (1960). ... Sacramento Kings franchise all-time leading scorer with 22,009 points and all-time assists leader with 7,731 (1960-61 through 1969-70).

COLLEGIATE RECORD

NOTES: THE SPORTING NEWS College Player of the Year (1958, 1959, 1960). ... THE SPORTING NEWS All-America first team (1958, 1959, 1960). ... Led NCAA Division I with 35.1 points per game (1958), 32.6 points per game (1959) and 33.7 points per game (1960).

Season Team	G	Min.	FGM	FGA	Pct.	FTM	FTA	Pct.	Reb.	Ast.	Pts.	AVERAGES RPG	APG	PPG
56-57—Cincinnati‡	13	...	151	...	...	127	178	.713	...	...	429	...	...	33.0
57-58—Cincinnati	28	1085	352	617	.571	280	355	.789	425	...	984	15.2	...	35.1
58-59—Cincinnati	30	1172	331	650	.509	316	398	.794	489	206	978	16.3	6.9	32.6
59-60—Cincinnati	30	1155	369	701	.526	273	361	.756	424	219	1011	14.1	7.3	33.7
Varsity totals	88	3412	1052	1968	.535	869	1114	.780	1338	...	2973	15.2	...	33.8

NBA REGULAR-SEASON RECORD

RECORDS: Shares single-game record for most free throws attempted in one quarter—16 (December 27, 1964, vs. Baltimore).

HONORS: NBA Most Valuable Player (1964). ... NBA Rookie of the Year (1961). ... All-NBA first team (1961, 1962, 1963, 1964, 1965, 1966, 1967, 1968, 1969). ... All-NBA second team (1970, 1971).

Season Team	G	Min.	FGM	FGA	Pct.	FTM	FTA	Pct.	Reb.	Ast.	PF	Dq.	Pts.	AVERAGES		
														RPG	APG	PPG
60-61 —Cincinnati	71	3012	756	1600	.473	653	794	.822	716	*690	219	3	2165	10.1	*9.7	30.5
61-62 —Cincinnati	79	3503	866	1810	.478	700	872	.803	985	*899	258	1	2432	12.5	*11.4	30.8
62-63 —Cincinnati	80	3521	825	1593	.518	614	758	.810	835	758	293	1	2264	10.4	9.5	28.3
63-64 —Cincinnati	79	3559	840	1740	.483	*800	938	*.853	783	*868	280	3	2480	9.9	*11.0	31.4
64-65 —Cincinnati	75	3421	807	1681	.480	*665	793	.839	674	*861	205	2	2279	9.0	*11.5	30.4
65-66 —Cincinnati	76	3493	818	1723	.475	742	881	.842	586	*847	227	1	2378	7.7	*11.1	31.3
66-67 —Cincinnati	79	3468	838	1699	.493	736	843	.873	486	845	226	2	2412	6.2	*10.7	30.5
67-68 —Cincinnati	65	2765	660	1321	.500	*576	660	*.873	391	633	199	2	1896	6.0	*9.7	*29.2
68-69 —Cincinnati	79	3461	656	1351	.486	*643	767	.838	502	*772	231	2	1955	6.4	*9.8	24.7
69-70 —Cincinnati	69	2865	647	1267	.511	454	561	.809	422	558	175	1	1748	6.1	8.1	25.3
70-71 —Milwaukee	81	3194	592	1193	.496	385	453	.850	462	668	203	0	1569	5.7	8.2	19.4
71-72 —Milwaukee	64	2390	419	887	.472	276	330	.836	323	491	116	0	1114	5.0	7.7	17.4
72-73 —Milwaukee	73	2737	446	983	.454	238	281	.847	360	551	167	0	1130	4.9	7.5	15.5

Season Team	G	Min.	FGM	FGA	Pct.	FTM	FTA	Pct.	REBOUNDS			Ast.	St.	Blk.	TO	Pts.	AVERAGES		
									Off.	Def.	Tot.						RPG	APG	PPG
73-74 —Milwaukee	70	2477	338	772	.438	212	254	.835	71	208	279	446	77	4	...	888	4.0	6.4	12.7
Totals	1040	43866	9508	19620	.485	7694	9185	.838	...	...	7804	9887	77	4	...	26710	7.5	9.5	25.7

Personal fouls/disqualifications: 1973-74, 132/0.

NBA PLAYOFF RECORD

Season Team	G	Min.	FGM	FGA	Pct.	FTM	FTA	Pct.	Reb.	Ast.	PF	Dq.	Pts.	AVERAGES		
														RPG	APG	PPG
61-62 —Cincinnati	4	185	42	81	.519	31	39	.795	44	44	18	1	115	11.0	11.0	28.8
62-63 —Cincinnati	12	570	124	264	.470	133	154	.864	156	108	41	0	381	13.0	9.0	31.8
63-64 —Cincinnati	10	471	92	202	.455	109	127	.858	89	84	30	0	293	8.9	8.4	29.3
64-65 —Cincinnati	4	195	38	89	.427	36	39	.923	19	48	14	0	112	4.8	12.0	28.0
65-66 —Cincinnati	5	224	49	120	.408	61	68	.897	38	39	20	1	159	7.6	7.8	31.8
66-67 —Cincinnati	4	183	33	64	.516	33	37	.892	16	45	9	0	99	4.0	11.3	24.8
70-71 —Milwaukee	14	520	102	210	.486	52	69	.754	70	124	39	0	256	5.0	8.9	18.3
71-72 —Milwaukee	11	380	57	140	.407	30	36	.833	64	83	29	0	144	5.8	7.5	13.1
72-73 —Milwaukee	6	256	48	96	.500	31	34	.912	28	45	21	1	127	4.7	7.5	21.2

Season Team	G	Min.	FGM	FGA	Pct.	FTM	FTA	Pct.	REBOUNDS			Ast.	St.	Blk.	TO	Pts.	AVERAGES		
									Off.	Def.	Tot.						RPG	APG	PPG
73-74 —Milwaukee	16	689	90	200	.450	44	52	.846	15	39	54	149	15	4	...	224	3.4	9.3	14.0
Totals	86	3673	675	1466	.460	560	655	.855	...	...	578	769	15	4	...	1910	6.7	8.9	22.2

Personal fouls/disqualifications: 1973-74, 46/0.

NBA ALL-STAR GAME RECORD

NOTES: NBA All-Star Game Most Valuable Player (1961, 1964, 1969). ... Shares career record for most free throws attempted—98. ... Shares single-game record for most free throws made—12 (1965).

Season Team	Min.	FGM	FGA	Pct.	FTM	FTA	Pct.	Reb	Ast.	PF	Dq.	Pts.
1961 —Cincinnati	34	8	13	.615	7	9	.778	9	14	5	0	23
1962 —Cincinnati	37	9	20	.450	8	14	.571	7	13	3	0	26
1963 —Cincinnati	37	9	15	.600	3	4	.750	3	6	5	0	21
1964 —Cincinnati	42	10	23	.435	6	10	.600	14	8	4	0	26
1965 —Cincinnati	40	8	18	.444	12	13	.923	6	8	5	0	28
1966 —Cincinnati	25	6	12	.500	5	6	.833	10	8	0	0	17
1967 —Cincinnati	34	9	20	.450	8	10	.800	2	5	4	0	26
1968 —Cincinnati	22	7	9	.778	4	7	.571	1	5	2	0	18
1969 —Cincinnati	32	8	16	.500	8	8	1.000	6	5	3	0	24
1970 —Cincinnati	29	9	11	.818	3	4	.750	6	4	3	0	21
1971 —Milwaukee	24	2	6	.333	1	3	.333	2	2	3	0	5
1972 —Milwaukee	24	3	9	.333	5	10	.500	3	3	4	0	11
Totals	380	88	172	.512	70	98	.714	69	81	41	0	246

RODGERS, GUY   G

PERSONAL: Born September 1, 1935, in Philadelphia. ... 6-0/185. ... Full name: Guy William Rodgers Jr.
HIGH SCHOOL: Northeast (Philadelphia).
COLLEGE: Temple.
TRANSACTIONS/CAREER NOTES: Selected by Philadelphia Warriors in 1958 NBA Draft (territorial pick). ... Warriors franchise moved from Philadelphia to San Francisco for 1962-63 season. ... Traded by Warriors to Chicago Bulls for draft choice, cash and two players to be named later (September 7, 1966); G Jim King and G Jeff Mullins sent to Warriors to complete deal. ... Traded by Bulls to Cincinnati Royals for G Flynn Robinson, cash and two future draft choices (October 20, 1967). ... Selected by Milwaukee Bucks from Royals in NBA expansion draft (May 6, 1968).
MISCELLANEOUS: Golden State Warriors franchise all-time assists leader with 4,855 (1958-59 through 1965-66).

COLLEGIATE RECORD

NOTES: THE SPORTING NEWS All-America first team (1958).

Season Team	G	Min.	FGM	FGA	Pct.	FTM	FTA	Pct.	Reb.	Ast.	Pts.	AVERAGES		
												RPG	APG	PPG
54-55 —Temple‡	15	...	...	...	...	...	...	...	...	...	278	...	...	18.5
55-56 —Temple	31	...	243	552	.440	87	155	.561	186	...	573	6.0	...	18.5
56-57 —Temple	29	...	216	565	.382	159	224	.710	202	...	591	7.0	...	20.4
57-58 —Temple	30	...	249	564	.441	105	171	.614	199	...	603	6.6	...	20.1
Varsity totals	90	...	708	1681	.421	351	550	.638	587	...	1767	6.5	...	19.6

NBA REGULAR-SEASON RECORD

Season Team	G	Min.	FGM	FGA	Pct.	FTM	FTA	Pct.	Reb.	Ast.	PF	Dq.	Pts.	AVERAGES RPG	APG	PPG
58-59 —Philadelphia	45	1565	211	535	.394	61	112	.545	281	261	132	1	483	6.2	5.8	10.7
59-60 —Philadelphia	68	2483	338	870	.389	111	181	.613	391	482	196	3	787	5.8	7.1	11.6
60-61 —Philadelphia	78	2905	397	1029	.386	206	300	.687	509	677	262	3	1000	6.5	8.7	12.8
61-62 —Philadelphia	80	2650	267	749	.356	121	182	.665	348	643	312	12	655	4.4	8.0	8.2
62-63 —San Fran.	79	3249	445	1150	.387	208	286	.727	394	*825	296	7	1098	5.0	*10.4	13.9
63-64 —San Fran.	79	2695	337	923	.365	198	280	.707	328	556	245	4	872	4.2	7.0	11.0
64-65 —San Fran.	79	2699	465	1225	.380	223	325	.686	323	565	256	4	1153	4.1	7.2	14.6
65-66 —San Fran.	79	2902	586	1571	.373	296	407	.727	421	846	241	6	1468	5.3	10.7	18.6
66-67 —Chicago	81	3063	538	1377	.391	383	475	.806	346	*908	243	1	1459	4.3	*11.2	18.0
67-68 —Chi.-Cin.	79	1546	148	426	.347	107	133	.805	150	380	167	1	403	1.9	4.8	5.1
68-69 —Milwaukee	81	2157	325	862	.377	184	232	.793	226	561	207	2	834	2.8	6.9	10.3
69-70 —Milwaukee	64	749	68	191	.356	67	90	.744	74	213	73	1	203	1.2	3.3	3.2
Totals	892	28663	4125	10908	.378	2165	3003	.721	3791	6917	2630	45	10415	4.3	7.8	11.7

NBA PLAYOFF RECORD

Season Team	G	Min.	FGM	FGA	Pct.	FTM	FTA	Pct.	Reb.	Ast.	PF	Dq.	Pts.	AVERAGES RPG	APG	PPG
59-60 —Philadelphia	9	370	49	136	.360	20	36	.556	77	54	39	3	118	8.6	6.0	13.1
60-61 —Philadelphia	3	121	21	57	.368	11	20	.550	21	15	16	2	53	7.0	5.0	17.7
61-62 —Philadelphia	13	482	52	145	.359	35	55	.636	7	88	57	3	139	0.5	6.8	10.7
63-64 —San Fran.	12	419	57	173	.329	33	47	.702	58	90	46	1	147	4.8	7.5	12.3
66-67 —Chicago	3	97	15	40	.375	4	5	.800	6	18	11	0	34	2.0	6.0	11.3
69-70 —Milwaukee	7	68	4	14	.286	9	12	.750	4	21	7	0	17	0.6	3.0	2.4
Totals	47	1557	198	565	.350	112	175	.640	173	286	176	9	508	3.7	6.1	10.8

NBA ALL-STAR GAME RECORD

Season Team	Min.	FGM	FGA	Pct.	FTM	FTA	Pct.	Reb	Ast.	PF	Dq.	Pts.
1963 —San Francisco	17	3	6	.500	1	2	.500	2	4	2	0	7
1964 —San Francisco	22	3	6	.500	0	0	...	2	2	4	0	6
1966 —San Francisco	34	4	11	.364	0	0	...	7	11	4	0	8
1967 —Chicago	28	0	4	.000	1	1	1.000	2	8	3	0	1
Totals	101	10	27	.370	2	3	.667	13	25	13	0	22

RUSSELL, BILL   C

PERSONAL: Born February 12, 1934, in Monroe, La. ... 6-10/220. ... Full name: William Felton Russell.
HIGH SCHOOL: McClymonds (Oakland, Calif.).
COLLEGE: San Francisco.
TRANSACTIONS/CAREER NOTES: Selected by St. Louis Hawks in first round (third pick overall) of 1956 NBA Draft. ... Draft rights traded by Hawks to Boston Celtics for F/C Ed Macauley and draft rights to F Cliff Hagan (April 29, 1956).
CAREER HONORS: Elected to Naismith Memorial Basketball Hall of Fame (1974). ... Declared Greatest Player in the History of the NBA by Professional Basketball Writers' Association of America (1980). ... NBA 25th Anniversary All-Time Team (1970) and 35th Anniversary All-Time Team (1980).
MISCELLANEOUS: Member of NBA championship teams (1957, 1959, 1960, 1961, 1962, 1963, 1964, 1965, 1966, 1968, 1969). ... Member of gold-medal-winning U.S. Olympic team (1956). ... Boston Celtics all-time leading rebounder with 21,620 (1956-57 through 1968-69).

COLLEGIATE RECORD
NOTES: NCAA Tournament Most Outstanding Player (1955). ... Member of NCAA championship teams (1955, 1956).

Season Team	G	Min.	FGM	FGA	Pct.	FTM	FTA	Pct.	Reb.	Ast.	Pts.	AVERAGES RPG	APG	PPG
52-53—San Francisco‡	23	...	...	...	...	...	...	...	...	...	461	...	...	20.0
53-54—San Francisco	21	...	150	309	.485	117	212	.552	403	...	417	19.2	...	19.9
54-55—San Francisco	29	...	229	423	.541	164	278	.590	594	...	622	20.5	...	21.4
55-56—San Francisco	29	...	246	480	.513	105	212	.495	609	...	597	21.0	...	20.6
Varsity totals	79	...	625	1212	.516	386	702	.550	1606	...	1636	20.3	...	20.7·

NBA REGULAR-SEASON RECORD
RECORDS: Holds single-game record for most rebounds in one half—32 (November 16, 1957, vs. Philadelphia).
HONORS: NBA Most Valuable Player (1958, 1961, 1962, 1963, 1965). ... All-NBA first team (1959, 1963, 1965). ... All-NBA second team (1958, 1960, 1961, 1964, 1966, 1967, 1968). ... NBA All-Defensive first team (1969).

Season Team	G	Min.	FGM	FGA	Pct.	FTM	FTA	Pct.	Reb.	Ast.	PF	Dq.	Pts.	AVERAGES RPG	APG	PPG
56-57 —Boston	48	1695	277	649	.427	152	309	.492	943	88	143	2	706	*19.6	1.8	14.7
57-58 —Boston	69	2640	456	1032	.442	230	443	.519	*1564	202	181	2	1142	*22.7	2.9	16.6
58-59 —Boston	70	*2979	456	997	.457	256	428	.598	*1612	222	161	3	1168	*23.0	3.2	16.7
59-60 —Boston	74	3146	555	1189	.467	240	392	.612	1778	277	210	0	1350	24.0	3.7	18.2
60-61 —Boston	78	3458	532	1250	.426	258	469	.550	1868	268	155	0	1322	23.9	3.4	16.9
61-62 —Boston	76	3433	575	1258	.457	286	481	.595	1790	341	207	3	1436	23.6	4.5	18.9
62-63 —Boston	78	3500	511	1182	.432	287	517	.555	1843	348	189	1	1309	23.6	4.5	16.8
63-64 —Boston	78	3482	466	1077	.433	236	429	.550	1930	370	190	0	1168	*24.7	4.7	15.0
64-65 —Boston	78	*3466	429	980	.438	244	426	.573	*1878	410	204	1	1102	*24.1	5.3	14.1
65-66 —Boston	78	3386	391	943	.415	223	405	.551	1779	371	221	4	1005	22.8	4.8	12.9
66-67 —Boston	81	3297	395	870	.454	285	467	.610	1700	472	258	4	1075	21.0	5.8	13.3
67-68 —Boston	78	2953	365	858	.425	247	460	.537	1451	357	242	2	977	18.6	4.6	12.5
68-69 —Boston	77	3291	279	645	.433	204	388	.526	1484	374	231	2	762	19.3	4.9	9.9
Totals	963	40726	5687	12930	.440	3148	5614	.561	21620	4100	2592	24	14522	22.5	4.3	15.1

NBA PLAYOFF RECORD

NOTES: Holds career playoff record for most rebounds—4,104. ... Holds NBA Finals records for highest rebounds-per-game average—29.5 (1959); and highest rebounds-per-game average by a rookie—22.9 (1957). ... Holds NBA Finals single-game records for most free throws attempted in one half—15 (April 11, 1961, vs. St. Louis); most rebounds—40 (March 29, 1960, vs. St. Louis and April 18, 1962, vs. Los Angeles); most rebounds by a rookie—32 (April 13, 1957, vs. St. Louis); and most rebounds in one quarter—19 (April 18, 1962, vs. Los Angeles).

Season Team	G	Min.	FGM	FGA	Pct.	FTM	FTA	Pct.	Reb.	Ast.	PF	Dq.	Pts.	RPG	APG	PPG
56-57 —Boston	10	409	54	148	.365	31	61	.508	244	32	41	1	139	24.4	3.2	13.9
57-58 —Boston	9	355	48	133	.361	40	66	.606	221	24	24	0	136	24.6	2.7	15.1
58-59 —Boston	11	496	65	159	.409	41	67	.612	305	40	28	1	171	27.7	3.6	15.5
59-60 —Boston	13	572	94	206	.456	53	75	.707	336	38	38	1	241	25.8	2.9	18.5
60-61 —Boston	10	462	73	171	.427	45	86	.523	299	48	24	0	191	29.9	4.8	19.1
61-62 —Boston	14	672	116	253	.459	82	113	.726	370	70	49	0	314	26.4	5.0	22.4
62-63 —Boston	13	617	96	212	.453	72	109	.661	326	66	36	0	264	25.1	5.1	20.3
63-64 —Boston	10	451	47	132	.356	37	67	.552	272	44	33	0	131	27.2	4.4	13.1
64-65 —Boston	12	561	79	150	.527	40	76	.526	302	76	43	2	198	25.2	6.3	16.5
65-66 —Boston	17	814	124	261	.475	76	123	.618	428	85	60	0	324	25.2	5.0	19.1
66-67 —Boston	9	390	31	86	.360	33	52	.635	198	50	32	1	95	22.0	5.6	10.6
67-68 —Boston	19	869	99	242	.409	76	130	.585	434	99	73	1	274	22.8	5.2	14.4
68-69 —Boston	18	829	77	182	.423	41	81	.506	369	98	65	1	195	20.5	5.4	10.8
Totals	165	7497	1003	2335	.430	667	1106	.603	4104	770	546	8	2673	24.9	4.7	16.2

NBA ALL-STAR GAME RECORD

NOTES: NBA All-Star Game Most Valuable Player (1963).

Season Team	Min.	FGM	FGA	Pct.	FTM	FTA	Pct.	Reb	Ast.	PF	Dq.	Pts.
1958 —Boston	26	5	12	.417	1	3	.333	11	2	5	0	11
1959 —Boston	27	3	10	.300	1	1	1.000	9	1	4	0	7
1960 —Boston	27	3	7	.429	0	2	.000	8	3	1	0	6
1961 —Boston	28	9	15	.600	6	8	.750	11	1	2	0	24
1962 —Boston	27	5	12	.417	2	3	.667	12	2	2	0	12
1963 —Boston	37	8	14	.571	3	4	.750	24	5	3	0	19
1964 —Boston	42	6	13	.462	1	2	.500	21	2	4	0	13
1965 —Boston	33	7	12	.583	3	9	.333	13	5	6	1	17
1966 —Boston	23	1	6	.167	0	0	...	10	2	2	0	2
1967 —Boston	22	1	2	.500	0	0	.500	5	5	2	0	2
1968 —Boston	23	2	4	.500	0	0	...	9	8	5	0	4
1969 —Boston	28	1	4	.250	1	2	.500	6	3	1	0	3
Totals	343	51	111	.459	18	34	.529	139	39	37	1	120

NBA COACHING RECORD

BACKGROUND: Player/head coach, Boston Celtics (1966-67 through 1968-69). ... Head coach/general manager, Seattle Supersonics (1973-74 through 1976-77).

Season Team	REGULAR SEASON				PLAYOFFS		
	W	L	Pct.	Finish	W	L	Pct.
66-67 —Boston	60	21	.741	2nd/Eastern Division	4	5	.444
67-68 —Boston	54	28	.659	2nd/Eastern Division	12	7	.632
68-69 —Boston	48	34	.585	4th/Eastern Division	12	6	.667
73-74 —Seattle	36	46	.439	3rd/Pacific Division	—	—	—
74-75 —Seattle	43	39	.524	2nd/Pacific Division	4	5	.444
75-76 —Seattle	43	39	.524	2nd/Pacific Division	2	4	.333
76-77 —Seattle	40	42	.488	4th/Pacific Division	—	—	—
87-88 —Sacramento	17	41	.293		—	—	—
Totals (8 years)	341	290	.540	Totals (5 years)	34	27	.557

NOTES:

1967—Defeated New York, 3-1, in Eastern Division semifinals; lost to Philadelphia, 4-1, in Eastern Division finals.

1968—Defeated Detroit, 4-2, in Eastern Division semifinals; defeated Philadelphia, 4-3, in Eastern Division finals; defeated Los Angeles, 4-2, in World Championship Series.

1969—Defeated Philadelphia, 4-1, in Eastern Division semifinals; defeated New York, 4-2, in Eastern Division finals; defeated Los Angeles, 4-3, in World Championship Series.

1975—Defeated Detroit, 2-1, in Western Conference first round; lost to Golden State, 4-2, in Western Conference semifinals.

1976—Lost to Phoenix in Western Conference semifinals.

1988—Replaced as Sacramento head coach by Jerry Reynolds (March 7).

DID YOU KNOW...

...that Oscar Robertson is the only player to record a triple-double in his first NBA game?
Magic Johnson did so in his fifth game; Damon Stoudamire his 11th.

SCHAYES, DOLPH　　　　　F/C

PERSONAL: Born May 19, 1928, in New York. ... 6-8/220. ... Full name: Adolph Schayes. ... Father of Dan Schayes, center with six NBA teams (1981-82 through 1995-96).
HIGH SCHOOL: DeWitt Clinton (Bronx, N.Y.).
COLLEGE: New York University.
TRANSACTIONS/CAREER NOTES: Selected by Tri-Cities Hawks in 1948 National Basketball League Draft. ... NBL draft rights obtained from Hawks by Syracuse Nationals (1948). ... Nationals franchise became part of NBA for 1949-50 season. ... Nationals franchise moved from Syracuse to Philadelphia and renamed 76ers for 1963-64 season.
CAREER HONORS: Elected to Naismith Memorial Basketball Hall of Fame (1972). ... NBA 25th Anniversary All-Time Team (1970).
MISCELLANEOUS: Member of NBA championship team (1955). ... Philadelphia 76ers franchise all-time leading rebounder with 11,256 (1948-49 through 1963-64).

COLLEGIATE RECORD

Season Team	G	Min.	FGM	FGA	Pct.	FTM	FTA	Pct.	Reb.	Ast.	Pts.	RPG	APG	PPG
44-45—New York U.	11	...	46	...	...	23	...	...	...	...	115	...	...	10.5
45-46—New York U.	22	...	54	...	...	41	...	...	...	...	149	...	...	6.8
46-47—New York U.	21	...	66	...	...	63	...	...	...	...	195	...	...	9.3
47-48—New York U.	26	...	124	...	...	108	...	...	...	...	356	...	...	13.7
Totals	80	...	290	...	...	235	...	...	...	...	815	...	...	10.2

NBL AND NBA REGULAR-SEASON RECORD

HONORS: All-NBA first team (1952, 1953, 1954, 1955, 1957, 1958). ... All-NBA second team (1950, 1951, 1956, 1959, 1960, 1961). ... NBL Rookie of the Year (1949).

Season Team	G	Min.	FGM	FGA	Pct.	FTM	FTA	Pct.	Reb.	Ast.	PF	Dq.	Pts.	RPG	APG	PPG
48-49—Syr. (NBL)	63	...	271	...	...	267	370	.722	...	...	232	...	809	...	...	12.8
49-50—Syracuse	64	...	348	903	.385	376	486	.774	...	259	225	...	1072	...	4.0	16.8
50-51—Syracuse	66	...	332	930	.357	457	608	.752	*1080	251	271	9	1121	*16.4	3.8	17.0
51-52—Syracuse	63	2004	263	740	.355	342	424	.807	773	182	213	5	868	12.3	2.9	13.8
52-53—Syracuse	71	2668	375	1002	.374	512	619	.827	920	227	271	9	1262	13.0	3.2	17.8
53-54—Syracuse	72	2655	370	973	.380	488	590	.827	870	214	232	4	1228	12.1	3.0	17.1
54-55—Syracuse	72	2526	422	1103	.383	489	587	.833	887	213	247	6	1333	12.3	3.0	18.5
55-56—Syracuse	72	2517	465	1202	.387	542	632	.858	891	200	251	9	1472	12.4	2.8	20.4
56-57—Syracuse	72	*2851	496	1308	.379	*625	691	.904	1008	229	219	5	1617	14.0	3.2	22.5
57-58—Syracuse	72	*2918	581	1458	.399	629	696	*.904	1022	224	244	6	1791	14.2	3.1	24.9
58-59—Syracuse	72	2645	504	1304	.387	526	609	.864	962	178	280	9	1534	13.4	2.5	21.3
59-60—Syracuse	75	2741	578	1440	.401	533	597	*.893	959	256	263	10	1689	12.8	3.4	22.5
60-61—Syracuse	79	3007	594	1595	.372	*680	783	.868	960	296	296	9	1868	12.2	3.7	23.6
61-62—Syracuse	56	1480	268	751	.357	286	319	*.897	439	120	167	4	822	7.8	2.1	14.7
62-63—Syracuse	66	1438	223	575	.388	181	206	.879	375	175	177	2	627	5.7	2.7	9.5
63-64—Philadelphia	24	350	44	143	.308	46	57	.807	110	48	76	3	134	4.6	2.0	5.6
Totals	1059	...	6134	...	...	6979	8274	.843	...	...	3664	...	19247	...	...	18.2

NBL AND NBA PLAYOFF RECORD

Season Team	G	Min.	FGM	FGA	Pct.	FTM	FTA	Pct.	Reb.	Ast.	PF	Dq.	Pts.	RPG	APG	PPG
48-49—Syr. (NBL)	6	...	27	...	...	32	42	.762	...	...	26	...	86	...	...	14.3
49-50—Syracuse	11	...	57	148	.385	74	101	.733	...	28	43	...	188	...	2.5	17.1
50-51—Syracuse	7	...	47	105	.448	49	64	.766	102	20	28	2	143	14.6	2.9	20.4
51-52—Syracuse	7	248	41	91	.451	60	78	.769	90	15	34	2	142	12.9	2.1	20.3
52-53—Syracuse	2	58	4	16	.250	10	13	.769	17	1	7	0	18	8.5	0.5	9.0
53-54—Syracuse	13	374	64	140	.457	80	108	.741	136	24	40	1	208	10.5	1.8	16.0
54-55—Syracuse	11	363	60	167	.359	89	106	.840	141	40	48	3	209	12.8	3.6	19.0
55-56—Syracuse	8	310	52	142	.366	73	83	.880	111	27	27	0	177	13.9	3.4	22.1
56-57—Syracuse	5	215	29	95	.305	49	55	.891	90	14	18	0	107	18.0	2.8	21.4
57-58—Syracuse	3	131	25	64	.391	30	36	.833	45	6	10	0	80	15.0	2.0	26.7
58-59—Syracuse	9	351	78	195	.400	98	107	.916	117	41	36	0	254	13.0	4.6	28.2
59-60—Syracuse	3	126	30	66	.455	28	30	.933	48	8	10	0	88	16.0	2.7	29.3
60-61—Syracuse	8	308	51	152	.336	63	70	.900	91	21	32	2	165	11.4	2.6	20.6
61-62—Syracuse	5	95	24	66	.364	9	13	.692	35	5	21	0	57	7.0	1.0	11.4
62-63—Syracuse	5	108	20	44	.455	11	12	.917	28	7	17	0	51	5.6	1.4	10.2
Totals	103	...	609	...	...	755	918	.822	...	...	397	...	1973	...	...	19.2

NBA ALL-STAR GAME RECORD

Season Team	Min.	FGM	FGA	Pct.	FTM	FTA	Pct.	Reb	Ast.	PF	Dq.	Pts.
1951—Syracuse	...	7	10	.700	1	2	.500	14	3	1	0	15
1952—Syracuse				Selected, did not play—injured.								
1953—Syracuse	26	2	7	.286	4	4	1.000	13	3	3	0	8
1954—Syracuse	24	1	3	.333	4	6	.667	12	1	1	0	6
1955—Syracuse	29	6	12	.500	3	3	1.000	13	1	4	0	15
1956—Syracuse	25	4	8	.500	6	10	.600	4	2	2	0	14
1957—Syracuse	25	4	6	.667	1	1	1.000	10	1	1	0	9
1958—Syracuse	39	6	15	.400	6	6	1.000	9	2	4	0	18
1959—Syracuse	22	3	14	.214	7	8	.875	13	1	6	1	13
1960—Syracuse	27	8	19	.421	3	3	1.000	10	0	3	0	19
1961—Syracuse	27	7	15	.467	7	7	1.000	6	3	4	0	21
1962—Syracuse	4	0	0	...	0	0	...	1	0	3	0	0
Totals	...	48	109	.440	42	50	.840	105	17	32	1	138

ALL-TIME GREAT PLAYERS

NBA COACHING RECORD

BACKGROUND: Player/head coach, Philadelphia 76ers (1963-64).
HONORS: NBA Coach of the Year (1966).

Season Team		W	L	Pct.	Finish		W	L	Pct.
				REGULAR SEASON				PLAYOFFS	
63-64 —Philadelphia		34	46	.425	3rd/Eastern Division		2	3	.400
64-65 —Philadelphia		40	40	.500	3rd/Eastern Division		6	5	.545
65-66 —Philadelphia		55	25	.688	1st/Eastern Division		1	4	.200
70-71 —Buffalo		22	60	.268	4th/Atlantic Division		—	—	—
71-72 —Buffalo		0	1	.000			—	—	—
Totals (5 years)		151	172	.467	Totals (3 years)		9	12	.429

NOTES:

1964—Lost to Cincinnati in Eastern Division semifinals.
1965—Defeated Cincinnati, 3-1, in Eastern Division semifinals; lost to Boston, 4-3, in Eastern Division finals.
1966—Lost to Boston in Eastern Division finals.
1971—Replaced as Buffalo head coach by John McCarthy (October).

SHARMAN, BILL   G

PERSONAL: Born May 25, 1926, in Abilene, Texas. ... 6-1/190. ... Full name: William Walton Sharman.
HIGH SCHOOL: Narbonne (Lomita, Calif.), then Porterville (Calif.).
COLLEGE: Southern California.
TRANSACTIONS/CAREER NOTES: Selected by Washington Capitols in second round of 1950 NBA Draft. ... Selected by Fort Wayne Pistons in 1951 NBA Dispersal Draft of Capitols franchise (did not report to Fort Wayne). ... Traded by Pistons with F Bob Brannum to Boston Celtics for NBA rights to C Charlie Share (1951). ... Signed as player/head coach by Los Angeles Jets of American Basketball League (1961).
CAREER HONORS: Elected to Naismith Memorial Basketball Hall of Fame (1975). ... NBA 25th Anniversary All-Time Team (1970).
MISCELLANEOUS: Member of NBA championship teams (1957, 1959, 1960, 1961).

COLLEGIATE RECORD

NOTES: The Sporting News All-America first team (1950). ... The Sporting News All-America third team (1949). ... In military service during 1944-45 and 1945-46 seasons.

Season Team	G	Min.	FGM	FGA	Pct.	FTM	FTA	Pct.	Reb.	Ast.	Pts.	RPG	APG	PPG
													AVERAGES	
46-47—Southern Cal	10	...	16	...	...	9	12	.750	...	...	41	...	...	4.1
47-48—Southern Cal	24	...	100	...	...	38	44	.864	...	...	238	...	...	9.9
48-49—Southern Cal	24	...	142	...	...	98	125	.784	...	...	382	...	...	15.9
49-50—Southern Cal	24	...	171	421	.406	104	129	.806	...	...	446	...	...	18.6
Totals	82		429			249	310	.803			1107			13.5

NBA REGULAR-SEASON RECORD

HONORS: All-NBA first team (1956, 1957, 1958, 1959). ... All-NBA second team (1953, 1955, 1960).

Season Team	G	Min.	FGM	FGA	Pct.	FTM	FTA	Pct.	Reb.	Ast.	PF	Dq.	Pts.	RPG	APG	PPG
															AVERAGES	
50-51 —Washington	31	...	141	361	.391	96	108	.889	96	39	86	3	378	3.1	1.3	12.2
51-52 —Boston	63	1389	244	628	.389	183	213	.859	221	151	181	3	671	3.5	2.4	10.7
52-53 —Boston	71	2333	403	925	.436	341	401	*.850	288	191	240	7	1147	4.1	2.7	16.2
53-54 —Boston	72	2467	412	915	.450	331	392	*.844	255	229	211	4	1155	3.5	3.2	16.0
54-55 —Boston	68	2453	453	1062	.427	347	387	*.897	302	280	212	2	1253	4.4	4.1	18.4
55-56 —Boston	72	2698	538	1229	.438	358	413	*.867	259	339	197	1	1434	3.6	4.7	19.9
56-57 —Boston	67	2403	516	1241	.416	381	421	*.905	286	236	188	1	1413	4.3	3.5	21.1
57-58 —Boston	63	2214	550	1297	.424	302	338	.894	295	167	156	3	1402	4.7	2.7	22.3
58-59 —Boston	72	2382	562	1377	.408	342	367	*.932	292	179	173	1	1466	4.1	2.5	20.4
59-60 —Boston	71	1916	559	1225	.456	252	291	.866	262	144	154	2	1370	3.7	2.0	19.3
60-61 —Boston	61	1538	383	908	.422	210	228	*.921	223	146	127	0	976	3.7	2.4	16.0
Totals	711		4761	11168	.426	3143	3559	.883	2779	2101	1925	27	12665	3.9	3.0	17.8

NBA PLAYOFF RECORD

Season Team	G	Min.	FGM	FGA	Pct.	FTM	FTA	Pct.	Reb.	Ast.	PF	Dq.	Pts.	RPG	APG	PPG
															AVERAGES	
51-52 —Boston	1	27	7	12	.583	1	1	1.000	3	7	4	0	15	3.0	7.0	15.0
52-53 —Boston	6	201	20	60	.333	30	32	.938	15	15	26	1	70	2.5	2.5	11.7
53-54 —Boston	6	206	35	81	.432	43	50	.860	25	10	29	2	113	4.2	1.7	18.8
54-55 —Boston	7	290	55	110	.500	35	38	.921	38	38	24	1	145	5.4	5.4	20.7
55-56 —Boston	3	119	18	46	.391	16	17	.941	7	12	7	0	52	2.3	4.0	17.3
56-57 —Boston	10	377	75	197	.381	61	64	.953	35	29	23	1	211	3.5	2.9	21.1
57-58 —Boston	11	406	90	221	.407	52	56	.929	54	25	28	0	232	4.9	2.3	21.1
58-59 —Boston	11	322	82	193	.425	57	59	.966	36	28	35	0	221	3.3	2.5	20.1
59-60 —Boston	13	364	88	209	.421	43	53	.811	45	20	22	1	219	3.5	1.5	16.8
60-61 —Boston	10	261	68	133	.511	32	36	.889	27	17	22	0	168	2.7	1.7	16.8
Totals	78	2573	538	1262	.426	370	406	.911	285	201	220	6	1446	3.7	2.6	18.5

NBA ALL-STAR GAME RECORD

NOTES: NBA All-Star Game Most Valuable Player (1955). ... Holds single-game record for most field goals attempted in one quarter—12 (1960).

Season Team	Min.	FGM	FGA	Pct.	FTM	FTA	Pct.	Reb	Ast.	PF	Dq.	Pts.
1953 —Boston	26	5	8	.625	1	1	1.000	4	0	2	0	11
1954 —Boston	30	6	9	.667	2	4	.500	2	3	3	0	14
1955 —Boston	18	5	10	.500	5	5	1.000	4	2	4	0	15

Season	Team	Min.	FGM	FGA	Pct.	FTM	FTA	Pct.	Reb.	Ast.	PF	Dq.	Pts.
1956	—Boston	22	2	8	.250	3	5	.600	3	1	2	1	7
1957	—Boston	23	5	17	.294	2	2	1.000	6	5	1	0	12
1958	—Boston	25	6	19	.316	3	3	1.000	4	3	2	0	15
1959	—Boston	24	3	12	.250	5	6	.833	2	0	1	0	11
1960	—Boston	26	8	21	.381	1	1	1.000	6	2	1	0	17
Totals		194	40	104	.385	22	27	.815	31	16	16	1	102

ABL REGULAR-SEASON RECORD

Season Team	G	Min.	FGM	FGA	Pct.	FTM	FTA	Pct.	Reb.	Ast.	Pts.	RPG	APG	PPG
												AVERAGES		
61-62—Los Angeles	19	346	35	80	.438	37	34	1.088	43	37	107	2.3	1.9	5.6

HEAD COACHING RECORD

BACKGROUND: Player/head coach, Los Angeles Jets of American Basketball League (1961-62). ... Assistant coach, New Orleans Jazz (1974-75 and 1975-76). ... Vice president of basketball operations, Los Angeles Clippers (1986 to present). ... General manager, Los Angeles Lakers (1975-76 through 1981-82). ... President, Lakers (1982-83 through 1989-90). ... Consultant, Lakers (1990-91 to present).
HONORS: NBA Coach of the Year (1972). ... ABA co-Coach of the Year (1970).

COLLEGIATE COACHING RECORD

Season Team	W	L	Pct.	Finish
62-63 —Cal State-Los Angeles	10	12	.455	4th/California Collegiate Athletic Association
63-64 —Cal State-Los Angeles	17	8	.680	2nd/California Collegiate Athletic Association
Totals (2 years)	27	20	.574	

ABL COACHING RECORD

Season Team	REGULAR SEASON				PLAYOFFS		
	W	L	Pct.	Finish	W	L	Pct.
61-62 —Los Angeles-Cleveland	43	26	.623		5	2	.714

NBA COACHING RECORD

Season Team	REGULAR SEASON				PLAYOFFS		
	W	L	Pct.	Finish	W	L	Pct.
66-67 —San Francisco	44	37	.543	1st/Western Division	9	6	.600
67-68 —San Francisco	43	39	.524	3rd/Western Division	4	6	.400
71-72 —Los Angeles	69	13	.841	1st/Pacific Division	12	3	.800
72-73 —Los Angeles	60	22	.732	1st/Pacific Division	9	8	.529
73-74 —Los Angeles	47	35	.573	1st/Pacific Division	1	4	.200
74-75 —Los Angeles	30	52	.366	5th/Pacific Division	—	—	—
75-76 —Los Angeles	40	42	.488	4th/Pacific Division	—	—	—
Totals (7 years)	333	240	.581	Totals (5 years)	35	27	.565

ABA COACHING RECORD

Season Team	REGULAR SEASON				PLAYOFFS		
	W	L	Pct.	Finish	W	L	Pct.
68-69 —Los Angeles ABA	33	45	.423	5th/Western Division	—	—	—
69-70 —Los Angeles ABA	43	41	.512	4th/Western Division	10	7	.588
70-71 —Utah ABA	57	27	.679	2nd/Western Division	12	6	.667
Totals (3 years)	133	113	.541	Totals (2 years)	22	13	.629

NOTES:
1962—Los Angeles Jets had 24-15 record when they folded after first half of season (January 10); Sharman then replaced John McLendon, who resigned as Cleveland Pipers head coach (January 28), and guided Pipers to ABL Championship.
1967—Defeated Los Angeles, 3-0, in Western Division semifinals; defeated St. Louis, 4-2, in Western Division finals; lost to Philadelphia, 4-2, in World Championship Series.
1968—Defeated St. Louis, 4-2, in Western Division semifinals; lost to Los Angeles, 4-0, in Western Division finals.
1970—Defeated Dallas, 4-2, in Western Division semifinals; defeated Denver, 4-1, in Western Division finals; lost to Indiana, 4-2, in ABA Finals.
1971—Defeated Texas, 4-0, in Western Division semifinals; defeated Indiana, 4-3, in Western Division finals; defeated Kentucky, 4-3, in ABA Finals.
1972—Defeated Chicago, 4-0, in Western Conference semifinals; defeated Milwaukee, 4-2, in Western Conference finals; defeated New York, 4-1, in World Championship Series.
1973—Defeated Chicago, 4-3, in Western Conference semifinals; defeated Golden State, 4-1, in Western Conference finals; lost to New York, 4-1, in World Championship Series.
1974—Lost to Milwaukee in Western Conference first round.

RECORD AS BASEBALL PLAYER

Year	Team (League)	Pos.	G	AB	R	H	2B	3B	HR	RBI	Avg.	BB	SO	SB	PO	A	E	Avg.
						BATTING									FIELDING			
1950	—Elmira (Eastern)	OF	10	38	5	11	2	0	1	11	.289	0	5	0	17	0	1	.944
	—Pueblo (Western)	OF	111	427	65	123	22	8	11	70	.288	42	47	11	214	16	10	.958
1951	—Fort Worth (Texas)	OF	157	570	84	163	18	5	8	53	.286	57	44	23	254	11	2	.993
1952	—St. Paul (A.A.)	OF	137	411	63	121	16	4	16	77	.294	29	32	2	215	15	3	.987
1953	—Mobile (South.)	OF	90	228	21	48	8	1	5	17	.211	30	26	0	136	6	2	.986
1954						Out of Organized Baseball.												
1955	—St. Paul (A.A.)	OF-3B	133	424	59	124	15	0	11	58	.292	34	33	3	183	100	11	.963

ALL-TIME GREAT PLAYERS

SIKMA, JACK — C/F

PERSONAL: Born November 14, 1955, in Kankakee, Ill. ... 7-0/250. ... Full name: Jack Wayne Sikma.
HIGH SCHOOL: St. Anne (Ill.).
COLLEGE: Illinois Wesleyan.
TRANSACTIONS/CAREER NOTES: Selected by Seattle SuperSonics in first round (eighth pick overall) of 1977 NBA Draft. ... Traded by SuperSonics with 1987 and 1989 second-round draft choices to Milwaukee Bucks for C Alton Lister and 1987 and 1989 first-round draft choices (July 1, 1986).
MISCELLANEOUS: Member of NBA championship team (1979). ... Seattle SuperSonics all-time leading rebounder with 7,729 (1977-78 through 1985-86).

COLLEGIATE RECORD

Season Team	G	Min.	FGM	FGA	Pct.	FTM	FTA	Pct.	Reb.	Ast.	Pts.	RPG	APG	PPG
73-74—Illinois Wesleyan	21	...	148	306	.484	28	37	.757	223	...	324	10.6	...	15.4
74-75—Illinois Wesleyan	30	...	265	537	.493	80	112	.714	415	...	610	13.8	...	20.3
75-76—Illinois Wesleyan	25	...	204	385	.530	93	126	.738	290	...	501	11.6	...	20.0
76-77—Illinois Wesleyan	31	...	302	324	.932	189	235	.804	477	...	837	15.4	...	27.0
Totals	107	...	919	1552	.592	390	510	.765	1405	...	2272	13.1	...	21.2

NBA REGULAR-SEASON RECORD

HONORS: NBA All-Defensive second team (1982). ... NBA All-Rookie team (1978).
NOTES: Tied for NBA lead with 11 disqualifications (1988).

Season Team	G	Min.	FGM	FGA	Pct.	FTM	FTA	Pct.	REBOUNDS Off.	REBOUNDS Def.	REBOUNDS Tot.	Ast.	St.	Blk.	TO	Pts.	AVERAGES RPG	AVERAGES APG	AVERAGES PPG
77-78—Seattle	82	2238	342	752	.455	192	247	.777	196	482	678	134	68	40	186	876	8.3	1.6	10.7
78-79—Seattle	82	2958	476	1034	.460	329	404	.814	232	781	1013	261	82	67	253	1281	12.4	3.2	15.6
79-80—Seattle	82	2793	470	989	.475	235	292	.805	198	710	908	279	68	77	202	1175	11.1	3.4	14.3
80-81—Seattle	82	2920	595	1311	.454	340	413	.823	184	668	852	248	78	93	201	1530	10.4	3.0	18.7
81-82—Seattle	82	3049	581	1212	.479	447	523	.855	223	*815	1038	277	102	107	213	1611	12.7	3.4	19.6
82-83—Seattle	75	2564	484	1043	.464	400	478	.837	213	645	858	233	87	65	190	1368	11.4	3.1	18.2
83-84—Seattle	82	2993	576	1155	.499	411	480	.856	225	*686	911	327	95	92	236	1563	11.1	4.0	19.1
84-85—Seattle	68	2402	461	943	.489	335	393	.852	164	559	723	285	83	91	160	1259	10.6	4.2	18.5
85-86—Seattle	80	2790	508	1100	.462	355	411	.864	146	602	748	301	92	73	214	1371	9.4	3.8	17.1
86-87—Milwaukee	82	2536	390	842	.463	265	313	.847	208	614	822	203	88	90	160	1045	10.0	2.5	12.7
87-88—Milwaukee	82	2923	514	1058	.486	321	348	*.922	195	514	709	279	93	80	157	1352	8.6	3.4	16.5
88-89—Milwaukee	80	2587	360	835	.431	266	294	.905	141	482	623	289	85	61	145	1068	7.8	3.6	13.4
89-90—Milwaukee	71	2250	344	827	.416	230	260	.885	109	383	492	229	76	48	139	986	6.9	3.2	13.9
90-91—Milwaukee	77	1940	295	691	.427	166	197	.843	108	333	441	143	65	64	130	802	5.7	1.9	10.4
Totals	1107	36943	6396	13792	.464	4292	5053	.849	2542	8274	10816	3488	1162	1048	2586	17287	9.8	3.2	15.6

Three-point field goals: 1979-80, 0-for-1. 1980-81, 0-for-5. 1981-82, 2-for-13 (.154). 1982-83, 0-for-8. 1983-84, 0-for-2. 1984-85, 2-for-10 (.200). 1985-86, 0-for-13. 1986-87, 0-for-2. 1987-88, 3-for-14 (.214). 1988-89, 82-for-216 (.380). 1989-90, 68-for-199 (.342). 1990-91, 46-for-135 (.341). Totals, 203-for-618 (.328).

Personal fouls/disqualifications: 1977-78, 300/6. 1978-79, 295/4. 1979-80, 232/5. 1980-81, 282/5. 1981-82, 268/5. 1982-83, 263/4. 1983-84, 301/6. 1984-85, 239/1. 1985-86, 293/4. 1986-87, 328/14. 1987-88, 316/11. 1988-89, 300/6. 1989-90, 244/5. 1990-91, 218/4. Totals, 3879/80.

NBA PLAYOFF RECORD

Season Team	G	Min.	FGM	FGA	Pct.	FTM	FTA	Pct.	REBOUNDS Off.	REBOUNDS Def.	REBOUNDS Tot.	Ast.	St.	Blk.	TO	Pts.	AVERAGES RPG	AVERAGES APG	AVERAGES PPG
77-78—Seattle	22	701	115	247	.466	71	91	.780	50	128	178	27	18	11	35	301	8.1	1.2	13.7
78-79—Seattle	17	655	102	224	.455	48	61	.787	39	160	199	43	16	24	40	252	11.7	2.5	14.8
79-80—Seattle	15	534	65	163	.399	46	54	.852	30	96	126	55	17	5	35	176	8.4	3.7	11.7
81-82—Seattle	8	315	57	128	.445	50	58	.862	21	76	97	24	9	8	16	164	12.1	3.0	20.5
82-83—Seattle	2	75	11	31	.355	8	12	.667	6	20	26	11	2	2	5	30	13.0	5.5	15.0
83-84—Seattle	5	193	49	98	.500	12	14	.857	11	40	51	5	3	7	9	110	10.2	1.0	22.0
86-87—Milwaukee	12	426	73	150	.487	48	49	.980	33	97	130	23	15	10	18	194	10.8	1.9	16.2
87-88—Milwaukee	5	190	35	76	.461	25	30	.833	24	38	62	13	2	4	15	95	12.4	2.6	19.0
88-89—Milwaukee	9	301	37	94	.394	23	28	.821	9	41	50	30	8	4	21	105	5.6	3.3	11.7
89-90—Milwaukee	4	117	6	23	.261	6	8	.750	0	14	14	7	2	4	12	20	3.5	1.8	5.0
90-91—Milwaukee	3	51	6	15	.400	1	2	.500	3	9	12	6	5	1	3	14	4.0	2.0	4.7
Totals	102	3558	556	1249	.445	338	407	.830	226	719	945	244	97	80	237	1461	9.3	2.4	14.3

Three-point field goals: 1979-80, 0-for-2. 1982-83, 0-for-1. 1983-84, 0-for-1. 1986-87, 0-for-1. 1987-88, 0-for-3. 1988-89, 8-for-28 (.286). 1989-90, 2-for-7 (.286). 1990-91, 1-for-2 (.500). Totals, 11-for-45 (.244).

Personal fouls/disqualifications: 1977-78, 101/7. 1978-79, 70/2. 1979-80, 55/1. 1981-82, 34/1. 1982-83, 7/0. 1983-84, 22/1. 1986-87, 56/3. 1987-88, 23/0. 1988-89, 41/2. 1989-90, 19/0. 1990-91, 4/0. Totals, 432/17.

NBA ALL-STAR GAME RECORD

Season	Team	Min.	FGM	FGA	Pct.	FTM	FTA	Pct.	REBOUNDS Off.	REBOUNDS Def.	REBOUNDS Tot.	Ast.	PF	Dq.	St.	Blk.	TO	Pts.
1979	—Seattle	18	4	5	.800	0	0	...	1	3	4	0	1	0	0	0	0	8
1980	—Seattle	28	4	10	.400	0	0	...	2	6	8	4	5	0	2	3	3	8
1981	—Seattle	21	2	5	.400	2	2	1.000	1	3	4	4	5	0	1	1	1	6
1982	—Seattle	21	5	11	.455	0	0	...	2	7	9	1	2	0	2	1	1	10
1983	—Seattle	17	4	6	.667	0	0	...	1	2	3	1	2	0	1	1	1	8
1984	—Seattle	30	5	12	.417	5	6	.833	5	7	12	1	4	0	3	0	0	15
1985	—Seattle	12	0	2	.000	0	0	...	0	2	2	0	1	0	0	1	1	0
	Totals	147	24	51	.471	7	8	.875	12	30	42	11	20	0	9	7	7	52

Three-point field goals: 1980, 0-for-1. 1981, 0-for-1. Totals, 0-for-2.

SILAS, PAUL — F/C

PERSONAL: Born July 12, 1943, in Prescott, Ariz. ... 6-7/230. ... Full name: Paul Theron Silas.
HIGH SCHOOL: McClymonds (Oakland, Calif.).
COLLEGE: Creighton.
TRANSACTIONS/CAREER NOTES: Selected by St. Louis Hawks in second round (12th pick overall) of 1964 NBA Draft. ... Played in Eastern Basketball League with Wilkes-Barre Barons (1965-66). ... Hawks franchise moved from St. Louis to Atlanta for 1968-69 season. ... Traded by Hawks to Phoenix Suns for F Gary Gregor (May 8, 1969). ... Traded by Suns to Boston Celtics (September 19, 1972) to complete deal in which Suns acquired draft rights to G Charlie Scott (March 14, 1972). ... Traded by Celtics to Denver Nuggets in three-way deal, in which F Curtis Rowe was traded by Detroit Pistons to Celtics, and G Ralph Simpson was traded by Nuggets to Pistons (October 20, 1976). ... Traded by Nuggets with F Willie Wise and C Marvin Webster to Seattle SuperSonics for C Tom Burleson, G/F Bob Wilkerson and 1977 second-round draft choice (May 24, 1977). ... Signed as veteran free agent by San Diego Clippers (May 21, 1980); SuperSonics received 1985 second-round draft choice as compensation.
MISCELLANEOUS: Member of NBA championship teams (1974, 1976, 1979).

COLLEGIATE RECORD

NOTES: Led NCAA Division I with 20.6 rebounds per game (1963). ... Holds NCAA record for most rebounds in three-year career—1,751.

Season Team	G	Min.	FGM	FGA	Pct.	FTM	FTA	Pct.	Reb.	Ast.	Pts.	RPG	APG	PPG
60-61—Creighton‡	21	...	225	...	...	96	119	.807	568	...	546	27.0	...	26.0
61-62—Creighton	25	...	213	524	.406	125	215	.581	563	...	551	22.5	...	22.0
62-63—Creighton	27	...	220	531	.414	133	228	.583	557	...	573	20.6	...	21.2
63-64—Creighton	29	...	210	529	.397	117	194	.603	631	...	537	21.8	...	18.5
Varsity totals	81		643	1584	.406	375	637	.589	1751	...	1661	21.6	...	20.5

NBA REGULAR-SEASON RECORD

HONORS: NBA All-Defensive first team (1975, 1976). ... NBA All-Defensive second team (1971, 1972, 1973).

Season Team	G	Min.	FGM	FGA	Pct.	FTM	FTA	Pct.	Reb.	Ast.	PF	Dq.	Pts.	RPG	APG	PPG
64-65—St. Louis	79	1243	140	375	.373	83	164	.506	576	48	161	1	363	7.3	0.6	4.6
65-66—St. Louis	46	586	70	173	.405	35	61	.574	236	22	72	0	175	5.1	0.5	3.8
66-67—St. Louis	77	1570	207	482	.429	113	213	.531	669	74	208	4	527	8.7	1.0	6.8
67-68—St. Louis	82	2652	399	871	.458	299	424	.705	958	162	243	4	1097	11.7	2.0	13.4
68-69—Atlanta	79	1853	241	575	.419	204	333	.613	745	140	166	0	686	9.4	1.8	8.7
69-70—Phoenix	78	2836	373	804	.464	250	412	.607	916	214	266	5	996	11.7	2.7	12.8
70-71—Phoenix	81	2944	338	789	.428	285	416	.685	1015	247	227	3	961	12.5	3.0	11.9
71-72—Phoenix	80	3082	485	1031	.470	433	560	.773	955	343	201	2	1403	11.9	4.3	17.5
72-73—Boston	80	2618	400	851	.470	266	380	.700	1039	251	197	1	1066	13.0	3.1	13.3

Season Team	G	Min.	FGM	FGA	Pct.	FTM	FTA	Pct.	Off.	Def.	Tot.	Ast.	St.	Blk.	TO	Pts.	RPG	APG	PPG
73-74—Boston	82	2599	340	772	.440	264	337	.783	334	581	915	186	63	20	...	944	11.2	2.3	11.5
74-75—Boston	82	2661	312	749	.417	244	344	.709	348	677	1025	224	60	22	...	868	12.5	2.7	10.6
75-76—Boston	81	2662	315	740	.426	236	333	.709	*365	660	1025	203	56	33	...	866	12.7	2.5	10.7
76-77—Denver	81	1959	206	572	.360	170	255	.667	236	370	606	132	58	23	...	582	7.5	1.6	7.2
77-78—Seattle	82	2172	184	464	.397	109	186	.586	289	377	666	145	65	16	152	477	8.1	1.8	5.8
78-79—Seattle	82	1957	170	402	.423	116	194	.598	259	316	575	116	31	19	98	456	7.0	1.4	5.6
79-80—Seattle	82	1595	113	299	.378	89	136	.654	204	232	436	66	25	5	83	315	5.3	0.8	3.9
Totals	1254	34989	4293	9949	.432	3196	4748	.673	...	...	12357	2572	358	138	333	11782	9.9	2.1	9.4

Personal fouls/disqualifications: 1973-74, 246/3. 1974-75, 229/3. 1975-76, 227/3. 1976-77, 183/0. 1977-78, 182/0. 1978-79, 177/3. 1979-80, 120/0. Totals, 3105/32.

NBA PLAYOFF RECORD

Season Team	G	Min.	FGM	FGA	Pct.	FTM	FTA	Pct.	Reb.	Ast.	PF	Dq.	Pts.	RPG	APG	PPG
64-65—St. Louis	4	42	4	10	.400	3	4	.750	18	1	6	0	11	4.5	0.3	2.8
65-66—St. Louis	7	80	5	18	.278	8	11	.727	34	2	11	0	18	4.9	0.3	2.6
66-67—St. Louis	8	122	9	36	.250	11	18	.611	52	6	17	0	29	6.5	0.8	3.6
67-68—St. Louis	6	178	22	51	.431	27	38	.711	57	21	17	0	71	9.5	3.5	11.8
68-69—Atlanta	11	258	21	58	.362	19	37	.514	92	21	32	0	61	8.4	1.9	5.5
69-70—Phoenix	7	286	46	109	.422	21	32	.656	111	30	29	1	113	15.9	4.3	16.1
72-73—Boston	13	512	47	120	.392	31	50	.620	196	39	39	0	125	15.1	3.0	9.6

Season Team	G	Min.	FGM	FGA	Pct.	FTM	FTA	Pct.	Off.	Def.	Tot.	Ast.	St.	Blk.	TO	Pts.	RPG	APG	PPG
73-74—Boston	18	574	50	126	.397	44	53	.830	53	138	191	47	13	9	...	144	10.6	2.6	8.0
74-75—Boston	11	405	42	92	.457	16	25	.640	46	84	130	40	12	2	...	100	11.8	3.6	9.1
75-76—Boston	18	741	69	154	.448	56	69	.812	78	168	246	42	24	6	...	194	13.7	2.3	10.8
76-77—Denver	6	141	14	33	.424	13	24	.542	16	24	40	16	2	4	...	41	6.7	2.7	6.8
77-78—Seattle	22	605	33	94	.351	41	60	.683	73	114	187	36	12	6	28	107	8.5	1.6	4.9
78-79—Seattle	17	418	21	54	.389	31	46	.674	40	58	98	19	9	5	34	73	5.8	1.1	4.3
79-80—Seattle	15	257	13	43	.302	11	13	.846	33	42	75	15	9	2	9	37	5.0	1.0	2.5
Totals	163	4619	396	998	.397	332	480	.692	...	...	1527	335	81	34	71	1124	9.4	2.1	6.9

Personal fouls/disqualifications: 1973-74, 51/2. 1974-75, 45/1. 1975-76, 67/1. 1976-77, 23/1. 1977-78, 59/0. 1978-79, 44/1. 1979-80, 29/0. Totals, 469/7.

NBA ALL-STAR GAME RECORD

Season Team	Min.	FGM	FGA	Pct.	FTM	FTA	Pct.	Reb	Ast.	PF	Dq.	Pts.
1972—Phoenix	15	0	6	.000	2	3	.667	9	1	1	0	2

Season Team	Min.	FGM	FGA	Pct.	FTM	FTA	Pct.	Off.	Def.	Tot.	Ast.	PF	Dq.	St.	Blk.	TO	Pts.
1975—Boston	15	2	4	.500	2	2	1.000	0	2	2	2	2	0	4	0	...	6
Totals	30	2	10	.200	4	5	.800	...	...	11	3	3	0	4	0	...	8

EBL REGULAR-SEASON RECORD

														AVERAGES		
Season Team	G	Min.	FGM	FGA	Pct.	FTM	FTA	Pct.	Reb.	Ast.	PF	Dq.	Pts.	RPG	APG	PPG
65-66 —Wil.-Barre	5	...	25	...	...	13	21	.619	85	9	...	...	63	17.0	1.8	12.6

NBA COACHING RECORD

	REGULAR SEASON				PLAYOFFS		
Season Team	W	L	Pct.	Finish	W	L	Pct.
80-81 —San Diego..	36	46	.439	5th/Pacific Division	—	—	—
81-82 —San Diego..	17	65	.207	6th/Pacific Division	—	—	—
82-83 —San Diego..	25	57	.305	6th/Pacific Division	—	—	—
Totals (3 years)	78	168	.317				

THEUS, REGGIE   G

PERSONAL: Born October 13, 1957, in Inglewood, Calif. ... 6-7/213. ... Full name: Reggie Wayne Theus. ... Name pronounced THEE-us..

HIGH SCHOOL: Inglewood (Calif.).

COLLEGE: UNLV.

TRANSACTIONS/CAREER NOTES: Selected after junior season by Chicago Bulls in first round (ninth pick overall) of 1978 NBA Draft. ... Traded by Bulls to Kansas City Kings for C Steve Johnson, 1984 second-round draft choice and two 1985 second-round draft choices (February 15, 1984). ... Kings franchise moved from Kansas City to Sacramento for 1985-86 season. ... Traded by Kings with 1988 third-round draft choice and future considerations to Atlanta Hawks for G/F Randy Wittman and 1988 first-round draft choice (June 27, 1988). ... Selected by Orlando Magic from Hawks in NBA expansion draft (June 15, 1989). ... Traded by Magic to New Jersey Nets for 1993 and 1995 second-round draft choices (June 25, 1990). ... Waived by Nets (August 15, 1991). ... Played in Italy (1991-92).

COLLEGIATE RECORD

											AVERAGES		
Season Team	G	Min.	FGM	FGA	Pct.	FTM	FTA	Pct.	Reb.	Ast.	Pts.	RPG	APG	PPG
75-76—UNLV	31	...	68	163	.417	48	60	.800	53	139	184	1.7	4.5	5.9
76-77—UNLV	32	...	178	358	.497	108	132	.818	145	136	464	4.5	4.3	14.5
77-78—UNLV	28	...	181	389	.465	167	207	.807	191	126	529	6.8	4.5	18.9
Totals	91	...	427	910	.469	323	399	.810	389	401	1177	4.3	4.4	12.9

HONORS: NBA All-Rookie team (1979).

NBA REGULAR-SEASON RECORD

								REBOUNDS								AVERAGES		
Season Team	G	Min.	FGM	FGA	Pct.	FTM	FTA	Pct.	Off.	Def.	Tot.	Ast.	St.	Blk.	TO	Pts.	RPG	APG	PPG
78-79—Chicago	82	2753	537	1119	.480	264	347	.761	92	136	228	429	93	18	303	1338	2.8	5.2	16.3
79-80—Chicago	82	3029	566	1172	.483	500	597	.838	143	186	329	515	114	20	348	1660	4.0	6.3	20.2
80-81—Chicago	82	2820	543	1097	.495	445	550	.809	124	163	287	426	122	20	259	1549	3.5	5.2	18.9
81-82—Chicago	82	2838	560	1194	.469	363	449	.808	115	197	312	476	87	16	277	1508	3.8	5.8	18.4
82-83—Chicago	82	2856	749	1567	.478	434	542	.801	91	209	300	484	143	17	321	1953	3.7	5.9	23.8
83-84—Chi.-K.C.	61	1498	262	625	.419	214	281	.762	50	79	129	352	50	12	156	745	2.1	5.8	12.2
84-85—Kansas City	82	2543	501	1029	.487	334	387	.863	106	164	270	656	95	18	307	1341	3.3	8.0	16.4
85-86—Sacramento	82	2919	546	1137	.480	405	490	.827	73	231	304	788	112	20	327	1503	3.7	9.6	18.3
86-87—Sacramento	79	2872	577	1223	.472	429	495	.867	86	180	266	692	78	16	289	1600	3.4	8.8	20.3
87-88—Sacramento	73	2653	619	1318	.470	320	385	.831	72	160	232	463	59	16	234	1574	3.2	6.3	21.6
88-89—Atlanta	82	2517	497	1067	.466	285	335	.851	86	156	242	387	108	16	194	1296	3.0	4.7	15.8
89-90—Orlando	76	2350	517	1178	.439	378	443	.853	75	146	221	407	60	12	226	1438	2.9	5.4	18.9
90-91—New Jersey	81	2955	583	1247	.468	292	343	.851	69	160	229	378	85	35	252	1510	2.8	4.7	18.6
Totals	1026	34603	7057	14973	.471	4663	5644	.826	1182	2167	3349	6453	1206	236	3493	19015	3.3	6.3	18.5

Three-point field goals: 1979-80, 28-for-105 (.267). 1980-81, 18-for-90 (.200). 1981-82, 25-for-100 (.250). 1982-83, 21-for-91 (.231). 1983-84, 7-for-42 (.167). 1984-85, 5-for-38 (.132). 1985-86, 6-for-35 (.171). 1986-87, 17-for-78 (.218). 1987-88, 16-for-59 (.271). 1988-89, 17-for-58 (.293). 1989-90, 26-for-105 (.248). 1990-91, 52-for-144 (.361). Totals, 238-for-945 (.252).

Personal fouls/disqualifications: 1978-79, 270/2. 1979-80, 262/4. 1980-81, 258/1. 1981-82, 243/1. 1982-83, 281/6. 1983-84, 171/3. 1984-85, 250/0. 1985-86, 231/3. 1986-87, 208/3. 1987-88, 173/0. 1988-89, 236/0. 1989-90, 194/1. 1990-91, 231/0. Totals, 3008/24.

NBA PLAYOFF RECORD

								REBOUNDS								AVERAGES		
Season Team	G	Min.	FGM	FGA	Pct.	FTM	FTA	Pct.	Off.	Def.	Tot.	Ast.	St.	Blk.	TO	Pts.	RPG	APG	PPG
80-81—Chicago	6	232	40	90	.444	37	43	.860	7	14	21	38	9	0	15	119	3.5	6.3	19.8
83-84—Kansas City.....	3	81	19	43	.395	9	10	.900	4	7	11	16	5	0	9	43	3.7	5.3	14.3
85-86—Sacramento	3	102	18	46	.391	9	12	.750	3	5	8	19	3	2	14	45	2.7	6.3	15.0
88-89—Atlanta	5	127	14	38	.368	9	12	.750	3	4	7	24	1	0	10	37	1.4	4.8	7.4
Totals	17	542	89	217	.410	64	77	.831	17	30	47	97	18	2	48	244	2.8	5.7	14.4

Three-point field goals: 1980-81, 2-for-9 (.222). 1983-84, 0-for-3. 1985-86, 0-for-1. 1988-89, 0-for-2. Totals, 2-for-15 (.133).

Personal fouls/disqualifications: 1980-81, 22/0. 1983-84, 9/0. 1985-86, 9/0. 1988-89, 18/1. Totals, 58/1.

NBA ALL-STAR GAME RECORD

							REBOUNDS								
Season Team	Min.	FGM	FGA	Pct.	FTM	FTA	Pct.	Off.	Def.	Tot.	Ast.	PF	Dq.	St.	Blk.	TO	Pts.
1981 —Chicago	19	4	7	.571	0	0	...	0	1	1	3	0	0	2	0	4	8
1983 —Chicago	8	0	5	.000	0	0	...	1	0	1	1	1	0	0	0	0	0
Totals............................	27	4	12	.333	0	0	...	1	1	2	4	1	0	2	0	4	8

ITALIAN LEAGUE RECORD

											AVERAGES		
Season Team	G	Min.	FGM	FGA	Pct.	FTM	FTA	Pct.	Reb.	Ast.	Pts.	RPG	APG	PPG
91-92—Ranger Varese................	30	1151	268	572	.469	288	340	.847	118	161	878	3.9	5.4	29.3

THOMAS, ISIAH   G

PERSONAL: Born April 30, 1961, in Chicago. ... 6-1/182. ... Full name: Isiah Lord Thomas III.
HIGH SCHOOL: St. Joseph's (Westchester, Ill.).
COLLEGE: Indiana.
TRANSACTIONS/CAREER NOTES: Selected after sophomore season by Detroit Pistons in first round (second pick overall) of 1981 NBA Draft. ... Announced retirement (May 11, 1994). ... Vice president, Toronto Raptors (May 24, 1994 to present).
MISCELLANEOUS: Member of NBA championship teams (1989, 1990). ... Member of U.S. Olympic team (1980). ... Detroit Pistons all-time leading scorer with 18,822 points, all-time assists leader with 9,061 and all-time steals leader with 1,861 (1981-82 through 1993-94).

COLLEGIATE RECORD

NOTES: THE SPORTING NEWS All-America first team (1981). ... NCAA Division I Tournament Most Outstanding Player (1981). ... Member of NCAA Division I championship team (1981).

Season Team	G	Min.	FGM	FGA	Pct.	FTM	FTA	Pct.	Reb.	Ast.	Pts.	RPG	APG	PPG
79-80—Indiana	29	...	154	302	.510	115	149	.772	116	159	423	4.0	5.5	14.6
80-81—Indiana	34	...	212	383	.554	121	163	.742	105	197	545	3.1	5.8	16.0
Totals	63	...	366	685	.534	236	312	.756	221	356	968	3.5	5.7	15.4

NBA REGULAR-SEASON RECORD

HONORS: All-NBA first team (1984, 1985, 1986). ... All-NBA second team (1983, 1987). ... NBA All-Rookie team (1982).

Season Team	G	Min.	FGM	FGA	Pct.	FTM	FTA	Pct.	Off.	Def.	Tot.	Ast.	St.	Blk.	TO	Pts.	RPG	APG	PPG
81-82—Detroit	72	2433	453	1068	.424	302	429	.704	57	152	209	565	150	17	†299	1225	2.9	7.8	17.0
82-83—Detroit	81	*3093	725	1537	.472	368	518	.710	105	223	328	634	199	29	*326	1854	4.0	7.8	22.9
83-84—Detroit	82	3007	669	1448	.462	388	529	.733	103	224	327	†1123	204	33	307	1748	4.0	11.1	21.3
84-85—Detroit	81	3089	646	1410	.458	399	493	.809	114	247	361	*1123	187	25	302	1720	4.5	*13.9	21.2
85-86—Detroit	77	2790	609	1248	.488	365	462	.790	83	194	277	830	171	20	289	1609	3.6	10.8	20.9
86-87—Detroit	81	3013	626	1353	.463	400	521	.768	82	237	319	813	153	20	343	1671	3.9	10.0	20.6
87-88—Detroit	81	2927	621	1341	.463	305	394	.774	64	214	278	678	141	17	273	1577	3.4	8.4	19.5
88-89—Detroit	80	2924	569	1227	.464	287	351	.818	49	224	273	663	133	20	298	1458	3.4	8.3	18.2
89-90—Detroit	81	2993	579	1322	.438	292	377	.775	74	234	308	765	139	19	*322	1492	3.8	9.4	18.4
90-91—Detroit	48	1657	289	665	.435	179	229	.782	35	125	160	446	75	10	185	776	3.3	9.3	16.2
91-92—Detroit	78	2918	564	1264	.446	292	378	.772	68	179	247	560	118	15	252	1445	3.2	7.2	18.5
92-93—Detroit	79	2922	526	1258	.418	278	377	.737	71	161	232	671	123	18	284	1391	2.9	8.5	17.6
93-94—Detroit	58	1750	318	763	.417	181	258	.702	46	113	159	399	68	6	202	856	2.7	6.9	14.8
Totals	979	35516	7194	15904	.452	4036	5316	.759	951	2527	3478	9061	1861	249	3682	18822	3.6	9.3	19.2

Three-point field goals: 1981-82, 17-for-59 (.288). 1982-83, 36-for-125 (.288). 1983-84, 22-for-65 (.338). 1984-85, 29-for-113 (.257). 1985-86, 26-for-84 (.310). 1986-87, 19-for-98 (.194). 1987-88, 30-for-97 (.309). 1988-89, 33-for-121 (.273). 1989-90, 42-for-136 (.309). 1990-91, 19-for-65 (.292). 1991-92, 25-for-86 (.291). 1992-93, 61-for-198 (.308). 1993-94, 39-for-126 (.310). Totals, 398-for-1373 (.290).

Personal fouls/disqualifications: 1981-82, 253/2. 1982-83, 318/8. 1983-84, 324/8. 1984-85, 288/8. 1985-86, 245/9. 1986-87, 251/5. 1987-88, 217/0. 1988-89, 209/0. 1989-90, 206/0. 1990-91, 118/4. 1991-92, 144/2. 1992-93, 222/2. 1993-94, 126/0. Totals, 2971/48.

NBA PLAYOFF RECORD

NOTES: NBA Finals Most Valuable Player (1990). ... Holds NBA Finals single-game records for most points in one quarter—25 (June 19, 1988, vs. Los Angeles Lakers); and most field goals in one quarter—11 (June 19, 1988, vs. Los Angeles Lakers). ... Shares NBA Finals single-game record for most field goals in one half—14 (June 19, 1988, vs. Los Angeles Lakers).

Season Team	G	Min.	FGM	FGA	Pct.	FTM	FTA	Pct.	Off.	Def.	Tot.	Ast.	St.	Blk.	TO	Pts.	RPG	APG	PPG
83-84—Detroit	5	198	39	83	.470	27	35	.771	7	12	19	55	13	6	23	107	3.8	11.0	21.4
84-85—Detroit	9	355	83	166	.500	47	62	.758	11	36	47	101	19	4	30	219	5.2	11.2	24.3
85-86—Detroit	4	163	41	91	.451	24	36	.667	8	14	22	48	9	3	17	106	5.5	12.0	26.5
86-87—Detroit	15	562	134	297	.451	83	110	.755	21	46	67	130	39	4	42	361	4.5	8.7	24.1
87-88—Detroit	23	911	183	419	.437	125	151	.828	26	81	107	201	66	8	85	504	4.7	8.7	21.9
88-89—Detroit	17	633	115	279	.412	71	96	.740	24	49	73	141	27	4	43	309	4.3	8.3	18.2
09-90—Detroit	20	758	148	320	.463	81	102	.794	21	88	100	163	43	7	72	409	5.5	8.2	20.5
90-91—Detroit	13	436	60	149	.403	50	69	.725	13	41	54	111	13	2	41	176	4.2	8.5	13.5
91-92—Detroit	5	200	22	65	.338	22	28	.786	3	23	26	37	5	0	16	70	5.2	7.4	14.0
Totals	111	4216	825	1869	.441	530	689	.769	134	390	524	987	234	38	369	2261	4.7	8.9	20.4

Three-point field goals: 1983-84, 2-for-6 (.333). 1984-85, 6-for-15 (.400). 1985-86, 0-for-5. 1986-87, 10-for-33 (.303). 1987-88, 13-for-44 (.295). 1988-89, 8-for-30 (.267). 1989-90, 32-for-68 (.471). 1990-91, 6-for-22 (.273). 1991-92, 4-for-11 (.364). Totals, 81-for-234 (.346).

Personal fouls/disqualifications: 1983-84, 22/1. 1984-85, 39/2. 1985-86, 17/0. 1986-87, 51/1. 1987-88, 71/2. 1988-89, 39/0. 1989-90, 65/1. 1990-91, 41/1. 1991-92, 18/0. Totals, 363/8.

NBA ALL-STAR GAME RECORD

NOTES: NBA All-Star Game Most Valuable Player (1984, 1986). ... Holds career record for most steals—31.

Season Team	Min.	FGM	FGA	Pct.	FTM	FTA	Pct.	Off.	Def.	Tot.	Ast.	PF	Dq.	St.	Blk.	TO	Pts.
1982 —Detroit	17	5	7	.714	2	4	.500	1	0	1	4	1	0	3	0	1	12
1983 —Detroit	29	9	14	.643	1	1	1.000	3	1	4	7	0	0	4	0	5	19
1984 —Detroit	39	9	17	.529	3	3	1.000	3	2	5	15	4	0	4	0	6	21
1985 —Detroit	25	9	14	.643	1	1	1.000	1	1	2	5	2	0	2	0	1	22
1986 —Detroit	36	11	19	.579	8	9	.889	0	1	1	10	2	0	5	0	5	30
1987 —Detroit	24	4	6	.667	8	9	.889	2	1	3	9	3	0	0	0	5	16
1988 —Detroit	28	4	10	.400	0	0	...	1	1	2	15	1	0	1	0	6	8
1989 —Detroit	33	7	13	.538	4	6	.667	1	1	2	14	2	0	4	0	4	19
1990 —Detroit	27	7	12	.583	0	0	...	1	3	4	9	2	0	3	0	1	15
1991 —Detroit							Selected, did not play—injured.										
1992 —Detroit	28	7	14	.500	0	0	...	0	1	1	5	0	0	3	0	3	15
1993 —Detroit	32	4	7	.571	0	2	.000	0	2	2	4	2	0	2	0	2	8
Totals	318	76	133	.571	27	35	.771	13	14	27	97	17	0	31	0	41	185

Three-point field goals: 1984, 0-for-2. 1985, 3-for-4 (.750). 1986, 0-for-1. 1989, 1-for-3 (.333). 1990, 1-for-1. 1992, 1-for-3 (.333). 1993, 0-for-1. Totals, 6-for-15 (.400).

ALL-TIME GREAT PLAYERS

THURMOND, NATE   C/F

PERSONAL: Born July 25, 1941, in Akron, Ohio. ... 6-11/235. ... Full name: Nathaniel Thurmond.
HIGH SCHOOL: Central Hower (Akron, Ohio).
COLLEGE: Bowling Green State.
TRANSACTIONS/CAREER NOTES: Selected by San Francisco Warriors in first round of 1963 NBA Draft. ... Warriors franchise renamed Golden State Warriors for 1971-72 season. ... Traded by Warriors to Chicago Bulls for C Clifford Ray, cash and 1975 first-round draft choice (September 3, 1974). ... Traded by Bulls with F Rowland Garrett to Cleveland Cavaliers for C/F Steve Patterson and F Eric Fernsten (November 27, 1975).
CAREER HONORS: Elected to Naismith Memorial Basketball Hall of Fame (1984).
MISCELLANEOUS: Golden State Warriors franchise all-time leading rebounder with 12,771 (1963-64 through 1973-74).

COLLEGIATE RECORD

NOTES: The Sporting News All-America first team (1963).

Season Team	G	Min.	FGM	FGA	Pct.	FTM	FTA	Pct.	Reb.	Ast.	Pts.	RPG	APG	PPG
59-60—Bowling Green‡	17	...	...	...	...	...	...	...	208	...	225	12.2	...	13.2
60-61—Bowling Green	24	...	170	427	.398	87	129	.674	449	...	427	18.7	...	17.8
61-62—Bowling Green	25	...	163	358	.455	67	113	.593	394	...	393	15.8	...	15.7
62-63—Bowling Green	27	...	206	466	.442	124	197	.629	452	...	536	16.7	...	19.9
Varsity totals	76	...	539	1251	.431	278	439	.633	1295	...	1356	17.0	...	17.8

NBA REGULAR-SEASON RECORD

RECORDS: Holds single-game record for most rebounds in one quarter—18 (February 28, 1965, vs. Baltimore).
HONORS: NBA All-Defensive first team (1969, 1971). ... NBA All-Defensive second team (1972, 1973, 1974). ... NBA All-Rookie team (1964).

Season Team	G	Min.	FGM	FGA	Pct.	FTM	FTA	Pct.	Reb.	Ast.	PF	Dq.	Pts.	RPG	APG	PPG
63-64 —San Fran.	76	1966	219	554	.395	95	173	.549	790	86	184	2	533	10.4	1.1	7.0
64-65 —San Fran.	77	3173	519	1240	.419	235	357	.658	1395	157	232	3	1273	18.1	2.0	16.5
65-66 —San Fran.	73	2891	454	1119	.406	280	428	.654	1312	111	223	7	1188	18.0	1.5	16.3
66-67 —San Fran.	65	2755	467	1068	.437	280	445	.629	1382	166	183	3	1214	21.3	2.6	18.7
67-68 —San Fran.	51	2222	382	929	.411	282	438	.644	1121	215	137	1	1046	22.0	4.2	20.5
68-69 —San Fran.	71	3208	571	1394	.410	382	621	.615	1402	253	171	0	1524	19.7	3.6	21.5
69-70 —San Fran.	43	1919	341	824	.414	261	346	.754	762	150	110	1	943	17.7	3.5	21.9
70-71 —San Fran.	82	3351	623	1401	.445	395	541	.730	1128	257	192	1	1641	13.8	3.1	20.0
71-72 —Golden State	78	3362	628	1454	.432	417	561	.743	1252	230	214	1	1673	16.1	2.9	21.4
72-73 —Golden State	79	3419	517	1159	.446	315	439	.718	1349	280	240	2	1349	17.1	3.5	17.1

Season Team	G	Min.	FGM	FGA	Pct.	FTM	FTA	Pct.	REBOUNDS Off.	Def.	Tot.	Ast.	St.	Blk.	TO	Pts.	RPG	APG	PPG
73-74—Golden State	62	2463	308	694	.444	191	287	.666	249	629	878	165	41	179	...	807	14.2	2.7	13.0
74-75—Chicago	80	2756	250	686	.364	132	224	.589	259	645	904	328	46	195	...	632	11.3	4.1	7.9
75-76—Chi.-Clev.	78	1393	142	337	.421	62	123	.504	115	300	415	94	22	98	...	346	5.3	1.2	4.4
76-77—Cleveland	49	997	100	242	.407	68	106	.642	121	253	374	83	16	81	...	268	7.6	1.7	5.5
Totals	964	35875	5521	13105	.421	3395	5089	.667	...	...	14464	2575	125	553	...	14437	15.0	2.7	15.0

Personal fouls/disqualifications: 1973-74, 179/4. 1974-75, 271/6. 1975-76, 160/1. 1976-77, 128/2. Totals, 2624/34.

NBA PLAYOFF RECORD

Season Team	G	Min.	FGM	FGA	Pct.	FTM	FTA	Pct.	Reb.	Ast.	PF	Dq.	Pts.	RPG	APG	PPG
63-64 —San Fran.	12	410	42	98	.429	36	53	.679	148	12	46	0	120	12.3	1.0	10.0
66-67 —San Fran.	15	690	93	215	.433	52	91	.571	346	47	52	1	238	23.1	3.1	15.9
68-69 —San Fran.	6	263	40	102	.392	20	34	.588	117	28	18	0	100	19.5	4.7	16.7
70-71 —San Fran.	5	192	36	97	.371	16	20	.800	51	15	20	0	88	10.2	3.0	17.6
71-72 —Golden State	5	230	53	122	.434	21	28	.750	89	26	12	0	127	17.8	5.2	25.4
72-73 —Golden State	11	460	64	161	.398	32	40	.800	145	40	30	1	160	13.2	3.6	14.5

Season Team	G	Min.	FGM	FGA	Pct.	FTM	FTA	Pct.	REBOUNDS Off.	Def.	Tot.	Ast.	St.	Blk.	TO	Pts.	RPG	APG	PPG
74-75—Chicago	13	254	19	38	.368	18	37	.486	24	63	87	31	5	21	...	46	6.7	2.4	3.5
75-76—Cleveland	13	375	37	.79	.468	13	32	.406	38	79	117	28	6	29	...	87	9.0	2.2	6.7
76-77—Cleveland	1	1	0	0	...	0	0	...	0	1	1	0	0	1	...	0	1.0	0.0	0.0
Totals	81	2875	379	912	.416	208	335	.621	...	...	1101	227	11	51	...	966	13.6	2.8	11.9

Personal fouls/disqualifications: 1974-75, 36/0. 1975-76, 52/2. Totals, 266/4.

NBA ALL-STAR GAME RECORD

Season Team	Min.	FGM	FGA	Pct.	FTM	FTA	Pct.	Reb	Ast.	PF	Dq.	Pts.
1965 —San Francisco	10	0	2	.000	0	0	...	3	0	1	0	0
1966 —San Francisco	33	3	16	.188	1	3	.333	16	1	1	0	7
1967 —San Francisco	42	7	16	.438	2	4	.500	18	0	1	0	16
1968 —San Francisco					Selected, did not play—injured.							
1970 —San Francisco					Selected, did not play—injured.							
1973 —Golden State	14	2	5	.400	0	0	...	4	1	2	0	4

Season Team	Min.	FGM	FGA	Pct.	FTM	FTA	Pct.	REBOUNDS Off.	Def.	Tot.	Ast.	PF	Dq.	St.	Blk.	TO	Pts.
1974 —Golden State	5	2	4	.500	0	1	.000	1	2	3	0	0	0	0	0	...	4
Totals	104	14	43	.326	3	8	.375	...	...	44	2	5	0	0	0	...	31

TWYMAN, JACK — F/G

PERSONAL: Born May 11, 1934, in Pittsburgh. ... 6-6/210. ... Full name: John Kennedy Twyman.
HIGH SCHOOL: Pittsburgh Central Catholic.
COLLEGE: Cincinnati.
TRANSACTIONS/CAREER NOTES: Selected by Rochester Royals in second round (10th pick overall) of 1955 NBA Draft. ... Royals franchise moved from Rochester to Cincinnati for 1957-58 season.
CAREER HONORS: Elected to Naismith Memorial Basketball Hall of Fame (1982).

COLLEGIATE RECORD

Season Team	G	Min.	FGM	FGA	Pct.	FTM	FTA	Pct.	Reb.	Ast.	Pts.	RPG	APG	PPG
51-52—Cincinnati‡	16	...	27	83	.325	13	27	.481	55	...	67	3.4	...	4.2
52-53—Cincinnati	24	716	136	323	.421	89	143	.622	362	...	361	15.1	...	15.0
53-54—Cincinnati	21	777	174	443	.393	110	145	.759	347	...	458	16.5	...	21.8
54-55—Cincinnati	29	1097	285	628	.454	142	192	.740	478	...	712	16.5	...	24.6
Totals	90	...	622	1477	.421	354	507	.698	1242	...	1598	13.8	...	17.8

NBA REGULAR-SEASON RECORD

HONORS: All-NBA second team (1960, 1962).

Season Team	G	Min.	FGM	FGA	Pct.	FTM	FTA	Pct.	Reb.	Ast.	PF	Dq.	Pts.	RPG	APG	PPG
55-56 —Rochester	72	2186	417	987	.423	204	298	.685	466	171	239	4	1038	6.5	2.4	14.4
56-57 —Rochester	72	2338	449	1023	.439	276	363	.760	354	123	251	4	1174	4.9	1.7	16.3
57-58 —Cincinnati	72	2178	465	1028 *	.452	307	396	.775	464	110	224	3	1237	6.4	1.5	17.2
58-59 —Cincinnati	72	2713	710	*1691	.420	437	558	.783	653	209	277	6	1857	9.1	2.9	25.8
59-60 —Cincinnati	75	3023	870	2063	.422	*598	762	.785	664	260	275	10	2338	8.9	3.5	31.2
60-61 —Cincinnati	79	2920	796	1632	.488	405	554	.731	672	225	279	5	1997	8.5	2.8	25.3
61-62 —Cincinnati	80	2991	739	1542	.479	353	435	.812	638	215	323	5	1831	8.0	2.7	22.9
62-63 —Cincinnati	80	2623	641	1335	.480	304	375	.811	598	214	286	7	1586	7.5	2.7	19.8
63-64 —Cincinnati	68	1996	447	993	.450	189	228	.829	364	137	267	7	1083	5.4	2.0	15.9
64-65 —Cincinnati	80	2236	479	1081	.443	198	239	.828	383	137	239	4	1156	4.8	1.7	14.5
65-66 —Cincinnati	73	943	224	498	.450	95	117	.812	168	60	122	1	543	2.3	0.8	7.4
Totals	823	26147	6237	13873	.450	3366	4325	.778	5424	1861	2782	56	15840	6.6	2.3	19.2

NBA PLAYOFF RECORD

Season Team	G	Min.	FGM	FGA	Pct.	FTM	FTA	Pct.	Reb.	Ast.	PF	Dq.	Pts.	RPG	APG	PPG
57-58 —Cincinnati	2	74	15	45	.333	7	12	.583	22	1	6	0	37	11.0	0.5	18.5
61-62 —Cincinnati	4	149	34	78	.436	8	8	1.000	29	12	18	0	76	7.3	3.0	19.0
62-63 —Cincinnati	12	410	92	205	.449	65	77	.844	98	30	47	1	249	8.2	2.5	20.8
63-64 —Cincinnati	10	354	83	176	.472	29	49	.592	87	16	41	1	205	8.7	1.6	20.5
64-65 —Cincinnati	4	97	19	48	.396	11	11	1.000	17	3	16	0	49	4.3	0.8	12.3
65-66 —Cincinnati	2	11	2	4	.500	1	2	.500	2	0	3	0	5	1.0	0.0	2.5
Totals	34	1095	245	556	.441	121	159	.761	255	62	131	2	621	7.5	1.8	18.3

NBA ALL-STAR GAME RECORD

Season Team	Min.	FGM	FGA	Pct.	FTM	FTA	Pct.	Reb	Ast.	PF	Dq.	Pts.
1957 —Rochester	17	1	8	.125	1	3	.333	0	1	1	0	3
1958 —Cincinnati	25	8	13	.615	2	2	1.000	3	0	3	0	18
1959 —Cincinnati	23	8	12	.667	2	4	.500	8	3	4	0	18
1960 —Cincinnati	28	11	17	.647	5	8	.625	5	1	4	0	27
1962 —Cincinnati	8	4	6	.667	3	3	1.000	1	2	0	0	11
1963 —Cincinnati	16	6	12	.500	0	0	...	4	1	2	0	12
Totals	117	38	68	.559	13	20	.650	21	8	14	0	89

UNSELD, WES — C/F

PERSONAL: Born March 14, 1946, in Louisville, Ky. ... 6-7/245. ... Full name: Westley Sissel Unseld.
HIGH SCHOOL: Seneca (Louisville, Ky.).
COLLEGE: Louisville.
TRANSACTIONS/CAREER NOTES: Selected by Baltimore Bullets in first round (second pick overall) of 1968 NBA Draft. ... Bullets franchise moved from Baltimore to Washington and renamed Capital Bullets for 1973-74 season. ... Bullets franchise renamed Washington Bullets for 1974-75 season.
CAREER HONORS: Elected to Naismith Memorial Basketball Hall of Fame (1987).
MISCELLANEOUS: Member of NBA championship team (1978). ... Washington Bullets franchise all-time leading rebounder with 13,769 and all-time assists leader with 3,822 (1968-69 through 1980-81).

COLLEGIATE RECORD

NOTES: THE SPORTING NEWS All-America second team (1967, 1968).

Season Team	G	Min.	FGM	FGA	Pct.	FTM	FTA	Pct.	Reb.	Ast.	Pts.	RPG	APG	PPG
64-65—Louisville‡	14	...	214	312	.686	73	124	.589	331	...	501	23.6	...	35.8
65-66—Louisville	26	...	195	374	.521	128	202	.634	505	...	518	19.4	...	19.9
66-67—Louisville	28	...	201	374	.537	121	177	.684	533	...	523	19.0	...	18.7
67-68—Louisville	28	...	234	382	.613	177	275	.644	513	...	645	18.3	...	23.0
Varsity totals	82	...	630	1130	.558	426	654	.651	1551	...	1686	18.9	...	20.6

NBA REGULAR-SEASON RECORD

HONORS: NBA Most Valuable Player (1969). ... NBA Rookie of the Year (1969). ... All-NBA first team (1969). ... NBA All-Rookie team (1969).
NOTES: Led NBA with .56085 field-goal percentage (1976).

Season Team	G	Min.	FGM	FGA	Pct.	FTM	FTA	Pct.	Reb.	Ast.	PF	Dq.	Pts.	AVERAGES RPG	APG	PPG
68-69 —Baltimore	82	2970	427	897	.476	277	458	.605	1491	213	276	4	1131	18.2	2.6	13.8
69-70 —Baltimore	82	3234	526	1015	.518	273	428	.638	1370	291	250	2	1325	16.7	3.5	16.2
70-71 —Baltimore	74	2904	424	846	.501	199	303	.657	1253	293	235	2	1047	16.9	4.0	14.1
71-72 —Baltimore	76	3171	409	822	.498	171	272	.629	1336	278	218	1	989	17.6	3.7	13.0
72-73 —Baltimore	79	3085	421	854	.493	149	212	.703	1260	347	168	0	991	15.9	4.4	12.5

Season Team	G	Min.	FGM	FGA	Pct.	FTM	FTA	Pct.	REBOUNDS Off.	Def.	Tot.	Ast.	St.	Blk.	TO	Pts.	AVERAGES RPG	APG	PPG
73-74—Capital	56	1727	146	333	.438	36	55	.655	152	365	517	159	56	16	...	328	9.2	2.8	5.9
74-75—Washington	73	2904	273	544	.502	126	184	.685	318	759	1077	297	115	68	...	672	*14.8	4.1	9.2
75-76—Washington	78	2922	318	567	*.561	114	195	.585	271	765	1036	404	84	59	...	750	13.3	5.2	9.6
76-77—Washington	82	2860	270	551	.490	100	166	.602	243	634	877	363	87	45	...	640	10.7	4.4	7.8
77-78—Washington	80	2644	257	491	.523	93	173	.538	286	669	955	326	98	45	173	607	11.9	4.1	7.6
78-79—Washington	77	2406	346	600	.577	151	235	.643	274	556	830	315	71	37	156	843	10.8	4.1	10.9
79-80—Washington	82	2973	327	637	.513	139	209	.665	334	760	1094	366	65	61	153	794	13.3	4.5	9.7
80-81—Washington	63	2032	225	429	.524	55	86	.640	207	466	673	170	52	36	97	507	10.7	2.7	8.0
Totals	984	35832	4369	8586	.509	1883	2976	.633	...	...	13769	3822	628	367	579	10624	14.0	3.9	10.8

Three-point field goals: 1979-80, 1-for-2 (.500). 1980-81, 2-for-4 (.500). Totals, 3-for-6 (.500).

Personal fouls/disqualifications: 1973-74, 121/1. 1974-75, 180/1. 1975-76, 203/3. 1976-77, 253/5. 1977-78, 234/2. 1978-79, 204/2. 1979-80, 249/5. 1980-81, 171/1. Totals, 2762/29.

NBA PLAYOFF RECORD

NOTES: NBA Finals Most Valuable Player (1978).

Season Team	G	Min.	FGM	FGA	Pct.	FTM	FTA	Pct.	Reb.	Ast.	PF	Dq.	Pts.	AVERAGES RPG	APG	PPG
68-69 —Baltimore	4	165	30	57	.526	15	19	.789	74	5	14	0	75	18.5	1.3	18.8
69-70 —Baltimore	7	289	29	70	.414	15	19	.789	165	24	25	1	73	23.6	3.4	10.4
70-71 —Baltimore	18	759	96	208	.462	46	81	.568	339	69	60	0	238	18.8	3.8	13.2
71-72 —Baltimore	6	266	32	65	.492	10	19	.526	75	25	22	0	74	12.5	4.2	12.3
72-73 —Baltimore	5	201	20	48	.417	9	19	.474	76	17	12	0	49	15.2	3.4	9.8

Season Team	G	Min.	FGM	FGA	Pct.	FTM	FTA	Pct.	REBOUNDS Off.	Def.	Tot.	Ast.	St.	Blk.	TO	Pts.	AVERAGES RPG	APG	PPG
73-74—Capital	7	297	31	63	.492	9	15	.600	22	63	85	27	4	1	...	71	12.1	3.9	10.1
74-75—Washington	17	734	71	130	.546	40	61	.656	65	211	276	64	15	20	...	182	16.2	3.8	10.7
75-76—Washington	7	310	18	39	.462	13	24	.542	26	59	85	28	6	4	...	49	12.1	4.0	7.0
76-77—Washington	9	368	30	54	.556	7	12	.583	24	81	105	44	8	6	...	67	11.7	4.9	7.4
77-78—Washington	18	677	71	134	.530	27	46	.587	72	144	216	79	17	7	36	169	12.0	4.4	9.4
78-79—Washington	19	736	78	158	.494	39	64	.609	90	163	253	64	17	14	30	195	13.3	3.4	10.3
79-80—Washington	2	87	7	14	.500	4	6	.667	7	21	28	7	0	3	3	18	14.0	3.5	9.0
Totals	119	4889	513	1040	.493	234	385	.608	...	...	1777	453	67	55	69	1260	14.9	3.8	10.6

Three-point field goals: 1979-80, 0-for-1.

Personal fouls/disqualifications: 1973-74, 15/0. 1974-75, 39/0. 1975-76, 19/0. 1976-77, 32/0. 1977-78, 62/2. 1978-79, 66/2. 1979-80, 5/0. Totals, 371/5.

NBA ALL-STAR GAME RECORD

Season Team	Min.	FGM	FGA	Pct.	FTM	FTA	Pct.	Reb	Ast.	PF	Dq.	Pts.
1969 —Baltimore	14	5	7	.714	1	3	.333	8	1	3	0	11
1971 —Baltimore	21	4	9	.444	0	0	...	10	2	2	0	8
1972 —Baltimore	16	1	5	.200	0	0	...	7	1	3	0	2
1973 —Baltimore	11	2	4	.500	0	0	...	5	1	0	0	4

Season Team	Min.	FGM	FGA	Pct.	FTM	FTA	Pct.	REBOUNDS Off.	Def.	Tot.	Ast.	PF	Dq.	St.	Blk.	TO	Pts.
1975 —Washington	15	2	3	.667	2	2	1.000	2	4	6	1	2	0	2	0	...	6
Totals	77	14	28	.500	3	5	.600	...	...	36	6	10	0	2	0	...	31

NBA COACHING RECORD

BACKGROUND: Vice president, Washington Bullets (1981-82 to 1995-96). ... Assistant coach, Bullets (1987-January 3, 1988). ... Executive vice president/general manager, Bullets (1996-97 season).

Season Team	REGULAR SEASON W	L	Pct.	Finish	PLAYOFFS W	L	Pct.
87-88 —Washington	30	25	.545	T2nd/Atlantic Division	2	3	.400
88-89 —Washington	40	42	.488	4th/Atlantic Division	—	—	—
89-90 —Washington	31	51	.378	4th/Atlantic Division	—	—	—
90-91 —Washington	30	52	.366	4th/Atlantic Division	—	—	—
91-92 —Washington	25	57	.305	6th/Atlantic Division	—	—	—
92-93 —Washington	22	60	.268	7th/Atlantic Division	—	—	—
93-94 —Washington	24	58	.293	7th/Atlantic Division	—	—	—
Totals (7 years)	202	345	.369	Totals (1 year)	2	3	.400

NOTES:

1988—Replaced Kevin Loughery as Washington head coach (January 3), with record of 8-19. Lost to Detroit in Eastern Conference first round.

DID YOU KNOW...

...that Eddie Johnson is the only player to score 18,000 career points and never play in an NBA All-Star Game?

WALKER, CHET   F/G

PERSONAL: Born February 22, 1940, in Benton Harbor, Mich. ... 6-7/220. ... Full name: Chester Walker. ... Nickname: The Jet.
HIGH SCHOOL: Benton Harbor (Mich.).
COLLEGE: Bradley.
TRANSACTIONS/CAREER NOTES: Selected by Syracuse Nationals in second round (14th pick overall) of 1962 NBA Draft. ... Nationals franchise moved from Syracuse to Philadelphia and renamed 76ers for 1963-64 season. ... Traded by 76ers with F Shaler Halimon to Chicago Bulls for F Jim Washington and player to be named later (September 2, 1969).
MISCELLANEOUS: Member of NBA championship team (1967).

COLLEGIATE RECORD

NOTES: The Sporting News All-America first team (1962). ... The Sporting News All-America second team (1961).

Season Team	G	Min.	FGM	FGA	Pct.	FTM	FTA	Pct.	Reb.	Ast.	Pts.	AVERAGES RPG	APG	PPG
58-59—Bradley‡	15	...	146	264	.553	56	93	.602	246	...	348	16.4	...	23.2
59-60—Bradley	29	...	244	436	.560	144	234	.615	388	...	632	13.4	...	21.8
60-61—Bradley	26	...	238	423	.563	180	250	.720	327	...	656	12.6	...	25.2
61-62—Bradley	26	...	268	500	.536	151	236	.640	321	...	687	12.3	...	26.4
Varsity totals	81	...	750	1359	.552	475	720	.660	1036	...	1975	12.8	...	24.4

NBA REGULAR-SEASON RECORD

HONORS: NBA All-Rookie team (1963).

Season Team	G	Min.	FGM	FGA	Pct.	FTM	FTA	Pct.	Reb.	Ast.	PF	Dq.	Pts.	AVERAGES RPG	APG	PPG
62-63 —Syracuse	78	1992	352	751	.469	253	362	.699	561	83	220	3	957	7.2	1.1	12.3
63-64 —Philadelphia	76	2775	492	1118	.440	330	464	.711	784	124	232	3	1314	10.3	1.6	17.3
64-65 —Philadelphia	79	2187	377	936	.403	288	388	.742	528	132	200	2	1042	6.7	1.7	13.2
65-66 —Philadelphia	80	2603	443	982	.451	335	468	.716	636	201	238	3	1221	8.0	2.5	15.3
66-67 —Philadelphia	81	2691	561	1150	.488	445	581	.766	660	188	232	4	1567	8.1	2.3	19.3
67-68 —Philadelphia	82	2623	539	1172	.460	387	533	.726	607	157	252	3	1465	7.4	1.9	17.9
68-69 —Philadelphia	82	2753	554	1145	.484	369	459	.804	640	144	244	0	1477	7.8	1.8	18.0
69-70 —Chicago	78	2726	596	1249	.477	483	568	.850	604	192	203	1	1675	7.7	2.5	21.5
70-71 —Chicago	81	2927	610	1398	.465	440	559	*.859	588	179	187	2	1780	7.3	2.2	22.0
71-72 —Chicago	78	2588	619	1225	.505	481	568	.847	473	178	171	1	1719	6.1	2.3	22.0
72-73 —Chicago	79	2455	597	1248	.478	376	452	.832	395	179	166	1	1570	5.0	2.3	19.9

Season Team	G	Min.	FGM	FGA	Pct.	FTM	FTA	Pct.	REBOUNDS Off.	Def.	Tot.	Ast.	St.	Blk.	TO	Pts.	AVERAGES RPG	APG	PPG
73-74 —Chicago	82	2661	572	1178	.486	439	502	.875	131	275	406	200	68	4	...	1583	5.0	2.4	19.3
74-75 —Chicago	76	2452	524	1076	.487	413	480	.860	114	318	432	169	49	6	...	1461	5.7	2.2	19.2
Totals	1032	33433	6876	14628	.470	5079	6384	.796	...	...	7314	2126	117	10	...	18831	7.1	2.1	18.2

Personal fouls/disqualifications: 1973-74, 201/1. 1974-75, 181/0. Totals, 2727/23.

NBA PLAYOFF RECORD

Season Team	G	Min.	FGM	FGA	Pct.	FTM	FTA	Pct.	Reb.	Ast.	PF	Dq.	Pts.	AVERAGES RPG	APG	PPG
62-63 —Syracuse	5	130	27	53	.509	22	30	.733	47	9	8	0	76	9.4	1.8	15.2
63-64 —Philadelphia	5	190	30	77	.390	34	46	.739	52	13	15	0	94	10.4	2.6	18.8
64-65 —Philadelphia	11	469	83	173	.480	57	75	.760	79	18	38	0	223	7.2	1.6	20.3
65-66 —Philadelphia	5	181	24	64	.375	25	31	.806	37	15	18	0	73	7.4	3.0	14.6
66-67 —Philadelphia	15	551	115	246	.467	96	119	.807	114	32	44	0	326	7.6	2.1	21.7
67-68 —Philadelphia	13	485	86	210	.410	76	112	.679	96	24	44	1	248	7.4	1.8	19.1
68-69 —Philadelphia	4	109	23	43	.535	8	12	.667	23	8	5	0	54	5.8	2.0	13.5
69-70 —Chicago	5	178	35	83	.422	27	33	.818	42	11	14	0	97	8.4	2.2	19.4
70-71 —Chicago	7	234	44	100	.440	17	24	.708	50	22	20	0	105	7.1	3.1	15.0
71-72 —Chicago	4	97	16	38	.421	13	16	.813	14	4	7	0	45	3.5	1.0	11.3
72-73 —Chicago	7	229	42	121	.347	33	37	.892	62	14	15	0	117	8.9	2.0	16.7

Season Team	G	Min.	FGM	FGA	Pct.	FTM	FTA	Pct.	REBOUNDS Off.	Def.	Tot.	Ast.	St.	Blk.	TO	Pts.	AVERAGES RPG	APG	PPG
73-74 —Chicago	11	403	81	159	.509	68	79	.861	26	35	61	18	10	1	...	230	5.5	1.6	20.9
74-75 —Chicago	13	432	81	164	.494	66	75	.880	10	50	60	24	13	1	...	228	4.6	1.8	17.5
Totals	105	3688	687	1531	.449	542	689	.787	...	...	737	212	23	2	...	1916	7.0	2.0	18.2

Personal fouls/disqualifications: 1973-74, 26/0. 1974-75, 32/2. Totals, 286/3.

NBA ALL-STAR GAME RECORD

Season Team	Min.	FGM	FGA	Pct.	FTM	FTA	Pct.	Reb	Ast.	PF	Dq.	Pts.
1964 —Philadelphia	12	2	5	.400	0	0	...	0	0	1	0	4
1966 —Philadelphia	25	3	10	.300	2	3	.667	6	4	2	0	8
1967 —Philadelphia	22	6	9	.667	3	4	.750	4	1	2	0	15
1970 —Chicago	17	1	3	.333	2	2	1.000	2	1	2	0	4
1971 —Chicago	19	3	9	.333	4	5	.800	3	1	1	0	10
1973 —Chicago	16	1	5	.200	2	2	1.000	1	0	2	0	4

Season Team	Min.	FGM	FGA	Pct.	FTM	FTA	Pct.	REBOUNDS Off.	Def.	Tot.	Ast.	PF	Dq.	St.	Blk.	TO	Pts.
1974 —Chicago	14	4	5	.800	4	4	1.000	0	2	2	1	1	0	0	0	...	12
Totals	125	20	46	.435	17	20	.850	...	...	18	8	11	0	0	0	...	57

ALL-TIME GREAT PLAYERS

WALTON, BILL   C/F

PERSONAL: Born November 5, 1952, in La Mesa, Calif. ... 6-11/235. ... Full name: William Theodore Walton III. ... Brother of Bruce Walton, offensive lineman with Dallas Cowboys (1973-75).
HIGH SCHOOL: Helix (La Mesa, Calif.).
COLLEGE: UCLA.
TRANSACTIONS/CAREER NOTES: Selected by Portland Trail Blazers in first round (first pick overall) of 1974 NBA Draft. ... Signed as veteran free agent by San Diego Clippers (May 13, 1979); Trail Blazers received C Kevin Kunnert, F Kermit Washington, 1980 first-round draft choice and cash as compensation (September 18, 1979). ... Clippers franchise moved from San Diego to Los Angeles for 1984-85 season. ... Traded by Clippers to Boston Celtics for F Cedric Maxwell, 1986 first-round draft choice and cash (September 6, 1985).
CAREER HONORS: Elected to Naismith Memorial Basketball Hall of Fame (1993).
MISCELLANEOUS: Member of NBA championship teams (1977, 1986).

COLLEGIATE RECORD

NOTES: THE SPORTING NEWS College Player of the Year (1972, 1973, 1974). ... Naismith Award winner (1972, 1973, 1974). ... THE SPORTING NEWS All-America first team (1972, 1973, 1974). ... NCAA Division I Tournament Most Outstanding Player (1972, 1973). ... Member of NCAA Division I championship teams (1972, 1973). ... Holds NCAA tournament career record for highest field-goal percentage (minimum of 60 made)—68.6 percent, 109-of-159 (1972 through 1974). ... Holds NCAA tournament single-season record for highest field-goal percentage (minimum of 40 made)—76.3 percent, 45-of-59 (1973).

Season Team	G	Min.	FGM	FGA	Pct.	FTM	FTA	Pct.	Reb.	Ast.	Pts.	RPG	APG	PPG
70-71—UCLA‡	20	...	155	266	.583	52	82	.634	321	74	362	16.1	3.7	18.1
71-72—UCLA	30	...	238	372	.640	157	223	.704	466	...	633	15.5	...	21.1
72-73—UCLA	30	...	277	426	.650	58	102	.569	506	168	612	16.9	5.6	20.4
73-74—UCLA	27	...	232	349	.665	58	100	.580	398	148	522	14.7	5.5	19.3
Varsity totals	87	...	747	1147	.651	273	425	.642	1370	...	1767	15.7	...	20.3

NBA REGULAR-SEASON RECORD

HONORS: NBA Most Valuable Player (1978). ... NBA Sixth Man Award (1986). ... All-NBA first team (1978). ... All-NBA second team (1977). ... NBA All-Defensive first team (1977, 1978).
NOTES: Led NBA with 3.25 blocked shots per game (1977).

Season Team	G	Min.	FGM	FGA	Pct.	FTM	FTA	Pct.	Off.	Def.	Tot.	Ast.	St.	Blk.	TO	Pts.	RPG	APG	PPG
74-75—Portland	35	1153	177	345	.513	94	137	.686	92	349	441	167	29	94	...	448	12.6	4.8	12.8
75-76—Portland	51	1687	345	732	.471	133	228	.583	132	549	681	220	49	82	...	823	13.4	4.3	16.1
76-77—Portland	65	2264	491	930	.528	228	327	.697	211	723	934	245	66	211	...	1210	*14.4	3.8	18.6
77-78—Portland	58	1929	460	882	.522	177	246	.720	118	648	766	291	60	146	206	1097	13.2	5.0	18.9
78-79—Portland								Did not play—injured.											
79-80—San Diego	14	337	81	161	.503	32	54	.593	28	98	126	34	8	38	37	194	9.0	2.4	13.9
80-81—San Diego								Did not play—injured.											
81-82—San Diego								Did not play—injured.											
82-83—San Diego	33	1099	200	379	.528	65	117	.556	75	248	323	120	34	119	105	465	9.8	3.6	14.1
83-84—San Diego	55	1476	288	518	.556	92	154	.597	132	345	477	183	45	88	177	668	8.7	3.3	12.1
84-85—L.A. Clippers	67	1647	269	516	.521	138	203	.680	168	432	600	156	50	140	174	676	9.0	2.3	10.1
85-86—Boston	80	1546	231	411	.562	144	202	.713	136	408	544	165	38	106	111	606	6.8	2.1	7.6
86-87—Boston	10	112	10	26	.385	8	15	.533	11	20	31	9	1	10	15	28	3.1	0.9	2.8
87-88—								Did not play—injured.											
Totals	468	13250	2552	4900	.521	1111	1683	.660	1103	3820	4923	1590	380	1034	865	6215	10.5	3.4	13.3

Three-point field goals: 1983-84, 0-for-2. 1984-85, 0-for-1. Totals, 0-for-4.
Personal fouls/disqualifications: 1974-75, 115/4. 1975-76, 144/3. 1976-77, 174/5. 1977-78, 145/3. 1979-80, 37/0. 1982-83, 113/0. 1983-84, 153/1. 1984-85, 184/0. 1985-86, 210/1. 1986-87, 23/0. Totals, 1298/17.

NBA PLAYOFF RECORD

NOTES: NBA Finals Most Valuable Player (1977). ... Holds NBA Finals single-game record for most defensive rebounds—20 (June 3, 1977, vs. Philadelphia; and June 5, 1977, vs. Philadelphia). ... Shares NBA Finals single-game record for most blocked shots—8 (June 5, 1977, vs. Philadelphia). ... Shares single-game playoff record for most defensive rebounds—20 (June 3, 1977, vs. Philadelphia; and June 5, 1977, vs. Philadelphia).

Season Team	G	Min.	FGM	FGA	Pct.	FTM	FTA	Pct.	Off.	Def.	Tot.	Ast.	St.	Blk.	TO	Pts.	RPG	APG	PPG
76-77—Portland	19	755	153	302	.507	39	57	.684	56	232	288	104	20	64	...	345	15.2	5.5	18.2
77-78—Portland	2	49	11	18	.611	5	7	.714	5	17	22	4	3	3	6	27	11.0	2.0	13.5
85-86—Boston	16	291	54	93	.581	19	23	.826	25	78	103	27	6	12	22	127	6.4	1.7	7.9
86-87—Boston	12	102	12	25	.480	5	14	.357	9	22	31	10	3	4	8	29	2.6	0.8	2.4
Totals	49	1197	230	438	.525	68	101	.673	95	349	444	145	32	83	36	528	9.1	3.0	10.8

Three-point field goals: 1985-86, 0-for-1.
Personal fouls/disqualifications: 1976-77, 80/3. 1977-78, 1/0. 1985-86, 45/1. 1986-87, 23/0. Totals, 149/4.

NBA ALL-STAR GAME RECORD

Season Team	Min.	FGM	FGA	Pct.	FTM	FTA	Pct.	Off.	Def.	Tot.	Ast.	PF	Dq.	St.	Blk.	TO	Pts.
1977 —Portland							Selected, did not play—injured.										
1978 —Portland	31	6	14	.429	3	3	1.000	2	8	10	2	3	0	3	2	4	15
Totals	31	6	14	.429	3	3	1.000	2	8	10	2	3	0	3	2	4	15

DID YOU KNOW...

...that Michael Jordan has scored at least 40 points five times in the NBA Finals?
The Boston Celtics, as a team, have two such performances.

WEST, JERRY　　　　　　　　　G

PERSONAL: Born May 28, 1938, in Cheylan, W.Va. ... 6-2/185. ... Full name: Jerry Alan West.
HIGH SCHOOL: East Bank (W.Va.).
COLLEGE: West Virginia.
TRANSACTIONS/CAREER NOTES: Selected by Minneapolis Lakers in first round (second pick overall) of 1960 NBA Draft. ... Lakers franchise moved from Minneapolis to Los Angeles for 1960-61 season.
CAREER HONORS: Elected to Naismith Memorial Basketball Hall of Fame (1979). ... NBA 35th Anniversary All-Time Team (1980).
MISCELLANEOUS: Member of NBA championship team (1972). ... Member of gold-medal-winning U.S. Olympic team (1960). ... Los Angeles Lakers all-time leading scorer with 25,192 points (1960-61 through 1973-74).

COLLEGIATE RECORD

NOTES: The Sporting News All-America first team (1959, 1960). ... NCAA Tournament Most Outstanding Player (1959).

Season Team	G	Min.	FGM	FGA	Pct.	FTM	FTA	Pct.	Reb.	Ast.	Pts.	RPG	APG	PPG
56-57—West Virginia‡	17	...	114	...	...	104	...	...	...	...	332	...	...	19.5
57-58—West Virginia	28	799	178	359	.496	142	194	.732	311	41	498	11.1	1.5	17.8
58-59—West Virginia	34	1210	340	656	.518	223	320	.697	419	86	903	12.3	2.5	26.6
59-60—West Virginia	31	1129	325	645	.504	258	337	.766	510	134	908	16.5	4.3	29.3
Varsity totals	93	3138	843	1660	.508	623	851	.732	1240	261	2309	13.3	2.8	24.8

NBA REGULAR-SEASON RECORD

RECORDS: Holds single-season record for most free throws made—840 (1966).
HONORS: All-NBA first team (1962, 1963, 1964, 1965, 1966, 1967, 1970, 1971, 1972, 1973). ... All-NBA second team (1968, 1969). ... NBA All-Defensive first team (1970, 1971, 1972, 1973). ... NBA All-Defensive second team (1969).

Season Team	G	Min.	FGM	FGA	Pct.	FTM	FTA	Pct.	Reb.	Ast.	PF	Dq.	Pts.	RPG	APG	PPG
60-61 —Los Angeles	79	2797	529	1264	.419	331	497	.666	611	333	213	1	1389	7.7	4.2	17.6
61-62 —Los Angeles	75	3087	799	1795	.445	712	926	.769	591	402	173	4	2310	7.9	5.4	30.8
62-63 —Los Angeles	55	2163	559	1213	.461	371	477	.778	384	307	150	1	1489	7.0	5.6	27.1
63-64 —Los Angeles	72	2906	740	1529	.484	584	702	.832	443	403	200	2	2064	6.2	5.6	28.7
64-65 —Los Angeles	74	3066	822	1655	.497	648	789	.821	447	364	221	2	2292	6.0	4.9	31.0
65-66 —Los Angeles	79	3218	818	1731	.473	*840	*977	.860	562	480	243	1	2476	7.1	6.1	31.3
66-67 —Los Angeles	66	2670	645	1389	.464	602	686	.878	392	447	160	1	1892	5.9	6.8	28.7
67-68 —Los Angeles	51	1919	476	926	.514	391	482	.811	294	310	152	1	1343	5.8	6.1	26.3
68-69 —Los Angeles	61	2394	545	1156	.471	490	597	.821	262	423	156	1	1580	4.3	6.9	25.9
69-70 —Los Angeles	74	3106	831	1673	.497	*647	*785	.824	338	554	160	3	2309	4.6	7.5	*31.2
70-71 —Los Angeles	69	2845	667	1351	.494	525	631	.832	320	655	180	0	1859	4.6	9.5	26.9
71-72 —Los Angeles	77	2973	735	1540	.477	515	633	.814	327	747	209	0	1985	4.2	*9.7	25.8
72-73 —Los Angeles	69	2460	618	1291	.479	339	421	.805	289	607	138	0	1575	4.2	8.8	22.8

| | | | | | | | | | REBOUNDS | | | | | | | AVERAGES | | |
Season Team	G	Min.	FGM	FGA	Pct.	FTM	FTA	Pct.	Off.	Def.	Tot.	Ast.	St.	Blk.	TO	Pts.	RPG	APG	PPG
73-74—Los Angeles	31	967	232	519	.447	165	198	.833	30	86	116	206	81	23	...	629	3.7	6.6	20.3
Totals	932	36571	9016	19032	.474	7160	8801	.814	...	...	5376	6238	81	23	...	25192	5.8	6.7	27.0

Personal fouls/disqualifications: 1973-74, 80/0.

NBA PLAYOFF RECORD

NOTES: NBA Finals Most Valuable Player (1969). ... Holds career playoff record for most free throws made—1,213. ... Holds single-series playoff record for highest points-per-game average—46.3 (1965).

Season Team	G	Min.	FGM	FGA	Pct.	FTM	FTA	Pct.	Reb.	Ast.	PF	Dq.	Pts.	RPG	APG	PPG
60-61 —Los Angeles	12	461	99	202	.490	77	106	.726	104	63	39	0	275	8.7	5.3	22.9
61-62 —Los Angeles	13	557	144	310	.465	121	150	.807	88	57	38	0	409	6.8	4.4	31.5
62-63 Los Angeles	13	638	144	286	.504	74	100	.740	106	61	34	0	362	8.2	4.7	27.8
63-64 —Los Angeles	5	206	57	115	.496	42	53	.792	36	17	20	0	156	7.2	3.4	31.2
64-65 —Los Angeles	11	470	155	351	.442	137	154	.890	63	58	37	0	447	5.7	5.3	40.6
65-66 —Los Angeles	14	619	185	357	.518	109	125	.872	88	79	40	0	479	6.3	5.6	34.2
66-67 —Los Angeles	1	1	0	0	...	0	0	...	1	0	0	0	0	1.0	0.0	0.0
67-68 —Los Angeles	15	622	165	313	.527	132	169	.781	81	82	47	0	462	5.4	5.5	30.8
68-69 —Los Angeles	18	757	196	423	.463	164	204	.804	71	135	52	1	556	3.9	7.5	30.9
69-70 —Los Angeles	18	830	196	418	.469	170	212	.802	66	151	55	1	562	3.7	8.4	31.2
71-72 —Los Angeles	15	608	128	340	.376	88	106	.830	73	134	39	0	344	4.9	8.9	22.9
72-73 —Los Angeles	17	638	151	336	.449	99	127	.780	76	132	49	1	401	4.5	7.8	23.6

| | | | | | | | | | REBOUNDS | | | | | | | AVERAGES | | |
Season Team	G	Min.	FGM	FGA	Pct.	FTM	FTA	Pct.	Off.	Def.	Tot.	Ast.	St.	Blk.	TO	Pts.	RPG	APG	PPG
73-74—Los Angeles	1	14	2	9	.222	0	0	...	0	2	2	1	0	0	...	4	2.0	1.0	4.0
Totals	153	6321	1622	3460	.469	1213	1506	.805	...	...	855	970	0	0	...	4457	5.6	6.3	29.1

Personal fouls/disqualifications: 1973-74, 1/0.

NBA ALL-STAR GAME RECORD

NOTES: NBA All-Star Game Most Valuable Player (1972).

Season Team	Min.	FGM	FGA	Pct.	FTM	FTA	Pct.	Reb	Ast.	PF	Dq.	Pts.
1961 —Los Angeles	25	2	8	.250	5	6	.833	2	4	3	0	9
1962 —Los Angeles‡	31	7	14	.500	4	6	.667	3	1	2	0	18
1963 —Los Angeles	32	5	15	.333	3	4	.750	7	5	1	0	13
1964 —Los Angeles	42	8	20	.400	1	1	1.000	4	5	3	0	17
1965 —Los Angeles	40	8	16	.500	4	6	.667	5	6	2	0	20
1966 —Los Angeles	11	1	5	.200	2	2	1.000	1	0	2	0	4

ALL-TIME GREAT PLAYERS

Season Team	Min.	FGM	FGA	Pct.	FTM	FTA	Pct.	Reb.	Ast.	PF	Dq.	Pts.
1967 —Los Angeles	30	6	11	.545	4	4	1.000	3	6	3	0	16
1968 —Los Angeles	32	7	17	.412	3	4	.750	6	6	4	0	17
1969 —Los Angeles					Selected, did not play—injured.							
1970 —Los Angeles	31	7	12	.583	8	12	.667	5	5	3	0	22
1971 —Los Angeles	20	2	4	.500	1	3	.333	1	9	1	0	5
1972 —Los Angeles	27	6	9	.667	1	2	.500	6	5	2	0	13
1973 —Los Angeles	20	3	6	.500	0	0	...	4	3	2	0	6
1974 —Los Angeles					Selected, did not play—injured.							
Totals	341	62	137	.453	36	50	.720	47	55	28	0	160

NBA COACHING RECORD

BACKGROUND: Consultant, Los Angeles Lakers (1979-80 through 1981-82). ... General manager, Lakers (1982-83 to present).

	REGULAR SEASON				PLAYOFFS		
Season Team	W	L	Pct.	Finish	W	L	Pct.
76-77 —Los Angeles	53	29	.646	1st/Pacific Division	4	7	.364
77-78 —Los Angeles	45	37	.549	4th/Pacific Division	1	2	.333
78-79 —Los Angeles	47	35	.573	3rd/Pacific Division	3	5	.375
Totals (3 years)	145	101	.589	Totals (3 years)	8	14	.364

NOTES:

1977—Defeated Golden State, 4-3, in Western Conference semifinals; lost to Portland, 4-0, in Western Conference finals.
1978—Lost to Seattle in Western Conference first round.
1979—Defeated Denver, 2-1, in Western Conference first round; lost to Seattle, 4-1, in Western Conference semifinals.

WESTPHAL, PAUL — SUNS

PERSONAL: Born November 30, 1950, in Torrance, Calif. ... 6-4/195. ... Full name: Paul Douglas Westphal.
HIGH SCHOOL: Aviation (Redondo Beach, Calif.).
COLLEGE: Southern California.
TRANSACTIONS/CAREER NOTES: Selected by Boston Celtics in first round (10th pick overall) of 1972 NBA Draft. ... Traded by Celtics with 1975 and 1976 second-round draft choices to Phoenix Suns for G Charlie Scott (May 23, 1975). ... Traded by Suns to Seattle SuperSonics for G Dennis Johnson (June 4, 1980). ... Signed as veteran free agent by New York Knicks (March 12, 1982). ... Waived by Knicks (June 20, 1983). ... Signed by Suns (September 27, 1983). ... Waived by Suns (October 12, 1984).
MISCELLANEOUS: Member of NBA championship team (1974).

COLLEGIATE RECORD

NOTES: The Sporting News All-America second team (1972).

											AVERAGES		
Season Team	G	Min.	FGM	FGA	Pct.	FTM	FTA	Pct.	Reb.	Ast.	Pts.	RPG	APG	PPG
68-69—Southern Cal‡	19	...	134	262	.511	87	119	.731	106	...	355	5.6	...	18.7
69-70—Southern Cal	26	...	147	277	.531	84	110	.764	68	45	378	2.6	1.7	14.5
70-71—Southern Cal	26	...	157	328	.479	109	150	.727	84	84	423	3.2	3.2	16.3
71-72—Southern Cal	14	...	106	219	.484	72	95	.758	74	71	284	5.3	5.1	20.3
Varsity totals	66	...	410	824	.498	265	355	.746	226	200	1085	3.4	3.0	16.4

NBA REGULAR-SEASON RECORD

HONORS: NBA Comeback Player of the Year (1983). ... All-NBA first team (1977, 1979, 1980). ... All-NBA second team (1978).

									REBOUNDS								AVERAGES		
Season Team	G	Min.	FGM	FGA	Pct.	FTM	FTA	Pct.	Off.	Def.	Tot.	Ast.	St.	Blk.	TO	Pts.	RPG	APG	PPG
72-73—Boston	60	482	89	212	.420	67	86	.779	...	...	67	69	...	...	...	245	1.1	1.2	4.1
73-74—Boston	82	1165	238	475	.501	112	153	.732	49	94	143	171	39	34	...	588	1.7	2.1	7.2
74-75—Boston	82	1581	342	670	.510	119	156	.763	44	119	163	235	78	33	...	803	2.0	2.9	9.8
75-76—Phoenix	82	2960	657	1329	.494	365	440	.830	74	185	259	440	210	38	...	1679	3.2	5.4	20.5
76-77—Phoenix	81	2600	682	1317	.518	362	439	.825	57	133	190	459	134	21	...	1726	2.3	5.7	21.3
77-78—Phoenix	80	2481	809	1568	.516	396	487	.813	41	123	164	437	138	31	280	2014	2.1	5.5	25.2
78-79—Phoenix	81	2641	801	1496	.535	339	405	.837	35	124	159	529	111	26	232	1941	2.0	6.5	24.0
79-80—Phoenix	82	2665	692	1317	.525	382	443	.862	46	141	187	416	119	35	207	1792	2.3	5.1	21.9
80-81—Seattle	36	1078	221	500	.442	153	184	.832	11	57	68	148	46	14	78	601	1.9	4.1	16.7
81-82—New York	18	451	86	194	.443	36	47	.766	9	13	22	100	19	8	47	210	1.2	5.6	11.7
82-83—New York	80	1978	318	693	.459	148	184	.804	19	96	115	439	87	16	196	798	1.4	5.5	10.0
83-84—Phoenix	59	865	144	313	.460	117	142	.824	8	35	43	148	41	6	77	412	0.7	2.5	7.0
Totals	823	20947	5079	10084	.504	2596	3166	.820	...	...	1580	3591	1022	262	1117	12809	1.9	4.4	15.6

Three-point field goals: 1979-80, 26-for-93 (.280). 1980-81, 6-for-25 (.240). 1981-82, 2-for-8 (.250). 1982-83, 14-for-48 (.292). 1983-84, 7-for-26 (.269). Totals, 55-for-200 (.275).

Personal fouls/disqualifications: 1972-73, 88/0. 1973-74, 173/1. 1974-75, 192/0. 1975-76, 218/3. 1976-77, 171/1. 1977-78, 162/0. 1978-79, 159/1. 1979-80, 162/0. 1980-81, 70/0. 1981-82, 61/1. 1982-83, 180/1. 1983-84, 69/0. Totals, 1705/8.

NBA PLAYOFF RECORD

									REBOUNDS								AVERAGES		
Season Team	G	Min.	FGM	FGA	Pct.	FTM	FTA	Pct.	Off.	Def.	Tot.	Ast.	St.	Blk.	TO	Pts.	RPG	APG	PPG
72-73—Boston	11	109	19	39	.487	5	7	.714	...	...	7	9	...	...	...	43	0.6	0.8	3.9
73-74—Boston	18	241	46	100	.460	11	15	.733	6	15	21	31	8	2	...	103	1.2	1.7	5.7
74-75—Boston	11	183	38	81	.469	12	18	.667	5	8	13	32	6	2	...	88	1.2	2.9	8.0
75-76—Phoenix	19	685	165	323	.511	71	93	.763	14	33	47	96	34	9	...	401	2.5	5.1	21.1
77-78—Phoenix	2	66	22	47	.468	8	9	.889	3	3	6	19	1	0	5	52	3.0	9.5	26.0
78-79—Phoenix	15	534	142	287	.495	52	66	.788	7	26	33	64	15	5	38	336	2.2	4.3	22.4
79-80—Phoenix	8	253	69	142	.486	28	32	.875	2	8	10	31	11	3	13	167	1.3	3.9	20.9

Season Team	G	Min.	FGM	FGA	Pct.	FTM	FTA	Pct.	Off.	Def.	Tot.	Ast.	St.	Blk.	TO	Pts.	RPG	APG	PPG
									REBOUNDS								AVERAGES		
82-83—New York	6	156	22	50	.440	10	13	.769	0	8	8	34	2	2	9	57	1.3	5.7	9.5
83-84—Phoenix	17	222	30	80	.375	28	32	.875	3	5	8	37	12	0	24	90	0.5	2.2	5.3
Totals	107	2449	553	1149	.481	225	285	.789	...	...	153	353	89	23	89	1337	1.4	3.3	12.5

Three-point field goals: 1979-80, 1-for-12 (.083). 1982-83, 3-for-8 (.375). 1983-84, 2-for-9 (.222). Totals, 6-for-29 (.207).

Personal fouls/disqualifications: 1972-73, 24/1. 1973-74, 37/0. 1974-75, 21/0. 1975-76, 61/1. 1977-78, 4/0. 1978-79, 38/0. 1979-80, 20/0. 1982-83, 13/0. 1983-84, 23/0. Totals, 241/2.

NBA ALL-STAR GAME RECORD

Season Team	Min.	FGM	FGA	Pct.	FTM	FTA	Pct.	Off.	Def.	Tot.	Ast.	PF	Dq.	St.	Blk.	TO	Pts.
								REBOUNDS									
1977 —Phoenix	31	10	16	.625	0	0	...	0	1	1	6	2	0	3	2	...	20
1978 —Phoenix	24	9	14	.643	2	5	.400	0	0	0	5	4	0	1	1	3	20
1979 —Phoenix	21	8	12	.667	1	2	.500	0	1	1	5	0	0	0	0	1	17
1980 —Phoenix	27	8	14	.571	5	6	.833	1	0	1	5	5	0	2	1	3	21
1981 —Seattle	25	8	12	.667	3	3	1.000	2	2	4	3	3	0	0	1	4	19
Totals	128	43	68	.632	11	16	.688	3	4	7	24	14	0	6	5	11	97

Three-point field goals: 1980, 0-for-2.

HEAD COACHING RECORD

BACKGROUND: Assistant coach, Phoenix Suns (1988-89 through 1991-92).

COLLEGIATE COACHING RECORD

Season Team	W	L	Pct.	Finish
			REGULAR SEASON	
85-86 —S'western Baptist Bible Coll.	21	9	.700	
86-87 —Grand Canyon College (Ariz.)	26	12	.684	NAIA Independent
87-88 —Grand Canyon College (Ariz.)	37	6	.860	NAIA Independent
Totals (3 years)	84	27	.757	

NBA COACHING RECORD

Season Team	W	L	Pct.	Finish		W	L	Pct.
	REGULAR SEASON					PLAYOFFS		
92-93 —Phoenix	62	20	.756	1st/Pacific Division		13	11	.542
93-94 —Phoenix	56	26	.683	2nd/Pacific Division		6	4	.600
94-95 —Phoenix	59	23	.720	1st/Pacific Division		6	4	.600
95-96 —Phoenix	14	19	.424			—	—	—
Totals (4 years)	191	88	.685	Totals (3 years)		25	19	.568

NOTES:

1987—Defeated Fort Lewis College (Colo.), 94-87, in NAIA District 7 first round; lost to Western State College (Colo.), 74-69, in NAIA District 7 championship.

1988—Defeated Southern Colorado, 68-62, in NAIA District 7 first round; defeated Colorado School of Mines, 113-79, in District 7 championship; defeated Hastings College (Neb.), 103-75, in NAIA Tournament first round; defeated Fort Hays State (Kan.), 101-95, in second round; defeated College of Idaho, 99-96, in third round; defeated Waynesburg State (Pa.), 108-106, in fourth round; defeated Auburn-Montgomery (Ala.), 88-86 (OT), in NAIA championship game.

1993—Defeated Los Angeles Lakers, 3-2, in Western Conference first round; defeated San Antonio, 4-2, in Western Conference semifinals; defeated Seattle, 4-3, in Western Conference finals; lost to Chicago, 4-2, in NBA Finals.

1994—Defeated Golden State, 3-0, in Western Conference first round; lost to Houston, 4-3, in Western Conference semifinals.

1995—Defeated Portland, 3-0, in Western Conference first round; lost to Houston, 4-3, in Western Conference semifinals.

1996—Replaced as Phoenix Suns head coach by Cotton Fitzsimmons (January 16).

WHITE, JO JO　　　　　G

PERSONAL: Born November 16, 1946, in St. Louis. ... 6-3/190. ... Full name: Joseph Henry White.

HIGH SCHOOL: Vashon (St. Louis), then McKinley (St. Louis).

COLLEGE: Kansas.

TRANSACTIONS/CAREER NOTES: Selected by Boston Celtics in first round (ninth pick overall) of 1969 NBA Draft. ... Traded by Celtics to Golden State Warriors for 1979 first-round draft choice (January 30, 1979). ... Contract sold by Warriors to Kansas City Kings (September 10, 1980). ... Played in Continental Basketball Association with Topeka Sizzlers (1987-88).

MISCELLANEOUS: Member of NBA championship teams (1974, 1976). ... Member of gold-medal-winning U.S. Olympic team (1968).

COLLEGIATE RECORD

NOTES: THE SPORTING NEWS All-America first team (1968, 1969).

Season Team	G	Min.	FGM	FGA	Pct.	FTM	FTA	Pct.	Reb.	Ast.	Pts.	RPG	APG	PPG
												AVERAGES		
64-65—Kansas‡	2	...	11	34	.324	11	15	.733	25	...	33	12.5	...	16.5
65-66—Kansas‡	6	...	35	88	.398	18	27	.667	32	...	88	5.3	...	14.7
65-66—Kansas	9	...	44	112	.393	14	26	.538	68	...	102	7.6	...	11.3
66-67—Kansas	27	...	170	416	.409	59	72	.819	150	...	399	5.6	...	14.8
67-68—Kansas	30	...	188	462	.407	83	115	.722	107	...	459	3.6	...	15.3
68-69—Kansas	18	...	134	286	.469	58	79	.734	84	...	326	4.7	...	18.1
Varsity totals	84	...	536	1276	.420	214	292	.733	409	...	1286	4.9	...	15.3

NBA REGULAR-SEASON RECORD

HONORS: All-NBA second team (1975, 1977). ... NBA All-Rookie team (1970).

Season Team	G	Min.	FGM	FGA	Pct.	FTM	FTA	Pct.	Reb.	Ast.	PF	Dq.	Pts.	RPG	APG	PPG
														AVERAGES		
69-70 —Boston	60	1328	309	684	.452	111	135	.822	169	145	132	1	729	2.8	2.4	12.2
70-71 —Boston	75	2787	693	1494	.464	215	269	.799	376	361	255	5	1601	5.0	4.8	21.3
71-72 —Boston	79	3261	770	1788	.431	285	343	.831	446	416	227	1	1825	5.6	5.3	23.1
72-73 —Boston	82	3250	717	1665	.431	178	228	.781	414	498	185	2	1612	5.0	6.1	19.7

Season Team	G	Min.	FGM	FGA	Pct.	FTM	FTA	Pct.	REBOUNDS Off.	Def.	Tot.	Ast.	St.	Blk.	TO	Pts.	AVERAGES RPG	APG	PPG
73-74—Boston	82	3238	649	1445	.449	190	227	.837	100	251	351	448	105	25	...	1488	4.3	5.5	18.1
74-75—Boston	82	3220	658	1440	.457	186	223	.834	84	227	311	458	128	17	...	1502	3.8	5.6	18.3
75-76—Boston	82	3257	670	1492	.449	212	253	.838	61	252	313	445	107	20	...	1552	3.8	5.4	18.9
76-77—Boston	82	3333	638	1488	.429	333	383	.869	87	296	383	492	118	22	...	1609	4.7	6.0	19.6
77-78—Boston	46	1641	289	690	.419	103	120	.858	53	127	180	209	49	7	117	681	3.9	4.5	14.8
78-79—Boston-G.S.	76	2338	404	910	.444	139	158	.880	42	158	200	347	80	7	212	947	2.6	4.6	12.5
79-80—Golden State	78	2052	336	706	.476	97	114	.851	42	139	181	239	88	13	157	770	2.3	3.1	9.9
80-81—Kansas City	13	236	36	82	.439	11	18	.611	3	18	21	37	11	1	18	83	1.6	2.8	6.4
Totals	837	29941	6169	13884	.444	2060	2471	.834	...	...	3345	4095	686	112	504	14399	4.0	4.9	17.2

Three-point field goals: 1979-80, 1-for-6 (.167).
Personal fouls/disqualifications: 1973-74, 185/1. 1974-75, 207/1. 1975-76, 183/2. 1976-77, 193/5. 1977-78, 109/2. 1978-79, 173/1. 1979-80, 186/0. 1980-81, 21/0. Totals, 2056/21.

NBA PLAYOFF RECORD

NOTES: NBA Finals Most Valuable Player (1976).

Season Team	G	Min.	FGM	FGA	Pct.	FTM	FTA	Pct.	Reb.	Ast.	PF	Dq.	Pts.	AVERAGES RPG	APG	PPG
71-72—Boston	11	432	109	220	.495	40	48	.833	59	58	31	0	258	5.4	5.3	23.5
72-73—Boston	13	583	135	300	.450	49	54	.907	64	83	44	2	319	4.9	6.4	24.5

Season Team	G	Min.	FGM	FGA	Pct.	FTM	FTA	Pct.	REBOUNDS Off.	Def.	Tot.	Ast.	St.	Blk.	TO	Pts.	AVERAGES RPG	APG	PPG
73-74—Boston	18	765	132	310	.426	34	46	.739	17	58	75	98	15	2	...	298	4.2	5.4	16.6
74-75—Boston	11	462	100	227	.441	27	33	.818	18	32	50	63	11	4	...	227	4.5	5.7	20.6
75-76—Boston	18	791	165	371	.445	78	95	.821	12	59	71	98	23	1	...	408	3.9	5.4	22.7
76-77—Boston	9	395	91	201	.453	28	33	.848	10	29	39	52	14	0	...	210	4.3	5.8	23.3
Totals	80	3428	732	1629	.449	256	309	.828	...	...	358	452	63	7	...	1720	4.5	5.7	21.5

Personal fouls/disqualifications: 1973-74, 56/1. 1974-75, 32/0. 1975-76, 51/0. 1976-77, 27/0. Totals, 241/3.

NBA ALL-STAR GAME RECORD

Season Team	Min.	FGM	FGA	Pct.	FTM	FTA	Pct.	Reb	Ast.	PF	Dq.	Pts.
1971—Boston	22	5	10	.500	0	0	...	9	2	2	0	10
1972—Boston	18	6	15	.400	0	2	.000	4	3	1	0	12
1973—Boston	18	3	7	.429	0	0	...	5	5	0	0	6

Season Team	Min.	FGM	FGA	Pct.	FTM	FTA	Pct.	REBOUNDS Off.	Def.	Tot.	Ast.	PF	Dq.	St.	Blk.	TO	Pts.
1974—Boston	22	6	12	.500	1	3	.333	2	4	6	4	1	0	2	1	...	13
1975—Boston	13	1	2	.500	5	6	.833	0	1	1	4	1	0	0	1	...	7
1976—Boston	16	3	7	.429	0	0	...	0	1	1	1	1	0	2	0	...	6
1977—Boston	15	5	7	.714	0	0	...	0	1	1	2	0	0	0	0	...	10
Totals	124	29	60	.483	6	11	.545	...	...	27	21	6	0	4	1	...	64

CBA REGULAR-SEASON RECORD

Season Team	G	Min.	FGM	FGA	Pct.	FTM	FTA	Pct.	Reb.	Ast.	Pts.	AVERAGES RPG	APG	PPG
87-88—Topeka	5	122	12	30	.400	4	6	.667	6	21	28	1.2	4.2	5.6

Three-point field goals: 1987-88, 0-for-3.

WILKINS, DOMINIQUE   F

PERSONAL: Born January 12, 1960, in Paris, France. ... 6-8/224. ... Full name: Jacques Dominique Wilkins. ... Brother of Gerald Wilkins, guard with Orlando Magic.
HIGH SCHOOL: Washington (N.C.).
COLLEGE: Georgia.
TRANSACTIONS/CAREER NOTES: Selected after junior season by Utah Jazz in first round (third pick overall) of 1982 NBA Draft. ... Draft rights traded by Jazz to Atlanta Hawks for F John Drew, G Freeman Williams and cash (September 2, 1982). ... Traded by Hawks with 1994 conditional first-round draft choice to Los Angeles Clippers for F Danny Manning (February 24, 1994). ... Signed as unrestricted free agent by Boston Celtics (July 25, 1994). ... Signed by Panathinaikos Athens of Greek League (August 12, 1995).
MISCELLANEOUS: Atlanta Hawks franchise all-time leading scorer with 23,292 points and all-time steals leader with 1,245 (1982-83 through 1993-94).

COLLEGIATE RECORD

NOTES: The Sporting News All-America second team (1981, 1982).

Season Team	G	Min.	FGM	FGA	Pct.	FTM	FTA	Pct.	Reb.	Ast.	Pts.	AVERAGES RPG	APG	PPG
79-80—Georgia	16	508	135	257	.525	27	37	.730	104	23	297	6.5	1.4	18.6
80-81—Georgia	31	1157	310	582	.533	112	149	.752	234	52	732	7.5	1.7	23.6
81-82—Georgia	31	1083	278	526	.529	103	160	.644	250	41	659	8.1	1.3	21.3
Totals	78	2748	723	1365	.530	242	346	.699	588	116	1688	7.5	1.5	21.6

NBA REGULAR-SEASON RECORD

RECORDS: Holds single-game record for most free throws without a miss—23 (December 8, 1992, vs. Chicago).
HONORS: Slam-Dunk Championship winner (1985, 1990). ... All-NBA first team (1986). ... All-NBA second team (1987, 1988, 1991, 1993). ... All-NBA third team (1989, 1994). ... NBA All-Rookie team (1983).

Season Team	G	Min.	FGM	FGA	Pct.	FTM	FTA	Pct.	REBOUNDS Off.	Def.	Tot.	Ast.	St.	Blk.	TO	Pts.	AVERAGES RPG	APG	PPG
82-83—Atlanta	82	2697	601	1220	.493	230	337	.683	226	252	478	129	84	63	180	1434	5.8	1.6	17.5
83-84—Atlanta	81	2961	684	1429	.479	382	496	.770	254	328	582	126	117	87	215	1750	7.2	1.6	21.6

Season Team	G	Min.	FGM	FGA	Pct.	FTM	FTA	Pct.	Off.	Def.	Tot.	Ast.	St.	Blk.	TO	Pts.	RPG	APG	PPG
84-85—Atlanta	81	3023	853	*1891	.451	486	603	.806	226	331	557	200	135	54	225	2217	6.9	2.5	27.4
85-86—Atlanta	78	3049	888	*1897	.468	577	705	.818	261	357	618	206	138	49	251	2366	7.9	2.6	*30.3
86-87—Atlanta	79	2969	828	1787	.463	607	742	.818	210	284	494	261	117	51	215	2294	6.3	3.3	29.0
87-88—Atlanta	78	2948	909	1957	.464	541	655	.826	211	291	502	224	103	47	218	2397	6.4	2.9	30.7
88-89—Atlanta	80	2997	814	1756	.464	442	524	.844	256	297	553	211	117	52	181	2099	6.9	2.6	26.2
89-90—Atlanta	80	2888	810	1672	.484	459	569	.807	217	304	521	200	126	47	174	2138	6.5	2.5	26.7
90-91—Atlanta	81	3078	770	1640	.470	476	574	.829	261	471	732	265	123	65	201	2101	9.0	3.3	25.9
91-92—Atlanta	42	1601	424	914	.464	294	352	.835	103	192	295	158	52	24	122	1179	7.0	3.8	28.1
92-93—Atlanta	71	2647	741	1584	.468	519	627	.828	187	295	482	227	70	27	184	2121	6.8	3.2	29.9
93-94—Atl.-LA Clip.	74	2635	698	1588	.440	442	522	.847	182	299	481	169	92	30	172	1923	6.5	2.3	26.0
94-95—Boston	77	2423	496	1169	.424	266	340	.782	157	244	401	166	61	14	173	1370	5.2	2.2	17.8
Totals	984	35916	9516	20504	.464	5721	7046	.812	2751	3945	6696	2542	1335	610	2511	25389	6.8	2.6	25.8

Three-point field goals: 1982-83, 2-for-11 (.182). 1983-84, 0-for-11. 1984-85, 25-for-81 (.309). 1985-86, 13-for-70 (.186). 1986-87, 31-for-106 (.292). 1987-88, 38-for-129 (.295). 1988-89, 29-for-105 (.276). 1989-90, 59-for-183 (.322). 1990-91, 85-for-249 (.341). 1991-92, 37-for-128 (.289). 1992-93, 120-for-316 (.380). 1993-94, 85-for-295 (.288). 1994-95, 112-for-289 (.388). Totals, 636-for-1973 (.322).

Personal fouls/disqualifications: 1982-83, 210/1. 1983-84, 197/1. 1984-85, 170/0. 1985-86, 170/0. 1986-87, 149/0. 1987-88, 162/0. 1988-89, 138/0. 1989-90, 141/0. 1990-91, 156/0. 1991-92, 77/0. 1992-93, 116/0. 1993-94, 126/0. 1994-95, 130/0. Totals, 1942/2.

NBA PLAYOFF RECORD

Season Team	G	Min.	FGM	FGA	Pct.	FTM	FTA	Pct.	Off.	Def.	Tot.	Ast.	St.	Blk.	TO	Pts.	RPG	APG	PPG
82-83—Atlanta	3	109	17	42	.405	12	14	.857	8	7	15	1	2	1	10	47	5.0	0.3	15.7
83-84—Atlanta	5	197	35	84	.417	26	31	.839	21	20	41	11	12	1	15	96	8.2	2.2	19.2
85-86—Atlanta	9	360	94	217	.433	68	79	.861	20	34	54	25	9	2	30	257	6.0	2.8	28.6
86-87—Atlanta	9	360	86	210	.410	66	74	.892	27	43	70	25	16	8	26	241	7.8	2.8	26.8
87-88—Atlanta	12	473	137	300	.457	96	125	.768	37	40	77	34	16	6	30	374	6.4	2.8	31.2
88-89—Atlanta	5	212	52	116	.448	27	38	.711	10	17	27	17	4	8	12	136	5.4	3.4	27.2
90-91—Atlanta	5	195	35	94	.372	32	35	.914	6	26	32	13	9	5	11	104	6.4	2.6	20.8
92-93—Atlanta	3	113	32	75	.427	23	30	.767	12	4	16	9	3	1	10	90	5.3	3.0	30.0
94-95—Boston	4	150	26	61	.426	16	18	.889	17	26	43	8	2	3	9	76	10.8	2.0	19.0
Totals	55	2169	514	1199	.429	366	444	.824	158	217	375	143	73	35	153	1421	6.8	2.6	25.8

Three-point field goals: 1982-83, 1-for-1. 1983-84, 0-for-1. 1985-86, 1-for-5 (.200). 1986-87, 3-for-10 (.300). 1987-88, 4-for-18 (.222). 1988-89, 5-for-17 (.294). 1990-91, 2-for-15 (.133). 1992-93, 3-for-12 (.250). 1994-95, 8-for-17 (.471). Totals, 27-for-96 (.281).

Personal fouls/disqualifications: 1982-83, 9/0. 1983-84, 13/0. 1985-86, 24/0. 1986-87, 24/0. 1987-88, 24/0. 1988-89, 5/0. 1990-91, 8/0. 1992-93, 8/0. 1994-95, 7/0. Totals, 123/0.

NBA ALL-STAR GAME RECORD

Season Team	Min.	FGM	FGA	Pct.	FTM	FTA	Pct.	Off.	Def.	Tot.	Ast.	PF	Dq.	St.	Blk.	TO	Pts.
1986 —Atlanta.............	17	6	15	.400	1	2	.500	2	1	3	2	2	0	0	1	1	13
1987 —Atlanta.............	24	3	9	.333	4	7	.571	3	2	5	1	2	0	0	1	2	10
1988 —Atlanta.............	30	12	22	.545	5	6	.833	1	4	5	0	3	0	0	1	0	29
1989 —Atlanta.............	15	3	8	.375	3	3	1.000	1	1	2	0	0	0	3	0	2	9
1990 —Atlanta.............	16	5	10	.500	2	2	1.000	0	0	0	4	1	0	1	0	0	13
1991 —Atlanta.............	22	3	11	.273	6	8	.750	3	0	3	4	2	0	1	1	2	12
1992 —Atlanta.............								Selected, did not play—injured.									
1993 —Atlanta.............	18	2	11	.182	4	4	1.000	4	3	7	0	2	0	1	0	1	9
1994 —Atlanta.............	17	4	9	.444	3	6	.500	2	0	2	4	1	0	0	0	1	11
Totals..........................	159	38	95	.400	28	38	.737	16	11	27	15	13	0	6	4	8	106

Three-point field goals: 1990, 1-for-1. 1991, 0-for-2. 1993, 1-for-3 (.333). 1994, 0-for-2. Totals, 2-for-8 (.250).

GREEK LEAGUE RECORD

Season Team	G	Min.	FGM	FGA	Pct.	FTM	FTA	Pct.	Reb.	Ast.	Pts.	RPG	APG	PPG
95-96—Panathinaikos.................	14	...	...	...	...	...	...	...	95	19	292	7.0	1.4	20.9

WORTHY, JAMES   F

PERSONAL: Born February 27, 1961, in Gastonia, N.C. ... 6-9/225. ... Full name: James Ager Worthy.
HIGH SCHOOL: Ashbrook (Gastonia, N.C.).
COLLEGE: North Carolina.
TRANSACTIONS/CAREER NOTES: Selected after junior season by Los Angeles Lakers in first round (first pick overall) of 1982 NBA Draft. ... Announced retirement (November 10, 1994).
MISCELLANEOUS: Member of NBA championship teams (1985, 1987, 1988).

COLLEGIATE RECORD

NOTES: The Sporting News All-America first team (1982). ... NCAA Division I Tournament Most Outstanding Player (1982). ... Member of NCAA Division I championship team (1982).

Season Team	G	Min.	FGM	FGA	Pct.	FTM	FTA	Pct.	Reb.	Ast.	Pts.	RPG	APG	PPG
79-80—North Carolina...............	14	396	74	126	.587	27	45	.600	104	26	175	7.4	1.9	12.5
80-81—North Carolina...............	36	1214	208	416	.500	96	150	.640	301	100	512	8.4	2.8	14.2
81-82—North Carolina...............	34	1178	203	354	.573	126	187	.674	215	82	532	6.3	2.4	15.6
Totals	84	2788	485	896	.541	249	382	.652	620	208	1219	7.4	2.5	14.5

NBA REGULAR-SEASON RECORD

HONORS: All-NBA third team (1990, 1991). ... NBA All-Rookie team (1983).

Season Team	G	Min.	FGM	FGA	Pct.	FTM	FTA	Pct.	Off.	Def.	Tot.	Ast.	St.	Blk.	TO	Pts.	RPG	APG	PPG
82-83—Los Angeles....	77	1970	447	772	.579	138	221	.624	157	242	399	132	91	64	178	1033	5.2	1.7	13.4
83-84—Los Angeles....	82	2415	495	890	.556	195	257	.759	157	358	515	207	77	70	181	1185	6.3	2.5	14.5

Season Team	G	Min.	FGM	FGA	Pct.	FTM	FTA	Pct.	REBOUNDS Off.	Def.	Tot.	Ast.	St.	Blk.	TO	Pts.	RPG	APG	PPG
84-85—L.A. Lakers	80	2696	610	1066	.572	190	245	.776	169	342	511	201	87	67	198	1410	6.4	2.5	17.6
85-86—L.A. Lakers	75	2454	629	1086	.579	242	314	.771	136	251	387	201	82	77	149	1500	5.2	2.7	20.0
86-87—L.A. Lakers	82	2819	651	1207	.539	292	389	.751	158	308	466	226	108	83	168	1594	5.7	2.8	19.4
87-88—L.A. Lakers	75	2655	617	1161	.531	242	304	.796	129	245	374	289	72	55	155	1478	5.0	3.9	19.7
88-89—L.A. Lakers	81	2960	702	1282	.548	251	321	.782	169	320	489	288	108	56	182	1657	6.0	3.6	20.5
89-90—L.A. Lakers	80	2960	711	1298	.548	248	317	.782	160	318	478	288	99	49	160	1685	6.0	3.6	21.1
90-91—L.A. Lakers	78	3008	716	1455	.492	212	266	.797	107	249	356	275	104	35	127	1670	4.6	3.5	21.4
91-92—L.A. Lakers	54	2108	450	1007	.447	166	204	.814	98	207	305	252	76	23	127	1075	5.6	4.7	19.9
92-93—L.A. Lakers	82	2359	510	1142	.447	171	211	.810	73	174	247	278	92	27	137	1221	3.0	3.4	14.9
93-94—L.A. Lakers	80	1597	340	838	.406	100	135	.741	48	133	181	154	45	18	97	812	2.3	1.9	10.2
Totals	926	30001	6878	13204	.521	2447	3184	.769	1561	3147	4708	2791	1041	624	1859	16320	5.1	3.0	17.6

Three-point field goals: 1982-83, 1-for-4 (.250). 1983-84, 0-for-6. 1984-85, 0-for-7. 1985-86, 0-for-13. 1986-87, 0-for-13. 1987-88, 2-for-16 (.125). 1988-89, 2-for-23 (.087). 1989-90, 15-for-49 (.306). 1990-91, 26-for-90 (.289). 1991-92, 9-for-43 (.209). 1992-93, 30-for-111 (.270). 1993-94, 32-for-111 (.288). Totals, 117-for-486 (.241).

Personal fouls/disqualifications: 1982-83, 221/2. 1983-84, 244/5. 1984-85, 196/0. 1985-86, 195/0. 1986-87, 206/0. 1987-88, 175/1. 1988-89, 175/0. 1989-90, 190/0. 1990-91, 117/0. 1991-92, 89/0. 1992-93, 87/0. 1993-94, 80/0. Totals, 1975/8.

NBA PLAYOFF RECORD

NOTES: NBA Finals Most Valuable Player (1988).

Season Team	G	Min.	FGM	FGA	Pct.	FTM	FTA	Pct.	REBOUNDS Off.	Def.	Tot.	Ast.	St.	Blk.	TO	Pts.	RPG	APG	PPG
83-84—Los Angeles....	21	708	164	274	.599	42	69	.609	36	69	105	56	27	11	39	371	5.0	2.7	17.7
84-85—L.A. Lakers	19	626	166	267	.622	75	111	.676	35	61	96	41	17	13	26	408	5.1	2.2	21.5
85-86—L.A. Lakers	14	539	121	217	.558	32	47	.681	22	43	65	45	16	10	36	274	4.6	3.2	19.6
86-87—L.A. Lakers	18	681	176	298	.591	73	97	.753	31	70	101	63	28	22	40	425	5.6	3.5	23.6
87-88—L.A. Lakers	24	896	204	390	.523	97	128	.758	53	86	139	106	33	19	55	506	5.8	4.4	21.1
88-89—L.A. Lakers	15	600	153	270	.567	63	80	.788	37	64	101	42	18	16	33	372	6.7	2.8	24.8
89-90—L.A. Lakers	9	366	90	181	.497	36	43	.837	11	39	50	27	14	3	22	218	5.6	3.0	24.2
90-91—L.A. Lakers	18	733	161	346	.465	53	72	.736	25	48	73	70	19	2	40	379	4.1	3.9	21.1
92-93—L.A. Lakers	5	148	32	86	.372	3	5	.600	7	10	17	13	5	0	7	69	3.4	2.6	13.8
Totals	143	5297	1267	2329	.544	474	652	.727	257	490	747	463	177	96	298	3022	5.2	3.2	21.1

Three-point field goals: 1983-84, 1-for-2 (.500). 1984-85, 1-for-2 (.500). 1985-86, 0-for-4. 1986-87, 0-for-2. 1987-88, 1-for-9 (.111). 1988-89, 3-for-8 (.375). 1989-90, 2-for-8 (.250). 1990-91, 4-for-24 (.167). 1992-93, 2-for-8 (.250). Totals, 14-for-67 (.209).

Personal fouls/disqualifications: 1983-84, 57/0. 1984-85, 53/1. 1985-86, 43/0. 1986-87, 42/1. 1987-88, 58/0. 1988-89, 36/0. 1989-90, 18/0. 1990-91, 34/0. 1992-93, 11/0. Totals, 352/2.

NBA ALL-STAR GAME RECORD

Season Team	Min.	FGM	FGA	Pct.	FTM	FTA	Pct.	REBOUNDS Off.	Def.	Tot.	Ast.	PF	Dq.	St.	Blk.	TO	Pts.
1986 —L.A. Lakers........	28	10	19	.526	0	0	...	2	1	3	2	3	0	0	2	1	20
1987 —L.A. Lakers........	29	10	14	.714	2	2	1.000	6	2	8	3	3	0	1	0	2	22
1988 —L.A. Lakers........	13	2	8	.250	0	0	.000	1	2	3	1	1	0	1	0	1	4
1989 —L.A. Lakers........	18	4	7	.571	0	0	...	0	2	2	2	0	0	2	0	0	8
1990 —L.A. Lakers........	19	1	11	.091	0	0	...	3	1	4	0	1	0	1	0	1	2
1991 —L.A. Lakers........	21	3	11	.273	3	4	.750	0	2	2	0	2	0	2	1	0	9
1992 —L.A. Lakers........	14	4	7	.571	1	2	.500	0	4	4	1	0	0	1	0	0	9
Totals..........................	142	34	77	.442	6	9	.667	12	14	26	9	10	0	7	4	4	74

Three-point field goals: 1986, 0-for-2. 1989, 0-for-1. Totals, 0-for-3.

YARDLEY, GEORGE   F

PERSONAL: Born November 23, 1928, in Hollywood, Calif. ... 6-5/195. ... Full name: George Harry Yardley III.
HIGH SCHOOL: Newport Harbor (Calif.).
COLLEGE: Stanford.
TRANSACTIONS/CAREER NOTES: Selected by Fort Wayne Pistons in first round of 1950 NBA Draft. ... Played with the San Francisco Stewart Chevrolets in the National Industrial Basketball League, an Amateur Athletic Union League, during 1950-51 season (finished third in the league in scoring with a 13.1 point average on 104 field goals and 53 free throws for 261 points in 20 games). ... In military service during 1951-52 and 1952-53 seasons. ... Signed by Pistons (1953). ... Pistons franchise moved from Fort Wayne to Detroit for 1957-58 season. ... Traded by Pistons to Syracuse Nationals for F/G Ed Conlin (February 13, 1959). ... Played in American Basketball League with Los Angeles Jets (1961-62).
CAREER HONORS: Elected to Naismith Memorial Basketball Hall of Fame (1996).

COLLEGIATE RECORD

Season Team	G	Min.	FGM	FGA	Pct.	FTM	FTA	Pct.	Reb.	Ast.	Pts.	AVERAGES RPG	APG	PPG
46-47—Stanford‡			22				Freshman team statistics unavailable.				52			2.9
47-48—Stanford	18	...	22			8	20	.400	...	...	52	...	...	2.9
48-49—Stanford	28	...	126	377	.334	93	131	.710	...	...	345	...	...	12.3
49-50—Stanford	25	...	164	452	.363	95	130	.731	...	...	423	...	...	16.9
Varsity totals	71	...	312			196	281	.698	...	...	820	...	...	11.5

NBA REGULAR-SEASON RECORD

HONORS: All-NBA first team (1958). ... All-NBA second team (1957).

Season Team	G	Min.	FGM	FGA	Pct.	FTM	FTA	Pct.	Reb.	Ast.	PF	Dq.	Pts.	AVERAGES RPG	APG	PPG
53-54 —Fort Wayne	63	1489	209	492	.425	146	205	.712	407	99	166	3	564	6.5	1.6	9.0
54-55 —Fort Wayne	60	2150	363	869	.418	310	416	.745	594	126	205	7	1036	9.9	2.1	17.3
55-56 —Fort Wayne	71	2353	434	1067	.407	365	492	.742	686	159	212	2	1233	9.7	2.2	17.4
56-57 —Fort Wayne	72	2691	522	1273	.410	503	639	.787	755	147	231	2	1547	10.5	2.0	21.5

Season Team	G	Min.	FGM	FGA	Pct.	FTM	FTA	Pct.	Reb.	Ast.	PF	Dq.	Pts.	AVERAGES RPG	APG	PPG
57-58 —Detroit	72	2843	673	*1624	.414	*655	*808	.811	768	97	226	3	*2001	10.7	1.3	*27.8
58-59 —Det.-Syrac.	61	1839	446	1042	.428	317	407	.779	431	65	159	2	1209	7.1	1.1	19.8
59-60 —Syracuse	73	2402	546	1205	.453	381	467	.816	579	122	227	3	1473	7.9	1.7	20.2
Totals	472	15767	3193	7572	.422	2677	3434	.780	4220	815	1426	22	9063	8.9	1.7	19.2

NBA PLAYOFF RECORD

Season Team	G	Min.	FGM	FGA	Pct.	FTM	FTA	Pct.	Reb.	Ast.	PF	Dq.	Pts.	AVERAGES RPG	APG	PPG
53-54 —Fort Wayne	4	107	16	33	.485	10	12	.833	24	3	10	0	42	6.0	0.8	10.5
54-55 —Fort Wayne	11	420	57	143	.399	60	79	.760	99	36	37	2	174	9.0	3.3	15.8
55-56 —Fort Wayne	10	406	77	183	.421	76	98	.776	139	26	25	0	230	13.9	2.6	23.0
56-57 —Fort Wayne	2	85	24	53	.453	9	11	.818	19	8	7	0	57	9.5	4.0	28.5
57-58 —Detroit	7	254	52	127	.409	60	67	.896	72	17	26	0	164	10.3	2.4	23.4
58-59 —Syracuse	9	333	83	189	.439	60	70	.857	87	21	29	0	226	9.7	2.3	25.1
59-60 —Syracuse	3	88	15	39	.385	10	12	.833	17	1	9	0	40	5.7	0.3	13.3
Totals	46	1693	324	767	.422	285	349	.817	457	112	143	2	933	9.9	2.4	20.3

NBA ALL-STAR GAME RECORD

Season Team	Min.	FGM	FGA	Pct.	FTM	FTA	Pct.	Reb	Ast.	PF	Dq.	Pts.
1955 —Fort Wayne	22	4	11	.364	3	4	.750	4	2	2	0	11
1956 —Fort Wayne	19	3	7	.429	2	3	.667	6	1	1	0	8
1957 —Fort Wayne	25	4	10	.400	1	1	1.000	9	0	2	0	9
1958 —Detroit	32	8	15	.533	3	5	.600	9	1	1	0	19
1959 —Detroit	17	2	8	.250	2	2	1.000	4	0	3	0	6
1960 —Syracuse	16	5	9	.556	1	2	.500	3	0	4	0	11
Totals	131	26	60	.433	12	17	.706	35	4	13	0	64

ABL REGULAR-SEASON RECORD

Season Team	G	Min.	FGM	FGA	Pct.	FTM	FTA	Pct.	Reb.	Ast.	Pts.	AVERAGES RPG	APG	PPG
61-62—Los Angeles	25	948	159	378	.421	148	122	1.213	172	65	482	6.9	2.6	19.3

ZASLOFSKY, MAX   G/F

PERSONAL: Born December 7, 1925, in Brooklyn, N.Y. ... Died October 15, 1985. ... 6-2/170. ... Full name: Max Zaslofsky.
HIGH SCHOOL: Thomas Jefferson (Brooklyn, N.Y.).
COLLEGE: St. John's.
TRANSACTIONS/CAREER NOTES: Signed after freshman season as free agent by Chicago Stags of Basketball Association of America (1946). ... Name drawn out of hat by New York Knicks in dispersal of Stags franchise (1950). ... Traded by Knicks to Baltimore Bullets for G/F Jim Baechtold (1953). ... Traded by Bullets to Milwaukee Hawks (November 1953). ... Traded by Hawks to Fort Wayne Pistons (December 1953).

COLLEGIATE RECORD

NOTES: In military service (1944-45 season).

Season Team	G	Min.	FGM	FGA	Pct.	FTM	FTA	Pct.	Reb.	Ast.	Pts.	AVERAGES RPG	APG	PPG
45-46—St. John's	18	...	59	...	...	22	38	.579	...	...	140	...	...	7.8

NBA REGULAR-SEASON RECORD

HONORS: All-NBA first team (1950). ... All-BAA first team (1947, 1948, 1949).

Season Team	G	Min.	FGM	FGA	Pct.	FTM	FTA	Pct.	Reb.	Ast.	PF	Dq.	Pts.	AVERAGES RPG	APG	PPG
46-47 —Chicago (BAA)	61	...	336	1020	.329	205	278	.737	...	40	121	...	877	...	0.7	14.4
47-48 —Chicago (BAA)	48	...	*373	1156	.323	261	333	.784	...	29	125	...	*1007	...	0.6	*21.0
48-49 —Chicago (BAA)	58	...	425	1216	.350	347	413	.840	...	149	156	...	1197	...	2.6	20.6
49-50 —Chicago	68	...	397	1132	.351	321	381	*.843	...	155	185	...	1115	...	2.3	16.4
50-51 —New York	66	...	302	853	.354	231	298	.775	228	136	150	3	835	3.5	2.1	12.7
51-52 —New York	66	...	322	958	.336	287	380	.755	194	156	183	5	931	2.9	2.4	14.1
52-53 —New York	29	...	123	320	.384	98	142	.690	75	55	81	1	344	2.6	1.9	11.9
53-54 —Bal-Mil-FW	65	...	278	756	.368	255	357	.714	160	154	142	1	811	2.5	2.4	12.5
54-55 —Fort Wayne	70	...	269	821	.328	247	352	.702	191	203	130	0	785	2.7	2.9	11.2
55-56 —Fort Wayne	9	...	29	81	.358	30	35	.857	16	16	18	1	88	1.8	1.8	9.8
Totals	540	...	2854	8313	.343	2282	2969	.769	...	1093	1291	...	7990	...	2.0	14.8

DID YOU KNOW...

...that Scott Burrell is the only athlete ever selected in the first round of two different pro sports drafts? He was chosen by the Seattle Mariners in the 1989 baseball draft and the Charlotte Hornets in the 1993 NBA draft.

NBA PLAYOFF RECORD

Season Team	G	Min.	FGM	FGA	Pct.	FTM	FTA	Pct.	Reb.	Ast.	PF	Dq.	Pts.	AVERAGES RPG	APG	PPG
46-47 —Chicago (BAA)	11	...	60	199	.302	29	44	.659	...	4	26	...	149	...	0.4	13.5
47-48 —Chicago (BAA)	5	...	30	88	.341	37	47	.787	...	0	17	...	97	...	0.0	19.4
48-49 —Chicago (BAA)	2	...	15	49	.306	14	18	.778	...	6	3	0	44	...	3.0	22.0
49-50 —Chicago	2	...	15	32	.469	15	18	.833	...	6	7	...	45	...	3.0	22.5
50-51 —New York	14	...	88	217	.406	74	100	.740	58	38	43	...	250	4.1	2.7	17.9
51-52 —New York	14	...	69	185	.373	89	110	.809	44	23	51	...	227	3.1	1.6	16.2
53-54 —Fort Wayne	4	...	11	36	.306	13	15	.867	3	6	7	...	35	0.8	1.5	8.8
54-55 —Fort Wayne	11	...	18	44	.409	16	20	.800	16	18	20	...	52	1.5	1.6	4.7
Totals	63	...	306	850	.360	287	372	.772	...	101	174	...	899		1.6	14.3

NBA ALL-STAR GAME RECORD

Season Team	Min.	FGM	FGA	Pct.	FTM	FTA	Pct.	Reb	Ast.	PF	Dq.	Pts.
1952 —New York	...	3	7	.429	5	5	1.000	4	2	0	0	11

ABA COACHING RECORD

Season Team	REGULAR SEASON W	L	Pct.	Finish	PLAYOFFS W	L	Pct.
67-68 —New Jersey	36	42	.462	T4th/Eastern Division	—	—	—
68-69 —New York	17	61	.218	5th/Eastern Division	—	—	—
Totals (2 years)	53	103	.340				

ATTLES, AL

PERSONAL: Born November 7, 1936, in Newark, N.J. ... 6-0/185. ... Full name: Alvin A. Attles.
HIGH SCHOOL: Weequachic (Newark, N.J.).
COLLEGE: North Carolina A&T.
TRANSACTIONS/CAREER NOTES: Selected by Philadelphia Warriors in fifth round (39th pick overall) of 1960 NBA Draft. ... Warriors franchise moved from Philadelphia to San Francisco for 1962-63 season.

COLLEGIATE RECORD

Season Team	G	Min.	FGM	FGA	Pct.	FTM	FTA	Pct.	Reb.	Ast.	Pts.	RPG	APG	PPG
56-57 —N. Carolina A&T						Statistics unavailable.								
57-58 —N. Carolina A&T						Statistics unavailable.								
58-59 —N. Carolina A&T	29	...	105	225	.467	56	91	.615	...	...	266	...	...	9.2
59-60 —N. Carolina A&T	24	...	190	301	.631	47	71	.662	80	...	427	3.3	...	17.8
Totals	53	...	295	526	.561	103	162	.636	...	...	.693	...	...	13.1

NBA REGULAR-SEASON RECORD

Season Team	G	Min.	FGM	FGA	Pct.	FTM	FTA	Pct.	Reb.	Ast.	PF	Dq.	Pts.	RPG	APG	PPG
60-61 —Philadelphia	77	1544	222	543	.409	97	162	.599	214	174	235	5	541	2.8	2.3	7.0
61-62 —Philadelphia	75	2468	343	724	.474	158	267	.592	355	333	279	8	844	4.7	4.4	11.3
62-63 —San Fran.	71	1876	301	630	.478	133	206	.646	205	184	253	7	735	2.9	2.6	10.4
63-64 —San Fran.	70	1883	289	640	.452	185	275	.673	236	197	249	4	763	3.4	2.8	10.9
64-65 —San Fran.	73	1733	254	662	.384	171	274	.624	239	205	242	7	679	3.3	2.8	9.3
65-66 —San Fran.	79	2053	364	724	.503	154	252	.611	322	225	265	7	882	4.1	2.8	11.2
66-67 —San Fran.	70	1764	212	467	.454	88	151	.583	321	269	265	13	512	4.6	3.8	7.3
67-68 —San Fran.	67	1992	252	540	.467	150	216	.694	276	390	284	9	654	4.1	5.8	9.8
68-69 —San Fran.	51	1516	162	359	.451	95	149	.638	181	306	183	3	419	3.5	6.0	8.2
69-70 —San Fran.	45	676	78	202	.386	75	113	.664	74	142	103	0	231	1.6	3.2	5.1
70-71 —San Fran.	34	321	22	54	.407	24	41	.585	40	58	59	2	68	1.2	1.7	2.0
Totals........................	712	17826	2499	5545	.451	1330	2106	.632	2463	2483	2417	65	6328	3.5	3.5	8.9

NBA PLAYOFF RECORD

Season Team	G	Min.	FGM	FGA	Pct.	FTM	FTA	Pct.	Reb.	Ast.	PF	Dq.	Pts.	RPG	APG	PPG
60-61 —Philadelphia	3	110	12	26	.462	5	14	.357	12	9	14	0	29	4.0	3.0	9.7
61-62 —Philadelphia	12	338	28	76	.368	17	31	.548	55	27	54	4	73	4.6	2.3	6.1
63-64 —San Fran.	12	386	58	144	.403	30	56	.536	37	30	54	5	146	3.1	2.5	12.2
66-67 —San Fran.	15	237	20	46	.435	6	16	.375	62	38	45	1	46	4.1	2.5	3.1
67-68 —San Fran.	10	277	25	62	.403	23	30	.767	53	70	49	2	73	5.3	7.0	7.3
68-69 —San Fran.	6	109	7	21	.333	1	4	.250	18	21	17	0	15	3.0	3.5	2.5
70-71 —San Fran.	4	47	4	7	.571	4	7	.571	8	11	13	0	12	2.0	2.8	3.0
Totals........................	62	1504	154	382	.403	86	158	.544	245	206	246	12	394	4.0	3.3	6.4

HEAD COACHING RECORD
BACKGROUND: Vice president/assistant general manager, Golden State Warriors (1987-88 to present). ... Assistant coach, Warriors (February 13, 1995-remainder of season).

NBA COACHING RECORD

Season Team	REGULAR SEASON				PLAYOFFS		
	W	L	Pct.	Finish	W	L	Pct.
69-70 —San Francisco.............................	8	22	.267	6th/Western Division	—	—	—
70-71 —San Francisco.............................	41	41	.500	2nd/Pacific Division	1	4	.200
71-72 —Golden State..............................	51	31	.622	2nd/Pacific Division	1	4	.200
72-73 —Golden State..............................	47	35	.573	2nd/Pacific Division	5	6	.455
73-74 —Golden State..............................	44	38	.537	2nd/Pacific Division	—	—	—
74-75 —Golden State..............................	48	34	.585	1st/Pacific Division	12	5	.706
75-76 —Golden State..............................	59	23	.720	1st/Pacific Division	7	6	.538
76-77 —Golden State..............................	46	36	.561	3rd/Pacific Division	5	5	.500
77-78 —Golden State..............................	43	39	.524	5th/Pacific Division	—	—	—
78-79 —Golden State..............................	38	44	.463	6th/Pacific Division	—	—	—
79-80 —Golden State..............................	18	43	.295	6th/Pacific Division	—	—	—
80-81 —Golden State..............................	39	43	.476	4th/Pacific Division	—	—	—
81-82 —Golden State..............................	45	37	.549	4th/Pacific Division	—	—	—
82-83 —Golden State..............................	30	52	.366	5th/Pacific Division	—	—	—
Totals (14 years)........................	557	518	.518	**Totals (6 years)**	31	30	.508

NOTES:
1971—Lost to Milwaukee in Western Conference semifinals.
1972—Lost to Milwaukee in Western Conference semifinals.
1973—Defeated Milwaukee, 4-2, in Western Conference semifinals; lost to Los Angeles, 4-1, in Western Conference finals.
1975—Defeated Seattle, 4-2, in Western Conference semifinals; defeated Chicago, 4-3, in Western Conference finals; defeated Washington, 4-0, in World Championship Series.
1976—Defeated Detroit, 4-2, in Western Conference semifinals; lost to Phoenix, 4-3, in Western Conference finals.
1977—Defeated Detroit, 2-1, in Western Conference first round; lost to Los Angeles, 4-3, in Western Conference semifinals.
1980—Missed final 21 games of season due to injury; replaced by assistant coach John Bach (6-15) for remainder of season.

AUERBACH, RED

PERSONAL: Born September 20, 1917, in Brooklyn, N.Y. ... 5-10/170. ... Full name: Arnold Jacob Auerbach. ... Name pronounced HOUR-back.
HIGH SCHOOL: Eastern District (Brooklyn, N.Y.).
COLLEGE: Seth Low Junior College (N.Y.), then George Washington.
CAREER HONORS: Elected to Naismith Memorial Basketball Hall of Fame (1968).

COLLEGIATE RECORD

Season Team	G	Min.	FGM	FGA	Pct.	FTM	FTA	Pct.	Reb.	Ast.	Pts.	AVERAGES RPG	APG	PPG
36-37—Seth Low J.C.					Statistics unavailable.									
37-38—George Wash.	17	...	22	...	...	8	12	.667	...	...	52	...	...	3.1
38-39—George Wash.	20	...	54	...	...	12	19	.632	...	...	120	...	...	6.0
39-40—George Wash.	19	...	69	...	...	24	39	.615	...	...	162	...	...	8.5
4-year-college totals	56	...	145	...	...	44	70	.629	...	...	334	...	...	6.0

HEAD COACHING RECORD

BACKGROUND: Head coach, St. Alban's Prep (Washington, D.C.). ... Head coach, Roosevelt High School (Washington, D.C.). ... Assistant coach, Duke University (1949-50).
HONORS: NBA Coach of the Year (1965). ... NBA 25th Anniversary All-Time team coach (1970). ... NBA Executive of the Year (1980). ... Selected as the "Greatest Coach in the History of the NBA" by the Professional Basketball Writers' Association of America (1980).

NBA COACHING RECORD

Season Team	REGULAR SEASON W	L	Pct.	Finish	PLAYOFFS W	L	Pct.
46-47 —Washington (BAA)	49	11	.817	1st/Eastern Division	2	4	.333
47-48 —Washington (BAA)	28	20	.583	4th/Eastern Division	—	—	—
48-49 —Washington (BAA)	38	22	.633	1st/Eastern Division	6	5	.545
49-50 —Tri-Cities	28	29	.491	3rd/Western Division	1	2	.333
50-51 —Boston	39	30	.565	2nd/Eastern Division	0	2	.000
51-52 —Boston	39	27	.591	2nd/Eastern Division	1	2	.333
52-53 —Boston	46	25	.648	3rd/Eastern Division	3	3	.500
53-54 —Boston	42	30	.583	T2nd/Eastern Division	2	4	.333
54-55 —Boston	36	36	.500	3rd/Eastern Division	3	4	.429
55-56 —Boston	39	33	.542	2nd/Eastern Division	1	2	.333
56-57 —Boston	44	28	.611	1st/Eastern Division	7	3	.700
57-58 —Boston	49	23	.681	1st/Eastern Division	6	5	.545
58-59 —Boston	52	20	.722	1st/Eastern Division	8	3	.727
59-60 —Boston	59	16	.787	1st/Eastern Division	8	5	.615
60-61 —Boston	57	22	.722	1st/Eastern Division	8	2	.800
61-62 —Boston	60	20	.750	1st/Eastern Division	8	6	.571
62-63 —Boston	58	22	.725	1st/Eastern Division	8	5	.615
63-64 —Boston	59	21	.738	1st/Eastern Division	8	2	.800
64-65 —Boston	62	18	.775	1st/Eastern Division	8	4	.667
65-66 —Boston	54	26	.675	1st/Eastern Division	11	6	.647
Totals (20 years)	938	479	.662	**Totals (19 years)**	99	69	.589

NOTES:
1947—Lost to Chicago in BAA semifinals.
1949—Defeated Philadelphia, 2-0, in Eastern Division semifinals; defeated New York, 2-1, in Eastern Division finals; lost to Minneapolis, 4-2, in World Championship Series.
1950—Lost to Anderson in Western Division semifinals.
1951—Lost to New York in Eastern Division semifinals.
1952—Lost to New York in Eastern Division semifinals.
1953—Defeated Syracuse, 2-0, in Eastern Division semifinals; lost to New York, 3-1, in Eastern Division finals.
1954—Defeated New York, 93-71; lost to Syracuse, 96-95 (OT); defeated New York, 79-78; lost to Syracuse, 98-85, in Eastern Division round robin; lost to Syracuse, 2-0, in Eastern Division finals.
1955—Defeated New York, 2-1, in Eastern Division semifinals; lost to Syracuse, 3-1, in Eastern Division finals.
1956—Lost to Syracuse in Eastern Division semifinals.
1957—Defeated Syracuse, 3-0, in Eastern Division finals; defeated St. Louis, 4-3, in World Championship Series.
1958—Defeated Philadelphia, 4-1, in Eastern Division finals; lost to St. Louis, 4-2, in World Championship Series.
1959—Defeated Syracuse, 4-3, in Eastern Division finals; defeated Minneapolis, 4-0, in World Championship Series.
1960—Defeated Philadelphia, 4-2, in Eastern Division finals; defeated St. Louis, 4-3, in World Championship Series.
1961—Defeated Syracuse, 4-1, in Eastern Division finals; defeated St. Louis, 4-1, in World Championship Series.
1962—Defeated Philadelphia, 4-3, in Eastern Division finals; defeated Los Angeles, 4-3, in World Championship Series.
1963—Defeated Cincinnati, 4-3, in Eastern Division finals; defeated Los Angeles, 4-2, in World Championship Series.
1964—Defeated Cincinnati, 4-1, in Eastern Division finals; defeated San Francisco, 4-1, in World Championship Series.
1965—Defeated Philadelphia, 4-3, in Eastern Division finals; defeated Los Angeles, 4-1, in World Championship Series.
1966—Defeated Cincinnati, 3-2 in Eastern Division semifinals; defeated Philadelphia, 4-1, in Eastern Division finals; defeated Los Angeles, 4-3, in World Championship Series.

DID YOU KNOW...

...that three active NBA coaches have coached teams in the NCAA Final Four? They are Larry Brown (UCLA, 1980), P.J. Carlesimo (Seton Hall, 1989) and John Calipari (Massachusetts, 1996).

COSTELLO, LARRY

PERSONAL: Born July 2, 1931, in Minoa, N.Y. ... 6-1/188. ... Full name: Lawrence Ronald Costello.
HIGH SCHOOL: Minoa (N.Y.).
COLLEGE: Niagara.
TRANSACTIONS/CAREER NOTES: Selected by Philadelphia Warriors in second round of 1954 NBA Draft. ... Sold by Warriors to Syracuse Nationals (October 10, 1957). ... Nationals franchise moved from Syracuse to Philadelphia and renamed 76ers for 1963-64 season. ... Played in Eastern Basketball League with Wilkes-Barre Barons (1965-66). ... Drafted by Milwaukee Bucks from 76ers in NBA expansion draft (May 6, 1968).
MISCELLANEOUS: Member of NBA championship team (1967).

COLLEGIATE RECORD

Season Team	G	Min.	FGM	FGA	Pct.	FTM	FTA	Pct.	Reb.	Ast.	Pts.	RPG	APG	PPG
50-51—Niagara‡					Freshman team statistics unavailable.									
51-52—Niagara	28	...	131	...	...	58	87	.667	...	...	320	...	...	11.4
52-53—Niagara	28	...	185	...	...	140	194	.722	...	...	510	...	...	18.2
53-54—Niagara	29	...	160	...	...	125	152	.822	...	...	445	...	...	15.3
Varsity totals	85	...	476	...	...	323	433	.746	...	...	1275	...	...	15.0

HONORS: All-NBA second team (1961).

NBA REGULAR-SEASON RECORD

Season Team	G	Min.	FGM	FGA	Pct.	FTM	FTA	Pct.	Reb.	Ast.	PF	Dq.	Pts.	RPG	APG	PPG
54-55—Philadelphia	19	463	46	139	.331	26	32	.813	49	78	37	0	118	2.6	4.1	6.2
55-56—Philadelphia						Did not play—in military service.										
56-57—Philadelphia	72	2111	186	497	.374	175	222	.788	323	236	182	2	547	4.5	3.3	7.6
57-58—Syracuse	72	2746	378	888	.426	320	378	.847	378	317	246	3	1076	5.3	4.4	14.9
58-59—Syracuse	70	2750	414	948	.437	280	349	.802	365	379	263	7	1108	5.2	5.4	15.8
59-60—Syracuse	71	2469	372	822	.453	249	289	.862	388	449	234	4	993	5.5	6.3	14.0
60-61—Syracuse	75	2167	407	844	.482	270	338	.799	292	413	286	9	1084	3.9	5.5	14.5
61-62—Syracuse	63	1854	310	726	.427	247	295	.837	245	359	220	5	867	3.9	5.7	13.8
62-63—Syracuse	78	2066	285	660	.432	288	327	*.881	237	334	263	4	858	3.0	4.3	11.0
63-64—Philadelphia	45	1137	191	408	.468	147	170	.865	105	167	150	3	529	2.3	3.7	11.8
64-65—Philadelphia	64	1967	309	695	.445	243	277	*.877	169	275	242	10	861	2.6	4.3	13.5
66-67—Philadelphia	49	976	130	293	.444	120	133	.902	103	140	141	2	380	2.1	2.9	7.8
67-68—Philadelphia	28	492	67	148	.453	67	81	.827	51	68	62	0	201	1.8	2.4	7.2
Totals	706	21198	3095	7068	.438	2432	2891	.841	2705	3215	2326	49	8622	3.8	4.6	12.2

NBA PLAYOFF RECORD

Season Team	G	Min.	FGM	FGA	Pct.	FTM	FTA	Pct.	Reb.	Ast.	PF	Dq.	Pts.	RPG	APG	PPG
56-57—Philadelphia	2	16	3	8	.375	0	1	.000	5	2	3	0	6	2.5	1.0	3.0
57-58—Syracuse	3	134	10	34	.294	14	14	1.000	25	12	6	0	34	8.3	4.0	11.3
58-59—Syracuse	9	361	54	121	.446	51	61	.836	53	54	40	2	159	5.9	6.0	17.7
59-60—Syracuse	3	122	20	47	.426	10	12	.833	14	20	15	1	50	4.7	6.7	16.7
60-61—Syracuse	8	269	42	103	.408	47	55	.855	35	52	39	3	131	4.4	6.5	16.4
61-62—Syracuse	5	167	22	51	.431	29	33	.879	16	28	21	0	73	3.2	5.6	14.6
62-63—Syracuse	5	134	16	37	.432	19	23	.826	4	23	27	2	51	0.8	4.6	10.2
63-64—Philadelphia	5	36	3	14	.214	10	10	1.000	3	4	14	1	16	0.6	0.8	3.2
64-65—Philadelphia	10	207	22	53	.415	11	16	.688	12	20	43	2	55	1.2	2.0	5.5
66-67—Philadelphia	2	25	6	8	.750	5	5	1.000	4	3	2	0	17	2.0	1.5	8.5
Totals	52	1471	198	476	.416	196	230	.852	171	218	210	11	592	3.3	4.2	11.4

NBA ALL-STAR GAME RECORD

Season Team	Min.	FGM	FGA	Pct.	FTM	FTA	Pct.	Reb.	Ast.	PF	Dq.	Pts.
1958—Syracuse	17	0	6	.000	1	1	1.000	1	4	2	0	1
1959—Syracuse	18	3	8	.375	1	1	1.000	3	3	1	0	7
1960—Syracuse	20	5	9	.556	0	0	...	4	2	1	0	10
1961—Syracuse	5	1	2	.500	0	0	...	0	0	2	0	2
1962—Syracuse					Selected, did not play—injured.							
1965—Philadelphia	11	2	7	.286	0	0	...	1	2	2	0	4
Totals	71	11	32	.344	2	2	1.000	9	11	8	0	24

EBL REGULAR-SEASON RECORD

Season Team	G	Min.	FGM	FGA	Pct.	FTM	FTA	Pct.	Reb.	Ast.	PF	Dq.	Pts.	RPG	APG	PPG
65-66—Wilkes-Barre	12	...	54	...	...	53	59	.898	22	83	...	.	167	1.8	6.9	13.9

HEAD COACHING RECORD

BACKGROUND: Head coach, Minoa High School, N.Y. (1965-66). ... Head coach, Milwaukee Does of Women's Professional Basketball League (1979-80).

NBA COACHING RECORD

Season Team	REGULAR SEASON				PLAYOFFS		
	W	L	Pct.	Finish	W	L	Pct.
68-69—Milwaukee	27	55	.329	7th/Eastern Division	—	—	—
69-70—Milwaukee	56	26	.683	2nd/Eastern Division	5	5	.500
70-71—Milwaukee	66	16	.805	1st/Eastern Division	12	2	.857
71-72—Milwaukee	63	19	.768	1st/Midwest Division	6	5	.545

ALL-TIME GREAT COACHES

Season Team	REGULAR SEASON				PLAYOFFS		
	W	L	Pct.	Finish	W	L	Pct.
72-73 —Milwaukee	60	22	.732	1st/Midwest Division	2	4	.333
73-74 —Milwaukee	59	23	.720	1st/Midwest Division	11	5	.688
74-75 —Milwaukee	38	44	.463	4th/Midwest Division	—	—	—
75-76 —Milwaukee	38	44	.463	1st/Midwest Division	1	2	.333
76-77 —Milwaukee	3	15	.167		—	—	—
78-79 —Chicago	20	36	.357		—	—	—
Totals (10 years)	430	300	.589	Totals (6 years)	37	23	.617

COLLEGIATE COACHING RECORD

Season Team	W	L	Pct.	Finish
80-81 —Utica	13	12	.520	Independent
81-82 —Utica	4	22	.154	Independent
82-83 —Utica	11	15	.423	Independent
83-84 —Utica	11	15	.423	Independent
84-85 —Utica	15	12	.556	Independent
85-86 —Utica	13	14	.481	Independent
86-87 —Utica	10	16	.385	Independent
Totals (7 years)	77	106	.421	

NOTE:

1970—Defeated Philadelphia, 4-1, in Eastern Division semifinals; lost to New York, 4-1, in Eastern Division finals.

1971—Defeated San Francisco, 4-1, in Western Conference semifinals; defeated Los Angeles, 4-1, in Western Conference finals; defeated Baltimore, 4-0, in World Championship Series.

1972—Defeated Golden State, 4-1, in Western Conference semifinals; lost to Los Angeles, 4-2, in Western Conference finals.

1973—Lost to Golden State in Western Conference semifinals.

1974—Defeated Los Angeles, 4-1, in Western Conference semifinals; defeated Chicago, 4-0, in Western Conference finals; lost to Boston, 4-3, in World Championship Series.

1976—Lost to Detroit in Western Conference first round. Resigned as Milwaukee head coach and replaced by Don Nelson (November 22).

1979—Replaced as Chicago head coach by Scotty Robertson (February 16).

CUNNINGHAM, BILLY

PERSONAL: Born June 3, 1943, in Brooklyn, N.Y. ... 6-7/210. ... Full name: William John Cunningham.

HIGH SCHOOL: Erasmus Hall (Brooklyn, N.Y.).

COLLEGE: North Carolina.

TRANSACTIONS/CAREER NOTES: Selected by Philadelphia 76ers in first round of 1965 NBA Draft. ... Signed as free agent by Carolina Cougars of American Basketball Association (August 1969). ... Signed as free agent by 76ers (1969). ... Suspended by NBA (1972). ... Restored by NBA (1974). ... Returned to 76ers (1974).

CAREER HONORS: Elected to Naismith Memorial Basketball Hall of Fame (1985).

MISCELLANEOUS: Member of NBA championship team (1967).

COLLEGIATE RECORD

NOTES: THE SPORTING NEWS All-America second team (1965).

Season Team	G	Min.	FGM	FGA	Pct.	FTM	FTA	Pct.	Reb.	Ast.	Pts.	AVERAGES		
												RPG	APG	PPG
61-62—North Carolina‡	10	...	81	162	.500	45	78	.577	127	...	207	12.7	...	20.7
62-63—North Carolina	21	...	186	380	.489	105	170	.618	339	...	477	16.1	...	22.7
63-64—North Carolina	24	...	233	526	.443	157	249	.631	379	...	623	15.8	...	26.0
64-65—North Carolina	24	...	237	481	.493	135	213	.634	344	...	609	14.3	...	25.4
Varsity totals	69	...	656	1387	.473	397	632	.628	1062	...	1709	15.4	...	24.8

NBA REGULAR-SEASON RECORD

HONORS: All-NBA first team (1969, 1970, 1971). ... All-NBA second team (1972). ... NBA All-Rookie team (1966).

Season Team	G	Min.	FGM	FGA	Pct.	FTM	FTA	Pct.	Reb.	Ast.	PF	Dq.	Pts.	AVERAGES		
														RPG	APG	PPG
65-66—Philadelphia	80	2134	431	1011	.426	281	443	.634	599	207	301	12	1143	7.5	2.6	14.3
66-67—Philadelphia	81	2168	556	1211	.459	383	558	.686	589	205	260	2	1495	7.3	2.5	18.5
67-68—Philadelphia	74	2076	516	1178	.438	368	509	.723	562	187	260	3	1400	7.6	2.5	18.9
68-69—Philadelphia	82	3345	739	1736	.426	556	754	.737	1050	287	*329	10	2034	12.8	3.5	24.8
69-70—Philadelphia	81	3194	802	1710	.469	510	700	.729	1101	352	331	15	2114	13.6	4.3	26.1
70-71—Philadelphia	81	3090	702	1519	.462	455	620	.734	946	395	328	5	1859	11.7	4.9	23.0
71-72—Philadelphia	75	2900	658	1428	.461	428	601	.712	918	443	295	12	1744	12.2	5.9	23.3

Season Team	G	Min.	FGM	FGA	Pct.	FTM	FTA	Pct.	REBOUNDS			Ast.	Stl.	Blk.	TO	Pts.	AVERAGES		
									Off.	Def.	Tot.						RPG	APG	PPG
74-75 —Philadelphia	80	2859	609	1423	.428	345	444	.777	130	596	726	442	91	35	...	1563	9.1	5.5	19.5
75-76 —Philadelphia	20	640	103	251	.410	68	88	.773	29	118	147	107	24	10	...	274	7.4	5.4	13.7
Totals	654	22406	5116	11467	.446	3394	4717	.720	...	...	6638	2625	115	45	...	13626	10.1	4.0	20.8

Personal fouls/disqualifications: 1974-75. 270/4. 1975-76, 57/1. Totals, 2431/64.

NBA PLAYOFF RECORD

Season Team	G	Min.	FGM	FGA	Pct.	FTM	FTA	Pct.	Reb.	Ast.	PF	Dq.	Pts.	AVERAGES		
														RPG	APG	PPG
65-66 —Philadelphia	4	69	5	31	.161	11	13	.846	18	10	11	0	21	4.5	2.5	5.3
66-67 —Philadelphia	15	339	83	221	.376	59	90	.656	93	33	53	1	225	6.2	2.2	15.0
67-68 —Philadelphia	3	86	24	43	.558	14	17	.824	22	10	16	1	62	7.3	3.3	20.7
68-69 —Philadelphia	5	217	49	117	.419	24	38	.632	63	12	24	1	122	12.6	2.4	24.4
69-70 —Philadelphia	5	205	61	123	.496	24	36	.667	52	20	19	0	146	10.4	4.0	29.2
70-71 —Philadelphia	7	301	67	142	.472	47	67	.701	108	40	28	0	181	15.4	5.7	25.9
Totals	39	1217	289	677	.427	179	261	.686	356	125	151	3	757	9.1	3.2	19.4

NBA ALL-STAR GAME RECORD

Season	Team	Min.	FGM	FGA	Pct.	FTM	FTA	Pct.	Reb.	Ast.	PF	Dq.	Pts.
1969	—Philadelphia..............	22	5	10	.500	0	0	...	5	1	3	0	10
1970	—Philadelphia..............	28	7	13	.538	5	5	1.000	4	2	3	0	19
1971	—Philadelphia..............	19	2	8	.250	1	2	.500	4	3	1	0	5
1972	—Philadelphia..............	24	4	13	.308	6	8	.750	10	3	4	0	14
	Totals	93	18	44	.409	12	15	.800	23	9	11	0	48

ABA REGULAR-SEASON RECORD

NOTES: ABA Most Valuable Player (1973). ... ABA All-Star first team (1973).

				2-POINT			3-POINT								AVERAGES		
Season	Team	G	Min.	FGM	FGA	Pct.	FGM	FGA	Pct.	FTM	FTA	Pct.	Reb.	Ast.	Pts.	RPG	APG	PPG
72-73—	Carolina.................	84	3248	757	1534	.493	14	49	.286	472	598	.789	1012	530	2028	12.0	6.3	24.1
73-74—	Carolina.................	32	1190	252	529	.476	1	8	.125	149	187	.797	331	150	656	10.3	4.7	20.5
	Totals	116	4438	1009	2063	.489	15	57	.263	621	785	.791	1343	680	2684	11.6	5.9	23.1

ABA PLAYOFF RECORD

				2-POINT			3-POINT								AVERAGES		
Season	Team	G	Min.	FGM	FGA	Pct.	FGM	FGA	Pct.	FTM	FTA	Pct.	Reb.	Ast.	Pts.	RPG	APG	PPG
72-73—	Carolina.................	12	472	111	219	.507	1	4	.250	57	83	.687	142	61	282	11.8	5.1	23.5
73-74—	Carolina.................	3	61	9	29	.310	0	2	.000	4	5	.800	16	6	22	5.3	2.0	7.3
	Totals	15	533	120	248	.484	1	6	.167	61	88	.693	158	67	304	10.5	4.5	20.3

ABA ALL-STAR GAME RECORD

			2-POINT			3-POINT							
Season	Team	Min.	FGM	FGA	Pct.	FGM	FGA	Pct.	FTM	FTA	Pct.	Reb.	Ast.	Pts.
1973	—Carolina.....................................	20	9	11	.818	0	1	.000	0	0	...	6	4	18

COMBINED ABA AND NBA REGULAR-SEASON RECORDS

								REBOUNDS							AVERAGES		
	G	Min.	FGM	FGA	Pct.	FTM	FTA	Pct.	Off.	Def.	Tot.	Ast.	Stl.	Blk.	TO	Pts.	RPG	APG	PPG
Totals	770	26844	6140	13587	.452	4015	5502	.730	...	...	7981	3305	...	...	...	16310	10.4	4.3	21.2

Three-point field goals: 15-for-57 (.263).
Personal fouls: 2845.

NBA COACHING RECORD

		REGULAR SEASON				PLAYOFFS		
Season	Team	W	L	Pct.	Finish	W	L	Pct.
77-78	—Philadelphia...............................	53	23	.697	1st/Atlantic Division	6	4	.600
78-79	—Philadelphia...............................	47	35	.573	2nd/Atlantic Division	5	4	.556
79-80	—Philadelphia...............................	59	23	.720	2nd/Atlantic Division	12	6	.667
80-81	—Philadelphia...............................	62	20	.756	T1st/Atlantic Division	9	7	.563
81-82	—Philadelphia...............................	58	24	.707	2nd/Atlantic Division	12	9	.571
82-83	—Philadelphia...............................	65	17	.793	1st/Atlantic Division	12	1	.923
83-84	—Philadelphia...............................	52	30	.634	2nd/Atlantic Division	2	3	.400
84-85	—Philadelphia...............................	58	24	.707	2nd/Atlantic Division	8	5	.615
	Totals (8 years)...............................	454	196	.698	**Totals (8 years)**	66	39	.629

NOTES:

1977—Replaced Gene Shue as Philadelphia head coach (November 4), with record of 2-4.

1978—Defeated New York, 4-0, in Eastern Conference semifinals; lost to Washington, 4-2, in Eastern Conference finals.

1979—Defeated New Jersey, 2-0, in Eastern Conference first round; lost to San Antonio, 4-3, in Eastern Conference semifinals.

1980—Defeated Washington, 2-0, in Eastern Conference first round; defeated Atlanta, 4-1, in Eastern Conference semifinals; defeated Boston, 4-1, in Eastern Conference finals; lost to Los Angeles, 4-2, in World Championship Series.

1981—Defeated Indiana, 2-0, in Eastern Conference first round; defeated Milwaukee, 4-3, in Eastern Conference semifinals; lost to Boston, 4-3, in Eastern Conference finals.

1982—Defeated Atlanta, 2-0, in Eastern Conference first round; defeated Milwaukee, 4-2, in Eastern Conference semifinals; defeated Boston, 4-3, in Eastern Conference finals; lost to Los Angeles, 4-2, in World Championship Series.

1983—Defeated New York, 4-0, in Eastern Conference semifinals; defeated Boston, 4-1, in Eastern Conference finals; defeated Los Angeles, 4-0, in World Championship series.

1984—Lost to New Jersey in Eastern Conference first round.

1985—Defeated Washington, 3-1, in Eastern Conference first round; defeated Milwaukee, 4-0, in Eastern Conference semifinals; lost to Boston, 4-1, in Eastern Conference finals.

DALY, CHUCK

PERSONAL: Born July 20, 1930, in St. Mary's, Pa. ... 6-2/180. ... Full name: Charles Jerome Daly.
HIGH SCHOOL: Kane Area (Pa.).
COLLEGE: St. Bonaventure, then Bloomsburg (Pa.) State.

COLLEGIATE RECORD

													AVERAGES		
Season	Team	G	Min.	FGM	FGA	Pct.	FTM	FTA	Pct.	Reb.	Ast.	Pts.	RPG	APG	PPG
48-49—St. Bonaventure‡..........							Freshman team statistics unavailable.									
49-50—Bloomsburg State							Did not play—transfer student.									
50-51—Bloomsburg State	16	...	...	...	...	...	...	...	...	...	...	215	...	...	13.4
51-52—Bloomsburg State	16	...	...	...	...	...	...	...	...	...	...	203	...	...	12.7
Varsity totals..........................	32	...	...	...	...	...	...	...	...	...	...	418	...	...	13.1

HEAD COACHING RECORD

BACKGROUND: Head coach, Punxsutawney High School, Pa. (1955-56 through 1962-63; record: 111-70, .613). ... Assistant coach, Duke University (1963-64 through 1968-69). ... Assistant coach, Philadelphia 76ers (1978-December 4, 1981). ... Broadcaster, 76ers (1982-83).

COLLEGIATE COACHING RECORD

Season Team	W	L	Pct.	Finish
69-70 —Boston College	11	13	.458	Independent
70-71 —Boston College	15	11	.577	Independent
71-72 —Pennsylvania	25	3	.893	1st/Ivy League
72-73 —Pennsylvania	21	7	.750	1st/Ivy League
73-74 —Pennsylvania	21	6	.778	1st/Ivy League
74-75 —Pennsylvania	23	5	.821	1st/Ivy League
75-76 —Pennsylvania	17	9	.654	2nd/Ivy League
76-77 —Pennsylvania	18	8	.692	2nd/Ivy League
Totals (8 years)	151	62	.709	

NBA COACHING RECORD

Season Team	REGULAR SEASON				PLAYOFFS		
	W	L	Pct.	Finish	W	L	Pct.
81-82 —Cleveland	9	32	.220		—	—	—
83-84 —Detroit	49	33	.598	2nd/Central Division	2	3	.400
84-85 —Detroit	46	36	.561	2nd/Central Division	5	4	.556
85-86 —Detroit	46	36	.561	3rd/Central Division	1	3	.250
86-87 —Detroit	52	30	.634	2nd/Central Division	10	5	.667
87-88 —Detroit	54	28	.659	1st/Central Division	14	9	.609
88-89 —Detroit	63	19	.768	1st/Central Division	15	2	.882
89-90 —Detroit	59	23	.720	1st/Central Division	15	5	.750
90-91 —Detroit	50	32	.610	2nd/Central Division	7	8	.467
91-92 —Detroit	48	34	.585	3rd/Central Division	2	3	.400
92-93 —New Jersey	43	39	.524	3rd/Atlantic Division	2	3	.400
93-94 —New Jersey	45	37	.549	3rd/Atlantic Division	1	3	.250
Totals (12 years)	564	379	.598	Totals (11 years)	74	48	.607

OLYMPIC RECORD

Season Team	W	L	Pct.	Finish
1992 —Team USA	8	0	1.000	Gold medal

NOTES:

1972—Defeated Providence, 76-60, in NCAA Tournament first round; defeated Villanova, 78-67, in second round; lost to North Carolina, 73-59, in regional final.

1973—Defeated St. John's, 62-61, in NCAA Tournament first round; lost to Providence, 87-65, in second round; lost to Syracuse, 69-68, in regional consolation game.

1974—Lost to Providence, 84-69, in NCAA Tournament first round.

1975—Lost to Kansas State, 69-62, in NCAA Tournament first round.

1981—Replaced Don Delaney (4-13) and Bob Kloppenburg (0-1) as Cleveland head coach (December 4), with record of 4-14.

1982—Replaced as Cleveland head coach by Bill Musselman (February), with record of 13-46.

1984—Lost to New York in Eastern Conference first round.

1985—Defeated New Jersey, 3-0, in Eastern Conference first round; lost to Boston, 4-2, in Eastern Conference semifinals.

1986—Lost to Atlanta in Eastern Conference first round.

1987—Defeated Washington, 3-0, in Eastern Conference first round; defeated Atlanta, 4-1, in Eastern Conference semifinals; lost to Boston, 4-3, in Eastern Conference finals.

1988—Defeated Washington, 3-2, in Eastern Conference first round; defeated Chicago, 4-1, in Eastern Conference semifinals; defeated Boston, 4-2, in Eastern Conference finals; lost to Los Angeles Lakers, 4-3, in NBA Finals.

1989—Defeated Boston, 3-0, in Eastern Conference first round; defeated Milwaukee, 4-0, in Eastern Conference semifinals; defeated Chicago, 4-2, in Eastern Conference finals; defeated Los Angeles Lakers, 4-0, in NBA Finals.

1990—Defeated Indiana, 3-0, in Eastern Conference first round; defeated New York, 4-1, in Eastern Conference semifinals; defeated Chicago, 4-3, in Eastern Conference finals; defeated Portland, 4-1, in NBA Finals.

1991—Defeated Atlanta, 3-2, in Eastern Conference first round; defeated Boston, 4-2, in Eastern Conference semifinals; lost to Chicago, 4-0, in Eastern Conference finals.

1992—Lost to New York in Eastern Conference first round.

Team USA defeated Angola, 116-48; Croatia, 103-70; Germany, 111-68; Brazil, 127-83; and Spain, 122-81, in preliminary round. Defeated Puerto Rico, 115-77, in medal round quarterfinals; defeated Lithuania, 127-76, in semifinals; defeated Croatia, 117-85, in gold-medal game.

1993—Lost to Cleveland in Eastern Conference first round.

1994—Lost to New York in Eastern Conference first round.

HANNUM, ALEX

PERSONAL: Born July 19, 1923, in Los Angeles. ... 6-7/225. ... Full name: Alexander Murray Hannum.
HIGH SCHOOL: Hamilton (Los Angeles).
COLLEGE: Southern California.
TRANSACTIONS/CAREER NOTES: Played for Los Angeles Shamrocks, an Amateur Athletic Union team and averaged 9.8 points per game (1945-46). ... Signed by Oshkosh All-Stars of National Basketball League (1948). ... Sold by Oshkosh of NBL to Syracuse Nationals of NBA (1949). ... Traded by Nationals with Fred Scolari to Baltimore Bullets for Red Rocha (1951). ... Sold by Bullets to Rochester Royals during 1951-52 season. ... Sold by Royals to Milwaukee Hawks (1954). ... Hawks franchise moved from Milwaukee to St. Louis for 1955-56 season. ... Released by Hawks (1956). ... Signed by Fort Wayne Pistons (1956). ... Released by Pistons (December 12, 1956). ... Signed by Hawks (December 17, 1956).

NOTES: In military service (1943-44 through 1945-46).

Season Team	G	Min.	FGM	FGA	Pct.	FTM	FTA	Pct.	Reb.	Ast.	Pts.	RPG	APG	PPG
												AVERAGES		
41-42—Southern California‡					Freshman team statistics unavailable.									
42-43—Southern California	15	...	23	...	...	9	20	.450	...	...	55	...	...	3.7
46-47—Southern California	24	...	...	...	...	...	...	...	...	...	251	...	...	10.5
47-48—Southern California	23	...	108	...	...	...	...	...	...	...	263	...	...	11.4
Varsity totals........................	62	...	...	...	...	...	...	...	...	...	569	...	...	9.2

NBL AND NBA REGULAR-SEASON RECORD

Season Team	G	Min.	FGM	FGA	Pct.	FTM	FTA	Pct.	Reb.	Ast.	PF	Dq.	Pts.	RPG	APG	PPG
														AVERAGES		
48-49 —Osh. (NBL)	62	...	126	...	...	113	191	.592	...	...	188	...	365	...	...	5.9
49-50 —Syracuse....................	64	...	177	488	.363	128	186	.688	...	129	264	...	482	...	2.0	7.5
50-51 —Syracuse....................	63	...	182	494	.368	107	197	.543	301	119	271	16	471	4.8	1.9	7.5
51-52 —Balt.-Roch..................	66	1508	170	462	.368	98	138	.710	336	133	271	16	438	5.1	2.0	6.6
52-53 —Rochester..................	68	1288	129	360	.358	88	133	.662	279	81	258	18	346	4.1	1.2	5.1
53-54 —Rochester..................	72	1707	175	503	.348	102	164	.622	350	105	279	11	452	4.9	1.5	6.3
54-55 —Milwaukee	53	1088	126	358	.352	61	107	.570	245	105	206	9	313	4.6	2.0	5.9
55-56 —St. Louis	71	1480	146	453	.322	93	154	.604	344	157	271	10	385	4.8	2.2	5.4
56-57 —F.W.-St.L.	59	642	77	223	.345	37	56	.661	158	28	135	2	191	2.7	0.5	3.2
Totals..............................	578	...	1308	...	...	827	1326	.624	...	...	2143	...	3443	...	...	6.0

NBL AND NBA PLAYOFF RECORD

Season Team	G	Min.	FGM	FGA	Pct.	FTM	FTA	Pct.	Reb.	Ast.	PF	Dq.	Pts.	RPG	APG	PPG
														AVERAGES		
48-49 —Osh. (NBL)................	7	...	12	...	...	16	26	.615	...	...	...	...	40	...	...	5.7
49-50 —Syracuse....................	11	...	38	86	.442	17	34	.500	...	10	50	...	93	...	0.9	8.5
50-51 —Syracuse....................	7	...	17	39	.436	8	10	.800	47	17	37	3	42	6.7	2.4	6.0
51-52 —Rochester	6	146	16	42	.381	8	13	.615	26	8	30	3	40	4.3	1.3	6.7
52-53 —Rochester	3	52	4	10	.400	3	8	.375	4	2	16	1	11	1.3	0.7	3.7
53-54 —Rochester	6	107	12	29	.414	15	24	.625	22	5	28	3	39	3.7	0.8	6.5
55-56 —St. Louis	8	159	21	66	.318	19	35	.543	29	10	36	3	61	3.6	1.3	7.6
56-57 —St. Louis	2	6	0	2	.000	0	0	...	0	0	2	0	0	0.0	0.0	0.0
Totals..............................	50	...	120	...	...	86	150	.573	...	...	...	...	326	...	...	6.5

HEAD COACHING RECORD

HONORS: NBA Coach of the Year (1964). ... ABA Coach of the Year (1969).

NBA COACHING RECORD

Season Team	REGULAR SEASON				PLAYOFFS		
	W	L	Pct.	Finish	W	L	Pct.
56-57 —St. Louis................................	15	16	.484	T1st/Western Division	8	4	.667
57-58 —St. Louis................................	41	31	.569	1st/Western Division	8	3	.727
60-61 —Syracuse................................	38	41	.481	3rd/Eastern Division	4	4	.500
61-62 —Syracuse................................	41	39	.513	3rd/Eastern Division	2	3	.400
62-63 —Syracuse................................	48	32	.600	2nd/Eastern Division	2	3	.400
63-64 —San Francisco........................	48	32	.600	1st/Western Division	5	7	.417
64-65 —San Francisco........................	17	63	.215	5th/Western Division	—	—	—
65-66 —San Francisco........................	35	45	.438	4th/Western Division	—	—	—
66-67 —Philadelphia............................	68	13	.840	1st/Eastern Division	11	4	.733
67-68 —Philadelphia............................	62	20	.756	1st/Eastern Division	7	6	.538
69-70 —San Diego..............................	18	38	.321	7th/Western Division	—	—	—
70-71 —San Diego..............................	40	42	.488	3rd/Pacific Division	—	—	—
Totals (12 years)............................	471	412	.533	Totals (8 years)	47	34	.580

ABA COACHING RECORD

Season Team	REGULAR SEASON				PLAYOFFS		
	W	L	Pct.	Finish	W	L	Pct.
68-69 —Oakland................................	60	18	.769	1st/Western Division	12	4	.750
71-72 —Denver..................................	34	50	.405	4th/Western Division	3	4	.429
72-73 —Denver..................................	47	37	.560	3rd/Western Division	1	4	.200
73-74 —Denver..................................	37	47	.440	T4th/Western Division	—	—	—
Totals (4 years)............................	178	152	.539	Totals (3 years)	16	12	.571

NOTES:

1957—Replaced Red Holzman (14-19) and Slater Martin (5-3) as St. Louis head coach (January), with record of 19-22. Defeated Fort Wayne, 115-103, and Minneapolis, 114-111, in Western Division tiebreakers; defeated Minneapolis, 3-0, in Western Division finals; lost to Boston, 4-3, in World Championship series.

1958—Defeated Detroit, 4-1, in Western Division finals; defeated Boston, 4-2, in World Championship Series.

1961—Defeated Philadelphia, 3-0, in Eastern Division semifinals; lost to Boston, 4-1, in Eastern Division finals.

1962—Lost to Philadelphia in Eastern Division finals.

1963—Lost to Cincinnati in Eastern Division semifinals.

1964—Defeated St. Louis, 4-3, in Western Division finals; lost to Boston, 4-1, in World Championship Series.

1967—Defeated Cincinnati, 3-1, in Eastern Division semifinals; defeated Boston, 4-1, in Eastern Division finals; defeated San Francisco, 4-2, in World Championship Series.

1968—Defeated New York, 4-2, in Eastern Divison semifinals; lost to Boston, 4-3, in Eastern Division finals.

1969—Defeated Denver, 4-3, in Western Division semifinals; defeated New Orleans, 4-0, in Western Division finals; defeated Indiana, 4-1, in ABA Finals. Replaced Jack McMahon as San Diego head coach (December), with record of 9-17.

1972—Lost to Indiana in Western Division semifinals.

1973—Lost to Indiana in Western Division semifinals.

ALL-TIME GREAT COACHES

HEINSOHN, TOM

PERSONAL: Born August 26, 1934, in Jersey City, N.J. ... 6-7/218. ... Full name: Thomas William Heinsohn.
HIGH SCHOOL: St. Michael's (Union City, N.J.).
COLLEGE: Holy Cross.
TRANSACTIONS/CAREER NOTES: Selected by Boston Celtics in 1956 NBA Draft (territorial pick).
CAREER HONORS: Elected to Naismith Memorial Basketball Hall of Fame (1985).
MISCELLANEOUS: Member of NBA championship teams (1957, 1959, 1960, 1961, 1962, 1963, 1964, 1965).

COLLEGIATE RECORD

Season Team	G	Min.	FGM	FGA	Pct.	FTM	FTA	Pct.	Reb.	Ast.	Pts.	RPG	APG	PPG
52-53—Holy Cross‡	15	...	97	...	...	70	...	...	...	...	264	...	...	17.6
53-54—Holy Cross	28	...	175	364	.481	94	142	.662	300	...	444	10.7	...	15.9
54-55—Holy Cross	26	...	232	499	.465	141	215	.656	385	...	605	14.8	...	23.3
55-56—Holy Cross	27	...	254	630	.403	232	304	.763	569	...	740	21.1	...	27.4
Varsity totals	81	...	661	1493	.443	467	661	.707	1254	...	1789	15.5	...	22.1

NBA REGULAR-SEASON RECORD

HONORS: NBA Rookie of the Year (1957). ... All-NBA second team (1961, 1962, 1963, 1964).

Season Team	G	Min.	FGM	FGA	Pct.	FTM	FTA	Pct.	Reb.	Ast.	PF	Dq.	Pts.	RPG	APG	PPG
56-57 —Boston	72	2150	446	1123	.397	271	343	.790	705	117	304	12	1163	9.8	1.6	16.2
57-58 —Boston	69	2206	468	1226	.382	294	394	.746	705	125	274	6	1230	10.2	1.8	17.8
58-59 —Boston	66	2089	465	1192	.390	312	391	.798	638	164	271	11	1242	9.7	2.5	18.8
59-60 —Boston	75	2420	673	1590	.423	283	386	.733	794	171	275	8	1629	10.6	2.3	21.7
60-61 —Boston	74	2256	627	1566	.400	325	424	.767	732	141	260	7	1579	9.9	1.9	21.3
61-62 —Boston	79	2383	692	1613	.429	358	437	.819	747	165	280	2	1742	9.5	2.1	22.1
62-63 —Boston	76	2004	550	1300	.423	340	407	.835	569	95	270	4	1440	7.5	1.3	18.9
63-64 —Boston	76	2040	487	1223	.398	283	342	.827	460	183	268	3	1257	6.1	2.4	16.5
64-65 —Boston	67	1706	365	954	.383	182	229	.795	399	157	252	5	912	6.0	2.3	13.6
Totals	654	19254	4773	11787	.405	2648	3353	.790	5749	1318	2454	58	12194	8.8	2.0	18.6

NBA PLAYOFF RECORD

Season Team	G	Min.	FGM	FGA	Pct.	FTM	FTA	Pct.	Reb.	Ast.	PF	Dq.	Pts.	RPG	APG	PPG
56-57 —Boston	10	370	90	231	.390	49	69	.710	117	20	40	1	229	11.7	2.0	22.9
57-58 —Boston	11	349	68	194	.351	56	72	.778	119	18	52	3	192	10.8	1.6	17.5
58-59 —Boston	11	348	91	220	.414	37	56	.661	98	32	41	0	219	8.9	2.9	19.9
59-60 —Boston	13	423	112	267	.419	60	80	.750	126	27	53	2	284	9.7	2.1	21.8
60-61 —Boston	10	291	82	201	.408	33	43	.767	99	20	36	1	197	9.9	2.0	19.7
61-62 —Boston	14	445	116	291	.399	58	76	.763	115	34	58	4	290	8.2	2.4	20.7
62-63 —Boston	13	413	123	270	.456	75	98	.765	116	15	55	2	321	8.9	1.2	24.7
63-64 —Boston	10	308	70	180	.389	34	42	.810	80	26	36	0	174	8.0	2.6	17.4
64-65 —Boston	12	276	66	181	.365	20	32	.625	84	23	46	1	152	7.0	1.9	12.7
Totals	104	3223	818	2035	.402	422	568	.743	954	215	417	14	2058	9.2	2.1	19.8

NBA ALL-STAR GAME RECORD

Season Team	Min.	FGM	FGA	Pct.	FTM	FTA	Pct.	Reb.	Ast.	PF	Dq.	Pts.
1957 —Boston	23	5	17	.294	2	2	1.000	7	0	3	0	12
1961 —Boston	19	2	16	.125	0	0	...	6	1	4	0	4
1962 —Boston	13	4	11	.364	2	2	1.000	2	1	4	0	10
1963 —Boston	21	6	11	.545	3	4	.750	2	1	4	0	15
1964 —Boston	21	5	12	.417	0	0	...	3	0	5	0	10
1965 —Boston					Selected, did not play—injured.							
Totals	97	22	67	.328	7	8	.875	20	3	20	0	51

HEAD COACHING RECORD

NOTES: NBA Coach of the Year (1973).

NBA COACHING RECORD

	REGULAR SEASON				PLAYOFFS		
Season Team	W	L	Pct.	Finish	W	L	Pct.
69-70 —Boston	34	48	.415	6th/Eastern Division	—	—	—
70-71 —Boston	44	38	.537	3rd/Atlantic Division	—	—	—
71-72 —Boston	56	26	.683	1st/Atlantic Division	5	6	.455
72-73 —Boston	68	14	.829	1st/Atlantic Division	7	6	.538
73-74 —Boston	56	26	.683	1st/Atlantic Division	12	6	.667
74-75 —Boston	60	22	.732	1st/Atlantic Division	6	5	.545
75-76 —Boston	54	28	.659	1st/Atlantic Division	12	6	.667
76-77 —Boston	44	38	.537	2nd/Atlantic Division	5	4	.556
77-78 —Boston	11	23	.324		—	—	—
Totals (9 years)	427	263	.619	Totals (6 years)	47	33	.588

NOTES:
1972—Defeated Atlanta, 4-2, in Eastern Conference semifinals; lost to New York, 4-1, in Eastern Conference finals.
1973—Defeated Atlanta, 4-2, in Eastern Conference semifinals; lost to New York, 4-3, in Eastern Conference finals.
1974—Defeated Buffalo, 4-2, in Eastern Conference semifinals; defeated New York, 4-1, in Eastern Conference finals; defeated Milwaukee, 4-3, in World Championship Series.

1975—Defeated Houston, 4-1, in Eastern Conference semifinals; lost to Washington, 4-2, in Eastern Conference finals.
1976—Defeated Buffalo, 4-2, in Eastern Conference semifinals; defeated Cleveland, 4-2, in Eastern Conference finals; defeated Phoenix, 4-2, in World Championship Series.
1977—Defeated San Antonio, 2-0, in Eastern Conference first round; lost to Philadelphia, 4-3, in Eastern Conference semifinals.
1978—Replaced as Boston head coach by Satch Sanders with club in third place (January 3).

HOLZMAN, RED

PERSONAL: Born August 10, 1920, in Brooklyn, N.Y. ... 5-10/175. ... Full name: William Holzman.
HIGH SCHOOL: Franklin K. Lane (Brooklyn, N.Y.).
COLLEGE: Baltimore, then City College of New York.
TRANSACTIONS/CAREER NOTES: Played in New York State League with Albany (1941-42). ... In military service during 1942-43, 1943-44 and 1944-45 seasons; played at Norfolk, Va., Naval Training Station and scored 305 points in 1942-43 and 258 points in 1943-44. ... Signed by Rochester Royals of National Basketball League (1945). ... Played in American Basketball League with New York (1945-46). ... Royals franchise transferred to Basketball Association of America for 1948-49 season. ... Royals franchise became part of NBA for 1949-50 season. ... Acquired from Royals by Milwaukee Hawks (1953).
CAREER HONORS: Elected to Naismith Memorial Basketball Hall of Fame (1985).
MISCELLANEOUS: Member of NBL championship team (1946). ... Member of NBA championship team (1951).

COLLEGIATE RECORD

Season Team	G	Min.	FGM	FGA	Pct.	FTM	FTA	Pct.	Reb.	Ast.	Pts.	RPG	APG	PPG
38-39—Baltimore						Statistics unavailable.								
39-40—City Coll. (N.Y.)						Did not play—transfer student.								
40-41—City Coll. (N.Y.)	21	...	96	...	...	37	...	...	...	...	229	...	...	10.9
41-42—City Coll. (N.Y.)	18	...	87	...	...	51	...	...	...	...	225	...	...	12.5
Totals	39	...	183	...	...	88	...	...	...	...	454	...	...	11.6

ABL REGULAR-SEASON RECORD

Season Team	G	Min.	FGM	FGA	Pct.	FTM	FTA	Pct.	Reb.	Ast.	Pts.	RPG	APG	PPG
45-46—New York	4	...	18	...	...	12	...	...	...	...	48	...	...	12.0

NBL AND NBA REGULAR-SEASON RECORD

HONORS: All-NBL first team (1946, 1948). ... All-NBL second team (1947).

Season Team	G	Min.	FGM	FGA	Pct.	FTM	FTA	Pct.	Reb.	Ast.	PF	Dq.	Pts.	RPG	APG	PPG
45-46 —Roc. (NBL)	34	...	144	...	...	77	115	.670	...	...	54	...	365	...	...	10.7
46-47 —Roc. (NBL)	44	...	227	...	...	74	139	.532	...	...	68	...	528	...	...	12.0
47-48 —Roc. (NBL)	60	...	246	...	...	117	182	.643	...	...	58	...	609	...	...	10.2
48-49 —Roc. (BAA)	60	...	225	691	.326	96	157	.611	...	149	93	...	546	...	2.5	9.1
49-50 —Rochester	68	...	206	625	.330	144	210	.686	...	200	67	...	556	...	2.9	8.2
50-51 —Rochester	68	...	183	561	.326	130	179	.726	152	147	94	0	496	2.2	2.2	7.3
51-52 —Rochester	65	1065	104	372	.280	61	85	.718	106	115	95	1	269	1.6	1.8	4.1
52-53 —Rochester	46	392	38	149	.255	27	38	.711	40	35	56	2	103	0.9	0.8	2.2
53-54 —Milwaukee	51	649	74	224	.330	48	73	.658	46	75	73	1	196	0.9	1.5	3.8
Totals	496	...	1447	...	...	774	1178	.657	...	...	658	...	3668	...	...	7.4

NBL AND NBA PLAYOFF RECORD

Season Team	G	Min.	FGM	FGA	Pct.	FTM	FTA	Pct.	Reb.	Ast.	PF	Dq.	Pts.	RPG	APG	PPG
45-46 —Roc. (NBL)	7	...	30	...	...	21	31	.677	...	...	10	...	81	...	...	11.6
46-47 —Roc. (NBL)	11	...	42	...	...	22	29	.759	...	...	22	...	106	...	...	9.6
47-48 —Roc. (NBL)	10	...	35	...	...	10	15	.667	...	...	6	...	80	...	...	8.0
48-49 —Roc. (BAA)	4	...	18	40	.450	5	6	.833	...	13	3	...	41	...	3.3	10.3
49-50 —Rochester	2	...	3	9	.333	1	2	.500	...	0	3	...	7	...	0.0	3.5
50-51 —Rochester	14	...	31	76	.408	23	34	.676	19	20	14	0	85	1.4	1.4	6.1
51-52 —Rochester	6	65	3	15	.200	1	6	.167	6	2	3	0	7	1.0	0.3	1.2
52-53 —Rochester	2	14	1	5	.200	1	4	.250	1	1	4	0	3	0.5	0.5	1.5
Totals	56	...	163	...	...	84	127	.661	...	...	65	...	410	...	...	7.3

HEAD COACHING RECORD

HONORS: NBA Coach of the Year (1970).

NBA COACHING RECORD

Season Team	REGULAR SEASON				PLAYOFFS		
	W	L	Pct.	Finish	W	L	Pct.
53-54 —Milwaukee	10	16	.385	4th/Western Division	—	—	—
54-55 —Milwaukee	26	46	.361	4th/Western Division	—	—	—
55-56 —St. Louis	33	39	.458	T2nd/Western Division	4	5	.444
56-57 —St. Louis	14	19	.424		—	—	—
67-68 —New York	28	17	.622	3rd/Eastern Division	2	4	.333
68-69 —New York	54	28	.659	3rd/Eastern Division	6	4	.600
69-70 —New York	60	22	.732	1st/Eastern Division	12	7	.632
70-71 —New York	52	30	.634	1st/Atlantic Division	7	5	.583
71-72 —New York	48	34	.585	2nd/Atlantic Division	9	7	.563
72-73 —New York	57	25	.695	2nd/Atlantic Division	12	5	.706
73-74 —New York	49	33	.598	2nd/Atlantic Division	5	7	.417
74-75 —New York	40	42	.488	3rd/Atlantic Division	1	2	.333

Season Team	REGULAR SEASON						PLAYOFFS		
	W	L	Pct.	Finish			W	L	Pct.
75-76 —New York	38	44	.463	4th/Atlantic Division			—	—	—
76-77 —New York	40	42	.488	3rd/Atlantic Division			—	—	—
78-79 —New York	25	43	.368	4th/Atlantic Division			—	—	—
79-80 —New York	39	43	.476	T3rd/Atlantic Division			—	—	—
80-81 —New York	50	32	.610	3rd/Atlantic Division			0	2	.000
81-82 —New York	33	49	.402	5th/Atlantic Division			—	—	—
Totals (18 years)	696	604	.535	Totals (10 years)			58	48	.547

NOTES:
1954—Replaced Fuzzy Levane as Milwaukee head coach with record of 11-35.
1955—Milwaukee franchise transferred to St. Louis.
1956—Lost to Minneapolis, 103-97, in Western Division 2nd place game; defeated Minneapolis, 2-1, in Western Division semifinals; lost to Fort Wayne, 3-2, in Western Division finals.
1957—Replaced as St. Louis head coach by Slater Martin (January).
1967—Replaced Dick McGuire as New York head coach (December), with record of 15-22 and in fifth place.
1968—Lost to Philadelphia in Eastern Division semifinals.
1969—Defeated Baltimore, 4-0, in Eastern Division semifinals; lost to Boston, 4-2, in Eastern Division finals.
1970—Defeated Baltimore, 4-3, in Eastern Division semifinals; defeated Milwaukee, 4-1, in Eastern Division finals; defeated Los Angeles, 4-3, in World Championship Series.
1971—Defeated Atlanta, 4-1, in Eastern Conference semifinals; lost to Baltmore, 4-3, in Eastern Conference finals.
1972—Defeated Baltimore, 4-2, in Eastern Conference semifinals; defeated Boston, 4-1, in Eastern Conference finals; lost to Los Angeles, 4-1, in World Championship Series.
1973—Defeated Baltimore, 4-1, in Eastern Conference semifinals; defeated Boston, 4-3, in Eastern Conference finals; defeated Los Angeles, 4-1, in World Championship Series.
1974—Defeated Capital, 4-3, in Eastern Conference semifinals; lost to Boston, 4-1, in Eastern Conference Finals.
1975—Lost to Houston in Eastern Conference first round.
1978—Replaced Willis Reed as New York head coach (November), with record of 6-8.
1981—Lost to Chicago in Eastern Conference first round.

JONES, K.C.

PERSONAL: Born May 25, 1932, in Taylor, Texas. ... 6-1/200.
HIGH SCHOOL: Commerce (San Francisco).
COLLEGE: San Francisco.
TRANSACTIONS/CAREER NOTES: Selected by Boston Celtics in second round of 1956 NBA Draft. ... In military service (1956-57 and 1957-58); played at Fort Leonard Wood, Mo.; named to Amateur Athletic Union All-America team as a member of 1957-58 Fort Leonard Wood team. ... Played in Eastern Basketball League with Hartford Capitols (1967-68).
CAREER HONORS: Elected to Naismith Memorial Basketball Hall of Fame (1988).
MISCELLANEOUS: Member of NBA championship teams (1959, 1960, 1961, 1962, 1963, 1964, 1965, 1966). ... Selected by Los Angeles Rams in 30th round of 1955 National Football League draft. ... Member of gold-medal-winning U.S. Olympic team (1956).

COLLEGIATE RECORD

NOTES: Underwent appendectomy after one game of the 1953-54 season and was granted an extra year of eligibility by the University of San Francisco; however, he was ineligible for the 1955-56 NCAA tournament because he was playing his fifth season of college basketball. ... Member of NCAA championship team (1955).

Season Team	G	Min.	FGM	FGA	Pct.	FTM	FTA	Pct.	Reb.	Ast.	Pts.	AVERAGES		
												RPG	APG	PPG
51-52—San Francisco	24	...	44	128	.344	46	64	.719	...	...	134	...	...	5.6
52-53—San Francisco	23	...	63	159	.396	81	149	.544	...	...	207	...	...	9.0
53-54—San Francisco	1	...	3	12	.250	2	2	1.000	3	...	8	3.0	...	8.0
54-55—San Francisco	29	...	105	293	.358	97	144	.674	148	...	307	5.1	...	10.6
55-56—San Francisco	25	...	76	208	.365	93	142	.655	130	...	245	5.2	...	9.8
Totals	102	...	291	800	.364	319	501	.637	...	....	901	...	...	8.8

NBA REGULAR-SEASON RECORD

Season Team	G	Min.	FGM	FGA	Pct.	FTM	FTA	Pct.	Reb.	Ast.	PF	Dq.	Pts.	AVERAGES		
														RPG	APG	PPG
58-59 —Boston	49	609	65	192	.339	41	68	.603	127	70	58	0	171	2.6	1.4	3.5
59-60 —Boston	74	1274	169	414	.408	128	170	.753	199	189	109	1	466	2.7	2.6	6.3
60-61 —Boston	78	1607	203	601	.338	186	320	.581	279	253	200	3	592	3.6	3.2	7.6
61-62 —Boston	79	2023	289	707	.409	145	231	.628	291	339	204	2	723	3.7	4.3	9.2
62-63 —Boston	79	1945	230	591	.389	112	177	.633	263	317	221	3	572	3.3	4.0	7.2
63-64 —Boston	80	2424	283	722	.392	88	168	.524	372	407	253	0	654	4.7	5.1	8.2
64-65 —Boston	78	2434	253	639	.396	143	227	.630	318	437	263	5	649	4.1	5.6	8.3
65-66 —Boston	80	2710	240	619	.388	209	303	.690	304	503	243	4	689	3.8	6.3	8.6
66-67 —Boston	78	2446	182	459	.397	119	189	.630	239	389	273	7	483	3.1	5.0	6.2
Totals	675	17472	1914	4944	.387	1171	1853	.632	2392	2904	1824	25	4999	3.5	4.3	7.4

NBA PLAYOFF RECORD

Season Team	G	Min.	FGM	FGA	Pct.	FTM	FTA	Pct.	Reb.	Ast.	PF	Dq.	Pts.	AVERAGES		
														RPG	APG	PPG
58-59 —Boston	8	75	5	20	.250	5	5	1.000	12	10	8	0	15	1.5	1.3	1.9
59-60 —Boston	13	232	27	80	.338	17	22	.773	45	14	28	0	71	3.5	1.1	5.5
60-61 —Boston	9	103	9	30	.300	7	14	.500	19	15	17	0	25	2.1	1.7	2.8
61-62 —Boston	14	329	44	102	.431	38	53	.717	56	55	50	1	126	4.0	3.9	9.0
62-63 —Boston	13	250	19	64	.297	21	30	.700	36	37	42	1	59	2.8	2.8	4.5

Season Team	G	Min.	FGM	FGA	Pct.	FTM	FTA	Pct.	Reb.	Ast.	PF	Dq.	Pts.	AVERAGES RPG	APG	PPG
63-64 —Boston	10	312	25	72	.347	13	25	.520	37	68	40	0	63	3.7	6.8	6.3
64-65 —Boston	12	396	43	104	.413	35	45	.778	39	74	49	1	121	3.3	6.2	10.1
65-66 —Boston	17	543	45	109	.413	39	57	.684	52	75	65	0	129	3.1	4.4	7.6
66-67 —Boston	9	254	24	75	.320	11	18	.611	24	48	36	1	59	2.7	5.3	6.6
Totals	105	2494	241	656	.367	186	269	.691	320	396	335	4	668	3.0	3.8	6.4

EBL REGULAR-SEASON RECORD

Season Team	G	Min.	FGM	FGA	Pct.	FTM	FTA	Pct.	Reb.	Ast.	PF	Dq.	Pts.	AVERAGES RPG	APG	PPG
67-68 —Hartford	6	...	15	...	...	9	18	.500	24	41	...	...	39	4.0	6.8	6.5

HEAD COACHING RECORD

BACKGROUND: Assistant coach, Harvard University (1970-71). ... Assistant coach, Los Angeles Lakers (1971-72). ... Assistant coach, Milwaukee Bucks (1976-77). ... Assistant coach, Boston Celtics (1978-79 through 1982-83 and 1996-97 season). ... Vice president/basketball operations, Celtics (1988-89). ... Assistant coach, Seattle SuperSonics (1989-90). ... Assistant coach, Detroit Pistons (1994-95).

COLLEGIATE COACHING RECORD

Season Team	W	L	Pct.
67-68 —Brandeis	11	10	.524
68-69 —Brandeis	12	9	.571
69-70 —Brandeis	11	13	.458
Totals (3 years)	34	32	.515

ABA COACHING RECORD

Season Team	REGULAR SEASON W	L	Pct.	Finish	PLAYOFFS W	L	Pct.
72-73 —San Diego	30	54	.357	4th/Western Division	0	4	.000

NBA COACHING RECORD

Season Team	REGULAR SEASON W	L	Pct.	Finish	PLAYOFFS W	L	Pct.
73-74 —Capital	47	35	.573	1st/Central Division	3	4	.429
74-75 —Washington	60	22	.732	1st/Central Division	8	9	.471
75-76 —Washington	48	34	.585	2nd/Central Division	3	4	.429
83-84 —Boston	62	20	.756	1st/Atlantic Division	15	8	.652
84-85 —Boston	63	19	.768	1st/Atlantic Division	13	8	.619
85-86 —Boston	67	15	.817	1st/Atlantic Division	15	3	.833
86-87 —Boston	59	23	.720	1st/Atlantic Division	13	10	.565
87-88 —Boston	57	25	.695	1st/Atlantic Division	9	8	.529
90-91 —Seattle	41	41	.500	5th/Pacific Division	2	3	.400
91-92 —Seattle	18	18	.500		—	—	—
Totals (10 years)	522	252	.674	Totals (9 years)	81	57	.587

NOTES:

1973—Lost to Utah in Western Division semifinals.

1974—Lost to New York in Eastern Conference semifinals.

1975—Defeated Buffalo, 4-3, in Eastern Conference semifinals; defeated Boston, 4-2, in Eastern Conference finals; lost to Golden State, 4-0, in World Championship Series.

1976—Lost to Cleveland in Eastern Conference semifinals.

1984—Defeated Washington, 3-1, in Eastern Conference first round; defeated New York, 4-3, in Eastern Conference semifinals; defeated Milwaukee, 4-1, in Eastern Conference finals; defeated Los Angeles, 4-3, in World Championship Series.

1985—Defeated Cleveland, 3-1, in Eastern Conference first round; defeated Detroit, 4-2, in Eastern Conference semifinals; defeated Philadelphia, 4-1, in Eastern Conference finals; lost to Los Angeles Lakers, 4-2, in World Championship Series.

1986—Defeated Chicago, 3-0, in Eastern Conference first round; defeated Atlanta, 4-1, in Eastern Conference semifinals; defeated Milwaukee, 4-0, in Eastern Conference finals; defeated Houston, 4-2, in NBA Finals.

1987—Defeated Chicago, 3-0, in Eastern Conference first round; defeated Milwaukee, 4-3, in Eastern Conference semifinals; defeated Detroit, 4-3, in Eastern Conference finals; lost to Los Angeles Lakers, 4-2, in NBA Finals.

1988—Defeated New York, 3-1, in Eastern Conference first round; defeated Atlanta, 4-3, in Eastern Conference semifinals; lost to Detroit, 4-2, in Eastern Conference finals.

1991—Lost to Portland in Western Conference first round.

1992—Replaced as Seattle head coach by interim coach Bob Kloppenburg with club in sixth place (January 15).

KUNDLA, JOHN

PERSONAL: Born July 3, 1916, in Star Junction, Pa. ... 6-2/180. ... Full name: John Albert Kundla.
HIGH SCHOOL: Central (Minneapolis).
COLLEGE: Minnesota.
CAREER HONORS: Elected to Naismith Memorial Basketball Hall of Fame (1995).

COLLEGIATE RECORD

Season Team	G	Min.	FGM	FGA	Pct.	FTM	FTA	Pct.	Reb.	Ast.	Pts.	AVERAGES RPG	APG	PPG
35-36 —Minnesota‡						Freshman team statistics unavailable.								
36-37 —Minnesota	15	...	53	...	...	34	53	.642	...	...	140	...	...	9.3
37-38 —Minnesota	20	...	62	...	...	41	77	.532	...	...	165	...	...	8.3
38-39 —Minnesota	17	...	71	...	...	40	63	.635	...	...	182	...	...	10.7
Varsity totals	52	...	186	...	...	115	193	.596	...	...	487	...	...	9.4

HEAD COACHING RECORD

BACKGROUND: Head coach, De La Salle High School (Minn.).

COLLEGIATE COACHING RECORD

Season Team	W	L	Pct.	Finish
46-47 —St. Thomas (Minn.)	11	11	.500	
59-60 —Minnesota	12	12	.500	T3rd/Big Ten Conference
60-61 —Minnesota	10	13	.435	T4th/Big Ten Conference
61-62 —Minnesota	10	14	.417	7th/Big Ten Conference
62-63 —Minnesota	12	12	.500	T4th/Big Ten Conference
63-64 —Minnesota	17	7	.708	3rd/Big Ten Conference
64-65 —Minnesota	19	5	.792	2nd/Big Ten Conference
65-66 —Minnesota	14	10	.583	T5th/Big Ten Conference
66-67 —Minnesota	9	15	.375	9th/Big Ten Conference
67-68 —Minnesota	7	17	.292	T9th/Big Ten Conference
Totals (10 years)	121	116	.511	

NBL COACHING RECORD

	REGULAR SEASON					PLAYOFFS		
Season Team	W	L	Pct.	Finish		W	L	Pct.
47-48 —Minneapolis	43	17	.717	1st/Western Division		8	2	.800

NBA COACHING RECORD

	REGULAR SEASON					PLAYOFFS		
Season Team	W	L	Pct.	Finish		W	L	Pct.
48-49 —Minneapolis	44	16	.733	2nd/Western Division		8	2	.800
49-50 —Minneapolis	51	17	.750	T1st/Central Division		10	2	.833
50-51 —Minneapolis	44	24	.647	1st/Western Division		3	4	.429
51-52 —Minneapolis	40	26	.606	2nd/Western Division		9	4	.692
52-53 —Minneapolis	48	22	.686	1st/Western Division		9	3	.750
53-54 —Minneapolis	46	26	.639	1st/Western Division		9	4	.692
54-55 —Minneapolis	40	32	.556	2nd/Western Division		3	4	.429
55-56 —Minneapolis	33	39	.458	T2nd/Western Division		1	2	.333
56-57 —Minneapolis	34	38	.472	T1st/Western Division		2	3	.400
57-58 —Minneapolis	10	23	.303	4th/Western Division		—	—	—
58-59 —Minneapolis	33	39	.458	2nd/Western Division		6	7	.462
Totals (11 years)	423	302	.583	Totals (10 years)		60	35	.632

NOTES:

1948—Defeated Oshkosh, 3-1, in NBL playoffs; defeated Tri-Cities, 2-0, in NBL semifinals; defeated Rochester, 3-1, in NBL championship series.

1949—Defeated Chicago, 2-0, in Western Division semifinals; defeated Rochester, 2-0, in Western Division finals; defeated Washington, 4-2, in World Championship Series.

1950—Defeated Rochester, 78-76, in Central Division first-place game; defeated Chicago, 2-0, in Central Division semifinals; defeated Fort Wayne, 2-0, in Central Division finals; defeated Anderson, 2-0, in NBA semifinals; defeated Syracuse, 4-2, in World Championship Series.

1951—Defeated Indianapolis, 2-1, in Western Division semifinals; lost to Rochester, 3-1, in Western Division finals.

1952—Defeated Indianapolis, 2-0, in Western Division semifinals; defeated Rochester, 3-1, in Western Division finals; defeated New York, 4-3, in World Championship Series.

1953—Defeated Indianapolis, 2-0, in Western Division semifinals; defeated Fort Wayne, 3-2, in Western Division finals; defeated New York, 4-1, in World Championship Series.

1954—Defeated Rochester, 109-88; Fort Wayne, 90-85; and Fort Wayne, 78-73, in Western Division round robin; defeated Rochester, 2-1, in Western Division semifinals; defeated Syracuse, 4-3, in World Championship Series.

1955—Defeated Rochester, 2-1, in Western Division semifinals; lost to Fort Wayne, 3-1, in Western Division finals.

1956—Defeated St. Louis, 103-97, in Western Division second-place game; lost to St. Louis, 2-1, in Western Division semifinals.

1957—Defeated Fort Wayne, 2-0, in Western Division semifinals; lost to St. Louis, 114-111, in Western Division tiebreaker; lost to St. Louis, 3-0, in Western Division finals.

1958—Replaced George Mikan as Minneapolis head coach (January 14), with record of 9-30 and in fourth place.

1959—Defeated Detroit, 2-1, in Western Division semifinals; defeated St. Louis, 4-2, in Western Division finals; lost to Boston, 4-0, in World Championship Series.

LAPCHICK, JOE

PERSONAL: Born April 12, 1900, in Yonkers, N.Y. ... Died August 10, 1970. ... 6-5/185. ... Full name: Joseph Bohomiel Lapchick.

TRANSACTIONS/CAREER NOTES: Played with independent teams, including the Original Celtics (1917 through 1920, 1924 through 1926, 1932 through 1936).

CAREER HONORS: Elected to Naismith Memorial Basketball Hall of Fame (1966).

MISCELLANEOUS: Did not play high school or college basketball.

PRO RECORD

Season Team	League	G	FGM	FTM	Pts.	Avg.
20-21 —Holyoke	IL	11	14	40	68	6.2
Schenectady	NYSL	5	2	10	14	2.8
21-22 —Schenectady-Troy	NYSL	32	12	95	119	3.7
Brooklyn	MBL	10	6	20	32	3.2
Holyoke	IL	16	13	40	66	4.1
22-23 —Brooklyn	MBL	33	34	109	177	5.4
Troy	NYSL	24	13	59	85	3.5
Holyoke	IL		Statistics unavailable.			
26-27 —Brooklyn	ABL	32	35	131	201	6.3
New York	NBL	17	20	66	106	6.2
27-28 —New York	ABL	47	103	110	316	6.7
28-29 —Cleveland	ABL	39	51	86	188	4.8

Season	Team	League	G	FGM	FTM	Pts.	Avg.
29-30	—Cleveland	ABL	52	47	92	186	3.6
30-31	—Cleveland-Toledo	ABL	30	22	49	93	3.1
32-33	—Yonkers	MBL	1	0	0	0	0.0
33-34	—Plymouth	PSL	1	1	3	5	5.0
	ABL pro totals		200	258	468	984	4.9
	MBL pro totals		44	40	129	209	4.8

COLLEGIATE COACHING RECORD

Season	Team	W	L	Pct.	Finish
36-37	—St. John's	12	7	.632	Independent
37-38	—St. John's	15	4	.789	Independent
38-39	—St. John's	18	4	.818	Independent
39-40	—St. John's	15	5	.750	Independent
40-41	—St. John's	11	6	.647	Independent
41-42	—St. John's	16	5	.762	Independent
42-43	—St. John's	21	3	.875	Independent
43-44	—St. John's	18	5	.783	Independent
44-45	—St. John's	21	3	.875	Independent
45-46	—St. John's	17	6	.739	Independent
46-47	—St. John's	16	7	.696	Independent
56-57	—St. John's	14	9	.609	Independent
57-58	—St. John's	18	8	.692	Independent
58-59	—St. John's	20	6	.769	Independent
59-60	—St. John's	17	8	.680	Independent
60-61	—St. John's	20	5	.800	Independent
61-62	—St. John's	21	5	.808	Independent
62-63	—St. John's	9	15	.375	Independent
63-64	—St. John's	14	11	.560	Independent
64-65	—St. John's	21	8	.724	Independent
	Totals (20 years)	334	130	.720	

ABL COACHING RECORD

		REGULAR SEASON				PLAYOFFS		
Season	Team	W	L	Pct.	Finish	W	L	Pct.
61-62	Cleveland	6	6	.500		—	—	—

NBA COACHING RECORD

		REGULAR SEASON				PLAYOFFS		
Season	Team	W	L	Pct.	Finish	W	L	Pct.
47-48	—New York (BAA)	26	22	.542	2nd/Eastern Division	1	2	.333
48-49	—New York (BAA)	32	28	.533	2nd/Eastern Division	3	3	.500
49-50	—New York	40	28	.588	2nd/Eastern Division	3	2	.600
50-51	—New York	36	30	.545	3rd/Eastern Division	8	6	.571
51-52	—New York	37	29	.561	3rd/Eastern Division	8	6	.571
52-53	—New York	47	23	.671	1st/Midwest Division	6	5	.545
53-54	—New York	44	28	.611	1st/Eastern Division	0	4	.000
54-55	—New York	38	34	.528	2nd/Eastern Division	1	2	.333
55-56	—New York	26	25	.510		—	—	—
	Totals (9 years)	326	247	.569	Totals (8 years)	30	30	.500

NOTES:

1939—Defeated Roanoke, 71-47, in NIT quarterfinals; lost to Loyola, 51-46, in semifinals; lost to Bradley, 40-35, in third-place game.

1940—Lost to Duquesne, 38-31, in NIT quarterfinals.

1943—Defeated Rice, 51-49, in NIT quarterfinals; defeated Fordham, 69-43, in semifinals; defeated Toledo, 48-27, in finals.

1944—Defeated Bowling Green, 44-40, in NIT quarterfinals; defeated Kentucky, 48-45, in semifinals; defeated DePaul, 47-39, in finals.

1945—Defeated Muhlenberg, 34-33, in NIT quarterfinals; lost to Bowling Green, 57-44, in semifinals; lost to Rhode Island, 64-57, in third-place game.

1946—Lost to West Virginia, 70-58, in NIT quarterfinals.

1947—Lost to North Carolina State, 61-55, in NIT quarterfinals.

1948—Lost to Baltimore in quarterfinals.

1949—Defeated Baltimore, 2-1, in Eastern Division semifinals; lost to Washington, 2-1, in Eastern Division finals.

1950—Defeated Washington, 2-0, in Eastern Division semifinals; lost to Syracuse, 2-1, in Eastern Division finals.

1951—Defeated Boston, 2-0, in Eastern Division semifinals; defeated Syracuse, 3-2, in Eastern Division finals; lost to Rochester, 4-3, in World Championship Series.

1952—Defeated Boston, 2-1, in Eastern Division semifinals; defeated Syracuse, 3-1, in Eastern Division finals; lost to Minneapolis, 4-3, in World Championship Series.

1953—Defeated Baltimore, 2-0, in Eastern Division semifinals; defeated Boston, 3-1, in Eastern Division finals; lost to Minneapolis, 4-1, in World Championship Series.

1954—Lost to Boston, 93-71; Syracuse, 75-68; Boston, 79-78; and Syracuse, 103-99, in Eastern Division round robin.

1955—Lost to Boston in Eastern Division semifinals.

1956—Resigned as New York head coach.

1958—Defeated Butler, 76-69, in NIT first round; defeated Utah, 71-70, in quarterfinals; lost to Dayton, 80-56, in semifinals; lost to St. Bonaventure, 84-69, in third-place game.

1959—Defeated Villanova, 75-67, in NIT first round; defeated St. Bonaventure, 82-74, in quarterfinals; defeated Providence, 76-55, in semifinals; defeated Bradley, 76-71 (OT), in finals.

1960—Lost to St. Bonaventure, 106-71, in NIT quarterfinals.

1961—Lost to Wake Forest, 97-74, in NCAA Tournament first round.

1962—Defeated Holy Cross, 80-74, in NIT quarterfinals; defeated Duquesne, 76-65, in semifinals; lost to Dayton, 73-67, in finals.

1965—Defeated Boston College, 114-92, in NIT first round; defeated New Mexico, 61-54, in quarterfinals; defeated Army, 67-60, in semifinals; defeated Villanova, 55-51, in finals.

LOUGHERY, KEVIN

PERSONAL: Born March 28, 1940, in Brooklyn, N.Y. ... 6-3/190. ... Full name: Kevin Michael Loughery.
HIGH SCHOOL: Cardinal Hayes (Bronx, N.Y.).
COLLEGE: Boston College, then St. John's.
TRANSACTIONS/CAREER NOTES: Selected by Detroit Pistons in second round (13th pick overall) of 1962 NBA Draft. ... Traded by Pistons to Baltimore Bullets for Larry Staverman (October 28, 1963). ... Traded by Bullets with Fred Carter to Philadelphia 76ers for Archie Clark and future draft choice (October 18, 1971).

COLLEGIATE RECORD

Season Team	G	Min.	FGM	FGA	Pct.	FTM	FTA	Pct.	Reb.	Ast.	Pts.	RPG	APG	PPG
57-58—Boston College‡	19	...	133	...	...	55	...	...	...	...	321	...	...	16.9
58-59—Boston College	19	...	128	...	...	65	...	...	...	...	321	...	...	16.9
59-60—St. John's						Did not play—transfer student.								
60-61—St. John's	25	...	106	252	.421	54	77	.701	116	...	266	4.6	...	10.6
61-62—St. John's	26	...	169	378	.447	65	76	.855	151	...	403	5.8	...	15.5
Varsity totals	70	...	403	...	...	184	...	...	...	...	990	...	...	14.1

NBA REGULAR-SEASON RECORD

Season Team	G	Min.	FGM	FGA	Pct.	FTM	FTA	Pct.	Reb.	Ast.	PF	Dq.	Pts.	RPG	APG	PPG
62-63 —Detroit	57	845	146	397	.368	71	100	.710	109	104	135	1	363	1.9	1.8	6.4
63-64 —Det.-Balt.	66	1459	236	631	.374	126	177	.712	138	182	175	2	598	2.1	2.8	9.1
64-65 —Baltimore	80	2417	406	957	.424	212	281	.754	235	296	320	13	1024	2.9	3.7	12.8
65-66 —Baltimore	74	2455	526	1264	.416	297	358	.830	227	356	273	8	1349	3.1	4.8	18.2
66-67 —Baltimore	76	2577	520	1306	.398	340	412	.825	349	288	294	10	1380	4.6	3.8	18.2
67-68 —Baltimore	77	2297	458	1127	.406	305	392	.778	247	256	301	13	1221	3.2	3.3	15.9
68-69 —Baltimore	80	3135	717	1636	.438	372	463	.803	266	384	299	3	1806	3.3	4.8	22.6
69-70 —Baltimore	55	2037	477	1082	.441	253	298	.849	168	292	183	3	1207	3.1	5.3	21.9
70-71 —Baltimore	82	2260	481	1193	.403	275	331	.831	219	301	246	2	1237	2.7	3.7	15.1
71-72 —Balt.-Phil.	76	1771	341	809	.422	263	320	.822	183	196	213	3	945	2.4	2.6	12.4
72-73 —Philadelphia	32	955	169	427	.396	107	130	.823	113	148	104	0	445	3.5	4.6	13.9
Totals	755	22208	4477	10829	.413	2621	3262	.803	2254	2803	2543	58	11575	3.0	3.7	15.3

NBA PLAYOFF RECORD

Season Team	G	Min.	FGM	FGA	Pct.	FTM	FTA	Pct.	Reb.	Ast.	PF	Dq.	Pts.	RPG	APG	PPG
62-63 —Detroit	2	26	1	10	.100	1	1	1.000	4	3	4	0	3	0.0	0.0	1.5
64-65 —Baltimore	10	297	53	137	.387	34	38	.895	34	30	36	0	140	3.4	3.0	14.0
65-66 —Baltimore	3	27	3	7	.429	3	6	.500	1	1	4	0	9	0.3	0.3	3.0
68-69 —Baltimore	4	173	29	79	.367	23	35	.657	18	21	16	0	81	4.5	5.3	20.3
69-70 —Baltimore	7	153	26	77	.338	15	21	.714	16	8	24	0	67	2.3	1.1	9.6
70-71 —Baltimore	17	500	84	212	.396	64	85	.753	38	52	57	2	232	2.2	3.1	13.6
Totals	43	1176	196	522	.375	140	186	.753	107	116	140	2	532	2.5	2.7	12.4

HEAD COACHING RECORD

BACKGROUND: Player/head coach, Philadelphia 76ers (February 1973-remainder of 1972-73 season). ... Broadcaster (1988-89 and 1989-90). ... Scout, Miami Heat (1988-89 and 1989-90). ... Assistant coach, Atlanta Hawks (1990-91). ... Vice president/director of player personnel, Heat (February 1995 to 1995-96) ... Vice president/consultant (1996-97 season).

NBA COACHING RECORD

	REGULAR SEASON				PLAYOFFS		
Season Team	W	L	Pct.	Finish	W	L	Pct.
72-73 —Philadelphia	5	26	.161	4th/Atlantic Division	—	—	—
76-77 —New York Nets	22	60	.268	5th/Atlantic Division	—	—	—
77-78 —New Jersey	24	58	.293	5th/Atlantic Division	—	—	—
78-79 —New Jersey	37	45	.451	3rd/Atlantic Division	0	2	.000
79-80 —New Jersey	34	48	.415	5th/Atlantic Division	—	—	—
80-81 —New Jersey	12	23	.343		—	—	—
81-82 —Atlanta	42	40	.512	2nd/Central Division	0	2	.000
82-83 —Atlanta	43	39	.524	2nd/Central Division	1	2	.333
83-84 —Chicago	27	55	.329	5th/Central Division	—	—	—
84-85 —Chicago	38	44	.463	3rd/Central Division	1	3	.250
85-86 —Washington	7	6	.538	T3rd/Atlantic Division	2	3	.400
86-87 —Washington	42	40	.512	3rd/Atlantic Division	0	3	.000
87-88 —Washington	8	19	.296		—	—	—
91-92 —Miami	38	44	.463	4th/Atlantic Division	0	3	.000
92-93 —Miami	36	46	.439	5th/Atlantic Division	—	—	—
93-94 —Miami	42	40	.512	4th/Atlantic Division	2	3	.400
94-95 —Miami	17	29	.370	5th/Atlantic Division	—	—	—
Totals (17 years)	474	662	.417	Totals (8 years)	6	21	.222

ABA COACHING RECORD

	REGULAR SEASON				PLAYOFFS		
Season Team	W	L	Pct.	Finish	W	L	Pct.
73-74 —New York Nets	55	29	.655	1st/Eastern Division	12	2	.857
74-75 —New York Nets	58	26	.690	T1st/Eastern Division	1	4	.200
75-76 —New York Nets	55	29	.655	2nd/Eastern Division	8	5	.615
Totals (3 years)	168	84	.667	Totals (3 years)	21	11	.656

NOTES:
1973—Replaced Roy Rubin as Philadelphia head coach (February), with record of 4-47.
1974—Defeated Virginia, 4-1, in Eastern Division semifinals; defeated Kentucky, 4-0, in Eastern Division finals; defeated Utah, 4-1, in ABA Finals.
1975—Lost to St. Louis in Eastern Division semifinals.
1976—Defeated San Antonio, 4-3, in semifinals; defeated Denver, 4-2, in ABA Finals.
1979—Lost to Philadelphia in Eastern Conference first round.
1980—Resigned as New Jersey head coach (December); replaced by Bob MacKinnon with club in fifth place.
1982—Lost to Philadelphia in Eastern Conference first round.
1983—Lost to Boston in Eastern Conference first round.
1985—Lost to Milwaukee in Eastern Conference first round.
1986—Replaced Gene Shue as Washington head coach (March 19), with record of 32-37. Lost to Philadelphia in Eastern Conference first round.
1987—Lost to Detroit in Eastern Conference first round.
1988—Replaced as Washington head coach by Wes Unseld (January 3) with club in fourth place.
1992—Lost to Chicago in Eastern Conference first round.
1994—Lost to Atlanta in Eastern Conference first round.
1995—Replaced as Miami head coach by Alvin Gentry (February 14) with club in fifth place.

MacLEOD, JOHN

PERSONAL: Born October 3, 1937, in New Albany, Ind. ... 6-0/170. ... Full name: John Matthew MacLeod.
HIGH SCHOOL: New Providence (Clarksville, Ind.).
COLLEGE: Bellarmine (Ky.).

COLLEGIATE RECORD

Season Team	G	Min.	FGM	FGA	Pct.	FTM	FTA	Pct.	Reb.	Ast.	Pts.	RPG	APG	PPG
55-56—Bellarmine						Statistics unavailable.								
56-57—Bellarmine	10	...	0	...	...	1	...	...	...	...	1	...	...	0.1
57-58—Bellarmine	8	...	2	...	...	3	10	.300	...	...	7	...	...	0.9
58-59—Bellarmine	5	...	2	...	...	4	...	...	...	...	8	...	...	1.6
Totals	23		4			8	...				16			0.7

HEAD COACHING RECORD

BACKGROUND: Assistant coach, DeSales High School, Ky. (1959-60 through 1961-62). ... Head coach, Smithville High School, Ind. (1963-64 and 1964-65; record: 16-24). ... Assistant coach, Cathedral High School, Ind. (1965-66). ... Assistant coach, University of Oklahoma (1966-67).

COLLEGIATE COACHING RECORD

Season Team	W	L	Pct.	Finish
67-68 —Oklahoma	13	13	.500	T3rd/Big Eight Conference
68-69 —Oklahoma	7	19	.269	8th/Big Eight Conference
69-70 —Oklahoma	19	9	.679	3rd/Big Eight Conference
70-71 —Oklahoma	19	8	.704	2nd/Big Eight Conference
71-72 —Oklahoma	14	12	.538	3rd/Big Eight Conference
72-73 —Oklahoma	18	8	.692	4th/Big Eight Conference
91-92 —Notre Dame	18	15	.545	Independent
92-93 —Notre Dame	9	18	.333	Independent
93-94 —Notre Dame	12	17	.414	Independent
94-95 —Notre Dame	15	12	.555	Independent
95-96 —Notre Dame	9	18	.333	13th/Big East Conference
Totals (11 years)	153	149	.507	

NBA COACHING RECORD

Season Team	REGULAR SEASON				PLAYOFFS		
	W	L	Pct.	Finish	W	L	Pct.
73-74 —Phoenix	30	52	.396	4th/Pacific Division	—	—	—
74-75 —Phoenix	32	50	.390	4th/Pacific Division	—	—	—
75-76 —Phoenix	42	40	.512	3rd/Pacific Division	10	9	.526
76-77 —Phoenix	34	48	.415	5th/Pacific Division	—	—	—
77-78 —Phoenix	49	33	.598	2nd/Pacific Division	0	2	.000
78-79 —Phoenix	50	32	.610	2nd/Pacific Division	9	6	.600
79-80 —Phoenix	55	27	.671	3rd/Pacific Division	3	5	.375
80-81 —Phoenix	57	25	.695	1st/Pacific Division	3	4	.429
81-82 —Phoenix	46	36	.561	3rd/Pacific Division	2	5	.286
82-83 —Phoenix	53	29	.646	2nd/Pacific Division	1	2	.333
83-84 —Phoenix	41	41	.500	4th/Pacific Division	9	8	.529
84-85 —Phoenix	36	46	.439	3rd/Pacific Division	0	3	.000
85-86 —Phoenix	32	50	.390	T3rd/Pacific Division	—	—	—
86-87 —Phoenix	22	34	.393		—	—	—
87-88 —Dallas	53	29	.646	2nd/Midwest Division	10	7	.588
88-89 —Dallas	38	44	.463	4th/Midwest Division	—	—	—
89-90 —Dallas	5	6	.455		—	—	—
90-91 —New York	32	35	.478	3rd/Atlantic Division	0	3	.000
Totals (18 years)	707	657	.518	Totals (11 years)	47	54	.465

NOTES:

1970—Defeated Louisville, 74-73, in NIT first round; lost to Louisiana State, 97-94, in quarterfinals.

1971—Lost to Hawaii, 87-86 (2 OT), in NIT first round.

1976—Defeated Seattle, 4-2, in Western Conference semifinals; defeated Golden State, 4-3, in Western Conference finals; lost to Boston, 4-2, in World Championship Series.

1978—Lost to Milwaukee in Western Conference first round.

1979—Defeated Portland, 2-1, in Western Conference first round; defeated Kansas City, 4-1, in Western Conference semifinals; lost to Seattle, 4-3, in Western Conference finals.

1980—Defeated Kansas City, 2-1, in Western Conference first round; lost to Los Angeles Lakers, 4-1, in Western Conference semifinals.

1981—Lost to Kansas City in Western Conference semifinals.

1982—Defeated Denver, 2-1, in Western Conference semifinals; lost to Los Angeles Lakers, 4-0, in Western Conference semifinals.

1983—Lost to Denver in Western Conference first round.

1984—Defeated Portland, 3-2, in Western Conference first round; defeated Utah, 4-2, in Western Conference semifinals; lost to Los Angeles Lakers, 4-2, in Western Conference finals.

1985—Lost to Los Angeles Lakers in Western Conference first round.

1987—Replaced as Phoenix head coach by Dick Van Arsdale (February 26).

1988—Defeated Houston, 3-1, in Western Conference first round; defeated Denver, 4-2, in Western Conference semifinals; lost to Los Angeles Lakers, 4-3, in Western Conference finals.

1989—Replaced as Dallas head coach by Richie Adubato (November 29).

1990—Replaced Stu Jackson as New York head coach (December 3), with record of 7-8.

1991—Lost to Chicago in Eastern Conference first round.

1992—Defeated Western Michigan, 63-56, in NIT first round; defeated Kansas State, 64-47, in second round; defeated Manhattan, 74-58, in quarterfinals; defeated Utah, 58-55, in semifinals; lost to Virginia, 81-76, in final.

MOE, DOUG

PERSONAL: Born September 21, 1938, in Brooklyn, N.Y. ... 6-5/220. ... Full name: Douglas Edwin Moe.

HIGH SCHOOL: Erasmus Hall (Brooklyn, N.Y.), then Bullis Prep School (Silver Springs, Md.).

COLLEGE: North Carolina, then Elon College (N.C.).

TRANSACTIONS/CAREER NOTES: Selected by Chicago Packers in second round (22nd pick overall) of 1961 NBA Draft. ... Signed by Packers (1961); Packers later refused to honor contract when Moe was implicated in college point-shaving scandal; Moe was exonerated but did not play basketball from 1961-62 through 1964-65. ... Played with Padua, Italy (1965-66 and 1966-67). ... Signed by New Orleans Buccaneers of American Basketball Association (1967). ... Traded by Buccaneers with Larry Brown to Oakland Oaks for Steve Jones, Ron Franz and Barry Leibowitz (June 18, 1968). ... Traded by Oaks to Carolina Cougars in three-way deal in which Cougars sent Stew Johnson to Pittsburgh Pipers and Pipers sent Frank Card to Oaks (June 12, 1969). ... Traded by Cougars to Washington Capitols for Gary Bradds and Ira Harge (July 24, 1970). ... Capitols franchise moved from Washington to Virginia and renamed Squires for 1970-71 season.

COLLEGIATE RECORD

NOTES: THE SPORTING NEWS All-America second team (1959, 1961).

Season Team	G	Min.	FGM	FGA	Pct.	FTM	FTA	Pct.	Reb.	Ast.	Pts.	AVERAGES RPG	APG	PPG
57-58—North Carolina‡							Statistics unavailable.							
58-59—North Carolina	25	...	106	265	.400	104	164	.634	179	67	316	7.2	2.7	12.6
59-60—North Carolina	12	...	60	144	.417	82	113	.726	135	...	202	11.3	...	16.8
60-61—North Carolina	23	...	163	401	.406	143	207	.691	321	...	469	14.0	...	20.4
Totals	60	...	329	810	.406	329	484	.680	635	...	987	10.6	...	16.5

ABA REGULAR-SEASON RECORD

NOTES: ABA All-Star first team (1968). ... ABA All-Star second team (1969). ... Member of ABA championship team (1969).

Season Team	G	Min.	2-POINT FGM	FGA	Pct.	3-POINT FGM	FGA	Pct.	FTM	FTA	Pct.	Reb.	Ast.	Pts.	AVERAGES RPG	APG	PPG
67-68— New Orleans	78	3113	662	1588	.417	3	22	.136	551	693	.795	795	202	1884	10.2	2.6	24.2
68-69— Oakland	75	2528	524	1213	.432	5	14	.357	360	444	.811	614	151	1423	8.2	2.0	19.0
69-70— Carolina	80	2671	527	1220	.432	8	34	.235	304	399	.762	437	425	1382	5.5	5.3	17.3
70-71— Virginia	78	2297	395	861	.459	2	10	.200	221	259	.853	473	270	1017	6.1	3.5	13.0
71-72— Virginia	67	1472	174	406	.429	1	9	.111	104	129	.806	241	149	455	3.6	2.2	6.8
Totals	378	12081	2282	5288	.432	19	89	.213	1540	1924	.800	2560	1197	6161	6.8	3.2	16.3

ABA PLAYOFF RECORD

Season Team	G	Min.	2-POINT FGM	FGA	Pct.	3-POINT FGM	FGA	Pct.	FTM	FTA	Pct.	Reb.	Ast.	Pts.	AVERAGES RPG	APG	PPG
67-68— New Orleans	17	715	140	335	.418	4	11	.364	107	149	.718	169	40	399	9.9	2.4	23.5
68-69— Oakland	16	593	115	280	.411	0	4	.000	87	111	.784	124	31	317	7.8	1.9	19.8
69-70— Carolina	4	168	25	72	.347	0	4	.000	12	16	.750	26	25	62	6.5	6.3	15.5
70-71— Virginia	12	421	89	174	.511	1	3	.333	31	41	.756	57	37	212	4.8	3.1	17.7
71-72— Virginia	11	245	37	84	.440	0	1	.000	22	25	.880	43	27	96	3.9	2.5	8.7
Totals	60	2142	406	945	.430	5	23	.217	259	342	.757	419	160	1086	7.0	2.7	18.1

ABA ALL-STAR GAME RECORD

Season Team	Min.	2-POINT FGM	FGA	Pct.	3-POINT FGM	FGA	Pct.	FTM	FTA	Pct.	Reb.	Ast.	Pts.
1968 —New Orleans	29	7	12	.583	0	1	.000	3	5	.600	7	5	17
1969 —Oakland	26	6	13	.462	0	0	...	5	8	.625	6	6	17
1970 —Carolina	36	0	5	.000	0	0	...	2	3	.667	8	6	2
Totals	91	13	30	.433	0	1	.000	10	16	.625	21	17	36

HEAD COACHING RECORD

BACKGROUND: Assistant coach, Elon College, N.C. (1963-64 and 1964-65). ... Assistant coach/director of player personnel, Carolina Cougars of ABA (1972-73 and 1973-74). ... Assistant coach/director of player personnel, Denver Nuggets of ABA (1974-75 and 1975-76). ... Assistant coach, Nuggets (1980).
HONORS: NBA Coach of the Year (1988).

NBA COACHING RECORD

Season	Team	REGULAR SEASON				PLAYOFFS		
		W	L	Pct.	Finish	W	L	Pct.
76-77	—San Antonio	44	38	.537	3rd/Central Division	0	2	.000
77-78	—San Antonio	52	30	.634	1st/Central Division	2	4	.333
78-79	—San Antonio	48	34	.585	1st/Central Division	7	7	.500
79-80	—San Antonio	33	33	.500		—	—	—
80-81	—Denver	26	25	.510	4th/Midwest Division	—	—	—
81-82	—Denver	46	36	.561	T2nd/Midwest Division	1	2	.333
82-83	—Denver	45	37	.549	T2nd/Midwest Division	3	5	.375
83-84	—Denver	38	44	.463	T3rd/Midwest Division	2	3	.400
84-85	—Denver	52	30	.634	1st/Midwest Division	8	7	.533
85-86	—Denver	47	35	.573	2nd/Midwest Division	5	5	.500
86-87	—Denver	37	45	.451	4th/Midwest Division	0	3	.000
87-88	—Denver	54	28	.659	1st/Midwest Division	5	6	.455
88-89	—Denver	44	38	.537	3rd/Midwest Division	0	3	.000
89-90	—Denver	43	39	.524	4th/Midwest Division	0	3	.000
92-93	—Philadelphia	19	37	.339		—	—	—
Totals (15 years)		**628**	**529**	**.543**	**Totals (12 years)**	**33**	**50**	**.398**

NOTES:
1977—Lost to Boston in Eastern Conference first round.
1978—Lost to Washington in Eastern Conference semifinals.
1979—Defeated Philadelphia, 4-3, in Eastern Conference semifinals; lost to Washington, 4-3, in Eastern Conference finals.
1980—Replaced as San Antonio head coach by Bob Bass (March 1). Replaced Donnie Walsh as Denver head coach (December), with record of 11-20.
1982—Lost to Phoenix in Western Conference first round.
1983—Defeated Phoenix, 2-1, in Western Conference first round; lost to San Antonio, 4-1, in Western Conference semifinals.
1984—Lost to Utah in Western Conference first round.
1985—Defeated San Antonio, 3-2, in Western Conference first round; defeated Utah, 4-1, in Western Conference semifinals; lost to Los Angeles Lakers, 4-1, in Western Conference finals.
1986—Defeated Portland, 3-1, in Western Conference first round; lost to Houston, 4-2, in Western Conference semifinals.
1987—Lost to Los Angeles Lakers in Western Conference first round.
1988—Defeated Seattle, 3-2, in Western Conference first round; lost to Dallas, 4-2, in Western Conference semifinals.
1989—Lost to Phoenix in Western Conference first round.
1990—Lost to San Antonio, 3-0, in Western Conference first round.
1993—Replaced as Philadelphia head coach by Fred Carter (March 7), with club in sixth place.

MOTTA, DICK

PERSONAL: Born September 3, 1931, in Midvale, Utah. ... 5-10/170. ... Full name: John Richard Motta.
HIGH SCHOOL: Jordan (Utah); did not play varsity basketball.
COLLEGE: Utah State (did not play basketball).

HEAD COACHING RECORD

BACKGROUND: Head coach, Grace Junior High School (1954-55). ... Head coach, Grace High School (1955-56 through 1959-60). ... Head coach, Weber Junior College (1960-61 and 1961-62). ... Broadcaster, Detroit Pistons (1988 through January 1990). ... Consultant, Dallas Mavericks (1990). ... Assistant coach, Denver Nuggets (1996-97 season).
HONORS: NBA Coach of the Year (1971).

COLLEGIATE COACHING RECORD

Season	Team	W	L	Pct.	Finish
62-63	—Weber State	22	4	.846	Independent
63-64	—Weber State	17	8	.680	2nd/Big Sky Conference
64-65	—Weber State	22	3	.880	1st/Big Sky Conference
65-66	—Weber State	20	5	.765	2nd/Big Sky Conference
66-67	—Weber State	18	7	.720	3rd/Big Sky Conference
67-68	—Weber State	21	6	.778	1st/Big Sky Conference
Totals (6 years)		**120**	**33**	**.784**	

NBA COACHING RECORD

Season	Team	REGULAR SEASON				PLAYOFFS		
		W	L	Pct.	Finish	W	L	Pct.
68-69	—Chicago	33	49	.402	5th/Western Division	—	—	—
69-70	—Chicago	39	43	.476	T3rd/Western Division	1	4	.250
70-71	—Chicago	51	31	.622	2nd/Midwest Division	3	4	.429
71-72	—Chicago	57	25	.695	2nd/Midwest Division	0	4	.000
72-73	—Chicago	51	31	.622	2nd/Midwest Division	3	4	.429
73-74	—Chicago	54	28	.659	2nd/Midwest Division	4	7	.364
74-75	—Chicago	47	35	.573	T1st/Midwest Division	7	6	.538
75-76	—Chicago	24	58	.293	4th/Midwest Division	—	—	—
76-77	—Washington	48	34	.585	2nd/Central Division	4	5	.444
77-78	—Washington	44	38	.537	2nd/Central Division	14	7	.666

Season Team	REGULAR SEASON W	L	Pct.	Finish	PLAYOFFS W	L	Pct.
78-79 —Washington	54	28	.659	1st/Atlantic Division	9	10	.474
79-80 —Washington	39	43	.476	3rd/Atlantic Division	0	2	.000
80-81 —Dallas	15	67	.183	6th/Midwest Division	—	—	—
81-82 —Dallas	28	54	.341	5th/Midwest Division	—	—	—
82-83 —Dallas	38	44	.463	4th/Midwest Division	—	—	—
83-84 —Dallas	43	39	.524	2nd/Midwest Division	4	6	.400
84-85 —Dallas	44	38	.537	3rd/Midwest Division	1	3	.250
85-86 —Dallas	44	38	.537	3rd/Midwest Division	5	5	.500
86-87 —Dallas	55	27	.671	1st/Midwest Division	1	3	.250
89-90 —Sacramento	16	38	.296	7th/Pacific Division	—	—	—
90-91 —Sacramento	25	57	.305	7th/Pacific Division	—	—	—
91-92 —Sacramento	7	18	.280		—	—	—
94-95 —Dallas	36	46	.439	5th/Midwest Division	—	—	—
95-96 —Dallas	26	56	.317	T5th/Midwest Division	—	—	—
Totals (24 years)	**918**	**965**	**.488**	**Totals (14 years)**	**56**	**70**	**.444**

NOTES:
1970—Lost to Atlanta in Western Conference first round.
1971—Lost to Los Angeles in Western Conference first round.
1972—Lost to Los Angeles in Western Conference first round.
1973—Lost to Los Angeles in Western Conference first round.
1974—Defeated Detroit, 4-3, in Western Conference first round; lost to Milwaukee, 4-0, in Western Conference semifinals.
1975—Defeated Kansas City-Omaha, 4-2, in Western Conference first round; lost to Golden State, 4-3, in Western Conference semifinals.
1977—Defeated Cleveland, 2-1, in Eastern Conference first round; lost to Houston, 4-2, in Eastern Conference semifinals.
1978—Defeated Atlanta, 2-0, in Eastern Conference first round; defeated San Antonio, 4-2, in Eastern Conference semifinals; defeated Philadelphia, 4-2, in Eastern Conference finals; defeated Seattle, 4-3, in World Championship Series.
1979—Defeated Atlanta, 4-3, in Eastern Conference semifinals; defeated San Antonio, 4-3, in Eastern Conference finals; lost to Seattle, 4-1, in World Championship Series.
1980—Lost to Philadelphia in Eastern Conference first round.
1984—Defeated Seattle, 3-2, in Western Conference first round; lost to Los Angeles Lakers, 4-1, in Western Conference semifinals.
1985—Lost to Portland in Western Conference first round.
1986—Defeated Utah, 3-1, in Western Conference first round; lost to Los Angeles Lakers, 4-2, in Western Conference semifinals.
1987—Lost to Seattle in Western Conference first round.
1990—Replaced Jerry Reynolds as Sacramento head coach (January 4), with record of 7-21 and club in seventh place.
1991—Replaced as Sacramento head coach by Rex Hughes (December 24) with club in seventh place.

NELSON, DON

PERSONAL: Born May 15, 1940, in Muskegon, Mich. ... 6-6/210. ... Full name: Don Arvid Nelson.
HIGH SCHOOL: Rock Island (Ill.).
COLLEGE: Iowa.
TRANSACTIONS/CAREER NOTES: Selected by Chicago Zephyrs in third round (19th pick overall) of 1962 NBA Draft. ... Zephyrs franchise moved from Chicago to Baltimore and renamed Bullets for 1963-64 season. ... Contract sold by Bullets to Los Angeles Lakers (September 6, 1963). ... Waived by Lakers (October 21, 1965). ... Signed as free agent by Boston Celtics (October 28, 1965).
MISCELLANEOUS: Member of NBA championship teams (1966, 1968, 1969, 1974, 1976).

COLLEGIATE RECORD

Season Team	G	Min.	FGM	FGA	Pct.	FTM	FTA	Pct.	Reb.	Ast.	Pts.	AVERAGES RPG	APG	PPG
58-59—Iowa‡					Freshman team did not play intercollegiate schedule.									
59-60—Iowa	24	...	140	320	.438	100	155	.645	241	...	380	10.0	...	15.8
60-61—Iowa	24	...	197	377	.523	176	268	.657	258	...	570	10.8	...	23.8
61-62—Iowa	24	...	193	348	.555	186	264	.705	285	...	572	11.9	...	23.8
Varsity totals	**72**	...	**530**	**1045**	**.507**	**462**	**687**	**.672**	**784**	...	**1522**	**10.9**	...	**21.1**

NBA REGULAR-SEASON RECORD

Season Team	G	Min.	FGM	FGA	Pct.	FTM	FTA	Pct.	Reb.	Ast.	PF	Dq.	Pts.	AVERAGES RPG	APG	PPG
62-63 —Chicago	62	1071	129	293	.440	161	221	.729	279	72	136	3	419	4.5	1.2	6.8
63-64 —Los Angeles	80	1406	135	323	.418	149	201	.741	323	76	181	1	419	4.0	1.0	5.2
64-65 —Los Angeles	39	238	36	85	.424	20	26	.769	73	24	40	1	92	1.9	0.6	2.4
65-66 —Boston	75	1765	271	618	.439	223	326	.684	403	79	187	1	765	5.4	1.1	10.2
66-67 —Boston	79	1202	227	509	.446	141	190	.742	295	65	143	0	595	3.7	0.8	7.5
67-68 —Boston	82	1498	312	632	.494	195	268	.728	431	103	178	1	819	5.3	1.3	10.0
68-69 —Boston	82	1773	374	771	.485	201	259	.776	458	92	198	2	949	5.6	1.1	11.6
69-70 —Boston	82	2224	461	920	.501	337	435	.775	601	148	238	3	1259	7.3	1.8	15.4
70-71 —Boston	82	2254	412	881	.468	317	426	.744	565	153	232	2	1141	6.9	1.9	13.9
71-72 —Boston	82	2086	389	811	.480	356	452	.788	453	192	220	3	1134	5.5	2.3	13.8
72-73 —Boston	72	1425	309	649	.476	159	188	.846	315	102	155	1	777	4.4	1.4	10.8

Season Team	G	Min.	FGM	FGA	Pct.	FTM	FTA	Pct.	REBOUNDS Off.	Def.	Tot.	Ast.	Stl.	Blk.	TO	Pts.	AVERAGES RPG	APG	PPG
73-74 —Boston	82	1748	364	717	.508	215	273	.788	90	255	345	162	19	13	...	943	4.2	2.0	11.5
74-75 —Boston	79	2052	423	785	*.539	263	318	.827	127	342	469	181	32	15	...	1109	5.9	2.3	14.0
75-76 —Boston	75	943	175	379	.462	127	161	.789	56	126	182	77	14	7	...	477	2.4	1.0	6.4
Totals	**1053**	**21685**	**4017**	**8373**	**.480**	**2864**	**3744**	**.765**	...	...	**5192**	**1526**	**65**	**35**	...	**10898**	**4.9**	**1.4**	**10.3**

Season Team	G	Min.	FGM	FGA	Pct.	FTM	FTA	Pct.	Reb.	Ast.	PF	Dq.	Pts.	RPG	APG	PPG
63-64 —Los Angeles	5	56	7	13	.538	3	3	1.000	13	2	11	1	17	2.6	0.4	3.4
64-65 —Los Angeles	11	212	24	53	.453	19	25	.760	59	19	31	0	67	5.4	1.7	6.1
65-66 —Boston	17	316	50	118	.424	42	52	.808	85	13	50	0	142	5.0	0.8	8.4
66-67 —Boston	9	142	27	59	.458	10	17	.588	42	9	12	0	64	4.7	1.0	7.1
67-68 —Boston	19	468	91	175	.520	55	74	.743	143	32	49	0	237	7.5	1.7	12.5
68-69 —Boston	18	348	87	168	.518	50	60	.833	83	21	51	0	224	4.6	1.2	12.4
71-72 —Boston	11	308	52	99	.525	41	48	.854	61	21	30	0	145	5.5	1.9	13.2
72-73 —Boston	13	303	47	101	.465	49	56	.875	38	15	29	0	143	2.9	1.2	11.0

Season Team	G	Min.	FGM	FGA	Pct.	FTM	FTA	Pct.	Off.	Def.	Tot.	Ast.	Stl.	Blk.	TO	Pts.	RPG	APG	PPG
73-74 —Boston	18	467	82	164	.500	41	53	.774	25	72	97	35	8	3	...	205	5.4	1.9	11.4
74-75 —Boston	11	274	66	117	.564	37	41	.902	18	27	45	26	2	2	...	169	4.1	2.4	15.4
75-76 —Boston	18	315	52	108	.481	60	69	.870	17	36	53	17	3	2	...	164	2.9	0.9	9.1
Totals	150	3209	585	1175	.498	407	498	.817	...	...	719	210	13	7	...	1577	4.8	1.4	10.5

HEAD COACHING RECORD

BACKGROUND: Assistant coach, Milwaukee Bucks (September 9-November 22, 1976). ... Head coach/director of player personnel, Bucks (November 22, 1976 through 1985). ... Head coach/vice president of basketball operations, Bucks (1985-May 27, 1987). ... Executive vice president, Golden State Warriors (1987-88). ... Head coach/general manager, Warriors (1988-89 to February 13, 1995).

HONORS: NBA Coach of the Year (1983, 1985, 1992).

NBA COACHING RECORD

Season Team	REGULAR SEASON				PLAYOFFS		
	W	L	Pct.	Finish	W	L	Pct.
76-77 —Milwaukee	27	37	.422	6th/Midwest Division	—	—	—
77-78 —Milwaukee	44	38	.537	2nd/Midwest Division	5	4	.556
78-79 —Milwaukee	38	44	.463	4th/Midwest Division	—	—	—
79-80 —Milwaukee	49	33	.598	1st/Midwest Division	3	4	.429
80-81 —Milwaukee	60	22	.732	1st/Central Division	3	4	.429
81-82 —Milwaukee	55	27	.671	1st/Central Division	2	4	.333
82-83 —Milwaukee	51	31	.622	1st/Central Division	5	4	.556
83-84 —Milwaukee	50	32	.610	1st/Central Division	8	8	.500
84-85 —Milwaukee	59	23	.720	1st/Central Division	3	5	.375
85-86 —Milwaukee	57	25	.695	1st/Central Division	7	7	.500
86-87 —Milwaukee	50	32	.610	3rd/Central Division	6	6	.500
88-89 —Golden State	43	39	.524	4th/Pacific Division	4	4	.500
89-90 —Golden State	37	45	.451	5th/Pacific Division	—	—	—
90-91 —Golden State	44	38	.537	4th/Pacific Division	4	5	.444
91-92 —Golden State	55	27	.671	2nd/Pacific Division	1	3	.250
92-93 —Golden State	34	48	.415	6th/Pacific Division	—	—	—
93-94 —Golden State	50	32	.610	3rd/Pacific Division	0	3	.000
94-95 —Golden State	14	31	.311		—	—	—
95-96 —New York	34	26	.567		—	—	—
Totals (19 years)	851	630	.575	Totals (13 years)	51	61	.455

NOTES:

1976—Replaced Larry Costello as Milwaukee head coach (November 22), with record of 3-15 and club in sixth place.

1978—Defeated Phoenix, 2-0, in Western Conference first round; lost to Denver, 4-3, in Western Conference semifinals.

1980—Lost to Seattle in Western Conference semifinals.

1981—Lost to Philadelphia in Eastern Conference semifinals.

1982—Lost to Philadelphia in Eastern Conference semifinals.

1983—Defeated Boston, 4-0, in Eastern Conference semifinals; lost to Philadelphia, 4-1, in Eastern Conference finals.

1984—Defeated Atlanta, 3-2, in Eastern Conference first round; defeated New Jersey, 4-2, in Eastern Conference semifinals; lost to Boston, 4-1, in Eastern Conference finals.

1985—Defeated Chicago, 3-1, in Eastern Conference first round; lost to Philadelphia, 4-0, in Eastern Conference semifinals.

1986—Defeated New Jersey, 3-0, in Eastern Conference first round; defeated Philadelphia, 4-3, in Eastern Conference semifinals; lost to Boston, 4-0, in Eastern Conference finals.

1987—Defeated Philadelphia, 3-2, in Eastern Conference first round; lost to Boston, 4-3, in Eastern Conference semifinals.

1989—Defeated Utah, 3-0, in Western Conference first round; lost to Phoenix, 4-1, in Western Conference semifinals.

1991—Defeated San Antonio, 3-1, in Western Conference first round; lost to Los Angeles Lakers, 4-1, in Western Conference semifinals.

1992—Lost to Seattle in Western Conference first round.

1994—Lost to Phoenix in Western Conference first round.

1995—Replaced as Golden State head coach by Bob Lanier (February 13) with club in sixth place.

1996—Replaced as New York head coach by Jeff Van Gundy (March 8) with club in second place.

DID YOU KNOW...

...that George Yardley, with 2,001 points in 1957-58, became the first
NBA player to score 2,000 points in a season?

RAMSAY, JACK

PERSONAL: Born February 21, 1925, in Philadelphia. ... 6-1/180. ... Full name: John T. Ramsay.
HIGH SCHOOL: Upper Darby Senior (Pa.).
COLLEGE: St. Joseph's, then Villanova, then Pennsylvania.
TRANSACTIONS/CAREER NOTES: Played with San Diego Dons, an Amateur Athletic Union team (1945-46). ... Played in Eastern Basketball League with Harrisburg and Sunbury (1949-50 through 1954-55).
CAREER HONORS: Elected to Naismith Memorial Basketball Hall of Fame (1992).

COLLEGIATE RECORD

Season Team	G	Min.	FGM	FGA	Pct.	FTM	FTA	Pct.	Reb.	Ast.	Pts.	RPG	APG	PPG
42-43—St. Joseph's‡						Freshman team statistics unavailable.								
43-44						Did not play—in military service.								
44-45						Did not play—in military service.								
45-46						Did not play—in military service.								
46-47—St. Joseph's	21	...	72	214	.336	20	32	.625	...	...	164	...	...	7.8
47-48—St. Joseph's	14		60			38	...	...	...	...	158	...	...	11.3
48-49—St. Joseph's	23		75	...	...	52	...	...	...	...	202	...	...	8.8
Varsity totals	58	...	207	...	...	110	...	...	...	...	524	...	...	9.0

EBL REGULAR-SEASON RECORD

Season Team	G	Min.	FGM	FGA	Pct.	FTM	FTA	Pct.	Reb.	Ast.	PF	Dq.	Pts.	RPG	APG	PPG
49-50 —Harrisburg	25	...	134	...	...	68	...	...	...	...	...	...	336	...	...	13.4
50-51 —Harrisburg	20	...	96	...	...	43	...	...	...	...	...	...	235	...	...	11.8
51-52 —Sunbury	26	...	159	...	...	86	...	...	...	...	...	...	404	...	...	15.5
52-53 —Sunbury	21	...	116	...	...	97	...	...	...	...	...	...	329	...	...	15.7
53-54 —Sunbury	28	...	112	...	...	101	...	...	...	...	...	...	325	...	...	11.6
54-55 —Sunbury	30	...	164	...	...	155	...	...	...	...	...	...	483	...	...	16.1
Totals	130	...	685	...	...	507	...	...	...	...	...	...	1877	...	...	14.4

HEAD COACHING RECORD

BACKGROUND: Head coach, St. James High School (Pa.) and later head coach, Mount Pleasant High School, Del. (1949-1955). ... General manager, Philadelphia 76ers (1966-67 and 1967-68). ... Head coach/general manager, 76ers (1968-69 and 1969-70).

COLLEGIATE COACHING RECORD

Season Team	W	L	Pct.	Finish
55-56 —St. Joseph's	23	6	.793	Independent
56-57 —St. Joseph's	17	7	.708	Independent
57-58 —St. Joseph's	18	9	.667	2nd/Middle Atlantic Conference
58-59 —St. Joseph's	22	5	.815	1st/Middle Atlantic Conference
59-60 —St. Joseph's	20	7	.741	1st/Middle Atlantic Conference
60-61 —St. Joseph's	25	5	.833	1st/Middle Atlantic Conference
61-62 —St. Joseph's	18	10	.643	1st/Middle Atlantic Conference
62-63 —St. Joseph's	23	5	.821	1st/Middle Atlantic Conference
63-64 —St. Joseph's	18	10	.643	T2nd/Middle Atlantic Conference
64-65 —St. Joseph's	26	3	.897	1st/Middle Atlantic Conference
65-66 —St. Joseph's	24	5	.828	1st/Middle Atlantic Conference
Totals (11 years)	234	72	.765	

NBA COACHING RECORD

Season Team	REGULAR SEASON				PLAYOFFS		
	W	L	Pct.	Finish	W	L	Pct.
68-69 —Philadelphia	55	27	.671	2nd/Eastern Division	1	4	.200
69-70 —Philadelphia	42	40	.512	4th/Eastern Division	1	4	.200
70-71 —Philadelphia	47	35	.573	2nd/Atlantic Division	3	4	.429
71-72 —Philadelphia	30	52	.366	3rd/Atlantic Division	—	—	—
72-73 —Buffalo	21	61	.256	3rd/Atlantic Division	—	—	—
73-74 —Buffalo	42	40	.512	3rd/Atlantic Division	2	4	.333
74-75 —Buffalo	49	33	.598	2nd/Atlantic Division	3	4	.429
75-76 —Buffalo	46	36	.561	T2nd/Atlantic Division	4	5	.444
76-77 —Portland	49	33	.598	2nd/Pacific Division	14	5	.737
77-78 —Portland	58	24	.707	1st/Pacific Division	2	4	.333
78-79 —Portland	45	37	.549	4th/Pacific Division	1	2	.333
79-80 —Portland	38	44	.463	4th/Pacific Division	1	2	.333
80-81 —Portland	45	37	.549	3rd/Pacific Division	1	2	.333
81-82 —Portland	42	40	.512	5th/Pacific Division	—	—	—
82-83 —Portland	46	36	.561	4th/Pacific Division	3	4	.429
83-84 —Portland	48	34	.585	2nd/Pacific Division	2	3	.400
84-85 —Portland	42	40	.512	2nd/Pacific Division	4	5	.444
85-86 —Portland	40	42	.488	2nd/Pacific Division	1	3	.250
86-87 —Indiana	41	41	.500	4th/Central Division	1	3	.250
87-88 —Indiana	38	44	.463	6th/Central Division	—	—	—
88-89 —Indiana	0	7	.000		—	—	—
Totals (21 years)	864	783	.525	**Totals (16 years)**	44	58	.431

NOTES:
1956—Defeated Seton Hall, 74-65, in NIT quarterfinals; lost to Louisville, 89-79, in semifinals; defeated St. Francis-New York, 93-82, in third-place game.
1958—Defeated St. Peter's, 83-72, in NIT first round; lost to St. Bonaventure, 79-75, in quarterfinals.

1959—Lost to West Virginia, 95-92, in NCAA Tournament first round; lost to Navy, 70-59, in regional consolation game.

1960—Lost to Duke, 58-56, in NCAA Tournament first round; lost to West Virginia, 106-100, in regional consolation game.

1961—Defeated Princeton, 72-67, in NCAA Tournament regional semifinal; defeated Wake Forest, 96-86, in regional final; lost to Ohio State, 95-69, in national semifinal; defeated Utah, 127-120 (4 OT), in consolation game.

1962—Lost to Wake Forest, 96-85 (OT), in NCAA Tournament regional semifinal; lost to New York University, 94-85, in regional consolation game.

1963—Defeated Princeton, 82-81, in NCAA Tournament first round; defeated West Virginia, 97-88, in regional semifinal; lost to Duke, 73-59, in regional final.

1964—Defeated Miami (Fla.), 86-76, in NIT first round; lost to Bradley, 83-81, in quarterfinals.

1965—Defeated Connecticut, 67-61, in NCAA Tournament first round; lost to Providence, 81-73 (OT), in regional semifinal; lost to North Carolina State, 103-81, in regional consolation game.

1966—Defeated Providence, 65-48, in NCAA Tournament first round; lost to Duke, 76-74, in regional semifinal; defeated Davidson, 92-76, in regional consolation game.

1969—Lost to Boston in Eastern Division semifinals.

1970—Lost to Milwaukee in Eastern Division semifinals.

1971—Lost to Baltimore in Eastern Conference semifinals.

1974—Lost to Boston in Eastern Conference semifinals.

1975—Lost to Washington in Eastern Conference semifinals.

1976—Defeated Philadelphia, 2-1, in Eastern Conference first round; lost to Boston, 4-2, in Eastern Conference semifinals.

1977—Defeated Chicago, 2-1, in Western Conference first round; defeated Denver, 4-2, in Western Conference semifinals; defeated Los Angeles Lakers, 4-0, in Western Conference finals; defeated Philadelphia, 4-2, in World Championship Series.

1978—Lost to Seattle in Western Conference semifinals.

1979—Lost to Phoenix in Western Conference first round.

1980—Lost to Seattle in Western Conference first round.

1981—Lost to Kansas City in Western Conference first round.

1983—Defeated Seattle, 2-0, in Western Conference first round; lost to Los Angeles Lakers, 4-1, in Western Conference semifinals.

1984—Lost to Phoenix in Western Conference first round.

1985—Defeated Dallas, 3-1, in Western Conference first round; lost to Los Angeles Lakers, 4-1, in Western Conference semifinals.

1986—Lost to Denver in Western Conference first round.

1987—Lost to Atlanta in Eastern Conference first round.

1988—Resigned as Indiana head coach (November 17); replaced by Mel Daniels with club in sixth place.

SHUE, GENE

PERSONAL: Born December 18, 1931, in Baltimore. ... 6-2/175.

COLLEGE: Maryland.

TRANSACTIONS/CAREER NOTES: Selected by Philadelphia Warriors in first round (third pick overall) of 1954 NBA Draft. ... Contract sold by Warriors to New York Knicks (November 29, 1954). ... Traded by Knicks to Fort Wayne Pistons for rights to G Ron Sobieszczyk (April 30, 1956). ... Pistons moved from Fort Wayne to Detroit for 1957-58 season. ... Traded by Pistons to Knicks for C Darrall Imhoff and cash (August 29, 1962). ... Traded by Knicks with C Paul Hogue to Baltimore Bullets for G/F Bill McGill (October 30, 1963).

COLLEGIATE RECORD

Season Team	G	Min.	FGM	FGA	Pct.	FTM	FTA	Pct.	Reb.	Ast.	Pts.	RPG	APG	PPG
												AVERAGES		
50-51—Maryland‡	14	...	...	...	...	53	75	.707	...	...	181	...	...	12.9
51-52—Maryland	22	...	91	243	.374	53	75	.707	...	...	205	...	...	9.3
52-53—Maryland	23	...	176	375	.469	156	223	.700	...	...	508	...	...	22.1
53-54—Maryland	30	...	237	469	.505	180	228	.789	...	...	654	...	...	21.8
Varsity totals	75	...	504	1087	.464	389	526	.740	...	...	1367	...	...	18.2

NBA REGULAR-SEASON RECORD

HONORS: All-NBA first team (1960). ... All-NBA second team (1961).

Season Team	G	Min.	FGM	FGA	Pct.	FTM	FTA	Pct.	Reb.	Ast.	PF	Dq.	Pts.	RPG	APG	PPG
															AVERAGES	
54-55—Phil.-N.Y.	62	947	100	289	.346	59	78	.756	154	89	64	0	259	2.5	1.4	4.2
55-56—New York	72	1750	240	625	.384	181	237	.764	212	179	111	0	661	2.9	2.5	9.2
56-57—Fort Wayne	72	2470	273	710	.385	241	316	.763	421	238	137	0	787	5.8	3.3	10.9
57-58—Detroit	63	2333	353	919	.384	276	327	.844	333	172	150	1	982	5.3	2.7	15.6
58-59—Detroit	72	2745	464	1197	.388	338	421	.803	335	231	129	1	1266	4.7	3.2	17.6
59-60—Detroit	75	†3338	620	1501	.413	472	541	.872	409	295	146	2	1712	5.5	3.9	22.8
60-61—Detroit	78	3361	650	1545	.421	465	543	.856	334	530	207	1	1765	4.3	6.8	22.6
61-62—Detroit	80	3143	580	1422	.408	362	447	.810	372	465	192	1	1522	4.7	5.8	19.0
62-63—New York	78	2288	354	894	.396	208	302	.689	191	259	171	0	916	2.4	3.3	11.7
63-64—Baltimore	47	963	81	276	.293	36	61	.590	94	150	98	2	198	2.0	3.2	4.2
Totals	699	23338	3715	9378	.396	2638	3273	.806	2855	2608	1405	8	10068	4.1	3.7	14.4

NBA PLAYOFF RECORD

Season Team	G	Min.	FGM	FGA	Pct.	FTM	FTA	Pct.	Reb.	Ast.	PF	Dq.	Pts.	RPG	APG	PPG
															AVERAGES	
54-55—New York	3	49	8	17	.471	6	7	.857	12	4	5	0	22	4.0	1.3	7.3
56-57—Fort Wayne	2	79	14	27	.519	4	4	1.000	7	8	3	0	32	3.5	4.0	16.0
57-58—Detroit	7	281	45	123	.366	40	43	.930	46	33	15	0	130	6.6	4.7	18.6
58-59—Detroit	3	118	28	60	.467	27	33	.818	14	10	7	0	83	4.7	3.3	27.7
59-60—Detroit	2	89	15	38	.395	18	20	.900	12	6	5	0	48	6.0	3.0	24.0
60-61—Detroit	5	186	35	72	.486	23	29	.793	12	22	11	0	93	2.4	4.4	18.6
61-62—Detroit	10	369	62	151	.411	37	48	.771	30	49	29	0	161	3.0	4.9	16.1
Totals	32	1171	207	488	.424	155	184	.842	133	132	75	0	569	4.2	4.1	17.8

NBA ALL-STAR GAME RECORD

Season	Team	Min.	FGM	FGA	Pct.	FTM	FTA	Pct.	Reb	Ast.	PF	Dq.	Pts.
1958—Detroit		25	8	11	.727	2	3	.667	2	0	3	0	18
1959—Detroit		31	6	12	.500	1	2	.500	4	3	4	0	13
1960—Detroit		34	6	13	.462	1	2	.500	6	6	0	0	13
1961—Detroit		23	6	10	.600	3	4	.750	3	6	1	0	15
1962—Detroit		17	3	6	.500	1	1	1.000	5	4	3	0	7
Totals		130	29	52	.558	8	12	.667	20	19	11	0	66

HEAD COACHING RECORD

BACKGROUND: General manager, Philadelphia 76ers (1990-91 and 1991-92). ... Director of player personnel, 76ers (1992-93-present).
HONORS: NBA Coach of the Year (1969, 1982).

NBA COACHING RECORD

		REGULAR SEASON				PLAYOFFS		
Season	Team	W	L	Pct.	Finish	W	L	Pct.
66-67 —Baltimore		16	40	.286	5th/Eastern Division	—	—	—
67-68 —Baltimore		36	46	.439	6th/Eastern Division	—	—	—
68-69 —Baltimore		57	25	.695	1st/Eastern Division	0	4	.000
69-70 —Baltimore		50	32	.610	3rd/Central Division	3	4	.429
70-71 —Baltimore		42	40	.512	1st/Central Division	8	10	.444
71-72 —Baltimore		38	44	.463	1st/Central Division	2	4	.333
72-73 —Baltimore		52	30	.634	1st/Central Division	1	4	.200
73-74 —Philadelphia		25	57	.305	4th/Atlantic Division	—	—	—
74-75 —Philadelphia		34	48	.415	4th/Atlantic Division	—	—	—
75-76 —Philadelphia		46	36	.561	T2nd/Atlantic Division	1	2	.333
76-77 —Philadelphia		50	32	.610	1st/Atlantic Division	10	9	.526
77-78 —Philadelphia		2	4	.333				
78-79 —San Diego		43	39	.524	5th/Pacific Division	—	—	—
79-80 —San Diego		35	47	.427	5th/Pacific Division	—	—	—
80-81 —Washington		39	43	.476	4th/Atlantic Division	—	—	—
81-82 —Washington		43	39	.524	4th/Atlantic Division	3	4	.429
82-83 —Washington		42	40	.512	5th/Atlantic Division			
83-84 —Washington		35	47	.427	5th/Atlantic Division	1	3	.250
84-85 —Washington		40	42	.488	4th/Atlantic Division	1	3	.250
85-86 —Washington		32	37	.464				
87-88 —L.A. Clippers		17	65	.207	6th/Pacific Division	—	—	—
88-89 —L.A. Clippers		10	28	.263		—	—	—
Totals (22 years)		784	861	.477	Totals (10 years)	30	47	.390

NOTES:

1966—Replaced Mike Farmer (1-8) and Buddy Jeannette (3-13) as Baltimore head coach (December) with record of 4-21.

1969—Lost to New York in Eastern Division semifinals.

1970—Lost to New York in Eastern Division semifinals.

1971—Defeated Philadelphia, 4-3, in Eastern Conference semifinals; defeated New York, 4-3, in Eastern Conference finals; lost to Milwaukee, 4-0, in World Championship Series.

1972—Lost to New York in Eastern Conference semifinals.

1973—Lost to New York in Eastern Conference semifinals.

1976—Lost to Buffalo in Eastern Conference first round.

1977—Defeated Boston, 4-3, in Eastern Conference semifinals; defeated Houston, 4-2, in Eastern Conference finals; lost to Portland, 4-2, in World Championship Series. Replaced as Philadelphia head coach by Billy Cunningham (November 4).

1982—Defeated New Jersey, 2-0, in Eastern Conference first round; lost to Boston, 4-1, in Eastern Conference semifinals.

1984—Lost to Boston in Eastern Conference first round.

1985—Lost to Philadelphia in Eastern Conference first round.

1986—Replaced as Washington head coach by Kevin Loughery (March 19).

1989—Replaced as L.A. Clippers head coach by Don Casey (January 19).

NBA Commissioners

**NBA President
Maurice Podolof
(1946 to 1963)**

**NBA Commissioner
J. Walter Kennedy
(1963 to 1975)**

**NBA Commissioner
Lawrence O'Brien
(1975 to 1984)**

**NBA Commissioner
David J. Stern
(1984 to present)**

NBA ALL-TIME TEAMS

CLUB	YEARS	RECORD	NOTE
Cleveland Rebels	1946-47	30-30	Finished only season third in Western Conference. ... Lost to New York, 2-1, in quarterfinals.
Detroit Falcons	1946-47	20-40	Finished only season fourth in Western Conference. ... .246 field-goal percentage was last in league.
Pittsburgh Ironmen	1946-47	15-45	Finished only season fifth in Western Conference. ... Led league with 1,360 personal fouls and finished last with 272 assists.
Toronto Huskies	1946-47	22-38	Finished only season 6th in Eastern Conference. ... First Canadian team in NBA.
Providence Steamrollers	1946-47 to 1948-49	46-122	Ernie Calverley led league with 3.4 assists per game during 1946-47 season. ... Compiled 17-64 road record in only three seasons.
Chicago Stags	1946-47 to 1949-50	145-92	Max Zaslofsky led league with 21.0 scoring average during 1947-48 season. ...Played in first NBA Finals (1946-47); lost 4-1 to Philadelphia Warriors.
St. Louis Bombers	1946-47 to 1949-50	122-115	29-19 record was best in league during 1947-48 season; lost to Philadelphia Warriors, 4-3, in semifinals.

Washington Capitols	1946-47 to 1950-51	157-114	Red Auerbach's first professional coaching job; 115-53 in three seasons. ... Bob Feerick led league with .401 field-goal percentage and was a member of original All-NBA first team during 1946-47 season.

WARRIORS FRANCHISE

Philadelphia Warriors	1946-47 to 1961-62	558-545	NBA champions (1947, 1956). ... Joe Fulks led league with 23.2 scoring average during 1946-47 season.
San Francisco Warriors	1962-63 to 1970-71	330-399	NBA Finals (1964, 1967) . ... Wilt Chamberlain led league in rebounding with 24.3 per game (1963) and in scoring with 44.8 and 36.9 points per game (1963, 1964) in two seasons with San Francisco Warriors.
Golden State Warriors	1971-72 to present	990-1,060	NBA champion (1975) ... During championship season Rick Barry led league in free-throw percentage with .904, steals with 2.85 per game, was second in scoring with 30.6 points per game and was named NBA Finals Most Valuable Player.
Totals	1946-47 to present	1878-2004	Warriors franchise has won three NBA championships.
Boston Celtics	1946-47 to present	2,422-1,465	16-time NBA champions (1957, 1959, 1960, 1961, 1962, 1963, 1964, 1965, 1966, 1968, 1969, 1974, 1976, 1981, 1984, 1986). ... 22 Hall of Fame players have played for the Celtics.
New York Knickerbockers	1946-47 to present	1,979-1,904	NBA champions (1970, 1973). ... In 1970 Knicks became first team to place three players on the NBA All-Defensive first team (Dave DeBusschere, Willis Reed and Walt Frazier).
Baltimore Bullets	1947-48 to 1954-55	161-303	NBA champion (1948). ... Won championship first year in league. ... Kleggie Hermsen led championship team with a 12.0 scoring average.
Indianapolis Jets	1948-49	18-42	In their only season, 25 players suited up for the Jets.

PISTONS FRANCHISE

Fort Wayne Pistons	1948-49 to 1956-57	313-306	NBA Finals (1955, 1956). ... Larry Foust led team with 17.0 points per game and 10.0 rebounds per game during 1954-55 season.
Detroit Pistons	1957-58 to present	1,470-1,687	NBA champions (1989, 1990). ... Compiled 72-10 home record during two championship seasons. ... During 1988-89 season Pistons had six players average more than 13 points per game (Adrian Dantley, Isiah Thomas, Joe Dumars, Mark Aguirre, Vinny Johnson and Bill Laimbeer).
Totals	1948-49 to present	1,783-1,993	Pistons franchise has won two NBA championships.

ROYALS FRANCHISE

Rochester Royals	1948-49 to 1956-57	357-263	NBA champion (1951). ... Championship team included three future Hall of Famers (Bob Davies, Bobby Wanzer and Red Holzman).
Cincinnati Royals	1957-58 to 1971-72	555-634	Oscar Robertson averaged triple-double during 1961-62 season.
Kansas City/ Omaha Royals	1972-73 to 1974-75	113-133	During 1972-73 season, Nate "Tiny" Archibald led NBA with 34.0 points per game and 11.4 assists assists per game. ... Phil Ford was named NBA Rookie of the Year (1979).
Kansas City Kings	1975-76 to 1984-85	381-439	Western Conference Finals (1980-81); lost to Houston, 4-1.
Sacramento Kings	1985-86 to present	325-577	Mitch Ritchmond is only Sacramento player to be named to an All-NBA team(second- 1994, 1995; third- 1996).
Totals	1948-49 to present	1,731-2,046	Kings franchise has won one NBA championship.

LAKERS FRANCHISE

Minneapolis Lakers	1948-49 to 1959-60	457-382	NBA champions (1949, 1950, 1952, 1953, 1954). ... First championship team included four future Hall of Famers (George Mikan, Jim Pollard, Slater Martin and coach John Kundla). ... Lakers had a 122-15 (.891) home record in five championship seasons in Minneapolis.
Los Angeles Lakers	1960-61 to present	1,835-1,103	NBA champions (1972, 1980, 1982, 1985, 1987, 1988). ... Kareem Abdul-Jabbar won an NBA-record six Most Valuable Player awards, including three with Lakers (1976, 1977, 1980).
Totals	1948-49 to present	2,292-1,485	Lakers franchise has won 11 NBA championships. ... 11 Hall of Fame players have played for the Lakers. ... Jerry West has been a player, coach and G.M. for Lakers.
Denver Nuggets	1949-50	11-51	Finished only season sixth in Western Division. ... Compiled 1-26 road record in only season.
Anderson Packers	1949-50	37-27	Finished only season second in Western Division. ... Lost to Minneapolis, 2-0, in Western Division semifinals. ... Led league with 87.3 scoring average.
Sheboygan Redskins	1949-50	22-40	Finished only season fourth in Western Division. ... Lost to Indianapolis, 2-1, in Western Division semifinals.

HAWKS FRANCHISE

Waterloo Hawks	1949-50	19-43	Finished only season fifth in Western Division. ... Jack Smiley played and coached in Hawks only season (6.6 points per game and 11-16 record as coach).

continued

HAWKS FRANCHISE (continued)

Tri-Cities Blackhawks	1949-50 and 1950-51	54-78	Frank Brian was named to All-NBA second team (1951).
Milwaukee Hawks	1951-52 to 1954-55	91-190	Bob Pettit was named NBA Rookie of the Year and All-NBA first team (1955). ... Finished last place all four years in Milwaukee while compiling a 92-190 record.
St. Louis Hawks	1955-56 to 1967-68	553-452	NBA champion (1958). ... During 10 of 13 years in St. Louis, the Hawks had one or more players on the All-NBA first or second teams; Bob Pettit (first- 1956, 1957, 1958, 1959, 1960, 1961, 1962, 1963, 1964; second-1965), Slater Martin (second- 1957, 1958, 1959) and Cliff Hagan (second-1958, 1959).
Atlanta Hawks	1968-69 to present	1,186-1,110	Coach Lenny Wilkens notched his record 939th career victory during 1994-95 season while with Atlanta. ... Dominique Wilkins won NBA Slam Dunk contest at 1985 and 1990 NBA All-Star weekends.
Totals	1949-50 to present	1,884-1,830	Hawks franchise has won one NBA championship.
Indianapolis Olympians	1949-50 to 1952-53	132-137	Alex Groza led league with .478 and .470 field-goal percentage and was second with 23.4 and 21.7 points per game during only two seasons in NBA (1950, 1951).

76ERS FRANCHISE

Syracuse Nationals	1949-50 to 1962-63	576-437	NBA champion (1955). ... Dolph Schayes was named to All-NBA first team six times (1952, 1953, 1954, 1955, 1957, 1958) and second team six times (1950, 1951, 1956, 1959, 1960, 1961).
Philadelphia 76ers	1963-64 to present	1,459-1,240	NBA champions (1967, 1983). ... Moses Malone was named the NBA Most Valuable Player during 1982-83 championship season.
Totals	1949-50 to present	2,035-1,677	76ers franchise has won three NBA championships.

BULLETS FRANCHISE

Chicago Packers	1961-62	18-62	Walt Bellamy averaged 31.6 points and 19.0 rebounds per game and was named NBA Rookie of the Year during 1961-62 season.
Chicago Zephyrs	1962-63	25-55	Future Hall of Famer Walt Bellamy led team with 27.9 scoring average and 16.4 rebounds per game.
Baltimore Bullets	1963-64 to 1972-73	401-412	NBA Finals (1971). ... Earl "The Pearl" Monroe was the NBA Rookie of the Year (1968) and was named to the All-NBA first team (1969).

continued

BULLETS FRANCHISE (continued)

Capital Bullets	1973-74	47-35	Elvin Hayes led the league with 18.1 rebounds per game and was named to the All-NBA and All-Defensive second teams during only season the team was called the Capital Bullets.
Washington Bullets	1974-75 to present	843-961	NBA champion (1978). ... Championship was only one for Elvin Hayes, who played in 1,303 NBA games, and coach Dick Motta who has coached in 1,883 NBA games
Totals	1961-62 to present	1,334-1,525	Bullets franchise has won one NBA championship.
Chicago Bulls	1966-67 to present	1,316-1,143	NBA champions (1991, 1992, 1993, 1996). ... Michael Jordan is only the second player—Willis Reed the other—in NBA history to be named NBA All-Star game, regular season and NBA Finals MVP in same season (1996).

ROCKETS FRANCHISE

San Diego Rockets	1967-68 to 1970-71	119-209	Former players Pat Riley, Rudy Tomjanovich and Rick Adelman have coached in 11 NBA Finals, winning six NBA titles (Riley 4, Tomjanovich 2).
Houston Rockets	1971-72 to present	1,049-1,001	NBA champions (1994, 1995). ...Hakeem Olajuwon was named NBA Most Valuable Player and Defensive Player of the Year during 1993-94 season.
Totals	1967-68 to present	1,168-1,210	Rockets franchise has won two NBA championships.
Seattle SuperSonics	1967-68 to present	1,253-1,1125	NBA champion (1979). ... Led NBA in scoring defense, allowing only 103.9 points per game during championship season. ... 1996 NBA Finals appearance was first since championship season.
Milwaukee Bucks	1968-69 to present	1,271-1,025	NBA champion (1971). ... Kareem Abdul-Jabbar won three Most Valuable Player awards while with Milwaukee. ... Bucks won seven consecutive division titles (1979-80 through 1985-86).
Phoenix Suns	1968-69 to present	1,246-1050	NBA Finals (1976, 1993). ... In their 28 seasons, the Suns have won 50 or more games 11 times. ... Charles Barkley won the Suns only Most Valuable Player award (1993). ... Owner Jerry Colangelo has been named NBA Executive of the Year four times (1976, 1981, 1989, 1993).

CLIPPERS FRANCHISE

Buffalo Braves	1970-71 to 1977-78	259-397	Braves put together three consecutive winning seasons from 1973-74 to 1975-76 (42-40, 49-33 and 46-36).
San Diego Clippers	1978-79 to 1983-84	186-306	World B. Free named to the All-NBA second team (1979).

continued

CLIPPERS FRANCHISE (continued)

Los Angeles Clippers	1984-85 to present	333-641	Current head coach, Bill Fitch, is team's ninth head coach while in Los Angeles. ... Only winning season came in 1991-92 (45-37).
Totals	1970-71 to present	778-1,344	In 26-season history, the Clippers' franchise has never had a winning record on the road.
Cleveland Cavaliers	1970-71 to present	953-1,179	Won only division title during 1975-76 season. ... Had three players on All-Rookie team following 1986-87 season (Brad Daugherty, Ron Harper and John Williams). ... Mark Price won the NBA Long Distance Shootout contest at 1993 and 1994 NBA All-Star games.
Portland Trail Blazers	1970-71 to present	1,129-1,003	NBA champion (1977). ... Of the 15 franchises to enter the NBA since 1970, the Trail Blazers are the only team to win an NBA championship.

JAZZ FRANCHISE

New Orleans Jazz	1974-75 to 1978-79	161-249	Never made playoffs while in New Orleans ... Pete Maravich was named All-NBA first team twice (1976, 1977) and second team once (1978) and Len "Truck" Robinson was named All NBA first team once (1978) while in New Orleans.
Utah Jazz	1979-80 to present	756-638	In the 11 seasons John Stockton and Karl Malone have been playing together, Utah has compiled a 563-339 record.
Totals	1974-75 to present	917-887	The Jazz have played in three Western Conference finals (1992, 1994, 1996).

NETS FRANCHISE

New York Nets	1976-77	22-60	Following ABA merger with NBA, the Nets sold Julius "Dr. J" Erving to 76ers in contract dispute.
New Jersey Nets	1977-78 to present	638-920	Nets have won only eight playoff games in NBA history.
Totals	1976-77 to present	660-980	At 7'6", Shawn Bradley is tallest player to play for Nets.
San Antonio Spurs	1976-77 to present	914-726	George Gervin's 33.1 points per game during 1979-80 season is highest scoring average for a Spurs player.
Indiana Pacers	1976-77 to present	737-903	Reggie Miller has made 1,203 three-point field goals, making him just the second player in NBA history—Dale Ellis the other—to have made more than 1,200 three-point field goal attempts.
Denver Nuggets	1976-77 to present	816-824	In eight of 11 seasons, Alex English averaged more than 25 point per game. ... David Thompson scored 73 points against the Pistons in 1978—the third-highest total ever.

Dallas Mavericks	1980-81 to present	541-771	Jason Kidd was the 1995 co-Rookie of the Year along with Pistons' Grant Hill.
Charlotte Hornets	1988-89 to present	272-384	The Hornets' first eleven draft picks—including Larry Johnson and Alonzo Mourning—are no longer with the team.
Miami Heat	1988-89 to present	247-409	At the 1995 NBA All-Star Weekend, Harold Miner won the Slam Dunk contest and Glen Rice won the Long Distance Shootout contest.
Minnesota Timberwolves	1989-90 to present	152-422	In their seven-year history, the Timberwolves have had five players named to the NBA All-Rookie first or second teams (Pooh Richardson, first-1990; Felton Spencer, second-1991; Christian Laettner, second-1993; Isaiah Rider, first-1994; and Kevin Garnett, second-1996).
Orlando Magic	1989-90 to present	278-296	NBA Finals (1995). ... Played in NBA Finals in only fifth season in league.
Toronto Raptors	1995-96	21-61	Damon Stoudamire was named NBA Rookie of the Year (1996). ... The Raptors handed the Bulls one of their ten losses during 1995-96 season.
Vancouver Grizzlies	1995-96	15-67	23-game losing streak is longest single-season mark in NBA history.

1995-96 NATIONAL BASKETBALL ASSOCIATION LEADERS

POINTS

(minimum 70 games or 1,400 points)

	G	FGM	FTM	Pts.	Avg.
Michael Jordan, Chicago	82	916	548	2491	30.4
Hakeem Olajuwon, Houston	72	768	397	1936	26.9
Shaquille O'Neal, Orlando	54	592	249	1434	26.6
Karl Malone, Utah	82	789	512	2106	25.7
David Robinson, San Antonio	82	711	626	2051	25.0
Charles Barkley, Phoenix	71	580	440	1649	23.2
Alonzo Mourning, Miami	70	563	488	1623	23.2
Mitch Richmond, Sacramento	81	611	425	1872	23.1
Patrick Ewing, New York	76	678	351	1711	22.5
Juwan Howard, Washington	81	733	319	1789	22.1

REBOUNDS

(minimum 70 games or 800 rebounds)

	G	Off.	Def.	Tot.	Avg.
Dennis Rodman, Chicago	64	356	596	952	14.9
David Robinson, San Antonio	82	319	681	1000	12.2
Dikembe Mutombo, Denver	74	249	622	871	11.8
Charles Barkley, Phoenix	71	243	578	821	11.6
Shawn Kemp, Seattle	79	276	628	904	11.4
Hakeem Olajuwon, Houston	72	176	608	784	10.9
Patrick Ewing, New York	76	157	649	806	10.6
Alonzo Mourning, Miami	70	218	509	727	10.4
Loy Vaught, L.A. Clippers	80	204	604	808	10.1
Jayson Williams, New Jersey	80	342	461	803	10.0

FIELD GOALS

(minimum 300 made)

	FGM	FGA	Pct.
Gheorge Muresan, Washington	466	798	.584
Chris Gatling, Golden State-Washington	326	567	.575
Shaquille O'Neal, Orlando	592	1033	.573
Anthony Mason, New York	449	798	.563
Shawn Kemp, Seattle	526	937	.561
Dale Davis, Indiana	334	599	.558
Arvydas Sabonis, Portland	394	723	.545
Brian Williams, L.A. Clippers	416	766	.543
Chucky Brown, Houston	300	555	.541
John Stockton, Utah	440	818	.538

STEALS

(minimum 70 games or 125 steals)

	G	No.	Avg.
Gary Payton, Seattle	81	231	2.85
Mookie Blaylock, Atlanta	81	212	2.62
Michael Jordan, Chicago	82	180	2.60
Jason Kidd, Dallas	81	175	2.16
Alvin Robertson, Toronto	77	166	2.16
Anfernee Hardaway, Orlando	82	166	2.02
Eric Murdock, Milwaukee-Vancouver	73	135	1.85
Eddie Jones, L.A. Lakers	70	129	1.84
Hersey Hawkins, Seattle	82	149	1.82
Tom Gugliotta, Minnesota	78	139	1.78

FREE THROWS

(minimum 125 made)

	FTM	FTA	Pct.
Mahmoud Abdul-Rauf, Denver	146	157	.930
Jeff Hornacek, Utah	259	290	.893
Terrell Brandon, Cleveland	338	381	.887
Dana Barros, Boston	130	147	.884
Brent Price, Washington	167	191	.874
Hersey Hawkins, Seattle	247	283	.873
Mitch Richmond, Sacramento	425	491	.866
Reggie Miller, Indiana	430	498	.863
Tim Legler, Washington	132	153	.863
Spud Webb, Atlanta-Minnesota	125	145	.862

BLOCKED SHOTS

(minimum 70 games or 100 blocked shots)

	G	No.	Avg.
Dikembe Mutombo, Denver	74	332	4.49
Shawn Bradley, Philadelphia-New Jersey	79	288	3.65
David Robinson, San Antonio	82	271	3.30
Hakeem Olajuwon, Houston	72	207	2.88
Alonzo Mourning, Charlotte	70	189	2.70
Elden Campbell, L.A. Lakers	82	212	2.59
Patrick Ewing, New York	76	184	2.42
Gheorge Muresan, Washington	76	172	2.26
Shaquille O'Neal, Orlando	54	115	2.13
Jim McIlvaine, Washington	80	166	2.08

ASSISTS

(minimum 70 games or 400 assists)

	G	No.	Avg.
John Stockton, Utah	82	916	11.2
Jason Kidd, Dallas	81	783	9.7
Avery Johnson, San Antonio	82	789	9.6
Rod Strickland, Portland	67	640	9.6
Damon Stoudamire, Toronto	70	653	9.3
Kevin Johnson, Phoenix	56	517	9.2
Kenny Anderson, New Jersey-Charlotte	69	575	8.3
Tim Hardaway, Golden State-Miami	80	640	8.0
Mark Jackson, Indiana	81	635	7.8
Gary Payton, Seattle	81	608	7.5

THREE-POINT FIELD GOALS

(minimum 82 made)

	FGM	FGA	Pct.
Tim Legler, Washington	128	245	.522
Steve Kerr, Chicago	122	237	.515
Hubert Davis, New York	127	267	.476
B.J. Armstrong, Golden State	98	207	.473
Jeff Hornacek, Utah	104	223	.466
Brent Price, Washington	139	301	.462
Bobby Phills, Cleveland	93	211	.441
Terry Dehere, L.A. Clippers	139	316	.440
Mitch Richmond, Sacramento	225	515	.437
Allan Houston, Detroit	191	447	.427